PENGUIN BOOKS

ENGLAND'S THOUSAND BEST CHURCHES

Simon Jenkins is Chairman of the National Trust and one of Britain's most prominent journalists. He writes a column for the *Guardian*, has edited both the *Evening Standard* and *The Times*, and has written many books on politics, history and architecture, including *England's Thousand Best Churches*, *England's Thousand Best Houses* and most recently *Wales: Churches, Houses, Castles*, all published by Penguin. He is also the author of *Thatcher and Sons*. He is a fellow of the Society of Antiquaries and lives in London and Aberdyfi.

D0333990

England's Thousand Best Churches

SIMON JENKINS

PENGUIN BOOKS

PENGUIN BOOKS

Published by the Penguin Group
Penguin Books Ltd, 80 Strand, London WC2R ORL, England
Penguin Group (USA) Inc., 375 Hudson Street, New York, New York 10014, USA
Penguin Group (Canada), 90 Eglinton Avenue East, Suite 700, Toronto, Ontario, Canada M4P 2Y3
(a division of Pearson Penguin Canada Inc.)
Penguin Ireland, 25 St Stephen's Green, Dublin 2, Ireland (a division of Penguin Books Ltd)
Penguin Group (Australia), 250 Camberwell Road, Camberwell, Victoria 3124, Australia
(a division of Pearson Australia Group Pty Ltd)
Penguin Books India Pvt Ltd, 11 Community Centre, Panchsheel Park, New Delhi – 110 017, India
Penguin Group (NZ), 67 Apollo Drive, Rosedale, North Shore 0632, New Zealand
(a division of Pearson New Zealand Ltd)
Penguin Books (South Africa) (Pty) Ltd, 24 Sturdee Avenue,
Rosebank, Johannesburg 2196, South Africa

Penguin Books Ltd, Registered Offices: 80 Strand, London WC2R ORL, England

www.penguin.com

First published by Allen Lane 1999
Published with minor revisions in Penguin Books 2000
Published with further revisions 2009
1

Set in Sabon
Typeset by Rowland Phototypesetting Ltd, Bury St Edmunds, Suffolk
Printed in England by Clays Ltd, St Ives plc

978-0-141-03930-5

www.greenpenguin.co.uk

Contents

Introduction:
The Museum of England

A serious house on serious earth it is,
In whose blent air all our compulsions meet,
Are recognised and robed as destinies.
And that much never can be obsolete.

Philip Larkin, 'Church Going'

The church of Culbone lies by a stream where the wooded slope of Exmoor falls towards the Bristol Channel. The nearest lane runs a mile away through the woods. A medieval settlement once spread under the trees, but this has long vanished, leaving only a house and the smallest church in England. This church is not dead. Each week a group of worshippers travels out from Porlock to celebrate communion. They come to kneel and pray to their God according to the rituals of the Church of England and among the shades of their collective ancestors.

On the outside wall of that church is a Saxon face, chiselled from a single block of sandstone and serving as a mullion between two openings. The face is indistinct but appears to depict a person. The mouth is lost but the eyes gaze out, all-seeing, ever smiling. The smile is not one of recognition, nor of faith, nor is it the smile of reason. I regard it as the smile of humanity eternal. It says simply, 'You will soon be gone, but I and our kind will be here for ever.' It has smiled on Culbone for a thousand years.

To me, a church is not a place of revealed truth but rather a shrine of impenetrable mystery, symbol of humanity's everlasting quest for explanation. Every civilisation has such places and we should respect them all. But the English churches contained in this book are more than that. They embody England's 'other' story, the history of a people mostly living far from London, far from commerce, court and parliament. Into these churches, English men and women have for centuries poured their faith, joy, sorrow, labour and love. Great cathedrals may speak the history of the rich and powerful. The local parish church is like Thomas Gray's tombstone. It tells of 'homely joys and destiny obscure . . . the short and simple annals of the poor'. This book is a celebration of those annals.

For many people today, the church is no more than a tapering spire rising above a skirt of trees and cottage roofs. It marks an ancient settlement and symbolises an ancient conformity. Manor house, vicarage and schoolroom are gathered round the old churchyard, as if for security in a hostile world. Gravestones lie tipsy amid ryegrass and sedge. The church enclave seems marginalised, an architecture too important for its present purposes, coming to life only for the rituals of marriage, christening and funeral. Yet until the past century the church was at the heart of every community. It marked each event in life's calendar, solemnising it with discipline and blessing it with charity. It registered, christened, taught, married, adjudicated, sustained, comforted and buried. Before the Reformation, the authority of the Church ran parallel to and often in conflict with that of secular power, both national and local. This authority was not always kind and not always impartial. The Church's behaviour mirrored that of the society of its day. But it was always there. The Church remains an overwhelming presence in England's history.

That Church found its public expression in architecture and art. It was also a patron of community ceremonial. Throughout the Middle Ages, churches were dominant consumers of materials and skilled labour. The early cathedrals were stupendous innovators, as well as arbiters of style. Not even the engineering projects of the 19th and 20th centuries can have been more costly in money, skills and materials than medieval church-building. This cost extended far beyond the buildings themselves, to carving, wall painting, glass staining, statues, screens, metalwork, embroidery and books. Some of this art was religious, adorning the rituals of the Church, but much was secular. Carvers used the fabric of the local church to depict kings, bishops, lords and commoners at work and play, often with irreverence. Two features alone, the corbel and the misericord, offer a record of medieval domestic life equalled only in illustrated Books of Hours.

These churches were and still are glorious. I regard them as a dispersed gallery of vernacular art, especially that of the Middle Ages, without equal anywhere in the world. This book is intended as a catalogue of that gallery. I have lost count of the number of church guides which assert, 'This building is not a museum, it is a place of worship.' I disagree. A church is a museum, and should be proud of the fact. No apostolic faith can renounce its past. Nor should any parish church forget that it owes its splendour to the love, labour and taxes not just of today's Anglicans but of its whole community through history. When the patrons of Adderbury in Oxfordshire decided to expand their church in the 15th century, all local tithes for a decade were diverted to the purpose. When the people of Bodmin in Cornwall rebuilt their church in 1469, no individual, guild or society was excused a contribution. Even the poorest home had to give a donation, if only a brick. An English church is more than a place of denominational worship. It is the stage on which the pageant of community has been played out for a millennium. The Church of England is the true

Museum of England, and its buildings should be the more treasured as a result.

Every breeze that blows over a meadow is said to leave some memory of its passing in the lie of the grass. To make the acquaintance of an English church is to witness the breeze of history make its imprint on stone, brick, wood and plaster. No church is identical with any other. Nowhere else in the world are places of worship so idiosyncratic as in England. Each arose from its particular landscape and culture, reflecting local materials, patronage and politics, even the liturgical views of the vicar. The humblest church is a casket of varieties.

Yet to most people today a church is a puzzling place, what Larkin called 'A shape less recognisable each week, / A purpose more obscure.' Even those acquainted with Roman Catholic ritual, for which medieval churches were designed, can be mystifed by the ledges, seats and openings arrayed round the chancel. Also obscure are the many parochial activities for which naves, towers and porches were intended. Ecclesiastical art and iconography can be no less mysterious. Why piscinas, stoups and misericords; why gargoyles, corbels and Green Men? A church is a song without words, an architectural Sanskrit. This introduction attempts some translation. The Museum of England needs not only a custodian but also a guide.

THE EARLY CHURCH

With the collapse of the Roman Empire, scattered Christian settlements may have survived in parts of the British Isles. But the rebirth of Christianity in Britain began with Patrick's arrival in Ireland from Rome in the 5th century and Columba's crossing from Ireland to Iona in 563, by which time missionaries were already penetrating Wales and Cornwall. In 597 Augustine landed in Kent and founded his church at Canterbury. Shortly afterwards Aidan came south from Iona to found the monastery at Lindisfarne. However, relics of these times are sparse and the missions were vulnerable to Viking assault in the 8th and 9th centuries. Many died out.

The arrival of Benedictine monks from the Continent in the 10th century led to the widespread rebuilding in stone of previously wooden structures. The newcomers built minsters from which subsidiary missions spread out over marsh and forest, and from which emerged the plan of the English church that was to last for six centuries. Attention in these early churches was focused on the altar, round which the rituals of the Mass were celebrated. Naves were simple. Towers often doubled as defensive structures, set to the west. But these churches remain elusive places. We can see relics at Breamore in Hampshire, Worth in Sussex and Great Paxton in Huntingdonshire but most are so altered as to have lost any original aura. Perhaps the church of St Laurence, Bradford-on-Avon (Wilts), comes closest to an original, but it too is stripped of the furnishings that would have crowded a Saxon interior.

The first great period of English church-building followed the Norman Conquest of 1066. Although Continental Romanesque forms were arriving in Saxon England from the early 11th century onwards, the Conquest signalled a burst of church-building that was not to be equalled until the late 15th century and perhaps not until the 19th. For a century, Norman barons, bishops and monks built stone structures on their newly conquered lands in the style then prevailing in northern France. The more elaborate were cruciform in plan, with a central tower and round it the chancel, transepts and nave. These churches had thick walls, round arches, small windows and, in the south-east, apsidal east ends. These features were adorned with abstract zigzag patterns or naturalistic shapes such as leaves, beasts and humans. The most developed examples of this carving, such as at Malmesbury (Wilts), Barfreston (Kent) and in the carved fonts of the Herefordshire School, drew inspiration from an astonishing range of European art, Viking, Spanish, even Byzantine. Norman was a truly European culture.

The next stimulus to church-building came as the Norman ascendancy evolved into a more settled internal unity in the 12th century, with greater prosperity and trade and with the growth of parochial organisation and discipline. The invaders became indigenous and English. After the murder of Thomas à Becket in 1170, Henry II sponsored new churches and monasteries. Thomas's image was depicted on murals and screens across the country (almost all obliterated by Henry VIII, who regarded Becket as a foreign traitor). By the start of the 13th century, pilgrimage had become a widespread practice, with paths, shrines and hostels to match. Thomas's Canterbury in particular became the destination for the pious who could not afford a costly and dangerous journey to Santiago de Compostela, let alone Jerusalem. It was such middle-class pilgrims that Chaucer recorded in his *Canterbury Tales*.

THE GOTHIC AGE

This spurt of patronage coincided with the arrival from France of the pointed (or broken) arch, signalling the 'transition' from Norman to Gothic in the last quarter of the 12th century. The pointed arch, originating in the Middle East, was the crucial engineering innovation of the Middle Ages. Instead of relying on the solidity of a load-bearing wall, a building's weight could now rest on a skeleton of piers, shafts and ribs. This enabled wall thicknesses to be reduced and window openings enlarged. The pointed arch was to hold the imagination of church architects into the 20th century, acquiring a symbolism far beyond its engineering. It was seen variously as two hands in prayer or two lines leading the mind to God. Ruskin wrote, 'Pointed arches do not constitute Gothic, nor vaulted roofs nor flying buttresses nor grotesque sculptures. But all of these things, and many other things with them, when they come together, have life.'

There were three stylistic phases of Gothic architecture, subsequently classi-fied and named by the antiquarian, Thomas Rickman, in 1817. They were Early English, Decorated and Perpendicular, inconveniently straddling rather than corresponding to centuries: roughly 1175–1250, 1250–1350 and 1350–1540. The overlap from Norman to the earliest Gothic is sometimes known as Tran-sitional, typified by new pointed arches rising above old zigzag decoration. Only Rickman's Early English has been queried as appropriate, since the style was emphatically French. I have followed recent usage and refer to it more correctly as Early Gothic.

The arrival of Gothic must have been sensational to 12th-century Britons, replacing the heavy proportions and dark interiors of Norman with an architec-ture of elegance, with undulating arches, rib vaults, lancet windows and steeples. From Norman scallop and water-leaf capitals a distinctive decoration evolved known as stiff-leaf composed of shapes drawn from nature. At Abbey Dore (Herefs) we can see unfinished fragments of earlier carvings, apparently abandoned by their carvers on the advent of the new style. At West Walton (Norfolk) the capitals look as if the stone leaves were straining to sprout and grow from the piers. Often this foliage is inhabited by animals and people, and by that most elusive figure of Gothic art, the Green Man, a figure of the woods, part-animal, part-human, good and bad in one. To enter the earliest Gothic churches is to sense mankind still accompanied on his journey through life to death by the ghosts of his forest origins.

Over the course of the 13th century most parish churches took on the appearance familiar today. The church tower and porch declared the pride of each community and the wealth of its senior citizens. The tower began as a place of security, often with a priest's room high off the ground and reached only by a ladder. It developed as a chamber for hanging bells, a landmark, a beacon and manifestation of civic dignity. The spires of the east Midlands and Lincolnshire, many dating from the 13th century, were the highest structures in England until well into the 20th century. The mighty towers of Somerset were still being built years after the Reformation, such was their civic significance. They parallel the *torre* of Tuscan hill towns, only finer by far.

Porches were equally significant. Since churches were usually locked to protect chancels and keep out vagrants and thieves, porches were where con-scientious clergy performed their parochial duties. The porch saw the start of many public rituals, such as of baptism and matrimony. Chaucer's Wife of Bath claimed to have had five husbands 'at the church door'. Here was a place of sanctuary, shelter, advice and instruction. It was the first home of the school and the church court. Altars were built in porches for the swearing of oaths. Towards the end of the Middle Ages, prosperous churches built upstairs rooms over their porches, known as parvises, for the conduct of clerical business. The most splendid is at Cirencester (Gloucs). Parish notices were required by law to be posted in the porch, as they are to this day.

Inside, the simple space of the Norman chancel became more distinctive and more lavish, especially after Rome's enunciation of the Doctrine of Transubstantiation in 1215. This required the vessels of the sanctuary to be kept purified and the chancel to be formally separated from the nave. The clergy built comfortable sedilia, or seats, next to the altar in which to sit during Mass. They built piscinas in which to wash the vessels that contained the 'blood of Christ' with special drains to prevent the water being misused (such as for witchcraft) afterwards. They built aumbries or cupboards in which to store them. Priests' doors enabled the clergy to enter and leave the chancel without having to pass through the nave. Round these features were set the carved Easter Sepulchre, the tombs of earlier priests, wooden stalls for clergy and, beneath the seats, half-seats or misericords on which bottoms could be rested when standing. Finally, large screens of stone or wood divided the chancel from the rest of the church. The chancel was thus an ever more elaborate stage on which the theatre of the Mass was performed, the screen its proscenium arch. It was decorated with ever greater richness.

If the chancel was the place of the clerical elite, the nave was the place of the people. From the 12th century onwards, the arrival in England of successive waves of Church reformers, notably the orders of friars, brought preachers who supplemented the Mass with biblical exegesis, supported by spectacular wall paintings. Aisles were added and naves rebuilt to meet a growing demand for space and comfort from congregations. These congregations, or at least those addressing them or leading them in the Mass, needed light. During the long reign of Henry III (1216–72) masons introduced tracery, a French innovation, to support ever larger window openings with mullions and wider expanses of stained glass. Like every feature of the church, what was first structural soon attracted ornament. Tracery first appeared at Westminster Abbey in 1245, and possibly earlier at Binham (Norfolk). It immediately took hold, beginning a new era of Gothic that yielded some of the masterpieces of English art.

DECORATED GOTHIC

The masons of the Decorated period displayed a licence to innovate and extemporise that was hitherto unknown in architecture. They took the structure of the church and the furniture of the liturgy and subjected it to astonishing enrichment. Window tracery was the pride of the style. Mullions rose from sills until feeling the constriction of the arch, then burst into astonishing shapes, of tulips, roses, eyebrows, daggers and teardrops. This tracery has been given confusing terms, formally known as Geometrical, Intersecting and Reticulated (*see* Glossary). Reticulated developed into a series of flamboyant curvilinear shapes that defy classification. Some shapes were peculiar to a particular church and mason. The tracery at Great Walsingham (Norfolk) is repeated only in a church in Catalonia, probably by the same hand. The windows at Leominster and Ledbury (Herefs) are works of remarkable artistic abstraction.

Decorated developed over the turbulent reigns of Edwards I, II and III and reached its apogee in the first half of the 14th century. It was most brilliantly expressed in stone carving, for instance the Percy tomb at Beverley (Yorks, ER), the Easter Sepulchre at Hawton (Notts) and the exterior adornment of Heckington (Lincs). The decorative feature known as ballflower, knobbly balls set in a crown of leaf, surrounded arches and windows for a brief period after 1300. Travel brought further enrichment. The S-shaped or ogee arch arrived in the 14th century, probably from the orient. The north porch of St Mary Redcliffe, Bristol, displays motifs believed to have come from Persia. The masons of the supreme work of the period, Patrington church (Yorks, ER), seem on first sight to have carved their masterpiece from a single giant block of limestone. English Gothic appeared to be breaking free of continental constraint and setting off in a direction and with an artistry all its own.

This adventure was stopped in its prime by the Black Death of 1349–50. To many historians, that calamity stifled joy and ended experiment. English men and women had been reminded of their mortality. Builders (those who survived) seemed to lose confidence in the freedom of expression they had enjoyed in the first half of the 14th century, as they also lost patrons. At Hythe (Kent) and in many other churches, we can see the break reflected in an immediate coarsening of design and materials. Masons abandoned the old flamboyance. They took refuge in engineering scale and in formalism, to create the most distinctively English Gothic, known as Perpendicular. This was to have its own majesty. But to the connoisseur, Gothic lost a subtlety, a harmony of language, in the mid-14th century that it never recovered.

PERPENDICULAR

The Perpendicular era of English church architecture lasted for two hundred years and, at its climax in the late 15th and early 16th centuries, saw the rebuilding of churches the length and breadth of the land. Its finest manifestation was along the limestone backbone of England, home of the sheep and thus of wool, and along the roads and rivers to the North Sea ports. Wool was the oil of medieval Europe, and the uplands of England were its principal oilfield. The Chancellor of England sat on a woolsack and the Royal Exchange had a fleece as its emblem. In the mid-15th century a wool merchant named John Barton arrived from Lancashire at the village of Holme (Notts) on the Trent. He settled, founded a chantry in the church and wrote over his door:

'I thanke God and ever shall / It is the sheepe hath payed for all.' It could serve as the motto of the Perpendicular.

As with Decorated, the Perpendicular style is best demonstrated in its windows. They expanded their openings, flattened their tops and became grids of vertical mullions and horizontal transoms. This tracery was known as Panel. In the 14th-century chancel at Dorchester Abbey (Oxon) we can see the masons changing style from Decorated to Perpendicular as they moved from north wall to south. There was a fashion for huge clerestories, the most spectacular being at Melton Mowbray (Leics). Windows grew bigger not just to depict the Bible story but to carry the arms and images of their donors. At Ludlow (Salop), the Palmers' window celebrates the wealthiest citizens, who could afford a pilgrim-age to the Holy Land. At Hillesden (Bucks) and Tattershall (Lincs) the walls appear as mere stone frames for the glass. 'Look-no-hands Gothic' was Osbert Lancaster's epithet for these great expanses. Such glass as survives, for instance at Fairford (Gloucs) and St Neot (Cornwall), hints at the magnificence that all England's church windows must once have displayed.

Perpendicular Gothic could be monotonous, not least when ostentation took the form of sheer bigness. The flint naves and towers of Norfolk and Suffolk can seem like Easter Island megaliths marching across an interminable plain. Yet this was also an architecture of audacity, halls of light with supports that appear to defy gravity. Nor were the churches merely big. The towers of Somerset and the angel roofs of East Anglia can be subtle in both proportion and decoration. Inside, Perpendicular masons turned their hand to wood and stone. The chancel screen was the message of the sanctuary conveyed to the congregation in the nave and was thus the most prominent of all church furnishings. The loft was fitted for musicians and players in the Easter Week ceremonies that formed the climax of the Church year. Above the loft was its focus, the rood group of the Crucifixion and attendant saints. Every English medieval rood was destroyed at the Reformation (though the Victorians replaced some). These churches were for public assembly as well as worship. They were theatre, satire, music and entertainment. They saw constant pro-cessions, parades and ceremonies. The bench carvers of Somerset were masters of ridicule. A capital in St Mary, Beverley (Yorks, ER) portrays a singing quintet, one of thirty-four carvings depicting musical activity. The town must have been alive with perpetual song.

The Perpendicular style reached its zenith in the second half of the 15th century, also the climax of the Wars of the Roses. Churches were filled with heraldry and magnificent alabaster tombs, as at Tewkesbury (Gloucs) and Harewood (Yorks, W). The Tudor victory at Bosworth in 1485 gave medieval patronage its final surge. The hope of peace and national unity made English churches active, crowded and colourful as never before. The focus of liturgy had emphatically shifted from the chancel to the nave: a shift from the religion of the Mass to that of biblical worship and preaching, from altar to pulpit, that was to continue through the Reformation. Roughly half the churches existing in England at the time of the Reformation (c.1534–50) had been rebuilt over the preceding five decades, including almost all those in the West Country and East Anglia. The Somerset historian, Kenneth Wickham, wrote that, 'Never before or since has so much money been spent on the parish churches of England as in the half century before the last bad years of Henry VIII.'

An increasingly wealthy laity now paid for ever larger naves and towers, crowded with the emblems and memorials of their donors. Grandees founded chantries for their souls, an early and urgent form of death duty. Local guilds, commercial, charitable and usually both, paid for chapels and windows much as a sponsor pays for a room in a museum today. Eamon Duffy's graphic story of the Reformation, *The Stripping of the Altars*, lists the items for which parishioners were expected to pay, from psalters and censers to candleholders and graveyard walls. At St Neot (Cornwall) each local guild is named at the foot of its window. A window in All Saints, York, depicts the donor enacting the rituals of charitable piety to ensure his place in Heaven. At the head of every early 16th-century will was a bequest to the local church. Few rich men and women sought refuge from their communities in private oratories or were buried in private mausoleums, as on the Continent. The medieval parish church could accommodate the richest and poorest within its walls, and in this lay its variety and its present character.

We find it hard today to imagine either the appearance or the atmosphere of these places. The closest parallels are the churches of eastern Orthodoxy or the Easter ceremonial of Catholic Latin America. The tiny painted churches of Romania's Carpathian Mountains come closest to showing how a Norman church might have seemed, dark, dank and thick with icons, screens and murmured Masses. I once attended Easter Mass in the Peruvian Andes. The small church was crowded with Indians who had come down from the mountains in thick shawls and hats, laden with offerings for the altars of their favourite saints and for shrines to the dead of the previous year. Walls and furnishings were encrusted with old Spanish paintings, carvings and dirt. Candles were everywhere. Mass was sung by a visiting priest and a few schoolboys from the village. Worshippers, many huddled on the floor, looked on in dumb wonderment.

Yet even these examples cannot evoke the full civic splendour of late-medieval ritual. For this I turn to the series of paintings of *The Guild of the True Cross*, executed by Carpaccio at the end of the 15th century and now in Venice's Accademia. They show members of the Guild on their annual procession through the streets of the city. Mysticism and ritual are combined with the vitality of a parade. The whole community is caught up in the ostentatious ceremony of the Guild, an institution both secular and religious. The costumes and vestments are as colourful as was the decoration of the church itself. This was England, too, on the threshold of the Reformation.

THE REFORMATION

The English Reformation was an upheaval to which no precise date can be put. Henry VIII's Act of Supremacy of 1534 severed the links between the English Church and Rome. In 1536 and 1539 the monasteries were dissolved and between 1538 and 1547 shrines and chantries were suppressed. But it was not until the reign of Edward VI, in 1549, that the Book of Common Prayer was promulgated and orders given for the removal of 'superstitious images'. These reappeared during the brief reign of the Roman Catholic Queen Mary, only to be emphatically banned under Elizabeth I, along with rood figures and lofts. It took more than a quarter-century for the old religion to be suppressed and its images and stone altars destroyed. Stained glass, statues, reredoses and carvings were defaced, vestments shredded and wall paintings whitewashed. Many chancels were put out of use, converted into schoolrooms or even demolished. Churches were brought under the authority of lay churchwardens.

This transformation was not sudden, but it was complete. There were protests against the new liturgy. In the West Country, Lincolnshire and the North, where the old Church was secure (and central authority less so) there were rebellions. Under Queen Mary and later under Charles I, latent Roman Catholicism within the English Church burst back to life. But the new Anglicanism took hold. English parishes accepted the Protestant Reformation as the spirit of the age. Priests were expected to preach and were now allowed to marry. For two centuries after the Reformation, Anglican church-building rested from the frenetic activity of the previous century. Outside London, barely a dozen buildings on my list date from 1535 to 1735. But the new rich who acquired most of the monastic estates and took over responsibility as parochial patrons did not altogether desert their duties. They adapted their churches to the new prayer book. They walled off many chancels and converted chantries to serve as family pews and mausoleums. Churches became Protestant 'preaching boxes', but they were not ignored – at least initially.

Catholic historians depict the 16th century as a period of reckless iconoclasm, when English art was desecrated at the moment of its greatest fruition. The desecration was undeniable, but to an increasing number of the country's rulers, and of the ruled, Catholic icons were the emblems of an alien and dangerous creed. For a time in the 1570s, the British Crown was sorely threatened by Scotland, France and Spain, all professing some allegiance to Rome. A vast quantity of furnishing was destroyed in the Reformation, including all roods, but enough survived to require a second burst of iconoclasm a century later under Cromwell. Even then, the greatest loss of medieval glass was probably due not to iconoclasm but to 18th- and 19th-century neglect, witness the experience of Cirencester (Gloucs). As I hope this book testifies, much medieval church art is with us still, if we know where to find it.

With this in mind, I see the Reformation more positively, as a political as well as a religious movement that pre-empted later upheaval. It forged a Church of England that survives to this day. England's medieval churches avoided the greater catastrophes suffered by Continental churches during the political revolutions of 18th- and 19th-century Europe. In the 1820s and 1830s it was the Low Countries and France that were looted for fittings to fill the churches of England, not the other way round. Nor is it the case that, after the events of the 1530s, all art in churches withered. It took to new forms and purposes. Craftsmen continued to be imported from the Continent, especially from Flanders and the Netherlands. What changed was the purpose of their commissions, from religious to secular, from decorating altars, roods and chantries to refurnishing the naves and adorning the memorials of the Elizabethan and Jacobean rich.

If I seem over-enthusiastic about such memorials, as about tombs in general, it is because they remain the outstanding works of art in English churches. They survive to an extent unknown elsewhere in Europe. Unlike religious carving, medieval tombs mostly escaped iconoclasm and the custom for this form of memorial continued undiminished by the Reformation. Nothing indicates the continuity of English society as much as the respect shown for family monuments: Elizabeth I expressly forbade their destruction. Nothing indicates the discontinuity of English art so much as the changing styles in which these monuments were executed. At the time of the Reformation, they were moving from Gothic to classical. This change can be seen on dazzling display in churches such as Framlingham (Suffolk), Bottesford (Leics) and Great Brington (Northants). Talents that might once have adorned roods and altars now celebrated members of the Howard, Manners and Spencer families. At Elstow (Beds), the new manorial owners replaced the reredos with a modest carving of themselves.

This was the age of preaching and thus of the furnishings. Listening congregations needed to be comfortable. Churches stripped of their altars were filled instead with the sound of carpentry. This reached a crescendo in the first third of the 17th century, when almost every church was given a new Jacobean pulpit, lectern and set of pews, often charging 'pew rents' like season tickets. Some also received decorative screens that rivalled those of the 15th century, notably at Croscombe (Somerset) and St John, Leeds (Yorks, W). The brief Anglo-Catholic revival under Archbishop Laud in the 1630s saw altars restored and surrounded with protective rails. Laud's follower, Bishop Cosin of Durham, inspired a flourish of 'Gothic-Baroque' furnishings in the north-east, as at Sedgefield (Durham). In London, where the Great Fire wiped out two-thirds of the medieval churches, the replacements were sumptuous in both architecture and fittings. So too were the churches built under Queen Anne's Act for the building of new churches of 1711 (*see* page 463).

The English church in the Hanoverian era was less distinguished. Rarely did Georgian magnates extend to their churches the magnificence displayed in their houses. But at Great Witley (Worcs) and Euston (Suffolk), estate churches were built to be worthy of their settings. The 18th century was also unsurpassed for monuments. Rich families throughout England summoned Rysbrack, Roubiliac, Scheemakers and others to form what is a collective national treasure-house of sculpture. Even modest churches such as St Mary, Knebworth (Herts), Babraham (Cambs) and Bletchingley (Surrey) contain statues of a quality that would merit display in any national gallery. In the early 19th century a new generation of patrons filled their churches with fittings from ravaged Continental monasteries. Cockayne Hatley (Beds) and Gatton (Surrey) are spectacular ecclesiastical antique shops.

The Georgian period was one of dwindling congregations and little need for new building. Faced with the challenge of Nonconformity, especially Methodism, the Church of England turned the 19th century defeatist and corrupt. Visitors recorded collapsed roofs, chancels open to the sky and absent or incompetent vicars. The Reformation may have reassured the rich that they need no longer fear damnation, and thus relieved them of considerable expense to the Church's benefit. But three centuries on, the stock of Anglican buildings, almost all medieval, was in no state to meet the Industrial Revolution and the population explosion of 19th-century England.

THE VICTORIANS AND AFTER

The Church of England at the dawn of the Victorian age was as in need of 'reformation' as its Tudor predecessor. It was a Church frightened by revolution in Europe and political reform at home, and frightened also by the awesome growth of cities, to which a pre-industrial parochial church seemed to have no response. It met the challenge. Already in 1818 an Act had been passed by parliament to provide new churches at public expense. This produced a number of 'Waterloo' churches, mostly in a tedious classical style. But the start of the Victorian Anglican revival came in 1833, when John Keble preached a sermon in Oxford that was not so much reformist as counter-reformist. Calling on the Church of England to resist pressure to liberalise its liturgy and secularise its government after the 1832 Reform Act, Keble demanded a return to the rituals of the medieval Church. In collaboration with Edward Pusey and

John Newman, he wrote a series of tracts advocating strict observance of the Anglo-Catholic liturgy and a national campaign to propagate it. The Oxford Movement, often referred to as 'Tractarian', did more than defeat the reformers. Coinciding with the writings and architecture of the Roman Catholic A. W. N. Pugin, it signalled a new burst of Gothic church restoration and building. The energy released by the Movement was astonishing, sending a gale of change through Anglican liturgy and church-building. Cambridge reacted to Oxford's initiative by taking up the same cause. The Cambridge Camden Society and its *Ecclesiologist* magazine became arbiters of church design.

The Oxford Movement galvanised the landed gentry, as if eager to grasp at any weapon to repel the encircling Methodists and Baptists. Money was suddenly available for church restoration. No less important, younger sons were sent to Oxford and Cambridge to take holy orders. Some were quite unsuited to them, like the hero of Trollope's *Framley Parsonage*. They were expected to take their Anglican vocation seriously and attend their parishes. Many devoted the same lifetime's evangelism to this task as their brothers were to devote to the burdens of empire. The eccentric poet Robert Hawker dedicated himself to the people of the isolated smuggling village of Morwenstow (Cornwall). Vernon Musgrave of Hascombe (Surrey) built a new church and filled it with wall paintings in the medieval style, as did Gambier Parry at Highnam (Gloucs). The aristocracy followed suit, employing architects as original in their day as any in Europe. The Marquess of Ripon commissioned William Burges to build Studley Royal (Yorks, N) and the Duke of Newcastle summoned G. F. Bodley for his mini-cathedral at Clumber (Notts). Hardly a county in England is without its magnificent Victorian church, buildings which deserve to rank among the masterpieces of English architecture.

Where the new patrons did not build they restored. As the century progressed, almost every church was besieged by eager patrons and no less eager architects. Ancient plaster was scraped from damp walls and 17th- and 18th-century furnishings, galleries and box pews torn out. The architect's preferred style, initially Perpendicular or Early Gothic, but later a more eclectic and Continental variety, was introduced. Tracery and carvings were retooled. Wood was mass-produced. Tiles and central-heating ducts replaced old flagstones. Many of the restored churches lost the patina of age and took on the atmosphere of modern civic institutions. The result can seem deadening to the modern eye. To enter an old church and find the hard-edged stone-work, machined windows and heavy woodwork of a Victorian restoration is to experience a swift loss of enthusiasm.

In fairness we can only guess at the ruins which confronted the restorers. Many churches had barely been touched for three centuries. By the mid-19th century, an English parish church was synonymous with tumbledown decay.

When J. L. Pearson arrived at Stow (Lincs) in 1865, he had to excavate a pile of rubble to find anything of the chancel to restore. He guessed the appearance of the great Norman church from fragments. Small wonder that with so much to be done, bad design mingled with good. But some Victorian restoration was excellent. At Brant Broughton (Lincs) the local vicar, aided by Bodley, devoted his life to returning the aura of medieval worship to his church; the result is a brilliant marriage of ancient and (relatively) modern.

Not until the foundation by William Morris and friends of the Society for the Protection of Ancient Buildings was serious attention given to protecting the fabric of medieval churches rather than merely re-creating their style. When Morris protested at the wrecking of Burford (Oxon), the vicar threw him out with the cry, 'The church, sir, is mine and I shall stand on my head in it if I choose.' But by the last quarter of the century, a new respect for the past came from architects themselves, such as Bodley, the Sedding family and F. C. Eden. The Seddings sensitively restored churches in the West Country in the Anglo-Catholic tradition. Some, such as Blisland (Cornwall), come as close as any English church to re-creating a sense of pre-Reformation colour and busyness, with crowded altars, chapels and screens.

The work of these men lived on into the 20th century, exemplified by Ninian Comper and in churches inspired by the Arts and Crafts Movement. These include E. S. Prior's Roker (Durham) and Sedding's Holy Trinity, Sloane Street (London). Comper's masterpiece in Wellingborough (Northants) is a giant of Perpendicular architecture. Roughly two dozen of the churches in this book date from the 20th century, though few from its second half. Most modern churches are in cities, usually inaccessible and lacking the appeal of ancient foundations. As Comper wrote in 1947 at the end of his life: 'The note of a church should not be that of novelty but of eternity ... Knowledge of tradition is the first requisite for the creation of atmosphere in a church.' Lest this seem prejudice on my part, I include the vigorous new church of St Paul, Harringay, in North London. It is a work of great beauty as well as novelty, yet not without intimations of eternity. It stands in direct line of descent from that little chapel at Culbone.

THE PRESENT AND FUTURE

Preparing this list has been a personal odyssey through the landscape of England. Old churches have survived best by being in parts of the country least affected by industry or suburbanisation. I like to think that any reader who contrives to visit all thousand churches in this book will have been guided to the loveliest corners of England. Nor are these always at the extremities. Some of the most remote churches are on the marshes of Essex and the coast of Dorset, in Norfolk's Breckland and the Sussex Downs. They are the more precious for being relatively accessible.

Such loveliness is ever more rare. Many superb churches are now swamped by suburban development which, with the virtual collapse of rural planning in the last quarter of the 20th century, has accelerated across England. I have struggled to restrict references to this sprawl, far worse than the notorious 'ribbon development' of the years between the two world wars, but sometimes anger gets the better of me. The march of the out-of-town estate and its ugly sister, the bypass hypermarket, spells ruin for towns as much as for the country-side, sucking economic activity from urban centres and leaving behind derelic-tion and poverty. This will be regretted not only by those nostalgic for the vitality of country towns and for the seclusion of country areas, but even by those suburbanites who were promised a rural idyll and find themselves only in a bleak 'out-of-town'. To stand in the churchyard of Willen (Bucks) and gaze out over the grid plan of Milton Keynes is to feel the chill of a ghastly mistake. There must be a better way.

The debates that divide the world of church conservationists are no easier to resolve. English churches, especially medieval ones, are far removed in appear-ance from their pre-Reformation state. Most were stripped in the 16th century, refurnished in the 17th and 18th centuries, and drastically restored in the 19th. They have been subject to constant change, each reflecting the taste and opinion of the age. Modern conservation, especially of the finer churches on my list, has veered against any further change. This has impeded any alterations to fabric and fittings, and insisted on minimal alteration to newly discovered relics of the past such as wall paintings.

My sympathies flow back and forth. The Church of England has done dread-ful things to what is the most precious stock of medieval architecture in Europe. Some alterations had to be stopped. But a church is primarily a theatre for its liturgy, which appears to be in constant flux. In addition, some churches are depressingly bare. Many have benefited greatly from modern refurnishing, such as Clifton (Notts) or Rotherham (Yorks, S). In my opinion greater freedom could be shown in such innovation. Churches whose walls were scraped down to bare stone by the Victorians would be much improved by the reinstatement of their plaster. They would also seem less like archaeological sites if meaning-less fragments of wall painting were not left stranded like flotsam in a sea of whitewash. A wall should have some visual integrity. If wall paintings are wanted, let us paint new ones, as the Victorians did so splendidly in the recently restored Garton-on-the-Wolds (Yorks, ER).

A related ambition should be to reinstate the statuary for which Gothic churches offered a rich platform. Whether reproduction or modern is no matter.

Empty niches, inside and outside a church, are as much an offence to the eye as to architecture. They look like paintings from which the faces have been removed, a triumph of archaeology over aesthetics. A campaign to 'fill the niches' is overdue. Nothing so demonstrates the Church of England's loss of self-confidence as its inability to encourage modern church art. However, this stricture does not apply to two ecclesiastical art forms which are at present alive and well, embroidery and calligraphy. The kneeler and the memorial slab shine out among the contents of churches as the 20th century at its best. Perhaps this is because both artefacts require skills that remain rooted in local craftsmanship.

A more complex challenge is stained glass. Ask people who seldom visit churches for the word that most characterises them today and they reply, gloom. Early medieval churches were dark, the only daylight coming from small window openings, themselves often thick with glass. This lent them an enclosure that suited the mysteries of the Mass. The Reformation swept away this mystery, bringing the English church into the light of day. The reredos at Shorthampton (Oxon) is formed, says the guide proudly, of 'the sky, the trees and the good earth outside'. Victorian restorers and those of the 20th century turned their backs on daylight, reinstating dark stained glass. This sometimes worked as an artistic programme, for instance the many installations of the Morris partnership for G. F. Bodley and his contemporaries. More often the insertions were piecemeal, insipid and dour. Most such glass should be removed and stored, for a future generation to reconsider.

Beyond such controversies of style, the Church of England's predicament is more serious. It is how to sustain a vast inheritance of buildings on the back of falling membership. A glimmer of hope has been offered by the availability of public funds for church restoration. This, together with valiant fights against redundancy by individual parishes, means that almost all the churches in this book are in good repair. Even those declared 'redundant' have a friend in the admirable Churches Conservation Trust, which keeps them consecrated, in repair and accessible even if unused. Losses – such as the burning of Brancepeth in Durham in 1998 – are mercifully rare. But money is not enough. Church conservation must appeal to a wider community than that of the Anglican faith, to people who will appreciate churches not as religious institutions alone, but as fine buildings and galleries of arts and crafts.

Because of this I cannot believe that, in a hundred years' time, parish churches will still be in the sole custodianship of the Church of England. Unless it can find within itself some new Victorian revival, to rekindle enthusiasm for church buildings among the faithful, this Church must rely on the faithless to look after and keep open its places of worship. I envisage some new version of the pre-Reformation division, with the Church guarding the chancel and its places of formal worship, and the wider community taking responsibility for the nave and the remainder of the fabric. In taking such responsibility, the community would also be regaining what it scarcely knows it once enjoyed, both a centre of community life and a gallery of community art. It might also find an enhanced purpose for secular parish councils. There are churches which already engage that spirit, for instance Blakeney (Norfolk) and Tamworth (Staffs), but they are rare exceptions. It is to this new support for parish churches that this book is dedicated.

CONCLUSION

At the start of the introduction I called my thousand churches a Museum of England. It is a museum united by highways and byways, by the memories of enthusiasts and, I hope, by this book. Many people have asked me whether I, not a practising Christian, really see a church as no more than that, a museum building in which a few people choose to worship. Are these churches just so many historic buildings? Could I not sympathise with Eliot's poem 'Little Gidding': 'You are not here to verify, instruct yourself, inform curiosity or carry report. You are here to kneel where prayer has been valid'? Could I not understand Iveson Croome's cry, on his memorial in North Cerney (Gloucs): 'Lord I have loved the habitation of Thy house and the place where honour dwelleth'?

I would once have given a simple answer, no. I could not understand the meaning of these words. I could not see in a church that quality believers call holiness. I could respect and honour it, but not share it. Now at the end of my journey, my response is more muted. Late one summer, I found myself outside the little church of Up Marden, a place of delicious remoteness in the Sussex Downs. The evening was warm and the gloaming was rising from the valley beneath. Through a churchyard hung low with trees I could sense the air filling with the ghosts of villagers climbing up the hill to that tiny building. I sensed their coming for a thousand years. As they arrived, they hurled their hopes against those walls, wept on altars and filled rafters with their cries. That shed called a church had received their faith, and offered in return a humble consolation. Now mute in death, these people communicated to me as they did to Eliot, 'tongued with fire beyond the language of the living'. I could not be immune to the spirits of such a place.

I do not experience these spirits in theatres or assembly halls, or in churches that lack the patina of age or the imprint of the breeze of history. Yet I can find them in a wild hillside chapel or in the echoing aisle of a Gothic minster. I find them curled up amid the incense of a Victorian baptistery or sunning themselves on the carvings of a Tudor nave in summer. They do not force me to my knees but they whisper to me to tread softly, as they did Philip Larkin, bidding him to 'take off my cycle-clips in awkward reverence'. Such places have a quality all their own. They have Ruskin's sense of 'voicefulness, of stern watching, of mysterious sympathy . . . which we feel in walls that have long been washed by the passing waves of humanity'. If this is religious awe, so be it.

For me the experience is not of faith, but rather of the memory of faith present in an old building. In these churches England's ancestors sought explanation for the travails of life in the rituals of their tribe, as ordered by their anointed priesthood. Such explanation has been sought by every society since the dawn of time. It has been sought in religion, but also in the creations of religion, churches which are shrines to the memory of faith. It has been sought in religious art since art is the most refined form of memory. That is why beautiful objects have always belonged to the rituals of the Church.

I have long understood the essentially humanist faith that drove Dostoyevsky's Alyosha to gaze on the night sky and then fall to embrace the earth, without knowing 'why he longed so irresistibly to kiss it, to kiss it all'. Yet I could also understand the priest who might lead the weeping Alyosha quietly into a church and there show him the same security in an awareness of the past, in the relics of his forebears and in the comfort of familiar ritual. We can all thank God for these securities, whatever we may mean by Him and by them.

I see my churches as witness to the bonds that have brought the English people together in village and town through a thousand years of history. They are memory in stone, and as such echo the memorial lines first written in a Berkshire churchyard: 'At the going down of the sun and in the morning, / We will remember them.' It is through the churches of England that we learn who we were and thus who we are and might become. Lose that learning and we lose the collective memory that is the essence of human society. We must remember.

The Thousand Best

There are roughly 8,000 extant pre-Reformation churches in England and about the same number of Anglican churches built since then. There are countless places of worship of other denominations. My original shortlist, drawn mostly from secondary sources, was of 2,500. All of these I visited. My criterion was to list churches which I would regard as 'worth a detour' and worth the effort of gaining access, although the harder they were to enter, the higher standard I demanded of the interior. That the final list was roughly a thousand was a happy coincidence.

My principal definition was that a church be in some sense parochial. I have therefore excluded cathedrals and private and college chapels. I am aware that cathedrals are giants towering over most of my entries, but they have guides enough. Consistency, therefore, leads me to omit a number of former town churches that have been elevated to cathedral status, such as Portsmouth and Newcastle. Equally I have included monastic foundations which were not made cathedrals at the Reformation but were acquired by their towns. These include Beverley, Selby, Tewkesbury and Sherborne. They may seem like cathedrals, but they are parish churches like any other.

Roman Catholic churches are also parochial, but since almost all are post-Reformation only a few rank among the 'best'. The same applies to Non-conformist chapels, few of which are accessible. There are about twenty non-Anglican churches on the list, including two Quaker chapels. Excluded are churches now in secular use, but so-called redundant churches are included where they remain consecrated, notably those in the care of the Churches Conservation Trust, marked [CCT] in the text, or English Heritage [EH]. Lastly I have permitted myself a handful of entries which do not conform to these criteria but which I simply like too much to omit, such as Burghclere (Hants). I apologise to those which feel unjustly excluded as a result.

The ranking of churches from one to five stars is more controversial. My intention is to give visitors some idea of relative appeal. One and two stars indicate churches worth visiting for just a few features, and these are bound to be rather arbitrary. Three stars and above should embrace all the outstanding (and open) parish churches in England. The top hundred, with four or five stars (*see* page xxxi), either demand a long visit or include works that would feature in the entrance hall of my 'virtual' museum. They deserve to rank among the masterpieces of English art. Needless to say, these judgements are entirely my own.

The descriptions of churches are of what can be seen inside and outside, together with something of their history. This includes their surroundings and churchyards. I have discussed liturgical furnishings where this seemed appropriate. I have not discussed church bells or the contents of towers or vestries: most are invisible and some are precious. Nor do I mention easily movable furniture, for obvious reasons.

I have ordered the book by counties. English churches are still typified by county more than in any other way. The enthusiast will recognise a Somerset tower, Kentish tracery or Suffolk flushwork. English topography is divided into counties because they mark the Saxon boundaries of England. These patterns were reflected in the building materials and styles of early churches. Counties still delineate our sense of locality and defy all attempts by central authority to obliterate them, although not to alter their borders. Since new maps show the latest boundaries I have placed churches within those boundaries. This may not equate with older maps or guides, notably the Pevsner volumes and *Shell Guides*. Particular care is needed where the more drastic changes have occurred, in Yorkshire and the Thames valley.

As for disappearing counties, the following arbitrary rules have been followed, chiefly to accord with what I take to be custom and common sense. I have merged old Cumberland and Westmorland into the new Cumbria, but retained Huntingdonshire and Rutland as separate entities. In Yorkshire I have used the new four-part boundaries and names. The non-county City of York is appended to North Yorkshire and the non-county City of Bristol is appended to Gloucestershire. Middlesex has gone, and London is divided into the City of London, the City of Westminster and the rest of Greater London. This is as simple as I could make it.

A number of corrections have been made since the first edition. Churches live and change. Further corrections are welcome.

Access

Accessibility is the single most vexing topic among church enthusiasts. Nothing is more infuriating after a long drive or even longer walk than to feel the cold, unyielding iron of the handle of a locked door. This guide would be useless if readers did not feel its churches could be entered and enjoyed in person. I found roughly half my recommendations were open at reasonable times of the day and the year. Most of the rest had a key at an easily discoverable location. Of those that were locked, most indicated the location of the key, though not always the presence of the keyholder. As a general rule I set myself a limit of half an hour to gain entry, with the aid of the latest siege equipment, usually including a car, a mobile phone and a copy of *Crockford's Clerical Directory*. If a church resisted even such assault, I have left it out. In particular, a church that demands prior written notice of a visit, as if it were a private house, is in my book 'not open to the public'.

On this subject the Church of England is institutionally unsympathetic. Almost no church has a sign outside giving opening hours, which might at least pre-empt a fruitless walk to the door. Vicarage phone numbers, if they are publicised, are frequently on answering machines. Notices giving the address of the keyholder, when they exist, are often illegible and lack a map. I know of no diocese that publishes a list of opening times and keyholders' addresses, even those, such as Lincoln, that produce admirable guides to their churches. (The Open Churches Trust does publish opening times in London.) The buildings in this book are all outstanding and eagerly sought by a growing band of enthusiasts. None should be inaccessible.

The customary excuse for locking a church is the threat of vandalism and the cost of insurance. Vandalism can be most distressing for those victimised. Fortification may be justified in a few inner city churches, though even they capitulate to vandalism far too easily. Most insurers do not insist on churches being locked, only on their being periodically supervised. In my experience, the chief difference between an accessible and a shut church is not its location or the value of its contents but the attitude of the vicar and churchwardens. Some are true enthusiasts who rightly regard the opening of their church as a pastoral and community obligation. To them and their frequent welcome, I offer heartfelt thanks. To a minority of vicars, sadly a substantial one, I and therefore the general public was a nuisance to be kept at bay.

To close a church is not to forestall trouble – closed churches are almost as vulnerable as open ones – but to let the vandal win. Churches have been 'robbed' throughout history: this was once a common reason for deportation to Australia. Rural England is nowadays wealthy enough to afford a keyholder or 'dropper-in', or at least the elementary courtesy of clearly displayed instructions on access. One effective defence, security cameras, is not expensive. But no security is as effective as a regular flow of welcomed visitors. A parish church is a church open to all. A church shut except for services is the private meeting house of a sect.

In return, I believe that visitors should pay. Nobody should visit and enjoy a church without contributing to the cost of that enjoyment. I cannot see why popular churches should not charge something for entry, as most cathedrals now do. The only churches in this list that charge are Stratford-upon-Avon for its chancel, and (half-heartedly) the magic shrine of St Clether's Well (Cornwall), where a faded 1913 notice still requests threepence to be left on the altar. Churches used to be less shy about asking for donations. As for how much to leave, I can only cite the chapel at Swell (Somerset). Even before the days of inflation and decimalisation, it exhorted visitors:

> *If aught thou hast to give or lend,*
> *This ancient parish church befriend.*
> *If poor but still in spirit willing*
> *Out with thy purse and give a shilling,*
> *But if its depths should be profound*
> *Think of God and give a pound.*

Sources

Three ghosts inhabit all English churches. They linger in every arcade, peep from every gallery and flit across every monument. They are those of John Betjeman, Alec Clifton-Taylor and Nikolaus Pevsner. No visitor is without their companionship. Betjeman's affection, expressed in the introduction to his *English Parish Churches* (Collins, 1958 and revisions), arose from a deep piety. To him a church was touched by the hand of God and blessed as a place of private worship. In my youth, he guided my eye and taught me that a great Gothic church should, by the sheer power of its oratory, 'force us to our knees in prayer'. Clifton-Taylor's enthusiasm was quite different, that of a lover of architecture, topography and geology. His eye was more prosaic, but his critical faculties no less keen. His love of 17th-century fittings was equalled by a loathing for most Victorian glass. His *English Parish Churches as Works of Art* (Batsford, 1974) remains the best general book on church appreciation. Over both Betjeman and Clifton-Taylor towers the magisterial Pevsner. His *Buildings of England* series (Penguin, 1951–74) is the principal source for any book on English churches. The series is being updated and the earlier volumes are less extensive and reliable than the revised ones. Pevsner was a stern recorder and his books are works of description rather than enthusiasm. But he is indispensable.

Next in line are church guide books. These are variable and tend to rely on Pevsner and local gossip. The best are superb, with the advantage of parish historians able to include most recent research. The great churches, such as Ludlow (Salop) and St Mary Redcliffe, Bristol, are the subject of books themselves. My prize for the best amateur guide goes to Navenby (Lincs), and for honesty to Greensted (Essex), for an insert confessing that recent tree-ring scholarship has lopped two centuries off its date. Of the national church guides, Robert Harbison's *Shell Guide to English Parish Churches* (André Deutsch, 1992) is the most idiosyncratic, Betjeman's *Guide to English Parish Churches* (HarperCollins 1958, revised 1993) the most exhaustive and Laurence Jones's *The Beauty of English Churches* (Constable, 1978) the most meticulous catalogue of church features. County guides to churches are too numerous to mention.

Of specialist books, those devoted to architectural periods tend to be available only in libraries, including John Harvey on Perpendicular Gothic, Nicola Coldstream on Decorated and Terry Friedman on the 18th-century church, supplementing Marcus Whiffen on the same topic. Maisie Anderson's

History and Imagery in English Parish Churches (Murray, 1971) is a delightful handbook to the old and the mysterious. John Martin Robinson's *Treasures of English Churches* (Sinclair Stevenson, 1995) pictures the many works of art buried in these buildings. Stephen Friar's encyclopaedia *A Companion to the English Parish Church* (Sutton, 1996) is impossible to fault. The best survey of Victorian churches is the Faber Guide (1989) of that name. Richard Morris's intriguing *Churches in the Landscape* (Dent, 1989) traces their geographical and topographical settings. Eamon Duffy's *The Stripping of the Altars* (Yale, 1992) gives a partisan but fascinating account of the Reformation.

I can only hope to have found a small gap on this crowded shelf.

The Top Hundred

FIVE STARS

Devon
Ottery St Mary

Dorset
Christchurch
Sherborne

Gloucestershire
Bristol, St Mary Redcliffe
Cirencester
Fairford
Tewkesbury, Abbey

Lincolnshire
Boston
Grantham

Norfolk
Walpole St Peter

Oxfordshire
Burford

Shropshire
Ludlow

Staffordshire
Cheadle

Suffolk
Long Melford

Warwickshire
Warwick

Yorkshire,
East Riding of
Beverley, The Minster
Patrington

Yorkshire, North
Selby

FOUR STARS

Berkshire
Langley Marish

Buckinghamshire
Hillesden
Wing

Cheshire
Nantwich

Cornwall
Launceston
St Neot

Cumbria
Cartmel
Wreay

Derbyshire
Ashbourne
Melbourne

Devon
Crediton
Cullompton

Dorset
Bournemouth, St Peter
Bournemouth, St Stephen
Milton Abbey
Wimborne Minster

Essex
Copford
Thaxted
Waltham Abbey

Gloucestershire
Bristol, The Lord Mayor's
    Chapel
Chipping Campden
Deerhurst
Highnam
Northleach

Hampshire
Romsey
Winchester, St Cross

Herefordshire
Abbey Dore
Kilpeck
Ledbury
Leominster
Shobdon

Huntingdonshire
Barnack
Castor

Kent
Barfreston
Stone (nr Dartford)

Lancashire
Liverpool, St Agnes

Lincolnshire
Brant Broughton
Heckington
Louth
Stow

London: The City
St Mary Woolnoth
St Stephen Walbrook

*London: The City of
    Westminster*
All Saints, Margaret Street
St Augustine, Kilburn
St Mary-le-Strand

*London:
    Greater London*
Chelsea, Spitalfields

Norfolk
King's Lynn, St Margaret
Norwich, St Peter
    Mancroft
Salle

Northamptonshire
Lowick
Stanford on Avon
Wellingborough

Northumberland
Hexham

Nottinghamshire
Clumber
Newark-on-Trent

Oxfordshire
Bloxham
Dorchester

Shropshire
Shrewsbury, St Mary

Somerset
Bath
Crewkerne
Dunster
Isle Abbotts

Staffordshire
Hoar Cross

Suffolk
Framlingham
Kedington
Lavenham
Mildenhall
Southwold

Sussex
Brighton, St Michael

Warwickshire
Stratford-upon-Avon

Wiltshire
Devizes
Edington
Malmesbury

Worcestershire
Great Malvern
Great Witley
Pershore

*Yorkshire,
    East Riding of*
Beverley, St Mary

Yorkshire, North
Bolton Abbey
Lastingham
Studley Royal
Whitby

Victorian and Later

Churches built since *c*.1830 with principal architect(s)

Bedfordshire		*Essex*	
Woburn	H. Clutton	Great Warley	C. Harrison Townsend
Berkshire			
Wickham	B. Ferrey	*Gloucestershire*	
		Daylesford	J. L. Pearson
Cambridgeshire		Highnam	H. Woodyer
Cambridge, All Saints	G. F. Bodley	Selsley	G. F. Bodley
Cheshire		*Hampshire*	
Stockport, St George	H. J. Austin	Cosham	N. Comper
		Lyndhurst	W. White
Cumbria			
Bampton	P. Webb	*Herefordshire*	
Wreay	S. Losh	Brockhampton	W. R. Lethaby
Derbyshire		Hoarwithy	J. P. Seddon
Derby, St Mary	A. W. N. Pugin		
		Hertfordshire	
		Ayot St Peter	J. P. Seddon
Devon		Knebworth, St Martin	E. Lutyens
Babbington	W. Butterfield	Watford, Holy Rood	J. F. Bentley
Dorset		*Lancashire*	
Bournemouth, St Peter	G. E. Street	Barton-on-Irwell	E. W. Pugin
Bournemouth, St Stephen	J. L. Pearson	Liverpool, St Agnes	J. L. Pearson
Cattistock	G. G. Scott, Jn.	Liverpool, St John	G. F. Bodley
		Manchester, Holy	
Kingston	G. E. Street	Name of Jesus	J. A. Hansom
Poole, St Osmund	E. S. Prior		
Durham			
Roker, St Andrew	E. S. Prior		

London:
The City of Westminster

All Saints, Margaret Street	W. Butterfield
Immaculate Conception, Farm Street	J. J. Scoles
St Augustine, Kilburn	J. L. Pearson
St Cyprian, Clarence Gate	N. Comper
St James the Less, Pimlico	G. E. Street
St James, Spanish Place	E. Goldie
St Mary Magdalene, Paddington	G. E. Street

Greater London

Brompton Oratory	H. Gribble
Holy Trinity, Prince Consort Road	G. F. Bodley
Holy Trinity, Sloane Street	J. D. Sedding
St Augustine, Queen's Gate	W. Butterfield
St Cuthbert, Philbeach Gardens	H. Roumieu Gough
St Jude, Hampstead Garden Suburb	E. Lutyens
St Martin, Gospel Oak	E. B. Lamb
St Paul, Harringay	Inskip & Jenkins

Norfolk

Booton	W. Elwin
Glandford	Hicks & Charlewood

Northamptonshire

Wellingborough, St Mary	N. Comper

Nottinghamshire

Clumber	G. F. Bodley
Coddington	G. F. Bodley

Staffordshire

Cheadle	A. W. N. Pugin
Denstone	G. E. Street
Hoar Cross	G. F. Bodley

Surrey

Hascombe	H. Woodyer
Lower Kingswood	S. Barnsley

Sussex

Brighton, St Bartholomew	E. Scott
Brighton, St Michael	G. F. Bodley, W. Burges

Wiltshire

Wilton	T. H. Wyatt

Worcestershire

Dodford	Bromsgrove Guild

Yorkshire, East Riding of

Scorborough	J. L. Pearson
South Dalton	J. L. Pearson

Yorkshire, North

Scarborough, St Martin	G. F. Bodley
Skelton (nr Ripon)	W. Burges
Studley Royal	W. Burges

Yorkshire, South

Doncaster, St George	G. G. Scott

Yorkshire, West

Leeds, St Peter	D. Chantrell
Saltaire Congregational Church	H. F. Lockwood

Acknowledgements

This book was first suggested by Andrew Franklin, then of Penguin. If publishing is the act of inspiration and recognition, he deserves first credit. It was seen to press by Anna South, Andrew Barker and their colleagues at Penguin, to all of whom I owe many thanks. Clive Aslet, editor of *Country Life*, first unleashed shortened versions of the entries on to the public, accompanied by the photographs of Paul Barker, in my view the finest church portraitist there is. The entries, though all written by myself, rest on two pillars. Valerie Scott researched and corrected those facts susceptible to checking. She saved me from many solecisms, kept me to the path of historical rigour and prepared the glossary. Jenny Dereham's text editing went far beyond the call of duty, embracing visits to many of the churches mentioned. I deeply appreciate the commitment they both brought to the task, rooted in their own love of English churches. Such was their professionalism that I hesitate to add the customary disclaimer, that all errors are entirely my responsibility, true though that is.

Friends at the Pevsner guides office, led by Bridget Cherry, were generous with their suggestions, as were the Churches Conservation Trust and innumerable correspondents, most prolific in East Anglia, Somerset and Gloucestershire. Of those who helped with shortlists I must pick out Michael Gillingham and the late James Lees-Milne. Patrick Garland wins the prize for best entry hitherto unknown to me, Didling (Sussex). A host of enthusiasts joined me on the sometimes lonely, always frenetic round of visits. I cannot thank them all individually, but particularly salute the adventurous spirits of Celina Fox, Tom Jenkins, Camilla Cavendish, Christopher Booker, Nicky Lusty, Richard Ryder and my wife Gayle Hunnicutt. Of the many clergymen who were approached for access or advice, I set aside those who locked me out of buildings that should be open to all. Instead I thank the hundreds whose devotion to the churches in their care continues to stand between salvation and disaster for the finest collective monument to the story of the English people.

Glossary

ambulatory: aisle surrounding the chancel on three sides.

anchorite: hermit of extreme holiness licensed to be walled up in a cell attached to a church chancel until dead.

Anglo-Catholic: Victorian High Church movement within Anglicanism but stressing the Church of England's Catholic continuity. *See* **Oxford Movement**

apse: semi-circular east end of the chancel, typically Norman.

Arts and Crafts: artistic movement, *c.*1870–1914, initiated by writings of John Ruskin and William Morris, in response to industrialisation and mass production. Initially inspired by Gothic and 'Pre-Raphaelite' designs, it evolved into the British manifestation of the European Art Nouveau style.

aumbry: cupboard, usually in chancel, to hold sacred vessels.

baldacchino: freestanding canopy over altar, supported by columns. Also called ciborium.

ballflower: rich Decorated Gothic ornament of *c.*1300, formed of three petals enclosing a ball.

bay: architectural division, usually the width of a window or arch.

beakheads: feature of Norman carving, a row of monstrous animal heads with beaks usually biting a roll-moulding.

bedesman: someone endowed to pray for the soul of the departed, sometimes depicted at the feet of a medieval effigy.

blind arcade: pattern of arches attached to a surface but with no openings. Sometimes called blank arcading.

boss: knob or projection, often richly carved, at the interesection of a roof vault rib.

broach: the triangular face whereby a square tower is converted into an octagonal spire.

Camden Society: *see* **Oxford Movement**

capital: the top of a column or pier below the entablature, its carving typically indicating its style and date. The commonest medieval capitals were cushion, scallop or trumpet, water-leaf, stiff-leaf, moulded (*see* illustration).

celure: bay of roof in front of the altar or rood, often painted to depict the sky over the Crucifixion.

chamfer: surface of arch formed by cutting off the square edge, typical of Early Gothic building.

chancel: east arm of a church reserved for the clergy, usually containing the choir, sanctuary and main altar.

chantry: medieval endowment for celebration of Masses for the soul of the founder, usually part of an aisle or small chapel. Suppressed after the Reformation in 1547.

ciborium: *see* baldacchino

clerestory: top storey of windows to lighten the nave (sometimes also transpets and chancel), commonly inserted in the Perpendicular period.

college, collegiate: complete church or part of church, with priests or canons to say Masses for soul of founder, or for educational or charitable role. Canons might be laymen. Before the Reformation, 'colleges' were thus different from parish churches, although they might include parochial naves or aisles.

corbel: stone bracket, often carved with angels or human heads. A series of such brackets round the external eaves of a Norman or Early Gothic church is a corbel-table.

'Cotswold' window: *see* woolgothic

crocket: decorative leafy knob on the outside of an arch, characteristic of 13th- and 14th-century Gothic design.

crossing: the central space, usually under an existing or former tower, of a cruciform church that has transepts as well as a chancel and nave.

Cushion

Scallop or Trumpet

Water-leaf

Stiff-leaf

Moulded

cruciform: church plan in the shape of a cross, with transepts and a central tower, typically Norman and Early Gothic. Central towers, being built over crossing spaces, often fell and were later replaced with western ones.

curvilinear: *see* tracery

cusp: a projecting point in Gothic tracery or arch. In Kent, the point was sometimes split, hence Kentish cusp.

dado: lower part of wall or screen, the latter often carrying paintings of saints.

Decorated: Gothic architecture and design of the period *c.*1250–1350, characterised by complex window tracery, naturalistic carving, ballflower and, later, ogee arches.

Dissenters: members of Non-conformist groups who refused to follow the

Church of England (or the Roman church) after the Reformation, such as Baptists, Unitarians, Congregationalists and Presbyterians.

dissolution of the monasteries: seminal act of the English Reformation, 1536 and 1539. Many monastic churches became parish churches.

Doom: painting of Last (or Day of) Judgement, often placed facing the nave above the chancel arch.

Early Gothic: often called Early English, the style dominant after the decline of Norman, c.1190–1250, characterised by the earliest pointed arches, lancet window with no tracery, stiff-leaf carving and shafts often of black Purbeck marble.

Easter sepulchre: recess usually in north wall of chancel where consecrated bread and wine were kept from Good Friday to Easter Sunday. Often richly carved with Easter scenes and central to Easter ritual.

entasis: slight bulging of a column or spire to give an appearance of added height.

flamboyant: *see* **tracery**

fleuron: decorative carved flower or leaf.

flushwork: flint used decoratively in conjunction with stone to form patterns on a wall exterior, typical of East Anglia.

gargoyle: waterspout on the eaves or tower of a church, often carved into fantastic human or animal shapes.

geometrical tracery: *see* **tracery**

Gothic: architectural style arriving from France in the late 12th century and initially typified by the pointed arch.

Gothic Revival: any use of Gothic after the arrival of classical forms in the 16th century, sometimes referred to as Gothic 'survival' in the early period. In the 18th century, the word is sometimes spelled Gothick. It became the dominant style of Victorian church building.

green man: enigmatic creature carved on fonts, capitals, arches and misericords, usually with foliage emerging from mouth, ears and even eyes. Much studied and debated, Green Men are assumed to be related to pre-Christian forest rituals, sometimes as symbols of evil, sometimes of fertility and rebirth. There are some Green Women but very few.

guild: religious society professing attachment to a saint or holy relic. Guilds evolved to become among the most powerful institutions in the medieval community. They embraced professional and trade groups, and endowed chantries, chapels and windows. Skill guilds were precursors of trade unions. The Palmers Guild was of those who could afford a pilgrimage to the Holy Land.

hatchment: diamond-shaped panel depicting the heraldry of a deceased person, corruption of 'achievement'.

hood mould: projected moulding above an opening to throw off water.

hunky punk: carved figure with no functional purpose on the exterior of a church tower, mostly in Somerset.

intersecting tracery: *see* **tracery**

ironstone: any stone whose staining indicates the prescence of iron traces.

lancet: Early Gothic window of a single light under a pointed arch with no tracery.

Laudian: church feature associated with the anti-Puritan Archbishop William Laud (d.1645), who sought under Charles I to restore aspects of the pre-Reformation liturgy, notably rails protecting the altar.

lierne: *see* **vault**

long-and-short work: self-explanatory feature of corners of Anglo-Saxon churches.

lucarne: small window opening in spire, usually decorative but perhaps to reduce wind resistance.

Middle Ages: period traditionally taken to begin with the Norman Conquest (1066) and end with either the Tudor victory at Bosworth (1485) or the start of the English Reformation (1534).

minster: Anglo-Saxon missionary community and church, origin of many great monasteries and cathedrals.

misericord: tiny shelf carved under a hinged choir-stall seat to support the occupant when standing. These were often elaborately carved, for some reason usually with secular rather than religious themes.

mullion: vertical stone divide between glass panes (or lights) of a window.

narthex: enclosed vestibule at west entrance of a church.

ogee: recumbent, S-shaped curve forming arches and gables in the late-Decorated period, probably originating in the Middle East. When thrust forward from the wall, the shape is a 'nodding ogee'.

Oxford Movement: High Church tendency founded by John Keble and others in 1833 advocating a return to the liturgy of the early Church of England and the architecture of the Middle Ages. Its followers were known as Tractarians and some as Anglo-Catholics. A similar movement in Cambridge founded the Camden Society and *The Ecclesiologist* magazine, devoted to church architecture and its relation to liturgy and dogma.

panel tracery: *see* **tracery**

panelling: almost any decorative pattern applied to a blank surface of stone or wood.

parclose screen: screen usually of decorative wood between a side chapel and other parts of a church.

parvise: room, usually for the occupation of a priest, above a porch.

patron: person holding the right to nominate a vicar to a church, who may be a bishop, nobleman, college, manorial lord or rector. The patron was normally responsible for the upkeep of the chancel, while the parishioners were responsible for the nave and tower.

Perpendicular: dominant style of Gothic architecture roughly from the Black Death to the Reformation, c.1350–1540, characterised by large windows with panel tracery, flattened arches and roof and tower battlements.

piers: usual term applied to columns or other supports dividing the nave or chancel of a church from its aisles.

piscina: small recess with basin and drain for washing holy vessels, usually in south wall of chancel but also found in chapels and chantries.

plate tracery: *see* **tracery**

poppyhead: carved top of a bench-end or choir stall. Nothing to do with poppies, possibly from French *poupée*, a doll, or Latin *puppis*, a ship's figurehead (or both).

Purbeck marble: not marble but stone from the Isle of Purbeck in Dorset celebrated for taking a glossy black stain, much used for Early Gothic shafts.

quarry: small panel of glass set into a window, usually monochrome or engraved and depicting a domestic scene.

rebus: a pictorial pun on a name, as in Kidlington (Oxon) depicted by a kid, fish and tun or barrel.

rector: the distinction between a rector and vicar is now purely historical. In the Middle Ages, the former was a patron or independent incumbent who received local tithes and was responsible for the chancel and rectory. A vicar was appointed by a monastic or other foundation and received lesser tithes. After the Reformation, many monastic livings were transferred to 'lay rectors' who appointed vicars to preach.

recusant: any person refusing to submit to the authority of the Established Church, usually a Roman Catholic but also a **Dissenter**, involving often severe penalties in the 16th and 17th centuries.

Reformation: in England, the separation of the official church from Roman Catholicism in the 1530s and the adoption of Protestant liturgy. *See* Introduction

reredos: painted or sculpted screen behind and above the altar.

reticulated tracery: *see* **tracery**

rib: *see* **vault**

roll-moulding: rounded moulding feature in Norman arches and doorways, sometimes bitten by a **beakhead**.

rood: Crucifixion group of Christ flanked by the Virgin and St John, usually carved, sometimes painted, above the screen dividing the nave from the chancel. All disappeared at the Reformation, but some were reinstated by the Victorians. The rood group was carried on a beam or more often on a complete screen. The latter normally carried a loft in which singers and musicians would perform the Easter Week rituals, and its base or **dado** was painted with saints.

sanctuary: part of the chancel round the altar, distinct from the choir and associated with the rituals of the Mass.

sedilia: group of (usually three) recessed seats in the south wall of the chancel, for the priest, deacon and sub-deacon who officiated in the High Mass, often richly decorated.

shaft: slender vertical column flanking a pier or window opening, characteristic of Early Gothic architecture.

sheela-na-gag: form of exterior carving, female and apparently obscene, believed to be associated with fertility.

spandrel: spaces between arches, roughly triangular in shape.

spire: *see* **steeple**

springer: the point at which an arch or rib departs from the vertical line of a wall or pier.

squint: an opening cut through an internal wall to enable priests at side altars to see the sanctuary and thus synchronise the ceremonies of the Mass.

steeple: vertical structure attached, or adjacent, to the nave and comprising the tower and often a tapering spire above it.

stiff-leaf: *see* **capital**

strapwork: flat decorative feature, like straps or ribbons, used to adorn early classical tombs and screens.

string course: a band of projecting stonework on a wall surface.

tester: flat canopy over a pulpit, also called a sounding board.

tierceron: *see* **vault**

tracery: stone ribs filling the upper parts of windows in Decorated and Perpendicular churches. Like pier capitals, they help fix the date and style of a church (*see* illustration). Blind tracery is the same when applied to walls or screens that have no openings. The customary sequence of tracery styles is, of the Decorated period, Plate (*a*), Geometrical (*b*), Y-tracery (*c*), Intersecting (*d*) and Reticulated (*e*), with the late Decorated tracery also referred to as curvilinear and flamboyant. Panel tracery (*f* and *g*) is that of the Perpendicular period.

(a)　　*(b)*　　*(c)*　　*(d)*　　*(e)*　　*(f)*　　*(g)*

Tractarian: *see* **Oxford Movement**

transepts: the arms projecting north and south from the crossing of a cruciform church.

Tree of Jesse: Christ's family tree, representing his descent from Jesse, father of King David. Most often depicted in windows.

trefoil: most common Gothic decorative form of three leaves, normally found in tracery. Likewise quatrefoil, cinquefoil, octofoil, etc.

triforium: middle tier in a three-tier church interior, with the nave arcade below and clerestory above, characteristic of Decorated period.

triple-decker pulpit: post-Reformation composition of pulpit, reading desk and clerk's desk, sometimes used even when only two components are present.

tympanum: space above a doorway or opening and below its arch. Tympanum partitions were often inserted over rood screens to carry paintings or, after the Reformation, texts and coats of arms.

vault: stone roof. Complete vaults are rare in parish churches, being usually confined to cathedrals, but they are found in porches, chapels and chancels. A barrel vault (also called a tunnel vault or, if ceiled, a wagon roof) comprises a simple semi-circular roof running the length of a nave or chancel. A rib is a projecting feature of a vault, sometimes structural and sometimes decorative. Tierceron ribs rise from supporting piers to the vault apex but do not cross other ribs. Lierne ribs join and cross other ribs and do not rise from piers. Fan ribs, typical of late-Perpendicular design, are self-explanatory, sometimes supporting decorative pendants in the middle of the vault. All these ribs give their names to vaults. Burial chambers are also sometimes called vaults.

vicar: *see* **rector**

wagon roof: *see* **vault**

water-leaf: *see* **capital**

weepers: small figures set round a medieval tomb chest representing grieving relatives, priests or even angels.

weeping chancel: custom of building a medieval chancel slightly north of the east–west axis, supposedly in imitation of Christ's head on the cross. A more prosaic explanation attributes such distortion to topography or some failure in the structure. A few chancels 'weep' to the south.

wildman: also referred to as a woodwose. Often found carved on fonts, arches, capitals and gargoyles and rooted in ancient folklore, wildmen are usually seen as evil devils of the forest. But, like **green men**, they seem also to have been symbols of fertility and rebirth.

'windblown' stiff-leaf: a self-explanatory variant of Early Gothic carving. *See* **capital**

woolgothic: term sometimes applied to the spectacular Perpendicular churches of the Cotswolds. A feature was a large 'Cotswold' window above the chancel arch, bringing extra light into the nave.

Y-tracery: *see* **tracery**

List of Illustrations

All photographs by Paul Barker from the Country Life *Archive*

Bedfordshire

Bedfordshire is not a glamorous county, yet there are surprising pleasures off its all-too-beaten tracks. The bigger towns are ruined, Luton spectacularly so, but the central greensand ridge is beautiful, with Woburn at its heart. Bedford retains some character in its centre and Leighton Buzzard some dignity, both thanks to the presence of fine churches. Dunstable's Norman priory church survives as a ghost of past greatness. Early Gothic enthusiasts visit the stiff-leaf carvings at Eaton Bray. But Bedfordshire's chief treasures are its eccentricities, the two 'antique shop' churches of Cockayne Hatley and Old Warden. Both were furnished by early 19th-century patrons who acquired art of outstanding quality looted from Continental churches during the Napoleonic Wars, notably medieval stained glass and woodwork.

Bedford *
Chalgrave *
Cockayne Hatley ***
Dunstable **
Eaton Bray **

Elstow **
Felmersham ***
Leighton Buzzard ***
Luton: St Mary **
Odell *

Old Warden **
Turvey **
Woburn *
Wymington **

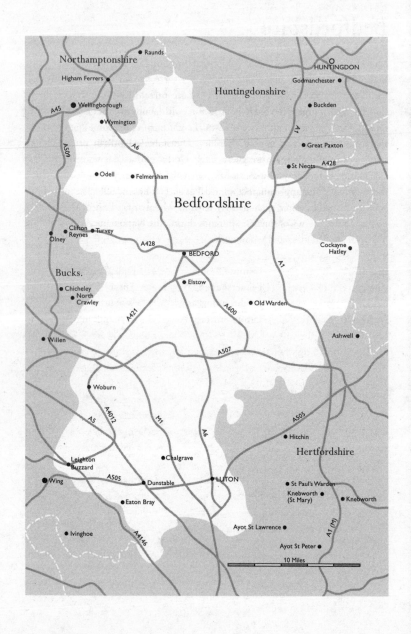

BEDFORD
St Paul *
Wesley pulpit, Bodley screen

Medieval Bedford boasted many fine churches; modern Bedford boasts hardly any. The area round St Paul's in the centre of the town struggles to uphold the old tradition in an otherwise dull town centre 'doughnutted' by modern development. Though the church exterior is of little interest, the interior is a fine monument to civic religion, with pews for the mayor, brasses of benefactors, regimental banners and memorials to local schools. St Paul's is a shrine to an old English borough at prayer.

The old entrance was by the south porch, with an Early Gothic arch. Here is the grave of the appropriately named Patience Johnson. She died in 1717 at the age of thirty-eight, giving birth to her twenty-fifth child. The present entrance is by the west front, into a modern narthex with engraved glass doors. The interior is enlivened by a Bodley chancel screen, brightly coloured and with a rood group above it. The church was refashioned in the 1880s with a new north aisle, its piers matching those opposite. Hence only the south arcade contains original piers. The entire north side of the church is Victorian, and gloomy Victorian at that.

Nineteenth century also but more accomplished is the chancel, incorporating fragments of medieval work. Some stalls and misericords are original, as is the ceiling, but the brightly painted angels with musical instruments are Victorian. The sanctuary is overseen by the genial aquiline features of Andrew Dennys, vicar in the time of James I.

The church's principal treasure, standing at the crossing, is the Wesley pulpit. Dating from 1680, it was used by Wesley when he preached his Assize Sermon in 1758. Methodism was, he would stress, not schismatic but a movement within the Anglican communion. The pulpit was ejected from the church in 1831 but returned in 1929.

The Trinity Chapel survives at the east end of the south aisle, built in the early 15th century for the Guilds of the Trinity and Corpus Christi. The brasses include those of such Bedford dignitaries as Sir William Harpur of 1573. He went on to become Lord Mayor of London and is portrayed in both armour and robes alongside his wife. The chapel was venue for the BBC's broadcast services during the Second World War.

CHALGRAVE
All Saints *
Wall paintings

The church lies in a circular, probably pre-Christian, enclosure in a field on the outskirts of Toddington near the M1. A copse of chestnuts guards flint chequerboard walls, a porch with a shrine alcove and a thick tower that has lost its top. When I visited it on a winter day with the trees coated in hoar frost, the place seemed enchanted.

Chalgrave boasts that its now vanished village was purchased from 'the heathen' Danes in 911, giving it the oldest written record of land transfer in England. The church was consecrated in 1219, and the manor was later the home of Sir Nigel Loring, knight in the Hundred Years War and Chamberlain to the Black Prince.

The interior is spacious and has excellent stiff-leaf capitals in the north arcade, similar to those at neighbouring Eaton Bray. Chalgrave's pride is its wall paintings of 'All Saints', the best in the county. They are faded, the clearest being the three apostles in the north aisle. A jolly St Martin divides his cloak with his sword over the south door while the customary St Christopher can barely be discerned over the north door.

In the spandrels of the nave arches are heraldic shields, including the arms of the Loring family. The church has two 14th-century effigies of knights, presumably Lorings, splendidly kitted out in chainmail. Lorings from across the world regularly return to Chalgrave to celebrate reunion with their ancestors in the church.

COCKAYNE HATLEY
St John ***
Continental woodwork and glass

This astonishing church lies lost in fields close to the Cambridgeshire border. The brown cobble exterior is of no significance. At the start of the 19th century, the building was all but derelict. Held since 1417 by the Cockayne family, it passed by marriage to the son of a Cambridgeshire grandee, one Henry Cockayne Cust. In 1806 he became both squire and rector of a property which, so he recorded, had snow falling through gaps in the roof on to the high altar.

Cust was both devout and a man of means. He set about a twenty-five-year campaign to put his new living on the antiquarian map. The existing structure was respected, original materials being used where possible. Wooden angels for the roof were brought from a church in Biggleswade. Memorials to Cockayne ancestors were rearranged and their brasses reset in the central aisle. The monument over the south door is to Sir Patrick Hume, Master of Hounds to James I and a distant relative of the Douglas-Home family. He married a Cockayne.

This might not be worth a detour, were it not for Cust's passion for collecting. No chancel in England quite compares with that at Cockayne Hatley, pre-eminent among the many being filled in the early years of the 19th century with the cast-offs of Continental churches and monasteries in the wake of Napoleon's armies. The invaders were followed by teams of antique dealers, with England their principal market. Neighbouring Old Warden, Gatton (Surrey) and Brougham Chapel (Cumbria) offer similar displays. Cust gathered medieval stained glass, screens, doors, anything that would add to the glory of his incumbency.

The principal acquisition was from a dealer in Charleroi in Belgium. This was the choir fittings of the Abbey of Oignies, wrecked during the Napoleonic invasion of Flanders. The stalls were fitted into the chancel and nave, and those to either side of the chancel arch bear the abbey arms and the date 1689. The backs of the stalls in the chancel are carved in high relief with busts of saints and popes. They include Aquinas and St Bernard with a chained devil. The images of post-Reformation popes must be unique in an Anglican parish church. The busts, apparently portraits, are surrounded by garlands and putti holding instruments. The work is heavier than contemporary 17th-century English carving. We might have stumbled on a papal conclave, banished to this wild Bedfordshire field for some unnamed collective crime.

In the nave the stalls are arranged in collegiate style, facing each other across the aisle. It is not clear where poorer parishioners can have sat during services. All the seats have misericords. Other acquisitions include the communion rail from Malines, depicting the harvesting of corn and grapes, and the gathering of water and manna. There is a west screen from Louvain. The organ pipes above are fakes set in a rococo frame.

The glass is the best in the county. The chancel windows inserted in 1829 are by Willement, an early-Victorian specialist in stained glass. His east window is designed round medieval fragments illustrating the life of Christ, also acquired by Cust. Old glass portraying St Peter appears in the west window. The finest glass is the 13th-century east window of the north aisle, brought from a demolished church in Yorkshire. It shows Saxon saints and kings. They are depicted in fresh primary colours under Gothic canopies, although some of the glass is later.

In the churchyard is the family tomb of the Henley family, friends of both Robert Louis Stevenson and J. M. Barrie. The one-legged poet, William Ernest Henley, was reputedly the original of Stevenson's Long John Silver. His daughter Margaret, who died aged five, was said by Barrie to have been the model for Wendy. The Henleys were not local. It was Cust's son Harry who had suggested to Henley that he and his daughter might like to be buried at Cockayne. The Custs even collected corpses.

DUNSTABLE
St Peter **
Norman west front, modern stained glass

The church sits awkward and alone on a suburban site where Roman Watling Street crosses the Icknield Way. The old priory and most of its church were demolished at the Dissolution. The nave survived, having been given to the town in 1392. All that remains of the priory buildings is a ghostly 15th-century gateway. It was at Dunstable that Cranmer decreed Henry VIII's marriage to Catherine of Aragon null and void. It can thus be regarded as witness to the start of the English Reformation.

The west front is the most evocative survival of the old priory church. It is asymmetrical, down-at-heel and intriguing. The doorway is late 12th-century Norman, its carvings severely eroded or bashed. The remainder of the front was built after 1222, when the west towers fell down and were not replaced. The present tower is 15th century, added after the nave had become a parish church.

Inside all is dark and uncertain in date. The lofty Norman nave is flanked by a Victorian north arcade, but the south arcade is original. Behind it is the old Norman south aisle, full of Romanesque shadows and gloomy Georgian monuments to Dunstable dignitaries. The whole church was upheaved in the 15th century when the top storey was removed and the old gallery glazed and turned into a clerestory. The north aisle was rebuilt and a wooden screen erected to the east. Its tracery has ogee arches and deep cusps, almost like thorns. A later, Tudor screen in the north arcade holds the arms of England and Castile. This is most rare and must date from Queen Mary's brief reign.

What might be an intolerably dark interior is enlivened by that rare thing, excellent modern glass. This is by John Hayward and was inserted in 1972. It is bold yet in keeping with the medieval atmosphere of the church. The west window portrays Henry I and Prior Bernard, founders of the monastery.

EATON BRAY
St Mary **
Stiff-leaf carving

Eaton Bray is celebrated among enthusiasts for Early Gothic carving, of which it offers a feast. The exterior, set in a dull suburban churchyard, is of little interest. It was rebuilt by Sir Reginald Bray in the 15th century after he won fame and the manor of Eaton for finding the crown of Richard III at Bosworth (whether or not in a thornbush) and placing it on Henry Tudor's head. Bray rebuilt the tower, chancel and nave roof, inserting a clerestory and replacing earlier windows with Perpendicular ones.

He wisely did not disturb Eaton's glory, the nave arcades. The south arcade is c.1220, with octagonal piers and leaves of a different design in each capital, wayward in style and still echoing Norman leaf carving. The north arcade is later, c.1240, and richer. Here clustered shafts rise to roll-moulded arches, curvaceous and feminine. Each capital is of the same design, the leaves deep-cut and swept sideways round the pier drum, known as 'windblown'. The two types of capital are reflected in the conical supports or responds, where the arches die into the walls. This is craftsmanship of outstanding quality, executed by carvers who stand comparison with Grinling Gibbons.

The font replicates the style of the north arcade and is again a work of a superb quality. The nave west wall is filled with a fine organ case and gallery rising its full height. This was installed between the two world wars and is like the bridge of a galleon. On either side are two long hooks, used for pulling the thatch from buildings when on fire. The hinges on the south door are of medieval craftsmanship, possibly by Thomas of Leighton, who designed similar scrollwork at Leighton Buzzard church.

ELSTOW
St Mary and St Helena **
Green Man carving, Bunyan memorials

An oasis of half-timbered houses and a village green survives in a desert of highway interchanges and industrial estates on the outskirts of Bedford. Here too are the remains of a Norman abbey church. Next door is a detached tower, in which the young John Bunyan rang the bells. He recalled being terrified that they would crash down on his head in punishment for his sins. The tower has been suggested as the original for Castle Beelzebub in *Pilgrim's Progress*, from which arrows were shot at arriving pilgrims.

The abbey was founded by a niece of William the Conqueror as a Benedictine nunnery. At its peak thirty nuns were in residence and by the Dissolution its laxity was notorious. One injunction ordered the nuns to stop eating with men in the buttery, and to wear gowns that closed in front 'and are not so deep voided at the breasts'. Elstow today is far more sedate. After the Dissolution it was briefly considered as a cathedral for Bedford, but passed instead to Sir Humphrey Radclyff. All but the nave was demolished and a new east wall built in c.1580, with three large Perpendicular windows. To this church the young Bunyan came as a boy, to be spellbound by the preaching of the vicar, Christopher Hall, who arrived in 1639 when Bunyan was eleven.

Elstow comprises a tall Norman nave with aisles, the height reflecting its monastic status. The two western bays are Early Gothic, with stiff-leaf capitals and lancet windows in the clerestory. On the east wall are sumptuous corbels, one a vigorous Green Man with foliage sprouting from his ears. In the centre of the wall, where one might expect a reredos, is an emphatic symbol of the Dissolution. The new owners, the Radclyffs, are depicted in a monument, kneeling above the altar at prayer.

Otherwise this is Bunyan's church. He is recalled in two Victorian windows in the south and north aisles. These portray the horrors (and rare delights) of *Pilgrim's Progress*. The north window shows *The Holy War*, with good and bad in rather obvious contention. A pious Bunyan is represented by a carving on the lectern.

FELMERSHAM
St Mary ***
Early Gothic west front

Felmersham church stands on a small bluff across the valley of the Ouse, magnificent for so small a village. It was here that the priors of Lenton in Nottinghamshire decided in 1220 to erect (or wholly rebuild) an outpost of their priory, treating nave and chancel with equal splendour. The 15th century added the tower, clerestory and embattlements, but most of the church is in its Early Gothic form, and as such is a Home Counties rarity.

The west front is Felmersham's pride, ornate for collegiate architecture that tended to concentrate on the chancel. It is three-tiered, with blind arcading topped by high, shafted windows. The only intrusion is Perpendicular mullions in the centre window. White doves flit in and out of the carved recesses. It is an exhilarating composition.

The interior is no less thrilling. Felmersham is cruciform and the view west from its crossing is of undulating waves of shafts and arches. The four bays of the nave alternate round and octagonal piers and are of unequal width. The corbels look as if they were carved by a medieval Epstein. The wooden angels are modern. The small transepts retain their Early Gothic windows and the arch to the chancel still has a 15th-century rood screen with original colouring.

The screen's central gable uses angels as crockets. Those who blame the Puritans for church iconoclasm should not lightly excuse the Victorians: they removed Felmersham's screen loft, which must have been as fine as the screen beneath. The chancel itself is empty and spare.

LEIGHTON BUZZARD
All Saints ***
Angel roof, Bodley reredos, Simnel graffiti

The buzzard is no bird but a Norman prebendary, Theobald de Busar. The brief postwar attempt to rename the town Leighton Linslade was unsuccessful. Leighton has avoided the rape and pillage that have wrecked Watford, Hemel Hempstead and Luton to the south. The church sits well behind a historic market place, the spire visible for miles around. Although the interior was gutted by fire in 1985, the walls and tower were saved and the restoration has been executed with panache.

The first impression of Leighton is of a bold Midlands church, with a rugged, battered and wizened exterior, dating from the late 13th century. The fine steeple is of 1290, the tower and ironstone belfry becoming octagonal before sending the spire shooting up into the sky. This has slight entasis to convey even greater height. The corner pinnacles were added in 1842.

The interior of Leighton, apart from the arcades, is all Perpendicular. Its East Anglian atmosphere is due to that ubiquitous 15th-century patron, Alice de la Pole, Duchess of Suffolk and enthusiast for all things angelic. The grand-daughter of Chaucer, she is buried in Ewelme (Oxon) where angels cover her tomb. The duchess paid for the insertion of new windows throughout the church, including the clerestory, and for the new roof. Most angel roofs have lost their statuary and their colour. At Leighton all has been restored, incorporating the fragments which survived the fire. The 18 corbels are each carved with an angel carrying an Instrument of the Passion. Above every second corbel and post is a large gilded angel projecting horizontally. Smaller angels flutter along the frieze. This decorative richness is repeated in the aisles, transepts and chancel, all restored by Joe Dawes.

The chancel is almost the same length as the nave, a nobly proportioned space much improved by the loss of Victorian glass in the fire. Bodley's lush reredos escaped the disaster and is of three alabaster panels, showing the Crucifixion, flanked by doors with angels on embossed leatherwork. The chancel stalls and misericords are original and probably came from St Albans. Here stands the earliest known eagle lectern in England, made of oak in the 13th century.

The crossing arches are adorned with intriguing graffiti. One is of a medi-eval window, perhaps drawn by a mason to instruct his staff. The other is of 'Simon and Nelly', a deep scratch-relief of two figures arguing over whether a Christmas pudding should be boiled or baked (hence 'Sim-Nel' cake). She grabs his ear and prepares to hit him with a spoon. Leighton was well-treated by Kempe's glassworks. The clerestory windows and large west window are of saints. The south transept contains a Kempe masterpiece, four archangels recently donated to the church by the glaziers Goddard & Gibbs to commemorate the fire. On the west door are 13th-century hinges by Thomas of Leighton. These are superb works of Early Gothic ironwork, their fantastic scrolls worthy of any rococo master.

LUTON
St Mary **
Baptistery, Barnard Chantry

The picture on the cover of the guidebook to Luton parish church is almost comical. The photographer contrives an angle that gives it a site in rural woodland. In reality, this fine Perpendicular church is set in some of the worst urban development that even the Home Counties have to offer, a horror of car parks, one-way systems and hostile shopping centres. Forget Slough, O friendly bombs, come to south Bedfordshire.

Though traces of earlier work abound, Luton is a conventional, large town church of the Perpendicular era, with tedious window tracery but attractive chequerboard exterior. The pattern, in stone and flint, is original on the tower and Victorian elsewhere. The interior is big, white and elegant, and a challenge to its surroundings. The two richest periods of English architecture, the 15th and 19th centuries, are in harmonious union. Of an earlier date are arches and stiff-leaf capitals in the north aisle, the Decorated tower window and arch with foliated capitals, and the extraordinary baptistery. The last stands free in the nave, a superb work of early 14th-century carving with an octagonal gabled canopy. The crockets on the gables are richly flamboyant. Painted white, they should be coloured and gilded.

Luton is filled with relics of a prosperous past. The chancel east window is Victorian Early Gothic, a lovely triplet of lancets above a mosaic of the Last Supper. On the south wall is a quartet of sedilia bearing the heraldry of a 15th-century abbot of St Albans. Next to it is a gem, the tiny Barnard Chantry of c.1490. This has a door, window, stone vault and piscina and must be the smallest chapel of its sort in England, with room for just one priest. The choir stalls outside are Victorian but reuse a set of superb 15th-century poppyheads. The corbel heads in the roof seem exceptionally rude.

In total contrast to the Barnard Chantry is the Wenlock Chapel, north of the chancel and guarded by a fine 16th-century screen. This was built, or rebuilt, in 1461 by Lord John Wenlock with an unusual double-arched stone screen dividing it from the chancel. The Perpendicular windows, tombs, statue niches and corbels are a magnificent evocation of late Gothic grandeur. The tomb of William Wenlock (d.1392), John's great-uncle, fills one of the dividing arches.

ODELL
All Saints *
Pulpit with hour glass

Odell church is set on a mound above a smartly turned-out commuter village. Its tower is clasped by corner buttresses that diminish as they rise past a frieze, to emerge as four pinnacles. The limestone is interspersed with ironstone in deference to neighbouring Northamptonshire. The church is entirely Perpendicular and unrestored, and charmingly atmospheric.

The interior is light with the nave dominant. The chancel retreats behind a chancel arch whose sweep matches the curve of the roof above. The box pews incorporate fragments of medieval panelling and the pews at the back of the nave appear to be original 15th-century seats. They face back and front and look most uncomfortable. The Jacobean pulpit has an hour-glass holder, acquired during the Commonwealth in 1654 when, according to Odell's historian, 'men preferred sound to sense and the length of a sermon was the criterion of its excellence'. Whether excellence lay in brevity or prolixity is not clear. Old flagstones litter the floor.

The story of this simple Midlands church includes one incumbent who must have been typical of many in these parts in the 17th century. Peter Bulkeley (b.1582) succeeded his father as rector in 1623, but as a Puritan was soon at odds with the Laudian ascendancy. He was forced from the living and sold his estate, emigrating with his family to America. Bulkeley went on to help found and be minister of the colony of Concord in Massachusetts. Soon Laud was dead and the Odell pulpit was occupied by preachers who needed hour glasses to stop them preaching the Puritan word. Yet Bulkeley prospered. His son was the first graduate of Harvard in 1642. His grand-daughter was mother of Ralph Waldo Emerson.

OLD WARDEN
St Leonard **
Imported Flemish woodwork

We turn from the crawling traffic of the Biggleswade bypass, following signs for two miles to the Shuttleworth aircraft museum. At Old Walden beyond, a row of thatched cottages gives way to a church with a Trollopian name but wholly un-Trollopian contents. Here in 1841 Robert Henley, Lord Ongley, imitated Henry Cust at Cockayne Hatley and filled his church with Continental fittings. The resulting atmosphere is that of an Alpine chalet built into an Edwardian public school. Yet the fittings are mostly from the 16th and 17th centuries and are superb. Old Warden is redeemed from Pevsner's charge of oppressive stuffiness by the sheer quality of its contents.

Virtually every fitting is 'imported', including two magnificent family pews, one in the nave and one in the chancel. The vicarage pew in the chancel has a relief of the Last Supper, Belgian in origin. The Shuttleworth pew in the nave is surrounded by an acanthus scroll, again Belgian. The south nave pews are set longitudinally to face the pulpit and the front bench is topped by two enormous carved snakes, rippling along its entire length. All the benches have this ripple effect, a theme repeated high in the rafters of the nave roof. This roof in turn looks ready to spill bats and trolls out over the congregation below.

Round the altar, which is flanked by two high Gothic pinnacles, is further carving, including panels said to be from Anne of Cleves's house in Bruges. It carries the initials AC. More reliefs of the life of Christ adorn the pulpit. Indeed no corner seems untouched by the Ongley zest for European carpentry. Even the stairs to the south aisle gallery have what must be the most elaborate staircase brackets in any church in England.

Never are we allowed to forget the progenitor of all this. There are Ongley hatchments and statues commemorating the family's residence at Old Warden Park. Sir Samuel Ongley (d.1726) stands at the back of the nave, garbed as a Roman emperor and looking down on his collection. 'Free from pride and ostentation' reads the inscription. The work is by Scheemakers. High over the south-east angle to the nave is a fine baroque monument to Caroline Shuttleworth (d.1899), portrayed as Faith.

The most remarkable treasure in the church is the 14th-century window in the north aisle, reset from Warden Abbey. It shows the Cistercian abbot of the abbey in a white habit, with St Margaret holding a dragon on a leash. Both are in the most vivid colours. This is the only known depiction of an abbot of this order.

TURVEY

All Saints **

13th-century wall painting, Mordaunt tombs

Turvey is smart Beds, smart houses, smart pubs and smart church. The church is attended by handsome yew trees, wicket-gate, well-kept churchyard and a tower with confident pyramidical spire and cross. Under a high porch is door ironwork attributed to the 13th-century Thomas of Leighton, whose work also survives at Eaton Bray and Leighton Buzzard. He achieved in iron scrolls a similar curvaceousness to those of the Early Gothic masons in stone, their stiff-leaf embalming nature in art. Such work reminds us how close the craftsmen of the 13th century must have felt to woods, trees and flowers.

Turvey is an ancient foundation. High in the nave walls are old window openings, said by the guide to be variously Anglo-Danish or Romano-Saxon. They are earlier than the battered Norman font inside the main door. The principal relics of the medieval period are sculptural. In the south aisle Lady Chapel is a sedilia and piscina group with, next to it, a well-preserved 13th-century fresco of the Crucifixion. This was described on its discovery in the 1930s as 'the finest painting of its subject and time in the country'. Christ is in the Giotto-esque pose of sinuous agony (well before Giotto).

More static are the Mordaunt monuments. The earliest is in the south aisle and shows Sir John (d.1506) in armour with his wife Edith, carved in alabaster on a Purbeck base. The corners have strange twisted columns. Sir John's head rests on a helmet with a crest of 'a screaming man', though perhaps he is merely biting, *'un homme mordant'*. The monument to the 1st Lord Mordaunt (d.1560) between chancel and south chapel travels half a century from Henry VII to Elizabeth and to 16th-century classicism. It is a bold two-tier monument. The effigies rest on a sarcophagus set under a broad semi-circular arch and flanked by an impeccable Doric order. A more conventional tomb lies in the north aisle, to the 2nd Lord Mordaunt (d.1571). Here Doric columns support what might be an eight-poster bed. He is strangely elevated above his two wives lying either side of him. Most medieval and Jacobean tombs were egalitarian in this respect. The helmeted figure is now a smiling negro. Yet another tomb, to the 3rd Lord (d.1601), at the west end of the north aisle, has a bare-breasted woman in place of screaming men.

Turvey was restored and extended eastwards by George Gilbert Scott for the lord of the manor, Charles Longuet Higgins, in 1852. Scott's organ chamber must have delighted his client, who played the organ here on Sundays. It is given a three-bay Purbeck and stone arcade with gaily painted organ pipes looming over the choir. Turvey's guidebook has one of the best church plans I have seen.

WOBURN
St Mary *
Cathedral of Bedford estate

This ugly duckling sits beside the road away from the centre of Woburn, as if banished from the picturesque village. Its elongated gargoyles seem to be sticking out their tongues in retaliation. St Mary's looks the more odd for having lost its spire, taken down as unsafe in the 1890s. Yet the interior is a tour de force of money-no-object Gothic. It was designed in 1865 for the 8th Duke by the Bedford estate architect, Henry Clutton. He was a scholar of French Gothic, and here evokes an Île-de-France cathedral. The space is light and airy with slender piers, yet covered throughout by a stone vault which flows uninterrupted from nave to chancel. Illumination is generous, with large windows spilling sun on to a lofty interior.

The focus of the composition is the chancel, which rises above flights of steps in the manner propagated by Butterfield at All Saints, Margaret Street (London). The spectacular reredos was designed in the early years of the 20th century by Caröe and carved in Oberammergau in Germany. The delicate rose window above is by Kempe. More striking is the St Francis window in the south aisle, inserted in 1938 to commemorate the then Duchess of Bedford's love of the flora and fauna of the Woburn estate. The crypt under the chancel was intended to take the tombs of the Bedford family, but they maintained family tradition and continued to be buried in the mausoleum at their older seat of Chenies (Bucks).

WYMINGTON
St Lawrence **
Curvilinear windows, Curteys tomb

This delightful church appears to have strayed from over the Northamptonshire border yet found itself, as Betjeman put it, 'on a slightly tighter budget' than was normal in that luxuriant county. From the outside the church is small both for its site and for its decoration. The patron was a wool merchant, John Curteys, who built in the late 14th century but mostly still in the earlier Decorated style. This is immediately noticeable in the windows, which are square-headed yet have curvilinear Decorated tracery. Some are lily-patterned, some have pleasing teardrops beneath 'eyebrows'. The tower has a strange spire covered in crockets and small gabled openings. The battlements all seem too big for the walls beneath, like a child wearing its father's hat. The porch too is rich, with a Green Man boss and a priest's room above.

The interior is homely. Aisles run the length of the building to the east wall, their chapels thus embracing the chancel. The tomb of Curteys himself stands beneath an ogival arch in the south chancel arcade. He died in 1391 after achieving the lucrative and important office of Mayor of the Staple (or wool market) at Calais. He is shown in civilian costume, apt for a merchant. The church fittings are rich, in particular the piscina and sedilia group. The piscina has a nodding ogee arch peering forward from the wall, a motif repeated in the south chapel. Above the chancel arch is a Doom fresco, for which there is a spotlight.

Like much of Bedfordshire, Wymington is blessed in its woodwork. The vestry in the north aisle has an original screen. The pews have 'draw-out' seats along the side of the central aisle. The pulpit is Jacobean and the font Decorated, with a frieze of ogees beneath the rim and a tall wooden cover. Wymington is praised by Clifton-Taylor for its freedom from stained glass. Seen from outside at dusk and lit from within, it is a radiant and inviting place.

Berkshire

Berkshire has more character than its status as perpetual slip-road to the M4 might suggest. It embraces the valleys of the Thames and the Kennet, a country of chalk down and heavy clay, little populated until the coming of the railways. Even today it is less blighted by suburb than most of the Home Counties, despite boundary changes which have added Slough to its Maidenhead–Reading conurbation. For us, this is a county of small churches set in water meadows and apparently lost for a village, as at Avington, Bisham and East Shefford.

Boundary changes also lost to Oxfordshire the fine 'White Horse' churches that lie in the lee of the Berkshire Downs. But the Downs themselves shelter Lambourn's massive Norman nave and the extraordinary de la Beche tombs at Aldworth. The Langley library in Slough is the loveliest in any church in England and is reached through one of the finest private pews. Wickham's Victorian elephant corbels are, as the description suggests, unique.

Aldworth *** Hamstead Marshall * Shottesbrooke **
Avington * Lambourn ** Warfield *
Bisham ** Langley Marish **** Wickham *
East Shefford * Newbury *

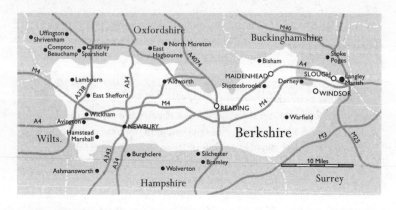

ALDWORTH
St Mary ***
De la Beche tombs

The church lies on a slope of the Downs near where the de la Beche family built their castle after the Conquest. The manor remained in the male line until the Black Death when, whether from piety or egotism or both, the family commissioned a set of memorial effigies and installed them in a new south aisle of the church. They have no parallel in England, although the Lumley tombs in Chester-le-Street (Durham) are similar.

The church has been heavily restored outside and in. There are eight tombs in total, of which six are under Decorated canopies along the side walls and two under the central arcade. In the early 14th century, the de la Beches appear to have been keen to emphasise their ancestry. The niche canopies were restored in the 1870s, so we cannot be sure whether the unusual forked cusps, reminiscent of Kentish tracery, are original. The exact dates of the various tombs and niches may differ, but most of the set would appear to date from that most innovative period of English architecture, the late 13th and early 14th centuries.

We are thus looking at faces, garments and weaponry of a dormitory of knights and ladies of the time leading up to the Hundred Years War. The men were known locally as the Aldworth Giants. A Cromwellian officer recorded them as nicknamed John Long, John Strong, John Never Afraid and (outside the church and now vanished) John Ever Afraid. Three of the group are unusually animated for the period. The knight in the north-east corner may be in the act of rising and drawing his sword to fight for Christ, in the manner of the effigy in Dorchester Abbey (Oxon). He is believed to be Sir Philip de la Beche, valet to Edward II. Seven feet tall, he is accompanied by a page at his feet to emphasise his height.

The paired effigy is of Sir John and Lady Isabella, builder of the chapel, both sadly headless. Her robe is earlier, 13th century in style, further confusing the dates. Under their feet are their dogs. Equally developed drapery graces the figure of Lady Joan de la Zouche in the south aisle. On my visit the tombs were covered in flowers hiding their more battered parts, a thoughtful touch.

Some benches have carved poppyheads, but these have, for some reason, been banished to the back of the nave. The ancient yew in the churchyard, thought to be a thousand years old, was blown down in 1976 but part of its ruin is (or on my visit was) sprouting again. Buried in the same spot is the poet Laurence Binyon, author of the poem 'For the Fallen'. It might be an epitaph for the de la Beches, indeed for all England's parish churches: 'At the going down of the sun and in the morning, / We will remember them.'

AVINGTON
St Mark and St Luke *
Norman font carvings

The church is isolated in a meadow on the banks of the River Kennet. When Arthur Mee visited it he deplored the proximity to the A4, now a side road due to the building of the M4. The hamlet is a manor, farm and row of cottages. A giant cedar throws a protective arm over the walls of this, the most complete Norman church in Berkshire.

The exterior apart from the porch is entirely Norman, with round-headed windows throughout. The south door has zigzag decoration over a 16th-century door. The aisle-less interior is not so much a church, more a tunnel. The great arch, once sealing the plebeian nave from the clerical chancel, is wholly dominant, not least because it has developed an alarming sag at its apex. It has a broad span and bold carving with an outer arch of fleurons, then a row of zigzag, then an inner arch of beakheads, monsters with their tongues out. The message of this common Norman motif remains obscure.

The chancel is puzzling. The intention was to build a stone vault, for which the ghosts of rib-ends are in place. Whether a vault was built but collapsed or was never completed is not known. The roof today is timber. There is a dark and brilliant stained glass window in the south wall of the chancel.

The treasure of the little church at Avington is its font, encircled by figures in a continuous arcade. The characters are unclear but one shows a couple kissing: either a man and woman or Judas kissing Christ. Another has the Devil tempting Judas. Figurative fonts of the early Norman period are rare, however crude the carving.

BISHAM
All Saints **
Hoby Chapel and tombs

Bisham lies on the water's edge where the Thames cuts through the Chilterns between Marlow and Henley. The west façade faces direct on to the river, with restored Norman round-headed windows, steep gables and an embattled tower. The setting is sublime, as the guide says, 'breathing the very spirit of sweet peace'.

The first impression of the interior is of Victorian rebuilding. This took place in a series of campaigns, culminating in the removal of internal walls and galleries and the extension of the chancel eastwards. Windows were all replaced in Decorated style. A reredos in the north chapel has a Gothic panel portraying four saints, a welcome relief from the relentless restoration.

The one part of Bisham left alone by the Victorians was the Hoby Chapel in the south aisle, its monuments and window a typical family shrine of the Tudor age. The farthest monument is to Sir Philip (d.1558) and Sir Thomas Hoby (d.1566), half-brothers and both diplomats. They are dressed in armour and lie in curious poses, with their heads resting on helmets in the medieval style, but also propped up by their arms in a less formal manner. The carving is refined, and exceptional for its date. It may have been the work of a sculptor at the French court where Sir Thomas was ambassador. His widow, Elizabeth, had the chapel built and the tombs erected. She also composed long epitaphs that are classics of Tudor funerary verse. The English translation of the Latin ends, 'When Fate shall call, my better house the grave / With yours my ashes shall united have; / Better, ah, better far with thee to sleep, / Than sadly solitary live and weep.'

Despite these sentiments, Elizabeth took a second husband, John, Lord Russell, and survived until 1609. Her own much more grandiose tomb stands to the west of her first husband's. She kneels at a reading desk beneath a Corinthian canopy in what is now a wholly Jacobean style. With her are three deceased daughters and a dead infant son. Outside the memorial are the children who survived her, a daughter and two sons. She wears a sweeping headdress with coronet. Shields and crests adorn what would make an admirable stage-set for a Shakespeare play. Her ghost is said to haunt the neighbouring Bisham Abbey, now a sports training centre. She allegedly beat a son to death for blotting his exercise book, a salutary warning to Britain's sporting stars.

Lady Russell's daughter-in-law, Margaret (d.1605), is commemorated in a monument of much rarer form. It comprises an obelisk, standing on a multi-storey pedestal which incorporates a cushion, topped by a flaming heart and attended by four splendid swans, supporters of the Hoby arms. On the north side of the Hoby Chapel is a poignant memorial to George Vansittart-Neale, a young Etonian who died at the age of fourteen in 1904. The epitaph reads, 'This little workman will never need to be ashamed. In his simple faith he found the rock of ages, in his wondering love he soared upward to the fatherhood of God and when the call reached him he was ready. He had finished a simple life.' The figure of his dog is apparently a portrait.

EAST SHEFFORD
St Thomas *
Fettiplace tombs

The church is supremely atmospheric, a chapel in a meadow by the River Lambourn, lost to any settlement beyond a farmer's cottage and a rebuilt farmhouse up the lane. The manor was once held by the ubiquitous Fettiplaces (*see* Childrey, Oxon). The big house was demolished in the 19th century and worship in the church ceased, but vigorous conservation has kept it open if redundant.

The church has no tower and is a simple unaisled box rising behind a pine tree which lost its top in a gale. The exterior is rather forlorn, the inside the more delightful. It was deftly restored by the Churches Conservation Trust in 1972 and is now bright and colourful. We are greeted on entry into the south chapel by the alabaster tomb of Sir Thomas Fettiplace and his Portuguese wife Beatrice, beautifully executed and with angels as weepers round the base, c.1450. A wide arch from this chapel opens into the remainder of the church, a double-cell of nave and chancel virtually as one. On the north wall of the latter is a Perpendicular tomb of John Fettiplace and his wife, dated 1524. It has no effigies but there are characters portrayed in small brasses in the niche. Two stained glass fragments of the same date are set into the otherwise clear east window, the right-hand one a primitive Annunciation. The floor tiles look original.

Over the low chancel arch facing the nave is a surviving mural of the Nativity with traces of kings. Above it and elsewhere are fragments of post-Reformation biblical texts used to overpaint the murals. In 1979 an old-fashioned mural was painted to commemorate Harold Armstrong, whose energies helped save the church when it was threatened with demolition in the 1950s. In the north wall is a curious relic of the old rood loft staircase, apparently designed for a dwarf. [CCT]

HAMSTEAD MARSHALL
St Mary *
17th-century furnishings

The old house of the Cravens was built on a small bluff over the River Kennet, designed by Balthazar Gerbier in the early 17th century. Gerbier was Master of Ceremonies to James I. The house was supposed to be an English version of Heidelberg Castle, though it bore no resemblance to that pile on a much taller hill. The house was eventually burned down. Only its magnificent gate piers remain, standing in the field behind the church like Ozymandias's 'trunkless legs of stone'. The Craven mausoleum is hidden by yews in the churchyard.

The church is a charming 18th-century conversion of an inconsequential medieval building, which kept in place much of the 17th-century furnishings. It is memorable for its atmosphere rather than any particular work of art. The form is Perpendicular, with two wide arches to a north aisle, containing an east window that appears to be half Decorated, half Perpendicular in style. The windows contain opaque glass which gives light but sadly no view of trees or sky.

Hamstead Marshall's furnishings are as good as any in Berkshire. The pulpit is of 1622 with a magnificent tester. The box pews are unaltered, each of a different height, indicating the dignity – and rent – of the owning family. One has a pretty openwork screen as its backing. The west gallery is raised on Doric columns with exaggerated entasis and a fine organ. The chancel was extensively restored in the 1920s with a Gothic reredos crowned with a mural of the Holy Ghost descending.

LAMBOURN
St Michael **
Hare-coursing arch, King Charles roundel

Here in a moist fold of the Berkshire Downs is 'the Valley of the Racehorse'. Stables and training gallops are on all sides. The grass is lush and the regulars at the George opposite the church are eerily short in stature. The lychgate is a memorial to William Jousiffe, who brought horses to Lambourn from Newmarket in 1878 and founded the neighbourhood's best-known industry.

There was prosperity long before. Lambourn is one of the few big early medieval churches in Berkshire, the tower visible in its hollow from the slopes of the Downs. Inside the porch a spiral staircase leads up to the parvise, the first of many curiosities in this intriguing building. The first impression of the interior is of impenetrable gloom. Vivid windows by Kempe in both north and south aisles are in themselves beyond reproach. But the east window is a poor work by Hardman & Co., a children's colouring book picture, and Willement's south chapel window is even more garish.

The nave remains impressive. It has strong Norman arcading and the crossing is Transitional, with stiff-leaf emerging from the Norman capitals. The hand of a 19th-century restoration by Street is heavy but, like most cruciform churches, Lambourn has exciting variations in perspective and mood. This is nowhere more evident than in the extraordinary 13th-century arch leading to the Lady Chapel. Set into the hollow of its chamfer is a scene of hare coursing, a sport popular on the Downs. It rests on two carved heads, one a lady in a wimple, the other a grimacing man with buttons on his sleeve, the whole a delightful composition of medieval craftsmanship.

In the north chapel is the alabaster tomb of Sir Thomas Essex (d.1558). At its head is a 17th-century font which saw service as a garden ornament until returned to the church in 1908. Other Lambourn curiosities include a set of village stocks in the north transept and an alabaster roundel of King Charles among angels in the south aisle. This recalls the cult of the King and Martyr that flourished briefly after his execution.

LANGLEY MARISH
St Mary * * * *
Kedermister pew and library

This is for connoisseur church-hunters. We are not just in Slough but in a sub-urban backstreet of Slough, minutes from the A4 and five from the M4. Cars are everywhere. The setting could hardly be less promising. Yet here lies one of the gems of English Church art, the Kedermister pew and library.

The church is basically medieval, a nave, chancel and large north aisle and chapel. A restored 15th-century screen divides nave and chancel. The floor includes a number of 14th-century tiles and a Green Man lurks on the north side of the chancel arcade. But all this is subsidiary to the work of Sir John Kedermister, whose alterations to the church in the early years of the 17th century are the glory of Langley. The Jacobeans could be as generous patrons of parish churches as were their 15th-century forebears.

Kedermisters were keepers of the Crown park of Langley in the Tudor period. The family discharged this task so well that by 1626 John Kedermister had been given a lease on the park and a knighthood. He not only rebuilt much of the church and endowed the adjacent almshouses, he also imitated many enlightened patrons in buying and installing a parish library, one of the few to survive. He died without heir in 1631 and the estate passed first to the Seymours and then to the Harveys. The latter's monuments feature prominently in the Kedermister Chapel.

The older Kedermister memorial in the chancel is a late-Tudor work, extravagant with strapwork and heraldry. Some of this is painted as a mural on the wall. Father and grandfather with their wives occupy two panels, kneeling in prayer with their families beneath them. The future Sir John is the eldest of the group of thirteen on the left. A similar memorial to his father-in-law is in Dorney church.

Sir John's most extensive changes were to the south transept, which is raised on a family vault and reached up a flight of steps. It is furnished with one of the most delightful works of Jacobean design, the Kedermister pew. This is approached through a Gothic Coade stone screen inserted by the Harvey family at the end of the 18th century, apparently keen to make their own mark on the work of their predecessor. Today it is the Harvey monuments that loom over the old chapel, in a variety of Georgian and Victorian funerary styles. The earliest, to David and Elizabeth Harvey of 1791, has a woman representing religion, holding a book and leaning on an urn.

The south wall is filled with the Kedermister pew. Such installations were a Reformation innovation. Previously the wealthy of the parish might sit in special seats in the chancel but they remained part of the congregation. As chantries and chapels were abolished, many were converted into private boxes, often reusing old screens for this purpose. As at Rycote (Oxon) these boxes might occupy most of the nave, confining the tenantry to the back benches or the gallery. But most pews were in some way open to the church, their owners signifying community leadership by their presence in the body of the church.

Not so the Kedermisters. Their pew is sealed from the church by a screen and ceiling. It might be the women's balcony of a mosque. The screen's upper panels are filled with lattice-work grilles, enabling the occupants to see the pulpit, though not the chancel. Private access was by a door at the rear. The screen is wooden but painted to look like marble, with panels and bosses, and topped by a Latin text and strapwork crest. The ceiling has ventilation panels. Above in the towering south window are the Kedermister arms in stained glass. Lest any family member think themselves too aloof from worship, Sir John had eyes (of God) painted throughout the interior.

The library is behind the pew. This is a small cabinet entirely walled with panels on which are painted cartouches, saints and landscape scenes. The panels open to reveal over 200 books, a collection completed by the 1630s and including valuable medieval manuscripts. These are no longer stored in the building. Such costly collections would normally have been confined to a squire's private library. This was a generous donation to the parish and remains the property of a local trust. The insides of the panels include portraits of Sir John and his wife and catalogues of the contents. It is the jewel of Slough.

NEWBURY
St Nicholas *
Hardman glass

Newbury church hides behind the market place just south of the Kennet
and Avon Canal. It is a rebuild of the early 16th century. The patron was
John Smallwood, son of a London draper and a typical self-made clothier of the
time. He was known as John of Winchcombe (the Cotswold wool town) as
well as Jack of Newbury and reputedly owned a hundred looms. When asked
to send six soldiers to Henry VIII's army in Scotland he sent a hundred with
himself at their head. Offered a knighthood, he asked instead for the right of
free trade with Europe. To him, an honour, like Falstaff's, was but air. You
could not cash a knighthood but you could a monopoly. His wealth was
prodigious and much was spent on the church of his adopted town, though not
completed until after his death.

The style is Perpendicular, with high windows, battlements and a strong
pinnacled tower all faced in ashlar. The same loftiness is displayed inside. The
16th century preferred scale and show to architectural invention. The chancel
was restored by the Victorian, Henry Woodyer, its arch a pastiche of Perpendicularity, with such touches as a burst of foliage at the bottom of the arch
chamfers. The Jacobean pulpit of 1607 has panels in green and gold. At the
back of the south aisle is an enjoyable but much eroded monument to Griffith
Curteys, the local MP who died in 1587. One Ionic canopy covers Curteys himself in one bay, while his family is crowded into the other, a fusion of Jacobean
and classical traditions in memorial art.

When Arthur Mee visited Newbury in the 1930s he enthused about the
local Stained Glass Society which had filled the church windows over a long
campaign from 1867 to 1935. 'Craftsmen have found in these windows', he
wrote, 'a joy akin to that of the medieval artists ... We have heard it said
that the day will come when the windows of Newbury will be as famous as
those of Fairford.' The glass, which extends across the entire nave and
clerestory, is by Hardman & Co. of Birmingham. Its chief virtue to the modern
eye is its unity of design and the vigour of the architectural settings of each of
the biblical scenes. It remains dark.

SHOTTESBROOKE
St John **
Needle spire, complete Decorated interior with tombs

Amid the web of motorways and estates of the Maidenhead–Reading conurbation, old England can still assert itself. The Shottesbrooke estate and the

Landmark Trust have preserved a group of cottages and farms in the Thames valley that might be deepest Gloucestershire. The church is reached past a Private sign on the road between White Waltham and Waltham St Lawrence. The spire is visible rising over the woods from a distance and is a splendid feature of the landscape.

Shottesbrooke was erected in 1337, a rare example of a church built from scratch in the Decorated style and unaltered since. It was founded by Sir William Trussell as part of a college, a gesture of lavish piety shortly before the Black Death. The chancel is substantially larger than the nave. Legend has it that his mason, pleased with his work, climbed the spire with a bottle, became drunk and fell to his death. The fine needle spire, its pure lines touched only by discreet lucarnes at the base, surely merited a mild intoxication if not a violent death.

The interior is no less lofty. Light pours in from all four points of the compass. Decorated windows are filled with curvilinear tracery, and a clear west end admits the evening light. The crossing is handsome, and the transept arches, with neither capitals nor bases, are reduced to the simplest forms. Street restored the church in 1852 but with a deferential hand. To him we attribute the sedilia and piscina as well as the choir stalls.

In the north transept a remarkable double tomb runs the entire length of the north wall. The canopy has eight crisp ogee arches and a miniature vault within. It is probably the tomb of Sir William Trussell and his lady, who survived the plague and died in 1363. One visitor is said to have seen through a crack in the tombs the knight wrapped in lead and her ladyship in leather. A smaller but equally extraordinary tomb stands against the north wall of the chancel. It is of William Throkmorton (d.1535), a warden of the pre-Reformation college. The effigy lies in a stone coffin and is curiously bisected by a stone tablet, as if someone feared he might rise up and escape.

The floors of Shottesbrooke are littered with splendid brasses still in place. One pair, of a priest and a layman of c.1370, has them both in prayer with singularly grim expressions on their faces.

WARFIELD
St Michael *
Decorated chancel carvings

The village is composed of large houses with walls round their gardens, seeming to turn their backs on each other and on the road. The church is undaunted, gathering round it a small close of old farm buildings. Even from outside, the building is clearly of importance. The east windows of chancel and chapel have the best curvilinear Decorated tracery in the county.

The inside is darkened by glass and by heavy wooden roofs with no clerestory. We pass swiftly to the chancel through one of two fine screens. That in the north aisle is Perpendicular with an intact rood loft. Beyond is one of the finest chancels in the Thames valley, paid for by the 14th-century priors of Hurley.

High on the north wall are three restored niches with Victorian statues in place, above a triple arcade to the north chapel. This is enlivened by classical wall memorials, although spoiled by its western bay being filled with the organ.

The reredos has blind arcading and sedilia. This work was restored by Street but the design is said to be original and the carving in the arch spandrels looks authentic. Every crocket and finial has broken into bud. To the right of the altar a Green Man starts out of the leaves, vomiting foliage.

No less fruitful was Thomas Williamson (d.1611), whose memorial hangs on the south wall. His innumerable children are so crowded into the background as to form a wallpaper tribute to his (and his wife's) fecundity.

WICKHAM
St Swithun *
Elephant corbels

No enthusiast for Victorian eccentricity can miss Wickham. It boasts a Saxon tower and contrasting interior by the Gothic revivalist, Benjamin Ferrey. The church is at the top of a hill to the south of the village, next to a huge rectory and park. It is surrounded by cedars and austere evergreens, giving its approach the gloom beloved of many Victorian churches.

The tower is Berkshire's one Saxon survival, with Roman tiles and small pillars in the tower windows. The tower was apparently a defensive structure, with a high door and beams to support a beacon inside. The interior is an astonishing confection of Victorian Gothic with much extravagant carved foliage. The nave is tall and short, of just three bays, with a wide north aisle and narrow south one. Leaves are everywhere. They drip from capitals, corbels, friezes. They erupt behind ogees and rise out of crockets, as if the whole building were a conservatory. In the nave spandrels are angels. This is all rich and vigorous. The west wall forms a reredos behind the font which, itself, is splendid, with a cover made in New Zealand.

But Wickham's surprise is hidden in the gloom of the north aisle. Ferrey designed the church in 1845, intending to use angels in the north aisle roof. His patron, William Nicholson, had other ideas. He had found four papier mâché elephants at a Paris exhibition and suggested these be used instead, copying the four to make eight. These beasts peering down from the darkness of Wickham rank among the sensations of English church architecture. They are huge.

Buckinghamshire

Buckinghamshire is essentially Chiltern country, forming a link between the Thames basin and the Midlands. The landscape is richer in great estates than in settlements, yet the county is surprisingly well-endowed with good churches. The old Saxon minster at Wing and the spectacular Norman church of Stewkley were both narrowly saved from airport extinction. The 12th-century fonts of the Aylesbury area are second only in fame to those of Herefordshire. The earlier Gothic periods are weak, but Hillesden is a superb last flourish of Perpendicular before the Reformation.

The county's strength is in post-Reformation patronage, witness that English church art did not die with the break from Rome. Almost every church is rich in monuments and furnishings of the 16th, 17th and 18th centuries, chief being those of the Russells at Chenies, the Dormers at Wing, the Wrightes at Gayhurst and Rysbrack's masterpiece at Quainton. The Georgians left fine churches at West Wycombe and Gayhurst and the Quakers built humble Jordans. Lastly, the county shelters the shades of Gray's celebrated elegy at Stoke Poges.

Bledlow *	Hillesden ****	Olney *
Chenies **	Ivinghoe *	Quainton **
Chetwode **	Jordans **	Stewkley ***
Chicheley *	Little Kimble *	Stoke Poges **
Clifton Reynes **	Little Missenden **	Twyford *
Dorney **	Nether Winchendon *	West Wycombe **
Gayhurst **	North Crawley *	Willen *
Haddenham *	North Marston **	Wing ****

BLEDLOW
Holy Trinity *
Aylesbury font

In such genteel countryside, this church is surprisingly wild. It is approached along a path that overlooks a water garden in a deep ravine. Georgian houses and cottages line the street opposite and Bledlow Ridge gazes down from the Chilterns above. A strong gable end remains on the tower to indicate a former roof. Inside, the atmosphere is that of a back parlour in a rundown country house. Everything needs attention but has mercifully failed to get it.

The nave is of roughcast walls and crumbling plaster. Most of the piers have foliated capitals with upright stiff-leaf carvings, but the chancel arch rests on later corbel heads, of men with flowing hair. There is carving everywhere, indicating not just 13th-century prosperity but a reluctance on the part of later generations to alter the work of their forebears. In the chancel are three stepped lancet windows to the east, and a window in the south wall with tracery and one foliated and one plain shaft. Old heraldic glass survives in the chapel of St Margaret.

Bledlow has a 12th-century Aylesbury font. This has an ample fluted bowl with a rim decorated with leaves, set on a base like an upside-down scalloped capital. This appealing style is ubiquitous in Buckinghamshire, its motifs inspired by workmen at St Albans Cathedral. Fragments of medieval wall paintings survive, including a St Christopher and a fine Adam and Eve in the south wall. But the charm of Bledlow is more than the sum of its parts.

CHENIES
St Michael **
Russell tombs

Chenies is a small Buckinghamshire estate village. The cottages were rebuilt in the 19th century but the 15th-century manor survives on a rise from the road. The house was the medieval home of the Russells, later Earls and finally Dukes of Bedford, and remained in the family until a death duties sale of 1954. Other 'seats' at Woburn, Moore Park and Bloomsbury drew the family away from Chenies when alive, but in death the Russells returned to their ancestral roots. The church is of interest only for the Bedford Chapel, though this is visible only through a screen.

The chapel built in 1556 is a monument to family longevity equalled only by the Spencers at Great Brington (Northants). The collection of funerary sculpture covers almost five centuries, with nineteen memorials in all. As at Brington we marvel at an aristocracy that continued to seek rest not in a cathedral or private mausoleum, but among the yeomen from whom they rose. That said, this chapel is very much distinct from those yeomen's graves, and is kept locked. The tombs are visible through double doors from the nave and through a third in the chancel. Half of the monuments are mostly invisible and the rest only in a dim light. Given the importance of the collection, proper access should be permitted or the wall redesigned to give a better view from the church.

Describing each of the monuments in turn would therefore be pointless and there is a list in the church. But even through the glass the spectacle is worth a visit. The House of Russell rests in morgue-like gloom, remembered in stone, alabaster and marble beneath a hammerbeam roof. The chamber is filled with banners. The earliest tomb is just visible at the back of the chapel. It is of a Russell predecessor, Sir John Cheyne, in medieval chainmail, its base for some reason left unfinished. The knight and his lady appear to be emerging from the raw stone. The most impressive group is at the east end, a set of seven alabaster tombs of the late 16th and early 17th centuries, arranged like ships in line astern for review. The effigies are still medieval, lying in prayer above tomb chests, but the decoration is early classical and highly coloured. At the feet of two sets of effigies can be seen the Russell goat.

At the west end of the chapel is a shock, a monument covering the entire wall. It is a vast Baroque memorial to the 5th Earl and 1st Duke of Bedford (d.1700), developer of Bloomsbury in London. Gone are the days of effigies in prayerful sleep. The memorial shows him in fashionable Stuart clothes and his wife in a Roman gown. Both are seated, leaning away from each other with the Order of the Bath between them. Round them rise columns, a canopy and an open pediment which almost touches the roof. Also at the west end are memorials by William Chambers, Richard Westmacott Jnr and Alfred Gilbert, in other words the pick of Georgian and Victorian designers. The windows are by Kempe and depict copious Russell heraldry.

CHETWODE
St Mary and St Nicholas **
Early medieval glass

Hidden in rolling farmland near the site of a large Augustinian priory is the best medieval glass in Buckinghamshire. Nave and transepts have gone, leaving just this fragmentary chancel as a parish church. A priory house is tacked on to its side and a curious west tower placed where the crossing would have been. The interior is minster-like, tall and battered but with a spectacular sanctuary. This is dominated by tall deep-set lancets, five to the east and three to the north and south. These are complemented by an enriched Early Gothic sedilia in the south wall, its middle bay pierced by a door.

The glass in the south windows (moved in 1842 from the east windows) dates from the 13th and 14th centuries. It includes some of the earliest heraldic glass in England, showing the arms of Henry III. The middle panel of the central lancet has a bishop, possibly St Nicholas, and above him St John the Baptist, 'swaying' in a manner common in glass of this period. His garment is broadly folded and suggests familiarity with contemporary glass at Westminster and in France. The pictures are set as roundels in abstract grisaille (or semi-clear) glass. When the Victorian, William Holland, came to set glass in the east window he used the same motifs and proportions to excellent effect.

Apart from this, there is little to detain us at Chetwode. The organ, given more prominence in the nave even than the pulpit, has a pretty Gothic case of 1842. A curiosity is the mini-transept in the north wall which contains two ancient family pews, one still with its fireplace. The occupants of these homes-from-home can hardly have seen the preacher, let alone the altar.

CHICHELEY
St Laurence *
Comper loft and ringers' chamber

The much restored church guards the lime avenue to the splendid Chicheley Hall. The adjacent M1 might be miles away. The plan is odd. There is a central crossing tower with nothing much to 'cross' and a large Perpendicular window in place of a south transept. The chancel was rebuilt in 1708 without an east window, its south windows having an unlikely combination of classical hoods and Gothic tracery. The private door in the south wall has a pediment holding the arms of Sir John Chester, builder of the Hall a hundred yards to the east. The designer was Chester's local mason, James Oldfield, though the guide attributes the work to none other than Christopher Wren.

The interior is a surprise. The familiar problem of what to do with the bell-ringers in a church with a central bell-tower is resolved by having the ringers' chamber as an open gallery. And since the gallery is here in the middle of the nave, Comper decided in 1907 to use it for a rood as well. The result is the only example I know of a three-in-one, a choir gallery, ringers' chamber and rood loft. The rood is a confident early work of Comper, his figures less effete and his style less Perpendicular than later. Beyond is a Doric screen and iron gates to the chancel, keeping both the medieval church and Comper at bay. The chancel has a plaster ceiling with flower motifs.

West of the loft, in the nave and north aisle, is very much 'below stairs'. In the aisle is the monument to Anthony Cave (d.1558). It is an early classical composition of 1576 with sarcophagus, Doric order, caryatids and a pediment, most unusual motifs for the date. The effigy is disquieting, with a naked cadaver of hermaphrodite features. Above it on the back wall a man, wife and children appear floating in mid-air. Next door is a more conventional monument. This is dedicated to Sir Anthony Chester of 1637, showing him kneeling in Stuart costume and facing his wife.

CLIFTON REYNES
St Mary **
Wooden effigies with medieval dog

This is a chocolate-box church, prettily sited above a hamlet near the River Ouse and well away from any suburb. The exterior is friendly Perpendicular, with prominent battlements and a square Norman tower. The interior proportions are presumably Saxon, eccentric, tall and narrow as if someone had squeezed the three-bay arcade upwards. The clerestory is so darkened by stained glass as to deny the name, though the glass appears to be original. The north aisle is late-Georgian and the south one has a fine Tudor window. The north chapel contains the various monuments to the Reynes family.

This chapel is a delight, a local family lying in state in their village cathedral. There are three tombs, two of them with unusual wooden effigies of knights and their wives. In the wall recess of *c.*1340 are Thomas Reynes and his wife carved in oak, he cross-legged and in armour, dated *c.*1300. The western arch contains a monument to Ralph Reynes, *c.*1330. Again the material is oak, wonderfully darkened by age. In the east arch to the chancel lies the stone tomb of Thomas Reynes III, *c.*1385. The chest has mourners round its base. More extraordinary is the dog on which his feet rest. It is named on its collar as 'BO', said to be the only medieval pet named in this way. (I am sure I have met others.)

Clifton Reynes's font is Perpendicular and of exceptional quality. Its stem is adorned with tracery, symbolising windows and thus light. Cherubs and flowers indicate innocence. Eight panels of saints round the bowl signify the sanctity conferred by baptism.

DORNEY
St James **
Palmer family pews

Some churches deserve a brass rhubarb for the rudeness of their custodians. 'I wouldn't let you in even if you asked,' was the opening salvo of Dorney's keyholder to a courteous enquiry if the church were open. Such is today's Church of England.

But Dorney is worth the effort. The group of Tudor house, farm and church is tucked down a cul-de-sac by the Thames, all picturesque and cottagey, and the village of Bray is just across the river. There are still Palmers at Dorney Court, 300 years after Barbara Palmer was a mistress to Charles II. Such oases amid the enveloping suburbia are very precious. The thick-set oblong tower of the church is built of English bond brickwork. Flemish bond is used in the small 17th-century Garrard Chapel north of the chancel and on the Dutch gable embellishing the porch, dated 1661. The approach down the lane might be from a de Hooch painting.

The interior seems little altered since the 18th century, with furnishings of every preceding period crammed into the small aisle-less nave and chancel. If the local Palmer family were grand, they were domestic in their grandeur. Walls tilt at odd angles. Box pews are jammed into every available space. The baptistery is tucked down steps under the gallery, surrounded by medieval benches. The gallery itself forms three sides to the west end of the church, and is set on chunky pillars.

The Palmer pew, with padded seats and threadbare carpet, faces the Jacobean pulpit. On its wall are what appear to be pewter memorial plates with beautiful lettering. Earlier pews crowd the chancel, with panels and poppyheads. To its north lies the exclusive Garrard Chapel, guarded by gates. Inside is a simple but colourful Jacobean memorial of 1607 erected by Sir William Garrard's son-in-law, Sir John Kedermister. It is in the style of his memorial to his own father in the chancel at Langley Marish (Berks).

GAYHURST
St Peter **
Baroque monument to the Wrightes

There is no finer landscape in Buckinghamshire than that of Tyringham and Gayhurst. The two houses face each other across immaculate parks on either side of the River Ouse. They might be the Backs at Cambridge. Gayhurst church is reached through the main gates to the big house. This house passed through the hands of Sir Francis Drake and Everard Digby (of the Gunpowder Plot) before the Wrighte family acquired it in 1704 and built a new church in the style of Wren.

The church, completed in 1728, dominates the group of house, stables and estate buildings. It is Baroque, in warm honey-coloured stone but strangely proportioned. The south façade is clearly intended to be seen as a unity, the centre balanced by the chancel to the east and the tower to the west. Its classicism is much abused by architectural critics, but I find its wilfulness charming in this picturesque setting. The tower cupola sits well among the trees when seen from over the park.

Inside, we are in the entrance hall of a grand house. As outside, the chancel and tower balance each other across the expanse of the nave. The walls have giant pilasters rising to a frieze decorated alternately with books and bishops' mitres. To the left of the chancel arch is the pulpit and tester. To its right is Gayhurst's masterpiece, the monument to Sir George Wrighte and his son. This is a superb work of Baroque modelling; to Pevsner it is 'not only one of the grandest but also one of the most successful of its type in England'. The artist is anonymous. The two men stand framed by Corinthian columns as if modelling their Georgian costumes.

The chancel is, in effect, a withdrawing-room. The ceiling is elaborately plastered, in a foliated pattern more 17th century than 18th. There is no east window; instead, the customary Georgian Corinthian reredos is guarded by wrought iron railings. The box pews are intact, that of the Wrighte family located directly under the statue of its illustrious member.

HADDENHAM
St Mary *
Duckpond churchyard, Aylesbury font

Haddenham village centre is happily isolated from the surrounding suburbia. The wide green is surrounded by old cottages with not a roof tile or wall coping out of place. A duckpond laps the churchyard wall and a wicket-gate points the way to a two-storey north porch and solid west tower. The latter's belfry has Early Gothic blind arcading.

The interior is bright and unspoilt. The nave is Transitional *c.*1200, its arcade piers rising to a modern plastered ceiling with no clerestory. East and west ends are blessed with three stepped lancets each and there are also lancets in the chancel. These windows are sadly blighted with modern glass, though old glass has been reassembled in the north chapel.

The font is Norman of the Aylesbury style, with incised bowl and dragons chasing each other round the rim. The fate of anyone dying unbaptised was to fall into the jaws of these monsters. Haddenham retains fragments of its old screens and has almost complete Perpendicular benches, some with their carved poppyheads.

HILLESDEN
All Saints ****
Perpendicular north chapel, Dutch glass

Hillesden owes its splendour to the monks of Notley Abbey, who initiated its rebuilding at the end of the 15th century, shortly before the Dissolution. They had been accused of allowing it to become ruinous, at a time when monasteries were being attacked for neglecting their parochial responsibilities. The lavish north chapel, later filled with Denton memorials, must have been part of this rebuilding. When the Dentons took the manor from the abbey in 1547, they thus acquired a building recently completed and one they swiftly adjusted to the celebration of family rather than church.

Dentons held Hillesden for barely a century. At the start of the Civil War, Alexander Denton fortified the house for the Royalist forces then at Oxford. Besieged by Cromwell in person, the village fell and many of the 140 prisoners taken were massacred. Despite promises of safe passage, Denton himself was forced to watch his house burned to the ground. He died two years later in prison. The house was rebuilt and Dentons returned, remaining until the middle of the next century, but the house they rebuilt has since disappeared. The church survived, with Cromwell's bullet holes still in its door. The young George Gilbert Scott, brought up nearby, declared that Hillesden was the church that first fired his enthusiasm for the Gothic. It was, he wrote, 'an exquisite specimen of the latest phase of Gothic art'. He later restored it free of charge.

The view of the church from the north is magnificent: a castellated, turreted casket of tracery and glass. The two-storey vestry has a staircase tower crowned with an extravagant ogival canopy covered with pinnacles and panels. Masons at the climax of the Perpendicular age seemed eager to dispense with walls altogether. Everywhere we see expanses of glass, designed for light and to carry the heraldic devices of those who sponsored it, including the princes and priors of the Church. This is the ultimate architecture of ostentation.

This sense of display is continued inside, as light and airy as a giant greenhouse. Tall shafted columns rise to chamfered arches above linenfold pews. The plan is cruciform. The north transept contains the Denton family pew decorated with cartouches. The clerestory is almost continuous, so light that the roof might seem about to blow away. There is a tall rood screen in place, its canopy deeply coved. The walls of both the chancel and the north chapel are stone-panelled.

The chapel, first built by the monks, is the more ornate, presumably dedicated by the monks to their patron. Round its ceiling is a frieze of half-angels with instruments. Soon after the Dentons took over the manor, their monuments invaded this chapel, the effect being of a miniature Beauchamp Chapel at Warwick. The tomb of the armoured Thomas Denton (d.1558) and his wife is of alabaster, much bashed presumably by Cromwellians. The later memorial to Alexander Denton (d.1576) has no effigy and marks the Elizabethan transition from medieval to classical. There are now Doric columns and strapwork and no sign of an effigy, only a sarcophagus.

Although Hillesden's glass was ruined in the Civil War, a number of panes survive in the upper panels. These are mostly of saints and priests and are primitive in execution. A treasure, however, is the magnificent window in the east wall of the south transept, illustrating eight scenes from the life of St Nicholas. This is Dutch work of the early 16th century and is wholly different from contemporary English work, for instance in Fairford (Gloucs). The Hillesden window is superb and admirably preserved. There are no architectural frames or stylised poses. Instead we have everyday scenes portrayed realistically. The figures might have stepped from a painting by Jan Steen or van Ostade – notably the quayside transaction of wooltraders.

The south window in the same transept is a good Victorian imitation of the style by Burlison & Grylls.

IVINGHOE
St Mary *
'Windblown' stiff-leaf carving

Ivinghoe lies in an appendix of Buckinghamshire, jutting into Bedfordshire, that has somehow survived boundary revision. The church is a cruciform structure, Perpendicular outside but containing a fine 13th-century arcade with excellent stiff-leaf capitals. These are almost as rich as those of what may be its sister church at Eaton Bray (Beds), carving for connoisseurs, deeply undercut and 'windblown' round the piers. The nave is whitewashed but must have looked dazzling when painted, presumably in all the colours of the forest. The remains of circular clerestory windows show through the plaster above the piers.

Ivinghoe's woodwork is mostly 15th century, including the roof, benches and lectern. The roof has angels, apostles and corbels of monsters and humans, the east bay further enriched with bosses. The pew poppyheads include Green Men and one near the south door has a playful mermaid. The modern kneelers are excellent, bold red but not garish. Most have abstract designs, a relief from the 'L. S. Lowry' style favoured by modern embroiderers.

In the chancel is a badly damaged effigy of a priest set in a wall tomb decorated with realistic faces. The church was deferentially restored by Street, whose principal contribution, a fine font, stands in the north aisle attended by a triptych. A final curiosity is the survival of the old fire hook set on the churchyard wall by the entrance. These hooks were used to pull burning thatch from roofs, originally in the days when church roofs were thatched rather than tiled. They lived on as primitive parish fire-fighting equipment.

JORDANS
Meeting House **
Early Quaker fittings

Jordans is the Quaker Westminster Abbey. James II's Declaration of Indulgence in 1687 (and the subsequent Toleration Act of 1689) offered all Dissenters freedom of worship, 'though we cannot but heartily wish, as it will easily be believed, that all people of our dominions were members of the Catholic church'. Quakers were now able to meet without fear of prosecution, if not of discrimination. They had been gathering in the Chilterns for many years before the building of this, their most famous Meeting House. Jordans Farm up the road had a Quaker as proprietor, William Russell. The present farm hints at close association with the *Mayflower*, indeed claims part of the ship's timbers and possibly part of a cabin door, a latter-day worship of relics.

In 1688, the foundations were laid for a new Meeting House in a clearing by the Beaconsfield road. The redbrick house, clad in wistaria, looks today as it did then, a subdued William and Mary mansion with shuttered windows, of the sort imitated throughout the American colonies. Jordans's high windows look out across the lawn to the Chiltern woods. The simple room is panelled in deal and surrounded with benches. Along the far wall from the gallery is a raised bench for visiting or itinerant ministers, an architectural feature that sits oddly with the Quaker principle of egalitarianism in prayer. In front of this are the Elders' benches. The floor is of brick.

The gallery, once used for women's meetings, now houses a William Penn museum much visited by Americans. Penn hailed from Buckinghamshire and was a frequent attender at the Meeting House, in whose grounds he was buried in 1718, according to his own wishes. The settlement of Pennsylvania, which he founded and inhabited for just four years, later sought to have his remains reburied in the state capital. On one occasion two men had to be stopped from trying to exhume them. The Friends replied that such a removal to America, 'amid the pomp and circumstance of a state ceremonial accompanied in all probability by military honours and parade, would be utterly repugnant to [Penn's] known character and sentiments'. And that was that.

LITTLE KIMBLE
All Saints *
Medieval wall paintings

This modest church with a small bell-turret nestles into the hillside beneath Great Kimble. Severe Victorian restoration gives the exterior the appearance of a cemetery chapel. The interior is a simple two-cell church with small Decorated windows and insipid yellow glass in the east window. Other windows have heraldic and naturalistic medieval glass, including oak leaves and acorns. There are poppyhead carvings in the chancel and a fine wooden eagle lectern. On the floor of the chancel are 13th-century tiles, carefully protected from passing feet. One shows a king with his dog and another two knights fighting.

Little Kimble's wall paintings are the most extensive in the county. They are unusually monochrome and date from the start of the 14th century, covering the nave walls and window splays. In a north splay is St Francis preaching to birds. On the west wall a devil can be made out pushing women into Hell and there is a St Christopher on the north wall facing the old south door. The rest of the pictures are mostly of saints. These have been well-restored and displayed. Little Kimble's wall paintings are more curiosity than art, but a pleasant surprise in this unpromising context.

LITTLE MISSENDEN
St John **
Wall paintings, Aylesbury font

Here the Chilterns are at their most immaculate, every inch tended and with not a leaf or blade of grass out of place. Next to the manor in the valley bottom is a church from a quite different context. It survived Tudor and Victorian alteration alike, and is rugged with fragmentary traces of ancient wall paintings, the picture book of the medieval unlearned.

The age of Little Missenden is a matter of controversy. Pevsner declares it Norman, rather than the Saxon preferred by the guide. The proportions of the nave are Saxon, tall with tiny windows. Roman tiles are set into the chancel arch. The round arches of the nave arcade are Norman but appear to be insertions into an earlier structure of which traces are visible high on the nave wall. This is all obscure but character-forming.

The chancel is incontrovertibly Early Gothic, with three beautiful east lancet windows of equal height divided by shafts on two planes. The tower arch and the tower itself are a Perpendicular contribution, while the big pointed south aisle windows are 18th century. Also Georgian is the curiously large dormer window visible on the outside of the nave roof. The wall paintings are mostly too faded to be recognisable, but there is a strong St Christopher on the north wall. There are also 17th-century texts in painted surrounds.

The baptistery contains an Aylesbury font, Norman with a rim of leaves above a fluted base. The 20th century has contributed a graceful addition, a neo-Georgian vestry house attached to the north exterior, by Raymond Erith and Quinlan Terry.

NETHER WINCHENDON
St Nicholas *
Flemish window roundels

Nether (or Lower) Winchendon sits beneath the Long Crendon ridge looking across the River Thame to the Chilterns. The village is a world apart. The centre is formed by a triangular green with a round Victorian pillar box set grandly in the middle. To the west rises the gable of a rambling mansion; medieval, Tudor and neo-Gothic, it has often been used for television sets. The church is small but heavily proportioned. Nave and chancel roofs retain steep pre-Perpendicular roofs, alongside which the tower sits squat and apologetic.

The exterior is of crumbling limestone, with restored early Decorated tracery in its windows. The interior is simple and without aisles. But 17th- and 18th-century woodwork is intact and the church's charm lies in this completeness. Box pews survive throughout, including the squire's pew painted with Gothic panels. The pulpit is of 1613, with clerk's desk and tester. It rises high in the south-east corner of the nave, where a south-facing window would have illuminated the priest at evensong.

Over the congregation hang many brass candelabras. The church is lit throughout with candles and oil lamps. In the chancel are handsome Jacobean armchairs and in the windows roundels from Holland. These form a particularly fine set, portraying domestic and farmyard scenes. They would have been brought by 16th-century Flemish refugees as identity cards, to prove their place of origin and status – the prettiest of passports. The glass was moved to the church from the house in 1958. The nave contains an ancient clock with a loud tick. Given in 1772 by Jane Beresford, it 'may remind all who hear it to spend their time in an honest discharge of their calling and in the worship of God: that repentence may not come too late'.

NORTH CRAWLEY
St Firmin *
Partridge carvings

St Firmin was born in Pamplona, home of the fighting bulls, and rose to become bishop of Amiens. What he is doing in north Buckinghamshire nobody seems to know. The dedication presumably dates from a Norman exile thinking of home.

The church is reached down a dark yew avenue from the forecourt of a busy pub. The nave arcades are of two periods, Early Gothic with stiff-leaf on the south side and Decorated on the north. The arches change their proportions as they go west. The Early Gothic chancel has an inscription outside the east window from a medieval rector, Peter of Guilford, addressed to St Firmin himself: 'Peter gives you a new chancel, Firmin, so when you praise God you will remember Peter.' That would today be called buying access.

North Crawley is distinguished not so much for its architecture as for its carpentry. The tie-beam roofs are magnificent, with apostles on the wall-posts, each standing on what appears to be a partridge. The significance of these birds is as obscure as St Firmin. The screen is complete and painted, the only one in the county. It has ogee openings and coving. Most remarkable are the painted panels of saints and prophets with inscriptions, a gallery of 15th-century figures and in good repair. North Crawley has box pews of 1827 which include 17th-century panels, while Tudor benches are arranged at the rear. There is an ancient font on colonettes with a wooden cover of 1640.

NORTH MARSTON
St Mary **
Doctor Schorne's 'Jack-in-the-Box'

The church standing proud above its village is a memorial to England's first popular doctor and his cure for gout. It faces south over the churchyard like a disjointed Tudor stage-set. Tower and nave are battlemented and the chancel also pinnacled. By the time of these alterations it had long been a shrine to its 14th-century rector, John Schorne (d.1314), regarded by many adherents in his day as a saint. Schorne's line was a claim to have imprisoned the Devil in a boot, thus enabling him to cure gout. This is allegedly the origin of Jack-in-the-Box, and of the many Boot inns found on routes leading to North Marston.

The guide suggests the small opening high on the north wall of the chancel, giving on to a priest's room above the vestry, may have contained a mechanical Jack to delight (or terrify) visitors. More to the point, Schorne appears to have discovered the value of local chalybeate spring water in curing eye infections. Chalybeate springs were widely credited with curative properties, though the virtues may have been no more than those of diligent cleanliness. Such was Schorne's reputation that he is portrayed among genuine saints on screens at Cawston (Norfolk) and Sudbury (Suffolk).

Schorne's reputation enriched North Marston in the late medieval period. His shrine is (or was) at the east end of the south aisle, represented by a Decorated window, an ornate piscina and tiny alcove near the floor. The window and frieze have fleuron decorations. The sedilia are unusually elaborate, with detached columns, as are the niches on either side of the altar. The choir stalls are original and have poppyheads and misericords.

In 1478 the canons of Windsor staged what appears to have been a tomb robbery. Eager to raise funds to complete St George's Chapel, they removed

Schorne's remains to Windsor, hoping that pilgrims and donors might make their way there instead. This testament to the mobility of medieval pilgrims presumably paid dividends, if the present St George's, Windsor, is the result. The enrichment of North Marston's chancel and exterior may have been paid for in compensation for the removal of the shrine.

Nor was this the end of the church's eccentricity. In 1852 a local landowner and miser, John Nield, left a huge fortune of £250,000 to Queen Victoria in person. She bought Balmoral with the money, but returned some to the village to pay for the church's restoration by Matthew Digby Wyatt. The guidebook remarks mournfully that 'the excitement of those times has died away'.

OLNEY
St Peter and St Paul *
Decorated steeple, Olney Hymnal

Northamptonshire churchbuilders are regularly accused of straying into neighbouring counties. Nowhere do they do so more emphatically than at Olney, childhood home of the architect George Gilbert Scott, residence of William Cowper and inspiration of the Olney hymns. The early 14th-century Decorated tower rises beyond a meadow by the River Ouse. It has none of the modesty of the Home Counties and all the self-confidence of the Midlands, and is a work of beauty and originality.

The tower is of three diminishing stages capped with octagonal pinnacles, and the spire is ribbed with four tiers of lucarne windows. The tapering of both tower and spire is perfectly judged. They dominate a nave and chancel restored by Scott in the 1870s. His large but delicate east window is a masterpiece of Victorian Gothic.

Olney's interior is spacious but dreadfully scraped and heavily restored. There is thus no telling if the Decorated window tracery is 14th century or Victorian. The nave has lost its clerestory and been reduced in height, leaving it curiously lower than the chancel. The latter is almost all by Scott. Fierce glass by William Holland fills the east window. Two chancel windows of the 1970s are ugly but include, at their bases, depictions of two Olney residents. One is a solicitor, the other a vicar, the latter in front of his vicarage and depicting the neighbouring fields. They might be scenes from Trollope.

Two distinguished Church figures lived in Olney in the late 18th century, John Newton and William Cowper. Newton was a preacher and hymn-writer whose pulpit stands dejected in the south-west corner of the church. His works include 'Amazing Grace' and 'Glorious Things of Thee are Spoken'. Cowper's pastoral verse reflects the soft air of the Ouse valley. To the Olney Hymnal he contributed 'God Moves in a Mysterious Way'. The church is best known nowadays as the finishing point in the local Shrove Tuesday pancake race, marked on the churchyard wall.

QUAINTON
Holy Cross and St Mary **
Dormer monument by Rysbrack

The church is well-sited with its rectory and almshouses on a slope of Quainton Hill. A rare windmill survives to challenge the eminence of the church tower. The 14th-century church was restored by William White with his customary bravura in the 1870s. White's work is recognisable chiefly for the heavy, almost Tyrolean, members of his hammerbeam roofs, most noticeable here in the chancel. Medieval brasses from the 14th, 15th and 16th centuries have been set, most unusually, into the backs of the sedilia, the inscriptions respectively in French, Latin and English.

Quainton is notable for its monuments. In the south aisle lies the tomb of Richard Winwood (d.1689) erected by his wife. The subjects are recumbent but not in repose. Winwood wears old-fashioned plate armour but is fully wigged and stares out into the church. His wife is propped up on her elbow behind him, her hands in pensive prayer. Winwood sheds a tear. The carver was Thomas Stayner.

An adjacent wall monument to Dr Richard Brett (d.1637) displays husband and wife kneeling opposite each other in prayer, their children assembled on each side. Brett helped with the King James Bible translation, his linguistic versatility demonstrated in the inscriptions. His epitaph ends, 'Instead of weeping marble, weep for him / All ye his flock whom he did strive to winn.' In the north aisle is a monument to Sir Richard Pigott (d.1685) and his wife and descendants, designed by the Venetian architect, Giacomo Leoni, some time after 1735. It consists of a tall classical frame in grey and white marble with, at its centre, a black sarcophagus.

Quainton's treasure, however, is usually kept locked beneath the tower. It is the wall monument to Judge Dormer's son, Fleetwood (d.1726), lately identified as by Rysbrack of *c.*1728. His son lies dead between the figures of his father and mother. She weeps, while the judge stands in full wig and gown, looking as if this was just another of life's inconveniences. The relation of the figures to the architectural background is superbly handled. The draperies are charged with energy, the textures of the judge's fur cloak, lace cuff and hairy wig finely differentiated. Rysbrack and his contemporaries represented the high point of 18th-century sentiment.

STEWKLEY
St Michael ***
Unaltered Norman interior

How Stewkley survived the centuries is a mystery. Perhaps the village was too poor or the population too sparse to merit a new church. Or perhaps the parishioners liked it as it was. Only when Street arrived in 1862 was a firm hand laid on its ancient stones, but only as restorer. The nearest Stewkley came to disaster was in the 1970s when neighbouring Cublington was proposed as a site for a third London airport. The authorities offered to move the church to another position.

The building is a late Norman spectacular of 1150–80. The west front to the main road displays the virtuoso zigzag carving that is Stewkley's signature. This primitive decoration covers the triple-arched west door and the west window above. The door's tympanum has two dragons unusually divided by a large dripstone. Zigzag adorns every window surround, arch and frieze. The massive central tower has intersecting blind arcading with tiny windows.

The interior is divided into three cells, those of nave, tower and chancel. For all Stewkley's architectural authenticity, the furnishings and thus the atmosphere are wholly different from those prevailing in Norman times. These spaces would then have been crowded with screens, icons, paintings, candles, dirt and wafts of incense. What we see today is 20th-century conservation of a Victorian reorganisation, a victory for architectural over liturgical archaeology.

Yet the succession of tower arch and chancel arch is breathtaking. The rhythm of zigzag arches, zigzag string course, zigzag window surrounds and zigzag ribs to the vault shows a frenzied fascination with this decorative form. There are only a few variations. Beakheads appear round the chancel arch and faces can be seen peering out between chevrons, apparently dancing in candlelight. The only pointed arches are over the piscina and another on the tower stair. Some alabaster fragments of a Virgin and Child, probably from a 15th-century reredos, have been set into the chancel north wall.

Street's contribution to Stewkley included the south porch, a round window unnecesssarily inserted high in the west wall and a neo-Norman pulpit. The place is now scrubbed and tidy. Street's reredos with marble inlay has been covered with a thick curtain, presumably as not in keeping with the remainder of the Norman chancel. This seems fastidious.

STOKE POGES
St Giles **
Gray's Elegy churchyard

The villages of the southern extremity of the Chilterns have mostly been transformed into commuter suburb disguised by woodland. But here, tucked away north of Slough between the M4 and the M40, is precious Green Belt. In its midst are the meadows that surround the churchyard celebrated by Thomas Gray. If any church merits an entry on the strength of a poem, it is this. Gray wrote his churchyard elegy here by his mother's tomb, backed by ancient brick and flint walls and gazing out over elms, yews and gravestones. The elms have gone and the lowing herd from o'er the lea is the soft murmur of a distant motorway. But Gray's context survives, commemorated by the preservation of the lea by the path leading to the church. The lea now belongs to the National Trust. The elegy is printed complete at the back of the guidebook.

Stoke Poges church presents a typical Thames valley scene. A battlemented bell-tower rises behind a ripple of gables in brick and flint, themselves floating on ancient headstones and chest tombs, framed by yews and redbrick walls. Despite the tramp of tourists, the churchyard is not tame and Victorian restoration is not too evident. The place is still of 'homely joys and destiny obscure', telling 'the short and simple annals of the poor'. Even the Tudor Hastings Chapel to the south of the chancel has a yeoman quality to it. The family crest on the door shows a bull with horns and its tongue hanging out.

The Victorians were less kind to the inside. The Norman chancel arch was replaced with an insipid Gothic one and the 13th-century nave scraped of its plaster to reveal roughcast flint and chalk walls. These coupled with the high roof make the nave look like a barn. Of greater appeal is the Hastings Chapel. This was built in 1558 by Lord Hastings to serve as an oratory for an adjacent almshouse, now removed. The chapel was then quite separate; an opening to the chancel was not cut through until the 18th century. The chapel is dominated by hatchments and monuments. The latter include an ornate Victorian brass to a member of the Howard Vyse family, and a bizarre cartouche with angels and skulls. The Penns, ubiquitous across Buckinghamshire, owned Stoke in the 18th and 19th centuries and had a family pew and vault here in the church.

Stoke has two extraordinary windows. One is that of the 'bicycling nude' in the west window, dated to the 17th century and apparently of a naked man with a horn riding an ancient hobby-horse. It is incorporated into a modern memorial window. The other of 1871 is even more odd. Located in the south aisle it commemorates a child Howard Vyse and has two lights, one showing the child slipping from the arms of its mother and the other its being received by an angel. The eerie figures rise into a night sky above a shoreline and a broken column. I have seen nothing like it.

Back in the churchyard, the memorial to Gray and his mother is immediately beneath the east wall. Dorothy Gray died in 1753 and is described simply as 'widow, the careful, tender Mother of many children, one of whom alone had the misfortune to survive her'. That one was Thomas.

TWYFORD
St Mary *
Wenman memorial

This modest country church greets visitors with holly and yew on either side of the gate and with gravestones drawn up in orderly ranks like a guard of honour. The 15th-century door is proud of its original hinges. It is set in a fine Norman arch with well-preserved beakhead decoration. The shafts have beasts for capitals.

The interior shows traces of its Norman origins in the chancel arch, but Twyford is a stylistic jumble and therein lies much of its delight. The north aisle is narrow and was apparently inserted in 1733 as a manorial pew. The south aisle has corbel faces, all with their tongues sticking out. The church retains its pre-Victorian furnishings. The dado of an original rood screen survives beneath a modern reconstruction. The pews are robust medieval carpentry which look as though they were hewn from solid chunks of wood. They might be benches in a back parlour.

The one touch of class is in the south aisle. Here stands the massive Purbeck marble altar tomb of Thomas Giffard (d.1550) and wife, lord of the local manor. His brass lies on top, the feet resting on a greyhound. Like many brasses, this is a palimpsest reused from a previous tomb, that of William Stortford of 1416. A tomb recess in the adjacent wall contains a strange carved figure holding a heart. Overlooking this medieval scene is the austere monument to a descendant of the Giffards, Richard, 1st Viscount Wenman (d.1640). He is commemorated within a classical frame with sorry-looking Ionic capitals. Everything is out of proportion, in a style I would describe as Jacobean Mannerist.

WEST WYCOMBE
St Lawrence **
Lavish 'Palmyra' interior

West Wycombe has a prominence enjoyed by few churches in England. On busy days cars must be left in the car park and the steep hill ascended on foot. Beneath are spread the soft Chiltern valleys, tamed by Sir Francis Dashwood, wealthy Georgian dilettante and collector. On the opposite hillside stands his house and garden. Below is the village, with hardly a building out of place. The Hell-Fire Club once met in caves beneath the hill, where Dashwood and his friends indulged in banquets, orgies and mystic rituals – or so it was alleged by their enemies, and some of their excluded but envious admirers.

Today we see only a romantic group of buildings set well in the landscape. The church is medieval in origin. The east window outline survives, as does the stone tower, with eight bells that can be seen on the climb to the balcony beneath the famous golden ball. Inside this ball, of gilded canvas, ten people could and presumably still can sit down to dinner. It is certainly by far the best look-out point in the Chilterns.

Dashwood rebuilt the interior in 1761–3. The designs have been attributed to his friend, Nicholas Revett, who also worked on the house. At the rededication in 1763, West Wycombe was hailed as 'the most beautiful country church in England'. To the modern eye the interior may seem ponderous and florid. It reflects the mid-Georgian fascination with the architecture of the eastern Roman empire. All four walls have engaged columns with an exceptionally rich Corinthian order. The shafts are painted in imitation porphyry, an exotic marble. The lavish decoration extends to the ceiling, with designs drawn from Robert Wood's *Ruins of Palmyra* (1752), hugely influential among mid-Georgian architects. The walls are decorated with a palm frieze in a rococo style, of fine workmanship, with garlands, flowers and doves.

The chancel is reached through iron gates and is more like a private chapel in a grand house. In the centre of the ceiling is a painting of the Last Supper by a Milanese artist, Giovanni Borgnis. The east window contains Flemish roundels of biblical scenes, a more satisfying decoration than the usual large Victorian compositions. Wycombe's font is also in the chancel. It takes the unlikely form of a pillar on a tripod up which a serpent makes its way towards a dish on the top. Here four doves dip their beaks into the waters of life. One dove is underneath, uncomfortably close to the snake, a child at risk through not being baptised. The nave enjoys some equally fine woodwork, the lectern and pulpit being 'school of Chippendale'. They are of rosewood and sit on pedestals, like monarchical thrones, adorned with eagles.

To the east of the church is the Dashwood mausoleum, a hexagon of walls open to the sky with memorials to the family ranged along the walls. Visitors can be seen peering through its gate, puzzled as to whether this enclosure really is a Hell-Fire Valhalla, or just a walled kitchen garden.

WILLEN

St Mary *

Classical gem in Milton Keynes landscape

Milton Keynes has swallowed up many a pretty church in its computer-generated surroundings. Getting to Willen is a grim expedition through bleak roundabouts and chill-dried housing estates. The old church overlooks an artificial lake like a friendly spaniel left out to die. It was built in 1680 for the headmaster of Westminster School, Richard Busby, by Robert Hooke, a friend of Wren and designer of The Monument in London. Hooke had been a pupil of Busby, which presumably explains this out-of-the-way commission. He was primarily a scientist, claiming that Newton had stolen his work on the discovery of gravity. If true, this was no mean theft.

The building is charming. It sits on a small hill, dominated by a west tower of brick with stone dressings and corners finished with pineapple finials. Inside is a simple room with a plastered barrel vault. The original chancel was replaced by an apse in 1861. The decoration is pink wash with white plasterwork adornments, principally acanthus leaves, cherubs and gold bosses of sunbursts and shells. The wall panelling and box pews are still in place, as is the two-decker pulpit. The font has a marble bowl decorated with winged cherubs' heads, crowned with a magnificent wooden cover carved with garlands and fruit.

Impressively, the church has been restored on the initiative of the local people. What is now required is the removal of its dark Victorian glass.

WING

All Saints ****

Saxon nave, Dormer monuments

Anglo-Saxon architecture is usually more remarkable for its age than its beauty. Wing is remarkable for both. It sits on a rise above the Vale of Aylesbury. Like Stewkley, it was threatened in the 1970s with development as London's third airport, a strange proposal in such undulating landscape. The church's status as one of the outstanding Saxon churches in England strengthened the protesters' case.

The best approach is from the south-east, where we are greeted by an apse that has a crypt beneath it. The presence of both in a church that also retains a Saxon nave, aisles and west wall is unique. Wing appears to have belonged to the sister-in-law of King Edgar, widowed in her teens. Its importance must have declined swiftly since the church avoided the attentions of Normans and Goths alike. Not until the construction of the south aisle in the 14th century and the tower, clerestory and apse windows in the 15th were alterations made to the original.

Wing's interior retains the lofty simplicity of the earliest English churches. The Saxons would have been baffled at our obsession with coating their interiors with whitewash, and ridding them of iconography. At Wing the arches are simple, mere openings cut through thick walls. The apse arch is one of the widest of its period in the country and is surmounted by a small double window. The Perpendicular roof is a Buckinghamshire masterpiece. Every surface is carved, with the wall-post figures comprising a gallery of medieval characters, saints and kings. Many of the figures are playing early musical instruments, including trumpets, sackbuts and clarinets.

The Dormers came to Ascott Hall in the 1520s and proceeded to fill the church with their memorials. The earliest is in the north aisle to Sir Robert Dormer (d.1552), though the monument may be of 1575. A huge canopy supported by Corinthian columns and pilasters shelters a tomb chest with bulls' heads. It is a superb work of early English classicism (though the designer may have been French). In the chancel is a monument to Sir William Dormer, apparently of 1590. The refinement of the earlier tomb is now debased. Sir William lies in armour with his wife beside but below him, both with their hands in prayer.

Opposite is another stylistic shift, a monument of 1616. By then the Dormers had risen from the supine and kneel, one behind the other, in prayer. Their children are no longer relegated to the base but cluster round them, a family now nuclear rather than extended.

The south aisle contains a simple brass to Thomas Cotes, porter at Ascott Hall. It reports that Cotes has now left his key, fire, friends and all to find new room in Heaven. There is his grave: 'Reader, prepare for thine, for none can tell, / But that you two may meet tonight. Farewell.'

Cambridgeshire

The administrative county embraces the old Huntingdonshire, but as most locals still refer to them as separate, I have respected the separation. Cambridgeshire proper owes its best churches to water rather than land. Medieval Wisbech was a seaport and the Fen waterways could bring ships from the Wash as far south as Cambridge. The draining of the Fen by Dutch engineers in the 17th century converted the marsh into fertile farmland, but the county is still flat. One or other of the great monuments of Ely Cathedral and King's College Chapel, Cambridge, is visible from any high point.

So too are the towers of the churches that lined the old 'coastal' settlements running down the Fen shore along the east boundary of the county. These include the Swaffhams, Isleham, Burwell and the magnificent Decorated church of Bottisham. The county has its share of East Anglia's Perpendicular wealth, such as the tower at Wisbech and the great angel roof at March. South of Cambridge, the contours climb towards Essex. Here are admirable works of art, including the restored 12th-century murals at Ickleton, the North tombs at Kirtling and the extraordinary Bennet memorial at Babraham.

The city of Cambridge is not distinguished for parish churches, but plays host to the most neglected Victorian church in this book, Bodley's All Saints, Cambridge.

Babraham **	Cambridge:	Kirtling **
Balsham **	Great St Mary *	March ***
Bottisham ***	Harlton **	Swaffham Prior *
Burwell **	Hildersham *	Trumpington *
Cambridge:	Ickleton ***	Walsoken ***
All Saints **	Isleham *	Wisbech ***

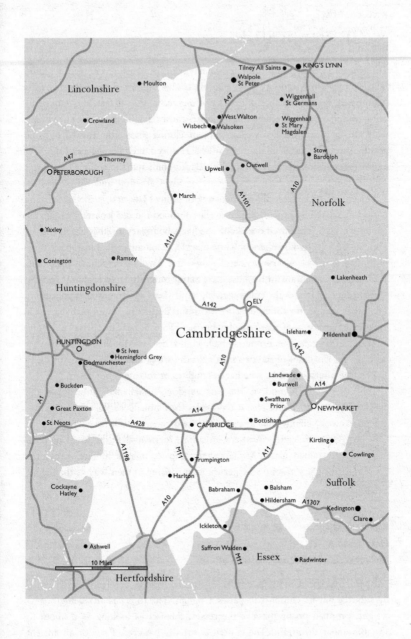

BABRAHAM
St Peter **
Baroque statues, Piper glass

The church in Babraham, pronounced Baybr'm, is down a lane next to Philip Hardwick's early Victorian Babraham Hall. This may be in what Pevsner calls 'ham-fisted' neo-Jacobean, but does not deserve its present fate, surrounded by pre-fabs and a housing estate. The planners must have been asleep. The church walls are a pleasing East Anglian mix of clunch and flint, washed by lime and the sun. The latter falls on 17th- and 18th-century benches and box pews and a Perpendicular pulpit with clerk's desk. The hatchments are of the local Adeane family.

The church is memorable for two works of art. The first is the astonishing Bennet memorial by Jasper Latham in the south aisle. It can be seen through the window even if the church is locked. The haggard figures of Sir Richard and Sir Thomas Bennet, two brothers in white marble, stand against a black backcloth. Both appear to be wearing funeral robes, are barefoot and have long hair. The faces, drawn and with big noses, are extraordinarily lifelike, almost surreal. One brother addresses the congregation, hands held apart as if in supplication. The other stands in profile, bent forward and appearing to speak to him. He looks most severe, as if reproving his brother. They appear to portray a Sceptic meeting a Mystic. The drama, which could be by Molière, is remarkably Baroque for the dates of the two men's deaths, 1658 and 1667. Two putti lean against the plinth weeping, whether in laughter or sorrow is not clear.

The other work is modern, the east window, designed by John Piper and executed by Patrick Reyntiens. It represents the emblems of St Peter, keys, fishing boat, cock, chains and anchor. The two men, who worked together at Coventry Cathedral and elsewhere, are the Morris and Burne-Jones of post-war English stained glass. At Babraham, Piper's images radiate across the church, forthright yet in no way garish, as surprising in their way as the Bennet statues.

BALSHAM
Holy Trinity **
Medieval choir stalls, ecclesiastical brasses

Balsham may be a straggling village, its picturesque cottages overwhelmed by suburb, but its church still packs a punch. The tower is an ageing heavy-weight, propped up by massive buttresses, themselves looking as if about to stumble under the strain. The church is equally battered. Parts of an ancient clock are distributed in the north aisle, as if in an antique shop. A carpenter-rector in the 1930s named John Burrell made a font cover, with a howitzer shell as counterweight. There are bats nesting in the chancel. This is an eccentric place.

The tower is Early Gothic but appears to be of Saxon origin. One man alone is said to have survived a Viking raid that wiped out the village. A Saxon coffin survives under the tower, whether his or not, who knows? The arcades and aisles are Perpendicular, the chancel early 14th century with a Reticulated east window. The late-medieval rood screen is among the best in the county, complete with loft and ribbed and coloured. The plastic sheeting that fills the chancel arch to keep the chancel warm in winter must surely be a temporary expedient.

The chancel at Balsham, though heavily restored by the Victorians, contains two medieval masterpieces. First is a magnificent set of choir stalls with tall traceried backs and two tiers of carved arm rests, one for use when standing, one when seated. These rests form rows of mini-gargoyles best seen in profile. Animals, dolphins, mermaids, dragons, even the occasional human, start out of the stalls as if straining to escape some cataclysm. In among them (on the north side) is a Fen Fowler on stilts with his dog. The rector in the late 14th century was John Sleford, chaplain to the Queen. The guide suggests that the stalls may have come from the Westminster workshops.

On the floor are two massive brasses to 15th-century rectors. One commemorates Canon Sleford himself (d.1401), the other John Blodwell (d.1462). They are among the finest ecclesiastical brasses in England – such memorials suffered more in the Reformation than those of soldiers. In Sleford's case the surround portrays his church offices, embracing Wells, Ripon, Westminster and royal appointments. He could clearly afford these stalls. A small chapel to St Nicholas stands in the north aisle. This was constructed by John Burrell in the 1930s from 17th-century panels taken from his rectory. It is a charming work of personal piety, with altar, altarpiece, reredos, parclose and screen. The saint's statue is on top.

BOTTISHAM
Holy Trinity ***
Decorated carvings, children's tomb

Burwell, the Swaffhams and Bottisham lie along the southern 'shore' of the Cambridgeshire Fen. Those sensitive to such topography can feel the aura of shore villages. Low cottages, wide greens and narrow lanes run down towards the level, as if craving the sea. Here at Bottisham, the prosperity of the sea trade is made stone in one of the county's most glorious churches. It stands substantially as the Decorated masons and their patron, Elias de Beckingham, left it *c.*1330. Beckingham was a man of parts, being a judge under Edward I. He died in 1305 and may have paid for the new church in his will.

The interior is reached through the west door under an Ely-style galilee. The nave is Decorated and unusually homogeneous. The arcades are, says Pevsner in a rare flurry of adverbs, 'steeply and nobly pointed and finely and richly moulded'. Every opening is opulent. In the chancel an earlier, Early Gothic church is dominant. The east window of three lancets was inserted in 1875. Its egregious stained glass commemorates Colonel Gambier-Jenyns, who survived the charge of the Light Brigade. Next to it are simple Early Gothic sedilia and a piscina.

The church is full of oddities. It has a plain stone rood screen, *c.*1475. At the east ends of the aisles are tall windows which would once have lit altars but now light superb post-Reformation monuments. They stand behind wooden screens that are presumably relics of a 14th-century rood. The left-hand monument is to Lionel and Dorothy Allington of 1638. Two infants lie under a canopy with two curtains parted by putti. The scene is sentimental yet moving. 'Stay passenger,' bids the inscription, 'and wonder whom these stones had learned to speake'. The grammar and punctuation are questionable, but the gist is that the children came into the world, 'tasted, liked it not and bad farewell'.

The second monument is a century later. Sir Roger Jenyns (d.1740) and his wife sit on a mat holding each other's hand, as if about to rise for a dance, a picture of marital bliss. On the south wall a grateful child records a gift by Jenyns – 'I was naked and ye clothed me' – the monument being dated 1730. The modern candelabra is aggressive, as is the restored Victorian reredos above a tiled dado. Time will weather them all. The west end was refurnished by Sir Albert Richardson in 1952.

BURWELL
St Mary **
Perpendicular stone carving, urine-bottle boss

Before the draining of the Fen, Burwell was a shore village and thus an important exporter of wool and importer of stone. The exterior is remarkable, with as much glass as wall and a 'woolgothic' wheel window above the chancel arch. The designer is said to be the Cambridge mason, Reginald Ely, architect of King's College Chapel. There is a dedication to John Benet and his wives, dated 1464, which is shortly after the completion of King's. The tower is partly Norman, with an unnecessary Georgian spirelet. Even outside, we can see from the handsome clerestory that the interior must be spectacularly high.

The interior is an essay in Perpendicular height and light. The nave has five bays, the piers soaring towards the panelled clerestory with capitals only on the minor shafts. The east wall of the chancel above the chancel arch, including the swirling wheel window, is of a splendour to rival such features of Gloucestershire churches. The chancel is lower but with windows of the same size as in the nave, giving it an almost dazzling brightness. Here the statue niches are crowned with a virtuoso display of carved crocketing, which extends to the reredos, restored by Street. The carving at Burwell is again attributed to Reginald Ely. The Perpendicular east windows in the chancel and aisles are unusually inventive, as are the chancel niches, each one slightly different. This is 15th-century carving at its best.

Where Ely stopped, Burwell's woodworkers took over. Much of the delight of the church is overhead. The wall plates and bosses are deeply carved, the subjects including elephants and castles, a tiger with a mirror and foxes with geese. The best known is above the north aisle and portrays a mermaid, a fox and a monkey with a urine bottle. The last was apparently an attack on the medieval medical profession.

CAMBRIDGE
All Saints **
Tractarian interior by Bodley, Morris windows

Everyone in Cambridge knows the steeple of All Saints, opposite the entrance to Jesus College. Few know that the steeple marks the city's most distinguished non-collegiate church. Fewer still can be aware of its deplorable state. That a work by the master of late-Victorian architecture, Bodley, should stand unused in the centre of a rich university city is shocking. All Saints stands forlorn in the care of the Churches Conservation Trust, while new halls, libraries and auditoriums rise all round it.

The church was a replacement in the 1860s for a local town church on a small plot of land donated by Jesus College. There was barely room for a churchyard and the tower had to be erected over the chancel. The architect equal to the challenge was the young Bodley, who invoked the aid of the equally youthful Morris, Burne-Jones and friends. All Saints predates their other early masterpieces at Selsley (Gloucs) and Scarborough (N.Yorks). It survives in its 19th-century Tractarian guise, including seats, hangings and candles round the altar.

The exterior is dominated by a fine ribbed spire, said to be based on that of Ashbourne (Derbys). The interior is composed of a nave and a single aisle, divided by a strong arcade. These are covered from floor to ceiling with stencilled murals in red, green and gold by Morris and later by Kempe. The paintings continue up to the rafters, and run through into the chancel. They are now dingy beyond appreciation, though not beyond restoration (compare them with restored Bodley murals at Tue Brook in Liverpool). The painted pulpit, rood screen and sanctuary furnishings, all by Bodley, miraculously survive in place.

The glass at least retains its colour. That in the east window is by Morris, Burne-Jones and Madox Brown. Portraying Old Testament prophets, it was completed in 1866 when the partnership was still in its early, tentative style. Morris's personal taste for backgrounds full of foliage and landscape was not yet dominant. His work in Jesus College Chapel across the road was ten years later. The two eastern windows in the nave north wall are by Kempe. But wake up, Cambridge.

[CCT]

CAMBRIDGE
Great St Mary *
Roof carvings, modern reredos

The churches of Cambridge are disappointing, as if cowering beneath the single splendour of King's College Chapel. They attracted too much attention in the 19th century and perhaps too little in the 20th. Great St Mary's is the University church, but like St Mary's in Oxford it must meet the needs of both town and gown. The exterior is meagre. An early 17th-century tower with crenellated turrets is poorly proportioned. The roof runs to only a handful of pinnacles and the white stone is without character.

The inside is more noble, rebuilt at the end of the 15th century with donations from both Richard III and Henry VII. The rebuilding was completed by 1519, shortly after King's College Chapel across the road. Perhaps wisely, the patrons of St Mary's did not compete, contenting themselves with a conventionally rich East Anglian interior, like that of Saffron Walden (Essex).

The church's principal feature is the nave arcade of five tall, slender bays leading to the wide chancel arch. All have tracery in their spandrels and a sumptuous frieze. The roof is original and is made from 100 oak trees donated by Henry VII. The bosses are magnificent if hard to discern in detail from the ground. There is no screen to the chancel, which gives a clear view of the church's most distinguished work of art, the Majestas of Alan Durst, installed as a reredos in 1960. It draws the eye down the length of the church, despite being forced to fight with the Victorian glass above. St Mary's has a charming Virgin and Child by Loughnan Pendred and an ancient parish chest of c.1522 outside St Andrew's Chapel.

HARLTON
St Mary **
Fryer monument, 20th-century altar carvings

The church is well-sited on a mound looking across flat country towards Cambridge, a landscape filled with radio dishes and east winds. On my last visit, a gale was blowing and Harlton's windows might have been on the bridge of a ship defying a storm. The soft clunch stone walls have been patched and repaired with cobbles and bricks so often they look like the sweepings of a builder's yard.

Inside, the lightness is dazzling. Harlton is late 14th century but with charming traces of Decorated about the tops of its windows. The masons seem so attached to the pre-Black Death style that they retained it for the apex of their Perpendicular openings. The east window has four-petal tracery. The windows, free of stained glass, allow the trees and landscape to enter the church and form its backdrop. They are so tall as to need no clerestory.

Tallness is also the essence of the tower arch, chancel arch, arcades, organ case, old stone screen, even the pews. On either side of the altar are two tall pinnacles over empty niches. The reredos has excellent modern carvings by local artist H. J. Ellison (1924) in the style of Eric Gill. They are a most satisfactory substitute for the originals. Would that he had filled the other niches.

No less tall is the Fryer memorial in the south aisle. The lord of the manor, Henry Fryer (d.1631), kneels flanked by his father, a doctor, in front and his mother behind, while below reclines his wife Bridget. The canopy is supported not by columns but by an unusual caryatid and a Persian in the act of wiping away a tear from his eye. This remarkable work is attributed to Maximilian Colt. The inscription mentions that 'the poore man's bowels were his chest', which may be understood as Fryer's wish that his wealth be used to feed the poor rather than left in a money box. He died in a duel in Calais (says the *Shell Guide*) or falling from his horse (says the church guide).

Harlton has fine modern kneelers, including the only double kneeler I have seen. Its size was either to encompass all of Ely Cathedral in its embroidery, or to honour the American saying, 'A family that prays together stays together.'

HILDERSHAM
Holy Trinity *
Painted Victorian chancel, *memento mori* brass

Hildersham should be visited for its village charm and that rare thing in a medieval church, a complete High Victorian chancel designed to match the original nave. The work was undertaken by two rectors, James Goodwin and his son Charles, in the 1890s, with the help of the firm of Clayton & Bell. Whether the Victorian revival of the liturgical atmosphere of Decorated Gothic was faithful to any original we cannot know. The stone and woodwork are machined and therefore hard in appearance. The colouring is mostly pastel.

Yet the chancel is a coherent and pleasant change from the naked, scraped Gothic of much of East Anglia. After falling into disrepair the church was restored in 1973 by S. E. Dykes Bower. The chancel is now glorious, its roof depicting sky, fleur-de-lis and stars. The murals, by Clayton & Bell in the style of Lord Leighton, represent biblical scenes. The alabaster reredos is of Christ backed by grapes and ears of corn. The east window above is of the Tree of Jesse.

The church possesses 15th-century brasses of the Paris family. Rubbings of their facsimiles helped pay for the 1970s' restoration, bringing in £1,000 a year. One is of a husband and wife in an unusual composition, kneeling before a cross with God sitting behind on a seat. Another shows a jolly knight in armour and another a *memento mori*, a gruesome cloaked skeleton commemorating Richard Howard (d.1499). This failed to deter the thieves who in 1977 stole the church's two 14th-century oak effigies of Sir William Busteler and his wife. Like many stolen English church furnishings, rumour claims that they are available for a price in Belgium – in which case they should be bought back.

In the tower vestry is a huge 13th-century ladder to the bell loft, its treads quartered logs of tree trunk. Do not climb it; the woodworm is horrendous.

ICKLETON
St Mary ***
12th-century wall paintings

Ickleton is a suburbanised village close to the Hertfordshire border. Its church has a Norman west door in its tower and a Norman interior. These were regarded as charming but relatively undistinguished when, in 1979, a pyromaniac set fire to the church and destroyed much of the roof and transept. In the course of restoration, the builders discovered a complete set of 12th-century wall paintings along the north and east nave walls. Murals of such an early date are rare, chiefly confined to Kempley (Gloucs), Copford (Essex) and the Lewes School of painters in Sussex.

Ickleton's nave might have been brought from the Umbrian hills. Simple arches devoid of mouldings rest on plain cushion capitals and cylindrical piers. Some of the arches contain fragments of Roman bricks, while the slimmer piers are actually reused Roman columns. The north aisle is narrow while the south, probably early 14th century, is broad, necessitating a wide Perpendicular arch to the transept, uncomfortably filled with the organ. The tall and graceful Perpendicular screen retains some of its paintings.

All this is subsidiary to the nave wall paintings. Great excitement attended their discovery after the fire. The main nave murals date from the end of the 12th century, that is from the end of the Norman period. The Doom over the east wall is believed to be later, of the 14th century. The north wall upper tier shows four traditional Passion scenes, of the Last Supper, the Betrayal, the Flagellation and Christ carrying the Cross. The Last Supper shows Judas taking a fish from the table, whether as a thief or because the fish represented Christ is not known. The Doom is much damaged, but depicts the Virgin baring her breasts to Christ in a gesture of supplication. Such nudity was later considered shocking and became a particular target for the iconoclasts. This is a rare surviving example.

ISLEHAM
St Andrew *
Repainted Peyton monuments

We need to half shut our eyes on a misty day and imagine a small settlement on an eminence in the Fen, surrounded by water and marsh. This 'ham' cannot have been on much of an 'isle', yet it was enough for the 11th-century Benedictines to found a priory above the water line. Their disused chapel still stands at the bend in the high street. St Andrew's is 100 yds down the road. The west tower is Victorian, but the rest of the church dates from the early 14th century, much altered in the late 15th, when the manorial lord, Christopher Peyton, rebuilt the upper parts. His work includes the unusual carvings in the spandrels and the high roof of 1495 which was, at one stage, peopled with 60 angels. The surviving angels are particularly well-carved, with charming hand gestures and flowing garments. The chancel still has medieval stalls with misericords and a magnificent Jacobean altar rail.

Peyton also commissioned the family monuments, now among the best in the county. The first is in the chancel, a chest tomb topped by a superb brass commemorating his father, Thomas Peyton (d.1484), flanked by two wives. The three engraved figures look like medieval teenagers in fancy dress, lying beneath an intricate Gothic canopy. The principal monuments are in the south transept, where they are being restored with help from Peytons all over Britain and America. Pride of place goes to the tombs of Sir Robert and Sir John Peyton (d.1590 and 1616 respectively), both flamboyant six-posters, the earlier with bulbous columns and the later with Corinthian ones. They have been fiercely and controversially repainted, but such memorials were always garish. Only the modern eye requires antiquity to be faded.

Isleham was singled out by Clifton-Taylor as having the most inappropriate Victorian glass in England. This is perhaps an exaggeration in what is a tough contest, but surely it must one day be removed.

KIRTLING
All Saints **
Norman carving, North tombs

Forget the village of that name, which lies a mile distant. Look instead across the rolling Cambridgeshire–Suffolk border for the gatehouse of Kirtling Tower, ancestral home of the North family. The Norths were descended from a 16th-century Nottingham merchant. His son Edward became a lawyer, married well and acquired Kirtling in 1526. He rose to become Royal Treasurer and Chancellor of the well-named Court of Augmentation. In this office his task was to be dispenser of the spoils of the Dissolution of the Monasteries, the greatest redistribution of wealth since the Conquest. The 16th century was a good time to be a lawyer – if ever there were a bad one. Even by Tudor standards North was sensationally rich. His London home was the Charterhouse.

Kirtling's church was already in its present form by then. Indeed over the 12th-century south door is a fine Norman carving of Christ in Majesty. The churchyard falls away to the north. To the south is a rectory, a wall and then a sudden change of scene from demure rusticity to grandeur. A moat encloses a mound and the remains of the old castle, guarded by peacocks and ducks.

The interior is comparatively bare, except for a set of superbly restored North family hatchments. The Perpendicular south chapel (confusingly called the North Chapel) has against its east wall the fine classical tomb chest of Edward North himself (d.1564), with pilasters and coats of arms in wreaths. Assiduous in life, he was sober in death. North's son Roger (d.1600), like many offspring of the upwardly mobile, appears to have been altogether more flamboyant. A diplomat and soldier active in the Dutch wars, he was one of the royal courtiers expected to entertain Elizabeth I on her progress, in a style that must have tested even the North finances. His tomb chest is similar to his father's but is covered by a huge six-poster canopy. Its columns are astonishingly lavish, covered with spirals of mulberry, oak and vine. The effigy has its feet on a ferocious dragon. The last of the North line, buried in the vault beneath, was Lady Valerie North (d.1965).

MARCH
St Wendreda ***
Finest English angel roof

March, like Needham Market (Suffolk), is a case of roof, all roof and little but roof. The church is situated a mile to the south of the town. The tower, predominantly Perpendicular, is tall and slender, the elegance of its spire spoilt by heavy buttressing. A processional path was inserted through its base. These intrusions remain a mystery but were probably to avoid festival celebrants having to use the adjacent public road. Except for the roof, the inside is pleasant but undistinguished.

But what an 'except'. The March roof may not equal Needham for engineering skill but it outshines all others for the unity and splendour of its carving. It survived the Reformation axe and the buckshot of the Cromwellians. It survived the Victorians. It survived even those modern iconoclasts, the worm, the beetle and neglect. The structure is still held together by most of its original wooden pins, helped only by a modern iron bar inserted to strengthen the walls across the nave.

The structure is a conventional double hammerbeam, built between 1470 and 1520. But the great beams disappear completely behind the heavenly host of angels. There are 118, in addition to saints and apostles. The roof was probably paid for by the seven guilds of the 15th-century town. There are angels' wings on the wall-posts, wings on the hammers and wings on the tops of the tie-beams. It is as if March could not bear to worship without a cloud of angels in attendance. We dare not clap our hands, lest they come to life and lift the entire roof slowly up into the sky. In a spandrel on the north side is a carved 'prince of darkness'; this is known as a 'spoiler' or cartoon and is intended to prevent the whole work seeming too perfect. He keeps the roof moored to the ground.

SWAFFHAM PRIOR
St Mary **
Twin Fenland octagons

East Anglia has other twinned churches but few occupy so spectacular a site as the two Swaffham churches, St Mary and St Cyriac, cohabiting in one churchyard. Their two octagons look over the Fens from the medieval 'shore', as if straining to catch the attention of Ely across the ghost of the water. In Norman times, the portion of Swaffham that was St Mary's belonged to the Prior of Ely; the other portion belonged to three knights. Each patron built a church on the mound overlooking the village. Both churches have seen vicissitude, rivalry and ruin, even after they were officially 'merged' in 1667. St Mary's has emerged the victor, with St Cyriac's in the care of the Churches Conservation Trust.

The octagonal tower of St Mary's must have predated Ely. It is hugely Norman, with wide internal arches rising on squinches in what looks more like a fortress than a church. The octagon is topped by a 16-sided Early Gothic lantern and then by a modern crown. The church was rebuilt in the Perpendicular period but fell into ruin after its spire was struck by lightning in 1767. The chancel was rebuilt by Arthur Blomfield in 1878 and the church revived in the form we see today.

The interior is more of a curiosity than beautiful. The aisle windows contain a complete set of 20th-century glass which was designed by T. F. Curtis and inserted c.1920 in commemoration of the Great War. The pictures are of comic-book simplicity, set in Gothic canopies to give a three-dimensional effect. The scenes embrace war in the trenches, the Cambridge countryside, the Bible and even the Statue of Liberty.

The second church, St Cyriac's, is a forlorn place up a path through a fine yew avenue. The dedication is rare, to the same saint as France's premier military academy. Of the medieval church only the tower remains, Perpendicular rising to another octagon. The rest of the church fell into ruin in the 18th century, but was revived after the lightning strike on St Mary's. In 1806 the nave and chancel were rebuilt as a bare neo-Gothic hall, with a dull exterior of Cambridgeshire yellow brick. This was the village church until Blomfield's rebuilding of St Mary's. The interior has a simple Georgian reredos and western organ gallery.

[Part CCT]

TRUMPINGTON
St Mary and St Michael *
Trumpington brass

This Cambridge suburb struggles to keep its heart rural, or at least villagey. Tall yews, thatched cottages and big houses in expansive grounds guard a distinguished church whose exterior bears the outward signs of heavy Butterfield restoration. Its interior was richly patronised throughout its history. A nave of five soaring bays displays the multiple shafts and chamfers of the Decorated period, most splendidly in the tower arch. The transepts are separated from the nave by two bays of the arcade.

The rest of the church would be anticlimax but for the magnificent canopy over the tomb of Sir Roger de Trumpington (d.1289) in the north transept. The canopy is later than Sir Roger's celebrated brass, which depicts a knight in chainmail. The Trumpington brass is very early, and compares with others of this period at Stoke D'Abernon (Surrey) and Acton (Suffolk).

A collage of medieval glass has been inserted in the rectangular opening behind the clerk's desk. The pulpit is an unusually austere Jacobean work from Emmanuel College.

WALSOKEN
All Saints ***
Seven-Sacraments font

Walsoken is another marsh church, now in a suburb of Wisbech. The tower's Early Gothic buttresses, pinnacles and short Northampton spire are similar to Tilney's. It is a marvellous work, so much more inventive than the Perpendicular towers familiar in these parts. The west door has colonettes with stiff-leaf capitals. The body of the church exterior is conventional, low-slung Perpendicular. But all this is deceptive. Inside is the most substantial Norman parish church in Cambridgeshire.

The arcades are of nine bays, two of them in the chancel. These have piers alternately octagonal and round, leading to a chancel arch which, though pointed, still has zigzag moulding. The west tower arch is Early Gothic, the roof 15th century with figures in canopied niches against the wallposts, a charming decoration and, in my experience, unique.

More eye-catching is a recent addition to the east wall of the nave, a large 17th-century carving of King David playing a harp. This faces a contemporary carving on the west wall of King Solomon. Paintings on either side depict him about to cut the baby in half, bizarre irruptions into the peace of the nave. I am surprised that Walsoken worshippers can ever keep their eyes to the ground.

Walsoken's other woodwork includes the parclose screen to the south aisle chapel, a delicate fretwork with much original carving. Adjacent is a beautiful Flemish statue of St Mary and St Anne. Even by neighbouring Norfolk standards, Walsoken's Seven-Sacraments font is spectacular, finely placed in the middle of the nave. Below the reliefs of the sacraments are groin-vaulted niches containing eight saints, all in excellent condition. The font dates from as late as 1544.

WISBECH
St Peter and St Paul ***
Detached tower, double nave with chancels

Medieval Wisbech (pronounced beach) was a seaport at the southern extremity of the Wash, commanding the junction of the Nene and Ouse rivers. The parade of Georgian buildings along the bank of the Nene forms a superb and celebrated tableau, but the rest of the town is disappointing. The church lies in the centre, but is somehow disjointed from the surrounding streets, like a feature in a municipal garden.

The chief external glory is the Perpendicular tower. Like many built on unstable East Anglian soil, it was detached to avoid any collapse also ruining the church. A former tower base remains at the west end of the nave, the super-structure having fallen into the nave in the 16th century. The new tower, along with the church itself, appears to have sunk beneath the level of the churchyard. It begins as a plain structure but grows more ornate, and plutocratic, with height, as if eager to show off the names of its patrons to seafarers arriving at the port. The crown is a flourish of shields and coats of arms, topped by pierced battlements and a flèche.

The interior is a marvellous jumble of additions. Wisbech has not one nave but two, each with a chancel and each with an aisle. Subsequent alter-ations further confuse the story, offering a challenge for any dating enthusiast. The plan is as follows. The first nave, to the north, has a Norman arcade to its north aisle with scalloped and water-leaf capitals. Its south arcade, dividing it from the second nave, is Perpendicular and must be later than the second, south, nave built in the 14th century. That nave's own south arcade is Decorated. Meanwhile the chancels were not left in peace. The original Norman north chancel was demolished and rebuilt longer and wider in the Decorated style. Since this is wider than the old nave, a most unfortunate 'crank' arch is set at the east end of the north aisle. The second nave has its own chancel, now holding the organ, and its own guild chapel of the Holy Trinity, now a vestry.

That is as clear as I can make it. Not surprisingly, the resulting church lacks focus. Its best feature is undoubtedly the north chancel. This has the appearance of a tunnel, culminating in a superb early Decorated east window above a Venetian mosaic, by Salviati, of Leonardo da Vinci's *Last Supper*. The window is of lancets topped by a circle, the latter filled with trefoils. The choir stalls, some of them with misericords, have candleholders and must look lovely when lit on a dark night for winter evensong.

Cheshire

The county was always prosperous and its churches ostentatious. They stand proud over their villages in the rolling country south of the industrial Mersey and the Manchester Ship Canal. Strong red sandstone is interspersed with the black-and-white half-timbering characteristic of Cheshire's domestic architecture. Its most celebrated interior, Lower Peover, is the oldest aisled wooden church in England.

Cheshire is essentially of the Perpendicular age. The naves of Astbury, Great Budworth and Malpas are of East Anglian quality, notably Malpas's superb angel roof. Equally outstanding are the monuments of that period, the Savages of Macclesfield and the Cholmondeleys and Breretons of Malpas. Over them towers the old salt town of Nantwich, its church tower, crossing, roofs and choir stalls putting it in the first rank of northern churches. The early Victorians gave Cheshire a curious gallery of Continental fittings at Birtles, and the late Victorians commissioned Hubert Austin's masterpiece at St George, Stockport.

Acton *
Astbury ***
Birtles *
Bunbury **

Chester: St John *
Great Budworth **
Lower Peover ***
Macclesfield ***

Malpas ***
Nantwich ****
Stockport: St George **
Warburton *

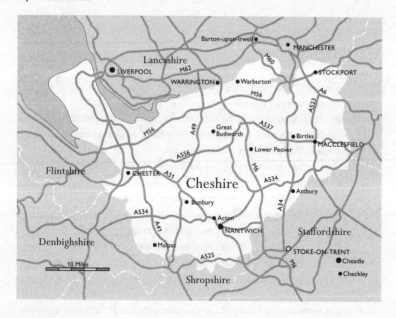

ACTON
St Mary *
Wilbraham monuments

The church lies off the Nantwich to Wrexham road and is a single flourish of 17th-century ostentation by Sir Richard Wilbraham. A Cholmondeley by birth, he decided in 1620 to adorn his local church with what today look like birthday cake trimmings. He crowned the sides of the chancel with a parapet made up of heart shapes, and the east end with a crest of shells and arrowheads. The Wilbraham arms are over the east window.

The 13th-century nave is wide, with narrow Perpendicular aisles. Each aisle has at its east end a superb tomb. In the north is that of Sir William Mainwaring of 1399. He lies battered and graffitied beneath a cusped and crocketed canopy, crowned by his emblem of an ass. An earlier Mainwaring lost his horse in battle and seized an ass to continue his charge. The *Dad's Army* captain of the same name would have approved. In the south aisle is an amiable contrast, the tomb of Sir Richard and Lady Wilbraham, the church's 17th-century patrons. They are beautifully attired in clothes old-fashioned for their day, assured rather than pompous, contented amid their good works.

The wide 14th-century chancel arch frames Wilbraham's new chancel. This houses a fine set of 17th-century furnishings. The east window is by Kempe.

ASTBURY
St Mary ***
All-through clerestory, mechanical font cover

The village is on the Cheshire plain but with the ridge of the Peak District filling the horizon. The church's apparent custodian told me sternly that it was 'not open to the public'. The pub opposite was equally unwelcoming. When will these great churches learn to engage the support of their communities? The lovely Queen Anne rectory was more helpful.

At first sight Astbury is an architectural mystery. From the north it appears as a Perpendicular chapel, adrift from an older, indeed Norman, tower. The latter is attached to the north-west of the church and has a fine octagonal needle spire. The west porch, of three storeys, almost amounts to a tower in itself and there is also a two-storey south porch. The church must have many secret rooms and its medieval clergy much business to do. The churchyard is full of interest, with a fine gateway and a medieval tomb canopy.

Inside, all is revealed and is sensational. The seven-bay red sandstone arcade continues through nave and chancel without a break. The plan narrows slightly from west to east to emphasise its length, a most unusual feature in a Gothic church. The wall shafts rise from corbels carved with faces of bishops and priests to a clerestory that is Astbury's glory. Each window is of four lights and is so high as to form a sort of church above a church. The clerestory runs uninterrupted to the east end. The east window of seven lights is almost as tall as the whole church. The composition is harmonious, the Perpendicular style at its least dull.

The architecture is rivalled by the fittings. The deeply coved rood screen has unusual open arches, ten in all, with filigree tracery confined to the heads. Above is a wooden roof with shallow beams, intricate pendants and golden bosses. The box pews are from the 17th century, as are the pulpit and wooden eagle lectern with rotund body and huge talons. The font and cover are Jacobean. The cover is extraordinary, a pedimented canopy raised by a lift with another, bigger pedimented canopy to contain it.

BIRTLES
St Catherine *
Victorian collector's treasure trove

I approached the church in Birtles from the Macclesfield to Knutsford road on a brisk spring morning with the sun rising over rolling country. Thick mist lay in the hollows. Suddenly over a crest appeared the Cheshire Hills Hunt, galloping towards me as if in cavalry formation. They were splendidly attired in pink and black. This is rich country of big houses and open estates, which once extended round the salt mines of Nantwich and the silk mills of Macclesfield and has retained its aura of secluded wealth.

In 1840, Thomas Hibbert of Birtles Hall indulged a then popular taste for ecclesiastical antique-collecting and built himself a church to match. The result is Cheshire's answer to Old Warden (Beds) or Gatton (Surrey), a veritable treasure trove of fittings acquired from the churches and monasteries of Europe in the wake of the Napoleonic Wars. The church sits next to its rectory on a hilltop, with Birtles Hall – a 1920s reconstruction – flying its flag in the distance. The small tower is octagonal and endearing, the windows Perpendicular.

Inside, the effect is of an antique shop or perhaps the private chapel of an old Dutch mansion, warm, dark and crowded. The dominant pulpit is apparently four pulpits in one. Superbly carved panels portray biblical scenes and are dated 1686. The sanctuary is panelled, as is most of the church. A fierce Continental eagle forms the lectern and the cornice of the clerk's desk is supported by stern putti. The nave pews are upholstered like theatre seats. The west wall contains a burst of relief carving, and is said to be constructed from Dutch stall backs. The hymn board is surmounted by an otter which is clasping an oak sprig in its mouth.

Birtles would deserve fame for its glass alone. The three figures in the east window are of the Virgin, an angel and St John. The rest of the glass mostly comprises miniature Dutch roundels of the 16th and 17th centuries. They are of scenes from the Bible, classical mythology or Dutch home life, reminiscent of the paintings of van Ostade or Avercamp. I find them charming and thoroughly in keeping with this comfortable Cheshire scenery. The baptistery that forms a balancing transept to the porch is also vividly panelled and painted.

BUNBURY
St Boniface **
Alabaster effigy of giant, 'bulging udder' woman

Bunbury sits on an incline, its south aisle blazing out over the houses below. The tower is massive and solid, and the light-hearted aisles seem to embrace it for protection. The Perpendicular interior expresses itself in clustered piers, high clerestory and double-deckered aisle windows. Yet there are fragments left from the Decorated period, as if to remind us of what went before. Thus we see a wide chancel arch, an east window of flamboyant design and a chancel surviving from a college founded by Sir Hugh Calveley in 1386. The whole interior is full of light.

On the walls of the nave are parts of an old parclose screen with crude paintings. Indeed the church is littered with pieces that appear to have fallen off the fabric at various stages, like an architectural casualty ward. The Ridley Chapel contains a stone screen with paintings on its dado and much surviving colour. It also has doors with wooden trellis panels. The altar in the north aisle has a curious frieze backed with a Green Man. Outside is a rare survival of a priest's house attached to its own chantry.

In the Decorated chancel is the spectacular tomb of Calveley himself (d.1394). He was said to be a giant and is here portrayed as such in chainmail. It was unusual for alabaster effigies of this period to be likenesses; most came from the Nottingham workshop and were ordered by status and heraldry. Perhaps for Calveley a particularly large one was ordered. Another fine tomb is of Sir George Beeston of 1601. He wears black armour and has a white head and beard. The modern east window is ugly, but must be the only one to have a railway signal incongruously sited beneath a near-naked John the Baptist.

At the back of the church is the standing memorial of Jane Johnson who died in 1741. She was the wife of a local dancing master and is shown with 'bulging udders' so large that they offended an 18th-century vicar. He had the statue buried. It was found again in 1882 and re-established, albeit inconspicuously. She looks most odd.

CHESTER
St John *
Shrouded skeleton memorial

St John's was Chester's cathedral from 1075 until 1095, and retained the name until Henry VIII raised the Abbey to that rank. The monastery went into abrupt decline, such that by the 19th century it was a ruin. The Victorians restored it with customary gusto, building on a new north-east bell-tower with a curious triangular cap. The old west tower fell in 1881, taking with it the original, magnificent Early Gothic north porch. This has now been rebuilt.

The forms and spaces of the interior are still those of an abbreviated Norman cathedral. The nave piers are massive drums rising to moulded capitals. The triforium and clerestory appear later, probably from the late 12th and early 13th centuries respectively. They are more intricate with clustered shafts and four pointed arches to each bay. To the east is the Norman crossing with wide arches on tall piers with clustered shafts. It makes a splendid proscenium for the short chancel, which is mostly Victorian.

The Lady Chapel occupies part of the south transept and has a charming late 17th-century reredos. Here is a monument to Diana Warburton (d.1693). A pretty white Corinthian niche with swags and putti forms the astonishing frame to a full-length standing skeleton behind a shroud. This work of ghoulish piety is by the sculptor Edward Pierce, pupil of Wren. At the back of the church are Saxon crosses and old tombstones. One of the latter carries the scissors of a glover, another the hammer and tongs of a smithy. The west window by Edward Frampton, from the Clayton & Bell firm, portrays events in the life of the Chester church, including King Charles escaping over the Dee in 1645.

GREAT BUDWORTH
St Mary **
Picturesque setting, burials price list

Great Budworth is a picture village clinging to an isolated hill on the Cheshire plain. A narrow high street and even narrower Church Street rise to a pub, an old tree, a disused pump and a church. Although many of the cottages are Victorian, by the Cheshire architect John Douglas, Victorian now merges so well into Tudor that few visitors care for the distinction and regard everything as quaint. The churchyard itself is among the best in the county, with yew and lime in abundance, stocks by the entrance and a former schoolhouse at the rear.

The sandstone church is worthy of its setting. Not all Perpendicular churches should be compared with those of East Anglia, but here the comparison favours Cheshire. The west tower is tall and strong, the outline embattled and the east end well-balanced with flanking chapels. The interior is beautifully composed. The arcades and aisle run the length of the church, with a tall clerestory. The south aisle windows are open to the sun, which brings to life the pinkness of the stone. This harmonious design is enlivened by excellent sandstone carving. Grimacing faces peer from otherwise simple capitals. The humour seems random: a face sticks out its tongue at the congregation, while an owl on the south wall of the nave keeps watch on any mice that might venture below.

The south transept comprises the resting place of the Warburtons of Arley. Here lies an alabaster effigy of Sir John Warburton (d.1575), sadly deprived of his arms and legs but still wearing delicately carved armour. Here too are medieval stalls and later benches with poppyheads. The north transept is a fragment of a former Decorated church, its windows Reticulated. This was used after the Reformation as burial place for the Leycesters, benefactors of Lower Peover. The chancel has good glass by Kempe.

In the south aisle is a price list for services performed by the 19th-century clergy, with a simple means test. Fees for interment of 'labouring classes' are two shillings to the minister and one shilling to the clerk. Fees for interment 'among the yeomanry' are double that rate. Whether the service supplied was different is not indicated.

LOWER PEOVER
St Oswald ***
Ancient wooden frame, 'rival' family pews

The village is pronounced Peever, derived from the Saxon for a 'sparkling stream'. The church lies down a cobbled lane from the main road, past old cottages, at the end of which is a 17th-century schoolroom and a restaurant called 'The Bells of Peover'. The ensemble is completed by a churchyard that gives on to meadows and trees. This is pure stockbroker Cheshire. Lest we forget, we can hear its pumping artery, the M6, a mile to the west.

The churchyard is dominated by a massive Perpendicular tower built in 1582. This is deceptive of what lies behind, a marvellous pile of black-and-white timbering. Peover is the ecclesiastical version of Cheshire's celebrated mansions, Little Moreton and Chorley Hall, a monument to the oakwood that long contributed so much to architecture in these parts. A poem on the west wall celebrates its virtues: 'Talk not of Syrian cedar, / Nor yet of foreign pine, / And mention not the timber / Of any other clime. / But see our native oak / In noble grandeur stand, / The dread of every sea, / The glory of our land.'

Peover is a church of six long bays rising on rough-hewn octagonal oaks with giant arch braces. There is no chancel divide. Until the 19th century, the roof ran down to the outside walls. Now the aisles have their own gable roofs, but the interior structural timbers are original. Original from when is a matter of controversy. It has been suggested that Peover's arcades could be as early as the 13th century, making it the oldest arcaded wooden-frame church in Europe. However, early 14th century appears the most likely date for the church. Peover has not yet been tree-ring dated. No matter, the wealth of ancient woodwork is exhilarating, more vital than stone and still carrying the aura of the forest.

The exterior of Lower Peover was restored by Anthony Salvin in 1852 but the interior (apart from the earlier arcades) is late medieval with Jacobean fittings. The nave is filled with dark box pews, divided from the choir by a pierced wooden screen. The Shakerley pews display the family crest. Their rivals, the Cholmondeleys, are portrayed on the pews now in the choir. The lovely pew facing the pulpit was that of a third local family, the Leycesters, who paid for much of this woodwork. The superb 17th-century pulpit has marquetry panels. The walls are wood-panelled and the choir stalls even have wooden candlesticks.

Round the aisle chapels are cage-like screens composed of simple uprights. The south chapel has the finer fittings, including an inner screen with finials, giant balls and two superb monuments to members of the Shakerley family. Outside is a hand of St Oswald, as well as a magnificent hollowed-out oak chest. Keys to its five separate locks were kept by five wardens, who had all to be present to unlock it. Church theft is not a novel problem. By the font is an old bread shelf for the poor, which is still kept filled on Sunday in accordance with its bequest.

MACCLESFIELD
St Michael ***
Pardon brass, Savage tombs, Morris glass

Macclesfield, like Nantwich, is the sort of attractive North Country town that southerners believe does not exist. The town was built on silk. At its heart is an 18th-century high street running along the crest of a hill with lanes running steeply down to a valley. At its north end this street opens into a square in front of the church, which thus forms a climax to the town centre, especially dramatic from below.

The church of St Michael was almost entirely rebuilt in Victorian Gothic by Arthur Blomfield in 1898–1901. But parts of the medieval church remain, making the west front a curious sequence of bays. The south-west tower, of blackened sandstone, is a restored original and most handsome. To its left rise the west windows of the Victorian nave, while to its right are the ends of the Legh Chapel and the early 16th-century Savage Chapel, with a tower that was once its entrance porch. This contained chantry priests' rooms above. The Savage tombs within are among the finest in the North of England.

The nave interior is all Blomfield gloom, with darkened sandstone and stained glass. We do best to make straight for the Savage Chapel. The Savages prospered mightily in the Wars of the Roses, Sir Thomas rising to become Archbishop of York at the end of the 15th century. He endowed the chantry chapel that bears his name and the local grammar school. Although his tomb is at York, his home church is filled with ancestors and descendants. The Savages appear to have had a high mortality rate, almost all called John. Interest lies chiefly in tracing the stylistic evolution of the alabaster effigies, from the first Gothic tombs of 1492 and 1495 (in the chancel) to those of 1527, 1528 and 1597. One change in the early tombs is in shoe style, evolving from pointed to rounded. Elizabeth, wife of the 1528 Sir John, in the chapel, has naturalistic rumples in her dress, and the tomb has fine weepers round its chest, battered but also with vivid drapery. Another of the chapel tombs has its centre section left uncarved.

The chapel itself is a world apart from the church. Much of its atmosphere derives from its glass. This is Morris partnership work throughout, albeit mostly from the firm's later production line. The east window is a Burne-Jones design executed in 1905. The small lights in the south wall are his familiar figures of Faith, Hope and Charity. On the chapel's west wall hangs the surviving half of the famous Pardon brass. This is dated 1506 and shows Roger Legh with his six sons. The instruction is in Latin to the priests to recite five Paternosters, five Aves and one Creed to grant pardon for 26,000 years and 26 days. This seems long enough for anyone, however rich.

Back in the chancel are yet more Savages. Against the south wall is the finest monument, to Katherine, wife of the 1495 Sir John. Her figure is the epitome of elegance and refinement, her headdress of almost Egyptian complexity. Directly outside the Savage Chapel is an effigy of a Savage descendant, Lord Rivers (d.1696), by William Stanton. He has all Stanton's facility at recreating cloth in marble, from the wigs and ruffs to the drapes of the tomb canopy.

Leaving the church we cannot avoid the west window by Powell & Sons. Its subject is not religious but imperial, a memorial to Victoria's reign installed in 1902.

MALPAS
St Oswald ***
Painted angel ceiling, Brereton and Cholmondeley chapels

Malpas is French for 'bad road', a reference to the wildness of this territory, always vulnerable to Welsh raids. The castle has all but vanished but the Perpendicular church would cut a dash in any county, towering over its village like a castle in its own right. The sandstone exterior celebrates donations at the turn of the 16th century by the Cholmondeley and Brereton families. The latter's emblem, a chained bear, can be seen as a corbel on the outside near the porch, adjacent to a corbel of Siamese twins. The 18th-century gates and vestry have been attributed to Vanbrugh, who did work in the neighbourhood.

The interior of Malpas is second only to Nantwich for splendour in this district. A single group of late 15th-century masons has been credited with most of the churches in the south of Cheshire. Common features include moulded capitals, a wide, low chancel arch and double-decker windows to carry masses of heraldic glass. At Malpas the nave is particularly graceful, with a fine contrast between the tall, narrow tower arch to the west and the open sweep of the chancel arch to the east.

The eye is immediately led to the nave roof, a work of about 1480, panelled and with a profusion of exquisite foliate bosses and angels. They have been restored to a dark rich oak with gold trimmings. The statues used to be replaced as and when they rotted or fell. They have now been stabilised and their wings replaced with fibre-glass. In future they should fly rather than fall. The chancel narrows slightly on the south side, allegedly a deliberate adjustment to lengthen the perspective – or to avoid the slope of the hill. The effect is expressive. The chancel contains old stalls and misericords.

Malpas's two treasures are the Cholmondeley and Brereton chapels, each divided from the nave by Perpendicular screens with tracery of lace-like delicacy. In each lies the effigy of its founder with his wife. They offer an admirable comparison of English sculpture eighty years apart, before and after the Reformation. The Brereton tomb is the earlier, of 1522, and shows a medieval knight, Sir Randal Brereton, and his lady. He is in armour, she in a gown with girdle and tassel. They are elegant, elongated figures in superb condition, with weepers round the chest inside undamaged niches. Opposite is Sir Hugh Cholmondeley (d.1605). The style is now classical and the chest plain with corner pilasters and crude weepers. The effigies are strangely stiff, and the folds in the lady's dress quite horizontal. In this case, artistic victory goes to the Goths.

By the entrance to the church is a superb 13th-century chest covered in ironwork. Such furniture has long disappeared from almost all English houses, yet is richly represented in England's churches.

NANTWICH
St Mary ****
Octagonal tower, medieval stall canopies

Nantwich, once capital of the Cheshire salt industry, is a discreet market town with a well-designed pedestrian area at its heart. Here the church overlooks a small green that gives on to the churchyard. Though the exterior is darkened by the poor ageing quality of Cheshire sandstone, the church's interior is the glory of the county. Apart from George Gilbert Scott's 19th-century west front, the building is essentially Decorated in form, a thrilling composition.

Crowning the exterior is the octagonal crossing tower, rising majestic over an enveloping canopy of trees. Beneath Perpendicular battlements and pinnacles, the bell-openings have Decorated ogee hoods. Most of the window tracery is also Decorated, either Reticulated or Intersecting, that in the chancel enriched with crocketed gables.

The church is entered through a vaulted porch blessed with a small Kempe window. The nave is only four bays long, but grand with tall arcades. Here the sandstone is less polluted, although Scott's scraping has left blotchy discoloration. The eastward vista is dominated by the low arches and mighty shafted piers of the crossing. Above the crossing is Scott's bold black-and-red lierne vault, the work of a medievalist with the courage of his convictions. Nantwich has two pulpits, one stone of the 14th century decorated with the most delicate Perpendicular panelling, the other of wood and Jacobean.

The vaulted chancel beyond is of cathedral quality, with lierne ribs and some 70 bosses. How much of this work preceded the Black Death and how much followed it is a puzzle. The east window is a complete work of the later period, while the north and south chancel windows are earlier. We fall back on the old answer to the mid-14th-century conundrum, that 'on-going work was interrupted by the plague'.

The principal adornment of the chancel is its stalls, as fine as those in Chester Cathedral and with a forest of canopies. In the darkness of a spring evening, I watched the shadows move through the pinnacles as through a thicket of cypresses. Shields, crockets and finials crowd above each clerical stall, while misericords beneath record the doings of Nantwich citizens. Here are all the old favourites: a woman beating a man with a spoon, a virgin and unicorn, and a mermaid with a mirror. The reredos was installed in 1919 in a style deferential to the stalls. The sedilia has nodding ogees.

We return to the nave via the transepts. The north is Decorated and holds the church's best window, by Kempe but incorporating medieval glass to form a Tree of Jesse. The other windows are early works by John Hardman. The south transept is Perpendicular, with a monument to Sir Thomas Smith (d.1614), Mayor and Sheriff of Chester, and his wife. Although the design is conventional, the work is unusually monochromatic, and the better for it. The materials are creamy alabaster and limestone.

The 20th century has been no less active in Nantwich. Across the nave's west end hangs the Jubilee curtain designed by Denise Bates in 1976. In the north aisle is a window of 1985 by Michael Farrar-Bell. It commemorates a local farmer by portraying all Creation in the Cheshire countryside. Its subject is seen peacefully walking his dog through the trees while the inhabitants of Noah's Ark swirl above his head.

STOCKPORT

St George **
Perpendicular mammoth by Austin, Art Nouveau carving

The north-west of England abounds in churches by the late-Victorian Hubert Austin, dominant partner in the Lancaster practice of Paley & Austin. The churches come big and small, spectacular and mundane. St George's is a masterpiece of the spectacular mode. It was commissioned by a rich brewer, George Fearn, who rejected such national figures as Pearson, Bodley or Norman Shaw in favour of a local firm. Austin fulfilled his confidence, building in 19th-century Perpendicular. The church rises over the Buxton Road south of the town and was dubbed by Archbishop Lord Fisher 'the finest parish church built since the Reformation'. The guide responds to this hyperbole with a modest, 'Probably he was right.'

St George's is big and rich, a re-creation of East Anglia's noblest in powerful red Runcorn stone. The plan is cruciform, with transepts, high clerestory, battlements and a massive tower with flying buttresses to its spire. The entire steeple is 236 ft high. Such is the purity of the Gothic revival that the exterior comes complete with gargoyles, saints' niches and figures of seated bishops. Austin was not a reproducer of Gothic, more a recreator. This is a Victorian building. For all its grandness, it has none of the scholastic coolness associated with Pearson or Street. St George's lifts the spirit in a neighbourhood that needs a lift.

The interior is dominated by the stately progress of the arcades from lofty west end to airy crossing and chancel. The roof is hammerbeam with intermediate tie-beams. The glass is clear, the furnishings sumptuous, tentatively rather than assertively Art Nouveau. Each bench end was individually designed and carved, the church seating 1,200 people. Nothing was cheese-pared. This richness increases with the chancel and north chapel. The chancel stalls would stand comparison with the best of the 15th century, heavy with wood carving, angels and foliage. On one bench-end is a delightful carving of a bishop holding a scourge. The ceiling is painted in reds and gold.

The north chapel contains a gem of Art Nouveau carving in its wooden reredos and ceiling. Balancing it to the south is the astonishing organ case, in which Austin contrived to combine Gothic, Tudor and Jacobean motifs. At the back of the church, the alabaster font has lush foliage round its bowl, on a base of pierced Gothic tracery.

WARBURTON
St Werburgh *
Timber frame, antique atmosphere

There are corners of rural England that even the harshest modernity cannot conquer. Motorways swirl across the Mersey plain, their noise seeming to penetrate the most rural corners. The approach to Warburton from the main road crosses a toll bridge over the Manchester Ship Canal. Here birds can be heard to sing and dogs bark defiance at the M6. A scruffy evergreen churchyard conceals an apparently Tudor structure with a small brick tower and obelisks. When Mee visited the spot after the Second World War, huge ships were passing eerily behind on the canal.

Warburton tower is set unusually to the east of the nave, with an old hearse house next to it. The windows are cheap Tudor and 17th-century insertions. Nobody seems to have had much money for this building. The inside might be a fragment of the old Mersey forest. Warburton is a simple wooden structure of tree trunks with the crudest of beams holding up the roof. This covers nave and aisles in a continuous sweep. The beams are smoothed only where needed for the joinery and bear the scars of many past changes. There are mortice holes for a vanished south gallery. The structure is hard to date.

The chancel area has Jacobean railings surrounding the altar table on three sides. Pulpit, lectern and half the box pews survive while a plan in the guide lists the farms and cottages to which each pew was allocated in the 18th century. At the back are 12th-century tomb slabs dating from an earlier church on the site. The building is redundant but accessible, a place of blown leaves, old flagstones and quiet antiquity.

[CCT]

Cornwall

Cornwall was the adopted home of John Betjeman, his 'sweet brown home of Celtic saints'. Its churches are as a group the oldest, smallest and most distinctive in England. They were founded by Celtic missionaries from Wales and Ireland and rebuilt by the Normans. Their poverty left them little touched until the late 15th and early 16th centuries, when a burst of restoration led to the rebuilding of almost all of them. Most take the form of a single nave/chancel, low-slung and with wagon roofs. They would be monotonous but for the charm of their always warm interiors and the magnificence of their wood carving.

Cornwall is a county of settings. For moorland and cliff we have St Neot's, Lanteglos, Tintagel and St Levan's. For wild, sandy shore, nothing can compare with Gunwalloe and St Enodoc's, or for picturesque waterside, St Just and St Winnow. But the typical Cornish church is a simple tower poking over the curve of the contour, marking some ancient settlement in the cleft beneath. The dominant building material is granite, sometimes silver-grey, sometimes oatmeal, sometimes pink, sparkling alike in sunlight and in rain. Nowhere is this material displayed more richly than on the exterior of Launceston. But granite is hard to work and thus lacks the crispness and variety of detail that gives such beauty to limestone.

For that reason, Cornish carvers measured their skill against more tractable wood, in roofs, rood screens and bench-ends, supreme at Altarnun and Launcells. Only neighbouring Devon and East Anglia can rival the Cornish for woodwork. The Victorians were kind to Cornwall, holding their hand until late in the 19th century and then sending F. C. Eden and the Seddings to restore or reinstate such fine screens as Blisland, Mullion and St Buryan.

Cornwall was Royalist in the Civil War and never adopted the full rigour of the Reformation. Many of its churches proclaim Charles the Martyr and still display the letter he sent from Sudeley, thanking them for support during the Civil War. Almost all seem more Roman Catholic than Anglican.

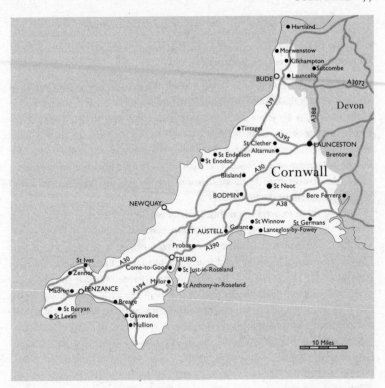

Altarnun ***

Blisland ***

Bodmin **

Breage *

Come-to-Good *

Golant *

Gunwalloe **

Kilkhampton *

Lanteglos-by-
  Fowey **

Launcells ***

Launceston ****

Madron *

Morwenstow **

Mullion *

Mylor *

Probus **

St Anthony-in-
  Roseland *

St Austell *

St Buryan **

St Clether *

St Endellion **

St Enodoc *

St Germans ***

St Ives **

St Just-in-Roseland *

St Levan *

St Neot ****

St Winnow *

Tintagel ***

Zennor *

ALTARNUN
St Nonna ***
Monster heads on font, 79 bench-ends

St Nonna was the mother of St David and left Wales to preach to the Cornish in
AD 527. So says the legend with impressive precision. Her church, the 'cathedral
of the moors', is a 15th-century structure with a tall west tower. Today it sits
within earshot of the main Bodmin Moor road, across from an ancient footbridge that looks as if it might shelter trolls. Altarnun's sacred well was a centre
for the treatment of madness. The treatment involved surprise immersion in
water, the patient then being rushed into the church for prayers, the action
being repeated 'until the fury abates'.

The first thing to greet the terrified victim would have been a fierce bearded
face on the Norman font, still with some medieval colour. One of a dozen
so-called 'Altarnun fonts' in the area of pagan origin, it is square with four
flowers surrounded by snakes and four mask-like faces at the corners. Altarnun
is no place for gentle religion. Its piers are not quarried but are 'moorstones',
monoliths gathered from the surface of the moor, roughly dressed and set on
end. The walls behind are scraped of their old limewash to reveal the slate slab
construction. The wagon roofs are unceiled.

Someone has begun to restore the rood coving at either end of the 19th-
century screen but, according to the guide, 'ran into financial difficulties'. Nor is
this the end of the oddities. The altar rail beyond the screen extends the full
width of the church, embracing the chancel and aisles in one sweep. It carries
the names of the 'minister' and churchwardens at the time (1684). Behind the
altar are two primitive but moving panel paintings of 1620.

The wide open space of nave and aisles is filled with early 16th-century
benches. Their 79 bench-ends are among the best in Cornwall. They are large
and bold in style, straddling the Gothic–classical divide, and include religious
and domestic symbols. Apart from the usual Instruments of the Passion are
jesters, violinists, moorland sheep, griffins, angels and coats of arms. There is a
rare 'vernicle' or portrait of Christ on a handkerchief, given him to wipe his face
by St Veronica (hence her name from Latin for true icon). A portrayal of a
bagpiper is, says Clifton-Taylor, 'at quite the wrong end of Britain'. Cornish
carvers met the challenge of oak as masons elsewhere met that of stone, and
used as their canvas the ends of parishioners' benches, where their work could
be seen by all. For once we have the name of a craftsman. On one end an angel
proclaims, 'Robart Daye, Maker of This Work'. The date is early 16th century.

BLISLAND
St Protus and St Hyacinth ***
Eden's re-creation of pre-Reformation interior

Such is the celebrity of this church in a cleft of Bodmin Moor that we should understand what it is not. Blisland is not a pre-Reformation survival of the Old Religion in a part of England long resistant to Protestantism. The church retains the Catholic ritual but its pre-eminent design is that of Victorian restoration. The architect responsible was F. C. Eden who, like the Sedding brothers, rebuilt Cornwall's churches with sensitivity and was a particular favourite of John Betjeman.

Blisland is mainly a Norman structure. Its Bodmin granite walls, green and moist, appear to have slithered downhill from the village green. The tower is set oddly against the north transept, as if trying to hold the place steady. Grinning faces in the vaulted porch are like theatrical masks preparing us for the drama within. The interior is dominated by Eden's Gothic screen of 1896–7. It seems to fill the entire church, ablaze with bold colouring. The one weakness is the carving of the rood characters themselves. Religious art at that time seemed unable to avoid insipidity.

The church is small and the north aisle truncated, so the screen seals the chancel and side chapels from the nave and aisle. This priestly enclosure is enhanced by the furnishings. The north chapel is almost a private alcove, with a crude slate memorial of 1624. The chancel reredos is by Comper, but this time in early classical style, with dainty shell-head niches and decorated pilasters. Surrounded by mosaics and fronted by black-and-white tiles, it is a composition more appropriate to a London oratory than Bodmin Moor.

The nave cannot match this. Its piers bend and buckle before Eden's chancels, distorted by medieval burials beneath the nave floor. The struts of the wagon roof are so out of line as to resemble crazy paving. Edward Collins was the Victorian rector who commissioned Eden, collaborating with him in respecting existing work. Eden also restored the late 17th-century pulpit, which stands at the junction of the nave, carved in the style of Grinling Gibbons and crowned by the sternest of testers.

BODMIN
St Petroc **
St Petroc's casket

The church stands boldly close to the heart of this tough moorland town. Bodmin was a crossroads of saintly passage across Dark Ages Cornwall, and was a natural centre of early monastic activity. It was here that the remains of the Welsh St Petroc (d.564) were moved from Padstow presumably for safety from the Danes. They were later stolen by French monks but returned in a beautiful Byzantine casket. This was lost, found in 1831, displayed in 1957, stolen again and eventually found on a moor outside Sheffield.

The church was rebuilt in 1469–72 and is unique in retaining a complete set of accounts listing every contribution to the new structure. The new work cost £268 and almost everyone in the town gave in some way. Forty guilds were involved, five of them crafts and the rest clubs and religious societies. The vicar gave a year's salary and those too poor to give money gave labour, or even a goose or pot to be sold. Those who refused to give were fined or had their goods seized. The pre-Reformation church was a true work of community co-operation – or at least taxation.

The result is a fine structure of Bodmin stone, dominating the town centre. An old Decorated chantry, now a ruin, was left in the churchyard. The interior has characteristic Cornish wagon roofs with sumptuous bosses to the nave and north and south aisles. The Victorian restoration is heavy but oppressive only in the glass. The casket is now set into the south wall and heavily secured. It is a work of ivory and gold and has been dated to c.1170.

The church is notable for two spectacular works, the Norman font and the Vivian tomb. The font is distinctive: a bowl supported on five pillars. The pillars rise not, as at Altarnun, to grotesques but to angels. The monsters are relegated to the underside of the bowl where they cavort amid giant tendrils of foliage. The font was the battleground of good and evil, the latter defeated in the ceremony of baptism.

The tomb stands between the chancel and north chapel and is of the most austere black Catacleuse stone. The effigy commemorates Thomas Vivian (d.1533), one of the last priors of Bodmin, and lies on a chest adorned with figures of evangelists. These are in panels divided by balusters in a primitive classical style. The work seems far detached from the subtleties of the Italian Renaissance, displayed on Henry VII's tomb at Westminster, on which this is said to have been partly based. Vivian lies here, surrounded by dark, brooding moorland, a symbol of the impending eclipse of Cornish monasticism.

BREAGE

St Breaca *

Christ of the Trades wall painting

Breaca came to Cornwall from Ireland and the village name rhymes with vague. The mid-15th-century church exterior is in familiar Cornish granite, with a porch that mimics the battlements of the tower. This tower has prominent pinnacles and is coated in lichen and moss which turn deep green on a moist day, as if the church were most used to being under water. Breage's interior is spacious, with two aisles and two transepts. The roofs are wagon style but the Victorians reinstated screens and choir stalls and produced a new reredos. The Sudeley letter, sent by Charles I to thank Cornwall for its support during the Civil War and displayed in many local churches, is prominently transcribed in the south transept.

Breage is celebrated for its wall paintings. These date from the mid-15th century and are mostly concentrated on the north wall. St Christopher is shown carrying Christ as a child through waters full of fish, with a mermaid holding a mirror. This is big and colourful. Next door is Christ in a loincloth, his wounds pouring blood. The meaning of this image has been much debated and is sometimes referred to as Christ of the Trades, as if blessing labour. A different interpretation is from Clive Rouse, who has discovered an identical mural in San Miniato outside Florence. The latter's inscription tells workers that if they use their tools on the Sabbath, God will consign them 'to everlasting damnation'. This appears to settle the matter. The painting is thus a Sabbatarian warning.

The tools depicted at Breage constitute a museum of medieval implements: hammers, saws, scythes, shears, musical instruments and a wheelbarrow. Similar images can be found at Ampney St Mary (Gloucs) and West Chiltington in Sussex, and there are fragments elsewhere in Cornwall.

COME-TO-GOOD
Quaker Meeting House *
Unaltered 18th-century interior

Local histories maintain that the name is a corruption of the Cornish *cwym-ty-coit* or valley by the dwelling in the wood. Recent research doubts this. There is no use of the name until the late 17th century and it almost certainly refers to the presence of Quakers. Today the name extends to a settlement that has grown up round one of England's most unassuming places of worship.

The Quakers were granted freedom of public worship in 1689, and this building was erected in 1710 to replace an earlier structure. It is of whitewashed cob with a deeply sloping thatched roof. At one end is still an open stable for horses. The windows are small casements with lozenge glass, apparently retained from an earlier building. The setting, within a small burial ground, is pleasing. The chapel is kept open.

The interior is a reflection of the exterior. The main room is bare of ornament and rises the full height of the thatched gable, which fills the room with the smell of straw. The furnishings are of light pinewood, including a gallery. Round the wall are panelled settles and at the east end is a raised dais for visiting ministers. These ministers could prolong services for up to three hours, by when the upright benches must have become most uncomfortable. There is no ornament. There is certainly no cushion.

GOLANT
St Samson *
Hillside setting

The Celts built their churches high on the bluffs that command views over the Fowey gorge. Their legends were a match for such sites. This is the landscape of Tristan and Isolde, of wandering saints, and of gold on its way from Wales to Brittany. St Samson, formerly Abbot of Caldey off the Welsh coast, is believed to have led a band of missionaries south, crossing Cornwall from St Kew to Golant on his way to the Rance valley in Brittany. A holy well lies next to the porch, which is furnished as an ante-room and was presumably a chapel to the well. The church is surrounded by stone crosses and wild flowers, a glorious location on a fine day.

Golant's interior is warm and welcoming. Nave and south aisle are divided by clustered arcading, some whitewashed, with a double wagon roof. That over the nave has had its ceiling panels removed, leaving nail holes showing in the unworked rafters. We can see from the aisle roof that the builders intended undressed wood to be ceiled and only the carved wood to be left visible. This ceiling should surely be reinstated.

The pulpit and reading desk panels portray saints and their emblems interspersed with local faces and utensils, a gallery of early 16th-century craftsmanship. High on the north wall is a huge coat of arms of James II, proof of the Royalist sympathies that continued in these parts to the end of the 17th century, and indeed since. Golant's stained glass is inoffensive and includes two figures of St Samson and St Anthony contemporary with the building of the church. An 18th-century slate memorial to Edmund Constable records briskly: 'Short blaze of life, meteor of human pride / Essay'd to live, but liked it not and died.'

GUNWALLOE
St Winwaloe **
Hermitage marooned on beach

There is no stranger site for a church. Gunwalloe is half on land, half on sea, lying in the lee of a small sand-dune between two halves of a beach. At high tide, rollers stream past on either side and the noise of the sea is overwhelming. Wind blows sand through cracks in the windows while the tide seems about to burst down the door. The preacher must have to grasp the pulpit to steady himself against the swell. Every year storms hit this little place and some have half demolished it. Most of the windows are boarded up. Yet Gunwalloe has been here since the dawn of English history. It shows no sign of giving up now.

The Cornish built most of their churches on hillsides above their harbours. This one was founded by St Winwaloe, a Breton missionary, specifically as the 'Church of the Storms'. Legend locates a hermit's cell in the dune behind the church, where a detached tower stands. Like most Cornish churches it was rebuilt in the 15th century with a north and a south aisle and side chapels. The Victorians added a firm roof, aisle screens and benches with linenfold panelled ends. There is even an altar by Comper, delicate for so wild a spot. The rood loft stairs still exist, for what must have been tiny musicians, and the south aisle retains its original wagon roof with carved timbers. By the north and south doorways are fragments of the old rood screen, which is said to have been made from a Portuguese galleon wrecked in 1527. The panels show the apostles with Moorish faces and boss-eyes.

Gunwalloe is reached across the fields below the village, the view spoilt by a large Edwardian hotel on a distant cliff. What should be wild headland is now manicured golf course. The suburbanisation of the Cornish coast continues unabated.

KILKHAMPTON
St James *
Grenville memorials by Gibbons pupil, 157 bench-ends

This church, its tower soaring over the north Cornwall plateau, is the equal of Altarnun for bench-ends. Kilkhampton has 157 in all. They are the product of a mid-16th-century rebuilding by the local Grenville family, which appears to have left little but a particularly splendid Norman doorway from an earlier church. The aisled interior is unusually high for Cornwall, with three wagon roofs extending its full length. The chancel is Victorian, as is the glass that fills every window and makes the interior uncomfortably dark.

The benches are complete and magnificent. They have turned black with age and each appears carved from a solid log of wood, including the shelves for prayer books. The carving is cruder than, for instance, Launcells. The themes are similar to the ends at Altarnun. Thus we find the Instruments of Christ's Passion, heraldic emblems, mermaids, tools of trades, grotesques and scrollwork. These were the first seats in the church. An order of 1567 survives for the 'plasing' of seats, with names attached. Some are of farms rather than individuals. Grander seats are in the Grenville Chapel, before the days of box pews and rents.

The Grenville (or Granville) memorials are the work of a local sculptor, Michael Chuke, a pupil of Grinling Gibbons. One is to the Civil War naval hero, Sir Bevill Grenville, and is framed by the paraphernalia of war: 'Thus slain thy valiant ancestor did ly / When he one Bark a Navy did defy.' Chuke also carved the royal coat of arms, more jolly than artistic.

LANTEGLOS-BY-FOWEY
St Wyllow **
Hilltop setting, Sedding restoration

Those who can find this church deserve a medal. It is nowhere near Lanteglos Highway and lies above Pont Creek between Polruan and Bodinnick, apparently to serve both communities. Worshippers must have endured the most punishing climb to reach it. The granite tower should be a distant marker, were it not buried behind Cornish hedgerows. There is a farm next door, but no sign of settlement, modern or ancient. This is a church for finding and keeping.

There must have been no shortage of parishioners. The churchyard is crowded and the interior spacious, to the scale of a town church. It is as if Bodinnick's boatbuilders had dragged three galleons up the hill and turned them upside down. The rounded arches are presumably not Norman as the piers are Gothic, but the sanctuary windows are set deep and bold.

Lanteglos was fortunate in escaping early Victorian restoration. Its guardian was the admirable E. H. Sedding, nephew of J. D., who found it 'a fascinating storehouse of Christian art . . . no other Cornish church contains more of its old woodwork'. Less of this remains, but the bench-ends are extensive and fragments of old carpentry have been incorporated into Sedding's work of c.1900. For the choir he turned to the Misses Rashleigh Pinwill of Plymouth. Daughters of the rector of Ermington in Devon, they were enthusiasts for traditional West Country woodwork. Their excellent carving is found throughout the region (see Launceston).

The medieval lords of Lanteglos were the Mohuns. Thomas Mohun lies in the south chapel under a brass with the incomplete date of 14. . . His survivors omitted to fill it in. The Mohuns lived on to become Royalist barons under Charles I. Their pew has been refashioned as panelling at the west end of the south aisle. The estate decayed through the high living and duelling habits of the Restoration Mohuns and was sold to Thomas Pitt. This governor of Madras was owner of the Pitt Diamond and of Boconnoc House, which lies inland near Lostwithiel. His grandson was the prime minister.

LAUNCELLS
St Swithin ***
Bench-ends, including 'Ascension' footprints

Launcells was Betjeman's 'least spoilt church in Cornwall'. It lies buried in a defile in the treeless north Cornwall plateau, the pinnacles of its tower peeping above the contours as if half buried. The church is reached down a lane devoid of habitation. Its entrance rises above a stream with a holy well dedicated to St Swithin, embraced by banks of wild flowers.

The interior is a lofty hall, with chamfered arches and capitals carved with fleur-de-lis. North and south arcades are of different stone, enabling us to see how easier to carve was the softer polyphant than the hard if beautiful granite. There are three high wagon roofs with deep-carved members. Even the Victorians were unable to insert a chancel into Launcells. A small sanctuary backed by a tall Gothick reredos fills the east wall. On its floor are 15th-century Barnstaple encaustic tiles, patterned with lions and pelicans.

Once again Cornish woodwork steals the show. In the north aisle is a stern row of Georgian box pews and a no less stern Georgian pulpit and tester. A large coat of arms of Charles II surmounts the entrance to a vanished rood loft on the north wall. The south aisle is jollier, with Jacobean screens, presumably from a family pew, placed against the east wall. Next to them is a friendly monument to Sir John Chamond (d.1624), lying uncomfortably in his armour, resting his head on his arm.

The Tudor bench-ends are among the best in the county. The Instruments of the Passion and other Christian emblems are displayed in Gothic frames, but there are no human forms. Each panel tells a Bible story by allegory: Christ the gardener as a spade and three spice boxes for the three Marys. The Ascension is portrayed by two footprints in a rock, the two feet disappearing at the top of the frame. This is elusive but enjoyable iconography.

LAUNCESTON
St Mary ****
Carved granite façades, 20th-century woodwork

Launceston is the premier church of Cornwall in the former county capital. The old town clusters round the castle walls like a mini-Windsor. The church lies down a lane from the market square, its carved wall decoration unparalleled in England. Apart from an older tower, the church is the creation of one man, Sir Henry Trecarrel, whose house is now a ruin at Trecarrel five miles to the south. The church was built in 1511–24 in the final burst of patronage that took place shortly before the Reformation. Whether Trecarrel intended to display his wealth or his piety is not known, possibly both. His coat of arms and that of his wife cover the church exterior.

The ornament is what Pevsner calls a 'barbarous profusion'. Not even masons in easy-to-work limestone attempted such ornament elsewhere in England. To chisel solid granite, however crude the result, must have involved a phenomenal effort and heavy expenditure. The carving covers all sides and includes the pinnacles on the buttresses. The motifs, apart from the Trecarrel arms, are quatrefoils, shields, flowers and mottoes. They are repetitive and not especially beautiful, but they are prolific. The work has been attributed to masons from St Mary, Truro, begun in 1504. On the outside of the east wall is a prone figure of Mary Magdalene. A local custom is to throw a stone which, if it rests on her back, will bring good luck. The porch has more complex imagery, including St George and the Dragon and St Martin dividing his cloak, as well as the herbal ingredients of St Mary's ointment.

The interior conforms to the usual Cornish plan. It has eight continuous bays with no division between nave and chancel and no sign of a rood loft or stair. The roof has carved members, tiny angels and apparently over 400 bosses. Launceston has four works of art that merit attention. The Gothic rood screen is by the Rashleigh Pinwills of Plymouth of 1911, and is as fine as anything imported by F. C. Eden or the Seddings from London. The Pinwills were also responsible for the woodwork of the reredos. The pulpit is Perpendicular, painted black but with gold details and a red and green ribbed stem. There is a profusion of foliage in the ogival panels. The bench-ends are, for once, not Tudor but Art Nouveau. Their theme is the Works of the Lord. One near the entrance proclaims, in what might be a theme for all Cornish bench-ends, 'O All Ye Green Things Upon The Earth'.

Against the north wall is that rare object in Cornwall, an accomplished Georgian memorial. This is to two friends, Granville Piper and Richard Wise, both mayors of Launceston. Their own presence is confined to two busts, while prominence is given instead to statues of the Virtues, standing between pairs of superimposed Corinthian columns in an imposing design.

MADRON
St Maddern *
Atmospheric interior, Nelson banner

The terraced churchyard of Madron offers us, on a clear day, the entire sweep of Mount's Bay as far as St Michael's Mount. The church lies in a suburb a mile out of town, presumably once a missionary shrine located apart from the pagan settlement that was the object of its attention. Penzance acquired its own parish church in the 19th century, but Madron retains the character of a town church, with a pleasing jumble of memorials, hatchments and banners. It rightly calls itself the mother church of Penzance.

Though the interior was much restored by the Victorians, the worst scraping was confined to the sanctuary. Arcade capitals have foliage carving and angels. The roof is alive with some 250 original wood bosses and the rood screen, restored in the 19th century by the Bolithos of Tregwainton, contains the remains of Tudor panels. The charm of the church lies in its atmosphere of general busyness, like a collector's attic of church contents. The south chapel has gnarled bench-ends topped with beasts. On the wall is an alabaster group of saints from a lost chapel reredos. Near to it is a coat of arms of Henry VII, reputedly commissioned by Benedict Tregos, the local parson who backed Perkin Warbeck's Cornish rebellion. In this fashion did he hope to make amends to the king.

On the south wall of the aisle is the Maddern memorial of 1621, childlike in its simplicity. An ancient Christian burial stone with text in Latin stands at the back of the same aisle. By the door hangs the Nelson banner. Early news of Trafalgar and of Nelson's death arrived in Penzance from a fishing boat that had met the first of the returning ships in the Channel. A thanksgiving and memorial service was quickly arranged and this banner was made to carry in the procession. On the outside of the church's east wall is a memorial to William Thomas of Tregwainton. He died in 1781 and the slab is an accomplished work of English rococo.

MORWENSTOW
St John the Baptist * *
Norman font, smugglers' church of poet-vicar

Morwenstow lies in Cornwall's north-east corner, in a no-man's-land of cliffs, windswept fields and isolated farms. To the west lies only America. The church clings to the side of a coastal combe, across which runs the South-West Coast Path. It is infused with the spirit of one man, the Victorian Robert Hawker, who was appointed to this distant living in 1834, having been an outstanding scholar and poet at Oxford. He wrote of his parish, 'So stern and pitiless is this iron-bound coast, that within the memory of one man upwards of 80 wrecks have been counted within a reach of 15 miles, with only here and there the rescue of a living man.'

Hawker's parishioners were mostly smugglers, wreckers and Dissenters. He dreaded wrecks for their harvest of corpses on the rocks, yet he insisted on burying sailors not according to tradition, in beach-side graves as if drowned at sea, but properly in his churchyard. The figure-head from the wreck of the

Caledonia is a gravestone in the churchyard. The single survivor, a French-speaking Guernsey sailor, wept loudly at the burial service for his comrades. Hawker recalled the stranger's cry as 'the touch that makes the whole world kin'.

The vicarage, lying near the church, is adorned with Gothic windows and chimneys said to be copied from churches Hawker admired elsewhere in the county. He became increasingly eccentric, carrying charms about his person and preaching against storms. He was said to have invented harvest festival services. Hawker was fond of opium and became a Roman Catholic on his deathbed. His volatile temperament was well-tuned to a parish that he grew to love. He married a woman twice his age. When she died he married a woman a third his age, who bore him three children, the last dying in 1950.

Morwenstow is rare in Cornwall in escaping Tudor reconstruction, apart from the west tower and south aisle. Norman beasts adorn the doorway and the Norman north arcade survives, green, damp and primitive, except for two Early Gothic arches closest to the chancel. The pews are either Tudor or Victorian Tudor and there are no modern chairs. Above the screen reassembled by Hawker is a 1930s rood. In the south aisle is the Hawker memorial window of 1902, with scenes from his life at Morwenstow, including Hawker himself with his dog. The Norman font is among the oldest known, a tub font with cable decoration round its waist. The hollowed bowl is in the shape of an open hard-boiled egg.

MULLION
St Mellanus *
Arts and Crafts screen

The Ministry of Defence has left us little to enjoy of the wind-blasted Lizard peninsula, but Mullion survives, an archetypal Cornish church above the cove. Huge granite blocks form the tower, with local serpentine stone for dressings. The north door is said to date from the 11th century. The south door has a dog flap at the bottom for the convenience of shepherds. Shepherds seem far removed from the present-day congregation, mostly retired people who form the bulk of the population of these coastal villages.

A fine screen and bench-ends again predominate. The former is by Eden in collaboration with Herbert Read of Exeter and was not completed until 1961. It runs across the nave and aisles, its dado is of Arts and Crafts panels with interlaced fronds. The loft parapet is classical. Eden's weakness is evident in the quality of the figures composing the rood group. Mullion's niches have been filled with modern saints' statues, which are as poor as those of Eden's rood.

The bench-ends are battered and knobbly, as if hacked from stone rather than wood. They portray the familiar Cornish mix of the Instruments of the Passion, biblical characters and village ribaldry.

MYLOR
St Mylor *
Waterside setting, Celtic cross

At Mylor, setting is all. The church rises above a busy quayside and marina in a creek off Carrick Roads opposite St Mawes. The churchyard, crammed with ancient stones, conceals the church in a delightfully unkempt jungle of vegetation. An ancient belfry, with later wooden bell-chamber, stands apart in the trees. Outside the south door is reputedly the largest Celtic cross in Cornwall, reaching 7 ft down beneath the ground surface. It seems sad that it cannot be re-erected to its full height. The porch next to it is adorned with an open ogee arch with panelled uprights, an effete insertion into this robust work. There are two Norman doorways to the church, the north one with a Maltese cross above it.

The interior has the familiar Cornish plan of a nave with only one aisle to the south. Its Perpendicular arcade is of a full six bays, including the chancel. The interior, though heavily restored, is of interest for its ancient furnishings. These include a fine 15th-century screen dado of coloured panels with flower patterns. The pulpit is Elizabethan and in the south aisle is another presumably Elizabethan work, a magnificent seat pieced together from various fragments. Experts have detected influences from both Ireland and Scandinavia. The motifs on the back and seat are classical. In the south chapel is a fine wall memorial to Francis Trefusis (d.1680).

PROBUS
St Probus **
'Somerset' tower

Probus stands at a crossroads in the valley of the River Fal, which it marks with Cornwall's tallest tower. The church rises from a churchyard coated in green lichen. On a wet day it looks as if it has spent most of its life under water. Its story is rooted in controversy. The local landowner, Nicholas Carminowe, a prominent Protestant, was averse to the parishioners wanting to build a new tower for the church. He even took the suit to the Court of Star Chamber in 1517 and said he would 'make them beg their bread' before he allowed it. But the villagers persevered. They sought help from as far off as Somerset, their design imitating that of North Petherton, even carrying on its exterior the weird

Somerset carvings known as hunky punks. They built one of the best towers in the county.

The tower displayed the traditional Somerset stages, the middle one with single perforated openings, doubled at the belfry stage above. The top has perforated panelling, a battlemented parapet and clusters of pinnacles at each corner. There are more pinnacles on the buttresses. By using elvan stone, a version of granite, Probus could not offer its carvers the malleability of Somerset limestone, but the tower is a final flourish of Perpendicular at the gateway to the western reaches of Cornwall towards Land's End.

Probus has one treasure. Enthusiasts for Georgian monuments must penetrate the south chapel, now used as a vestry. Here lies Thomas Hawkins (d.1766), owner of the local mansion of Trewithen. He went out in style. A maiden leans on his pyramid gazing in adoration at a medallion. Her other hand rests on a shield and her foot drops over the edge of the monument. Overhead an angel performs an astonishing dive from the heavens to hold aloft the celebratory inscription. We might be in Westminster Abbey rather than a Cornish village. Probus was heavily reworked by Street in 1851, who used the Tudor bench-ends for screens and installed iron gates and dark pews. The chancel is like a private chapel.

ST ANTHONY-IN-ROSELAND
St Anthony *
Early Gothic restoration by the sea

The church is reached either by driving the length of the St Anthony peninsula on the southern tip of Roseland or by ferry from St Mawes opposite. In the latter case, the approach is up a creek dominated by the yellow 1840s façade of Place House, ancestral home of the Sprys. This is set above a lawn, surrounded by trees, and looks French, with a turreted central bay. Behind the house and with its south transept built on to it, is the old church. The Victorian broach spire was apparently intended to echo the turret of the house, and be all that could be seen of the church from the water.

St Anthony's is a rare Victorian restoration of a 12th-century monastic church, a cell of the priory at Plympton in Devon. It was built cruciform, with a uniform set of lancet windows, and survived unaltered throughout the 15th and 16th centuries. The chancel, however, fell into ruin and was used as a chicken run. The Spry family acquired the estate in 1649. Samuel Spry, MP for Bodmin, rebuilt the church after 1849 on the advice and apparently to the designs of Clement Carlyon, rector of St Just.

Carlyon respected the Early Gothic structure and also restored the fine Norman south doorway, surviving from a previous church on the site. His most vigorous intrusions are the wooden roofs, Minton floor tiles and stained glass. He also contributed his own version of lumpy Cornish bench-ends. The crossing is serenely proportioned, with Plantagenet arms decorating the tower interior. The lancets are beautiful, with mouldings and shafts. Even the Victorian glass is inoffensive. There are charming Art Nouveau altar rails. The Spry memorials are gathered in the north transept, recording deeds of maritime valour. Descendants of the Sprys, the Grant-Daltons, remain at the big house, though the church is redundant.

[CCT]

ST AUSTELL
Holy Trinity *
Tower carvings

St Austell is in every way a strange place. The town is surrounded by disused china clay workings, leaving giant spoil tips and hills gouged open to the sky. In certain lights these seem like moonscapes. The town is composed of tedious industrial suburbs but has, at its heart, a tight cluster of old streets and buildings. Its church, like the best town churches, is not detached in a close but is part of the street scene.

St Austell is chiefly distinctive for its tower, the finest in the county. The guide describes it, like its rival at Probus, as of the Somerset type. I prefer to think of it as good Cornish. Perpendicular in style, it rises in three stages to a battlemented and pinnacled crown, flanked by four-light Perpendicular aisle windows. Most spectacular are the carvings. Lions, apostles, angels and beasts crowd every corner. On the west face is a set of carved figures reminiscent of Cullompton (Devon), described with delightful redundancy by A. L. Rowse as 'the masterpiece of the unknown craftsman who fashioned it'. The top figure, in excellent preservation, is God the Father with Jesus between his knees. Beneath is a tender Annunciation and on the third tier are local saints flanking the Resurrection.

The interior is unutterably gloomy. So enveloping is the Victorian stained glass that no detail can be seen without electric light. To walk down the aisle is like swimming in an aquarium. Much of this is the fault of Street, 19th-century restorer of the church. But Street had his virtues, which emerge as the eye adjusts to the darkness. While adding his own pulpit and reredos, he kept the original, superb wagon roofs, except in the chancel and chapels where he inserted his own. These were further embellished in the 1920s with angels in the arches dividing them from the nave and aisle. To the east, Street left a 13th-century chapel. This is Early Gothic, with thick walls and lancet windows.

Under the tower arch appears to be another survivor, of an old rood screen.

This has tracery of the most beautiful filigree pattern, not so much Gothic as imitation lace.

ST BURYAN
St Buriana **
Original painted screen

The extremities of the British Isles are shaved close by the wind. Nothing grows at Land's End above six feet. Yet the builders of St Buryan defied the elements and called their church the cathedral of the west. On a clear day it can be seen from the Isles of Scilly. The church was founded by St Athelstan in thanks for his defeat of the Danes. A dean and prebends were appointed and paid, though allowed to be absentees. This was as well for them as the parish was declared an extended sanctuary, meaning that criminals escaping justice could be at liberty within a mile of the church if they paid a fine under Church authority. This was presumably an early form of convict settlement, to garrison this bleak corner of the kingdom. The result was constant trouble, with visitations, mutinies and complaints of dissent throughout the Middle Ages. In 1328, the bishop had to excommunicate most of the villagers to bring them to heel, and even that took eight years to accomplish.

St Buryan possesses one of Cornwall's best medieval screens. It was donated by the Levelis family, who held land at Trewoofe at the head of Lamorna Cove. On the west wall of the church is a primitive slate memorial to the last Levelis, who appears to have died childless: 'This worthy family hath flourished here since William's Conquest full six hundred year ... This gentleman, last of his name, hath by his vertues eterniz'd the same much more than children could or bookes, for love records it here in hearts.' He also left the screen, its colour preserved, glowing red, green and gold.

The screen was restored by E. H. Sedding, but the work facing the nave is original. Each level is admirably decorated with painted dado panels, filigree tracery in the openings, and covings with lierne ribs and bosses. Finest of all are the rood beams, with rows of decorative motifs, the principal one a masterly composition of vines and foliage entwining a Noah's Ark of creatures. The composition flutters across the interior like a flock of birds beneath the whitewashed wagon roof.

The rector responsible for restoring the screen was Canon Martyn, whose memorial is the 1920s reredos by the Rashleigh Pinwills of Plymouth. He was a tough parson. Local labourers were challenged to boxing matches if they failed to come to church, and members of the congregation were berated from the pulpit if they failed to pay attention. Gentler hands have produced new hassocks, an excellent set portraying ships, local farms and even cricket, all on a vivid maroon ground.

ST CLETHER
St Clederus *
Holy well in isolated setting

St Clether is in the valley of the River Inney north of Altarnun. It must, at least on my last visit, be the only valley along the north Cornish coast where no building, caravan or wind farm intrudes. The church would not qualify for an entry but for its neighbouring holy well and chapel, still consecrated. This is reached by walking half a mile up a gorse-filled valley behind the village, carpeted in wild daffodils in spring. Thousands of such holy wells proliferated across England before the Reformation, worshipped by pagans and Christians alike. Some had chapels associated with them, whose monks profited from their restorative fame. St Clether's well presumably survived because of its remoteness.

The well chapel ranks with St Aldhelm's in Dorset as among the simplest entries in this collection, and by the same token is strangely moving. A gabled cell was built directly over the old spring. Reduced to a roofless ruin in the 19th century, it was restored by the antiquarian, S. Baring-Gould, and rededicated in 1909.

The water from the well no longer runs directly under the altar, which is composed of four monoliths with a fifth set on top of them. On it are the chapel's only furnishings, two modern slate candlesticks and a cross. To its right is the niche where the water still gathers, with a shelf on which pilgrims were expected to leave offerings. The priest would gather them through a trap door. On the wall is an old sign of 1913 asking all visitors to donate 3d. This is the only church I know with the courage to name a specific entry charge.

ST ENDELLION
St Endelienta **
Carved Gothic altar, 'Betjeman' bells

'St Endellion, St Endellion,' wrote Betjeman, 'the name is like a ring of bells.' The church tower is stumpy rather than graceful, but is of Lundy granite. On a clear day this granite can see the island of its birth, out in the Bristol Channel.

St Endelienta was the daughter of a Welsh prince who came to live as a hermit in the Tretinney valley. Legend holds that she lived on nothing but cow's milk. When a local lord killed her cow, her godfather, none other than King

Arthur, came and killed him. She then proved her sanctity by bringing both lord and cow back to life. On her death she ordered an ox cart to carry her body on the road until it stopped. There should be her shrine. Here indeed it is.

The interior is unremarkable. The arcades are slim and graceful, the wagon roofs wide with no chancel division. Like many Cornish roofs, they have had their ceilings removed and crude rafters exposed. As a result, the modern angels, carved and painted by local villagers, are hard to discern. But the fawn hassocks designed to match the angels are more than compensation.

The church's principal treasure is a Gothic altar of c.1400 in the south chapel, possibly the shrine of St Endelienta, in a much-prized West Country stone called Catacleuse. This dark material could be finely worked, unlike the harsh Cornish granite, and even polished to look like marble in the manner of Purbeck stone. The chest has eight empty niches with tiny vaults. The work is by 'the Master of Endellion', who also carved the holy water stoup inside the south door. They are of quite remarkable quality and it seems a pity that we cannot rise to the challenge of filling the chest niches in honour of this unsung master. The altar in the north chapel is a simple modern rectangle composed of mortared stone blocks.

The church has a celebrated tradition of bellringing. A primitive panel on the north wall portrays six ringers and their admonitory rhyme: 'Who therefore doth Damn, Curse or Swear / Or strike in quarrel tho no Blood appear, / Who weares a Hatt or Spurr, o'erturns a Bell, / Or by unskilful handling spoils a peal / Shall sixpence pay for every single crime . . . / I will make him careful against another time.'

Betjeman used the next, final, lines in his poem on the wedding of the Prince and late Princess of Wales: 'Let's all in love and friendship hither come, / Whilst the shrill treble calls to Thundering Tom. / And since bells are for modest recreation, / Let's rise and Ring and fall to Admiration.'

St Endellion is the venue for Cornwall's festival of summer music and the distinguished string quartet is named in its honour. I watched an orchestra arrive for rehearsal one spring evening. They stomped in through the porch lugging their instruments into the gloom, recalling a day when strolling players must have trodden this same path. Music was always heard over these Cornish hills.

This is a church of contrasting stone. From the local Delabole slate quarries are superb gravestones in the churchyard, with exquisite lettering. The row of stones lining the path to the door offers a gallery of English lithography over two centuries, an art form that is insufficiently appreciated.

ST ENODOC
*

Dunes setting, Betjeman's grave

The walk to St Enodoc's by the sea is a pilgrimage for any lover of English churches, since it was the holiday home of the young John Betjeman, subject of his finest church poem and finally his burial place. His mother is also buried here and a memorial to his father Ernest is in the nave. His gravestone is by the path in the churchyard.

St Enodoc's embodied all that Betjeman valued in English life and landscape. Landward are the secure Edwardian villas of Trebetherick, hidden among the Scots pines and cedars. Holidaying children play adventures in large gardens and along sandy footpaths. Between the beach and the site of the church is a golf course that barely harms the scenery. The church path crosses the 13th fairway, as Betjeman wrote, 'ignoring Royal and Ancient, bound for God'. This is not the wild Cornwall of Tintagel or Gunwalloe but the tranquil coastline of middle-class vacation.

The church is set among the dunes on Daymer Bay, from where walkers can look out across the mouth of the River Camel towards Padstow. St Enodoc's looks out nowhere, as only the top of its 13th-century stone spire is visible above the dunes, crooked like a dunce's cap. For most of its life the dunes have threatened to engulf it. By the mid-19th century drifts were filling the nave and covering the walls. The vicar had to be lowered through a hole in the north transept roof to hold an annual service and thus keep the church in being. A comprehensive restoration took place in 1864, in the words of the vicar's son, 'by the masons and workmen of the parish with loving care, and nothing was destroyed needlessly or removed if it was of use or interest'. The excavated church is still in a hollow, surrounded by a thicket of tamarisk to keep the elements at bay. Beneath part of this hedge is a shed once used as a mortuary for sailors wrecked on the beach.

The Victorianised Norman interior is more charming than distinguished. The nave is unaisled but the south chancel aisle has a granite arcade and forms almost a second nave with its own screen. The dado of the old rood screen survives in place. It has boldly carved and coloured panels that might be from the transom of a man-of-war. The font and piscina are Norman.

I first visited St Enodoc's at the end of a warm spring day. The golfers were clearing the last green and the rooks growing restless in the pines. Dogs were walking on the distant beach. Only an insistent blackbird on the steeple broke the calm, singing its heart out. Betjeman's gravestone is embellished with florid lettering out of character with both the man and the place, but he would not have complained. He had already written: 'Oh kindly slate, to give me shelter in this crevice dry. / These shivering stalks of bent-grass, lucky plant, / Have better chance than I to last the storm.' And so they had.

ST GERMANS
St Germanus ***
Norman exterior, Rysbrack monument, Burne-Jones windows

St Germans is unlike any other church in Cornwall. It was rebuilt as a Norman outpost on the borders of Kernow, ancient Celtic name for Cornwall, and lies sandwiched between Port Eliot House and the River Tamar. The original church was the seat of the Saxon bishops of Cornwall, but what we see today is mostly Norman and Perpendicular. Despite Victorian restoration, St Germans retains the aura of a collegiate priory, its flagstones echoing to chanting canons and clanking knights, a church of soaring vaults, receding chapels and dark recesses.

The Norman west front is worthy of a cathedral. The west doorway consists of no fewer than seven orders of arches, most of them with zigzag decoration surmounted by a wide gable. The composition is so eroded that it might have been etched from a single cliff of stone. The two towers have different upper stages, that to the south being 15th century and square, that to the north being 13th century and octagonal. The square one was altered to become the home of the parish church bells.

The interior is the nave of the old priory church, stripped of its chancel after the Dissolution. The style changes as we move east. At first all is decidedly Norman, a building of cylindrical piers, scalloped capitals, rounded arches and deep shadows, the sort of place to plan an ecclesiastical murder. Further east the work is late medieval, much restored. The large east window is Perpendicular, inserted after the collapse of the disused chancel in 1592. In the days of the priory, the present south aisle served as the parish church. Its east end had once been a chapel of the sacred relics of St Germanus, brought here in 1358. Its east wall, with three Decorated windows, has been ruthlessly scraped to look like a dry-stone wall.

St Germans has two treasures. The east window is a Burne-Jones masterpiece, a ten-light composition in his most mature style. The background is a soft green-yellow, leaving figures in red and blue to glow even more vividly in the half-light. Burne-Jones also designed a window in the south wall of the aisle. The south aisle is filled with memorials to the Eliot family, who acquired the old priory after the Dissolution and who hold it still. Their finest monument, however, is in the north-west corner of the church. This is to Edward Eliot (d.1722) and is by Rysbrack. It shows Eliot in Roman costume being mourned by a maiden with weeping putti. Only the Hawkins memorial in Probus church is its equal in Cornwall.

ST IVES
St Ia **
Medieval choir stalls, Hepworth statue

St Ia was Irish and landed in Cornwall, with the panache of her race, sailing on a leaf. Her early 15th-century granite church lies at the foot of the old town where it meets the water's edge. Seen from the harbour, the quartet of gables along the east front appears to rise directly from the beach. The church is as firm as any in Cornwall in its Anglo-Catholicism. An admonition greets the visitor: 'Some people will tell you that at the Reformation the Church of England ceased to be Catholic and became Protestant. Do not believe them.' The church is exuberant in its candles, icons and ritual, perhaps in penance for standing out from most of Cornwall and supporting Cromwell in the Civil War. Located at the hub of tourist St Ives, it hums with activity.

The interior has two aisles with arcades of sandstone. The carvers took the opportunity of this un-Cornish material to produce eccentric capitals. Overhead, three wagon roofs are decorated with angels and bosses, the richest being in the chancel. The pulpit is faced with bench-ends. The medieval choir stalls portray local scenes and one names a local blacksmith, Ralph Clies, shown with his wife and surrounded by the tools of his trade. Such artisans were men of some distinction, readily commemorated in their local church.

St Ives has fewer modern works of art than might be expected in this self-proclaimed cultural capital of the west. The 15th-century granite font, showing demons cast out by baptism, is set in a graceful baptistery designed by S. E. Dykes Bower in 1956. The Lady Chapel of *c.*1500 forms a second south aisle, and accounts for the fourth gable seen outside. It holds Barbara Hepworth's Madonna and Child, given in memory of her son killed in the RAF in 1953. We are encouraged to touch the soft white stone. Hepworth also designed the steel candlesticks which stand before it. More such pieces should be spared from the town's many art galleries and from its Tate Gallery outpost.

ST JUST-IN-ROSELAND
*
Waterside setting in exotic garden

Roseland is a secret appendix that might be called Going-Nowhere. Neither as wild as the Lizard nor as barren as Land's End, it remains a bleak extremity apart from its western shore along the Fal estuary. Here it is indented with fjords so deep and sheltered that, in the 18th century, they were proposed as a royal dockyard. The Fal is still used for mooring mothballed supertankers. Where the river broadens into an estuary, a side road descends from the Roseland plateau to the picturesque creek of St Just-in-Roseland.

In this micro-climate, the earth sprouts palm trees, cedars and bamboo. The sub-tropical vegetation is, like Portmeirion in North Wales, the work of an Edwardian enthusiast, the botanist John Treseder. Returning with specimens from Australia in 1897, he decided on St Just as the ideal place to attempt their propagation in England. The resulting garden, now merged with the church-yard, is filled with such exotics as camellia, rhododendron, fuchsia, magnolia and, round the church itself, palm trees. The palms stand well against the Gothic tower. In summer this might be Cap d'Antibes. H. V. Morton in the 1920s thought he had blundered on the Garden of Eden.

The church interior is mostly Perpendicular and unremarkable. The plan is of nave and chancel, with a single aisle. The roof bosses are modern, designed by John Phillips in 1990 and made by a local carver, Charles Moore. The crudely-worked Victorian bench-ends, which might be by a local ship's carpenter, offer a dash of vigour in this rather precious setting. St Just's is usually crowded with tourists. It is best visited late in the day or off-season, when birdsong and the lapping of the tide can be heard and when Treseder's fusion of hemispheres can seem complete.

ST LEVAN

*

Cliff-side setting, screen carvings

St Levan's is the most westerly church in my list, buried beyond Porthcurno and its Minack amphitheatre clinging to a rock above the sea. Not even Epidaurus can offer so dramatic a backdrop for a stage, where the human voice must cry above screaming gulls and crashing waves. St Levan's lies a mile by coast path beyond Minack or two miles south of Land's End. Its tower rises from within the defile down to Porthchapel.

The path to the door passes the St Levan stone, shaped like two halves of a loaf of bread. The stone was venerated as holy in pre-Christian times. It allegedly acquired its shape when the saint sat on it to rest from fishing and smote it with his stick, cutting it in two. The stone still lies split. Next to it is a Celtic cross 7ft high, intended to neutralise the pagan power of the rock. Such legends seem more substantial when the scene is visited under black storm clouds overhead and an occasional crack of thunder. This is nether England and no place to trifle with the shades of ancient Kernow.

The tower is 15th century, rebuilt with pinnacles and battlements. How such rebuilding was financed in these desperately poor corners of England, when no such money was available for instance in Tudor Sussex or Kent, is a mystery. The arcade has simple, rough-hewn lumps of granite fashioned into six bays. There are traces of paint still in the south aisle roof. While the pews are late Victorian, they incorporate bench-ends of battered antiquity. These include portrayals of St Levan's fishes, a jester and a pilgrim.

The dado of an old screen is of higher quality, its carving as good as any in Cornwall. Here is complete stylistic freedom. The entwined ropes, leaves, monsters and serpents seem more Celtic than Gothic, their forms taken from daily life and imagination, rather than from any carver's pattern book.

ST NEOT
****

Medieval glass

St Neot's contains the principal treasure of Cornish religious art. The church sits, a granite jewel-case, on a southern slope of Bodmin Moor. The porch is protected from the Devil by a cluster of Cornish crosses. The unusually rich south wall carries six uniform bays of Perpendicular windows, divided by pinnacled buttresses. The stone has been dressed and weathered by the Bodmin wind, as if rubbed down with emery paper. On the tower hangs a sprig of oak, in honour of Charles the Martyr, a 'saint' still venerated in these parts.

The church is second only to Fairford (Gloucs) in the completeness of its medieval glass. The interior is an inside-out casket in which rays of daylight, whether sunny or grey, are transformed by glass into a moving kaleidoscope of tone. William Morris held that medieval glass could capture, store and then give off the rays of the sun. Its primary colours were thus purer than those of factory-produced Victorian glass. The interior of St Neot's is free of the jarring light of even the best 19th-century glass. (However, its east window is Victorian and can be inspected for contrast.)

Unfortunately, the master of St Neot's appears to have run out of money before he could complete his work. Medieval windows were placed round a church to a set pattern, like the frescos in an Italian monastery. The set begins at the east end of the south aisle. This portrays the Creation, with God and his mathematical instruments and a serpent with the head of a man. The first window in the south aisle is of the Old Testament, principally of Noah. These scenes are superb, by an English Bruegel, full of incident and movement. Four of the panels show detailed knowledge of 16th-century ship design. Like the carvings at Tiverton (Devon), they form the basis of our knowledge of medieval seafaring.

Now the pattern goes astray. Imported glass was expensive and more space in the windows had to be given to portrayals of sponsors and their families, a common problem among fundraisers. Thus we see Tudor ostentation slowly getting the better of piety. The next window has the Borlase family with St Christopher, then windows celebrating donations by families named as Martyn, Motton, Callaway, Tubbes and, in the north aisle, Harys. In each case the donor's family is shown at the foot of the window.

The rest of the north aisle windows are dedicated to saints and appear to have been paid for by the young men and women of the parish. The last is a superb work depicting scenes from the life of St Neot.

ST WINNOW
*

Waterside setting

Cornwall's coastal churches are either placed where missionary saints first landed and blessed the ground, or high on a cliff where they might be safe from pagan attack. St Winnow shrewdly ran his ship aground on an idyllic spot, on the banks of the Fowey estuary, surrounded by wooded hillsides and the sound of birds. The place is utterly peaceful.

The interior is typical of Cornish Perpendicular churches. The nave and south aisle have ornamented wagon roofs, their members distorted by settlement. E. H. Sedding restored the old screen at the end of the 19th century. It is so covered in carved foliage that new leaves seem to be growing daily in front of our eyes. Two east windows have original glass, much in need of cleaning. They show saints and characters in medieval costumes. The bench-ends depict vernacular scenes, including a fine sailing ship in a storm and a man drinking. The best monument, of 1651 in the south aisle, is to one William Sawle. He announced his going with an anagram of his name: 'I was ill: am wel.'

TINTAGEL
St Materiana ***
Wild hilltop setting

Most of Cornwall's coastal churches hide in ravines or lurk on beaches. Tintagel's Norman church stands brave on a cliff, a short distance from the famous castle on its offshore rock. The church is the most defiant I know, hurling itself at wind and sea. The castle was probably built at the same time as the church but is now a wreck of a building, evoked by its custodians with artists' impressions. If the medieval knights returned to their castle they would be horrified at its state. If they returned to Tintagel church they would be at home. It needs no props to the imagination. It still boasts the old religion that gave it birth. Damp chapels hold statues, icons and candles of the Roman rite. Cornish churches may be 'of England', but Protestant they are not.

Most churches benefit from a fair setting. Tintagel benefits from a foul one. On a sunny day it is rather dull. But see it in a storm, by moonlight or, as I once did, in the densest of fogs, and the Celtic saints rise from the graveyard and beckon us through the creaking door. The church plan is so confusing that I walked round it twice before giving up trying to guess which was the chancel.

The church is Norman not just in origin but in atmosphere. The doorways are round-arched and the windows designed more to keep out the elements than to let in the light. The first spectacle inside is a set of grotesque Norman heads on the large font. Beyond is a plethora of altars, all dressed and with candles, including chapels dedicated to St Faith, St Symphorian, St Denys and the Blessed Sacrament. Most have statues of saints in the appropriate niches or on brackets: some of them good modern work, including two Oberammergau statues of Christ, and some dreadful. There are candles on the rood screen in front of the crucifix.

In the Blessed Sacrament Chapel hangs a fine copy of the National Gallery's Perugino altarpiece. The east window is modern, by Alfred Fisher, depicting children and the components of the Communion. It honours Arthur Canner, vicar until 1976. The chancel contains a bishop's chair and what appears to be an old school desk with an inkwell and recess for pens. This would be a relic of the post-Reformation use of chancels as schoolrooms. Few scholars can have enjoyed a more splendid desk, or studied in a wilder spot.

ZENNOR
St Senara *
Mermaid legend, tomb of last Cornish speaker

The little church lies at the end of the St Ives to Zennor coast walk, and is sister refuge to the Tinners Arms opposite. This is the heart of mining country with a ruined chimney stack on every horizon. The pub has an effigy of a miner over its door.

Every Cornish church has its saint's legend, and most are best left to the guidebooks. St Senara's life was unusually tough. Married to a Breton king, she was accused of infidelity and, though pregnant, was nailed into a barrel and thrown into the sea. She was fed by angels, gave birth in the barrel and was washed on to the Irish coast with her child, Budoc. Setting off home to Brittany and a possibly repentant husband, mother and son sojourned at Zennor. Young Budoc was also beatified for his troubles.

The church has roughcast walls and a primitive arcade of local Zennor granite. Large corbels in the chancel appear to be relics of a Norman structure.

The woodwork is mostly Victorian and the east window lancet horribly modern. A squint from the little south transept gives a view of the altar and it is here that the church's principal curiosity is found, a mermaid bench-end with a legend as exotic as that of St Senara. A local girl used to sit in the church of an evening listening to a boy chorister, Matthew Trewhella, whose voice infatuated her. One day she lured him down to neighbouring Pendour Cove, and from there out into the sea, never to be seen again. It is a rare case of a mermaid working her lethal magic on dry land. The two still sing together far across the water on quiet nights. They sing here too, on their bench-end.

On the outside wall by the porch is a memorial to John Davey (d.1891). He was, according to the inscription, the 'last to possess any considerable knowledge of Cornish language'. This challenges the common view that the last Cornish speaker was Dolly Pentreath, who died in the 18th century. Davey's father 'and instructor' was the local schoolteacher, which suggests that his interest in Cornish was scholarly rather than vernacular. Cornish is now widely studied and appears in local phrasebooks and on souvenirs. The Lord's Prayer in Cornish is displayed in many churches and is similar to, but not the same as, Welsh. It begins: *Agan Tas-ny, us yn nef, Benygys re bo do Hanow.*

Cumbria

Cumbria is a land of lakes and fells, Wordsworth and Helvellyn, surely the most enchanted county in England. Its true cathedral is Cartmel, once in Lancashire, now granted to its proper setting. The sight of the old church tower across Morecambe Bay, with a late sun catching white stone against black fells, is English landscape at its most glorious.

Otherwise, the county was not rich during the great church-building eras. Its most characteristic places of worship are upland chapels such as Wasdale Head or Torpenhow. The former counties of Westmorland and Cumberland retain many reminders of their noble families. The church of the Lonsdales at Lowther has outlasted the big house. We have Lady Anne Clifford to thank for the excellent restorations at Brougham and Appleby, where her tomb is a superb work. The Howards asked Philip Webb to build a new church at Brampton, filled with excellent Morris glass. Cumbria has no treasure to compare with Sarah Losh's astonishing labour of love at Wreay. It is a church unique in England.

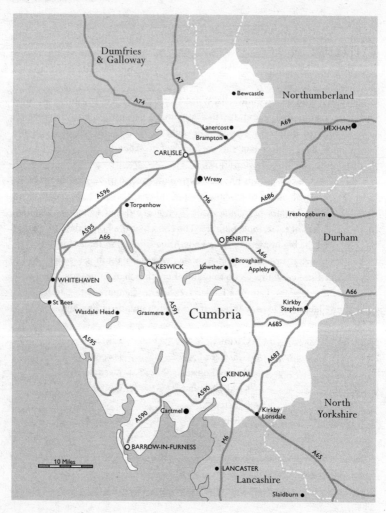

APPLEBY

St Lawrence **

Anne Clifford's tomb, Baroque organ case

The small towns of the far north are without equal in England. Spared by the 19th century and impoverished in the 20th, they have few of the suburbs and out-of-town shopping centres of the south. Appleby shares with Kirkby Stephen an attractive market square offset by a church partly hidden behind an architectural screen. The screen is by Robert Smirke, designer of neighbouring Lowther

Castle. The church lies at the foot of Boroughgate, downhill from the old castle, one of many restored in the 17th century by Lady Anne Clifford, whose story is told under Brougham Chapel. She 'caused a great part of Appleby Church to be taken down and rebuilt', and was probably responsible for the present chancel and north-east chapel.

The church exterior appears to have survived fire and storm, its carvings bashed, its stone scorched, its angles deepened by soot and wind. The church was indeed burned by the Scots in 1388. The dogtooth decoration on the Norman porch is much broken. The interior, unlike the austere Kirkbys, is homely. It is mostly early 14th-century Decorated work, with a nave of five sandstone arches, enclosing box pews. The chief treasure stands at the west end, an organ brought from Carlisle Cathedral in 1683 after Lady Anne's death. Its case is said to date from the 16th century and to be one of the oldest in the country. Three crested turrets rise above a cluster of pipes and cherubs, a magnificent piece.

In the north-east corner of the church stands the memorial chapel of Lady Anne herself (d.1676). Its most prominent monument is the alabaster and stone tomb chest to her mother, Margaret, Countess of Cumberland. It is restrained for its Jacobean date (1617) with a beautifully carved effigy wearing a metal coronet. The inscription reads that 'thou seest in sight the cover of her earthly part. But passenger know Heaven and Fame contains the best of her.' The draping of the mantle is similar to that on the tomb of Elizabeth I in Westminster Abbey and is attributed to the same sculptor, Maximilian Colt. There are skulls round the chest, including some incorporated into classical Ionic capitals.

Lady Anne's own memorial is a wall tomb of 1655 attributed to Thomas Stanton. The back is covered in heraldry intended to validate a lineage that was source of much litigation in her life. The tomb chest has no effigy and is guarded by a slab with iron rings.

BEWCASTLE
St Cuthbert *
Carved Celtic cross

First you must get there. A minor road leads north from Brampton past the fortified manor of Askerton. The moorland broadens out, and the streams become fiercer. This is wild border country. Suddenly the road descends over Kirk Beck with, on the far hill, a Norman keep on the site of a Roman fort. Hadrian's Wall is to the south.

The churchyard is surrounded by drystone walls and fields. The church is modern and of little interest, although the small museum near the farmhouse is worth a visit. The appeal of Bewcastle lies in the presence in its churchyard of one of the earliest truly English works of art. Pevsner's accolade is unreserved. Bewcastle Cross, and Ruthwell Cross in Dumfries, are 'in art the greatest achievement of their date in the whole of Europe'. Often such relics have lost the power to move us. Not so Bewcastle.

The cross, which has mislaid its cross-piece, is dated to the late 7th century, by when Christian missionaries had already pushed south from Iona into England and were sending out missions from Lindisfarne. Their masons were imported from southern Europe, or were acquainted with the motifs of early Christianity. The swaying vine leaves and scrolls inhabited with animals, found in both Roman and Nordic Christianity, were vividly re-created in the Lindisfarne Gospels. The joy in nature and disciplined composition might also be said to reflect Roman designs, which might have adorned colonists' villas in these moorlands.

Each of the four faces of the cross has different carvings. All survive intact. Three sides are mostly decorated with vine scrolls, birds and knots. The fourth shows St John the Evangelist at the bottom, Christ stamping on a lion and an adder, and, at the top, St John the Baptist with a lamb. Birds inside scrolls can similarly be found in churches in Ravenna and in Coptic relics.

What lines of communication can have brought such art across Europe in the so-called Dark Ages? As so often in this survey, I am amazed at how cosmopolitan were these early Christian artists. Those who wish to see a less eroded version of Bewcastle Cross, with free insertions by the artist Sarah Losh, can find one in the churchyard at Wreay.

BRAMPTON
St Martin *
Pre-Raphaelite glass

Brampton was blessed in the late 19th century with the patronage of the Howards, Earls of Carlisle. In the 1870s, some townspeople decided to ask the family for a new church, others for a tram system. Those being pious days, the church party won, and Brampton lost for ever the blessing of a tram. George Howard, nephew of the then Earl, enthusiastically supported the project. He was himself an artist and agreed to pay half the money on condition that he could choose the architect. William Morris's associate, Philip Webb, had already built Howard a house on Palace Green in London. In Brampton he was to receive his only church commission. He demanded complete artistic autonomy and commissioned his friend Morris to do the glass. The vicar, a Londoner named Henry Whitehead, supported him. Bereaved donors were discouraged from giving plaques or monuments in memory of their loved ones, only Morris windows.

The work, designed in 1874, is unusual for being a Victorian church not built in a Gothic style. It is an irregular design which eludes stylistic categories. The north side, with battlements and a row of gables, has a domestic character. The interior is equally inventive, a wide space with much painted woodwork. Yet it is lugubrious, as if Webb's usually joyful Queen Anne style were too wilful for these northern hills. He is rescued by his choice of Morris and his comrade-in-arms, Burne-Jones. Brampton offers one of the most explosive displays of Pre-Raphaelite colour in the country, a testament to the confidence with which the Morris partnership could by now handle this medium.

The contract was not a happy one. Burne-Jones's bitter comment on Brampton was: 'a masterpiece of style, a chef d'oeuvre of invention, a capo d'opera of conception, a Herculean labour, hastily estimated in a moment of generous friendship for £200'. He went on, 'If the firm regards as binding a contract made from a noble impulse, and in a mercenary spirit declines to reopen the question, it must remain equally a monument of art and ingratitude.' Twelve of the 14 windows are by Burne-Jones, works of his maturity, mostly 1878–98. Most of the windows are rather small. The finest is the five-light east window, dedicated to Charles Howard, George's father, whom Burne-Jones called a 'dignified and kind-hearted old man'.

Whitehead was 'broad church' and Brampton has few of the familiar scenes of Nativity or Crucifixion. Instead we see Christ the Good Shepherd above the sacred pelican, with angels and saints chosen because they have the names of members of George Howard's family. Big swaying figures fill the frames, the reds, blues, pinks and purples burning from the glass. Behind them is a dense background of leaves, flowers and animals, without space or perspective. The effect is intensely powerful. Similar figures fill the windows in the north aisle. Those in the south aisle are memorial compositions in dark landscape settings. They include a version of one of Burne-Jones's favourite subjects, Faith, Hope and Charity, using as models women well-known to the Brotherhood – and often exchanged between them.

BROUGHAM
St Wilfred **
Flemish choir stalls and screen

Cumberland was a land of border magnates, of Cliffords, Dacres, Lowthers and Nevilles. Each had their hours of fame, but few had more than the Cliffords. Their Norman ancestors were rich in exotic names such as FitzPune, Veteriponts, FitzGeoffrey. They later supplied some of the darkest characters of English history, Black-Faced Clifford and Butcher Cumberland. But in the 17th century the family fortune fell on one daughter, Anne, who married first the

Earl of Dorset and then the Earl of Pembroke. In 1643 at the age of fifty-three she inherited the northern estates of her father (and, by a complex route, her uncle). Six years later in 1649 she escaped the Civil War and travelled north to attend to her inheritance.

This included the border castles of Appleby, Skipton, Brough, Pendragon, Wharton and Brougham, all of which she set about restoring. When told that Cromwell would not permit such militarism and would destroy her castles, she replied, 'As often as he destroys them I will rebuild them while he leaves me a shilling in my pocket.' Her style of restoration was medieval. She spent the rest of her life travelling between her properties like an ancient magnate with a retinue of retainers. She visited every corner of her estates, reviving the communities that lay in her charge. Her progress was meticulously recorded in her diary. Lady Anne died at Brougham, her favourite castle, in 1676. Her monument is in Appleby church.

Lady Anne rebuilt the chapel that lies on the hill above her ruined Brougham Castle, next to Brougham Hall. The Hall passed in due course to William Brougham, later 2nd Baron Brougham and Vaux, who shared with many Regency young men a taste for collecting Continental antiques. In the 1840s he turned his attention to the small chapel that lay outside the walls of his house, to which it is joined by a curious bridge. He 'Normanised' the interior, notably the windows, and filled it with the plunder of his agents.

The collection might form the contents of a college or private house chapel, mostly 16th- and 17th-century French and Flemish woodwork. The stalls have poppyheads and are covered in flamboyant panelling with intricate relief carvings. Those on the north side have lofty Gothic canopies. On the south side is a pulpit with carved panels. Most astonishing of all is the screen which divides off the west end of the chapel. It has 21 tall colonettes, as densely packed as sardines, and minutely carved. They are thought to come from bishops' stalls and four-poster beds. Sadly the church's greatest treasure, a Flemish 15th-century triptych, is now in Carlisle Cathedral. The authorities might in return have restored the medieval glass in the east window, which is in a bad state. The chapel is a remarkable treasure house to find in the wilds of Cumbria.

BROUGHAM
St Ninian, Ninekirks **
River setting, 17th-century woodwork

This is surely England's most unobtrusive church. A small lay-by must be found on the A66 two miles down the River Eamont from Brougham Castle. From there an indistinct track leads across fields to a bend in the river. There is no sign of any settlement and the fainthearted might accept defeat long before a small meadow is reached over the brow of a hill. At the far side lies an overgrown churchyard, among whose wild flowers the church sits in utter tranquillity. It is redundant but kept open.

St Ninian's, also known as Ninekirks, is the old parish church of Brougham, favourite home of Lady Anne Clifford, whose tale is told under Brougham Chapel. She recorded that it 'would in all likelihood have fallen down it was soe ruiness if it had not bin repaired by me'. The date of this work, 1660, with her initials, is in the plaster of the east gable. The church is similar in outline to Brougham Chapel. Long and low with big buttresses it has the appearance of an almshouse. The walls are of sandstone, forming a single cell with arch-braced roof. The windows are small and the interior atmospheric. Plain oak furnishings installed by Lady Anne appear to be as she left them. There are box pews, screened for families from the castle and the Hall. These screens are a bit like cages. The double-decker pulpit still has its tester. Under the chancel floor is an ancient coffin lid carved with a cross and a sword.

The ancient tombstones in the churchyard are covered in lichen and attended by wild flowers. Here there are no sounds but those of nature.

[CCT]

CARTMEL
St Mary and St Michael ****
Norman chancel, Jacobean screen and choir stalls, Harrington tomb

Cartmel was granted to the monks of Lindisfarne by the King of Northumbria in the 7th century and to Cumbria by government officials in the 20th. It was protected by the Lakeland mountains to the north and by the treacherous sands of Morecambe Bay to the south. Crossing these sands to Cartmel by coach was a favourite, if risky, pastime of the Victorians.

Today, the village is of Dorset prettiness, full of tourists in summer and dominated by the eccentric tower of its church. It has the curious feature of a belfry set diagonally to the base of the tower. Its limestone is eerily white, especially against the often lowering clouds of the fells behind. The priory was a Norman foundation which, though often altered and rebuilt, survived the Reformation without extensive demolition. The reason is that the founders insisted from the start that the building also serve the local parish.

Cartmel is the most beautiful church in the north-west, its interior both domestic and serene. The Perpendicular nave is that of a small parish church, just three bays long with lean-to aisles. The walls have been scraped down to rough stonework and cry out for limewash, though the stone is at least warm in colour. Everything changes at the crossing. Suddenly we are in the church of a great priory, talking the language of international Norman and Gothic and showing traces of frequent rebuildings. Deep Norman windows jostle with high Perpendicular ones, and there are chamfered arches and blind doorways.

Even the crossing is outshone by Cartmel's chancel. This is reached through a dark Jacobean screen thick enough to be a wall, pierced by openings of oriental delicacy. The screen was the gift of George Preston, a local landowner who came to the rescue of the post-Dissolution church. The chancel arcades rest on massive Norman piers, but rise to a rhythmic Early Gothic triforium. This would once have been darkly mysterious, with narrow windows in the east wall. Now it is lit by a big Perpendicular window filling the east wall completely. The whole chamber is a textbook in medieval architecture. The spotlighting is excellent.

The Perpendicular style also contributed choir stalls with misericords. The stalls are superb, as good as those of Lancaster, while the misericords include a Green Man, a mermaid and an elephant and castle. The backs are Jacobean, with filigree panels like the screen, and are divided by colonnettes carved with vine leaves. Rudely interrupting the sedilia is the tomb of the first Lord Harrington (d.1347), dividing the sanctuary from his chantry, known as the Town Choir. The tomb is a vigorous example of Decorated design. The uprights of the canopy are covered in heraldic shields and small bedesmen line the chest, bashed but still proclaiming Harrington's munificent glory. Small weepers are bowed over the effigy, a touching and unique form.

The Town Choir Chapel beyond is Decorated of c.1340. Its east window is curious, with Reticulated tracery rising either side of Perpendicular mullions, as if the mason were struggling to move from one Gothic period to the next. The window would once have contained glass depicting the Tree of Jesse, some of which survives. It is of a high quality. The figure of the Annunciation angel in a centre panel was once exhibited in the Louvre.

Cartmel has an excellent guide to its glass. The architectural west window is by Burlison & Grylls; the Pre-Raphaelite panels beneath the adjacent Te Deum window are by Shrigley & Hunt. The church has sustained its artistic patronage. The Gothic reredos is by the Warham Guild, of 1932. By the chancel screen and at the back of the nave are two sculptures by Josefina de Vasconcellos, one of St Michael and the other entitled 'They Fled by Night' portraying the rest on the flight to Egypt.

GRASMERE
St Oswald *
Roof restoration celebrated by Wordsworth

There is no escaping Wordsworth in Grasmere, venue for heavy-duty poetry tourism. Yet his cottage and the village contrive to keep their heads and resist the onslaught without too much damage. The lake and surrounding fells are untarnished. A stream flows unspoilt through the village centre and encircles the churchyard, gently watering Wordsworth's grave, round which nothing more than railings have been set. Grasmere is still a delightful place.

The medieval church in which Wordsworth worshipped is much restored and its exterior clad in dreary grey pebbledash. There is only one distinctive feature of the interior, the north aisle added in 1562 to receive parishioners from adjacent Langdale. That aisle is eccentric. The builders were not over-worried about stylistic nicety and apparently knocked holes in the existing north wall to extend the roof as best they could. The division took the form of a rudimentary two-storey arcade that does not rise to the roof but supports a zany lattice of beams. The high collar-beams span both nave and aisle, passing over the top of the dividing arcade. The lower tie-beams rest on the upper arcade. What are technically king-posts and queen-posts leap off the walls at odd angles. They are of dark wood against whitewash and might be the loft of a dockland warehouse. The north aisle is still called the Langdale aisle.

When the Victorian parishioners came to renovate this structure, they were blessed with a verse by Wordsworth in its honour. It comes from his poem 'The Excursion':

> *Not raised in nice proportion was the pile,*
> *But large and massy, for duration built,*
> *With pillars crowded and the roof upheld*
> *By naked rafters intricately crossed,*
> *Like leafless underboughs in some thick wood.*

Not every church alteration merits a Wordsworth stanza. There is a small plaque to the poet near the chancel and a booklet on his connection with the church. The guide rightly congratulates the parish on clearing the east window of Victorian glass in 1937, 'allowing a magnificent natural view of the fells and admitting plenty of light'.

KIRKBY LONSDALE
St Mary **
Massive Norman arcade

Kirkby Lonsdale is a Pennine town almost without blemish. The church sits surrounded by 17th- and 18th-century streets near the market square, yet with fields and fells visible on all sides. The streets have names such as Mill Brow, Jingling Lane and Devil's Bridge, and the churchyard contrives tranquillity amid bustle. Ruskin called it 'one of the loveliest scenes in England – therefore in the world'. In celebration of the view north and east over the River Lune the Victorians built a gazebo in the churchyard.

The west front of the church has a late Norman core, including a splendid doorway, with Perpendicular battlements, tower top and outer north aisle. The interior is still more mixed. The remarkable three bays of the north arcade are among the most exciting survivals in any church of the early Norman period. They stand like giant Romanesque stalagmites in a cave of later architecture. Clustered piers alternate with cylindrical piers carved into trellis patterns, reminiscent of Durham Cathedral. The scalloped capitals are carved with a variety of animals and abstract patterns. It seems likely that a grander church was planned but abandoned, to be resumed on a more modest scale.

The rest of the building conforms to that modesty. The late Norman south arcade seems modern in comparison to the massive earlier work. The outer north aisle and arcade are Perpendicular. The church has a font cover of rich oak carving. The choir screens are Victorian metalwork and there is a Jacobean cupboard at the back of the church. A savage restoration and scraping in 1866 have left their mark.

KIRKBY STEPHEN
St Stephen *
Stone carving of Norse devil

Kirkby Stephen church, like Appleby, is screened from its market place by a Georgian loggia. The churchyard, sadly bare of its gravestones, shelters behind attractive Georgian houses. The building itself is long and low, except for a Perpendicular west tower, but with large east chapels looming like attached barns.

Kirkby Stephen's interior is unexpectedly grand for so modest a town. The tower arch seems meant for a taller structure. The fine nave is Early Gothic. Eight sandstone bays lead us to the crossing and Victorian chancel. Here we find a sumptuous pulpit donated by the town to the church in 1872 in memory of a popular vicar. It is of Shap granite and Italian marble. In the chancel is a resited piscina–sedilia set, the latter with floral motifs on its capitals.

The tombs make a motley collection. Those in the Wharton Chapel include the tomb of Thomas, 1st Lord Wharton (d.1568), a late example of an early classical tomb, with balusters and shell-head niches round the chest. A more remarkable work is at the back of the nave, known as the Loki stone. This is an Anglo-Danish cross shaft of a 'chained devil', the Norse god Loki. This creature is described in the guide as 'one of the earliest Christian symbols of the devil in human shape'. It is the only example in Britain and is strangely powerful.

LANERCOST
St Mary **
Early Gothic nave, Morris glass

Lanercost is a glorious oasis to find in these northern wastes, especially on a wild, wintry day. A frontier church in every sense, the old Augustinian priory was built by the Norman Vaux family *c.*1166 from the stones of Hadrian's Wall and intended as both a military and a religious bulwark against the Scots. It was regularly raided and pillaged, most drastically by William Wallace in 1297. At the Dissolution the property passed to the Dacre family, who established a parish church in the north aisle, converted part of the priory into a residence and left the rest to decay. In 1740, however, the old nave was restored, roofed and reunited with the north aisle. Today, the former crossing, tower and chancel survive outside, unroofed and as ruins. They play host to a fine gallery of tomb chests. The remains are in the hands of English Heritage.

The exterior of the restored nave makes an immediate impact with its superb Early Gothic west front facing the car park. Three lonely lancets linked by blind arcading rise above a west portal topped by a small niche with a statue of St Mary. Inside is a cool, sophisticated Early Gothic nave and north aisle. There was never a south aisle, this being the site of the old cloister. Above runs a magnificent clerestory, with a shafted wall passage, decorated with nailhead and dogtooth, but with one capital on the south side curiously decorated with beautiful stiff-leaf, that is in a later Early Gothic style. How did this happen? Did an itinerant mason arrive one day, offer to run up a 'modern' carving to show how it was done and then disappear?

The east end of the nave has Georgian windows in the new wall, giving sight of the ruined chancel beyond. The north aisle has exciting glass by the Morris partnership, though I wonder if any of its members came this far north to install it. On my visit the church resounded to recorded plainsong, a wholly suitable enhancement. In the ruined chancel are exposed tombs of the Vaux family. They are sadly eroded by the weather. Here too is a small terracotta effigy of a baby. This is a Victorian memorial to a Dacre child who died in 1883.

LOWTHER
St Michael ***
Ravine setting, Lonsdale statue by Stanton

England offers few churches more splendidly situated. St Michael's stands at the end of the vista below Lowther Castle on a bluff overlooking a ravine. Askham Hall rises on the far bank and wild fells stretch to the horizon. Sir John Lowther acquired the site in the 1680s, moved the old village from the park south of the church, built a house and rebuilt the church. He was a man of parts, rising to be First Lord of the Treasury, Lord Privy Seal and Viscount Lonsdale by the time of his death in 1700. The house later burnt down but was rebuilt for another eccentric Lowther by Robert Smirke in 1806. Smirke's house is now a picturesque ruin, magnificent on its hill, but the church in which generations of Lowthers are buried is still active.

The exterior is ungainly, the result of 17th-century additions to an ancient core. The inside is delightful, dating back to a time when this bluff was inhabited by both Vikings and Normans. An old Norse tomb is displayed in the porch, showing two Viking ships with warriors. The short, four-bay arcade is Norman, the north side being adorned with capitals with carved heads. The crossing is later, formed of graceful Early Gothic arches. With the short transepts, this creates a most exciting volume at the heart of the building.

Lowthers are everywhere. The earlier ones are in the south transept, three tombs displaying the evolution of memorial art during the Stuart era. Sir Richard Lowther (d.1608) lies in alabaster, medieval-style in armour and in prayer. Against the west wall is a monument to two Sir Johns (dd.1637, 1675). The tomb is of the latter date, and is attributed to Jasper Latham. Here the form is of two busts with a skull on a cushion between them, backed by a black curtain.

The third monument is to the creator of the Lowther estate, the 1st Viscount Lonsdale, by William Stanton. We have now reached the early 18th century and the contrast is complete. A late Stuart courtier rests comfortably on one arm, languidly balancing his viscount's coronet in the other hand. His stocking is rolled to the knee, with every twist of lace and fur portrayed. The statue is the equal of Stanton's Lytton masterpieces at Knebworth (Herts).

In the north transept are later memorials to the family. They include a Victorian brass of Henry, Earl of Lonsdale, who died in 1876. He is shown in military dress, with moustaches and lock of hair, his breastplate of steel. In the chancel is a Pre-Raphaelite plaque to Emily, wife of the 3rd Earl, with her dog beneath. In the churchyard, noble over the ravine beneath, is the Lowther mausoleum of 1857.

ST BEES
St Mary and St Bega *
Norman west front, Art Nouveau screen

The old abbey stands in a valley with the sea in the distance. It seems miraculously detached from the coastal sprawl of suburban estates and caravan parks. The sandstone church and Elizabethan school commemorate an Irish girl named Bega who sailed single-handed across the Irish Sea to escape a forced marriage to a Viking chief. Though much of the present church dates from

Butterfield's Victorian restoration – and worth seeing for that – the west front is original and forms a rugged cliff of Norman architecture. The magnificent doorway has three arches which appear to have been hacked direct from a megalith of sandstone, like the arches at Petra. Some of the carved capitals remain without their shafts, resplendent in mid-air. Opposite is more Norman carving on a gateway lintel.

Inside, tall lancet windows illumine an Early Gothic nave, with Norman piers alternately octagonal and cylindrical. One shafted pier on the north side has a pilgrimage shell above its capital. The aisles and windows are all by Butterfield, mostly with awful glass. Like most priories, St Bees lost its east end at the Reformation. For once the chancel was not demolished but converted for secular use. A fine set of lancets thus survives in what is now a school library.

The new chancel inserted into the nave by Butterfield is guarded by St Bees' treasure, his Art Nouveau metalwork screen. This is a splendid piece. Swirling fronds soar upwards to fill the entire archway, a remarkable display of iron-work virtuosity. A small museum occupies part of the south aisle.

TORPENHOW
St Michael *
Imported Baroque ceiling

The northern Lake District is a lost corner of England. Here Vikings settled along the Solway Firth amid a moorland wilderness beneath the heights of Skiddaw. The 20th century has made little impact on this region. Villages seem sparse and underpopulated, including that of Torpenhow, pronounced Trepenna. But its Norman church is a delight, if only for its name, chancel arch and ceiling.

The name is curious. The guide suggests three Celtic tongues all gave it their word for hill: tor, pen and how. The church is long and low and has no tower. The south porch contains a reset Norman door. The interior was scraped by the Victorians, but not so as to weaken the power of what is Cumbria's most complete Norman interior. A short nave of three bays leads to a broad rounded chancel arch decorated with strong zigzags and with inventive capitals. On the (evil) north capital are devils holding arms; on the (good) south are tiny heads on scallops, humans and animals gazing across the arch from Heaven towards Hell. It forms a simple parable in stone.

The walls are thick and the windows are small and flat topped. The east window has Intersecting tracery. The nave ceiling is a complete anachronism, if such a word can ever be used of an English church. It was donated by one Thomas Addison in 1689. He had just acquired a local house or 'Seat answerable to his present Quality', and presumably worried that the church might be beneath his dignity. The ceiling is said to be from a demolished livery hall in the City of London. It is Baroque in style, of wood painted with cherubs and scrolls. It could hardly be more out of character with the church or, I suppose, the neighbourhood.

WASDALE HEAD
St Olaf *
Mountain chapel, climbers' graves

Half the pleasure (or pain) of Wasdale Head lies in reaching it. The road creeps up Wasdale between looming fells past Wastwater, into the heart of the central massif of the Lake District. This is serious climbing country, at the hub of the great wheel of Pillar, Great Gable and mighty Scafell Pike.

By the end of the 19th century Wasdale Head had become the centre of Lakeland mountaineering. The settlement had barely fifty souls, and today has shrunk to just a church, a few farms and the Wastwater Inn. Here climbers and lesser mortals brood silently over vast bowls of soup – and usually curse the weather. In winter this must be a bleak spot. Even in summer it bespeaks the solemnity of England's most earnest sport.

The church sits in an enclosure of yews across a field some distance from the inn. It is tiny but a notice claiming it as England's smallest church is contested by graffiti citing Culbone (Somerset) and Dale Abbey (Derbys). The churchyard contains graves of mountaineers lost on the surrounding peaks, with many headstones declaring, 'I will lift up mine eyes unto the hills.' The church is plain with a single low sweeping roof and small bellcote. The date is uncertain, the earliest reference to it being in 1550. The dedication to St Olaf is as recent as 1977, in honour of the Vikings to whom legend attributes the early settlement of these dales.

The present interior is mostly the result of an 1890s' restoration. According to the guide, there was previously an earthen floor, no seats and no window glass. The present appearance is of a 17th-century chapel with high-backed pews and balls on the bench-ends. The oil lamps have electric bulbs. Outside is the grave of Alexandrina Wilson, last teacher in the dale, who died in 1947.

WHITEHAVEN
St James **
Sumptuous Georgian interior

Whitehaven's early prosperity was based on coal for Ireland. In the mid-17th century, west Cumberland offered the most accessible coal for the booming city of Dublin. This was exploited by the lord of Whitehaven, the enlightened Sir

John Lowther, who is buried at Lowther church. He had a taste for classical planning and promoted the expansion of the town on a rectangular street pattern. Eighteenth-century growth was swift, extending the stately streets up on to the surrounding hills. Equally swift was the 19th-century decline when Welsh coal came to dominate the Irish market. Whitehaven was left as one of the few substantial planned and unaltered towns in England.

The former parish church of St Nicholas was rebuilt by the Victorians, but Georgian St James survives, well-situated at the top of the hill above Queen Street. The plan was prepared in 1752 by the Lowther agent, the splendidly named Carlisle Spedding. The pedimented tower façade, in two shades of stone and rendering, surveys the town with supreme confidence. It is one of the few churches I know with engraved glass doors that open automatically. The engravings are of Buddhist symbols, in honour of a Sri Lankan vicar, Russell Rebert, incumbent from 1984 to 1994. The rest of the exterior looks domestic and rather forbidding.

The church has Cumbria's most impressive 18th-century interior, demonstrating the ambition that the Lowthers and Whitehaven still had for their town in the 1750s. The colours are soft 'Wedgwood' creams, pinks and blues. The ceiling would not be out of place above the ballroom of a stately home. There are galleries on three sides with Doric and Ionic columns. The fourth side has a huge chancel arch, and an apse containing an Ionic reredos, which echoes the Doric entrance portal. The font is said to be from the Florence Duomo. Can this be true?

The ceiling contains two admirable stucco roundels, one of the Annuciation, the other of the Ascension. They are composed of relief cloud trails and sunbursts, with figures sculpted in the round. Beneath is a delightful rococo pulpit, daringly supported on a single Doric column complete with its own tiny entablature. In the Lady Chapel we are brought literally down to earth: a lump of coal and a miner's lamp commemorate a pit disaster in 1947.

WREAY

St Mary ****

Sarah Losh's Lombardic Revival

This is one of the most eccentric small churches in England. The hamlet of Wreay, pronounced ree-ah, sits round a formal green of beeches, firs and cherry trees, and is near Carlisle (another Wreay is by Ullswater). Here stands a church which, but for the severity of its stone, might be on a hillside in northern Italy.

The church was commissioned and designed by a local woman, Sarah Losh, in memory of her sister and parents. Her portrait hangs inside the door. Many visitors have wondered how a provincial lady, even of good education (her father knew Wordsworth), could have acquired such detailed knowledge of Italian Romanesque and Early Christian architecture. There are other 'Lombardic' churches in England, for example at Wilton (Wilts), designed by T. H. Wyatt for the Countess of Pembroke. Wilton was begun in 1841, and Wreay in 1835.

The answer must lie in the talent and education of Miss Losh herself. She was the daughter of an educated ironmaster, John Losh, owner of a Newcastle factory. Sarah and her sister Catherine were taken to Italy in 1817. She knew French, Latin and Greek and when her sister died in 1835, the fifty-year-old Sarah determined to pour into her memorial all she had acquired of art and architecture. We know of no assistant in the venture; the building appears to be entirely her work. The only other inspiration was a Major William Thain, a local hero and soldier, who fought at Waterloo and died on the Afghan frontier in 1842. He sent Sarah a pine cone, her last missive from him before he died. The motif appears everywhere in the church.

The shape is a simple box, with a steep gable on the west front. The round arched openings are decorated with flora and fauna, boldly carved, slightly abstract, and larger than life size. Among other motifs are the caterpillar, chrysalis and butterfly as symbols of life, death and resurrection. On each corner of the side elevations is a monstrous gargoyle.

Inside, the nave is plain, unaisled and outwardly dull, until we examine the details. The clerestory has small arched windows in triplets, containing lovely stained glass. The middle opening uses black glass in which are set brilliantly coloured leaves. The glass in the nave windows is of fragments brought back from the ruined archbishop's palace in Paris by Sarah's cousin, William. The furnishings border on Disneyesque, except that they are stylistically harmonious and superbly executed.

The font is adorned with butterflies and pomegranates and was mostly carved by Losh herself. Pevsner calls it 'Byzantino-Naturalistic'. Stone lilies float in water of glass. Losh's eagle lectern and pelican reading desk rise out of trunks covered in bark. The pulpit is a hollowed-out trunk. The adjacent candleholder is, I think, a giant thistle. The chancel arch has a frieze of angels and palm trees, a work of great elegance.

The chancel is even more remarkable. It has an arcaded apse with closely spaced columns and painted surrounds. The deep clerestory has windows with metal stencils of fern fossils. All this work appears to be without any academic or aesthetic forerunner. Historians have failed to find any pattern-book (except possibly by a German scholar) from which Losh could have derived her inspiration. We know only that her gardener did much of the wood carving and a local mason, William Hindson, the stonework. It is said that Hindson was treated to a trip to Italy by Losh to improve his technique.

The mausoleum for Catherine and Sarah Losh is in the churchyard and is of stones laid casually in a 'cyclopean' style. Next to it is a good Victorian reproduction of the Bewcastle Cross, which is better than the original in that it is now less eroded. Unlike almost all the works in this book, Wreay appears to have been the creation of a single original mind. Sarah Losh was an individual genius, an architectural Charlotte Brontë. The Arts and Crafts Movement took half a century to catch up with her.

Derbyshire

This is a county of peak and dale, of aristocratic palaces and modest villages. The churches reflect this diversity. Most are of granite and pink stone. Every period of church architecture is represented. The crypt at Repton dates from the 9th century. Melbourne is a Norman mini-cathedral, built by the bishops of Carlisle. The walls of Wirksworth and Bakewell are alive with Saxon and Norman carvings, rescued from history and set out as galleries of ancient art.

The Goths contributed the superb Decorated chancels at Norbury and Sandiacre. Excellent medieval glass survives at Morley. But Derbyshire's prize is its alabaster, the Carrara marble of English sculpture. The effigies of the Cockaynes at Ashbourne, the Sacheverells at Morley and the Fitzherberts at Norbury are as fine as any in England. They form an encyclopedia not only of English history, but of armour, fashion, art and family life. This tradition was later crowned by the Victorian Boothby effigy of a girl sleeping in death at Ashbourne.

Derbyshire received less attention from the 18th and 19th centuries. The furnishings at tiny Dale are unforgettable, good Victorian glass can be found at Ashbourne, and admirable 20th-century wood carving revives medieval craftsmanship in the bench-ends at Tideswell.

Ashbourne ****	Derby: St Mary RC *	Sandiacre **
Ashover *	Eyam *	Steetley *
Ault Hucknall *	Melbourne ****	Tideswell **
Bakewell ***	Morley ***	Whitwell *
Chesterfield ***	Norbury ***	Wirksworth ***
Dale **	Repton ***	Youlgreave **

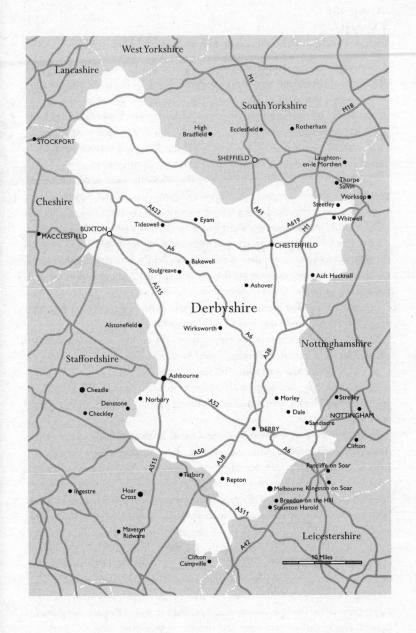

ASHBOURNE
St Oswald ****
Cockayne and Boothby tombs, 19th- and 20th-century glass

Ashbourne sits at the southernmost tip of the Peak District and thus of the spine of England. Here we bid farewell to the soft flatlands of the south and head for Dovedale and the harsh Pennine Way. The town has a high street and square largely devoid of 20th-century intrusion. The church, which was to George Eliot 'the finest mere parish church in the kingdom', lies at its western extremity, its spire soaring over a churchyard which, on my last visit, was carpeted with daffodils. A verger assured me there were more than 100 varieties.

The exterior of pink limestone is odd, the cruciform plan somehow out of proportion. There is a long Early Gothic collegiate chancel and massive 212-ft crossing tower and spire. There are wide eastern aisles to the transepts. Yet the nave is hardly worth the name, short with a single aisle to the south. Ashbourne church was for clergy and gentry, but apparently not for locals. Small wonder the Methodists were so popular in these parts. Yet the building contains some of Derbyshire's finest monuments and its best stained glass. It is possible that parts of the spire and nave aisle were by a local mason, Henry Yevele, who left Ashbourne for London in the mid-14th century, to become the master architect of English Perpendicular and builder of Westminster Hall.

The interior is as eccentric as the exterior. No corner is without interest: carved kings and queens, bell ropes, Green Men, a lush chancel roof of 1963 by S. E. Dykes Bower and a reredos with scenes from Dovedale. A window in the north transept has even been set at an angle to catch the rays of the evening sun. Here is a church with grand and intimate spaces, a church of something for everyone.

Pride of place goes to the Cockayne Chapel in the east aisle of the north transept, which is filled with their tombs. John Cockayne was steward to John of Gaunt, whose wife, Blanche, was daughter of the local Earl of Derby. Cockaynes were active in national politics throughout the Wars of the Roses and into the Tudor period. They remained powers in the district, at Ashbourne Hall, until the 1670s when debts forced a sale to the Boothby family. The tombs range from the early 15th to the late 16th centuries and include brasses, chests, incised slabs and wall memorials. The finest medieval work, to Sir John Cockayne (d.1447) and his wife, is of Derbyshire alabaster, he in armour, she in a magnificent medieval costume, with angel weepers holding shields round the chest. Near them are buried two centuries of Cockaynes, a mortuary of ages, a gathering of the clan, so common in England yet without equal elsewhere in Europe, and symbol of continuity and stability in local land tenure.

At the southern end of the group is a gem, Thomas Banks's figure of Penelope

Boothby, who died aged five in 1791. The child lies as if asleep within her marble effigy. Her figure is visible under her gown with unashamed poignancy, her little toe gingerly covered. The sash of velvet is chiselled to a different texture from the cloth of the dress. Queen Charlotte was said to have broken into tears on seeing the statue at a Royal Academy exhibition. Evincing such a reaction was regarded as a challenge to late-Georgian sculpture.

After the tombs, the windows. If these great churches must be rendered gloomy by Victorian glass let it be the best. Ashbourne's glass is excellent. The east and west windows are by Kempe, the latter a Tree of Jesse, its figures in perpetual Kempeian motion. Another Kempe is in the north wall, with his wheatsheaf signature. In the south aisle is a 1904 work by Christopher Whall, commemorating a wife and daughter who died in a local fire. This is Arts and Crafts at its most ethereal. Girls play the organ dressed in medieval clothes with flowers and crowns in their hair, the celestial city visible through a thicket of thorns. Whall's signature was his own thumbprint, seen in the clearer panes. In the west wall of the south transept is a work of 1933 by the Bromsgrove Guild, brilliantly coloured but hard to see. Ashbourne church is one of the finest works of art in the county, and should rank alongside the magnificent historic mansions.

ASHOVER
All Saints *
Norman lead font, Babington tomb

Ashover lies in a secluded valley north of Matlock Moor on the road to Chesterfield. The church is typical of Derbyshire, with generous proportions but a short tower and a narrow spire. In the uplands, steeples were never a navigational aid, as on the plains. The church is surrounded by handsome stone houses, lawns, walls and a sense of prosperity. On my visit it smelled strongly of polish. The walls have been scraped, so crudely as to resemble a dungeon. But the church contains two works of art without equal in the county.

One is the Norman lead font at the rear of the nave, one of only 30 left in England that avoided being melted for bullets at some stage in its life. Others are found at Dorchester (Oxon) and Brookland (Kent). Here the bowl is encircled by an arcade which frames apostles holding books, a beautiful composition. The other treasure is the Babington tomb. Ashover men fought under Thomas Babington, lord of the manor, at Agincourt and returned to name their inn after St Crispin, the day of the battle. (Another theory holds that Crispin was patron saint of the local cobblers.) A Babington rebuilt much of the church in the 15th century and another Thomas, who died in 1518, lies on a tomb outside the chancel. The effigies are painted and rest their heads on tasselled cushions. Below is a superb carved chest, with ogee canopies and weepers intact.

That both font and tomb should have survived when Cromwellian troops were burning down the local pub for refusing them beer is remarkable. The font was saved by being buried in a kitchen garden. There is a fine Arts and Crafts reredos in the north chapel, executed by a local carver, George Eastwood, who also made the bench-ends in Perpendicular style.

AULT HUCKNALL
St John *
Norman tympanum, Hobbes memorial

Ault Hucknall is less than a mile from Hardwick Hall and the little church is a relief after the excitement of the great house. It sits on the escarpment overlooking the Amber valley and the mighty torrent of the M1 beneath. The church stands in a village of just four houses, outnumbered by the yews in the churchyard. Its material is bold white limestone. Embedded in the outside of its west wall is a Norman arch and tympanum so indistinct that it could depict either a centaur or St Margaret emerging from the body of the Devil.

The interior is odd. There are two Norman arches knocked through a wall to form a north aisle, and three Gothic ones to the south. The most prominent feature is the view east through a wide Norman chancel arch to a narrow Saxon one beyond. The first arch has beakhead and other decoration, jumbled and evidently a reassembling of older carvings. It is said to tell the Bible story. The other arch is a simple entry to the old sanctuary, forming a dark and mysterious space beyond the crossing.

The Cavendish Chapel in the south aisle hardly merits the name, containing just one tomb of the family. Most Cavendishes were buried at Edensor on the Chatsworth estate. Here we have Anne, 1st Countess of Devonshire (d.1598), commemorated in a monument dated 1627. It is an unusual tomb chest crowned with a row of allegorical figures, three of them decapitated allegedly by a clumsy workman. They should surely be replaced by copies. Here too is a memorial to Hardwick's most distinguished employee, the political philosopher, Thomas Hobbes, tutor to the Cavendish children. His first book was not on philosophy but on the wonders of the Peak District. He was buried here in 1679 at the age of ninety-two.

BAKEWELL
All Saints ***
Saxon wall carvings, Vernon monuments

Bakewell is a jolly Peak District town built of the blackest stone. The church tower rises over the town, pinning it to the dale as if fearful that the Devil might steal it in the night. The visitor should not be deterred. Bakewell's joys are buried in the darkness of All Saints.

The church's principal contents are built into its fabric. The north Midlands is rich in Saxon relics. In the 1840s a Victorian collector, Thomas Bateman, opened a crypt and discovered, according to Pevsner, 'the earliest and most varied collection of early medieval monuments in the United Kingdom'. The best known, the Bakewell Cross, is in the churchyard, a storybook of saints embraced in circles, knots and scrolls. The south porch wall is thick with fragments of ancient capitals, drums, friezes and cornices, as is the west wall inside. Most of this carving is crude and hard to discern. But as we gaze on them, their ancient faces become alive and start out at us from the gloom.

The east aisle of the south transept is Bakewell's grandest space. The Vernons of Haddon Hall were once kings of the Peak. This mausoleum commemorates them with, sequentially, an early 15th-century stone knight, a late 15th-century tomb chest to John Vernon, 16th-century alabaster effigies of Sir George Vernon and his wives, a late Elizabethan wall monument to Dorothy Vernon and her husband, and another to her son, Sir George Manners (d.1623). The upper part of this last work is conventional, but in the lower part the usual chest is replaced by two tiers of arcades framing kneeling children. They include a baby which died at birth and looks remarkably smug. Against the east wall of the south aisle is the Foljambe memorial of 1385. This is an unusual half-length wall memorial of a knight and his wife. They appear to be praying together in bed.

The church is well-endowed with poppyheads and misericords. More recent craftsmanship is on the east face of the chancel screen, beautiful carvings of the six acts of charity installed by Giles Gilbert Scott. He incorporated medieval bench-ends and misericords in new chancel furnishings.

CHESTERFIELD
St Mary and All Saints ***
Twisted spire, Foljambe tombs

Chesterfield is universally known for its twisted spire, the most famous architectural distortion north of Pisa. Most leaning spires require a particular angle of vision. Chesterfield's rotation can be seen from every side, as well as from the train and the bypass. The cause remains unknown. One theory is that the Devil rested on his way from Sheffield to Nottingham, another that a virtuous maiden sent the spire wild with admiration.

A less romantic theory holds that lead plates laid herringbone over unseasoned timber led the wood to twist but not snap under the weight. The structure turned and sank, but then 'set' without collapsing. It lasted from the 14th century to the 19th when it was declared unsafe and experts advised demolition. Rubbish, said the citizens of Chesterfield and merely strengthened it. Today it rises 228 ft and leans 7½ ft to the south and 3½ ft to the west. Especially when floodlit at night, the spire has an eerie beauty, like a work by the Barcelona architect Antoni Gaudí.

The interior is vast, rich and gloomy with Victorian and modern glass. The aisled nave offers a spacious vista, dominated by a fine panelled pulpit. This is very much a space for civic assembly. Beyond the crossing, we enter a different church, of aisles and chapels filled with dark tombs behind aloof screens. One screen of filigree delicacy protects the north chapel; a beefy Elizabethan one protects the south chapel. Chesterfield is High Church. There are five subsidiary altars, each one dressed, with candles in abundance.

Most spectacular of the memorials are those to the Foljambe family (also present at Bakewell). These cram the south chancel chapel like saints in an overwrought Italian cathedral, all brown and dusty. To the left is a Gothic tomb with a knight kneeling at prayer over it. His head inside the helmet appears to be that of a girl. In the centre are Elizabethan tomb chests, classical but with a Dutch robustness. On the east wall is an astonishing memorial of three allegorical figures, representing Youth, Old Age and Death, with beneath them a shrouded corpse. Below are a skull and gravedigger's tools, a most ghoulish portrayal of death. Several of these monuments are by Garret Hollemans, father of Jasper Hollemans who sculpted the Spencer family memorials at both Great Brington (Northants) and Yarnton (Oxon).

The altar reredoses are mostly by Temple Moore in the 1890s. They are among his best work. That in the north chapel is based on a central panel from Oberammergau.

DALE
All Saints **
Chancel furnishings

Here we have a gaunt ruin, a hermit's cave, an old willow tree and a tiny church under the same roof as a gabled Tudor house. Round the lawn are ancient stone walls and gravestones used as croquet hoops. This is a place of eccentric mystery. We learn that in the 12th century a baker in Derby saw a vision in which he was told to leave his work and become a hermit in Depedale. A knight took pity on him and paid for a chapel. A woman, known as the 'Gome of the Dale', took more pity, extending the chapel and persuading a nephew to found an abbey nearby. The abbey prospered and the older buildings became the infirmary and infirmary chapel. Apart from some ruins down the hill, these buildings are all that remain.

The interior of the chapel ranks with Whitby (Yorks, N) and Minstead (Hants) as a gem of pre-Victorian church furnishing. It is just 25 × 26 ft and is only larger than Culbone (Somerset) and Stockwood in Dorset by having an aisle. Its 'nave' must be the smallest by far. The structure is attached to the old infirmary, which became an inn, then a farmhouse and is now a private house. In its first incarnation, the sick would attend service in the upper gallery, entered from an outside staircase. When it was an inn, the Blue Bell, the clergy used to dress in the bar, entering the church through a now-blocked door.

Today we see two small chambers, separated by what may once have been a solid wall between the canons' oratory and the parish nave. In the late 15th century the church was reordered, with the wall replaced by a wooden screen and a gallery inserted. What passes for a nave – it is more like a parlour – was suggested by Arthur Mee as a junk shop for the goblins of the dale. It has just three pew benches and a small harmonium. The chancel is for the Mad Hatter. The pulpit leans out of a far corner as if about to topple on to the clerk's desk. This desk is located behind what passes for an altar, surely a unique arrangement. A large chair imported by Lord Stanhope as his 'bishop's throne', a box pew, assorted screens, beams and seats are crammed in a space too small to swing a cat.

In the nave is a wall painting, reproduced in the south aisle, that shows two saints kissing, reputedly Mary and Elizabeth.

DERBY
St Mary RC, Bridge Gate *
Restored Pugin interior

Derby's fine old parish church is now a cathedral. But St Mary's rises defiantly to the east of the town, brutally cut off by a gorge filled with a torrent of motorway traffic. It forms a fine vertical foil to the town centre and cathedral steeple. One of A. W. N. Pugin's few complete works, it was designed in 1837 in the Perpendicular style, which soon afterwards he denounced as degenerate Gothic, in the course of his conversion to Decorated. The church was enhanced by the charming north Lady Chapel added by his son, E. W. Pugin, and by an admirable modern restoration.

The tall luminous nave with large clerestory culminates in a vaulted apse. The fittings are excellent, with a lovely iron chancel screen by John Hardman and a rood on an independent arch. The decoration is equally splendid. A blue roof is studded with stars. Carved Stations of the Cross are set in the aisle walls. Stained glass is mostly by Hardman. The nave walls are painted with saints in roundels and angels in the spandrels. Every opening has a painted decorative border. Statues fill niches everywhere. The sedilia is in black and gold and the floor is of sumptuous marble. Pugin's patron was the Earl of Shrewsbury, for whom he also created Cheadle (Staffs).

The Lady Chapel may be too much for Protestant taste. The east wall is of transcending piety, the Madonna on the altar picked out by a spotlight.

EYAM
St Lawrence *
Plague church museum

I have included few churches for history alone, but cannot exclude Eyam. The surrounding scenery is magnificent and the church, partly rebuilt in the 19th century, tells a story that has drawn visitors for centuries.

In 1665, clothes arrived in the village from a London tailor, infested with plague larvae. After the first deaths, the inclination of the population was to flee. The young rector, William Mompesson, and his predecessor Thomas Stanley, who had recently been ejected from the living for Puritanism, won the villagers' agreement that nobody should leave until the infection passed. Otherwise all Derbyshire might succumb. Messages were sent to other villages, pleading for food to be left at an appointed spot. The village was turned into a quarantined fortress. This state lasted a year, during which three-quarters of the villagers perished, including Mompesson's wife. But Derbyshire was saved. Mompesson and Stanley both survived, and entered the annals of English heroism.

The church is part a museum dedicated to the plague and the village's story. Here too are Mompesson's pulpit and his chair as well as relics of the plague year. A modern window adds its contribution to the story. The nave walls retain some unusual painted cartouches and texts of the 16th and 17th centuries. Light relief is found in the churchyard: the tombstone of a Derbyshire cricketer, Harry Bagshawe, who died in 1927. The gravestone shows a ball breaking his stumps and an umpire's finger pointing upwards to Heaven.

MELBOURNE
St Michael with St Mary ****
Norman bishops' nave, 'misogynist' crossing arch

Melbourne lies comfortably in the valley of the River Trent, yet it is unmistakably a tough northern church. The settlement was made the seat of the Norman bishops of Carlisle – well behind the 'front line' – when their city was threatened by Scottish raiding parties. They built a church commensurate with their status, a mini-cathedral large enough for later generations of worshippers and thus saved from rebuilding. It survives as one of the finest Norman churches of England.

The church sits in an enclave to the south of the village, emerging from among the stables and servants' quarters behind Melbourne Hall. It is firmly 'below the salt', away from the Hall's splendid park of lawns, cedars and lake. Yet the church is a match for them all. Of the three bold limestone towers, that over the crossing has a 17th-century belfry. The east end has lost its three apses as well as the upper part of the chancel, but their skeletons can be seen in the walls. Everywhere are blocked arches and round-headed windows, with shafts and zigzag carving. Some of this has been retooled by the Victorians, some is crumbling to nothing. Two west towers have been reduced to stumps, but the door beneath them is a fine composition of four arches with an outer fan of zigzag.

The interior is sensational, Norman in both character and detail. The nave arcades are elephantine, circular piers rising to scallop or scroll capitals surmounted by tall horseshoe arches with zigzag. The clerestory has a cathedral-like wall passage and there is a west gallery above a vaulted narthex: lavish for a 12th-century parish church. Even richer is the crossing. Here four Norman arches rest on carved capitals. These are deeply incised and include the 'Melbourne cat', which could be a lion, and a rare sheela-na-gig. This primitive fertility monster has her legs apart to form the lobes of the capital and vine leaves emerging from her mouth, an astonishing image. The west piers of the crossing retain fragments of wall painting. To the north is a devil in breeches treading on two women, who seem to be holding a ball with little devils on their backs. The meaning is obscure, but this appears a thoroughly misogynist crossing.

Above rises the organ loft, whose ropes ring Melbourne's famous peal of twelve bells. Aisles and chapels proliferate, in a cool white stone that contrasts with the dark wooden roofs. The altar frontals are excellent and even John Hardman's east window is inoffensive. In the north aisle hang the flags of Australia and Melbourne. The link is tenuous. The Lamb family became Viscounts Melbourne in the 18th century, a son becoming Queen Victoria's first prime minister. She gave her name to a new province in Australia, he to its capital. He never visited the place, but the link has continued ever since.

MORLEY
St Matthew ***
Wall of medieval glass, Sacheverell tombs

Morley is for monuments and glass. The spire rises over a churchyard filled in spring with crocuses and daffodils. It is surrounded by a tithe barn, dovecote and former rectory. A 13th-century Richard de Morley passed the manor through the female line to Ralph Stathum in 1378 and on to the Sacheverells. The first Sacheverell tomb commemorates John, killed at Bosworth Field in 1485. The male line survived until the 17th century, the female lives on under the name of Sitwell, the two reunited in the name of the historian Sacheverell Sitwell.

The interior is much restored and is architecturally of little interest. The eye moves swiftly to the north aisle, where a wall of stained glass runs almost its entire length in a magnificent tapestry of light. This wall was erected after the destruction of neighbouring Dale Abbey in 1539, specifically to receive the glass from its refectory, purchased by Sir Henry Sacheverell. The Sacheverells were long-standing recusants and this chapel was built to celebrate Catholic Mass, a tradition that survived through the 17th century. The windows were covered in shutters to stop outsiders seeing Mass or smashing the glass. They were nearly lost in the 18th century through neglect, but restored in 1847.

The windows depict the story of St Robert of Knaresborough and of the Invention of the Holy Cross. Roughly half of each sequence is original, the rest Victorian re-creation but loyal to the original. The difference is not always easy to detect and is, like carefully restored architecture, perhaps best ignored. Old and new glass alike is charming.

After the glass come the tombs and brasses in the north chancel aisle, to Stathums and Sacheverells galore. This is a collection to rival Ashbourne, with the added pleasure of medieval tiles on the floor. The tiles, like the glass and possibly the niches and piscinas, come from Dale. The best brass is in the arcade, and commemorates the builder of the chapel, Henry (d.1558) and Isabella Sacheverell. In the north corner of the chapel is an effigy of his daughter, Katherine Babington (d.1543), grandmother of the Babington plotter against Elizabeth, portrayed here as serene and confident in her faith.

The tomb is of a quality, says Pevsner, to merit a place in Westminster Abbey. Whether the Abbey authorities would have admitted her is more doubtful. The 17th century donated incised slabs to Sacheverell children set into the floor and a big monument to Jacynth (d.1656) against the east wall.

In the south chapel is a sad memorial to Jonathas (*sic*) Sacheverell. He decided as heir to the estate to become a Protestant (in 1662) in the hope that this would protect its fortune from possible seizure, 'it being a principle constantly acted upon, for the government to strain every point to give succession to those of the Establishment'. He may have been right about the government, but he was wrong about his elder brother, who was still in a position to alter his will. This he did, bequeathing the estate to a separate branch of the family, loyal Catholics.

NORBURY
St Mary and St Barlok ***
South tower over porch, Fitzherbert tombs

The hall and refectory, churchyard yews and slate tombs offer a setting for a Derbyshire narrative from the Normans to today. Fitzherberts held the lordship of the manor from 1125 until it passed to the National Trust in 1987. The form of the church is curious, with a tower rising over the south porch. This tower is flanked on each side by an aisle and clerestory bay such that the whole south aspect of the church looks like a deliberately symmetrical composition. Gothic architecture is full of surprises. To the east is a magnificent Decorated chancel, of which the patron Nicholas Fitzherbert was most proud. His inscription runs, 'This church he made of his own expence / In the joy of heaven be his recompence.' Fitzherberts remained Catholic through the Reformation and Civil War, suffering far more for it than did the Sacheverells of Morley.

The nave interior is modest. There is an Early Gothic font on clustered shafts and, in the south chapel, a 14th-century tomb chest bearing a Fitzherbert with crossed legs and sheathed sword. These features, much debated by medievalists, are not related to the crusades but probably indicate no more than life's journey at an end. The glass in the east window of the south chapel portrays Nicholas and his wife with their children behind them, and St Anne teaching the Virgin to read. The south window depicts St Barlok, an obscure Irish saint.

The chancel is a cool, spectacular work. The huge windows are filled with Intersecting tracery with unusual rosettes at their centres, like the tracery at Checkley (Staffs). This is Perpendicular scale without Perpendicular tracery, and must date from the last period of Decorated Gothic in the mid-14th century. The glass is mostly original. The east window, recently restored, shows apostles, saints and Fitzherberts with roughly equal status. The side windows are as yet unrestored and dirty, but will one day form the finest collection of glass in the county.

On the chancel floor are two large tombs of Fitzherberts, Sir Nicholas (d.1473) and Sir Ralph (d.1483), the latter alongside his wife. Both have

Yorkist collars of suns and roses, thus predating the Tudor accession after Bosworth in 1485. The effigies are superb works of Midlands alabaster, both uncannily similar and assumed to be by the same carver. Every detail is immaculate, even the fingernails and strands of hair. The chests have weepers beneath ogee canopies, admirably preserved and each one slightly different. Other members of the family are commemorated in incised floor slabs and brasses. The choir stalls are ancient, as are the oil lamps. In the nave floor is a Saxon shaft carved, most unusually, with a human figure blowing a horn.

REPTON
St Wystan ***
Saxon crypt

Repton sits on a hill overlooking the River Trent, its church topped by a needle spire and flanked by the famous school. The church exterior is much altered and includes an apparently original square-headed Decorated window next to the porch. Nothing was sacred to 14th-century masons, not even the pointed arch.

Repton begins with its chancel. While the windows are later insertions, the walls and proportions are Anglo-Saxon, dated to the 8th or the 9th century, possibly both. The exterior is unbuttressed and rises from below present ground level, the large blocks of early masonry contrasting with later stonework. This encloses the crypt, reached from inside the church by a staircase on either side of the chancel arch. It is a precious relic of pre-Conquest architecture. Repton crypt is possibly two centuries older than the crypt at Lastingham (Yorks, N) and more intimate than such heavy restorations as Escomb (Durham) or Worth (Sussex). Square and round piers with spiral fluting and square capitals stand on old flagstones and support arches and vaults.

The scholarly guide debates at length the purpose of this chamber and concludes that it probably held the tomb of King Ethelbert and perhaps King Ethelbald, before doubling as a pilgrimage shrine for St Wystan. The steps are deeply worn by thousands of pilgrims. The crypt seems to have been complete by the end of the 9th century and thus qualifies as one of the oldest unaltered places of worship in England. Such humble shrines once existed in their thousands across Europe, from Compostela to Constantinople, but so rarely survive.

The rest of the interior has been badly scraped: the nave east wall looks like the cliff face of a stone quarry. The arcade is gracefully arched, the two eastern bays being 19th-century replacements for decayed Saxon bays. The clerestory and nave roof are 15th century. Among an eccentric collection of memorials is, in the south chapel, a tablet showing an old man being helped to Heaven by his muse. This lady assisted its subject John Macaulay (d.1840) to a 'profound, exact, extensive, elegant, peculiar, philological acuteness'. Lucky man. In the north chapel is a Baroque bust of Francis Thacker (d.1710). He looks out confidently over the medieval gloom, with flamboyant cravat, shirt open and a coat of arms toppling above his head.

SANDIACRE
St Giles **
Grime-encrusted Decorated windows

Arthur Mee begins his entry for Sandiacre: 'Here engines of enormous power are made which work in every continent, in mill and mine, making power and light in distant cities and pumping drains under the streets of London.' This may explain the awful prospect south of the church, a Derbyshire next to Nottinghamshire that few know and fewer visit.

The church looms up as a soot-covered beacon on a hill overlooking the scene. It is reached up a lane from the valley below and at once demonstrates a split personality. The west end is Norman and plebeian. A Saxon–Norman tower rises like a military keep, with a broach spire of dark stone added in 1300. Behind is an unaisled nave with Norman door and mostly round-headed windows. The chancel is a total contrast, a pinnacled and enriched Gothic chamber, higher than the nave and bellowing its glory out over the valley.

The interior mirrors this contrast. The nave is thin and simple with corbels high on the walls, relics of an earlier roof. The chancel arch is of the same period, crudely moulded and with the Sandiacre 'imp' high on its wall. The chancel was the work of Roger de Norbury, Bishop of Lichfield in the mid-14th century and a great builder of chancels at the time of the Black Death. A six-light east window with lily-pattern tracery forms the backdrop. The remaining Decorated tracery is formal Reticulated on the south side and a free curvilinear on the north. The sedilia and piscina have beautifully elongated canopies. The priest's door is adorned with the heads of Edward III and Queen Philippa.

Sandiacre font has Decorated patterns round its bowl, oak and vine leaves that might come from a William Morris wallpaper. The church records its incumbents by name and character. Thus a 17th-century curate, William Viccars, was 'an able man and of good conversason'. He was succeeded by Joseph Moore, 'whose Youth was not despicable, being Grave, Serious and Savoury'. He was ejected for Nonconformity in 1662.

STEETLEY
All Saints *
Norman chapel restored by Pearson

Steetley is a chapel in the parish of Whitwell, off the main road next to a large field full of poppies in summer. It is a Norman survivor, albeit much restored. The guide shows the church before Victorian rescue, as a roofless ruin covered in romantic creeper. Nobody today would dare reconstruct a medieval building so drastically. The gentler word 'reconciled' was used at the time of its reconsecration in 1880.

J. L. Pearson was a scholarly restorer, as we know from his work at Stow (Lincs) and elsewhere. He took few liberties with Norman carving. He replaced most of the south portal which had almost crumbled away but left the corbel-table in its eroded state, the limestone now as porous as cheese. The interior is saved from gloom by a jolly Decorated window in the south chancel wall. Otherwise the fenestration is confined to original Norman slits. Pearson also left almost untouched the carved arches east and west of the chancel. Their capitals include Adam and Eve, a lion and a soldier with a shield, possibly St George and the Dragon. Happily the Norman apse survives unscathed, with its vault, wall shafts and carved capitals. The nave has been scraped but, for some reason, not the apse.

Steetley has good modern glass of abstract design in the east and south windows. The latter is dedicated to the Thornton family and celebrates local village life. In both windows the blue of water rises to greet red flames above.

TIDESWELL
St John **
Medieval and modern wood carving

Tideswell calls itself the 'cathedral of the Peak', another parish church to claim territorial status by virtue of its size. The tower undoubtedly dominates the small town. Indeed the nearer we approach, the smaller seems the town and the larger the church. The first impression is of Decorated grandeur, especially the curvilinear tracery of the south transept. The tower has a heavy base, undistinguished belfry and, as if to compensate, massive polygonal turrets and pinnacles forming the crown.

The interior comes closest to justifying the cathedral epithet. Nave, crossing, transepts and chancel are the 14th century at its most ambitious, flirting with Continental flamboyance before settling back into English Perpendicular. This is a church of generous proportions. The chancel was rebuilt in the late 14th century and although the side windows still have Decorated tracery with quatrefoils, they have the square heads of the Perpendicular period.

The church's glory is its woodwork, which dates from all periods. There are medieval misericords in the north transept and, elsewhere, Victorian and 20th-century carvings of the highest quality. The chancel contains Victorian stalls by Tooley of Bury St Edmunds, the ends carved with saints performing deeds associated with their legends. This tradition was continued in the 20th century, with work by local craftsmen named Advent and William Hunstone. They contributed stalls, bench-ends and an organ case of astonishing virtuosity. Their bench-ends include representations of baptism, ordination, confirmation and visiting the sick. Complex tableaux are executed with none of the stagey piety of much modern religious work. An excellent guide explains each one.

Tideswell is rich in monuments, some more successful than others. In the centre of the chancel is a tomb chest with a brass on top, a rare portrayal in this form of the Holy Trinity. A skeleton lurks beneath. The east end has four large statues, installed in the 1950s. They were not carved by the Hunstones, more is the pity.

WHITWELL
St Lawrence *
Decorated sedilia group

This 'best kept' village lies south of Whitwell Wood on the border of Derbyshire and Yorkshire. Its Scotland Street recalls the boundary not just of the two counties but of the ancient kingdoms of Mercia and Northumbria. I suppose it was a Midlander's last sight of home territory before embarking on dangerous foreign soil.

The church is a friendly structure set in a sloping churchyard. The tower has a Norman base and west door over which that once-ubiquitous adornment of churches, creeper, has for once been left in place. The interior is formed of a spacious Norman nave with its original clerestory and corbel-table. The arch to the chancel is more developed, with water-leaf capitals. The nave is whitewashed but the north aisle scraped.

The rest of the church is Decorated in style. The north transept contains a wall tomb with, next to it, a monument of 1632 to the 'right noble, learned and religious knight, Roger Manners'. His face peers from beneath an armoured visor. In the south transept are some good modern statues of saints. The most notable medieval survival is the piscina-sedilia group in the chancel. This has elaborately elongated canopies and is carved with fulsome cusps, crockets and gables. Pevsner attributes this to the carvers of Hawton (Notts), which is praise indeed.

WIRKSWORTH
St Mary ***
Carved Saxon coffin lid, miner's graffito

The town lies in a dale from whose surrounding hills men have hacked lead since the Dark Ages. Scratched into a stone in the church is a graffito of an ancient miner with his pick, the only medieval portrayal of such labour other than at Newland (Gloucs). The church rises big and dark in the centre of the town, its pink stone discoloured by soot, like the hide of a wild boar.

Wirksworth is as grand a church as Ashbourne, albeit heavily restored by George Gilbert Scott in the 1870s. The plan is cruciform, the tower supported inside by a flurry of shafted piers. The chancel aisles are so generous as to make the chancel seem like a nave and the sanctuary the chancel. The transepts have rare aisles. The walls are scraped down to pink stone. Yet there is a raw dignity to this church which Scott has preserved, even if the atmosphere is blighted by bad Victorian glass.

The contents of Wirksworth include one of the finest Saxon coffin lids extant. This is set into the north wall of the nave, its relief carving portraying eight scenes from the life of Christ. We can discern Christ washing the disciples' feet, the Entombment and, on the lower tier, the Ascension. This lid is among the most evocative images of Dark Ages art. Its inspiration is similar to the 'Byzantine' carvings at Breedon (Leics) to the south. The figures could hardly be more primitive, more aloof from the Saxon tradition, yet they radiate life. As we look round the church and our eyes grow accustomed to the dark, the walls seem to move. Beasts, faces, flowers start out from the walls in which their restorers have imprisoned them. None is special but the whole is a unique ensemble. The ancient miner, known as 't'owd man', is on the corner of the south transept. It came from nearby Bonsall church.

In the north chancel aisle are two Elizabethan tomb chests to members of the Gell family. These are beautifully executed in alabaster, each strand of the fur collars picked out in stone.

YOULGREAVE
All Saints **
Pilgrim figure, Flemish alabaster panel

I reached Youlgreave over the moor from Elton. The massive 100-ft gritstone tower, stained black but with touches of weathered pink, dominated its settlement like a Crusader keep. Yet the churchyard was full of spring flowers and farm smells, the church open and welcoming.

The interior has strong Norman piers and scalloped capitals. Embedded in the tower arch is a carving of a tiny Norman wayfarer, carrying his bag and staff. This was presumably in honour of locals setting out across the Peak as on a pilgrimage. The north aisle has a window of fragments of medieval glass from the ruined Ypres Cathedral, gathered by the brother of a boy killed at Gallipoli. Also in this aisle is an alabaster panel of the Virgin, intended as a memorial to Robert Gilbert (d.1492). He and his seven sons are on the left, his wife and ten daughters on the right, the Virgin in the centre. This simple but exquisite example of late-medieval art was possibly executed by a Fleming working at the famous Burton alabaster works, whose products were distributed nationwide.

The chancel was restored by Norman Shaw and is dominated by a Burne-Jones window. Evangelists and angels are portrayed in rich golds, yellows and oranges. The head of St Mark is crowned with the most dramatic of lions. Beneath the window lie two monuments. One is to Sir John Rossington, holding his heart in his hands. The other, in the centre of the chancel, is to Thomas Cokayne (d.1488). According to the guide, he died in a fight with another man over a family settlement. Because he predeceased his father, he was portrayed smaller than life size, just three and a half feet long. He is depicted in chainmail, a collar of Yorkist suns and roses and beautifully armoured feet resting on a lion.

Youlgreave font is Norman with a rare feature, a water stoup cut out of the same lump of rock and supported by a salamander.

Devon

Devon churches are West Country picturesque. They punctuate the landscape with stone towers set against the soft curves of the hillsides. Most, like those of Cornwall, were rebuilt in the 15th or 16th century, often with a low roof and no division between nave and chancel. What they may lack in architecture, they make up for in interior woodwork. This is a county of wagon roofs, broad screens, lofts, pulpits and bench-ends. Many Devon churches are set in classic English villages enveloped in thatch and with the sea in the distance. Yet on the north coast are also wild churches of cliff and moorland, trapped, said Sir John Fortescue, 'between the hammer of the west wind and the anvil of the yellow clay'.

The jewel of pre-Reformation Devon is undoubtedly Ottery St Mary, built by Bishop Grandison in what seems a facsimile of Exeter Cathedral. Only the battered old minster of Crediton, rich in sandstone and carvings, is its rival in splendour. Next in rank is Cullompton, with a majestic screen, roof and fan-vaulted aisle. For the most part, Devon is a county of gentility, demonstrated by the delightful Georgian furnishings of Molland and Parracombe. A different, wilder Devon is displayed at Widecombe on Dartmoor, or tucked into the combes of Tawstock or Hartland, running down to the Bristol Channel, resting-place for many shipwrecked vessels.

The county was lucky in its restorers, notably the Sedding family, their work best exhibited in the Arts and Crafts furnishings of Holbeton. William Butterfield made a spectacular excursion to Babbacombe. Twentieth-century wood carving is best represented by Herbert Read, whose work is found in church after church, often indistinguishable from the Perpendicular screens of which he was a master restorer.

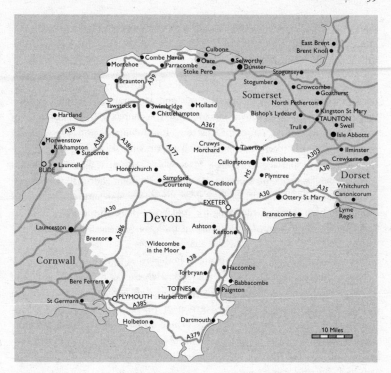

Ashton **

Babbacombe *

Bere Ferrers **

Branscombe *

Braunton *

Brentor *

Chittlehampton **

Combe Martin *

Crediton ****

Cruwys Morchard *

Cullompton ****

Dartmouth ***

Haccombe **

Harberton *

Hartland ***

Holbeton **

Honeychurch *

Kentisbeare **

Kenton *

Molland ***

Mortehoe *

Ottery St Mary *****

Paignton **

Parracombe **

Plymtree *

Sampford Courtenay *

Sutcombe *

Swimbridge ***

Tawstock ***

Tiverton **

Torbryan *

Totnes *

Widecombe in the
   Moor *

ASHTON
St John the Baptist, Upper Ashton **
Village setting, painted screen

The Ashton villages lie in a backwater off the Teign valley road on the eastern rim of Dartmoor. The moor here is gentle and agricultural, offering a spring-time idyll of streams, meadows and cottages. The church at Upper Ashton, set at the top of the valley, is huge for its setting. It is dominated by a granite tower rising like a ship's prow, creaming through a springtime sea of blossom.

This is a typical Devon church, a place where setting is all, or almost all. A Perpendicular work of the 15th century, the interior walls are covered in cream limewash, the arcades of Beer stone, the tower arch unusually high. The ceiling has been stripped, rendering the roof bosses hard to see. Perpendicular bench-ends are surrounded with strange palm leaves, overseen by a pulpit and tester.

Over all watches the screen, spanning both nave and aisle, restored in the 1900s by the master of Devonian woodwork, Herbert Read. Its staircase is still in place, though not the loft to which it once led. It is rich in vine and other motifs. The dado has a celebrated group of panel paintings of 32 Church doctors and saints, with their emblems. These do not compare with the East Anglian masters, but are identifiable by the objects which they hold, usually the method of their martyrdom. Thus St Sidwell holds a scythe and St Apolionia a peculiarly horrible pair of pincers.

The north aisle chapel belonged to the Chudleighs and was richly decorated. Here the later screen paintings include bold half-figures of prophets carrying scrolls with Latin inscriptions. The scheme continues on the parclose screen. The north wall has a mural of Christ with the Instruments of the Passion. Chudleigh arms appear in medieval glass in the windows. A memorial stands in the north aisle to Sir George Chudleigh (d.1657), boasting that his wife Mary had nine sons and nine daughters, for which achievement he appears to take principal credit.

BABBACOMBE
All Saints *
Butterfield luxury in suburban Torquay

Retirement homes now spread over the once-wild cliff of South Devon. Babbacombe was a poor fishing village without even a breakwater to shelter its boats, but the 19th century brought a different tide, sweeping up from Torquay. The Anglo-Catholics seized the moment and commissioned Butterfield, now in his prime, 'to maintain a strong and resonant Catholic tradition' in the booming resort. He produced a gloomy masterpiece, its bold tower dominating the landscape of toy streets and tidy villas.

The tower marked the completion of the church in 1874. This is of white stone and strangely fussy. The buttresses seem wilful, the bell-opening tracery unconventional and the lucarnes in the spire so elongated as to make the spire seem diminutive, a steeple that seems to be starting and stopping again. But in these surroundings this is a class act. In its day, Butterfield's polychrome interior would have seemed in keeping with the seaside gaiety.

Age and stained glass have made it solemn, but a keen eye can still detect the rich range of materials. Babbacombe is built of no fewer than 50 varieties of Devon marble, in addition to marbles from Belgium and Sicily. These can be seen in the nave piers and in the sumptuous chancel with its stiff-leaf capitals. Not an inch of wall is without geometrical or naturalistic decoration.

The pulpit and font are Butterfield masterpieces. They are based on the theme of a double arcade rising to a Gothic arch, the marble colonettes ringed with white stone. While the rest of the church bears the patina of time, they seem pristine compositions of marble design, ornate yet restrained, as good as can be found in any Victorian church. The lectern and chancel railings are also by the architect. The stone reredos carries mosaics by the Italian, Antonio Salviati, whose former works can still be seen on the Grand Canal in Venice.

BERE FERRERS
St Andrew **
Ferrers monuments and glass

The Ferrers were leading courtiers of William the Conqueror. Henry de Ferrers was chairman of the Domesday Commission and the family was rewarded with estates across England. Their emblem was three horseshoes, symbol of the farrier. Bere must have been a commanding site, on a promontory upstream of Plymouth. Today it is a cul-de-sac, sited at the end of a spit dividing the River Tamar from the River Tavy.

The church lies on the bank of the latter, the tide lapping the churchyard. The tower is almost pathetically small, rendered and stained with red lichen. Old slate tombs recall the terrors of sea and disease. One by the footpath records simply 'Cholera 1849' with no names. The interior, however, is a song to granite. The capitals of the piers are hacked from this unyielding stone, some of them little more than hunks of rock. The windows have a rare selection of tracery for a Devon church, Intersecting in the east window, Reticulated in the transepts and Perpendicular elsewhere. This was a rich church in the 13th century, as silver mining drew labour to Devon from all over England.

Later generations offset the granite with woodwork. Tudor bench-ends fill the nave, with Ferrers heraldry on one of them. The rood screen has various defaced saints. The early 14th-century stained glass in the east window was given by Sir William de Ferrers, builder of the present church. Christ is portrayed in the centre with a Ferrers husband and wife in the outer lights; he is in prayer, holding a model of a church. The colouring is vivid, and rare in Devon. A fine Ferrers monument fills the chancel tomb recess, with a Decorated canopy, high pinnacles and faces on the ends of the cusps. Another Ferrers lies in the north transept, portrayed as a knight in chainmail. The Purbeck chest to Lord Willoughby de Broke (d.1522) is said to be the first in the county to have classical ornament, in the form of laurel wreaths.

BRANSCOMBE
St Winifred *
Picturesque hillside setting

Hidden inland from marauding Danes, Branscombe is also hidden from marauding trippers. The hamlet nestles in a valley between Sidmouth and Seaton and still boasts a working blacksmith. The church lies under the side of a hill, a curious site shaded with evergreens. The tower is four-square and Norman, with slit belfry openings. It contains a priest's chamber, including a small window for keeping watch on the altar.

Part of the nave is also Norman. The church was gradually enlarged in the 13th and 14th centuries with transepts, and an extended nave and chancel. The confined site produces a pleasantly elongated interior, there being little room for nave aisles. In the chancel are two shuttered lepers' windows below the 'clerk's window', supposedly to allow those unable to enter the church to witness the Sacrament at the altar.

The church has excellent post-medieval woodwork. The chancel screen of 1660 is in the sort of vernacular Gothic appropriate to a Devon farm parlour. A fragment of the original rood was recently discovered in a local house and fashioned into a new cross for the Millennium. The 18th-century three-decker pulpit is rare in Devon. The north transept contains the tomb of Joan Wadham (d.1583), a West Country girl married first to John Kellaway and then to John Wadham, their son Nicholas being founder of the Oxford college. She had twenty children.

BRAUNTON
St Brannock *
Bench-ends, piglets boss

Braunton is almost a suburb of Barnstaple, its church being on the Ilfracombe road out of town. A strong broach spire stands well against the hillside and a stream runs alongside the churchyard. St Brannock's is a large seafaring church. It was reputedly the landing place, burial place and shrine of one of Devon's earliest Welsh missionaries, St Brannock, which means that the church must go back as far as any church in the county. The tower appears Norman in origin, but has a Saxon tomb set into the lintel of its west window.

The interior has no aisles and a massive wagon roof. Take out the west wall and it might have seen service as a dry dock for an old Barnstaple man-o'-war. The view east to the chancel suggests an Early Gothic rebuilding of a Norman structure. There are three lancets in the north wall of the chancel, lancets on either side of the Early Gothic chancel arch and low arches to north and south transepts. The nave walls look even older, thick with deep splays to the windows.

The furnishings include a forest of Devonian bench-ends, mostly monograms and trade emblems, but with a good Samson's head towards the front of the centre aisle. These date from the 16th century, each one a work of personal craftsmanship. The seats between these ends are hunks of crudely adzed wood. The north transept gallery of 1619 was the private pew of the Snow family. The Victorian restorers did a bad job with the stained glass but an excellent one with the ceiling bosses. One directly above the font has a fat pig feeding a litter.

BRENTOR
St Michael *
Wild Dartmoor setting

Of all the St Michaels founded to ward the Devil from the tops of hills, Brentor is the most spectacular. On a sunny day it is a friendly outcrop of stone on a limb of Dartmoor, with glorious views over the moor. In rain and a thick Dartmoor mist it has an aura of menace. On my first visit the tor proved an invisible marker, and only by chance did I see the tower itself loom out of the mist. Finding my way back to the road was equally hazardous. Visitors (unguided by any signs) could easily lose themselves and vanish into the surrounding bog.

The church was founded in the 12th century by the Giffard family as an outpost of the church in neighbouring Tavistock. The intention appears to have been symbolic rather than parochial. In 1625 a visitor, Tristram Risdon, wrote that it was 'a church full bleak and weather beaten, all alone, as if it were for-saken'. It stands today on a bluff surrounded by rocks, with a modest wall delineating the churchyard from the moor. There are some gravestones, of those who have liked the idea of being buried in such a spot, but the guide warns that there is little earth. Burials have been discontinued.

The church's walls and tower are ageless, probably 14th century, but were comprehensively restored in the 19th century. The inside is heavily restored, but thousands make the journey to visit it none the less. A modern window of St Michael has been inserted in the east window, but not so as to obliterate the view of sky.

CHITTLEHAMPTON
St Hieritha **
'Somerset' tower, Giffard monument

First, a matter of names. A chittle is Saxon for hollow. St Hieritha, usually known as St Urith, is a unique dedication. She was allegedly a local girl hacked to death with scythes for her Christianity at the instigation of a pagan step-mother. A spring gushed forth on the spot where she fell, as was customary for Dark Ages martyrs (often thanks to the marketing zeal of the spring-owners). She also appears on the screens at Upper Ashton and as far away as Bere Ferrers.

As befits a shrine, St Hieritha's is a grand affair with aisles and transepts. The dominant feature is the splendid tower, which might have wandered across Exmoor from Somerset. Since Urith was a popular saint, the tower may be the gift of the 16th-century absentee vicar, Richard Woolman, Dean of Wells and Henrician politician. It is fine even by Somerset standards, with stages lengthening as they rise to the fretted bell-openings. The buttresses are surmounted by pinnacles drawing the eye upwards to ornamented battlements. The town square below was once enclosed by houses. These were demolished in the 19th century and the tower can now be seen in full glory with a lime arbour leading to its elaborate south porch.

The heart sinks on entry to see the scraping. The walls of Chittlehampton are like the fake rustication on a privatised council house. Just a little money could restore the limewash and ceiling plaster. The chancel roof is ceiled and altogether more happy. To the north of the chancel is the alcove containing the shrine of St Urith, with an incised slab which may once have covered her remains. The Gothic niche attached to a pier once contained her statue, which was a casualty of the Reformation. Her image survives on the north side of the stone pulpit, where she holds the palm of martyrdom.

The pulpit is of the Devon type, with heavy uprights and Latin doctors peering from ogee canopies. In the north transept is a standing wall monument to the Giffard family. It is a rough and battered memorial commemorating John Giffard, his father (d.1622), grandfather, son and grandson, as well as innumerable daughters. One of the last is said to have died pricking herself with a fern which she is portrayed as holding.

COMBE MARTIN
St Peter *
Twentieth-century furnishings

The village lies in the bottom of a sheltered combe that runs from Exmoor to the sea. For Devon, it is a dull place, its main street ending in old boarding houses near the beach.

However, the village was once rich, and prospered from silver and lead mining in the Middle Ages, which helped pay for the finest tower in the district. Though a perfectionist might consider the buttresses set too far from the angles and the pinnacles weak, the gargoyles are excellent and statues fill the niches. The north side of the church is a symmetrical showpiece, with three projections of transept, chapel and vestry.

Inside, the church's chief interest is its screen. This has a dado with paintings of saints intact. It is divided in the centre, with modern statues in the niches, and has a loft completed by the admirable Herbert Read in 1911. This is a superb example of the marriage of ancient and modern craftsmanship that is a feature of many Devon churches. The restored wagon roof is painted sky blue with vivid coloured bosses. Combe Martin has been a continuous patron of modern design. The reredos, a confident neo-Gothic work of light oak, is by a local artist, Doris Downing, of 1972. There is also a 1962 rood group above the screen, made by Colin Shewring from a picture in a Book of Hours.

CREDITON
Holy Cross ****
Carved sedilia, Buller memorial screen

Crediton's housing estates sprawl unplanned across its slopes and industry invades its centre. But the four tall pinnacles of the church of the Holy Cross still hold the place together. The russet sandstone reminds us that Devon is not just a county of lanes and picture villages. Crediton might be a church in the North Country, its red walls stained and sooted.

There have been at least four churches on this site. The first was a Saxon foundation associated with St Boniface, born Winfrith. This son of Crediton became a missionary, travelled to the Continent and was there celebrated for felling the Great Oak of Thor in a German forest. In doing so he converted so many pagans to Christianity that his fame spread across Europe. In the 10th century Crediton succeeded St Germans as seat of the new diocese of the West Country, and a new cathedral church was duly built. When the see moved to Exeter in 1050, the church was awarded collegiate status and rebuilt in stone.

The tower, crossing, Lady Chapel and southern vestry survive from the Norman period. The tower is like an old Norman struggling to escape from a Perpendicular prison. The structure was comprehensively rebuilt in the 15th century, creating the Perpendicular fabric we see today. At the Dissolution it was bought by the townspeople and became parochial, but it retained its old Chapter House and associated offices, known as the Governors' Room, off the south choir aisle. This is now used as a museum.

Today the church contains a number of 20th-century works of art, which so dominate the interior as to demand first notice. In the centre of the impressive view west to east down the nave is an extraordinary screen, completely covering the tower arch and east wall. This was inserted in 1911 by W. D. Caröe as a memorial to General Sir Redvers Buller. This controversial soldier was described by the West Country historian, S. H. Burton, as 'one of the least distinguished generals ever to command a British Army corps'. His performance during the Boer War in Natal was catastrophic and cost the army dear. Yet he was always a favourite of Devonians. (A statue of him greets travellers on the road from Crediton into Exeter.) Caröe's style is a mix of Perpendicular and Pre-Raphaelite in what could be a backdrop for an Arthurian romance. The symbols of the Cross and Christ in Majesty are surrounded by military saints, coats of arms and shields. It is a confident work of late-Gothic revivalism, a style of enduring appeal to English designers.

A similar revivalism is displayed in the south transept, filled in 1926 with memorial glass of various local families. At the corner of the transept is a wooden sculpture of St Boniface by Witold Kawalec, given in 1979. Continuing eastwards we reach Crediton's more authentic Gothic treasures. In the south choir aisle is a fine tomb recess, and behind it are three sedilia. Both recess and sedilia date from the 15th century and, although mutilated, retain vaulting, figure sculpture and medieval paint. The adjacent medieval tomb chest, with effigies of a knight with his lady in a wimple headdress, is believed to be that of Sir John Sully, who lived to be 105. He died in 1387 but has survived many vicissitudes since.

The Lady Chapel was reused after the Reformation as the town's grammar school. It is now back to its former use and is gloomy with Victorian glass. The north-east chapel is more cheerful, dedicated to Sts Nicholas and Boniface, its altar a Flemish merchant's chest. This is magnificently carved with blind tracery and a Nativity in the centre. The sanctuary contains two monuments that might dominate a less assertive space. One is a Jacobean memorial to Sir William Perryam, the other the battered but lovely tomb of the Tuckfield family, erected in the 1630s, with an early seated effigy as the centrepiece, framed by an elaborate stone and marble portico and sitting well inside its Gothic arch. On leaving the church, note the porch gates, made by a local 17th-century blacksmith, Simon Leach. This is a church of all the arts.

CRUWYS MORCHARD
The Holy Cross *
Named pews

The church merits an entry for family longevity alone. In 1175 there arrived in the foothills of Exmoor a Norman adventurer, Robert de Cruwys. Since then, seven centuries, thirty-three monarchs, forty-two rectors, pestilence, insurrection, war and peace have not moved the de Cruwyses. Their descendants are here still. The big house lies in unkempt woodland next to the church, embodying the continuity of English land tenure down the ages. These were not noblemen but simple gentry. Cruwyses were rectors of the church, with few gaps, from 1740 to 1950 and the building is their memorial. Cruwys Morchard is a place of names.

The church has a pinnacled Gothic tower visible above the trees and is approached through an unusual revolving lychgate. The churchyard seems on the brink of yielding to surrounding jungle. The interior is of c.1689–1702, after a lightning fire almost completely destroyed the medieval structure. Local people managed to save the porch with water and used long pikes to drag out the chest, which local report said was 'all in flames where the communion plate was, some of which began to be discoloured'. The bells had melted on their mounts in the tower and molten metal ran down the tower walls.

Most of the fabric of the church, dating from the 14th and early 16th centuries, survived the fire. The woodwork suffered worst, and virtually all had to be replaced. The new interior was saved from Victorian alteration and today is little changed from the reign of Queen Anne, except that the nave box pews are lower than the original ones. The chancel screen is a chaste classical composition with tiny Corinthian columns above the dado, and large ones flanking the doorway, topped by a pediment containing a crown on a cushion. The screen continues as a parclose at right angles.

The naming of the pews in the nave and aisles at Cruwys Morchard is claimed as unique, though I have found it at Thurning (Norfolk) and West Grinstead (Sussex). A 1700 plan shows 193 seats to be rented at 6d or 1s a year to specific local families, to pay for the rebuilding after the fire. Pews are also marked for 'girls under 14 years of age' and for 'boys under 16 years'. The church's one significant memorial is, for some reason, hidden behind the organ. It is to John Avery (d.1693), his memory obscured not, we trust, because he failed to be a Cruwys. The family burials are mostly in the churchyard near the house. There is an obelisk to Henry Shortrudge Cruwys, a rector who died in 1804. He 'lieth buried in a small house which he borrowed of his Bretheren the worms, in the hope of the Resurrection to Life eternal'.

CULLOMPTON
St Andrew ****
Carved screen, Perpendicular roof, aisle fan vault

There is nothing complex to Cullompton. It is a monument to English Perpendicular Gothic, as straightforward as its neighbour, Ottery St Mary, is confused. The tower, roof, screen and Lane Chapel are well preserved. The restorer's decision to reinstate bright colours to the wood surfaces, offset by white walls and pale stone dressings, is admirable.

The church sits away from the centre of the town, down its own lane. The tower is later than the rest of the church, dated 1545–9, with Ham stone dressings on a sandstone structure. It is highly decorated, with small pinnacles and gargoyles sitting on the tops of two buttresses. The exterior is most remarkable for the ostentatious Lane Chapel attached to the south side of the church *c.*1526–9. The buttresses have the patron's shears and ships, and many depictions of J L (John Lane). The rival Moore Chapel on the north-east side of the church is a more modest affair.

The first impression of the interior, approached from the west under the tower, is superb. The nave is prefaced by a low gallery of 1637, set on charming Ionic columns, with evangelists between blind arches. This increases the drama of Cullompton's famous roof and screen. The roof is wagon shaped but with the panels and cross-braces that are normally features of a flat roof. They are richly worked, rising from angel posts. The chancel divide is marked only by a carved rood beam with a coat of arms. The colours throughout are blue, red and gold, renewed in the chancel but not in the nave. These roofs would do credit to a Tudor banqueting hall. The pattern is repeated in the aisles.

The Cullompton screen is remarkable for its completeness and the purity of its decoration, despite frequent renewal. The colouring is unashamedly fresh, with blues, reds, greens and gold detailing. The coving projects in a series of fans and the original cornice has vine leaves and other foliage, all still crisp. The church possesses the remains of the old rood Golgotha, a stark mass of rocks, skulls and bones. Now at the back of the south aisle, it would have formed the base for the Crucifix above the rood loft. Why not restore it?

The chancel is divided from the side chapels by further screens. These reflect the rivalry between the local Moore and Lane families. The Moores of Moorehays House were traditional landed wealth, John Lane an *arriviste* cloth merchant. The screen to the Moore Chapel is in a flat Perpendicular, crowned by angels holding Moore family shields. The roof bosses are particularly splendid. Lane's response was to construct a completely new south aisle, with fan vaulting of a lavishness rare in a parish church. The guide suggests that a wooden roof was replaced by a stone one specifically to compete with the Moores. Or perhaps Lane saw the new Dorset aisle at Ottery St Mary, built at the same time, *c.*1520. Either way, expense can have been no object. There are carved saints and angels everywhere, even filling the buttress panels and vault pendants. The whole chamber shimmers with sunlight and forms a splendid climax to the interior. A rare West Country Burne-Jones window is an added delight.

The extraordinary preservation of Cullompton is due to William Froude, Brunel's engineer on the local section of the Great Western Railway. He lived in the town in the 1840s and paid for the restoration and recolouring of the chancel. He left the nave roof, to which he felt the parishioners should contribute. They declined, their meanness evident to this day. The tower holds a complete set of ten bells. These can be seen in the course of a climb up to the tower roof, from where there is a view out over the soft Devon hills.

DARTMOUTH
St Saviour ***
Nautical town church, medieval door, Devon pulpit

Seaport churches have a character of their own. An aura of salt, ropes and fish hangs about their rafters. Memorials and windows tell of tragedies at sea. The woodwork is that of mast and spar rather than of plough and barn roof. Stand in the gallery at Dartmouth, half shut your eyes and you could be on the poop deck of a schooner.

The church is moored, as if in retirement, in the back lanes of the old port. It was once the subject of a power struggle between Church and Crown. St Saviour's was founded at the behest of Edward I in 1286. The bishop was offended at this infringement of his prerogatives, and the church was not consecrated until 1372. The building at that time consisted only of the two west bays, still clearly distinct from the later eastern ones. Their arcades are raised on odd capitals, the arches encrusted with a sort of primitive ballflower, a design all of its own. The decoration might be crustaceans stuck to the underside of a ship.

Dartmouth's first treasure is inside its south porch, a superb door covered in medieval ironwork. This is in the form of a tree of life with the lions of Edward I, dating from the 13th century and remounted on the present woodwork in

1631, when the church was extensively rebuilt. At that time, a west gallery was inserted, incorporating panels from Spanish ships, Armada flags, coats of arms and a clock. The staircase carries all manner of paraphernalia, including the former reredos, charity boards, a carved open Bible and a painting by a 19th-century Totnes artist, William Brockendon. If this is a poop deck, it has just weathered a bad storm.

The nave has 17th-century bench-ends, but also choir stalls with ogee backs, apparently from the chancel. The screen is original, darkly coloured in black and gold. The coving is perfect. Next to it stands a magnificent Devon pulpit, looking as if carved from marzipan with black and gold leaves of monstrous proportions. The preacher emerges from the top like a tulip from a bunch in a vase. Both screen and pulpit date from the last decade of the 15th century, that final burst of energy in English medieval art. They have an unrestored density and colour that make them among the most enjoyable of all Devon works in wood.

In the chancel is the brass of John Hawley (d.1408). Three times Mayor of Dartmouth he paid for extensions to the church at the turn of the 15th century, including the new chancel. He is represented as a medieval knight, lying between his two wives and holding the hand of one of them. The altar is a curiosity. It is late Victorian but incorporates four carved evangelists of 1588. They were the legs of the communion table which replaced the stone altar at the Reformation. The chancel was restored by E. H. Sedding and is one of his most discreet and effective compositions.

HACCOMBE
St Blaise **
Estate setting, medieval brasses

The church sits under a wooded hill at the end of the valley where the Carews had their seat from 1066 to 1942. The house is now divided into flats and the park spills down the hill in allotments, but the setting survives and the church offers a rare Devon example of a pre-Perpendicular chapel. It was built by a Carew ancestor, Sir Stephen de Haccombe, in thanks for his safe return from the Fifth Crusade in 1233. The dedication was to the Armenian, St Blaise, who was martyred by being flayed with a woolcomb, making him a popular if eccentric object of veneration by clothiers.

Almost a century later, a college of secular priests was established in the church, which was accordingly enlarged by the addition of a north aisle. The church was presided over by an 'archpriest' who had the right not to recognise a visit of the bishop and to wear lawn sleeves and a fur stole. This title survived the Dissolution and persisted into the 20th century.

Today the church is well lit, well tended and filled with treasures. It has a tiny west porch, no tower, just a bellcote. Lancet windows are bright with Flemish glass roundels, mostly secular and moved from the big house. Fine memorials fill the interior, including a splendid set of Carew brasses under the carpet in front of the altar. The tomb of the founder, Sir Stephen de Haccombe, lies between chancel and aisle, the effigy retaining traces of original paint, including the black stripes of the Haccombe shield. Next to him is a diminutive effigy of alabaster, just 2 feet long and superbly carved. Its size probably indicates a 'heart burial'. Nearby are two female tombs, also with traces of colour.

Haccombe has a fine collection of medieval tiles and some original glass in the south wall window. Since a Carew went down with the Tudor *Mary Rose*, some timber from the raised ship was given to the church for its processional cross in the 1980s.

HARBERTON
St Andrew *
Metalwork Victorian screen, Devon pulpit

This typical Devon Perpendicular church stands well on a steeply rising churchyard outside Totnes. The village seems to huddle out of sight. When a benefactor, Sir Robert Harvey, donated the tower clock in 1898 he did so on condition that there was no face on the side of the tower facing his neighbour, with whom he was in dispute. The tower is in dark red sandstone with an exterior stair turret and what Clifton-Taylor calls a 'lofty austerity'.

The interior, as so often in Devon, is dominated by a late 15th-century screen with a magnificent cornice. The Victorian restorers, rather than repaint the saints' panels, replaced them with metal plates on which saints and angels were shown in contemporary style, though sadly not in contemporary costume. They are extraordinarily lifelike. Some of the original wooden panels are displayed in a case in the north aisle. Even more remarkable is the pulpit. It is an octagonal structure with rich foliate carving on the uprights and ogee canopies, painted the richest black and gold. In the niches are plump figures of apostles, possibly Flemish and replacing those lost in the Reformation. Their style is not so much late Gothic as 'Baroque-gothic'. The Victorian reredos is a sumptuous work of mosaic and alabaster, set amid an Art Nouveau surround. Stained glass is ubiquitous and pernicious.

Apart from the tower clock, the Harveys of Dundridge House left a fine series of memorials. One is to an eleven-year-old boy named Tito who died in 1895, showing him asleep with a lily laid on his body. The adjacent window has Christ with his hand on Tito's shoulder. The family mausoleum is in the churchyard, again with a sad effigy of Tito with his parents. The Italianate composition was inspired, suggests Pevsner, by Lady Harvey's Roman Catholic background. Outside the porch stands a sandstone Saxon cross decorated with palms.

HARTLAND
St Nectan * * *
Norman font, original screen

The north Devon coast beyond Bideford is as fierce as anywhere in England. The west shore faces out to the Atlantic, long a graveyard of wrecks. Even in the days of steam, any ship that failed to round Hartland Point into Bideford Bay in an onshore wind was said to be doomed. Today, crowds racing to Cornwall pass far to the south. The adventurous ones may reach Clovelly or even Morwenstow, but Hartland is more remote. Nor is Hartland village the location of its church. Two miles west in the direction of the sea we reach Stoke and even then we do not see the church. This lies above the site where the Saxon Countess Gytha, mother of King Harold, founded an abbey in 1050 in thanks for the salvation of her husband in a storm.

The church is approached down a path from the village of Stoke over the widest step-stile I know. It would keep an elephant at bay. The tower of Perpendicular granite is 130 ft high and the second tallest in Devon, testament to the church's status as a beacon to mariners. The dedication is to St Nectan, whose medieval statue survives on the tower's east face. The interior is graciously proportioned with stone rather than granite arcades and an all-through wagon roof. Part of this is ceiled with reproduction panels based on original (or at least Victorian) patterns and colours. The evidence for this is some old panels now stored in the small museum above the north porch, called the Pope's Chamber.

Hartland's masterpiece is its 15th-century screen, one of the most complete in Devon. It spans the entire building. While the tracery is simple and the dado of conventional West Country design, the coving and cornice are magnificent. Four bands of fretwork can be made out. Between the coving ribs are stylised flowers and shields. On the nave side, the dominant vegetation is berries, on the chancel side grapes. The colouring has been touched up over the centuries and is mostly early Victorian, though much of the cornice colour is original. The uprights are banded red and white like barbers' poles.

Hartland is a miniature gallery of vernacular art. The square Norman font is highly decorated, with intersecting arches on the bowl and foot and zigzag on the stem. The north chapel has a reredos of Belgian Gothic panels and a 14th-century altar screen has been built into the south chapel. The windows include three Flemish roundels, one portraying a medieval town in the background. In the chancel is a magnificent late Gothic tomb chest of polished black stone, surrounded by pinnacled niches. This came from the neighbouring abbey. The old Tudor benches in the south chapel are more comfortable than the 18th-century pews, which seem intolerably hard. Perhaps worshippers brought cushions.

In the churchyard is the grave of Allen Lane, founder of Penguin Books, sponsor of Nikolaus Pevsner and thus begetter of this survey.

HOLBETON
All Saints **
Arts and Crafts furnishings by J. D. Sedding

The guide cites no fewer than sixteen spellings of the name of this small village near the River Erme. It lies on a slope overlooked by a fine church whose churchyard is worth a visit in itself. Lovely lychgates to the east and north of the building give on to a tumbling hillside of slate and lichen-clad tombstones. The pleasure of the church lies in J. D. Sedding's Victorian restoration for the Mildmay family. Sedding succeeds admirably both in reviving the spirit of antiquity and in bringing to it a flavour of the Arts and Crafts Movement, well displayed outside in the flowing brass studs on the west and south doors.

The skeleton of Holbeton is that of a simple granite nave with spacious aisles, the capitals poorly carved in the Cornish style, which means in no style at all. The rest is almost all Sedding, including most of the stone and woodwork. The 1880s seem to have produced as vigorous a craftsmanship as the 1480s, so much so that original and replaced elements are hard to distinguish. Pride of place must go to the screens. The heraldry dates these to after the Reformation, and they were thus designed without rood lofts. The motifs are said to be Italian or even Spanish, with simple dividers rising to close-knit, almost dense tracery. Legend has it that some of these designs may have come from wrecked Spanish ships, source of much craftsmanship in these coastal churches.

Next in order of precedence are Sedding's bench-ends. Here are birds and animals, leaves and flowers. More Sedding designs surround the altar and fill the chancel roof, and he also designed the wooden sedilia. Stone makes an appearance only for the pulpit and the Victorian font. In the north chapel is a memorial to Restoration fecundity. Sir Thomas Hele, who died in 1670, is portrayed with three generations of his offspring, twenty-two in all, depicted as praying figures. Only the glass is dire, shutting out the wild Devonian sky which would bring this lovely interior even more to life.

HONEYCHURCH
St Mary *
Norman farmers' chapel

The sign on the door says simply, 'This door is never locked'. It should be the motto of the Church of England.

Honeychurch is one of Devon's few 'atmosphericks'. The building is tiny, simple and devoid of architectural features, lying on a farm lane and never anything but a farmers' chapel. Apart from Perpendicular windows and west tower, it remains more or less pure Norman. The interior comprises a small nave and smaller chancel, divided by a simple granite arch, its capitals so crude as to be barely worth the name. On either side of the south door are two monster corbel heads removed from outside the church.

The interest of the church, and most of its atmosphere, derives from its 15th-century carpentry. The nave is filled with seats so worm-eaten that the rear ones would wear holes in all but the stoutest flannel. By the door is a small poor-box. The pulpit is primitive, as are the floorboards that substitute for flagstones or tiles. Overlooking this scene is a coat of arms apparently painted over a St Christopher mural.

The only curiosity in what passes for the chancel are some medieval cooking pots. These are stored, for some reason, under a table next to the altar. Pevsner suggests that these may have been acoustic pots, to be set in the walls of chancels allegedly to enhance the sound of singing.

KENTISBEARE
St Mary **
Refined screen carving

The church sits over the crest of a hill on the road from Cullompton, discreetly hidden behind the Wyndham Arms. The pink-grey tower has a stair turret of white Beer stone in chequerboard pattern with red sandstone, a fetching combination. Inside, sun streams through Perpendicular windows on to Perpendicular piers, illuminating one of Devon's best screens.

The south aisle was the gift of a Tudor Merchant Venturer, John Whiting (d.1529). His carved table tomb is in his chapel, warmed with Elizabethan panelling. A capital in the south arcade is carved with a woolsack bearing Whiting's merchant's mark, and the coat of arms of the Merchant Venturers. Whether Whiting contributed also to the screen we do not know. It may defer to neighbouring Cullompton in scale but compensates in refinement. Some of its colouring is original, justifying the restorers in not repainting it. The tracery is delicate, almost oriental. A small angel watches from the north wall, as if deputed to the task from the dozens that crowd the roofs and walls. Facing the screen at the west end of the nave is a fine 17th-century gallery, its parapet painted and inscribed.

On the north wall of the chancel is a memorial to George Scott, cousin of the novelist Walter and rector of the church. He died here aged twenty-six in 1830. An urn is attended by a cherub with a modest verse by Walter Scott himself: 'To youth, to age alike, this tablet pale / Tells the brief moral of its tragic tale . . .' In the north aisle hangs a bold landscape of the village by local children.

KENTON
All Saints *
Twentieth-century wood carving

Kenton is a castle of a church near the River Exe. The predominant sandstone has Beer stone dressings with apparently random patching, the effect being of a building covered in blotched rouge. The battlements, pinnacles and gargoyles seem effete additions, but are all part of a Perpendicular whole. The two-storey south porch has carved square-headed doorways and elaborate statue niches, unusual for Devon.

The interior is more spacious than the Devon norm. Its most prominent feature is a superb screen heavily restored by Herbert Read, with a profusion of carving. He re-created the rood loft, with five angels below tall, intricately worked canopies. The coving and cornice, dominated by a beam carved with viticulture, are also renewed. The rest of the screen is wholly overpowered by the loft. Its saints' panels are primitive in execution, combining work by Flemish craftsmen and local carvers. The restoration was installed in 1899, the more modest side screens in the 1930s. The central cross is by the Arts and Crafts artist Henry Wilson and was originally intended for Exeter Cathedral.

The pulpit, similar to that at Harberton, is much restored but still wonderfully lavish with heavy leaves round the panels. On the altar is yet more spectacular carving, including a relief from the Oberammergau workshops much favoured by late-Victorian designers.

MOLLAND
St Mary ***
Rare screen with solid tympanum

This is farming Exmoor, on the western fringes overlooking the River Yeo and far from the tourist trail. The church was in the domain of the recusant Courtenay family, passionate Royalists in the 17th century.

The three magnificent Courtenay monuments of the late 17th and early 18th centuries make no reference to this. But the memorial to Daniel Berry, the 17th-century vicar, is unequivocal. His 'zeal for the martyred King Charles the First', reads the inscription, led to his being 'sequestered by the then rebels and ever after persecuted till he died'. The monument was erected by his son after the Restoration to honour the memory of 'all orthodox and loyal men of the late times'. Such sentiments are found in churches throughout the West Country.

For all this, Molland's charm lies in its Georgian furnishings, the most complete set in Devon. They survived because the 19th-century lords of the manor were still Roman Catholics, with little interest in the condition of their Protestant parish church or with ripping out its rented family pews and up-dating its liturgy.

The nave is filled with box pews that seem to rise up the richly shafted stone arcade like a surging tide. The piers are almost buried in woodwork. On one of them, a medieval statue niche contrives to keep its head above water. The screen is a great rarity, being topped by a solid wall tympanum with coat of arms and Ten Commandments, as at Parracombe across the moor and at Ellingham (Hants). The three-decker pulpit has a monumental tester. As an added incentive to good behaviour, a set of stocks is preserved in the nave.

I visited Molland at Easter. It was filled with flowers that seemed to pour in through doors and windows from the hills outside, invading every shelf and ledge in the place. In the churchyard are monumental gravestones with excellent Georgian lettering.

MORTEHOE
St Mary .*
Modern mosaic and stained glass

Beyond Ilfracombe on the north Devon coast lies the Atlantic, broken only by the cliffs of Morte Point and the hamlet of Mortehoe above Woolacombe. The inland road reaches a rocky, treeless outcrop that might be the Hebrides. Opposite a pub called The Ship Aground is a church also aground, simple but lovable. On my visit, the little combe echoed with the efforts of the bell-ringers, which were extraordinarily loud.

The church rises beyond a lychgate surrounded by banks of flowers. The interior has been much restored, its heart an Early Gothic structure, represented by a chancel arch and lancet windows. The two-bay arcade to the north aisle is built of rough stone, yet the opposing south arcade is curiously delicate, with a strange diagonal passage between transept and nave, lit by Perpendicular windows.

The nave is dominated by a 1905 mosaic filling the chancel arch. It shows four large archangels and the Lamb of God against a gilt background. It was designed by Selwyn Image, Slade Professor of Art at Oxford, executed by the same craftsmen who did the mosaics in St Paul's Cathedral. The mosaic was donated by a churchwarden in memory of his wife. There is no forgetting her now.

Image also designed the stained glass in the 'diagonal' windows, illustrating the same four archangels. A better window is by Henry Holiday in the east wall of the north aisle, of Christ stilling the storm. There are fine bench-ends in the nave.

OTTERY ST MARY
*****

Miniature Exeter Cathedral, painted roof, fan-vaulted aisle

Ottery St Mary sits cosily in its nest on the banks of the River Otter. At first sight it might be a French monastery that came to Devon on a visit, fell in love with the place and decided to stay. Twin towers, high gables and triple lancet windows are those of a Norman collegiate foundation. But closer inspection indicates a thoroughly English church, combining dash with domesticity. The stone is honey-coloured, fertilising colonies of lichen. Nothing is lacking.

The church's origins were indeed French, the patrons being secular canons from Rouen. The present structure owes its appearance to Bishop Grandison of Exeter, who wrested the church from Rouen in 1335 and two years later founded a college of forty members at Ottery. Grandison commenced rebuilding in 1342, using the new cathedral at Exeter as a model. He erected a 'posh' east end, two bays larger than the west end, lengthened even further by a Lady Chapel, and furnished with a second pair of transepts.

Also unusual are the two towers over the main transepts, features otherwise found only at Exeter. One tower has a spire with a medieval weathercock fitted with tubes to 'whistle' in the wind, now defunct. Equally distinctive is the absence of 14th-century tracery. The windows of many lights within a single arch are Early Gothic in style, a form of 'classical' Gothic sometimes used by senior prelates at this time.

The interior of Ottery offers connoisseurs a test of taste. The church received the attention of successive Victorians, including Edward Blore and William Butterfield, but their restoration was overlaid in 1977 by vigorous and controversial repainting. The colouring of the roofs, vaults and screens, though not the carved stone, is startling and distracting. Yet as at Cullompton, the intention was to reinstate the visual impact of a medieval church, however upsetting to the modern eye. I found Ottery's colours grew on me. The Lady Chapel, restored by the Victorian Henry Woodyer and now a century old, is visually subdued in comparison.

The view east from the nave extends through the crossing and into the chancel. The arcades are plain but nave and aisle roofs are bright with white, red and blue paint, adorned with magnificent bosses. The crossing vault has bosses worthy of their Exeter inspiration. The boss depicting Grandison himself is at the centre. The vault of the chancel, the visual climax to the view from the nave, is curvilinear. Here the motif is a four-petalled rosette, the ribs serving simply as decoration. Pevsner attributes this work to William Joy of Wells. The carvers of the Ottery bosses are from Exeter, of unsurpassed excellence. In the nave arcades are two magnificent Decorated tombs, of Bishop Grandison's brother, Sir Otho (d.1359), and his wife Beatrix (d.1374). The canopies are both giant ogees, decorated with no fewer than 50 shields for their coats of arms. I am surprised nobody had the courage to paint these.

We now enter the Dorset aisle, running parallel to the north aisle and the only substantial addition to the old church. This is a magnificent work, built in the early 16th century. The arcading is luxuriant, with capitals formed of scrolls, vine leaves and corbel heads portraying an owl, a Green Man and even an elephant. The aisle is most remarkable for its fan vault, with curious openwork pendants, some of them twisted. The west window is a fierce Victorian work by Wailes, best seen against the setting sun.

The south transept is a contrast. Its mosaic wall tiles are by Butterfield and were installed by the Coleridge family. The vicar of Ottery at the end of the 18th century was the poet's father. The serene late-Victorian memorial is to a Lady Coleridge (d.1878). The great clock is believed to be Grandison's original, with one of the oldest mechanisms extant. The outer rim has 24 hours, not 12.

The chancel is dominated by the great stone reredos. The basic structure is 14th century, but it was extensively wrecked in the Reformation. The architectural sculpture was replaced by the Victorians and the figures were contributed by Herbert Read in the 1930s. Again, modern colour is dominant. The sedilia is superb, lofty and richly crocketed.

The cathedral plan continues east of the reredos, though with almost toylike smallness. Here is an ambulatory, a stone screen and loft and finally a Lady Chapel. This has an east window with no fewer than eight lights. There are corbels carved with the heads of Grandison and his sister, and bosses with scenes from the life of the Virgin. Much of the woodwork is original, including oak stalls and a wooden eagle lectern, one of the earliest in the country.

PAIGNTON
St John **
Kirkham Chantry screen

Paignton is down-market Torbay, with some of the ugliest bungalow and caravan estates that even South Devon can offer. But its centre has a period charm, and hidden behind the high street is an exotic survival: the red walls and crumbling tower of what might be the house of a San Gimignano princeling. This was a palace of the bishops of Exeter, set next to what was, believe it or not, their lordships' deer park. The palace is no more, only the walls remain. But beyond is the church, which is emphatically still here, built of vivid red sandstone.

The exterior is notable for its length, the interior for its jolly use of red piers and white plaster. The effect is appropriately seaside. In the south aisle is one of the most remarkable monuments to survive in any church in England, the Kirkham Chantry screen, now guarding the entrance to the south transept and St Michael's Chapel. It ranks with the Babington Chantry at Kingston on Soar (Notts) and the Bedingfield tombs at Oxborough (Norfolk), works of pre-Reformation ecclesiastical sculpture left intact by 16th-century iconoclasts.

The screen dates from the late 15th century and consists of an arched entrance dividing two bigger arches, containing tombs of the Kirkham family. These arches have ornate fan vaults and pendants. Above them rises a forest of gables and statues, embracing apostles, evangelists, doctors of the Church and angels galore. There are no inscriptions. Some of the statues have been bashed about and a verger tells me others have fallen in among the carvings on top. The overall effect is of a giant cake awaiting a wedding that was called off at the last minute.

The church has a fine pre-Reformation stone pulpit with ogee panels and thick Devonian uprights. The chancel sedilia is a superb Victorian reconstruction of the Decorated Gothic original, in 'full Technicolor'.

PARRACOMBE
St Petrock **
Georgian fittings, screen with tympanum

One of the best-known churches of Exmoor, St Petroc sits on a hillside off the A39 near Churchtown, accessible down a dirt track from the main road. Protesters led by John Ruskin saved it from demolition in 1879, when a Victorian replacement was built farther down the hill. The church is now redundant but accessible.

The exterior is unremarkable, with Early Gothic chancel and tower, and a low Perpendicular nave and south aisle. Inside is a complete Georgian refurnishing. Windows flood the pews with southern light. Nave and aisle are divided by an arcade of piers with four shafts and four hollows, and foliated capitals of the standard Devon type. Between the nave and the chancel is a most unusual gated screen topped by a huge tympanum. On this is painted the royal arms, surrounded by the Lord's Prayer, the Creed and the Commandments. The post-Reformation Word thus takes the place of the pre-Reformation rood. The chancel is an enclosed sanctuary of a sort now extremely rare, as at Molland.

There are 15th-century benches in the body of the church and 17th-century box pews at the back. These rise in five tiers for the musicians and children, as in an early theatre. One pew had a chunk cut out of it for the bow of a bass viol. There are hat pegs on all sides. Parracombe is free of stained glass and visitors can see out and in. There are wall memorials to the local Lock family. The old slate floor might be hewn from the ground itself and, on my visit, wild flowers decorated the font.

[CCT]

PLYMTREE
St John *
Gilded screen, alabaster panel

The pretty village surrounds a church well-guarded by a giant yew tree. The tower is adorned with a statue of the Virgin and Child, much eroded but still gentle and full of movement. The interior is charmingly intimate, the arcade capitals in the form of painted flowers. Beneath are old benches complete with panelled ends resting on a wood and flagstone floor. This is one of Pevsner's 'most attractive' Devon interiors.

The church's pride is its screen, one of the finest even in this county of screens. It is crowned with bands of intricate carving, covered in faded gilding. The dado displays 34 painted saints, unsophisticated but well preserved. St Margaret can be seen re-emerging from the mouth of the dragon and St Sebastian is much pierced by arrows. My favourite is the charming Annunciation, with lovely lilies, a simple artist's evocation of a sublime religious moment. At the back of the south aisle behind the font is another treasure: an alabaster panel depicting the Resurrection, apparently relocated from a former altarpiece. It is typical of Flemish carving distributed across England in the 16th century.

SAMPFORD COURTENAY
St Andrew *
Tree-trunk chest

This cream-tea village of white cob and thatch is further blessed by a Devonshire tower soaring over it. This is Devon at its most homely. The church sits on the edge of the village, its churchyard sloping down to surrounding fields. The church was held by the Courtenays, lords of Tiverton much executed during the Wars of the Roses and the disputes of the Tudors. The village's worst moment came at Whitsun 1549, when the inhabitants rose against the Protestant prayer book ordained by Edward VI. They joined those of Clyst St Mary in the disastrous siege of Exeter. Like other prayer book revolts, this one was ruthlessly suppressed, which may explain the loss of Sampford's screen.

The interior is charming as a whole rather than in its parts. The nave has granite piers, some with softer polyphant stone from Cornwall which allowed detailed carving of the capitals. The roof has fine bosses, including a pig with a litter, a Green Man and a three-rabbit motif. The ceiling is cream rather than white and should be an example to all West Country roofs awaiting the return of ceilings stripped out by the Victorians. In 1923 Herbert Read supplied a small screen to the south chapel, using fragments of an original work. The only stained glass is medieval fragments in the tracery of some of the windows, prettily colouring the sunlight.

The pulpit is mahogany and unusually solid for Devon. The guide suggests that the old church chest, hollowed from a single trunk of oak, was the one ordered to be used in 1549 'for the receipt of Communion Alms' that would otherwise have gone for the Mass. Such an order drove dozens of the men of this parish to their deaths.

SUTCOMBE
St Andrew *
Pulpit, wood carvings

Here is deserted north Devon, with no tourists, few pubs, no caravan sites. Only the towers of churches rebuilt by the early Tudors poke above the wind-blasted hedgerows. Sutcombe is a small Perpendicular church of repointed sandstone close to the Cornish border. It has Cornish features, such as light granite piers in the north arcade, an all-through wagon roof and carved bench-ends. The granite in the church particularly appealed to Clifton-Taylor, 'sparkling cream-grey with a specially grainy texture'. The unscraped north wall is mostly of square-headed Tudor windows.

The nave presents a wealth of wood carving. The early 16th-century bench-ends are in lighter wood than in Kilkhampton over the border, their bottoms restored rather than left worm-eaten. The bench-ends commemorate local families who presumably paid for the restoration of the church: Giffard, Le Cornu, Spencer, Prideaux and De Esse, Norman names living on into the 16th century. In the south chapel, once belonging to Thuborough Barton House, are memorials to the Prideaux. The best carving is on the 16-sided pulpit, a swirl of scrolls, sea creatures and sheaves of corn, by a local Grinling Gibbons. Even the eagle lectern is of wood. I found this a church of remarkable silence.

SWIMBRIDGE
St James ***
Perpendicular roofs, 'cupboard' font cover

Swimbridge will always be Jack Russell's church. The transformation of 19th-century churches by energetic parsons from Oxford and Cambridge has often been noted. Few were as vigorous as Devon's 'hunting parson', John Russell, who officiated at Swimbridge for forty-six years from 1833. An athletic young man, he loved country pursuits and went from Blundell's School to Exeter College, Oxford, where he scarcely read a book. Not until his last term did the fields round Oxford see him abandon the hunt and struggle to learn his Latin. On one such occasion, he was distracted by a terrier bitch that caught his fancy, which he bought off its milkman owner. Naming it Trump, he crossed it with a local dog and the first litter founded the breed that took his name.

Russell came to Swimbridge at the age of thirty-eight, where he kept a pack of hounds and hunted the hills of north Devon incessantly. When asked by the austere Bishop Phillpotts of Exeter to sell his pack since 'hunting parsons' were bringing the diocese much ridicule, he agreed. He transferred his pack to his wife's name, and continued hunting. Yet he was a conscientious vicar. He restored the church and expanded its work and its school, and was widely venerated on his death. His grave is in the churchyard and the pub overlooking it is named after him and his dogs. Jack Russell societies still meet here.

The church is situated in a basin of hills, long, low and West Country in all but its steeple. This has a 14th-century lead-covered broach spire, one of a group with Barnstaple and Braunton in the north of the county. The rest of the church is Perpendicular, an easy place to imagine Russell's parishioners crowding to hear his short, simple sermons, while his groom stood by the door with his horse saddled and ready.

The church interior is remarkable for its roofs, despite Pearson's removal of much of the ceiling in the 19th century. The screen is outstanding even for Devon. It spans both nave and aisles, every inch richly carved with stylised foliage in the fan-vaulted coving, and with panels both Tudor and Art Nouveau. The Devon pulpit has panels of saints beneath ogee arches, divided by heavily carved verticals. Traces of the original red and green survive.

The font cover is one of the most remarkable in England. It consists of an elongated 18th-century octagonal cupboard, with a Gothic openwork top, and a canopy like a pulpit tester. It includes panels with early Renaissance scrollwork dated to Henry VIII's reign. The font itself, almost an afterthought, is a simple bowl enclosed inside the cupboard doors. Altogether a curious contraption.

The best monument is that to John Rosier (d.1658) with his cheek resting on his hand. He was a lawyer and his epitaph reads: 'Loe with a Warrant sealed by God's decree / Death his grim Seargant hath arrested me / No bayle was to be given, no law could save / My body from the prison of the grave.'

TAWSTOCK
St Peter * * *
Family pew, Bourchier and Wrey monuments

The church is tucked cosily in a combe below Tawstock Court with the Taw valley opening out beyond. The house, now a school, was home of the Bourchier family, later Earls of Bath and later still, by marriage, of the Wreys. Their monuments fill the church, the most impressive collection of any church in Devon. Over the priest's door outside the south chapel is the Bourchier coat of arms, set between Tudor windows.

Tawstock is rare in the county in being a cruciform church with crossing tower. It is even rarer in the manner of its construction. When the early 14th-century architects came to add aisles to the old nave, they did not rebuild the interior with arcades of piers. They appear simply to have knocked through the outer walls and inserted arches in them. These arches die into their uprights, resting on carved faces or foliage. The cause is unclear, unless work was curtailed by the Black Death and resumed without benefit of earlier plans. The resulting heaviness is further emphasised by the lowness of the crossing arches. This gives the church a domestic intimacy at its core, exaggerated as the floor level steps downhill towards the chancel.

The north transept contains a wooden gallery brought from Tawstock Court in the 18th century, where charity boards meticulously record the donations of the local gentry for the relief of the poor. One, Mary Peard, has her name immortalised for a gift of just ten shillings. Another monument celebrates Sir John Wrey, who died in 1597 and was grandfather of the Wrey who married into the Bourchier family. Towards the crossing is a manorial pew, almost an enclosed box, with a hint of classical in the Ionic balusters which support a canopy with rosettes. In the crossing are old benches with Tudor ends. On one of these is a hunky-punk, a legendary inhabitant of Dartmoor with one arm and one leg that either helped travellers to avoid bogs or led them into them. They also adorn Somerset towers.

The chancel contains a rare wooden effigy of a medieval lady, possibly the 14th-century Audley who brought Tawstock to the Bourchiers by marriage. Near her is the Renaissance tomb of the 3rd Earl of Bath (d.1623). In the south chapel is the monument to Frances, Lady Fitzwarren, one of the first classical tombs in Devon, at the late date of 1589. Nearby is the 5th and last Earl's tomb (d.1654), without effigy and in the form of a black marble sarcophagus, supported by griffins and flanked by obelisks. His wife (d.1680) is commemorated by an independent standing figure between chapel and chancel. The contrast between the earlier and later pairs of tombs is striking. The south transept is for the Wreys, who established themselves at Tawstock in the 17th century. Their memorials are less spectacular. The transept ceiling is of the most exquisite plasterwork.

TIVERTON
St Peter ★★
Maritime stone carvings

Tiverton church stands on a bluff overlooking the River Exe in this dramatic town on a hill. At first sight it is in conventional Perpendicular style with tower pinnacles and battlements. On closer view the southern side seems to have been touched by a wand. The south aisle exterior and porch are decorated with extraordinary free Gothic carving, inspired by 15th-century seafaring prosperity.

The story of Tiverton church, as it survives today, is the story of one man, John Greenway. He was born humble but rose to wealth as a London Merchant Venturer and Draper. While the local Courtenay family, lords of the manor and denizens of the adjacent castle, were fighting and dying in the Wars of the Roses (*see* Sampford Courtenay), Greenway and his fellow merchants busied themselves making money. Greenway built his chantry in 1517, and with his friends built and adorned the south aisle and the porch. Rarely is old wealth in starker contrast with new than in Greenway's church next to the ruin of the Courtenays' castle.

The outside of the Greenway Chapel rises proud above the rest of the south aisle, with a tall parapet of carved friezes. The lower frieze has a sea of wavy lines bearing every kind of ship in the Merchant Venturer's employ. Each one is different and carefully described. They are shown well armed with cannons and archers aloft in crows' nests to ward off pirates. Between them are spread the tools of the trade, anchors and ropes, bales of wool and animals, notably monkeys, from the lands with which Greenway traded. It forms an encyclopedia of English maritime history. Above is a narrow frieze, now much eroded, with tiny scenes from the life of Christ. Above again is a deep tier of heraldic carving.

The carving extends to the south porch, although it is much restored. Above the door is an Assumption, with Greenway and his wife on either side. The vault is a wonder of swirling tracery and nautical and natural motifs. In the east wall is set a door to the chapel itself. This is a curiosity, half Gothic, half classical.

Of the restored interior of the church little need be noticed. In the south aisle is a fine mayoral pew with a lion and unicorn rampant, as if facing down the preacher in the adjacent pulpit. There are two tomb chests, one on either side of the chancel. That on the south side for John Waldron (d.1579) is entirely Gothic, and therefore extraordinary for its date. That on the north is for George Slee (d.1613) and is covered in Renaissance strapwork. They are just thirty years apart.

TORBRYAN
Holy Trinity *
Box pews, original screen

There are many churches like Torbryan in South Devon, but its isolation in its combe gives it especial charm. Now restored, the 15th-century tower is of the local type, with its stair turret built up the tower south wall. This was once covered in cement rendering, but the care of the Churches Conservation Trust has replaced this with correct lime plaster covering.

The church is entered through a south porch decorated with a delightful fan vault. The interior is plain but spacious. Nave and chancel have no architectural divide, the arcades being of six bays with generous aisles, foliated capitals and a bold wagon roof running from west to east. The box pews survive, encasing earlier pew seats. The church's forte is a magnificent Devon screen and pulpit. The screen has lost its loft and coving but benefits from being unrestored. Its colouring is dull and old, the saints' panels apparently unretouched. Unusually, it embraces the arcade piers.

The pulpit is composed of the upright parts of an old screen, with bulges in the middle where the screen would have encased a pier. Can nothing be done to make more use of such an evocative place?
[CCT]

TOTNES
St Mary *
Perpendicular stone screen

Totnes has one of the most attractive high streets in England, its famous arch house recently restored after a fire. The church, so prominent a feature of the town when seen from afar, disappears completely until it emerges in a small close near the castle. The tower with tall octagonal pinnacles was financed by a local tax in the 1450s. A wharf was even built at the foot of the high street for importing the stone. The south porch has a most unusual inner door. This looks early 16th century, with Gothic linenfold in the lower panels, but early classical motifs in the upper ones.

The interior is largely Victorian restoration but is dominated by a great rarity, an original stone screen with surviving colour. 'One of the most perfect in England,' says Pevsner. It was contemporary with the tower, 1459, a time of civic pride in Totnes. It is a magnificent work, spanning the nave and both aisles. In the aisles it combines Perpendicular tracery and ogee arches, which are prettily decorated with cusps on the underside and battlements above. For some reason the younger George Gilbert Scott removed the loft in the 1870s' restoration, despite the protests of his assistant. The screen is further adorned, when seen from the west door, by an 18th-century candelabra.

In the chancel is a relic from a former screen. This is the entrance to a rood loft staircase, still painted and decorated. One of its niches has an animal slinking round the foot of a tree. The north aisle contains a refined memorial to Christopher Blackhall (d.1633), a simple Renaissance recess with pilasters in which the husband kneels with his four wives below him. Although formalist in style, the figures are different. Could they be attempts at portraits?

WIDECOMBE IN THE MOOR
St Pancras *
Moorland setting, three-rabbit boss

Widecombe is capital of the moor. It is a wild settlement in a fold of the hills, over which loom the tors of Honeybag, Bell and Chinkwell. This is stranger country than the deceptively soft contours imply. Widecombe was known for tin miners and impenetrable dialects, and was the venue for Uncle Tom Cobbleigh's notorious ride on a ghostly white mare. In its square is a fine set of ancient almshouses, the nearest old Dartmoor came to a welfare state.

The church has pride of place. Its tall Perpendicular tower is one of the grandest in Devon, and has been a beacon to generations of moorland wanderers. It might seem more appropriate to Tiverton or Totnes than an isolated moorland village. The interior is simple, with arcades of granite monoliths and white ceiled roof with painted bosses. Third from the east is a three-rabbit boss. This rare symbol of the Trinity is formed of three animal heads sharing just three ears.

The dado of the old screen survives, with 32 painted apostles, Church fathers and saints. Pews fill half the nave, leaving space at the back for a small village museum. This includes a plough, a chest, some old crosses, prayer sheets and a feather duster.

Dorset

Dorset's attractions are scenic, of village, farm and manor set against tight limestone contours and wooded vales. In the north-west, the charm of these settings is enhanced by Ham stone, brought over the border from Somerset. It adds glory to the great church at Sherborne with its fan vault, to Milton Abbey in its sweeping valley, and to tiny Cerne Abbas. To the north-east the building materials are poorer. At Wimborne and Bere Regis limestone is mixed with brown 'earthstone' in chequerboard patterns. But along the dramatic coastline to the south are the Portland and Purbeck outcrops, whose products were exported nationwide.

Dorset has a small but admirable selection of all periods of English architecture. For lovers of Norman, Christchurch is one of England's least known medieval masterpieces. The transition from Norman to Early English is exemplified at Whitchurch Canonicorum and Wimborne. Of the Decorated style, few churches can compare with the great windows of the crossing at Milton Abbey. Perpendicular is nowhere richer than at Sherborne. After the Reformation, the 18th century is on its best behaviour at Blandford and Charlton Marshall. But for unredeemed wildness nothing can compare with St Aldhelm's, on its clifftop at Worth Matravers, with nothing between it and the pounding sea.

Boundary changes have brought Dorset Bournemouth's Victorian twins, G. E. Street's St Peter's and J. L. Pearson's St Stephen's. They offer a superb essay in Gothic Revival contrast. The 20th century has left Laurence Whistler's only complete set of engraved windows, an artistic triumph at Moreton.

Affpuddle *
Beaminster *
Bere Regis **
Blandford Forum **
Bournemouth:
    St Peter ****
    St Stephen ****
Cattistock *
Cerne Abbas *
Chalbury *
Charlton Marshall **
Charminster *

Christchurch *****
Iwerne Minster *
Kingston (Isle of
    Purbeck) **
Lyme Regis *
Milton Abbey ****
Moreton **
Poole: St Osmund ***
Portland: St George,
    Reforne *
Puddletown ***
Sherborne *****

Studland **
Tarrant Crawford *
Trent **
Whitchurch
    Canonicorum **
Wimborne
    Minster ****
Winterborne
    Tomson **
Worth Matravers:
    St Aldhelm *
    St Nicholas *

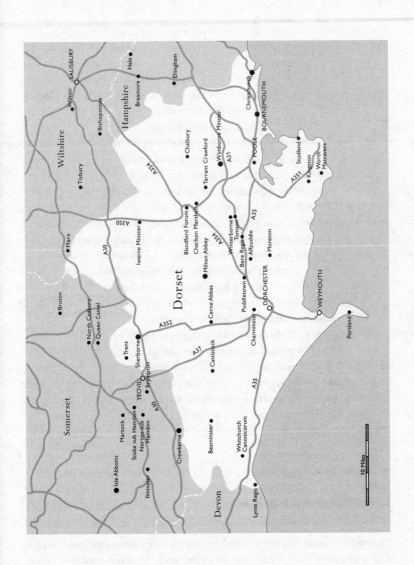

AFFPUDDLE
St Laurence *
Medieval door, evangelist pulpit

The village name derives from a Saxon donor, Affrith, and the adjacent river. The church lies down the road from Tolpuddle in a willowy glade by the Piddle. The surrounding fence is tumbledown and the small gate almost disintegrated in my hand. Beyond is a churchyard laid out as a war memorial, the stream on one side and the rectory on the other, a perfect village setting. The chequerboard flint and stone tower is a miniature of that at Bere, its pinnacles, battlements and turret the only dash of ostentation.

The church is basically of the 13th century, with a 15th-century tower. It contains three works of art. One is the south door, formed of an Early Gothic trefoil arch with two faces gazing from the moulding and with stiff-leaf in the spandrels. Next are the bench-ends, not of Devonian quality, but with lively linenfold and floral patterns carved in 1547, shortly after the church passed from the ownership of Cerne Abbey to a local landowner, Sir Oliver Lawrence. Such work demonstrates that all artistic patronage in English churches did not die out with the Reformation, but found new forms of vernacular expression. Affpuddle's pulpit is of the same period. This delightful work is in a most unusual polygonal form, with human figures and balusters, divided by tall panels containing reliefs of the evangelists. There are also pelicans in roundels, a wonderful fusion of medieval and Renaissance forms.

The screen against the north aisle chapel comprises bits of the old rood screen. In the same aisle is a battered Norman font, like a squashed truckle of cheese. The Lawrence family arms, shown in the chancel, are reputedly the origin of the American flag, George Washington's mother having been a Lawrence whose arms were quartered with stars and stripes (others are at Great Brington, Northamptonshire). The windows are of curious green glass. The effect is to make it seem as if the Piddle had flooded and submerged the church.

BEAMINSTER
St Mary *
Pinnacled tower, Strode monuments

Beaminster starts and almost finishes with its tower, one of the finest in Dorset. The town is Hardy's Emminster. Arthur Mee records a sign on the approach hill that once read: 'Drive slowly or break your neck.' In those days (the 1930s) Beaminster still had a town crier and three blacksmiths.

The west tower of *c.*1500 is lavishly embellished by some 40 pinnacles erupting from every surface. Pinnacles line the top, rising from the steps of the buttresses and capping the canopies of the tiny statue niches. The west front is a superb composition, with a series of reliefs of the Virgin and Child, Resurrection and Ascension, all weathered but still in place and therefore rare. On either side of the reliefs are figures of saints with, beside the top panels, two curious characters, one apparently a pilgrim with stick and scallop shell, the other a fuller with the tools of the Beaminster flax business.

The church is mostly Perpendicular. The aisled nave has capitals carved with vine leaves. Its Victorian corbel heads were carved by the same firm as those for the House of Commons. The chancel is a more modest affair, while off to its north is the vestry, converted from an old mort house or ossuary. Here the bones of villagers dug up to make space for others would once have been stored. The chancel screen is 20th century, by the Devonian, Herbert Read.

Beaminster's treasures are the two wall memorials to the Strode family in the north aisle. That to Thomas Strode (d.1698) portrays him standing in the pose of a swaggering lawyer under a classical canopy with weeping putti. Adjacent is the tomb of George and Catherine Strode by Scheemakers in 1753. Half a century has muted the bravado. The marble sarcophagus and obelisk are now addressed by virtuous maidens while the wife points out a holy text to her reclining husband – unless they are arguing over some domestic account. The joy of such 'conversation pieces' is that we can make up our own conversation.

BERE REGIS
St John **
Hammerbeam roof, Turberville tombs

We must avert our eyes from the bland council houses that besiege Bere church-yard and look instead at a tower with traceried bell-openings, standing proud above the village. The building material is reminiscent of Wimborne, banded and chequerboard, using the familiar east Dorset mixture of flint and limestone, with insertions of brown stone and sometimes brick. At Bere, the walls have attracted the same lichen as the graves. From the north-east, stones and walls merge in one glorious patina of whites, greys and yellows.

Bere is a jumble of styles, with Norman and Perpendicular dominant. A Saxon arch forms the east bay of the north arcade and similar fragments are embedded in the chancel arch wall. The remainder of the nave arcade is late Norman. The earlier south side displays bizarre carvings in its capitals, includ-ing a bear-baiting monkey and grimacing faces, one apparently suffering toothache. The north arcade is simpler, showing Early Gothic discipline. The chancel is of the latter period, with Plate tracery in the east window.

Bere roof is a Dorset original. The structure is arch-braced with illusory hammerbeams, all of oak. There is a full complement of bosses: kings and saints rub shoulders with twelve large apostles, each at least 3 ft long and brightly coloured. The central bosses are huge, the easternmost being the head of Cardinal Morton, patron of the rebuilding and founder of the north chapel. Morton was born in the parish of Bere and rose to become a master politician during the Wars of the Roses, holding numerous bishoprics as well as the two highest offices of archbishop and Chancellor. A shrewd devotee of the Tudor cause, he dominated the reign of Henry VII and gave his name to the miser-king's notorious tax-extortion, 'Morton's fork'. His roof is like the man, strong, multicoloured, a survivor through terrible times. Bere has no clouds of East Anglian angels.

The Tudors contributed the handsome Skerne tomb in the chancel and added to those of the Turbervilles, lords of the manor for some 500 years. Their extinction in the 18th century intrigued Hardy and inspired his tale of Tess. In it he described a scene of tombs 'defaced and broken, their brasses torn from the matrices, the rivet-holes remaining like martinholes in a sand-cliff', all a metaphor of departed glory. In the wall, set within a panelled frame, is the Turberville window of heraldic glass.

So oppressive is the Victorian glass at Bere that my first longing was to go round with a hammer. The best is by John Hardman, an east window of the Crucifixion in dazzling blues and reds.

BLANDFORD FORUM
St Peter and St Paul **
Georgian interior, rebuilt after fire

Blandford church forms the centrepiece of one of the most celebrated disaster reliefs in England. In 1731 a fire engulfed the entire heart of the town and led to a national appeal for its restoration. The town was lucky in having as leading citizens the Bastard brothers, William and John, architects and builders. Their father had already rebuilt Charlton Marshall church to the south. The fire gave the sons their opportunity and they took it with panache. They were known to be friends of the London architect, Thomas Archer (see St Paul's, Deptford in Greater London). Their style reflects the 'vernacular Baroque' of the new churches built in London in the reign of Queen Anne.

The building sits happily overlooking the main street, now free of most through-traffic. Its classical tower is Blandford's most prominent landmark, the crowning cupola an addition referred to by the Bastards as 'a temporary wooden structure', pending money for a spire. The money never materialised. A memorial to the fire stands outside the churchyard, where there is also an obelisk to the Bastards. Few town churches in England are as in keeping with their surroundings as Blandford's. It is an ill fire that blows no good.

The interior is imposing. A grand arcade of widely spaced Ionic columns supports a heavy entablature. The nave is covered, oddly, by a tripartite vault in a Gothic style, with elaborately decorated groins. The apse was moved east on rollers in 1895 to lengthen the chancel, the relocated apse being given stained glass and blue paint and thus a yellowish glow.

The church happily retains its numbered box pews. The Bailiff's pew, in which John Bastard must have sat with pride when holding that office in 1750, is half way down on the right. It is as fine a chair as you will see in any church in England. A convex organ gallery of the late 18th century fills the west end. The pulpit came from a lost Wren church in London, St Antholin's. The charity boards in the north transept have had all reference to Blandford blacked out from the text. This was a 'Dad's Army' effort to prevent an invading German army from discovering where it was, never rectified.

BOURNEMOUTH
St Peter ****
Colourful Gothic interior by Street

Bournemouth is England's most exotic large-scale resort, largely due to the hills and ravines that cut through its centre. Its prosperous late-Victorian residents, many of them retired, sought only the best in the churches that served their booming town. St Peter's was begun in 1854, on the foundations of an 1840s predecessor. It is a marvel of Gothic polychrome and decoration, mostly from the hand of Street, who was to design four other churches in the town. His patron was its Anglo-Catholic vicar, Alexander Morden Bennett, who dominated Bournemouth's religious life much as the Wagners dominated Brighton, and was also suspected of popery.

Thirty years later, after Bennett's death, St Stephen's was erected in his memory across the valley, designed by Pearson. No two churches better convey the contrasting styles of 'High Church' Victorian Gothic. The first is essentially an exercise in colour and decoration, the second in architectural form. The first is jolly, the second austere, the first a hymn, the second a psalm.

St Peter's was built over twenty-five years from 1854 as small donations came in, and the plan is accordingly disparate and complex. The exterior has a high tower of stone, ostentatiously rising over the shopping area and best seen from afar. The nave is approached through a western vestibule with a massive strainer arch, revealing a high hammerbeam roof. This forms a trefoil over the chancel arch, decorated with a Clayton & Bell mural of the Crucifixion. The south aisle survives from the earlier church, the north is a superb corridor, like the arm of a cloister with 12 apostle windows.

This is mere preamble. The glory of St Peter's is the chancel and south transept, recently and magnificently restored. It today constitutes one of the richest Gothic Revival interiors in England, to compare with A. W. N. Pugin's Cheadle (Staffs). Every pier, rib and vault seems to drip with stiff-leaf and angels, in stone, alabaster and marble. No inch is devoid of colour. Choir stalls designed by Bodley erupt in a profusion of foliage, one of them occupied by Gladstone at his last communion in 1898. Above rise iron and brass screens, then shafted pillars, then crocketed arches, then roundels filled with relief carvings, then a vaulted roof with huge bosses. North and south of the chancel are double arcades in alabaster of astonishing richness. The south arcade forms a sedilia whose decoration would have made the 13th century gasp.

The south chapel commemorates John Keble, who retired to Bournemouth and worshipped here. If anything, its sanctuary designed by T. G. Jackson is richer even than the chancel. The transept murals have been admirably restored in tones of soft green and gold. The pulpit was designed by Street and carved by his master carver, Thomas Earp, who was also responsible for the reredos. Burne-Jones supplied the south chapel window. In the churchyard is the grave of Mary Shelley, reputedly with Shelley's heart laid beside her, it having been removed from his funeral pyre on an Italian beach.

BOURNEMOUTH
St Stephen ****
Serene Gothic interior by Pearson

St Stephen's could be a Cistercian reaction to the effusion of St Peter's. It was founded as a memorial to the vicar of St Peter's, Alexander Morden Bennett, who died in 1880. The church reflects the more restrained Gothic Revival that Pearson shared with George Gilbert Scott, in contrast to the more decorative style of Butterfield, Street and Bodley. Among his masterpieces, St Stephen's ranks with St Augustine, Kilburn (London) and St Agnes, Liverpool (Lancs). It is a quiet, serene interior that would not seem out of place in a French monastery. The church was incomplete on Pearson's death and was finished by his son. Its vicar at the time, A. S. Bennett, was the son of the man whom it commemorated.

The exterior is dominated by a high north-west bell-tower for which a spire was planned but never built. It is balanced by a tall flèche over the nave and further turrets over the transepts. The interior instantly displays Pearson's mastery of Gothic space. It is controlled by a single design, vaulted throughout and lit by a clerestory of lancet windows with arcades that continue even round the west end. The easternmost bay of the nave arcades turns inward to the crossing to prepare the eye for the chancel. This is a remarkable dramatic touch. The view east is memorable, with unfolding arches, slender shafted piers and vault ribs studded with ballflower. The transepts north and south are handled differently. The north is open, with a rose window, the south enclosed, with the organ loft above a vaulted chapel. Of all Victorian architects, I am sure the 13th century would have awarded Pearson the palm.

St Stephen's is also a monument to how modern lighting can enhance the qualities of a Gothic church, picking out the recesses and emphasising the shadows. The restored altar triptych, of gold with red background, draws the eye to the sanctuary yet never overpowers the architecture. In the north transept is a serene sculpture of a Madonna and Child by Benjamin Clemens. The glass is all by Clayton & Bell, the clerestory rightly left clear.

CATTISTOCK
St Peter and St Paul *
Font cover, Morris glass

Cattistock is not to every taste. The church is mostly Victorian, including the tall tower and the grey-green lichened stone. The approach is through a gloomy churchyard dark with yews and a porch that seems (on a wet day) worthy of Charles Addams. The interior is no less dark. This is George Gilbert Scott's Decorated Gothic of the 1850s, which means heavy proportions and dark stained glass. Scott built a south aisle, polygonal apse and stone pulpit reached by a door in the chancel. Cattistock benefited from a succession of wealthy Victorian parsons, and Scott's son, also George Gilbert, took over the work in the 1870s. He produced the tower and north aisle in a Perpendicular style, anathema to the previous generation. The church is thus a study in changing Victorian taste.

The tower is impressive. The later phase of Victorian revivalism was more responsive to local traditions. The pattern is taken from Charminster yet given a Somerset flourish. Scott junior has put the bell-openings in a single giant frame rising almost the full height of the tower. Not even the Somerset masters were this bold. It is, says Pevsner, 'the finest Perp tower of Dorset, even if second-hand Perp'. In the base of the tower, Scott installed a baptistery, covered in stencilled wall paintings. These include a large mural of St George and his dragon. Its centrepiece is a towering Gothic font cover designed by Temple Moore in 1904.

The jewel of Cattistock is the Morris glass of 1882 in the south aisle. From wherever you stand in the church, this window asserts its presence, glowing like a fire in the corner. It portrays six angels, the top two by Burne-Jones and the lower four by Morris. Some are adapted from windows in Jesus College Chapel in Cambridge and others from Tue Brook in Liverpool. The colouring and background are brilliant.

CERNE ABBAS
St Mary *
Stone chancel screen

The village needs no introduction, a lovely Dorset backwater enfolded in its own valley. Golden Ham stone glows with sunlight and looks cheerful even in rain. The Benedictine abbey is now a ruin on the hillside, but in the late 13th century the monks built the villagers a church for their own use, possibly based on a former chapel. The dedication to St Mary came at a time when the cult of the Virgin was strong. The present church sits in the centre of the town opposite a street of cosy timbered cottages.

The exterior, except for the Ham stone tower, is a chequerboard of Ham and local flint. The tower is all Perpendicular finery: three bold stages with ornate battlements and pinnacles. The gargoyles are admirably primitive. On the west front is a statue of the Virgin and Child, eroded but still delicate. Beneath is an old stocks.

The interior is full of light. Its most prominent feature is a rare stone chancel screen. Its dado is solid stone and, before truncation in the 19th century, it rose the full height of the chancel arch. Thus, apart from the doorway and small openings, it would have cut off the chancel completely from the nave. This arrangement can still be seen in an 1870s photograph on the tower screen. The aisle walls are covered with biblical texts where once there were pre-Reformation murals. The remains of the text frames can still be seen above the Victorian chancel arch.

The colourful hood to the font is modern, of 1963. On the other side of the south doorway are the remains of a fireplace. Perhaps when the porch was too cold the villagers were allowed in to gather here round a fire. The chimney leads outside to a gargoyle west of the porch. It must have been particularly grotesque when smoking.

CHALBURY
All Saints *
Georgian furnishings

The church is worth a visit for the view alone. Despite being almost in Wiltshire, Chalbury offers a view of the hills of Purbeck, the Channel and the Isle of Wight, with the rolling Dorset countryside beneath. An elm nearby was once used by sailors for navigation. Otherwise, the church is remarkable for its Georgian woodwork, perfectly preserved. The building is a simple box of nave and chancel with tiny bellcote. The windows indicate a medieval original.

The charm is inside, an unaltered 18th-century arrangement of box pews and three-decker pulpit, with clear light streaming in through Georgian glass. The pews come in all shapes and sizes, high, low, for the squire, the clerk and, in the west gallery, the musicians. The chief curiosity is the chancel arch, a double screen like an internal Venetian window, deep enough to have more seats inside.

The seating allocation is recorded. The bench on the south side of the chancel was for the rectory servants. The long, theatrical bench raised on the chancel's north side was for the Earl of Pembroke, owner of the land in these parts, presumably when he and his family deigned to come over from Wilton. Of the nave boxes, the biggest was for Chalbury Farm, the next biggest for Didlington Farm and the next for Uppington Farm. Despite brightly embroidered covers, the pew benches are cramped and very upright, posture rigorously enforced.

Chalbury has been gaily repainted in mushroom and magnolia, fashionable in the 1970s, while wreaths of dried flowers in matching purple and yellow bid visitors welcome. Outside in the churchyard are Victorian gravestones with crocketed tops. Most are coated in a mosaic of lichens, an especially fine one being just under the east window. As for windows, compare the pleasing Georgian fenestration of the church with the ugly plate glass permitted in a converted barn next door. Planners sleep while England burns.

CHARLTON MARSHALL
St Mary **
Interior in style of Wren

The church nudges up against the main road south of Blandford and is, in my view, a more attractive classical composition than its more famous neighbour. It was designed for the local rector, Dr Sloper, in 1713 probably by John Bastard, father of the architects of Blandford. Apart from the medieval tower, which he adorned with small pediments and obelisks, Bastard completely rebuilt the church. Yet he left it with much of its medieval character, with pitched roof, flat east end, buttresses and gabled south porch. Even the north arcade, whose arches have been classicised, has square piers rather than classical columns. The round-arched windows have clear glass and admit, as the vicar told me, 'the light of reason on all sides'.

The woodwork is exceptional for a church of this size and appears to be original and complete. The huge reredos covers the entire east end and is worthy of the best City of London chancel. The pulpit has a tester crowned with cherubs and a pelican 'in its piety'. Every detail of the marquetry, panelling and coving is given a baroque flow. The font is in the form of an Ionic column with a pine-cone cover. The church was recently saved from redundancy. On my visit the congregation was full of life, apparently conducting a vote on what hymns they would sing at the start of Sunday service.

CHARMINSTER
St Mary *
Trenchard tombs

The Trenchards were big landowners in the 16th century, building nearby Wolfeton House and endowing the old village church with a west tower and aisles. The tower is the best feature, rugged and magnificent, its buttresses liberally carved with the letter T. This was medieval arts patronage of the most ostentatious kind.

The interior is dominated by a vigorous late-Norman arcade and Norman chancel arch. The capitals are scalloped but the arches pointed, with nailhead decoration rising to an odd mixture of alternating Norman and Perpendicular clerestory windows, as if the 16th-century restorers could not run to a full set. When the Victorians did this sort of restoration we are offended, when the Tudors we are charmed.

The chancel was demolished, as were so many, in the 17th century and not rebuilt until the 19th but with an original window reinserted, apparently the wrong way round. The Trenchards lie mostly in the south chapel or Wolfeton aisle, under defaced table tombs and floor slabs. The jolliest memorial is on the wall, to Grace (Trenchard) Pole, portrayed kneeling at prayer in a lace collar. She has copious cherubs for company, perhaps to console her for the loss of her own children before she died. She was brightly repainted in 1970. We repaint church sculpture: why not church architecture? Charminster is a friendly building, full of the corbel faces of those who must have built it and worshipped in it. Under the tower is a fine window by Kempe.

CHRISTCHURCH
Priory *****
Norman exterior, Decorated screen, Perpendicular tombs and chantries

Of all the great churches of England, Christchurch is probably the least well known. Its tower rises beyond the water meadows of the River Avon near the coast, which has taken more punishment from planners than any. The continuous ribbon of retirement suburbs from Lymington to Poole is a landscape without redemption. I prefer the desolate mills and blasted tips of the north of England to this endless drabness. Christchurch Priory is like Gulliver awakening from a long sleep on the shore and now struggling to escape the bonds of modern life.

The church is sensational. The view of the reredos as climax to the Norman nave and crossing arch is a *coup de théâtre* of church architecture. The sanctuary is adorned with Gothic treasures, culminating in the Salisbury

Chantry. Christchurch, like Sherborne and Beverley Minster (Yorks, ER), has the proportions of a cathedral, being transferred from priory to parish church at the Reformation. Little damage was done at the time, except to the monastic buildings. The church survived virtually intact and even Benjamin Ferrey's Victorian restoration seems unobtrusive.

The sequence of tower, nave, chancel and Lady Chapel forms the longest parish church in England. The central tower fell in the 15th century and was replaced by the present west tower. The Norman nave and transepts survive, the former with Early Gothic windows. They convey enormous strength, alleviated by the north transept's sumptuous blind arcading. This north transept is one of the most spectacular works of Norman design in England, despite the reckless intrusion of a Perpendicular window. The stair turret is most celebrated, a series of graceful arcading on the ground floor, colonettes on the second, a bold trellis pattern on the third and then more blind arcading at the top. Could anyone pull off such a composition today?

Continuing round the exterior, we suddenly meet Perpendicular for the rebuilt chancel and Lady Chapel. The former has four-light clerestory windows, the latter a most unusual upper storey. This was used as a grammar school and is now a museum.

The church is entered through the north porch. This is no mere parish shelter, but a ceremonial meeting place for the prior and the burgesses of the town. It is in the richest Early Gothic style, with the double doorway into the church flanked each side by no fewer than six Purbeck shafts. The tierceron vault and effusive bosses are Victorian restorations in the Decorated mode. The interior is an essay in contrasts. The Norman nave is massive. The aisle and clerestory windows are Early Gothic insertions and the wooden roof is Victorian reproduction. But the great vista eastwards dominates the scene. This is modulated first by the dark height of the old crossing, the earliest part of the church, then by the chancel, a blaze of light crowned by a lierne vault.

Glimpsed over the crossing pulpitum is the enormous 14th-century stone reredos, a masterpiece of English Decorated carving. It depicts a Tree of Jesse surmounted by a crowded Epiphany. The composition is full of movement and vigour. The remaining niches need filling, the more so since the composition is itself surmounted by a 1967 mural of Christ the Saviour by Hans Feibusch. If murals can be so confidently replaced, why not statuary?

This reredos must have been re-erected when the new Perpendicular chancel was built almost two centuries later. At its heart is the Great Quire, filled with some of the finest stalls and misericords in the region. The latter include such favourites as a fox in a pulpit preaching to a flock of geese. High above the stalls, the shafts end in foliated capitals that have been painted and gilded, recreating the richness of the Perpendicular originals.

A different eastwards view is down the south aisle towards the chancel. This is framed by a slender lancet, erupting in a complex lierne vault. The aisle is lined with memorials and two chantry chapels, to Robert Harys (in 1525) and John Draper (prior in 1520). These date from the last burst of Perpendicular before the Reformation, Draper's chantry already showing Renaissance motifs. He was the prior who had to surrender the foundation's wealth to Henry VIII, but was allowed a pension of £133 a year and a comfortable home. Perhaps it is to his diplomacy that Christchurch owes its survival.

The north aisle chantries are richer still. The masterpiece, the Salisbury Chantry, was built in 1529 for Margaret Pole, Countess of Salisbury and owner of the manor of Christchurch. She was to be executed by Henry VIII for the outspoken Catholic views of her son, then studying in Rome. She claimed Plantagenet title to the throne as daughter of the Duke of Clarence. The chantry's fan vaulting, canopied niches, tracery and panelling are worthy of her.

The Lady Chapel stands out to the east of the ambulatory, its wall arcading and reredos of the utmost richness. The priest's doors in the north wall and the stops to the lierne vault overhead are elaborately decorated. The church retains three Saxon crypts.

IWERNE MINSTER
St Mary *
Lady Chapel by Pearson

Iwerne is a curious place, so chiselled and changed by the past hundred years as to have lost much of its ancient patina. It is worth visiting with Pevsner in hand, if only to see the old man fussing over who did what to which in the course of restoration. Since one of the Victorian restorers was the drastic T. H. Wyatt and the other was J. L. Pearson, no one can tell whether any of the Norman fragments that give Iwerne such charm are in their original location. Yet the result is so uniform that, in another hundred years, the place will presumably seem as ancient as before the Victorians took hold of it.

The interior is Transitional Gothic. The north arcade is Norman with scallop capitals, the south already has pointed arches. In the north arcade is a Norman arch into a transept chapel, but here we find a most confusing Norman window of two lights separated by a delightful Purbeck shaft with a Gothic stiff-leaf capital. Then comes a complete surprise, Pearson's reconstruction of the south, Lady Chapel. This is a gem of Victorian design. It has a Decorated arcade dividing it from the nave and is roofed with a stone vault, with lierne ribs and intricate floral bosses. How far this work is based on archaeological evidence of a former chapel and how far on Pearson's own highly developed Gothic imagination is unknown.

The chapel can be lit by a switch in the choir. The only pity is that Pearson did not complete the job by painting it. The chapel stained glass is reproduction 16th-century Flemish and a delight.

KINGSTON
St James **
Street's hilltop homage to Gothic

Beyond Corfe Castle the wilder reaches of the Isle of Purbeck run towards the cliffs of Worth Matravers. Here we find a tower that commands views over half the county and a Victorian church widely regarded as a most perfect re-creation of early 13th-century architecture. Kingston already had one medieval church and cannot have needed another. Yet the 28-year-old Earl of Eldon responded to the agricultural recession of the 1870s with an act of pious ostentation. He asked Street to build him a large church at whatever cost, using local materials and local staff. The architect spent £70,000 over seven years from 1873 to 1880, a huge sum at the time.

Street was immensely proud of this creation, referring to it as his 'jolliest' church, an extraordinary adjective from the designer of the vivacious St Peter, Bournemouth. It is certainly not an adjective I would use. Clifton-Taylor referred to it as 'Gothic architecture at its most classical and least quirky; if it is chilly it is the chilliness of perfection'. The structure is of Purbeck stone and looms massively over the old village. The roof slates are carefully graded. Street designed all his windows as lancets, except at the west end where a rose window sits above a narthex. This window, together with the narthex and apsidal east end, reveal Continental influence.

The interior is a severe but respectful homage to the Gothic tradition, vaulted in stone except in the nave. The arcades and much of the architectural detail are picked out, as in an Early Gothic cathedral, in the local limestone celebrated for taking a black polish and thus known as Purbeck 'marble'. The shafts are given stiff-leaf capitals. The furnishings are sparse but of high quality, notably the ironwork screen. The apse, with its Purbeck outlines, soaring rib vault and magnificent arch is a work of harmony and nobility.

If not a work of warmth, Kingston is certainly one of beauty. The product of one recession, it has survived many since, and calls from the heights of Purbeck to Corfe and the Dorset hills beyond.

LYME REGIS
St Michael *
Norman porch, Mary Anning window

The church sits at the unfashionable end of this charming resort, east of The Cobb. It is tucked in behind a rising cliff as if for protection from the sea. Erosion has brought the shore less than 100 yds from the church, where concrete battlements protect it from further danger.

A previous Saxon–Norman structure survives in the curious west porch and tower facing the road. The porch, a noble stone chamber, is part of the nave of the former church. Two bays remain, as if hacked from walls that seem a geological museum of every building material in Dorset. Next to it is a stained glass window commemorating the Lyme origins of Thomas Coram, founder of the Foundling Hospital in London.

Both the aisles and the nave run through to the east wall in the Cornish style, with a one-bay projection for a chancel. The nave has a wagon roof that continues into the chancel at a lower level. Since the floor rises at this point, the effect is a theatrical lengthening of the perspective. Above the chancel arch is a Victorian mural of the Raising of the Cross. We can sense the nearness of the sea, yet the windows are filled not with the grass, sky and seagulls but heavy-duty Victorian stained glass.

The first window on the north side (by Wailes) commemorates Mary Anning, a local shopkeeper's daughter who, in the 19th century, was the first person to begin digging fossils from the lias cliffs. In 1812, when she was just ten, she found the first ichthyosaurus on this site. Mary became a celebrity when her collection passed to what is now the Natural History Museum, for a meagre £23 plus a small annuity. Other treasures in the nave include a fine Jacobean pulpit and tester and an outstanding 16th-century Flemish tapestry, spotlit on the north wall.

MILTON ABBEY
****

Decorated crossing and windows, Pugin glass

The abbey church was an ancient Benedictine foundation burnt in 1309 but not rebuilt beyond its crossing. It owes its picturesque setting to the Earl of Dorchester's decision in 1771 to demolish the old abbey buildings and erect a new house on the site. He moved the village to a valley a mile away. The village street once stretched south and east of the abbey, where there is now a school cricket field and golf course. The sweep of the church, William Chambers' house and Capability Brown's grounds, set in a glade amid wooded slopes, is one of the great set pieces of English landscape.

The abbey church still belongs to the diocese. It is built of warm Ham stone, Chilmark stone and flint and consists only of an aisled chancel and crossing with tower and transepts. It is thus a 14th-century fragment of what was intended to be a massive structure. Blind arcades to the east indicate a vanished Lady Chapel while the west front has springers for nave arcades that were never built. What stands is reminiscent of a college chapel, serene in the height and uniformity of its elevation and with magnificent transept windows.

These windows dominate our first impression of the interior, since we enter directly into what was meant to be the crossing. Most of the work is Decorated Gothic of the mid-14th century. The sensational south window has seven lights below a screen of Reticulated tracery, four tiers of cusped lozenges, like a giant net hung down from the gable. The glass is a Tree of Jesse by A. W. N. Pugin. The later north transept window is no less spectacular but here the Perpendicular style has taken over. The east and west windows of the transepts are astonishingly high, Perpendicular engineering at its most spectacular. The lierne vault becomes a fan under the tower. The walls, in contrast to the sophistication of the fenestration, are strangely roughcast, of stone, Purbeck marble and flint. This whole space is one of the glories of English Gothic.

In the north transept stands the monument to the couple who destroyed the original village but perhaps saved the church, Joseph Damer, later Earl of Dorchester, and his wife. The tomb was designed by Robert Adam, the effigies carved by Agostino Carlini. They portray a husband gazing down lovingly on his dead spouse, both lying comfortably on a bed. Next door stands an unusual Art Nouveau font by J. A. Jerichau. Two large angels dominate the composition; the water bowl is hardly noticeable at their feet.

The chancel is divided from the crossing by a restored pulpitum screen which carries the organ. On its east side are two panel paintings dating from the 15th century, of the founder of the monastery, King Athelstan, and his mother Egwynna. The choir culminates in a vast Perpendicular reredos, restored in plaster by James Wyatt in the 18th century. This is painfully lacking in statuary, surely a fit project for a modern benefactor. High on the north wall is a rare medieval tabernacle of carved wood. This would once have hung before the reredos to house the Sacrament.

In the south aisle is a memorial to a member of the Tregonwell family, who acquired the abbey after the Dissolution and before its sale to the Damers. John Tregonwell bequeathed his library to the church in thanks for being saved when he fell from its roof as a child. His pantaloons allegedly filled with air and broke his fall. I assume that this was the first successful parachute.

MORETON
St Nicholas **
Engraved windows by Whistler

The Dorset countryside conceals the oddest delights. Here among woods and fields lies a gallery of light that might grace a street in Bath. Moreton church was built in 1776 by James Frampton in the Gothic style and extended by his descendant, William Frampton, rector in 1840–98. Wrecked by a wayward bomb in the Second World War, it was restored with engraved rather than stained glass by Laurence Whistler. The glass is the only complete project of such engraving and is Whistler's masterpiece. The cemetery contains the grave of T. E. Lawrence 'of Arabia', although his memorial is in a church in Wareham.

The church is a rectangular structure with a north aisle and south chapel. The apsidal chancel has more the character of a conservatory bay window, looking out to the woods. The roof is adorned with bosses and heavy shields, the pews with candleholders and blue kneelers. Pride of place goes to the twelve windows, executed gradually over thirty years from 1955 to 1985 as private funds were available. The theme of Whistler's work is light, declared by ubiquitous large candles. The five windows in the apse were the first to be installed.

The central window shows the Instruments of the Passion. On either side the harvest on land and sea and the church bombed and restored are represented in medallions. The outer pair of windows show a Christmas tree and an ash tree. The window of 1982 in the Trinity Chapel is a surreal composition of a crashed fighter plane, magnolia, butterflies, clouds, buzzards and Salisbury Cathedral, and commemorates a pilot shot down in the Second World War. The west, Galaxy window of 1984 is a whorl of bursting light, suggesting colour without colour, the fire of the explosion spreading out into blossom. This is as exciting a work of 20th-century art as Chagall's windows at Tudeley (Kent).

In the side chapel is a memorial to the first Mrs Frampton (d.1762), expressed in terms florid even for the 18th century. She was 'a rare Example of true *Conjugal* Affection and of those amiable Qualities on which alone are founded the Charms of Domestic Happiness'.

POOLE
St Osmund, Parkstone ***
Arts and Crafts interior

Among the terraced and semi-detached sprawl of Poole rises a miniature Albi Cathedral, a giant basilica of moulded brick. Rose windows start out of walls, saints gaze down from niches and the west front is powerful enough to ward off the worst Albigensian attack. As the Victorian straitjacket of strict Gothic was thrown off towards the turn of the 20th century, there was a vogue for Byzantine churches. Most splendid was the Roman Catholic Westminster Cathedral, possible inspiration for St Osmund's. The plans were first drawn up in 1904 by a local architect, G. A. B. Livesay, to whom we owe the east end, including the baldacchino.

The west end came later, 1911–27, to designs by Arthur Grove and E. S. Prior, the latter a leader of the Arts and Crafts Movement and pupil of Norman Shaw. The shallow crossing dome, west turrets and rounded openings sustain the Byzantine flavour of the east end. The west front is a masterpiece of eclecticism, with Frankish turrets, Lombard arcading, Saxon patterning, above a shallow Art Nouveau arch of terracotta with a vine trail moulding. All this was executed in handmade bricks, says the guide, 'made by the wire-cut extrusion process, powered by portable steam engine and textured by hand, brushing and pressing grit and coal dust into the surface'.

The interior, not surprisingly, is a stylistic jumble. Prior's nave is the most disciplined part, with arcades of round arches and piers with pilaster strips and Byzantine capitals. The theme is repeated in the aisles. The capitals are of deep red terracotta, erupting at the crossing arch into four astonishing angels whose wings stick out over the space like the horns of a giant antelope. The chancel beyond is superbly theatrical, with walls curving up to the baldacchino, which is composed of four columns surmounted by a miniature Roman temple. This might be a set for *Aida* (but compare St Bartholomew, Brighton, in this respect). The church has many well-crafted fittings of the 1920s.

The south transept chapel is lined with black and white marble, with simple altar rails, reredos and an Arts and Crafts grille by Macdonald Gill, brother of Eric, who contributed the lettering. The hand-beaten bronze lectern is by W. Bainbridge Reynolds, who also designed the candelabra and altar crosses. The abstract stained glass is by Prior.

PORTLAND
St George, Reforne *
Georgian church above quarry

Portland is an appendix of Dorset left to the mercy of the philistine Royal Navy. Its quaint streets and cliffs have been battered less by storms and centuries of quarrying than by dreadful naval buildings. Yet high on the Reforne bluff looking out towards Devon is a surprise. St George's was built in 1754–66 by a local architect, Thomas Gilbert, in the grandest style, for what must have been a booming community of Portland quarriers.

The tower appears to imitate a west tower of St Paul's Cathedral. The church is cruciform with pedimented transepts, a curiously flattened dome and two tiers of windows throughout. The interior has shallow plaster vaults but is chiefly of interest for being unaltered. Twin pulpits, or at least a pulpit and reading desk, stand under the crossing. The original box pews are still in place, worshippers to the east having to turn west to face the pulpit and away from the altar. The 'rectory' pews nearest the altar have high backs, entirely cutting it from view.

The churchyard is full of lichen-clad Portland gravestones and monuments, sheltered only by the meagrest of trees on this windswept spot. In the background, cranes still quarry London's favourite stone.

[CCT]

PUDDLETOWN
St Mary ***
Atmospheric interior with 17th-century furnishings

Puddletown church is a like a Dickensian law court. We can make out the jury box, the dock, the witness box, and the pulpit for the presiding judge. Galleries for onlookers stack up to the west. The south transept could even serve as a prison pen. Yet when I visited the church one autumn evening it was filled with the remains of a harvest festival. Stooks of corn leaned against the pews and branches stretched like cobwebs across the windows. It had been transformed into a lovable shrine of community endeavour. Puddletown was Weatherbury in Hardy's *Far from the Madding Crowd*.

The nave is wide, with a superb panelled roof and an aisle only to the north. The peculiar character of the church is due to the lord of the manor, J. G. Brymer, deciding in 1910 to expand the old chancel and north chapel in the Perpendicular style, reusing stones from cottages demolished in the process. What might have been a dark interior was thus given a baroque spaciousness. The new chancel has a light barrel roof and three-sided altar rails. The mural texts are well preserved and include one with two hands holding the Bible.

None of Brymer's work disturbed furnishings dating back to 1634. The box pews are secretively high, with two grand ones facing the pulpit. The latter is a magnificent three-decker, panelled with Doric columns, and with a high tester. A clerk's pew and library shelves are immediately beneath it. Opposite across a sea of box pews is a west gallery of the same period. This is fronted with balusters and a large wooden coat of arms apparently taken from a wrecked ship.

The Athelhampton Chantry contains the tombs of the Martyns of Athelhampton Hall. That of Sir William Martyn divides the chapel from the nave. It is of alabaster and dates from the 1470s. Others are more mutilated but together form a charming mausoleum. Nicholas Martyn's brass indicates his death without male heir in 1595. The eldest of his four daughters, Elizabeth, continued the line in the Brune family.

SHERBORNE
Abbey of St Mary *****
Complete fan vault, carved bosses, misericords

Sherborne, like Beverley, Selby and Tewkesbury, requires a disclaimer. Prior to the Reformation it ranked with the great monastic churches that are now cathedrals. Indeed it was a cathedral until 1075 and a monastery church until the Dissolution. Since then, like most former monastic foundations, it has been parochial. The town was fortunate in what it inherited and has been careful in conserving that fortune. The abbey lies in the centre of the town, surrounded by ancient buildings. Abbey and town are both of Ham stone, a glorious material warmer than even the most creamy Cotswold. The church thus sits well in context, its size lightened by windows of the Perpendicular style at its gayest and most confident.

Sherborne's Saxon–Norman origins explain the heavy central tower and the asymmetry of the first bay of the nave arcade. The porch is Norman, as are the main crossing transepts. The 13th century added the Early Gothic Lady Chapel with Purbeck shafts and stiff-leaf capitals, and Bishop Roger's Chapel off the north choir aisle. Key to the abbey's character is the transformation of the remaining core by its abbots in the 15th century. The cause was a revolt by the local citizens against the abbot in 1437, during which the nave roof and tower were burnt. For this the town was punished by being compelled to pay for the reconstruction, and pay for the best. It took the abbot half a century to complete the task.

His monks did not enjoy the finished work for long. Just seventeen of them were left to surrender Sherborne to the king on its dissolution in 1539. The new church was purchased and then sold to the townspeople by a local magnate, Sir John Horsey. The abbey on which they had had to spend so much money duly became their church. They understandably respected it. Only a westward extension, which had been the parish's church of All Hallows, was demolished. The eastern chapels were converted for the use of Sherborne School, remaining so until restored to the main church in the 1930s.

The interior is uniformly Perpendicular, with the exceptions noted above. Both nave and choir have immense panelled piers, those in the choir continuing uninterrupted up to the vaults. Sherborne has some of the finest fan vaults in England. They cover virtually the whole interior, except for the nave vaults which have liernes, and the south transept, which is not vaulted. There is evidence that the design existed even before the fire of 1437, making it the first high fan in England. The nave vault, built at the end of the century, is sufficiently similar to suggest the same hand or at least the same design. John Harvey comments that the work 'is very distinctive and must be the creation of a great master; it is quite possible that his name is known, but unconnected with any existing work through which the authorship of Sherborne could be traced'. Harvey's best guess is William Smyth, who was working at Wells in the second half of the 15th century.

The essence of the Sherborne fans is that, unlike the more decorative fans of Gloucester, Bath or Cambridge, they do not overlap and thus cut each other off. Nor do they have pendants or other foibles. The components are structural. Each fan is a complete semicircle (in fact a polygon). Individual ribs leap from the fan to cross the central vault, intersecting in a series of lozenges. This gives to the starburst of the fan the tautness of earlier lierne ribs. The choir vault is narrower than that of the nave: its diagonal ribs buckle and twist and the fans come closer to touching, like exotic palm trees. The vault in the north transept, different again, might be that of a bedchamber, all frills and lace.

The vault intersections are punctuated with bosses. They are masterpieces of medieval carving, easier to study in the guide than with the naked eye. Most represent the dominant themes of late 15th-century Sherborne, the red and white roses of the civil war, the abbot's rebus, the coat of arms of Henry VII. They also portray simple scenes of domestic life and legend. Dogs chew on a bone. A pelican 'in her piety' plucks blood from her breast to feed her young. An owl is mobbed by birds. In the south transept the corbels, more crudely carved, are of men and women in the fashions of the period. There are a number of Green Men with foliage issuing from their mouths. The well-known boss of the mermaid holding a mirror and comb is high in the eastern bay of the nave. This is sophisticated and enlightened decoration. I would pit Sherborne's roof against any contemporary work of the Italian Renaissance.

More medieval carving is to be found in the choir. Ten misericords survive under the Victorian stalls, including the well-known woman beating her husband and master beating a boy. In the latter case the carver even portrays the weals in the boy's bottom. The pupils all have faces of monkeys. One of the bench-ends has a poignant old man selling cherries. After this vitality, Sherborne's extensive memorial sculpture can seem stilted. In the Wykeham Chapel is the monument to Sir John Horsey and his son, purchaser of the abbey at the time of the Dissolution. He died in 1546, when knights were still portrayed in armour but forms were appearing in Renaissance tomb canopies.

Forty years later and across in St Katherine's Chapel, John Leweston was commemorated in Elizabethan classicism, though still recumbent and in prayer.

A century later, memorial art had changed again. The south transept contains the standing monument to John Digby (d.1698), grand, pompous, splendid and very much alive. His calf is well turned, his wig is in place and his adoring wives are on either side. Beneath is his eulogy: 'He was naturally inclined to avoid the hurry of a publick life, yet careful to keep up to the port of his quality, was willing to be at ease, but scorned obscurity.' Beside the supporting columns are two putti weeping stone tears, whether of mirth or sadness is not clear.

The present Chapel of St Mary le Bow was the headmaster's drawing-room and study of Sherborne School. The old fireplace can still be seen in the east wall. Next door in the Lady Chapel is a lovely engraved glass reredos by Laurence Whistler of 1968.

STUDLAND
St Nicholas **
Coastal setting, Norman interior

Here begins the great sweep of south-west England, from Poole Harbour to Land's End. Studland might be a Cornish enclave, isolated on its promontory, cut off from the subtopia of Poole and west Hampshire. In Saxon days it guarded the approaches to Wareham. Today it is where walkers start on that splendid scenic pilgrimage, the South West Coast Path. Here they might bless their rucksacks and take strength for the trials ahead.

The church is reached through the trees at the end of a gentle lane, where the churchyard offers a panorama of Poole Harbour and the Isle of Wight. In summer this is a peaceful scene of birdsong and sailing boats. The church is a rough stone building dominated by a low central Saxon–Norman tower, much buttressed and its upper stage unfinished. The north windows are mere slits. The roof is of Dorset stone tiles and rests on a corbel-table of carved Norman grotesques and abstract shapes. Some of these are reminiscent of Kilpeck (Herefs).

The shock is inside. Studland's interior is black and sinister even in summer sunlight. Little has been altered since the 12th century, apart from an Early Gothic east window and 17th-century windows let into the south wall. The place must once have been dark as a tomb. The whitewash may be anachronistic, but is a relief. Two great horseshoe arches dominate the crossing. The scalloped capitals have excellent details while the arches have roll-mouldings. 'How is one to date them?' wails Pevsner. They are clearly early, given the absence of the characteristic late Norman motif of zigzag. We are here at the first dawn of post-Conquest England.

The Norman font is unadorned. Jolly banners rest against the walls. Outside on the green by the main road is a modern (1976) version of an old Saxon cross that once stood here, its motifs taken from such crosses elsewere in Dorset. Wouldn't it be nice if there were more such works on every crossroads in England?

TARRANT CRAWFORD
St Mary *
Gothic wall paintings

This place of ghosts lies at the end of a lane leading to a Georgian farmhouse and outbuildings. It was the site of one of the richest Cistercian nunneries in England, founded in the 1220s by Bishop Poore, builder of Salisbury Cathedral, who returned to be buried. Here too lay Queen Joan of Scotland, daughter of King John of England. Her effigy was reputedly of gilded marble, possibly the work of Elias of Dereham, builder of Salisbury Cathedral. The tomb was much treasured by the nuns. All this is gone, leaving only a simple peasants' chapel. This is now redundant but easily accessible.

The structure dates from before the founding of the nunnery, for which it may have been a lay chapel. It consists of nave and chancel, with barely any architectural division between them. Only the upper part of the tower, with its jutting parapet, has a touch of sophistication.

The window recesses are deep and there is a Perpendicular light set in the north wall, with fragments of old glass. During the church's restoration in 1911 the box pews were reduced and portions used to panel the east end. The pulpit, altar rails and font cover all date from the 17th century.

Tarrant Crawford's 14th-century wall paintings on the south wall are crude and indistinct but form an extensive decorative scheme. The upper level depicts 14 scenes from the life of St Margaret of Antioch. Below is a frieze of the three living and three dead kings, the latter as skeletons warning the former of their fate. These reflections on the mortality of the rich greatly comforted medieval worshippers. To the east is a large Annunciation. The old tomb slab in the chancel is said to be that of Bishop Poore.
[CCT]

TRENT
St Andrew **
Gerard tombs, medieval screen

Trent stands proud in this northern spur of Dorset, rare in the county in having a spire, indeed a spire that dominates the church. It rises above the south transept and leaves the chancel almost as an adjunct. The material is limestone, the period 14th century, and the style more Midlands than Dorset, perhaps because the church belonged to Studley Priory in Warwickshire. The windows are mostly Decorated. In the 15th century the church benefited from a bequest for a chantry, of which no trace remains but which presumably occupied the north transept. The house of the chantry priest remains in the churchyard.

Trent has a happy interior. There are no aisles. The view east is dominated by one of Dorset's finest screens, with rib-vaulted coving, tracery and rich foliated bands along the top, attributed to the craftsmen of Glastonbury. Other woodwork includes the late-medieval bench-ends and font cover and the 17th-century lectern and pulpit. A number of alterations were made c.1840 by the vicar, the Reverend William Turner. They are Victorian in date but Regency in spirit. He installed the light-hearted ceiling and decorated the chancel with stars, shields and angels. He also covered the lower walls with faience tiles and the floor with Minton tiles. His arms are shown on some of the bench-ends.

Most of Trent's monuments are behind another screen in the north transept. Here are two wall recesses with knights' memorials. Stranger still is the memorial that forms the transept arch itself. This was inserted by one of the Gerard family, lords of the manor after the Reformation, to his wife Anne who died in 1633. The inside of the arch carries a loud inscription: 'All flesh is grass and the glory of it is as the flower of the field.' On the east support is a small memorial of columns and angels. In the south transept is a tablet to Lord Fisher, a postwar Archbishop of Canterbury who retired to Trent, became a curate and chose to be buried here, rather than at Canterbury, on his death in 1974.

WHITCHURCH CANONICORUM
St Wite **
Saint's shrine, Norman capitals

The shrine of St Wite, a plain chest, lies in the north transept of her church. She specialised in cures. Her bones are inside, and there are still three holes to enable pilgrims to push injured limbs inside to touch her holy form. Building work in 1900 broke open the casket and revealed the bones of a small woman about forty. Such a bodily survival in England is extremely rare, the other known case being that of St Edward at Westminster Abbey. Who was St Wite (or Candida or Blanche) is a mystery discussed at length in the guidebook. She appears to have been a Breton saint brought over by Saxon colonists and allegedly murdered by the Vikings. High on the tower wall is a small panel depicting a Viking ship.

The church erected in her name was owned, as its name suggests, by the canons of Sarum. Its chief treasures are a collection of late-Norman and Early Gothic capitals, which adorn nave and transepts and are Dorset's best. We enter through a Norman south door into an aisle surviving from the Norman church.

Here the cylindrical piers are crowned with diminutive scalloped or huge water-leaf capitals. The north arcade has pointed arches and capitals with both trumpet-scallops and stiff-leaf. The middle bay has deeply incised zigzag round its entire arch. This superb profusion of carving continues in the capitals of the north transept and the shrine of St Wite, some stiff-leaf, some 'wind-blown' or spiral leaf. Here are masons struggling to break free of Norman formalism into the new Gothic.

This all forms a most remarkable gallery. The windows are mostly Early Gothic lancets bringing extra light into the transepts. The church is bare of ornament but a tomb survives in the chancel, that of Sir John Jeffrey, who died in 1611.

WIMBORNE MINSTER
St Cuthburga ****
Moses carving, Uvedale monument

The old minster sits in the centre of this market town like a mini-cathedral, much loved and much visited. Even the stand on which the churchyard sign is mounted is a work of art. The exterior looks eccentric, with two towers, one Norman at the crossing and another Perpendicular at the west. The stone is odder still, Dorset limestone interspersed with what Clifton-Taylor calls a 'dark rust-brown conglomerate of the Tertiary period', dug from the heaths north of the New Forest. The effect, seen also at Ellingham (Hants) and Bere Regis, is of a quilt of coloured rags. It is not unpleasing, but detracts from the vertical line of the Gothic building. If the desire was for economy, the brown stone presumably being cheaper, it is odd that the masons did not concentrate this stone rather than disperse it at random.

Inside are all the components of an English church: Norman core, Early Gothic east end, Decorated aisles and adornments and Perpendicular 'topping and tailing'. Wimborne was a Saxon nunnery wrecked by the Danes but revived as a college of canons by Edward the Confessor. The Norman nave and crossing are powerful, Saxon in plan. The nave arcades are late Norman, with zigzag arches and carved heads peering out of the mouldings. The clerestory is Perpendicular.

At the west end behind the tower screen is a fine Norman font resting on Purbeck marble shafts, with a Victorian font cover. High on the wall is an astronomical clock, its mechanism dating from the early 14th century with the earth at the centre of the universe. It is not linked with the 'Quarter Jack' on the tower outside, where a model soldier strikes each 15 minutes. Erected in 1612, he was originally a monk, but became a patriotic Grenadier during the Napoleonic Wars.

We pass east through the two crossing arches to the chancel, where three large Early Gothic windows rise the full height of the east wall. The lancets are barely pointed, with black Purbeck marble shafts. From the nave, they make a perfect foil for the Norman arches. The stained glass is Flemish 16th century, compatible with Early Gothic windows. The central window was given by the Bankes family of Kingston Lacy, and represents the Tree of Jesse.

In the north chancel aisle stands the superb Jacobean monument to Sir Edmund Uvedale (d.1606). It is unusually restrained, the effigy lying, head on hand, staring into the future while garlands and ribbonwork play round the inscription above. For some reason he has two left feet. Near him is a Saxon oak chest hewn out of a solid trunk of undressed wood, a superb survivor. On the south side of the chancel lies the tomb of John Beaufort, Duke of Somerset (d.1444), and his wife, grandparents of Henry VII. Alabaster effigies are set on a chest of Purbeck marble, portrayed solemnly holding hands. Next to them is Wimborne's famous Moses corbel, dating from the late 12th century and therefore earlier than the arch in which it is set. The head has flowing hair and plaited beard.

In the south chapel is another Wimborne curiosity, the Ettricke tomb. The chest is of a local lawyer who, in a temper, said he would not be buried inside or outside the church of his native town. He contrived eventually to be buried in the wall. Convinced he was dying in 1693 he even had the date inscribed on his tomb. It had to be changed when he survived another ten years, the masons not trying too hard to erase the former date. In the sanctuary wall is a small brass put up in the 15th century to King Ethelred the Unready, defender against the Danes and buried in the old convent on the site. This is the only royal brass known in England. Wimborne has a fine chained library.

WINTERBORNE TOMSON
St Andrew **
Farmyard setting

In an earlier age, Winterborne Tomson would have been another old chapel converted to a barn. To us it is a precious relic, lying hidden off the side road to Anderson. To its east lies 17th-century Tomson House and to the north a farm fills the church with farmyard smells. The structure is Norman single-cell, most unusual in retaining an intact apse. The roof has tiles with slates at the edges. The walls are battered, narrowing as they rise, and have Norman buttresses to the apse. The only light is from three late-Perpendicular window openings in the south wall.

The interior, now redundant, is bare apart from its furnishings, but these are a delight. They are of bleached oak, donated by an early Georgian Archbishop of Canterbury, William Wake. They include beautifully crafted box pews, a pulpit with tester, a screen, turned altar rails and a west gallery with staircase. The opening in the screen giving access to the pulpit is raised by a little arch to save the preacher's head. Across the front of the gallery a salvaged portion of the old rood loft survives, so worm-eaten it is hardly recognisable. The wagon roof is still plastered.

Winterborne Tomson has few monuments. A wall plaque to A. R. Powys, with lettering by Reynolds Stone, commemorates the Dorset architect who found the church as an animal pen in 1929 and raised money for its restoration. Much of this money came from selling a manuscript of that lover of all Dorset churches, Thomas Hardy. On the warm autumn afternoon when I was last there, the cows were noisy outside and a trapped bee buzzed against the window pane.

[CCT]

WORTH MATRAVERS
St Aldhelm *
Wild clifftop chapel

I used to consider Worth Matravers the loneliest village in the south. In summer it is gentle and silent. In winter great waves crash against the cliffs of the Isle of Purbeck, as if determined to carry it off to sea. The wind rushes low over open fields and trees crouch beneath high walls. This was smuggling and stonecutting country. The soil is thin. The old Square and Compass pub, with its beer in casks and its warren of rooms, is fiercely defended by real-ale enthusiasts and resistant to alteration. On one wild winter evening, I had the place entirely to myself.

St Aldhelm's is two miles beyond Worth on a headland accessible by the bridlepath to the coastguard station. This is the farthest corner of Purbeck. At the clifftop is a plateau beneath which the sea polishes Purbeck's stone to the eponymous 'marble'. From this headland in 1140, according to legend, a Worth man watched his daughter and her newly wed groom set out in a boat to their new home along the coast. As the couple drew abreast of the headland a sudden storm caught the boat, capsized it and all hands were lost. The distraught father built this chapel in their memory and it remains unaltered to this day. This is the only chapel in England with no east wall, since the corners are the points of the compass. The present altar table has had to be set across the east corner.

This fact, and the prominent location, have led some to suggest that the building was not originally for worship but was a castle, a lighthouse or a hermitage. The guide is sure that the purpose was religious, possibly a chantry suppressed in the 16th century. It was used as a 'sea marke' in the 17th century but returned to partial worship in 1874. There are now services at Easter and on some Sunday evenings in summer. It was once also a 'wishing chapel', with good luck coins dropped into the central column.

St Aldhelm's is a buttressed square box with a stone pyramid roof and a modern cross on top. There is one small window and another blocked. The interior is like a Byzantine water cistern, dripping wet and dominated by a powerful central column from which eight ribs soar into the darkness. Four form arches to the sides, four to the corners. This is Norman at its most primitive: no carving or decoration, no bases or bosses. The blackened lime-stone, reminiscent of Studland, seems to suck water up from the ground like a capillary. There are a few Victorian benches and a fussy font. Otherwise there is nothing but wind, sea, screaming birds and mystery.

WORTH MATRAVERS
St Nicholas *
Norman carving

St Nicholas's is a strange church. It sits on a slope in the middle of the village, its walls thick and heavily roofed, as if determined to prove a match for any weather. The structure is Norman, with round-arched windows high in the nave and a corbel-table of carved heads running round the exterior beneath the eaves. The origin of these carvings is confusing. The corbel-table, south door and even the chancel arch are said to have been brought here and reset from a Dissolved monastery elsewhere. Yet there seems no reason to refuse local masons the credit for the south doorway and arch. They are similar to those at Studland, suitable for a modest church such as Worth, though they may have been moved in the course of rebuilding.

The doorway is now much eroded. The tympanum portrays the Coronation of the Virgin, a theme that did not occur in Europe until the end of the 12th century, making this work the latest of Norman. The interior, though much restored, retains the proportions of the 12th-century structure. The chancel arch, horseshoe in shape, is ferocious with zigzag, its jagged line like a shark's jaw waiting to clamp on worshippers beneath. Behind the pulpit is a small cross brought by the vicar on his retirement from a previous posting, the Maldives in the Indian Ocean. As the guide says, he could hardly have been appointed to a greater contrast from those 'sultry coconut islands'.

Durham

County Durham is chiefly remarkable for scarce Saxon remains in industrial settings. Bishop Biscop founded the first churches on the Tyne in the late 7th century, a century after St Augustine's foundation at Canterbury. What survives of those days includes fragments of the monastic churches at Monkwearmouth and Jarrow, while the earlier Escomb stands more or less complete.

The Middle Ages were less generous to this county of cold seas and rolling hills. There are fine Early Gothic buildings at Darlington and South Church and the evocative pile built by the Bruces at Hartlepool. Otherwise the period is recalled in details, the anchorage at Chester-le-Street, the Lumley effigies in the same church and the Neville monuments at Staindrop.

Not until the arrival of the Laudian Bishop Cosin in the 1630s did County Durham leap forward from the 13th century. The tragic destruction by fire of his work at Brancepeth in 1998 leaves only Sedgefield as his memorial in this list. The Victorians treated the county quietly until the arrival of E. S. Prior at the turn of the 20th century. His Roker is one of the few churches that merit the title of cathedral, in this case of the Arts and Crafts Movement.

Chester-le-Street ***   Jarrow **   Sedgefield **
Darlington ***   Lanchester *   South Church *
Escomb **   Monkwearmouth *   Staindrop **
Hartlepool **   Roker: St Andrew ***
Ireshopeburn *   Seaham *

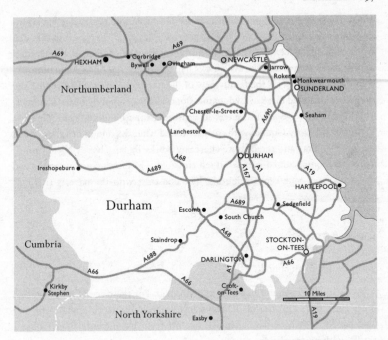

CHESTER-LE-STREET
St Mary and St Cuthbert ***
Anchorage, Lumley tombs

The west front of Chester-le-Street looks out across bleak suburbs. The tower rises through four stages, with an octagonal belfry, before reaching a stone spire. To the left is a rare surviving anchorage, now a museum called the Anker House. This was inhabited by an extreme form of hermit, an anchorite who would be walled up for life in a space adjacent to a church. He or she had only a squint giving a view of the altar and an opening for food. Immediately outside was a grave open and ready for burial. It was the most saintly of callings, a state of transition from this world to the next, permitted only to those authorised by a bishop. The cell has been much altered. There is an odd window to the street, carved of a single block of stone and much eroded. Whether this existed before the Dissolution, when anchorages were abolished, is not clear. The squint can be seen inside the porch.

The church itself is long and narrow with a tall nave and badly scraped arcades. The north aisle has another Chester curiosity, a continuous line of Gothic effigies of the Lumley family. They were assembled in the 1590s from Durham Cathedral graveyard or from Dissolved monasteries, or were carved to order. There was nothing a Tudor grandee liked more than to prove his ancestry. Only five are genuinely medieval. Some have heads or feet cut off so they can fit the available space. The best is the third from the west, chainmailed and cross-legged, dated to *c.*1260. The aisle looks like a casualty station at Agincourt.

In the north chapel is the family pew of the Lambtons, Earls of Durham. The chapel was inserted in 1829 by Ignatius Bonomi above a family burial chamber. The Lambtons were more discreet in death than the Lumleys. The chancel is Victorianised Early Gothic, with early traceried windows and intact piscina and sedilia. The altar and reredos are charming works by Sir Charles Nicholson of 1928, the frontal carved in relief in red and gold. The niches contain statues and the walls have 20th-century murals. The constrast with the nave is rich and colourful.

DARLINGTON
St Cuthbert ***
Early Gothic town church

The centre of Darlington has been transformed. For the price of a devastating inner ring road, the core of the town has been cleared of through-traffic and landscaped. It is now like a citadel, cut off from its outskirts by a moat of traffic, with its drawbridge raised.

The town was an important staging post between York and Durham. The church was begun as a college by Bishop Puiset of Durham in the 1180s. The east end was almost complete by the early years of the 13th century. Nave and aisles were built by the 1240s. The town belonged to the bishops of Durham, and they held the post of mayor into the 19th century. Having constructed so large a building so early, they felt no need to expand it at a later date. Darlington thus possesses a miniature Salisbury Cathedral, darkened by time and Victorian glass but beautifully proportioned.

The west front, a balanced composition of blind arcading, lancets and elaborate doorway, welcomes shoppers down a cobbled avenue into a cool Gothic retreat. Above the door is a modern statue of St Cuthbert. The church is cruciform with an exterior of pink-grey stone. The tower has belfry openings with a simple but soaring needle spire. The restoration of this and the rest of the church by George Gilbert Scott in the 1860s was sensitive. The Gothic tower had settled a full 8 inches, tilting the nave piers and requiring the windows to be filled with masonry. The guide relates that Scott found the church damp and rat-infested, with huge cracks in the walls. He stripped off the plaster, took up the floor, removed a hundred skulls in a single day, and raised the medieval ceiling to its old height. Those who deplore Victorian restoration need to remember the dilapidation it had to confront.

The aisled nave and crossing have fine Early Gothic arches. The chancel and transepts are enriched by shafts and blind arcading. The view towards the short chancel is impeded by a 14th-century stone screen but uplifted by a delicate organ case. To find Early Gothic transepts surviving in a town church is rare. The more austere north transept contains relics of chantries. On its east wall is a First World War monument to a Brigadier-General. He was killed in 1917, by when the attrition rate of officers was so great that he had been made a general at the age of just twenty-five.

The chancel is 'Scott-ish' but has 15th-century stalls and 11 misericords, including one of a naked man in high boots. The reredos is a mosaic of the Last Supper by a local artist, John Dobbin. It was donated in 1875 after being offered to Westminster Abbey and rejected.

ESCOMB
St John **
Well-preserved Saxon remains

The church of Escomb is subsidiary only to Jarrow and Monkwearmouth as an Anglo-Saxon shrine on Tyneside. It is better preserved than either. Though not mentioned by Bede, the fabric is 7th century with reused Roman stone. Archaeologists suggest that Escomb may be even earlier than Bishop Biscop's 'Roman' settlement at Monkwearmouth. The circular (or Celtic) churchyard and sloping walls are evidence of Irish influence prior to the Synod of Whitby in 664.

The church lies at the foot of a hill surrounded by mediocre council houses allegedly meant by their architect to defer to their historic setting. From the outside it is a double-cell chapel, with no tower and only a south porch as a later addition. Next to the porch is a rare Saxon sundial, capped by snakes and with three marks to show times of services. Another dial on the porch is 18th century. The south wall offers a gallery of English fenestration: a window each to Saxon, Norman and Gothic traditions, each struggling to admit more light without losing security or wall stability.

The walls are partly built of Roman stones brought from the old camp at Binchester. However, they are arranged Saxon fashion in long-and-short work. The inside is dominated by the chancel arch which includes traces of medieval wall painting. There is some old cobbled flooring in the nave that could be Saxon, and a quantity of ancient crosses set against walls and in the porch. Escomb's churchyard used to be unkempt and overgrown, offering some barrier to its surroundings. It is now mown and manicured.

HARTLEPOOL
St Hilda **
Water-leaf capitals, Bruce mausoleum

St Hilda's, on the headland beyond West Hartlepool, is another of my lost
corners of England. The church overlooks what is left of an old town, once
the port for the city of Durham but now submerged amid characterless housing
estates. From here even West Hartlepool looks enticing. Yet the church,
founded by the earliest Lindisfarne missionaries and rebuilt by the Brus (or
Bruce) family in the 13th century, is a battered titan of the Early Gothic
style.

The church is well sited in an extensive churchyard with views out over the
water. Its size appears to reflect the Bruces' desire for a prominent burial place.
The west tower is astonishing. Its core is Early Gothic with an embattled later
top, but there must be more masonry in the buttresses than in the tower itself.
They lean on the tower like giants trying to stop it sliding downhill and into the
bay. There is even room between the buttresses for a Galilee Chapel, probably
of processional significance.

The exterior of the nave is graceful Early Gothic. Only the south doorway
looks like a survival from the Norman building. The original arcaded clerestory
has lancet windows flanked by blind arches. The interior has the proportions
and enrichment of an abbey. Early Gothic arcading strides rhythmically
towards the chancel arch, which is of five orders with water-leaf carving on the
capitals. Some of these capitals are lovely.

The Bruce mausoleum was rebuilt behind the altar in the 1920s by Caröe.
The chapel contains monuments and relics. Many of the tombs are eroded from
having been outside for centuries. They are of another world from modern
Hartlepool.

IRESHOPEBURN
Methodist Chapel *
Dale chapel, original interior

Upper Weardale is forgotten England. The road through the North Pennines
passes hills with names like Black Hill, Great Stony Hill and Chapel Fell. This
is country where the fires of Methodism took hold, fanned by an absentee
Anglicanism. There are as many chapels in these parts as there are in Wales.
Many are early and handsome, and Ireshopeburn is the best. Part has become a
local museum, a model of what should be done with many half-used English
churches.

The chapel lies on the river bank next to the Weardale Inn, on the outskirts of the village. The bold Georgian façade greets travellers down the main road, as effective a landmark as any church steeple. The church is of grey stone with round-arched windows and a date of 1761 in its pediment. It was extended and refitted in 1872, yet retains the aura of an 18th-century meeting house. The walls are cream and the woodwork brown.

As with most Wesleyan chapels, the fittings focus all attention on the pulpit. This gives the chapel a sense of crescendo, as at Wesley's New Room in Bristol. The preacher speaks from what amounts to the poop deck, addressing the crew amidships beneath him, ranged on balconies, panelled boxes, benches and pews. Above him is nothing more symbolic than a giant clock, the Word tempered only by time.

JARROW
St Paul **
Bede's monastery, Piper window

In the right light, Jarrow appears to be struggling to recapture its past glory. Here is early Christianity's most celebrated shrine, that of the 7th-century monk, the Venerable Bede. We must blot out the pylons, the factories and the modern estates, indeed blot out a millennium and a half of history. Who can say if the present church was better surrounded by yesterday's industrial dereliction than by today's bleak lawn and the 'Bedeland theme park'? For that matter, what would Bede have wanted? Perhaps he would have approved of 'interpretation'. We just creep inside and sit quietly in the chancel.

St Paul's was founded seven years after Monkwearmouth by a group of monks under instruction from Bishop Biscop. It became Bede's home, from the age of eight in 681 until his death at the age of sixty-three. Here he wrote his history of the English Church, then already a century old, as well as some 60 works of biblical interpretation. His influence, and thus that of Jarrow, spread throughout medieval Europe. The monastery was destroyed by the Vikings but rebuilt by the Normans in 1074. The original dedication stone of 685 survives above the chancel arch and is the oldest in England – saving the blushes of St Martin, Canterbury (Kent).

The present church is in three parts. The nave is partly 18th century and partly Victorian by George Gilbert Scott, replacing the unstable Saxon nave which was lost in the late 18th century. The tower includes fragments from the original 11th-century structure. The chancel, however, is mostly 7th-century Saxon and thus offers at least a relic of the fabric of Bede's church.

The west door leads into the nave, with a wide north aisle that contains an exhibition about Bede's monastery. The various prominent carvings of Christ, St Michael and Bede himself date from 1973 and are by Fenwick Lawson.

Under the tower is a board with what must be the longest list of incumbents in the land, from 674 to today.

The essence of Jarrow is its Saxon chancel, for long the only part of the church in use for worship. Much of the stone is Roman, possibly from the camp at South Shields. The south wall is evidently pre-Conquest, with high small windows, some open, some filled in and some with ancient stone shutters. One of the windows contains Saxon stained glass, excavated from the site and inserted in 1980. This is reputedly the oldest such glass in western Europe.

In the north wall is glass by John Piper, depicting the Jarrow double cross set against a deep blue background, the two Bs standing for Benedict Biscop, not Bede. The window was unveiled by the then Princess of Wales in 1985. The chancel also contains a medieval bishop's chair and some fine poppyheads of men with their tongues sticking out. A jaded floor carpet adds an unnecessarily domestic touch to this remarkable shrine.

LANCHESTER
All Saints *
Early Gothic tympanum, Roman monument

Lanchester speaks both Norman and Early Gothic. Ostensibly it is cold and over-restored, but the Norman chancel arch, thick with zigzag, forms a splendid frame for the exceptionally tall east wall lancets beloved of the Early Goths in the north-east. The church contains much Roman stonework, mostly from the Roman fort after which the village is named.

The nave is heavily restored Norman Transitional but the piers of the north arcade are Roman monoliths from the camp, ancient giants pressed into the service of history. Beyond its splendid arc, the chancel is Early Gothic. Over the vestry door is a minor gem, a carved tympanum in the cusped arch to the vestry door, much bashed but still showing a Christ with angels, and griffins below. Carved heads flank two sanctuary windows. Lanchester's walls are plastered and demonstrate how much better carved stone appears when set in a limewashed background. The chancel retains some of the original choir stalls and there are fragments of medieval glass in a south window.

In the porch is a Roman altar dedicated to Garmangabis with the name of the relevant emperor (Gordian) scratched out. It was supposedly erected by mercenaries from the Suebi tribe in Germany, used to garrison Britain in the 3rd century. I noticed that at the time of my visit the Durham Light Infantry was repaying the compliment by serving on garrison duty in Germany. The more things change the more they are the same.

MONKWEARMOUTH
St Peter with St Cuthbert *
Tower fragments of Saxon foundation, Kempe window

The church and monastery were founded by Bishop Biscop in 674, ten years after the Synod of Whitby had decided on the rite of the English Church against the Irish missionaries from Iona and in favour of Rome. Biscop was a Northumbrian nobleman firmly in the spirit of the new Church. He made no fewer than six pilgrimages to Rome, returning as an ardent bibliophile and lover of Continental art. He used Gallic masons to build his churches. At Monkwearmouth he undertook to copy the Latin Bible for English use, assisted by his pupil Bede at Jarrow. One copy of this Bible, believed to be original, was recently identified in Florence.

Only the wildest imagination can re-create those times in this suburb of modern Sunderland – despite the admirable museum that is now part of the church. The building is marooned amid housing estates, protected only by a moat of roads on the far side of the River Wear. Ancient history can surely have no more improbable setting.

The church is mostly a Victorian rebuilding. Only the west tower and wall remain of the earliest foundation. Seen from inside, this wall is but a ghost of glories past. There are Saxon openings in the tower and simple carvings beside the west doorway. These are of monsters with fish-tails and long beaks. Above, at first floor level, is a course of animals. The figure in the gable end, where evidence elsewhere suggests would be a Rood, is said to be of St Peter. Here, says the guide with some desperation, 'you are treading in the footsteps of the saints'. The rest of the interior is well restored, notably the Decorated east window.

The museum in the south-west corner of the church contains fine carvings from the site, as well as photographs of a terrible arson attack in 1984. An excellent Kempe window has been relocated in the museum south wall, so positioned that it can be studied in detail.

ROKER
St Andrew ***
Gallery of 'Arts and Crafts'

Roker surpasses Monkwearmouth in the modest canon of Sunderland churches. This once-prosperous suburb to the north of the town has a church that was commissioned in 1903 by a labourer turned shipyard millionaire, Sir John Priestman. It was built in 1906–7.

This adventurous patron invited a design from E. S. Prior, then doyen of the

Arts and Crafts Movement. The resulting church, though little-known, deserves to rank with J. D. Sedding's Holy Trinity, Sloane St (London) and C. Harrison Townsend's Great Warley (Essex) among the masterpieces of early 20th-century art. St Andrew's is no humble seaside chapel. It is huge, boasting the same title, 'cathedral of the Arts and Crafts Movement', claimed by Holy Trinity.

The exterior of St Andrew's is massive and strong, as if Roker were still warding off Vikings. The east tower has polygonal corner turrets, its cold grey stone defying the North Sea wind. The interior is spectacular. Sweeping concrete arches run the length of the nave, rising in an elliptical curve from floor to apex. This feature was used by W. R. Lethaby, architect of Brockhampton (Herefs), with whom Prior worked in the office of Norman Shaw. It also occurs in contemporary American work by Frank Lloyd Wright. Sunderland people like to see the ellipse motif as the ribs of an upturned ship, as was always implied by the word nave.

St Andrew's is a rich gallery of ecclesiastical art. The font is by A. Randall Wells, with four foliated legs supporting a deep bowl, topped by a cover by Thompson of Kilburn (in North Yorkshire, not London). The nave includes a number of plaques with lettering by Eric Gill. The lectern is the masterpiece of the Arts and Crafts artist, Ernest Gimson. It is wood, inlaid with ebony, ivory and mother-of-pearl, an outstanding work.

The church tapers towards the east with steps rising to its climax, the chancel set under the tower. Here the reredos and ceiling painting were inserted by Prior in 1927. The reredos is a tapestry of the Adoration by Burne-Jones. The chancel mural of the Creation is by Gill's brother, Macdonald, curving upwards to a sun in the centre of the ceiling. The components of this firmament, water, trees, birds and stars, are wholly original, not Pre-Raphaelite nor Impressionist nor even Post-Impressionist, but a perfect foil for the architecture.

The east window depicts the Ascension, by H. A. Payne of Birmingham. It was singled out by Clifton-Taylor, stern critic of modern glass, as 'having the quality of rich tapestry and glows like jewellery'. Both stained glass and clear glass were meticulously specified by Prior. By day or night, this is a most successful re-creation of the medieval tradition in church design. The ships may have gone from Sunderland and the money with them, but their wealth remains in this fine memorial.

SEAHAM
St Mary *
Kempe windows

What is to become of these coastal settlements, developed on hostile cliffs to house workers digging coal from under the sea? The pits have closed but the people remain trapped on their estates. Miners were well paid and well housed. Some are now trying to give Seaham tourist appeal. But the one thing that might have drawn visitors was the old pithead and that has been ruthlessly demolished. There remains only the North Sea crashing on a sandless shore.

There is also a church, dating from days long before the discovery of coal. St Mary's lies north of the town over a small dell. It is a relic of an early Saxon mission and still has Saxon fragments. The interior is scraped and Victorianised but this has not destroyed its aura. In the nave are deep-splayed Saxon windows, and the chancel has a double piscina, surrounded by nailhead decoration. There are pre-Victorian fittings, including box pews, a rector's and a squire's pew and an Elizabethan pulpit.

St Mary's also has a touch of class, two Kempe windows complete with his wheatsheaf signature. They represent St Mary and St John, St Peter and St Andrew, and are outstanding works. Outside is the old vicarage, a massive pile defying the wind and the sea and protecting the old church from being blown away across the hills.

SEDGEFIELD
St Edmund **
Jacobean screen, shroud brasses

This is smart County Durham. Sedgefield is an old market town within commuting range for middle managers from Teesside. Unlike the similar settlement of Norton, it has not been enveloped by suburb. The centre is well disposed, with houses and pubs round an extensive green. In the centre stands the church, with the old rectory to one side. The fine west tower has bold angle buttresses.

Since the destruction of Brancepeth, Sedgefield is the only church in the north-east to display fittings installed under the influence of Bishop Cosin during the Laudian period in the 1630s. As such it is precious. The interior structure is Early Gothic, the arcade capitals carrying some of the best stiff-leaf in the county. Friendly faces peer out of the foliage and the north-east capital carries a menagerie of mythical beasts.

The fittings, like Brancepeth, were a stylistic marriage of Jacobean and Gothic Revival. Outstanding is the screen, a work of 17th-century carving to rank with St John, Leeds (Yorks,W) and Croscombe (Somerset). Gothic are the canopies and pinnacles, classical the balusters, strapwork and rustication. The detail displays vividly the carver's power to manipulate wood. The same facility is shown in the pews and choir stalls and backs. The reredos is no less remarkable. Giant swags appear to celebrate some celestial fruiterer. The wall panelling is plainer and more classical, and probably dates from *c*.1670.

Sedgefield has two unusual brasses fastened to the nave wall. They depict skeletons tied up in shrouds, a ghoulish form of commemoration.

SOUTH CHURCH
St Andrew, Auckland *
Early Gothic interior, Celtic crosses

On one side of Bishop Auckland rise the palace and the old castle of the Prince Bishops of Durham, proud over the gorge of the River Wear. On the other side, the road towards Shildon and Newton Aycliffe offers a sadder sight. But spirits are lifted by the tower of the largest parish church in the county. It soars over the bypass, with a churchyard rich in tall North Country gravestones and equally noble yews.

South Church is remarkable even in a region blessed with Early Gothic buildings. Its 13th-century design is complete, but for a Perpendicular clerestory and top to the tower. Even the south porch dates from the original building, with two storeys, a stone vault and traceried windows.

The interior is exciting more for its architecture than its atmosphere. The arcades are superb, with shafted piers and complex moulded arches. There is no change in rhythm at the crossing and transepts. The windows are almost all lancets, some grouped, some high and low, most with rere-arches. The stone is warm and the excellent 15th-century choir stalls wonderfully dark.

The roofs are Perpendicular. Only the stained glass lets the side down. That in the south transept is awful, of a 'comic book' quality. The church contains one of the best collections of early Christian stone carvings in the county. Some of this has been refashioned into a single cross, an archaeological liberty that would not be allowed today, but which is wholly enjoyable.

STAINDROP
St Mary **
Neville effigies

Staindrop guards the road into the Pennines from the Tees valley. It is the church of Raby Castle, a Neville fortress, and the family treated it to a medieval college of priests and a chantry. The bulky outline is that of a 12th-century foundation, softened and lightened by Perpendicular additions. When I pushed open the door one winter's Sunday morning, I found an elderly congregation receiving a ferocious sermon on sex. They sat motionless, as if entombed in the place since the 17th century.

Staindrop's porch has an unusual tunnel vault with ribs. The nave arcades are Transitional, the eastern bays with scallop capitals, the western carved out of solid wall. The surfaces have been ruthlessly scraped, some to a soft yellow, some to grimy grey. The south aisle contains a beautiful set of Decorated piscina, sedilia and tomb arch. The screen is said to be the only one surviving from the Middle Ages in the county.

All this is overshadowed by the Neville monuments, which are of the highest quality. Ralph Neville, Earl of Westmorland (d.1425), lies in alabaster, with his two wives in richly flowing costumes. This is one of the most notable alabaster tombs in the country, to rank with those of Harewood (Yorks,W) and Lowick (Northants). The effigy cuts a splendid figure, with moustaches and a chainmail camail or headdress, considered out of date by the early 15th century. At his feet is a rare feature, bedesmen not counting rosaries but kneeling at lecterns. The weeper panels are beautifully crafted. Another Neville, the 5th Earl (d.1560), has an effigy of wood, so old, black and hard that it might be Purbeck marble. The church has monuments of all periods of a quality rare in the northeast, including 19th-century work by Nollekens, Westmacott and, in the churchyard, a mausoleum of 1850 by William Burn.

Essex

Essex is an unfashionable county. It has few big towns, no rolling hills and no dramatic coastline. Barred from the capital by London's rambling eastern suburbs, it is mostly *terra incognita* to those not raised within its borders. Yet for picturesque beauty, the villages of north Essex can equal those of Suffolk. Even the estuarial flatlands have a bleak mystery. Essex churches are full of interest. Stone was never plentiful, even East Anglian flint, and builders often resorted to wood and brick. As masters of brick they were in a class of their own.

The county had the distinction of seeing the first mission of the Northumbrian monks to the south, when St Cedd came to Bradwell. His church, or that of his followers, still lies isolated on a wild eastern shore. Equally distinguished from the pre-Gothic period are the old wooden walls of Greensted, the oldest log-built church in Europe, and the superb wall paintings of Copford. The Norman arcades at Waltham Abbey stand by the M25 as a fragment of one of England's most famous monastic foundations. The Goths left the glorious Reticulated window at Tilty, the screen at Finchingfield and the wealthy churches at Thaxted and Saffron Walden. The wooden towers of Blackmore and Margaretting are unique to the county, as are the brick towers of Ingatestone, Fryerning and Layer Marney.

Essex offers a feast of lesser treasures: the French glass at Rivenhall, the acrobats frieze at Lawford and the Tree of Jesse window at Margaretting, each a work of art in itself. At Great Warley, the Edwardian C. Harrison Townsend created a masterpiece of the Arts and Crafts Movement that deserves to be better known.

Blackmore **
Bradwell-on-Sea **
Brightlingsea *
Castle Hedingham **
Chickney *
Copford ****
East Horndon *
Finchingfield **
Fryerning *
Great Bardfield *

Great Bromley **
Great Warley ***
Greensted **
Hatfield Broad Oak *
Ingatestone *
Lambourne End *
Lawford **
Layer Marney ***
Little Dunmow **
Little Easton **

Maldon **
Margaretting *
Radwinter *
Rivenhall *
Saffron Walden ***
Stebbing *
Thaxted ****
Tilty **
Waltham Abbey ****

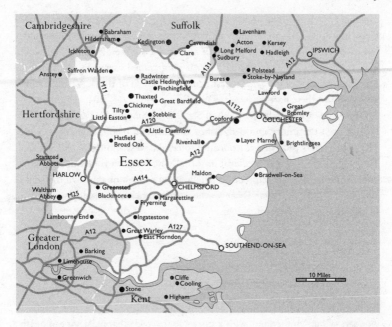

BLACKMORE
St Laurence **
Wooden Gothic tower

The church, relic of a Norman priory, is isolated at the end of a lane next to a house called Jericho. Its glory is its tower, to Pevsner 'one of the most impressive, if not the most impressive, of all timber towers of England'. Dating from the 1480s, this structure rises in three diminishing stages to a broach spire, each stage with a lean-to roof and sheltering eaves. The bottom stage is timber-framed and plastered, the others shingled. These storeys are more than just roofs, for this is true woodland architecture. Its builders were seeking to rival in wood the work of contemporaries in brick and stone.

The church is approached from the north, where a long tiled nave roof sweeps down to the tops of Tudor windows. Inside, we turn at once to the tower chamber, guarded by a Norman wall that was once the west wall of the priory church. Its origins are indicated by a high arched doorway, two deeply splayed windows and a circular gable window. Beyond is all engineering: a maze of oak beams and cross-braces towers above a base of ten central posts. The beams are supported on Gothic arches of wood.

The remainder of the church is less spectacular. This was the nave of the former priory church. It has a Decorated north arcade that runs through to the sanctuary, with Norman arches at either end. Its chief curiosity is north arcade piers of stone and south ones of brick, presumably a cheap 16th-century insertion. At the east end of the south aisle is the outline of a door that would have led to the old priory cloister. Over it is an animal variously described as a rat, a salamander or a boar, the last being an emblem of the de Veres, a family ubiquitous in these parts.

Opposite is a fine alabaster tomb of Sir Thomas Smyth (d.1594) and his wife. He acquired the priory and demolished the east end of the church in *c.*1580. The parishioners took him to court to protect the west end from a similar fate. The effigies are stiff and medieval in form, lying on mats rolled up as pillows under their heads. The sculpture is detailed and of high quality. On the wall is a tablet of 1881 to Edgar Disney, who also secured memorials to himself at Ingatestone and Fryerning.

BRADWELL-ON-SEA
St Peter-on-the-Wall **
Saxon mission, wild coastal setting

Bradwell is lost England. Arthur Mee coloured it purple: 'one of the forgotten wonders of our Motherland, with a story and spectacle that must stir our hearts. We are here at the dawn of our history.' Amen to that. The Essex between the Blackwater and Crouch rivers is as isolated as anywhere in England. Cabbage fields and a scattering of weekend cottages lead only to the sea. There is nothing else beyond Burnham to the south and Maldon to the north, not surprisingly considered a suitable site for a nuclear power station. The land sinks to flatness. Trees shrivel and the sky assumes command.

Here the Romans built an extensive fort, probably *Othona*, later settled by the Saxons but eventually lost beneath the beach. It was here that St Cedd came from Lindisfarne to convert the heathen southerners to Christianity. King Oswald of Northumbria (604–42) had earlier invited Aidan and his monks from Iona to convert Northumbria, a mission so successful that Cedd, one of Aidan's followers, was sent south to Essex in 654. Augustine had already landed in Kent in 597 but his mission at Canterbury did not proselytise with the same zeal as the northern monks. Cedd returned to the north for the Synod of Whitby in 664 and died of plague soon after.

The chapel would have had a tower and apse. Both must have collapsed and at some indeterminate time the nave became a barn. It was not restored until the 1920s and stands today half a mile across the fields from the nearest road, overlooking the saltings and beach. The church retains lofty Saxon pro-portions, though the roof is modern. The walls are rubble, patched and scarred over the ages to the point where the liturgical significance of the structure is obscure. The stone comes from the old fort, with some Roman tiles reused as dressings. The outlines of openings in the side walls indicate nothing more exciting than old doorways for farm vehicles. The deep-splayed windows in the south wall are original.

Fragments of an original chancel arch can be seen in the east wall, dividing the apse from the nave. It appears that there were two arches, rather than the usual single or triple arch. This suggests that the nave may have been divided into two by a curtain, with men worshipping on one side and women on the other, a pattern known in other Celtic churches. The present church has a simple modern crucifix in the Celtic style and an altar inlaid with stones from Iona, Lindisfarne (Northumb) and Lastingham (Yorks, N), sister communities of Cedd's ministry.

Is Bradwell the oldest church in England? The guide claims so. But St Martin, Canterbury (Kent) is dated by Bede as pre-Augustinian. Jarrow and Monkwearmouth (both Durham) are of the 670s, but this assumes that Bradwell was built, or a church on this site consecrated, on Cedd's arrival in the 650s. Escomb (Durham) also claims to be before the Synod of Whitby. It is possible that Saxons built Bradwell after Cedd's death. Who knows? We are safe in saying it is very old. Less old is the ugly vestry hut built next to it.

BRIGHTLINGSEA
All Saints *
Essex tower, 'insurance' sculpture

This is a land of reed and marsh, of long sea views and seagulls. I was once stranded here in a dinghy as a boy and had to wade ashore through thick mud, aiming for the tower of 'Brittlesey' church in the distance, a beacon of blessed dryness. The church lies a mile inland from the old quay, on what in Essex qualifies as a hill.

The tower is one of the finest in the county. The diagonal buttresses have statue niches and the west front is the equal of Stoke-by-Nayland (Suffolk). An ogee hood crowns the door and finishes proud of the window. On top of the tower is that rare thing for Essex, a pierced battlement, built in 1490. The church's principal benefactor was the Beriffe family, merchants who brought the port its 15th-century prosperity. In 1531 John Beriffe left to the Lady Chapel 'three-quarters of the ship called Trinitie, if God send her well home'. Presumably He did.

The exterior walls include fine flint flushwork. The interior is spare and simple. A Victorian frieze round the nave commemorates every Brightlingsea sailor who died at sea, a grim harvest when recorded en masse. The glass is clear, which compensates for the lack of a clerestory. The Beriffes are well represented by brasses in the north chapel. In the chancel is one surprise they would have appreciated, a huge monument to a German insurance broker, Nicholas Magens, who died in 1764 'worth £100,000'. It is composed of a winged female holding a scroll and leaning on a globe, attended by ships and cherubs. The sculptor is the little-known Nicholas Read. The insurance business was never so well portrayed.

CASTLE HEDINGHAM
St Nicholas **
Hammerbeam roof, de Vere heraldry

On the hill stands what remains of the castle of the de Veres, Earls of Oxford but lords of Essex and Suffolk, their pennant fluttering in the wind. Down in the smoke of the village lies the church, its tower echoing the keep on the hill. Both are big, aristocratic buildings, which today look disdainfully out over the housing estates of the upper River Colne.

From the entrance to the churchyard, the church presents a Norman chancel with an east wheel window and steep roof. In front of it stands a tall Norman cross, its decoration apparently carved on a Saxon upright. The contrasting tower is a Tudor affair with buttresses, battlements, pinnacles and a stair turret with 18th-century cupola. Over the west window are the badges of the 16th-century John de Vere, including his whistle and chain (as High Admiral), his chair of estate (as Great Chamberlain), the ox and ford (the rebus of Earl of Oxford) and the de Vere five-pointed star.

The interior is big and Norman, lifted into the air by its magnificent double hammerbeam roof (*c.*1535), every bit a match for the boisterous Norman of the nave below. The nave displays a mix of rounded and pointed arches, lightened above by a spacious clerestory. The church is proud of its doors, of which it still has three intact from the Norman period. The south door is known as the 'skin' door, for traces of human skin were once found pinned to it. This ancient and horrible practice is believed to have been a punishment, clearly ineffective as a deterrent, for stealing from a church.

The chancel is reached through a superb screen of *c.*1400. It has open ogee arches rising through Panel tracery to an embossed frieze. But the cusping inside the arches and the spandrels pierced like lace collars suggest a carver of almost oriental delicacy. The Norman chancel has windows united by continuous arcading. Here too is another de Vere, the 15th Earl of Oxford (d.1539), whose tomb chest has a relief of a man and a woman carved on the black marble top. It is unusually deep-cut, half way between an effigy and an incised slab.

CHICKNEY
St Mary *
Isolated setting, figurative carvings

This must be Essex's most improbable church. It lies detached from any village beyond an asparagus farm. Pheasants rise shrieking from an overgrown church-yard, which is sheltered by chestnuts and sycamores. Nothing else moves or breathes. The church has a dunce's cap for a spire. The interior is small and atmospheric, with a chancel askew and a nave that is not quite a rectangle. The original windows, one of which is Saxon, are so narrow that light relies on two later Perpendicular openings. The font, with ogee canopies, is superb.

The chancel is almost as wide as the nave. The stone altar was recovered from some pre-Reformation concealment. Above it are fine carvings of a man and a woman. These tiny fragments are a delight, vernacular art displayed in the simplest yet most public way. The chancel is filled with furniture, like an old attic. An iron candelabra stands ready with candles over the nave, should anyone require nocturnal worship. Though redundant, the church is still supplied with candles and fresh flowers. Chickney is not unloved.
[CCT]

COPFORD
St Michael ****
12th-century wall paintings

The sumptuousness of Copford is explained by the presence of Copford Hall, ancient manor of the Bishops of London. Its great cedars offer a splendid backdrop to the approach to the church from the road. Even they are scant preparation for the interior. Copford's Norman wall paintings are among the best in England, ranking with those of Ickleton (Cambs) and Kempley (Gloucs).

Copford is a 12th-century church, heavily restored. The inside is at first sight odd. The nave walls have three springers of a lost tunnel vault, rare in a parish church. The removal of the vault was probably to avert a collapse, since the roof is clearly 15th century. The south arcade appears to be mainly late 13th century, but its arches are so varied that it is hard to believe they are of the same date. The eastern one appears Transitional Norman, the middle one looks late 13th century and is partly of brick. If so, this is among the earliest medieval brick in England, some of it possibly reused Roman brick.

Paintings cover almost all the wall surfaces. As at Kempley they were applied to wet plaster, and were thus more robust than later medieval works. None-theless, all have been restored with varying degrees of vehemence after their discovery in the 19th century under layers of Reformation whitewash. Those in the apse were overpainted by Daniel Bell in the 1870s. It is known that he added a number of details of his own, including a crown on Christ's head. The Annunciation above the chancel arch is a completely Victorian work. All have recently been restored 'as found', with overpainting left in place.

The details of the paintings are covered in the guide. Those in the chancel are the familiar Byzantine/Romanesque characters of the saints and apostles surrounding Christ in Majesty. Here Bell's decorative flourishes can seem intrusive, especially round the windows, which are filled with fierce Victorian glass. The underside of the chancel arch carries the signs of the zodiac, as a link between the Earthly and Heavenly realms. The Copford masterpiece is in the nave above the pulpit, a rare example of the Raising of Jairus's Daughter, clearly still in its 12th-century form. This story was often taken as a metaphor of the Resurrection, with the father pleading with Christ, who gazes into the distance. Much of the nave painting is abstract, almost Art Deco.

A huge wooden frame supports the bell loft at the west end of the nave. The original Perpendicular screen survives and the Victorian pulpit includes a charming St Michael on its newel post. On the floor are original tiles and, in the chancel, mosaics. I am told that those by the pulpit were designed by women from Abingdon prison.

EAST HORNDON
All Saints *
Tyrell family pews

An easy church to see but hard to reach. Despite its prominence on a hill behind the Halfway House Inn, it must be gained from the lane to the north and then across a field. On a clear day East Horndon has a marvellous view south to Tilbury and the Thames. Perhaps due to its proximity to London, Essex has had the most unscrupulous church wreckers in England. East Horndon appears to have been their favourite spot, as the guide never ceases to point out. But in the 1970s the church was rescued from decay and brought to its present happy if somewhat denuded state within the care of the Churches Conservation Trust. A statue by Nollekens has had to be removed to the Victoria and Albert Museum for safe keeping.

The church is entirely of 15th- and 16th-century brick with a prominent south chapel and eccentric tower parapet. On a sunny day, the inside is all brightness and jollity, thanks to a German bomb that removed its Victorian glass in the war. The church was rebuilt by the Tyrell family in the 1440s, their work including the roofs, south chapel (for their memorials) and transept galleries. The galleries may have been to house chantry priests, but later became family pews and are not unlike opera boxes, looking down on the nave. The

Tyrell Chapel retains one unstolen work, the inscribed limestone slab of Alice Tyrell (d.1422), wife of the Speaker of the Commons. It portrays a woman in 15th-century dress, in the style of a brass but mercifully more durable. She lies flanked by saints in niches beneath a vaulted canopy.

The guide recounts the tale of a Tudor rector of East Horndon, Robert Hunter, whose long incumbency saw him charged with slander, bigamy, beating, chaining his wife to a post and illegal logging. None of this appears to have undermined his job security. A hundred years later a visitor reported that the church was in decay, its monuments 'all torne or worne out, their sepulchres like all the rest foulie defaced'. Perhaps our times are not the worst.
[CCT]

FINCHINGFIELD
St John **
Picturesque setting, jolly corbel heads

Finchingfield is a village to rank with Suffolk's finest. Rows of medieval cottages look across the stream which bisects the green. Ducks waddle over a hump-backed bridge. On one side is the pub, on another a windmill and on a third, the church. The composition is flawless.

The church lies up a steep rise, from where its thick Norman tower looms like a bastion. The exterior is of flint, stone and brick, used apparently at random. The interior is rendered dim by tinted rather than stained glass. On a sunny day this conveys an impression of being under water. The screens are the best in Essex. The earliest, in the south aisle, has Decorated tracery with a gallery of grotesques and a figure playing bagpipes. The rood screen is Perpendicular but of great complexity. The arches have bunches of grapes for crockets.

In the south chapel beneath a wall entirely composed of painted organ pipes is the Berners tomb of 1523, topped by brasses of a man and wife in 'playing-card' costumes. Their faces are caricatures from the engraver's assembly line, with wide eyes and large noses. There are weepers round the chest. Finchingfield has excellent corbel heads, leaping from the walls, smiling, grimacing, in various forms of headgear, but all with faces that seem real. They were presumably based on the people of the village, a genre of local art that was respected by iconoclasts throughout England.

FRYERNING
St Mary *
'Essex' brick tower, Airey Neave window

We could be nowhere but Essex. The church sits on a small eminence attended by a grove of Scots pines amid open fields. The walls are of any material that came to hand, puddingstone, chalk, brick and flint, like a fruit cake. The tower is big, of redbrick with a blue brick diaper pattern. The link with neighbouring Ingatestone is both architectural and historical. The church was acquired by Sir Nicholas Wadham, whose wife was a daughter of William Petre of Ingatestone. Wadham College, Oxford, still holds the living.

The tower appears to predate Ingatestone and the Petre connection. It replaced a wooden tower, presumably like those at Blackmore and Margaretting, in the early 16th century when the church was still owned by the Knights Hospitallers. The architect may have been Girolamo de Trevizi, the Italian who worked at Hampton Court for Wolsey and at neighbouring Layer Marney.

The 16th-century church was refashioned from the ghost of an 11th-century foundation. Five Norman windows are still visible on the outside wall, as are the round arches on the doors. The interior is unspectacular, with a number of 20th-century insertions. The Norman font has ancient symbols, including a Tree of Jesse and a cross and crown. Two Norman windows have vivid 20th-century glass.

The church contains a memorial to Airey Neave MP, a native of the parish who was killed by the IRA in 1979. The window, set in the north wall, was designed by Neave's cousin Penelope and portrays St Michael and St Christopher. Roundels show the two buildings with which his career was most associated, Colditz Castle, in which he was imprisoned during the war, and the Houses of Parliament.

GREAT BARDFIELD
St Mary *
Stone rood screen

North Essex has a genius for attractive villages and Great Bardfield is one of them. A combination of Victorian poverty and 20th-century prosperity has preserved its charm. As often, the cottages developed on common land away from the medieval manor and church, the latter now somewhat isolated from the village. The tower is like a Norman keep but with a vivid Oxford dark blue clock on its north face, for some reason repainted from an earlier Cambridge light blue.

The nave is gloomy, darkened by glass that not even the clerestory can outwit. This at least sheds mystery on Bardfield's treasure, its screen. Great Bardfield and its neighbour, Stebbing, claim to possess the only two complete stone screens surviving in England, though there are others, including Totnes (Devon) and Westwell (Kent). Great Bardfield has two Perpendicular shafts dividing it into three parts and the tracery has several subsidiary ogees. It is plainly late 14th century and a fine work. The rood figures are Victorian, added by Bodley.

GREAT BROMLEY
St George **
Carved capitals, Red Indian window

The church is moored on its mound across a small meadow like a pocket battleship, tall, compact and powerful. The tower is a stocky version of neighbouring Brightlingsea, with a double-stepped parapet and pinnacles. It has a familiar Essex support of diagonal and angle buttresses. The porch might be a work apart, a casket of flint and stone flushwork. The inner door is guarded by flying figures of Adam and Eve.

Great Bromley's interior is dominated by one of the county's finest roofs (with Castle Hedingham). This is a double hammerbeam, still with much of its paintwork. Every inch is carved, including the spandrels, the frieze, and the saints on the posts and corbels. Sadly the angels on the lower hammerbeams are missing, removed in the 19th century as dangerous. Even more remarkable are the three Decorated capitals of the south arcade. They are mostly of acanthus, but the westernmost is a gallery of superb grotesques, low enough to be studied properly. A dragon is swallowing a man; a man with his tongue out is being bitten on the cheeks by a frog and a fish monster; two angels are holding hands. Such intimate delights make church visiting a joy.

The north aisle contains a shrine to the Stone family, who left for America in 1634 and regularly return to pay homage to their Essex forebears. The stained glass window duly depicts a Red Indian. The tower chamber includes a row of bowler hats belonging to past bell-ringers. The earliest is 1716 and the most recent 1972. There is much wall yet to fill.

GREAT WARLEY
St Mary ***
Arts and Crafts

In 1876 a young stockbroker named Evelyn Heseltine acquired a cottage called Goldings in Great Warley and proceeded to establish himself as a latter-day lord of the manor. In 1902 he agreed to donate both land and £5,000 to a build a new church, with C. Harrison Townsend as architect and William Reynolds-Stephens as interior designer. The result is one of the most exciting Arts and Crafts interiors in England. That its treasures require it to be kept locked is sad, mitigated by the eagerness of the wardens to open it to those asking for admittance.

The exterior appears to be a modest neo-Gothic chapel with shingled spire and belfry, set in a well-tended churchyard of yews. Only the ironwork on the drainpipes hints at something special within. The interior plan consists of nave and transepts but no aisles, with an apsidal east end. There is a wagon roof. The interest of the church lies in the furnishings, as complete a programme of early 20th-century design as anything by Charles Rennie Mackintosh or Otto Wagner.

The nave is panelled in wood with marquetry. The electroliers are of cast iron but decorated with enamel and glass beads. The roof has broad ribs of aluminium leaf, decorated with reliefs of giant rose trees, each resting on a panel of lilies, symbol of the church's patron saint, the Virgin Mary. Font, pulpit and lectern are Art Nouveau, the first of marble, the second and third of metal panels beaten into extraordinary natural shapes. The pulpit is cruciform, with stylised bronze trees supporting the arms of the Cross recalling the purest Gothic naturalism.

Moving east we find the parclose screen is of walnut and the chancel screen composed of brass rose trees, rising from their roots and ending with angels in their flowers. The rood cross is inscribed with the word 'love'. Yet even this is surpassed by the organ case, a variety of metal panels with rose trees and hearts in abundance. Beyond stands the reredos, Reynolds-Stephens's climax. Here on a marble base are brass, pewter, mother-of-pearl against a background of aluminium leaf and decorated with grapes, symbol of the Eucharist. On to this falls light from windows also designed by Reynolds-Stephens, in the Morris style. A wondrous church.

GREENSTED
St Andrew **
Oldest wooden nave in Europe

Greensted church lies in a delightful glade, within striking distance of the London Underground, yet as rural as any in Essex. An ancient lane leads through the woods to a small clearing filled with wild flowers in spring. The white weatherboarded tower, shingled broach spire and steeply pitched nave roof are picturesque, not at all the image of an East London suburb.

The age of Greensted is controversial. To past experts this is not just the one surviving 'log church' in England, but also very old, indeed Saxon. It was said to be one of the shrines at which St Edmund's body rested in 1013, on its ceremonial journey from London to Edmund's grave at Bury in Suffolk. The oldest parts of the structure are the dark split logs forming the nave walls. The rest of the building is Tudor and Victorian. These are the only split log walls in England, though many exist in Scandinavia.

Tree-ring dating carried out on the timbers in 1960 suggested a date of c.850. This would be some two centuries after St Cedd landed at Bradwell, adding extraordinary antiquity to Greensted's unique construction. On that basis, tourists have flocked to Greensted, drawn by the force of the child's question, 'Could these trees have been acorns when Jesus was on earth?' But later tree-ring dating in 1995 suggested a date around the Conquest, in the late 11th century. More research is under way and there is a helpful and honest *erratum* in the guidebook. In the meantime, Greensted is still the oldest wooden church in the world and probably the oldest wooden building standing in Europe.

The church remains charming. The chancel is Tudor and of brick, the nave roof is late Victorian, as is much of the remaining woodwork. The chancel stained glass is dreadful. Set into the roof is a Victorian beam, its carving depicting the legend of St Edmund's head, which was guarded by a dog after decapitation.

HATFIELD BROAD OAK
St Mary *
Queen Anne woodwork, modern 'acorn' kneelers

The village is set in the rolling countryside between the Rodings and Hatfield forest. A well-treed churchyard surrounds a church that survives from the remains of a Norman Benedictine priory. Following a quarrel between monks and parishioners, the church was divided c.1378, and the parochial west end survives as the present church. The monastic part was demolished after the Reformation, but traces can be detected beyond the present east wall. This is de Vere country. A de Vere founded the priory and another lies in effigy in the centre of the choir, carved in chainmail in the act of drawing his sword. There was an inexhaustible supply of de Veres to be interred in the family's many East Anglian churches.

This is a church of furnishings. The Perpendicular interior is dominated by a single work, the 18th-century candelabra which hangs low over the nave. This must have been even more prominent when ablaze with candles on a dark night. Above is a gallery of fine corbel heads. The chancel reredos and altar rail were carved by John Woodward (c.1700) in the style of Grinling Gibbons. A settle by the same hand is at the back of the south aisle by the font. At the same time, the early 1700s, a library was built on the east side of the church and this still exists, a rare survival in a parish church (the most valuable books are in the county archive).

Hatfield Broad Oak has an exceptionally fine set of 180 modern kneelers, made in 1988–9. Their dominant terracotta colour was taken from the chancel tiles. The pictures are partly biblical, partly local, as was the medieval tradition of church craftsmanship. All carry the local emblem of acorns and oak leaves.

INGATESTONE
St Edmund and St Mary *
Brick tower, Petre monuments

When Arthur Mee passed through Ingatestone before the last war, he noted 'the windmill is still at work crushing oats and beans with stones turned by wooden cog wheels'. No more. The modern village has lost its charm and the church is an aristocrat lost amid the housing estates.

That said, nothing can detract from its tower. Essex towers are not the timid brick turrets of the Thames valley. They are huge, reflecting the ostentatious power of the county's Tudor potentates. This one is magnificent, a unified Perpendicular composition of redbrick with black Tudor diapering. Strong angle buttresses rise to a heavy battlemented crown, the bell-openings plain. The guide suggests that it is made of a million bricks. The brick even trespasses inside, forming half the piers in the six-bay arcade.

On the Dissolution, Ingatestone passed to Sir William Petre, Secretary of State to Henry VIII. He rebuilt the south chapel for the use of the almshouses and as a vault for family burials. Petre served three Tudor monarchs and must have been lucky to die in his bed in 1572. He lies between chancel and chapel, celebrated in alabaster, clad in armour and with his wife by his side. Both gaze up in admiration at the family's coat of arms. The tomb is of the best early classical craftsmanship, attributed to the court mason, Cornelius Cure. The church is filled with Petres. Also in the south chapel are two fine wall memorials, one to Robert Petre (d.1593), the other to a sea captain, John Troughton, of thirty years later. It is by Epiphanius Evesham, one of the most distinguished of early 17th-century sculptors.

LAMBOURNE END
St Mary *
Manorial setting, Georgian chancel beam

Lambourne End lies in the armpit of the M11 and M25, yet here the suburbs retreat and a country lane leads uphill through fields and oak woods. We pass Lambourne House and, beyond a scatter of cottages, Lambourne Hall.

Opposite the Hall, in what now seems deepest country, sits a church that is faintly New England in character. It has been patched together from Norman, Gothic and 18th-century fragments. The spacious churchyard merges into the surrounding parkland and includes a magnificent cedar tree.

The west gable and bell-tower are white clapboard, the spire broached. The inside is a surprise. Under a 17th-century gallery over the west door are wooden struts holding up the tower. The nave is bridged by a wide Georgian chancel arch crowned with a coat of arms and two hatchments. Behind, the chancel beams are cloaked in Georgian decoration, their king-posts covered in acanthus. The chancel walls are 12th century, yet remodelled in the early 18th, 'boldly, naively, and very successfully' says Pevsner in a curious run of epithets.

A sign outside proclaims 'no artificial flowers'. Why then do they allow composition headstones, bane of English churchyards?

LAWFORD
St Mary **
Decorated chancel, tumblers window

The church lies up a rural lane on the outskirts of Manningtree, set in an immaculate churchyard. The tower is eccentric even by Essex standards, a cocktail of grey-black flint, ginger septaria stone, brown puddingstone and various colours of brick. Given that these materials decay at different rates, the structure must be in a state of perpetual convalescence.

The nave is 14th century and of little interest, but the chancel is exquisite. Lawford displays all the originality and verve of Decorated Gothic at its peak. It contains nine big windows, all with unconventional tracery. The mullions seem to acquire a life of their own as they reach the head of each opening. The windows are framed by shafts and arches carved with foliage, interspersed with owls, thrushes and squirrels. Each is part of a pattern, yet each a design on its own. Around the easternmost north window is a celebrated sequence of village tumblers, each holding the leg of the one above. This acrobats window is unique, as delightful as any figure carving in an English church.

The piscina-sedilia group is of miraculous detail, only slightly defaced by iconoclasm. We are left wondering, was each piece the work of a separate, perhaps rival, mason or was a single master in charge of the whole? As with the sepulchre at Hawton (Notts) or the corbels at Patrington (Yorks, ER), we long to see into the minds of these craftsmen. The art displayed in England's churches in the decades immediately before the Black Death has not been equalled since.

LAYER MARNEY
St Mary ***
Marney Chapel and tombs, St Christopher mural

With the end of the Wars of the Roses and the advent of the Tudors, many simple country squires rose to become powers in the land. Sir Henry Marney was one such. As Lord Marney he became privy councillor to Henry VII and Henry VIII, head of the latter's bodyguard, Sheriff of Essex and Lord Privy Seal. Here at his country estate he planned a gatehouse and palace to rival Hampton Court. Begun *c.*1520, it rose higher than any domestic building in England, decorated with similar Italian terracotta to that on the gateway at Hampton. It is one of the last ostentations of the Middle Ages. By 1525 both Marney and his son were dead. The palace was left unfinished.

A church worthy of this setting was built to the rear of the house. The approach is across wide East Anglian contours from the Colchester road. This is brick country and the church, like the gatehouse, has brick walls, buttresses, porches, mouldings and battlements. The brick tower is similar to those at Ingatestone and Fryerning, Perpendicular with Tudor arches to the windows and bell-openings. The most unusual feature is, on the north side, a complete priest's extension with chimney.

The interior is light and open in its spaces, the nave bare except for a wall painting of St Christopher of uncertain date. This is in good repair (or good restoration) and shows a river bank on which a man sits fishing while the saint performs his miracle. It is one of the most charming depictions of the story. The screen is poorly carved, as is the Tudor pulpit and tester.

The excitement is in the Marney Chapel, divided off by a linenfold panelled screen. Here a large Tudor fireplace has recently been uncovered, supplied by Marney for the comfort of the two priests and five bedesmen paid to say Mass here each day. They must have made a jolly community round their fire and we wonder if they survived the later suppression of chantries under their patron's boss, Henry VIII.

The tombs are an excellent collection. One, dating from an earlier church, is of Sir William Marney (d.1414). With Gothic posts and leopards standing guard, it was moved from a former position in the middle of the chancel. Fourteenth-century grandees were accustomed to rising at the Resurrection directly facing the altars they had financed. The tomb of Lord (Henry) Marney (d.1523), builder of tower and church, lies between chancel and chapel. It is richly worked, with an elaborate canopy, decorated with early classical forms including balusters and dolphins. Most audaciously it has a Gothic vault with classical Ionic capitals as pendants. The effigy is in black marble but the chest is terracotta, similar to that used on the gatehouse decoration. It is, as Pevsner implies, a struggle between new style and old, Renaissance with 'a Gothic hangover'.

The third tomb is to Henry's son John, who travelled with him to the Field of the Cloth of Gold and who died just two years after him. This is similar, though without a canopy, and is probably by the same hand, the face being that of a young man. The east window is filled with Marney heraldic glass. The chapel is a splendid memorial to a transient glory.

LITTLE DUNMOW
Priory of St Mary **
Flitch Chair, Fitzwalter monument

First the story of the flitch. In the Middle Ages, when marriage was taken less seriously than today, the Church tried to encourage couples to sanctify what were usually informal relationships with the bond of 'holy wedlock'. Many incentives to win the Church this matrimonial monopoly were tried. The priors of Little Dunmow hit on the idea of offering any couple who agreed to be married in church and remain 'unregreted' for a year the reward of a side (or flitch) of bacon. Such marriages were said to have 'brought home the bacon', or been a success. The tradition stopped only with the Dissolution of the priory. The manorial lord revived the quaint custom in the 18th century, but stopped it again when a couple sold slices of the bacon to tourists, presumably as a 'marital aid'. The tradition is commemorated in the local pub.

The priory has gone the way of the bacon but its south chapel, now the parish church, still stands, incongruous on a lawn next to a housing estate. It became ruinous but was heavily restored in the 19th century, with five large south buttresses and an effete bell-tower. The buttresses separate four superb Decorated windows, testament to the wealth of the 14th-century monastery.

Inside, the original north arcade separating the present church from the old chancel survives and displays some of the richest Norman Transitional carving in Essex. Even finer is the arcading between the windows on the south wall. This rises the full height of the walls. Spandrels are adorned with animals, flowers and human faces. The piscina even has a floral plughole. The window tracery is more conventional than at Tilty or Lawford, but still diverting.

In the chancel stands the Flitch Chair, once used in the bacon ceremony. It is made of an old stall and was exhibited at the Victoria and Albert Museum in 1930. A monument at the back of the church has superb alabaster effigies to the last of the Fitzwalters, one-time barons of Magna Carta. They are of Walter (d.1432) and his wife Elizabeth, he in fine armour, she in medieval costume. Another effigy of a lady is earlier and, though serene, is less accomplished. Since her identity is unknown legend runs rife. She is variously Fitzwalter's mother, a

Fitzwalter who died resisting the advances of King John, or even Robin Hood's Maid Marion.

LITTLE EASTON
St Mary **
Bourchier brass, bomber window

Victorian almshouses stretch along the road. A rambling 17th-century manor house stands next door. This is the valley of the River Chelmer north of Dunmow, which some visitors say is 'like Suffolk', but Essex people say is 'like Essex'. The church is externally disappointing, apparently Victorian with neo-Norman windows to the south chapel. The first impression of the interior is little better, except that few churches of this size are so richly endowed with furnishings.

These start with two 12th-century wall paintings, apparently of Christ in a style like that of a Sienese icon. Opposite are eight Gothic panels, depicting the Passion. Though blackened by time they are in a good state, replicated in drawings below. The chancel contains a sumptuous wall monument to Lady Alianore Bourchier, who died *c.*1400. Instead of an effigy there is a tiny stone knight, faceless and without his hands, oddly incongruous in this grand setting. Opposite are the iron gates to the Bourchier/Maynard Chapel, apparently moved from the manor. The tomb chest of Henry, Viscount Bourchier (d.1483), is crowned by a superb brass, including traces of its original coloured enamelling. His successor at the manor, Henry Maynard (d.1610), is shown with his six sons and two daughters. The children who died in infancy are portrayed holding skulls.

By the time the tomb of William Maynard and his wife was erected, probably in the late 17th century, style had been transformed. The figures now stand life-size, in Roman costume. The inscription describes Maynard as a Royalist. He was 'well calculated to supply the place of a prince, the defender of the peace, the laws and the Anglo-Catholic faith. When the madness of fanatics daily increased, when even religion itself was banished, then he bid adieu to a restless, rebellious and ungrateful country.'

Also on the west wall is a bust of the grand-daughter of the last Lord Maynard, Frances Evelyn, Countess of Warwick (d.1938). A famous beauty, she was also a socialist and local benefactress, depicted here by Edward Boehm. A curious abstract panel behind the pulpit, by the Art Nouveau artist Alfred Gilbert, recalls visits to the house by Ellen Terry. The theatre that she created from the barn behind the church survives in use to this day.

The north transept forms a memorial to the American bombers based here during the war. The windows are garishly militaristic. Christ is shown blessing a sky thick with warplanes, while the emblems equate the crews with medieval crusaders.

MALDON
All Saints **
Decorated arcading, Washington window

Maldon is an isolated town on a bluff at the head of the Blackwater estuary. To the north lies a rolling landscape towards Suffolk. To the south lie flatlands and marshes towards the Thames.

The much-battered church is broadside to the High Street and retains two curiosities. One is the only triangular tower in England, apparently the result of an acute street alignment. It is topped by a hexagonal spire and a curious canopy for a sanctus bell. The church's south-wall buttressing is adorned with Victorian niches displaying statues of Essex worthies, including St Cedd of Bradwell, the Saxon warrior Brithnoth and the 15th-century grandee, Sir Robert D'Arcy.

The second curiosity is the inner face of this same wall. Most of the church was spoiled in the 18th century, when the north aisle and nave were rebuilt as a single large space. The south aisle survived, divided from the nave by a fine Purbeck marble arcade of c.1340. Its south wall plays host to a magnificent procession of Decorated arcading. The lower tier embraces the sedilia and has ogee canopies along the entire length of the wall, as in a cathedral chapter house. The upper tier of arcading frames the windows and fills the spaces between them. The work was commissioned by the 14th-century D'Arcy family, or possibly also the town guilds.

The south chapel contains the Washington window of 1928, presented by the citizens of Maldon, Massachusetts. The American town was founded by Joseph Hills of Maldon and the window portrays Columbus, the Pilgrim Fathers, Washington signing the Declaration and, for no apparent reason, Joan of Arc. The town was strongly Puritan and was home to a Washington ancestor and to the captain of the *Mayflower*.

Another local character was a preacher, Joseph Billio, whose phenomenal energy in the pulpit, and presumably his loquacity, gave rise to the phrase 'going like Billio'.

The gloomy north chapel contains the monument to Thomas Cammock (d.1602). He eloped with the daughter of his employer by the two of them swimming their horse across the River Crouch to escape pursuit. The father relented in honour of their courage. By two wives he produced twenty-two children, who crowd the memorial like a packed school assembly. Cammock looks down from his memorial, understandably smug.

MARGARETTING
St Margaret *
Interior pargeting, Jesse window

Half the fun of Margaretting is in getting there. It lies some way from its village on the far side of a level crossing whose sole purpose is to serve the church and rectory next door. The church has a rare 15th-century wood-framed tower. It rests on ten posts with arched braces and contains a peal of original bells. The belfry and spire are shingled. The wooden porch is Tudor, with traceried open sides and a steep gable.

Inside there is one treasure, the astonishing east wall. This is covered in pargeting, familiar on Essex cottages but not on church walls, here depicting the Feeding of the Multitude. Dated 1678, it frames an almost complete 15th-century Tree of Jesse window. Vines rise out of Jesse's body, representing the wine of the Eucharist. The figures are set in roundels, animated against floral backgrounds, the colours muted but complete. Such glass was manufactured by Flemish glaziers, either on the Continent or in England.

The churchyard is a peaceful place, so much so that on my visit the tower had been taken over by a large bees' nest. Only the intermittent roar of a passing train disturbed their work.

RADWINTER
St Mary *
16th-century Flemish reredos

The church is outwardly unappealing, mostly the work of a Victorian vicar eager to visit his Anglo-Catholic principles on whatever parish fell to his lot. J. F. W. Bullock arrived in 1865 and stayed fifty-one years. His architects were first Eden Nesfield and then Temple Moore, though Bullock seems to have been the dominant influence.

The church, with a thick tower and needle spire, sits by the main road. Nesfield restored an unusual Tudor porch with oversailed chamber above. Surviving from the old church are the nave arcades, roof and corbels. These last are carved with idiosyncratic heads, one blindfold and another with medieval spectacles. The rest is Nesfield. He rebuilt the chancel and covered the walls with murals, carvings and cupboards, including a splendid one in the tower chamber. The font cover is a soaring concoction of angels and prophets. The rood screen has a crucifix and candles lit by electricity. The Victorian stained glass appears to conform to a narrative programme, as in the Middle Ages.

The church masterpiece is the reredos, a set of six 16th-century Flemish panels between 19th-century wings. The carving is of superb quality, with background reliefs and free-standing figures illustrating the life of St Mary.

RIVENHALL
St Mary *
French medieval glass

The church has the best European stained glass that Victorian money could buy. It lies at some distance from the village, a flag flying from its white turreted tower. The nave was rebuilt in the 19th century round a core of Saxon flint walls, the footings of the former tower visible to the west of the existing one. Original windows survive behind deep splays. The plaster in these splays apparently dates from 980.

Rivenhall's 12th-century glass was brought to the church in 1840 by its curate, Bradford Hawkins. His father had moved to Tours in France 'for financial reasons', and it was from a church in the district that he bought a dirt-encrusted window for the then huge sum of £65. At the time, wealthy English clergymen were combing Europe for furnishings for churches they were eager to restore. Hawkins put the glass in the east window at Rivenhall. It is among the earliest surviving in Europe, some fragments dating from *c.*1150. The images of saints and archbishops have the swaying outline characteristic of Early Gothic work. One is a touching portrayal of the Virgin and Child. In the bottom right-hand corner is a knight on horseback, apparently riding backwards. The glass was buried during the war and reassembled afterwards.

SAFFRON WALDEN
St Mary ***
King's Chapel turrets, Audley tomb

Think of a big East Anglian church, then double it. St Mary's towers over the centre of this handsome town, set on a hill with a wooded churchyard sloping down to the streets below. It is the largest church in Essex and is the third on the site. The present structure was begun in the late 15th century and the spire erected in 1832. The work is attributed to Simon Clerk and John Wastell, successive master masons of King's College Chapel, Cambridge.

Saffron Walden is Perpendicular by name and perpendicular by nature. The exterior, says Norman Scarfe in the *Shell Guide*, 'rears its long line of decorous battlements in all-round defence against the forces of darkness'. The south porch is a church in itself, two-storeyed, vaulted and turreted. The east end has two turrets with ogee domes, like those which Wastell added to King's. Similar turrets adorn the west tower.

From outside we can already glimpse the lofty nave arcades, forming spaces across which light from the huge windows dances in silence. Their spandrel carvings include saffron flowers, on which the town's early wealth depended. The original wooden roof is filled with carved bosses of Tudor roses and emblems of donors. Despite its architectural richness, Saffron Walden is a bare church with Victorian fittings. The brasses have been collected and fastened to the north wall.

The one outstanding monument is to Thomas Audley (d.1544) by Cornelius Harman. The tomb chest has classical pilasters and wreathed roundels, and is a rare example of the provincial influence of Henry VII's Italian tomb in Westminster Abbey. It is carved from the blackest Tournai marble. It was Audley, then Lord Chancellor, who won the church after the Dissolution. Thomas Fuller wrote of the tomb in his *Worthies of England* (1662) that the marble was 'not blacker than the soul, nor harder than the heart, of the man whose bones lie beneath it'.

The rood screen and loft were designed in 1923 by Sir Charles Nicholson and the organ made in 1824. It now has 3,500 pipes, a row of which bursts forth from the south chapel towards the nave in what is known as a 'trompeta real'. A 19th-century organist, John Frye, appointed by open competition when he was only eight, is commemorated in the east window of the north aisle. The tower has 12 bells, making it one of the largest peals in the country. The local society of ringers claims a 300-year history. Everything about Saffron Walden is big.

STEBBING
St Mary *
Stone rood screen

The church lies at the entrance to the village, its 'Hertfordshire spike' visible from a distance over the valley. The exterior is a mixture of brick and stone in a pleasant churchyard. The church's treasure is inside, a rare surviving screen made of stone. This one is earlier than the screen at neighbouring Great Bardfield, with the flowing Decorated tracery of the first half of the 14th century.

The church is a fit setting for the screen, with noble nave and discreet angels carved on the nave roof. The window glass is almost all clear, though with medieval fragments surviving like jewels against the waving trees outside. The screen is composed of three big arches filling the chancel opening. The heads of the arches have a confection of ogees robust in outline and adorned with ball-flower crockets. These, however, are Victorian restorations, as is clear from Buckler's *Essex Churches*, which shows the screen denuded of tracery in 1856.

Certainly in its present form Stebbing gives an echo of the faintly oriental Gothic found occasionally in the Decorated period, as at Cley (Norfolk) and St Mary Redcliffe, Bristol. These shapes were found in psalters and pattern books brought by traders from the Levant. They came to fascinate designers in the decades before the Black Death.

THAXTED
St John ****
Flying-buttressed spire, Perpendicular windows, Adam and Eve glass

The town of Thaxted is queen of Essex and her crown is the church. The steeple stands out over the surrounding fields. The town streets all seem to bend in its direction over ancient cobbles and past timber-framed houses. This was a place of thatchers, hence its name, then of cutlers, hence the name of its town hall, and finally of cloth, to which the church owes its richness. Thaxted is a corrective to those who find East Anglian Perpendicular monotonous. We do not know who built this church, but we do know of the remarkable vicars, Conrad Noel and Jack Putterill, who for most of the 20th century made it a centre of Anglo-Catholic evangelism. Gustav Holst came to live in Thaxted and played the organ. The town's name was given to the tune from *The Planets*, later used for 'I Vow to Thee, My Country'.

The tower is almost as high as the church is long, perfectly proportioned from base to spire. This latter is supported by flying buttresses and has ribs with crockets. The side walls of the chancel and aisles are filled with beautiful windows, those in the chancel having straight tops, entirely filling the walls with glass. Ferocious gargoyles abound. The porches are richly decorated, the north one especially so. The south porch has unusual entrances in all three sides and a star vault. Both porches have upstairs rooms. The room above the north porch is a private chapel dedicated to John Ball, 'priest-martyr' and organiser of the 1381 Peasants' Revolt.

The interior is saved from blandness by its proportions and by the ingenuity with which the transepts throw shadows across the central space. The plan dates from *c.*1340, leaving a late Decorated nave with beautifully rhythmic arcades. From this core the Perpendicular architecture seems to blossom outwards. The nave aisles are wider than the nave, while the transepts are so short as almost to be 'false'. The chancel has aisles of its own, only slightly narrower than those in the nave, with arcades with charming pierced spandrels. Above soar Thaxted's clerestories, and roofs of Tudor oak.

The church is a gallery of medieval stone carving. Grotesques, monsters, bishops, saints adorn the rafters in happy congregation. The carving in the north transept is truly astonishing. Nodding ogee arcading is infested with angels, popping out of every nook, smiling and playing instruments. Conrad Noel filled the empty niches and dressed every altar. Gaudy banners hang in the chancel, restoring some of the colour of the pre-Reformation church. In the south transept is a lovely 14th-century German Madonna.

The glass is mostly clear throughout. As a result, when I visited on an early spring day, the windows were filled with the sight of cherry blossom. This perfectly matched the flowers of the Garden of Eden, depicted in the lovely medieval window (c.1450) of Adam and Eve in the south aisle.

TILTY
St Mary **
Reticulated east window tracery

The Decorated style challenged masons and craftsmen to break the rules. The east window of Tilty church is one such breach. It can be seen from across the valley of the River Chelmer, like a skein of silk hung out to dry.

This was once no more than a chapel outside the gate of the 12th-century Cistercian abbey, which is now an adjacent ruin. The Cistercians were strict against allowing outsiders into their monastery churches. This is a typical chapel 'outside the gates', to serve the community of the abbey and those visiting.

The nave is Early Gothic, covered in mustard-coloured plaster. Seen from the west end, with its three small lancets, it might be a chapel-of-ease somewhere on the Sussex Downs. Some time in the early 14th century the monks must have decided that visiting clergy deserved a more sumptuous chancel. It is wider and considerably more lavish than the nave. The church thus presents a contrast of priest and peasant, rich and poor, a charmingly incompatible couple.

The east window is filled with gloriously flamboyant tracery. It has five lights, rising to a rose filled with tear-drop openings, pointing in all directions. Tracery bends and swirls, yet the craftsman never loses control. It is an uplifting composition. The sedilia is richly canopied, perhaps even by the same hand as the window. The pulpit is surprisingly narrow, leaving no scope for theatrical gestures on the part of the priest. The clear glass allows fine views over fields. Light floods the interior in return.

WALTHAM ABBEY
Holy Cross ****
15th-century Doom, Burne-Jones windows

Waltham was one of England's greatest monasteries. Built on the site of a shrine to the Holy Cross by King Harold in 1060, it was here that he sought blessing before the Battle of Hastings. After his death, his former love, Edith Swan-Neck, was the only person to recognise his mangled body, which was brought here for burial. The abbey was later tripled in size, as one of Henry II's penances for Becket's death. Its splendour rivalled Canterbury. But denied cathedral status at the Dissolution, Waltham's fall was great. After the destruction of the monastery in 1540, only the old Norman nave of the monastic church was left standing as a parish church. The footings of the old abbey can be traced in the adjacent park.

What is left is still magnificent. Waltham lies surrounded by village streets and the Lea Valley Park, just five minutes from the M25. Modern grandiloquence should dub it the 'cathedral of the M25'. The exterior is undistinguished, patched and restored over the ages, as if by a Cockney jobbing builder. The tower was erected in the reign of Mary Tudor to stop what was left of the nave from collapsing. Its bells were those heard one stormy night by Tennyson and are said to have inspired 'Ring out wild bells' from *In Memoriam*.

The impact of the interior is wholly Norman, including that of the sumptuous east end inserted by Burges in 1860. The nave is a ghost of the Norman naves of Durham and Peterborough Cathedrals. The arcades, galleries and clerestory survive, given a theatrical uplift by the absence of floors to the galleries. Some of the piers have spiral and chevron grooving, believed once to have been filled with precious metal. Their majesty is spoilt only by being covered in gaudy banners. Burges's east wall was built half way down the nave of the old abbey, an indication of the latter's enormous size. In honour of this dignity, Burges had Peterborough's medieval roof re-created at Waltham, in full Gothic colour and with the signs of the zodiac representing the months of the year.

Burges's carver, Thomas Nicholls, produced the superb reredos of the Nativity in polychrome relief, with a frieze of Aesop's fables. Above rises the glory of the east end, Burne-Jones's earliest and finest windows. These were designed when he was still working for Powell & Sons in 1861, before he joined William Morris. The lancets depict a Tree of Jesse and, above it in the wheel window, God the Creator and the seven days of the Creation. The artist portrays landscape with almost abstract effect. These are windows to match the best of the Middle Ages, curtains of colour, light absorbed and magnified by glass, what Philip Larkin called 'sun-comprehending glass'. They remind me of the paintings of Samuel Palmer.

South of the choir is a relic of the Gothic 14th-century abbey, the Lady Chapel. Until the 19th century, this was a derelict room, its windows bricked up and used as a store. The bookshop in the crypt was even a prison, a common fate for lockable church rooms in the Middle Ages. During restoration, a complete 15th-century Doom painting was uncovered above the altar. With gilded angels on the altar and light pouring in through the Decorated south windows, the chapel today is a complete contrast to the heavy Norman next door. The 14th-century Waltham Madonna rests in an opening into the chancel.

Waltham's finest tomb lies next to the Lady Chapel. Sir Edward Denny (d.1600) acquired the manor on the Dissolution. His tomb has the usual Elizabethan heraldry and strapwork but has lost its columns. Ten children pray beneath, the two on the right holding hands to indicate twins. Denny and his wife lie with their heads resting on their hands, as if watching Shakespeare on television. In the north aisle is a baroque tomb chest for a ship-owner, Robert Smith (d.1697). On its front is an allegorical relief of the Ship of Industry evading the Rock of Sloth. The Latin inscription below translates, 'By industry small means increase / Large ones by indolence decrease.'

Gloucestershire

with Bristol

Gloucestershire is an aristocrat among counties. In the late Middle Ages it was among the richest in England and its wealth was wool. Shepherds and drovers prospered in its villages, clothiers and merchants in its towns. Gloucestershire tycoons migrated to London and Calais, honouring their home county with churches that are masterpieces of 'woolgothic' architecture. This Perpendicular style was characterised by high towers, lavish porches and rich fittings. Above the chancel arch was often a 'Cotswold window', bringing extra light on to the rood and nave.

The style is displayed most brilliantly at Cirencester, Fairford, Chipping Campden and Northleach. These churches are in glorious Cotswold limestone, rich gold in the south, cool and milky in the north. But Cotswold churches are not all grand. Earlier and simpler memorials to wool fill the hills and hidden valleys, such yeomen's churches as Bibury and Duntisbourne Rouse, and Buckland with its shepherds' pews. They are set in villages that have become symbols of idyllic England to generations of Britons abroad.

The county is not all Cotswold. The earliest Saxon missionaries made their way inland up the River Severn, where relics of their incursions are found at Deerhurst and in the frescos at Kempley. Over the vale towers the abbey church of Tewkesbury, with one of the great Norman naves of England. Tewkesbury's Despenser tombs of the 14th and 15th centuries form the finest collection of medieval monuments outside Westminster Abbey.

By the 17th century, Gloucestershire's age of splendour was over. But the county was fortunate in its 19th-century benefactors. They contributed Henry Woodyer's Highnam, J. L. Pearson's Daylesford and G. F. Bodley's Selsley, the last recently restored as a gallery of early Morris glass.

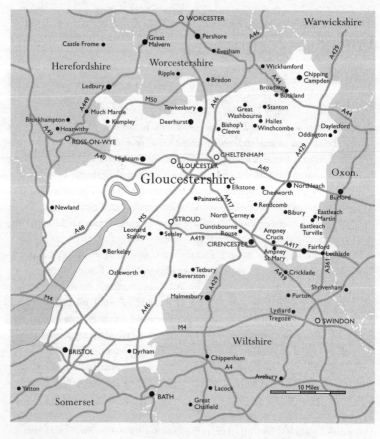

AMPNEY CRUCIS
Holy Rood *
Memorial cross, Lloyd tomb

The Ampneys are immaculate Gloucestershire, stone-walled, stone-roofed and manicure-verged. The church is on the western extremity of the village, enfolded by an angle of Ampney Park House. Indeed the north side of the church looks directly into the east wing of the house, the manor first of the Lloyds, then of the Pleydells. The church sits in a grove of trees, as it has since Saxon times. In the churchyard is a medieval Gothic cross with relief carvings of the Crucifixion and the Virgin and Child. Churchyard crosses commemorated the dead in the days before gravestones. Ampney Crucis has one of the few complete examples to survive.

The church has a Perpendicular west tower but a Norman core. Inside the church and directly opposite the door is the ghost of a Saxon arch composed of long and short quoins. The dominant feature of the church is its Transitional crossing, with a zigzag-carved chancel arch and graceful Norman capitals.

The Lloyd tomb in the north transept is surmounted by a classical pediment which was apparently removed and discovered this century in the cellars of the manor. George Lloyd (d.1584) and his wife, he in armour, she in contemporary dress, lie in prayer with their children arrayed round the chest. He has full moustaches. The south transept is devoted to the later Pleydells, by when monumental art was more subdued. Memorial tablets give the time as well as the date of death, as if to lend precision to any future astrologer. Under the tower is a copy of a mural of the martyrdom of St Erasmus, found in the north transept. His innards are being wound out of him on a spit. The picture may give small children nightmares.

AMPNEY ST MARY
St Mary *
Norman carving, Christ of the Trades mural

The church lies isolated from its village on the far side of the main road, allegedly a victim of a plague resettlement. It is watched over by an old cedar and was known, until stripped of vegetation in 1913, as the Ivy Church. The double-cell building is mostly of the early 12th century, with an Early Gothic chancel and Decorated additions. It has neither transepts nor aisles and is largely unscathed by later alteration, a plain church full of minor incidents.

The first is the carved Norman lintel on the outside of what was once a north door. An elongated Lion of Righteousness is shown stamping on two jolly serpents (or one two-headed one) representing evil. A griffin looks on. The interior is reached through a south door composed of a slab of elm. Open on a fine day, it admits sun on to simple pews and ancient flagstones. The Norman font is decorated with zigzag. The pulpit is tiny. The entrance to the chancel is guarded by a stone screen base, without any superstructure.

St Mary's is best known for its wall paintings. These are much eroded and date from the 12th to the 15th century, covering most of the wall surface. They are hard to decipher and many seem little more than medieval graffiti or 'stoning', in imitation of blocks of stone. The rarest work is on the south wall, a Sabbatarian mural in the spirit of Mrs Proudie. It shows Christ's wounds bleeding when forbidden tasks are undertaken on a Sunday. The picture shows implements that should not be used, including those of the wheelwright. Another such 'Christ of the Trades' is found at Breage (Cornwall).

In the south wall is a window carved from a single large block of stone, possibly Saxon. The rebates appear intended for skin, which would be stretched across the opening in place of glass. The church concludes with a flourish, the west wall illuminated by an eventful Decorated window of flowing lines and tumbling mouchettes.

BERKELEY
St Mary ***
Early Gothic west front, Berkeley memorials

This is a rugged church in sandstone looking down on the no less rugged castle and the Severn estuary beyond. Its bell-tower was built well away from the church to the north, thus offering less of a threat to the castle should it be captured in a siege. Berkeley's glory is the west front, filled by five tall lancet windows and propped up by two large buttresses. A small masterpiece on the south side is the priest's doorway to the Berkeley Chapel, early Perpendicular with ogee hood and family shields, a work of proud but pious patronage.

Inside, the Early Gothic arcades have stiff-leaf capitals, some so deeply cut that the leaves seem about to blow in the wind. On the south arcade is a carving of two women gossiping near a toad, said to be a warning against rumour-mongering. The remains of a Doom painting are discernible over the chancel arch. Medieval stone screens divide off the chancel and the Berkeley Chapel, while in the chancel is a stone reredos by Comper of 1918. Berkeley seems to bring out ruggedness even in the most delicate of designers.

Pride of Berkeley is the Berkeley Chapel and the alabaster effigies to successive barons. The 8th Lord, who fought at Crécy in 1346 and died in 1361, lies under the south nave arcade in battledress and chainmail, his wife at his side. It was to him that the unfortunate Edward II was entrusted, and then murdered in his castle in 1327. The couple have their hands raised in prayer. Students shine torches through them to test the purity of the alabaster.

In the Berkeley Chapel itself lies the 11th Lord, James (d.1463), with his younger son, who is presented as smaller to indicate his youth. They are still in armour but bareheaded and their hands in prayer point towards their chins. Exceptional figure sculpture survives round the chest. Subsequent Berkeleys offer a parade of English monumental sculpture and dress. The last of the line, who died in 1942, was commemorated with a memorial by Comper.

Edward Jenner, son of the vicar and himself a local doctor, invented vaccination in 1823 by trying out his serums on his own family in the parish. The east window is his memorial. In the churchyard is the tomb of Dicky Pearce, believed to be England's last court jester, who worked for the Earl of Suffolk. He died in 1728 and his epitaph reads, 'What signifies to cry, / Dickys enough are still behind to laugh at by and by.'

BEVERSTON
St Mary *
Saxon Resurrection carving

Beverston hovers under the walls of an outlying castle of the Berkeley domain, patronage that brought parishioners fine carving and a handsome tower and rood. Fallen into ruin, the church was rescued by the Victorians and is now in active use. It is reached at the end of a muddy lane. High on its tower wall is an eroded but still discernible Saxon carving, apparently of the Resurrection.

The bright interior has a 13th-century south arcade; its cylindrical piers rise to trumpet-scallop capitals, like an Elizabethan ruff, beneath pointed arches. Most of the surrounding windows are of the mid-14th century, when the Berkeleys refortified the adjacent castle. Though this had a chapel of its own, the family maintained their patronage of the church and even endowed a Berkeley Chapel in the north transept, with an unusual walk-through squint to the chancel.

Beverston has been able to salvage much of its screen. The medieval woodwork was found in the 1880s acting as a pergola in the rector's garden. It was reinstated with a rood group above it. A Tudor panelled stone pulpit also survives. Overhead, the Victorian restorer Lewis Vulliamy constructed a strange new roof, with transverse beams jutting sideways as if lost for somewhere to go. It reminds me of the eccentric 'Wordsworth' roof at Grasmere (Cumbria).

BIBURY
St Mary ★★
Picturesque setting, Saxon carvings

The village of Bibury is strung along the Coln stream, picturesque with its trout farm, almshouses and summer tourist crowds. The church has wisely retreated up a valley behind the school. This is pukka Gloucestershire. The church is waited on by cedars and rose bushes and the lawn is neatly mown. The path leads straight to a Norman north doorway with zigzag mouldings and Decorated windows on either side. A small Perpendicular north-west tower forms a corner with a rickety lamp attached to it. Beyond is an abundance of clothiers' rolltop tombs and stones with carved cherubs.

Bibury church is Saxon at heart and must have been substantial even before the Conquest. A fragment of an old Saxon cross shaft is embedded in the exterior north wall of the chancel. The interior is dominated by the tall Saxon chancel arch, which was raised by the Normans so that it cut through an old Saxon string course. Aisles were added and arcades opened up, bearing a text-book selection of Norman motifs, zigzags, scallops, trumpets and water-leaf. The chancel was also lengthened and given triple lancets. It contains no fewer than ten aumbries and must have been a hive of liturgical activity.

Each era thus left its mark on Bibury, Early Gothic chancel, Decorated north aisle windows to add to the Norman doorways, and small Perpendicular windows to accompany the tower. It is all an enjoyable Cotswold congeries. I expected a jolly monk to come bouncing out of the chancel after Sunday service and invite himself to sherry with the village's second-homers.

BISHOP'S CLEEVE
St Michael ★★★
Norman west front, chest with Norman locks

Here on the outskirts of Cheltenham is a big church that may have begun life as a Saxon minster. It was rebuilt big by the Normans and has stayed big ever since. It could hardly be less 'Cheltenham', although if Cheltenham ever wanted a cathedral, this should be the place. Bishop's Cleeve is a building full of eccentricities.

They begin with the west front. This is a late-Norman ensemble of gable, turrets and doorway with zigzag surround and a serpent moulding. One of the carvings is of a boy with his legs crossed and carrying something under his arm, allegedly trying to get on to the roof. The south porch has Norman arcading, a rib vault with zigzag carving and a doorway surround decorated with two serpents, their tails joined and their heads eating birds. A Green Man peers from the left-hand capital. This is a superb composition to find in a parish church, and has been attributed to the same masons as Elkstone.

The nave interior is at first odd rather than beautiful. The old Norman bays were taken down in the 16th or 17th century and replaced by half their number of wider bays. This spoils their proportion and makes the later Gothic arcade to the south aisle chapel appear almost delicate. This chapel, like the chancel and much else at Bishop's Cleeve, is of the early 14th century, a period which now takes over and contributes much of the church's glory. Bishop's Cleeve is covered in ballflower decoration. It is rich also in window tracery of the period. The west window is Reticulated and the south transept a stylish swirl of Intersecting. The transepts were bricked up after the collapse of the central tower in the late 17th century.

The Jacobean west gallery stands almost free of the walls on columns with an intricately carved entablature. This has been revived for musicians and choir. The church still has the old accounts for 18th-century musical instruments, including cellos, fiddles and bassoons. A chest at the back of the church was hacked from a single lump of wood, possibly of the early 13th century; its locks are apparently Norman.

Bishop's Cleeve has tried valiantly to act as patron of good modern art, but not succeeded. Modern paintings include a set of Stations of the Cross donated by a former master from the local secondary school. The altarpiece is also a 20th-century work, and the new rood is in acrylic by the 'internationally known local artist', P. J. Crook. Its material alone is out of place. The stained glass is equally bleak.

A small museum of the church's history housed over the south porch is reached past a charming flurry of fan-vaulting in the aisle. It contains murals by a Georgian schoolmaster called Sperry, who used the bare walls as a blackboard. Thus we see a giant tiger, a battle scene, a skeleton and arithmetic tables.

BUCKLAND
St Michael **
Shepherds' pews, medieval cope

Forget for a moment the Cotswold wool churches, endowed by the tycoons who grew fat on the textile trade. Remember instead the farmers, shearers and drovers who reared their sheep in the folds of the Cotswold escarpment. Their isolated settlement had churches which few could afford to rebuild in the new Perpendicular style. One such is Buckland, a simple structure set in a secluded village. Perpendicular tower top, aisle windows and chancel conceal a 13th-century nave. Victorian restorers scraped off the plaster and medieval wall paintings, but at least left the woodwork.

The interior is filled with Cotswold carpentry. There are wooden pews, wainscoting, gallery, reredos, chests and roofs. The unusual nave roof has king-posts with painted beams and pendant bosses, a feature repeated in the aisles. During restoration in 1981 these paintings were discovered on what were rotting beams, so the surface layer was cut and bonded on to new beams laid in their place. The benches and pews date from the 15th to the 19th century. Against the south wall are 17th-century oak benches with carved testers. These were known as the shepherds' pews, since shepherds and their dogs occupied them, entering from the west door rather than through the porch. If they were so 'below the salt', why such beautiful pews? Behind them on the window ledges are brass memorial plates with beautiful 18th-century lettering.

The west gallery nearly went the way of the wall paintings. It had been installed in the late 17th century by the lord of the manor, James Thynne, to house a school. When it was proposed for removal, the parishioners restored it at their own expense. The reredos is a Great War memorial to Charles Brough Scott, with a St Michael and 'The Happy Warrior'. Above is a stained glass window, composed of 15th-century fragments depicting a bishop officiating at the Sacrament, reset by Morris in 1883. Near the north door a small museum displays Gothic panels with carvings and painted angels from nearby Hailes Abbey. Inside a case is a rare medieval cope in blue velvet, again probably from Hailes.

CHEDWORTH
St Andrew **
Perpendicular window display

Beautifully set in a valley basin and enveloped in drystone walls and birdsong, Chedworth is a surprise. From the valley and manor house next door it looks like an architectural stage set. To the left spread the modest wings of a Norman tower and to the right an Early Gothic chancel, while centre stage is held by a monumental piece of scenery: a battlemented wall with five large Perpendicular windows. These were built around an earlier porch without replacing it. Over the top is ranged a row of terrifying gargoyles, one of a monster being sick.

In most Cotswold churches such windows indicate a lofty Perpendicular interior. Not here. This is indeed a piece of scenery with, behind it as if back-stage, a Norman interior. The patron was the Yorkist magnate, Richard Neville, whose unfortunate daughter married Richard III. The turret containing the rood stair carries the date of 1485, the year of Bosworth, so it is possible the church fell victim to this climax to the Wars of the Roses. Work must have stopped when money ran out, before demolition had been started on the north side.

Whatever the story, the interior contains a Norman north arcade with intricately scalloped capitals. This divides the nave from what might be termed a farther backstage, the north aisle. There is no south aisle and the nave is lit by the clear glass of the tall south windows. The chancel arch is Early Gothic, with stiff-leaf capitals so undercut they seem about to fall to the ground. Next to it rises a staircase to a vanished rood loft, with a Perpendicular pulpit apparently carved from a single block of stone.

In the north aisle is a modern Madonna and Child in the style of Michelangelo, carved by Helen Frazer Rock (1911). It is a restrained work of the sort that could fill a thousand empty niches in English churches. The church is adjacent to one of England's best-preserved Roman villas, in which has been found the chi-rho symbol of early Christianity. It is possible that the colonists founded a small church near their home. If so, this could be an 'earliest Christian site' to rank with Lullingstone (Kent), and predate St Martin, Canterbury.

CHIPPING CAMPDEN
St James ****
Cotswold tower, clothiers' tombs, altar hangings

Chipping Campden rivalled Cirencester, Northleach and Chipping Norton (Oxon) as capital of the 15th-century Cotswold wool trade. A dozen of its merchants rose to become lord mayors of London. They put a sheep on top of the Royal Exchange and a Woolsack under the Chancellor. Chipping is a corruption of cheaping, or market place, and the town's status derived both from the sheep downs and from its place on the wool route over the Cotswolds from the Welsh Marches. Prosperity seems to have been unaffected by the Hundred Years War and enhanced by the Wars of the Roses. Not until the rise of cloth manufacture in the valleys were these hill communities challenged.

The wealth is still displayed in the procession of houses along the high street, and in the almshouses and domed gatehouse to the old manor near the church. Campden was lucky in its 20th-century preservation, and is rightly celebrated as a Cotswold town that has settled gracefully for village status in its old age. Today the church tower rises above a bridge of twelve apostle lime trees and an arboretum of evergreens. Its massive outline is softened by thin pilaster strips rising the full height of each face. With pinnacles topping the diagonal buttresses and a pierced parapet with ogee arches, the composition soars over the landscape, an outstanding symbol of England's medieval wealth.

The nave was built from 1488 and is similar to that at Northleach. Concave-sided octagonal piers rise to shallow arches and wide clerestory windows. Over the chancel arch is another large window to light the rood, known as a Cotswold window. The detail is simple, compared for instance with the multiple shafting of the nave at St Mary Redcliffe, Bristol. The impact of Chipping

Campden is not decorative but spatial, deriving from the proportion of height to length, the grandeur of the clerestory, and the harmony between arcades, chancel arch and tower arch.

The church is well endowed with monuments to its many benefactors. The largest brass in Gloucestershire lies directly before the altar, eight feet tall. It depicts William Grevel (d.1401), 'formerly a citizen of London and flower of the wool merchants of all England'. Having retired to Gloucestershire after a career in the City (how little changes!), he died before the building of the present church. He lies with his wife Marion in an attitude of prayer. On the north wall of the chancel is a Renaissance tomb of Thomas Smythe (d.1593), complete with two wives and thirteen children. With pediments and strapwork cartouches, it is modelled on George Lloyd's tomb at Ampney Crucis.

Smythe's sons sold the manor in 1610 to Sir Baptist Hicks, another wealthy London merchant. Hicks donated the pulpit, eagle lectern and chancel roof. The church gave him the south chapel for his family tombs. His own tomb is a grand twelve-poster, of black and white marble, attributed to Nicholas Stone. It shows Hicks (d.1629), by then Lord Campden, in state robes with his wife. The portrayal of both in old age looks realistic. The other principal monument is to his successor, Lord Campden, and his wife, by Joshua Marshall. It is in sharp contrast to the confidence of the earlier work. This Campden died in the Civil War and stands with his wife, shrouded in their tombs, awaiting the call to Heaven.

Beneath the tower can be seen what is claimed to be England's only complete set of medieval altar hangings, dating from the late 15th century. Faded and restored, they are precious survivals of what must once have been a common possession of every English church, even poor ones.

CIRENCESTER
St John the Baptist *****
Perpendicular porch, fan vaults, merchants' tombs

Cirencester is the cathedral of 'woolgothic'. It is not just a masterpiece of Perpendicular art, but a town church whose history can be read and enjoyed with ease. In the 14th and 15th centuries, upland wool was the oil and coal of England. The wealth of the merchant houses of London was built on its trade, and the wool towns of Gloucestershire, Yorkshire and East Anglia were its Manchesters and Birminghams. Here the new rich of England formed their guilds and built and endowed their chantries.

Cirencester, as its name implies, was a Roman centre at the junction of Fosse Way and Ermine Street. Remains of what appears to be the longest Saxon church in England have been uncovered in the abbey grounds next door. The present church was founded in the 12th century, but only the eccentric ground plan reflects this early structure. The chancel survives from the 13th and 14th centuries. Rebuilding began at the start of the 15th century and was still underway a hundred years later.

The church was a joint work of the town and abbey. The abbey owned the wool market and taxed its produce. The abbot was frequently in conflict with the increasingly wealthy merchants, represented by their guilds. The guilds paid for the church tower and new nave, and filled the latter with glass. The tower is the least successful part of the composition, despite its handsome profile over the rooftops of the old town. It does not soar – a planned spire was not added as the walls were considered too weak – but sits on a heavy lower stage, with giant buttresses supporting its east side. The best view is from the east, where the upper storeys sit above the undulating gables and pinnacles of the chapels and aisles like a barque in a heavy sea.

Cirencester is most celebrated for its south porch. This was built by the abbey in 1490, presumably to appease or at least accommodate the merchants in the market. As was noted in the Introduction, such medieval porches were of great local importance, for here the conduct of both church and secular business took place. Cirencester's is the largest and most complex in England. It is exceptionally grand, three bays wide, three deep and three storeys tall, though the top storey was rebuilt in the 1830s. The guilds occupied the first and second storeys. It might qualify as England's first office block. The exterior is in the most elaborate Perpendicular Gothic; restless tracery pushes up through panels and oriel windows towards the parapet. Nothing is still.

Cirencester's nave was rebuilt in 1516–30 with soaring Perpendicular arcades and a seven-light Cotswold window above the chancel arch. This is overseen by the arms of Henry VIII. A modern opera house merely lists its patrons by name: a wool church does so with angels carrying their coats of arms high above the nave. Everywhere are the devices and arms of the leading families of the town, the Garstangs, Rychards and Tappers. Opening off the nave are chantry chapels established by individual benefactors, c.1430–60. At the east end of the south aisle is the Garstang Chapel, erected within the church and surrounded by a fine mid-15th-century wooden screen. Its mullions are carved with the Garstang arms and trademarks in an alternating sequence. The family came from the north, as did many Cotswold merchants. Social mobility did not begin with the Victorians. Henry Garstang's tomb is dated 1464.

The second chantry chapel is a large, four-bay structure built on to the north aisle. It was financed by two courtiers to Richard of York, Richard Dixton and William Prelatte. Both were members of the Weavers' Guild of the Holy Trinity, after which the chapel is named. It is divided from the north aisle by a stone screen and crowned by a fine timber roof. Brasses to the two founders survive, with Prelatte flanked by his two wives. The two aisles north of the chancel were rebuilt c.1450, and a chantry established shortly after, its cheerful fan vault financed by the abbey in 1508. It had provided a similar fan in the south porch slightly earlier. This was followed by a new rood screen in the 1520s. Such commissions were the final burst of abbey patronage before the Dissolution.

Cirencester's stained glass was reputedly the equal of Fairford's. It survived the Reformation and even the Civil War, but fell victim to decay. What remained in the late 18th century was gathered together in the main east and west windows. Further fragments survived into the 19th century but were thrown into a railway ditch. Some of these fragments were recovered and reinstated in the south chancel, in a window above the sedilia.

DAYLESFORD
St Peter *
Immaculate Pearson interior

The church seems at first sight a gloomy Victorian conceit, poking an urban nose over the fields of the Daylesford estate. Yet it is one of Pearson's most perfect small works, built in 1859–63 for Harman Grisewood, successor to Warren Hastings as owner of the big house. Like Pearson's Scorborough (Yorks, ER), which was being built at the same time, the church is a bold design in the French Early Gothic idiom. It is built on a cruciform plan, with diminutive chancel and transepts round a massive central tower with a sturdy pyramidical spire. To the north is a Plate tracery window in the nave and a wheel window in the transept. Equal care is taken with the smaller decorations.

The interior, at least on a sunny day with light filtered through the windows, has the character of a dark and mysterious jewel box. The stained glass is by Clayton & Bell, as vivid and confident in style as the work of the Morris partnership was shortly to become. The roof is cedar, the benches and stalls oak. Decorating the small crossing are multiple shafts and floriated capitals. Daylesford was designed on Tractarian principles, to bring worshippers close to the ceremonies of the chancel. Accordingly Pearson reserved the richest decoration for the chancel, which has a stone vault and marble and mosaic inlay.

Outside, to the east of the church, is a Coade stone memorial to Warren Hastings (d.1818).

DEERHURST
St Mary ****
Saxon fragments, angel sculpture

Deerhurst's church, a former Anglo-Saxon monastery, and the adjacent Odda's Chapel form a picturesque group on the bank of the Severn. Here the Saxons would have sailed up-river to found a mission, before pushing on to Tewkesbury and Worcester. Odda's Chapel, founded in 1056, is up a lane a hundred yards to the south and, now disused, is in the care of English Heritage. The church is still functioning, a museum of styles and treasures from almost every period of English architecture, especially Anglo-Saxon. Deerhurst is a delight to the detective.

The approach, past the farmhouse lawn, is deceptive. We see a Perpendicular clerestory above a long row of Tudor aisle windows. However, a closer look reveals earlier work. In the south-east corner is the herringbone pattern of a Saxon wall above a blocked doorway leading from the church to the old cloister. There is more herringbone in the clerestory, and in the tower, which is virtually all Saxon work. Nothing seems to have been demolished, merely patched by each generation like a pauper's garment.

The interior of Deerhurst has been much restored. The limewashed walls look new and white, the archaeological fragments obviously left as curios. It is an exceptional survival, the Saxon work evident in the tall narrow nave and the west and east walls. The west wall is entirely Anglo-Saxon, with openings at three levels. At the top level are two windows with the triangular heads characteristic of Saxon work. The east wall retains the Saxon chancel arch. There are some 30 Saxon doorways and other openings at Deerhurst. The Early Gothic arcades have a superb collection of capitals, from stiff-leaf to arabesque. A man's face stares out from the foliage on the south side, as if tormented by the pressure of the shafts.

In the north aisle are two ancient brasses, one of the Virgin, the other of Sir John Cassey and his wife, with her dog Terri at her feet. In the south aisle west window is 15th-century glass, including the much-reproduced depiction of St Catherine with her wheel under a flamboyant canopy. The church has several treasures of Saxon sculpture. On the interior wall of the tower is a relief of a Madonna and Child, dated to the 8th century. It once had painted details. The font is also Saxon, covered in trumpet-spiral ornament and reputedly one of the oldest surviving in England.

Outside the east end of the church, seen from the farmyard, are the footings of the Saxon apse. Arrows point upwards to an angel in relief, high on the wall, a rare survival of 10th-century carving. On the day of my visit, a pigeon had died and the ground beneath the angel was strewn as if with her fallen feathers. This is a church of constant delight and surprise.

DUNTISBOURNE ROUSE
St Michael **
Isolated hillside chapel with crypt

We are in the deepest Cotswolds. 'This is country lagging a century or two behind,' says the guide, 'more primitive, almost savage, as if the shepherds had never left and the binder never come.'

Like the downland churches of Sussex, Duntisbourne Rouse never had a patron rich enough to rebuild its Saxon nave and Norman chancel. Only a modest bell-tower was added in the Tudor period. The church clings to the side of the hill with a valley, fields and woods falling away to the east. This gives the east end a bold outline, with room for a tiny crypt beneath the chancel. The small cross on the floor is lit by the sun's rays in the early morning.

Inside, the windows and the Norman chancel arch were sadly scraped and restored as recently as the 1930s. There are no windows on the north side and, apart from one early Perpendicular opening, only tiny round-headed and lancet windows elsewhere. There are box pews, a Jacobean pulpit, an Early Gothic font and traces of mural in the chancel. The only surprise is the late-medieval choir stalls with four misericords of heads surrounded by vine leaves. These look too sophisticated for Duntisbourne and were presumably brought from elsewhere.

When I was last at this church, an autumn wind had blown leaves into a flurry round the medieval cross in the churchyard. Someone had used the same leaves inside, mingled with old man's beard, to decorate the pews, a delightful gesture of nature turned to art.

DYRHAM
St Peter *
Setting, Elizabethan tomb

William Talman's magnificent 1698 Dyrham Park gazes out across the Cotswold escarpment towards the Severn valley. The church is perched above a wall overlooking the lawn, seemingly buttressed by magnificent yew hedges. The approach to the church is from the village down the hill, or through the house itself, when open by the National Trust. The exterior appears a simple Perpendicular structure. The interior glows with Tudor warmth, as light floods in from the garden, enhancing the pink limewash on the walls. On a summer's day, with flowers on the pulpit and bees humming about the rafters, the interior might still be a set for *The Remains of the Day*, which was filmed at Dyrham.

The Early Gothic nave and north arcade are flanked by 16th-century aisles. The most distinguished tomb is at the east end of the south aisle, to George Wynter (d.1581). This is English Renaissance, the canopy top-heavy and lavishly carved, with piers and Corinthian columns. When it was installed, in the reign of Elizabeth I, the big house outside would still have been two-gabled and medieval. Nearby is the Russell brass of 1416, of which a replica is available for rubbing. This is of limited quality but remarkable for being life size (5ft 4ins). The knight and his lady lie stiff and expressionless, hands together in prayer. They now adorn many a student's wall.

Dyrham has six fine bells, one of which is apparently from the reign of Edward I, making it over six centuries old. There is a battered but decorative Flemish triptych on the altar.

EASTLEACH MARTIN
St Michael and St Martin *
EASTLEACH TURVILLE
St Andrew *
Twin churches facing each other across a glade

This is the Cotswolds of which exiles dream, ancient stones hung with wild rose and hawthorn, set in valleys of deepest green and full of the smell of cut grass. Two small churches, one redundant, face each other across a small stream. On my last visit, worshippers were leaving St Andrew's and wending their way over the little River Leach towards St Michael's and their cars, as if enacting Samuel Palmer's painting, *Evening Church*. Each church was founded by a separate manorial lord, the one by Richard Fitzpons, the other by Roger de Lacy. Both are Norman in origin.

St Andrew's is still active. The dates of its component parts are largely immaterial, since the charm of the church lies in the whole. A Norman tympanum surmounts the south door. Alterations were carried out in Early Gothic and Decorated styles. In the 17th century a north aisle was demolished as well as a chantry chapel off the chancel. The chancel arch and triple lancet east window are Early Gothic, adorned with rare Cotswold stiff-leaf. The tomb recess even has decorative ballflower. The furnishings are almost all 17th century.

The church of St Michael and St Martin lies across the glade, redundant but pristine in its restoration. It sits on a grassy expanse beyond a stone wall. The west tower with a hipped roof is relieved by Perpendicular tracery in the window. The north transept appears longer than the nave. Inside, the atmosphere is sadly more of a museum than a church. The windows run the gamut of

Gothic tracery: Geometrical, Reticulated and Intersecting from the Decorated style and Panel tracery from the Perpendicular. What fun the masons must have had adapting their craft to changing fashion. John Keble was curate at Eastleach (1815–25) and the little bridge linking the two churches is still known as Keble's Bridge.

[St Michael's CCT]

ELKSTONE
St John ***
Norman chancel, columbarium in chancel roof

This is not tourist Gloucestershire, but high country where wind is wild, landscape bare and the stone hard and grey. The village of Elkstone has been spoilt by modern cottages, but at its heart, amid pines full of noisy rooks, rises a church that is worth the climb up the escarpment or from the valleys to the east.

The original Norman church had a crossing tower that was lost in the 13th century, hence the buttress towards the east end. The east window surround is, according to the guide, a unique pattern of 'battlemented sunk-fret' ornament. The carved heads of the nave corbel-table survive on north and south walls, not of the quality of Kilpeck (Herefs) but still a fine gallery of faces. A new west tower was built *c*.1370. It is Perpendicular with gargoyles which include instrument players.

The Norman tympanum over the south door has Christ in Majesty, with the emblems of the evangelists and the hand of God above Him. Above is a deep beakhead, a grotesque monster apparently in contention with Christianity. On the left an upside-down monster holds a beak in each hand, as if to keep them shut; on the right is a lyre. In the middle, a snake looks at a lion while it eats its own tail. Among these monsters we see the head of a man and a woman, apparently the sponsors of the work.

The interior is a shock. To the west rises a tall 15th-century tower arch with a pretty lierne vault supporting it. The nave is Victorianised, but the chancel, low and narrow, has vaults unaltered since the 12th century. Two robust arches decorated with zigzag enclose what might be a monk's cell, which formerly supported the tower. The chancel arch ends in two dragon's heads, one descending right behind the preacher's head. Beyond is the sanctuary, also unaltered, where four grotesque faces form the junction of the ribs. The east window has an intricately carved surround and vividly coloured glass dated 1929, by Henry Payne of Stroud but in the style of Burne-Jones. The ensemble is suffused with gold light from the glass.

Elkstone has fine woodwork, including box pews. Decorated panels adorn the altar rail and pulpit, part of whose tester has been reused as a reading desk.

The chancel exterior is noticeably higher than the interior, as the roof space contains a rare surviving columbarium. This priest's dovecote was apparently reached by the same north stair which served the central tower and rood loft.

FAIRFORD
St Mary *****
Complete set of medieval glass, stone carvings, misericords

Fairford is one of England's outstanding galleries of church art. I first visited it as a boy on one of the final runs of the old Oxford to Fairford railway as jets from the American air base roared overhead. The jets still roar, but Fairford seems immune to their thunder. It displays England's only complete set of medieval narrative glass, that of St Neot (Cornwall) being incomplete.

The glass, and indeed most of the church, was the creation of a Cirencester wool merchant, John Tame, in the 1490s, and of his son Edmund (d.1534). The church is unusual in being built new from the foundations, and is thus a perfect Perpendicular structure. It is approached from the south-east across a churchyard of tumbled tombs and chests. The church exterior is enriched with carved stonework: corbels, gargoyles and string courses alive with the faces of men, women and beasts. Four dwarfs in hats guard each corner of the tower, along with the arms of Tame and other holders of the Fairford manor. These depict shears and gloves, horseshoes and pincers. On the wall outside the south aisle is the carved figure of a boy apparently climbing over it.

The interior is dominated by 28 large windows, as though the building were intended to be their frame. The best viewing time is either on a winter's day or with the sun low at dusk. Then the rest of the interior retreats into darkness and the window colours appear to take fire. Each fragment possesses the quality, noted by Ruskin, of absorbing and refracting light in its own way. Fairford is like a vast illuminated missal.

The glass is not just rare but of the highest quality, attributed to the royal glazier, Barnard Flower. He was of Flemish origin and worked at Westminster Abbey and King's College, Cambridge. Flemings were the master glaziers of late-medieval Europe and the Fairford windows almost certainly include work by other Flemish immigrants. The colours are strong and primary. Detail is confined to areas of clear glass on which the only tones are black and yellow. Glass enamelling had not yet been introduced. The designs are derived from illuminated books; scholars have traced many of the Fairford compositions to specific texts circulating in the late 15th century, particularly the popular Pauper's Bible. While each pane has been cleaned and protected, only the west window was substantially reglazed after being blown out during a storm in the

18th century. Repair and restoration was by Hardman & Co. of Birmingham, who had to replace much of the glass in the upper half.

The narrative sequence is typical of a pre-Reformation church, and of frescos in France and Italy. The theme is the history of the Christian Church. Round the east end is the Life of Christ, with the pivotal event, the Crucifixion, dominating the east window. In the north-east are scenes from the Virgin's life, and in the south-east are the incidents of Christ's life. In the nave, Old Testament prophets in the north aisle face New Testament apostles in the south aisle. In the clerestory, the persecutors of early Christians line the north side as vividly portrayed villains. On the south side are their victims, the saints. All this reaches its climax in the great west window, which portrays Christ in Majesty, with the Day of Judgement and its graphic depictions of Heaven and Hell beneath. On the left of this window is another showing the Judgement of David and on the right the Judgement of Solomon. The sequence is superbly modulated by the different weights of the windows: three lights in the clerestory, four lights in the aisles, five at the east end and seven lights in the west. The sequence is a major work of medieval art, of which Flower was a master. His monsters and demons are as terrifying as anything by Taddeo Gaddi or Bosch. They are an astonishing masterpiece to find in this gentle Cotswold backwater.

This is not the end of Fairford's treasures. The choir screens are superb, on the north side embracing the canopy to the tomb of Tame senior, in a Renaissance Purbeck marble chest with brasses on top. On the other side of the Lady Chapel is the effigy of his grandson's wife and her last husband, Robert Lygon, in medieval armour. The stalls survive, possibly brought here from Cirencester Abbey at the Dissolution. Their misericords are fine enough to merit a guidebook of their own. The subjects include a woman beating a boy with a bat, two women discussing the merits of a dead fowl and a woman appearing to hit a man who is trying to fit her with a new shoe. Why such scenes should adorn the underside of a monk's seat during Mass is an enduring mystery of ecclesiastical art.

GREAT WASHBOURNE
St Mary *
Gothic squints

The church is surrounded by cottages, some timbered, some of stone in the shadow of Alderton Hill. Its initial appearance suggests a Saxon rather than Norman foundation. There is no tower, merely a bellcote, and the aisleless nave is high and narrow. North and south doorways are both round-arched and the south one has an incised tympanum with a Maltese cross in the middle. The chancel was rebuilt in the 17th century. An inscription on the outside proclaims that 'James Cartwright did newly build up this chancel, 1642.'

The predominant feature inside is the wall dividing nave and chancel with, as its centrepiece, a small early Norman arch matching the north and south doorways. On either side of the arch are two fine Gothic squints – openings for viewing the altar – that on the right an Early Gothic trefoil arch, that on the left Decorated, with a small ogee. They might be taken from a textbook on styles of church architecture.

The chancel beyond is enclosed, as if a private sanctuary. Sunlight falls on a Perpendicular font which stands, unusually, in the centre of the chancel, a most dramatic effect. The church has a two-decker pulpit and smart altar frontals. The whitewashed walls show fragments of wall paintings. These are a puzzle. If there are more behind why not reveal them? If not, the fragments look merely surreal.

HAILES

*

Rare chancel seating

Undedicated and predating the ruined abbey across the road, Hailes is an unassuming chapel in the lee of the Cotswold escarpment. It is a simple cell of nave and smaller chancel, the one with a timber bellcote. Apart from some Decorated windows, the church was disturbed only once, by Puritans in the 17th century. With tourists teeming past to the abbey ruins opposite – why are dead ruins more appealing than a living church? – this is a calm, forgotten place.

Nave and chancel are divided by a Norman pointed arch with scalloped capitals, now filled with a Perpendicular screen of simple, severe lines. The nave has a king-post roof, the chancel a plastered wagon roof. The chancel, however, is unlike any other. While the Reformation usually deserted the chancel and concentrated worship in the nave, at Hailes it was the chancel that was converted into what might be a Nonconformist meeting house. The walls are panelled with seating backed up against them. The 17th-century altar was positioned in the middle of this chamber, like a dining table, but the chancel has since been rearranged to a more conventional three-sided arrangement. On the floor are medieval tiles, apparently from the old abbey.

The nave looks rather out of things. There are original benches, a pulpit and sounding board, all as if in another church. The nave has wall paintings, mostly of the early 14th century. These include a St Christopher and heraldic devices of various local patrons, as well as a hare hunt.

HIGHNAM
Holy Innocents ****
Woodyer's Gothic memorial

Highnam is the result of two labours of love, the first of creation, the second of restoration. The church was founded by Thomas Gambier Parry in 1849, to commemorate his late wife Isabella. The dedication is a reference to their many children who died in infancy. Only one, the composer Hubert Parry, lived to adulthood.

Like many of his generation, Parry was an enthusiast for the Anglo-Catholic revival and for its architectural concomitant, the Gothic Revival. He was a friend of the architect Henry Woodyer, a young follower of A. W. N. Pugin, who was to develop a lucrative church practice in Surrey. Parry asked Woodyer for a new church for the scattered community at Highnam, the project embracing a parsonage, lodge and schoolhouse. It was to be a model of such extended village patronage. Parry himself executed the church frescos in 1850–71.

Together with the later Hascombe (Surrey), Highnam was Woodyer's masterpiece. The church fell into decay after Parry's death and was restored in the 1980s by his descendant as patron, T. J. Fenton. The frescos had been obliterated and their cleaning proved a vindication of the spirit-based mural paint which Parry invented, to adapt the Italian fresco technique to the English climate. Woodyer's ensemble is now partly blighted by traffic and Parry's landscaping is wild and scrappy, but the west tower and spire still soar 200 feet over the neighbourhood. A grove of cypress, yew and monkey puzzle guards the church like spinster aunts.

The church is in the Decorated style, the austerity of its exterior stone relieved by plentiful crockets and pinnacles. The interior is gloomy even in daylight, every window being filled with stained glass and the lofty roof lost in darkness. The church is therefore best seen with evening light shining through its windows, catching each painting in turn, or with the aid of the admirable floodlights. Parry's wall paintings dominate the nave. Not an inch of wall is without decoration, the themes being borrowed from his European travels. The chancel arch rises to a benign Last Judgement which, on my visit, was lit by a ray of bright sunlight piercing the stained glass of the dormer window. The chancel is like the banqueting hall of a French prince. The east wall depicts vines entwining roundels filled with angels.

The furnishings were designed by Parry and Woodyer, and executed by Hardman. They include a sumptuous iron screen to the south chapel and an intricately carved stone reredos. Hardman even designed ornamental covers for the radiators. The floors are covered with Minton tiles. The glass is consonant with the architecture. Parry commissioned Wailes to do the north side and

Pugin the south, allegedly 'to pit one against the other that they might do their best'. The east window is a softer work by Clayton & Bell, portraying the Life of Christ. This replaced an earlier window by Hardman which Parry felt old-fashioned within ten years of its execution.

No expense was spared at Highnam. Parry concealed the cost even from himself by having all bills go directly to his bank manager, a practice not to be recommended when dealing with architects. When his masterpiece was complete in April 1851, Parry's son wrote that, on the eve of consecration, 'when all his guests had gone to bed and the new church stood gaunt and silent under the moon, father made his way there alone. He carried in his arms the bust [of Isabella] . . . and placed it in the niche in the chapel where it now stands.' This is a church at one with its maker.

KEMPLEY
St Mary ***
Norman wall paintings

Kempley church lies more than a mile beyond its village, in what seems the back of beyond. It is classified as redundant and is well cared for by English Heritage. The 13th-century fortified tower has a simple pyramidical roof. The door, like the rest of the church, is early Norman. The carvings of the doorway and tympanum are intact and even the massive hinges on the door are original. Recent dating has declared Kempley's roof timbers the oldest in England, c. 1120–50.

The appeal of the church lies in its wall paintings, those in the sanctuary reminiscent of the catacombs of ancient Rome. The structure is a double-cell divided by a Norman arch with vigorous carving. The only later work is a Decorated window in the south nave and a pulpit and oak pews. Kempley's nave murals are 14th century and fragmentary. They include saints with St Michael weighing souls in the north window splay, the plumes of a knight and, on the north wall, a vivid Wheel of Life. Over the arch is a Doom, also a chequerboard pattern.

The chancel is of a different order, the most complete set of Romanesque wall paintings in England, at least in an unrestored state. They were painted c.1130–40, covered in whitewash at the Reformation, and uncovered and varnished over by John Middleton in 1872. This varnish was destructive and in 1955 Eve Baker removed it. The murals had been executed in true fresco, painted into wet plaster, and had remained sound over the centuries. The colours shine more strongly, it is said, when the air is damp after rain. The predominant tones are red and ochre.

The murals portray the customary scenes of the early Christian rite. Overhead in the barrel vault are Christ in Benediction, with seraphim, the Virgin and St Peter. On the walls are the twelve apostles, pilgrims, a bishop and angels in roundels, some in excellent condition. Most rare is that almost the whole surface area is still covered. The impression of Kempley chancel is the same as would have confronted the 12th-century worshippers. I should love to see it, however briefly, lit by the original candles and hung with icons. The Kempley murals, according to Clifton-Taylor, are 'unquestionably the most worthy of a visit' in England.

[EH]

LECHLADE
St Lawrence ***
Tower carvings, roof bosses and corbels

Lechlade is a cadet branch of the 'woolgothic' aristocracy, and the most self-effacing. It sits in the corner of a market place, its churchyard pleasant rather than noble. Yet the carving on the exterior of the tower is a match for that at Fairford and Winchcombe. Guarding the tower is a magnificent monster holding a sword, looming over approaching visitors. The church was almost completely rebuilt in the 1470s on an earlier foundation, with spire, nave roof, clerestory and porch added in the early 16th century. An arcade of four sweeping bays with aisles lends an airiness to the interior. A heavy Victorian screen shields the chancel and thus obstructs the view of the east window.

Lechlade's speciality is the bosses and corbels adorning its roofs. These are not easy to see on a dark day, and photographs are helpfully displayed on the wall. The bosses form a gallery of domestic and religious activity. There are two wrestlers directly above the east window. Ten angels bear the Instruments of Jesus's Passion, including a blacksmith with nails. The stone corbels are carved with Church fathers and symbols of the evangelists. The east wall of the north aisle has a portrayal of St Agatha with a sword through her naked breasts. She was the patron saint of women suffering from breast cancer and here demonstrates the only known treatment at the time. A wall monument to Anne Simmons (d.1769) has a sobbing putto nearly smothered by a cascade of drapery. On the north wall of the nave is a small door with Panel traceried woodwork and an ogee surround, a gem of late-Gothic art.

Lechlade inspired a verse by Shelley in 1815. The poet saw the church as dusk fell on a summer's evening, 'Clothing in hues of Heaven thy dim and distant spire, / Around whose lessening and invisible height / Gather among the stars the clouds of night.'

LEONARD STANLEY
St Swithun **
Norman biblical carvings

In the lee of the Cotswold escarpment lies an ensemble of mansion, farm and priory church that is more French than English. The mansion is now a farmhouse but might pass for an 18th-century convent. An old Saxon chapel survives among its buildings, which probably served as the parish church until the 15th century. The priory church, pleasantly pervaded with a smell of manure, is Norman in its crossing tower and in the doorways on three sides. The doorway to the north is adorned with two dragon heads.

Leonard Stanley has an aisleless nave and a 14th-century wagon roof. It appears that the monastic and parochial parts of the church were once divided by an old rood screen, for some reason located half way down the nave. There is a similar confusion at Dunster (Somerset). The steps and openings for this screen can be seen on the south wall of the nave. Whether the canons were too numerous for the chancel or their chantries and altars were bursting for space we do not know.

Beyond the crossing, the chancel roof was raised by the Victorians, leaving two superbly-carved Norman capitals below the arches. The figures are unique in Gloucestershire. That on the north side shows Mary Magdalene anointing Christ's feet; that on the south shows a Nativity, with Mary in bed having given birth to Jesus, while an angel draws back the curtain and an ox looks on. They are vivid and expressive works. Above an adjacent aumbry is a more primitive carving of Adam and Eve as animals, Eve offering her apple while stamping on the serpent. The guide offers this as 'one of the most remarkable sculptures that the Middle Ages have handed down'. It is indeed outstanding.

NEWLAND
All Saints ***
Forester tombs, miner's brass

The Forest of Dean is Gloucestershire that has declared its independence and drifted off towards Wales. In the Balkans it would be a nation state. Its medieval mining and foresting communities were too poor to rebuild their Norman churches, which left them vulnerable to Victorian restorers. Newland is the finest, though hardly merits its acclaimed title of 'cathedral of the Forest'.

The setting is magnificent. The sandstone church sits on a small plateau amid wooded hills, its tower seeming to soar from one direction, nestle from another. Round it are gathered oaks, cedars, firs and pines. Toppling chest tombs fall about themselves in the churchyard, a space bounded by almshouses and with views over the forest. The interior is originally of the 13th and 14th centuries but was rebuilt in the 19th century by William White, architect of another forest church, Lyndhurst (Hants). The guide says that the old church was so ruinous there he had no alternative. White complained about the perverseness of the workmen employed at Newland who, 'in answer to his remonstrations for acting contrary to express orders ... told him that anyway they had erred on the right side'.

This is an emphatic White interior, characterised by bold new windows and a heavy chalet-style roof. What survives from the former structure is the spaciousness of the aisles, creating a large, domestic hall that would once have been crowded with miners, farmers, foresters and their families, choir chanting and dogs barking. The church possesses a large collection of tombs, a true parade of local history. Some are recumbent in stone, some lurk beneath brasses or inscribed pavings, some peer out from wall memorials or are depicted in the small exhibition in the north aisle. There are the Joyces, man and wife, her headdress a severe rectangle, his chainmail resting on a helm with a Saracen's head crest. Near the font is 'Jenkin Wyrall, Forester of Fee', in his woodman's costume, complete with horn, sword and knife. The south aisle boasts a tombslab with the outline of a bowman in a large-brimmed hat.

Most odd is the unique brass in the south aisle chapel. The Free Miners of the Forest of Dean enjoyed similar privileges to those of wool and other merchants. Above the brasses of the Gryndours is a crest of a miner standing on a helmet surrounded by leaves. The man carries a pick and a hod on his back, with a candle between his teeth. This may seem a curious image to find on a 15th-century knight's helmet but illustrates the importance of mining in the economy of the Forest. The only other image of a medieval miner is one carved in stone on a wall at Wirksworth (Derbys).

Newland has a fine tradition of modern embroidery. The Lady Chapel was decorated by Beryl Dean and a team of helpers, with a blue altar frontal and reredos curtain, colourful pennants and a dark brown and gold pulpit cloth.

NORTH CERNEY
All Saints **
Antiquarian restoration

North Cerney is the jewel of the Churn valley. The church glows amid the trees across the main road from the Bathurst Arms. It is both a medieval building and a 20th-century labour of love, that of William Iveson Croome, early doyen of the church conservation movement. This was his home church, on whose restoration he worked with the Gothic revival architect, F. C. Eden. Croome, who died in 1967, left his mark on every corner. His memorial tablet in the south transept states, 'Lord, I have loved the habitation of thy house and the place where honour dwelleth.'

The exterior is a picturesque if puzzling jumble. The churchyard is kept neat by local sheep, though this appears to require ugly electric fencing. The cruciform church and saddle-backed west tower are mostly Norman. In the late 15th century the transepts were added and the nave roof was renewed. A small Cotswold window above the east wall of the nave was blocked in the course of a later renewal.

Inside, Croome and Eden take over. Their most prominent creation is a rood loft, one of the few into which it is possible to climb and look out over the nave. This was completed in 1925. The carving is all local work, apart from the Crucifixion, which Croome bought in an antique shop in Italy. It dates from 1600. Eden also designed the screen to the south transept chapel and the main reredos. The altar frontal was surplus to requirements at Chartres Cathedral at the turn of the century.

Croome's attention is evident everywhere. The chancel arch is restored Norman, the pulpit Perpendicular, the reading desk made from an old box pew. The south transept squint is converted into a corridor. A new organ has its own gallery overlooking the nave. Contemporary glass can be found in the north and south transepts. On the west wall of the latter are four handsome monuments, each belonging to a different century and together illustrating the stylistic changes of the ages. Their dates are 1647, 1704, 1855 and 1967, the last to Croome, a simple slate roundel. In my view, the most modern is also the most beautiful.

On the exterior, where chancel meets transepts, are two huge gargoyles. Near the southern one, carved into the wall, is a manticora, a beast with human head and arms and the body of a lion. Another is at the foot of the tower. Like the fertility emblems found on the outside of some Norman churches, their origin is a mystery. What vision were they meant to ward off, or what god propitiate?

NORTHLEACH
St Peter and St Paul ****
Perpendicular porch, wool merchants' brasses

Northleach was for more than a hundred years the pre-eminent Cotswold wool town. Annals of the merchants of the Calais Staple are filled with references to this market. Its wool was the finest and claimed the highest prices in Calais and Flanders. Accounts of life in the 15th century describe merchants constantly in transit between Northleach, the wharves of Stepney and the market at Calais. The town developed its own middlemen, the Midwinters, Busshes and Elmes, with whom the London dealers traded. Money flowed through the town, much of it finding its way to adorn a church that ranks with those of Cirencester and Chipping Campden.

The town today is a shadow of its mighty past, but not so its church. A sleepy square slopes upwards towards a churchyard that is hidden from view behind the town lock-up. Suddenly we are confronted with a bull-neck of a tower. This was built c.1380–1400 for an earlier church and rises over a later battery of pinnacles, battlements and tracery. The tower is decorated only on its upper stage, as if designed to be seen from a distance. Huge diagonal buttresses offer support, including two inside the nave itself.

Next we approach the great porch. Northleach porch may not be as ostentatious as Cirencester or as exotic as St Mary Redcliffe, Bristol, but its ogee hoods, buttresses and pinnacles are a perfect late-Gothic composition. The porch vault is of two bays, a flourish of ribs. Supporting it is a complete set of medieval corbel heads, including a cat playing a fiddle, above blind arcading. Overhead is a priest's chamber, with a fireplace and chimney hidden within a buttress and pinnacle. If such porches could talk, they could surely tell the history of a different England from that in any written record.

Northleach's interior is not worthy of its exterior. It has been maltreated by both the last two centuries, particularly the 20th. The original proportions survive. The ratio of height to length and width must be unprecedented in England, reminiscent of a Continental hall church. This impression is exaggerated by the clerestory, the huge tower arch and octagonal piers with concave faces. This design is rare but occurs elsewhere in the county, at Chipping Campden and Rendcomb. The nave was completed in the first half of the 15th century, possibly by Henry Winchcombe, a mason who carved his name on a pier base in the south arcade.

The clerestory was added by the wool magnate John Fortey. He raised the nave nearly half as high again as he found it. The Lady Chapel came later still, in 1489, at a time when many chantries were founded in thanks for the end of the Wars of the Roses and the marriage of Henry Tudor to Elizabeth of York. The timber roofs and carved bosses are original. To lean back and gaze up at them (or use the mirror supplied for the purpose) is to experience the full majesty of English Perpendicular.

Northleach's brasses comprise the best collection in the county, having survived the iconoclasts, the vandals and the brass robbers. These mass-produced images reflected the status and interests of their patrons. Those at Northleach show not knights but merchants in contemporary dress, and appear to make some attempt at truth to life. Some are bald, some bearded, some with lined faces, some still young. The figures are shown in prayer and most stand on the emblems of their wealth, the sheep and the woolpack.

Fortey himself (d.1459) is near the pulpit, splendid in a fur-lined gown and adorned with his woolmark. My favourite is the brass of John Taylour and his wife in the south aisle. They gaze towards each other, their fifteen children arrayed at their feet. His shoes are no longer pointed nor his hair long, indicating a later date for his death. Scholars have traced all these families and their inter-relations. They constitute, as the guide says, 'members of an international trading organisation' as important to northern Europe as were the banking families of contemporary Florence or of Victorian London.

Northleach's modern furnishings are a mess. The new altar and the low-backed seating designed by Basil Spence in 1961 are out of character and insipid. A fussy iron screen divides the nave from the chancel. Perhaps a future age will find them less offensive to the eye.

ODDINGTON
St Nicholas **
Ancient woodland setting, Doom mural

Oddington is hidden, like an old sea chest shoved away in an attic. It lies down a track half a mile from the village, its original settlement probably deserted by plague. The churchyard is filled with yews, behind which rises a thick wood of beeches. The church, ruined for many years and restored only in the twentieth century, is too grand for a mere village. This is an abbey-in-the-woods near what was a residence of a 13th-century Archbishop of York. A visit by Henry III led to the addition of an Early Gothic nave and chancel alongside the old Norman ones.

The structure is thus easy to read. The old nave is now the south aisle, divided from the new nave by a three-bay arcade. A new tower was built over the old chancel, with its chancel arch filled in for added strength. In the 14th century two handsome Decorated windows were inserted into the aisle wall and a huge painting of a Doom covered a new north wall. This was discovered in 1913 but not fully restored until the 1970s. The work is faded but the figures of Christ and the apostles can be seen at the top, with below them angels, trumpets, hellfire and the damned being boiled in water or hanged from a gibbet. The Puritans covered it with whitewash, but to compensate at least contributed a battered old pulpit attached to the nave wall, still with its tester.

In the chancel is a stone reredos erected by the vicar responsible for the 1912 restoration, to commemorate his son who fell at Ypres. Outside the east end of the church is a stone effigy of a woman, dating from the 1690s, with feet sticking out beneath her dress. Outside the west end are Victorian headstones in a lettering known as Grot (short for grotesque). Villagers preferred to be buried here even after the 1850s, when a new church was built in the village. The old shades called them back. In the spring and summer, some kind friend of Oddington fills the church with wild flowers.

OZLEWORTH
St Nicholas *
Hexagonal tower

This is smart Cotswolds. Cedars glide across terraced lawns. Pheasants strut past horseboxes and look disdainfully at King Charles spaniels. Ozleworth, hidden away in its secluded valley above Wotton-under-Edge, is beautiful. It is one of the corners of England whose occupants have used their wealth to grant themselves a respite from ugliness, despite a microwave tower just over the horizon.

The church is part of what must have been an ancient hill settlement, since the churchyard, most unusually, is in the form of a circle, indicating a 'Celtic' site. It now forms one side of an elegant stableyard behind the house of Ozleworth Park. The church's most eccentric feature is at once apparent, a short Norman hexagonal tower dividing the nave and chancel. The only other such tower is at Swindon near Cheltenham, also owned by the Norman grandee, Roger de Berkeley, who built Ozleworth in the early 12th century. It is believed that the structure was originally a simple six-sided oratory, presumably with an eastern apse. The east side of the tower is wider than the other sides.

This building was altered in the Early Gothic style with the addition of a chancel to the east and a nave to the west. There are neither transepts nor aisles. Heavy restoration in 1873 by the then vicar, William Lowder, stripped the interior of any medieval patina, but the renewed stonework offers at least an intimation of what was clearly remarkable carving. The south doorway is adorned with six large sprays of stiff-leaf round its arch. Inside, the arch dividing nave and tower has 13th-century zigzag decoration, so deeply undercut as to be almost free-standing.

The fittings are all Victorian, but in the south-west face of the tower is a window containing charming Flemish glass, probably of the 16th century. [CCT]

PAINSWICK
St Mary **
Churchyard tombs and yews

Painswick church is omitted from many guides because the interior is a disappointment. Shot to pieces in the Civil War, burned, struck by lightning, Victorianised and recently modernised, it has been ill-treated by history. Yet the town is among the loveliest in the Cotswolds and its churchyard is one of the most remarkable in England. It forms part of a sloping square surrounded by 17th- and 18th-century façades. Everything is in a soft, lustrous stone that glows in the long evening shadows produced by Painswick's steep contours. It is a glorious spot, with blackbirds in constant and noisy attendance.

The churchyard is peopled by two distinct tribes, the yews and the tombs, 99 of the first, 33 of the second. The yews were mostly planted in the 1790s, and are clipped each year in August. There are 99 by tradition because whenever a 100th was planted it died. The trees stand smart and to attention, pretending to watch over the tombs like Lewis Carroll's guardsmen. The tombs will have none of it. They are a complete contrast. Some are upright, stern and regimented, others are tilting, bashed and drunken. Those on the north side are in the better order, those to the south seem ready to escape the hillside entirely. Together they form a truly surreal landscape.

Painswick's richly carved table tombs are Gloucestershire treasures. They demonstrate the wealth of cloth living on into the 17th and 18th centuries, long after the boom years were over. Men and women no longer sought salvation in chantries or alabaster memorials. They were content to rest under the Cotswold sky, protected by angels and putti, their names carved in stone. These names reflect the trades on which Painswick's wealth was based: Packers, Pallings, Greenings and Smiths. The earlier tombs are of men calling themselves 'clothiers', middlemen between wool merchants and drapers. As the century progressed, the Pooles called themselves 'gents'. One tomb stands out from the others. It is number 32, the pyramidical resting place of John Bryan. He was neither clothier nor gent but a carver, creator of many of these works around him.

The church's nave and tower date from the late 15th century and are conventionally Perpendicular. The spire was not built until 1632 and has been rebuilt more than once since. Within twelve years it was besieged by Royalist troops who used cannon and firebombs to drive out the Parliamentarians quartered inside. Most of the interior fittings date from successive restorations in the late 19th or 20th centuries, although the excellent classical reredos in the south chancel aisle is of 1743, also by Bryan. Painswick has fine kneelers, some 300 in all, today's chief contribution to church craftsmanship. The project took four years and involved some sixty people working to an overall design by Anne Yeo, a sacristan. The kneelers depict Bible scenes, local societies and charities, views of the town, animals, birds and memorials to local people. They are more in tune with the medieval tradition of local craft than the bought-in stained glass.

RENDCOMB
St Peter *
Tudor interior, Herefordshire font

Up the Churn valley from North Cerney stands the un-Cotswoldian Rendcomb House, an Italianate mansion now a school. Sheltering beneath it is a rebuilt

Tudor church that was dedicated in 1517, the year of Luther's Articles. It must rank among England's last medieval churches before the Reformation. The patron was Sir Edmund Tame, whose father built Fairford. Traces of that great church are detectable even in this modest work. The exterior is conventional Perpendicular, with heavy battlements and pinnacles on the tower. The church-yard has a friendly jumble of tomb chests looking out across this lovely valley.

The first thing to catch the eye on entering is the font. This is of the 12th-century Herefordshire School, brought from Gloucester to adorn the garden of the big house. It has twelve apostles, or rather eleven with one left blank for Judas. Another font is by the pulpit, filled with flowers on my visit. Rendcomb comprises a nave with south aisle, divided by an arcade with concave-sided octagonal piers in the manner of Northleach and Chipping Campden. Buried in the north wall are the remains of an Early Gothic arcade to a lost north aisle, three piers revealed in the plasterwork.

The church has no clerestory and no divide between nave and chancel, but the chancel roof is distinct, a richly embossed Victorian structure of sycamore. The Victorians also reinstated the rood screen, using parts of an old one and grafting on to it a frieze of cast iron. This composition straddles both the chancel and the south chapel. The latter has an iron altar rail with the chained swan emblem of the Guise family, who succeeded the Tames as lords of the manor. The roofs rest on corbels, those in the south aisle carved with angels playing instruments and holding heraldic shields. Their faces are realistic enough to be members of the congregation.

The glass in the east window is dire, but some 16th-century glass survives in the north windows. It has early Renaissance forms which imply a different designer from Fairford, and a later date of *c.*1520.

SELSLEY
All Saints **
Gallery of early Morris glass

The church has a magnificent location on a ridge overlooking the approach to Stroud. Selsley is the product not of parochial history but of Victorian munificence, that of Sir Samuel Marling, merchant of Stroud. He is said to have demanded a design modelled on a church at Marling in the Austrian Tyrol. His architect in 1862, the young G. F. Bodley, erected a work in French (rather than Austrian) Gothic style, rugged and powerful with a saddleback tower, Plate tracery, apsidal chancel and steeply-pitched roofs. In winter, Selsley might be on a limb of the Alps. The exterior is austere, the interior no less so. A single, north aisle is divided from the nave by two heavy arches on a single short red granite pier, boldly adorned with leaf capitals.

The main interest of the church lies in its glass. At Selsley as in his other early commissions, such as St Michael, Brighton (Sussex) and St Martin, Scarborough (Yorks, N), Bodley commissioned glass from his friend, William Morris. In 1861 Morris had established a partnership in Red Lion Square with Burne-Jones, Ford Madox Brown, Dante Gabriel Rossetti and Philip Webb. Their capital was £20 each plus £100 from Morris's mother. Bodley's commissions were crucial to their early success, though a vicar at Middleton Cheney (Northants) also secured a superb and little-known set of windows.

Selsley was the firm's first ecclesiastical work, with most of the partners involved. The outcome is an exquisite early Pre-Raphaelite gallery, the windows following the medieval tradition, from the Crucifixion over the altar to Christ in Majesty in the west window. Selsley is to Victorian stained glass what Fairford, much admired by Morris, is to late Gothic. Madox Brown wrote that church glass was not about refined drawing: 'What it does admit of and imperatively require is fine colour, and what this can admit of and does very much require is invention, expression and good dramatic action.'

Much debate has surrounded who did what in early Morris windows. Here the consensus has the overall design by Webb, with the figurative scenes in a band running round the middle of the windows and white glass above and below. The simplified style and pure colours suit the architecture. The individual windows are by various members of the partnership. In general, Webb is master of animals and birds, Morris of foliage and background, and Burne-Jones, Rossetti and Madox Brown of the figurative composition, with Burne-Jones dominant. But the guide assigns individual windows to individual artists. Thus the Annunciation in the south chancel is given to Morris, apparently based on van Eyck's Ghent altarpiece. The Resurrection at the north end of the apse, attributed to Burne-Jones, echoes Piero della Francesca's version. My favourites are the vivid Creation scenes in the west window. The church has been immaculately restored.

STANTON
St Michael *
Comper furnishings

This jolly church with a needle spire sits between village and manor house under a glorious sweep of the Cotswolds. The eye is drawn at once to the Perpendicular windows in the south aisle, with two tiers of tracery above the main lights. They flank the porch within a frame of trees on either side, like a snug Tudor hostelry welcoming the passing traveller inside.

The interior is of all periods. The north arcade is Norman, with the elongated stiff-leaf of Early Gothic. The small transepts are 13th century, with squints to enable worshippers to see into the chancel. From the Perpendicular south arcade rude faces stare down from the spandrels, one poking out his tongue at the congregation. Stanton's woodwork includes a rare 14th-century pulpit now used as a lectern, balancing one with a Jacobean tester. There are early benches with carved poppyheads at the back of the nave, next to the Perpendicular font.

The church has furnishings by Comper, including an admirable screen of 1923, with rood and loft. He also restored the chancel and designed the gilt reredos. The east window is made of fragments of 15th-century glass brought from nearby Hailes Abbey, and surrounded by the shields of local dignitaries. Comper's strawberry mark is in the window. He also designed the west gallery and organ loft, and the war memorial in the churchyard. His work is a model 20th-century handling of a lovable old building. It was paid for by a wealthy Lancashire architect, Philip Stott, who bought Stanton Court in 1906.

TETBURY
St Mary *
Georgian Gothic interior

A tall spire rises over the gentle contours of the Gloucestershire plateau. The Prince of Wales, an admirer of this church, can see it from Highgrove and has described it from that distance as looking like Salisbury Cathedral. The old town is charming if rather precious, with the church set to the south of the main street. Apart from the restored medieval steeple, it is 18th-century Gothic and most unusual.

Approached from the town, the church is immediately eccentric. The west tower is normal, but the aisles appear to have shrunk while the clerestory has developed elephantiasis. Its large Perpendicular windows wholly dominate the composition and suggest a Tudor rebuild gone mad. All is revealed inside. Apart from the tower, Tetbury was completely redesigned in 1771 by a Warwick architect named Francis Hiorn, and reopened in 1781. The parish specifically requested a Gothic rather than a classical work. They got one.

Tetbury is in an exaggerated late Perpendicular style, strongly reminiscent of a German hall church and with no formal division between nave, aisles and chancel. It might almost be Methodist. The dominant characteristic of the interior is spaciousness, emphasised by the splendidly elongated and shafted piers supporting the roof. These are of cast iron clothed in wood, and look like the pillars of a Victorian conservatory. They rise to a shallow ceiling with a plaster rib vault.

The church is galleried and filled with box pews. The outer aisles are closed from the central space, entered by doors from the pews. They form an ambulatory with vestries and other rooms. The windows above are enormous but spoilt with stained glass that is made worse by appearing in some windows but not in others.

Visitors are greeted by a fierce modern mural by Pat Panton and Peter McLennan in the narthex, a sadly crude work for such delicate architecture.

TEWKESBURY
Abbey of St Mary *****
Norman nave, 'Sun of York' bosses, Despenser tombs, medieval glass

Tewkesbury Abbey is one of England's most splendid churches. It stands memorial to the grandest of the Marcher lords, burial place in turn of Fitzhamons, de Clares, Despensers, Beauchamps and Nevilles. Today it ranks with Beverley Minster (Yorks, ER) and Sherborne (Dorset) as the finest legacy left by monastic Catholicism to parochial Anglicanism after the Reformation. Some might regard these as not parish churches, but they are as parochial as a hundred other legacies of the Dissolution. Tewkesbury was fortunate in the extent of its survival. While neighbouring Worcester and, later, Gloucester were granted cathedral status, Tewkesbury was offered by Henry VIII to the townspeople, who bought it for £453.

With commendable restraint, they demolished only the Lady Chapel and the monastic buildings, leaving in place the biggest Norman tower in Europe and a vault that is a glory of English architecture. Even today the north and west of the abbey is still enclosed by buildings, giving a rare impression of what these great churches would have been like when pressed round by houses. Our enthusiasm for setting churches in a sea of lawn was not envisaged by their original architects, nor is it always appropriate.

The abbey is a Norman fabric with Decorated east end, windows and vaults. It is dominated by its huge central tower, the three upper stages ornamented with zigzag and blind arcading. Only the battlements and pinnacles of 1660 are a later intrusion, the wooden spire having blown off in 1559. A walk round the east end reveals the six chapels that form a corona round the ambulatory, above which rise superb Decorated windows. The Norman west front is based on a huge arch flanked by six shafts rising the full height of the nave. A pair of west towers was probably planned but not built. In its day this must have been one of the tallest arches in Christendom.

To enter the abbey is to encounter an enchanted forest. Eight bays of huge Norman drum piers, 6 ft 6 ins wide and over 30 ft tall, rise to a roof added in the 14th century. The Norman arcades, triforium and clerestory were left in place, but the new vault ribs were allowed to spring from lower down, like palm branches rising direct from the capitals. As a result, they burst upwards in splays of delight, meeting and intersecting in a dance of liernes and tiercerons. The central bosses portray the Life of Christ, the lesser ones angels.

At the crossing, the liernes perform their dance against a white background with a huge red and gold centrepiece. This is architecture of extraordinary beauty, pride of the families to whom the 'honour of Tewkesbury' was granted by successive monarchs: the de Clares, Despensers and Beauchamps. None deserved more credit than Eleanor de Clare, wife of Hugh le Despenser, who was hanged at Hereford in 1326 as favourite of Edward II. After his death, she embarked on a stupendous building programme at Tewkesbury, including the present choir and ambulatory of c.1340. She was to convert the old Norman structure into a Decorated casket for her family memorials.

The piers of the Norman choir aisles were truncated and a grandiose Decorated vault erected above, its ribs against a background of white, red and blue. Round the choir were then arrayed the chapels and chantries of her great dynasty. The earliest are to the north. Most splendid is the tomb next to the altar, of the second Hugh le Despenser, Eleanor's son (d.1348) and his wife Elizabeth Montacute (d.1359). The dainty canopy is carved with such crispness and precision that it resembles metalwork. Ogival arches swirl upwards in four diminishing tiers to brush against the hard stone of the vault, a phenomenal work of 14th-century design. Next door is the chantry of 1397 to the founder of the abbey, Robert Fitzhamon (d.1107), Eleanor's ancestor.

In the north ambulatory the tomb of Sir Guy de Brien (d.1390) attempts a copy of the Despenser tomb, but does not capture its ethereal beauty. Further east is the superbly decorated Wakeman cenotaph (or empty tomb), composed in the mid-16th century of filigree stonework worthy of an oriental mosque. Inside is that bizarre medieval foible, a decaying cadaver being eaten by vermin.

Eleanor's nephew, Edward le Despenser (d.1375), built the Holy Trinity Chantry in the south choir arcade and is portrayed on top of it in the celebrated 'kneeling knight' statue. Of this romantic individual, the French chronicler Jean Froissart wrote that he was 'much beloved of ladies; the most noble said that no feast was perfect if Sir Despenser was not present'. Edward's grand-daughter, Isabella Despenser, married first Richard Beauchamp, Earl of Worcester, and then his cousin of the same name but mightier title, that of Earl of Warwick. This took the dynasty into a new family and a new, grim century. After Warwick's death, Isabella erected a chantry chapel for him, c.1430, in the north choir arcade. It is an exceptionally elaborate two-tier structure with a fan vault at the lower level and a lierne vault above.

Their daughter married Richard Neville, Warwick the Kingmaker. Thus were two of the great families of late-medieval England united, their shifting allegiances lying at the root of the mayhem that was the Wars of the Roses. They finally and fatally aligned themselves with the Lancastrian cause, which met its end at the bloody Battle of Tewkesbury in 1471. At this battle, Margaret of Anjou, whose husband Henry VI was already ten years dead, was captured and her son, the Prince of Wales, killed and buried in the abbey. The victorious Yorkists under Edward IV inserted 'sun' bosses in the vault over the old Despenser choir. They shine down to this day, celebrating an event of which Shakespeare later wrote: 'Now is the winter of our discontent / Made glorious summer by this sun of York.' The speaker was Gloucester, later Richard III, one of the victors of Tewkesbury. The Yorkists enjoyed only fourteen years of ascendancy, before Richard fell to Henry Tudor at Bosworth.

These tombs and chantries are widely agreed to be second only to Westminster Abbey as a collection of funerary monuments. Each is a variant on a Gothic theme, a textbook of design over the four centuries that divided the Conquest from the Reformation. Above them rises magnificent ancient glass, most of it from the time of Eleanor's patronage and thus much earlier than most surviving medieval glass. Over the choir and in the east window is glass equalled only at Great Malvern (Worcs), Ludlow (Salop) and, of course, Fairford.

In the bottom right of the east window can be seen Eleanor herself, naked and 'stripped of all earthly trappings'. The armoured ranks of noblemen of the Despenser line fill the two west windows of the choir clerestory. This depiction of a great family in stained glass is unique for the period. The vestry door is covered with metal beaten from the armour of knights slain at the Battle of Tewkesbury. Flemish altarpieces, medieval statues, Victorian radiator covers and chests start out at us from every corner of this church, still deafened by the din of Britain's longest and most senseless civil war.

TEWKESBURY
Old Baptist Chapel *
Chapel in converted medieval house

The chapel is open to the public and still available for worship. It lies in a small courtyard off Church Street, directly opposite the abbey. A medieval timber-framed house was converted for chapel use probably in the 1620s. It retains beams that date from the 15th century. This is one of the earliest Baptist chapels in England.

That said, the main façade is mostly 18th century. The interior was altered in the 1720s to provide a minister's room on the upper floor. It was then that the elegant windows were installed, bringing light to the interior. The Baptistery is a (concealed) pit directly in front of the pulpit. The guide points out that the gradual adaptation of a family dwelling to a place of worship illustrates 'the belief that religion should be centred around the family and home as opposed to the monumental churches and rather impersonal clergy'. The raised pulpit, the gallery and minister's room evoke a tradition of group worship in which the congregation takes full part in the ceremony. The warm sunlight pouring in through high Georgian windows makes it a tranquil respite from the bustling town outside.

WINCHCOMBE
St Peter **
Gallery of gargoyles, Tudor embroidery

Winchcombe is a lesser sister of the great wool churches. The building is prominently set on the main street of a busy market town, guarded by forty of the country's finest gargoyles, big and ugly. Some are devils, some known people, some eccentrics in strange garb, including a top hat. Outside the south aisle is one of Sir Ralph Boteler, lord of Sudeley in the 15th century and benefactor of the church. He appears with a helmet and splendid moustache. The overall effect is extraordinary, of a gallery of jesters laughing, jeering and poking out their tongues at passers-by. The tower has eight pinnacles and a large golden weathercock, given by St Mary Redcliffe, Bristol, when the latter's spire was restored in 1874.

Winchcombe was built new on older foundations in 1454–70. The abbot of the monastery built the chancel and the townspeople the nave. In 1690, the chancel was rebuilt and its roof raised. The only relic of the former chancel arch is a finely executed wooden arch brace two bays from the east end, with wheels in its spandrels. The interior is thus a single large space, where the only difference between nave and chancel is in the tracery. Light floods in from the great seven-light east window and from the broad aisle and clerestory openings.

The furnishings are mixed. The east window glass, by John Hardman in 1885, is considered one of his masterpieces and portrays Christ calming the storm, surrounded by his disciples aboard a large ship. The sedilia are Perpendicular. Across the chancel is a curious memorial to Thomas Williams (d.1636). He is kneeling, supposedly to face his wife, but she is not there. She apparently survived to marry a second time and wished instead to join her second husband in death.

Behind a curtain in the north aisle is a former altar cloth, beautifully embroidered. The border shows the pomegranate emblem of Catherine of Aragon, who stayed at neighbouring Sudeley. The cloth was made up from 14th-century priests' copes. This is a great treasure, as are the carvings on the west screen, which include one known as the Winchcombe Imp.

Bristol

Bristol once ranked with York and Norwich as centres of medieval church building outside London. The Blitz took a dreadful toll on the city, but worse by far was insensitive post-war demolition and development, destroying much of what survived the bombing. Shorn of most of its pre-war street pattern and of the informal uses that retain life in city centres, Bristol finds it hard to look after even the churches that remain and many are inaccessible. But St Mary Redcliffe, its best church after the Cathedral, is in excellent condition, despite the traffic swirling past. So too is the Lord Mayor's Chapel, rich in stained glass and civic furnishings.

Lord Mayor's Chapel ****   St Mary Redcliffe *****
St John **   The New Room **

LORD MAYOR'S CHAPEL
St Mark, College Green ****
European medieval glass, civic tombs

The west front of the chapel, across College Green from the cathedral, is so small as to be near invisible. It is squeezed between later buildings and the tower is buried at the rear. The chapel originally served as an almshouse, but after the Dissolution it was bought by the Corporation and is now the only church in England that belongs to a local authority. It consists of a late 13th-century nave and an early 14th-century south aisle with a Perpendicular chancel. Yet this is one of the richest civic churches in England, a treasure house of memorials and stained glass of superlative quality.

The first impression of the interior is of the Perpendicular nave roof, its bosses picked out in gold. It covers the nave like a sumptuous quilted tent. On the walls are the hatchments of 18th- and 19th-century mayors of Bristol; on the walls are their sword rests. The nave glass is superb, most of it bought by the Corporation at the 1823 sale of the contents of Fonthill Abbey. The north wall carries an unusual display of secular glass from France, the best displaying the emblems of the royalist house of Montmorency, a curious subject for a proud civic church. More French glass of biblical scenes fills the windows in the south wall opposite.

To the south of the nave lies the south aisle and its chapel. Both are filled with the tombs of Bristol worthies, from the 13th century to the 20th. The most unusual is a figure of a scholar, John Cookin, down on one knee, his books behind him. He died at the age of eleven, a most studious young man. Above the arch between aisle and chapel is glass depicting Becket, by Benjamin West. The chapel is a gallery of English monumental art. In the centre are the supposed effigies of the founders of the original almshouse, de Gaunt and de Gournay. On the walls round them are the memorials of a great city, happily not in the cathedral but in a place of specifically civic worship. The chapel glass is composed of 16th- and 17th-century Flemish and German roundels.

This is but a prelude to the chancel and its adjacent Poyntz Chapel. These are exquisite spaces. The chancel is little more than a sanctuary, wholly dominated by a large Perpendicular east window filled with early 16th-century glass. Some of this is local but the main lights are from Cologne. In the centre are portrayals of St Catherine and St Barbara. On the right is a lovely picture of Mary and Joseph with, below, St Anthony and the raven. Adjacent on the north wall are two fine tombs. The larger commemorates Sir Maurice Berkeley (d.1464) and his wife. Over the effigies is a canopy with an elaborate ogee arch. This culminates in a huge finial standing proud above the monument. The wallplate has Perpendicular panelling.

To the south of the chancel and well hidden lies the Poyntz Chapel, a gem of late Perpendicular architecture erected by Sir Robert Poyntz (d.1520) and adorned with the arms of Poyntz and his king, Henry VIII, whom he attended at the Field of the Cloth of Gold. The room is decorated with fan vaulting and niches. Its lovely east window has stained glass from Venice, Germany and England, portraying saints and heraldic devices. These are surrounded by small quarries, well set, orderly and not overpowering. There can be no finer room in Bristol, now set aside for quiet contemplation.

ST JOHN
Broad Street **
Setting over city gate

The line of Broad Street rising towards Christ Church is one of the few neighbourhoods of Bristol still identifiably ancient, rather than a fragment-with-traffic. At the foot of the street lies a Gothic city gate, flanked by part of the old wall. The grooves of the portcullis can still be seen. Over the gate rises the west tower and spire of the now redundant St John's church, a picturesque composition. Underneath the outside wall, that is outside the ancient city, is the entry to a crypt which runs the length of the church. This remarkable chamber contains a vault with Decorated bosses and displaced medieval tombs.

The church is early Perpendicular and graceful, with the dimensions of a collegiate chapel. It has no aisles or transepts, just a simple single-storey nave, divided into six tall bays by lofty shafts rising to a wooden roof. There are excellent 17th-century fittings. The west gallery front is sumptuously carved, with panel pictures of saints above handsome doors and a list of past Bristol mayors. The font is decorated with a mass of cherubs' faces and has a cover of a dove on bold wooden supports. Even the almsbox is decorated in pretty Jacobean strapwork.

St John's windows are opaque, the upper tracery filled with fragments of medieval glass. The bay nearest to the chancel arch has a clerestory window, to direct light on to the vanished rood. Today the arch is decorated only by a magnificent Georgian sword-holder and a lion and unicorn, both arrogantly turning towards the wall. The chancel beyond contains the medieval tomb of the church's benefactor, Walter Frampton (d.1388). The reredos is a Tudor structure, oddly castellated, dividing off the vestry.
[CCT]

ST MARY REDCLIFFE
Redcliffe Way *****
Twin porches, Perpendicular interior, 1,200 roof bosses

'The fairest, goodliest and most famous parish church in England,' Queen Elizabeth is reputed to have said on a visit in 1574. Few would disagree, though some have questioned whether she said it. For centuries, St Mary's on its 'red cliff' welcomed home Bristol adventurers as they sailed up the Avon. Some are believed to have reached America before Columbus, based on a reference in Columbus's diaries.

St Mary's was the start and end of every such journey and no expense was spared on its adornment. Here the West Country tycoons, the Cabots, the Jays, the Canynges, the Ameryks, the Medes, sought glory in this world and security in the next. They built chantries to guard their souls in purgatory. They raised altars to their favourite saints. They financed clergy to sing Masses, twenty at the height of St Mary's prosperity. In 1416 a merchant named Belinus gave precious books in Latin to be read by the vicar and chaplains at their leisure. Fabrics, paintings, statues, icons and relics would have been carried up to the great porch from the forest of masts moored along the quay.

St Mary's is a masterpiece of English Gothic. It began as a shrine to Our Lady, on rising land by the river outside the city walls. Even today its spire of 292 ft (second only to Louth in Lincolnshire), restored in the 19th century after collapsing in the 15th, can hold its own among Bristol's tower blocks. But the tower must take second place to the north porch, a double-chambered structure facing what would have been the harbour. The inner porch, contemporary with St Mary's earliest phase, is Early Gothic while the outer porch, presumably built because the inner was overcrowded, is Decorated of the mid-14th century.

The outer porch is thus reached first. It is polygonal in plan and has an astonishing seven-pointed entrance arch. Scholars regard this as oriental, its origins lying in documents brought back by travellers from the Near East and Moorish Spain. Jean Bony, historian of English Decorated, describes the stonework as 'undercut in the manner of oriental ivories and criss-crossed by a pattern of large diamonds, suggesting ivory box lids'. Michael Quinton Smith, in his history of the church, sees in the porch's deep-carved motifs all the 'luxuriance of Seljuk portals in Asia Minor or the stucco-work of Islamic Spain'. By the early 14th century, English taste was no longer slave to France. It was open to the trade winds.

Who designed this marvel? We know that its motifs recur in medieval psalters. We know that one 'Robert the Sculptor' was in the retinue of an expedition sent to Persia by Edward I, which visited the Masjid Camii at Isfahan. That Persian temple vault is strikingly similar to the Lady Chapel at Wells. Others detect the hand of the master mason of late Decorated, William Ramsay. There is a similar 'oriental' door, possibly by Ramsay, at Cley next the Sea (Norfolk). He died in the Black Death in 1349, and this exotic cosmopolitanism vanished into English Perpendicular.

The richness of this porch can be seen in every detail. The polygonal buttresses are embellished with nodding ogee arches. The outside niches carry contorted images of pilgrims, cripples and peasants, a photographic record of those who would have loitered on this spot six centuries ago. The window tracery is like angels' wings. Inside, the hexagonal vault is so ribbed as to appear spinning free of the corners. Nor is the inner porch any less impressive. The view into it from the outer porch is as down a tunnel into history. The black Purbeck shafts and the 'windblown' stiff-leaf capitals are superb, the alcoves only awaiting the return of distant sailors and their offerings.

The first impression of the interior is of sheer Perpendicularity. Every line searches upwards to the roof, where it fractures into a maze of vault ribs. Yet the structure is a combination of inconsistencies, joins, changes in style and level. These add to St Mary's appeal, each age making its distinctive mark. The plan is that of an Early Gothic church, but a massive rebuilding on the old foundations began in the early years of the 14th century, yielding a Decorated south aisle and transept. The rest of the church dates from the end of that century and is Perpendicular. Yet these periods seem immaterial. The whole interior is a forest of soaring arches and vaults with aisles swerving away on all sides, including in the transepts.

The church is vaulted throughout. Palm-like pier shafts push upwards to the vault, interrupted by only a hint of a capital. The vault ribs form astonishing patterns, lozenges in the nave, hexagons in the south aisle, squares in the transepts and rectangles in the choir. The patterns are punctuated, so we are told, by no fewer than 1,200 bosses. It is as if the master masons had sat with their sketchbooks and doodled a dozen cat's cradles, then tossed the plan to their carvers and told them to 'go and decorate it'. In the north nave aisle is a boss in the form of a circular maze.

Facing the entrance on the south wall of the nave aisle are three tomb recesses, their canopies similar to the 'oriental' north doorway. These recesses are Gothic at its most exhilarating, swaying and bouncing concave lines swooping out to huge foliated stops. They were intended to house the tombs of priests of the 14th-century foundation. One contains that of John Lavyngton (d.1411). Similar tomb recesses are in Bristol Cathedral, where they are painted.

The church's principal benefactor, William Canynges, lived from 1402 to 1474 and thus saw both the completion of the interior and its restoration following the collapse of the old tower in 1446. Canynges was a merchant in cloth, shipping and property. He was Mayor of Bristol five times and its Member of Parliament. His list of ships is recorded in the church, and he employed 800 men in Bristol alone. On the death of his wife in 1467 he decided to become a priest and was ordained. As a result, he is portrayed twice: once alongside his wife in their tomb in the south transept, in the rich garments of a 15th-century merchant, and again nearby as a priest. At the feet of Canynges as merchant lies a dog; at the feet of Canynges as priest is an infidel's head.

The stained glass at St Mary's is Victorian, apart from some medieval fragments near the tower and a rather insipid modern window in the Lady Chapel by H. J. Stammers. My preference is for the Comper work in the south transept, but the glass throughout detracts from the architecture. An iron screen of 1710, once dividing nave and chancel and now beneath the tower, is the masterpiece of William Edney. To Sacheverell Sitwell it was 'one of the splendours of the ignored baroque art of England'. The finial is of two elongated arms holding a snake and a balance.

St Mary's in the 18th century also produced the tragedy of Thomas Chatterton. Above the porch is the room where the boy poet is alleged to have delved among church records to write his 'forged' document on medieval Bristol. He moved to London on the strength of its initial success, committing suicide at the age of seventeen. Chatterton's father was sexton to St Mary's.

THE NEW ROOM
Horsefair, Broadmead **
Early Methodist meeting room

The origins of the New Room are written in the annals of Methodism. George Whitefield had been preaching to vast gatherings of coal miners at Kingswood outside the city. In 1739 he sent word to Wesley in London to come and help him. His audiences were rising from 2,000 to as many as 20,000, at which point it is hard to believe that more than a few followers heard him.

The building that Wesley erected that year in the centre of the old city was not to meet this problem. It was intended not for preaching but for bringing together the elders of the Society for discussion. Dissenting groups had enjoyed the licence to gather in places of worship of their own since the Declaration of Indulgence of 1687. Wesley had resisted establishing Methodist churches because he did not hold himself to be a Dissenter but a true Anglican. Indeed, his brother Charles so disagreed with the setting up of the New Room as to write a note of protest on the back of the licence certificate. Charles none the less was a minister at the church for many years afterwards and lived here in 1748.

The room saw many of the theological disputes that wracked the movement during and after Wesley's life. It has since become a place of pilgrimage for Methodists the world over. It is American Methodism's site 'number 16'. The door is reached down an alley from the newly pedestrianised Broadmead next to the Arcade. Here stands a statue of Wesley on horseback, prayerbook in hand, leaning slightly forward and looking intense. Against the chapel wall is a shed still marked The Preacher's Stable.

The interior is that of a simple Georgian chapel, though with four strong Doric columns supporting a cupola lighting the third bay. There are box pews in the body of the chapel, with galleries on three sides and benches beneath. The joinery is excellent and such fittings as hatpegs and candleholders still survive. In the centre is the pulpit. The composition is 'three-decker' but symmetrical, raising the preacher to extraordinary prominence. To add to this grandiosity, the pulpit and subordinate lectern are reached not from the body of the church but from the private apartments beside and above.

The whole chamber has been redecorated in white and blue, and is filled with a serene silence. The adjacent apartments form a pleasant sequence of 18th-century rooms, and are now a museum with original furniture and mementoes of Methodism. Each chamber is named after an early dignitary. One of the rooms looks down through the cupola on to the pulpit beneath, Methodism's answer to Philip II's squint at the Escorial.

Hampshire

with Isle of Wight

Hampshire is a county of fierce contrasts. The central spine of the M3 down to Southampton and Portsmouth culminates in some of the dreariest development in Britain, especially the sprawl along the south coast. Inland there is a surprising wildness, both to the east, overlooking the Meon valley, and west to the Hampshire Downs. The heavily protected New Forest is still a blessed oasis.

The coastal churches date back to the earliest Saxon and Norman monastic foundations and many were of great wealth. These survive most spectacularly at Romsey and Winchester, St Cross. Inland from the coast, building materials were poor and settlements equally so. This was not wool country and the most endearing churches are tiny pre-Gothic structures hidden amid forested downland, as at Breamore, Corhampton and East Meon. Hampshire has surprisingly little Gothic church building, indeed probably the least in England, and almost nothing distinguished of the Perpendicular age.

Not until the 18th century does much new work emerge. The Georgians left the splendid Brydges church at Avington, and the charming fittings at Minstead. The Pre-Raphaelites decorated William White's glorious creation at Lyndhurst. Ninian Comper produced his last complete work in a modest backwater of Cosham. At Burghclere, Stanley Spencer created one of the outstanding mural cycles of the 20th century.

Ashmansworth *
Avington ***
Beaulieu *
Boarhunt *
Boldre *
Bramley *
Breamore **
Burghclere **
Corhampton *
Cosham **
Crondall **

East Meon ***
Ellingham *
Fawley *
Hale *
Headbourne Worthy *
Idsworth *
Lyndhurst ***
Minstead ***
Portchester **
Romsey ****
Selborne *

Silchester *
Southwick *
Stoke Charity **
Titchfield **
Winchester: St Cross
****
Wolverton *

Isle of Wight see page 300

ASHMANSWORTH

St James *

Private pews, Whistler glass

The Hampshire Downs can seem far from the rich estates of the Kennet valley. Ashmansworth is a small village of dormitory and weekend cottages. A drive marked with white stones leads to its church, with a weatherboarded bell-turret atop a red-tiled roof. Most of these downland churches were rebuilt in the 19th century, but St James retains a tranquil antiquity.

The church is a simple two-cell Norman building. The nave is dominated by rough, apparently medieval, woodwork. Huge wooden beams seem to be supporting not just the tower but the whole west end of the church. In the middle of the two tie-beams are carved bosses said to be from Winchester Cathedral. One is decorated with leaves, the other with grimacing monsters. At the west end are two galleries. That on the left is marked for the Earl of

Portsmouth, supposing he ever used it, and that on the right for the rector. Neither has any obvious means of access.

The nave is whitewashed apart from patches covered in barely decipherable wall paintings. The chancel arch appears to be Norman, though it may be a reworking of a Saxon opening. On either side are no less primitive squints, giving views of a small chancel with ancient tiles on the floor and deeply recessed windows, Norman to the north and lancets to the south. The furniture is rich. Two twisted candlesticks attend the altar and a set of Jacobean chairs arranged as if in a meeting house.

The porch contains a rare treasure, an engraved window by Laurence Whistler in celebration of English music. It is a memorial to the composer Gerald Finzi, erected by his widow in 1976. It portrays the tree of music with musical notes for leaves and composers' names for roots, a charming idea. Outside the porch is Finzi's tomb with an inscription carved by Reynolds Stone.

AVINGTON
St Mary ***
Rich Georgian interior

The once-gentle chalk valley of the Itchen has been devastated by the M3. Sheltering under its shadow to the north-east of Winchester is the Georgian park, house and church acquired by the 3rd Duke of Chandos in 1751. The church was built in 1768–71 by an unknown architect for the duke's wife, and recalls the church at the family's Middlesex estate at Stanmore (London), built half a century earlier. Avington shows no trace of the later style of William Chambers or Robert Adam and is, despite its date, the purest early 18th-century church in the county.

The church sits back from the road and forms part of the estate wall. There is a private entrance from the 'house side' next to the Brydges (Chandos) pew. Were the holly not so thick, the windows on this side would have a fine sight of the house across the lawn. The church is of redbrick, a simple embattled rectangle with a flat east end, west tower and round-headed Baroque windows.

The interior is lent a boudoir raffishness by the colouring of walls and ceiling, the former white, the latter a vivid powder-blue. Box pews with bowed corners are carefully graded from east to west according to the status of their occupants. That of the big house has the highest screens and the most ornate panelling. The woodwork is beautifully finished in costly Spanish mahogany. The pulpit is a three-decker, with desks for clerk and reader beneath and a tester topped by a dove. It must have taken a vicar secure in his living to lecture His Grace sitting so far beneath him.

At the east end is a Venetian window, a favourite Palladian motif, and a

Baroque reredos with a broken segmental pediment. It is flanked by a memorial to Margaret, wife of the Duke of Chandos and builder of the church, who died in 1768. She is described as a lady of 'beneficent actions, religious without enthusiasm, just without severity . . . But reader, commiserate not her fate, who doubtless now is completely blessed.' At the opposite end of the church is a small music gallery with a Gothick barrel-organ dating from the early 19th century.

The church is in good hands. With Avington divided into flats and with horses trotting confidently round its parkland, its once-uncertain future seems secure.

BEAULIEU
Blessed Virgin and Holy Child *
Stairway to refectory pulpit

The parish church of Beaulieu was once the abbey refectory, and therefore does not face east. The setting is superlative, across a green from the river and immaculately positioned next to the village and the abbey ruins. The other conventual buildings, heavily restored, lie adjacent to the church, together with a church hall added in 1992 and fitting well into the side of the church. The crowds of the motor museum seem far away.

The refectory was built *c*.1230 and became the church after the Dissolution in 1538. Both exterior and interior show its non-ecclesiastical origins. The building is tall, with a single huge buttress dividing two lancet windows in the 'east' wall. Three lancets survive in the 'west' wall. The interior is a single large space, high and graceful, with a wagon roof. This has its original bosses, primitive but lively and set in plaster panels painted bright red in 1959.

The most distinctive feature of the church is a six-bay arcade in the 'south' wall, with deeply moulded arches and coupled shafts of Purbeck marble. It opens on to a vaulted staircase of 18 steps built into the thickness of the wall. This leads to the pulpit, which is post-medieval but supported on the original large bracket, carved with stiff-leaf foliage. Here in the former refectory was the lectern for daily readings to the monks eating in silence below, as Cistercian rule required. This is a unique feature in an English parish church.

BOARHUNT
St Nicholas *
Saxon chancel, Henslow memorial

Portsdown Hill offers a blessed rampart against the awfulness of the Portsmouth coast, a landscape ruined beyond redemption by the philistinism of

20th-century defence. Inland we are in deepest country, with the ecclesiastical 'peculiars' of Southwick ('Suthick') and Boarhunt ('Borrunt'). The latter stands on an isolated hillock beyond a farm pond, where I saw a real heron cavorting with a fake one. The church is ancient and modest, a Saxon relic overlooking the Meon valley, reputedly one of the last outposts of paganism in England (*see* Corhampton and Titchfield).

The building is almost all Saxon, albeit without a tower and with a Victorian roof and west bellcote. Most remarkable from this date is the double-splayed window, now blocked, in the north wall of the chancel, best seen from outside. The guide suggests this may have been the only window in the original church. The ghosts of north and south doorways can be detected in the walls. The other windows are later. A rounded Saxon chancel arch dominates the interior. There are no carved capitals. The corbel face behind the altar, despite looking like an ancient Roman startled by a Saxon marauder, is Norman.

The furnishings are Victorian in date (1853) but Georgian in style, with three-decker pulpit, squire's pews and west gallery. On the north wall of the chancel is a handsome Tudor memorial dated 1577 to the local Henslow family, still owners of the huge Southwick estate. It has a plain chest topped by four Corinthian columns. Statues of the theological Virtues balance precariously on three pediments. They have been decapitated and should surely be given new heads. These minor works of art deserve proper restoration. By today's Henslows?

BOLDRE
St John *
20th-century glass

The church lies isolated from its village at the southern extremity of the New Forest, where the land drops down to the Lymington River. It seems to guard the remotest part of the forest from the encroaching agriculture of the valley. Boldre was once the mother church of both Brockenhurst and Lymington. It is best approached from Beaulieu.

The church is picturesque and asymmetrical, with a solid tower placed as at Fawley to the south of the chancel. The interior is largely unaltered from the 12th and 13th centuries. The eastern bays of the southern arcade are Norman, the remainder Early Gothic. The three-bay north arcade opens into a chapel, built in the late 13th century by Isabella de Fortibus, Countess of Devon. Restoration has not damaged the atmosphere, and the wagon roof has excellent 14th-century bosses. These form an inventive collection, now brightly painted. Many look like oriental masks.

The furnishings include a pleasant stone pulpit by Norman Shaw, architect of

Boldre Grange. The modern east window, by Alan Younger, is a rare success of semi-abstract religious art, a vigorous Christ in Majesty. Younger also designed the west window in the south aisle, again a striking work and one that does not exclude the daylight. The north chapel contains a monument to William Gilpin, painter and enthusiast for picturesque topography. He was vicar at the end of the 18th century, greatly improving the morals of parishioners who, on his arrival, were 'little better than a set of bandits'. Gilpin was one of many who opened the eyes of city dwellers to the charm of the English countryside, not least of the New Forest.

After the Second World War, Boldre became a memorial to HMS *Hood*, the cruiser sunk by the *Bismarck* in 1941. The vice-admiral aboard was a local man and, when no other memorial was established to the ship's company, Boldre became its shrine. An annual service is still held in its honour.

BRAMLEY
St James *
Becket mural, Soane transept

This is a jolly, patched-together church. It greets us across the churchyard with a large, Perpendicular south window, next to a deferential porch which could belong to an old farmhouse. This split personality continues inside, with Tudor benches and an 18th-century pulpit and west gallery, yet with a transept appropriate to a modest cathedral.

The church is mostly late Norman, with an all-through roof with decorated celure at its east end. Beneath is a 15th-century screen crowned by a Victorian beam and rood group, the latter designed by Temple Moore. Bramley's most ancient treasure is its wall painting. St Christopher on the north wall is magnificent, with mermaids and fish round his feet and sailing ships behind Christ's head. On the south wall is a vivid Thomas à Becket, painted so the guide says within fifty years of the event and lucky to survive iconoclasts. They made a particular target of the Becket cult, since Henry VIII regarded him as a traitor and enemy of the English monarchy. Maisie Anderson points out that the Bramley Becket avoids the mistake of depicting him dressed for Mass at the altar. It has him in cassock and furlined mantle 'which he probably wore when the frightened monks hurried him into the cathedral'. These and other paintings peer out from the covering plaster, over which biblical passages were later written and which also survive in part.

The south transept was built in 1802, a rare ecclesiastical work by Sir John Soane. It is occupied by the Brocas Chapel and the walls carry hatchments of the Brocases. Sir Bernard died in 1777 and his memorial is a tomb chest with a recumbent effigy, a rare form for the period. It is extravagantly sentimental, the dead man being cradled by a maiden at the moment of his demise. The glass is Flemish of the late 15th century and was said to have been hidden in a local moat during the Commonwealth. The panels depict biblical scenes but in everyday Flemish settings, like pictures by Bruegel.

BREAMORE
St Mary **
Saxon church and rood

Breamore is a Saxon church set in an uncluttered parkland of streams, woods, greens and cottages, where the valley of the Christchurch Avon meets the modest heights of the New Forest. Built *c.*1000, its age is indicated by the tall and narrow proportions of the nave. The walls are of whole flints with long-and-short stone quoins, the windows deeply splayed. Since the early 11th century the only substantive changes appear to have been the loss of a north transept, the partial rebuilding of the chancel and crossing, and the addition of a large Norman porch, though this may have been relocated. The church is celebrated as one of the most complete pre-Conquest structures in the south of England.

The upper part of the south porch was added in the 15th century, enclosing the Saxon rood. The rood itself has been defaced by iconoclasts, like those at Headbourne Worthy and Romsey. It portrays Christ in Agony, whereas the Romsey rood has Christ Triumphant. The upper part of the porch retains a piscina, traces of wall painting and corbels indicating a higher floor level, although the floor itself has gone. It must originally have contained an altar. The lower part of the porch is lined with benches. On its wall is a Great War Roll of Honour: among the dead or wounded were eight Witts, eight Candys, five Keepings and four Dommetts. Not since the plagues of the Middle Ages can such tragedy have been visited on an English village.

That is just the porch. The church interior is generously proportioned, the most exciting part being the crossing, or at least what remains of it after the arches were widened in the 15th century. They keep their Saxon decoration, with naturalistic corbels of flowers, leaves and a human head. A Saxon arch survives to the south transept, low and narrow, with square abaci. It has a Saxon inscription, translating as 'here the covenant is explained to thee'. No fewer than seven Saxon windows survive. The north side of the church is windowless, to keep out the Devil and give wallspace for long-vanished murals. Of the chancel, rebuilt in the 14th century, less need be noted, except the lovely Reticulated tracery in the east window.

BURGHCLERE
Sandham Memorial Chapel **
Stanley Spencer murals

Although this is officially an almshouse chapel, the Sandham Memorial Chapel is accessible, thanks to the National Trust, and is used annually for parochial worship. It also houses one of the 20th century's epics of religious art, Stanley Spencer's memorial to the dead of the Great War. The work covers all the walls of the chapel in a manner explicitly modelled on Giotto's Arena Chapel at Padua. Nor was that Spencer's only parallel. A number of the compositions echo Michelangelo's Sistine Chapel and the depiction of Man in contention with Fate. But the spirit is Spencer's own. He regarded this as his most important work.

The commission came from the Behrend family in honour of a brother who had died of illness in Macedonia, where Spencer had himself served as hospital orderly. The couple met Spencer in 1923 and decided on an oratory near their home in Burghclere. He pondered using fresco but decided instead on oil on canvas. For the smaller scenes, he worked on easels, but for the larger ones the canvas was glued to the wall and had to be worked directly from scaffolding. The chapel was begun in 1927 and unveiled in 1932.

The side walls depict scenes from Spencer's own experiences in the Medical Corps at home and on the Macedonian front. The domesticity and routine of the common soldier's life is contrasted with the awfulness of war. Soldiers scrub floors, sort laundry, tidy kit, make urns of tea and read maps. They are the living preparing for death, 'an in-dwelling peace to spite it all', as he later put it.

The chapel is dominated by the east wall painting of the Resurrection of the Soldiers, as the Sistine is by the Day of Judgement. This wall took Spencer a year to complete and has as its centrepiece a collapsed mule wagon. The mules, for whom Spencer developed a particular affection, turn to look at Christ as He gathers up the crosses that litter the field of battle. The dead rise from their graves to greet those still living. The war to end all wars is itself at an end. There is peace.

The work exhausted Spencer, and exhausted his marriage. It was greeted as an English masterpiece in the tradition of Hogarth and Blake, yet also compared with German post-war expressionists such as Max Beckmann. Though Spencer was appointed a war artist again in 1939, he concentrated on war factories and never produced another Burghclere. It sits alongside the poetry of Owen and Sassoon and Britten's *War Requiem* among the most moving monuments to 20th-century war.

CORHAMPTON
*
Unaltered Saxon chapel

Corhampton is unusual in having no dedication. It never had one, any more than it had a wealthy patron prepared to destroy the work of Saxon masons on this ancient burial mound in the Meon valley. The wooded district of 'Meonwara' was, according to Bede, among the last parts of England to be converted to Christianity, a task given to St Wilfrid from his mission at Titchfield. Even today there is a shyness to this church, hiding behind a massive yew tree above a mill stream. It is a place of antique calm.

The present structure presumably replaced Wilfrid's wood-and-mud shelter and has been dated to the early 11th century. The corners have long-and-short Saxon quoins, while the walls have elongated pilasters, known as lesenes. The two doorways, one now blocked, have Saxon arches. The interior is a simple double-cell of nave and chancel, linked by a semicircular arch. It rests on rectangular abaci with a single course of stone defining the rim. The chancel has extensive 12th- or early 13th-century wall paintings on its west wall, including drapery as if to imitate wall-hangings. The subject is apparently the life of St Swithun, first Bishop of Winchester, including an incident in which a woman spilled her eggs in front of the saint. He obligingly restored them whole to her basket.

East of the porch is a Saxon sundial, which divided the days into eight tides rather than twelve hours. The yew tree is extremely old, the girth suggesting a date at least as old as the church.

COSHAM
St Philip **
Comper's last Gothic interior

Cosham lies on the mainland opposite Portsmouth and must rank among the dreariest of the South Coast's 'suburbs without urbs'. South of the station an estate runs down to a dead-end by the railway tracks. It is the last place I expected to find an architectural gem. Yet Comper was always ready to surprise. Having chosen Wellingborough (Northants) for his cathedral, he blessed Cosham with its miniature. It was his last complete church and is the only parochial building worth struggling to enter in the Portsmouth area.

The land was a muddy creek dividing the coast from Portsea Island, developed in the 1930s as a private estate for dockyard workers. A new church was built, thanks to an anonymous donor, with Comper, as the leading church architect of the day, asked for a design. The guide remarks that when it was under construction in 1936–7, local people thought it was the new telephone exchange, the more so as Comper abandoned the proposed tower in favour of spending more on the interior, a wise priority. The exterior is a simple brick box with gabled roof. Six pinnacles alone adorn the parapet, with a small classical bellcote on the gable. The windows have good Intersecting tracery.

The interior is as bright and uplifting as any church built in the 20th century, with simplicity of form offset by richness of detail. The nave is wholly original, achieving the architect's professed desire for 'unity by inclusion' of different styles. Classical Corinthian columns support the most graceful of Gothic vaults. Walls, pillars and vaults are all in white plaster. The floor is of polished stone. The east end of the nave is dominated by Comper's particular forte, a large baldacchino. This is a canopy over the altar, reintroduced by Comper into Anglican architecture and sometimes called a ciborium. The latter is technically a canopy of wood, stone or metal over an altar; a baldacchino is the same, though once of cloth, the name deriving from the cloth of Baghdad. Cosham's is a beautiful structure, with four Corinthian columns rising to a canopy with rounded arches, angels in its spandrels and eagles at its corners. The underside of the canopy is blue with stars. The whole is gilded and has been well restored, a medieval manuscript in three dimensions.

Cosham's organ stands in the west gallery, the pipes lining its back and front. The organ is by Harrison & Harrison. Comper promised that it was 'incapable in competent hands of making too much noise'. The church, like too many of Comper's interiors, is spoiled by ugly seating.

CRONDALL
All Saints **
Norman nave, Transitional chancel carvings

This burly Norman church lies in a prosperous village near Aldershot. As in many overgrown dormitory settlements, the church offers an oasis of rurality amid the surrounding estates. Its exterior is much battered. Subsidence has meant huge buttresses propping up the west and south sides. In 1659 the old crossing tower had to be demolished, and the existing one was built detached from the church. This is a rare instance of church building of any sort during the Commonwealth. The new tower is massive and is linked to the church by curious wooden galleries, as if part of a Shakespearean theatre.

The interior is a complete surprise, a Victorian restoration by Giles Gilbert Scott of a late Norman church, with hardly a pointed arch in sight. The original fabric must contend with the hand of the restorer, but for once the Victorian does not emerge the winner, especially in the chancel. Fragments of untouched work survive in the nave aisles, including scalloped capitals, while the nave has water-leaf. The original clerestory shows a hint of Transitional points to the window arches.

The chancel is spectacular, lit by at least one clear glass window. This is the end of the Norman era, *c.*1200. Dogtooth abounds, arches are pointed, capitals have stiff-leaf and shafts the rings of Early Gothic. The rib vault is magnificent, excellently offset by Scott's restored east windows. At the apex of the vaults are stone bosses, one depicting the Lamb of God. Two ancient tomb recesses face each other across the chancel. The font is Saxon, as shapeless as a Henry Moore.

EAST MEON
All Saints ***
Tournai font

East Meon lies near the headwaters of the Meon valley, well stocked with the Saxon foundations of St Wilfrid's mission in the 7th century (*see* Corhampton). Few are as satisfying as East Meon, clutching at its hillside on the South Downs above the old village. Soon after the Conquest, a Saxon structure probably of wood and mud would have been demolished and a cruciform church taken its place. Subsequent poverty meant that little disturbed this replacement. Today's church is essentially that of the conquerors. The only additions are the Early Gothic south aisle and Lady Chapel, and the handsome broach spire on the Norman tower.

The tower has Norman decoration similar to that of Winchester Cathedral, whose bishop owned the manor of East Meon. His court house survives opposite the church. As the guide states, both 'must have been a constant and powerful reminder of the authority of East Meon's episcopal overlord'. The interior is light and spacious. This is due to the fine Early Gothic south arcade and aisle, whose Plate tracery windows admit more sun than any Norman would have dared. The chancel arch and crossing are Norman and darker, but the east window inserted this century by Comper brings light into the chancel. Comper is much in evidence at East Meon, both in the chancel and in the alabaster reredos in the Lady Chapel. Only his stained glass is a disappointment.

The Georgian pulpit came from Holy Trinity in the Minories in London. The kneelers are particularly good. But the treasure of East Meon lies to the right of the entrance door. The Tournai font is one of seven that survive in England, four in Hampshire, two in Lincolnshire and one in Ipswich. There are roughly fifty in Belgium and northern France. They came in about 1150 from Flanders and were carved by Flemish masters, in a Romanesque style still almost univer-sal throughout Europe. This one is believed to have been a gift to the church by the then Bishop of Winchester, Henry of Blois, powerful half-brother of the hapless King Stephen.

All Tournai fonts are of superb black marble, but each design is distinctive. East Meon's concentrates on the Creation and Adam and Eve. Of the four sides, two depict the flat Earth, on one of which dogs of war chase doves of peace, while the other shows composite animals, birds, reptiles and fish. The other two sides are more narrative, one depicting the Garden of Eden, the other the Gate of Paradise including an angel teaching Adam to dig and Eve to spin.

Many of these scenes were taken from religious dramas. The Expulsion is thus (improbably) from a majestic Romanesque city and the serpent is portrayed as a large dragon, which is how an actor would have dressed the part on stage. Equally 'dramatic' is the portrayal of God re-entering the church after giving orders to Adam. The Temptation was enacted with an artificial serpent. This is a Bayeux Tapestry in stone.

ELLINGHAM
St Mary *
Chancel screen with double tympanum

Ellingham is a friendly, picturesque church. It sits on the banks of the River Avon across a churchyard of springtime daffodils and lichen-clad gravestones. Its walls are a patchwork of pink brick, red tile and the guide's 'rustic, russet ironstone and honey-coloured rubble'. The south porch, with a painted sundial in the gable, is Georgian, while the bellcote and window in the south chancel are 19th century. This sort of domestic accretion is in keeping with the Tudor windows and 13th-century interior.

The attraction of Ellingham lies in its extraordinary screen, almost without equal in England, though a similar one can be found at Parracombe (Devon). This is a complete divide, shutting the chancel off as a separate space. We can gain only a glimpse through a rough Perpendicular grille above which is a giant double-thickness tympanum filling the entire chancel arch, partly wattle and daub, partly lath and plaster. There is a space of 2 ft between its east and west faces, once the old rood loft. What we appear to have is, to the east, the original 15th-century tympanum carrying the backdrop to the rood group, and to the west a post-Reformation insertion covered in biblical texts. These include the Lord's Prayer, the Ten Commandments, the Creed and Charles II's arms dated 1671. Unlike many such overpaintings, these are beautifully lettered and some carry Baroque frames.

To the left of this remarkable survival is a rare canopied pew, dated 1712. It has been moved round the nave over the years, coming to rest in 1883. The pulpit is 17th century; with the 18th-century chandeliers, it completes a fine collection of church fittings. The isolated chancel is strongly Victorian, but with a modern altar frontal. Ellingham also possesses a reredos in the style of Grinling Gibbons, which is no longer behind the altar but stands at the west end of the nave. This was designed to hold the Flemish painting that forms its centrepiece. The south windows are all by Kempe, better than the rest but a poor substitute for the sky outside.

FAWLEY
All Saints *
Eccentric location, Norman doorway

Modern Fawley looks as if Martians landed some years ago carrying with them alien chimneys, oil tanks, power stations, refineries and social clubs. Reputedly the largest oil plant in Europe fills the air with throbbing, yet the ancient church stands proud on its mound, looking out over Southampton Water towards the Hamble. It has a fine squat tower and an undulating graveyard that rolls from view under a copse of yew trees. The church is long, low and wide. It will be there when the Martians leave.

The core of the interior is a sizeable Norman structure, with a magnificent west doorway. The early 14th-century aisles extend the length of the church, encasing the Norman chancel and creating a triple gable to both west and east ends. They give the interior a sense of light and spaciousness. This was enhanced by careful postwar restoration after the chancel took a direct hit from a bomb.

Little was added to Fawley after the 1300s. There is a 19th-century window to light an old west gallery, some wall arcading for the baptistery under the tower and a Victorian porch. The Jacobean pulpit has perspectival panels, yet is hidden in the chancel. On my visit, autumn leaves had been woven into a frieze to fill the bare capitals of the nave arcades, a lovely touch. Fawley was the temporary resting place of islanders from Tristan da Cunha in 1961, when their volcanic home was threatened by an eruption. A model of one of the fishing boats in which they escaped is kept in the south chapel.

HALE
St Mary *
Baroque chapel in a dell

The church lies down a charming path beside the lime avenue to the great house and is not immediately visible. It is a minor work by the Queen Anne architect, Thomas Archer, and also his monument. He was also designer of St Paul, Deptford (London). The setting is idyllic. On my visit, early daffodils were carpeting the lawn up to the house and the scene was alive with evening birdsong. Below the church, woods descended to the River Avon. There was not a road within earshot.

The church is a curiosity. An original church of *c.* 1631 may have been designed by Inigo Jones, most evident in the bold west gable. This was altered, with transepts, by Archer during his tenure of the manor house in 1717. Some brown ironstone survives in the exterior walls, puncuated by Victorian windows. The extravagant north doorway has great volutes in the spandrels, and the south doorway has a Baroque frame and pilasters with exaggerated entasis. It looks like a frowning monster waving his arms in the air. Perhaps Archer meant it as a heavy joke.

The interior was altered by the Victorians, but in the north transept are three Georgian monuments, dominated by Archer's own. He is portrayed in Roman toga, a garment traditionally indicating an intellectual rather than an aristocrat, without wig and with a book in hand. His two wives attend him on either side. The stained glass is 19th century and modern. I would prefer the sky.

HEADBOURNE WORTHY
St Swithun *
Saxon rood

This is principally an entry for ghosts. The Worthy (or 'enclosure') churches crowded the banks of the River Itchen. They were intended less for parishioners than for pilgrims approaching the shrine of St Swithun at Winchester, or leaving it along the Pilgrims' Way to St Thomas's Shrine at Canterbury. These were the spiritual motorway service stations of their day. Headbourne Worthy lies in a meadow below the old road into the city, charmingly surrounded by streams, ducks and moorhens.

The church is a Saxon foundation and preserves one of the most important carved fragments of the pre-Conquest period. This is the giant rood at the west end of the old church, now reached through the vestry door. It was mutilated at the Reformation, leaving only the silhouette, but the shadow of Christ, the Virgin and St John can still be made out, all larger than life size. The hand of God comes down from a cloud above, as in the rood at Romsey Abbey. Pevsner claims that there is no work of comparable size anywhere at this date (*c.*1000), rendering the Headbourne rood a treasure of international status. If so, it is but a shadow of greatness.

The rest of the church is simple. The window openings date from every period, the glass almost all Victorian. The chancel is Victorian with, behind it, an unusual sedilia of three seats under a single arch. High on the nave wall is a brass of a Winchester scholar, John Kent, who died in 1434. He has a medieval version of a cartoon balloon coming out of his mouth, declaring 'My song shall be always of the loving kindness of the Lord.'

IDSWORTH
St Hubert *
Hillside chapel with St Hubert wall painting

How to choose between these downland churches? Idsworth belongs properly to Sussex, indeed to the Mardens group just over the border. A Saxon–Norman foundation of 1053, Idsworth was poor in the Gothic period, poorer in the 18th century and destitute in the late 19th when the lord of manor was so appalled by the building of a railway through his valley that he demolished his house and moved away.

The church was left alone in the middle of a sloping field, two miles north of Rowlands Castle. There is no village, no manor, no access road, no tombstones, no memorials. Yet it is open for worship and has a prosperous, confident air. The reason is that Idsworth was taken in hand by the twenty-five-year-old H. S. Goodhart-Rendel in 1912. His interventions were emphatic – to that extent in the Victorian tradition – yet with archaeological respect. The hand of the 20th century sits light on Idsworth. A scholar has been at work.

The chapel is approached along a grassy path up the hillside. The nave floor slopes upwards towards the chancel, continuing the rise of the contour. A crude pointed arch divides nave from chancel and there is a tiny Saxon–Norman window in the north wall. The nave has box pews and a Jacobean pulpit and sounding board. As to how much of the interior is original or is Goodhart-Rendel, neither Pevsner nor the guide offers a clue.

Rendel must have been responsible for the medallions that cover the chancel ceiling, but he would not have interfered with Idsworth's treasure, the early 14th-century mural of St Hubert on the chancel wall. This is a rarity both in its age and in its state of preservation. On the upper tier the miracle of St Hubert is clearly visible while the lower depicts the story of St John the Baptist and Salome. The dominant colours are red and ochre and the artistry is vigorous, the swaying trees particularly satisfying. A small painting displayed beneath the mural reconstructs the original. There should be a society for putting such admirable guides in all painted churches.

LYNDHURST
St Michael and All Angels ***
New Forest gallery of Pre-Raphaelite art

Lyndhurst is the masterpiece of George Gilbert Scott's wayward pupil, William White. Commissioned for the newly popular 19th-century resort in the New Forest, it was to be a gallery of White's Pre-Raphaelite associates. Built in 1858–69 of polychrome brick and stone and filled with contemporary art, it reflects the equally imaginative patronage of other Victorian resorts such as Scarborough and Brighton. The church sits bold on a slope opposite an Edwardian hotel above the high street, a torrent of through-traffic desperate for relief.

The interior is astonishing. Redbrick and dark wood predominate. Gothic arches broken by zigzag brickwork rise above piers with eight Purbeck shafts and freely-carved foliated capitals. The roof corbels have carved heads of Reformation dignitaries. Above them rise life-size angel musicians on the roof brackets. Every corner of Lyndhurst conveys White's attention to detail. Stone musicians adorn the chancel screen dado and stone saints adorn the pulpit.

A mural reredos runs the width of the chancel. It is by Lord Leighton, excellently lit, portraying the parable of the wise and foolish virgins. According to the guidebook, the bishop disapproved of the theme but was overruled by the parishioners. The big east window is by Burne-Jones, from the Morris workshop, representing the Heavenly City. The foliage, Pre-Raphaelite faces and flowing hairstyles are a vivid contrast to Kempe's surprisingly insipid west window. Burne-Jones also designed the south transept glass. The small Morris windows in the north aisle are charming, portraying ladies in soft colours against lush landscapes, an idealised Arcadian New Forest.

Behind the marble font in the baptistery is an extravagant neo-classical monument by Samuel Pepys Cockerell to his wife Anne. For a more modest memorial, the churchyard contains the grave of Alice Hargreaves, the inspiration for *Alice in Wonderland*. She married locally and lost two sons in the Great War. How many visitors to the New Forest race past Lyndhurst, unaware of this treasure house in its midst?

MINSTEAD
All Saints ***
Unaltered Georgian interior with family pews

Minstead is a 13th-century New Forest church which was refurnished, as were hundreds, in the 18th century. Yet so few survived without Victorian or later alteration as to leave it as a memorial to those that fell. The churchyard offers views over the Forest, through oaks and yews, its graves of local stone with a patina of friendly lichen. The lychgate commemorates a century of rectors from the Compton family. The last died in 1932.

The church exterior is like that of a rambling country cottage. The nave and chancel are mainly 13th century, with a Georgian brick tower of 1774, and a south transept of 1790. The tower has an apologetic spirelet. Inside, the 13th-century structure is noticeable only in a late Norman doorway, a lancet window and the pointed chancel arch. For the rest we have a parish church which nobody could afford to rebuild, and so local families merely paid for a new gallery or private pew for themselves and their staff and tenants as and when needed. Thus there is the manor pew, the castle pew and the lodge pew. These are in effect separate rooms, each with its own fireplace and furnishings. After centuries of accretion, Minstead is a church in which it is hard to know who is preaching to whom, much like St Mary, Whitby (Yorks, N).

The Minstead Lodge pew, north of the nave, has its own entrance and was not ceded to the parish by the Congleton family until 1968. It now houses the organ. The Castle Malwood pew, also reached from outside the church, retains its fireplace, seats with twisted balusters and kneelers. It is like a drawing-room with one side missing. Most remarkable is the Minstead Manor pew, now the south transept. It was once furnished with table, seats and even a sofa but was expanded to accommodate the manor's tenants as well as the family. All that survives of this distinction today is a red plush bench at the rear. The extension is supported by an early example of a cast-iron column, inserted in 1790.

The church also has a two-tier west gallery. The lower level was erected in the late 18th century for musicians, and the upper tier in 1818 for children from the Poor School. There is a long hat rack beneath the lower gallery. The pulpit is a three-decker and the font appears to be pre-Norman, depicting the Baptism of Christ on its west face. Minstead is all of a piece, a church where dates do not matter and time does not pass. In the churchyard, the author, Sir Arthur Conan Doyle, is buried alongside his wife.

PORTCHESTER
St Mary **
Norman font, Early Gothic carvings

The church is snugly positioned inside Portchester Castle, against the walls of the Roman outer bailey. These are real walls, some of the most complete Roman fortifications in England. Through the gate in the far side of the outer bailey lies the tidal marsh inland of Portsmouth. Under this wall, barges would for centuries have unloaded supplies from France. When Henry I restored the castle he built a keep and inner bailey, and in 1133 founded an Augustinian priory between the two baileys. The priory moved to Southwick ten years later and the newly built priory church reverted to parochial use. Perhaps canons and soldiers did not live well together.

The cruciform Norman church is an outstanding survival, hardly altered except for the loss of the south transept and north chapel, and the truncation of the chancel. With the departure of the priory this plainly became a poorer church, with few wealthy townsmen to endow chantries or pay for other adornments. It is impressive rather than lovable. A stern yew tree guards its entrance. The short crossing tower and pyramidical cap are severe, as if awaiting the murder of a saint. The west front has two plain buttresses flanking a richly decorated doorway with spiral shafts. The nave is vast and without aisles. Traces of round arches in the south wall indicate access to the former priory cloister.

The crossing piers are massive and their capitals are the principal decoration at Portchester. They have a wide variety of carved patterns, including foliage designs, and volutes reminiscent of a Corinthian capital. Were they inspired by classical work surviving from the Roman fort? Or perhaps here on a damp Wessex shore in the mid-12th century we see carvers turning their chisels from Norman to the freer spirit of the new Gothic. Some capitals in the north transept are particularly rich, but many are probably Victorian replacements. The nearest to Norman jollity is the font, a work of uninhibited 12th-century carving. The drum is a zoological garden of leaves, men and beasts above intersecting arches.

On the north wall of the nave is a huge coat of arms, commemorating a subsidy from Queen Anne's Bounty to repair the church after a fire in 1705, an impressive thank-you letter. Peering from the east wall of the chancel is a bust of a bearded man in armour. He is Sir Thomas Cornwallis, governor of the castle in the early 17th century. The sculptor was the admirable Nicholas Stone. Great efforts have been made by today's parishioners to warm the place. Tapestries hang on the walls and kneelers are embroidered with military motifs.

ROMSEY

Abbey of St Mary and St Ethelflaeda ****
Saxon roods, Norman arcades, carved capitals

The abbey was founded by King Alfred's son Edward as a nunnery in 907. It was sacked by Danes, rebuilt by Saxons and again by Normans, each time as a centre for female worship and education. At the Dissolution the abbey was acquired by the town. This saved it from demolition and, because of its size, from any need for subsequent expansion. Its setting is marred by mediocre town houses and shops pressing on three sides. The exterior, mostly crumbling or

1. England's smallest church, St Culbone, Somerset

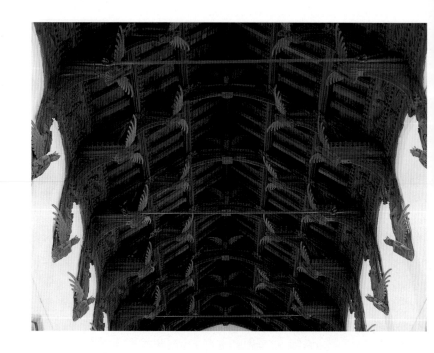

2. March's finest English angel roof, Cambridgeshire

3a. St Enodoc submerged in its dunes, Cornwall

3b. Salviati's saints in St Peter, Leeds

4. Episcopal Norman at Melbourne, Derbyshire

5. Devon ostentation: Cullompton's Lane aisle

6. England's earliest complete church at Escomb, Durham

7. Soaring 'woolgothic' at Chipping Campden, Gloucestershire

8. Flemish mastery at Fairford, Gloucestershire

restored Norman work, is patchy and the interior strangely empty. The abbey lacks the bustle of a cathedral yet is too big for the bustle of a small parish. Yet Romsey is one of England's grandest Norman churches.

On the outside wall of the south transept is the Romsey rood, a pre-Conquest relief of Christ, His arms spread in welcome not in crucifixion. The hand of God appears from a cloud above His head. Next to it is the magnificent doorway that once led to the abbess's cloisters, adorned with rosettes and twisted shafts. Apart from the later east and west windows, the interior retains its Norman appearance. Chancel, crossing, transepts and nave are tall and white, and massively proportioned. Arches pile on one another in three decks of arcade, gallery and clerestory. The piers have multiple shafts, one of which runs the entire height of the bay. The gallery has odd sub-arches with wall passages.

There is an intriguing evolution of style as we progress westwards from the crossing down the nave. The first two bays are divided by a cylindrical pier of two tiers. This form did not last long, since the next bays appear to have reverted to the standard Norman design. The westernmost bays, however, are Early Gothic, their piers resting on smart Purbeck bases and rising to capitals of stiff-leaf interspersed with faces. Gothic also are the two final bays of the gallery and almost the entire nave clerestory.

A closer look at the details reveals Romsey's phenomenal variety. Capitals are decorated with heads, beasts or flowers. Corbels erupt with faces peering down on the congregation. Two capitals in the chancel aisles tell stories, one of two kings pulling each other's beard, the other of kings and angels, with an inscription stating that its carver was called Robert. Everywhere are signs of 12th-century masons eagerly trying new styles and motifs imported from France.

Romsey offers a rich gallery of art of all periods. In the chancel south aisle chapel is a screen containing another Saxon rood, a finely executed Crucifixion with angels and saints in strong relief. Two soldiers are at the foot of the cross, one offering the sponge with vinegar. Romsey can justly claim this as one of the finest Saxon works extant in England. In the retro-choir is the coffin lid of a medieval abbess, her hand eerily emerging from beneath it to hold fast to her wand of office.

The north aisle and transept were, until the Dissolution, used as a parish church by the townspeople and an outer aisle was added, the transept acting as a chancel. Screens divided this area off from the rest of the abbey to stop the nuns 'escaping'. By the time of the Dissolution they numbered only nineteen, while the parish aisle must have been packed. When the old abbey was bought by the town (for £100) the additional aisle was demolished and Perpendicular windows inserted in the old north wall. Such was the parlous state of these buildings in the 18th century that the north transept was used as a fire station and the north aisle was a school. I sometimes wonder if many under-used modern churches might not benefit from being placed at the service of their wider community today.

Today the north transept retains a rare painted reredos of the early 16th century. Near the north door is a memorial effigy to a little child of the town named Alice Taylor, who succumbed to scarlet fever in 1843. She died clutching a rose her father gave her from his garden, and is portrayed on her deathbed, the rose still in her hand. In the south transept is the simple floor plate to Lord Mountbatten whose house was nearby at Broadlands.

SELBORNE
St Mary *
Gilbert White memorabilia, Flemish altarpiece

Selborne church is a shrine to the 18th-century naturalist Gilbert White, as indeed is most of the village. White's grandfather was vicar and White himself served the church as curate. The churchyard begins in the heart of the village beneath the celebrated hangar (or steep hill), and falls away eastwards to distant fields and woods. Birds are constantly in song. White's tombstone lies just north of the chancel, marked as he wished with the simplest of inscriptions, 'G.W. 26th June 1793'.

The flint building was restored by the naturalist's great-nephew, the architect William White, in 1856. His contribution is noticeable chiefly in the roofs. Were it not for the White association it might be just another amiable Hampshire church. But the ancient door and the Norman arcades form a serene retreat from the noisy churchyard on a warm summer day. The windows and fittings seem well suited to the role of a naturalist's shrine. The walls are plastered and limewashed and the chancel is a wide Early Gothic structure, White having replaced two east lancets with three.

Selborne has one great treasure, a Flemish altarpiece attributed to Jan Mostaert and given to the church in the late 18th century as a memorial to White. Why not an English work? It looks wonderfully rich on the altar and is well illuminated (and protected). The White memorial on the wall beside the altar wrongly locates the grave as 'fifth from this wall'. The chancel also contains a battered old reading desk and bench and, against the chancel arch, a Flemish relief carving of the Deposition.

The two White memorial windows are in the south aisle. That on the south wall is a big, rather fussy work of 1920. It portrays the village and church, with St Francis preaching to every bird mentioned in the diaries. Above is an architectural canopy at variance both with White and with St Francis. The east window is more moving. Erected in the 1930s, the glass is clear and permits a view of nature beyond, but includes roundels of rabbits, a turtle, a hedgehog and a bat. It is among the loveliest of 20th-century windows.

Outside lies the ruin of the great yew of Selborne. It fell in the storm of January 1990, and died despite frantic attempts to prop it up. The top was lopped and made into a font cover, an altar and other memorabilia, including a lute. A cutting from the stump was replanted opposite the church door and appears to be taking.

SILCHESTER
St Mary *
Screen with angels

The Roman town of Silchester was excavated at the turn of the 20th century and then reburied. Any finds of value were taken to Reading Museum. The site was remarkably complete and reburial seems strange. Only a half-mile length of wall remains, flanking the lane. The old manor house and church sit on a mound by a pond outside what would have been the town gate.

The church's location is charming, with an old yew and bench outside the porch. The building is plastered white on the outside while the interior is dark and cosy, comprising short nave and even shorter aisles. The north aisle has a single pier with a Norman scallop capital. The windows are mid-14th century, when the church was restored under the patronage of Eleanor Baynard. Hers is believed to be the effigy in the south aisle wall tomb.

Silchester is a carpenter's church. At the west end, two big wooden arch braces support the bells. The bench-ends are of 1909, Art Nouveau in style. The pulpit tester of 1639 is a dome with a dove on top, rather like an eccentric's umbrella. Most remarkable of all is the screen. Above the traceried openings is a frieze of angels, feathered and holding a text, motifs taken from a medieval coin known as a St Michael. The screen also carries roses and pomegranates, twin symbols of Henry VIII and Catherine of Aragon. This masterpiece was thus completed just before the Reformation, and must have been lucky to survive it.

There is no other architectural divide of nave from chancel. The chancel windows are lancets, their splays adorned with medieval paintings. A Perpendicular east window leaves the outer frames of the previous lancets still visible. There are a few fragments of medieval glass but, for the most part, the trees outside supply movement and shadow to Silchester's pleasant interior.

SOUTHWICK
St James *
Georgian chancel and reredos

The locals proudly refer to it as 'St James-Without-the-Priory-Gate, the Peculiar of Southwick', and pronounce it 'Suthick'. Southwick is an ancient downland settlement. To the south looms an escarpment cutting it off from Portsmouth, its crest lined with Ministry of Defence monsters. Here in the momentary peace of an old Hampshire village lies a church rebuilt, in the Gothic idiom, in 1566, and since then threatened only by the ravages of woodworm.

The appeal of the church once lay in its retention of a complete pre-Victorian interior. But woodworm attacked the nave box pews and in the 1950s these were ripped out and replaced not by copies but by the dreariest pews and chairs. The surviving west gallery has strong twisted columns, which presumably proved a match for the worms. The chancel is superb and might be the private chapel of a stylish Georgian mansion. Its box pews survive and are upholstered throughout, including one the size of a small drawing-room. The three-decker pulpit is also upholstered as if vicar and manor were rivals in comfort.

All eyes go to the reredos, a classical aedicule which frames an 18th-century painting of putti surrounding a dove, with little else that might qualify as religious. The chancel walls are panelled and adorned with numerous brass and alabaster memorials to the Thistlethwaite family. To the left of the reredos stands the tomb of the man who rebuilt the church after the Dissolution, John Whyte. He was servant to Thomas Wriothesley (of Titchfield), aide to Thomas Cromwell and later Earl of Southampton. Thus did the agents of the Henrician Reformation enrich their followers from its proceeds. Whyte acquired the old Southwick Priory, moved here from Portchester in the 12th century. The chest tomb appears to have come from the priory and is 14th century. The figures on the brasses are *c.*1520 and extra children and inscriptions were added as required.

STOKE CHARITY
St Mary and St Michael **
Tombs everywhere

The church sits in the middle of a field, surrounded by a scatter of cottages, woods, and a small lake now polluted with Canada geese. The exterior is flint with a tile-hung tower and splayed spire. The interior is astonishing, brightly scrubbed Norman, not over-restored and with a wealth of medieval monuments. The principal feature is an early Norman arcade of two wide bays divided by a huge pier with a scalloped capital. The chancel arch is later but still

Norman, with zigzag moulding and foliated capitals. The arch dividing the north aisle from the Hampton Chapel, next to the chancel, appears to be Saxon.

The delight of Stoke Charity is the monuments which so litter the place that the visitor is in danger of falling over them. A table tomb divides the chancel from the Hampton Chapel. Topped by Purbeck marble it has inlaid brasses of Thomas Hampton, who died in 1483, and his wife with six daughters and two sons. Two of the daughters have their hair hanging loose, to indicate they were unmarried. The brass is similar to that commemorating Thomas Wayte in the nave south wall. Pevsner points out that 'There was certainly no craving for originality among suppliers of funerary monuments or their customers' in the 1480s. Against the wall of the chapel is a Tudor tomb to John Waller of 1526 in full Perpendicular colour.

In the corner of the Hampton Chapel is a rare surviving carving of the Mass of St Gregory, dated to c.1500. Although not a sophisticated work, the piece is remarkable in having escaped the iconoclasts, presumably by being hidden. The surrounding walls and floors are rich in medieval fragments, tiles, carvings, mouldings and archaeological bric-à-brac. A light, happy museum of a church.

TITCHFIELD
St Peter **
Saxon remains, Wriothesley mausoleum

Titchfield is located off a pleasant village street but surrounded by a swirl of highways and some of the ugliest suburbs that even south Hampshire can offer. Yet its dignity survives. This was the southern outpost of the 7th-century mission of St Wilfrid of Northumbria. Wilfrid was sent to convert what Bede described as the last pagan area of England, the valley of the River Meon. The Saxon porch and west front of Titchfield are said to be Northumbrian in style. If they were indeed built under Wilfrid's influence, they rank with Bradwell (Essex) as the earliest Christian fragments in southern England.

The abbey was acquired at the Dissolution by Thomas Cromwell's assistant, Thomas Wriothesley. He rose to become Earl of Southampton and founded a dynasty that patronised Shakespeare, married into the Russell family and developed London's Bloomsbury estate. His tomb is the chief glory of the church.

The west front has a course of reused Roman tiles. Given the antiquity of the west porch, the 12th-century zigzag arch to the door and the tower above it are relatively modern. The proportions of the nave are Saxon, long and high, but derive their character from later changes. Most notable is the graceful Perpendicular north arcade and aisle, an unusually spacious gesture for the diminutive churches of the South Coast. Above the chancel arch is a painting by

Kempe of the Crucifixion, a fine substitute for a rood. Facing it on the west wall is a Victorian mural of the Draught of Fishes.

To the south of the chancel lies the Wriothesley mausoleum, with a memorial so large as to defy all efforts to use it as a chapel. It is now a museum of the history of the church. The monument itself is a triple tomb chest, a magnificent piece of carving. It was executed in 1594 by a Flemish sculptor, Gerard Johnson. The first Countess of Southampton has pride of place on the upper tier and is larger than the portrayals of her husband and son lower down on either side of her. The reason for this matriarchy is not known. The effigies of alabaster resting on marble are superb. The 1st Earl is clad in state robes and the 2nd in a suit of armour. Round the chest are children kneeling in prayer. The whole composition is united by four huge corner obelisks and attended by heraldic beasts and shields galore.

Equally fine is the monument to the four-year-old Lady Mary Wriothesley on the south wall. This is a charming effigy of a child in adult clothing, executed by Epiphanius Evesham in 1615.

WINCHESTER
St Cross ****
Norman almshouse church rich with zigzag

Forget the M3 and its tributaries. Forget booming Winchester, its college and wrecked city centre. Wander downstream beside the River Itchen to the water meadows beneath St Catherine's Hill. Here lies England's oldest and most perfect almshouse. It was begun in 1136 to house thirteen poor men and feed a hundred local people a day. The founder was the twenty-eight-year-old Henry de Blois, half-brother of King Stephen. His motive was either a moving encounter with a starving girl in the meadow, or, more plausibly, a desire to enhance his adjacent bishopric at Winchester. The resulting almshouse was remarkable in the wealth of its endowment – one seaside parish had to donate an annual dolphin – and in being lay rather than clerical. This saved it from Dissolution in 1536.

St Cross is a Norman cathedral in miniature. These are the lofty vaults, heavy piers and rounded windows of the Angevin kings, monarchs of thick forests and desperate civil wars. Yet despite periods of poverty and corruption – one inspiring Trollope's *The Warden* – the almshouse still honours its founder's intentions, dispensing 'a morsel of bread and a horn of beer' as the Wayfarer's Dole to passers-by. Two Tudor quadrangles serve a dozen brothers and the church doubles as the local parish church of St Faith. It has avoided suburban encroachment and remains surrounded by meadows, streams and woods. I can think of no medieval foundation in England in so unsullied a setting.

The structure is almost entirely of the late Norman period. Only the 14th-century west end and clerestory, and the 15th-century nave vault, are of later dates. The clerestory has Early Gothic Plate tracery. The nave is dominated by massive Norman piers, their capitals becoming less Norman as they proceed westwards. The first are scalloped, the next are moulded, while the west responds carry stiff-leaf carving. The earlier chancel and transepts have late-Norman zigzag carving to the point of obsession. Zigzag covers window surrounds, arch mouldings and rib vaults.

This restless, rather crude form of decoration rises above late-Norman shafts and early leaf capitals. It is hard to imagine what might have been its original impact without the original colour. In the north transept, zigzag keeps company with pointed windows. Nowhere better than at St Cross do we watch Norman give way to Gothic as walls and windows strain to discover new shapes and volumes to carry their sculptural inventions.

The furnishings at St Cross are seemly rather than than extensive. In the south chancel Lady Chapel is a Jacobean communion rail, not of the usual balusters but of openwork in a double-butterfly pattern. Here too is a Flemish triptych. The church has some 15th-century glass, the latter surviving in the east window and south transept. The church was extensively but carefully restored by Butterfield in the 19th century.

WOLVERTON
St Catherine *
Double altars, double pulpits

Here is a church to puzzle over. It looks towards Wolverton House over a parkland filled with cedars and other ornamental trees. The tower is of friendly Georgian redbrick, to which is attached a diminutive nave and chancel, apparently concertinaed. An early 18th-century exterior encases an eccentric interior.

The church has an altar at both ends. There are two identical pulpits left and right of the chancel arch, backed by squint passages with seats in them. They carry canopies with arches and pediments set at baroque angles, as if executed by a student of Nicholas Hawksmoor. In the chancel the wall panels incorporate Ionic pilasters that match the reredos, yet they stop uncomfortably short of the wall-posts of the Gothic roof. Gloomy Victorian glass makes it hard to appreciate the excellent Georgian furnishings.

The altar at the west end is a different matter. Its sanctuary lies under the bell-chamber, its niches strangely elongated and its reredos painted in the Italian style. Wolverton retains its box pews, each one adorned with a twisted brass candlestick still used for evening services. Bossy brass plates in the pews tell worshippers to turn up on time, sing heartily, kneel for prayers and stay kneeling at the end of the service. Above all they should keep their thoughts on holy things.

On my visit, the church was filled with glorious flowers. In the churchyard I noticed the nearest to a black tulip I have ever seen.

Isle of Wight

Christianity arrived in the Isle of Wight in 686 at the hands of King Caedwalla of Wessex. He said he would rule only Christians and massacred three-quarters of the island's population when they resisted his blandishments. The resulting Saxon churches were understandably robust, as were the succeeding Norman ones. Constant French raids left the buildings much battered but there are a few treasures, notably the Lily Crucifix of Godshill, the 'Louis XIV' sculpture of Yarmouth and Queen Victoria's royal pew at Whippingham, parish church for the Osborne estate.

Brading **	Shalfleet *	Yarmouth *
Carisbrooke *	Shorwell *	
Godshill ***	Whippingham **	

BRADING
St Mary **
Rollo child memorial

In the Middle Ages the sea came to the edge of Brading churchyard but is now distant across fields. The church's most distinctive feature is the rare processional passage under the west tower. The reason for such passages remains a mystery, lost somewhere between medieval ritual and medieval land law. The church has an unaltered nave of *c.*1200, leading to a chancel with a triple lancet window, all with cheerily plastered walls in what might be called seaside Gothic.

The monuments are excellent, the best filling the south chancel chapel. This is a mausoleum to a local family, the Oglanders, who fill walls, windows, floor and roof. There are Oglanders in stone, marble, alabaster and wood. Sir William (d.1608) is depicted in black and gold oak, lying on his back in prayer, his ruffs showing above his armour. Opposite is a stylised effigy of Sir John (d.1655). The figure lies on his side, resting on one arm and with his legs tangled as if in a complicated Highland reel. The flat-topped tomb chest of Oliver Oglander (d.1536) is surrounded by weepers carved in the round, a wonderful piece.

A monument in the aisle is to a child, Elizabeth Rollo (d.1875), at the age of one. The sculptor has depicted every detail, including her chubby hands and the lie of the leg under the gown. The work is reminiscent of the Boothby memorial in Ashbourne (Derbys).

CARISBROOKE
St Mary *
Carved singers on tower

The church is a perfect foil for the mighty castle, calling to it across a small valley in the centre of the island. Tower is answered by tower, turret by turret, battlement by battlement. The old white limestone of the church is crowned with red tiles. The stone is weather-beaten and the gargoyles wizened. The Perpendicular tower looks as if its builder simply slammed it on to the Norman nave and covered it with carvings. Some of these are eroded but those that are still distinct include a group of singers high on the west face. There is good stiff-leaf carving round the south doorway.

The present building is the nave of the old priory church. The monastery was dissolved in the early 15th century and the cloisters and chancel survive only as ghostly arches in the walls. The pulpit with back and tester is dated 1658, sober and Commonwealth in demeanour as opposed to the florid Jacobean of a generation before. The best monument is the canopied tomb chest of Lady Wadham (*c.*1520) under the north window. It is Tudor Gothic, square rather than soaring and with much panelling and cusping.

GODSHILL
All Saints * * *
Lily Crucifix

Godshill is deservedly the best-known church on the island. It claims to be one of the ten 'most-visited' in England, thanks to its location on the main tourist route south from Newport to Ventnor. The village is charming, with the church high above it and views out over the Downs.

The church has a rare double nave. The reason was probably that the church belonged to the prior of Carisbrooke and may have had separate naves for the public and the clergy, perhaps even for gentry and peasants. What is odd is that both are 'all-through' structures, with no architectural division between nave and chancel, yet with transepts on either side. The principal chancel today seems to be the south one. High Church icons are ubiquitous and the old flagstones echo with tourists.

Godshill's celebrated Lily Crucifix is in the south transept chapel, which is hung with rosaries and incense burners like a Catholic shrine. The mural form is extremely rare. Such lilies occur elsewhere in this book only on the painted roof at Abingdon (Oxon), a misericord in Tong (Salop) and a stained glass window at Long Melford (Suffolk). The Godshill Crucifix was overpainted at the Reformation and rediscovered in the 19th century. Though not especially ancient, dating from c.1440, it is the most moving of such images. Christ's body is contorted in agony on the naturalistic boughs of the flower, which seems to have grown over the years. There are fragments of other foliage in the ochre surround.

The church is thick with Worsley memorials. Their forebears, the Leighs, are commemorated in the Gothic tomb between chancel and north chapel. The canopy arch is extravagantly cusped, while the alabaster figure of Sir John Leigh (d.1529) lies beneath. His feet rest on a pig, reputedly the cause of his death by making his horse stumble. Also on the tomb is another Godshill rarity, two heavily hooded bedesmen praying for his soul. Lady Leigh has a remarkably fine headdress down to her shoulders.

In the north transept is the tomb of Henry and Robert Worsley (d.1747) with two busts and a sarcophagus under a bold classical canopy. They look a little pompous, but not as much as the tomb in the west end of the church of Richard Worsley (d.1805). This is the 'bath' sarcophagus, a 30-ton monster of Napoleonic scale that has understandably been moved from its former place in the centre of the church and is now hidden by the organ. I wish a similar ruthlessness were shown towards the church's stained glass.

SHALFLEET
St Michael *
Fortress tower

The most noticeable feature of Shalfleet on the road to Yarmouth is its Norman tower, relic of the days when the French visited the island regularly on raiding trips. Take away the church and we have an 11th-century keep, its walls 5 ft thick. As a castle it would be on every map: as a church it is overlooked. Nor did the Normans bequeath only a tower. Above the north door is the best tympanum on the island: 'A bearded man in a lay robe grips by their heads two affronted lions,' claims Pevsner, with a better eye than mine.

The interior is a spacious chamber with exceptionally good Decorated tracery. This is Intersecting in the north wall (apparently an early 19th-century wooden insertion), Geometrical in the chancel and Plate in the south aisle. The last takes the form of lancets topped by a round opening and two 'weeping' oval ones. I have seen this nowhere else. The rest of the interior is all of a piece. The south arcade has slender piers, the roofs have strong king-posts and the box pews are still in place. The chancel is furnished with linenfold panelling both on the dado of the screen and on the reredos.

SHORWELL
St Peter **
St Christopher mural

Shorwell is my Isle of Wight favourite. It clings to a slope above North Court, which was long the home of the island's celebrated Leigh family. The Perpendicular church has an unusual symmetry, with what it calls its 'three naves and three chancels'. These reflect the pre-Reformation distinction between the rector and the vicar, the former being ultimately responsible for the church, receiving tithes and paying for the chancel, the latter a subordinate normally looking after the nave. Here, as at Godshill, the patronage of Carisbrooke Priory appears to have led to separate naves being built as well as separate chancels.

The interior is as fussily decorated as an Indian restaurant. The Jacobean bench-ends carry fleur-de-lis poppyheads carved by a Victorian occupant of North Court, Sir James Willoughby Gordon. Above them rises a curious stone pulpit attached to one of the north arcade piers and reached actually through the pier from steps in the north aisle. There is a detached tester above it, dated 1620, so positioned that it surely cannot amplify the preacher's voice. The font cover is of the same period. The 15th-century roof beam between nave and chancel is supported on two splendid corbels representing Sin and Death.

The Leigh monuments are in the north chapel, including the kneeling figure of Sir John (d.1629). His infant great-grandson, who died at the same time, is portrayed in a similar pose behind him. Next to it is a fine classical memorial to Elizabeth Leigh of 1619, with swags and cartouches in shallow relief. The altar in the south chapel was apparently used as a travelling communion table by Sir James Willoughby Gordon in the Peninsular campaign. Its reredos is, of all things, an Icelandic painting of the Last Supper.

Shorwell possesses a St Christopher wall painting (c.1440) over the north door, admirably restored. All the saint's accoutrements are present, including the fish, the hermitage, the blossoming staff and the martyrdom. This is a great treasure. Why, I wonder, do so many St Christophers survive when other saints were destroyed? Perhaps the travelling iconoclasts could not bring themselves to deface their one-time patron saint.

WHIPPINGHAM
St Mildred **
Royal pew, Battenberg memorial

On the edge of the Osborne estate is the church where Queen Victoria worshipped when staying at her favourite house. Like Osborne, it was designed in 1854 in part by her husband, Prince Albert. He used Thomas Cubitt as co-architect and contractor for the house; at Whippingham church he used A. J. Humbert, who was also architect of Sandringham. Such early Victorian work tends to be valued chiefly for its eccentricity and the quality of its craftsmanship. That is certainly true here.

The outward appearance is odd, a cross between a college chapel and an asylum laundry. A cruciform plan with overweight crossing tower is given garish verticality by a cluster of turrets and spirelets. Of the former Norman church on the site there is no trace, except for a Saxon carving set into the west wall of the porch. The nave has no aisles but there are chapels with arcades on either side of the chancel. One of these is the royal pew, the other the Battenberg memorial chapel.

Despite this being a parish church, the atmosphere of the interior is still that of the sad later years of Victoria's reign. We feel we are intruding on a family in grief, so plentiful are the memorials. The crossing is crowned by a high lantern, decorated with the Order of the Garter. The walls are white, with red stencilling. The rose windows in either transept copy that of Notre Dame in Paris.

The memorial chapel contains the monument to Prince Henry of Battenberg, Victoria's son-in-law, who died of malaria in Africa at the age of thirty-eight. The chapel had been the pew of the royal household, but the staff and servants were ousted to make way for a huge tomb chest, with the Prince's sword and regalia on the walls. The masterpiece of the chapel, indeed of the church, is Alfred Gilbert's bronze screen in the chancel arcade, in flowing Art Nouveau. The bronze angel on the east window sill was designed by one of the Queen's daughters, Princess Louise, who also designed the font.

Opposite is the royal pew, whose entrance is in the south wall of the chancel, with a monogram of Victoria and Albert above the door. Victoria's own upholstered chair is in the centre. A memorial to her husband fills the west wall, oddly combining Greek Revival reliefs in white marble with a polychrome Gothic Revival frame. The scene only lacks figures from 'Madame Tussaud's'.

YARMOUTH
St James *
'Louis XIV' statue

Yarmouth is the prettiest of the island enclaves, its harbour not too obtrusive and the old streets of what was once the principal town still discreet. The church sits comfortably amongst them, its rubble walls and shrubs marred only by a huge No Entry sign. Can nobody stop this urban clutter?

The church is noticeable for its 1831 tower extension, an odd stone addition to the limestone base, erected as an aid to shipping and graced with an octagonal clock. The interior was rebuilt many times, after various French raids and fires. The present structure dates from the Jacobean period and was dedicated in 1626. It has the atmosphere of a cosy drawing-room, especially during a Sunday service in winter. The nave and chancel are wide, with dark woodwork and a west gallery displaying a curious row of 17th-century paintings.

The principal interest lies in a small mortuary chapel on the south of the chancel. This is dedicated to the Holmes family. Sir Robert, Governor of the Isle of Wight from 1668–92, apparently retained as a perk of office a share of any 'enemy' ship caught off his shores. One of his captures was a statue being shipped to Louis XIV, with its sculptor aboard. The statue had already been completed apart from the head, which the sculptor was to work from life when he arrived at the French court. Holmes decided to keep the work, ordering the sculptor to substitute his own head for the king's. Whether he paid for the loot or the new head is not known. He placed the result in his church. It is a splendid work, delightfully at odds with its modest surroundings.

Herefordshire

Herefordshire's soft hills rise over the valley of the River Wye, beyond the Severn. Though in the Marches, the county has few of the fortress churches that are a feature of Shropshire to the north. It is mostly a land of intimate churches, of soft pink sandstone nestling against green slopes.

Herefordshire's gift to art is the 12th-century Herefordshire School of stone carving, best displayed at Castle Frome, Eardisley and, above all, at wild Kilpeck. This Norman work stands comparison with any of its date in Europe. The motifs are drawn from Scandinavia, Germany, Spain and Italy, and display the Severn Vale as a cultural crossroads of Romanesque richness.

The transition from Norman to Gothic is admirably demonstrated at Cistercian Abbey Dore, handsomely restored in the 17th century. By the start of the 14th century, the county was also the home of exceptionally fine window tracery. At Leominster and Ledbury the Decorated style achieved a flamboyance to rank with the best of the East Midlands and Lincolnshire. This is complemented by the Much Marcle effigy of Blanche Mortimer, a jewel of English late Gothic.

The county is rich in post-Reformation eccentricity. Three churches are outstanding for their periods: the 'Strawberry Hill' Gothic of Shobdon, Hoarwithy's Romanesque revival loggia and W. R. Lethaby's delightfully rustic Arts and Crafts church at Brockhampton.

Abbey Dore ****	Garway *	Madley *
Brinsop *	Hereford: All Saints **	Moccas **
Brockhampton ***	Hoarwithy **	Monnington-on-Wye *
Castle Frome *	Kilpeck ****	Much Marcle **
Eardisley **	Ledbury ****	St Margaret's **
Eaton Bishop *	Leominster ****	Shobdon ****

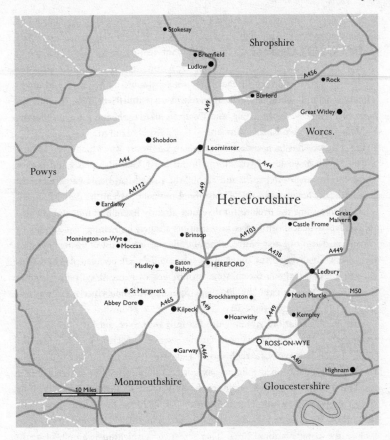

ABBEY DORE
****

Transitional capital carvings, 17th-century screen and gallery

The first impression of Abbey Dore down the Golden Valley is of a corner of France delicately dropped into an English meadow. The dark Hereford sandstone is speckled with white lime. The nave has gone, but the transepts, crossing and chancel of the old Cistercian abbey church loom high and austere. The French order was dedicated to asceticism, locating its monasteries far from settlement or temptation. Today, Abbey Dore is in a most sublime spot.

The monastery was founded in 1147, but most of what we see today is a rebuilding begun in 1180. The church is thus Herefordshire's exemplar of the transition from Norman to Early Gothic. While the exterior is red, the interior is of cool, grey limestone, brought to flaming life when a late sun shines low across the transept. Although the exterior is bare, the interior, with its 17th-century fittings, is sumptuous. The dominant feature is the east end, which shows Early Gothic at its most developed. A low arcade behind the altar has clusters of shafts, fourteen to each bay, with a double ambulatory and lancet windows behind. These all soar upwards in an astonishing rush, to meet the main east window, a lofty triple lancet with similar lavish shafts and mouldings. If this is ascetic, then I am Cistercian.

The chancel has a wonderful stone-flagged floor, on which rise arcades adorned with a wealth of late Norman and Early Gothic capitals and bosses. These can be seen both *in situ* and among the ruined fragments gathered in the ambulatory. They capture the 'Transitional moment', when the carvers' motifs were Norman but the architectural setting already had rib vaults and pointed arches. Norman scallops flower into trumpet shapes, into water-leaf and finally into the stiff-leaf of Early Gothic. The ambulatory is a forest of ancient carving, with the walls dividing the outer aisles into chapels left unfinished. On a dark evening we can imagine the masons sitting here with the latest pattern-books from France, talking over the designs, chipping with their chisels and pushing forward the frontiers of their art.

After the Dissolution, Abbey Dore fell into ruin. Not until the 1630s did it revive, when the local Scudamore family rescued it for the parish under the High Church influence of Archbishop Laud. A battlemented tower was raised, a touch of England on the French exterior. Stained glass was inserted in the east lancet windows. The Scudamores happily chose a talented carpenter, John Abel (1577–1664), whose Herefordshire work included Leominster town hall. He crafted the mighty wooden chancel roof and raised a screen, *c.*1633, to enclose the congregational area. This screen is a splendid example of 17th-century classicism, heavy and rich, a squirearchy Baroque in celebration of the manor, the church and the (Stuart) crown.

Against the west wall is a wonderfully solid oak gallery, warming what might otherwise be a gaunt space.

BRINSOP
St George *
Norman tympanum, Comper restoration

There can be few lovelier settings, even in Herefordshire, than Brinsop. The approach is off the main road past a pub with a weeping willow, then up a farm track, then through a gate, then towards a lake and a churchyard, and only then is there a church. It is filled with simple treasures, a nave with a north aisle, chapel and chancel, each component separated by wooden screens.

Set into the north wall is a strangely isolated Norman tympanum of St George and the Dragon, with further Norman carving over a north doorway. These presumably came from a previous church on the site and are attributed to the Herefordshire School of about 1150. A similar tympanum occurs in Poitou in France. Above the south door is the ghost of a painted medieval Crucifixion.

Brinsop chancel was extensively embellished by Comper between the wars. The angels on the screen are his, as is the golden canopy over the altar. The east window displays medieval stained glass in the central panels amid a Victorian surround. St George appears in full armour with shield and lance against a shimmering blue and red background, a splendid composition. The south window is a Comper memorial to Wordsworth, a frequent visitor. The reredos portrays birds plucking at the nails in Christ's hands. On either side are strong brass statues, one of St George, the other of St Martin.

BROCKHAMPTON
All Saints ***
Thatched Arts and Crafts church, 20th-century furnishings

The joy of most English churches is variety, the steady accretion of tradition and style to form a casual unity. Churches of one era lack this harmony and tend to shout. Not so 20th-century Brockhampton. Its architect, W. R. Lethaby, was a medievalist steeped in the writings of Ruskin and Morris. To him a place of worship had to be a work of art. At Brockhampton he built an expression of past time, yet without imitation or pastiche. The result was, to Pevsner, 'one of the most convincing and most impressive churches of its date in any country'.

At All Saints his client was Alice, daughter of Ebenezer Jordan of Massachusetts, who had been given the Brockhampton estate by her father on her marriage to a Yorkshireman, Arthur Foster. The church was Alice's memorial to her parents. Its design dates from 1901 and proved a troubled tale of architect–client relations. Lethaby had risen from humble origins to become a leading light of his profession, a socialist with a belief in the sanctity of craftsmanship. He was not a prolific architect and was determined that All Saints be built in accordance with his creed. He would be his own contractor, living and working on site and buying materials in consultation with his craftsmen. This was disastrous. Costs escalated, cracks appeared in walls and Lethaby was forced to pay for repairs and eventually refused any fee. He lived three more decades but never built another church.

The setting is glorious, the churchyard full of yew and box trees. The thatched lychgate might be topiary rather than architecture. The exterior appears a jumble, part medieval manor, part tithe barn, part Norman church with central crossing tower. It is heavy with sweeping eaves and thatch, as many English churches were in the early Middle Ages. But although Brockhampton seems engulfed in straw, there is still room for creeper to climb over the porch. There are carved doves of peace over the door, whose hinges are plaited. Even the nails were made locally. Stone seats, wooden belfry and cedarwood roof tiles contribute a gentle welcome.

Inside, the entire space is covered by a vault, supported by large wishbone arches, like crucks. These arches were beloved of Arts and Crafts designers, also found at E. S. Prior's Roker (Durham) and in the early work of Frank Lloyd Wright. Here the vault is steeply pitched and the ribs meet at an acute angle. They plunge from the apex to near the floor, making an especially powerful impact at the crossing. The nave and chancel windows are small, indeed poky, yet splayed to admit light.

Although Lethaby claimed to champion local crafts, he called in a galaxy of London artists. The tapestries flanking the altar are by Burne-Jones with Morris. The stained glass is by Christopher Whall, whose book on the subject Lethaby edited. The carved panels of the choir stalls, each of a different wild flower, are by the teacher of carving at the Royal College of Art, George Jack. On every side is embroidery, carving, pictures and icons. Even the hymn-book covers are embroidered. These, together with the altar front and seat covers, were apparently given by an anonymous donor. He or she walked in on a warm summer day in 1960 and left them on the altar, as tribute to the wild flowers carved on the stalls and in thanks for the church being kept open for visitors.

CASTLE FROME
St Michael *
Herefordshire font

A tiny Victorian broach spire beckons across the valley from the slopes of the Malvern Hills. The church architecture is Norman but of little interest, the reason for a visit being the font. This is a wonder of the Herefordshire School, its carving equalled only by that of the font at Eardisley and by the doorway decorations at Kilpeck.

These Norman fonts are as far in mood from the Gothic which followed as is an Inca statue from a post-Columbian altar. Dr Zarnecki, scholar of Norman carving, has traced the inspiration of these carvers to work as distant as Italy and Spain. Yet the abstract patterns in the font's borders at Castle Frome also suggest Viking and Saxon origins. The font, carved from a single piece of rock, rests on three giant figures. A snakelike pattern adorns the stem and the rim is plaited.

Most powerful are the relief figures. Christ stands for His baptism in a lake, with four fish and stylised ripples in concentric circles. The hands of God and John the Baptist touch His head. Next are bold sculptures of the angel of St Matthew, the eagle of St John, the lion of St Mark and the ox of St Luke. The work is *c.*1170, the final flourish of such uninhibited primitivism before the arrival of Gothic. Elsewhere in the church is a touching alabaster tomb of the Unett family of 1630.

EARDISLEY
St Mary **
Herefordshire font

This pretty village in a corner of the Welsh Marches contains the second of the surviving font masterpieces (with Castle Frome) of the Herefordshire School. The manor and castle were owned by the Norman Baskervilles, from the Conquest to the Restoration. They were succeeded by the Barnsleys, whose family litigation was one of many said to have inspired Dickens's Jarndyce versus Jarndyce.

A memorial to a Barnsley daughter is cryptically headed 'Bubbles Broken, but Death's the Gate to Life'. Such lines may appear original, but crop up with endearing frequency on tombs and memorials throughout England. I assume monumental masons kept books of them.

The font stands inside the south door, where a switch turns on a spotlight. It appears to be the work of one hand, probably the same as carved the doorway at Kilpeck. The bowl shows two narrative scenes. The first has two knights fighting, one stabbing a lance through the other's leg, entangled in foliage swirling up from the decorative stem. The magnificent owl is a medieval symbol of ignorance. The guide suggests that the scene may refer to a fatal duel between a 12th-century Baskerville and his father-in-law, Lord Drogo. Baskerville won and was forced by the church authorities to do penance, which may have included commissioning the font.

In the second scene, the Harrowing of Hell, Christ with a dove on His shoulder, representing the Holy Spirit, leads Man out of a forest of tentacles towards God. The great lion may represent the power of evil. This portrayal of the complete Trinity is said to be unique in medieval art. The style of the Eardisley font is far removed from the disciplines of classical statuary. It is said to display Celtic, Saxon and Norman motifs. Faces, limbs, gestures and backgrounds seem to have been culled from cultures untouched by the previous Roman Empire. It is as if European art were struggling to rediscover its roots and its inspiration from the primitive images of forest, marsh and mountain, which also inspired Gothic architecture.

As a contrast, the 1990s contributed the Steephens memorial window, a collage of vivid reds. The central figures appear to be in the style of the perform-ance artists, Gilbert and George – most strange.

EATON BISHOP
St Michael and All Angels *
Medieval glass

Eaton Bishop's glass is the best in the county. It fills the east and south windows of the Decorated chancel, inserted *c.*1330. The joy of these windows lies in their colour and completeness. Early glass was rough and uneven in thickness, absorbing and refracting daylight. Its effect derived from the juxtaposition of colours rather than from pictorial sophistication. The colours were left to glow, in Ruskin's phrase, 'like flaming jewellery'.

The early glaziers obtained most of their material from France, which made it costly and precious. Greens, yellows and browns predominate, with red and blue for particular effect. The compositions are full of emotion. In the east window a child tickles the face of the Madonna, her pose sinuous, her hand holding a flower. Below kneel the donors, tonsured like monks and looking piously upwards. The contorted shape of Christ on the cross in the south-east window is similar in style to those being painted in the same era by Cimabue or Simone Martini on the walls of Italy. Would that Eaton Bishop were as celebrated. Or is it better kept a secret?

GARWAY
St Michael *
Relic of Templar church

This is wild frontier country with an aura of barbarians roaming over the adjacent border. The district was Welsh-speaking until the 20th century and a 14th-century vicar was admonished by his superior for not speaking the language, since his congregation could speak no English. At the Conquest the land had been awarded to the Knights Templar for a defensive settlement against the Welsh. They built their typical round church here which, after their suppression in 1312, passed to the Knights Hospitallers. The district continued rebellious. It resisted episcopal authority from Hereford and was long suspected of papism.

The Templar foundation explains Garway's distinctive shape. A huge defensive tower once stood alone, separate from the round nave and square chancel. This church became ruinous and was demolished, its outline recently excavated in the churchyard. The one surviving feature is the Norman chancel arch, huge and with an inner moulding that appears oriental in inspiration. Is it conceivable that these Templars, travellers to the Near East, returned with architectural pattern-books? The arch capitals include a Green Man similar to one at Kilpeck.

The present church is mostly the one built by the Knights Hospitallers in the early 14th century, after the Templar suppression. The interior is washed pink. In the chancel open steps lead up to the absent rood loft. Garway retains much of its old woodwork, including a medieval nave roof decorated with stars and chunky 17th-century benches. Next door is a large 14th-century dovecote once belonging to the church.

HEREFORD
All Saints **
Twisted spire, medieval choir stalls

The ribbed steeple of All Saints is more dominant over the centre of Hereford than is that of the cathedral. As at Salisbury and Wells, here is a town church eager to outstrip its episcopal neighbour. It could hardly be more urban. There is no churchyard, only bustling pavements and pedestrianised streets around it. After years of dejection, All Saints has been restored and is now a paragon of parochial activity. There is a coffee bar and modern restaurant, the 'Café @ All Saints', occupying the west end and gallery. A fine oak banqueting table fills the south chapel. On my last visit a Russian Orthodox service was taking place in the Lady Chapel.

The much-buttressed tower had its celebrated twist corrected in 1992. Like the bulk of the church, it is 13th century. The interior, best viewed from a table in the coffee bar, seems almost as wide as it is long, the massive Early Gothic piers rising like tree trunks between the strong aisles. The roofs are exceptionally high, German Gothic in proportion, with hammerbeams in the nave and a wagon ceiling in the chancel. In the south chapel the ceiling has been removed, revealing the long wooden pegs that hold the members together. It looks uncomfortably naked.

The roofs give tremendous presence to the chancel and its spare, limewashed walls. The chancel is decorated only with a faded mural of the Annunciation by the east window and with superb choir stalls and misericords. These are free-standing and canopied, worthy of any cathedral. The stained glass of the 1930s in the east window is described as 'a bold attempt to create a fresh idiom'. The boldness and freshness did not grow on me. In the south chapel is an unusual Queen Anne reredos, in the rich style of a Wren City church. The chapel used to house a collection of chained books, but these were sold and are now located in the cathedral library. At the back of the church is an original charity bread shelf. On my visit, two fresh loaves awaited collection.

HOARWITHY
St Catherine **
Complete Romanesque Revival

On a summer day the loggia of Hoarwithy hangs over the valley of the Wye as an Umbrian church might over the Tiber. The building was commissioned by the vicar of neighbouring Hentland, William Poole, in the 1870s to replace a chapel that was 'as bare as the palm of the hand'. Poole was an idiosyncratic parson. His wealth enabled him to build the school, employ teachers and church staff, act as local magistrate and hold autocratic sway over the community. He was not popular. A later vicar, on visiting a dying parishioner in the 1940s, heard the man confess his terror at going to Heaven and meeting, not his Maker, 'but Mr Poole'.

The architect was J. P. Seddon and the style Italian Romanesque. The south-east campanile rises over the trees, the long rise of steps from the road under yew trees culminating in a cloister walk. This runs the length of the church from the tower, turns a corner and becomes a narthex attached to the west front. The churchyard, once lined with cypresses, is enlivened by a giant monkeypuzzle tree. The cloister roof is red-tiled, the arches small and rounded and their capitals carry Romanesque motifs. On the floor are mosaics. Everything is quiet and charming.

The interior is of a piece with the outside, a work of scholarly sophistication. Poole apparently sought inspiration from San Vitale in Ravenna and Le Puy and Laon in France. Seddon lined the north wall with large paired windows (including two ferocious stained glass saints), the south wall with a clerestory. The chancel is a complex space breathing Byzantine inspiration. Four columns support a small dome over the middle bay, with an apsidal sanctuary beyond. Side bays carry barrel vaults and lead on to half-apses.

The columns throughout are Cornish and French marble, with elaborate Byzantine capitals and purple porphyry bases. The altar is marble inlaid with lapis lazuli. Eleven windows of saints illumine the side apses, with a fine mosaic of Christ Pantokrator above the central apse. The choir stalls are decorated with more saints, claimed as Herefordshire Celts. This is a complete work of revivalist art, rare for its date and an astonishing creation to find in a backwater of Herefordshire.

KILPECK
St Mary and St David ****
Norman carving

Kilpeck is widely regarded as England's most perfect Norman church. It sits unobtrusively on a mound next to a castle ruin between the Wye and Dore valleys. The view is west to the Black Mountains and east to the Malverns. Lit by a setting sun, Kilpeck's red walls seem to take fire and fill the Marches with rich glowing embers.

The church was adjacent to a Benedictine priory and remains as built, a Norman structure of nave, chancel and apse, with no aisles or tower. Nothing appears to have been added or subtracted over the centuries, apart from the furnishings. This means that the carvings are *in situ* and in context. They cover the south and west doorways, the chancel arch and the corbel-table that runs round the entire church. Dating from the mid-12th century, they are master-pieces of the Herefordshire School, ranking with the fonts at Eardisley and Castle Frome. For their survival we must thank the durability of Old Red Sandstone, salvation of Herefordshire architecture, which seems impervious to weather.

The Kilpeck carvings demonstrate the vigour of the Saxon–Norman sculptural tradition. Themes and styles are drawn from the pilgrim routes across northern Europe, from Vikings, Saxons, Celts, Franks and Spaniards, the entire 'Northmen' diaspora. The south doorway has a Tree of Life tympanum. Oriental warriors peer through the foliage in the shafts and the dragons in the jambs. No less intriguing, if less accomplished, are the grotesques of the corbel-table, best preserved round the apse. Some are abstract, some figurative, some mythical. Here is an explicit sheela-na-gig of a woman holding open her vagina, a pig upside down, a dog and rabbit, two doves, musicians, wrestlers and acrobats. All the life of a busy and bawdy Herefordshire village is depicted on its church, with no respect for decorum or piety.

The interior is whitewashed in the post-Reformation style, and is Norman in style but not atmosphere. The carvings remain superb. In the shafts of the chancel arch are elongated saints, three to each side. These are quite different from the figures on the outside, stylised, serene, almost Gothic. This super-imposing of sculpted figures on the shafts is found at Ferrara in Italy but not in England. Next door is a water stoup, apparently depicting a pregnant woman holding her belly. The font is so big it could be used as a bath.

At the west end of the church is a Jacobean gallery, perhaps the most English artefact in the place.

LEDBURY
St Michael ****
'Floating' Norman chancel, Decorated baptistery chapel

Ledbury is an attractive town, set tight against a limb of the Malverns. From a distance its church spire appears to be pinning Ledbury to the slope. Once we are in the town, the church is suddenly unobtrusive, shut off from the hubbub of the high street and reached through a rabbit-warren of tiny lanes.

The steeple is a work of architecture in its own right, detached from the church to the north. It dates from the early 13th century, its spire replaced in the 18th by a Worcester architect named Nathaniel Wilkinson. Ledbury is thus a church of all periods. The west front is basically Norman, with turrets and zigzag carvings round its doorway. Inside, the eye is immediately drawn to the piers of the 12th-century chancel arcades which stand like tree trunks, holding up rough-hewn limestone walls with porthole clerestory windows. This chancel was left stranded by succeeding generations of builders, and looks like a church within a church. It is in the most bloodthirsty Norman style, framed by a sub-sided chancel arch that seems about to give up the ghost.

Round this chancel, the Gothic masons conduct their courtly dance. The aisles are large and airy, the same width as the nave but appearing bigger and grander by continuing on both sides of the chancel and thus embracing it with majestic windows. The whole interior is dominated by these windows, marvels of the Decorated era. They are mostly in the familiar Herefordshire style of 'three-light Reticulated' or 'stepped-lancet'. Most are filled with Victorian and later stained glass.

Even finer windows light the north chancel chapel. It was designed as a chapter house in 1330, at a time when the Benedictines hoped to convert Ledbury into a collegiate church. The chapel was later used as a baptistery. The windows are splendid accumulations of quatrefoils piled on trefoils, with ball-flower enlivening every shaft. The exterior is as ornate as the interior. Only Leominster can compete with this richness.

Every corner of the church has a distinctive character. The nave is floored with inscribed memorial slabs. An effigy of a Benedictine monk at prayer stands under a canopy in the chapel. There are two fonts, one 17th-century Baroque, the other Gothic by George Gilbert Scott. In the sanctuary is a monument to the Skynners, with Mrs Skynner in an Elizabethan ruff but a hat that might pass muster at Ascot. There are also monuments by Westmacott, Flaxman and Thornycroft.

Ledbury has a remarkable sanctuary opening, visible only from a specific point in the nave near the chancel. A red glass window is set above the east window, thought to have been a substitute for the red sanctuary lamp banned at the Reformation. In the north aisle is the modern Heaton window by John Clark. It rises up the wall like a furious flame, paying no respect to its surroundings. The churchwarden denied it was controversial, but conceded that it was 'much discussed'. Next to it is one of the many Georgian copies of the Sir Joshua Reynolds windows at New College, Oxford, with Lady Reynolds as Faith and the actress Mrs Siddons as Hope.

LEOMINSTER
St Peter and St Paul ****
Norman tower, Decorated south aisle windows, ducking stool

The old priory lay away from the centre of the town. What is left of the priory church is tucked down a quiet cul-de-sac in what amounts to its own park. It is a fragment, but a superb one. The west end, consisting of Norman north nave and aisle, and adjacent parochial south nave and aisle, survived the Reformation. The present church thus comprises three large chambers plus a north aisle, each dating from a distinct era of English architecture. The view from the south-west displays every period in a magnificent array of building styles.

The prominent Norman tower does not soar, but is a magnificent part of Leominster's splendid western aspect. It stands to the left, its base is complete with arched windows and carved doorway, apparently of the Herefordshire School. The 'school' trademark includes monsters and a strange man with quilted trousers. To its left are the Early Gothic lancets of the north aisle; to its right is the Perpendicular window of the south nave; farther right again is the Decorated west window of the south aisle, its arches studded with ballflower. These last decorative flourishes enjoyed a brief burst of fashion as Decorated reached its apogee around 1300.

The south elevation of the church is a coherent Decorated design. Five majestic windows, again framed in ballflower, are filled with Geometrical tracery, but with the circular lights cusped into a series of stars. The effect has the delicacy of lace yet the strength of stone. These are windows of the first rank.

The interior of Leominster is as exciting as the exterior. To the north lies the old Norman nave, built for the parishioners while the monks occupied the now-vanished chancel. This part of the church is flanked by elephantine arcades topped by expanses of raw masonry. Height is achieved by simply piling tier upon tier. The 13th century brought the new south nave for the parish, and the 14th saw the addition of the present south aisle. The dividing arcade was rebuilt in the 17th century and again in the 19th. It contains a superb 14th-century piscina and sedilia group, again enriched with ballflower but with triangular hoods rather than the ogees of the late Decorated style.

Most of the early furnishings were lost in a great fire which virtually gutted the church in 1699. However, Leominster possesses the last ducking stool to be used in England, kept in the north aisle. In 1809 Jenny Pipes was ducked in the local river, whether as a 'scold' or as a saleswoman caught for selling adulterated goods is not recorded.

MADLEY
Nativity of the Virgin *
Decorated apse, enclosed family pew

This is an austere place, even on the sunniest day. The tower is a powerful structure situated at an angle in the lane from the main road. The original church was Norman. It received an Early Gothic nave and clerestory, but found its glory, like most of Herefordshire, in the early years of the 14th century. This gave it a rare polygonal apse in the French style, with a crypt underneath, and a wealth of Decorated tracery. This tracery is Madley's glory. Most is in the customary Herefordshire form, of tall three-light openings with quatrefoils above. The east window of the south chapel has spectacular Reticulated tracery, the ribs snaking restlessly upwards towards the apex. The apse sedilia is surrounded with ballflower decoration.

Madley has, after Eaton Bishop, the best medieval glass in Herefordshire, dating from the early 14th century. Located in the chancel windows it is a reinstatement and not coherent, but the colours are vivid and create a pleasing sense of modernist collage. The church guidebook asks if anyone is good at jigsaw puzzles. In the north aisle stands the Lulham pew, made from the old chancel screen, with 17th-century additions. Its high sides and curtains enabled the family to remain wholly separate from the service. It even retains a small door through which the family could receive Communion without having to associate with the parishioners. This custom was, I suppose, one step better than having the grandees retreat altogether to a private chapel of their own.

Madley claims to have one of the largest fonts in England.

MOCCAS
St Michael **
Effigy of a knight

There is no village, just an Adam mansion set in a deer park sweeping down to the banks of the Wye. 'Remember those who have trodden this place before,' bids the vicar in his guide. Today we tiptoe gently across what is a private estate, past a genteel wall of clipped box. Moccas takes its name from the Welsh for a pig and a moor (*mochyn* and *rhos*).

The small, neat church consists of nave, chancel and apse in a descending sequence. The inside is Norman at its most theatrical. The view from the west end is of retreating arches with zigzag mouldings. The stone is tufa limestone, almost pumice. In the centre of the chancel lies the star of the show, an effigy of a medieval knight. His legs are crossed and there is a dog at his feet, the first wrongly supposed to indicate a crusader, the second that he died in his bed. He lies with light shining on him from the chancel windows. Winter evening services must be eerie events, as if the congregation were summoned to await the knight's resurrection and admonition, like Don Giovanni's Commendatore.

George Gilbert Scott Jnr's jolly organ case fills the west end of the church, recognising the role that colour once played in medieval architecture.

MONNINGTON-ON-WYE
St Mary *
Barley-sugar fittings

Monnington church sits next to the ancient manor house on a bend of the River Wye, reached by a winding path through the woods. It is a church of 1679 executed mostly in the medieval style but with classical fittings. The patron was Uvedale Tomkins, who lived next door. We can imagine him stomping up and down his lawn like a Henry Fielding squire, declaring to his builder that any style that was good enough for Edward III was good enough for him. His descendants lived at Monnington until 1962, when the estate was sold to the Bulmer cider family. There are now apple orchards on every side.

Churches of the late 17th century are rare in England and architects, other than in London, seem to have been baffled as to what style to choose. The exterior of Monnington, like the tower, is dressed in an odd form of Perpendicular. The windows are square-headed, except the east window, a strange composition with a rounded head and two tiers of triple lights. It is a lesson for all who might think that designing Gothic churches is easy.

The interior is a remarkably intact survival of its period. The fittings are a series of variations on a barley-sugar theme, otherwise known as twisted balusters. There are jolly barley-sugar columns to the screen, the communion rail, the pulpit and even the frame of Charles II's coat of arms. Nothing that could be twisted seems to have been left straight, and all was done by hand. The font and benches are also original. The only monument of note is of an ill-looking Francis Perrott (d.1667), who served the Venetian republic in the suppression of Barbary pirates. Such ventures seem far removed from the placid shores of the Wye. Perrott stares out of his bust: 'Stay passenger – if thou hast one tear / Bestow it on the noble dust laid here.'

MUCH MARCLE
St Bartholomew **
Blanche Mortimer effigy, Kyrle Chapel

Much Marcle contains my favourite English effigy. The interior has a simple Early Gothic nave, a substantial chancel and the even more substantial north Kyrle Chapel. The nave arcades are bold, lit by a strong clerestory and even stronger west window.

The effigy lies in a tomb against the north wall of the chancel, with an image as lovely as any bequeathed us by a medieval church. In a recess beneath a 14th-century canopy lies Blanche Mortimer, wife of Sir Peter Grandison and daughter of the 1st Earl of March. We know little more about her, except that she died childless in 1347, three years before the death of her husband. Women were always portrayed in death as aged thirty, supposedly Christ's age at the Resurrection. This implied the possibility of marriage to Him in the afterlife. The effigy would not have been intended as a likeness – though would that it might have been.

We see a face, only slightly damaged, that is serene, the eyes closed and the lips parted. Delicate fingers play with a rosary. The body is clothed in a tight-sleeved, loose-fitting gown with headdress. The gown is allowed to fall over the edge of the tomb, a happy effect also seen in a contemporary tomb at Ledbury. The effigy might be the original for Sleeping Beauty. It is a work of supreme craftsmanship, yet it lies open to inspection and even touch. Such are the treasures hidden in England's parish churches.

Much Marcle contains other fine tombs. In the nave is a rare wooden funerary effigy, carved from a solid block of oak and vividly repainted in what experts maintain are the original colours. The date is *c.*1360. He is a local gentleman, not a knight, and offers a record of civilian dress of the period. He wears a knee-length jerkin with hose, sword and purse. His face is remarkably bold.

North of the chancel is the Kyrle Chapel, regrettably locked, containing two more tombs. One is late 14th century, of a knight and his lady with winged angels filling the panels of the chest. Dogs are tugging at the foot of the lady's gown, as if willing her to wake up. The central tomb is that of Sir John Kyrle and his wife, of the mid-17th century. This is in alabaster and marble, the folds of the woman's dress lying thick, while the ruffs and the locks of her hair are brilliantly executed. His feet rest on a hedgehog, hers on a paw with a coronet. The shields of the chest are placed in classical wreaths. Kyrle was a Parliamentarian supporter of Cromwell. Much Marcle shows that Roundheads could be as magnificent as any Cavalier.

In Much Marcle's churchyard stands an ancient yew tree, much celebrated for its indeterminate age. It has a seat comfortably placed inside it.

ST MARGARET'S
St Margaret **
Tudor rood loft

First prize goes to those who can find this church, two miles down the road from its village and isolated in a field next to a farm. The site is glorious, with the Golden Valley laid out beneath. The church exterior is unremarkable except for a big weatherboarded bell-turret, but inside is one of the most satisfying rood lofts still standing.

The loft, accessible up a stair from the chancel, dates from the 1520s and retains all its original carving and panelling. It is big enough to take a large group of actors and musicians. The carving is worthy of a great house, with foliage, faces and shields in three bands. An elaborate coving rests on two intricately carved posts. All is in warm silvery oak. The St Margaret's loft does not have a subsidiary screen. It therefore lacks the intricate subsidiary panels and tracery of the best West Country screens, but makes up for this in the scale and richness of its carving.

The loft is attached to a solid wall through which a small opening leads to the chancel. It thus emphatically divides the chancel from the nave and suggests a dominance of parochial ceremony (in the nave) over clerical ritual (in the chancel), before the Reformation. The rest of the church is small and delightfully furnished, with painted biblical texts on its walls. The pulpit and organ are tucked apologetically away beneath the loft. In the chancel is a blue window of the path to the heavenly city, by the 20th-century designer Archibald Davies.

SHOBDON
St John ****
Rococo Gothic interior

Nothing quite prepares the visitor for Shobdon. Some have seen it as a pastiche of the Countess's boudoir in *The Marriage of Figaro* or even a Los Angeles wedding parlour. The *Shell Guide* describes it as an inconceivable place to hold a funeral. Yet Shobdon is a complete masterpiece, English rococo executed with confidence at a time when new churches in the Gothic style were rare.

The previous Shobdon church apparently ranked with Kilpeck and Eardisley in the canon of the Herefordshire School. Its demolition by Lord Bateman, the Georgian antiquary, was a tragedy hardly mitigated by his relocating fragments a quarter of a mile away, as a folly on a hill. The chancel arch and door tympanum, said to be by the same hand as Kilpeck, are now pathetically eroded. A plaster cast of the tympanum survives in the Victoria and Albert Museum.

The Batemans were Flemish immigrants. They bought Shobdon in 1705 when Sir John was a rising figure in the City of London. His son became a viscount and his grandson, Richard, assumed the stewardship of the Herefordshire estate. Richard was a friend of Horace Walpole, with a villa upstream of Walpole's Strawberry Hill at Old Windsor. One of Walpole's team of architects, Richard Bentley, was almost certainly responsible for Shobdon, although William Robinson and even William Kent have been suggested. The church was built in 1752–6.

The church is reached down an avenue of limes past estate buildings with sweeping views to the Welsh hills. The first impression of the interior is of icing-sugar whiteness, offset by sky blue. The basic form is traditional, of nave, transepts and chancel, yet this form is overwhelmed by the decoration. The three arches to the chancel and transepts each take the form of three ogees with pendants, embroidered with crockets and finials picked out in blue. All the windows have ogee frames and ogee lights. For good measure the wall panelling also has ogee arches. The bench-ends are pierced with cusped quatrefoils. The pulpit is a triple-decker confection, with a neo-Jacobean tester covered in open-work and with rich red hangings. The sanctuary chairs, even the flower stands, are in the ruling Gothic.

In the south transept, the manorial pews come complete with fireplace. Manorial servants were relegated to the north transept. The only severely jarring note is the glass in the east window. This is of 1907 and replaced Georgian glass now in the north transept. I am told it is to go. A fine Nollekens monument to Viscount Bateman, Richard's brother who died in 1802, hangs on the nave wall. Those with a taste for irony will enjoy the one survivor from the old church. The font was returned after seeing service as a garden ornament. It is Norman with a crude lion on its base, and lurks like Caliban at the court of Milan.

Hertfordshire

One of the smallest English counties, Hertfordshire finds excitement hard to come by. Its rolling chalk hills have been overwhelmed by suburban development, with little concern for landscape conservation. Everywhere are roads, housing estates, industrial zones and new towns. Such corners of green belt as survive seem to be gasping for breath.

The style of Hertfordshire churches is East Anglian. The building material is mostly flint, and craftsmanship tends to be concentrated on furniture and monuments. The county's only contribution to architectural history is the endearing 'Hertfordshire spike', a small, usually copper-covered apology for a spire, examples of which are found also in adjacent counties.

Of monuments the best are outstanding, notably the Lytton memorials at St Mary, Knebworth, and the Earl of Salisbury's tomb at Hatfield. Otherwise, Hertfordshire is a place of curiosities: the Norman mermen at Anstey, the folly church of Ayot St Lawrence, the ceramic arch at Ayot St Peter and Lutyens's humoresque at St Martin, Knebworth. For these small gifts we are thankful.

Anstey **
Ashwell *
Ayot St Lawrence **
Ayot St Peter **
Hatfield ***

Hitchin **
Knebworth:
  St Martin *
  St Mary ***
St Paul's Walden *

South Mimms *
Stanstead Abbots *
Watford:
  Holy Rood RC **

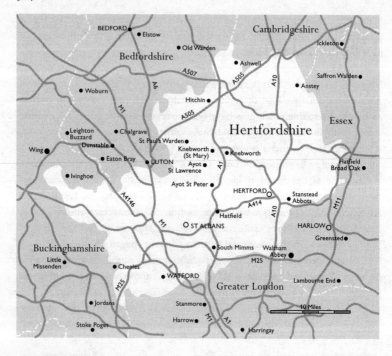

ANSTEY

St George ★★

Mermen font

On the far side of Anstey church lies a moat, probably of a vanished castle, into which a fully loaded bomber crashed one night during the Second World War. For some reason its bomb-bay did not explode. Had it done so there would be no Anstey.

The church that escaped is full of Norman mystery. It is cruciform with a crossing tower, lending the interior exciting pools of light and shade. Everywhere are examples of the carver's art. The tower arches have unusual rings. The chancel and transepts are Early Gothic with a triple lancet in the south transept. The nave arcades appear Decorated, with busily chamfered arches. Every corner is crowded with piscinas, sedilia, brackets, effigies. The church is furnished with gnarled record chests, fragments of a screen and medieval choir stalls and misericords. On many of the piers are graffiti of heraldic devices. This is a church in which children could play hunt-the-motif.

Pride of place goes to the font, adorned with the rarest of pagan emblems. The bowl stands on four supports, its rim depicting mermen, each one holding his split tail as if to create the effect of a boat. It is, says the guide, 'possibly symbolic of the ark of Christ's church'. The only other known portrayal of mermen on their own is in St Peter, Cambridge. My lexicon says that mermen were 'club bores', who would 'rise from the water and address anyone who happened to be near'. Similar creatures are depicted on Romanesque fonts in the Auvergne. They are of an age that must have seemed impenetrably ancient even to the Gothic era.

ASHWELL
St Mary *
Architectural graffito

Ashwell's tower thunders out over this prim commuter village. Every cottage seems in place and every glazing bar correct. I cannot imagine today's parish-ioners commissioning anything as crude as a tower built, in the words of the Shell Guide, 'like a Brooklyn skyscraper'. Its roughcast mass of crumbling stone and flint is supported by deep buttresses and has two elongated bell-openings on each side. The crowning Hertfordshire spike is lifted on a short octagon.

The inside is also massive. Built shortly after the Black Death, its aisle windows and clerestory pour light into the interior. The modern choir begins half way down the nave, with four new candlesticks and inoffensive new choir stalls. Its poppyheads include a fish and a griffin. The chancel is a large open chamber with Perpendicular windows and a richly carved piscina and sedilia. Over the altar hangs a modern Crucifixion by John Mills.

Ashwell's principal claim to fame is inside the tower. Low on the north wall is a graffito portraying old St Paul's Cathedral in London. Whether intended as instruction to the masons or as a boast by an itinerant London builder is unknown. Nearby is a Latin reflection on the plague of 1350: 'Miserable, wild, distracted, the dregs of the people alone survive to bear witness.' It was possibly scratched by a priest despairing at what was left of his parish after the Black Death.

AYOT ST LAWRENCE
St Lawrence **
Greek Revival church, 'his and hers' tombs

The 18th-century lord of the manor of Ayot St Lawrence, Sir Lyonel Lyde, decided that the Palladian vista from his house would be improved by a Doric temple and a Gothic ruin. So he reduced the existing village church to a pictur-esque wreck and asked his architect, Nicholas Revett, to design a temple as a new church at the far end of his park. When the Bishop of Lincoln, in whose diocese Hertfordshire then fell, heard what Lyde was doing he ordered a halt, but too late. The old church was already a crafted ruin. It survives buried in woodland opposite the pub.

Revett's temple rises splendid across the fields to the west. It is fronted by a portico that might be the entrance to a stately home, flanked by screens and pavilions. Revett was, with James Stuart, the pioneer of Greek Revival architecture in England. He visited Greece and published drawings of its classical antiquities, then little-known in the West. St Lawrence is of interest because it is one of the earliest Georgian buildings in the Greek, rather than Roman, style. The portico (built in 1778) is the first use of a Greek Doric order for a parish church. But church is thoroughly subordinate to scenery. Its back and side walls are of brick and there is not even a footpath to the door. The orientation is also reversed, so that the doorway and interior fittings, including the altar, face the house and village.

The interior struggles to live up to the setting. Though small, it is a handsome double cube with columned vestibule, coffered ceiling and a western apse, here Roman rather than Greek. St Lawrence suffers from a clutter of modern chairs in its nave. The organ is the original Georgian instrument. Commemorative urns to Sir Lyonel Lyde and his wife stand in the two side pavilions. He allegedly insisted that, since their life together had been so dogged by discord, the Church that had united them in life should make amends by separating them in death.

AYOT ST PETER
St Peter **
Arts and Crafts interior, naturalistic pottery arch

There are no signs pointing to this village in rolling countryside outside Welwyn, which is thus well isolated. Indeed, it is near impossible to find without a good map. The building was designed in 1874 by J. P. Seddon, architect of Hoarwithy (Herefs), to replace a recent Pearson church destroyed by fire. The exterior is an unconventional design, in redbrick with bands of blue and white and with an apse, tower and spire. The clock face is a large panel of blue mosaic with gold scrolls, boldly 'aesthetic' in an otherwise stern wall.

The interior is a delightful variant on late Victorian Gothic, thanks to its modest size and rich Arts and Crafts furnishings. Ayot St Peter was a statement to Seddon's London friends as much as to the people of Hertfordshire. Most extraordinary is the chancel arch. From a distance this looks like Purbeck marble, but on close examination is of ceramic, the only example of an arch of this material that I know. It portrays birds, flowers and foliage and was made by the potter Walter Martin of Southall in London. The work is complemented by a later iron screen of filigree delicacy; the whole space is topped by a low trefoil-shaped roof.

The font is equally original. The bowl sits on multi-coloured shafts and is surrounded with a mosaic pattern of fish, flowers and sea. Everywhere Ayot St Peter glories in colour. There is colour in the painted organ pipes, the chancel floor tiles and roof panels with paintings of saints and angels. The undistinguished stained glass (some of it by Seddon himself) is not obtrusive.

At the back of the church is a small defaced headstone to Elizabeth Horn (d.1688), wife of a rector, with beneath her name a skull and crossbones in the style of the time. Though modern in a medieval church, such memorials are charmingly old-fashioned in a Victorian one.

HATFIELD
St Etheldreda ***
Cecil and Brocket family chapels

Hatfield church would always have a fight on its hands. It stands hard by the walls of the great house, at the top of a street of redbrick and blossom. The churchyard gates are magnificent and yews hug the walls, as if protecting it from criticism for being over-restored.

Like most English magnates, Cecils were not too proud to be buried in their local church, even if it needed adjustment to their ever more exalted status. Hatfield had belonged to the bishops of Ely. After the Dissolution, Henry VIII used the palace as a nursery for his children, and it was here that Princess Elizabeth later received the news of her accession to the throne in 1558. In 1607 the house passed to Robert Cecil, son of Elizabeth's Lord Burghley. He built a new Hatfield House and extended the church as his mausoleum.

Apart from the tower, the west end of the church is mostly Victorian, including the small dormer windows that serve for a clerestory. As a result, the first impression of the interior is disappointing. Interest is concentrated east of the nave. The south transept retains stiff-leaf capitals and arcading, as well as a splendid Burne-Jones window of 1894, rich in foliage and colour. The saints appear lost in dense greenery while the tracery openings are alive with the flapping wings of angels.

This south transept leads into the Brocket Chapel, a battered chamber that was once private to the owners of Brocket Hall. It retains the atmosphere of a Tudor chapel, its roof and walls covered in heraldry and decorative colour. A wall memorial to Sir John Brocket (d.1598) has no effigy but a copious heraldic record. His helmet is suspended high above him. Another monument to his wife and her mother is more explicit, with two effigies reclining on their elbows. Near the window is a Rysbrack memorial to their descendants, the Reades.

The north chapel is a total contrast. Built by the Cecils in 1618, it was redecorated in 1871 by the 3rd Marquess of Salisbury, prime minister to Queen Victoria. If Brocket's Chapel is the roast beef of old England, Cecil's is European haute cuisine. Guarded by exquisite 18th-century ironwork gates from Amiens, it has a Gothic arcade dividing it from the north transept and a classical one dividing it from the chancel.

In the middle spreads the majestic tomb of the 1st Earl, who died in 1612. He lies on a marble slab, holding his emblems of office, with below him a skeleton. The composition is a radical departure from precedents. Unlike the canopied polychrome tombs familiar from the Elizabethan and Jacobean eras, this one is made of black and white marble and has no columns. Instead, the effigy is supported by the four Cardinal Virtues, Prudence, Justice, Fortitude and Temperance. A similar composition was later designed by Inigo Jones for James I's catafalque in 1625 and considered most advanced.

HITCHIN
St Mary **
Rich civic furnishings

The centre of Hitchin is spoilt by poor-quality development, but at its heart is a battered pile of brick, stone and glass, the largest and jolliest church in Hertfordshire. The outside looks as if passing citizens have periodically stuck a flint into the walls to keep them standing. Originally a collegiate church, it had a central tower, which collapsed and was replaced by a west tower in the 1190s. This was buttressed after an earthquake in 1298. The fine south porch has image niches, panelling, pinnacles and vault and was an addition of the 15th century.

The interior is ablaze with light. The Norman core was successively widened, lengthened and surrounded. Arcades and aisles were added to the nave in the early 14th century. Then in the 15th century the chancel was given chapels and a retro-choir, creating an ambulatory encircling the sanctuary. The church is filled with assorted treasures. There is a 12-sided font, its apostles defaced by Cromwell's troops. Corbels in the south aisle depict a beggar with a rat, and a girl being tempted by the Devil while trying to listen to an angel.

The church has magnificent woodwork, particularly in the south chancel chapel which was created for a guild. The screen has a cornice with angels holding the Instruments of the Passion, and splendid tracery. Its east side retains the stalls of the guild wardens. The roof has more angels, with musical instruments and the insignia of the Calais Staple, ubiquitous sign of medieval wealth from wool. Below are later memorials to the Radcliffe family as well as a fine collection of brasses. The retro-choir, a rarity in a parish church, is backed by a

19th-century mosaic reredos with scenes from the Life of Christ. Bashed late-medieval knights lie on the north chapel window sills, gazing out at a different Hitchin from the one they blessed with their patronage.

KNEBWORTH
St Martin *
Witty Lutyens interior

Edwin Lutyens married a Lytton of Knebworth and designed this curiosity in the centre of the town. As at Hampstead Garden Suburb, he wished to bring a noble classicism to new democratic estates. The result is a 20th-century church of rare character, though it may seem frigid to those unaccustomed to Lutyens's architectural humour. The church was begun in 1914 but not completed until 1964, by Albert Richardson.

The exterior is vernacular Gothic, with big, sweeping roofs and overhanging eaves familiar from Lutyens's Hampstead, and indeed from New Delhi. It is as if Knebworth citizens needed shelter from a fierce tropical sun. The boldness of line immediately distinguishes the church from its mediocre surroundings. The contrasting interior is classical. The spaces are variations on the theme of an arch, reminiscent of a Christian basilica but very unorthodox. Two large Doric columns rise in the middle of the north and south transepts, blocking them and directing the eye forward to the chancel. This rises up chequered steps, a *trompe l'oeil* effect, to a wide apse. Above are heavy, dark roof beams.

The aisle and transepts contrast with the nave. Smaller arches dash off in surprising directions, creating intimate corners for chapels and the font. The furnishings are mostly by Lutyens, including the pulpit and lectern on either side of the steps. The organ pipes are made to seem like a collection of walking sticks in a country house lobby. The modern pews are a fierce yellow and the apse a no less aggressive pastel blue.

KNEBWORTH
St Mary and St Thomas ***
Lytton monuments

When Lutyens married Emily Lytton of Knebworth in 1897, the reception had to be held in a tent on the lawn. The house had been rented out to save money. Today it is back in family ownership but gazes across at the horrors of Stevenage from hillsides that have been used for generations of pop concerts. There is no road to the church, which is reached by a path in front of the house.

The exterior is undistinguished, as is the restored nave. The furnishings include a complete set of 15th-century oak pews and a Georgian pulpit inlaid with Flemish 16th-century panels. The Adoration is superbly executed. In the chancel is an early 15th-century brass to Simon Bache, who had the difficult task of being treasurer to the future Henry V in his Falstaffian youth.

The treasures of Knebworth lie in the Lytton Chapel to the north of the chancel. This was enlarged c.1705, possibly by Hawksmoor. The screen was designed by Lutyens in honour of a Lytton who died in an air crash in 1933. The chapel is full of Lyttons, on the floor, walls, windows and bursting through the gap to the chancel. Here is the best of 17th- and 18th-century monumental art on parade: effigies awakening from supine sleep, first to pray, then to lie semi-erect and eventually to emerge into the prime of life, until later crushed into urns and beneath obelisks. Three of the Knebworth tombs are among the finest 18th-century monuments in England.

The two most spectacular are of Sir William Lytton (d.1705) and Sir George Strode (husband of Judith in the chancel) of 1707. Both lie semi-prone on cushions. The sculptor was a Londoner, Edward Stanton, whose work can also be seen in Lower Strensham church (Worcs). The figures are lifelike, corpulent, confident and richly dressed. The double-chinned William has a look of self-satisfaction. He is given a true Baroque canopy with arch and full columns.

Next in time is Lytton Strode Lytton, who died at the age of twenty-one in 1710. He stands as if caught in the act of conversation, his coat half unbuttoned and wearing a long peruke wig, a fine record of Queen Anne costume. Two weeping putti rather spoil the naturalism. The monument is framed by pilasters with a pediment embracing the family coat of arms. The sculptor is thought to be Thomas Green of Camberwell. The last major work is in the new Palladian taste. It has no columns but is a sarcophagus with allegorical relief sculpture, including a scene of children playing with an hour glass. The effigies, of William Lytton Strode (d.1732) and his wife, are marginalised and curiously archaic, kneeling in prayer.

ST PAUL'S WALDEN
All Saints *
Queen Mother's church, Baroque screen

The pretty Perpendicular church with battlements, Hertfordshire spike and south chapel sits on a mound within an immaculate churchyard. The parish was home of the Bowes-Lyon family. Queen Elizabeth, the Queen Mother, was baptised here in 1900. The church is remarkable for its chancel, created in 1727 by a local man, Edward Gilbert, who married into the Bowes family of Durham and whose daughter married John Lyon, Earl of Strathmore.

The screen is extraordinary, in 'wedding-cake' Baroque. Three bays of dainty columns and arches, with decorative cresting which defies description, are tricked out in green and cream with Jacobean finials. The chancel ceiling is stuccoed and the reredos rises the full height of the chancel and matches the screen. Nobody knows the name of the designer. Its impact on an otherwise timid Perpendicular interior is like the crash of a Bach chorale in the midst of a Tudor galliard.

In the tower is a rare survival, a window with medieval glass depicting the Virgin and Child, barely visible behind the gallery. The Virgin has lost her face but the colours and figure survive, moving and vivid. On the doorpost is a small dagger carved into the stone, believed to be a relic of the Peasants' Revolt. The east window, a surreal Christ donated by the Queen Mother and her brothers in 1946 in honour of their parents, is unworthy of the church.

SOUTH MIMMS
St Giles *
Frowyk tombs

The church defies a pandemonium of motorways and service stations near the intersection of the A1 and M25. It was restored by Street in 1877 and contains the proprietary chapel to the local Frowyk family, City goldsmiths and lords of the manor for three centuries. The nave is that of a conventionally prosperous Home Counties church. Street inserted a new pulpit and screen, the former with coloured panels reflecting his pupillage with Morris. The north aisle windows have remains of old glass, principally depicting donors, presumably saved from iconoclasm as being secular.

The two Frowyk monuments form a delightful contrast in Tudor styles, despite being just thirteen years apart. The first lies in the north chancel chapel, originally the Frowyk Chantry. It is to Henry Frowyk the Younger and was endowed in 1527, Perpendicular in style and with an effigy. The chapel is surrounded by its original screen, magnificently carved and with ogee arches. These have Green Men and leopards on their cusps, the latter the emblem of the Frowyks.

The monument to his father, Henry the Elder, who died after him *c.*1540, is in the chancel and is an extraordinary work, with bulbous corner posts which turn into balusters swathed in acanthus leaves near the top, an embryonic classical form. They support a canopy with a flattened Tudor Gothic arch, and flank a Gothic tomb chest. Pevsner wrote of this piece, 'a remarkable example of the gusto with which craftsmen at some distance from the Court threw themselves into the new Italian fashion'. The church is Anglo-Catholic, with a fine collection of vestments and a modern altar frontal portraying the legend of St Giles.

STANSTEAD ABBOTS
St James *
Openwork porch, 'spying' pews

This simple church sits on a hillside outside the modern village with Stanstead Bury house across the park behind. The 15th-century tower and Hertfordshire spike are conventional but the porch is a curiosity, a charmingly agricultural structure with cusped barge-boards and open timber-framed sides. It might be a village horse pound. The whitewashed interior of the church is little altered since the 18th century and is now in the care of the Churches Conservation Trust.

The chief feature of the nave is the high box pews, with a three-decker pulpit badly in need of its tester. This languishes as part of a screen behind the organ. The hatchments have been well restored with vivid hogs' heads, memorials to the local Booth family, of gin fame. The original crown-post roof survives. At the west end is a delightful early Victorian organ case in Puginesque Gothic.

North of the chancel is the Baeshe Chapel of 1577, a late date for such chapels. It commemorates the various occupants of Stanstead Bury, the Baeshes, Fieldes, Jocelyns and, since the 19th century, the Trowers. The tomb of the builder of the chapel, Sir Edward Baeshe (d.1587), is a characteristic Elizabethan monument with kneeling figures and attendant children. The Trower window is a striking composition of St Simeon and St Anna by Selwyn Image. The holes drilled in the pews are said to have enabled the masters to spy on the servants at prayer on the benches in front of them.
[CCT]

WATFORD
Holy Rood RC **
Bentley screen and furnishings

Watford is a dire warning to all who believe that developers and road engineers can together create tolerable new towns. It has joined Hemel Hempstead and Luton as cases of old market towns being converted into mall fortresses. A fragment of a high street survives with a dark parish church containing fine tombs, but to its west lies a jollier work. It is a rare church by J. F. Bentley, architect of the Roman Catholic Westminster Cathedral, begun in 1883. It is a true town church, with a compact plan in which numerous projections – tower, turret, transepts, aisles, chapels, vestries – are neatly contained within a rectangle. It is built of traditional local materials, of flint walls and stone bands.

Inside is displayed the art at which the late Victorians excelled, that of church furnishing. We enter through the tower, which contains an octagonal baptistery with a central pier. The font has an ornate cover, while vivid corbel heads support the vault. The nave is plain, a prelude to the burst of decoration and colour of the chancel and side chapels. Dominating all is Bentley's massive rood beam, floating free with no subsidiary screen and with a florid rood group above. The three figures are borne aloft on a tree-like cross, massively assertive.

The chancel is embraced by two levels of arcading, lending depth to the view from the nave. Every surface is enriched: the walls, sedilia, reredos and statue niches. The roofs and vaults are painted with tendrils and other motifs. Bentley designed almost all the stained glass. The light fittings are mostly Art Nouveau, installed in 1899.

Huntingdonshire

Huntingdonshire is here kept separate from its administrative county of Cambridgeshire, but amalgamated with the formerly separate Soke of Peterborough. As I explained in the Introduction, Fenland boundaries may have mattered as little to modern bureaucrats as to Saxon warlords but, to most local people, Huntingdonshire and Peterborough still form a natural entity. Here the Saxons established their great monastery at Peterborough in c.650 and set out to convert the marshes of east Mercia, with the Bible of Christ and the stone of Barnack.

Three monuments survive from these early days of Christianity in Britain: the tower at Barnack, the arch at Wittering and the interior at Great Paxton. A more intimate pre-Conquest art is depicted in the 11th-century carving of Christ in Majesty at Barnack, an outstanding treasure. The coming of the Normans saw the rebuilding of Peterborough, and the building of neighbouring Castor, with a tower of the most elaborate richness.

Of later churches there is little of distinction. The Early Gothic period survives in the chancel at Alconbury. Yaxley's tower is splendidly sited overlooking the Fens. Buckden and St Neots offer contrasting versions of Perpendicular rebuilding, the one a bishop's chapel, the other a confident town church. My Huntingdonshire favourites are the 17th-century interiors of George Herbert's Leighton Bromswold and Nicholas Ferrar's Little Gidding. These two sons of the English Reformation were friends, came to Huntingdonshire, but soon went in very separate ways.

Alconbury *
Barnack ****
Buckden *
Castor ****
Conington **
Godmanchester *

Great Paxton **
Hemingford Grey *
Leighton Bromswold **
Little Gidding **
Ramsey **
St Ives *

St Neots *
Thorney **
Wittering *
Yaxley ***

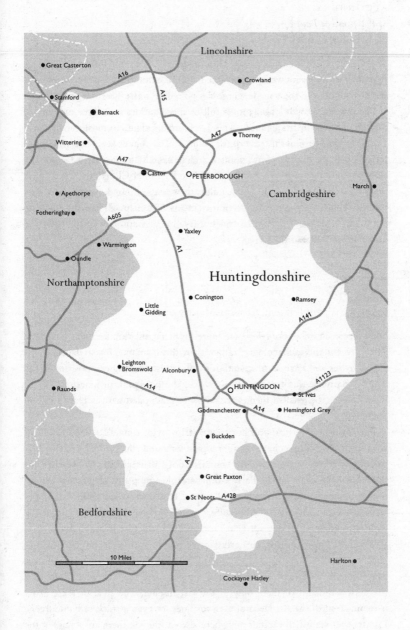

ALCONBURY
St Peter and St Paul *
Early Gothic chancel

The Great North Road bypasses Huntingdon by Alconbury Brook, a village
that shelters under its well-proportioned church, with Early Gothic steeple and
serene chancel. On the outside, gargoyles poke fun in the direction of the A1.

The interior, mostly of *c.*1300, is full of space and light. But the pleasure of
this church lies in the chancel. This is an immaculate composition of Early
Gothic, a style rare in this part of the country. The church is entered through a
large but simple doorway with pointed arch flanked by single shafts. Beyond are
six graceful bays, plus two half bays, of blind arcading along north and south
walls. The half bays are a mystery, unless the carvers wanted more opportunity
to display their skill at carving decorative heads. The east wall has three delicate
lancets with shafts. The roof has finely carved angels and monstrous bosses. It
looks unrestored and full of age.

BARNACK
St John ****
Saxon tower, stiff-leaf font, Christ in Majesty carving

Most Saxon churches are celebrated more for being old than for being beautiful.
They are for the archaeologist rather than the layman. Not so Barnack. Its
Saxon tower and Early Gothic spire form the most pleasing composition in the
county. Barnack was famous for its stone, the pale pinkish limestone of the
western Fens, beloved of medieval carvers in these parts as was Ham stone in
Somerset.

The tower has vertical and horizontal strips, with triangular windows in its
west front. The corners have familiar Saxon long-and-short stones and the door
surrounds come with discordant capitals above their pillars. Above rises the
disciplined symmetry of the Early Gothic steeple, composed of pinnacles rising
out of broaches round an octagonal belfry. This is crowned with a short but
virile stone cap. 'If it is called a spire,' writes Pevsner, 'it must be one of the
earliest in England.' It dates from *c.*1200 and is a structure of real power.

We enter through a superb Early Gothic porch, with a steeply-pitched roof
and fine stiff-leaf capitals to the doorway. Inside, the tower arch resumes the
Saxon theme. It rests on abaci between the piers and the arch which look as if
the mason thought of them only at the last minute. The style of these abaci
is reminiscent of the Art Deco of a 1930s liner, or even a stack of hamburgers.
I have never seen such capitals anywhere else – although there are echoes in the
arch at neighbouring Wittering.

The remainder of the interior seems not quite under control. The nave is Transitional. The north arcade has late-Norman stiff-leaf capitals and a few human heads. The south arcade moves easily into Early Gothic, with more stiff-leaf, clustered shafts, chamfered arches but nothing so vulgar as human heads. The restoration by Leslie T. Moore is dominated by the Victorian pews and rood screen, the latter using 15th-century panels for a dado. In the chancel is a wall memorial to Francis Whitstone, who died in 1598. Four of his seven sons ranged behind him are carved, the others meriting only paint.

Not an inch of wallspace in this church seems to lack some point of interest. The chancel piscina has a nodding ogee arch, projecting so far that it must have banged the head of the priest. Monsters peer out from the sedilia. The Lady Chapel has big niches either side of the altar, both early 16th century. The statue of the Virgin and Child is modern, but the Annunciation is original and of the finest quality. The font is outstanding, and rare in displaying stiff-leaf foliage. Patterns cover the bowl surface with almost rococo delicacy. It is set on a stem with a graceful, trefoil-headed arcade. The bowl itself is deep and may have been intended for the total immersion of the infant.

At the east end of the north aisle is Barnack's masterpiece, a seated Christ in Majesty discovered under the floor in 1931. Now generally dated before the Conquest, its strong face and flowing garments are among the most striking sculptures of the period in England.

BUCKDEN
St Mary *
Animal roof carvings

A good setting brings the simplest church alive. We are here on what was once the Great North Road, in the shadow of the palace of the bishops of Lincoln. This was a stopping point for the bishops on their way north to their diocese, and was as far as many of them reached. Hence the palace's lavish gatehouse and towers in Tudor brick. Hence also the ironic title of the celebrated Bishop Barlow (d.1691) as 'Bishop of Buckden'. The bishops were patrons of the church.

St Mary's is half a century earlier than Buckden Palace and is not of brick but of limestone and brown cobble. A tall Northamptonshire tower rises over neat gravestones of local stone and a well-composed Perpendicular nave. The two-storey porch is ostentatious, with stone vaulted roof and a boss of the Virgin surrounded by rays of light. Its battlements have relief carving.

The interior has been fiercely scraped, with rough blocks of mortared limestone fighting the graceful lines of the architecture. But this unnecessary harshness is relieved by the absence of Victorian stained glass. This leaves the church flooded with daylight, illuminating the glorious array of angels and corbel heads crowding the roofs. The angels are sedate enough with their musical instruments, but the south aisle corbels are a riot. One is a fierce tusked boar, another looks oddly like a Womble, figures that must give as much pleasure to a bored congregation as to their creators.

In the chancel is the memorial of Bishop Barlow, a black marble tablet with high relief carving in the style of Grinling Gibbons. There are also two black slabs in the nave floor with lovely Georgian lettering and rococo decoration.

CASTOR
St Kyneburgha ****
Exterior Norman carvings, angel roof, St Catherine wall painting

Castor sits in a discreet suburb of Peterborough, on the slope of a hill above the bank of the River Nene. It was an outpost of neighbouring Peterborough Cathedral and is a minor masterpiece of Norman architecture, dominated by a magnificent crossing tower that merits the title of sister to that of Peterborough. The tower is ornamented with two tiers of arcading, some blind and some with paired openings, all carved with zigzags, billets, fish-scale, lozenges: in other words the full Norman works.

The rest of the exterior is equally rich in Norman carving. In the south chancel wall is a priest's doorway, with a niche and simple tympanum giving the date of dedication as 1124 (though the 24 appears to have been scratched in later). It is flanked by a Perpendicular window, an Early Gothic lancet and windows with Geometrical and Y-tracery. Castor is thus a textbook of medieval architecture. Above the south porch is a Norman Christ in benediction. Inside is a gnarled oak door, the sort that is a pleasure to find unlocked and push open.

The interior is worthy of the exterior. The nave arcades are Transitional, with piers beneath just-pointed arches. The low crossing is pure Norman, with clustered piers and capitals depicting beasts and vegetation. These are more than mere faces. One depicts a man gathering fruit while another shows the legend of St Kyneburgha: when she was being chased by two thugs intent on rape, the contents of her basket spilled out and sprang instantly into bushes. These most conveniently trapped the men in their branches.

The roof is alive with freshly painted angels carrying musical instruments and the keys of St Peter. They look like primitive fairground ornaments but are said to be accurate to their 15th-century originals. The south transept has tall windows and clear glass, revealing the sky over the Nene. This transept contained the village school until the 1890s. The north transept held the shrine of St Kyneburgha and is divided from the north aisle by a heavy-traceried stone screen of the 1330s.

Castor's chancel contains many treasures, including a Norman piscina, an Early Gothic piscina and sedilia, and a delicate Saxon carving of an apostle. At the back of the north aisle is an admirably clear wall painting of St Catherine on her wheel, with the philosophers whom she is said to have converted being executed. It is the only picture I know of philosophers being put to death.

Castor sets its embroidered kneelers on the pew shelves. This fills the nave with colour, as the angels do the roof.

CONINGTON
All Saints **
Cotton monuments

This Huntingdonshire idyll lies off the Great North Road and through a series of meadows, beyond which a grove of tall trees suggests a great estate. We are in Cotton country, one-time home of the Stuart antiquary and politician, Sir Robert Bruce Cotton. He was a pioneer collector of books and manuscripts, and the Cotton papers with their personal cataloguing system formed the basis for the British Library.

The old castle has long been demolished and the present adjacent house is no match for the Perpendicular church, built *c.*1500. Its tower rises from a grove of holm oaks, yews and holly trees, lifted from the ordinary by a four-light bell-opening with four pinnacles, added by a Cotton in 1638. The nave fenestration is superb, with graceful Panel tracery. Conington may now be redundant and down-at-heel, but it still cuts a dash.

The interior has the familiar greenhouse effect of late Perpendicular: dazzlingly bright in summer and impossible to heat in winter. The roofs are flat and the aisles wide, with high-backed early Victorian pews. The arcade piers have clustered shafts with wildly complex cross-sections.

This is a church of heredity. Sir Robert was obsessed with his descent from the Scottish Bruces and filled his church with heraldry to that effect. Most of the monuments are Cottons, erected in the early 17th century by Sir Robert in memory of his 16th-century forebears, including one to the King of Scotland. The later bust of Sir Robert himself (d.1631) is a vigorous work by Edward Marshall of 1655. It is uncompromising and direct. The tablets of Sir John Cotton and his wife (both d.1702) are attributed to Grinling Gibbons, since he signed similar fine Cotton monuments at the other Conington in Cambridgeshire.

[CCT]

GODMANCHESTER
St Mary *
Bold tower, Kempe window

Some locals apparently call it Gumster, but I have not heard them do so. The old market town suffers from having a crossroads driven through its heart, but its bold church tower is visible across the Fens from miles around. Though Perpendicular, the tower was not built until 1623 and is faced in ashlar, sleek and grey against the brown cobbles of the rest of the church. It looks like a music-hall gent who has lost his trousers. To the right of the south porch is a mass dial with eight 'hours', in the Saxon manner.

The interior has arcades whitewashed and strangely bare. The church was heavily restored by Bodley, whose work includes a rood screen and handsome reredos. He preserved the choir stalls, which apparently came from Ramsey Abbey. Fine misericords are hard to see under the seats. Godmanchester offers a gallery of Kempe and Morris glass of variable quality. The Morris window is in the south aisle, depicting Justice, Courage and Humility, and is rather turgid. The Kempe window to its left is more inventive, full of animation, colour and Kempe's love of architectural settings. The figures are twisted and dressed in the most luxuriant garments.

The guide draws attention to one curiosity in the churchyard. On the (Devil's) north side of the church is a row of tombstones set at right angles to the rest. This section was reserved for Nonconformists, keen rivals to Anglicans in Huntingdonshire.

GREAT PAXTON
Holy Trinity **
Saxon nave and crossing

As long as English churches offer surprises such as Paxton they will survive. The old church sits on a mound looking across the Ouse valley and East Coast railway towards the Great North Road. The churchyard is reached over a small brook. The exterior of the church is Perpendicular and only two round-headed clerestory windows set into the brown cobbled nave offer a clue to what lies within. Great Paxton is said to be the only Saxon church in England to survive with both nave arcades and a crossing.

The church was built in about 1020 as a 'minster', or large pre-parochial church at the centre of a mission to the pagan forest and marsh dwellers. The Saxon features of the interior include the low, three-bay nave arcades and crossing. Clustered piers rise to bulbous capitals, like old pillows crammed under plain arches. At the crossing, all four piers survive, but above only the north transept arch remains. It is extraordinarily high, indicating that the Saxon church originally had equally high transepts to both north and south. The central tower has gone, but there is enough remaining here to show that this was a substantial church with complex liturgical requirements.

Great Paxton was little altered by the Victorians, but the modern rood is ugly, dominating the view of the 13th-century chancel. The benches are 15th-century originals.

HEMINGFORD GREY
St James *
Riverside churchyard, Early Gothic piscina

'Do not fish from the churchyard,' is the admonition on the gate to St James's. This is sad, since I can think of no happier place to drop a line into the Ouse. Water meadows stretch to the distant spire of Hemingford Abbots. Next door is the William and Mary façade of Hemingford Grey House, now a conference centre but once the vicarage. The church itself stands away from the village by the river. The spire was blown down in 1741, a stone from it being hurled 20 yards through a window of the house next door. The Georgians refashioned the stump and placed ball finials on it and on the battlements, creating what looks a curious anachronism. Next to it is a magnificent oriental plane tree, said to be one of the largest in England.

The interior is cosy. The nave arcades have three Norman arches and three Early Gothic ones, but these seem allocated at random. Two of the piers have scalloped Norman capitals, one of them going only half way round but richly carved. On the wall of the south aisle are two pretty corbels of women in medieval headdresses. The chancel contains a rare double piscina with Intersecting tracery on Purbeck shafts. This is a strangely rich feature to find in so simple a church. Opposite is an equally rare double aumbry – all most exotic.

St James's has jolly cartouche memorials on the walls, to which were added in the 1950s three tapestry panels by Augusta Watt, once patron of the living. Though the east window glass is poor there is an exceptional window by Kempe in the south aisle, with a brilliantly coloured landscape background.

On a summer day I found it hard to stay inside the church. The sand martins were diving across the river, the water and its bankside rippling with life. The guidebook describes not just the building but also the flora and fauna of the churchyard. This is a service much to be copied.

LEIGHTON BROMSWOLD
St Mary **
George Herbert's church, Jacobean woodwork

Leighton Bromswold is a surprise. The village stands on a hill with a solid church tower, Perpendicular in form but classical in decoration, like a yeoman farmer dressed up for town. The tower is the product of the brief incumbency of the poet, George Herbert, who arrived here in 1626 under the patronage of the Duke of Lennox, at a time when his clerical career was in difficulty. He was encouraged to take up the living and restore the derelict church by a former college friend, Nicholas Ferrar, who was at that time forming a religious community at Little Gidding, two miles to the north.

Herbert appears to have been a vicar here only briefly. When, in 1629, he met Jane Danvers in Wiltshire and married her, his Herbert relatives secured for him his more celebrated living of Bremerton near Salisbury. He left Leighton with the tower as yet unbuilt. Though he and Ferrar corresponded, it is believed that he never visited the Little Gidding community. Yet I like to imagine it was in these rolling Huntingdonshire hills that Herbert wrote his hospitable lines (to Jane or to God?): 'Love bad me welcome ... sweetly questioning / if I lack'd anything ... / You must sit down, says love, and taste my meat. / So I did sit and eat.'

The church is approached down a wide chestnut avenue, and is entered through a fine Early Gothic doorway. The interior is big, as if designed with the arrival of a man of Herbert's distinction in mind. The length of the chancel relative to the nave suggests an earlier collegiate foundation. The nave, like the tower, was rebuilt in the 17th century, but the Early Gothic chancel survives. It has an excellent double piscina with interwoven arches.

The church is a perfect setting for the 17th-century woodwork that is its most prominent feature. On either side of the chancel arch are two almost identical pulpits, for preacher and reader. This is a most un-Catholic emphasis on preaching for the High Church Herbert, though it may post-date him. The only difference I can detect between the two pulpits is the coving of the tester. There are turned balusters typical of the 17th century everywhere, on the stalls, benches, screens, indeed virtually any bit of woodwork to which a turner's lathe could be applied. The arrangement is symmetrical and comforting.

LITTLE GIDDING
St John **
Ferrar's Stuart commune

Nicholas Ferrar was the son of a City merchant trading with America. Though sickly and deeply pious, he rose to be an MP, manager of his father's business, Stuart courtier and potential statesman. He was offered the lucrative hand of Lord Southampton's heiress in marriage. But his father's death, a business reverse and his own ill-health persuaded him in 1624, at the age of thirty-two, to retire to Huntingdonshire and found an Anglo-Catholic commune. The time was that of the brief Laudian ascendancy. His mother duly bought the Little Gidding manor and Ferrar was ordained a deacon two years later. They persuaded his brother, brother-in-law and no fewer than thirty relatives and children to join them. Unlike Ferrar's friend, George Herbert at Leighton Bromswold, they remained true to their adopted county and never left.

Little Gidding at the time consisted of a hut, a ruined manor and a church used as a barn. These were rebuilt. Though later attacked by the Puritans as an Anglican nunnery, the community was strict and cohesive. The family rules were based on intense devotion, with 'watch' kept round the clock in the church. Members worked as bookbinders, and village children were taught and cared for. They received food and a penny on Sunday if they could recite a psalm. Ferrar died ten years later, but his brother continued the community for a further decade until it was denounced as popish.

The community was sacked by Cromwellians during the Civil War. Some Ferrars remained at Little Gidding, and the church was restored in the 18th century. Today Ferrar House has been refounded as the Community of Christ the Sower, and the church is open to the parish and public.

Unlike Leighton, Little Gidding church makes no pretence to grandness. It lies down a long country lane near the Northamptonshire border and across the lawn by the manor house. The Baroque façade was added in 1714 but the two-cell interior is as it was in Ferrar's time. There are two large windows on either wall plus a Venetian east window. The nave and chancel are lined with wood panelling of arcades on balusters, rising to the wagon roof. Seating is in the form of two single rows of stalls, facing each other across the aisle. The interior is lit by candles in wall sconces and by a splendid brass chandelier.

Little Gidding was High Church in liturgy. 'It is the right, good old way that you are in,' Ferrar was told after a visit by Charles I. Yet today the church in its simplicity looks more like a Puritan place of worship. A later admirer, T. S. Eliot, entitled one of his *Four Quartets* after the settlement. He took a different line from the King and Martyr: 'We cannot revive old factions / We cannot restore old policies / Or follow an antique drum.' But he concluded, as might any English church visitor, that 'The end of all our exploring / Will be to arrive where we started / And know the place for the first time.'

RAMSEY
St Thomas **
Norman carved capitals, Morris glass

This church is a monastic relic. Next door is the gatehouse of the ancient abbey, in a Fenland much populated by Saxons and much raided by Danes. The abbey was a Saxon Benedictine foundation, alongside neighbouring Thorney, Crowland and Spalding. These were, wrote Dom David Knowles, 'the coronal of English monasteries, set on islands and river banks round the edges of the Fen ... with its lofty timber and blossoming fruit trees and sacred isolation'. This inspiration, and the ease of waterborne transport for stone, yielded buildings of unrivalled richness. Ramsey itself still had thirty-four monks at the time of the Dissolution and was rated one of the ten richest abbeys in England. It passed to the Cromwell family and then the Fellowes.

The Norman tower was rebuilt in 1672. It faces out across a green with confidence, surrounded by almshouses and lawns and with a ruined gatehouse to the south. Behind the church stretches a wild churchyard with willows, planes and splendid 18th-century headstones lost in tall grass. It is thought that the nave was the hospitum, or guest house, of the abbey, with the chancel as its chapel. Yet it was a parish church by the late 13th century and has been so ever since.

The chancel has a rib vault with, detectable from outside, a priest's chamber above. The fine east end has three round-arched windows and an almond window above. Inside, the slightly later chancel arch is faintly pointed, but the nave arcades are thoroughly Norman. Each pier and each capital is delightfully different, a Pevsnerian riot of 'keeling, quatrefoils, scallops, waterleaf and crockets'.

The chancel has excellent glass by Morris & Co. The east windows depict saints against a blue background with a frieze of lilies beneath. The east window of the south aisle is a more ambitious Adoration from the same firm, with Perpendicular tracery fragmenting the scene but not diminishing its impact.

ST IVES
All Saints *
Theatrical Comper interior

St Ives is a hidden pleasure in this most hidden county. Seen from the eastern bypass, it appears a serene and unsullied market town with two fine spires rising over the rooftops. The medieval bridge stands with its chapel still consecrated. The parish church, however, is strangely inaccessible, on the far side of town and best reached along the river bank rather than through an ugly housing estate. Its glory is its steeple, high, elegant and with a gracefully tapering spire. Like most English spires it has been much rebuilt, most recently in 1918 when an aeroplane knocked it through the nave roof. The view from the south-east is best, with the tower rising above Intersecting tracery.

The interior in incorrigibly dark. But All Saints is for enthusiasts of High Church furnishings. It is a 'smells and bells' church, with a blast of incense at the door and saints filling every altar and niche. Not surprisingly the place is from the hand of Comper, who worked here in the 1890s. He filled the chancel arch with a screen rising its full height and set statues against the nave piers. The image brackets are 15th century, carved with animals, faces and foliage, a naturalism that contrasts with the piety of the figures.

Comper's sense of theatre is faultless. The location of the rood screen, with loft and organ above, makes an impact similar to Bodley's at Stratford-upon-Avon (Warwicks). The screen itself is Perpendicular, the tracery like lace, the loft panels painted alternately red and green, and the coving with a central pendant. The effect is Baroque rather than Gothic, a blast of the organ crashing out over the nave. Unfortunately Comper omitted to give the organist any sight of the choir, forcing the church to build another organ in the north chapel. Only the shell remains above the screen.

St Ives's font is Norman, with intersecting arches on attached columns. The blocked piscina in the south aisle is a gem of Early Gothic, a round dogtoothed arch with two intersecting chamfered arches. There is an admirable Kempe window in the chancel south wall.

ST NEOTS
St Mary *
Carved roof menagerie, good Victorian glass

St Neots has a big, eclectic church, as if the citizens had set out to copy the best tower in Somerset and the best nave in East Anglia. They boast of it as the 'cathedral of Huntingdonshire'. The tower is beyond reproach, both in proportion and decoration. Eight corner buttresses rise in six diminishing stages to independent pinnacles above panelled turrets. The structure was not completed until the 1530s, the final climax of Perpendicular.

The interior is certainly grand. The chancel arch is high, the tower arch even higher. The oak roof spreads out like a splendid carpet, its wallplates carved with angels, foliage and animals. This zoo includes camels, horses and dragons, presumably to imply the cosmopolitan reach of the town's trade. The chancel roof is more luxurious yet more restrained, with floral bosses at each intersection. Gothic screens divide the chancel from the chapels and nave aisles, that in the north aisle adorned with carved vine leaves and grapes. On the wall is a superb 14th-century niche, astonishingly rich in foliage, a reminder of a pre-Perpendicular church.

The 19th century gave St Neots a jolt. In the chancel is the extraordinary Rowley monument of 1893 by F. A. Walters, a soaring confection of ogival Gothic, rising above so thick a brass grille that the effigy behind is near invisible.

The Victorian stained glass, though dark, is undeniably impressive, in particular the sequence by Clayton & Bell in the north aisle. The story of Christ's life is told against a backdrop of blue sky and clouds, rich landscapes and lush palm trees. The work of this firm, often overshadowed by that of Morris & Co., can be no less exciting. Windows in the south aisle are also lavish. John Hardman's window of the Woman of Samaria was shown at the 1878 Paris exhibition. The golden colours catch the evening sun and suffuse this chilly church with warm light.

THORNEY
St Mary and St Botolph **
Ghost of Fenland abbey

Thorney was one of Saxon England's mighty abbeys, founded after Peterborough, *c.*670. It lasted two centuries before obliteration by the Danes, but was refounded by the Benedictines in 1108. Accessible only by boat, the site was an island 'of thorns' in the Fens, well equipped with anchorites, saints and relics, alleged to include those of Tancred the Martyr and Huna of Chatteris. The Norman abbey church was five times bigger than the one we see today, the tower reputedly higher even than Boston's Stump (Lincs). After the Dissolution the Earl of Bedford, to whom the land was given, was able to donate 40 tons of Thorney stone for new building at Cambridge's Trinity College and 146 tons for Corpus Christi. His descendant drained the Fens in these parts and rendered Thorney no longer an island.

Not until a century later, in 1638, were the remains restored as a parish church. As at Crowland across the border in Lincolnshire, we are left with a ghost. The aisles were demolished and the arcades filled in, the clerestory removed and the roof lowered. The line of the original roof can be seen on the west front of today's church. The present west front is a wonderful mishmash, of Norman flanking towers, Perpendicular frieze with statues in niches and a 17th-century west window that is rather lost in a bigger arch.

The interior reminds me of an Italian church, like Syracuse, in whose walls are embedded the remains of a Roman temple. The nave has five bays of Norman arcading with a cavernous gallery, and full-length shafts. The present transepts and crossing were erected by Edward Blore in 1840–41. At this time Anglo-Norman was mercifully in style and Blore was deferential to the originals. Rounded arches frame what would have been the entrance to the chancel but is now a blank east wall. The east window is a simple but large lancet inserted by Blore, a copy of a 12th-century window in the east end of Canterbury Cathedral.

WITTERING
All Saints *
Massive Saxon arch

Wittering lies off the Great North Road, a Saxon settlement near the old Ermine Street. There is little of that history left today. The legacy of fire, plague and the rural district council has been supplemented by a Royal Air Force base, yielding a miserable spread of council and defence properties. Why can nobody design modern villages that treat high street, green and church as did the Middle Ages? To add insult to injury the 14th-century tower was hit by lightning in the 19th century, and replaced by a truncated cap.

But Wittering has its astonishing Saxon arch. This arch, dated from the mid-10th century, wholly dominates the interior. It was joined in the 12th century by two more arches forming a north arcade. Norman in style, they are like two promiscuous daughters overlooked by a disapproving grandparent. The Saxon arch, like that under Barnack's tower, is not of any obvious family and appears to have been roughly fashioned by masons on the spot. It displays tremendous flair. Three large roll mouldings frame the opening with another as a strip outside the arch. These mouldings are broken by a massive abacus, or early capital, a crude block of masonry but with sloping sides. This is not so much decoration as assertion.

The Norman arches, in contrast, are carved with vigorous zigzag and rest on finely developed scallop capitals. They make a handsome pair, cleaned but not over-restored. The north chapel is dedicated to the RAF base: it has a modern window depicting St Michael and various generations of airmen. The candelabra is made from aircraft propellers.

YAXLEY
St Peter ***
Fenland tower, heart burial monument

Yaxley is a thrilling discovery, especially when approached from the south across the Fens. This is a country of water and cabbages, of long fields and huge skies, drained in the 1630s by the 4th Earl of Bedford. It is interlaced by dykes with names such as Monk's Lode, Bevill's Leam and Black Ham. A bluff that once overlooked a bend in the Nene (now redirected) ill-conceals the chimneys of Peterborough and modern housing estates. But rising over the scene is a tower to defy them all. Four stages culminate in pinnacles with flying buttresses and then a spire.

The tower and nave are mostly Perpendicular, the chancel Decorated. The interior is broad and spacious, its vistas modulated by transepts and aisles which run the length of the church, flanking the tower in the west and the chancel in the east. The windows are of all periods: narrow lancets in the transepts, triple lancets in the north aisle, Reticulated in the south transept, and a great five-light east window with curvilinear tracery. This last is a masterpiece, rendered even finer by ogival niches on either side. The only discordant note is Comper's stained glass and Temple Moore's screen and organ loft.

Every wall of Yaxley seems busy with piscinas and aumbries, relics of altars departed and shrines forgotten. In the north transept is a heart burial monument, with a relief wall tablet representing the box in which the heart was placed and two hands in prayer holding it aloft. If we cannot have church interiors that recall the bustle, colour, chaos and dirt of the Middle Ages, we can at least have one as charming to the eye as this.

Kent

Kent is surprisingly rich in old churches, many of them very old. The story begins with Augustine's mission at Canterbury and the Saxon minsters and collegiate foundations of Sheppey and Thanet, offering some of the most eerie church locations in England. The Normans did more than conquer Kent, they initiated wave after wave of stylistic innovation from France. Norman carvings adorned the Cinque Ports of New Romney and Sandwich and the great doorways at Barfreston and Patrixbourne. The county was home to Thomas à Becket, and the churches of the Pilgrims' Way still retain traces of his cult. The Middle Ages left the superb Early Gothic chancels at Minster-in-Thanet and Hythe, the exquisite early Decorated interior at Stone and England's finest gallery of brasses at Cobham.

A different Kent is found in the lush orchard landscape of the Weald. Here the Perpendicular age found money to spend on rich churches at Maidstone, Tenterden and Cranbrook, and the lavish Culpeper tombs at Goudhurst. It also rebuilt many of the delightfully intimate churches of Romney Marsh, a group distinct from the rest of the county and in the care of the Romney Marshes Historic Churches Trust.

The Restoration contributed the charming church of King Charles the Martyr at Tunbridge Wells and the Georgians the soaring spire of Mereworth. Kent was not rich in the 19th century, and Victorian architects are remarkable by their absence. But the Kent story ends in a blaze: Marc Chagall's glorious windows at Tudeley.

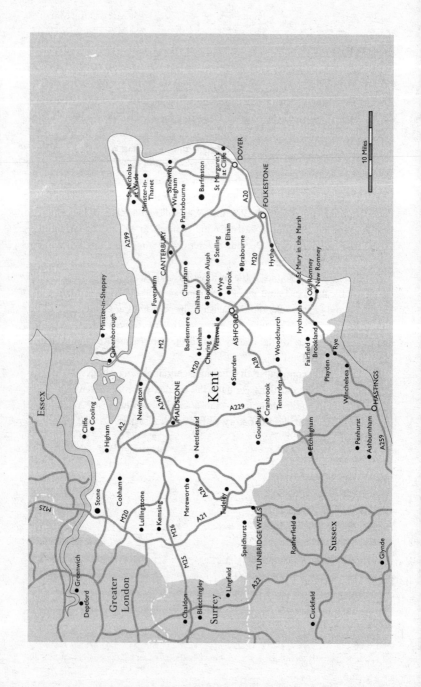

Badlesmere *

Barfreston ****

Boughton Aluph **

Brabourne **

Brook **

Brookland ***

Canterbury:

  St Martin *

Charing *

Chartham **

Chilham **

Cliffe **

Cobham ***

Cooling *

Cranbrook **

Elham **

Fairfield *

Faversham **

Goudhurst **

Higham *

Hythe ***

Ivychurch **

Kemsing *

Lenham *

Lullingstone ***

Maidstone **

Mereworth **

Minster-in-Sheppey

  ***

Minster-in-Thanet ***

Nettlestead **

Newington (nr

  Sittingbourne) *

New Romney ***

Old Romney **

Patrixbourne **

Queenborough *

St Margaret's at Cliffe *

St Mary in the Marsh *

St Nicholas at Wade **

Sandwich:

  St Clement **

Smarden *

Speldhurst *

Stelling *

Stone (nr Dartford)

  ****

Tenterden *

Tudeley **

Tunbridge Wells:

  King Charles the

  Martyr **

Westwell **

Wingham **

Woodchurch **

Wye *

BADLESMERE

St Leonard *

Unaltered Georgian fittings

East of the Faversham to Ashford road a lane runs across fields to a small farm. The Baron of Badlesmere was governor of Leeds Castle under Edward II. Failing to read the political wind correctly, he refused to lower his drawbridge to Queen Isabel in 1322 and was duly beheaded at Canterbury. After that fall from grace, this little church was hardly touched until the 18th century. Badlesmere has what some term an 'atmospherick' interior, aisleless and simple, a Georgian adaptation of a medieval nave and chancel. Hat pegs surround the walls. Old hymnals and Bibles litter the pews. A bird or two regard it as home. The church is redundant, still 'living' but only just.

The medieval period is represented in the chancel by two widely spaced lancets which form the east window and the small Decorated north window. The crown-post roof is 15th century. Otherwise the charm is in the furnishings. There are box pews throughout, their sides higher for the squire and rector. Those at the back of the church rise in tiers to enable children to see the service. The three-decker pulpit survives intact, as do the Protestant biblical texts on the walls. A simple wooden reredos is crowned by an acanthus finial.

Next to the altar rail is a set of bench-ends of *c.*1415. They have intricate

Perpendicular carving, including an emblem of the Trinity. It is hard to believe these 15th-century treasures were intended for here, and they may have come from Badlesmere property elsewhere.

BARFRESTON
St Nicholas ****
Complete Norman decoration

The village sits snugly in a defile a mile from the North Downs Way. I visited it on a winter day when the hill outside the church was so clogged with snow as to have become impassable. The adjacent pub with log fire and hot soup was as welcome as the sight of Barfreston's celebrated carvings. The church is situated on a small bluff with its west end giving directly on to the pub garden. It is a simple, double-cell chapel covered with Norman decoration, earning it the title of the 'Kilpeck of the South'. Heavy but apparently necessary 19th-century restoration has deprived Barfreston's interior of some of its aura of antiquity.

The south doorway can scarcely be rivalled in England for rich and well-preserved late Norman carving. In the tympanum, Christ is flanked by a king and queen, angels and graceful figures in foliage. The first and second surrounding orders have more carved foliage, and roundels with animal musicians and other chimeras. The outer order has ovals with the signs of the zodiac and the Labours of the Months. These are important to scholars of Norman iconography, and also appear round Thomas à Becket's shrine at Canterbury. Becket may even be the bishop at the apex of the middle order. Churches this near to Canterbury would have been in the thick of his cult.

The outside walls have an almost continuous arcading, some blind, some fenestrated. Above is a complete corbel-table of carved heads. The east end has three round-headed windows buried in lesser arches and above a wheel window of eight spokes composed of tiny columns. On either side are fragments of evangelists and even a knight on horseback. To one side is a lion. This wall is one of Kent's cheeriest compositions.

The tall interior is a casket of Norman art. The chancel arch has twisted columns, rippling foliage and 'swallow-tail spur' bases, of the sort which occur in the choir at Canterbury. On either side are high niches for now-vanished altars. The nave has two carved string courses, at sill and window arch height. These appear to have abstract decoration, but on closer inspection reveal wilful variety. A frieze of animals breaks into the pattern on the north wall, while more animals form stops to the south windows. The chancel courses are even richer. The wheel window surround is decorated with a wealth of abstract and animal ornament.

Barfreston is dated to the last quarter of the 12th century, the last flourish of

Norman art before the advent of Gothic. We can already see in the capitals of the chancel arch traces of the transition from water-leaf to stiff-leaf. But mostly this church looks back not forward, to the France of the Norman Conquest rather than the Gothic one.

BOUGHTON ALUPH
All Saints **
Lonely setting, heraldic glass

The place is named after its 13th-century lord, Alulphus of Boctune, and to find the church visitors must ignore the village and rely on instructions or a good map. It sits isolated on a mound next to a picturesque manor, its solitary churchyard looking out across rolling orchards towards Wye. The building is a rare instance of an English church as most would have appeared before the arrival of Victorian restorers. The Middle Ages hang heavy on its walls and in the glass of its windows. On my visit it looked dilapidated.

The exterior is not easy to read. Transepts and buttresses, tower and stair-turret seem to take off at odd angles. Inside all is clear, a lofty, rambling un-restored space with a straightforward plan. The nave, aisles and short transepts are 14th century, while the east end with a low chancel and Moyle Chapel is 13th. This chapel has two Early Gothic lancets and two Decorated windows. The chancel east window is eccentric, a late Decorated centre panel surrounded by the slender panels of conventional Perpendicular tracery. One reason for this shift to a less expressive style of tracery was the need for vertical shapes to accommodate the human figures associated with late heraldic glass. This survives at Boughton in the upper panels, of good quality with reds, whites and yellows and much architectural framing.

In the south transept is an old pedal organ with blue pipes, bringing some jollity to an otherwise forlorn place. The south porch has its own fireplace to warm passing pilgrims on their way to Canterbury. Churches were locked then too.

BRABOURNE
St Mary **
Scot tombs, Norman glass

The village of Brabourne nestles prettily in the lee of the North Downs where once the sea stretched far inland. Like neighbouring Brook, it would have been a seaside village and its massive tower would have served as a navigational aid. From the south this tower now looks a crippled thing, its top storeys having been removed for safety and its walls massively buttressed.

The interest of Brabourne is inside. The nave is tall and severe. A south aisle was added in the 13th century with handsome piers of Bethersden 'marble', Kent's answer to the hard-polished Purbeck stone of Dorset. The nave is lit by one Perpendicular window in the north wall, an out-of-character Victorian window in the south aisle and a gloomy little clerestory. But the eye is soon drawn east to the tall Norman chancel arch. This is enriched by superb carvings round the capitals, one apparently of an Egyptian dragon. Beyond is a decorated string course and attached pillar, apparently intended for a stone vault.

We now encounter the Scot family, lords of the manor in the Middle Ages. The unusual altar of c.1600 is a Scot tomb, recording their marital alliances and adorned with their shields. It eulogises the family with an inscription to the effect that 'the memorial of the just shall be blessed, but the name of the wicked shall rot'. One Scot helped defeat the Armada and another was founding father of 'the scholarship of magic'. Set into the north wall is an Easter Sepulchre that would once have been the tomb of Sir John Scot, courtier to Edward IV. A helm is fixed to the wall above.

More Scot monuments cover the walls and floor. In the south chapel the family's brasses have been admirably reset in the floor beneath protective carpets. They are exceptional, especially those to the women. Isabel, Lady Clifton, has flowing hair, while Sir William Scot stands rather uncomfortably on a greyhound. In the south chancel aisle is a curious and rare 'heart shrine'. This is believed to have been for the heart of John de Baliol, who died in 1269, though the tomb is dated c.1300. Its backing has rare Kentish split cusps, see Chartham.

Lastly a treasure. The glass in the small Norman window high in the north wall of the chancel is original 12th century. It is a complete and abstract pattern, of the sort normally seen only in stone carving. Semi-circles intersect in soft browns, ochres and greens, much faded, antique and serene.

BROOK
St Mary **
Norman tower, early wall paintings

Brook is not a church to be trifled with. It stands beneath the escarpment of the Downs looking out across what would once have been an expanse of inland water towards Tenterden. The church tower has the appearance of a massive Norman keep and it is hard to believe that security was not a concern of its architect. It rises in stepped stages, like a Mayan ruin. Within is a winding staircase to a first-floor chapel, altar and wall paintings. Such tower chapels are common in Germany but almost unknown in England. However, the tower is locked so its interior is now private.

There is more to Brook than its tower. This is among the earliest of Norman churches. It dates from immediately after the Conquest when Normans would have been eager to secure a foothold on the shores of this valuable inland lagoon. There is no visible trace of nailhead or zigzag and the Norman windows that penetrate its thick walls are tiny and high. Nave and chancel are unaisled and linked by an unadorned arch, a taller arch supporting the tower. In the chancel is a curious almond-shaped opening, allegedly for an anchorite's cell or possibly for relics. Next to it appears to be a leper's hole.

Brook is now lit by later and larger windows. This is as well, since the church contains some of the most remarkable wall paintings in Kent. Those in the nave are of poor quality. A St Christopher is visible above the north door and a frieze round the walls has been uncovered, partly obscured by Reformation texts. The paintings in the chancel are of a different order, roundels of the Life of Christ set in panels and alternating white-on-black and black-on-white. The technique is said to have been borrowed from an illuminated manuscript. These scenes must have been hard to see before the insertion of later windows. As in the caves of Lascaux the artists must have drawn as much for the pleasure of their craft as for public visibility.

The furnishings are mostly Victorian, though not the pulpit. This is a most unusual work of Tudor woodwork, including spiral colonettes that are simple but of great dignity.

BROOKLAND
St Augustine ***
Detached bell-tower, Norman lead font

This is no place to find without warning on a dark winter night. Brookland's separate, triple-coned bell-tower might have flown in from Transylvania, with bats in its eaves and worse inside. It is the stuff of many legends. One holds that it detached itself from the church in amazement when a 'confirmed old bachelor married a local spinster well stricken in years'. The truth appears to be a decision to house the bells on a wooden scaffold away from the church. This was then covered in wood shingles for protection. This explanation is too pedestrian for any Romney Marsh romantic. The tower inside is a latticework of medieval woodwork, comparable with the best of Essex.

While Brookland's exterior is a jumble of strange extensions, the interior is spacious and uniform. Seven wide bays of Early Gothic arcading in the nave lead without interruption to three bays of chancel. The nave retains its box pews and is overseen by a double-decker pulpit sadly without its tester. In the curious south chapel, denuded of adornment, are old 17th-century rails protecting a tomb chest and a lower floor. In the corner of this chapel is a fine wall painting of the murder of Thomas à Becket. It has the grouping and sense of drama of a painting by Uccello.

The back of the church serves as a museum of quaint objects, including one of the few surviving sets of tithe weighing scales. There is also a 'hudd', or graveside shelter, to protect the vicar when he was conducting burials in the rain (before the invention of the umbrella). In the north-west corner is a tiny chamber with a Tudor window, built as a schoolroom after the Reformation. It is now a chapel. Some original glass survives in the south aisle east window and the north aisle west window, the latter of excellent preservation.

Brookland possesses one outstanding work, its lead font of c.1200. There are only thirty surviving lead fonts in England, most having been melted down for pots or ammunition. Many of those in the south are believed to have come from Normandy or have been worked by Norman carvers. A local legend holds that Brookland's was stolen from a Normandy church by Romney raiders. The bowl is circular and covered in arcading, each arch containing a sign of the zodiac and the rural activities associated with that time of the year. They portray the simple tasks of farming life, a vernacular Book of Hours.

To leave Brookland and be faced with a row of new bungalows directly opposite is as depressing as are the caravans which defile the view of Fairfield. Nobody is guarding Romney Marsh these days.

CANTERBURY
St Martin *
Earliest church, Norman font

St Martin's status as the oldest church in continuous use in England is hard to contest. Bede recorded that a church dedicated to Martin had been built to the east of Canterbury in Roman times and that Queen Bertha, Frankish (and Christian) wife of the Saxon King Ethelbert of Kent, had worshipped here prior to Augustine's arrival in AD 597. This thesis is witnessed by archaeological evidence in the neighbourhood and is commemorated in the baptistery. The church is further honoured by inclusion in the UNESCO list of World Heritage sites.

At this point I dare not leave it off my list, even if little sense of antiquity hangs about the place now. More vivid ghosts of early Christianity can be sensed at Escomb (Durham) or Bradwell (Essex). Yet St Martin's is a renowned and much-visited shrine. It sits well on its hillside overlooking Canterbury from its least offensive quarter, with a tiered cemetery rising up the slope above it.

The exterior is a mosaic of building materials, some plainly old, a geological encyclopedia. Here are aged walls of Roman tile, ragstone, flint, brick and anything that came to hand. There are two blocked doorways in the south wall, one of which the guide protests 'could have been Roman' or at least Saxon, as are the buttresses. The whitewashed interior has Saxon proportions. Both nave and chancel are tall, divided by a high wishbone arch. The west wall is a splendid façade of ancient stone and window openings.

The church does contain one treasure, the Norman font reputedly brought from Canterbury Cathedral. Its components have apparently been stacked on top of each other in the wrong order, the interlocking rings not matching with those below.

CHARING
St Peter and St Paul *
Decorated tracery

Charing is an unobtrusive village on the slopes of the North Downs, fiercely proud of its appearance. It was a centre of resistance to the high-speed rail link to the Channel Tunnel. A narrow lane leads off the high street to the site of a former archbishop's palace. The palace is now a farm but impressive remains survive behind a tall flint and brick wall. This is pilgrim country, a day's walk from Canterbury, and the churchyard in spring is bathed in blossom, birdsong and beech.

The church faces us with a bold tower of *c*.1500. The west doorway is a unified composition of window and doorway under a square hood with decorated spandrels. Given the presence of an archbishop's residence, the interior is strangely simple. There are nave, transepts and chancel but no aisles. The windows are a textbook selection of Early Gothic, Decorated and Perpendicular tracery. A square-headed window on the south side of the nave has Reticulated tracery as wild as any in Kent. The central light is composed of an 'octofoil'.

The elaborate roof was restored after a fire in 1590, the beams being stencilled and painted rather than carved. The rood screen is a modern work of 1921 by the Devon carver, Fellowes Prynne. Charing's coat of arms originated with Charles I, but the C was converted into a G in the Hanoverian period and redated 1716. The original date of 1635 is visible at the end of the motto. For some reason Charing's best pews, from the 16th century, have been relocated under the tower.

How much better they would look in the front, especially adorned with the parish's modern seat-liners. These were sewn by local ladies in thanks for their safe return from the Holy Land – by package tour in 1983. The pilgrim spirit lives on in Charing.

CHARTHAM
St Mary **
Kentish tracery, Rysbrack monument

Chartham is a satellite village of Canterbury, set on the River Stour. Its church was constructed with a lengthy chancel reflecting its close links with the monks at Canterbury. The rector in 1292 was Thomas of Chartham, treasurer to the See of Canterbury. Edward I was a donor for its building in 1294. Hence the unity of the composition and the splendour of the chancel and transept windows. These are best appreciated from outside and especially from the east.

The church is best known as the home of Kentish tracery, a late 13th-century variant of the Decorated style known as split cusping. Its distinctive feature is the splitting of the cusps or 'spikes' inside the lights of the tracery. The tips of the cusps are pealed back like pieces of an orange. The designer appears to be straining after ever greater elaboration within the simple discs of earlier Geometrical tracery. He failed to 'discover' the flamboyant curve, eventually to emerge in the net-like pattern of Reticulation.

Kentish tracery turned out to be a stylistic blind alley. Split cusps are rare even in Kent, found in one or two instances at Rochester and Canterbury Cathedrals and, for unknown reasons, round the tombs at Aldworth (Berks) and Whitby Abbey in North Yorkshire, all dated to *c.*1300. At least in Chartham's east window, the effect is sensational, as if three fireworks had shot skywards at once to explode as a starburst.

The interior retains the proportions of a great 13th-century church, long with small transepts and a sense of climax in its sanctuary. The roof beams and rafters are exposed throughout, like those of a barn. A huge boss marks the crossing. The nave timbers are reconstructions by the Victorian, G. E. Street. He also restored as much as he could find of the original chancel glass, including grisaille and flower patterns in the borders of north and south windows.

The south transept is dominated by monuments to the Fagg family. Towering over them all is a Rysbrack of 1751 commemorating Sarah Young, née Fagg, who died at the age of eighteen. Her husband stands in characteristic mid-Georgian pose, like a Roman senator. She looks up admiringly while a cherub with a shell and extinguished torch gazes pensively at the ground.

Opposite under a protective carpet is an early brass, that of Sir Robert de Septvans (d.1306). A facsimile for rubbing leans against the north wall of the nave. The figure is of a knight lying cross-legged in chainmail. His head is uncovered and his hair and facial features are depicted. He has been widely reproduced.

CHILHAM
St Mary **
Digges memorials

Chilham is one of Kent's picture-book villages. No part is prettier than the square that separates the church from the Jacobean house built by the Master of the Rolls, Sir Dudley Digges, in 1616. Many later grandees moved their villages away from their gates. Not so Digges. House, village and church remain in cosy intimacy, enhanced by the presence of the White Horse Inn, the Copper Kettle and the Tudor Lodge.

The church is mostly Perpendicular, of flint and chequered stone. The tower, porch and transept face the churchyard, where the stump of an old yew tree is held to be 7th century. The interior is mostly Victorian and savagely so. The chancel was rebuilt by David Brandon in 1863 who, in the process, demolished two classical mausoleums to the north and south and replaced them with Gothic chapels.

These contain the principal reason for visiting the church. In the south chapel is the memorial to Lady Mary Digges, erected by her husband, the builder of the 'new castle', and designed by Nicholas Stone in 1631. It consists of an Ionic column attended by the four Cardinal Virtues, Justice, Temperance, Prudence and Fortitude, all on tall pedestals. Pevsner relates the design to that of Inigo Jones for James I's catafalque in 1625, the vanguard of contemporary taste (but *see* the Cecil monument in Hatfield/Herts for a similar design).

In the north chapel is a monument by Francis Chantrey to James Wildman (d.1822). A family mourns the death of a husband and father in grieving poses. Adjacent is a monument by Alexander Munro to two sons of the big house, Arthur and Edmund Harvey (d.1858). They read a book, *Babes in the Wood*, while their shuttlecock and bat lie discarded on the ground.

In the nave is a memorial to Sir Dudley Digges's sister, Lady Palmer (d.1619), which makes a sober comparison with Lady Digges's tomb of similar date. It is a free-standing monument comprising a tomb chest, inscription plate and canopy on Corinthian columns. The material is Bethersden 'marble', a Kent stone whose pattern is achieved by carving and then polishing the relief until dark, leaving the background matt and light. The inscription displays the piety expected of such memorials. The lady was 'fayrer than most women, wiser than most men'.

CLIFFE
St Helen **
Reticulated windows, carved sedilia

Cliffe is the closest that the end of the world gets to London. It looks out across the marshes to the distant chimneys of Canvey refinery in Essex, and is a sort of appendix between the Medway estuary and the Thames. The villages of the Hoo peninsula are sad, lost places, their public and private buildings unusually mean. Inside the church guidebook is a prayer for kindness that concludes, 'for I shall not pass this way again'. I fear that this may be true. Cliffe is on the way to nowhere.

It cannot always have been thus. Cliffe church once had wealthy patrons, and is generous in size and rich in decoration. It would make a more handsome community centre than any other building in the neighbourhood. The walls have strong 'liquorice allsort' banding of ragstone and knapped flint, into which are set some of the best windows in north-west Kent. These are Decorated in style and though restored by the Victorians are of the original design. Their richness was probably due to the patronage of the 14th-century Canterbury Cathedral. The mullions of the windows rise from the sills and, as if sensing the constriction of the arches, split wilfully into branches. The east window is a work of great delicacy, its bars like veins in a vast leaf.

The core of Cliffe is an Early Gothic cruciform church, with deep transepts and a nave clerestory. The piers have painted zigzags, discovered during restoration. This implies an unusually wealthy religious foundation, predating the 13th century.

The transepts have piscinas indicating pre-Reformation chapels. On their east walls are well-preserved wall paintings, the most vivid a martyrdom of St Edmund. The Jacobean pulpit is spacious – room for the most athletic preacher to prance about inside – with an hour-glass holder of 1636.

The Decorated chancel is that of a college, presumably reflecting Canterbury influence. It boasts medieval choir stalls, apparently from a priory in Leicestershire, with misericords. On the south wall is one of the finest sedilia in Kent, with intricately carved uprights and exaggerated crockets on the ogee arches, flowing upwards across the chancel wall. Someone, some time, thought Cliffe deserved nothing but the best.

COBHAM
St Mary ***
Largest brass collection in England, Renaissance tomb

Like so much of Kent, the village of Cobham is charming yet unknown. It sits on a hill on the old Dover road looking down towards Gravesend. Dickens visited the Old Leather Bottle in *Pickwick Papers*. Opposite, Sir John de Cobham founded a religious college in the 14th century. His family built one of Kent's finest houses a mile up the road. The village still has Cobham almshouses and a Cobham school. But only from the church, and especially its chancel, can we capture a true sense of the past of this place.

The church sits on a rise in the centre of the village. It was heavily restored in the 19th century by George Gilbert Scott, but he respected the chancel and its treasury of medieval art. Even before Cobham's collegiate foundation in 1362, this chancel was a grand place. Tall Early Gothic lancets light the three walls. An old rood screen once filled the east end directly above the altar, a most unusual location. We must imagine it covered in statues and candles, towering over the sedilia lining the walls and illuminating the knights commemorated in brass and stone beneath. Sir John's masons moved the Early Gothic piscina (with dogtooth decoration) down the wall, and inserted a Perpendicular one in its place.

The eye is drawn at once to the centrepiece of this great hall. On the floor is the largest display of brasses in one place in England, remarkable in quantity and quality. The most notable are of Sir John de Cobham himself (d.1408), portrayed holding a church, and of Sir Nicholas Hawberk (d.1407). The latter is regarded as Cobham's finest, with the Trinity set in a canopy over the knight's head and his son on a pedestal at his feet. The brass of Joan, Lady Cobham is one of the earliest female brasses, *c.*1320.

Adjacent stands the tomb chest of the 9th Lord Cobham (1561) and his wife, restored after being shattered by a falling beam in the 18th century. It lies plumb in front of the chancel altar. The alabaster effigies are beautifully carved, their hands in prayer, attended by heraldic beasts. The Gothic carving marries happily with its classical chest. The latter has Ionic columns with shell recesses, standing on a plinth in the strange form of a Doric entablature. The mourners are a delight, ten sons and four daughters, each slightly different and one, for some reason, about to get up from his knees. Perhaps he was the great man's heir. The work is proof, if proof were needed, that English church art did not die with the Reformation.

COOLING
St James *
Early Gothic arcading, 'Pip's churchyard'

Cooling is exciting in fact and fiction. We are on the northern extremity of the Hoo peninsula into the Thames estuary. In 1789 Hasted wrote that it was 'an unfrequented place, the roads of which are deep and miry and it is as unhealthy as it is unpleasant'. Dickens visited the church on his Kent honeymoon, enabling Cooling to lay claim to the title of Pip's village and the churchyard as Magwitch's domain. The church is best approached on a cold misty day with the opening of *Great Expectations* in mind: 'The dark flat wilderness beyond the churchyard, intersected with dykes and mounds and gates, with scattered cattle feeding on it, was the marshes; and that low leaden line beyond was the river . . . and that small bundle of shivers growing afraid of it all and beginning to cry, was Pip.'

Next to the church are the isolated remains of Cooling Castle, erected by Sir John de Cobham to keep marauding French from his land. The castle, still an impressive ruin, protects a farm, a pub and some ugly cottages. But the church (now redundant) is open, and in the churchyard are the blank headstones marking the graves of unnamed infants that may well have inspired Dickens's lament for Pip's lost siblings.

The church is big for a settlement of never more than 200 souls. It comprises a stocky tower, nave and chancel with restored Decorated windows. The interior is not spoilt by Victorian restoration, although the 19th-century glass comes close to doing so. Why not restore clear glass to the windows and let nature supply the view?

The chief interest of the interior lies in the Early Gothic chancel. Both walls have restored blind arcading with Purbeck marble shafting. The arcade forms a piscina and sedilia on the south side and is as opulent as the chancel at neighbouring Cliffe. The Cobhams acquired the manor in 1214, so presumably they were responsible. What must a priest have done to be posted to 13th-century Cooling, to sit in these lovely arcades and sing mass in this cold chancel? [CCT]

CRANBROOK
St Dunstan * *
Green Man bosses, immersion font

Cranbrook is regarded as the capital of the Weald, a hillside village grown big round its winding high street and smock windmill. Unlike its rival, Tenterden, it was not a prosperous trading port in the early Middle Ages. When the 15th-century clothiers came to rebuild their church they had little to keep of what went before.

The result is a big church up a slope at the elbow of the high street. Its crumbling honey-coloured stone is protected from the west wind by a rampart of yew, holly and magnolia. The tower is curiously stocky, as if waiting for an oast to be placed on top. The west wall is hung with the emblems of the families who paid for it. High on the tower's south face is a Baroque clock frame.

Cranbrook's interior is impressive rather than lovely. Six bays of high Perpendicular arcades with clerestory were not completed until the 1520s. Clothiers' symbols adorn the arcade piers, beneath half-angels. This is a busy church, with not a corner wasted, its pleasures lying in its furnishings. By the south door is a stone font designed for total immersion. An 18th-century vicar introduced the practice lest he lose parishioners to the Baptists. For whatever reason it was not a success; the register indicates only one use.

On the wall of the tower are three huge wooden bosses dated to about 1300, each a Green Man. They are magnificent examples of this eerie iconography, their faces glaring at us from deep in the past of the Wealden woods. The south chapel contains tombs to the Roberts dynasty of Glassenbury, including its genealogy. It records the large progeny but short lifespans of so many medieval families: 43 persons over eleven generations, yet the family died out in the 18th century.

A tablet west of the south door was erected by American descendants of William Eddye, vicar in 1591–1616, two of whose children departed for the new English colonies in America in 1630. The west end of the church is crowded with monuments, including a mannered death scene of the painter, Thomas Webster, lying with his brushes and attended by putti. Three south aisle windows are by Kempe at his most architectural.

ELHAM

St Mary **

20th-century furnishings by Eden, Becket icon

Elham has a long high street with pretty shops and houses, off which the church is granted its own small square with adjacent pub. The interior is at first sight a conventional Early Gothic nave and chancel with Decorated north aisle. On closer inspection it is that most delightful obeisance paid by the 20th-century to the Middle Ages, not a restoration but a re-creation of a Gothic interior by a scholar with a feel for the past. The scholar in this case was F. C. Eden, re-creator also of Blisland (Cornwall) and North Cerney (Gloucs). Elham is a church of furnishings, a treasure house of woodwork, art and statuary, more like a wealthy Wren church in the City of London than a modest Kent parish.

Eden panelled the nave and chancel in oak. He supplied the font with a Baroque cover and wall panel, and dressed the aisle chapels. The south aisle altar is decorated with a 15th-century alabaster triptych of St Catherine. This is a rare survival of a medieval icon. In the left panel, it represents Henry I with armed retainers confronting Becket at the Council of Northampton in 1164, and in the right panel is Becket's murder. This is regarded as the best surviving depiction of the scene. Almost all Becket icons were destroyed in the 16th century on the orders of Henry VIII, who regarded Becket as a traitor.

Against a north-east pier is a canopied altar and reredos of embossed Spanish leather. Beyond lies the Jesus Chapel, decorated with an extraordinary modern statue of Christ flying towards us, in a style that might be termed ecclesiastical socialist realist.

Eden enriched the oak of the chancel with limewood carving in the manner of Grinling Gibbons. At one point he turns the panelling into a handsome priest's sedilia. The reredos was painted by Ripley Wilmer in 1907 and the floor is tiled black and white. There is a filled and operational hour glass on the pulpit, the only one I know.

I wonder if the 21st century will be able to treat churches such as Elham with the same creative sensitivity as did Eden.

FAIRFIELD
St Thomas à Becket *
Timber frame church in marsh setting

Fairfield is one of the best-known churches in Kent, if only for its evocative isolation. It appears as if deposited by the tide on a mound in Romney Marsh, with the bluff of the Kent 'mainland' visible in the distance. There is no settlement near and until this century access was usually by boat. Sheep graze round the door and keep noisy guard on the enclave. Even in the 19th century fewer than a dozen dwellings could be ascribed to Fairfield parish, which has made no return since 1931. Yet a church here is recorded in the 13th century, still timber-framed when encased in brick in the 18th century. By 1913 it was on the point of collapse and the present church was restored by W. D. Caröe.

Fairfield evokes intimate worship. The church is small and the outside, despite its Georgian style, has a 20th-century feel to it. Caröe used cement to infill the timbering where he should have used plaster. But the atmosphere is suitably primitive. The nave roof is supported on a single crown-post, as is that of the chancel.

The interior has a complete set of box pews with, we are told, the best three-decker pulpit in Kent. In the chancel the small altar table, dressed and decorated with dried flowers, is surrounded by a rail with benches on either side. Under the tower is a picture of the church surrounded by floodwater in 1960. A poem to Fairfield by Joan Warburg appeared in *Country Life* in 1966:

> My parish is a lonely marsh,
> My service at the water's edge,
> Wailing of sea birds, sweet or harsh,
> The sussuration of the sedge,
> Bleating of a hundred sheep
> Where pilgrims and crusaders sleep.

FAVERSHAM
St Mary **
Medieval painted pier, original misericords

St Mary of Charity announces itself with a tapering crown that rises white and slender over the roofs of Faversham. The tower was rebuilt in the 18th century, based on St Dunstan-in-the-East in the City. The church guide calls it 'fanciful rather than academic', though the terms could equally be reversed. St Mary's is in parts medieval, Georgian and Victorian, but those parts are most eccentrically arranged.

The church sits away from the town centre behind the brewery and above the old creek. The tower, with a thin openwork spire and corner pinnacles, looms over a neighbourhood of attractive Georgian streets. It was built in the 1790s, prior to two separate campaigns of 19th-century rebuilding. Of these the second was by George Gilbert Scott, who encased the exterior in flint in the 1850s. This flint is relentless.

The interior is a surprise. Faversham is a patchwork of architects half-respecting the work of predecessors. The wide Georgian nave was designed by George Dance Snr in 1754 and is composed of five bays of severe Doric columns with a classical entablature and plaster ceiling. It has a conventional clerestory which Scott later decided to leave as Georgian inside but transforms into Gothic outside, a bizarre decision. At the west end of the nave, Dance left standing portions of an old Norman church. To the north, this means rounded arches and slit windows.

The crossing and aisled transepts at Faversham are Gothic, totally different in atmosphere and on a sensational scale. This part of the church was rebuilt in the Decorated style after its predecessor was destroyed by the townspeople, in reaction to an attempt to evict their vicar by the owner of the living, St Augustine's Abbey, Canterbury. The new church, according to a guidebook, could seat 1,398 people. Only Maidstone is bigger in the county. The piscinas dotted about the transepts indicate a wealth of 14th-century guilds, patrons and altars. These transepts are gloomy places, but the northern one is enlivened by a surviving wall painting on a pier. This runs round the entire shaft and depicts scenes from the Life of Christ in vivid reds and greens. The work is by an artist of great skill and, as so often, leaves us wondering at the other glories that such buildings must once have contained.

The chancel is Victorian, with an east window like a bad comic strip that ruins the fine reredos by Ewan Christian of 1867. It cannot ruin the superb choir stalls, which include some of the best misericords in Kent. Here is a devil eating a man's innards and an outstanding Green Man. Another is said to show a wolf cunningly chewing at its own paws, so it could stalk its prey more quietly.

GOUDHURST
St Mary **
Culpeper monuments

Just as Cranbrook is a town struggling to look like a village, Goudhurst is a village with the airs and graces of a town. Its ridge dominates this corner of the Weald and the church tower completes the view up a spacious street from the pond. From its top, vistas stretch in all directions across tile-hung houses and Scots pines to oasts, hops and orchards: a quintessential Kent scene.

The tower was struck by lightning in 1637 and rebuilt in a Gothic style three years later. The curious west window is identical to windows at St Katharine Cree (London) and at Berwick (Northumb), a transition from Gothic to classical, fashionable in churches at the time. The doorway boasts a classical surround, but the door hinges are Gothic. The remainder of the exterior is robustly Perpendicular. Inside, the nave arcade is at best a curiosity, botched together as and when funds were available. Surviving from a former Early Gothic church are the eastern bays of the north arcade. The chancel has Early Gothic lancets but has been ruthlessly scraped.

The glory of Goudhurst is the Culpeper memorials, located in the south chapel and south aisle. The Culpepers were based at Bedgebury, one of the oldest recorded manors in England with deeds dated AD 815. John of Bedgebury's brass (d.1424) is on the floor of the Lady Chapel, south of the chancel. His widow married Walter Culpeper. The most celebrated memorial is that of 'Old Sir Alexander' Culpeper (d.1537) and his wife Constance, in the south aisle under a bay window clearly designed for the purpose. The effigies are not in stone but in wood, with gesso detailing and colouring. Watching over them is a two-tiered relief in the window splay, portraying God, the Virgin and Child, St George and the Dragon and more kneeling Culpepers. The alcove is of honey-coloured stone which on a fine day both absorbs and radiates the southern sunlight.

Their son Alexander (d.1599) is next in line for memorial. His family is commemorated in a conventional wall monument of 1608. Father is in a niche above, son Alexander with wife and son kneel beneath a classical canopy, while assorted children line the chest. The family were by now ironmasters and their Bedgebury foundries made the guns for Drake's navy against the Armada. The tomb symbolises the power of Elizabethan England. Those seeking relief from Culpepers can turn to the Campions. A charming Stuart memorial to William Campion (d.1665) and his wife adorns the sanctuary wall. A later William Campion (d.1702) is commemorated in a monument attributed to Francis Bird, with an excellent, animated bust.

HIGHAM
St Mary *
Medieval door

The charm of Higham is better experienced than described. Now redundant, it sits on an isolated site on a bluff overlooking the Hoo marshes, with views on a clear day over the Thames to Essex. The church had an adjoining nunnery of some Tudor notoriety. At the start of the 16th century there were just five nuns left, two of whom were recorded as being pregnant by the priest. Perhaps as a result, the nunnery had the distinction of being the first in Kent to be dissolved, ten years before the formal Dissolution.

The church exterior has strong horizontal bands of stone and flint, as at Cliffe, although its Decorated window tracery is less wayward and may be Victorian. The south porch shelters the church's treasure, a superb medieval door. It has traceried blind arches, and is studded with flowers, animals and heads. The interior is wide and white. The effect is confusing, as of a double nave, since the old nave has become the north aisle, with the previous south aisle becoming the nave and chancel.

The space is rich with mellow late-medieval woodwork. The pulpit and carved flowers round its top may be by the same hand as the door. Similar tracery appears in the rood screen, a rare survival in Kent. In the Lady Chapel is a large chest sitting on a bier.

[CCT]

HYTHE
St Leonard ***
Early Gothic chancel, ossuary

Here is a church worthy of a Cinque Port. The building rises, a massively buttressed cliff of stone, on the steep hillside above the old town. It is mostly 13th century, as its lancet windows testify. The interior also offers an architectural drama rare in any parish church, with a chancel fit for a minster. Beneath it lies a crypt that is now England's most celebrated and gruesome ossuary.

The church is reached up a flight of twenty-two steps that seem to continue through porch, choir and sanctuary as if the masons could not resist climbing. The short, 14th-century nave is a confusion of medieval rebuildings, the arcades neither matching each other nor, on the north side, quite fitting together. The guide attributes this, as with most erratic church building, to the Black Death. Certainly the stone is of poorer quality in the western (later) bays. But these arches are still richly moulded for a small town church and make a satisfying contrast with the earlier work. On the sides of many of the piers are masons' and pilgrims' marks, graffiti by travellers leaving for or returning from a crusade or a shrine. They include sailing ships as well as crosses. Some hundred have been discovered in the church and others are still coming to light.

We now turn to Hythe's great Early Gothic chancel. The choir rises on nine steps directly out of the crossing, with another three rising to the altar. Above soars a stone vault. The effect is theatrical, echoing the late 12th-century choir at Canterbury Cathedral. The elevation of arcade, gallery and clerestory is exceptional for a parish church. The upper tiers have wall passages. The rich decoration, with dogtooth carving and multiple shafts, indicates the prosperity of the Cinque Ports at the turn of the 13th century. The north gallery and vault of the chancel were not completed at the time. A collapse in trade with France after 1206 halted the import of Caen stone, and local sandstone was substituted.

Hythe was fortunate in its restorer, Pearson, who worked here in 1886. His contribution is worthy of the original. He was also responsible for the fine choir stalls. The early double piscina and (rare) double sedilia look new but are said to be careful restorations, with trefoil arches and delicate shafts. The Victorian pulpit was designed by Street, and has mosaics by the Italian, Salviati. It brings a dash of southern sun to this dark northern temple, made darker by the mass of Victorian glass that shuts out the Kent sky. In the south chapel is a reredos also by Street. This was originally in the sanctuary and is a flowing Pre-Raphaelite rendering of the Entombment. Next to it are two modern candlesticks in memory of the novelist, Elizabeth Bowen.

Hythe's 'crypt' is located under the sanctuary, and was built as part of a processional route when the extension of the chancel in the 13th century left insufficient room in the churchyard. The same solution occurs at Walpole St Peter (Norfolk). Today it houses one of England's two surviving ossuaries, the other being at Rothwell (Northants). These stores were used to honour the bones of the dead where existing churchyard graves had become overcrowded. Bones are stacked on the left and skulls on the right, all in neat rows. Visitors can pick them up and poke their fingers in their eyes.

IVYCHURCH
St George **
Rough marshland fittings

Ivychurch is sad yet composed. It stands on the eastern edge of Romney Marsh, its eroded tower looming over an adjacent pub. The exterior ragstone is so battered by wind and rain it looks as if a serious gale would reduce it to a mound of sand. Yet its long low outline with no break for the chancel is graceful, and unusual in a structure as early as the mid-14th century. The interior is the only Marsh church that looks in urgent need of conservation.

The architectural unity of the interior is accentuated by the pleasing rise and fall of the seven-bay arcades, which run uninterrupted from west to east, Cornish fashion. The walls retain their plaster. The roof has rough-hewn beams and the clerestory has been bricked up, as is the east window of the north aisle. The surviving windows are a delight, mostly with clear glass showing the trees bending in the wind outside. Those to the west are in a good state of repair and the west window in the north aisle is particularly fine. A central ogee light pushes upwards into a flower burst of five quatrefoils, still filled with original glass of particular intensity. Medieval glass also survives in the south aisle's east window.

In what passes for a chancel, fragments of the old screen and pews put on a brave show of a choir. The carpentry is rough. Only the pulpit and altar rails look as if they come from a sophisticated workshop. Even rougher is what remains of a stone seat along the south aisle wall. The nave arcade spandrels are hung with stern biblical admonitions. One over the south door says, 'He was afraid and said, how dreadful is this place!'

KEMSING
St Mary *
Comper furnishings, village tapestry

The church nestles under the North Downs near the Pilgrims' Way, one of dozens of such places of worship, shelter and commerce along the route to

Canterbury. The rich would travel to Jerusalem or Santiago de Compostela. Canterbury was for poorer pilgrims. Of these Chaucer's picture of a contented bourgeoisie is not the only one. As Maisie Anderson wrote, 'The sick and maimed dragged themselves towards the shrines where lay their last hope of cure, and lunatics were driven foward, bound and beaten, to wake the echoes of the great churches with their eldritch screams.' No sign of those crowds remains. Only the churchyard marks the relics of anonymous wayfarers laid to rest by the path. Today this churchyard rises up the escarpment into a long hanger of woods, from where it looks down on a grim spread of housing estates.

Though a Norman foundation, the church was heavily restored in the 20th century and it is this restoration that merits a visit. The Gothic revivalist Comper did little work in Kent, but at Kemsing he was lucky, as a young man, to find a vicar, Thomas Skarratt, who was both rich and enthusiastic. Skarratt had already commissioned restorations by other architects and is commemorated with his own brass in the chancel.

Comper's contribution dates from 1900, though he was continuing earlier work by T. G. Jackson and W. F. Unsworth, the latter being responsible for the screen and rood loft. Comper decorated the chancel and supplied the reredos and canopy. The result is a Comper spectacular: rood screen decorations of coats of arms, dragons, angels, painted walls and window splays, Gothic panelling and shields of local families, including Skarratts, Theobalds and Collets. A canopy of gold overtowers the altar with its Pre-Raphaelite reredos. There is even a singing gallery and an aumbry cupboard that looks like a safe in a Medici bank. It is an uncommonly harmonious work of 20th-century art.

The rest of the church is of less interest. Next to the font is a large and confident plaque of the Madonna and Child in bronze (of 1923) by J. D. Sedding's pupil, Henry Wilson. Wilson also designed a collection of memorials in the north-east corner of the churchyard by the wood. The modern stained glass, mostly by Comper, is weak. A window in the south wall appears to include a depiction of William Morris, as does the east window. A large framed tapestry hangs in the nave, with a set of 28 roundels of Kemsing scenes and institutions. This was designed by a local artist, Al Hart, and was completed in 1991.

LENHAM
St Mary *
Elizabethan pulpit, memorial to fertility

Lenham is an appealing village. The church square is a triangle with picturesque houses and tile-hung cottages, spoiled only by parked cars. A large medieval tithe barn survives to the south of the churchyard, a second having burned down in 1962. The church is secluded, with yews, headstones and a timbered gable to its porch. Inside is a simple Early Gothic north arcade with scraped walls. The west end of the nave has a surprisingly tall tower arch, with huge doors giving on to nothing more dignified than a kitchen. These doors were apparently carved by a Victorian vicar.

Lenham's pleasures are principally those of an active village church not stripped of contents or atmosphere; on my visit it had ladies filling every ledge with flowers. The old box pews retain their brass candleholders, overseen by Lenham's treasure, a lofty and opulent Elizabethan pulpit with superb carvings of vine leaves, arcading and putti. The tester is dated 1622, though some experts make it contemporary with the pulpit, which is of 1574. On the south wall is a mural of St Michael weighing souls of *c*.1350.

In the chancel are 15th-century misericords, though difficult to see. A curious tomb of a priest lying on his side is set into the north wall, for some reason the middle of his figure left uncarved. By the altar a floor memorial records a grandson of one of Lenham's most prolific daughters, Mary Honywood. She died in 1620 at the age of ninety-two, leaving at the time of her death 16 children, 114 grandchildren, 228 great-grandchildren and 9 great-great-grandchildren, thereby increasing Lenham's population by 367. I doubt if many English villages (or women) could beat that.

LULLINGSTONE
St Botolph ***
Hart tombs, font in a cupboard

Lullingstone claims to be the site of the oldest continuous Christian worship in England. The Roman villa preserved half a mile down the River Darent includes the remains of a Christian chapel dated to *c*.380. This had a church built on top of it, but that closed and the present church is a Norman foundation. St Martin, Canterbury, holds fast to title of 'oldest church'. The villa is a now a tourist attraction, but the church and castle remain tucked into a stretch of the valley down a private drive that is none the less a right of way.

Lullingstone Castle is a Tudor and Queen Anne house set in parkland on the banks of the stream. The enclosure is entered by a large Elizabethan gatehouse, and the church lies across the lawn, framed by majestic cedars. Despite the apparent aloofness, the church declares itself emphatically not a private chapel but the parish church. The exterior is restored Gothic, with Decorated windows and an early 16th-century north chapel. A pleasing contrast is offered by the 18th-century bellcote and classical porch.

The interior is full of surprise. The 14th-century church was transformed by Sir John Peche in the early Tudor period and by Percyvall Hart in the reign of Queen Anne, when the castle was also rebuilt. It is to these two transformations that the church owes its charm. Of Peche's work the only survival is the excellent rood screen, light and taut with spiky tracery and a pendant vault. It bears Peche's rebus, a peach with a letter E. The classical balustrade probably belongs to Hart's alterations. So too does the curious font-in-a-cupboard just inside the entrance. This is a most unusual object, with a pyramidical top like an up-market pillar box.

In common with the rest of the church, the chancel is a mixture of Tudor and Queen Anne. The former is represented by the extravagant tomb of Sir John Peche (d.1522) dividing the chancel from the north chapel. Sir John himself lies demure under a slab, still medieval in appearance (complete with page-boy haircut), with a helmet under his head and a beast with broken teeth under his feet. The canopy is grandiloquent, reaching almost to the chancel roof.

Now for the splendid north chapel itself. The centrepiece is the tomb of Sir George Hart (d.1587), great-nephew of Peche. Hart's tomb is quite different from the tombs in the chancel, designed some time after 1603. It is simple with well-carved, naturalistic effigies and a plain chest. At each corner is an allegorical figure: Resurrection, Labour, Repose and, as a gruesome skeleton, Death. The glass above the tomb is finest Flemish, with vivid rural scenes.

The memorial to the 18th-century Sir Percyvall Hart (d.1738) covers the entire west wall of the chapel. Although his decoration of the church was in the classical taste of Queen Anne's reign, by the time of his death a freer rococo prevailed. His memorial is thus a feather-light structure decorated with exotic bamboo shoots and palm fronds. Hart was of Jacobite views – much to Queen Anne's taste – and his epitaph is shot through with resentment at the Whig politics of the succeeding House of Hanover: 'His steady attachment to the Old English Constitution disqualified him from sitting any more in parliament ... having always preferred the interest of Great Britain to that of any foreign state.'

Glass in the south wall of the nave has a 16th-century portrayal of St George killing the Dragon, and a gruesome martyrdom of St Erasmus. His entrails are being extracted by means of a winch, like so much spaghetti.

MAIDSTONE
All Saints **
Widest English interior, cookery misericord

Maidstone church forms a charming group with its old collegiate buildings and former archbishop's palace. They sit on a low bluff on the east bank of the River Medway, defying the gyratory traffic scheme by which the council has spoiled the rest of the town. Here is an oasis of medieval walls, buttresses, chestnuts and flowing water. The domain was that of William Courtenay, Archbishop of Canterbury in 1395, who built a college of secular canons and a church to match. We are in the reign of Richard II, a high point of English medieval art. The church is pure Perpendicular, with a grandeur and unity of style rarely seen outside the wool counties.

Maidstone's exterior never quite soars, in part because of the loss of its spire in 1730. The nave is reputedly the widest in England yet the width is not equalled by the height and the clerestory is diminutive. The restoration by Pearson included the roof and rood screen. The chancel has a dramatic sequence of four steps from the nave, a further four up to the sanctuary and a Gothic reredos by Pearson, piled high behind the altar. This does its best to outshine the poor Victorian glass in the east window. Pearson also supplied a set of murals on either side of the altar, which give the composition some panache.

The choir stalls are original, with a celebrated misericord portraying the cook with her ladle. The four-seated sedilia with lofty canopies is appropriate to an archbishop's foundation. Behind is the 1417 tomb of the first master of Courtenay's college, John Wootton, in full Perpendicular pomp and with much of its colouring intact. A mural shows Wootton apparently arriving in Heaven. A more exotic memorial in the north aisle is that of John Astley, 17th-century resident of the Old Palace next door and donor of 70 seats for the poor in the nave. Designed by the visionary sculptor, Edward Marshall, it shows four figures in death shrouds standing in niches, each making enigmatic gestures. This style was introduced by Nicholas Stone for Donne's monument in Westminster Abbey.

MEREWORTH
St Lawrence **
Baroque tower, *trompe l'oeil* decoration

Classical churches are such a rarity in the English landscape that we stop and marvel at them. When John Vane, 7th Earl of Westmorland, demolished Mereworth's castle, church and village between 1722 and 1744, he determined to commemorate his Grand Tour with a suitable monument in the Kent countryside. Colen Campbell was commissioned to rebuild Mereworth Castle after Palladio's Villa Rotonda at Vicenza. The church was more of a problem, as it already served the village and contained the tombs of ancestors. Westmorland decided to demolish the old one, and erect a new church away from the house. History does not name the architect, but attributions include Campbell himself, James Gibbs, Thomas Archer and Roger Morris, the current favourite.

The grand Baroque tower looks as if it should be seen at the end of a processional way, despite sitting on an abrupt bend in the road. The spire rises to an exaggerated height and bears a close resemblance to that of St Giles-in-the-Fields in London. The body of the church is more severely Palladian. It has a Tuscan portico and wide eaves in the manner of St Paul, Covent Garden (London). The nave seems to crouch at the foot of the tower and throw its arms round it in supplication. Horace Walpole described the tower as being 'so tall that the poor church curtsies under it'.

The entrance is through a vestibule in the tower base, between a pair of graceful curving staircases. Most churches of this period were either demure preaching boxes or took their cue from Wren's English Baroque. Mereworth's interior is the latter, yet impressive rather than beautiful. Engaged Doric columns line all four walls, while the aisles are formed by two lines of free-standing columns. They support a heavy entablature with Hebrew mottoes and a coffered barrel vault. All the details here are not carved but painted *trompe l'oeil*. Similarly the columns are painted to look like marble and the west end has an eerie painting of organ pipes and angels. Most of the glass is awful.

In a chapel at the west end of the south aisle are a number of monuments from the old church. There is a brass of John of Mereworth and memorials to Westmorland predecessors. It is dominated by the tomb of Sir Thomas (d.1589) and Lady Fane (d.1626), erected in 1639. It has a splendid Corinthian canopy with a putto flying over a cloudy sky.

MINSTER-IN-SHEPPEY
St Mary and St Sexburga ***
Twin naves, Shurland tomb with horse, Northwood brasses

Those who make the adventurous journey over the bridge to Sheppey see a modest hill ahead of them. On this isolated corner of north Kent a minster has stood since the arrival of the earliest Christian missions in the 7th century. A nunnery was founded here by Sexburga, Queen of Kent, after she was widowed in 664. It was much battered by Vikings and rebels, and rebuilt in the early 12th century with a new parish church alongside. Thanks to this parochial adjunct, the building survived the Dissolution. The gatehouse is visible west of the nuns' nave and chancel. The whole ensemble of empty churchyard, rambling woods and vicarage hidden amid a flower garden looks vaguely French, as indeed it once was.

The church building is complicated on first view, since it is still two churches in one. The north side is the old nunnery church, the south a 12th-century parochial nave. The massive west tower, which booms out over the estuary, is 15th century and crowned with an unsuitable wooden bell-turret. The lovely Norman west doorway was a Victorian relocation.

Inside, the two sides of the church would once have been separated by a thick wall, later pierced by the present arcade. The north side is older and more sombre. Here are remains of a Saxon structure as big as that of Brixworth (Northants). The traces of window openings, Roman tiles and Saxon quoins are a jumble, the proportions alone giving some idea of past grandeur. The 13th-century chancel arch is a lovely work, rising above a fine screen. Walls and floor are littered with Gothic fragments, including a mutilated stone reredos.

The south, parish side offers a more domestic environment. Despite later windows, this is an Early Gothic church with lancets at its east end. These have graceful splays, but poor stained glass. On either side are saints' niches, one of them still with medieval painting. Against the south wall is the highlight of Minster, a large Gothic tomb of Sir Robert de Shurland (d.1300). Its canopy has exaggerated ogee cusping and two superb heads, of a man and a woman, at each end of its hood. Might they be portraits? The effigy's legs are crossed and he lies on his side in a pose charged with movement, wearing a coat over his armour. Behind him is the head of his horse, which reputedly carried him out into the estuary to seek a pardon from Edward I, who was sailing past at the time.

Minster's other noted monument lies between the two chancels, the tomb of Shurland's Tudor descendant, Sir Thomas Cheyne (d.1558). His patriarchal head and clothing, though much eroded, are finely carved. The tomb chest has pilasters and classical mouldings. The two huge Northwood brasses can be studied in replica under the organ loft. That of Joan, Lady Northwood, is said to be among the earliest female brasses in England, c.1330 (but see Cobham).

MINSTER-IN-THANET
St Mary ***
Early Gothic chancel, anti-feminist misericords

The Canterbury to Ramsgate road enters Thanet beyond Monkton, offering a view over the River Stour to Pegwell Bay. Here the early Saxons landed in the 5th century. This most historic corner of Kent is now submerged by uncontrolled development. Below in a valley can be made out the spire of Minster-in-Thanet, 7th-century sister church to Minster-in-Sheppey and one of the county's most ancient foundations. The present building was refounded by the Normans on a spectacular scale and then extended in the 13th century with new crossing and chancel.

The entrance is approached across a wide churchyard. Here the headstones have been removed to the outskirts, but the chest tombs were left in place, a strange class distinction. The initial appearance is of a Perpendicular parish church, with square-headed aisle windows and a battlemented nave and tower. Only the lancets of the chancel and transepts intimate the antiquity of the structure.

This is more apparent from the west entrance, which leads through a huge Saxon wall into the Norman nave. The view is nothing short of majestic. Ahead we see the crossing arch and the Early Gothic chancel, with a triple lancet as its eastern climax. There is no interrupting screen. The nave is powerful, with stately arcades of rounded arches. The two western bays are the earliest and most primitive.

The nave thus forms a theatrical prelude to the later crossing and chancel beyond. Here the mood changes abruptly. Minster's eastern half is an aristocrat among England's Early Gothic churches, with high rib-vaulting throughout. In the crossing, the ribs of the vaults spring from piers below the level of their capitals. This eccentricity gives tremendous tension to the composition. Was it deliberate?

The church was completed by 1230, after which it remained substantially unaltered. In the 15th century choir stalls with misericords were installed. The best-known, a 'scold' bridled with a bit in her mouth, is third from the east on the south side. Another shows a demon peering between a woman's headdress of horns, reflecting ecclesiastical disapproval of 'devilish' fashions. Various relics of the church are displayed in the nave, including the remains of a chained Bible and a wooden chalice.

Minster had a lively series of vicars. During the Commonwealth, Richard 'Blue Dick' Culmer, wrecker of Canterbury Cathedral's stained glass, was incumbent and tore the cross from the steeple with his own hands. He was so unpopular that he dared not collect his tithes. His name is even omitted from the list of incumbents inside the porch. An 18th-century vicar, John Lewis, historian of Thanet, was said to have written a thousand sermons. He ordered them to be destroyed on his death 'lest they should contribute to the laziness of others'.

NETTLESTEAD
St Mary **
Gallery of Plantagenet glass

Nettlestead church stands next to a medieval house but is cut off from any settlement. It is reached by a path across a moth-eaten cricket pitch near the River Medway. In 1496, the manorial lord, John Pympe, left money to rebuild the nave of the church for his collection of stained glass. The result is a simple Kentish ragstone chapel from whose nave three Perpendicular bays seem ready to burst. An earlier tower and chancel are barely able to hold them in place.

Alas, Pympe's great windows were all but destroyed in a gale in 1763, after which the bits were gathered up and put back with little attempt to resolve the jigsaw. This seems to have been most casual. The middle window on the north side is apparently original, apart from the heads, and the window to its left is also medieval, depicting Thomas à Becket's return to Canterbury shortly before his martyrdom.

The glass on the right is said to be a 'forgery' of 1894, in which case it is a good one. Glass in the tracery panels was better able to survive the wind but it is quaint rather than beautiful. Angels covered in feathers have shields over their private parts.

Nettlestead, old and restored, gives a passable impression of the home church of a wealthy Plantagenet. On either side of the chancel arch are graceful memorials of ladies at prayer. The interior is suffused with warm yellow light on a sunny day, and would make a fine film set for a medieval drama.

NEWINGTON (nr Sittingbourne)
St Mary *
Orchard setting, giant font cover

London does not give way easily to Kent down the old Dover road. Suburb seems to follow suburb, but by the time we reach Newington and its cherry orchards, we are in country. The church sits down a small lane of its own, with fruit trees and fields for a backdrop. In the blossom season it is apparently the 'most photographed church in Kent'. The tower is big, with diagonal buttresses and the banding of stone and knapped flint beloved of north Kent masons. It rises crumbling but magnificent above the orchards.

The west doorway has a restrained but beautiful Decorated arch. The interior is that of a prosperous rural community, able to build afresh as it grew. Only the chancel shows fragments of old work, with an Early Gothic arcade opening into the south chapel. The chapel roof is of archaeological interest as an early example of crown-post construction, embellished with foliage decoration. The screen parclose is restored, its tracery again Decorated. The tomb chest is, according to the guide, the 'shrine of St Robert of Newington', possibly a murdered pilgrim, c.1350.

Newington has two rarities. First are the extensive wall paintings in the north aisle, though deciphering them is not for the faint-hearted. Over the north altar is a Last Judgement and there are plentiful saints in the window splays. The other treasure is the font cover, one of the largest in Kent. The cover is fixed and the font is thus reached through doors in its side. The crown is Perpendicular, with crocketed finial, but the main body has Ionic balusters, 'transitional' between Gothic and classical. The 18th-century chandelier in the nave is so low that a tall verger might crack his head on it.

NEW ROMNEY
St Nicholas ***
Norman arcades saved by Morris, Reticulated windows

Romney, Hythe, Dover, Sandwich and Hastings were the original Cinque Ports, and immensely proud of it. They were founded by William the Conqueror after they had rebuffed his initial landings in 1066 and their trading privilege was a straight bribe. The five became seven with the addition of Rye and Winchelsea and then degenerated, as Romney might say, with the addition of 'corporate' members from all along the coast. Romney was 'lead' port. Under the tower of St Nicholas met the merchants who enjoyed the right to carry the canopy over the monarch at his Coronation and sit at his side during the Coronation banquet. This right, along with the banquet, has gone. But the Cinque Ports still have special duties at coronations and a member of the Royal Family is honorary Lord Warden.

This fame was of no avail during the great South Coast storm of 1287. It inundated the port with four feet of sand and shingle, and overnight moved the Rother estuary west to Rye. A huge tide of debris covered the old town, which understandably went into decline. Many buildings were rebuilt on the new level but the church was made of stronger stuff. The steps down to the west door of the tower indicate the scale of the catastrophe, as does the staining of the Norman piers. It is hard to imagine that ships once moored at the edge of the churchyard. But then it is equally hard to envisage the entrance and nave crowded with traders, fixing prices and guarding monopolies while priests sung mass behind the screen.

The tower is a powerful pre-storm structure of tier upon Norman tier. The west door, the inside vault and the bands of windows and arcading were meant to ward off both Danes and storms. The turrets, each one different, are later, and once sheltered beneath a spire, demolished in 1772. Inside, the impression is of 12th-century robustness in the nave, gradually softening as we move eastwards towards the chancel, a progress from Norman darkness to Gothic light. The two westernmost bays are complete in their Norman state, saved from Victorian demolition by the intervention of William Morris in 1880. This was the first time such traces of the past – Morris's 'grave and satisfying simplicity' – were felt to be worth preserving.

The glory of New Romney is its east end, in particular the three great windows inserted in the early 14th century. They are symmetrical. North and south chapel windows have two decks of Reticulation above three lights. The chancel window is of three decks above five lights. Inside and out this tracery contrives to be both refined and robust, a true high point in English art. The same refinement is seen in the chancel arcades. The sun pours in through the windows and dances across the open spaces.

The modern seating in the chancel is a dreadful mess of cheap timber and plastic. Only in the nave do box pews survive. If comfort is really the order of the day, why not bring these pews forward into the chancel, where services are now held, and upholster them?

OLD ROMNEY
St Clement **
Painted box pews, font with carved animals

Old Romney is the jewel of the Marsh and is some way inland from New Romney. From the west, the church presents an outline of spreading yew, conical shingled spire and steep gable with Reticulated tracery. Like all Marsh churches it sits on a mound (probably artificial), dentilated with headstones and tended by sheep. Its comforting ragstone porch must have been a haven of refuge on a wild Marsh night.

From outside, the location of the tower and the various abutments and extensions conceal the orientation. Inside, the plan is clearer. The nave forms a central chamber, almost a foyer, with a high king-post roof of rough-hewn timber. Two simple arches give on to a south aisle and a north chapel. The church has excellent 18th-century fittings. Most noticeable are the box pews, repainted a soft 'interior decorator's' pink, and also a minstrels' gallery supported on Doric columns.

The chancel is divided from the nave by a small Norman arch with no fewer than three squints and 18th-century twisted rails. The altar has a classical reredos with Commandments, and biblical quotations dot the church walls. The north chapel was erected in the 1430s for the guild of Our Lady and still has its original stone altar. Even in a parish as small as Old Romney, the guild tradition was strong. Old Romney has an extraordinary font, a square block of stone set on four pillars. These have eccentric capitals carved with monkeys, Green Men, priests and other symbols. There was no limit to the inventiveness of English carvers at the turn of the 14th century.

PATRIXBOURNE
St Mary **
Norman doorways, Swiss glass

Patrixbourne may suffer in comparison with Barfreston as a gallery of late Norman carving, but only in comparison. The church sits in the shadow of the A2, surrounded by a neat estate village of Victorian cottages. Its south door is a masterpiece.

The church exterior declares itself immediately with the famous wheel window glowing from its east wall, battered but with its spokes disappearing into the mouths of monsters at the rim. There are two Norman south doors. The first, a priest's door to the chancel, is crowned by an eroded statue of a bishop with his hand raised in blessing. Like that above the door at Barfreston, this is probably Becket, whose martyrdom at Canterbury was about the time of the construction of the church.

The south door under the tower has an arch of five orders fanning out above a tympanum. This has Christ seated with creatures of the Apocalypse, including two wyverns and angels. The arches contain familiar Norman motifs, including foliage knots and the heads of humans, birds and beasts. One of the men has a moustache and a hat. Above is a rare triangular gable with zigzag ornament and a niche containing a Lamb of God. The interior is over-restored. The west wall has an unusual set of identical memorials to members of the Hughes-Hallet family. Adjacent in the nave is a finely carved 16th-century screen. It was once behind the altar and could surely return there.

Highlight of the interior is the 16th- and 17th-century Swiss glass. This is enamelled and more lush than the more common Flemish imports of the same period. One set is buried within Victorian surrounds in the east windows, illustrating biblical scenes with, at the bottom of the south window, Samson killing the lion. This is apparently an exact copy of a Dürer woodcut. A second set, less disturbed, hangs in the Bifrons Chapel in the south aisle. These pieces depict secular subjects, most of them set against bright alpine landscapes. One shows the legend of Pyramus and Thisbe, Pyramus with a sword through his body. They are gems of European art.

QUEENBOROUGH
Holy Trinity *
Panoramic tower view, painted roof

Any visit to the Isle of Sheppey should include a detour to this little village. It was built, or rebuilt, to serve one of England's forgotten castles, built by Edward III against the French in 1361, the town being named after his queen, Philippa of Hainault. The castle was demolished in the Civil War – the railway station is on the site – though it cannot have caused anyone much trouble. Today the old high street runs prettily down to the water, looking across the estuary to Southend.

The 14th-century church is an ungainly pile of Kentish rag, its tower that of an earlier Norman structure. The key unlocks the tower and the best reason for a visit is the view from the top over the marshes of Sheppey and the Thames. The interior is essentially Perpendicular, the pews and windows restored by the Victorians. The one real treasure is the ceiling, a surviving late 17th-century painted wagon roof covered in clouds and sky. The Angel of the Apocalypse sounds the Last Trump. A fire in 1930 defaced it, but it cannot be beyond restoration.

The font is of 1610; its carvings represent Queenborough Castle, then still standing. The nave contains two paintings from a 17th-century reredos, or possibly from a passing ship. There is a pretty organ loft over the south door. On my visit, the interior was ablaze with flowers, always sign of a loved church.

The churchyard is crammed with tombs, mostly of seafarers. By far the biggest, indeed one of the biggest in Kent, is to the Greet family, doyens of the town. The tomb, of 1829, is a baroque chest rising to a finial and obelisk, a fine memorial to a once-royal port.

ST MARGARET'S AT CLIFFE
*

Norman interior, galleon graffiti

This must once have been a superb site. The church stands on a bluff over-looking the sea at St Margaret's Bay with the South Foreland and the cliffs of Dover to the south. A pretty village street goes past the church, but beyond is all undignified South Coast tattiness. What remains of the old church is consider-able. Norman blind arcading runs round the exterior at clerestory height. The two doorways, north and west, carry fine Norman carving. The west doorway has a steep gable containing patterns, foliage and heads, with seated figures of saints in roundels. The north doorway is better preserved under a porch, though less complex.

St Margaret's interior is intact Norman; the restoration is not overpowering. The nave aisles are surprisingly grand for a Norman church, due to St Margaret's ownership by St Martin's Priory at Dover. The arcades are decorated with zigzag and other relief carving. The capitals are all scalloped but with grotesque faces peering out of their corners, faces repeated in the bottoms of the spandrels. The more we look, the more faces we see, like little mice peeping out of the lace ruffs of a sleeve. On the piers are numerous maritime graffiti, including an invaluable record of an early galleon on the pillar near the font. It includes a stern-hung rudder and a bush on the bowsprit. I am told the sail reefing points can even be made out.

ST MARY IN THE MARSH
*

Flemish altarpiece

The church lies isolated between Ivychurch and the sea, with only the Star pub, a few houses and the shades of E. Nesbit, author of *The Railway Children*, for company. She came here late in life to settle in two army huts with her nautical husband, who carved her memorial on a displaced barge-board by the churchyard path. The church is cottagey and well tended, with pretty flowers in troughs by the porch. On my visit on a spring day, the organ was being played and its sound spilled out over the road to the pub opposite.

The interior is simple Early Gothic, with a three-bay nave and two-bay chancel. Shafts flank the chancel lancets but the east window is a Decorated insertion, framing a lime tree that dapples light over the interior. St Mary's once enjoyed a sculptor with skill and a sense of humour: corbels in the north arcade and on the sedilia portray a man and monsters. The royal coat of arms is a fine rendering of a style that is a speciality of the Marsh churches. Equally fine is a small painted altarpiece in the south aisle, which I take to be a Flemish copy.

ST NICHOLAS AT WADE
**

Norman arcade carvings, Decorated tower arches

The village stands between the A28 and the A299 at the gateway – once the 'wading' place – to the Isle of Thanet. Place names round here are bizarre: to the north, Plumpudding Island and to the south, Plucks Gutter. The church itself is a proud structure that might have strayed across the estuary from Essex. The setting is agricultural, opposite a farmhouse with a Dutch gable.

The prominent tower would once have looked out over marshes towards Reculver Castle, one of England's most historic defences and now a dramatic ruin. It stands at the south-west corner of the church, balancing the chancel with its Decorated east window. This window is a magnificent work, the curvilinear tracery embracing two giant petals in the centre.

We enter by the south porch, whose niche has been filled by a modern statue of St Nicholas by Darsie Rawlins. The interior is dominated by the astonishing Norman south arcade. When the Norman masons came to build it, they appear simply to have pierced the old south wall of the nave to make arched openings. As if to compensate for this economy, the arches were then richly decorated. Their capitals carry figures apparently squeezed out of the mortar under pressure. Some have Early Gothic stiff-leaf carving, others have Green Men, including what appears to be a Green King. I have not encountered this before.

At the west end of the south aisle is another surprise: the tall Decorated arches supporting the tower. Their solemn piers might be underpinning the tower of a large town church. A vault was evidently planned within the tower, but money, time or fashion appear to have run out.

The Jacobean pulpit fills an angle of the chancel arch. It has an ornate backboard and looks out across the nave to a no less splendid Georgian chandelier, with a crown and a mitre on its chain.

The chancel has a two-bay Norman arcade to the north chapel which houses monuments to the local Bridges family. Among other luminaries, the family produced a poet laureate (Robert, d.1930) and a cabinet secretary (Lord Bridges, d.1969).

SANDWICH
St Clement **
Norman carvings, Tudor octagonal font

The town of Sandwich was once the most important naval base in England. The silting of its port in the late Middle Ages left it high and dry. The walled settlement of mostly Tudor buildings had no further reason for development, apart from the refacing of its houses in brick in the 18th century. River, ramparts and streets are intact. Many churches were damaged by subsidence and are heavily restored or inaccessible, but St Clement's, the main parish church, suffered least. It lies east of the town centre at the end of a charming Georgian terrace.

The central tower is Norman with three splendid tiers of blind arcading. This is supported by an Early Gothic chancel and Perpendicular nave. Wide aisles engulf the old transepts. The interior is enlivened by a roof whose oak rafters are decorated with bosses and small gold angels in the East Anglian style. The angels have huge wings and are positioned on their beams as if ready to fly east or west on command.

The crossing is pure Norman, with tall arches and unusual blind arcades high above them. The capitals are carved with strange dog faces. Round this space are grouped most of the church's best features. By the north-east pier is a beautifully carved Norman doorway to the belfry stair, with a tympanum containing a carving of a stag. Facing the south transept is a medieval terracotta statue of St John. In the same transept a lion's face peers up from a piscina drain, as if in a Renaissance fountain.

The chancel has three modest lancet windows in the east wall, unworthy of its scale. The Perpendicular choir stalls are still in place, looking engagingly scuffed, presumably by pupils when it served as a schoolroom after the Reformation. Underneath these stalls appears to be an ancient brick heating system. The finest work in St Clement's is the font, a large octagonal bowl set on a stem with (sadly empty) statue niches but with large heraldic shields and Tudor roses on each face of its octagon.

SMARDEN
St Michael *
Scissor-beam roof, medieval alms box

Another 'best-kept' Kent village of just one sleepy street, but with a shock of a church opening off a small close. From the road, the exterior looks merely big, a huge sloping slate roof to the nave with the tiled roof of the chancel to the right. Inside, we might be in a medieval airship hangar. Smarden is nicknamed 'the Barn of Kent', and barn is what it seems. It appears to have been built after 1332 when a local market was licensed and much business anticipated.

There are no aisles or arcades, just a long sweep of roof gable. This roof is of scissor-beam construction, since the space is too wide to be spanned by the single trusses of a tie-beam. To support this, the walls are thick and the window openings have heavy arches. This is ponderous but impressive, presumably as wide as a 14th-century engineer felt he could achieve with no arcade on which to rest the weight of the roof. Even the tracery, late Decorated and early Perpendicular, is heavy-boned. The nave has modern pews and panelling, which warms and relieves the vastness of the space.

The Victorians made some efforts to tame Smarden. They put curious ogival reredoses over altars on either side of the plain chancel arch. These have murals of angels, the Annunciation and the Passion. Modern incumbents have also put angels in the various niches and flowers in the piscinas and water stoups. This is like putting an Amazon in curlers.

Smarden has a rare medieval alms box on a semi-octagonal base carved from a trunk of oak. It was intended to be too heavy for any thief to cart away. On the top are the remains of a copper plate cut away for enamel decoration, dating from the 13th century and most rare.

SPELDHURST
St Mary *
Glass by Morris & Co.

Speldhurst clings to a hillside outside Tunbridge Wells overlooking the upper Medway valley. The church is surrounded by substantial houses (and the George and Dragon pub) with confident and comfortable stone walls to their gardens. It was rebuilt almost entirely by John Oldrid Scott in 1871 and is stylish but dull. The reason for visiting it is the glass, from Morris & Co. in its prime. Speldhurst is a good example of what so much Victorian glass is not, part of an aesthetic whole with the architecture. It glows on all sides.

That said, the various compositions are in contrasting styles. The west window of the north aisle is the most celebrated work. Known as the Window of Praise, it depicts a congregation of angels playing instruments. The angels, said to be based on a Filippo Lippi, are pale against deep green and blue backgrounds. Facing them is the superb aisle east window, in softer shades set against a white background with geometrical patterns. At the west end of the south wall are the Virgin and St Elizabeth, again in pale costumes against blue and red.

In the chancel, Burne-Jones offers two pictures, the Baptism of Christ and the Cleansing of Naaman. These are more naturalistic, with rich Italianate landscapes. The large east window of the Crucifixion is a late work of Burne-Jones, installed posthumously in 1905 from his designs and replacing an earlier window. It is less successful, the figures doused in pink. These pictures are granted a worthy setting. On either side of the altar are two magnificent brass candelabras.

STELLING
St Mary *
Rustic Georgian interior

I found Stelling only after getting lost and twice slithering into an icy ditch. In winter, Kent is the coldest county in southern England and the Downs round Stelling must be its most Arctic point. The church has no prominent tower or spire. Yet when found it is all innocence, a farm to one side and small cottages to the other, plus a friendly yew.

The exterior of is no great moment, Early Gothic in origin but with Decorated east windows. The church has an unusual T-plan, the stem forming the south aisle and the cross bar the nave and chancel. The charm of Stelling lies in its interior. When we enter through the south door, everything that catches the eye is 18th century. A wide columned gallery is overhead, with a sweeping arch opening on to the nave. This frames the three-decker pulpit, on either side of which are original box pews. We might be in a Methodist chapel.

Only from the middle of the nave is the eccentricity of the plan apparent. Seen from the door it is looks Georgian. Seen from the nave it is medieval. The nave and chancel are Early Gothic, with deeply splayed window openings. The nave roof is crown-post, the chancel roof is unceiled. Clear windows permit daylight to fill the interior, illuminating gently peeling walls. The floor tiles are old and unpolished. The 18th century at Stelling sits well with the 13th.

STONE (nr Dartford)
St Mary ****
Gothic carvings from Westminster workshop

Stone is one of Kent's most dramatic churches. In its day it must have cut a dash, starting out above the trees on a chalk bluff overlooking the Thames. For medieval sailors it would have marked the point where the estuary became a river. Canterbury pilgrims would have passed through, avoiding the forest tracks inland. Even so, it is hard to see why a church of such ostentation, and in a French style then confined to Westminster Abbey, should have been built here. Stone bears little comparison with its adjacent cathedral at Rochester.

Today the squat tower is visible on the south bank just downstream from the M25 Dartford crossing. The church exterior is dull, apart from the impressive height of the chancel. The inside is a complete work of the late 13th century, in transition from Early Gothic to new Decorated forms. It has a chancel of extraordinary richness with the same Geometrical tracery and rich foliage carvings then being introduced, *c.*1260, at Westminster. The outcome is worthy of the finest parish churches. While Stone, in what is now a sad corner of outer London, may have a charm elusive to all but the most determined connoisseur, for them it is a treat.

The nave is predominately Early Gothic. The arcades have slender piers with alternating shafts of plain stone and Purbeck marble. The mouldings of the arches grow richer from west to east, and the same hierarchy governs the treatment of the aisle windows. First come simple paired lancets with a quatrefoil above; in the middle bay the same form is framed by shafts and a moulded arch; then nearest the chancel are windows with detached rere-arches and trefoils. The sequence is clearly meant as a crescendo and is supremely decorative. The tower arches are later, masterpieces of mature Decorated carving. Their capitals are thick with oaks, acorns and maple. This is some of the best stonework in England.

Yet the glory of Stone is its chancel, entered by an arch that appears deliberately narrow, as if to dramatise the impact of its interior. Here is a minor chapter house, with ribbed stone vaulting and blind arcades of trefoils ornamented with foliage. The panels probably came from Westminster: the end ones are cut off short as if measured for somewhere else. It is possible that Stone was the beneficiary of over-ordering by the Westminster architects – a production surplus in the trefoil department. Here too are three early Decorated windows, a simple Geometrical design of perfect poise. Above the arcade level, the chancel is entirely a restoration by Street, but his work is said to be authentic to the original, whether in fact or only in spirit, who can tell?

In the north aisle are the indistinct remains of murals. One of them is a murder of Thomas à Becket. How many modern pilgrims racing round the M25 know the treasure lying just a mile from their path?

TENTERDEN
St Mildred *
Whitfield monument

Tenterden church gets a poor write-up from church guides. Yet its mighty 15th-century tower is worthy of any in the Cotswolds. It rises in four tall stages with deep angle buttresses and two-light openings in the belfry. The top has battlements and small corner turrets, with more tiny battlements and crocketed pinnacles, an extraordinary combination. The tower forms a beacon on the crest of Tenderden ridge. Its predecessors would presumably have guided ships into this 'corporation' Cinque Port (*see* New Romney). On a clear day France can allegedly be seen from the top of the tower.

The church sits neatly behind the main square on the high street, of grey stone with splashes of brown ironstone enlivening the walls. At the foot of the west tower is a magnificent entrance, with a huge Perpendicular window above a double doorway. A stone string course between first and second stages is humped to emphasise the height of the window. The whole composition is superbly balanced.

The interior of Tenterden is blighted by the insensitive Victorian restoration that afflicts so many town churches. However, the Whitfield monument in the north chapel is a handsome Jacobean work. Tenterden began life as a seaport, sustained itself on the cloth trade before converting, like Goudhurst, to iron. The Whitfields of Cumberland, like many 15th-century *arrivistes*, migrated south as iron-founders. Herbert Whitfield (d.1623) would thus have been eager to protest his distinguished lineage, which he does with no fewer than eighteen different coats of arms. He faces his wife in prayer across a lectern, with no hint of his industrial background.

TUDELEY
All Saints **
Chagall glass

Sarah, the daughter of Sir Henry and Lady d'Avigdor Goldsmid, was drowned in a sailing accident near Rye in 1963. The grief-stricken family commissioned the Russian artist, Marc Chagall, to design a new east window for their local church in memory of their daughter. The church is a modest structure, rebuilt in the 18th century and with a curious tiled turret sitting on the tower. The new window was installed in 1967 and was so admired that more windows for the entire church were commissioned. Seven arrived in 1974 and the final four in 1985, the year of Chagall's death. The glass was made and fitted by Charles Marq of Rheims, a modern collaboration as successful as that between John Piper and Patrick Reyntiens. The removed Victorian windows are on display under the tower. (This is what should happen with all bad Victorian glass.)

The glass at Tudeley is a superb work of 20th-century church art, ranking with Stanley Spencer's murals at Burghclere (Hants). The church is small and, with every one of its windows radiating deep blues and yellows, the visitor is submerged in Chagall's water world. The theme is set by the east window, in which a young girl floats in the trough of a wave. Beside are a grieving family. Above are a horseman and a messenger mounting the ladder to Heaven. There Christ looks down from the Cross, portrayed as what the guide calls 'the radiant and personable young man in whose company young people delight'. The blue is overpowering but not lugubrious.

The windows in the south wall of the nave are not blue but yellow to receive the rays of the sun on this side of the church. These 'glorious golden hues ... radiate joy and hope for mankind and the promise of life eternal'. To find Tudeley open in the depth of winter added to my delight in discovering it, unsignposted, on the outskirts of Tonbridge.

TUNBRIDGE WELLS
King Charles the Martyr **
Restoration interior in style of Wren

Tunbridge Wells was to the Restoration court what Brighton was to the Regency. The wells were an outpost of Tonbridge five miles away and had no place of Anglican worship until 1678, when a subscription was raised for a new chapel. The sponsors' list included the then Queen and the future Queen Anne, as well as Clarendon, Rochester, Pepys, Evelyn and a bevy of dukes and earls. The site might be modest, squeezed in at the end of the Pantiles, but the best plasterers were summoned from Wren's workshops in London. The dedication was in the High Church mood of the day, to King Charles the Martyr.

Today the chapel is almost invisible amid the passing traffic, but this adds to its quaint urbanity. A small tower and cupola poke up above the old roofs of the Pantiles. Steep gables mark the roof ends and classical doorways dress a redbrick façade of round-arched windows. We might be in Bruges, with tarmac instead of water.

The chapel is as built except for a Victorian chancel inserted by Ewan Christian in 1882. The interior is warm and friendly, much closer in atmosphere to a Wren hall church than an Anglo-Catholic shrine to a martyred king. Indeed, the altar was originally tucked away under the north gallery. The plan is a spacious square, bisected by two Ionic columns of oak clad in plaster. These were inserted when an extension was completed in 1696, the original rectangular chapel being doubled in width to form the present square. The galleries survive except to the east, as do benches with beautifully carved ends. This contrasts uncomfortably with Christian's chancel, a frigid composition of Venetian arch and pictorial stained glass window.

Above stretches the glorious ceiling, mostly the work of John Wetherell and Henry Doogood over the period 1682–96. It has a wealth of delightful saucer domes, and naturalistic plasterwork in the manner of Grinling Gibbons. Cherubs cavort amid the fronds, flowers and fruit dripping from every panel. An experienced eye is apparently able to distinguish Wetherell's more stylised manner from the freer hand of Doogood. The whole is as voluptuous as any aristocrat's saloon, here floating delightfully in air above the alleys of old Tunbridge.

WESTWELL
St Mary **
Free-standing stone screen

A pilgrim's church nestles under the Downs, with duckpond and ancient houses for company. The exterior is buttressed, drearily rendered and has a weak spire on its tower. We must not be deterred. Damp, rot and deathwatch beetle brought Westwell near to disaster in the 1960s. It is now well tended: the churchwarden, a former Royal Marine, told me the beetle was unquestionably the 'toughest campaign' of his career.

The core of the church is Early Gothic with alternating round and octagonal piers to its arcade. The tower arch has shafts with vigorous stiff-leaf capitals and corbels with human heads. An ancient wooden ladder leads to the belfry. But the eye is immediately drawn to the extraordinary stone chancel screen, of two graceful piers supporting three soaring trefoiled arches. This is Gothic at its most diverting and beautiful. The chancel itself has a stone vault and more arcades north and south. Seen from near the altar, Westwell's forest of arches is faintly oriental. Not surprisingly, this aerial structure has long been unstable. The south aisle piers tilt alarmingly and require braces and buttresses to hold them up.

The east window is a tall triple lancet of 13th-century origin. The glass of the central lancet is a masterpiece of conservation. The top area apparently survived iconoclasm while the bottom was reconstructed to match the original, from medieval fragments and modern imitation. The result is colourful and admirably deceptive. The sedilia is worthy of its setting, with arm rests and a king's head, probably of that 'Decorated' monarch, Henry III. The old choir stalls have crude poppyheads.

WINGHAM
St Mary **
Oxenden monuments

This is a church full of delightful oddities. The Archbishop of Canterbury founded a college here in 1282 and to this we owe the spacious chancel and celebrated tracery. But poverty rather than wealth greets us on entering. The south arcade piers are of plain wood, the only other example of wooden piers in a stone church being at Radley (Oxon). The reason is that the old nave was ruinous after the Reformation. In 1555 a local brewer, George Ffogarde, was given the task of collecting money for a new one but, having raised £224, he embezzled the lot. Wood was the only material that could be afforded after this disaster. The pillars were given a coating of plaster to look Doric, but the Victorians removed this as unauthentic.

The much-restored chancel is higher than the nave. The windows in the south wall of the chancel and east wall of the aisle are the most elaborate, a version of Geometrical in which three large roundels sit on top of three Intersecting lights, a pattern peculiar to Kent. The west window is simpler and later, with Reticulated tracery in the form of two giant spoons. The church furnishings include a stone reredos of the 15th century, apparently from Troyes in France and donated to the church in 1934. The scenes portrayed are from the New Testament, but need to be seen close to.

Wingham has fine monuments. In the south transept is the astonishing Oxenden memorial of 1682, in the form of an obelisk rising above four horned oxen, the family crest. The carving is exquisite, with cherubs in various grieving poses, one hooded and holding a skull, another grappling with a helmet, another in tears. The faces of the obelisk are decorated with fruits and flowers in high relief. The work is in the style of Grinling Gibbons and is attributed to his master, the Dutchman Arnold Quellin.

The north chapel contains a work that can be 'compared and contrasted' with the Oxenden obelisk. It is Nicholas Stone's monument to Sir Thomas Palmer of 1624. Two effigies lie on a chest with a conventional pedimented memorial behind. Because the chapel is locked, this monument and others can be seen only by doing what should not be done, standing on the misericord seats of the choir.

WOODCHURCH
All Saints **
Early Gothic chancel, priest brass

The church stands on a mound, surrounded by pubs, wistaria and old clapboarded houses, its churchyard bringing a refreshing unkemptness to an immaculate Kent village. With few exceptions, Woodchurch is a complete Early Gothic building. The broach spire is heavily buttressed and dressed in cedar shingles, attended by a retinue of evergreens.

The interior arcades rest on thick waxed stone piers. Rough-hewn tie-beams hold the roof in place. The nave is gloomy, with no clerestory, but the chancel is superb. If the nave speaks 'forthright prose', says Pevsner, 'the sanctuary speaks exalted poetry'. Here eight lancets pour light through wide splays, past shafts waxed to look like Purbeck, on to walls that mercifully retain their plaster. On the south wall, triple sedilias run into a double piscina.

Woodchurch is well furnished. The east window glass is by Kempe at his most restrained, with foliage decorating roundels of saints, and enough clear glass to admit daylight. A window in the south aisle has a medieval portrayal of the Entombment of the Virgin, much battered by time. The church possesses a most unusual brass of 1333. This shows a priest, Nichol de Gore, in a large circular frame with a French inscription, from which project four large finials with fleur-de-lis decoration.

WYE
St Gregory and St Martin *
Queen Anne chancel

The churchyard looks northwards across meadows towards a gap where the River Stour pierces the North Downs. The church is handsomely situated at the end of a wide street, which seems to have been planned with the tower as its climax. The foundation was granted collegiate status in the mid-15th century, by an Archbishop of Canterbury, John Kempe, who was a native of Wye. The college became the town's grammar school at the Reformation, and is now an agricultural college, part of London University.

With the college came a large cruciform church that survived until 1686, when a collapse of the tower demolished the crossing, transepts and chancel. So nervous were the townspeople in rebuilding the tower that they made it truly massive, covering the whole of the old south transept. From the outside, this wholly overshadows their new chancel.

The interior retains four surviving bays of Archbishop Kempe's Perpendicular nave. The rest of the church is early 18th century, built in 1701–6, and its charm lies in the contrast of the medieval and Queen Anne elements. The 18th-century chancel might be that of a royal chapel of ease, with a three-window apse and blue, white and mauve panelling. It is sumptuous, and most un-ecclesiastical.

Wye prides itself on its 20th-century art. There is a Mother and Child on a pier by the Lady Chapel, by Neil Godfrey. Beside the lectern is a pier statue of St James, by John Forsyth.

Lancashire

Lancashire is two counties. The south, reputedly the most densely populated region in Europe, is a landscape of sad towns and even sadder suburbs. Of the Middle Ages accessible to the public, there is barely a trace other than the screen at Sefton. Architectural excitement in Liverpool and Manchester had to await the Victorians, though they arrived splendidly in the persons of J. L. Pearson and G. F. Bodley. Yet most of their works are locked, such as Bodley's great church at Pendlebury which I therefore have to exclude from my list. Visiting the churches of south Lancashire demands an adventurous spirit.

The north of the county has more to offer, not least the spectacular scenery of the Pennines to the east and Morecambe Bay to the west. The old priory church on the rock at Lancaster has superb woodwork in its choir, and Whalley boasts some of the best misericords in the country. Having accepted the administrative move of Cartmel into Cumbria, I have compensated Lancashire by receiving Slaidburn and Great Mitton from Yorkshire. They are fine hill churches.

Barton-upon-Irwell
  RC **
Great Mitton **
Lancaster **
Liverpool:
  St Agnes, Sefton Park
  ****

Liverpool:
  St John, Tue Brook
  ***
Manchester:
  Holy Name of Jesus
    RC, Moss Side **
  St Ann **

Sefton ***
Slaidburn *
Standish **
Warrington *
Whalley ***

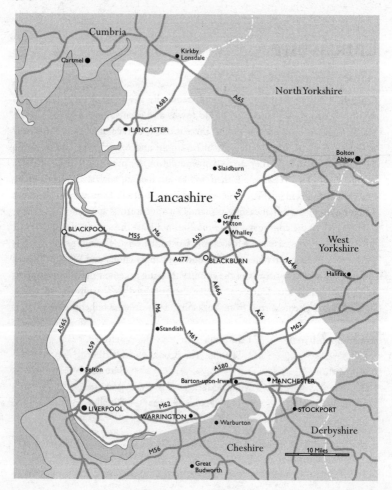

BARTON-UPON-IRWELL
All Saints RC **
E. W. Pugin interior, wedding-cake reredos

The de Trafford family were in Lancashire under King Canute. Throughout the Reformation they stood fast by the old religion, one being hanged in 1538 for 'opposing the sacrilegious havoc of churches and monasteries and standing up for his own'. Trafford Hall became a warren of priests' holes and private chapels. But by the end of the 18th century, tolerance and the growth of Roman Catholic Manchester had led the small community at the Hall to consider 'missionary' patronage in the local community. This took the form of a mission at Barton, converted in the early Victorian period into a full church under Sir Humphrey de Trafford. The family chaplain, John Kershaw, doubled as the local priest.

In 1863 de Trafford and Kershaw commissioned the Catholic architect Edward Welby Pugin, son of A. W. N., to build a family chantry and, attached to it, a new parish church in Barton. Money was no object and the resulting building was, to Pevsner, 'the masterpiece of [Pugin's] life without any doubt'. Two decades later the Manchester Ship Canal was driven through the parish immediately to the north of the church, cutting the parish in two. Its swing bridge frequently left parishioners stranded and services had to wait while the bridge was reopened. The church never fully recovered and is now attached to a small Greyfriars community, through which access may be gained.

The exterior is that of a French Early Gothic church. There is an eastern apse, a western rose window, Plate tracery in the other windows and a small bellcote in place of a demolished tower. The interior is extraordinary. The small nave has arcades of banded painted stone with the most effusive floral capitals imaginable. Above are naturalistic carved heads and a polished wood ceiling. At the west end is a large gallery with gaudy modern window glass. Pugin's forte is the east end. Here the chancel reredos is like a wedding cake, adorned with so many angels it looks on the point of take-off.

The de Trafford Chapel lies to the north of the chancel, from which it is divided by an unusual arcade in two planes, of thick piers to the chancel and thin ones to the chapel, both carrying vaults. The north chapel is a charming space – the Victorians were at their best when decorating small – with sumptuous floor tiling and an imposing reredos with a figure of the dead Christ beneath the altar. This carries a modern statue of St Maximilian wearing his Auschwitz concentration camp shirt.

GREAT MITTON
All Hallows **
Shireburne tombs

The old village lies between Whalley and Clitheroe at the confluence of the Ribble and Hodder rivers. The church is mostly Early Gothic with lancet windows, but the variously spelled Shireburne Chapel was added in 1440 and rebuilt in 1594. It was to house the tombs of the 'popish' Shireburnes of neighbouring Stonyhurst. The house was eventually given to the Jesuits as a school after their expulsion from Belgium in 1794. The tombs are among the best in the county (albeit Great Mitton was formerly in Yorkshire). Of the rest of the church we need note only the fleur-de-lis bench-ends and the fine 15th-century screen from Sawley Abbey.

The earliest tomb is of Sir Richard (d.1594), with an effigy of an alabaster knight in prayer and a wife with voluminous petticoats. The next group against the wall are a century later and commemorate four more Richards in succession. The sculptor was the famous William Stanton of London, who normally carved his figures standing up. These are affectedly medieval: the effigies, though wearing contemporary dress, are lying down with hand on heart and legs crossed, like ancient knights. These poses must have been at the order of Isabel, widow of one of the Richards, who paid £253 for the group in 1699. They are probably the last tomb chests with recumbent effigies until the Victorian era.

Three years later, Stanton carved yet another memorial: this was to the Shireburne heir, another Richard, who died from eating poisonous berries aged nine, thus carelessly leaving the estate without succession. This monument is quite different. The boy stands in a classical frame contemplating the emblems of death, a skull, hour glass, sickle and bones galore. More macabre are two skeletal hands emerging from the earth as though trying to rise from the dead.

LANCASTER
St Mary **
Flamboyant choir stalls

Lancaster no longer lives up to its superb location. The centre and its environs are gap-toothed and lifeless. The fortress is grimly embattled to serve as a prison, looming over the town like Kafka's castle. Some attention has been paid to modern building on the river slope of the castle mound. But oh for planners who cared!

Yet the old priory church outguns even the castle, a beacon over a wilderness of warehouses, roads and estates beyond the River Lune beneath. It was established for the Benedictines by Roger, cousin of William the Conqueror and potentate of the north-west. The present church is predominantly Perpendicular and the best of that style in the county. The material is blackened sandstone. The aisled interior is spacious but with just four bays to the nave and a similar length of chancel. The walls are thankfully plastered – other Lancashire churches please note – except for the area above the chancel arch. It looks as if the builders wandered off to another job before finishing. The west gallery is still in place and the nave has a beautiful set of chandeliers, possibly 17th century. Most of the glass is terrible.

Lancaster's treasure is the set of choir stalls, with some of the most remarkable woodcarving in the north of England. The canopies of the stalls are tall gables thick with foliage and monster heads, framing tracery of Spanish flamboyance. Indeed, they remind me of the towers of Gaudi's church in Barcelona. They may have come from Cockersands or Furness Abbeys after the Dissolution. Set into their backs are modern tapestries, a drastic intrusion but one which works surprisingly well. They were designed by Guy Barton and worked by ladies of the parish in 1962–75. The soft reds, blues and gold in Gothic settings offer an excellent foil for the surrounding stalls. One of the embroideries depicts the famous Victorian coach dash against the tide across Morecambe Bay sands.

LIVERPOOL
St Agnes, Sefton Park ****
Pearson's Early Gothic interior

The church's patron was a rich Liverpool stockbroker, Douglas Horsfall. The architect was Pearson and the year 1882. Never was there greater contrast between an interior and exterior. St Agnes's presents itself to Ullet Road as a gaunt, dark, redbrick structure, Victorian Gothic at its grimmest and least inspiring. Yet the interior is a masterpiece to rival Pearson's St Augustine, Kilburn (London). The style is Early Gothic, almost lighthearted in comparison with Kilburn. Like most Liverpool churches, the liturgy is 'high'. On a Sunday morning the incense and chants mingle with the light bursting through the clerestory, bringing to life Pearson's stone vaults, subtle planes and secret chapels. The dominant building material is stone, light and almost white in places, with Purbeck shafts for contrast.

Pearson is a genius of English architecture. The form of the church is complex, aisled throughout with two sets of transepts. The nave walls have a three-tiered elevation that includes a triforium and wall passage. But the eye is constantly drawn upwards and eastwards to the chancel, where steep-pointed arches seem to rise and fall with increasing restlessness. The arcade arches are picked out with dogtooth ornament and are doubled round the apse.

In the north-east transept Pearson inserts a beautifully arcaded stone octagon to carry the organ. This is set above a small forest of eleven piers, including central ones supporting a vault, all in white stone and Purbeck. Off the south-east transept is a Lady Chapel with its own aisles. These architectural eddies and diversions produce shafts of light illuminating stone, alabaster and brass. St Agnes's is an essay in the art of shadow.

The polygonal apse, another feature beloved of Pearson, has an ambulatory which creates further vistas. Below the clerestory windows are relief panels of saints, while the tall stone reredos has sculpture of more seated saints in the round, flanking a Crucifixion, in white on a red background. Near the organ is a rebus of the patron, Horsfall, showing a horse falling. Those seeking relief from this excitement can go next door along Ullet Road to a Unitarian church by Percy Worthington. It is full of Art Nouveau, nowhere better than in the design of the west door, which is everything that Pearson was not.

LIVERPOOL
St John, Tue Brook ***
Complete Bodley interior

G. F. Bodley's Liverpool masterpiece lies set back from the interminable West Derby Road. Access is hard but worth the effort. The decoration and fittings are one of his most successful Gothic revivals, a sumptuous affirmation of art in a lost Liverpool suburb. He applied himself with characteristic fervour to every detail, from floor to ceiling, and commissioned some of the earliest mural paintings by Kempe, then working at the firm of Clayton & Bell.

The church was designed in 1868–70. The exterior is of unattractive banded red and yellow stone, delicately referred to in the guide as 'cream relieved with pink'. The interior, especially in sunlight, is dazzling. The simple plan comprises a narrow nave with wide aisles and a low chancel partly concealed by a bold rood screen.

Every inch is decorated. Whereas much Gothic revival left decoration subordinate to architecture (as sometimes did Bodley), here decoration is all. St John's has a lightness and colour reminiscent of the showrooms of Bodley's friend, William Morris. Though the wall paintings degenerated, said a critic, 'to the state of a much worn Persian carpet', they have been brilliantly restored.

The bottom of the aisle walls starts with painted masonry joints, rising to stencilled flowers, then to stencilled IHS symbols. These also decorate the clerestory. The nave is crowned by a white roof dressed in red and green. Roses fill the spandrels of the arcade. Over the chancel arch is a mural by Kempe depicting the Crucifixion. Below is a magnificent screen, of black oak with coving ribs picked out in gold. The loft has painted foliage panels and angels, all in frames of exquisite richness.

The chancel is no less ablaze with colour. Every inch is painted. The choir stalls, like the screen, are stained oak and decorated. Bodley's organ case and screen are among his finest works. He also designed the reredos, with above it a Morris & Co. window in poor condition. The best window, by Burne-Jones, is at the west end of the south aisle above the children's altar. It depicts St Ursula and St Nicholas.

MANCHESTER
Holy Name of Jesus RC, Moss Side **
Hansom's white terracotta spectacular

The Moss Side district south of Manchester city centre was laid waste by the city council in the 1960s, an act of devastation worse than anything wreaked by war and now regarded as one of the great planning disasters of 20th-century Britain.

The resulting neighbourhoods, seem immune to the millions of pounds since spent 'rescuing' them. Only Manchester University maintains a massive presence. The more precious are the pre-devastation relics. Down the Chorlton boundary runs Oxford Road with, towering over it, a Gothic west front that might be spoiling for a street fight. The Holy Name of Jesus would lay Albi Cathedral flat with one blow.

The church is a Jesuit foundation of 1869 and was designed by the Order's favourite architect, J. A. Hansom, inventor of the Hansom cab. The style is French Gothic, though the plan is wider than that suggests, with a short apsidal sanctuary in the Jesuit manner. There are bulging transepts, chapels and turrets galore. A colossal west front rises from a gabled double doorway past four traceried lancets to an octagonal bell stage, which boasts a single massive opening. Its 'eye' looks out over the surrounding wilderness like a Cyclops. This top stage was not by Hansom, who had wanted a spire, but is a 1928–32 addition by Adrian Gilbert Scott. This descendant of the great architect was then working on Liverpool's Anglican cathedral.

The interior is utterly different in mood from the exterior. It is a hall of shimmering white terracotta, the nave of five slender bays rising to a ribbed vault. Arcades lead to aisles, and beyond to a line of chapels with exquisite tracery screens. Aisle and clerestory windows are lined with inner and outer arches, an ostentatious gesture. The height of the crossing offers a tremendous sense of 'released space'. This height and the ubiquitous white terracotta give the Holy Name an aura unlike any church I know. It is like a gigantic grotto, haunted with incense.

The west of the church is filled by two tiers of cavernous galleries that could, and I hope do, house a complete choir and orchestra. Beneath is a baptistery of the most serene terracotta, the font of alabaster and the cover of oak. At the east end of the church rises the altar reredos of Caen stone, with soaring canopies and niches containing Jesuit saints. The pulpit is covered in mosaic depicting English Catholic martyrs, including Sir Thomas More. The impression is of no expense spared, of a busy, popular church that has retained the loyalty of its benighted quarter, and should one day make joyful witness to its revival.

MANCHESTER
St Ann **
Baroque town church

Central Manchester has much to do to revive its former glory, but the area
bounded by Deansgate, Market Street and the Town Hall is now pedestrianised
and civilised. Behind the statue of Richard Cobden stands the Baroque church
of St Ann, looking north over its square. Here is a quarter of Manchester that
has not been humiliated by the 20th century. The church was founded in 1709
by a local aristocrat, Lady Ann Bland, in honour of her own own name and that
of the then Queen. Her house, Hulme Hall, lay across Deansgate and the church
stood on what were the outskirts of the town, facing a large cornfield. Those
were the days.

The best feature of this classical church is its north side to the square. Two
storeys of handsome round-arched windows of equal height are separated
by coupled pilasters. The north doorway has coupled columns and a pediment,
and the west tower is dignified, with pilastered bell-stage and balustrade. The
building is in a soft pink-mauve stone and looks well in sunlight. Though
Mancunians like to see the hand of Wren the work is now attributed to a
Derbyshire architect, John Barker.

The interior is stately. Its original design, influenced by the strongly
Protestant Lady Ann, was as a 'preaching box', with the pulpit centrally placed
in front of the altar. The galleries are supported by sturdy Tuscan columns,
which in 1837 replaced the original square pillars. The upper Doric arcade is
18th century. Walls and ceilings are unadorned. The richness of the interior
comes from the lush darkness of the wood seating and of Alfred Waterhouse's
1887 restoration, or rather insertion, of a chancel. This raised the floor at the
east end and moved the pulpit to a more modest location in the nave.

The pews still have their numbers and some even their names. Everyone had a
fixed position. One regular member of the congregation commented after the
Victorian alterations that it was the first time he had actually seen the parson
preaching. On the pew ends are umbrella stands and small buckets to catch the
water. Much of the stained glass, admitted by the guide to be 'something of a
departure' from the church's style, was removed by the IRA bomb of 1996, to
be replaced by 18th-century replicas.

SEFTON
St Helen ***
Medieval screens, hour-glass pulpit

Sefton is not to be confused with Sefton Park in Liverpool. The village is a blessed relief for the south Lancashire church visitor. Located on the outskirts of the Merseyside conurbation, it seems to snatch at a few fields for protection as the housing estates and shopping centres march towards it, leaving central Liverpool empty.

Sefton is more than an oasis. Its pre-Reformation oak woodwork is spectacular, the only medieval church in this part of the county that I left uplifted rather than disappointed. The exterior is of soft Perpendicular sandstone heavily impregnated with black. The 14th-century tower has strong buttresses and a spire oddly accompanied by four pinnacles like upturned bells, added later. The bulk of the church was rebuilt by the Molyneux, lords of Sefton, in the early 1500s. The porch has in its niche a charming modern statue of St Helen, a gift of the Caröe family.

The interior is an airy Tudor composition of nave, aisles, chancel and chapels but with no chancel arch. The whole space is dominated by the most admirable woodwork. The roofs are modern craftsmanship excellently imitating what I assume were original beams. The benches are unusual in their completeness. Large poppyheads fill the nave, with carved bench-ends including the Instruments of the Passion and ornate letters of the alphabet. At the back near the door is a special pew for the dog-whipper, whose job was to keep dogs out and the congregation awake. There are pews for the churchwardens, and a 'mayor's' pew, followed by one for 'the corporation'. These were members of a local bowling society who pretended to grandeur and worshipped separately at their 'cathedral' – a Sefton in-joke.

The chancel screen is among the best in the north of England. Of light oak it has deep coving to its canopy and an ornamental grille instead of tracery. The canopy and the top of the dado are minutely and exquisitely carved. The side screens, no fewer than six, are equally intricate. To the north is the Blundell pew, guarding the entrance to the Lady Chapel, and to the south the Sefton pew. All are separated by individual screens, as if rival hands were determined to produce the most splendid work. The pulpit of 1635 is no less finely worked, delicate on an hour-glass base, with board and tester in place. Molyneux memorials in alabaster, stone and brass fill the chapels, recording the family's valour from the Crusades through Flodden Field to the Battle of Jutland.

SLAIDBURN
St Andrew *
Jacobean screen, Georgian woodwork

The village is delightfully lost in the Hodder valley above Clitheroe, where the Forest of Bowland descends towards Ribbledale. The church sits proud on a mound, with a former village grammar school beyond it. The interior is notable for its 17th- and 18th-century woodwork, inserted after the stripping out of the pre-Reformation furnishings. Even the limewash has survived together with a record of its bill of 1762, 'for six loads of lime' at a cost of six shillings.

Most prominent of the fittings is the Jacobean screen. This superb work is believed to have been carved by Francis Grundy, maker of the famous screen at St John, Leeds (Yorks,W) for John Harrison, whose family had ties with Slaidburn. The robust classical uprights and delicate pierced cornice are carved with vines, grapes and heads. Equally fine are the subsidiary screens, box pews and family pews and an old chest by the organ. The Georgian pulpit has a lofty tester and velvet hangings, more appropriate to an Oxford college than this rough moorland.

STANDISH
St Wilfrid **
Elizabethan roofs, embryonic classical arcades

The church stands big and black, defying the surrounding housing estates, motorways, flyovers and superstores. Damn the lot of them, it seems to cry, and erects a battlemented gatehouse as if to keep them out. The tower is 19th-century Gothic and prominently spired with an octagonal bell-stage. It is of grey-black ashlar while the rest of the church is yellow-black 'gritstone'. The nave and chancel are of an unusual date for English parishes, Elizabethan 1582–4, a time of 'Gothic survival' rather than revival. The nave arcades seem undecided between Gothic and classical. They have tentative columns of a Tuscan order, while the arches above are Gothic, a most strange 'transitional' form.

The Perpendicular interior is blighted by savage scraping and then, as if to hide the outrage, the gloomiest of Victorian glass. The east window is modern, by H. J. Stammers. Yet all is forgiven for the finest roof in Lancashire, worthy of Somerset's best. This is a Tudor work of panels and cross-braces covering nave, aisles and, most elaborate, the chancel. The vicar has studied the bosses and claims that no two are the same. Other woodwork contemporary with the church includes the pulpit, altar rail and some bench-ends.

The tomb on the north side of the chancel is of Richard Moody (d.1586), rector of the Elizabethan church, whose initials also appear on the roof. Like the church, his monument is in an embryonic classical style, although it has hijacked a 14th-century effigy of a priest. However, the church is predominantly about Standishes, who have their own chapel. A Standish apparently killed Wat Tyler in front of Richard II during the Peasants' Revolt, and is celebrated in a Victorian window. Another, Myles, was Captain of the Guard on the *Mayflower*. A descendant of this Standish arrived from America in 1846 to lay claim to the local estates, but discovered that Myles was from a junior branch of the family and had to return empty-handed. The pew ends in the Standish Chapel display the family crest of an owl with a rat.

WARRINGTON
St Elphin *
Victorian rebuild of 14th-century nave and tower

The steeple of St Elphin's stands high over the Mersey plain, for once devoid of tower blocks or other challenges to its prominence. Seen from the M6 bridge over the Ship Canal it rises like another Grantham, 280 ft high and the third highest spire in England (after Louth/Lincs and St Mary Redcliffe, Bristol). It sits behind the Ring o' Bells pub and a row of Georgian houses, amid an otherwise bleak expanse of estates. Only the chancel survives of the medieval church, the remainder being an 1860s rebuilding by the architects Frederick and Horace Francis in deep red sandstone. When the rebuilding took place, two ancient chasubles were discovered in the chancel crypt. These were generously given to the local Roman Catholic church, where they remain.

The interior is that of a confident town church. Its nave retains earlier 19th-century galleries and a spectacular west organ screen and pipes, dated 1908. The crossing piers are equally magnificent, with thick foliage round their capitals. Only in the chancel, erected by Sir William le Boteler in 1354, are the Middle Ages left to themselves, though with a Victorian vault. The windows have Decorated tracery with strangely contorted Reticulation. In the north transept is an alabaster tomb of Sir John le Boteler (d.1463) with his wife, fine late Perpendicular sculpture with saints and scenes from the Bible carved on the chest. A. W. N. Pugin designed the east window.

WHALLEY
St Mary ***
Medieval choir stalls and misericords

The church is tucked away near a row of cottages in the centre of the village, near the site of an old abbey. It is in weathered pale limestone with a squat, oblong tower. Outside the porch are three ancient 'Celtic' crosses of Anglo-Saxon date. Whalley contains excellent medieval and post-Reformation woodwork, in particular a magnificent set of choir stalls inherited from the dissolved monastery. Indeed, the church could qualify as a museum of ecclesiastical seating.

At the west end of the nave is a fine panelled gallery now serving as an organ loft. Then in eastwards succession come a churchwardens' pew, a constable's pew, benches dated 1638, a rectory pew of 1702 and, most spectacular of all, 'The Cage'. This last is a flourish of pierced woodwork made up of bits of screens and pews completed in 1697. Over its two doors are the initials of the Fort and Taylor families who for years contested ownership of the pew. A court decided they should both occupy it. On this decision at least they could agree: they would endure no such humiliation. Both built themselves private galleries elsewhere in the nave, which have now vanished.

The chancel dates from the early 13th century. It has lancet windows and contains Whalley's treasure, a set of clergy choir stalls. They were carved in about 1430 and, rare among medieval works, the name of the carver survives, a Mr Eatough. Restored in the 19th century, the stalls, poppyheads, misericords and cathedral-like canopies give this little church a grandeur well beyond its station. The misericords are beautifully executed and deserve nationwide repute. They include two eagles carrying Alexander to Heaven, a blacksmith shoeing a goose, a girl with a weeping satyr, a wife beating her husband with a pan, and a splendid George and the Dragon.

The 20th-century reredos is a lovely work with reliefs of biblical figures, carved by George Jack in 1928. Above rises the east window, filled with heraldic shields set in clear glass. Installed in 1816 it commemorates the families of the neighbourhood, with such exotic names as the Lords of Blackburnshire, the Duchess of Buccleugh, Ormerod of Ormerod, Starkie of Twiston and Parker of Brownsholme, Forester of Bowland. With great trees waving outside, the window forms a fitting climax to a spectacular scene.

Leicestershire

Leicestershire has always been a comfortable county. Its churches originated in the early Saxon missions sent from Peterborough, and have benefited from being on the route from the Midlands to the east coast ever since. There is no distinctive Leicestershire style, more a mix of Lincolnshire and Northamptonshire. From the earliest days we have the superb 9th-century carvings at Breedon, Byzantine rather than Saxon in style. The Norman era left little but fragments in St Mary, Leicester, unless we include the exquisite French glass collected in the chancel at Twycross. But Leicestershire is rich in Decorated Gothic: at Stoke Golding and Gaddesby the designers of windows and the carvers of corbels showed themselves equal to any in England.

This is a county of towers. Perhaps the best in the Midlands is that of Market Harborough, crowned by its superb broach spire. To this must be added the tower at Hallaton and England's most astonishing clerestory at Melton Mowbray, where 48 windows seem to lift tower, nave and transept into the sky. From the 18th century, Leicestershire has two masterpieces: the sober church at King's Norton, with its central pulpit, and the more joyful work built for the clerical Earl of Harborough next to his mansion at Stapleford. He located his pulpit in the west wall and his hassocks are still in the gallery. Leicestershire is oddly poor in monuments, except for one collection that is beyond compare, the tombs of the Earls of Rutland crammed into Bottesford chancel beneath the heights of Belvoir Castle.

Bottesford ***
Breedon on the Hill ***
Claybrooke Parva *
Gaddesby ***
Hallaton **
King's Norton **

Leicester: St Mary de
  Castro **
Lubenham *
Market Harborough *
Melton Mowbray ***
Peatling Magna *

Stapleford ***
Staunton Harold ***
Stoke Golding ***
Thornton *
Twycross **

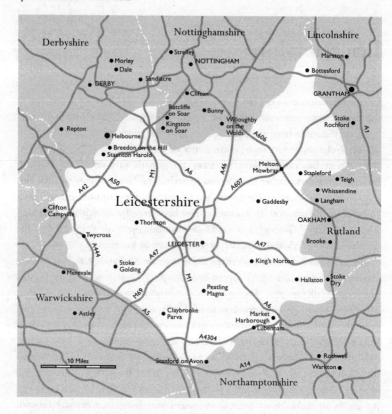

Nottinghamshire

Derbyshire

Lincolnshire

Morley
Dale
DERBY
Sandiacre
Strelley
NOTTINGHAM
Clifton

Marston
Bottesford
GRANTHAM

Repton
Ratcliffe on Soar
Bunny
Kingston on Soar
Willoughby on the Wolds
Stoke Rochford
A1

Melbourne
Breedon on the Hill
Staunton Harold

A42
A50
M1
A6
A46
A606
A607

Melton Mowbray
Stapleford
Teigh
Whissendine
Langham

Leicestershire

Clifton Campville
Thornton
Gaddesby

OAKHAM
Rutland

Twycross
LEICESTER
A47
Brooke

Merevale
A444
A47
Stoke Golding
M1
M69
King's Norton
Hallaton
Stoke Dry

Warwickshire

Astley
A5
Claybrooke Parva
Peatling Magna
Market Harborough
A6
Lubenham

A4304
Stanford on Avon
A14
Rothwell
Warkton

Northamptonshire

10 Miles

BOTTESFORD
St Mary ***
Manners/Rutland mausoleum

The church should be approached from the south. A gentle stream flows through a natural arboretum of weeping willow, copper beech and pine. Water-birds play on the bank. Beyond rises an old ironstone church with smart ashlar dressings. The 210-ft steeple is unspectacular in detail but beautifully pro-portioned. Round the nave roof is an ornamental parapet with pinnacles. This is the parish church for Belvoir Castle, whose walls ride white and magnificent on a distant bluff, and is the resting place of the lords of Belvoir. The church is known as 'the Lady of the Vale'.

The nave is of little interest, scraped Perpendicular arcades but with carvings apparently of the Deadly Sins, including gluttony and lying. The pulpit is dated 1631 and is admirably carved, but all eyes are drawn to the chancel, its arch crowned with the coat of arms of Queen Victoria. At the Reformation, the chancel became the mausoleum of the de Roos and Manners families, Earls and later Dukes of Rutland. In 1828 a new mausoleum was built at Belvoir and later members of the family were buried there. What survives at Bottesford is a 'dormitory' of twenty-four memorials, including the tombs of earls in unbroken succession from the 1st to the 8th. If the crowding is too rich for some, it was too much for the present congregation. The altar has had to be moved to the west end of the chancel.

The collection has a remarkable symmetry, but is best appreciated in locational not chronological order. On entering the chancel, we see two Elizabethan wall monuments facing each other north and south. These are to the 3rd and 4th Earls, made in 1591 by Gerard Johnson of Southwark at a cost of £100 each. Next, riding like ships at anchor down in the centre of the chancel, are the 1st and 2nd Earls. The latter has an extraordinary tomb, the two effigies being displayed under a dining table, representing a communion altar, while kneeling weepers appear above. This is the tomb type favoured by 16th-century French kings, including Louis XII. The table is supported by balusters elaborately carved in alabaster. Beyond is the Earl's father, Thomas Manners (d.1543). This tomb is traditional, with two effigies and weepers round the chest, but the corner balusters are incipient classical forms. The two monuments demonstrate the advent of classical design in England.

Next we reach two later tombs, again facing each other across the chancel, those of the 7th and 8th Earls (d.1641 and d.1679) by Grinling Gibbons. By this date the architectural canopies of earlier works are giving way to figure sculpture. The 8th Earl and his wife are in Roman dress with symbols of death, including an urn and a skull. Next come the earlier, Jacobean 5th and 6th Earls, who died in 1612 and 1632 respectively. The 6th's is one of the most grandiloquent tombs in England. The husband lies prone with one wife slightly above and another slightly beneath him, as if on a slope. The canopy is on a truly monumental scale. Above a coffered arch supported by four columns on either side rises a further canopy with columns projecting out into space. Above again, the family arms are displayed, touching the roof.

The 6th Earl's effigy is the first in civilian dress. The long inscription boasts his travels and achievements, and mentions the celebrated deaths of two of his sons 'in infancy by wicked practice and sorcerye'. The two boys sit at his feet holding skulls indicating their early deaths. Three women servants at Belvoir were accused of the boys' deaths, a mother and her two daughters. The mother asked for bread to prove her innocence, and duly choked to death on it. She was confirmed as a witch. The other two confessed to murder and were hanged in Lincoln gaol in 1618.

BREEDON ON THE HILL
St Mary and St Hardulph ***
Rare Saxon carvings, Shirley family pew

Approached from the north and east, Breedon is like a lighthouse on an island at low tide. The hill has been all but eaten away by centuries of quarrying and the church must be reached by climbing a path from the village or by a circuitous road from the west. The exterior is heavily buttressed and the tower has nothing so risky as a spire. Much of the exterior stone is deeply weathered, as if the wind were in league with the carvers whose work has made the place famous. The hills of Derbyshire can be seen in the distance, with occasional cooling towers. In the churchyard are slate gravestones, some with exquisite rococo lettering.

There was a church here from the earliest years of Christianity in these parts. Breedon was settled *c.*676 as a monastic outpost of the abbey at Peterborough. Over the next two centuries, local or imported carvers produced some of the most exciting sculpture to survive in England, almost ranking as a stone equivalent to the Lindisfarne Gospels. The church was probably rebuilt when a Norman priory was established in the ruins by Augustinian canons before 1122 and a new chancel built in the 13th century. The nave and other priory buildings were lost in the Reformation, when the Shirley family purchased the priory from Henry VIII. What survives is thus the old 12th-century crossing and 13th-century chancel, albeit much restored. The crossing tower is now the west tower. Remarkably, the Saxon carvings were kept through all these vicissitudes.

The interior is bright and lively, with red and blue carpets and tall lancets in the east wall. Georgian box pews, west gallery and pulpit survive. In the north aisle stands the magnificent Shirley pew, a wooden room within a room like a gilded zoo cage, with plain panels, thickly balustered openings and a roof above a carved frieze and cornice. On top are extravagant shields, dated 1627. Beyond is an equally lavish Shirley tomb of 1598. This has a two-storey canopy of columns sheltering a skeleton below, and the kneeling family above.

The Saxon carvings were set into the new porch (formerly the south transept) after the Reformation. They have since been moved elsewhere within the church, looming out of the walls only after our eyes are used to the interior light. We can see them behind the south aisle altar, on the frieze behind the main altar and embedded in the walls above the arcades. The carvings date from the 9th century and fall into two groups. The wall friezes are mostly of 'inhabited vines' filled with animals and humans, a picture book of contemporary life. The second group is of individual saints and angels within panel frames. The most famous of these is in the tower ringing chamber (invisible except in illustration) and shows the Archangel Gabriel giving a blessing in the Byzantine style, with his third finger touching the thumb.

Many of the subjects and poses look Greek rather than Celtic or Saxon. Pevsner says of the Breedon carvings that 'The figures, inexplicable from Anglo-Saxon or contemporary Continental art, come close to a faithful imitation of a Hellenistic style. It is perhaps the most impressive English figure sculpture of its time.' As for who brought these artists, their patterns and motifs, to this lonely spot so long before the Norman invasion, history is silent.

CLAYBROOKE PARVA
St Peter *
Decorated chancel tracery

Claybrooke should one day be restored in pre-Reformation colours. The exterior sits happily on a bend in the road, with walls of soft-coloured limestone and the tower a solid 17th-century construction. Inside, the nave is Perpendicular. Pink stone piers rise harmoniously to soft limestone arches and plastered walls, with a well-restored roof and a full complement of carvings, including imps and monsters.

The jewel of the church is its chancel, unusually spacious for so modest a place and among the finest in the county. The clear glass enables the sunlight to dance through the swirling Decorated tracery. North and south windows are all on a theme of unfurling flower petals, artistry created by an unknown hand. The east window, a Victorian insertion by Street in 1878, is more restless, its tracery pattern bent and buckled as if under the weight of the roof. There are two lovely original doorways in the north side of the chancel.

The church appeals for money for repairs to the structure, and also for its 'Send a Cow to Uganda Scheme'. How on earth to choose between these two causes?

GADDESBY
St Luke ***
Extravagant Decorated exterior, Waterloo monument

Gaddesby shares with Stoke Golding the palm among Leicestershire village churches. But where Stoke is a serenely harmonious work, Gaddesby is a jumble of variations on one explosive theme. That theme is immediately apparent up the hill on the approach. The Decorated west end of the south aisle appears to have been designed at the end of a riotous 14th-century party. It is one of the most eccentric compositions on any English church.

The exterior is of a custardy ironstone with limestone patching and dressing.

The clerestory windows have unusual Plate tracery and ballflower decoration. But all is overshadowed by the western extension of the south aisle, seldom an interesting part of a church. It was commissioned by an unknown patron, possibly associated with the Knights Templar, who held the manor at the time. The Knights were a flamboyant lot but, as so often, we long to know more of the people associated with a church. The lavishness, being on the exterior, was presumably intended as much for show as for devotion. But the Templars were disbanded in 1312, and the Gaddesby work looks later, c.1340.

The composition is of the richest Decorated Gothic. It comprises a west door, as if to a separate chapel, topped by a 'spherical triangle' window. This contains three spherical quatrefoils, linked to the door by a strange garland of ballflower. Above are three niches topped by a frieze of ogee canopies crowned by an ornamental parapet. The south-west corner next to it has angle buttresses with pinnacles of even greater richness. Along the south wall, the largest pinnacle appears to have spawned a small one, as if trying to calm things down. The whole work is faced in ashlar and covered in figurative carving. There are ladies in wimples and men sticking out their tongues. Monsters are everywhere. The work is reminiscent of Portuguese late Gothic, of stone worked like a living material dredged from the sea.

The interior is more modest by far, almost uncannily so, but no less delightful. Wide windows are left free of stained glass so their elegant tracery is the more visible. A five-bay arcade is enclosed to east and west by a steep Decorated arch. Wooden roofs survive and limewash covers the walls. The floors are paved with ancient stones, tiles and medieval bricks in a delightful jigsaw. The nave pews are medieval, gnarled, with high sills for the rushes that once kept feet warm and clothes out of the mud. The aisles are cluttered with paraphernalia of all ages, a piscina here, a tomb recess there, a battered knight, a row of corbel heads, an incised alabaster slab, an ancient organ. The font is a Decorated composition of niches and flowers.

In the chancel is Gaddesby's last surprise, the memorial to Colonel Edward Cheney (d.1848) of the Scots Greys. His fame lay in having four horses shot from under him at Waterloo. The sculptor portrays him life size rising from the saddle of one of the dying horses, a most arresting image.

HALLATON
St Michael **
Village setting, Kempe windows

The village is the prettiest in Leicestershire and knows it. At its centre, modern housing gives way to immaculate cottages set round a sloping green with a cross and a butter-cross in the middle. This is limestone country near the rolling

Rutland border, but the cottages are in a variety of materials, stone, brick, timber, and covered with slates, tiles and thatch.

The church is worthy of its setting. It shows to its village a lavish north aisle whose north-east corner turret has a set of empty niches with enriched canopies, holding the shields of the Bardolf and Endgaine families, manorial lords and patrons in the 14th century. Its pinnacle, together with the adjacent window, almost rivals Gaddesby for Decorated splendour. The window tracery is like a cluster of balloons kept aloft only by the ingenuity of the masons. Round the corner, the south porch contains a rare Norman tympanum showing St Michael spearing a dragon.

For once a Midlands church can be recommended for its glass. The chancel east window is a Kempe masterpiece, including his wheatsheaf signature. It portrays the Nativity, with richly clothed figures. Kempe's restless style is reflected in the background of dark sky and verdant landscape and in the ups and downs of the Gothic canopy. The angel window in the chancel south wall is also by Kempe, as are the excellent archangels in the east of the south aisle. The north arcade has Norman capitals, carved with different types of water-leaf. Outside the north wall of the chancel is a fine rococo memorial to an 18th-century rector, George Fenwick, badly in need of restoration.

KING'S NORTON
St John **
Intact Gothic Revival interior

Everything about this church is remarkable. From the south, across the valley from Illston, the tower and nave rise on their hill with all the splendour of a Fotheringhay. We assume we are approaching a great work of English 14th-century Decorated. Closer to, the church retains its magnificence but changes its character. It is not medieval but Gothic revival, built for William Fortrey, the lord of the manor, by a local architect named John Wing.

Most remarkable is the year of its design, 1760. Authentic Gothic works of the mid-Georgian period are almost unknown: asked to date King's Norton, most would choose the 1830s. Architects at this time normally opted for a more whimsical style, sometimes spelled Gothick, as at Shobdon (Herefs). King's Norton borders on severity. The only whimsy here is the ogival hoods to the windows. The tower, despite losing its spire in the 19th century, is a beautifully balanced work. The windows, narrow and lofty, are like a row of hooded monks.

The interior of King's Norton is as fine a space as is offered by any 18th-century church, displaying the Georgian genius for simplicity without tedium. A rectangular chamber is filled with an even light from clear windows. The roof is of wood, the walls white. There is no distraction. Certainly there is none from the fittings, which although nearly all classical are monastic in their austerity. Happily untouched by restoration, the original box pews survive, as does the west gallery on fluted columns.

Just two extravagances are permitted. One is classical and original: a three-decker pulpit remains, most unusually, in its intended position in the middle of the nave. It symbolises the Protestant centrality of the Word. Today it is like a theatrical dais, wheeled on for a recital. The other is a Gothic intruder and the only discordant note, the font. This is Victorian Perpendicular with concave panels. No infant would dare cry in such a setting.

LEICESTER
St Mary de Castro **
Norman sedilia carvings

Oh, to have seen Leicester in its prime. The church guide shows the spire of St Mary's rising above a sea of gravestones framed by trees. The photographer must have contorted himself: the location is just off the central ring road. Modern Leicester is dire, but the church is at least protected by an enclave of half-timbered and Georgian buildings near the remains of the castle. Nor is it a tedious town church, but an eccentric medieval building containing the county's best Norman survivals.

The exterior was heavily restored by the Georgians (the spire) and the Victorians (most of the rest). Medieval fragments start out of the exterior walls. There is a fine corbel-table on the north wall of the chancel and the north door-way is a mass of zigzag. The interior is ghostly, architecturally shambolic and fascinating. At its core is an elongated Norman nave and collegiate chancel. Nobody, not even the Victorians, quite had the courage to clear this away, so Norman relics pop up on all sides. They emerge as window and door openings, arches embedded in walls, relics of chapels and shrines long forgotten.

After the Normans came the large parochial south aisle in the 13th century. This supplied so much space that no later expansion seems to have been necessary. Both nave and aisles are adorned with carved animals, some original, some Victorian where masons chose to re-create the monsters that so intrigued their forebears. At the west end of the nave, a man appears trapped between the arches, as if exhausted with the task of holding up the roof.

We now penetrate the old chancel, guarded by a Jacobean screen. Here lies Leicester's treasure, the Norman sedilia of three arches surrounded by zigzag decoration, enriched with deeply undercut foliage and abstract patterns resting on colonettes. Overhead is Victorian stained glass created in the 12th-century style by Wailes, depicting biblical roundels in an abstract field. There was a move in the 1930s, apparently resisted, to lighten the interior by removing at least some of this glass.

St Mary's has long been a High Church bastion. Altars are dressed, candles burn in every corner and not a shelf lacks an icon of sorts. My reaction is that if a church wishes to go down this route it should at least go the whole hog. Put back the screens, chantries, wall paintings and priests in constant attendance.

LUBENHAM
All Saints *
Georgian box pews

A large Victorian house shelters a small church of intense charm. A stubby tower hides behind a large fir tree, beneath which the nave is stretched out like a cat asleep. Each bay might be a separate cottage, so diverse are the components, a Norman arch here, a Tudor window there, some with upstairs rooms, others without.

The church is entered through an old chapel that is now a vestry-cum-parlour. It is a shock to see among the hymn books, cassocks and coffee mugs a Norman monster peering out next to a delightful Decorated squint. The squint might be used today for passing a cup of tea to the priest. Lubenham (pronounced Lubbenham not Loobenham) is entirely covered inside in whitewash. The first impression is of an isolation ward, yet somehow the white contrives to stay domestic and warm.

The nave arcades are from a medieval junk shop. The north side has two Norman arches resting on a cylindrical pier with a stiff-leaf capital and monsters. The church retains its Georgian box pews and a three-decker pulpit with tester. The churchwarden protested to me that these are not 'user-friendly' since no children and few adults can see over the top of them, but English Heritage had insisted they stay as a grant condition. Quite right. In the south aisle is a Jacobean family pew said to have been used by Elizabeth II during a visit to a local friend in the 1950s.

Wall paintings have recently been revealed through the whitewash on the chancel arch. The best is the head of an angel visible behind a hinged panel at the back of the pulpit.

MARKET HARBOROUGH
St Dionysius *
Decorated tower

There are few churches included in this book purely for their exterior and setting but Market Harborough is one. The church sits in the centre of the old town. It fills a square with, for company, a 17th-century grammar school, a Victorian factory and the town's main shopping street. This church is not aloof from its surroundings, behind a churchyard or close. It is a gregarious member of the club.

The tower is a work of finest 14th-century Gothic. The components appear perfectly balanced. To the north and south, the sequence is as follows: the lower stages are plain, the middle stage has three Gothic niches, while the upper stage has twin two-light bell-openings, tall and grand. The two top registers have friezes. The angle buttresses emerge as tiny broaches jutting slightly at the top of the walls. Finally, the spire: this rises, softly crocketed, as if four faces had become eight without us noticing. It is built with entasis, to exaggerate its height when seen from below.

There is nothing here that is inferior to the architecture of the Italian Renaissance. The mason of each stage must have plotted its balance, proportion and decoration with meticulous care, debating how much weight to give each element. If the medieval tower is among the glories of English art, then Market Harborough, built in the most inventive period of that art, c.1300, stands in the first rank. The rest of the church is disappointing. The tower is ashlar but nave and aisles are of rough ironstone, as if built as an afterthought for the servants' quarters. The interior is uninteresting, except in retaining galleries mostly of the early 19th century of the sort normally removed by the Victorians. The east window is by Hardman & Co., in the illuminated manuscript school of Victorian glass.

MELTON MOWBRAY
St Mary ***
Continuous 48-window clerestory

Melton Mowbray is a crowded market town, capital of the rich, rolling country of east Leicestershire, beloved of hunting people, cheesemakers and the pork pie. On a winter Saturday horses jostle with four-wheel-drivers on the roads round about. The area was as wealthy in the 14th century as it is today, though with less help from European subsidies (unless you call a wool monopoly a subsidy, as well you might). The result was St Mary's, a grand cruciform church with transepts and a crossing tower. The tower of scrubbed limestone dominates the town, spoilt only by a clumsy stair turret and spirelet in place of a spire. It is beautifully proportioned, with two storeys of bell-openings rising to a Perpendicular crown.

The tower is offset on closer view by the astonishing Perpendicular clerestory that runs continuously round nave and transepts. Seen from the west, the tower appears to float on glass, as does the roof. There are 48 of these windows and, with a low sun, they appear to slice the church into two layers. No less handsome is the earlier Geometrical and Intersecting tracery in the aisle windows. The west porch is adorned with nodding ogee niches and a doorway with fine shafts and mouldings. Ballflower bursts from every curved surface. The porch was a chapel in itself and has its own piscina. Melton is Leicestershire's most sophisticated church, even before we go inside.

The nave and transepts are both aisled, an unusual feature in a parish church. This creates a heady sense of space in the crossing. Inside, as outside, the clerestory dominates. It lifts the Decorated arcades and aisles upwards as if determined to deposit them in the sky. Such magnificence had to be paid for: in this case not by the owner, the Priory of Lewes, but by the merchants of the town. The priors were responsible only for the modest chancel. This is now mostly Victorian, scraped, dark, but rich in fittings, with a gleaming brass altar rail. Almost every window is messed about with a jumble of modern stained glass.

PEATLING MAGNA
All Saints *
Incised slab monuments

The village sits on a hillside south of Leicester and overlooking the path of the Grand Union Canal. Hidden below the main street and the pub, the church rubs shoulders with the Manor Farm, its approach shrouded in trees. The church is unaisled, like a banqueting hall with a wide Perpendicular nave roof with bosses intact. Ancient Commandment boards and hatchments line the walls. The tower arch is neat and Decorated, with no capitals. This is a yeoman's church in a lovely setting.

Only in the chancel is there something special, two alabaster tomb chests of members of the local Jervis family. In place of effigies on their tops are unusual inscribed images. Dated 1597 and 1614, these include dozens of children, in a sort of commemorative kindergarten. Opposite and high on the chancel wall is a memorial to William Jervis of 1618. He appears with his wife in voluminous, almost ludicrous, costume.

Peatling's chief claim to fame is the marriage of Elizabeth Jervis to Dr Samuel Johnson in 1735. She was twenty years older than he, painted her cheeks and was described as of 'good understanding and great sensibility but inclined to be satirical'. Johnson adored her.

STAPLEFORD
St Mary ***
Georgian interior in stately setting

The church hides amid the woods of the big house like something out of *Hansel and Gretel*. A cloud of blossom surrounds it in spring, with yews and cedars hovering behind. The drive is guarded by a stern gate and a row of almshouses. The house itself, with its astonishing 'Flemish' wing, is a hotel patronised by clients eager for a taste of ersatz English country life. The church survives all this, apparently untouched since it was built for the clerical Robert Sherrard, 4th Earl of Harborough, in 1783 by the architect, George Richardson. The same patron and architect created Teigh (Rutland). The church, now redundant, is in pretty Georgian Gothic, its stone contriving the same pink/white shade as the blossom.

The interior is all of a piece, with light oak pews set collegiate fashion, facing each other across the aisle. All the woodwork is panelled with a frieze of tiny blank Gothic arches. The delight of the church lies in the confidence of its plasterwork, a patchwork of ogees round the walls and ribs forming lozenges on the ceiling, all on pink and blue backgrounds. Yet there are none of the 'wedding-cake' fancies of the earlier Shobdon (Herefs). The church was originally built without a pulpit. The parson, often the Earl himself, preached from the family 'pew' in the west gallery, with its private fireplace. There is a similar pulpit at Teigh.

At the east end, the church unbends a little, rising to the sanctuary and the flanking Sherrard tombs. On the right of the sanctuary is the monument to the 1st Lord Sherrard (d.1640). It is a late example of a tomb chest with recumbent effigies. They lie in elaborate costumes and with eight children in prayer: 'fully good enough for Westminster Abbey', writes Pevsner. Opposite is Rysbrack's monument to the 1st Earl of Harborough (d.1732). He lies like a recumbent Roman senator at a banquet. He is pointing to his wife, who appears to be covering their child in a blanket. Above are two medallions and a coat of arms, a work of panache. In the gallery are some original Georgian kneelers.
[CCT]

STAUNTON HAROLD
Holy Trinity ***
Commonwealth church on mansion lawn

Pride of this church is a setting and a quote. The setting is incomparable. Behind a wall on the lawn of the great house, the church massively affirms the primacy of faith over landscape in the middle years of 17th-century England. The land falls away towards the lake past what is now a Ryder Home, marred only by caravans and Canada geese. But the trees are in place, as is the picturesque bridge over the water. The Gothic battlements of the church mingle with pine, fir and monkeypuzzle.

Over the west doorway is told the story of the church: 'In the yeare 1653 when all things sacred were throughout ye nation Either demollisht or profaned, Sr Robert Shirley Barronet Founded this Church whose singular praise it is to have done the best thing in ye worst times And hoped them in the most callamitous.' Shirley, an ardent Royalist and Laudian, died in the Tower of London three years later. He had built the church in defiance of Cromwell, and in the Gothic style. It is therefore unlike the other well-known 1650s church at Berwick (Northumb), whose partly classical design was approved by Cromwell.

Shirley's church is a testament to the old-style religion, or at least that of the Laudian version of the Reformation. It is mostly Perpendicular Gothic, with pinnacles, battlements and a strong west tower: Revived Gothic rather than Survived Gothic. The architect deliberately chose motifs from various medieval periods, rather than continuing the Perpendicular tradition into the 17th century. Thus the aisle and chancel windows have Decorated tracery. Only the west portal is classical, with pilasters decorated by swags, lion heads, angels and a crest of a coat of arms. But this work is not of Shirley's time, and dates from 1662–5 when the church was completed.

The interior is rich but restrained, with much woodwork. A magnificent wooden screen and gallery fill the west tower arch and support the organ. Wood panelling extends round all the walls, including the chancel and even the piers of the arcades. These panels are wonderfully complete. Nave and aisles are filled with box pews. The roof is painted on the theme of Creation out of Chaos, bulbous clouds with light shining through. A helm and gauntlets hang somewhat incongruously above the chancel arch. The wrought-iron gates in the chancel are 18th century, perhaps the only fitting not original in this ensemble.

STOKE GOLDING
St Margaret ***
Decorated tracery and carvings

Stoke Golding has never lacked admirers. 'A building of exceptional perfection', enthused Betjeman. 'Among the most beautiful in this or any county', exults the *Shell Guide*. Even Pevsner allowed that it was 'grand and noble'. The church hugs a hillside in the village overlooking the Ashby Canal, south of Bosworth Field and just off the A5. Its beauty lies in its unrestored state and the unity of its interior design.

Stoke Golding is essentially a Decorated church, and admirably illustrates the development of the style. The exterior is at its most sophisticated on the south side, as seen from the approach. Here windows display Geometrical and Intersecting tracery of the later 13th century. On the north side the tracery flowers into a flowing curvilinear of the early 14th century. Quatrefoil parapets embellish the south side and the tower top.

The first impact of the interior is made by the central four-bay arcade. Its clustered piers carry a forest of richly moulded arches and carved capitals, variations on a theme of heads amid forest foliage. It forms a veritable convention of Green Men. The furnishings are of all periods, the screen a pleasant Victorian work, the box pews generous in their legroom and with deep cushions. The font rests on a group of saints, including St Margaret with a donor. The south aisle contains a spectacular church chest of 1636.

The only blemish on this serenity is the Victorian rebuilding of the chancel, but even this is redeemed by the magnificent east window of five lights. Stoke Golding's crumbling limestone exterior is matched by a softly limewashed interior. Infused with sunlight, this is the Middle Ages on its best behaviour. It should be a model for church restorers nationwide.

THORNTON
St Peter *
Interior woodwork

The village is set along the crest of a ridge with the M1 in the distance and a reservoir close at hand. The churchyard runs down towards the water's edge, displaying rows of magnificent slate tombstones. Over this scene the green-black of the Perpendicular tower keeps stern watch, capped by a stone spire with lucarnes. The setting is most picturesque.

The church is entered through a splendid medieval wooden door. The interior welcomes visitors with a full set of Tudor benches, their bench-ends thick with linenfold panelling. These are rare in that we know the name of the carver, one Robert Baker. In the east window of the south aisle is some 14th-century stained glass, including a delightful Flight into Egypt. It is a pleasure to find such a modestly lovely work in so unassuming a place. In the tympanum above the chancel entrance is a fine set of Regency Commandment boards. These are in a classical frame and are written in the most beautiful lettering.

The chancel was rebuilt by the Victorians, perhaps as the old one was sliding downhill. The stone carving on the arch corbels is a riot of fruit and flowers. The guide notes that the church's walls are covered with 25 different varieties of lichen. But why not tell us more about them?

TWYCROSS
St James **
French medieval glass

There is little to bring us to Twycross village and only one thing to its church. This is the north Midlands at its least exciting. Apart from having an unusual Decorated north arcade, with no capitals at all, the church is heavily restored. The pew of the Howes of Gopsall Hall survives to the north of the chancel, with subsidiary pews 'for indoor and outdoor staff'. It is to the Howes that Twycross owes its celebrated east window. This medieval glass, some of the finest in England, was acquired by George III at the time of the French Revolution and distributed to various friends by his son, the future William IV. These included the Howes, who put it into their local church in 1840.

The east window at Twycross is, like the fine medieval glass at Wilton (Wilts) and Rivenhall (Essex), French in origin. It appears to have come to the Royal Family through the enterprising Georgian antique dealer, Christopher Hampp of Norwich. He was first of a succession of dealers who followed (or preceded) the revolutionary armies across Europe, 'saving' works from possible looting. The glass at Twycross is believed to come from the Sainte-Chapelle in Paris and from St-Denis in the Paris suburbs. Its fame is due to its age, charm and excellent preservation.

The best glass is the Presentation in the Temple. This came from St-Denis. That church was built in 1145, making this panel the earliest glass in England, although Dorchester (Oxon) lays claim to this title. The roundel is intact, with Jesus appearing to fly from Mary's hands. Another fine panel is a Deposition, from the Sainte-Chapelle, with deep reds and blues, Christ's arms and body conveying the sinuous line of Italian Early Gothic. Below, two 'spies' carry a huge bunch of grapes from the Promised Land.

Nobody seems to have considered returning these Elgin Marbles of the stained glass world to their original home.

Lincolnshire

Lincolnshire has the finest collection of medieval churches overall of any county in England. Its towers may not rank with those of Somerset, or its naves be a match for East Anglia's. But for quality in depth, Lincolnshire churches cannot be bettered. Above all, they are a pleasure to visit. The county is one of England's least known and least appreciated. It offers the opportunity, rare in modern England, of seeing unsung treasures in an uncluttered landscape.

From the south, the county could not have a more splendid gateway than Stamford, with as many entries as Bristol and a custodianship programme that is a model for the nation. The county's churches are almost all rural, dividing into four geographical areas which roughly correspond to architectural groups. To the south are the open Fens round the Wash. Here are fine churches similar to those of north Norfolk, their roots in the great monastic houses of Norman England, later rebuilt in the Perpendicular style on the wealth of the wool trade. Towering over them is Boston and its famous Stump.

To the east is a lost Lincolnshire of the coastal marshes and the slopes of the Wolds. This is a bleak landscape, blessed with tiny churches barely altered in the past two centuries, such as Addlethorpe, Theddlethorpe and Saltfleetby. Down the spine of the county run the Wolds, a sweeping chalk downland with huge views and modest villages, punctuated by the splendid tower of Louth. Finally, there is rich inland Lincolnshire of the Humber and Trent valleys, overlooked by the remarkable limestone scarp of the Lincolnshire Edge. Here we find the Saxon remains of St Peter, Barton, and the superb Decorated carvings of Heckington and Brant Broughton, the windows of Swaton and Sleaford, and a masterpiece of Early Gothic architecture, Grantham tower.

The Georgians left some endearing creations, such as Well and Hannah. But the Victorians needed to do little to Lincolnshire except tidy it up, as J. L. Pearson did most spectacularly in his restoration at Stow.

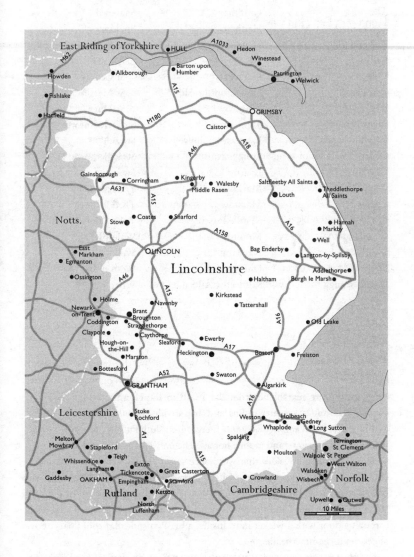

Addlethorpe *

Algarkirk ***

Alkborough *

Bag Enderby *

Barton upon Humber:

  St Mary **

  St Peter **

Boston *****

Brant Broughton ****

Burgh le Marsh **

Caistor *

Caythorpe **

Claypole **

Coates *

Corringham *

Crowland **

Ewerby **

Freiston **

Gainsborough *

Gedney **

Grantham *****

Haltham *

Hannah *

Heckington ****

Holbeach **

Hough-on-the-Hill *

Kingerby *

Kirkstead ***

Langton-by-Spilsby **

Long Sutton ***

Louth ****

Markby *

Marston *

Middle Rasen *

Moulton *

Navenby **

Old Leake *

Saltfleetby All Saints *

Sleaford ***

Snarford **

Spalding **

Stamford:

  All Saints **

  St George *

  St Martin **

  St Mary ***

Stoke Rochford **

Stow ****

Stragglethorpe *

Swaton **

Tattershall ***

Theddlethorpe

  All Saints *

Walesby **

Well **

Weston *

Whaplode **

ADDLETHORPE
St Nicholas *
Ancient screens

The Lincolnshire marshland from the Wash to the Humber estuary contains some of the saddest country in England. It is divided between intensive farming and intensive caravanning. Skegness merges into Butlin's and on into a spreading stain of bungalows and mobile homes. The only escape is inland, to the mile-wide fields and empty skies that were once said to drive men mad. Marshland churches dot this landscape like visitors from another planet. Addlethorpe was once a prosperous church. Its stone is ashlar, rather than the poorer local greenstone, the tower bold and the porch richly carved. A deeply grooved step leads through a door with a wicket in it. Inside, a big Perpendicular roof floats above angels on its hammerbeams.

The church was deprived of its chancel in 1706 on grounds of local impoverishment, in part due to the erosion of the coast and the famous 'sinking' of eastern Britain. The east wall is thus of brick, with a rood screen stuck on to it to form a reredos. Yet the church retains a forest of other, lesser screens, fashioned into a substitute for the lost chancel. Those to the north and south chapels are painted dark pink; the screen to the tower arch has ogees and a delightful central arch. More screens occupy the vestries and even the backs of the old pews. These pews have curious corkscrew candleholders on their ends. There is no stained glass, allowing the soft light of the marshes to flood the interior.

ALGARKIRK
St Peter and St Paul ***
Victorian reinstatement to Early Gothic interior

The village lies north of the River Welland and close to the Wash, yet seems to have been safe from inundation. The land hereabouts used to grow woad and chicory for the dyeing trade. The cruciform church is a rich fusion of medieval and Victorian work. The hereditary squarson (a squire-cum-parson) in the 1850s, Basil Beridge, commissioned the architect of Lancing Chapel, R. C. Carpenter, to restore the interior on Tractarian principles. The restoration was widely celebrated: 'so good it could hardly be improved upon,' wrote one review at the time.

Sitting on a mound, the church exterior is a typical Fenland marriage of Decorated 'ground floor' and Perpendicular clerestory. The big Decorated windows are variously of the 14th century and faithful restorations by Carpenter. From outside we can see the south windows of seven lights whose tracery loses itself in waving Reticulation. The nave clerestory has ten three-light windows.

Inside, Early Gothic arcades continue down the nave and into the transepts, sure sign of a rich church. The crossing is immodestly grand. Nothing is quite in order: the south transept is broader than the tower and the chancel wider still. Capitals are embellished with water-leaf and stiff-leaf carving, most superb on the south crossing arch. Carved grotesques are everywhere, a particularly engaging one attached to an arch in the north transept.

The chancel is obviously restored, yet in no sense overpowering. The lancet window splays are painted, the reredos of stone and the choir stalls graceful. Carpenter's work at Algarkirk was completed in 1854 and is a model of historical deference. The stained glass, mostly by Clayton & Bell, is simple, uniform and ungarish.

ALKBOROUGH
St John *
Roman maze

The village lies in one of those lost corners in which eastern England specialises, an outcrop at the junction of the Rivers Trent and Ouse at the head of the Humber. On a clear day, the view from the tower encompasses York, Lincoln,

Beverley and Hull, although the village, says the *Shell Guide*, 'has a Yorkshire bleakness'. A band of Cavaliers occupied the church during the Civil War but were attacked by Roundheads, killed and buried under the floor. When this was later excavated, one skeleton was found to be over seven feet tall.

The exterior is unspectacular, the Victorian chancel slightly taller than the nave yet carefully balancing the tower. The rest is all eccentricity. In the churchyard is the relic of a Saxon cross, so eroded by centuries of sword and scythe sharpening as to look like a Henry Moore sculpture. On the floor of the porch is an iron plan of an ancient maze, the original being located in the village and first recorded in the 17th century. The pattern has been traced back to Roman times. There are Roman fragments built into the base of the tower.

The fine Early Gothic doorway has triple shafts and a richly moulded arch, in a form similar to the nave arcades. On the south side are excellent stiff-leaf capitals, deeply undercut. The church nave boasts two grand pianos, used for occasional recitals by two concert pianists living in the village.

BAG ENDERBY
St Margaret *
Font with carved hart

The village lies isolated in the Wolds beyond Harrington Hall. At first sight, the church looks derelict. Tower and nave are of dark greenstone, crumbling and moist as if eager to sink back into the long grass of the churchyard. Only the nearby farms seem determined to keep it standing. The interior is more alive. It claims attachment to Tennyson, whose father held the living and who was reputedly rejected by the daughter of neighbouring Harrington Hall. A small exhibition is devoted to the link: 'Birds in our wood sang / Ringing through the valleys / Maud here, here, here / In among the lilies.'

The interior is utterly simple, with windows clear to the sky and a primitive screen to the chancel. On the chancel wall hangs a classical relief to the family of Andrew Gedney, with the date 1591. The joy of the church is the Perpendicular font, worth crossing Lincolnshire to see. The carvings on the octagonal bowl include a moving Pietà, a hart licking the bark of a tree sprouting from its back, and what looks like a saint playing a banjo.

BARTON UPON HUMBER
St Mary **
Contrasting medieval arcades

Barton once outranked Hull as a Humber port. Then the sea retreated, other ports claimed pre-eminence and the town moved uphill. Two ancient churches were left as they are now, adrift of the market place and rather forlorn, relics of what was a prosperous town in the early Middle Ages.

The approach to the church is from the south and shows the splendid porch and tower, both Early Gothic with much dogtooth and stiff-leaf carving. Inside, the nave arcades offer an excellent textbook of the radical change in church architecture at the end of the 12th century from Norman to Early Gothic. The north row is late Norman, with cylindrical piers and zigzag decoration. The south row is Early Gothic, with water-leaf capitals and piers with shafts and rings. The south piers resemble those of St Hugh's choir in Lincoln Cathedral of *c.*1200.

The chancel is fiercely scraped but displays stiff-leaf and Green Men in its arcade capitals. It is flooded with light and contains a strange memorial to Jane Shipsea (d.1626) in the form of a column interrupted by a tablet. In the floor of the chancel is a brass to Simon Seman (d.1433), a local vintner who rose to become a High Sheriff of London. He is shown in civilian dress standing proud on two barrels of wine.

BARTON UPON HUMBER
St Peter **
Saxon tower

Old St Peter's, as it is known locally, is one of England's premier Saxon survivors. The tower, which stands over the nave, is unaltered from the 10th century. Its western projection, possibly a baptistery, might be even older. In the 14th century St Peter's was extended eastwards and lost its Saxon chancel, but the old tower and baptistery were respected. Less respect is shown today. The church was occupied for years by English Heritage archaeologists, who used it as an excavation dump and now as a museum. The church is technically still consecrated, but has been stripped of ecclesiastical character. This, says a handout, permits 'unparalleled access to the fabric'. I am not clear what this means. The church is open only during the early afternoons.

The tower at least is visible from outside. Here are the familiar features of Saxon architecture. Windows are small, with twin openings of round or triangular heads, divided by a shaft. The walls are covered in purely decorative pilasters, complete down to the ground. Inside, the tower openings form a pleasantly antique backdrop to the Gothic rest of the church.

This is now bare of furnishings. The interest lies solely in the Decorated tracery and carving. The south windows are Geometrical, the north Reticulated. The arcade capitals and corbels, some reused from earlier incarnations, include excellent carvings, especially the Green Men against the west wall. Most unusual of all, in the north aisle inside the church, is an old window with carvings in its uprights forming part of a rare 'window rood'.

[EH]

BOSTON
St Botolph *****
The Stump, lantern interior, 62 misericords

Boston's famous Stump is not only Lincolnshire's most celebrated landmark and lighthouse to the Fens. It is also a wonder of medieval engineering. At 272 ft it is the highest church tower, not counting spires, in England. When the tower was planned in the 1300s, the town was the premier wool port in England after London. Status required a church and a beacon to match. Though massive in its foundations, the tower remained vulnerable to Fenland clay and was not felt to be strong enough to support a spire: hence the octagon and the nickname.

The Stump is traditionally photographed from along the banks of the River Witham, the structure rising vertically from the sloping foreshore. This view has been spoiled by concrete piling of the banks and by the building of a modern bridge and police station directly opposite. Today the view from the market to the east is happier, with the added advantage that from here the tower rises above a forest of pinnacles and does not overpower the nave.

Work on a new church was begun in 1309, with the Decorated style in full flower, but the tower was not finished until two centuries later. The tower's diminutive west doorway is Decorated, but Perpendicularity, in every sense, soon asserts itself. Blind panelling soars upwards past three windows on the north, west and south faces. Then come two ogee windows for the original bell-chamber. From here a spire should have taken over, as at Louth. At this point, says Pevsner, 'hubris gripped the Bostonians and they decided to heighten their tower . . . an undeniable coarsening'. The higher bell-stage is a rough-and-ready work of architecture. Although there is no specific evidence of a planned spire, having not built one, the masons seem to have gone on building up for the sake of sheer height. But once the disappointing bell-stage is passed, the crowning octagon is a superb work, adorned with pinnacles and flying buttresses. This was not completed until well into the 16th century.

If the remainder of the exterior is spectacular, the interior is overwhelming. The original south doors to the nave are among the finest medieval doors to survive anywhere. Boston is 14th-century design at its most generous, mobile and symmetrical. The view east from the west end of the nave is of grand arcades and colourful roofs. The eye is led through a graceful Decorated chancel arch into what is almost an optical illusion, the sham vault of the chancel. This was rebuilt in the 18th century and a new east window inserted in the 19th. Its tracery is Lincolnshire Decorated, its lines swirling upwards with manic freedom, in contrast to the static Panel tracery of Perpendicular, copied apparently from the tracery on the south doors.

The view west is no less exhilarating. The tower interior is as grand as the exterior, a vaulted lantern open to the top of the second stage and encompassing a breathtaking space. The view upwards in the early evening light is like peering into the canopy of a rain forest. The famous climb to the top of the lantern has the same number of steps as there are days of the year. The entrance is guarded by an 18th-century iron screen.

The medieval and Victorian furnishings of Boston are rich. In the north aisle is a black marble slab commemorating a merchant from Munster, who died at the height of the town's prosperity in 1312. A window in the east chapel includes scenes from Boston history, including the departure of its citizens in 1630 to found Boston in Massachusetts. They were seen off by the town's Nonconformist vicar, John Cotton, who was to follow them in 1633. His magnificent pulpit still stands in the nave, minutely carved with Ionic columns, picked out with finials and gilding. From here he would preach two-hour sermons and conduct five-hour catechisms.

A year after Cotton's departure to America, Archbishop Laud arrived to reassert the old rite, founding a splendid library above the porch. The chapel at the west end of the south aisle was named after Cotton in 1857. When George Gilbert Scott wanted to paint its ceiling with stars and stripes the vicar felt this was going too far.

Finest of the furnishings are in the chancel. Here George Pace in the 20th century added canopies to the 14th-century stalls. There is a superb collection of 62 original misericords, one of a monk birching a boy. In the aisle roof is a roof boss of a white elephant, recalling the bring-and-buy sale by which money was raised for its restoration. Boston has one of the most extravagant Victorian fonts in Decorated Gothic style in the country. It is by E. W. Pugin and could be a centrepiece for a fruiterer's wedding.

BRANT BROUGHTON
St Helen ****
Porch carving and gargoyles, interior by Bodley

Brant Broughton is remarkable for two contrasting reasons. The exterior is enlivened with superb 14th-century decoration, a gallery of Gothic carving to rank with Heckington and Sleaford. The interior is of the same period, but deferentially restored by a Victorian rector in collusion with the architect, G. F. Bodley. Together they represent a model of original Gothic and Gothic revival in harmonious alliance, both carried out by local craftsmen. Brant Broughton is an example of what might have been done with so many 19th-century ruins that were butchered or destroyed.

The steeple is magnificent, a fine tower rising to a soaring, exhilarating spire. It is set back minimally behind the parapet. The crocketed outline and attendant pinnacles, slightly askew, shoot the eye upwards when seen from directly below. Even the lucarnes are kept small to avoid interrupting the ascent. These structures have as much art and artifice as a Greek column. The Decorated tower, built just before the Black Death, is balanced by a symmetrical composition of nave and aisles added in the Perpendicular style. Even the porches match, north and south. Everywhere is ballflower and fleurons, scattered like petals across the face of the church.

These porches are gems of 14th-century architecture. They are stone vaulted with bosses and encrusted with animated carving. The bosses are so big as almost to fill the vault. Green Men guard the doors. These carvings are more than a menagerie, rather an imaginative realm in which mischief, humour and repulsion seem as important as piety. So lifelike are many of the faces, so simple their tasks, like a sower or a drummer boy, that they must surely be portraits. Yet they lie alongside monstrous beasts and distorted flowers. Over the south porch a man has his shirt raised and bottom exposed, apparently defecating at the viewer. What on earth was in the carver's mind? All of human life is in these carvings from the most vital period of English vernacular art.

The second Brant Broughton is inside, the careful application of Victorian restoration to medieval architecture. As at Algarkirk, the stimulus was a new Victorian squarson, the Anglo-Catholic Canon Frederick Sutton, who arrived in 1873. His architect was Bodley and his later partner, Thomas Garner. Together they played a brilliant variation on a Decorated theme. The only sadness is that a 20th-century restoration did not correct one Victorian blindspot, the scraping of the walls. These remain partly scraped and unnecessarily stained and gloomy. They need limewash.

Sutton and Bodley's innovations in the nave mostly took the form of iron candelabras and the insertion of window glass. The ironwork was made at the local Coldron forge in the village, which is still in business. Sutton's glass is most accomplished. He took advice from Kempe but designed the works himself and prepared the glass in a kiln set up in the adjacent rectory. The only exception is the east window by Burlison & Grylls, and some of the south windows are later. But the uniformity of design and the simplicity of the colours are gloriously at peace with the architecture.

The chancel is more obviously Bodley's work and replaced a Georgian structure standing at the time of Sutton's arrival. Bodley was then working on his masterpiece at Hoar Cross (Staffs) in a spirit of Tractarian grandeur. Behind the screen rises a typically Bodleyesque lierne-ribbed vault, wooden and brilliantly painted. By him too are the choir stalls, organ case, pulpit and reredos, the last framing a 15th-century German painted panel given by Sutton. It is a serenely sophisticated space to find in such robust surroundings. Under the tower is a superb fragment of a 14th-century Trinity sculpture.

BURGH LE MARSH
St Peter and St Paul **
Jacobean woodwork

The hill on which Burgh sits is so welcome in the flat marshes that I leapt out of the car and walked up its main street for the sheer pleasure of meeting a contour. The Saxon invaders built a church here, and the 18th century a cockpit. Beneath the tall bell-openings on the north side of the tower is a Victorian clock face. It warns, 'Watch and pray for ye know not when the time is.' The churchyard offers views over the marshes through a pleasant grove of yew trees.

The interior is a variation on a theme of Lincolnshire woodwork. The roof has no fewer than eleven Green Man bosses, surely a record. The chancel screen is decorated with crocketed ogees rising into a lace-like filigree of Perpendicular tracery. This is topped by a truly awful 1960s rood group with angels. These look like tasteless souvenirs. The screen beneath the tower is Gothic, as is the one now used as a reredos behind the altar. A fine Jacobean screen surrounds the south chapel, with delicate colonnettes and openwork obelisks on top. The same carver was apparently responsible for the superb pulpit of 1623.

The font cover, again Jacobean, has doors and scrolls and is crowned by a bird holding two containers in its beak. These are a mystery. Arthur Mee suggests that they are an inkwell for entering baptisms and a sandsifter for drying the ink. To Pevsner this explanation 'will hardly do'. The guide is silent. The magnificent wooden eagle lectern was carved in 1874 by an eccentric local barber, Jabez Good. Apart from cutting hair, he wrote a standard work on Lincolnshire dialect.

CAISTOR
St Peter and St Paul *
Gad whip

The fine old church sits on a steep slope in the centre of the hillside town, based on a Roman camp. Like Blandford in Dorset, much of the town was destroyed in a fire, in 1681. The church survived, though only to be severely restored by Butterfield from 1856. The tower retains much Norman work, in a pleasantly crumbling ironstone, and the south doorway is Early Gothic, with dogtooth ornament. The doors are covered in 13th-century ironwork, a beautiful swirl of curves with no sign of a pointed arch.

The nave is of four Early Gothic bays with a variety of capital motifs. The hand of Butterfield is heavy on the pulpit, benches and the chancel. With such Victorian work the best thing is sometimes to take a deep breath and appreciate it. For instance, much of the stained glass is excellent, including an Adoration by Kempe in the north aisle, and windows by Burlison & Grylls in the south aisle. Under a cusped recess in the north chapel is a fine effigy of Sir John de Hundon, mid-14th century, with a moustache and angels.

Caistor is home of the Gad whip, a fearsome object of 6 ft of stock and 7 ft of lash. This was to be cracked by a tenant of the manor in the porch every year during the reading of a Palm Sunday lesson. The whip was next held over the vicar's head, then laid to rest in the manorial pew. Nobody appears to know the reason, but it was presumably a penance for some ancient land dispute. The ceremony was last performed in 1846 and the whip now rests in a glass case. Next to it is a stone, supposedly made of blood and bones from the Holy Land: a reminder, says the guide cheerily, 'that our faith has had its faults too'. Rough place, Caistor.

CAYTHORPE
St Vincent **
Geometrical tracery, Arnhem window

The stone of the village varies from pink to ochre, depending as much on light and shade as on the stone itself. Roofs are pantiled, and oaks and yews shade the path to the church door. Above rises one of the county's most exotic steeples, a Decorated tower crowned by a pierced parapet of wavy tracery, pinnacles and pierced flying buttresses. The octagonal spire, crocketed its entire height, seems impossibly tall for its support. It has a pronounced bulge to give an illusion of added height, a bulge that was bigger, and the spire even higher, before being hit by lightning and rebuilt by George Gilbert Scott in the 1860s.

The church walls are composed of bands of limestone and ironstone. Most remarkable are the windows, almost all of them with rare Geometrical tracery, dating from 1290–1300. Though heavily restored, they show the 13th-century masons enlarging the windows and piercing their heads with a variety of sub-sidiary openings. From this to the Perpendicular in the north transept windows seems a long journey.

The interior is a shock, a most unusual case of an arcade running straight down the middle of the nave. The effect is almost an optical illusion, as if the architect had lost confidence in his ability to keep the roof up. This is a pity since the arcade seems unnecessary and interrupts the sight line to the charming crossing under the tower, a forest of waving shafts on all four corners.

A modern window in the north aisle commemorates the Airborne Signals unit billeted in the village before being flown to Arnhem and destruction in 1944. It shows the unit in action during the parachute drop.

CLAYPOLE
St Peter **
Decorated leaf capitals

From a distance, Claypole is a fine steeple crowning a bigger church than its little settlement seems to justify. Decorated windows with flower tracery fill the walls but only the south porch gives a real clue to what we are to find inside. It is flanked by eroded foliate capitals, the leaves seeming to sprout from the stone itself.

The interior of Claypole cannot be missed by lovers of 13th-century leaf carving. The use of foliage to decorate capitals straddles the Norman, Early Gothic and Decorated periods, dying out in the 14th century with the approach of Perpendicular formalism. Claypole appears to have been built, apart from its Perpendicular windows in chancel and transepts, mostly in the late 13th century, when the stylised stiff-leaf of the Early Gothic was giving way to the naturalistic foliage of the Decorated. Here it adorns almost every pier in the nave arcade, as well as the larger arches to the transepts and aisles at the cross-ing. Cruder and perhaps earlier work adorns the west, tower arch.

The motifs used are richly varied and deeply undercut. Many are oak and vine leaves, the tree of the countryside and the tree of the Sacrament. Each capital is different, as if the masons had each been left to evoke nature in his own way. One pier of the south arcade has two Green Men either side, leaves pouring from their mouths. In the north aisle is an ugly woman in a huge wimple, with a man and another woman on either side of her. Even more odd, inside the chancel arch, are two corbel heads of a man and woman. They have one hand under the chin, the other on the brow. Can we ever know what this means?

The chancel has fine sedilia and a beautiful aumbry. Otherwise Claypole is badly in need of limewash. The walls are stained and ugly and ill-display the art of the piers.

COATES
St Edith *
Only rood loft in Lincolnshire

The little church is well signposted, on a farm lane behind a row of poplars not far from Stow. It is the sort of church that must once have been known only to its immediate settlement. There is no tower. The interior is tiny, the structure essentially Norman. The south doorway has dogtooth decoration and the window openings inside are deeply splayed.

The charm of the church is in its woodwork. This comprises an open king-post roof, ancient benches, intact rood screen and a tympanum above. The loft, the only one to survive in Lincolnshire, can be reached by a stair. The screen tracery was restored by Pearson, who worked unobtrusively to restore the church in the 19th century. The bench-ends have simple poppyheads and a family pew lies at the back, the candelabras still with their candles. In the chancel is a medieval Easter Sepulchre, with a small Tudor brass to members of the Butler family. The floor is of old bricks. No more need be said of this charming place.

CORRINGHAM
St Laurence *
Norman capitals, Bodley restoration

This is an example of the magic that Bodley and his partner Thomas Garner could bring to even the most modest village church. Corringham is an un-attractive linear village, but the church is well isolated on its outskirts. The tall west tower is Saxon–Norman, its interior arch a series of roll-mouldings, looking like a stack of blankets.

The church is worth a visit if only for the Norman capitals on two bays of the north arcade. These are finely carved in a leaf-crocket design. The south arcade is Early Gothic with extensive stiff-leaf carving. But it is Bodley and Garner's work that catches the eye. To them we owe the aisle and north transept roofs, and the decoration of the chancel. Everything is of the highest quality. The reredos, screen with rood and organ case are worthy of a wealthy city church. The painted roofs are especially lively.

To complete Corringham's revival, Kempe supplied both the east window and another in the south transept. The latter is wonderfully original, a Tree of Jesse alive with prophets in active poses and set against thick oak leaves.

CROWLAND
Croyland Abbey, St Guthlac **
Abbey ruins, tower arch

Croyland was one of many Benedictine monasteries that the Saxons founded on islands in the Fens, supposedly near the spot where St Guthlac first grounded his boat on English soil. It saw periodic ruin and rebuilding but by the 15th century was a large institution extending over three quadrangles beneath a huge church. At the Dissolution the chancel and transepts were demolished and the south aisle and nave also fell into progressive decay. These now stand as ruins. A single Norman arch survives from the old crossing, exposed to the sky. Surviving too is the west front, standing like a stage set still covered with statues in niches and with the superb St Guthlac relief in its doorway.

What remained for the parishioners was only the north nave aisle. It had already been remodelled for parochial use in the 15th century and given a fine if truncated tower and a hilarious spire. The latter is minute, with lucarnes. It appears to have dropped by for a visit from a village church and decided to stay. The interior is graceful, with a long tierceron ribbed vault like that in Lincoln Cathedral. The ribs spring from their piers uninterrupted by capitals, rising from floor to apex like giant palm trees. Chapels lead off to the north, but the old south arcade is now filled with Tudor windows.

The best interior view is, unusually, from east to west. The tower is heralded by an arch worthy of the old abbey, jutting up higher than the vault, lit by a huge window and concealing a forest of bell-ropes. Set into one of the piers is a strange font, presumably an old holy water stoup. Here too is a rare thing, a memorial to a church mason. His name is William de Wermington (d.1427). The motto puns his tools: 'Live within your means [or compasses] and upon the square.'

EWERBY
St Andrew **
Tower carvings, Decorated screen and font

Ewerby ranks with Sleaford and Heckington as masterpieces of the Decorated style in the northern Fens. Built after the Black Death in a period of wealthy piety, these churches show a command of the curvilinear style and a fascination with carved decoration. Nor is there any sameness to these works. Each church is different, as if the masons were eagerly rivalling each other in their variations on a Gothic theme.

The church sits in the middle of a small village, its beautifully proportioned tower rising serene over the surrounding country. Here the spire is dominant, its long broaches rising direct from the walls. (This form was abandoned as impossible to repair without encasing the tower in scaffolding: spires were later recessed behind parapets.) The buttresses are so slight as to appear almost decorative, gargoyles springing out at each stage. With binoculars, it is apparently possible to find a man baring his bottom somewhere near the top (*cf.* Brant Broughton). The porch is equally splendid, with foliage sprouting round the doorway.

The interior is initially disappointing. The Victorians scraped the walls, revealing dry limestone rubble that might be the inside of a barn. High and dark roofs are marred by hanging lights and overhead heaters. But there are delights in the gloom. The tracery is Reticulated in the south windows, but roams wilder elsewhere.

There is no architectural divide between nave and chancel, just an intricate screen with grille-like tracery. This forms a fascinating pattern in the heads of the screen doors, one half of each arch Reticulated, the other a swirl of mouchettes. The font is Decorated – a charming piece with six miniature window designs, each being different, like a mason's pattern-book.

FREISTON
St James **
Norman nave, 'apprentice-boy' font cover

This is a ship of the Fens, set amid fields between the main road and the Wash. To outward appearance, Freiston is a bold Perpendicular structure, with massive tower, ostentatious west window, long nave and generous aisles. On closer inspection, oddities emerge. The clerestory is too big for the aisles, so much so that aisle and clerestory windows look to have been exchanged. Above the clerestory is a frieze of carvings, apparently a relic of a Norman church. Even odder is the east end, where we see the outline of a large pointed arch facing a pasture.

Freiston was a priory outpost of Crowland in the rich farming country of south Lincolnshire. East of the present church ran a transept and chancel. This makes more sense inside, where a severe Norman nave is embedded in the Perpendicular rebuilding. The church was steadily expanded as the community grew, the old nave extending westwards with three Early Gothic bays. The most sensational extension was upwards, with a mighty eight-window clerestory and roof, thick with stone and wood carvings. The north aisle was built of brick, an early use of this material presumably in the Tudor period. Was this, asks the guide, a sign of changing fashion or of declining wealth?

The furnishings include a superb Perpendicular font cover, an intricate confection of woodwork soaring upwards. Legend holds that it was carved by an apprentice. When his master saw its beauty, he flew into a jealous rage and struck the boy dead. The boy could ask for no finer monument.

GAINSBOROUGH
All Saints *
Town church based on St Martin-in-the-Fields

Those who deplore the declining respect for church property today should ponder Gainsborough. Victorian reports told constantly of thefts of prayer books and money, and of 'unspeakable degradations in the churchyard' committed by gypsies, marauding dogs and children. Five pounds (a huge sum) was offered to any who could apprehend vandals. The churchyard was unkempt and 'resembled a jungle'. Today the church rises from a pristine lawn, somewhat antiseptic.

The church reflects the wealth of the town as a port for trans-shipping goods from barges to sea-going vessels on the Trent. The former church was rebuilt 1736–44, apart from the tower. The architect was the Warwick architect, Francis Smith, and the model was James Gibbs's St Martin-in-the-Fields (London). It does not share St Martin's famous tower and portico, but has similar elevations with giant pilasters and Gibbs surrounds to the windows, continued round the eastern apse.

The interior is spectacular rather than lovable. A mighty parade of Corinthian columns marches towards the apse, where they turn into pilasters flanking a Venetian east window. The orders rise the height of the church and, in contrast to St Martin's, support a continuous straight entablature. The church retains its box pews and chandeliers, and galleries that were lowered in the 19th century to give them a steeper rake. The pulpit, wholly out of character with the rest of the interior, is by Pearson.

Gainsborough church is as blighted as any by Victorian glass. The elderly Bodley visited it in 1903 and declared 'all the windows atrocious'. He duly designed his own, equally atrocious, for a side chapel. Even the guide comments that 'its merit over that of the others is not apparent', adding that 'the glass in this church is of little intrinsic interest'. It argues that this is 'immaterial to the appreciation of the classical structure'. I disagree. The glass should go.

GEDNEY
St Mary **
Clerestory windows, medieval door

From Cambridge to the Wash, the Fenland churches ride the landscape like galleons on the Spanish Main. Gedney was once eager for a Lincolnshire spire.

The marshy subsoil thought otherwise, permitting no more than a dunce's cap spirelet. The massive tower, of Perpendicular piled on Early Gothic, and the famous clerestory and aisle windows render the whole building transparent, almost airborne. When caught by the evening sun Gedney is a church ablaze.

The aisle tracery is Intersecting or curvilinear, the choice apparently left to the whim of the mason. The aisle east windows are superb compositions, tall lancets supporting exotic fleur-de-lis. The interior is as spacious as the exterior suggests. The roof was much mutilated with repairs, a strange mix of crenellated tie-beams and two hammerbeams, but the bosses survive. The clerestory is of twelve closely spaced windows, each of three lights and Panel tracery. The windows are out of alignment with the arcade beneath, as if they came off an assembly line and were 'cut to fit'.

Gedney's furnishings are disappointing, especially the schoolroom chairs which fill the nave. There is a restored rood screen with tiny medieval heads carved on it. In the north aisle is supposedly a 14th-century Tree of Jesse window, though it was not in place on my visit. What is in place is a superb medieval south door, ranking with that of Stoke-by-Nayland (Suffolk). Its wicket door is a component of the design rather than hacked through afterwards.

GRANTHAM
St Wulfram *****
Steeple and west front, Decorated tracery, corbel-table carvings

Here is the finest steeple in England. When seen from the railway or across the flatlands of west Lincolnshire, Grantham's slender spike is one of the most exhilarating images of English Gothic. Nothing subsequently erected, even in glorious Somerset, is quite its equal among churches. Only the spire of Salisbury Cathedral can stand comparison. Yet Grantham has always been a parish church, its majesty civic, not ecclesiastical. The 19th century was hard on the interior and 20th-century glass adds aggression to the offence. The church is more awesome than lovable. But the steeple is to be savoured, best approached from the west, past a prettified close of gardens and trees.

The quality of English church towers lies in the mason's ability to resolve horizontal and vertical elements. The best towers in the east Midlands were earlier than those of East Anglia and Somerset, yet seem to have achieved this resolution in advance. At Grantham, the tower begins as a classic work of the turn of the 14th century. The multiple mouldings of the west doorway are echoed in the main west window, which has Intersecting tracery. Both are embellished in ballflower decoration of c.1300. The flanking end windows of the north and south aisles are filled with the most elaborate Geometrical tracery.

The tower now rises free of the roofline of the aisles, with two tiers of blind arcading. Then come two stages of bell-openings, one with two windows, the next with just one, as if to increase the tension. The tower is carefully tapered, with lines accentuated by angle buttresses. Four pinnacles now effortlessly conceal the shift from square tower into octagonal spire, which rises from its small broaches in a single final thrust. The taper of the spire seems perfectly judged, with its ribs and three tiers of diminishing lucarnes covered in ballflower, as if infested with golden snails. Grantham's tower ranks with any masterpiece of English art. Such was the effect on Ruskin that he (allegedly) swooned on first seeing it.

The interior of Grantham is a single vast rectangle, its atmosphere dominated by George Gilbert Scott's Victorian roofs and rood screen and by the gloomy stained glass that fills most of the windows. The arcades are a dignified jigsaw puzzle, the central four bays surviving in part from an earlier Norman church that was ruined in a mighty fire when hit by lightning in 1222. These include Norman piers and capitals, with water-leaf and scalloped carvings.

Greatest of the post-fire innovations, apart from the steeple, were the aisle windows. These present a sequence of English tracery through its finest era, roughly from 1280 to the advent of Perpendicular, c.1350. The earliest are six Geometrical windows of c.1280 in the north aisle. Contemporary with these is the north doorway (inside the later north porch, now the bookshop): this is a sumptuous portal of shafting and stiff-leaf. The tracery in the south nave aisle is Intersecting, first cusped and then, as we move eastwards, curvilinear with ballflower. The south chancel aisle windows are of 1330–50, each a variant on the most flowing Gothic style. The eye can hardly follow the line desired by the mason: we would love to have seen these patterns being planned and replanned in the workshop sand.

After this excitement the rest of Grantham may seem an anticlimax. Much of the Victorian glass is of high quality. The Kempe work is recognisable. Wailes contributed the west windows and Blomfield the reredos, a work that matches the grandeur of its setting. Above the south porch is a chained library, open in summer.

Less noticeable is the remarkable corbel-table also retained from the pre-fire church. It surrounds most of the exterior wall, especially on the south side, offering an extraordinary gallery of medieval carving. These grotesques are everywhere, extending beyond the customary gargoyles and corbels to include figures inserted apparently at random. Some are tiny, some monstrous, some human, some embracing each other. Some have fingers in their mouths, some are smiling, others sneering. Gazing up at them – Ruskin's 'monstrous and loathsome heads in clownish stupidity' – we can only wonder at what inspired their creators to take such trouble over what appear such trifles.

HALTHAM
St Benedict *
Dymoke family pews

This endearing church sits hidden from the main road past the Marmyon Arms. It is redundant and seems about to cede all access to the surrounding vegetation. There is no tower, but a modest bellcote. The most distinguished feature of the exterior is the splendid curvilinear east window, like a pot of tulips in full bloom. As fine, if more curious, is the eroded Norman tympanum over the south door. A job lot of emblems are arranged round a central Greek cross.

The remaining charm of Haltham is inside. Here is a simple chapel with room for rector, squire, tenant farmers, their workers and few others. There is a nave, chancel and small north aisle, divided from the nave by an arcade with restored stiff-leaf capitals. An extraordinary four-angled parclose screen separates the Dymoke family pews from the rest. It extends into the north aisle with high sides, crested top and lights subdivided by heavy pendants. Nobody could doubt which was top family in the neighbourhood. Dymokes were Hereditary Champion of England. The remaining seats are medieval with simple poppy-heads, overlooked by an 18th-century three-decker pulpit with tester.

All these furnishings appear decrepit, including the bedraggled cloth on the pulpit and the bat droppings in the chancel. At the back of the church is a large wooden chamber concealing the bell mechanism, reached by means of a worm-eaten ladder. On the outside of this chamber is painted the coat of arms of Charles I and a biblical text, as if by way of some decoration.
[CCT]

HANNAH
St Andrew *
Tiny Georgian interior

Hannah is a poor man's Well. Down the slope of the Wolds and across the Marshes, a small eminence above the fields allows room for just a chapel and overgrown churchyard, surrounded by a stockade of trees. The building is faintly incongruous, of greenstone with a red tiled roof, a peasant chapel yet with Georgian window openings and a Venetian east window. The church was rebuilt in 1753.

The interior is reached through a small porch in which, on my visit, a bunch of dried wild flowers had been immaculately arranged, an overture of poppies, sedges and grasses. The single-cell nave with chancel is so tiny that it seems that the entire congregation could shake hands at the same time. The box pews are intact and the double-decker pulpit has a tester crammed against the ceiling.

Into one of the pews is built the font, with a carved wooden cover that might be the warming-lid on a dinner dish.

The east end is curiously grand. Beneath the east window, the three-sided altar is surrounded by a complex altar rail with a projection in the centre to enable more communicants to celebrate at the same time. For some reason this has been painted blue. A recent vicar fought to save Hannah church against the destructive wiles of the diocesan authorities. He won and vowed that the church would always be open. It is.

HECKINGTON
St Andrew ****
Decorated figure carvings, Easter Sepulchre

The exterior of Heckington ranks with Brant Broughton among Lincolnshire's galleries of vernacular art. It stands in the centre of its village, a testament to the imagination of the early 14th century, to the years of ingenuity and plenty before the Black Death. The principal benefactor was its rector, Richard de Potesgrave, chaplain to Edward III and thus a man of means. The true heroes of Heckington are the carvers themselves, men of humour, intelligence and artistic licence. We have no knowledge of who they were, but they speak to us from every gargoyle and corbel head. A frame in the chancel shows a collection of the masons' marks. Imagine a modern artist consenting to remain so anonymous.

Of the tower a harsh critic might say that it is too solid. Heavy buttresses hold it to the ground, and the broach pinnacles, each a delightfully ornamented octagon, are too heavy for the spire. That said, the structure sustains a wealth of carvings, including 38 statues. The south elevation of the church itself is alive with figures, the porch likewise, inside and out. Monsters leap from foliage. Angels jostle peasants. A series of figures seem to be skiing downhill under the gargoyles. Many of the faces appear true to life. This must be a satirical magazine as well as an art gallery. The windows are equally superb and best appreciated from outside. In each the upward line seems to follow a different path. The climax is the chancel east window. Its tracery is curvilinear, describing tulips or pincers according to imaginative fancy.

The interior of Heckington is at first a disappointment. The scraped walls are black, streaked and crying out for plaster. Here is one Lincolnshire church which the Victorians did not handle well. The nave is redeemed by the Decorated font, as richly foliated as the porch but sadly stripped of statues. Some relief is in the chancel. It contains the tomb of Richard de Potesgrave, with the county's finest grouping of Easter Sepulchre, sedilia and piscina. The Sepulchre is a masterpiece. Unlike Hawton (Notts), the composition is vertical, with the figures recessed behind architectural features. The soldiers sleeping outside the tomb are almost hidden inside their canopies. The superstructure is a mass of foliage, as if the masons wanted to hide the shrine in a forest.

The same hands were clearly at work on the sedilia opposite. Here the imagery varies from pretty statues of saints to scenes from village life. We see a mediator trying to settle a domestic quarrel, a woman with a squirrel and a boy feeding a bird. At the back of the church is an excellent exhibition of its history.

HOLBEACH
All Saints **
Decorated window tracery

Holbeach is a smart little town off the Sleaford road. For travellers from King's Lynn, it is their first sight of a Lincolnshire steeple. This has a tall needle spire with broaches and lucarnes, above a tower with unusually large Decorated windows in each of its sides. This loss of support is compensated for by big angle buttresses, a happy arrangement. The church is set on the main street, with market stalls leaning against the churchyard wall on Saturdays, over-shadowed by larch and ash trees. The north porch is flanked by quaint towers, as if welcoming us to a castle that has lost its drawbridge.

The interior is large but gloomy. Even on a sunny day, the flower ladies had to turn on the lights to see what they were doing. Victorian glass fills almost every window. There is one clear glass window in the south aisle, through which we glimpse the trees outside as might the inmates of a prison. The most exciting space in the church, where the unusual Decorated windows illuminate the chamber beneath the tower, has been obstructed with bell-ringing equipment.

None the less, Holbeach is that rare thing, an almost complete Decorated church. The tracery is mostly curvilinear. The four-light window on the north side of the chancel has extraordinary swirling mouchettes, darting across its face at all angles.

In the north aisle is a sandstone tomb of Sir Humphrey Littlebury of the late 14th century. He lies with his feet on a lion and his head on his crest, a lady's head. The deep niches round the tomb chest are empty but beautifully carved with nodding ogee arches. A big royal coat of arms is crammed over the modern glass north door.

HOUGH-ON-THE-HILL
All Saints *
Saxon tower

The hill is the Lincolnshire Edge, as rich in churches as the wool villages of the Cotswolds. The churchyard, exotic with monkeypuzzle and Wellingtonia, offers views out over cottage roofs in all directions. Hough's delightful church is Saxon, a rare period in these parts, with a stair turret embedded in the west side of the roughcast tower. The nave interior is also Saxon in origin, of a height best appreciated by standing on the steps of the chancel and looking west towards the tower interior. The arcades, somehow inserted in Saxon walls, are each formed of two bays with big Early Gothic arches.

The roof and aisle roofs soar upwards, above blessedly unscraped walls. Since the clerestory is Perpendicular, it is hard to assess whether this loftiness is the work of the Saxons or of 15th-century masons eager to let light into the interior. However, the triangular-headed doorway high on the inside wall of the tower suggests that the height was indeed that of the Saxon church. If so, it must have seemed awesome to the tiny huts crowded round its base.

Most of the windows are clear, allowing us to appreciate both the church inside and the trees outside. Two are by Kempe and of good quality.

KINGERBY
St Peter *
Knight with flowing hair

Kingerby church sits redundant in the lee of the Wolds, a place of gigantic views and solitude. Its settlement has long been reduced to a few meandering lanes amid the farms. The local manor belonged to recusant Catholics who neglected the church after the Reformation, much to our advantage. This is a part of England which the 20th century rendered less rather than more crowded. The old church roof has gone, replaced by bright pantiles, which make the tapering 12th-century tower of ironstone and brick look faintly Umbrian from a distance.

The interior is atmospheric, with deep window splays and gently faded plaster wash on the walls. The fenestration is of different periods, including a quirky Decorated east window. A simple two-bay arcade leads to a south aisle, where the east window has two medieval panels of St Catherine and St Cecilia. Two dismembered knights rest at the west end of this aisle, one with excellent carved chainmail and belts.

In the chancel is an eroded but remarkable knight's tomb, apparently of a Disney. (Could it possibly be an ancestor?) The effigy is carved not in the round but in low relief. Only the torso and head with flowing hair and beard, and then the feet emerge from the slab. In place of the lower body is a large carved cross with shields. The tomb is apparently late 14th century but the low relief is more characteristic of the 12th century. Or is the whole thing unfinished? The Lincolnshire historian, Henry Thorold, writes, 'Time has moved slowly here and laid a gentle hand on Kingerby.'

[CCT]

KIRKSTEAD
St Leonard ***
Early Gothic fragment in a meadow

Across the empty fields south of Woodhall Spa rises an eerie pillar of ruined masonry. Many are the Fenland monastic ruins of which Shelley might have written, 'Look on my works, ye Mighty, and despair.' This trunkless leg of stone of a Lincolnshire Ozymandias is the remains of Kirkstead Abbey, the rest having disappeared under the plough. Yet a remnant of the settlement survives in a grove of trees down a track beyond the Abbey Farm. This is the old chapel outside the gates, of the sort often built by monasteries for lay visitors. It was converted in the 18th century for Nonconformist worship, and is now redundant.

A gem of Early Gothic, the building is one of the most surprising churches in England, its west front and interior of remarkable quality for a wayfarers' chapel. The date is c.1230, high point of Early Gothic before the advent of Decorated. The west doorway is adorned with stiff-leaf capitals and dogtooth, repeated in the blind arcading above. Opening the door we might expect to find a friendly Puritan chapel. Instead we have what could be the aisle of a cathedral.

The chamber is serene, in warm stone interspersed with white plaster. Light is from six uniform lancet windows on each side and a triple lancet at the east end. The roof is vaulted, the tierceron ribs springing from low corbels at head height. Most impressive is the attention given to decorative carving. Roof bosses, corbels and window-shaft capitals have stiff-leaf in abundance. At the east end, leaves sprout from shafts as if growing from living trees. The ribs and arches have dogtooth, but there is almost no other decoration. The chancel is defined by a wooden screen with simple trefoil arches. It appears contemporary with the rest of the chapel. Chancel screens did not appear in churches until the early 13th century, so this is presumably one of the oldest wooden screens in England.

Kirkstead contains a monument to an early 13th-century knight, again one of the oldest recorded. The helmet is of the ancient 'coal-scuttle' form, a cylinder with a slit. Since no face can be seen, this seems an anonymous way to want to be remembered.

LANGTON-BY-SPILSBY
St Peter and St Paul **
Unaltered Georgian interior

Langton is a puzzling church. An immaculate Georgian structure, it stands peaceful on a mound by a farm. The parish cannot have been big nor its parishioners wealthy, apart from the Langton family who have lived here for eight centuries and do so to this day. Yet the church, built by Squire George Langton *c*.1725, is arranged on the plan of a college chapel. The entire congregation is seated in tiers of box pews, with reading desks and candleholders, facing each other across the aisle. Did simple farmers in muddy boots really troop in here with their wives and servants to hear service? We do know that Samuel Johnson, friend of George's grandson, Bennet Langton, visited this church often. Langton was one of the doctor's favourites and earned his accolade: 'I know not who will go to Heaven if he does not.'

The church is a redbrick box with heavy overhanging eaves, yet another country church apparently drawing on Inigo Jones's widely copied St Paul, Covent Garden (London). Five round-arched windows light each side but only an octagon remains of what was once a more substantial steeple. The interior is unchanged Georgian and all of a piece. The woodwork of dark oak is immaculate, with a three-decker Doric pulpit towering over the congregation and a tall reredos with Corinthian pilasters. The west gallery survives, converted into the Langton family pew in 1850 after the installation of the organ in their original pew. There appears to be no electric light, just candles. In the porch is a Victorian photograph of the local bellringers, a splendid group.

LONG SUTTON
St Mary ***
Early Gothic spire, St George window

History claims that Long Sutton church, belonging to the monks of Castle Acre in Norfolk, was rebuilt in the 1170s by Lady Nicola de la Haye to rival neighbouring Whaplode. Lady Nicola was a friend of King John and hereditary constable of Lincoln Castle. She took the post seriously and personally supervised the castle's defence against barons rebelling against the King. After John's death at Newark in 1216, she continued to defend it for his son Henry III. As a reward she was granted the right to hold a market at Long Sutton. Thus enriched, she was probably responsible for the church's splendid Early Gothic tower.

This tower was built detached from the church, resting on a set of open arches which may have been used for a market. These were filled in for stability during the 18th century. The upper stages have blind arcading, the spire rising directly and without any parapet, in the Early Gothic fashion. This transformation of square tower into octagonal lead spire with four balancing turrets gives Long Sutton its charm. The spire is said to be the oldest lead spire in the country. When its ground floor was open it must have seemed to float across the Fens.

The church interior is Norman and big, big enough not to have required rebuilding as the population grew in size and wealth. But it was heightened with a Perpendicular clerestory, set on top of the old Norman clerestory, which became the middle stage in a three-tier elevation. The aisles were also heightened, their roofs reaching to the top of the Norman work. This Norman core is like a set of stage props, round which Decorated and Perpendicular masons supplied a theatre. The financing of the later work has been attributed to an even more distinguished owner of the Sutton manor, John of Gaunt, occasional resident at neighbouring Bolingbroke Castle.

Such patronage at the height of the Middle Ages gave the churches of the Fens a splendour to rival that of the Cotswolds. Records tell of five altars at Long Sutton paid for by Castle Acre priory and four by local guilds, supporting a total of eighteen priests in all. Of this little survives, but in the south chancel aisle is medieval glass, including a superb image of St George and the Dragon. It is rare to find a complete work of this scale. According to the guidebook, the figure is really John of Gaunt. He is not known to have killed any dragons, though some might say he created one in his son, Henry IV.

Long Sutton is blessed with a churchyard heavy with blossom in spring and crowded with Georgian headstones. Those near the south door boast Baroque cartouches and rococo coping, as if each were seeking to outdo the next. One is to an unnamed thatcher, with the tools of his trade displayed above a large heart.

LOUTH
St James ****
Tallest steeple, nave corbel heads, medieval chests

Louth possesses the most perfect Perpendicular Gothic steeple in England, rivalling Suffolk's Stoke-by-Nayland and the aristocrats of Taunton Vale (Grantham being two centuries older). Louth's steeple is also the tallest; at 295 ft it is 3 ft higher than St Mary Redcliffe, Bristol. It was built in 1501–15 by masons from Lincoln, and completed shortly before Lincolnshire's rebellion against the Reformation. Louth's vicar was to be executed at Tyburn, and much of the church's furnishing destroyed by iconoclasts.

The tower is a superb composition, the upward line perfectly modulated by horizontal divisions. The deep west doorway projects forward of the west front, its ogee gable carried up to the level of the west window. This window rises to a pair of windows and then to paired openings for the bell-chamber with more ogees. Finally we reach the astonishing enrichment of the battlements. The pinnacles are 50 ft high, readying the eye for a spire supported by open flying buttresses. This soars on upwards, its mason even spacing the crockets more widely as the apex approaches, thus syncopating the perspective. Not an element is out of place. The work is in every way a match for the contemporary Renaissance architecture of southern Europe.

The interior of Louth is almost domestic in comparison, 'friendlier than Boston' asserts the verger. The tower arch reflects the splendour of its exterior. Inside the tower a 'starburst' vault is set above the windows, creating a magnificent lantern. Below is surely the most spectacularly roofed coffee bar in England.

The rest of the interior was heavily treated in the 19th century but more sensitively by the 20th. The nave is dominated by its late Georgian pine roof, a magnificent composition of tie-beams and panels, restored in 1988 by Richard Benny of Lincoln. He stripped the wood and repainted the angels in red and blue. The corbel heads supporting the wall-posts are original, and stare out like monsters on the congregation below.

The south chapel contains beautiful Decorated sedilia, while fixed to the wall of the north chapel are two medieval angels rescued from the former roof and here visible at close quarters. Louth has a superb collection of old 'hutches' or chests. Most date from the Middle Ages, but my favourite is a 20th-century work with swirling neo-Gothic patterns in the side panels.

MARKBY
St Peter *
Thatched roof

I cannot omit Markby, the kind of church that uninhibited Americans describe as adorable. It sits, rather dejected, by the road from Alford to Hannah.

The best feature is immediately apparent from the approach, the only ecclesiastical thatched roof in Lincolnshire and one of barely a dozen to survive in England. Yet an old guide tells us that when the church was built, of fragments of the dissolved Markby Priory, the roof was of tiles. It was not thatched until 1672, when a local churchwarden took a fancy to the tiles and offered a thatched roof in return. More such helpful offers, please.

The church is of stone, double cell and without a tower or bellcote. The only embellishment is some reused fragments of dogtooth set into the chancel arch, clearly work from the old priory. Box pews and two-decker Georgian pulpit are preserved, although unattractively varnished. The communion rail is three-sided. The chief pleasure of the church lies in its survival. Long may it live.

MARSTON
St Mary *
Heavy broach spire, Thorold tombs

Marston is a 13th-century structure well restored, with a chancel mostly of the late 19th century. The most prominent feature is the tower, crowned by a pastiche of an east Midlands broach spire. It is pock-marked with lucarnes, and its broaches run fully half way up its height, as if never quite trusting the spire to look after itself. But then it had a serious duty to perform, protecting the church of the Thorolds, a great Lincolnshire family.

The doorway has Early Gothic stiff-leaf, which recurs on one capital inside. The nave arcades are Early Gothic on the south side, Decorated on the north, but they are merely a foretaste of the chancel. This was installed for the Thorolds in 1878–80, presumably with some reference to earlier work, by a local architect, Charles Kirk. It is a sumptuous work in the Decorated mode, including aumbry, piscina, sedilia and reredos. The last is a rich composition with a backdrop of deeply-cut foliage that would do credit to a 14th-century carver.

Thorolds came to Marston in the 14th century and are here still. In the south chapel lies the treasure of the church, the tomb of the Elizabethan Sir Anthony Thorold (d.1594). He is portrayed in alabaster with a sword at his side, as High Sheriff of Lincolnshire. He was every inch a landed gentleman, the sort who kept England in correct order through the turbulent reign of Good Queen Bess. Other Thorolds fill the church with their memorials. The tomb of William Thorold is remarkable for being a pure Gothic design despite the fact that he died in 1569. In the churchyard is reputedly the biggest and oldest laburnum tree in England.

MIDDLE RASEN
St Peter *
Norman doorway

The most extraordinary feature of this church is the brown ironstone of which it is constructed. The crumbling exterior appears to be fashioned of large cubes of solidified honey, held together by limestone and puddingstone insertions. One feels a strong punch would force an entry anywhere in the wall. The proper entry is to the south, through the most monumental Norman doorway in Lincolnshire, though not as the guide states 'in the country'. (Church guides out-do politicians for hyperbole.) Heavily restored, it is composed of bands of zigzag, crenellation and beakhead.

Much of the church is made from parts of another local church, St Paul's, demolished in the 19th century. How much is not clear, but certainly this includes a Decorated window in the chancel and a tomb with a fine effigy of a priest in flowing vestments under a canopy with its gable thrust forward. The chancel arch mouldings are Norman but the arch is pointed. The Norman font at the back of the north aisle came from a church in Grimsby in 1972.

On my last visit, I watched a woman in the congregation capture a butterfly that was distracting the vicar. She carefully scooped the insect in her hands, carried it out into the sun and freed it into a large bush of lavender in the churchyard, before tiptoeing back to the service. Such is English country worship. All God's creatures have their place. A butterfly's is in a lavender bush.

MOULTON
All Saints *
Adam and Eve font

The twin glories of the village of Moulton are its windmill and its church tower. The former, now without its sails, is or was reputedly the tallest in England. The latter is one of the most ornamented steeples in Lincolnshire. The western aspect is lush, with niches and panels rising to battlements and square pinnacles. These are topped by flying buttresses supporting a crocketed spire with lucarnes. Two of the niches still have their original figures.

The tower is of a different period and character from the earlier nave and chancel. The interior transition from the one to the other at the west end of the church is brutal. The nave arcades are Transitional with early stiff-leaf capitals and some heads hidden among the foliage. The rest of the interior, especially the aisle windows, is heavily restored. The screen, however, is a beautiful piece, with intricate tracery and deep coving, with a richness rare in Lincolnshire.

Moulton's principal treasure is its Adam and Eve font. The two figures stand against the stem, with biblical reliefs carved around the bowl. The sinuous lines could as well be Decorated Gothic or Baroque or even Art Nouveau. The guide suggests that the font was carved (in the second of these traditions) by William Tydd in 1719. Others claim it as a 19th-century copy of the Grinling Gibbons font in St James, Piccadilly (London), than which there is no higher praise.

NAVENBY
St Peter **
Easter Sepulchre carvings

The church sits behind the main street of this pretty Edge village, as if about to tip over into the valley of the River Brant. The exterior is unpromisingly Victorianised, although retaining a three-headed corbel under the south clerestory. The charm lies within, one of the marriages of medieval and Victorian architecture with which most English churches are cursed but some in Lincolnshire are blessed.

The church was restored once before, in the 1320s, when the builders decided to leave in place one pier of an Early Gothic arcade, apparently to keep its stone ledge as seating for the elderly. Behind it under the tower lies the baptistery, a 19th-century creation in green and mauve, entered under an arch displaying the arms of Queen Anne. The designer of this and the other Victorian work in the church was a Sleaford architect named Charles Kirk, who shared with the Fowlers of Louth responsibility for much careful 19th-century restoration in the county. The font cover was shown at the London Exhibition of 1862.

The chancel has a screen by Temple Moore, revealing an east window reconstructed by Kirk from a Decorated original. The window tracery is extraordinary. Curves are jagged and the central ogee is crushed under the apparent weight of three huge cusped circles. Such tracery is not so much curvilinear, more prickly. Beneath lies Navenby's treasure, a surviving group of founder's tomb, Easter Sepulchre, piscina and sedilia, all respected by Kirk even in their decay. The Sepulchre is in a class to rank with that of Heckington. The sleeping soldiers at the foot are in medieval costume, the women in the spandrels beautifully carved in flowing garments. Dated to the 1320s, the Navenby Sepulchre has been suggested as a test run, perhaps even a competition entry, for masons working on Lincoln Cathedral.

OLD LEAKE
St Mary *
Clerestory frieze

Old Leake is a big structure on the main road north of Boston, where fine Fenland churches come thick and fast. Sailors navigating the Wash must have been architectural experts, able to distinguish one tower from another through the mists of the marshes. Today the church rests in a churchyard denuded of character by having its tombstones all laid flat, a sad practice.

The principal interest of Old Leake is its clerestory, one of the finest in the county and, like much of the church, apparently an attempt to rival neighbouring Boston. The original church was Norman and also big, traces of it visible in the shafts at each end of the nave interior. But the structure was rebuilt at the end of the 13th century, yielding a flourish of early and late Decorated windows, followed by more alterations and additions in the Perpendicular period.

Outside we see a clerestory of two-light windows, with tracery alternating between Decorated and Perpendicular, the former with charming 'eyebrow' mouchettes. Between each window is an image niche, now empty. The whole composition forms an elaborate frieze above the nave. The east end has an openwork parapet with a bold wave of stonework. A south-east turret and spirelet are in delicate contrast to the splendidly robust tower.

Inside is a wide and sunny nave, the vagaries of the clerestory complemented by a strange arcade. Its rhythm is broken at the west end where the arches appear forcibly squeezed to accommodate the presence, and presumably the weight, of the tower. The restored chancel finds the openness of the nave altogether too naked. It resorts to opaque glass to shut out the world. Old Leake has what it claims are England's only poor-boxes hollowed from a single log.

SALTFLEETBY ALL SAINTS
*

Vernacular screens

The church stands well inland of sea defences that came too late to save its predecessor from inundation. A former church has gone the way of Dunwich in Suffolk, and disappeared into the North Sea. The present structure is no less redundant, and looks as if another serious tide would sink it for good. The greenstone tower is leaning outwards to the west, as if straining to escape inland. The roof looks ready to slide off its beams. Chunks of wall come away to the touch.

Yet Saltfleetby is an endearing church to find lost in mile-long fields, where agribusiness mingles with caravan sites. The interior is in the Churches Conservation Trust 'house style', of whitewashed walls, unceiled roofs and no fittings later than the 18th century. A single early 13th-century arcade of round piers divides the nave from the south aisle with later Y-tracery windows. The roofs are ancient, their timbers crudely tooled. In the south chapel is a rare stone reredos.

As with most Marsh churches, Saltfleetby's charm is in woodwork that is pleasing but unsophisticated. The screens appear to have been carved by amateurs trying to imitate professionals, with rough-cut crockets, cusps and arches. Some members retain traces of colour, though not as vivid as the later parclose screen between chancel and chapel.

The furnishings are random, gathered from other redundant churches in the area. There are two post-medieval pulpits. One is in its normal place, but another stands at the back of the nave. For some reason donated by Oriel College, Oxford, in the 19th century, it stares out like a dowager at the back of church, awaiting recognition by the parson.
[CCT]

SLEAFORD
St Denys ***
Decorated tracery, Comper loft, Morris glass

Sleaford church is superbly sited in the town centre, its tower and west front gazing directly over the market square. Nothing about it is dull. The church was never rebuilt, merely added to over the ages. Its connections with the bishops of Lincoln ensured patrons and chapels galore, an architectural diversity which even the Victorians were unable to erase.

How they tried. The prominent west front, which looks like an architectural textbook, is deceptive. The central doorway is reproduction and the circles and blind arcading above are not original but Victorian replacements of a Perpendicular window. The top of the tower is also a 19th-century rebuild. Only the Early Gothic belfry openings and lopsided buttresses are 13th century. Sleaford's stone spire is said to be one of the earliest of this type in England, its broaches rising directly from the buttresses (as at Long Sutton). Behind the tower, the church roofscape offers a forest of pinnacles, bell-turrets and niches.

These are outclassed by the superb window tracery. This is Lincolnshire at its most curvaceous, best displayed in the north transept north window. Words can barely do justice to this work. Six lights soar upwards until squeezed by the narrowing arch. The mullions react by splitting and twisting left and right as if frantic in the constricting space. Ogees break into quatrefoils, cusps and tiny holes, until the composition resolves itself into a pair of giant pincers containing four large quatrefoils. This is a work of infinite complexity, with variations repeated throughout the church.

The interior is big, scraped and needlessly gloomy. The north aisle is entirely Victorian, as is the strainer arch supporting the tower. Even the clerestory cannot resist darkened glass. That said, two windows by Holland of Warwick in the north and south walls of the chancel are good, as is a Morris window, with saints and giant oranges, which leaps out of the south aisle.

The church has an admirable rood screen and loft. The screen is original but the loft is by Comper in 1918, as inventive as ever. His wood is unusually dark and unpainted, as are the rood figures and angels. The loft blooms out over the crossing. Left and right of the chancel arch are two superb monuments to members of the local Carre family (d.1590 and 1618). The Carre name appears on other 17th-century memorials, culminating in the curly headed bust of Sir Edward Carre, who died in 1683 at the age of seventeen.

SNARFORD

St Lawrence **

St Paul tombs

This is lonely country of mean hedges and few woods. It is surely no place in which to be sad. We must seek out the church down a side road off the A46 north of Lincoln and now redundant. It huddles inside a clump of trees and looks externally of little interest. Yet it contains three spectacular monuments to the St Paul family.

The St Pauls – or Saintpaules or St Polls according to generation – were successful Tudor lawyers who prospered at court, acquired property on the Dissolution and were duly titled and landed. They appear to have been eager to turn Snarford into a miniature Bottesford (Leics). The most prominent monument, that to Sir Thomas (d.1582), stands directly behind the altar. It is in the form of a huge six-poster bed, with thick tapering uprights and the effigies lying asleep inside. The chest is encrusted with classical motifs and family heraldry. It deserves to rank with the Great Bed of Ware in the catalogue of English slumber. It might almost be a Hindu shrine. Delightful statues of kneeling children decorate the top.

Against the north wall are other St Paul memorials. That to Sir George (d.1613) has effigies which no longer lie medieval-style on their backs in prayer, but on their sides awake, heads propped on elbows. What strange shift in taste or piety dictated this evolution? The tablet memorial to Robert, Lord Rich (d.1619), shows a further innovation: relief medallions believed to be by Epiphanius Evesham. The man is portrayed not quite full-face while his wife is behind him in profile. Henry Thorold describes them as being 'like faces at a carriage window'. Snarford has a Perpendicular font with an unusually fine head of Christ.

[CCT]

SPALDING

St Mary and St Nicolas **

Forest of aisles, Victorian glass

Spalding was once an attractive town on either side of a straight river course with prominent houses lining either bank. It was regarded as 'Dutch' in character and was a centre of the English tulip industry. The planners have spoiled its

Georgian unity by permitting ugly modern development at every turn. Yet the church still rides proud over the rooftops, its tower detached from the nave presumably for structural security, for safety, with a pinnacled and crocketed spire as its climax.

The exterior of the church is near impossible to read. Walls, roofs and chapels seem to take off in all directions and none. The pattern inside is hardly more clear. There are piers everywhere, reminiscent of the pillared cisterns of subterranean Istanbul. The Early Gothic nave has double aisles on either side, the outer ones added in the 14th and 15th centuries. To add further vistas, the transepts themselves have eastern aisles, Early Gothic relics of chantries and shrines in what was a wealthy Fenland community. Above all this is a Lincolnshire hammerbeam roof, lit on special occasions by a superb 18th-century chandelier taking 36 candles.

The chancel looks most odd. It retains its Early Gothic proportions beyond a simple chancel arch and restored Perpendicular screen. A Victorian aisle (yes, another one) opens to its north side. Three Victorian lancets light the sanctuary, which has a painted ceiling of the 1950s by S. E. Dykes Bower. As often, the postwar restoration looks like a funfair, but cheers up a dark interior. The glass in the west window is of apostles by Clayton & Bell, so often purveyors of gloom to the worshippers of Lincolnshire. It is coherent and certainly spectacular. A jollier work is in the south aisle, where H. W. Harvey of York designed a colourful glass of Christ at Work and Play in 1966.

STAMFORD
All Saints **
Early Gothic arcading, Browne brasses

Stamford lies on the Great North Road at the fulcrum of the flow of wool and other produce from the north to the ports of East Anglia. It has the finest collection of medieval churches of any small town in England and makes impressive efforts to keep them open. All Saints sits in the heart of the town, facing the main road. Its designers took full advantage of their location.

The church is on ground which rises to the north. It therefore offers a south elevation with a lower tier of Early Gothic blind arcading, with Perpendicular aisle windows above, then a clerestory, and the tower rising behind. The blind arcading is beautifully executed, with alternating moulded and stiff-leaf capitals. The south porch is sumptuous under an ogival crocketed gable. The whole composition faces the main square in a bravura display of Gothic architecture, expressing Stamford's confidence in its mercantile wealth.

The interior has been much restored, but still offers evidence of its past glory.

The Early Gothic south arcade has the richest of stiff-leaf capitals. After the Wars of the Roses, the brothers William and John Browne, merchants of the Staple of Calais, richly endowed the church in which their parents were buried. They rebuilt the aisles, clerestory and steeple in a comfortable Perpendicular style, which seemed to lend itself well to Victorian restoration.

The Browne family brasses of the late 15th century are in the north aisle. They would not have been likenesses but were clearly commissioned to express the confident prosperity of wool. The men stand on woolpacks. The windows are filled with Victorian glass, of a lavishness that would surely have met with the Brownes' approval.

STAMFORD
St George *
Garter knights heraldic glass

St George's is tucked away in an unfrequented part of the town, in a square of the same name. The oblong west tower facing the square is a spatchcock of rebuilding, mostly of the 17th century but with a Decorated window. Much of the interior is Victorian but the atmosphere is modern. St George's gives an impression of busy activity.

The crucial date for the church is 1449, when the will of the first Garter King of Arms, Sir William de Bruges, left money for refashioning the chancel of his local church. He was an enthusiast for all things heraldic and also wished to commemorate the arms and mottoes of the 200 founder members of the Order of the Garter, whom he had served in his office. These were brought together in the great chancel window in 1732 and today comprise the most impressive collection of heraldic glass in the country. A guide relates the story of each knight.

The church is full of excellent 18th-century monuments from Stamford's last era of prosperity, especially to members of the Cust family. The best is a work by John Bacon of 1797 to Sir Richard Cust. A Grace is leaning on a broken column supporting a bust of the deceased against an obelisk background.

STAMFORD
St Martin **
Cecil tombs, Lambert grave

St Martin's lies on the hill that leads into the town from the south past the George Hotel. The scene was subject of Turner's famous depiction of a stage coach arriving at Stamford in a furious storm. The tower of the church dominates that picture, as if defying the weather to do its worst. So detached was St Martin's from the town centre that, while the town lay in the Diocese of Lincoln, St Martin's lay in the Diocese of Peterborough.

Though the tower does not shimmer white in the rain, as portrayed by Turner, and the hill is a horrible stream of traffic, the church juts superbly into the road, with ashlar-faced houses on all sides. This might be a Norfolk tower that had wandered up the Great North Road. The interior is that of a typical town church of the late 15th century, heraldic evidence giving a date of 1485–94. The nave is tall, narrow and spare, the arcades adorned with large heraldic angel stops. The chancel is similar.

The principal treasures are the Cecil tombs in the Burghley Chapel. The family mansion of that name lies on this side of town a mile distant. The collection is not large, but its masterpiece is the alabaster and marble six-poster monument to William Cecil (d.1598), most celebrated of Queen Elizabeth's courtiers and advisers. The columns are slender, supporting a canopy with twin barrel vaults, and the heraldry restrained, still a refined Elizabethan classicism with no trace of Jacobean vulgarity. The work is attributed to Cornelius Cure. Another work said to be by him is the more modest wall monument to William's father and mother, Richard and Jane Cecil, of the same date.

Best of the 18th-century memorials is to John Cecil, 5th Earl of Exeter (d.1700). This is a sarcophagus-and-obelisk composition by a Frenchman, Pierre Monnot. Here for the first time the architectural framework that had long dominated monumental art disappears, the obelisk becoming a backdrop. This form became the norm for tomb design throughout the 18th century into the 19th. The effigies are similarly transformed. The earl and his wife lie on a sarcophagus, semi-reclining and at ease, as if chatting with friends, while Victory and Art mourn their passing.

The glass in the east window was brought mostly from Tattershall in the 18th century. The fragments were set not in new glass of the same style but in a carpet of abstract geometric patterns, softly coloured and well controlled. We see Moses, Samson, David and Goliath as well as New Testament scenes, a most satisfying composition. In an extension of the churchyard to the east is the appropriately large tombstone to Daniel Lambert, who died in Stamford in 1809. He weighed almost 53 stone and remains unchallenged as the heaviest ever Englishman.

STAMFORD
St Mary ***
Arts and Crafts furnishing, 14th-century Madonna

The tower of St Mary's is a glorious Early Gothic work. It was built in the 13th century, before the days of Stamford's greatest wealth, and must have soared over the thatched hovels round it, the painted saints in their niches keeping watch over the town. St Mary's turns the angle from St Mark's Hill into Cheyne Lane with a truly massive Early Gothic tower, dressed with tier upon tier of blind and open arcading. This culminates in tall lancet bell-openings. The broach spire is heavy but stylish, with lucarnes clustered round the top. It may look comfortable above streets of limestone houses but it must have towered over those of wattle and daub.

The interior is that of a confined but lofty town church. The tower vault and nave arcades are Perpendicular. So is the exquisite ceiling of the north chapel, like a wagon roof over which has been stretched a richly embossed quilt. Between the chapel and the chancel is the tomb of Sir David Phillips (d.1506), bashed but with its essentials intact. These include a chest with delicate ogee niches framing saints and apostles, and a canopy with a superbly undercut stone frieze. Sir David was a Welshman who fought with Henry VII at Bosworth. The Welsh dragon appears in the heraldry.

In 1890 St Mary's saw a further restoration, this time at the hands of J. D. Sedding and his Arts and Crafts colleagues, at the invitation of the Anglo-Catholic vicar, John Mildmay, to whose tradition the church continues its allegiance. Sedding brought to what must have then been a bare shell of a medieval building a vivid set of High Church furnishings. They included new Perpendicular screens to the chancel and north chapel, lovely compositions of lancet lights, their heads filled with tracery. Sedding also designed a new chancel ceiling, altar front and the choir stalls with angel medallions. These stalls are similar to those supplied by Sedding to Chelsea's Holy Trinity, Sloane Street (London).

The chancel east window is a spectacular work by Wailes of 1860. The north chapel window by Christopher Whall is no less spectacular. Also in the north chapel are ogee tomb recesses and, recovered from one of them, a superb 14th-century Madonna. She has flowing drapery and was featured in the Age of Chivalry Exhibition at the Royal Academy in 1987.

STOKE ROCHFORD
St Mary and St Andrew **
Double-bed tomb

The church sits in a secluded valley just off the A1 south of Grantham, where the Great North Road diverges from Ermine Street. These lanes must have seen busy times, especially as the church served both the Turnor family's Rochford Hall (now a conference centre) and the Cholmeley family's Easton estate across the main road. A straggle of pretty cottages lies below the churchyard to the north. In one of them the keyholder at first refused to answer the door, fearing I was a canvasser 'from the politics' during an election.

The church is an eccentric building of all periods, starting with the Norman nave. The aisles lead without visual interruption into wide chantry chapels, rendering the interior cheerful and bright. The roofs are ceiled, that in the chancel with modern stencilled patterns at its corners. The chancel rises up the hill slope. To its north is a chapel containing a most extraordinary monument set into the floor and now covered in green mould. A man said to be Sir John Neville (d.1316) lies with his wife under a blanket, with both their busts and their feet left exposed.

The church, and therefore the monuments, were shared between the Turnors and the Cholmeleys. The south chapel is dominated by an ostentatious monument to Henry Cholmeley (1641). He and his wife are kneeling in prayer, attended by their children and heraldic achievements. The sanctuary reredos is by Mrs G. F. Watts, wife of the Victorian painter and a considerable artist in her own right. There is also a delightful painted font cover of 1937 by Jesse Bayes depicting the childhood of Christ. The seating is schoolroom modern, particularly ludicrous with box pews in the aisles looming up like cattle pens.

STOW
St Mary ****
Saxon and Norman remains, Pearson restoration

That this is a big church is already evident on the road from Lincoln. The outline is of a Saxon minster, despite the pinnacles added to the crossing tower. The Normans added a new nave and chancel, the latter in the grandest style. Since then, dereliction and restoration have given us a Victorian reinstatement of what the Norman masons would have rebuilt had they been available in the 19th century. Stow conveys the proportions and aura of a minster of the Saxon–Norman era as conceived by a later generation.

The architect was Pearson in 1865, but Stow has not been converted, like many churches of this period, into a whitewashed museum of church archaeology. The exterior has the familiar lofty walls and steep-pitched roof (once thatched) of a Saxon building, the nave and chancel reinforced by wall buttresses on all sides. Set into the south transept wall is a charming lesson in window history: one window round-headed (Saxon), one circular (Norman) and one Decorated Gothic. The south doorway has zigzag ornament and shows how hard must have been the decisions taken by the restorers. What to leave decayed but evocative, what to replace as too far gone?

The interior is not so much dominated as overawed by the mighty Saxon arches of the crossing. These would have supported an earlier tower and are remarkable both for their size and for the spacious crossing they enclose. The effect is marred only by later Gothic arches erected to support the 15th-century tower. These have worked their way into the old structure like four sturdy youths sent to help their elders bear the burden. In the west wall of the north transept is a complete Saxon arch with long-and-short work. Opposite is a carving of medieval musicians.

The chancel is predominantly Pearson's work and as such is controversial. He apparently found a semi-ruined structure with a Gothic east window and a wooden roof. But he also discovered traces of Norman work in the walls and under the floor, including parts of an original stone vault. From these he excavated fragments and then extrapolated what he assumed to be the form of the previous Norman building.

Scholars, including Pevsner, have given Stow a reasonably clean bill of architectural authenticity. The chancel arcading, window surrounds and vault ribs are carved with zigzag and crenellation. The vault itself was a triumph of stone engineering, covering a remarkably wide chamber with little external buttressing. My only question is why, having gone so far, Pearson did not go on to repaint the walls with Norman murals. Stow has a magnificent Early Gothic font, its bowl resting on colonnettes, with pagan emblems on its eight faces. One of these is a Green Man.

STRAGGLETHORPE
St Michael *
Saxon farmyard chapel

This is the sort of church of which there must have been thousands in pre-Conquest England. It sits among the cottages of the small village and is reached through the yard of Brant House Farm. The structure is essentially Saxon–Norman, with a 'modern' aisle added in the 12th century. Traces of Saxon-style stonework can be seen in the north-west corner and, inside, in a blocked triangular-headed doorway. For whatever reason, later generations had neither the money nor the inclination to rebuild the church, at least until after the Reformation. They merely inserted an occasional window when the eyesight of the priest needed one.

The only later insertion is box pews of the 18th century. There is a double-decker pulpit and some bench-ends. These somehow look more in keeping with the medieval church than the earlier tablet memorial to Richard Earle (d.1697) in black and white marble. It is in the form of two busts with drapes revealing a pious poem of the 'Stay, Reader, and observe Death's partial doom' variety. A charming place.

SWATON
St Michael **
Gallery of Gothic tracery

What did Swaton do to deserve this aristocrat of a parish church? Its tall pinnacles rise from afar across a landscape filled with such towers. Swaton is cruciform, with a 13th-century chancel and 14th-century nave of unusual scale and richness. The interior is spare of detail but of magnificent proportions. The nave is twice the length of the chancel and the width of the nave is exactly half its length. This is a church of volumes, height, light and shade.

The Reticulated window tracery towers over the nave in exotic buds on slender stems, variously of two, three and four lights and free of stained glass. The west end contains some of the most impressive windows in Lincolnshire, ranking with those of Sleaford and Grantham. The arcades are high and noble, rising from a forest of 15th-century and Victorian benches with carved poppy-heads. Ochre plaster covers the walls. A south aisle wall painting appears to be a wheel of life, including a child in a basket and a ladder. The Decorated font is beautifully adorned with diapering and with ballflower on its stem.

The chancel is earlier and feels it. The windows here are lancets to the north and south and Geometrical to the east. There is a calm poise to this early Decorated style, contrasting with the restless flamboyance of the later west end. The glass is mostly clear and reveals the sky and trees outside.

TATTERSHALL
Holy Trinity ***
Perpendicular giant matching adjacent castle

Tattershall is a church to admire rather than love. It rises next to the famous castle across the Fens near the River Witham. The castle is of brick and was designed for Ralph Cromwell, Treasurer of England, in the 1440s. Brick was then still an unusual building material, a full half-century before Layer Marney (Essex). The church supplementing Cromwell's chantry college was not begun until a decade after his death in 1456.

The church is huge, stone-built and set across the moat from the castle. It was constructed, in 'production-line Perpendicular', in the 1460s. The result is spectacular but bare. The exterior is of uniform outline, with Panel-traceried windows but no decorative cusping. The transepts are huge, almost churches in themselves, and have clerestories which continue from the nave. The tower is short, but well proportioned, plainly that of a collegiate rather than a parochial foundation.

The north door entrance is through a tiny wicket, so diminutive as to be like something from *Alice in Wonderland*. This at least has great dramatic effect. I watched one visitor after another bend through the door, straighten, and gasp at the scale of the interior. It is like a massive conservatory, and would indeed make a splendid one. There are few shadows and fewer surprises at Tattershall. It is not adorned with carved bosses or corbel heads, just a reserve squadron of angels deputed to scare the bats from the roofs. The walls have none of the memorials of a town church. Space and volume are all. Perpendicular has here become the 'Modern Movement' of the Middle Ages, rejecting the idiosyncrasies of earlier Gothic and deferring only to the wonder of engineering.

The stone pulpitum dividing the parochial nave from the collegiate chancel is a precious survival. It has two niches for altars on the west side, and a projection for a lectern on the east. The chancel offers one mild excitement. In its huge east window is gathered the church's remaining 15th-century glass, the rest having been taken to St Martin, Stamford. At the time of its completion every window was apparently full of this glass. The effect must have been sensational. Even today, feathered angels jostle with kings, saints and heraldry. Everywhere is the Treasurer's emblem, the purse. The Treasurer himself, Lord Cromwell, is recalled in a damaged brass in the north transept.

THEDDLETHORPE ALL SAINTS
*

Forlorn setting, ancient screens

Self-styled 'cathedral of the Marsh', Theddlethorpe is for lovers of decayed redundancy. The church stands inland from the coast road in a churchyard so overgrown as to constitute a nature reserve. The walls of the church seem about to join the gravestones in the enveloping vegetation. The building material is soft and spongy greenstone, patched with brick and concrete in so many places that the green looks more organic than structural. The east wall of the south aisle is composed of every material imaginable.

All Saints is none the less a dignified early Perpendicular church of c.1380. The interior stonework round the clerestory tells the same story as the exterior, a patchwork surface like a chequerboard. The nave is tall, the white plaster ancient. Fragments of a stone reredos survive in the south aisle. The screen to the chancel has the same slender tracery as at neighbouring Saltfleetby.

More remarkable are the two screens to the side chapels. Dated 1535, they have classical rather than Gothic motifs, including faces in profile along the frieze. Whenever I encounter these oddities I long to know who created them, on whose commission and with what pattern-book. Georgian memorials adorn the chancel, including one with two busts on a black sarcophagus, engagingly out of place in this setting. On my visit there seemed as many birds inside the church as outside.

[CCT]

WALESBY
All Saints **
Hilltop setting, Ramblers window

The old church at Walesby sits high on the Wolds, apparently overlooking the entire valley of the Trent. The village once lay next to the church. Today the old houses have vanished and the church must be approached on foot up a sloping meadow. Its warm ironstone rises above the grass like a slice of honey pudding. Guarding the approach is a flare beacon. The Viking Way along the Wolds passes this spot and the church has become a sanctuary with a corner dedicated to ramblers.

The windows give the church a date of about 1300, with Y-tracery, some of it Intersecting. The interior, now redundant but well restored, is much earlier and a charming surprise. The north and south arcades are Transitional. The north arcade has round arches, one scallop capital but already some stiff-leaf. The south arcade has mostly octagonal piers and capitals, but one capital has stiff-leaf and primitive carved heads. The whole ensemble was later given a small clerestory.

The restorers in the 1930s added a white-painted rood screen and jolly loft. Next to it stands a Jacobean-style pulpit, brought from redundant Kirkstead and now not needed here either. The only solecism is in the south aisle, an insipid Ramblers Association window of 1953. Surely the walkers in these parts would have preferred to worship before a view of the hills outside.

WELL
St Margaret **
Georgian church set in parkland

The village is tucked into the side of the Wolds facing the North Sea. Its main street leads directly into the drive of the big house, a plain Georgian mansion possibly by Thomas Archer or even James Gibbs. The church, built by the Bateman family in 1733, lies on the far hill, on an axis with the west front of the house and above a chain of lakes. It has a portico with Tuscan columns, strong pediment and deep eaves, like Langton-by-Spilsby and in the manner of St Paul, Covent Garden (London). The style is better suited to country than to town and forms a picturesque scene. The church can be approached only on foot.

The interior is satisfyingly Georgian, with a stately Venetian window above the altar, here positioned at the west end. As at Langton, the pews face each other across the aisle and are decorated with fluted pilasters. A huge triple-decker pulpit is built so high that an overactive preacher risks falling to his death from its eminence. Above is a plasterwork ceiling of angels, swags and acanthus, in white on a colour best described as cantaloup. The hatchments on the gallery are mostly of Batemans.

Well is still an active church, despite its isolation. Inter-denominational services are held out on the hillside in summer. Behind the church are traces of the Burgh-le-Marsh trackway, a pre-Roman route that once lay along the side of the Wolds.

WESTON
St Mary *
Early Gothic arcades, foliated font

Weston is a curiosity. From the outside, a long steep roof crowns an apparently Norman clerestory from which prominent corbel heads peer down at us. But this is essentially an Early Gothic church and of rare completeness. The porch greets visitors with an unusually narrow Early Gothic arch and contains blind arcading. The interior of the church has exquisite arcades, reminiscent of work at Lincoln Cathedral. Piers of four detached shafts and capitals display an abundance of Lincolnshire stiff-leaf. The east end has blind arcading and a shafted triple lancet window. So perfect an Early Gothic interior is rare. Weston is a parochial Kirkstead.

Early Gothic tends anyway to be dark, but that will not stop a Victorian from trying to make it even darker. The temptation was not resisted at Weston, though at least the glass is Clayton & Bell, relieved by jolly 1950s glass in the lancet behind the vicar's stall. The Victorians also contributed a pleasant pulpit with openwork panels, rather Muslim in appearance.

The font is a wonderfully vigorous Early Gothic piece. Huge flowers decorate each panel of the bowl. The most lively feature of the church is the kneelers; they offer a carpet of colour by being placed on the pew shelves.

WHAPLODE
St Mary **
Transitional capitals, Irby monument

Whaplode is the gem of the Lincolnshire group that extends from the Walpoles in Norfolk towards Spalding. An exhibition inside the church declares proudly that this was a 12th-century boom town, belonging to the Benedictines of neigh-bouring Crowland Abbey. The monks persistently neglected their chancel and left the townspeople to build and maintain the nave, a distinction evident in the building today. We are the beneficiaries of that neglect. Though altered in the 17th and 18th centuries, Whaplode was hardly touched by the Victorians.

The church is approached down a well-pollarded lime avenue, past an obelisk to a Georgian eccentric. This holds a phial of seeds which were intended to 'vegetate' should the tomb decay and the obelisk return to nature, a fate that has yet to occur. The tower is almost detached from the church and is massive, Early Gothic in style but with Norman zigzag ornament in the lower stage. Like many Fenland towers, it was probably sited to minimise the risk of progressive collapse should the foundations prove inadequate.

The interior is built round a Norman core. The eastern nave capitals are scalloped, the later western ones have stiff-leaf, the piers also evolving over time from cylindrical to quatrefoil. The resulting stylistic rhythm is charming. Whaplode suffered many vicissitudes, including battles between the parishioners and the monks over tithes. The chancel fell into decay and by the 17th century much of the tracery and the entire north transept needed replacement.

The transept duly became the village school, traces of an old fireplace surviving under the north window. (Would that schools continued to enliven under-used churches in this way.) The chancel was cheaply rebuilt in the early 19th century. Despite these changes, Victorian records indicate that the interior had to be 'stoved' with sulphur (i.e., smoked) to kill some 500 bats. Not until after 1900 was serious restoration begun, including most unusual Art Nouveau tracery in the north transept window. This is made of oak.

Whaplode's most prominent feature is the Irby monument in the south aisle. The Irbys were local magnates and hereditary MPs for Boston. Sir Anthony (d.1610) was a Puritan who left a spectacular tomb for himself under a ten-columned canopy. The five weepers were his sons, all of whom fought for Cromwell against the king. The colouring is brilliant. If we can bring ourselves to colour Jacobean monuments in this way, why are we so reluctant to do the same to Gothic ones? At the back of the north aisle is a 1907 Pre-Raphaelite painting, the artist using local schoolchildren as models.

London

The City of London

The churches of the City of London stand comparison with those of any European city other than Rome. This is due to London's continuous status as a commercial capital and to the accident of the Great Fire of 1666. Some medieval relics survive, notably at St Bartholomew's and the Temple, but central London churches are pre-eminently those initiated by two events. The first was the Great Fire of 1666 and the rebuilding of three-quarters of the old City within the walls. The second was a desire on the part of Queen Anne's new Tory government of 1710 to provide churches for the booming suburbs, as well as to initiate the hoped-for return to court and country of High Church principles. In 1711 an Act was passing allocating a new coal tax to 'the Building of Fifty New Churches' in London and its suburbs. A separate sum of money, known as Queen Anne's Bounty, was devoted to enhancing clergy stipends. Only twelve churches were completed, but they were among the finest works of architecture of their age. One of them, Nicholas Hawksmoor's St Mary Woolnoth, comes within the scope of this chapter, others in the section that follows.

The City's churches were thus transformed in the short period of 1670–1720. While church-building in the provinces was moribund, London of necessity saw a flowering of ecclesiastical architecture. The new buildings were classical in style and their architects were of extraordinary talent: notably Sir Christopher Wren, with Hawksmoor and Robert Hooke as assistants. They gave to the City places of worship that needed little expansion in the 19th century, even had land been available for the purpose. Most were damaged in the Blitz but have been restored, with varying degrees of success, even when their parishes vanished. A recent campaign has been launched to ensure their regular opening.

I have listed the churches by the names by which they are most familiarly known, followed by their addresses.

All Hallows by the
  Tower **
St Bartholomew-the-
  Great ***
St Bride Fleet Street **
St Helen Bishopsgate
  ***

St Katharine Cree **
St Magnus-the-Martyr
  ***
St Margaret Lothbury
  **
St Martin within
  Ludgate ***

St Mary Abchurch ***
St Mary Aldermary **
St Mary-at-Hill *
St Mary Woolnoth ****
St Stephen Walbrook
  ****
Temple Church ***

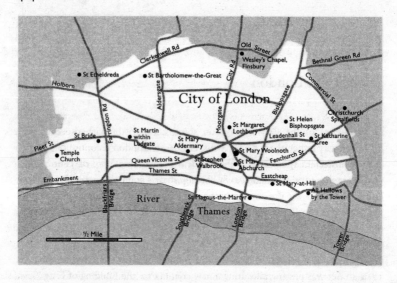

ALL HALLOWS BY THE TOWER (All Hallows, Barking)
Great Tower Street, EC3 **
Gibbons font, Roman pavement

The church sits high on Tower Hill and is blighted on one side by traffic and on the other by one of the City's most insensitive modern buildings. A civilised age will demolish this neighbourhood and start again, opening up the church on its slope down to the river.

The medieval church survived the Great Fire but not the Blitz. After the war, most Continental cities reinstated their ruined churches. Britain rarely did so. Today's All Hallows is the creation of the architect, Lord Mottistone (of Seely & Paget), under the aegis of the formidable vicar from 1922 to 1963, Tubby Clayton. It was at this church that Clayton founded the Toc H movement, dedicated to sustaining the wartime spirit of comradeship and community through into peacetime.

At first sight, Mottistone's exterior is dull 1950s reproduction Gothic, and the nave is little better. The church guidebook discreetly omits any view of it. The arcades rise to curious classical motifs above pews that are equally weak. Mercifully the generous windows admit plenty of light and the plan is spacious. That said, the church is a treasure house of furnishings and has outstanding subterranean archaeology. The furnishings include references to the church's links with City commerce. The church was that of the Port of London, and the south aisle contains a mariners' chapel and models of old ships. In the nave are fine Georgian sword rests of Sussex iron with rococo patterns. These patterns are repeated on the restored lectern.

On the north wall is an Elizabethan memorial to an Italian trader, Hieronimus Benalius (c.1584), surmounted by a fine cartouche. An adjacent canopied altar tomb to John Croke (d.1477) received more deferential treatment than was granted to the rest of the church. Blasted to pieces in the war, it was carefully reassembled from 150 fragments. In the north aisle hangs a magnificent Flemish altarpiece of c.1500. It was originally a triptych but the central panel of the Adoration is now missing. London churches are sadly short of such art. This one is well protected. The pulpit is a splendidly carved work of the 17th century, held aloft on a wine-glass stem. It was brought here from the ruined St Swithin, Cannon Street.

In a small baptistery to the south-west of the nave is All Hallows' treasure, a glorious font cover by Grinling Gibbons, with fruit, flowers and vegetables piled into a confection on which rests a dove. Ecstatic cherubs seem ready to climb up to reach it. All Hallows also has a set of fine pre-Reformation brasses. The best is a Flemish brass in the sanctuary, commemorating Andrew Evyngar and his wife (d.1533), an elaborate work with an intricate architectural canopy. In the nave is an effigy of Clayton, laid out medieval style.

The 14th-century undercroft has been converted into a sequence of three chapels and museum spaces illustrating the history of Christianity since Saxon times on the site. At the east end is the old Vicar's Chapel, with an altar made of stones from a crusader castle in Palestine. The walls contain openings to receive the ashes of the dead, stacked in little boxes. Access is over part of a Roman tessellated pavement, a precious survival and more evocative than such relics removed to a museum.

ST BARTHOLOMEW THE GREAT
Cloth Fair, Smithfield, EC1 ***
Norman choir, Rahere tomb

London has few remains of the religious foundations that in the Middle Ages crowded the City walls. The Charterhouse off Smithfield is closed to the public, but St Bartholomew the Great is accessible. Here is one of the last places where a fragment of the City's pre-Victorian townscape can be savoured. The monastery and the adjacent hospital were founded in 1123 by Rahere, a courtier of Henry I, in thanks for surviving malaria on a visit to Rome. Though the church has lost its monastery, is heavily restored and is crowded by modern office blocks, at its heart are the most impressive Norman remains in inner London after the Tower of London. Henry VIII's wreckers demolished the nave and outer buildings, but left the choir as a parish church.

St Bartholomew's suffered many fates. The Lady Chapel behind the choir became a Tudor house, then a printing works. The north gallery became a Nonconformist school, the north transept a smithy and the cloister became stables. Not until the late 19th century was restoration begun, including the building of new transepts and a new apsidal sanctuary in the Norman style by Sir Aston Webb. What exists today is a congeries of London church history, with only the choir and aisles in their original Norman state.

The exterior is forbidding, with Victorian flint lowering over the flint houses of Cloth Fair. A heavy 17th-century tower with jolly seaside lantern overlooks the vanished nave and the remains of the cloister, now a small garden. The entrance to the precinct from Smithfield is under a Tudor gatehouse and through one of the original west doorways of the lost nave. A path leads along the former south aisle beside the nave, now occupied by a graveyard, raised high by the pressure of the numbers buried underground.

The interior of St Bartholomew's is among London's most atmospheric. Not here the clean lines or cleared spaces of a Perpendicular or Georgian preaching house. This is a church of accretions and secret places, of incense, sudden heights and unexpected shafts of light. The plan is at first baffling since the entrance is under the 17th-century tower and leads into the rebuilt south transept, with the Norman arches of the former crossing opening to the left, and beyond the rebuilt north transept. It is all most confusing.

The plan soon becomes more clear. The core of St Bartholomew's is a four-bay Norman choir, with a bold arcade rising to a gallery and a later clerestory. The gallery to the north is still bricked up for the old schoolroom. To the south, one bay has a delightful oriel window, installed in the 16th century for Prior Bolton, with his arms in the panel beneath. Opposite on the ground floor is the tomb of the founder Rahere (d.1144), erected for pilgrims to admire in 1405. The effigy, vividly painted, is unusual in that the tiny bedesmen are placed not at his feet 'praying for his soles' as some have suggested, but by his legs reading to him. The tomb is much restored. I cannot see why parts have been recoloured and the rest left white.

The seating is collegiate. This enables the congregation to appreciate both the high altar to the east and the spendid composition of choir, stalls and organ to the west. Behind the ambulatory is Aston Webb's reinstated Lady Chapel. This is a serene space, a retreat from the hubbub of the City, its blank east end filled most effectively by stone niches. The church has an excellent collection of Tudor and Jacobean monuments. My favourite is that of Elizabeth Freshwater (d.1617) in the south transept. She kneels under an small arch, surrounded by voluptuous classical features that would be gross on a larger scale but here look rather jolly.

ST BRIDE FLEET STREET
Bride Lane, EC4 **
Wedding-cake spire

The church lies in a tranquil court, a few paces off Fleet Street. It remains the parish church of the newspaper industry even after the journalists have mostly departed the neighbourhood. It is approached from all sides down alleys and tunnels.

The steeple is Wren's tallest, still visible from afar, and from the west a brilliant foil to the dome of St Paul's. The spire with its five octagonal stages has been described variously as a wedding cake, a telescope and a 'madrigal in stone'. The tower beneath has an unusually well-developed lower stage, with pedimented west doorway, followed by a pedimented then a round window. Above this is a sophisticated bell-stage with corner columns and pilasters and a pinnacled parapet above. Only then does the famous spire take over. The composition, of 1671–8, is one of Wren's best-known creations, a shrine floating across a sea of roofs. I used to lift my gaze from many a tedious Fleet Street meeting and see St Bride's pinning London to the realm of sanity.

St Bride's was gutted in the war and rebuilt by the ubiquitous restorer of City churches, Godfrey Allen, in 1957. As so often, Allen decided not to reinstate Wren's design but to go for 20th-century 'neo-Wren'. His new St Bride's is a success, being all of a piece and retaining Wren's proportions. The bold arches of the arcades rise on coupled Doric columns to support a barrel vault pierced with clerestory windows.

The lightness of the columns is masked by Allen's exceptionally assertive furnishings. He dispensed with the old galleries and instead installed collegiate stalls, just two rows deep and backed by high classical screens. These isolate the aisles from the nave and sanctuary, leaving some guests at Fleet Street memorial services feeling very much below the salt. The style of the stalls is continued in an even bolder reredos, modelled on Wren's Chapel Royal at Hampton Court. A huge pedimented centrepiece is flanked by screens, with an extraordinary *trompe l'oeil* window in the east wall behind. Its sensationalism is worthy of old Fleet Street.

In the crypt are the remains of earlier foundations dating back to Saxon times. The area has been comprehensively excavated and is now used for an exhibition of London west of the Fleet.

ST HELEN BISHOPSGATE
EC3 ***
Twentieth-century restoration, City tombs

First the controversy, of a ferocity visited on few recent church restorations. Two IRA bombs, in 1992 and 1993, severely damaged this church and all but wiped out its sister, St Ethelburga's, to the north. The restoration was by the neo-classical architect, Quinlan Terry. He produced an interior suited to the new evangelical preaching style of the then incumbent. This involved replacing the medieval and Victorian jumble of floor levels, seating and screens with a single uniform stone floor throughout, higher than before and with modern chairs set in a semicircle facing the pulpit. This turned the old church into what is visually a single white chamber, its monuments dotted about as in a museum. The rearrangement evoked intense protest from conservationists, but churches do not have to conform to historic buildings laws. St Helen's is a vivid assertion of Anglican independence.

The church had escaped the Great Fire and most of the Blitz, its exterior the most lovably antique in the City. Two embattled 15th-century bays with large windows face west, crowned with a charming bell-tower, while to the south is a bleak car park towards modern Leadenhall Street. The side walls contain stone dating back to the 13th century, although the collection of windows, some lancets, some Decorated, some Perpendicular, are not all reliably original. The entrance courtyard has a collegiate atmosphere, dominated by a monumental doorway dated 1633. Its exaggerated and distorted classical forms are emphatically Mannerist.

The interior is now dominated by Terry's rearrangement. To him are due the white walls and the neo-Georgian west gallery. His raised flooring leaves many of the monuments looking as if a tide of whitewash has filled the church and covered their bases. No less drastic, the components of what was a warren of chancel, aisles and chapels are now liturgically eccentric. The congregation in the chancel must sit with its back to the altar.

St Helen's was originally two churches in one. The north aisle, wider than the nave, was the church of a pre-Reformation nunnery, the conventual buildings then extending to the north. The arcade that now runs down the centre of the church would then have had a screen to divide the monastic and parochial sections. After the Reformation the two parts were united and St Helen's collection of tombs, some from the demolished St Martin Outwich (also in Bishopsgate), were redistributed round the walls.

These tombs are the best in the City: indeed the church was dubbed the City's Westminster Abbey. The most prominent are in the nunnery aisle. On the north wall is the memorial to Martin Bond (d.1643). He commanded the City's

Trained Bands, or territorial army, at Tilbury at the time of the Armada and is seen in his tent. In the centre of the aisle is the famous tomb chest of Sir Thomas Gresham (d.1579), founder of the Royal Exchange, with fluted panels and large cartouches. In Pevsner's words 'it speaks eloquently of the informed personal taste of a well-travelled merchant prince'. Next to it is a contemporary tomb of Sir William Pickering (d.1574), more conventional in style with a bold effigy and elaborate superstructure of twin coffered arches.

Between the chancel and the south transept is a conventional alabaster tomb of Sir John Crosby (d.1476), whose neighbouring house was scandalously demolished in 1908 and re-erected in Chelsea, where it stands today buried in later buildings. Even lovelier is the tomb of John de Oteswich and his wife in the south transept. This is a late 14th-century work of alabaster, with highly refined effigies, the faces serene, the hands delicate in prayer, the robes folded and the buttoned sleeves meticulously carved.

ST KATHARINE CREE
Leadenhall Street, EC3 **
Eccentric transitional nave

This is the City's most curious church. It was rebuilt in 1630 after the partial collapse of a dissolved priory church, and is therefore a rare English ecclesiastical work of the early 17th century. It luckily stood beyond the eastern limit of the Great Fire. The building was consecrated in 1631 by Archbishop Laud, an important event in the Laudian Counter-Reformation. It contains a Laud Chapel and is patronised by the Society of King Charles the Martyr. The design reflects the transition from Gothic to classical in ecclesiastical architecture, perhaps better described as an interlude when the two styles were freely combined.

As with most buildings of this period, the name of Inigo Jones has been associated with St Katharine's, or more plausibly one of his assistants, Edmund Kinsman. The few English churches built immediately before the Civil War tend to refer for inspiration to the example of 'St Katharine Cree in London'. Even the Cromwellian frontier church at Berwick-upon-Tweed (Northumb), built two decades later, is virtually a copy.

The tower retains fragments of the pre-Reformation structure. It pokes its cupola cheekily out over modern Leadenhall Street and the surrounding office blocks. The former floor lay some 5 ft below that of the present church, as can be seen from a surviving pier inside the door. The oddness of the interior is immediately apparent. The plan is conventional, with six-bay arcades and aisles. But the arcades are classical, with Corinthian columns and round coffered arches. Above is a Gothic clerestory, and both nave and aisles have shallow plaster rib vaults. The nave vault springs from classical pilasters but the windows have Gothic tracery. As if to emphasise the oddity, these decorative features are picked out in pale blue on a cream background. The central bosses are heavy with City company emblems and form an excellent collection.

The chancel east wall is filled with a large wheel window inside a square frame, its glass depicting the life of St Katharine. This is said to be original, evidence of the vividness bordering on garishness of early 17th-century church decor. The Victorian glass beneath is comparatively subdued. In the Laud Chapel is a survival of the earlier church, the magnificent tomb of the Elizabethan diplomat, Sir Nicholas Throckmorton (d.1570).

ST MAGNUS-THE-MARTYR
Lower Thames Street, EC3 ***
Wren's Ionian splendour

This magnificent church is forever associated with T. S. Eliot's nostalgic evocation of old Billingsgate Market next door, 'Where fishermen lounge at noon; where the walls / Of Magnus Martyr hold / Inexplicable splendour of Ionian white and gold'. The fishermen have gone east, a bleak new bridge looms overhead and the exterior of St Magnus is just another riverside church horribly besieged by the Thames Street racetrack.

Wren's church of the 1670s has had innumerable alterations. In the late 18th century the north façade to the road was given porthole windows and the aisles were shortened by two bays to allow a footpath over old London Bridge to pass through the base of the tower. The archway constructed for the purpose is a fragment of the old bridge approach.

Once inside we can forget the location and allow one of Wren's most majestic compositions to speak for itself, though here again much has altered. A 1980s' fire has led to the restoration of enough 'white and gold' to give the aisled church the richness of a St Petersburg palace. The large south windows are sufficiently bright to have Wren's fluted Ionic columns and gilded tunnel-vault shimmering with light. This, together with the extensive Anglo-Catholic furnishings, makes St Magnus one of the most sumptuous of City churches.

The furnishings include a lofty two-tier wooden reredos with inset texts and paintings, surmounted by angels and a rood group. The upper tier is mostly by Martin Travers in 1924. The iron altar rails are original, as is the huge tester lowering over a diminutive pulpit which was once a three-decker. The west gallery forms, with the organ, a magnificent composition filling the west wall. It is attended by a forest of wardens' staves by the organ case. The gallery is reached from the lobby, which, even by City standards, is luxurious. It has a fine doorcase and twin staircases curving upwards on either side. In the south aisle is a statue by Travers of St Magnus with his axe, for some reason attended by potted palms.

ST MARGARET LOTHBURY
EC2 **
Wren church with imported screens

The church is tucked away behind the Bank of England and was designed by Wren in 1686. The crush of medieval churches in this district is indicated by the fact that St Margaret's 'parish' includes the old St Martin Pomeroy, St Mary Colechurch, St Christopher-le-Stocks, St Bartholomew-by-the-Exchange, St Mildred Poultry, St Olave Jewry and St Stephen Coleman. All have vanished. Yet St Margaret's still has existing churches a hundred yards in almost every direction. Continuing pleas for money for its restoration seem pathetic, given its position, surrounded by the greatest concentration of cash in Europe.

The street front includes both the south wall of the aisle and the plain tower, with a grand classical portal attributed to Robert Hooke. Inside, the plan is of a nave and single aisle, divided by two Corinthian columns. Two spectacular screens, one to the chancel and another to the aisle, give the church its principal appeal. Both are from other churches. The main screen was designed by Wren for All Hallows the Great, once in Upper Thames Street but demolished in 1894. It is among the most splendid in the City or anywhere, stretching the breadth of the church and composed of the most ornate openwork carpentry. A massive eagle with outstretched wings is suspended from the central broken pediment, which is crowned by the coat of arms of William and Mary, a superb architectural creation. The tall uprights are formed of twisted colonnettes, delicately intertwined.

The pulpit is excellent, crowned by a giant tester also from All Hallows the Great. The reredos is no less sumptuous. Indeed St Margaret's is full of the finest woodwork from churches less lucky to survive the centuries. The south aisle screen is made partly from altar rails from St Olave Jewry and is partly 19th century. The Pre-Raphaelite altarpiece in the south aisle is by Sister Catherine Weeks and dated 1908.

ST MARTIN WITHIN LUDGATE
Ludgate Hill, EC4 ***
Surviving 17th-century fittings

The black spire is forever memorable in the foreground of the view of St Paul's up Ludgate Hill. It has been given greater prominence by the removal of the adjacent railway bridge. The Portland stone south front rises sheer from the pavement, supporting the south tower with exaggerated volutes. The spire thus punctuates the soft bend of the western approach to the cathedral. How many millions pass St Martin's door without realising what lies inside?

The church is another example of Wren's genius at conjuring a maximum of grandeur from a minimum of volume, although the current edition of Pevsner is inclined to attribute its design to his assistant, Robert Hooke. The plan is a Greek cross within a square, the cross defined by four columns rising on elongated pedestals that supply upward thrust. The entablatures are richly carved. This simple composition is supplemented by a three-bay south vestibule, divided off by an arcade of piers and pilasters. The vestibule contains three superbly carved wooden doorcases, beneath a deep gallery backed by three windows.

The sense of height in the nave is further enhanced by the furnishings, by panelling, reredos and pews. These fill the lower part of the church, where they form a tidemark of dark wood beneath the foaming white of plaster. The pews and choir stalls, many with intricate openwork carving, were refashioned from the old box pews. The railing to the pulpit stair shares with the altar rails and seats a love of twisted balusters. The church also possesses an unusual double-seat with cane base for two churchwardens, and a lovely font contemporary with the church. This is virtuoso architecture. It could serve as church, ballroom or theatre.

ST MARY ABCHURCH
Abchurch Lane, EC4 ***
Wren interior, Gibbons reredos

This small church off Cannon Street offers a complete Wren interior, losing only its box pews to Victorian 'improvement'. It lies at a dignified distance from the street, beyond a courtyard of trees and pigeons, with space for its windows and steeple to be appreciated. We might be in the backwater of a Dutch provincial town, surrounded by a warren of the alleys in which this part of the City delights.

The interior is still more beguiling. The church was built in the 1680s when Wren was experimenting with domes for St Paul's Cathedral. St Mary's is thus four walls supporting a dome, with a much simpler handling of space than at St Stephen Walbrook. There are no columns and no aisles, and the dome is carried on eight modest arches. This was painted by William Snow in 1708, with Virtues and sky upholding the Name of God in Hebrew. Though damaged in the Blitz, enough survived to be restored, most recently in 1994.

The reredos is by Grinling Gibbons and dated 1686. It is a superbly architectural work, with coupled Corinthian columns supporting a pediment adorned with urns, broken by a central panel of fruit and garlands. The whole work drips with naturalistic carving. A bomb in 1940 reputedly reduced it to 2,000 pieces, each one meticulously gathered, saved and reassembled. Of the same period are the extravagant pulpit with its huge hexagonal tester, the evangelists on the font cover, the magnificent vestry doorcases and the sword-rests on the pews. At least some of the latter appear to be original. The whole composition is a precious survival of a 17th-century woodwork interior, rivalled only by that of St Mary-at-Hill, currently in store after a fire.

The walls are adorned with Georgian and later memorials, placed as if they were family portraits in the gallery of a great house.

ST MARY ALDERMARY
Queen Victoria Street, EC4 **
Wren's fan vaults

The church lies sandwiched apologetically between Queen Victoria Street and Cheapside, notable externally for its magnificent tower. This is unlike that of any other City church, a tall Perpendicular structure with panelled corner buttresses rising to four pinnacles like Burgundy bottles. It has affinities with the 15th-century turrets of King's College, Cambridge, and with Hawksmoor's later west towers of Westminster Abbey. Hawksmoor has even been suggested as the tower's designer. It appears, like the rest of the church, to be a partial reconstruction by the Wren office of a Tudor original of *c.*1520. Whether the adherence to the earlier Gothic design was requested by the parishioners or was a fancy of Wren's is not known. It may be no more than the result of much of the fabric having survived the Great Fire. Whatever the tower's genesis, the interior of St Mary's is of extraordinary originality.

The normal late Perpendicular plan is rectangular, apart from the angled east wall, with six-bay arcades and wide aisles. There is no chancel, just a one-bay sanctuary. But all eyes turn upwards, to the only complete fan vault on a parish church in England (other than such monastic survivors as Sherborne or Bath). Whether Wren was adapting a lavish pre-Fire vault or designing afresh is not known. Either way, the result is remarkable. The cartouches in the spandrels of the nave arcades are Wren-like, indeed some might be by Gibbons, and the vault detail hardly appears a medieval restoration. An attribution to Wren is therefore reasonable.

The vaults are plaster and cover the nave and both aisles. The fans do not extend across the vaults in the usual Gothic manner but embrace large traceried saucers enriched with cusping. The effect is more Regency Brighton than Tudor or Restoration London. It is hard to better Pevsner's enthusiasm: the interest of the vault lies not in the extent to which Wren was copying an original, but in its 'originality, the freedom with which he treated precedent and the fun which he evidently had in playing with Gothic forms'. Above the sanctuary Wren employs a more orthodox barrel vault, now brightly painted.

St Mary's retains its Victorian wall panelling and pews. The windows are modern and poor. The splendid old organ, dating from 1781, has lovely stencilled pipes peering out of the gloom.

ST MARY-AT-HILL
Lovat Lane, EC3 *
Wren's gutted masterpiece awaiting restoration

The most charmingly situated and most atmospheric of Wren's City churches survived the war almost intact. It was then hit by a disastrous fire in 1988 and a disastrous inertia ever since. The fabric was swiftly repaired but most of the precious fittings, which survived the fire, were put in store and are still there at the time of writing. The intention is to reinstate them and I therefore cannot omit the church from this list. Indeed the charm of St Mary's restored ceiling and windows alone merits inclusion.

The church lies on Lovat Lane and runs back to the street of St Mary-at-Hill along an alley. Here above old Billingsgate is another fragment of the pre-Blitz City. Ancient doorways conceal smart banks and law firms. A handful of people still live in the neighbourhood. There is little sense of overpowering modernity. St Mary's was once, and perhaps will be again, a church that not only Dickens but Wren himself would have recognised.

What survives of the interior is of great architectural interest. The plan is roughly square, with a central dome resting on four columns of a strange composite design. Some guides refer to them as an invention of the masons, but the revised Pevsner attributes them to drawings from Serlio's popular *Book of Architecture* (1537). The ceiling panels, later than Wren, are richly worked. The furnishings in store include the only complete set of box pews remaining in the City, part 17th-century, part 19th-century re-creations, as well as a fine pulpit, reredos and mayoral sword rests. Swift must be their return.

ST MARY WOOLNOTH
King William Street, EC4 ****
Hawksmoor's City masterpiece, Schmidt organ

St Mary's is Christ Church, Spitalfields, compressed on to a triangular City site, yet in no way tamed. This is Hawksmoor and he is never retiring. The church dominates the angle of Lombard Street and King William Street, the best approach being up the steps from Bank Station, its booking-hall fashioned from the church's former crypt. The west front is square and rugged with a rusticated ground floor, like a Piranesian wall, and has a tower-cum-portico rising above it. This idiosyncratic façade has much in common with Vanbrugh's house of Seaton Delaval in Northumberland, which dates from the same time, c.1718. It is a powerful match for the commercial towers round about.

The interior is the most remarkable in the City in the majesty it conjures from a limited space. The plan is a square within a square. The inner square has a lantern above an entablature, raised on twelve mighty Corinthian columns, grouped in threes at each corner. The entablature is broken only by the royal arms (of 1968) above the altar reredos. The lantern has semicircular clerestory windows, thus leading the eye not eastwards, as at Spitalfields, but upwards to the heavens. The outer square is formed by walls with pilasters. The aisles between the two squares were once filled with galleries, thankfully removed by Butterfield in the 19th century.

Apart from the galleries, Hawksmoor's woodwork survived both Butterfield's restoration and the war. The reredos is a magnificent Bernini-esque baldacchino, with barley-sugar columns and cherubs galore. The pulpit billows outwards towards the congregation, crowded by a graceful tester supported on gilded pillars. The 17th-century Schmidt organ adorns the west gallery, the only such organ still in place. It should be in continuous use, trumpeting the glories of this place to the passing bankers and clerks.

ST STEPHEN WALBROOK
EC1 ****
Elegant Wren interior, Henry Moore altar

This is regarded as Wren's most brilliant City church. Like Baroque churches in Rome, the structure is constrained by a small site and the need to squeeze formal classical proportions into the dimensions of a medieval city. This Wren did by designing from the inside out, and leaving the walls to themselves. Of the outside of St Stephen's only the tower shows panache, a charming pavilion topped by another. It is like a folly in a country house garden, riding over the rude landscape below.

The interior is one of London's most perfect spaces, marrying Roman dome, possibly the first in England, to a traditional Protestant preaching house. It is a cube of sixteen Corinthian columns. A large dome rests on an inner circle of eight columns and arches and is lit by a large central lantern. The dome has excellent plasterwork, its coffers filled with flora and foliage. The design dates from the early 1670s, when Wren was working on the dome of St Paul's. The straight entablature above the columns does not follow the circle of the dome, but links up with the outer columns. The resulting configuration of right angles, with advancing and receding clerestory walls, creates an infinite variety of vistas. The arches are like restless, celestial waves.

The appeal of St Stephen's lies entirely in this single, complex architectural effect. I first visited this church with an American photographer when the church was closed for restoration. He spent hours lying on his back amid the dust, cheering one photographic perspective after another. The church has long captivated admirers. The Georgian James Elmes referred to the columns as 'a band of elegant young dancers, at the close of a quadrille'. To David Piper in the *Companion Guide to London*, St Stephen's surpassed St Paul's in satisfaction, 'of almost abstract lucidity and elegance, yet also the most subtly sensuous delight'. It is a space, he said, that one must 'move about in, as through a sculpture turned inside out, to see it shape and reshape itself'.

St Stephen's was fortunate to protect its original fittings during the Blitz. It retains its Wren reredos, rails, font and pulpit. The pulpit canopy has been restored with a deep ogee dome, like a candle-snuffer poised to descend on a verbose preacher. Children prance round its rim. To the west, the organ case rises above a carved gallery and is decorated with appropriate trumpeters. Only the pews were unfortunately removed in the 19th century.

Though the appearance of St Stephen's is of a square church, the extra west bay and slightly wider bays on the centre line clearly indicate an east–west processional axis, which is also detectable in the vault. Hence the controversy that attended the installation of St Stephen's most incongruous fitting, the Henry Moore altar in the centre under the dome. This was the outcome of a lengthy court case in 1987 waged by the property developer, Lord Palumbo, who had paid for the altar and the church's restoration.

The location defied Wren's longitudinal plan and converted what was a preaching church, focused on the east end and pulpit, into a centralised place of worship concentrated on the altar. The ecclesiastical court judged the altar, a lump of Travertine stone, inappropriate. A higher court overturned this judgement. The stone, variously dismissed as a lump of cheese and a pagan shrine, looks wrong in this serenely grammatical architecture. Whether it is inappropriate is best left to theology.

TEMPLE CHURCH
The Temple, EC4 ***
Templar tombs, Early Gothic choir

The Blitz destroyed most of the Temple enclave as well as the roofs and fittings of the Temple church. But left intact were the walls and enough fragments for the restorers to reinstate the City's only work in a complete Early Gothic style.

The old Templars' church, with its circular nave and later rectangular chancel, forms a serene retreat in the heart of London.

The Knights Templar were an order of soldier monks founded in Jerusalem after the First Crusade to protect pilgrims to the Holy Land. Their churches were built circular after Jerusalem's Church of the Holy Sepulchre. They established their English headquarters on the north bank of the Thames, and the church was opened in 1185, the date of the Norman west doorway. Henry III so favoured the Templars that he wanted to be buried here. The choir was therefore rebuilt on a grand scale in 1240 as his mausoleum, and is now used as the church proper.

The Templars were suppressed in 1312 and their property granted to another, similar order, the Knights Hospitaller of St John. Since the Dissolution, the Temple has belonged to the Crown. Societies of lawyers have long rented the 'Inns' of the old Templars, and use the church to this day. While not technically a parish church, it is regarded as such by local residents. Here London's lawyers may kneel and confess their many sins.

The circular nave has a Norman exterior, of which the most evidently original feature is the vast west doorway, a complex work of colonnettes carved with lozenges and other motifs. For some reason the Victorians did not recut or restore it. The interior is one of the earliest examples of Early English style in England. Arcades, triforium and clerestory all follow the same circular plan. The arcade piers have Purbeck shafts, showing this superb stone at its most sophisticated. The interior was resurfaced after the Blitz, and all of the Purbeck was replaced. On the floor is a renowned collection of battered medieval effigies, some claiming to be early Templars, others anonymous.

The long-aisled choir opens from the east of the nave through a well-modulated vault. Architecture is now released from the constraints of the circle to create a majestic hall of slender piers and vaults. To Pevsner this was 'one of the most perfectly and classically proportioned buildings of the 13th century in England'. It was given wall paintings by the Victorians in imitation of its original appearance, but they were lost in the war. The vault was also lost but replaced, the white plaster revealing the gracefulness of the dark shafts and vault ribs.

The windows are triple lancets with Purbeck shafts. The glass is clear except for the east windows, which are successful postwar compositions by Carl Edwards in a medieval style. Included are roundels showing knights on a winged horse and London burning during the Blitz. The reredos was designed at least under the supervision of Wren, and was banished to County Durham's Bowes Museum by the Victorians until being returned after the war. It sits oddly in so pure a Gothic context.

Between nave and chancel lies an Elizabethan tomb of Edmund Plowden (d.1584), Treasurer of the Middle Temple, with, opposite, a Jacobean one of Richard Martin (d.1618), the former lying, the latter kneeling. The modern pews are arranged college-style, with Inner Temple lawyers sitting on the south and Middle Temple on the north.

The City of Westminster

London without its City churches may seem a monarch without a crown. Yet outside the City were always the Church, Court and Parliament, all based at Westminster. Apart from the Abbey, these institutions produced surprisingly little church-building in the Middle Ages. Westminster was a neighbourhood of noble mansions and executive headquarters but not a true town. St Margaret's, in the lee of the Abbey, was the parish church, as well suited to a modest market town as to a great capital. The early suburbs made do with such modest places of worship as Inigo Jones's eccentric St Paul, Covent Garden, and Wren's St James, Piccadilly.

Matters were improved by the 1711 Fifty New Churches Act (see London: The City). Westminster's quota included Gibbs's masterpiece, St Mary-le-Strand, once within the boundaries of Holborn but now part of the expanded City of Westminster. At the other end of the Strand is the same architect's celebrated St Martin-in-the-Fields in Trafalgar Square, not built under the Act but swiftly established as the town church of the Hanoverian monarchs. No less confident were the Victorian builders, pre-eminent among whom was Butterfield at All Saints, Margaret Street, perhaps the most influential church of the whole 19th century. Boundary changes which incorporated the old borough of Paddington into Westminster have added Pearson's St Augustine, Kilburn, and Street's St Mary Magdalene, Paddington, to form a dazzling trio of Gothic Revival churches.

All Saints, Margaret Street ****

Immaculate Conception, Farm Street RC **

St Augustine, Kilburn ****

St Cyprian, Clarence Gate ***

St James, Piccadilly *

St James, Spanish Place RC **

St James the Less, Pimlico **

St Margaret, Westminster *

St Martin-in-the-Fields, Trafalgar Square ***

St Mary-le-Strand ****

St Mary Magdalene, Paddington ***

St Paul, Covent Garden *

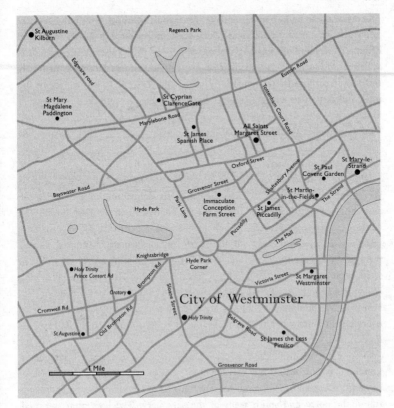

ALL SAINTS, MARGARET STREET
W1 ****
Butterfield's seminal Gothic Revival

All Saints is architecturally England's most celebrated Victorian church. It excites mixed emotions, sitting black and unappealing in a no-man's-land just north of Oxford Street. The exterior badly needs cleaning. Only the spire, higher than the towers of Westminster Abbey and horizontally banded, gives an intimation of greatness inside. There is a blast of incense at the door.

The church was commissioned by the High Church MP, Beresford-Hope, and built in 1849–59 on the site of a chapel already converted to the Anglo-Catholic rite in the 1830s. His architect was William Butterfield, from whom he demanded a church based on the Anglo-Catholic maxims of the Tractarian Oxford Movement. The chosen architecture was 13th-century Gothic, a distinct but visible chancel, an upward progression to the altar, profuse decoration and structural colour. A church, said Beresford-Hope, should have room for processions, candles, chanting and the veneration of saints: a means 'whereby many arts were made subservient to one great end, and the greatness of the end demanded the employment of the highest art'.

Beresford-Hope was to spend £70,000 on All Saints, making it probably the most costly Anglican church of the 19th century. It was certainly the most influential, its original impact hard to appreciate, given the change in architectural style that it initiated. At the time of its design, in the 1840s, new Gothic churches were mostly of grey Kentish ragstone rising over white Italianate terraces. Not until later did England see the wonders of Pearson, Bodley, Street and Burges.

The site is as small as that of a Wren City church. Butterfield was as successful as his forebear in exploiting it to the full, fitting in a clergy house and choir school to serve the busy parochial activities of the new church. The interior achieves its power through height and decoration. The arcades are just three bays, enormously tall and richly embellished with coloured shafted piers, deeply carved capitals and moulded arches. The tower is set over the south-west corner, with the baptistery installed below. The walls are alive with blind arcading, mosaics and murals. Even the floor and roof are decorated. However, the predominant colours are maroon and green, which merge into an overwhelming brown. This can make the nave seem oppressively dark to the modern eye.

Despite the small site, the chancel is one of the most spectacular chambers in London. The east wall is filled with a great reredos, a gorgeous painted tableau of saints, executed by William Dyce but renewed by Comper in 1909. It extends round the north and south walls of the sanctuary. The high altar is raised. A lofty chancel arch and low marble screen ensure that these features are visible from the nave and thus dominate the interior. Crocketed gables, coloured shafts and gilded finials burst from the reredos and rise towards a starry painted vault. The only daylight is from the clerestory because the site is surrounded by other buildings. This adds to the dramatic effect.

Comper also designed the suspended pyx over the altar and the rich gilded canopy to the Lady Chapel in the north chancel aisle. Both pulpit and font are made of inlaid coloured marble and elaborately carved. The church is kept open and is at its best when candle-lit at night.

IMMACULATE CONCEPTION, FARM STREET RC
W1 **
Gothic Revival nave, Pugin reredos

The Jesuit church at Farm Street is Gothic Revival at its most sumptuous. It was built early in the Revival, in 1844–9, and the architect was J. J. Scoles, a little-known builder of Roman Catholic churches in the capital. Later architects embellished both the aisles and the sanctuary.

To Scoles we owe the remarkable scene that greets us on entering: a complete Decorated nave of eight beautifully proportioned bays, with shafted marble piers and richly moulded arches leading to the wide chancel arch and sanctuary. They and the aisle vaults are dramatically uplit.

The chancel was later altered and raised, giving it an even more theatrical impact. The climax is the reredos, of gilded stone by A. W. N. Pugin in 1848. The sanctuary is lined in green marble and is flanked by chapels; that on the right (Farm Street is aligned north–south) is by Henry Clutton and decorated with thick marble arcading and angels by the architect of Westminster Cathedral, J. F. Bentley. It is an exotic chamber to find buried away in the heart of sedate Mayfair.

The ceilings are stencilled and painted throughout, except the nave aisles, which carry ornate lierne vaults. Not an inch of wall surface is without decoration – and this in the austere 1840s, not the colourful late-Victorian era. The right aisle carries large panels portraying the Stations of the Cross, the left aisle has side chapels and confessionals, ingeniously carved within the piers. In the west window above the gallery is excellent modern glass by Evie Hone of 1953, with the richness of colour of a Burne-Jones.

ST AUGUSTINE, KILBURN
Kilburn Park Road, NW6 ****
Pearson's London masterpiece

The church built by Pearson for Father Kirkpatrick in Kilburn is one of London's most original and magnificent places of worship. It was commissioned in 1871 as a focus of Anglo-Catholicism (and challenge to Roman Catholicism) in one of the capital's poorest, mostly Irish, communities. Pearson was at the peak of his powers. The congregation had been worshipping temporarily at All Saints, Margaret Street, and would have expected something no less splendid. They were given majesty, colour and High Church furnishings.

Externally Pearson's design is a balance of high nave and soaring steeple, a composition of which, at South Dalton (Yorks, ER), he had shown himself a master. Even today, surrounded by high-rise flats, St Augustine's is visible from every local vantage point. The nave culminates in a west front with a huge wheel window and tiny lancets below, flanked by turrets with pinnacles. The spire rises above a lofty belfry, supported by clasping pinnacles that counter-balance the west front. Only the redbrick detracts from the beauty of the structure, black and soot-stained and desperately in need of cleaning.

The interior of brick with stone articulation requires a moment's contemplation before its details are appreciated. The space is essentially a long, ten-bay hall, vaulted throughout. Aisles continue round all four sides of the church, with galleries above, which leap over the transepts as bridges. The galleries have internal dividing walls which act as buttresses, a form which Pearson apparently borrowed from the French cathedral of Albi. It gives the space an illusion of height and adds mystery to its depths. At the transepts, the intersecting planes seem to enfold each other in a brilliant dance of light and shadow.

The interior was intended to be coloured throughout, a programme only completed for the south transept, the lower stages, and the chapels. The upper level is decorated by stained glass in alternate windows and, vividly, in the west rose window. Both painting and glass are by Clayton & Bell. The vaults are perhaps more cavernous and evocative unpainted. The chancel is much richer, enclosed on all four sides by densely carved stone arcades. It is as if the sanctuary were a casket of stone inside a shell of brick. The reredos takes the form of a giant sculpted screen with a central niche.

To the north is the small Lady Chapel, to the south the exquisite Chapel of St Michael. The latter has been painted throughout, its ribs and arches picked out in reds, greens and golds. The murals are brilliantly restored and lit. This must be one of London's loveliest rooms.

The Anglo-Catholic tradition continues at St Augustine's in a rich collection of embroidery on altar frontals, banners and vestments. These were designed by such masters as J. D. Sedding, Street and Comper, forming a collection unequalled in any English church of the period.

ST CYPRIAN, CLARENCE GATE
Glentworth Street, NW1 ***
Norfolk Perpendicular interior by Comper

I first visited St Cyprian's, hidden behind the north end of Baker Street, with John Betjeman in the 1970s. It was a warm summer day and bees were buzzing against the window panes. He fell theatrically to his knees on entering, crying, 'Ah, Norfolk, Norfolk in Baker Street.'

The church was commissioned in the 1890s after Viscount Portman, the ground landlord of this Regent's Park hinterland, rejected Street for his misplaced 'churchmanship'. Portman wanted no truck with the Frenchness of the older revivalists. He preferred a young man, Ninian Comper, then eagerly publicising English Perpendicular as the true style of the Anglo-Catholic Gothic Revival. Betjeman adored Comper and became his most vociferous champion.

Comper's amalgam of a light and open architecture with 'pontifical' sanctuary fittings yielded some of the most brilliant churches of the early 20th century, not just here but later at Wellingborough (Northants) and Cosham (Hants). St Cyprian's was finished in 1903 and was Comper's first complete church. Its exterior to Glentworth Street is of no interest. The interior is a beautifully handled hall of tall, slender Perpendicular arcades, entirely surrounded with high aisle windows and further lit by a low clerestory. The model was the nave of Attleborough (Norfolk).

The roof is superbly painted, with a variety of tracery in the spandrels of the beams, very East Anglian. Across the nave and aisles runs an equally fine gilded screen. This has painted dado figures, vault, exquisite openwork loft and gilded rood group. Beyond is the customary paraphernalia of a Comper sanctuary. These include altar hangings, light fitting, niche statues and stained glass. Everything is of gold or bright colours, a rich composition shimmering in the daylight.

These fittings represented, to Comper, 'the best developments of our national English architecture, which is no less medieval than is Shakespeare. Both were developments of the Middle Ages, but both usher in the modern world.' The contrast with the stern French Gothicism of Butterfield and Pearson could not be greater. In his maturity, Comper came to favour an ever broader synthesis of styles, and the later fittings at St Cyprian's reflect this, particularly the classical 1930s' font cover. The church has no pews and has been defaced with ugly chairs.

ST JAMES, PICCADILLY
SW1 *
Adam and Eve font by Gibbons

One wartime bomb took away the vestry and east end, another set fire to the rest. Wren's one surviving West End church was restored by Albert Richardson, and for once a postwar restorer respected the master's style. The superb Gibbons fittings, removed before the Blitz, have been returned.

St James's was built by the Earl of St Albans to serve his new and, he hoped, incomparably fashionable suburban estate based on St James's Square. It was begun in 1676 but not consecrated until 1684. The curiously unobtrusive aspect to the north is due to Piccadilly not existing when the church was built, its entrance being in Jermyn Street. Today the church has made a virtue of this with a lively market in its churchyard. The spire is a postwar fibreglass replacement.

The interior is a fine space, big and open and admirably suited to the concerts for which it is celebrated. There are two tiers of windows north and south, and a magnificent Venetian east window is divided by a transom into two tiers. The wide nave is barrel-vaulted, with galleries rising on squat Doric pillars below and lofty Corinthian columns above. The plasterwork of the vaults has been restored. Only Richardson's grim light fittings inject a grating modernity. The church can allegedly hold 2,000 people.

St James's treasures are the works by Gibbons, the figures on the organ case, the reredos carvings and the marble font. The font is supreme, a work to rival the same artist's font cover at All Hallows by the Tower. The stem represents the Tree of Life and the serpent, flanked by figures of Adam and Eve. Above is a bowl with reliefs of Noah's Ark and the Baptism of Christ. The font is surely among Gibbons's masterpieces.

ST JAMES, SPANISH PLACE RC
W1 **
Royal choir stalls, Bentley sanctuary

The church owes its name to the presence of the Spanish embassy on the site now occupied by the Wallace Collection. There had been a Catholic chapel here in 1791, under the chaplaincy of the embassy. Funds were raised for a new Catholic church, which opened in 1890, to designs by Edward Goldie. His insertion of what amounts to a French cathedral in the back streets off Marylebone High Street is masterful. Without tower or other notable features, the simple ragstone exterior conceals an astonishing space within, culminating in one of London's most successful sanctuary decorations.

The interior is pure Early Gothic in style. The vaulted nave rises 60 ft, with arcades of eight graceful bays opening into double aisles and an apsidal sanctuary. The grand three-tier elevation includes a gallery which bridges the transepts, as at Pearson's St Augustine, Kilburn. The effect is lofty and serene. The sanctuary was decorated by J. F. Bentley and later by Bodley's partner, Thomas Garner, who was responsible for the reredos and canopy. The apse wall has a blind arcade of seven narrow arches, richly gilded and containing murals, responding perfectly to the lancets and vaulting above. The choir stalls are surmounted by two gilded crowns, awaiting the attendance of the King and Queen of Spain. The floor is of golden mosaic.

Equally polished is Bentley's Lady Chapel; the reredos is considered his masterpiece. St James's is not so much infused as marinaded in incense, which fills its central vessel with a soft mist, an aura of Iberian mystery.

ST JAMES THE LESS
Thorndike Street, Pimlico, SW1 **
Street's Italian Gothic exterior

St James's once towered over the smoking chimneys of Pimlico, south of Vauxhall Bridge Road. When built it was described by the *Illustrated London News* as 'a lily among weeds'. Today the lily is all but overwhelmed by the maroon cliffs of a housing estate called Lillington Gardens. But a view of the church has been opened to Vauxhall Bridge Road: from here we can see a campanile rising above a group of church, hall and school enclosed by an ornamental iron railing. The steeple, says the *Faber Guide to Victorian Churches*, is 'sheer and stern ... perhaps the finest Ruskinian steeple ever to rise in Victorian England'.

The church was commissioned and paid for in 1859 by the three Monk sisters, daughters of the Bishop of Gloucester. The architect was Street, who later built St Mary Magdalene, Paddington. Street was a more cosmopolitan Goth even than Butterfield or Pearson and drew inspiration not only from northern France but also from Italy and elsewhere. Here the east end has a continental apse. Italian influence is reflected in the lively coloured brick and stone of the exterior, and the free-standing bell-tower with its stocky spire. A cloistered porch leads to an elaborate north entrance.

The nave is broad rather than high. The roof is painted timber, brick vaults covering the aisles and chancel. We might be in a town hall in the Tuscan hills, were St James's not so emphatically dressed as a church. The three-bay arcades rest on short piers with fantastically carved capitals. Their huge arches have serrated edges. The aisles are narrow and tracery is limited to the simplest Plate form. All is rugged Early Gothic, the surfaces a seeming confusion of polychrome brick, marble, carving and mural. A painting after G. F. Watts fills the space above the chancel arch. The glass is by Clayton & Bell. The exterior wrought ironwork is continued *fortissimo* in that which covers the font.

ST MARGARET, WESTMINSTER
Parliament Square, SW1 *
Milton window, Charles I statue

This church is so overshadowed by its surroundings that it must shout to be heard, and prefers not to bother. It is Westminster Abbey's country cousin, left out on the grass between the Houses of Parliament and the Abbey's north transept. The long nave and aisles might be somewhere in East Anglia. Only the memorials suggest that this is the parish church of Parliament. It was here that the House of Commons gave thanks after two world wars and holds its memorial services.

The church was founded at much the same time as the Abbey, to serve the burgeoning population round its walls and thus obviate incursions into the Abbey itself. In this, it was like a hundred similar churches '*ad portas*' or outside the gates near monastic foundations. Pastoral care was undertaken by a monk from the Abbey, and St Margaret's remains under its jurisdiction, not that of the Diocese of London. Early buildings on the site were replaced by the present church in the early 16th century and completed in 1523. The tower was rebuilt in 1735 by John James. With four stages and long bell-openings, it recalls Magdalen Tower, Oxford.

Both outside and inside, the architecture of St Margaret's shows the lifelessness of late Perpendicular Gothic by the start of the 16th century, although this has been exacerbated by insensitive restoration. The battlemented west porch added by Pearson in the 19th century has more vigour. But St Margaret's is lifted by its furnishings. The east end of the church has been extended and rebuilt and is now modern. A relief copy of Titian's *Christ at Emmaus*, by Seffrin Alkin of *c.*1757, is set in a splendid reredos triptych by Kempe. Above rises St Margaret's famous east window. This is a 15th-century Netherlandish work believed to have been part of the dowry of Catherine of Aragon. Gothic in much of its detail but Renaissance in its unity of composition, the work is fiercely coloured.

The west windows are no less vivid. That in the centre commemorates Walter Raleigh, with the Milton window on its right, both by Clayton & Bell. The north aisle windows are mostly fragments surviving war damage but the south aisle was completely refenestrated by John Piper in 1966, working with his glazier, Patrick Reyntiens. These are inoffensive abstract designs, intended by Piper in no way to compete with the east window. The pulpit is a Victorian confection so colourful it might have fallen off a fairground ride. The wall memorials remind us that outside the Abbey and Parliament was a vigorous community at Westminster, going about its business as if this were no more than the county town of Middlesex.

Outside the east wall is a much-ignored statue of Charles I. He gazes across the traffic directly at the statue of Cromwell in the lee of Westminster Hall.

ST MARTIN-IN-THE-FIELDS
Trafalgar Square, WC2 ***
Steeple-on-a-portico, Italian plasterwork

St Martin's rises on its corner of Trafalgar Square like an elderly maestro trying to bring order to the cacophony below. This is England's most loved, most photographed and most imitated church. Across the British Empire, and across much of North America, James Gibbs's eccentric composition of tapering steeple atop a classical portico has been reproduced over and again. This arrangement has long been the despair of critics – 'a doubtful blessing' said Pevsner, a 'misplaced eye-tooth' said David Piper. Yet it marries the soaring quality of a steeple with a portico's reassuring security, restless Gothic verticality with classical repose. Millions who know nothing of the rules of architecture have found this marriage deeply satisfying.

The church was built in 1722 by Gibbs on the site of an earlier foundation when the area west of Covent Garden was developing as a smart suburb. An earlier church on the site had been located so that diseased corpses need not be carted past Henry VIII's Whitehall Palace to St Margaret, Westminster. Gibbs won the commission on the strength of his earlier St Mary-le-Strand. It was not until a century later that Trafalgar Square was built as London's nearest equivalent to a Grande Place, and St Martin's thrust into a new prominence. That it could stand this transformation from narrow street front to fulcrum of a large open space is a measure of Gibbs's greatness.

The portico is stupendous, one of the finest on any English church. The orders continue round the walls, with the columns turning into pilasters and forming the church into a classical temple, with a Venetian east window towards the Strand. From the west entrance, steep steps run down to the pavement on three sides, offering a grandstand view over the square. This is today a meeting place for young and old, souls lost and found.

The interior of St Martin's is almost as celebrated as the exterior. Influenced by Wren's City churches, it is the archetypal 18th-century design. The central barrel vault and the lateral saucer domes have theatrical plasterwork by the celebrated Italian double-act of Artari and Bagutti. The pair were brought specially from Italy by Gibbs and stayed to complete many an early Georgian palace. A wide nave is flanked by giant columns supporting galleries on three sides. At the east end the galleries turn into royal boxes, flanking a narrower chancel. The box pews date from 1799 but have been lowered. This was the parish church for Buckingham Palace and George I was a first churchwarden.

St Martin's saw the ministry of Dick Sheppard, an army chaplain in the Great War. The church was the first encountered by many troops returning from the trenches on the boat trains into Charing Cross. Sheppard would welcome them under his portico, which acquired the nickname of 'the church of the ever-open door'. Since then, the crypt has been a shelter for the homeless and a centre of charity for what was once the poor Covent Garden neighbourhood to its north.

ST MARY-LE-STRAND
WC2 ****

Gibbs's palazzo interior, vestry doors

St Mary's is the finest 18th-century church in London, a match for the best of Rome. Spared by the Blitz, it was neglected for years until a campaign was launched by John Betjeman in 1977 to restore it. The church is now open but besieged by traffic and is much in need of further restoration.

St Mary's was one of the first churches to be started after the 1711 Fifty New Churches Act. It was built behind the old aristocratic palaces on the banks of the Thames. When the church was under construction, the original Thames 'strand' or beach was found underneath at a depth of 17 ft.

It was James Gibbs's first major work, designed on his return from Rome, where he was trained under the Baroque architect, Carlo Fontana. The church cost the then astronomical sum of £16,000 and was built in 1714–17, though the interior was not finished until 1723. The exterior is a classical box with superimposed Ionic and Corinthian orders on all sides. In this it is unusually rich for a church in the centre of town, where it would have been crowded close by other properties. These were removed only with the creation of the Aldwych at the turn of the 20th century. With Wren's St Clement Danes (blitzed and rebuilt), the two churches have been likened to two stately barques, gliding west out of the City down the Strand, buffeted by swirling traffic.

There are windows only in the upper tier, keeping out the noise of the street. The exterior is enriched with carved fruit and cherubs, most lavishly on the east end. The west front is finely proportioned. Not here the steeple that Gibbs was to erect above the portico of St Martin-in-the-Fields. Instead, a tall classical tower soars above a façade in which the components seem perfectly matched: semi-circular porch in the lower tier, pedimented portico in the upper tier, topped by a balustrade. Where Wren's St Clement's to the east is English and rather plodding, the church of St Mary's is Italian and soaring.

The interior is one of the loveliest in London, even in its present discoloured state. It is a single space and might be the ballroom of a palazzo. The elliptical plaster vault is hugely ornate, with coffering alternately square and lozenge, and *trompe l'oeil* distortion at the ends. The chancel arch is a theatrical proscenium of columns and pediment containing the arms of George I. Beyond is an apse with a vault in stone rather than plaster. The effect is partly spoilt by vivid modern glass.

The fittings were luckily spared by the Blitz, despite the vicar having refused to put them into store. They include two magnificent vestry doors either side of the sanctuary and an exquisite pulpit which has lost its tester. It billows out from its base, dark wood inlaid with light. The work has been attributed to

Grinling Gibbons. The guidebook announces that this is 'the Wrens' church'.
The reference is to the Women's Royal Naval Service, who adopted it after the
last war.

ST MARY MAGDALENE, PADDINGTON
Woodchester Street, W2 ***
Street's London masterpiece, crypt by Comper

Travellers into London on the Westway flyover will recognise the thin, red-and-
white banded spike of St Mary Magdalene, carefully so called to distinguish it
from the neighbouring St Mary, Paddington. The church is tall and outwardly
grim, built high to fit on to a narrow site sloping up to the Grand Union Canal.
Its surrounding streets have been demolished and replaced by characterless
housing estates. As a result the church's proportions look mildly absurd.

No matter. This is the best example in London of Street's work, soaring,
rich and north European, where his St James the Less, Pimlico, is low, domestic
and Italian. Work began in the new suburb of Paddington in 1865 and continued for ten years, under the aegis of the Anglo-Catholic vicar, Richard
Temple West, late of All Saints, Margaret Street. West had endured a series of
brushes with ecclesiastical authority for his Tractarian principles, including
accusations of using Roman Catholic prayers and hearing confessions. Street,
like Butterfield, Pearson and Bodley, was happy to oblige a patron eager for the
most sumptuous of liturgical fixtures and fittings.

The church makes brilliant use of its site. There is room for an aisle only on
the south side, where the steeple is also squeezed in next to the small transept.
The east end is apsidal with large Geometrical windows. The other windows
are simple lancets. The interior flair is immediately apparent: a south arcade of
shafted piers, and a north arcade (to a negligible north aisle) including paired
subsidiary arches with the Stations of the Cross in their spandrels. Both arcades
have saints in niches in the main spandrels. Above is a high wagon roof lavishly
painted with more saints. The south aisle Lady Chapel was redecorated by
Comper, with a 1920s reredos by Martin Travers. The west end is an excellent
Early Gothic composition of three arches supporting three windows, one a rose.

The chancel is as fine as any by Street. The walls are covered in alabaster
panels and mosaics from the Salviati works in Venice. The windows, depicting
scenes from the Life of Christ, are especially fine, not radiant as were those of
Morris & Co., but well drafted and with simple clear colouring. Here and
throughout the church, they are by Henry Holiday.

In the crypt of St Mary's is a minor Gothic masterpiece, the memorial chapel
to West inserted after his death in 1893. The designer was the young Ninian
Comper, working in the purest Perpendicular style (*see* St Cyprian, Clarence

Gate) to re-create a medieval sanctuary chapel in memory of a celebrated Anglo-Catholic. The church was at the time 'under ban' for using incense and reserving the Sacrament. The crypt still has the air of a Catholic recusant's secret chapel. The low vault is of deepest blue with stars. The furnishings are brilliant with gold. It is a magic place, too hard of access.

ST PAUL, COVENT GARDEN
Entrance in Bedford Street, WC2 *
Actors' church by Inigo Jones

When the Earl of Bedford was developing London's first suburban estate on his 'convent garden' land, he was told by the King that it should be well designed and have a church. He duly commissioned the royal architect, Inigo Jones, but told him to keep it cheap, 'not much better than a barn'. Jones was said (by Horace Walpole) to have replied, 'You shall have the handsomest barn in Europe.'

Jones gave him a Tuscan temple that straddled the west side of the Covent Garden piazza. It was flanked by splendid gates, with its entrance originally at the east end, through the famous portico. This is composed of a deep and unadorned pediment above four Tuscan columns and pillars. Finished in 1633, St Paul's portico introduced a new scholarly classicism to England. It was built at a time when English churches were still pondering Gothic 'survival' or 'revival', and is contemporary with Staunton Harold (Leics) and St Katharine Cree. The portico featured in the paintings of Hogarth and in hundreds of 18th-century prints. It was the setting for Eliza's first encounter with Professor Higgins in the film, *My Fair Lady*. The composition was often echoed by later church architects. The Georgian churches at Langton-by-Spilsby (Lincs) and Mereworth (Kent) bear its imprint.

The strong pediment is repeated at the back, above a bold doorway flanked by pavilions. Here is the entrance to the church through a delightful garden entirely surrounded by buildings. The church interior is more or less as Bedford demanded: barn-like. Three huge windows light each side, with a simple reredos at the east end and a gallery at the west. On the gallery are fixed examples of the work of Gibbons, who was buried in the church. Otherwise, the chief interest lies in the record of members of the theatrical profession whose memorial services were, and still are, held here. At such times the otherwise quiet church takes on an ostentatious display of sobriety, as stars gather 'to see who is with us still'.

The wall plaques appear to leave out nobody: Chaplin, Coward, Neagle, Rambert, Thorndike, Wolfit, Redgrave, Helpmann, Robson and dozens more. What is not clear is who rates a mere panel and who a full plaque. The loveliest memorial is an embossed silver urn to Ellen Terry (d.1928).

Greater London (except the Cities of London and Westminster)

London beyond the boundaries of the two Cities was always an also-ran. The adjacent counties of Middlesex, Essex, Kent and Surrey saw the tramp of armies and merchants, the growth of market gardens and the eventual swamping of suburbs. The medieval vestries were seldom up to the job of regulating this, and were successively overtaken by the counties, the metropolitan boroughs and the Greater London Council, now Authority. This chapter embraces the boundary of the last. For the purposes of identification I have listed churches by the local neighbourhood with which they are familiarly associated.

Of pre-Reformation work there is little of note, apart from that valiant Early Gothic survivor, St Etheldreda, Ely Place. Queen Anne's Fifty New Churches Act was generous to East London, with Hawksmoor masterpieces in Spitalfields, Limehouse and Greenwich, and Thomas Archer's Baroque extravaganza in Deptford. The Victorians were no less lavish in patronising West London. Fine churches were built by Butterfield in Queen's Gate, by Bodley in Prince Consort Road and by J. D. Sedding in his treasure house of the Arts and Crafts in Sloane Street. Even the 20th century made its mark, with Lutyens in Hampstead Garden Suburb and Peter Jenkins in Harringay.

Too many of these buildings are neglected and hard to see. That prosperous suburbs cannot open their churches to visitors as readily as can villages and country towns is surely a disgrace.

Barking: St Margaret **

Chelsea: Holy Trinity, Sloane Street ****

Deptford: St Paul **

Finsbury: Wesley's Chapel *

Gospel Oak: St Martin *

Greenwich: St Alfege **

Hampstead: St John **

Hampstead Garden Suburb: St Jude **

Harefield: St Mary **

Harringay: St Paul *

Harrow: St Mary *

Holborn: St Etheldreda, Ely Place RC *

Kensington: Brompton Oratory RC **

Holy Trinity, Prince Consort Road **

St Augustine, Queen's Gate **

Kensington: St Cuthbert, Philbeach Gardens ***

Kew: St Anne *

Limehouse: St Anne **

Petersham: St Peter *

Spitalfields: Christ Church ****

Stanmore: St Lawrence ***

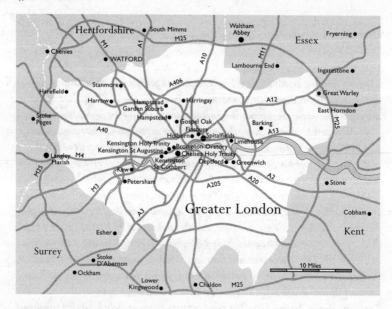

BARKING
St Margaret, Abbey Road, Barking **
Jolly East End interior

The church sits on a slope overlooking the River Roding, which runs down to the Thames at Barking Creek. Surrounding hypermarkets have knocked the stuffing out of the adjacent Barking town centre, but the gatehouse and 'curfew tower' of the old abbey survive, as does the churchyard. This is a handsome corner of East London. The exterior of the church is mostly Perpendicular and of limited interest. This was not the abbey church but the parish church associated with the abbey, hence the modesty of the chancel. Until 1894 the church bell was rung at dawn and dusk in winter to guide travellers across the Roding marshes. Today's equivalents are the garish signs on the adjacent North Circular Road.

The interior, reached through a dignified modern extension to the south, is a charming jumble of colour and old woodwork. Bits remain of all periods, including a Norman north chapel and a 13th-century north chancel arcade. The church has an inner and an outer north aisle, giving it an opulent spaciousness. The pews with large poppyheads and the pulpit appear 18th century. The pretty chancel screen is Victorian. In the south aisle a Chapel of Youth has a screen embellished with small statues of characters associated with the church. They include Captain Cook, who was married here, and the Quaker reformer, Elizabeth Fry.

The jollity of Barking is due in large part to the stucco vault of the old chancel, which 'weeps' slightly to the south. This was inserted in the 18th century and is white with coloured bosses and a classical cornice. In the chancel is an excellent incised slab to Martin (d.1328), the first recorded vicar of the parish church. Opposite is a curious memorial to Sir Charles Montague (d.1625) in the form of a relief panel. It shows Sir Charles asleep inside his tent while musketeers keep watch outside. In the background soldiers prepare for battle.

CHELSEA
Holy Trinity, Sloane Street, SW1 ****
Complete Arts and Crafts interior

Holy Trinity is pre-eminent among the monuments of the Arts and Crafts Movement, ranking with Roker (Durham) and Great Warley (Essex). It was built by the Master of the Art-Workers Guild, J. D. Sedding, entirely at the expense of the ground landlord, Earl Cadogan. The style is late Perpendicular. The church was consecrated in 1890, a year before Sedding's premature death and before the furnishings were installed. These were completed by Sedding's pupil Henry Wilson and colleagues from the Guild. If any collection deserves to stand as a monument to the flowering of Art Nouveau in England, it is Holy Trinity. This is the Chelsea of Pont Street and Oscar Wilde, of Belgravia moving into King's Road, of money meeting art.

The exterior is plutocratic rather than distinctive. A giant Perpendicular west window is flanked by two turrets gazing down on the boutiques of Sloane Street. The interior is huge, the nave being wider than that of St Paul's Cathedral. The arcades are heavy and hard, with curious Perpendicular panelling lying askew in the arch spandrels. But the eye is immediately drawn to the carving, which covers corbels, roof bosses and even the plaster of the aisle walls. It is as if every 'art worker' had come to leave his mark in honour of the Master.

Appreciation of the furnishings should begin with the stained glass. It is dominant and to a coherent plan, rare in a late Victorian church. That in the north aisle is by William Richmond, showing the lives of the saints and biblical characters in the vivid but dark tones of the Morris tradition. The south aisle glass is by Christopher Whall. It was Whall whom Sedding asked of Holy Trinity, with aesthetic feyness, 'Is it too naughty? I hope it's not too naughty.' Or did he hope otherwise?

The east window is the masterpiece of Burne-Jones's last period. In the main lights are 48 figures depicting the principal saints of the Bible story. At the top are scenes including the Temptation, the Crucifixion and the Nativity. The settings are by Morris. It is the largest and most splendid late work of the Morris partnership. Beneath is a museum of 'Arts and Craftsmanship', in iron, brass and beaten copper. The screens to chancel and chapels, the choir stalls, the organ case and railings glow in the dark, rich in detail and overwhelming in impact.

The chancel gates, in virtuoso wrought iron, are Sedding's most dazzling work, with acanthus swaying and drooping over subordinate foliage and embracing brass cartouches. Like all Sedding's work, the design is eclectic rather than abstract. He was an English Goth attaining the genius of a Gaudí. Betjeman regarded these gates as among the finest works of art in London. Other works are by Sedding, Wilson and friends of varying degrees of celebrity. The stone pulpit with marble inlay and a wilful staircase is by Sedding. The angel lectern is by H. H. Armstead. Hamo Thornycroft carved the stone corbels. Onslow Ford designed the font.

The highly original choir stalls display bronze relief panels including naturalistic designs on the fronts and saints in the lunettes on the canopies. To the north are the worthies of the Anglican Church, beginning with Bede and ending with John Keble. They are by F. W. Pomeroy. The altar cross and candlesticks are Sedding's. The south chapel guarded by two carved wooden columns is panelled in walnut. This was designed by Sedding's less iconoclastic successor, F. C. Eden, who was to carry the Anglo-Catholic decorative tradition on into the 20th century.

DEPTFORD
St Paul, Deptford High Street **
Baroque façades, 'Royal box' pews

Deptford was once a charming riverside village and shipyard, a stopping place for Londoners on their way to Greenwich. The old church, built by Thomas Archer under the 1711 Act, is now a dejected sight off the high street which, like everything else round here, seems to give it the cold shoulder.

Yet St Paul's is the kind of building foreigners can never credit to the English. The exterior is Baroque of astonishing vigour, with giant classical orders on all sides. The north and south elevations have pedimented porticos with heavily rusticated pilasters, set on magnificent double-flight staircases rising from the churchyard. These are presumably for scenic effect alone. The entrance front to the west is ingenious. Archer resolved the familiar 'tower on a portico' problem with a semicircle of columns above a fan of steps. On top is no pediment but a balustrade with a circular tower and spire, a completely happy composition. The east wall has an apse echoing the west portico with a Venetian window.

The interior is spectacular, almost a match for Hawksmoor's Christ Church, Spitalfields, and as theatrical. It is centrally planned with vestries in the angles. The overwhelming impact is created by the giant Corinthian columns and a deep entablature, encrusted with plasterwork. As Pevsner says, St Paul's comes 'closer to Borromini and the Roman Baroque than any other English church of this date'. Archer had studied in Rome.

The galleries are in place, as are the pews. Four private pews, like Royal boxes, jut from each corner on columns. The other furnishings are disappointing and not by Archer. The pulpit is weak and the font a strange Norman-style work. When properly lit, the sanctuary forms a fine classical composition round the Venetian window, with *trompe l'oeil* curtains opening above.

FINSBURY
Wesley's Chapel, City Road, EC2 *
Methodist shrine

The chapel is the self-styled 'Cathedral of World Methodism'. It was built next to the old Foundry in which Wesley had preached since what he termed his 'conversion' in 1738. The Moorfields Foundry had been taken over by the Methodists in 1739 but new premises were required and a purpose-designed chapel was begun in 1777, after a nationwide appeal. Wesley's architect at Moorfields was that of the Mansion House, George Dance the Younger. He called for something 'perfectly neat but not fine'. The gallery columns, of wood from Deptford dockyard, were given by no less a benefactor than George III. They have since been replaced with marble.

The church opened in 1778 and Wesley began his first sermon here attacking the fashionable hats of his startled congregation, 'the dangers of affluence among his followers being an obsession of his closing years', according to the church guide.

The exterior is simple and late Georgian, surrounded to the south and east by a graveyard and to the west by a courtyard with Wesley's old house on the right. Wesley's tomb is in the graveyard and his statue is in front of the main entrance. With the Nonconformist cemetery of Bunhill Fields opposite, the enclave is a welcome respite from the modern City, though the hagiography of the Wesley family in house, crypt, museum and gift shop is overpowering.

Of the original chapel interior little remains. The 18th-century pulpit rises in the middle of the nave although it was truncated in the 19th century. Behind in the conventional sanctuary are the original Georgian altar rail, reredos and altar, a composition quite unlike that of the Methodist Old Room at Bristol. Part of Dance's gallery survives, and the Adam-style ceiling, a most unMethodist touch, is a replica of the original raised to a higher level. It was said at the time of construction to be the widest unsupported ceiling in England. The gallery was flat but has been given a rake. Most of the fittings are 19th century and the heavy stained glass and ponderous memorials to famous Methodists give the interior a heavily Victorian atmosphere.

To the rear of the chapel is the tiny Foundry Chapel. This has benches from the old Foundry and the organ on which John's brother Charles composed his celebrated hymns. It might be the billiard room of a Victorian country house.

GOSPEL OAK
St Martin, Vicar's Road, NW5 *
Eccentric Gothic interior

The rich of Victorian London prided themselves on building churches for the poor. The evangelical glove-maker, John Allcroft of Stokesay in Shropshire, offered E. B. Lamb the chance to design a lavish place of worship for the new estates rising between Camden Town and Hampstead. Its lofty Kentish ragstone tower once soared over the surrounding streets, but is now lost among council flats. Lamb was a prominent 'rogue Goth' of the 1860s and St Martin's, built in 1866, falls firmly into the category of 'love them, or hate them' London churches. It is the antithesis of the stern Gothic of the Ecclesiologists or of variants espoused by Bodley and J. D. Sedding.

The style of St Martin's is castellated Perpendicular, its exterior irregular and picturesque. The porch might be the entrance to a fairyland castle, with vaults and battlements. The interior is large, but the space, almost a square in plan, is well controlled. The nave begins aisleless, but opens into aisles around the transepts, and ends in a spacious chancel. The windows are high Perpendicular, flooding the interior with light. The massive wooden roof, a wild web of struts and hammerbeams, is carried on strange colonnettes that start out of the walls like strips of piping. The roof dominates the space and gives it the character of a Tudor great hall. Corbels and capitals have lively carvings. The reredos in the north chapel is also boldly carved, a foretaste of Art Nouveau.

St Martin is Low Church, and there is no strong division between nave and chancel, yet the chancel furnishings are rich. The pulpit, chancel rail and reredos are of exquisite alabaster. Mosaic panels decorate the walls and the roof is brightly painted. The sanctuary is in the form of a polygonal apse, shimmering colourfully beyond the dark wood recesses of the nave. The guide relates that the first vicar was appointed by Allcroft in gratitude for his having saved Allcroft's son from a lion in Africa. Despite these heroics, he became an alcoholic recluse. The congregation must have found Lamb's interior a pleasant distraction from his sermons.

GREENWICH
St Alfege, Greenwich High Road, SE10 **
Hawksmoor's east front

Were it not for the curse of traffic, St Alfege would reign supreme over London's most coherent town centre. From a distance, the tower perfectly complements the masts of the *Cutty Sark* and the towers of the great hospital. The church was one of the first under the Fifty New Churches Act of 1711.

The church has been turned back to front. The east end, one of the finest classical compositions in London, was the entrance but is now closed. The new entrance is from the west. Oh, to close the street and reverse this arrangement. The east front consists of a complete Doric portico, the outer bays blind with pilasters and the central ones open with full columns. These are crowned by an open pediment with urns. Flights of steps led up to the original doors. The classical orders continue on all sides of the grand exterior. The tower at the far end was added by John James fifteen years after Hawksmoor's nave was completed. In comparison, it is a wimp of a thing.

The interior lacks the drama of Spitalfields or even Limehouse. It is dominated by a flat ceiling with a giant oval panel supported by weak corbels. The original galleries and woodwork, apparently by Gibbons, were lost in the war. They were all replaced by Albert Richardson in the 1950s, including the pulpit, which imitates the original. The pulpit is an alarmingly lofty structure, with the preacher peering down as if from a high diving board. There is superb wrought ironwork fronting the east galleries.

Greenwich must have the finest benefactor boards in England, beautifully lettered and hung on either side of the sanctuary with the king's coat of arms above them. This is a local welfare state with royal blessing. The sanctuary has *trompe l'oeil* coffering and a dire modern east window of 1953. Can nothing be done about this?

HAMPSTEAD
St John, Church Row, NW3 **
Baroque chancel, Constable's grave

The tableau of St John's at the end of Church Row was Georgian London's modest answer to Bath. Hampstead in the mid-18th century was eager to fend off the challenge of Richmond and Twickenham as a London resort. Church Row houses would be hired for a week or month in the summer by City bourgeoisie, to enjoy the air and the springs in Well Road. In 1744 the parishioners decided the time had come to rebuild the old medieval church in the field west of the town.

The distinguished local architect, Henry Flitcroft, duly submitted a model and offered his services free. But the cheese-paring parish Vestry rejected his design and decided on a competition in the hope of securing a cheaper one. The angry Flitcroft declined to enter. The result was a design from another parishioner, the unknown John Sanderson, which relocated the tower at the east end of the church behind the altar, to reduce the expense of piling. The cost would be met by selling pew rents at £50 for life. The church opened in 1747, its gates acquired at the sale of Canons House in Stanmore. The Vestry was obsessed with cost, allowing the better gates to go to New College, Oxford.

By the 1870s a further expansion was needed, and further controversy. This involved rebuilding the west end of the church and relocating the altar there. There was also a proposal to rebuild Sanderson's old east tower, instigating London's first and fiercest architectural conservation battle. This being Hampstead, those involved included the competing architects, S. P. Cockerell, Giles Gilbert Scott (who lived in Church Row) and Arthur Blomfield, as well as a galaxy of local and national artists, including William Morris, Norman Shaw, Bodley, Basil Champneys, Rossetti, Holman Hunt, Trollope and du Maurier. The tower was saved but a new west end culminating in a 'Greek cross' by Cockerell won the day.

Today therefore we enter St John's from the east. The interior is that of a sumptuous Georgian town church, yet with a Baroque swirl at its west end. The nave is clearly based on Gibbs's St Martin-in-the-Fields. Giant Ionic columns rise through galleries to a plaster vault. The wooden pews are painted and have pretty pedimented ends. To the west lies a crossing with small transepts and, beyond, a startlingly dramatic classical sanctuary. This has arches north and south, with pillars and oculi. We might be in a scaled-down St Paul's Cathedral.

The churchyard is a blissfully peaceful spot, with views south over London. John Harrison, the inventor of longitude, is buried near the south transept. Constable lies in the northern extension over the road.

HAMPSTEAD GARDEN SUBURB
St Jude, Central Square, NW11 **
Lutyens interior, 20th-century murals

Hampstead Garden Suburb is rightly so called. Despite the efforts of its philanthropic founder, Henrietta Barnett, to create a garden city and her employment of Sir Edwin Lutyens, it remains a suburb without an urb. Lutyens, the architect of imperialism and domestic grandeur, was unable to humanise the heart of the hilltop settlement. He set two churches, an institute and (later) houses in a landscaped park, as if this were Delhi's Rajpath in miniature. The area of the central square is dead, an architectural mausoleum. There is no pub or shop within reach. The suburb lives only in the introversion of its houses.

That said, the Anglican church, St Jude's, built in 1909–11 (completed 1935) is as fascinating in detail as it is disappointing in context. It contains one of the few complete church mural schemes of the 20th century. The exterior is Wren in style to the east, with brick walls and round-headed windows, and English vernacular to the west, with a huge roof that sweeps low over the eaves. These eaves are relieved by dormers, hips and gables on which Lutyens expended extraordinary care. The leaded panes of glass are delightful, the windows and doors framed with carved stone and brick. The tower with its tiers of open brick arches introduces a Byzantine note.

The interior is designed on cathedral proportions if not scale. The brickwork, round arches, barrel vaults, saucer domes, apses and decoration share the Byzantine theme of the tower. Yet the aisles might be those of a simple Tudor parish church with painted beams and low walls. The piers are of brick with rendered pilasters, the vaults mostly covered in Walter Starmer's majestic murals of traditional biblical scenes. Executed in the 1920s and taking nine years to complete, they are his masterwork, although more remarkable for their completeness than their intrinsic merit.

The best furnishings are at the east end, including superb 18th-century iron parclose screens. The north Lady Chapel has paintings of 'worthy Christian women', their identities listed inside the door. The south chapel was founded by the Harmsworth family, sometime Hampstead residents and founders of the newspaper dynasty. The first vicar of St Jude's, Basil Bouchier, was a noted yachtsman, social climber and High Churchman, through which contacts he won many endowments for his church. Derided for many decades, St Jude's is now appreciated as one of Lutyens's most distinctive creations.

HAREFIELD
St Mary, Church Hill, Hillingdon **
Yeomen's tombs

Only at Harefield, wrote Pevsner in 1951, can one 'reach open country and forget about the outer dormitory ring of the metropolis'. Not any more. But at St Mary's, suburban London does make a determined effort at rurality. A lane leads across a quiet stream and up a wooded hillside, on which sits a typically squat Middlesex yeomen's church. Like most of its fellows, it did not come into money until the 16th century. By then local families, here the Newdigates, Ashbys and the Countess of Derby, were putting their wealth into furnishings rather than fabric.

The strong tower is of flint rubble with brick facings. The 19th-century exterior carvings are excellent. A face on the south aisle wall rudely sticks out its tongue. On the north wall is an Ashby family memorial to a gamekeeper, Robert Mossendew, and his spaniel Tray: 'This servant in an honest way / In all his actions copy'd Tray.' Inside, the chancel dates from the 13th century, with an 18th-century ceiling, but the overall character is that of a heavy restoration in 1841, including curvilinear window tracery.

Harefield is to be visited for monuments, a crowded hall of local fame. Here the wealthier denizens of Harefield are portrayed in marble, stone and plaster, not dead but praying, sleeping, smiling, peering down on the congregation. They live on in theatrical tombs, hatchments, coats of arms, flags, windows. There is hardly an inch of space left uncovered. The two finest monuments flank the altar. On the right is the tomb of Alice, Countess of Derby (d.1637). Her three daughters are set into an arcade in the chest beneath. She lies as if in prayer in a vividly coloured four-poster bed with the curtains drawn back. The bed canopy rises to form a baldacchino guarded with carved crests. To the left of the altar lie her descendants, Sir Richard and Mary Newdigate (d.1692), in a monochrome tomb of similar design by Gibbons. The single effigy reclines on her arm in a white Roman robe.

The north, Breakspear, chapel is dedicated to the Ashbys. Here is a magnificent Jacobean monument to Sir Robert Ashby (d.1617) and family. The Latin inscription pleads that though he lies 'in this open tomb, I pray that my sins may be hidden'. The nave is filled with Ashbys and Newdigates who could not be fitted into the chancel or chapel. The churchyard offers a pleasant hillside walk. There is a poignant plot set aside for children who have died at the local Harefield hospital, a sad but peaceful place.

HARRINGAY
St Paul, Wightman Road, N4 *
Striking modern interior

The church, opened in 1993 to replace a previous one gutted by fire, was immediately celebrated as one of London's most successful since the war. With its simple rectangular body and pitched roof, it makes a distant allusion to a Greek temple. Its steep gables soar over the slopes of Wood Green, much as St Bartholomew's towers over Brighton. The roof is pierced by a single porthole window and its gable ends are glazed. At the west end the gable projects over the entrance. The walls are warm redbrick, with thick white bands by the doorway and thin ones round the side walls. The effect is of strength, unity and sophistication. The architect was Peter Jenkins of Inskip & Jenkins.

The entrance is detached from the nave by a lobby or narthex, sliced diagonally like two butterfly wings, revealing two tall windows rising the height of the structure and giving views into the interior. The inside is thus made visually accessible to the outside, yet is also enclosed and intimate. I can think of no classical building with as successful an entrance as this 'post-modern' flourish.

The interior is lofty and serene, its cool colours a striking contrast to the exterior. The side windows are deeply splayed and tiny, but the chamber is flooded with light from above. The walls are of white-painted brick, with a polished stone altar and, above it, a reredos of a Crucifixion in the form of an inverted and fragmented stained glass window made of giant mosaic pieces. It is by Stephen Cox. Above is an inscription in Greek. The neighbourhood was predominanly of Greek immigrants, but is now largely West Indian.

Apart from the altar, great attention has been paid to the stone and the colour. The font is a beautiful bowl of porphyry. The poor-box is of carved wood and on the walls are stone crosses and statues. The floor is paved with grey stone beneath black seats. This does not appear an expensive church, yet is rich in both proportion and material.

HARROW
St Mary, Harrow-on-the-Hill *
Harrovian memorials, Byron inspiration

Hard inside and flinty outside was Betjeman's comment on George Gilbert Scott's 'fierce' restoration of this prominent suburban church. It merits a visit chiefly for its setting. It stands with a tall octagonal spire on Harrow Hill, 400 ft above the Middlesex plain and with views on all sides. The buildings of old Harrow School cluster round its feet. Lamb pointed out to Wordsworth that this made the spire higher even than Salisbury's. The churchyard is famous for the spot, south-west of the tower, where the schoolboy Byron sat for hours on the Peachey tombstone. It has since been railed off to protect it from tourists in search of similar inspiration.

The church belonged to the Archbishop of Canterbury and dates back to the Conquest, though only fragments in the base of the tower survive of that period, including a Norman west doorway. Scott rebuilt most of the chancel in a Decorated style, for which there was no reference in the church, but this end is more confident than the restored 13th-century nave. In the 18th century the walls were reportedly cracked and not a pane was left in the windows. We tend to forget the problems facing Victorian restorers.

Harrow contains many treasures. The original carved Norman font, found in a local garden, is back in use. There is a richly-carved 17th-century pulpit sitting on scrolled brackets, with a sounding board. The nave roof is original 15th century, a fine work in the East Anglian tradition. Grimacing corbels support saintly apostles on the roof posts, and angels with instruments on the panels. An attractive small brass of John Lyon (d.1592), founder of the school, is fixed to the first pier of the north arcade. Above is Flaxman's memorial to Lyon, a classical relief of 1815 showing him teaching boys but not wearing Elizabethan dress. There are other memorials to schoolmasters who, for some reason, preferred to be remembered here rather than in the school chapel. This stands down the road and is also by Scott.

HOLBORN
St Etheldreda RC, Ely Place, EC1 *
Early Decorated nave

This valiant survivor is hidden from view near the end of a cul-de-sac, Ely Place, off Holborn Circus. The church was the chapel of the medieval palace of the Bishops of Ely. The property had a chequered history, having been seized from the Bishop by Christopher Hatton, a handsome young man with whom Elizabeth I became sufficiently infatuated to make him Lord Chancellor. Bishops of Ely sued the Hatton family for centuries but never regained more than the use of the palace itself, while the Hattons developed the garden for the street of that name.

The house was let to the Spanish ambassador in the 17th century, who converted the chapel for Roman Catholic use. After his departure and the demolition of the house for development in the 18th century, the chapel was used by Welsh Nonconformists for drovers to the adjacent Smithfield Market. In 1874 it was purchased by the Catholic Rosinian Order of Charity and has since become a Catholic parish church. (It is thus not, as is often claimed, the only Catholic church in London to 'survive' the Reformation.)

The church is of c.1300 but much restored. It retains the form of a private chapel, of a single space with an undercroft. The upper storey is remarkable, an early Decorated chamber of five bays of sweeping arched window openings. The windows have new tracery, reinstated on the pattern of the surviving east and west end windows. The east window is splendid, of five lights rising to Intersecting tracery enriched with a variety of foils and mouchettes. Niches contain statues of Catholic martyrs. The east window glass is by Joseph Nuttgens of 1952. The crypt, dating from the 13th century, is an evocative corner of medieval London.

KENSINGTON
Brompton Oratory RC, Brompton Road, sw7 **
Italian Baroque statues

What is a miniature Baroque cathedral doing apparently lost in the Brompton Road? It was here in the mid-19th century that the Oratorian, Father Faber, set up a religious house for his order. The order decided in 1878 to build a Roman Catholic church to challenge the Gothic splendours of the Anglo-Catholic revival. Theirs would be a cathedral to the Counter-Reformation, and in the favoured style of that movement, Italian Baroque. The church was begun in 1880 to designs by Herbert Gribble, modelled on the Gesù church in Rome. Gribble had worked on the Duke of Norfolk's cathedral of St Philip Neri at Arundel, and the Duke helped finance the Oratory. It was to cost £100,000 by 1896, the most expensive church of its date in London.

The entrance front on Brompton Road belies this grandeur, in part because two intended corner towers were never built. The dome over the crossing – the church is aligned north–south not east–west – adds some dignity, but the composition is modest compared to the Edwardian blowsiness of the Victoria and Albert Museum next door. The interior is completely Italian, cruciform, domed, with side chapels and altars opening off the nave, and exuberant decoration. Unlike Westminster Cathedral in Victoria Street, its decorative programme was finished. The walls are covered in stucco reliefs and murals, marble panelling, mosaics and statuary. The style is distinctly late Victorian, most noticeable in the Amazonian angels in the spandrels.

The church is crowded with statuary. Much of this, with the furnishings, was brought from the Gesù church in Rome and forms an important, if little appreciated, London museum of Italian sculpture. Against the nave piers are 17th-century figures rescued from the clearing of Siena Cathedral in 1890. At the north end is a copy of the statue of St Peter in the basilica in Rome, its foot much eroded by kissing. Each of the chapels is individually designed and decorated. The complete restoration of the church in the 1980s has greatly lightened what was an intolerably gloomy place. The pulpit is a splendid work of 1930s Baroque, its gigantic tester dripping with cherubs. An altarpiece in St Wilfrid's Chapel to the right of the chancel is by Rex Whistler.

KENSINGTON
Holy Trinity, Prince Consort Rd, sw7 **
Bodley's late-Gothic fittings

When Bodley was given the opportunity he rarely missed a beat. Holy Trinity is tucked away behind the Royal Albert Hall. It is aligned north–south (like a remarkable number of London churches), due to the shape of the plot given to replace an earlier church in Knightsbridge. Bodley, by then the grand old man of church architecture, was asked for a design, and it proved to be his last complete church, begun in 1901 but not finished until after his death in 1907. While Holy Trinity was being built, Bodley was exhausting himself designing cathedrals as far flung as Washington, San Francisco and India.

Holy Trinity is a modest masterpiece. The front to the road has three doorways and a big south window flanked by empty niches, rising to a gable with a simple bellcote. The elevation has been well restored, the present golden ashlar showing what a disservice is done to Gothic architecture by leaving it dirty. The interior is a contrast, a Gothic hall church of majestic proportions. It is lit by a huge north window and by three superb candelabras down the centre of the nave.

Bodley was a master of space and light. He delivers a surprise in a second, left-hand, aisle which sends the eye drifting sideways through the arcades. On the end wall is his own memorial, executed by a pupil, E. P. Warren. It is in a Jacobean style quite foreign to his own, recalling the monuments of 17th-century yeomen. Was this meant as a joke?

The furnishings, of pulpit, choir stalls and reredoses in both the sanctuary and Lady Chapel, are all by Bodley. He may have designed grander pieces, but few more lovely. All feature gilded high-relief figures on an olive background. The pulpit has a wine-glass stem and tester, with an ornamental staircase, as fine of its sort as any in England. The great triptych reredoses are more sumptuous, the one centred on a Crucifixion with figures sculpted in the round, the other a painted Annunciation. Were these not in a church, but a few hundred yards away in the Victoria and Albert Museum, crowds would daily sing their praises.

KENSINGTON
St Augustine, Queen's Gate, SW7 **
Anglo-Catholic Gothic

St Augustine with its blunt west front cocks a snook at the white stucco terraces of South Kensington. The dirty stone and brick exterior, badly in need of a clean, contrasts with the immaculate Holy Trinity in neighbouring Prince Consort Road. The state of the exterior is sad, given the restoration of the interior. This was Butterfield's most reckless exercise in Technicolor design, of 1871. He sought to bring the message of polychrome Ecclesiological Gothic to the pagan white Italianate of South Kensington, a style for which, according to the guide, 'he had a particular dislike'.

The interior is the apotheosis of polychrome. There are large expanses of wall because the lower level has no windows, and every inch is decorated. Most of the decoration is abstract, including the spandrels, described as 'Pether's buff patent bricks with moulded fleur-de-lis'. There is also figurative work: the arcade spandrels have mosaic scenes in quatrefoil frames, while comic-book cartoon tile murals cover the windowless aisle walls. The whole scheme was whitewashed over in the 1920s but recently restored.

The chancel is still more elaborate, rising up a series of steps as at Butterfield's All Saints, Margaret Street. The walls have the same polychrome brick and stonework but are here pierced by cinquefoils and a quatrefoil frieze. It is topped by a brilliantly coloured ceiling. The vast gilded Baroque reredos comes as a surprise. It is a later addition, by Martin Travers in 1928, more suited to south Italy than South Kensington but in tune with the surrounding effusiveness. Betjeman loved this church and wrote of Travers's work here, 'Those were waking days, / When faith was taught and fanned to golden blaze.'

KENSINGTON
St Cuthbert, Philbeach Gardens, SW5 ***
Baroque reredos in Arts and Crafts setting

Anywhere but in modern Earls Court, this church would be packed with visitors and guarded by proud parishioners. Instead, St Cuthbert's is neglected, hidden next to the exhibition halls at the end of Philbeach Gardens, its stark redbrick exterior contrasting with the surrounding stucco. The church is now roofed in copper, and a high green flèche rises in place of a tower. This is visible from the Hammersmith flyover approach into London.

None of this is a match for the interior, a work of extraordinary richness, even for late Victorian London. St Cuthbert's has outstanding Arts and Crafts furnishings. Though Church of England, the church guide rejects Anglicanism as a 'sixteenth-century sect' and emphasises its Catholicism by boasting three relics of its patron saint. The architect of the church, which opened in 1883, was Hugh Roumieu Gough, of no other distinction. He designed a high nave and continuous chancel in rich Decorated Gothic style, the nave piers composed of shafts of solid marble in various colours. The aisle walls are panelled in the same material, hung with large Stations of the Cross. Both nave and aisle walls are diapered, their patterns borrowed from various sources, and at the rear of the church is a charming baptistery with excellent windows by Kempe. The rood beam and group were copied from Granada Cathedral.

Gough's work is primarily a container for the craftsmanship of others, principally a member of the congregation, W. Bainbridge Reynolds, whose speciality was metalwork. To Reynolds, who worked here through the 1870s, we owe the lectern, of wrought iron and copper supporting a 'penthouse' to which leather supports for the books are lashed by thongs. Two majestic candleholders swing out on either side. Reynolds loathed mass production and executed everything by hand. Also by him are the superb metal screens at the ends of the north and south aisles, the altar rails, the candlestick by the curious double-throne sedilia, and any other metalwork we might encounter.

Even Reynolds is overshadowed by the astonishing reredos. This structure of unpainted wood rises the full height of the east end of the church and is comparable in scale only with reredoses found in Spain and Mexico. It was designed by the Reverend Ernest Geldart in 1914 and appears to be on a theme of incense. In the centre is Christ surrounded by a cloud of angels, all with smoking censers. The ornamented shafts on either side rise 44 ft and are covered in carvings of saints. St Cuthbert's is the sort of church that was out of fashion throughout the 20th century, yet it demonstrates a Victorian love of art that was unequalled since the Middle Ages. It will one day be appreciated as such.

KEW
St Anne, Kew Green, Richmond *
Royal pew of 'mad' George III

A church in honour of the namesake of the then Queen was first built on Kew Green in 1714. As Kew became a centre of Hanoverian court life, the church required constant expansion, first under George II, then under George III and William IV. A simple Georgian box became a grand Georgian box with Tuscan arcades and a royal gallery. This in turn was extended to include a royal mausoleum and apsidal sanctuary. But Kew never lost the character of modest chapel to a well-heeled but bourgeois coterie weekending out of town. It still sprawls across the centre of the green, like a courtier lazing on a rug.

The east end is a late-Victorian extension. The west front facing Kew Gardens is Georgian, with portico and octagonal cupola. The interior is a beautifully proportioned chamber with five-bay 'arcades' of Tuscan columns rising to a straight architrave and a simple barrel vault. Light floods through tall windows on to original pews and the aisle royal gallery that fills the west end. This gallery would have been used by George III towards the sad end of his life, while semi-incarcerated at Kew.

In the 1880s the church was extended eastwards to form a top-lit domed chancel and apsidal sanctuary. The decoration was now more lavish. Scagliola columns were inserted, the floor raised and the apse given a mosaic reredos and some ferocious stained glass by Kempe. The space was subsequently restored by Comper, the simple box given a lid of imperial panache.

St Anne's is well dressed with memorials, including to the Hookers, father and son, who founded the present Kew Gardens. Here too lies Gainsborough who, though he never lived here, asked specifically to buried at Kew. The church displays a fine modern icon of the Crucifixion, in a free interpretation of the Byzantine style, by the artist Brother Aidan.

LIMEHOUSE
St Anne, Commercial Road, E14 **
Hawksmoor in Docklands

When Hawksmoor built his Limehouse church as one of Queen Anne's 'Fifty New Churches' in the 1720s, it must have seemed as overwhelming to local residents as does the adjacent Canary Wharf today. Its white façades and huge tower would have arrived as creatures from another land. Yet while Canary Wharf is merely vast, St Anne's, and especially its west front, is a controlled explosion of architectural form. Like its sister at Spitalfields, it was long semi-ruined. By 1975 there were only twenty-four names on its electoral roll. Yet the exterior has been restored, and the church is still in use and regularly open. The churchyard has also preserved a sense of enclosure, with terraces and cottages to east and west and the Dockland Light Railway trundling past to the south.

The church's forte is its entrance front. Hawksmoor freely interpreted Wren's requirement that the Queen Anne churches have porticos 'both for beauty and convenience . . . together with handsome spires and lanterns rising in good portions above the neighbouring houses'. St Anne's can scarcely be said to have a portico at all, but a semicircular domed vestibule with giant pilasters, flanked by transepts and reached up a narrowing flight of steps, an optical illusion of grandeur. Inside, the vestibule itself is a superb chamber, like a lofty gazebo. Above rises the tower, a typically Hawksmoor sequence of square and polygonal shapes, restlessly altering the planes as it approaches the crown. The body of the church is plain.

The interior is not Hawksmoor's best, especially today in the bleak furnishings and colours of Blomfield's 1891 restoration, reinstated after the Blitz. But it retains Hawksmoor's sense of interior space, with corner columns turning a rectangle into a Greek cross, and a deep circular panel appearing to float in the ceiling. Lonely cherubs adorn various corners, desperate for company. The reredos offers a graceful arch over coupled columns but with an unspeakable modern window. The whole place awaits a return to Hawksmoor's original design. Come on, the tycoons of Canary Wharf, dig into your pockets.

PETERSHAM
St Peter, Richmond *
Riverside Georgian box

Despite the enveloping suburbs, the village of Petersham lies protected by green belt in a crook of the Thames, as if London had stopped at Richmond. The houses of Georgian courtiers look out towards Twickenham and cows graze in the meadows beneath Richmond Hill. Only the Star and Garter veterans' home is an intrusion, albeit a massive one.

The church sits in a spacious churchyard which contains, among fine chest tombs, that of George Vancouver, discoverer of western Canada. The building expanded what must have been a tiny medieval chapel in the fields. Its two transepts appear to have reoriented the entire building, the chancel now little more than an alcove. The atmosphere of the interior is that of an unaltered Georgian chapel, with high box pews. These are intact and carpeted and the church retains its galleries. Benches fill the centres of the aisles, with embroidered covers and jump seats at their ends.

The pulpit presides over all this from high on a corner of the chancel, balanced by a reading desk and clerk's pew. Behind is one good Jacobean monument, to George Cole and his wife of 1624, flanked by columns and with a grandson kneeling above. The glass is clear, except in the chancel, which is suffused with a strange yellow light.

SPITALFIELDS
Christ Church, Commercial Street, E1 ****
Hawksmoor's Baroque masterpiece

Christ Church offers one of London's architectural spectaculars. It was built by Nicholas Hawksmoor over fifteen years, 1714–29, one of the six Fifty New Churches Act commissions that he won. He was already fifty and had been Wren's assistant at St Paul's and in many City post-Fire rebuildings. Despite working in Wren's shadow, Hawksmoor's churches are in a class of their own, powerful and eccentric, with a drama that has rarely been surpassed in English architecture. That this masterpiece should have been left to rot for over thirty years is a desperate comment on British conservation. A huge but painfully slow restoration has been under way since 1970, when the church was near to collapse. It is far from complete.

Today the tower has been restored and once again blows its mighty blast across Spitalfields, challenging the offices on the City's eastern fringe to do their worst. The 18th-century streets of its immediate hinterland are among the most graceful in central London, while the adjacent Brick Lane, now home to the

Bangladeshi community, is certainly the most exotic. The church's west front, set back above steps from Commercial Street, is a soaring compilation of architectural shapes, apparently intended purely as theatre. A Tuscan portico appears to front a classical stage-set beneath a mighty tower of the same width.

Not all have admired this front. Pevsner said it 'could not be called anything but ugly' and protested at the device of using north–south tower buttresses purely for visual effect when seen from the west. Others regard Christ Church as the supreme work of London's classical architecture. The historian H. S. Goodhart-Rendel doubted whether, 'of its date and type there is any finer church than this in Europe'. It stands comparison with its rivals, Wren's St Stephen, Walbrook, and Gibbs's St Mary-le-Strand.

The interior is no less exhilarating than the exterior, though still in desperate condition. The walls are scraped back to their bricks. The vast flat ceiling seems to rest on faith, gloom and dust. Yet other classical churches in London are meek in comparison. Christ Church seems perpetually awaiting the curtain to go up on a grand opera. The plan is rectangular: symmetrical east–west and north–south, with giant columns on all sides. The aisles have five bays of windows, arranged in three tiers to light galleries which were removed in the 19th century. Great columned screens run east and west across the church, the east one carrying the royal coat of arms. Beyond it, above the reredos, is a large Venetian window.

The western wall of the interior is even more astonishing. Here the screen is broken by the huge Richard Bridge organ, still awaiting restoration. The instrument is a rare survivor of the Handelian organmaster. On either side of the organ rise two tiers of galleries, which originally continued round the other sides. Once again we might be at the opera, with grand boxes filled with ladies fluttering fans. This is London Baroque at its most self-confident.

STANMORE
St Lawrence, Whitchurch Lane, Harrow ***
Interiors with Baroque murals, Grinling Gibbons screen and monument

The vanished house at Canons is Middlesex's most celebrated ghost. James Brydges, later Duke of Chandos, rose to be Paymaster General to the Duke of Marlborough. In 1696 at the age of thirty-two he had married Mary Lake of Canons and was elevated to a dukedom. Rich on the proceeds of office, he rebuilt his wife's house in a palatial Baroque style and filled it with art and music. By the time of his death in 1744 the estate was already encumbered with debt and his son, the 2nd Duke, was obliged to pull down the house and sell its contents. The sale was among the most sensational in English art history. Chandos relics occur throughout this book, notably the stuccowork and windows now adorning Great Witley (Worcs).

While the house has vanished, the park remains, pathetically municipalised and surrounded by suburban estates. But there is still the parish church. Apart from the medieval tower, this was rebuilt for Chandos by John James in 1715, with a mausoleum later added to the north side, facing the park and house. James built the body of the church as if it were a private chapel, which is odd since the Duke had another chapel at the house. The church saw the earliest performances of Handel's Chandos anthems. The organ is one on which Handel played during his brief time in the Duke's service, with the black and white keys reversed. The splendid Corinthian chancel screen is by Grinling Gibbons.

The church, low, wide and aisleless, has the character of an early theatre, with its west gallery as royal box, the screen as proscenium arch and the sanctuary as the stage. Stanmore lacks the panache of Great Witley among 18th-century churches and has been criticised as too static and English a Baroque, yet it remains a rarity outside central London, a church with sumptuous decoration in the Italian style. The artists responsible for the interior paintings were Louis Laguerre for the ceilings, possibly Francesco Sleter for the grisaille depictions of Evangelists and Virtues on the side walls, and the Venetian Antonio Bellucci for the big murals east and west, including the Nativity and the Descent from the Cross. These ornate decorations, which might be those of a Venetian palazzo, contrast voluptuously with the simple box pews below. Only the font, a gift of the 1st Duke, is a match for the glories above.

More complete in atmosphere is the mausoleum north of the sanctuary, designed by James Gibbs twenty years after the building of the church. It is reached through an antechamber which was itself the original mausoleum. Again, every inch of wall and ceiling is covered in *trompe l'oeil* painting. Pride of place goes to the Duke's own monument by Gibbons. His two wives kneel on either side while he stands in Roman dress beneath drapes and a canopy crowned by urns. Two monuments to Chandos wives fill the south wall. In the north wall is a simple window giving on to what survives of the park, a sigh of transient grandeur.

Norfolk

Norfolk is a landscape of towers. From the tower of Happisburgh on the far east coast, I once counted twelve companions across the horizon. They bestride this flat country as the towers of Somerset bestride the Levels, castles of flint attached to greenhouses of glass. Norfolk has some 600 medieval churches, more prolific even than Lincolnshire. Choosing between the lesser ones is hard. There are churches everywhere, beckoning the eye with great windows, high clerestories and rich carvings and beckoning the ear with bells.

Most of these are of the Perpendicular era. Of earlier churches there are only modest survivors. Norfolk was among the first counties to be colonised by the Saxons, with round flint towers built as much for stability as for security. For early medieval art, Norfolk contains some works of national eminence: the 'Labours of the Month' Norman font at Burnham Deepdale, the Early Gothic leaf carving at West Walton, and the curvilinear windows at Snettisham, Cley and Great Walsingham.

Norfolk is primarily a county of the great Perpendicular rebuilding. The wool and cloth trade with the Continent in the 15th century brought it to the fore-front of commercial prosperity and thus of ecclesiastical architecture. Salle and Cawston in the east and Walpole St Peter in the west are favourites among enthusiasts. The churches of the Ouse delta form probably the finest concentration of late-medieval craftsmanship in England. To them must be added such accomplished works as the font canopy at Trunch, the exquisite paintings at Ranworth and the Flemish brass at St Margaret, King's Lynn.

Small wonder that, rare in English counties, there was little for the Georgians or Victorians to do but gaze in admiration and leave well alone.

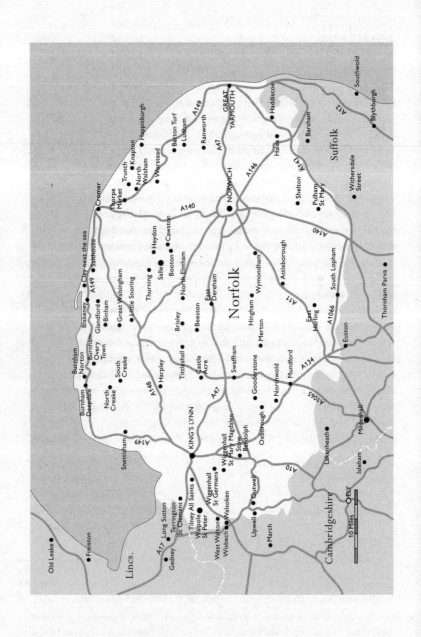

Attleborough ***

Barton Turf *

Beeston *

Binham **

Blakeney ***

Booton **

Brisley *

Burnham Deepdale *

Burnham Norton *

Burnham Overy Town *

Castle Acre *

Cawston ***

Cley next the Sea ***

Cromer *

East Dereham **

East Harling **

Glandford *

Gooderstone **

Great Walsingham **

Great Yarmouth:
   St Nicholas ***

Haddiscoe *

Hales *

Happisburgh *

Harpley *

Heydon *

Hingham **

King's Lynn:
   St Margaret ****
   St Nicholas *

Knapton *

Little Snoring *

Ludham **

Merton *

Mundford *

North Creake *

North Elmham *

North Walsham *

Northwold **

Norwich:
   Octagon Chapel *
   St Andrew *
   St Peter Mancroft ****

Outwell *

Oxborough **

Pulham St Mary **

Ranworth ***

Salle ****

Salthouse **

Shelton **

Snettisham **

South Creake *

South Lopham **

Stow Bardolph *

Swaffham **

Terrington St Clement ***

Thorpe Market *

Thurning *

Tilney All Saints **

Tittleshall *

Trunch **

Upwell **

Walpole St Peter *****

West Walton ***

Wiggenhall St Germans **

Wiggenhall St Mary Magdalen **

Worstead ***

Wymondham ***

ATTLEBOROUGH
St Mary ***
Vaulted screen, paintings of saints

The church sits on the outskirts of an undistinguished town near the main road to Norwich. It was settled by monks of the Holy Trinity in the 14th century who built a new Decorated church, now a Norfolk rarity. Their structure was based on a Norman foundation. Fragments of the earlier church survive beyond the chancel screen.

This screen dominates the nave and is the most complete in Norfolk. It was paid for, like the fine north porch, not by the church but by the Ratcliffes of Attleborough Hall. The screen was overpainted in the early 16th century with biblical texts, and again in the 17th century when it was adorned with the shields of all 24 bishoprics in England. The Ratcliffe family not only patronised the pre-Reformation church but took ownership after the ejection of the monks at the Reformation. In 1525, Robert Ratcliffe was Lord Fitzwalter and 1st Earl of Sussex. This may explain the survival of the screen. The Attleborough estate was later sold to the Bickley family, London drapers whose monuments adorned the transepts.

The screen, dating from the late 15th century, spans both nave and aisles, and its loft is supported not on ribbed coving but most unusually on a full vault with pendants. There are paintings of saints both in the main panels and in the dado. The vaulting is superb, the whole a supreme work of late-Gothic carving. The screen was moved to the west end of the nave in 1845 but restored in 1931.

By then the remains of the west wall mural had been uncovered and two fake Norman windows inserted where once had been a cross. The result is one of those curiously unsatisfactory works of conservation, the partial reinstatement of a mural. It should either be coherently completed in reproduction, or covered and replaced. The figures are unclear but the lower ones appear to be feathered angels playing basketball.

The late-Stuart pulpit is said to be by a pupil of Gibbons. The rare Regency iron lectern comes from King's Lynn, with steps in the form of a serpent with a long leaf for a railing. There is a trace of a St Christopher wall painting on the north wall and medieval stained glass high in the west window. The early 20th-century glass in some of the aisle windows lends a gloom quite out of character with the rest of the church.

BARTON TURF
St Michael *
Paintings of saints and kings

The church lies apart from its village in a grove of trees. It is outwardly Perpendicular, of flint with a fine tower and flushwork porch of two storeys, the ogee niches empty of statues. The interior is visited for its screen paintings, second only in quality to Ranworth's. The principal chancel screen has a central arch decorated with crockets, its dado panels set behind traceried frames.

Though not easy to appreciate except on hands and knees and with a magnifying glass, the paintings are of superb delicacy. The 12 panels depict the Virgin, saints and the nine orders of angels, the only example of the latter in Norfolk, perhaps because of their theological obscurity. The armour has enabled the paintings to be dated to *c*.1490. The artist of these works lacks the sophistication found at Ranworth, but shows the same fascination with symbolism, costume and colour. These are jewels of medieval art, glowing with pride in faith, in this quiet corner of England.

Other paintings, on a screen in the south aisle, are of four 'royal saints'. These are St Edmund, Edward the Confessor, St Olaf of Norway, murdered for trying to convert his people to Christianity, and finally Henry VI. Henry's sanctity was short-lived, promoted chiefly by his supporters after his defeat in the Wars of the Roses. Outside the church is a poignant memorial to the four Doyley boys, all drowned on The Broads on Boxing Day 1781, such being 'the changes and chances of this fleeting world'.

BEESTON
St Mary *
Openwork screens

Beeston church lies a mile from its village, alone on a hillock by a farm. It has a spire, unusual in Norfolk, rebuilt in 1873. Apart from the clerestory, the building is almost entirely 14th century. The best view of the interior is east towards the chancel from the steps under the tower. The slender chancel arch is crowned by the faded frame of a coat of arms that would have displaced the rood.

Beneath it and silhouetted against the east window is the mutilated outline of the screen. This looks curiously naked, without cornice or beam or any other top. Its points thrust up into the air like spikes. On either side are glimpses of fine Reticulated tracery in the aisle chapels, separated by superb parclose screens. The screen to the north chapel is densely and exquisitely carved. This is a vista of rare 14th-century purity.

Beeston is happy in its colouring. Pale stone is offset by plaster beneath honey-coloured oak roofs to the nave and aisles. These roofs rest on tall wall-posts with fine carved saints, their faces damaged by iconoclasts. The hammerbeams too are composed of saints. The pews have pierced backs and poppyheads.

The north aisle was reroofed with steel after the theft of its lead. I visited it during a storm, and the noise was like the arrival of a Salvation Army band.

BINHAM
Priory of St Mary **
Controversial west front

Binham was one of the great religious houses of Norman Norfolk. The Reformation put a stop to its rebuilding and the present church remains a ghost, a fragment of a priory in a field surrounded by ruins. Though the interior remains mostly Norman, the west front facing the road is 13th century. This façade has been so bashed about that it looks like a set for a Great War battle scene. The fenestration lost its impact with the collapse of its tracery in 1809, and the windows were later filled with brick.

What survives has long excited architectural historians. The reason is that the Early Gothic blind arcading on the lower storey rose not, in the fashion of the early 13th century, to simple lancet windows, but to early Geometric tracery, the earliest form of Decorated Gothic. The ubiquitous chronicler of medieval England, Matthew Paris, said that the front at Binham was built to full height by Prior Richard, who we know left Binham in 1244. This would make its window tracery the earliest in England. What would otherwise be the earliest was the tracery built in the chevet chapels at Westminster Abbey by English masons in 1245.

Some who have studied the Binham masonry at close quarters believe the tracery was a later insertion of c.1270, replacing lancets seen by Paris. The French historian of English Decorated, Jean Bony, concluded (in 1979) that Binham was not a 'precocious East Anglian initiative . . . but rather a peripheral manifestation of the proto-Decorated of Northamptonshire'. But the new edition of Pevsner reverts to the Paris identification, pointing out that Binham was unlikely to have built a new west front both in the 1240s and in the 1270s. Either way, a Georgian print shows the tracery in all its glory. It is now a ghost and I cannot see why it should not be reinstated. The aesthetic unity of the original is surely better than a ruin.

Binham's interior is quite different in character. When the priory was demolished at the Dissolution, just seven bays of the old nine-bay nave were left as the local church. The cool Norman interior is unlike a conventional Norfolk church. The three tiers with huge gallery openings are rich with shafts and mouldings. The nave has lost its aisles, and thus has few of the shadows that give Norman architecture its visual excitement. Yet as compensation it is gloriously flooded with daylight. There is a well-preserved font in a dominant position in the nave and Binham displays a few surviving misericords.

BLAKENEY
St Nicholas ***
Twin towers, seven-lancet window

Norfolk's coastal churches mostly rest on rising land, like galleons waiting to weigh anchor and set off to sea. Blakeney sits on a prominent site, strong, confident and incongruously large for the harbour that nestles beneath. The churchyard is filled with sailors' headstones, tall and bold. But the church's chief curiosity is its extra tower, an octagonal lantern at the east end of the chancel and cause of much speculation.

This chancel tower is normally considered to be a lighthouse, odd since the west tower is higher. The structure is too light to carry a bell, too heavy to be a sanctus bellcote and too strangely placed to have been a stair turret. Visitors are given slips of paper to come up with suggestions. Mine is that the lantern was a private venture by a local patron, an act of ostentation to rival whoever sponsored the main tower. Either way, it is a pleasing folly, an aft-mast to Blakeney's mainmast.

The earliest and most interesting part of the interior is the chancel, dating from a Carmelite friary founded here in 1296. This has a rib vault and a rare stepped seven-lancet east window, which is unusual for this late date. The only other medieval seven-lighter extant is at Ockham (Surrey). Here the monks would have conducted their Mass in intimate splendour, while the parishioners worshipped in the nave beyond. The nave is Perpendicular and architecturally conventional. Gazing over it is the original rood beam and Nativity figures, with a restored screen beneath them. The 20th-century stained glass in the south aisle windows portrays the history of early Christianity in Britain, and there is a leaflet to supply the key.

Blakeney today conveys a sense of vigorous activity. On my first visit, the churchwardens were lined up on parade to greet the parson, flowers in vases, hymn books at the ready, music sheets in hand. Each bay of the aisles was devoted to a local institution: the lifeboat station, the sailing club, the primary school, the bookshop, war veterans and church history. There was also an exhibition of the church's restoration over the years.

In other words, Blakeney offered a rare example of what every large historic parish church should aspire to being, also a community centre, market place and museum. Visitors could make themselves cups of coffee and take windfall apples from a basket. They were made to feel welcome, for whatever reason they had come.

Blakeney boasts that it was Norfolk's 'tourist church of the year, 1994'. A churchwarden is quoted from 1892: 'We do not want our churches to be picturesque ruins. We want them restored to the glory of which they were shorn in the days of intolerance and vandalism.'

BOOTON
St Michael **
Gothic Revival extravaganza by Pocahontas descendant

Where would the parish churches of England be were it not for the arrival of rich and sophisticated clergymen from Oxford and Cambridge in the 1830s and 1840s? Some were devout, some ambitious, some eccentric, some merely younger sons, but they were committed to ministry as few had been since the Reformation.

Whitwell Elwin of Booton was all these. He was a local man but descended, like others in the neighbourhood, from the Red Indian princess Pocahontas. He went to Cambridge and came to the Booton living in 1849, remaining there until his death in 1900. He edited the High Tory *Quarterly Review* (from 1853 to 1860), a task requiring so large a correspondence that the Post Office installed one of its earliest letter boxes in the village. He enjoyed a wide circle of friends and correspondents, including senior politicians and young ladies. He was also an ascetic. The austere redbrick rectory, which he built with his wife's dowry, remained undecorated, uncarpeted, unheated, and furnished only with hundreds of books.

The church, now redundant, was begun in 1875 and paid for by a lady friend of Elwin's who spent £1,500 a year on it for twenty years. She raised the money by slowly selling her land to a railway company. Elwin appears to have designed as he went along, consulting books from his library. All but the inner walls of the former church were demolished and replaced by do-it-yourself Gothic Revival. Today its thin, pinnacled turrets beckon across the fields from Salle and Cawston. Closer to, they are joined by other pinnacles, finials, crockets and even a minaret. Features are borrowed from other churches and cathedrals. Most prominent are the two western towers, triangular in plan, set at an angle to the west front but rather throwing the composition off balance.

The interior is less successful, blighted by the customary Victorian frigidity. But Elwin's eccentricity is some compensation. The chancel arch is topped by a triangular window that dominates the arch itself and leaves an uncomfortable space above it. The chancel has thick walls – apparently those of the old church – and two-light window openings. The pulpit is in the form of a bishop's throne, from which the chancel is invisible.

All this is raised from banality by the roof and the glass. The first has big East Anglian hammerbeams apparently based on Trunch. The angels are the work of an accomplished carver. Of equal quality is the excellent stained glass. The chancel glass is by the firm of Cox, Sons & Buckley, with a vividness rare in glass other than by Morris. The Isaac and Jacob in the south window is particularly fine.

The nave windows form a procession of angels playing musical instruments, executed to Elwin's designs by Purchase & Booker. They walk through lush fields and flowers, hair flowing and with lifelike faces. Some of these angels are reputedly portraits of the 'Blessed Girls', as Elwin called his many young female friends. Edwin Lutyens married one of them, calling this church 'very naughty but built in the right spirit'.

[CCT]

BRISLEY
St Bartholomew *
Stately box pews

The church is a Norfolk giant, dominating its small village across the church-yard. All is flint and fine proportion, the tower just strong enough to balance the two-tier nave and chancel. The west face of the tower is a superb composition of door and west window in a single frame.

The interior is spacious and unscraped. Plaster peels from ageing and damp walls. Here archaeologists have searched for wall paintings and found a small St Christopher, unusually on a south wall. (St Christopher was normally on the north wall, to greet travellers as they entered from the south porch opposite.) The screen is a soaring composition, hiding a beautifully canopied piscina and sedilia in the chancel. The three-decker pulpit retains its sounding board. Rectory and manor pews lead a stately sequence of box pews and benches. These appear to be of the same design, which suggests that the carvers intended a class gradation from the start.

The bench-ends include what looks like a mastiff eating a goose. On the floor are old red tiles that might have been lifted from a de Hooch painting and scrubbed for ages. Beneath the chancel is a crypt, once apparently used for prisoners being escorted overnight on their way to Norwich jail.

BURNHAM DEEPDALE
St Mary *
Labours of the Months font

The Burnhams have six medieval churches within two miles of one another. This coastline was the first landfall of the east winds from central Europe and thus of the Saxon invaders from across the North Sea. We do not know how many of Norfolk's round towers were begun by Saxons, but even those founded by the incoming Normans would have been built with Saxon hands and Saxon voices. With no stone for quoins, a round tower was probably standard for early Norfolk churches. The oft-cited need for towers as defence against Viking raids is improbable. These towers came later and anyway could not have with-stood much of a siege. Nelson was brought up at Burnham Thorpe and would have wandered the quays at Burnham Overy Staithe, admiring the square-riggers that once docked there.

Deepdale church is mostly Victorian and uncomfortably adjacent to the main road. The round tower has Saxon traces. Inside the church are two treasures, the Norman font and the medieval glass. Both are outstanding. The font is square and its carving secular, three faces containing panels of the Labours of the Months. January is drinking from a horn, February has his feet up by the fire, March is digging. We go on through pruning, weeding, mowing, reaping, pig killing and, in December, feasting. The carving is crude and eroded, but the naturalism of the poses offers a picture window on the past.

The glass is less immediate in its appeal. It is fragmented and scattered in a number of windows, with Victorian work in between. The best fragments are in the north aisle west window, including a beautiful roundel of the Trinity. A small abstract pattern surrounding a red cross is half-hidden behind the pulpit. There are fragments in the vestry and under the tower. Most charming, in the porch, are the 'sun' and 'moon' windows, the latter a jolly character with a Mona Lisa smile.

BURNHAM NORTON
St Margaret *
Wineglass pulpit

Norton stands lonely on a hill looking out towards the marshes and the coast. The tower is round, probably Anglo-Saxon in origin. Norton's font appears to be of the same family as Deepdale, square though with abstract rather than figurative decoration. The battered and restored rood screen includes 15th-century painted panels.

The wineglass or 'goblet' pulpit is one of the best in Norfolk in this delightful style. Shaped like a glass with stem but no base it must have been unstable should the preacher grow too agile in his oratory. 'Pray for John Goldale and Katherine his wife, they had it made in 1450', says the inscription. The panels portray the four Latin Doctors, Ambrose, Augustine, Jerome (mending his pen with his penknife) and Gregory. The pulpit was overpainted by the Victorians but recently restored to its medieval state. These wooden pulpits, which recur at South Creake, Blakeney and elsewhere, are among the most charming evocations of Norfolk Perpendicular.

The east window of the chancel is a gem of early 20th-century English glass, by an unnamed artist. Dated 1927, it depicts the two St Margarets, of Antioch and of Scotland. The style is Art Deco, one figure in profile, the other full face, both vivid with colour.

BURNHAM OVERY TOWN
St Clement *
Serene chancel

The church of Burnham Overy is a mile inland from the old harbour on a rare Norfolk hill near Burnham Market. Two windmills stand nearby. The church has a central tower with a pretty 17th-century cupola which stands like a ship's funnel on a long super-structure of nave and chancel. The tower was lowered when in danger of collapse. Traces of former high rooflines of chancel and transepts can be seen on the exterior. Today the transepts have gone, but this must once have been a substantial cruciform church.

What appears outside as three cells becomes two inside, with an odd corridor linking them. This was created when the crossing arches were filled with masonry to give strength to the tower. On the nave north wall is a diminutive St Christopher, apparently wading in Burnham Creek, with the church in the background. The north wall also holds a memorial to Robert Byford (d.1704). This is an accomplished work to find in so humble a church, a Baroque cartouche with projecting broken pediment above and a jumble of skulls beneath.

The chancel is now a separate and beautiful space. The arcade to an old south chapel has been retained, almost as an architectural folly, leaning outwards against the wall. At the foot of one of the piers is a curious 'floor piscina' of a sort I have not seen elsewhere.

CASTLE ACRE
St James *
'Ride-in' door, font cover

Castle Acre is a big church, proudly situated between the outer limits of the old castle and the precinct of the priory. This must once have been a thriving community, alive with soldiers, monks, tradesmen and pilgrims. Today it is a picture village. The church survives while its associated military and civilian settlement has diminished.

St James is flinty and Perpendicular, its churchyard running down to the priory ruins. The exterior is unexciting except for an oddity on the south chancel wall, a high Norman arch showing in the brickwork above an Early Gothic door. This clearly predates the rest of the church and may have been an opening high enough for a knight in full armour to ride into the sanctuary for blessing before battle. Since complex machinery was needed to winch heavily-clad soldiers on to horses, dismounting and remounting at a church door would have been a nuisance. Castle Acre thus qualifies as the world's first 'drive-in church'.

The interior is high, white and bright. At the rear of the nave a superb font cover rises on the slenderest of wooden supports. It is plain but remarkable for its height and medieval colouring. The church's other treasure is its wineglass pulpit, with painted Doctors of the Church and texts emanating from their mouths. This pulpit looks uncomfortably small, just two feet across, and the benches are equally diminutive. Historians used to suppose that medieval people were smaller than today, though this has since been disproved. They were just more accustomed to discomfort.

The only interruption in the clear glass is a medieval St George with his shield, in the east window of the south chapel. At the back of the church is a map showing pilgrims the way from this St James to the shrine of the same saint at Compostela. This is not just a drive-in church but has its own Continental motorway map.

CAWSTON
St Agnes ***
Hammerbeam roof, guild chapels

Cawston is a monument to cloth, of the sort that has dominated this landscape for half a millennium. Who crafted these churches we do not know, but we do know who paid for them. They were built not to be filled with people but to display the piety, generosity and ostentation of their wealthy patrons, here principally of Michael de la Pole, Earl of Suffolk and benefactor of many East Anglian churches. He paid for the tower after a previous one was blown down in a gale in 1412.

The tower is a massive keep, with angle buttresses sliced off at the top without parapet or battlement. As at Salle, the material was costly stone, some of it apparently from Caen. The stages are carefully modulated, with an elongated bell-chamber giving verticality to what would otherwise seem excessively heavy. The west front has its doorway and window contained in a single great arch. The doorway spandrels display the crest of the de la Poles: the head of a wildman facing a dragon. The north porch was the gift of the Oxburgh family, whose name is above the door.

Other benefactors are on display inside. The north transept is the work of the St Edmund Guild. The south transept was built by the Guild of St Mary, whose members are portrayed in the bosses. The piscina repeats the dragon and wildman motif, suggesting that de la Pole was a member of this fraternity. Another guild, that of the Plough, was responsible for the bell gallery under the tower arch, and for an annual 'ale' or fête to which the inscription refers. Alternatively the ale may be a local barley tax for church expenses. Plough guilds and associated inns were common in the Middle Ages. When Cawston's Plough Inn closed, it donated its sign to the church.

The church interior is dominated by one of the finest hammerbeam roofs in Norfolk, complete with the customary host of saints. Angels stand proud on the beam ends, as if about to dive into space. The spandrels behind are delicately traceried. Restored fragments of the rood cross mural can be seen above the chancel arch. Lute-strumming angels from the old clerestory windows have been relocated to a window in the south aisle.

Cawston's other treasure is one of the highest screens in the county, rising almost the height of the arcade arches. From the nave, its tracery is beautifully silhouetted against the Intersecting east window behind. The screen retains its original doors, and the dado panels have a set of painted images in excellent preservation. They are attributed to Flemish artists. A favourite is St Matthew with spectacles reading a book. The unusual figure on the farthest right is John Schorne (d.1314), a quack who claimed to cure gout by removing the Devil from boots. His shrine was at North Marston (Bucks) and his fame was so great that he appears in screens alongside saints.

Cawston's pulpit, font, misericords and poppyheads date mostly from the 15th century, since when little has been touched.

CLEY NEXT THE SEA
St Margaret * * *
Two-storey porch, oriental doorway, medieval carvings

Cley is a sea church stranded inland. East Anglia in the 14th century was rich and Cley port was one of its glories. The porch would once have been filled with the icons of sailors whose vessels crowded the quay south of what is now the churchyard wall. Today the old harbour is a rolling meadow.

The rebuilding of the church began at the start of the 14th century under the aegis of the de Roos family. They completed the new nave and transepts in the Decorated style. The old tower and chancel were still standing when, in 1349, the town was hit by plague, which killed much of the population. The port silted up and the town never fully recovered. What survives today is mainly a memorial to that bleak year.

Most of the splendours of Cley are to be seen from the south, originally the harbour, side. The Decorated south transept is now ruined but still has its walls intact. It is crowned by a crocketed and pinnacled gable framing one of Norfolk's most beautiful and eccentric windows. Four lights rise to support two circles containing quatrefoils. These in turn uphold a lozenge with four more quatrefoils. The nave clerestory windows are similarly wilful, alternating conventional two-light openings with roundels, apparently for no reason beyond the sheer joy of variety. The church's west door is framed by a cinquefoil with deep cusping. This echoes the oriental motifs brought to England by European and eastern merchants. Similar designs are displayed in the north porch of St Mary Redcliffe, Bristol.

The spectacular south porch was rebuilt in the early 15th century. This has two storeys, the upper one variously a storeroom, a library, a school and a priest's chamber. The ground storey is vaulted, with a lady chasing a fox carved in the central boss. The south face is an elaborate design with panelling, image niches and a pierced parapet. Round the entrance are the arms of the various patrons, the Vaux, de Roos, Nerford and de la Pole families. Clearly all was not lost to Cley by the Black Death if the church could command such patronage into the 15th century.

Inside, Perpendicular blandness is relieved by the brilliance of the light, with fragments of medieval glass surviving in the clerestory. Between the arches of the nave arcades are image niches, standing on corbels which form a gallery of medieval carving. One is of a musician, another of a lion chewing on a bone, another of St George fighting what looks like a domesticated village dragon. Similarly imaginative carving is on the Tudor bench-ends, whose monsters seem eager to climb from the maritime slime to ascend the glories above.

CROMER
St Peter and St Paul *
Tallest Norfolk tower, Burne-Jones window

Since Cromer was little more than a fishing village into the 19th century, the scale of its medieval church is astonishing. The 160-ft-high tower is the tallest in the county. Huge Perpendicular windows loom over the old town. When Victorian tourists arrived, they found a demolished chancel and much of the church ruinous. The wardens even bought hedgehogs to keep down the vermin. Blomfield rebuilt the nave and supplied a new chancel in 1887–9. He also restored the original porch, the richest part of the building.

The interior is therefore mostly Victorian and is spectacular. The hammer-beam roof has angel decoration and the tower arch is enormous. The aisles rank with those at Great Yarmouth for scale, lined with seven bays of transomed four-light windows. These run the entire length of the nave and chancel. Most of the windows are filled with tinted lozenge glass, filtering but not obstructing the daylight and with small quarries of yellow. There are modest memorials in modern glass to Cromer's seafaring characters.

The east window of the south aisle is by Burne-Jones, its brilliance radiating vividly across the interior.

EAST DEREHAM
St Nicholas **
Twin towers, Seven-Sacrament font

The dedication is to Nicholas but the church, and indeed the town, are in thrall to St Withburga. She was a daughter of the 7th-century King Anna of the

East Angles, whose progeny included Etheldreda, Sexburga and Ethelburga. St Withburga performed various miracles, not least of which was that her body did not decay on death. In the 10th century, monks from Ely stole it from this church, but her grave spouted a spring of pure water which flows to this day.

The church is oddly located below the centre of the town towards the river. There are two towers. One was built in 1536 and stands separate from the main church, Tudor and rather dull. The other is over the crossing, with a cupola and weathervane portraying Withburga's deer on top. We know that a Norman crossing tower collapsed in the 14th century and the replacement tower was presumably not considered strong enough for bells. Hence the new one in the churchyard. The nave was probably lengthened by building a new crossing east of the old one. The two towers now form an odd couple, as if married but agreeing to live apart.

The interior is eccentric. The nave is a simple unscraped space mostly of the Decorated style, yet with fragments of all architectural ages. The south piers are early 13th century and the north piers late 13th. The pride of East Dereham is its Perpendicular font, showing the 'Seven Sacraments'. This is one of the best in the county. Most such fonts were destroyed by Puritans objecting to the plurality of sacraments, so a complete work is rare. The sacraments are Mass, Ordination, Matrimony, Extreme Unction, Baptism, Confirmation and Penance. It has carved figures in four tiers and the details are beautifully executed; the Crucifixion is included to form the eighth side. The panels and saints niches have miniature lierne vaults, while the bowl is supported by angel corbels.

From the nave we pass to the transepts, with delicate painted ceilings of the 15th century, the southern one on the theme of the Lamb and the Book with Seven Seals. Below is a screen from Oxborough church. Its saints' faces are unmutilated, including an indistinct one of St Withburga. The north transept is a shrine to the poet William Cowper (d.1800) with a Heaton & Butler window of 1905. This depicts the poet piously gazing at his dog. 'His virtues formed the magic of his song,' says the inscription. Here too is a charming early Renaissance chest with a Nativity as its centrepiece.

The chancel is ferociously glazed, no chink of daylight being allowed ito intrude on the gloom.

EAST HARLING
St Peter and St Paul * *
Medieval glass, Harling and Lovell tombs

The tower of East Harling looks as if it has been telescoped into its base to avoid a thunderstorm. Light a fuse under it and it would rise like a rocket. The sequence is of robust base, delicate bell-stage and flèche of oak covered in lead. The south face of the nave is an essay in Perpendicularity, from the flush-work of the porch to the astonishingly tall mullions of the aisle and clerestory windows.

The interior retains Decorated work in the nave piers but again the Perpen-dicular dominates. The clerestory has nine triple-light windows, rising to a steep-pitched hammerbeam roof. Delicate carving fills the spandrels. The church is rich in medieval art, notably the 15th-century glass in the magnificent east window. The top row shows the Annunciation, Visitation and Nativity, the next the Life of Jesus, the next the Crucifixion and the bottom the Resurrection and Ascension, depicted with Christ's footsteps. Here too are the donors, Anne Harling's husbands, Wingfield and Chamberlain. The glass was removed for safe keeping during the Commonwealth and again during the last war and is thus a rare survival.

Anne Harling's tomb, with that of her first husband, lies between the chancel and the north chapel. More severe, classical monuments on either side of the altar are to the Lovells, who held the manor in the 16th and 17th centuries. The original choir stalls have animals climbing up their arm-rests, including a horse and lion in ungainly poses. Harlings and Lovells are commemorated again in the south aisle in two fine tombs, one Gothic, the other classical. Sir Robert Harling died in 1435, 'mangled by force of arms in Paris'. The tomb of Sir Thomas Lovell (d.1604) and his wife is a Jacobean masterpiece, beautifully coloured and with their emblems of feathers and a Saracen's head at their feet. This aisle also has a fine Tudor parclose screen round it, with vaulted coving and much original colour.

GLANDFORD
St Martin *
Victorian restoration as memorial to patron's mother

Down the road from Cley and over a challenging ford lies a Victorian model village, built by the Jodrell family of Bayfield Hall. A grassy slope next to the school leads up to the chapel refashioned from a ruin by Sir Alfred Jodrell in memory of his mother, Adela Monckton. Sir Alfred was a generous man, also restoring Salle church. St Martin's is a work of late-Victorian piety, warm and intimate, unlike such cold contemporaries as Daylesford (Gloucs). In summer the sounds and smells of the countryside slip easily into the nave.

The church was designed in 1899 by the little-known firm of Hicks & Charlewood and is a perfect example of a richly decorated High Church private chapel, although now a parish church. The short nave arcade is retained from the former church. The chancel is divided off by a complete rood screen, and has a hammerbeam roof. The chancel stalls are, as the guide boasts, worthy of an abbey. Above them rises an embossed roof with Italian candelabra, brought from Italy by Sir Alfred himself. The north chapel is a gem, with screens and rood loft stairs. Its ceiling is copied from Salle.

The font is a Norfolk Seven-Sacrament design, but re-created in Italian marble. In marble also is the Florentine memorial to Sir Alfred's mother. The glass is by Kempe and excellent.

GOODERSTONE
St George **
Painted screen panels

The church lies in the centre of its village beyond Oxburgh Hall. Its structure from outside is that of a traditional Norfolk mongrel, ancient base to the tower, Perpendicular nave, Decorated aisle and Early Gothic chancel with lancets and steep roof. Yet the church is full of eccentricities. The porch has unusual round windows in both walls, filled with tracery, almost as if a mason were setting his apprentices an exercise in fenestration.

The interior is charming. The nave, with only a south aisle, is exceptionally lofty, balanced by a chancel that is almost as high. The view east is superb. The two spaces, both flooded with light from clear windows, are divided by a Perpendicular screen rising almost to the top of the arch. This screen is the treasure of the church, both for its elegant tracery and for retaining on its dado paintings of saints and Church Doctors, albeit defaced. They are of good quality, though much in need of restoration.

The screen is lit by the north wall windows, a row of Perpendicular double-deckers, wonderfully high and light. The guide mentions donations by the guilds of St George, Corpus Christi and Holy Trinity. Whether each gave a window we do not know, but presumably this expanse was to carry stained glass in honour of the sponsors. The windows are reminiscent of those surviving in part at Nettlestead (Kent). Below the windows, 15th-century benches survive with poppyheads and low traceried backs. They cannot be comfortable but look happily appropriate to this setting.

GREAT WALSINGHAM
St Peter **
Rare 'bulb' tracery, carved bench-ends

The church is a serene contrast to the tourist-packed shrine of Little Walsingham down the road. When I asked the way to St Peter's a local man could not believe I wanted Great Walsingham rather than Little – indeed, he did not know why the epithets were not the other way round. He assured me that his local church contained nothing of interest.

St Peter's sits on a knoll outside the village, surviving virtually intact from the time of its building, c.1320, with some of Norfolk's most intriguing Decorated tracery. The gargoyles on the tower are so long as to make it look like an old steam funnel supported by rigging. The church has lost its chancel but seems none the worse for that. The principal windows are filled with tracery of the most distorted and fantastical form. Each ogival bulb has a smaller bulb seeming to grow inside it. Jean Bony, historian of English Decorated, finds this pattern only in neighbouring Mileham and in a cloister of a Cistercian abbey at Santes Crues in Catalonia. An English mason, Reynard Fennell, is known to have visited the latter church in the 1330s. Rarely do named artists pierce the anonymity of Gothic architecture.

The inside is a comforting chamber of roof, walls, seating and tiled floor, all bathed in an ochre tint, as if in an early photograph. The church is renowned for its 40 bench-ends, with poppyheads comprising a village art gallery. They include saints, flowers and mythical beasts and in the south aisle there is one of a dog begging. The benches have linenfold panelling in the front rows, pierced tracery backs and raised floor sills which were filled with straw in winter to take the chill off the feet. Great Walsingham also retains a rare aumbry on the north aisle wall, used for storing church treasures. Its original door, hinges and lock survive.

GREAT YARMOUTH
St Nicholas ***
England's largest parish church

Great Yarmouth is on the way to nowhere. With North Sea fishing in decline, the town's future must seem as uncertain as the flatlands that surround it are bleak. Yet the old town retains its historic core, including an astonishing church, the largest by floor area in England. St Nicholas was gutted by fire bombs in June 1942 and a wrangle ensued over the style of restoration. Should it be a new church, as at Coventry Cathedral, or a reinstatement, as in the previous Victorian rebuilding?

The answer was a bit of each, but mostly a restoration by S. E. Dykes Bower, completed in 1961. Pevsner in 1962 was appalled: 'What an opportunity was lost thereby! A modern interior, airy, noble, of fine materials could have arisen ... How defeatist does the imitation-Gothic interior appear.' I disagree, and the later edition of Pevsner is more moderate. But another opportunity was also lost. St Nicholas, after the Reformation, was divided into three churches, with separate areas for Independents, Presbyterians and Anglicans. After the bombing it was rebuilt solely for Anglican use – or under-use. The Church of England can be its own worst enemy.

The exterior is essentially Victorian. The west front to the main road is an eccentric composition of two large aisles with oversized turrets and pinnacles and three windows apiece. In the middle it squeezed the tiny nave end, which looks as if it has shrunk in the wash. Inside, all is Dykes Bower. White walls, leaping curves and honey-coloured stone arches dart off in all directions. The carving is crisp and the volumes clean. Yarmouth has a touch of a Sixties Habitat interior, most noticeable in the colours of the roofs.

The size of the church lies in width, not height. Dykes Bower sought to make the space of the aisles proportional to the nave by halving the number of bays in the nave arcades. He then commissioned Brian Thomas to create vividly coloured east and west windows. Dykes Bower himself designed the front of the great organ case in the north transept. This is a triumph of 20th-century Gothic, ranking with Comper's best. The blue, red and gold fascia glows out into the church, both bold and full of subtlety.

HADDISCOE
St Mary *
Saxon round tower, coachman's grave

In my experience England's most isolated spots are not at its extremities. They are cul-de-sacs such as Haddiscoe. It lies on a peninsula in a sweep of the River Waveney south of The Broads. Here Saxon invaders landed and formed their earliest settlements and here the first Christians placed their round-tower churches. Haddiscoe sits on its mound, as if waiting for another invasion that will come only if a new bridge is built across the Waveney. The place is so tranquil that we can still imagine the longboats pulled up on the banks of the marsh by what is now the churchyard, intent on some mild rape and pillage.

The round tower is small, at least to an eye used to later towers. The diameter is just 8 ft. The church would then have been of wattle and daub, with a thatched roof. The windows are typically Saxon, with triangular heads and a central shaft, but the chequerboard top stage is a 15th-century addition. The nave doorways are both Norman and therefore unusual in Norfolk, that on the south side with zigzag decoration and above it a relief of Christ in Majesty in a niche. The door is covered in wonderfully vigorous old ironwork.

The interior is disappointing. The north arcade was cut through the old Norman wall. The chancel contains a double piscina but the sedilia must have gone to make way for a Perpendicular window. The floor is tiled and the seats comforted with doormats. On the north wall is a faint St Christopher. Martin Travers's south window of 1931 celebrates the flower painter, Mia Arnesby

Brown. The churchyard wall holds a memorial to a coachman, William Salter, who died in 1776 when the Norwich stage crashed at this spot: 'His horses could they speak would tell / They loved their dear old master well ... / Take the reward of all his pains / And leave to other hands the reins.'

HALES
St Margaret *
Meadow setting, Norman apse

Hales tower can just been seen from the Norwich to Beccles road, a mile south of the present village. To sit in its overgrown churchyard surrounded by nothing but meadows and birdsong is to vanish from the modern world. Redundant but accessible, Hales's thatch has been renewed, its walls restored and its antiquity left undisturbed. Not much has happened round here since the Black Death.

The tower is round and the double-cell structure still has a Norman apse, making it the most intact pre-Gothic church in Norfolk. The apse has blind arcading, though interspersed with later lancets. There are Norman doorways north and south, the north particularly rich with a surround of zigzag and wheel-patterns. The capitals have rams' head and other decorations.

The interior contains an old pulpit, fragmentary screen, 15th-century font and brick altar. On my visit this was adorned with the most lovely dried flowers. Traces of murals are being uncovered, including a St Christopher and a St James.

[CCT]

HAPPISBURGH
St Mary *
Seaside setting, Evangelist font

This hulk of a church sits on a hillock at what could be the end of the world, an East Anglian Cape St Vincent looking due east out over the sea. Locals pronounce the place 'Haresbro'. The church has only a lighthouse and pub for company. Yet from its tower a dozen others are visible along the coast. Buttresses rise the full height of the tower, to help it withstand the easterlies that reputedly blow direct from the Urals. The flints embedded in walls might have been flung up from the beach by a storm.

Inside, the church is gaunt even by Norfolk standards. Best of the furnishings is a wonderfully intricate screen, offering a welcome touch of drawing-room urbanity. The font is also excellent. Against its stem are four lions and four wildmen, woolly, fierce and carrying clubs, surmounted by Gothic crocketed finials in relief. The bowl has reliefs of the symbols of the Evangelists, interspersed with angels playing musical instruments. Each panel is a delight.

The guide tells of a rector in 1793 who was concerned at the under-use of this font. He discovered that the reason was that poor parishioners could not afford the communal entertaining associated with a baptism. The rector undertook to pay for a large party himself, and on Whitsunday that year baptised 170 villagers at one session.

HARPLEY
St Lawrence *
Bench-end carvings

This odd little church lies up a lane away from its village and is almost enveloped in undergrowth. Outside is a tomb entirely encased in a blackberry bush. The church is a superb work of Decorated Gothic craftsmanship. Crocketing adorns the east-end gable, the windows and the lovely ogival priest's doorway. The south doorway is carved with saints and bishops. All this was the gift of the local Knollys family.

The interior is a musty space that might be lost in a stone forest. The benches are Perpendicular and complete, with poppyheads of bishops, monkeys, bears and mythical beasts. The front bench-end is signed John Martin 1638, but the rest look earlier. Harpley has a good screen with high Perpendicular tracery, but the dado figures have been repainted, like insipid characters from a children's Bible. The roof is restored but still has angels along its ridge and cornice; Harpley's angels, however, have folded wings which do not flap and they seem bored with life. There is an old bier at the back of the church, for carrying the coffins of the poor.

HEYDON
St Peter and St Paul *
Reformation fittings, black tomb chest

After crossing a prairie landscape with church towers rising like menhirs from the fields, we reach what seems a mirage. Heydon is a cosy estate village not of flint but of redbrick, with stables, almshouses and a well. The Earle Arms pub points to the gates of Heydon Hall. The scene is like a stage-set for Suffolk picturesque, yet in raw north Norfolk. The Heydons held the manor in the Middle Ages but left in 1447, to settle in their other manor of Baconsthorpe (and rebuild Salthouse church).

The tower is in the manner of neighbouring Salle, with Y-tracery in the bell-openings, battlements and crocketed pinnacles. The south porch has a vault with carved bosses and a priest's room above. The interior is little changed since a 17th-century refurnishing. The pews have poppyheads and there is a wine-glass pulpit. The manorial pew, with its own bible box, blocks any view of the altar from the north side of the church.

In the north aisle is one of the biggest tomb chests I have seen, belonging to Erasmus Earle. The black slab is 12 ft by 6 ft and reputedly broke three bridges and one man's back on its way here. Earle was a Cromwellian judge, born at nearby Salle, who bought the manor of Heydon and died here in 1667. Adjoining the tomb along the north wall are paintings surviving from the 13th-century church. They depict a traditional scene of 'three living and three dead', albeit truncated by the later windows. The crowned survivors are well preserved, a warning that mortality comes even to kings. This theme was a source of great comfort to the medieval poor – and is thus regularly reproduced.

Throughout my visit a bat darted up and down the nave, undeterred by a stuffed owl placed to scare it on the rood screen.

HINGHAM
St Andrew **
Morley tomb, German east window

Hingham is a typically big Norfolk church, towering over a small village. When these settlements were no more than wattle huts, the dominance must have been awesome. The exterior rhythm of tower, nave and chancel is serene, as is the interior rhythm of lovely 14th-century arcades. The nave height is immense, crowned by a superb hammerbeam roof.

Hingham's treasure, the Morley tomb, lies in the chancel, an astonishing work of red sandstone, rising the full height of the chancel and doubling as an Easter Sepulchre. To Pevsner this is 'one of the most impressive wall monuments of the 15th century in the whole of England', though he dates it well after Morley's death in 1435. The central arched recess is flanked by buttresses and every inch is carved. There are shields along the chest, weepers in relief against the back wall and Christ filling the centre pinnacle above. More figures appear in the arch. It is all a splendid flourish of manorial pomp that would not look out of place in Norwich Cathedral.

The east window was donated to the church by the lord of the manor in 1813, when Europe was being combed for treasures for the restoration of English churches. The glass is c.1500 from the Rhineland and comprises four separate windows merged into one. The style is distinctive, with a contorted Crucifixion reminiscent of Dürer. In the middle is St Anne, holding the Virgin holding Jesus. The colouring is garish.

The altar frontal has embroidery by Jeanette Durrant in 1986. It depicts the seasons in bright colours 'to balance the impact of the window above'.

KING'S LYNN
St Margaret * * * *
Norman west front, chancel carvings, 'peacock feast' brass

Poor King's Lynn, so dreadfully treated by the 20th century, still has corners of delight. Like most such corners, this one surrounds its church. St Margaret's remains the glory of the town, over which its twin towers stand like guardian angels. Despite the loss of the south-west spire, which crashed into the nave during a storm in 1741, and despite the bashings of every age, the church is a place of urban dignity. In the words of its excellent guide, its 'sturdy, muddled architecture has no claim to elegance'. Yet the church offers a stately progression, from Norman walling in the west front to Victorian reredos, that includes work of every period.

The church was founded (with Great Yarmouth) by Bishop Losinga of Norwich in 1101, as penance for his corruption in buying the See. The town was called Bishop's Lynn until after the Reformation and is just Lynn to its inhabitants. The church setting is 'town', with buildings huddled close on all sides. The two west towers rise above cliffs of Norman masonry, embedded in additions that appear to have no feature in common. This diversity is even more evident inside the west entrance. Norman wall shafting, like corrugation, continues round the tower supports. That on the north side leans markedly, as a result of medieval subsidence. The shafting on the south encloses a wall passage large enough to belong to a cathedral.

The nave is 18th-century Perpendicular, built by Matthew Brettingham of Holkham after the tower collapse. The charm of the interior lies east, in the 13th-century crossing and chancel. The piers have stiff-leaf on every capital. The arcades here form a gallery of medieval sculpture, a strip cartoon of Lynn's domestic life. A demon hugs a man, a woman is trapped in a scold's bridle and there are Green Men aplenty. The restored east window is a huge composition, a rose formed of Panel tracery. This was reconstructed in the 1870s from fragments found on the site and is somewhat tenuously claimed as the 'biggest Perpendicular rose in England'. The cheap painted glass is an insult and should be removed. The window forms a halo above Bodley's golden reredos of 1899. This is a masterpiece, with Christ blessing Gregory, Jerome, Augustine and Ambrose above beautiful reliefs of Bible scenes.

St Margaret's is a forest of screens and stalls. The former are mostly pre-Perpendicular, a rare display in wood of such Decorated motifs as steep gables, sharply pointed arches, trefoils, and ogees both flat and nodding. In among them are faces replicating those on the walls above. The misericords are excellent. The 16th-century eagle lectern once had its beak open to receive Peter's Pence, but this was later closed. Elizabethan screens shield the organ, its case a spectacular rococo work of 1754. The organist at the time was Dr Burney, father of Fanny and friend of Mozart.

The church's other treasures are the brasses in the south aisle. They are of Adam de Walsoken and Robert Braunche, of 1349 and 1364 respectively, among the largest and most elaborate brasses anywhere and normally credited to Flemish artists working in Bruges. While the faces and canopies are stylised, the clothes and panels appear to be specific to their subjects. The magnates of medieval Lynn were men of business and politics, not war. Under Braunche's feet is a depiction of a celebrated feast of peacocks he staged for Edward III in 1349.

KING'S LYNN
St Nicholas *
Two-storey porch, angel roof

The church in St Ann's Street, now redundant, was a chapel of ease for St Margaret's. It was not even allowed its own font until the 17th century. Though founded in the Norman period, St Nicholas was completely rebuilt in the early 15th century, its principal features being a magnificent south porch and a splendid Perpendicular nave and East Anglian angel roof. The spire was added by George Gilbert Scott in 1871, a period when, by my reckoning, he must have been working on literally hundreds of churches the length and breadth of England.

The two-storey porch is worthy of Gloucestershire's best. The façade is covered in beautiful niches and panelling, as if for the sheer fun of it. Inside the porch is a superb lierne vault. The church interior is spacious if rather bleak but has a fine roof, recently restored, of queen-posts interspersed with rich wooden tracery and decorated with squadrons of angels.

St Nicholas has lost its most famous bench-ends to the Victoria and Albert Museum – they depict sailing ships in full rig – but retains a beautiful poppyhead depicting Our Lady Star of the Sea surrounded by rich crocketing. The walls are adorned with the customary jolly 17th-century monuments of a busy town church, sadly busy no longer.
[CCT]

KNAPTON
St Peter and St Paul *
Angel roof

This is a land with towers on every horizon, sitting on small eminences like Corsican menhirs or Spanish windmills. They do not soar, as in Lincolnshire or

Somerset. They are more castle keeps, square, strong and plain. But they are visible, defining every ploughman's field and every village community. Knapton on its hill is neat, its walls of flints gathered from the fields round about. On the tower is a large weathervane designed by the artist John Sell Cotman when staying nearby.

Inside is a superb work of English carpentry. Knapton claims its roof to be 'probably the handsomest parish church roof in the country'. There are many challengers for this title, but the double hammerbeam erected in 1504 is faultless in its engineering. No deflection has ever been detected in the walls. The distribution of roof weight down the walls not only solved the problem of splay, but gave the carvers a gallery for their art. A 15th-century roof was, like a rood screen, a liturgical theatre. The saints, apostles and angels would have ready meaning for medieval worshippers, as would the emblems and scrolls in their hands. The roof was a 'cloud of witnesses'.

The work was repaired and repainted in the 1930s and a lower tier of angels added, making a total of 138 (Pevsner) or 160 (church guide). I fear I kept losing count. Knapton has little else of distinction. The font cover dates from 1704 and has a Greek palindrome which translates as 'Wash my sins, not my face only.'

LITTLE SNORING
St Andrew *
Round tower, fighter memorial

The name derives from an Anglo-Saxon invader named Snear. The church is attractively positioned on a slope over the stream from the village. This gives it a lush backdrop of green when approached from the south. A Norman round tower is detached from the body of the church and has a conical cap with dormer windows, like a dovecote. On closer view, we can see that a church extended east from this tower, its arch being now filled in except for a small door.

The present church is some yards uphill, and is mainly Gothic. Yet the porch and south door are Norman. This suggests there were two pre-Gothic churches on the site. The guide declares a mystery, and assumes the old tower to be Saxon, the nave having been burnt or grown too small and been demolished. Perhaps the old church began to subside, and a new one was built with the old tower left in place. Or perhaps the Norman door of the newer church was moved from the old on rebuilding. Who knows? Such are the puzzles that intrigue the church visitor. Above the doorway a grotesque face grimaces down at us, as if in tease.

Little Snoring is a friendly structure. Its outside walls seem to have been made of any materials that came to hand, pierced with windows of every period from Norman to Tudor. The nave has high screens near the door to keep out draughts. At its west end is a record of the local fighter squadron which used the church during the war, including details of each mission over Germany. The font is Norman and beautifully carved in a bold curvilinear pattern. Above the door is an unusual hatchment for James II dated 1686.

The chancel opens from the nave, lit by a triple deep-set lancet in the east and later Perpendicular openings. The north window is on a level with the upward sloping field and seems threatened by any passing tractor.

LUDHAM
St Catherine **
Painted tympanum, Evangelist font

Ludham is a Broads church in a spacious churchyard surrounded by old village houses. The exterior is of flint. The flushwork porch leads to a 14th-century interior, narrow, tall and with an emphatic screen and tympanum dividing it from the chancel. Before the insertion of the Perpendicular clerestory, the Reticulated east window must have glowed through the screen to a dark nave. No longer. The glory of Ludham is its nave roof and furnishings, bathed in sunlight and little affected by later restoration. Ludham is an immaculate survival. Even the old russet floor tiles are in place.

The nave is dominated by a hammerbeam roof, containing in its spandrels the wheel emblem of St Catherine. The screen has lost its vaulting but retains excellent paintings, almost up to Ranworth standard. The faces are little defaced and the hands expressive, all within richly traceried frames. Above is a celebrated tympanum, filling the arch over the screen with an extremely rare rood group defaced but visible in outline on the nave side. The arms of Elizabeth I face the chancel. After the Reformation, the rood group had been turned to face the chancel and the coat of arms painted, as is normal, facing the nave. This arrangement was reversed in 1867.

The Evangelist font is reminiscent of Happisburgh's, on a beautifully carved stem of wildmen in skins and with clubs, one of whom appears to be a woman. Female examples are rare (see Clare in Suffolk), especially in this case where the woman is obviously the companion of the male. The benches are medieval with carved poppyheads.

MERTON
St Peter *
Wilful Decorated tracery, angel-wing font

The church is set apart from its village, as if exiled in disgrace to the park of Merton Hall. The hall itself is some distance away over the lake, attended by green fields, horses and geese. The church is romantic – some might say dejected – its churchyard overgrown by bushes and high grass. Nature seems on the point of encasing the south porch entirely in vegetation.

Eccentricity is already apparent outside. The Norman round tower looks like something a local builder might have run up in an afternoon. The rest of the church is Decorated, under a steeply pitched roof. The window tracery of c.1300 is by those free-spirited masons of the period, twisting tracery into fantastic shapes, including an extraordinary version of cusped Intersecting in the chancel. At the rear of the dark interior the fine font has steps for statues, now vanished, and huge angel wings enveloping shields round the bowl. The piscina–sedilia group appears to be by the same hand as the windows. The Jacobean fittings are largely intact, including a two-decker pulpit, family pew and three-sided altar rail.

The screen is excellent, its Reticulated tracery a swirl of cusped openings so intricate as to suggest thorns on a rose tree. The doorway arch is alive with riotous ogees, as if in response to the surrounding vegetation.

MUNDFORD
St Leonard *
Comper furnishing

The church sits in its small churchyard on the outskirts of what was once a pretty village of variegated houses, but is now a series of uniform housing estates. Flint walls and a flèche on the saddleback roof of the semi-detached tower give no hint of the interior. This was blessed in 1911 by the arrival of the young Ninian Comper at the invitation of Captain Montagu of Lynford Hall. The result is an almost complete Comper set of 20th-century furnishings.

The masterwork is the screen, apparently constructed over an original frame. The loft and rood group rise above a vaulted arcade, supported in front on an extra row of shafts. In the place of musicians, Comper installed the pipes to his organ. The whole is painted in his usual vivid colours. This is the essence of Gothic Revival, a wilful originality of form and detail, a speciality of English church design throughout history.

Also by Comper is the jolly pulpit, from which a preacher seems more likely to crack jokes than lead a service. In the chancel are Comper stalls, retable, painted roof and a reredos whose figures complement those of the screen.

NORTH CREAKE
St Mary *
Gaudy roof angels

The church presents a massive Perpendicular tower to the Burnham road rushing a few yards from its west door. To reach the porch we venture beneath what seems the wall of a giant keep. Why so small an East Anglian church needs a tower and wall of such weight is a mystery. They were probably not defensive, nor were the bells so heavy. We must refer to those familiars of medieval tower building, fashion and rivalry.

The interior of North Creake, apart from its roof, is mostly an 1890s restoration of a Decorated chancel and Perpendicular tower and nave. The restoration is said to be faithful, but has deprived North Creake of much of the patina of age. The most noticeable feature of the nave is the roof, which retains some of its old paint. This fine East Anglian hammerbeam has gaudy angels that look rather oriental. The aisle roofs are simpler but also original. Even the restored chancel roof apparently uses the original members, though its angels look modern.

Above the chancel arch are the remains of a Doom painting, defaced by the chip marks of its plastering. This is a mess and would be better receiled. Beyond is a Decorated chancel containing a fine group of piscina, sedilia and Easter Sepulchre. This church needs three hundred more years to mature.

NORTH ELMHAM
St Mary *
St Cecilia screen painting

I am biased in North Elmham's favour after visiting it on the day of the August flower festival. Not a surface was without a display of blooms, each one chosen to illustrate a biblical phrase. The church stands bold against the road near the site of Norfolk's first cathedral, before the See moved to Thetford and then Norwich. The ruins of a chapel of the Saxon cathedral are still visible a hundred yards to the north.

The present structure is externally Perpendicular, with a big tower of stone-dressed flint and buttresses so prominent as to look like splints round a broken limb. A most unusual west porch is jammed in between them. In the north side of the church is a small 13th-century doorway with an equally unusual flourish of leaf carving beneath its hood. The interior makes free use of every period of

English architecture. The nave is ostentatiously high, built on an Early Gothic arcade of alternating round and octagonal piers. Above is a 15th-century clerestory, its height elongating the pillars beneath and carrying the eye far into the ceiling.

The church is noted for its screen panel paintings. These are of the highest quality, the faces only lightly scratched by iconoclasts. The portrait of St Cecilia is particularly fine, apparently original, as is St Dorothy next door. Elmham has Tudor benches with ends intact, and patches of medieval glass, gently effective in the north aisle tracery. But see it with flowers!

NORTH WALSHAM
St Nicholas *
Vaulted porch, Gothic font cover

The church is tucked away behind houses above the Market Place, in the town yet aloof from it. The old tower was almost as high as Cromer's, but on a stormy night in 1724 half of it came crashing down. The remainder survived another century before it too gave up the effort, its fall shaking the town so badly that many thought there had been an earthquake. Such were the massive temples built by medieval masons. The tower is now a ruined scar, with a fragment of a Saxon church visible on one side and the bell-loft still clinging to the wall inside.

The porch is most enjoyable, embellished with flushwork panelling and nodding ogee niches. It is 14th century, carrying the arms of John of Gaunt and Edward III and with a newly painted vault. If this looks vulgar to the modern eye, complain to the Middle Ages. The gate grille is of oriental intricacy. The interior displays familiar East Anglian characteristics, the roof offering no break for the chancel, which is flanked by aisles on both sides. The splendid font cover of *c.*1450 leaves no surface without cusp or pinnacle, rising the full height of the nave to a crowning pelican. It is more delicate and in many respects a finer work than more famous covers at Castle Acre or Trunch. The screen dado survives, with defaced saints.

The chancel contains a monument to Sir William Paston (d.1608). It was commissioned and built before his death, and displays the restrained classicism of the reign of Elizabeth I. Under the tower is a coat of arms of Charles II with an unusual Cromwellian device on the back. Beneath are two gargoyles salvaged from the tower. Seen close to, these grotesques might be by Epstein or Gill.

NORTHWOLD

St Andrew **

Stiff-leaf carving, Easter Sepulchre relic

Those who believe wild England is confined to uplands and seashores should explore the frontier between the Breckland and the Fens. Sand and Scots pine give way to the most desolate of landscapes. Northwold is a fine guardian of this country. It was birthplace of Bishop Hugh of Ely (d.1254), 'flower of the Benedictine order', and was thus beneficiary of his enthusiasm for church-building. To Hugh we owe Northwold's treasure, its 13th-century nave arcades adorned with clusters of stiff-leaf.

The church's most prominent outward feature is its tower, built *c.*1470, whose diagonal buttresses take no fewer than eight steps to the top. There they support lofty pinnacles above flushwork battlements. The intricate brick and flint clerestory is of the same 15th-century period.

The interior is enlivened not just by stiff-leaf carving on the capitals of the arcades but, most unusually, by carving on the bases as well. The walls carry traces of paintings, with skeletons much in evidence. Here the theme of 'three living and three dead' is depicted as three kings who went hunting and met three forebears, who said to them: 'As you are, so were we / As we are, you will be.'

The roof is excellent, of alternate hammerbeams and angels with six gold wings at the intersections. Even they are outshone by the Easter Sepulchre in the chancel. This has a canopy with three lierne vaults, each one different and tilted for visibility. The tomb chest beneath has a relic of a superb composition of Roman soldiers all in agitated attitudes, with trees as a background. Much of the sepulchre is of chalk, an easy target for the ravages of time and iconoclasm.

NORWICH

Octagon Chapel, Colegate *

Wesley's 'most elegant Meeting House'

Norwich has two of the most impressive Dissenter chapels in England, within 100 yds of each other along Colegate. The Old Meeting House, a Congregational foundation of 1693, has the more exciting exterior; this is in the richest William and Mary taste but is inaccessible. The neighbouring Octagon Chapel is more welcoming. The building is later, erected in 1756 for the Presbyterians, but handed to the Unitarians in 1820.

The chapel is shaped as its name implies and stands at the end of a small courtyard with alleys on either side and a graveyard behind. The exterior presents a wide portico to the yard. Ionic columns lead worshippers up spreading steps to an arched doorway. The roof is lit by circular dormer windows, ridiculed by some Anglicans as 'the Devil's cucumber frame'. It might indeed be the gazebo of a Georgian stately home. The roof is supported by arches resting on eight Corinthian columns, intersected by galleries. The pulpit holds centre stage, with the organ behind.

Wesley greatly approved of the Octagon, which seemed to him a stylistic advance on the New Room at Bristol (Gloucs), which he had built in 1739. It was, he said, 'the most elegant Meeting House in Europe ... furnished in the highest taste and as clean as any gentleman's saloon'. The Octagon was much imitated for Methodist churches in the 19th century. The church boasts five mayors of Norwich on its mace rest.

NORWICH
St Andrew, St Andrew's Street *
Dance of Death glass

After the Second World War Norwich still had 35 medieval churches, more per square mile than any city north of the Alps. In the 1970s the majority, 24, were declared redundant. Despite a vigorous campaign of salvation and reuse, the outcome has been a sadness for a city whose economy is bound to rely ever more on visitors. A tour of all these churches, had they been properly restored, would have been a superb experience. Instead, some were sold to new owners and few are accessible to casual visitors. Norwich has been unable to emulate York or Stamford (Lincs) with an active programme of church opening. As a result, precious survivors of the city's medieval past lie across the face of the city like so many black holes.

But not St Andrew's. Built in the prosperous late 15th century, it rises above the old town and is second only to St Peter Mancroft in size. Although extensively restored by the Victorians, it retains an aura of civic importance, a 'maximum of space with minimum of materials', says the guide. Monuments cover every inch of wall, especially in the Suckling Chapel in the north aisle. This is a gallery of late Elizabethan and Jacobean memorial art, a forest of slabs, balls, finials and skulls. The monument to Sir Robert (d.1589) has the figures kneeling and facing each other. By 1613 another Suckling, Sir John, is lying in less pious fashion, gazing over his wife, uniformed and with baton in hand. The tomb inscription is written in five languages.

The church has excellent fragments of 15th-century glass in the south aisle. These include one of my favourite works, a splendid Dance of Death in which the Devil is cavorting with a bishop across a chess board.

NORWICH
St Peter Mancroft, Market Place ****
Embellished tower, medieval glass of Bible scenes

St Peter is, like St Cuthbert, Wells (Somerset) and St Mary Redcliffe, Bristol (Gloucs), the town church of a great merchant city. It is the creation of commercial wealth rather than episcopal tithes, expressing civic achievement in architecture and cocking a snook at the cathedral. Here merchants met and worshipped in their guilds, civic rituals were performed and burghers were married and buried. Such churches are often compared to cathedrals but to no point. They were specifically not cathedrals. They were the apotheosis of the community church.

St Peter's towers over the crowded streets of Norwich's core. It was built in one campaign in 1430–50 and is thus English Perpendicular at its most mature. This is not a church of accretions but a single statement, one style, one place and one space. The exterior is dominated by the tower, intended to overtop Boston's but nowhere near as high. It was not completed until Street added a Victorian flèche in the 1890s. The tower remains a massive work, one of the most enriched in England, its walls covered in panelling and blind arcading and with huge three-light bell-openings. The crown carries a superb stone frieze rising to pointed battlements. The church has vaulted porches north and south. The north porch has had its niches filled with good modern statues: so why not the tower niches as well?

Few who enter St Peter's for the first time can stifle a gasp. The sense of space and light is overwhelming. To those who find Perpendicular bland or lacking in shadow and mystery, Norwich answers with a blaze of daylight, as if the sky itself had been invited in to pray. Shafted piers rise upwards past canopied saints between clerestory windows to a wooden ribbed coving concealing a hammerbeam roof. The eye is then taken further, through an angel frieze with outstretched wings to reach a climax of rose bosses. This is a supreme work of 15th-century carpentry, full of subtle refinement.

The east window entirely fills its wall, and is itself filled with mostly original glass of a 'people's Bible', with donors below. This glass includes moving New Testament scenes – such as a woman trying to strangle a soldier impaling her baby – and would have been the only illustration seen by most medieval citizens. It was reassembled after a Civil War explosion nearby, but missing panels have turned up at Felbrigg Hall and at the Burrell Museum in Glasgow. They should be returned at once. The replacement central panels are by Clayton & Bell. The reredos is by Seddon of 1885, completed and gilded by Comper. The aisles are one bay shorter than the nave, again culminating in walls of illuminated glass.

The font is a simple Seven-Sacrament work, much battered. Its canopy takes the form of four Perpendicular supports rising to angels flanking (empty) niches. St Peter's tower has a celebrated peal of twelve bells. The ringers, or 'scholars', can refresh themselves afterwards with a pewter beer jug capable of holding 33 pints.

OUTWELL
St Clement *
Family chapels, mini-hammerbeam

The road from Wisbech to Downham Market reaches the Well Creek off the Old Bedford River. This was the scene of extensive drainage in the 17th century, initiated by the Earl of Bedford and evident today in long dykes and Dutch-style bridges. Tall trees protect the church's east end from the road and the harsh Fenland sky. The crumbling gargoyles seem too relaxed to offer any menace and are almost welcoming.

Outwell's windows are of three, five, six and even seven lights, and lend the interior the aura of an old country house conservatory. The roof is populated by red and gold angels on the tie-beams and hammers. The charm of the church lies in its chapels, now dressed for Anglo-Catholic ritual with saints, icons and candles. The south chapel was for the Beaupré family, and has fine 18th-century iron gates and 16th-century monuments. The east window retains some medieval glass. The north chapel was for the Finchams and now contains the organ.

The small north aisle or Lynne Chapel has an excellent small hammerbeam roof, with sun and the shadows of trees pouring in from all sides. This is a place for those who like their churches cobwebby and romantic.

OXBOROUGH
St John **
Bedingfield monuments

At first sight the church is a ruin outside the estate wall of the magnificent Tudor house, Oxburgh Hall. The ruin is recent. One April morning in 1948, the old Perpendicular spire collapsed into the nave, while children in an adjacent playground watched aghast. The parishioners decided enough was enough and did not rebuild, leaving the nave a ruin. Only the chancel, south chapel and north aisle survived, the latter's corbel heads now gazing desperately out into the air. The chancel remains as the parish church, of domestic proportions and well converted. The original piscina and sedilia survive, still with some original colouring.

Oxborough's treasure is the Bedingfield Chapel next door. This is a typical work of early Tudor piety, endowed by Sir Edmund Bedingfield (d.1496) and his wife Margaret (d.1513) to contain their tombs. Bedingfield was Marshal of Calais. His wife was sister to Lord Marney, Tudor courtier and creator of Layer Marney Tower in Essex. Oxborough is an earlier structure but displays the same ostentatious brickwork. Like Marney's Essex tomb, the Bedingfield tombs are terracotta, but more classical. They have tomb chests and tall pedimented canopies with pilasters, and are covered in relief decoration. Both the material and the motifs are associated with the north Italian Renaissance of the early 16th century. But they crowd the tiny space more like the shrines of an Indian temple. Indeed Sir Edmund's tomb might be a model of the Temple of the Winds in Jaipur.

The chapel contains three other Bedingfield monuments, with the family crest of a fetterlock horseshoe, used to stop horses from straying. Seventeenth-century Bedingfields were Royalists and the inscriptions testify to their loyalty to their king. Sir Henry 'was tall and comely, endowed with rare parts both naturall and acuired'.

PULHAM ST MARY
**

Flushwork porch with carvings

The churches inherited by the Victorians in the early 19th century were mostly semi-ruins. Some were patched and left in peace. Most were modernised, with new pews, windows, roofs and chancel furnishings. Some Victorian patrons went further and created, in effect, new churches from the remains of old ones. This is what Bodley achieved at Pulham St Mary.

The exterior displays a fine flint tower and one of the best flushwork porches in the county. Panels and niches rise in tiers to a parapet of pierced quatrefoils topped by a wildman with a club. Although the niches have lost their images, much relief sculpture remains, including the head of St Edmund guarded by a wolf. The entrance arch spandrels contain scenes from the Annunciation.

Bodley arrived in 1886 to restore the roof and chancel arch, install new furnishings and repair the old screen. In the roofs we can still detect the original carpentry, for instance in the aisles. The chancel roof painting is clearly by Bodley, as is the font cover. His principal work is the screen, to which he gave a new loft with vaulted coving and filigree tracery in dark wood. The ribs are picked out in red, green and gold. The frame and the saints' pictures are (restored) originals. A medieval double piscina survives in the chancel, Early Gothic with intersecting round arches of a most graceful and unusual design. This is a medieval church re-created in the hands of a master craftsman.

RANWORTH
St Helen ***
Screen paintings

The 'parish church of The Broads' declares its welcome with a sign in the street booming OPEN. The tower summit offers a splendid view over the inland waterways, with sails fluttering into the distance. Taize's 'Resurrexit' was playing on a tape during my visit. Coffee was available, as was an excellent guide to England's finest church screen paintings.

Ranworth is of limited architectural interest. Ancient woodwork includes misericords, a linenfold pulpit and a rare medieval cantor's desk, decorated with fragments of plainsong. All eyes turn to the screen, a masterpiece of English medieval painting dating from the end of the 15th century. Its structure is simple, running the width of the nave and including the aisle chapels, where it forms a reredos. The coving of the loft survives as does the loft and loft stair, though without any parapet. Many of the surfaces have a delightful floral decoration on a white background, a pattern of which Robert Adam might have claimed authorship.

The painted panels themselves are so superior to most English screen painting at the time as to suggest a single artist, possibly from abroad. Pevsner relates the Ranworth paintings to others at Barton Turf and Southwold, but this is chiefly for the backgrounds. The quality of the figures at Ranworth is unique. They are mobile and developed, the faces full of expression. This is no workshop facsimile of an illuminated psalter, but the product of a personal vision. Aymer Vallance, in his 1936 study of church screens, is in no doubt that the artist was Spanish, a similar work existing in Barcelona. To him the Ranworth St Michael (with St George not far behind) is superb: 'Debonair and fantastic as he strides jauntily amid the serpent's coils ... the gaiety of his dancing draperies and the glitter of his dazzling gems are altogether of the South.'

SALLE
St Peter and St Paul ****
Norfolk's rural cathedral, font cover, carved bosses and choir stalls

Salle is a favourite of Norfolk church enthusiasts, isolated, wild and vast. Pronounced Saul, it booms out to travellers across the north Norfolk plain like an architectural foghorn. Its tower was erected on the wealth of wool and is now sustained on the love of its group of loyal parishioners. Salle might be a church of the Castilian plain, enriched with the gold of the Americas and far beyond the means or needs of its community. It is as much a testament to economic history as to faith.

The church was rebuilt in the early 15th century, paid for by Uffords, Mautebys, Morleys and Brewes. Rather than use cheap local flint, they brought costly Barnack stone from Peterborough, and were duly blessed for their generosity with two feathered angels waving censers over their coats of arms above the west door. By the middle of the century they had been joined by another cloth tycoon, Everard Brigg, whose E is worked into the tower parapet. The south transept was built by the St James's Guild, with the letter T for Thomas Brigg on its façade. The Brigg arms are also above the central niche of the south porch. The porches at Salle are big and double-storeyed.

Now for the inside. Entry is by the west door and the spectacle from the entrance is superb. The nave is as calm as the fields outside. Arcades rise and fall towards the chancel arch. An interior of immense height and volume frames the crockets of an elegant font cover. This is suspended from a huge bracket projecting from the bell-ringers' gallery in the tower, both embellished with tracery. Beneath this cover rests one of the best Seven-Sacrament fonts in Norfolk, its panels excellently preserved. Beneath each scene is a small angel holding the symbol of the sacrament above, such as the scourge as symbol of penance.

The roofs are no less splendid. The nave has a plain arch-brace with angels at the junctions of the rafters. The shallow transept roofs have charming cusped panels, while that of the St James's Guild Chapel in the south transept is allegedly the original for the roof of the House of Lords. Finest of all is the chancel roof, lifted into the sky on the wings of 160 angels, punctuated by a set of carved bosses worthy of any cathedral. Since they are near-invisible, there is a helpful photographic display of them on the wall. They show scenes from the Life of Christ, each ingeniously fitted into a circle. In a most explicit Circumcision, the baby seeks Mary's breast for comfort.

The nave contains a contemporary 15th-century wineglass pulpit, painted red and green, fashioned into a three-decker by a 17th-century clerk's desk and a reading desk. The furnishings include original choir stalls and misericords. The arm-rests and seats are a gallery of 15th-century vernacular art: dolphins, swans, squirrels, dragons and the heads of Green Men, all peering from flowers, fruit and leaves of familiar trees. The chancel also retains much original glass. On the north side are portrayals of patriarchs and even three cardinals in wide hats. They must have done well to survive the Reformation. The main east window glass is fragmentary but includes some vivid colouring, including pieces of dragons' wings.

A door in the north-west corner of the church gives access to the parvise of a porch. This was variously a priest's home, chapel and schoolroom. It has superb coloured bosses. The view from its window over the Norfolk countryside on a clear winter evening is one of utter tranquillity.

SALTHOUSE
St Nicholas **
'Lighthouse' windows

There is not a shoreline in England as rich in churches as the north coast of Norfolk. I was last at Salthouse during Sunday evensong when a late sun was flaming its glass and hymns were echoing across the sandy hillside. It was in every sense a lighthouse. This was always a treacherous shore. When the Norfolk magnate Sir Henry Heydon rebuilt the church at the turn of the 16th century, he put it as high as he could, to be safe from floods and to act as a lantern to ships at sea. The soft grey stone remains a beacon today. It is reached up a track from the shore, lined with high flint walls emitting an aroma of lavender and sage.

Heydon based his church on an earlier structure of which the Decorated tower and some windows remain. The aisle windows are unmistakably Perpendicular, rising tall and thin to the simplest of tracery. Inside, the vertical impact of these windows is exaggerated by the generous clerestory and no divide between nave and chancel. The chancel east window is also made to seem higher by the Y-tracery in the aisle east windows.

The furnishings of Salthouse suffered grievously at the Reformation. Fragments of a rood screen have been erected at the back of the nave. Others form divides for the choir stalls. They retain old paint, stencilwork and graffiti of ships scratched by clerks and schoolchildren. Such vandalism would seem outrageous today, yet these doodles are delightful mementoes of a community with the sea always on its mind.

SHELTON
St Mary **
Medieval donor windows, William III coat of arms

Perhaps it was the early summer haze, but Shelton seemed on my visit to typify the small Norfolk church. Fields and woods surround its enclosure, the only sound being of birds and the occasional bee. The manor built by Sir Ralph Shelton in the prosperous 1480s has gone, its site overwhelmed by nature. But his church survives. When seen from the road, the building is formed of a set of rectangles: diminutive tower, nine-bay clerestory, three-bay south aisle clad in diapered brickwork, and a high porch. The porch windows are like two eyes and a mouth.

The interior is as noble as the exterior is homely. It is formed of a single space, uninterrupted by any chancel arch, the walls white and the stonework a soft peach colour. Narrow arcades are linked to the clerestory by stone panelling and flattened niches in the spandrels. The nave is now ceiled, since the original roof was taken for a tithe barn in the 18th century, leaving angel corbels as ghosts. Iconoclasts were not the only wreckers of English churches.

The east windows contain a complete set of donor's glass. Sir Ralph and his wife pray to the Virgin. His son Sir John prays below, with King Edmund and Henry VII above them. Sir John was unable to complete his father's tomb, on which a start was made under the north wall. Politics intervened. His wife was aunt to Anne Boleyn, whose bull emblem is seen in the heraldry. After Anne's beheading, her daughter Elizabeth (the future queen) was hidden at Shelton, possibly in the tower, to avoid arrest. Almost every window in the church contains Shelton's scroll, his initial R and a rebus of a shell and a tun.

In the south aisle is a crude 1623 monument to the Houghton family, probably rearranged but now kneeling as a foursome with a rough and ready skull and crossbones painted above them. Above the tower arch is a superbly carved coat of arms of William III, given to the church in the 19th century.

SNETTISHAM
St Mary **
Decorated west window

Here is a corner of Lincolnshire that has wandered across the Wash. Approached from the west, Snettisham comes as no surprise. From the east it might be a foreign country, a land of stone rather than flint, of spires and thick-waisted pinnacles. Snettisham may have lost its chancel but the amputation makes it seem even bigger. It was designed *c.*1340 in the last phase of English Decorated at the time of the Black Death.

The church has a central tower, leaving the west end free for one of the finest windows in England. It greets the visitor climbing the incline from the road with a tracery pattern as complex as anything produced by the late Middle Ages. The lines flow sinuously upwards, the network of Reticulated ribs gradually taking life and breaking into naturalistic shapes, English Gothic flirting with Continental flamboyant. The pattern might be of roses encircling tulips, a glorious summer bouquet in stone. The tracery of the other windows is static in comparison.

Snettisham's interior has no truck with angels and hammerbeams. Soaring arcades greet clerestory windows of alternating rectangles and circles. The roof rafters are steeply pitched. Most of the furnishings are Victorian, but the eagle lectern is 15th century, fiercer and more realistic than the many 19th-century imitations. There is a wineglass pulpit, much restored. Many of the east and south windows were replaced after a bomb was dropped by a Zeppelin in 1915. This was apparently the first church in England to be attacked from the air.

SOUTH CREAKE
St Mary *
Anglo-Catholic furnishings

Which Creake is better? is as lively a question in Norfolk church circles as Which Burnham? South Creake is the more interesting, set in a wild churchyard of chestnut and cherry trees interspersed with headstones, and creeping ivy everywhere. The tower is stubby, lacking a parapet, like a head without a hat. The interior is a 15th-century conversion of an earlier structure, with a long chancel and a mix of periods in the window tracery. The removal of the pews reveals the stone seats round the pier bases and the remarkable height of the nave.

Today South Creake has been completely refurnished in the Anglo-Catholic rite. A 15th-century rood screen arrived in 1982 from a redundant church in Colchester. The Stations of the Cross are fibreglass, the font cover is blue and white. Above all this float painted angels on the roof hammerbeams. These were installed to celebrate the Battle of Agincourt in 1415 and hold shields of the Black Prince, musical instruments and Symbols of the Passion. They were repaired and repainted in 1958 and look vigorous.

Every available shelf or alcove is devoted to a statue or a shrine. Some are attractive, some less so. A figure of St Michael is dire. A shrine to St Edmund contains a statue of St Sebastian full of arrows. There are burning candles and the smell of incense everywhere. The windows mostly contain lugubrious glass. The cumulative impact of South Creake is of a richly endowed place of worship as it might have been before the Reformation cleared it of colour and clutter. The church has a much abused Perpendicular Seven-Sacrament font.

SOUTH LOPHAM
St Andrew **
Norfolk's best Norman tower

South Lopham is dedicated to St Nicholas but a 19th-century guide gave it to St Andrew by mistake and the new name stuck. So much for dedication. The church tower rises cool and magnificent over its grove of trees, isolated in the south Norfolk landscape. The trees form a virtual arboretum of evergreens, including a fine Wellingtonia.

The central tower is the most complete Norman work in the county. It does not appear to have had transepts. The exterior walls have blind arcading with minimal decoration, implying that this is an early work, possibly within a generation of the Conquest. It rises through no fewer than five stages, mostly with blind arcading, and might be a castle keep. Inside, the piers carry simple capitals, with no scallops or zigzag motifs.

The nave has no north aisle, only a solid north wall with one Perpendicular window. As compensation the Decorated south aisle and the clerestory suffuse the nave with light. Above is a hammerbeam roof. The chancel is likewise lit only on the east and south sides, but has big Decorated windows and mostly clear glass. The fine east window rises to a strangely squashed octofoil light. There is a scattering of good choir stalls. At the back, a splendid dug-out chest claiming to be 900 years old survives from the church's earliest days.

STOW BARDOLPH
Holy Trinity *
Hare effigy

The church overlooks the main road to King's Lynn on an eminence above the Great Ouse marshes. The exterior is of crumbling brick and rubble but the interior has been extensively restored. The object of a visit is on the north side, the 17th-century Hare Chapel, which hides Stow's chief attraction (or repulsion).

The chapel is now a Sunday school room. Pompous Hare monuments gaze down in lofty dismay on school tables covered in oilcloth. The monuments are curious rather than beautiful. That to Susanne Hare (d.1741) by Scheemakers has her in classical gown, lounging on the chest and looking up to Heaven. More grandiose is the earlier monument to Sir Thomas Hare (d.1693). He reclines on a cushion, bewigged but in a Roman soldier's uniform, as if an imperial consul. On the east wall are two fine Victorian brass plaques above a chest tomb to Sir Ralph Hare (d.1623), which, on my visit, was used as a shelf for the storage of coloured pencils and Sellotape.

This hardly prepares us for what lurks inside a cupboard against the chapel wall. This should be opened with care, for inside is a wax bust of Sarah Hare, the only monument of this material outside Westminster Abbey. Her will of 1743 was most explicit. She was to be buried by six poor men of the parish paid five shillings each for their pains. In addition, 'I desire to have my face and hands made in wax with a piece of crimson satin thrown like a garment in a picture, hair upon my head and put in a case of Mahogany with a glass before.' This instruction was carried out precisely. The effigy survives, having been conserved by Madame Tussaud's in 1984. Tussaud's should have been allowed to make more display of their handiwork, which is hidden and unmarked.

SWAFFHAM
St Peter and St Paul **
Hammerbeam roof, shopkeeper bench-end

We are at the northern limit of the Breckland wilderness, where the tower and flèche of Swaffham church are visible from afar. The Victorian spike might be a seaside fantasy but the creamy Barnack stone tower is conventional late Perpendicular, well set in a wooded churchyard. The church was the work of two men commemorated inside, the merchant John Chapman and the rector, John Botright (1435–74).

Their interior is beautifully proportioned, tall and slender with a happy sequence of arches formed by the chancel and east window beyond. Swaffham's roof is in Norfolk's first rank, of chestnut with one true and one decorative hammerbeam tier and a squadron of 88 flying angels. Dozens more angels decorate the wallplates. When restored they were found to be full of shot, said to be a relic not of iconoclasts but of shooting parties seeking to rid the nave of nesting birds.

The church's other treasures are more discreet. Medieval wood carving survives embedded in the Victorian benches and choir stalls. These include the emblems of the medieval liturgy and the celebrated Swaffham pedlar, supposedly John Chapman himself. Legend has him going to London to make his fortune, but being told by a shopkeeper that he is in the wrong place, and that his fortune lies in a pot of gold under a tree back in Swaffham. We must assume this was true. A lady, perhaps the shopkeeper, is depicted on another bench-end in the choir.

The carvings give a human touch to an otherwise austere interior. There is a fine Art Nouveau iron altar rail.

TERRINGTON ST CLEMENT
***
Font cover, Jacobean Commandments board

The view of Terrington St Clement from the south-west is of a majestic abbey, its buttresses and pinnacles stepped towards the sky. A detached tower rises to the left, a refuge for villagers during marshland floods. The medieval masons evidently dared not risk attaching a tower to the structure of the church on this soft soil. The tower came into its own during a flood in 1670 when the community gathered there and were fed by boat from King's Lynn. Centre stage is the nave, with a west window flanked by pinnacles that are spires in all but name. Beneath crouches the south porch, panelled even round its ponderous buttresses. The south transept has curious fenestration, three decks of six windows rising 3-2-1. Only the east end lapses from grace, with unusual brickwork taking over from stone.

The interior is to match. That a big church stood at Terrington before the 15th century is clear from the Norman bases in the crossing. The beginnings of a stone vault for a crossing tower are also visible, inserted before wiser counsel prevailed. The clerestory has an array of ogival niches, resting in turn on stone figures and repeated above the crossing arch. The iconoclasts must have risked life and limb to break the contents of these niches. They could not deprive the church of the view eastwards, with the window above the chancel arch spilling light into the crossing, to mingle with that pouring in from the transepts. This church is a hymn to light.

Pride of place among the furnishings goes to the beguiling 17th-century font cover. The body is in the form of a tiny round temple with classical columns, painted blue, but rising to a pure Gothic canopy. The font itself is reached through hinged doors, the inner faces of which carry paintings of the Baptism and Temptation in ethereal landscapes. In the chancel is a fine Early Gothic piscina and sedilia group, surviving from a former church. Terrington contains a Lord's Prayer and Commandments board in superb lettering and frame of 1635. The scrollwork, with faces and classical motifs, is worthy of an Adam notebook.

THORPE MARKET
St Margaret *
Regency music room interior

Thorpe is a relief from towers and hammerbeams, from fluttering angels, sweeping arcades and rich patrons. An 18th-century landowner's normal response to a ruinous church was to let it gently decay, and await Victorian restoration. Lord Suffield of Thorpe Market was more ambitious. In 1796 he asked a Mr Wood to erect something in 'a handsome and substantial manner'. He was given a flint-covered box, gabled and with pinnacles on each corner. Small porches balance each other over the doors to the chancel and nave. With their finials like minarets they have a hint of a mosque to them.

The result has received mixed reviews. 'More like a Vauxhall arbour than a church' and 'The ugliest place of worship I ever entered' were two Victorian comments. Pevsner called it 'gimcrack', but Betjeman and the *Shell Guide* were more generous. The windows have Gothic Y-tracery and are filled with soft-coloured glass that is not jarring. The ceiling is that of a Georgian music room, pale blue coving with coloured ribs resting on cherubs' heads.

The interior is dominated by two screens, composed of slender bamboo-like wooden fronds sustaining the oriental note of the exterior. They support glass panels. The west screen has the arms of the Harbord/Suffield family and of George III in the glazing. The east screen has pictures of Moses and Aaron.

In the small chancel are four 18th-century memorial tablets in keeping with the style of the church, presumably relocated from an earlier building. One, to Lady Elizabeth Rant (d.1697), is attributed to William Stauton. New benches have curved ends. The church could serve as a set for the last act of *Il Seraglio*.

THURNING
St Andrew *

Cambridge college furnishings, named box pews

Thurning presents a gentle face to the world. Its modest tower pokes above the trees and, as so often with Norfolk churches, there is little sign of adjacent habitation. Three Decorated windows adorn the south aisle, Perpendicular ones the north. The east end has flowing Reticulated tracery reset from an earlier chancel.

The character of Thurning lies in its woodwork, enough to delight any addict of pre-Victorian furnishing. Most comes from the 1823 demolition of the chapel of Corpus Christi College, Cambridge, of which a fellow, Henry Blake, became the local rector. He brought with him the chapel's 17th-century fittings, including altar rails, panelling and pulpit with tester. Box pews fill the north aisle, with others at the back of the nave for servants. Each is still named for its occupants. Of farm pews we have Lime Tree Farm, Roundabout Farm, Rookery Farm and then the larger Hall pew (for the squire) and pews for the Rectory, its servants and even coachmen. They were still being used as indicated in the 1920s.

In the middle of the nave are benches for 'others', women on the left and men on the right, with a row of pegs for hats. What they made of a Fellow of Corpus booming down from his monster pulpit we do not know. Three medieval heads still face the pulpit from across the nave, on the theme of hear no evil, speak no evil, see no evil. In the churchyard an old stable survives for the use of ponies during the service.

TILNEY ALL SAINTS
**

Jacobean screen with obelisks

The churches of the Ouse marshes form one of England's most magnificent displays of medieval art. Made of flint and Barnack stone, they reflect the wealth of these waterway communities at a time when England's most profitable commodity, wool, was carried westwards to North Sea ports and the

Continent from the uplands of the Pennine–Cotswold spine. The Fens were to the medieval economy what the railway junctions of the Midlands were to the 19th century.

The landscape here is so flat as to make the rest of Norfolk seem alpine. The collapse of local planning control has left many churches marooned amid cheap bungalows. Visitors must try to ignore them. Tilney is first beacon on the road west of King's Lynn. Its tower has projecting corner buttresses, giving it the appearance of being wider than it is long. From north or south the needle spire seems in proportion. When seen from the west, it is too small.

Inside, the arcades are Norman, a rare thing in Norfolk, with seven bays running through nave and chancel. The pier capitals display a full range of carving styles, stiff-leaf, water-leaf and scallops, while two piers are shafted. The later roof is as enjoyable as any in Norfolk, unrestored and alive with angels spilling over into the aisles. These angels, dusty and battered, seem to be coming at us from every direction, holding shields, texts, Symbols of the Passion, whatever came to hand. The vicar suggests that these roofs were prefabricated in Suffolk and brought up by waterway, which seems possible. We know that cathedral workshops turned out Perpendicular windows by the dozen for local churches.

Tilney is busy with screens and other woodwork. The parclose screens are Perpendicular, the rood is Jacobean of 1618. The latter is extraordinary, with original gates and decorated with foliage carving instead of tracery. There is a top deck, of balusters and obelisks. Inside the chancel are stalls with ancient misericords. The church appears to be gently decaying, despite recent help from the American Tilneys. Perhaps they were moved by an epitaph in the churchyard:

> The world's a City, full of crooked streets:
> Death is the Market Place, where all men meet,
> If Life were merchandise, that men could buy,
> Rich men would always live and poor men die.

TITTLESHALL
St Mary *
Coke monuments

The little church sits on the outskirts of its village, the churchyard pleasantly overgrown and the nave bare. Yet here the mightiest family in the county, the Cokes, Earls of Leicester, chose to be buried, before the erection of their mausoleum at Holkham in the 1890s. The old mausoleum at Tittleshall, on the north side of the chancel, is now closed but other family monuments are worth seeing.

These date from the late 16th century to the 18th. That of Bridget Coke (d.1598) is a superb work. She kneels in prayer with serene face and exaggerated trumpet ruffs to her collar. Children kneel below with individual expressions, the whole far more lively and naturalistic than most late-Tudor monuments. The tomb chest of Robert Coke (d.1679) is unusually funereal and sober, of black and white marble with fine arabesque engraving on its back plate. Later still is a chaste classical composition in honour of the first Earl (d.1759) and his Countess. The flanking busts of the couple are designed by Roubiliac.

To complete the set is a relief by Nollekens of Jane, wife of Thomas Coke 'of Norfolk' (d.1800). Its flowing lines and poignant emotion cost a staggering 3,000 guineas in 1805.

TRUNCH
St Botolph **
Gothic font canopy

Norfolk's old churches are so plentiful that each needs a unique selling proposition. Trunch has its font canopy. The church is Perpendicular, with a fine hammerbeam roof and angels and intricate tracery in the spandrels. After the Reformation the chancel became the village schoolroom. The choir stalls thus have inkwells drilled in the desks and boys' initials carved on them. The screen that would once have divided off the school is a worm-eaten, lovable old thing of 1502. Six panels survive on either side of the traceried arch, with saints and their emblems. Matthew has his axe and James his shell. The upper part has ogival arches and a cornice with some original paint.

The font is at the rear of the nave. Its bowl is c.1350, octagonal with steps. The huge hexagonal canopy, which would once have housed the font cover, is of c.1500. It is in the form of a gazebo on six legs rising from the floor to an intricate ogival crown. These legs are carved with foliage and animals such as squirrels, a monkey, a pig and a dog. Higher up is a wolf with its jaws open and tongue hanging out. The canopy proper has canopied niches which turn into a crown of flying buttresses encrusted with crockets. The composition is more decorative than artistic, and great fun.

UPWELL
St Peter **
Roof with giant angels

The first pleasure of Upwell is the delightful view of it from the bridge over the River Nene. A pool of architecture glows amid the tattiness of the Marshland housing. An octagonal tower rises above battlemented parapets which cover the roofline. The west wall has a fine Intersecting window and the porch looks ready to crumble to the touch.

The interior has two remarkable features. One is the roof, dark at first but gradually revealed as remarkably bold. The structure is single hammerbeam but the huge angels, their wings almost touching the beams, fill it with life, spreading into the aisles and the chancel. Other angels are on subsidiary panels and on the richly carved beams, which appear to be borrowed in style from those over the Suffolk border at Mildenhall.

The other feature is the complete late-Georgian fittings, with west and south galleries still in place. These partly spoil the line of the graceful Perpendicular piers, which soar upwards without a break for a capital. But there is a stately completeness to the nave interior, of pews with poppyheads, coats of arms and a pulpit with conical tester. The brass eagle lectern is 15th century, of a design much copied in the 19th.

The churchyard on the south side is packed with 17th- and 18th-century gravestones, uniformly covered in lichen. They form a magnificent gallery of this neglected English form of craftsmanship.

WALPOLE ST PETER
*****
Nave woodwork, font cover, 'bolt-hole' tunnel

The 'Queen of the Marshlands' deserves more respect than she has been accorded. The Walpoles may be safe from flooding, but are inundated by bungalow estates. St Peter's is to west Norfolk what Salle is to the east, a church for the connoisseur of this noble county. It is a place not of curiosity but of subtle proportion, of the play of light on stone and wood. If English churches were Dutch Old Masters, this would be St Pieter de Hooch.

The exterior is supremely graceful, early Perpendicular of *c.*1400, with ogees still in some of the window tracery. Wherever we look there is decoration, on the buttresses, the string courses, the battlements, even the sanctus bellcote, the last a gem of Gothic detailing. The porch is sumptuous, of two bays and two storeys. This is stone vaulted with a full set of bosses, each a meticulous example of 15th-century carving. The Perpendicular oak door is original. A sign warns worshippers to remove their pattens, or wooden shoes, before entering, with an old pair hanging by the door to illustrate the point.

Inside there is hardly a disappointment. We are met by a font with nodding ogees round its base and a Jacobean cover. Its fretwork rises like some exotic Ottoman smoking machine. The rear of the nave is enclosed by a 17th-century screen running the width of the building. This has three pediments and turns the rear of the nave into a foyer, as if guarding the entrance to a theatre. The nave arcades are early Perpendicular – the guide even hazards 'Transitional-Perpendicular' as if eager to invent a 14th-century style of its own – with piers shafted and arches steeply pointed. They hold the key to the charm of this church. Within its Perpendicular embrace survives the form of an earlier, more mobile Gothic of the decades before the Black Death.

The roof is surprisingly simple, with no decoration above the corbel level, but with a huge chandelier of 1701. Beneath is spread a carpet of light oak furniture. The pews date from the 15th to the 17th centuries and are enriched throughout. Those in the south aisle face laterally into the nave, rising in three tiers, as if meant for schoolchildren. Overlooking this array is a high pulpit on a spindly stem with tester above. The nave is completed by two aisle chapels, with a coloured Perpendicular screen in the south one. St Peter's has a rare 'hudd', or portable cubicle to protect the priest from rain when conducting burials before the invention of umbrellas.

The chancel is marked only by the dado of an old screen, still with painted panels. On either side are two doors to the vanished rood loft, both immaculate Decorated compositions with ogee arches. The chancel sanctuary eventually rises a total of 24 steps from the nave, granting it an overpowering presence. This has blind arcading, forming sedilia where appropriate. Each bay has tiny imitation rib vaults in its canopy. The corner niches are crowned with dogs. The saints' niches on the walls have lovely nodding ogee canopies.

Finally there is the tunnel. This is not just a 'bolt hole', its local nickname, but a passage with cobbles underfoot, tierceron vault and no fewer than 12 bosses. It must form the handsomest covered street in England. The purpose is unknown, but it was probably an ancient processional route of such significance that nobody dared divert it when the chancel was rebuilt above. Next to the church is the yew hedge of the old rectory, with a tree clipped into the shape of a cross.

WEST WALTON
St Mary ***
Early Gothic bell-tower, 'windblown' stiff-leaf capitals

Churches surviving in Norfolk from the Early Gothic period are rare and those with detached towers are rarer still. As at Terrington St Clement, the masons of West Walton did not trust the subsoil to hold bell-tower and church together. The tower has a Perpendicular crown, but the dogtooth decoration of the arches testifies to the Early Gothic, *c.*1250. The open ground floor was probably to provide shelter and a meeting place for the townspeople. Today the tower is too decayed for its bells to be rung with safety. It is now looked after by the admirable Churches Conservation Trust.

The widening of Walton's aisles in the late Middle Ages involved the truncation of the original porch, which now has a stepped brick gable. This is a ghost of what must have been a superb work. Two giant pinnacles flank the outer arch. 'Windblown' stiff-leaf capitals flank the inner one. These capitals are a foretaste of the nave capitals inside, some of the finest in England and a wonder of Early Gothic. The arcades are composed of multiple-moulded arches, sitting on cylindrical piers with four detached shafts of Purbeck marble. This is a French form also found at Westminster Abbey. These shafts rise to leaf capitals which seem to break free from the whole composition and grow a botanical life of their own. They are sensational, a breath of air in a landscape of so much staid Perpendicular.

The nave arcade spandrels contain 17th-century texts and emblems of the tribes of Israel. The clerestory is equally interesting, with windows and wall spaces united with arcading. There are traces of 13th-century wall painting. The aisles are a complete contrast. As often in country churches, the north aisle (or Devil's aisle) is visibly poorer than the south. The latter has the one original window, with Geometrical tracery and a remarkably ornate surround.

WIGGENHALL ST GERMANS
St Germaine **
Carved bench-ends

The four Wiggenhall churches once stood alone on their dykes like windmills in a Dutch landscape, swirls of brick, reed and sky. Modern development has stripped them of this romance. St Germaine's shelters under the lee of the River Ouse by a bridge from which walkers can look down on its roof. A sparse copse offers some protection from the east wind. The tower is 13th century, its interior arch having dogtooth decoration. The rest of the church is Perpendicular. Large aisles embrace the nave and chancel, and the roofs are original.

St Germaine's has some of the best benches in East Anglia, with a vitality that surpasses even those of the West Country. They fill the nave and aisles, ball-flower poppyheads leaping up on all sides like Grenadiers on parade. The ends are not simple relief panels, as in the West Country, but carved in the round, with saints and bishops in the panels and monsters and domestic scenes crowding round their tops. The figures are animated, with loving couples, drunkards, musicians and even a falling tree. Though eroded by time, worms and the hands of worshippers, these are minor sagas of medieval art.

The older benches have backs pierced by quatrefoils. The Stuart pulpit and lectern seem prim in comparison. The old font lies in the south aisle, but a Victorian replacement, with relief carvings of the Passion, stands facing the nave.

WIGGENHALL ST MARY MAGDALEN
**

Medieval woodwork, rare saints

This is the best of the Wiggenhall group, although part of its charm lies in its decayed state. St Mary Magdalen should not be confused with Wiggenhall St Mary, which has fine bench-ends but an ugly new roof. St Mary Magdalen sits in the middle of its village. The walls are of brick, freestone and any other material that might have served as ballast for barges passing down the Ouse.

The interior is mostly bare of ornament and monument. Its atmosphere derives from its lofty proportions, lightness and profuse woodwork. The aisle windows have early Perpendicular tracery, with ogees rising into panels. The east window is blessed with Decorated Y-tracery. The original roof rests on unrestored medieval corbels and battered angels. The benches below have simple abstract poppyheads. Did the parishioners decide not to compete with St Germaine's and St Mary's, or were these earlier, or later?

The chancel has a pronounced 'weep' to the north and is panelled with Jacobean vine carving, painted white when it reaches the reredos. Vines also decorate the door to the vanished rood loft. It has a profusion of medieval glass in the north aisle, albeit only in the upper panels. Iconographers have been intrigued by the rarity of the saints, who include St Callistus, St Britius, St Leger and St Romanus. Who they?

WORSTEAD
St Mary ***
Medieval screens, Reynolds copies

Worstead the name, worsted the cloth and worsted the wealth. This great wool church gazes out across the Norfolk flatlands and dreams of sheep. Its cloth was produced by Flemish immigrants fleeing political turbulence at home. They wove the local long-staple wool to a finely twisted thread, combed to mix warmth with strength. Good worsted was said to be as soft to the touch as silk. It now comes from Yorkshire and there are no traces of the craft in the place of its birth. The last Worstead weaver died in 1882.

The church was constructed afresh after 1379. Churches in this part of Norfolk boast their wealth by the intricacy of the tracery in the bell-chamber openings, and Worstead's is intricate indeed. The tower base is adorned with flushwork, with the flints carefully shaped and stuck into the mortar between the dressed stone. There are even traces of ballflower on the tower. The church appears still to have its original statue of the Virgin above the two-storey south porch.

The interior is spacious and bare. The hammerbeam roof is without angels, adding to the enveloping silence. The old box pews are still in place, while a screen at the back has fluted uprights. Under the tower is a ringers' gallery, paid for by the medieval Bachelors' Guild above a carved Gothic screen gallery, surely one of the most superb of its sort in the country. The panels in the dado below are early 19th century, copied from Reynolds's stained glass windows in New College, Oxford. Figures such as Faith, Hope and Charity are a surprise after the robust saints of most Norfolk screens.

A quite different style of screen divides the nave from the chancel and aisle chapels. The guide claims that, at the time of its erection in 1512, 'with its gilded gesso and painted flowers it must have been as lovely as anything in medieval art'. Even today, its filigree silhouette is beautiful against the Reticulated tracery of the east window. The dado panels have been painstakingly restored, the saints framed with cusps, ogees, flowers and foliage. Art imitates nature, to the glory of God and of wool. A woodcut on the cover of the guide depicts the church resting on the back of a sheep, the sky above strangely filled with a dogfight between angels and jet fighters. The reference is to a local wartime airbase.

WYMONDHAM
The Abbey ***
Abbey ruins, Comper screen

Pronounced Windom, Wymondham is a dowager duchess of a church. It is an eerie place, the adjacent abbey ruins alive with rooks at twilight. The ghosts of pilgrims flit through the mounds of lost cloisters and tumbled graves. Wymondham was notorious for the running disputes between the monks and townspeople over who had rights to which parts of the building. In 1249 the case went to Rome for settlement, with the town being granted the nave and northern aisle.

The church's appearance reflects this dispute. When the (monks') Norman crossing tower collapsed, the monks in 1409 built the new octagonal tower west of its foundations, using three bays of (the town's) nave and supporting it with a solid wall that cut directly across the nave. This caused pandemonium. The townspeople blocked and unblocked entrances. They hung bells in their (old) west tower and rang them to disrupt monastery services. The monks retaliated with chiming bells in their new octagon. They even increased its height to make their bells louder. Whereupon in 1448 Sir John Clifton, lord of the manor, offered to help the townspeople build a new west tower higher than the octagon. He added a clerestory to the nave and a new north aisle and north porch. These stand today. At the Dissolution, the chancel and abbey buildings were destroyed. The town had won.

The core of the interior is the old Norman nave, much retooled. The nave arcades and gallery survive, as do Clifton's clerestory and roof. These are out of character and scale with the lower tiers, like a modern lid on an ancient casket. Yet the roof has both grace and adornment. The hammerbeams are in the form of angels, the bosses in the form of starbursts. Here is a heavenly universe alive with constellations and flapping angels.

The crude east wall inserted by the monks is now relieved by one of Comper's finest screens. Two decks of saints in exquisitely carved niches rise above the altar, flanking the Virgin and a Christ in Majesty. A canopy with gilded angels stands guard over the scene. Higher still is a rood. To the right of the altar is an unusual early-Renaissance sedilia group, dated c.1530 and crammed inside a Norman arch. The north aisle was the original 'town' aisle and is wider than the nave, with a superb carved roof. Some of the corbel heads seem to be of local characters, including a man playing the bagpipes. The chapel reredos is a lovely Arts and Crafts triptych, with a plaster Crucifixion by R. Anning Bell.

Northamptonshire

Northamptonshire is a county of rolling country, ironstone walls and elegant steeples. Climb any rise and you will see a spire on the horizon. It may be broached, recessed or octagonal, but a Northampton church without its spire is naked.

The Nene valley, inland from the great Saxon minster at Peterborough, was rich in churches from earliest times, notably the two Saxon giants of Brixworth and Earls Barton. The work of Norman carvers is seldom better than round the extraordinary capitals at St Peter, Northampton, and the font at Crick. Then came the tower builders, masculine Early Gothic at Raunds, encrusted with French sculpture at Higham Ferrers, feminine Decorated at Oundle and King's Sutton, eccentric Perpendicular at Lowick and Fotheringhay.

Few of the county's naves quite measure up to their steeples, partly due to the ferocious restorations of George Gilbert Scott in the 1860s. But this is a county of excellent furnishings. Stanford offers a gallery of woodwork, monuments and glass commemorating the continuous patronage of the Cave family. Passenham retains a complete Laudian chancel. Proximity to the alabaster workshops of Nottingham gave Northamptonshire the superb Greene tombs at Lowick. Of later periods of funerary art are the tombs of the Spencers at Great Brington and the Montagus at Warkton. Finally, there is no 20th-century church in England to compare with Ninian Comper's masterpiece at Wellingborough.

Apethorpe *
Aynho *
Brixworth ***
Cottesbrooke *
Crick *
Croughton *
Earls Barton ***
Finedon *
Fotheringhay ***

Great Brington ***
Higham Ferrers ***
King's Sutton **
Lowick ****
Middleton Cheney **
Northampton:
  All Saints**
  St Peter **
Oundle *

Passenham **
Raunds **
Rothwell ***
Stanford on Avon ****
Warkton **
Warmington *
Wellingborough:
  St Mary ****

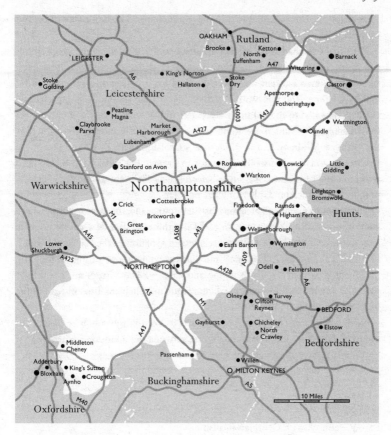

APETHORPE

St Leonard *

Mildmay tomb in tiny chapel

Apethorpe is visited only for its setting and the Mildmay tomb, but what a setting and what a tomb. Amid pale limestone walls and thatched roofs on the banks of the Willow Brook is the ideal of a secluded Midlands village. The church lies off the approach to the manor house, some distance from the mansion that was the home of the Mildmays, Earls of Westmorland.

The church has a Northamptonshire tower with lucarnes in dark limestone. The nave interior is small and bare. The chancel is wood-panelled, its most distinctive feature is a faded Georgian east window of stained glass whose colouring appears not to have been properly fixed. An earlier window dated

1621 using the same technique is in the south chapel. The best that can be said of these windows is that they are rare.

They are overshadowed by the Mildmay tomb, located in the chapel built for it in the 1620s. The incongruity almost defies description. It is as if the removal men had left an object destined for a palace in a suburban front hall by mistake. The tomb either arrived bigger than the builders expected, or the Mildmays were too mean to erect a chamber worthy of the work, unless they deliberately wanted the tomb to look ridiculously grand. The subject is Sir Anthony Mildmay (d.1617). He was son of Elizabeth I's Chancellor of the Exchequer and was himself ambassador to France. His wife, lying beside him, was renowned for scattering silver before her as she went about the village, a practice that understandably made her popular.

The tomb has a circular canopy as of a four-poster bed, with curtains tied back to reveal the effigies. It is an early and theatrical use of a device popular later in the century. At the corners are allegorical figures of the Cardinal Virtues, Fortitude, Temperance, Prudence and Justice, while above on the canopy are the Theological Virtues, Faith, Hope and Charity. The Virtues are beautifully executed and the effect serene, black and white marble being used instead of the usual garish Jacobean polychromy.

Next to the tomb is a memorial to the son of Lord Burghersh, who died at the age of one in 1816. It is a charming work, showing the infant on a marble cot in his bonnet with a podgy leg emerging naked from the blanket.

AYNHO
St Michael *
Baroque church with Georgian furnishings

Aynho is a church, a house, a village and a landscape on the Oxfordshire–Northamptonshire border. This setting arose on the ruins of Aynho left by the Civil War. The Cartwright family rebuilt the house over a period of forty years and survived here until 1954, when two generations of Cartwrights, father and son, were both killed in a car crash. The big house is now divided into flats. The churchyard is an ornamental lawn, adjacent to the drive and looking out over the park to the Cherwell valley and M40 in the distance.

The church's architect in 1723 was a local carpenter-cum-mason, Edward Wing, designing in the English Baroque of Archer and Hawksmoor. Thomas Archer himself had worked at Aynho House, and Wing's north and south elevations to the church might be practice runs for the façade of a country house, with a central pediment and doorway. The interior is less interesting. The ceiling is a dreadful 1960s insertion and the grisaille glass shuts out what should be the glory of this church, a view of the trees and walls of the churchyard. But a west gallery and handsome box pews survive, with a fine wooden lectern, candleholders and painted organ pipes.

Two windows by Kempe in the south aisle are some compensation. The east window is a later work by Willement in 1857, bright with blues and yellows. Outside, well-tended herbaceous borders reach up to the base of the medieval tower and roses were in full bloom in October.

BRIXWORTH
All Saints ***
Saxon tower and nave shell, eagle carving

The ever colourful Arthur Mee describes Brixworth thus: 'One of our famous places, where there comes to us a solemn sense of the age-old continuity of our island life. Here, gaunt and solitary among farm buildings, stands a church older than King Alfred.' Mee visited the church in the 1940s. Today a crude housing estate crowns the hill, spoiling the church's once serene dominance over the older part of the village. Inside, restorers have scrubbed and whitewashed every surface. As at Deerhurst (Gloucs) and Worth (Sussex), England's Saxon churches have proved irresistible to postwar interior decorators.

For age and size, Brixworth has few rivals in northern Europe. The original building is probably late 7th century, from the reign of the Mercian King Offa. It would have stood with Earls Barton in the Nene valley as inland missions of the Saxon minster at Peterborough. The exterior mixes many styles, but Saxon predominates. The brick arches of tower, nave and clerestory contain Roman tiles. Subsequent rebuilding has revealed thirty different types of stone in the walls.

The Saxon exterior would have looked different from the present more vertical structure. A low crossing tower was located at the east end, and a two-storey narthex or porch would have closed the west end, now the base of the tower. The present west stair turret is late Saxon. Low chapels (or porticus) lined the sides. The interior is pristine white with the splendid tiled heads of the arches on all four walls left in red. Though the proportions remain Saxon, the blocking of the arcades and removal of the aisles have changed the nave, and the loss of the west wall of the chancel has transformed the east end. The chancel was once a separate chamber for the priests, as in an Orthodox church today. Those in the nave could hear services but see little. The church now has a Gothic south transept used as a Lady Chapel and guarded by a colourful Perpendicular screen.

The apse is not original but is a work of Victorian archaeology. Brixworth was fortunate in having for forty years a vicar, C. F. Watkins (1832–73), committed to restoring his old church. He demolished a square medieval chancel and rebuilt what he assumed to be the Saxon apse. He did not rebuild the low ambulatory. Most of the furnishings are Victorian. The glass is mercifully restrained, mostly opaque abstract designs. Sunk in a wall inside the south door is a superb Saxon carving of an eagle, its wings raised in triumph.

COTTESBROOKE
All Saints *
Langham family gallery and mausoleum

On my visit the churchyard echoed to the sound of the local hunt. Riders were galloping across fields, down lanes and through spinneys in this hidden valley between Brixworth and Naseby. The great house of the Langhams, 17th-century London Turkey merchants, is out of sight. The church has only an old rectory and a row of almshouses for company, guarded by a magnificent cohort of cedars.

The building is of soft limestone with a tower but no spire. Its interior has a nave devoid of aisles, with an 18th-century ceiling and a painted coving. The three-decker pulpit is high, simple and austere, with its tester intact and no Jacobean frills. Most extraordinary is the family pew of the Langhams across the south transept. It has tenants' seats in front, then a curving staircase up to a gallery like a box in the theatre. The family would sit in lofty splendour on cushioned seats with a fire in the grate, mirror on the wall and doubtless a decanter under the shelf, keeping watch on their servants below.

Behind the pew is the family's mausoleum and chapel, a Perpendicular structure with restful views of cedars and hills beyond. This contains the tomb of the Langhams' predecessors at Cottesbrooke Hall, the Redes. Against the east wall is the monument to Sir John Rede (d.1604), on a rolled mat in Tudor armour with his ten children mourning in front. In the centre of the chapel and emphatically upstaging Rede is the tomb of Sir John Langham (d.1671) and his wife. The effigies are vigorous, clad in rich costumes and immaculate shoes. The sculptor in 1676, Thomas Cartwright, was paid the huge sum of £290 for it. There was money in Oriental trade.

On the walls of the nave are more discreet and pious monuments to Langham women. Most are by the younger John Bacon and form a remarkable gallery of his work, reflecting the sobriety of late Georgian design. Urns are draped with cloth. Columns lie broken. Roundels carry wreaths, some of them withered. At the back of the nave is an extraordinary memorial to Sir William Langham (d.1812) in the form of a large urn and a miserably drooping bunch of stone flowers.

CRICK
St Margaret *
Decorated tracery, monster carvings

The church is near the junction of the M1 and the M45, and near the gentler course of the Grand Union Canal. I suppose locals once regarded the canal as no less intrusive than we do the motorways. Yet the solid tower can hold its own. This was the church of the Astley family from the 13th to the 15th centuries and their five-leaf flower emblem features in the tracery. The church is almost all Decorated. The tower is of the masculine group of Northampton towers, the broach spire heavy and rooted firmly to its base. The windows have a life of their own. The east window of the south aisle has tracery taking off in all directions, while that of the chancel is like a florist's Easter spray, 'leading the eye a wayward dance'. The Astleys spent money on Crick.

The limewash walls of the interior are a relief from the jumping, swaying and chattering windows. Two bays of the south arcade are Early Gothic, having cylindrical piers and capitals with stiff-leaf carving. The nave is floored in old stone and the box pews are tall but without their doors. The joy of Crick is its carving. Monsters, men and women peer down from every corner of the building. The stops to the chancel windows have deeply incised foliage and figures, including a spectacular Green Man with teeth.

The Victorian stalls are dark and rich, including a fine reading desk opposite the pulpit. Next to the south door stands a parson's burial shelter, to keep him dry while awaiting the invention of the umbrella. The Norman font is unlike any I have seen, a bowl covered in hemispherical stone beads and resting on three monsters, apparently a primitive Italian motif.

CROUGHTON
All Saints *
14th-century murals

The exterior of the church is massive and strong, out of character with this immaculate Midlands village. The interior is a treasure house of medieval wall paintings, above a nave filled with bench-ends that might have strayed from Devon. The paintings have been defaced where they carried religious symbols but left intact where naturalistic. A book by the master on this subject, Professor E. W. Tristram, is available for visitors to read in the church. Dating from the 14th century, they were discovered in 1921 and restored in the 1960s. The detailed execution is not sophisticated, frequently seeming little more than graffiti, but the swaying poses are remarkable.

So too are the subjects. In the south aisle is a most rare surviving sequence of the Life of the Virgin. Almost all depictions of this subject were obliterated after the Reformation. Here too is the Massacre of the Innocents and a lovely Flight into Egypt. In the north aisle are scenes from the Life of Jesus, including a Last Supper, Scourging and Bearing of the Cross. The Last Supper is reproduced on the chancel reredos. Tristram compares these murals with contemporary and later work in Italy, even invoking the name of Giotto. Many of the figures demonstrate the characteristic Gothic movement, of aggression or agony. Here, as in so many places, I wonder how celebrated these works would be were they in an Italian church rather than an English one.

EARLS BARTON
All Saints ***
Saxon tower decoration, saints in modern dress

The tower of Earls Barton is one of the principal monuments of Anglo-Saxon architecture. Surrounded by the wattle and mud huts of the 10th century, it must have seemed a massive assertion of both faith and security. Even today it dominates a council estate crudely sited to its north and the small village to the south. What is remarkable about Earls Barton tower is not its antiquity – there are others as old – but its decoration. The surface is adorned with masonry strips that serve no function but to delight. The lozenge patterns appear to be the work of masons designing purely for their pleasure and that of their clients.

The tower is older than the church and may have originally contained the place of worship in its ground storey. It is of four stages topped by a 15th-century battlement. The latter is an anachronism that spoils the delicacy of the tiny five-light arcade beneath, a feature unique in English architecture and possibly Roman in inspiration. The subordinate strips (known as lesenes) form both the verticals and the lozenges, rising from the base in what appears a coherent decorative programme. The west doorway has a primitive arch. An even more simple two-light window occurs in the south wall and above it a doorway, apparently to give ladder access to villagers in the event of attack. There are no buttresses: this is a fine work of engineering as well as architecture.

The main body is by no means an anticlimax. Norman origins are evident in the south doorway. The doorway arch has grotesque beakheads pecking at its moulding, some with curious feathered headdresses. A rare Norman piscina and sedilia group survives in the chancel. The south aisle has graceful ogee windows. Of the furnishings, a 17th-century pulpit is overshadowed by the Perpendicular screen, restored in the 1930s when Henry Bird painted butterflies in the coving and saints in modern dress in the panels. These include Peter with a book, Paul with a sword and Philip with a basket of loaves. Apparently the bishop at the time demanded their removal, finding the modern dress sacrilegious, but the parishioners fought the case and won. Good for them. If medieval worshippers could handle religious figures in contemporary dress, why is it so off-putting today? Or is sanctity now a strictly antique concept?

FINEDON
St Mary *
Strainer arch

Finedon church sits above its little village, with a Tudor school and Jacobean vicarage forming a close round it. The stone is rich ironstone but clad in a lichen that gives it a white sheen, almost of hoar-frost. The building is cruciform, with tower, nave, aisles, transepts and chancel in perfect proportion. The windows might seem monotonous, were the tracery not Reticulated, uncusped and singularly graceful. This is 'drawing-room' Decorated, and is immaculate.

Inside, the eye is immediately caught by a feature rare in English parish churches, an inverted or strainer arch supporting the crossing, like a giant pair of pincers. The arch is ingeniously decorated to lessen its dominance, with tracery in the spandrels and fussy crenellation along the top. The two adjacent aisle arches are robust in contrast.

The chancel arch has a stone screen, a 19th-century restoration. The sedilia retain their stiff-leaf carvings and other fragments of past beauty. The font is Norman but looks as if successive generations of worshippers have come and sliced pieces from it, as from a lump of cheese. Like many old fonts, it saw service as a cattle trough until its 19th-century rescue. Finedon has a splendid organ case of 1717, with swirling volutes flanking the base pipes and broken pediments on either side.

FOTHERINGHAY
St Mary ***
Tower octagon, Yorkist shrine to Richard III

On a warm summer's day, Fotheringhay is a magic place. The church seems to float on its hill above the River Nene, a galleon of Perpendicular on a sea of corn. The octagonal tower piles into the sky on its square base, dominating a structure that seems entirely of glass. The aisle windows of Fotheringhay have tracery of the most refined delicacy. Here rests the memory of Fotheringhay's tragic heroine, Mary Queen of Scots, beheaded in the adjacent castle on the orders of Elizabeth I. Today the fears and rivalries of those times are remembered only in the shields and heraldry that crowd the nave interior. The sad castle has vanished.

The church was begun, a century and a half earlier, in 1411 when a collegiate foundation, formerly inside the castle, was transferred to the fields outside. Its patron was Edward, 2nd Duke of York, who fell at Agincourt in 1415 with the new college still under construction. He was buried in the now vanished choir, the nave not being completed until 1434. The contract for the nave survives, paying William Horwode 'Freemason of Fotheringhay' £300 for the work if it was satisfactory and a fine of imprisonment if he failed to deliver on time and budget. (Oh, happy days!) After the suppression of chantries the college was transferred to the Duke of Northumberland, who demolished the collegiate buildings and the east end of the church, leaving just the nave and tower for the local parish. He took 93 chained books from its library.

The surviving nave is high and short, of five bays. The expanse of what would once have been the chancel arch is a blank white wall with a small window towards the top. Below is the altar with insipid Georgian Commandments boards. Fotheringhay needs a latter-day Comper to fill this wall with a giant Perpendicular window. The small sanctuary has two Renaissance monuments to the founders of the college and builders of the church. They were erected as the result of Elizabeth's insistence, on a visit in 1573, that tombs formerly in the choir be relocated in the parish church. They commemorate the two Dukes of York, the 2nd Duke and founder, and Richard, the 3rd Duke, killed at Wakefield in 1459.

Under the tower is a fine fan vault, culminating in a falcon and fetterlock, emblem of the Yorkist faction triumphant at the time of its insertion. The only colour, apart from the warmth of the yellow stone, lies in the shields that decorate the nave and pulpit. The latter is a superb work supposedly donated by Edward IV. Its rib-vaulted tester and red, green and gold panels display the polychromy of a late-medieval church. Fotheringhay has recently become a Yorkist shrine, especially to the much-abused Richard III. A chapel was dedicated to his memory in 1982 and a York window commissioned, incorporating his heraldic glass. The bookstall sells literature supporting the reputations of Richard III and the more romantic, and marketable, Mary Queen of Scots.

GREAT BRINGTON
St Mary ***
Spencer chapel and tombs, Washington memorial

A continental grandee would have erected a family mausoleum within the boundaries of his estate, as has Earl Spencer for his sister Diana, Princess of Wales. Previously the Spencers of Althorp chose to be buried in their local parish church and visitors continue to visit it, at least as an afterthought to the celebrated island grave in the park. Yet Great Brington's north chapel houses one of the most remarkable set of monuments in England: twenty generations of Spencers, which must be a record for any church.

The church exterior is undemonstrative. Its honey-coloured walls rise modestly on the side of a hill beyond the village, the churchyard embracing a 'butterfly conservation area'. The first impression on entering is of a forest of poppyheads on the bench-ends, carved on one side only. But attention is swiftly drawn to the north arcade and tombs bursting into the chancel from the Spencer Chapel. The chapel was built by Sir John Spencer in 1514 and is a gem of Tudor architecture. Though locked, the most important tombs can be seen from various angles through the screens. The chamber is decorated with some 400 coats of arms, tracing the family's long history in plaster, wood, paint and glass.

The Spencer monuments, canopied and covered in carved reliefs, form one of the finest collections of 16th- and 17th-century tomb sculpture in the country. Most prominent are the three built into the chancel arcade. The earliest is of Sir John (d.1522) and Isabel Gaunt: still medieval in form, it carries a delightful Renaissance angel fixed to the underside of the canopy, like a classical sprite come to warn us of a style to come. The effigies are formal, with small individual canopies on the chest. The lady lies in an extraordinary winged headdress.

The next two tombs are by the Dutch sculptor Jasper Hollemans of another Sir John (d.1586) and Lord Robert (erected in 1599). The one has the tomb chest and large pediment covered in shields of arms, and obelisks covered in strapwork. The other has a canopy with strange pendants, topped by three obelisks nudging the arch above. The ladies' hoods are even more bizarre, surely of unmanageable dimensions.

Inside the chapel is another Hollemans monument, against the north-east wall, this one a four-poster bed erected like its predecessor in 1599. The pillars supporting the canopy are decorated with arabesques, and subsidiary columns carry heraldic supports. The lady is dressed in another huge hood, presumably the fashion in the late-Tudor court. The centre of the chapel gives pride of place to the most sophisticated of the memorials, the tomb of William, Lord Spencer (d.1638) by Nicholas Stone. This is a Baroque work in black and white marble, the effigies serene and the canopy raised on eight Corinthian columns. Stone was paid the handsome sum of £600 for the work, passing on just £29 to the effigy carvers.

Other monuments in the chapel are by John Flaxman, Joseph Nollekens, Francis Chantrey and, oddest of all, John Stone. The last portrays Sir Edward Spencer (d.1656) rising dramatically, fully clothed, from the Urn of the Resurrection. He places his left hand on the Bible, set on the column of Truth.

Much scholarship has gone into tracing Great Brington's other claim to fame, the Washington–Spencer link. A memorial to Laurence Washington (d.1616), ancestor of the president and buried in the chancel, is inside the church door. There is a poppyhead of the Washington coat of arms, with the famous stars and stripes. For Washington enthusiasts, other ancestors can be found at Wickhamford (Worcs) and Maldon (Essex).

The chancel east window depicts the Adoration of the Lamb and is by Burne-Jones. A south window has rare 16th-century glass of John the Baptist, with a canopy of cherubs playing bagpipes.

HIGHAM FERRERS
St Mary ***
Early Gothic tower carvings, St Maur brass

The smaller the Midlands town, the more unspoilt it is likely to be – and the finer its church. This town was home to Archbishop Chichele of Canterbury, founder of All Souls College, Oxford, a distinction likely to stand any 15th-century town in good stead. But the superb church preceded Chichele, who merely added to it his lustre. It lies up a small alley from the charming main street, set in an irregular close with a medieval bede house and old school.

Higham Ferrers' tower is Early Gothic, its spire an addition of the mid-14th century. The west front of the tower is little short of sensational, a gallery of medieval decoration attributed to French masons from Westminster. The twin doors are framed with carvings and a Tree of Jesse rising from a central shaft. The unusual roundels in the tympanum, based on illuminated manuscripts, are of New Testament scenes. Sculpture dots each front, including on the north a charming man making music while locked in the stocks. Some of the niches have excellent modern statues in them.

The spire rises from the pierced parapet of the tower, supported by delicate flying buttresses. It is one of the finest in a county famous for spires. The form is 'feminine', elongated, ribbed and crocketed. The lucarnes are particularly rich, with twin-lights, crockets and tracery. All this was rebuilt after a collapse in the 17th century.

As so often in Northamptonshire, the body of the church finds it hard to live up to the tower. There are two naves and two aisles, those to the south built, like the tower, in the 13th century, those to the north in the 14th. The space is wide but not tall, and thus lacks drama. A screen extends across both naves and aisles, crowned with a delicate Comper rood and loft. The church is 'high', its altars dressed, screens restored and niches filled, albeit with the ugly statuary of the Anglo-Catholic tradition. The best modern work is the embroidery of the altar frontals. A fine old pulpit has been banished to an aisle.

The chancel is a relief. The Decorated tracery is excellent, varied and set under swaying ogee arches. To Clifton-Taylor these are 'among the best Reticulated windows in England', high praise. A tomb chest in the north chancel aisle has an elaborate brass of Laurence St Maur or Seymour (d.1337), for whom the north extension of the church was made. It has an architectural frame with saints in niches and an angel above holding a heart in a napkin and is regarded as 'one of the finest English brasses', this time by Pevsner. Higham Ferrers is not short of admirers.

Chichele's old choir stalls are still in place, with his portrait on the college master's stall. The bede house and school are open to the public, the latter in beautiful Perpendicular Gothic with high pierced parapet and pinnacles. But we need to find active uses for these splendid old buildings.

KING'S SUTTON
St Peter and St Paul **
'Syncopated' tower, rib-cage memorial

The upper Cherwell valley is a landscape of churches, their steeples marching northwards from the Thames valley into the Midlands. The stone is warm ironstone and the spires beautifully situated on picturesque inclines. At King's Sutton, stone and timbered cottages enclose a village green, with the church at its apex. The tower does not dominate but merely punctuates the village, before the contours fall away into the valley beneath.

After Adderbury and Bloxham (*see* Oxon), King's Sutton spire was famous 'for beauty'. It rises almost 200 ft, and has a porch added to its west door. Above the bell-openings is a frieze, then an eruption of pinnacles, each one supported by its own flying buttress. The first lucarnes are kept low, the spire then rising free of interruption until almost the top, where lucarnes reappear. Lucarnes are normally to ventilate a spire and reduce wind resistance, and therefore should be evenly spaced. Here the effect appears to be purely aesthetic, to stretch the composition up into the sky. I would be intrigued to know the mason's explanation for this subtle syncopation.

The rest of the church is less impressive. The Norman origins of the chancel can be seen in the corbel-table outside and the blind arcading inside, but the church is mostly Decorated. The east window to the south aisle is exceptional, of five lights rising to a circle pierced by trefoils. The interior was heavily restored by George Gilbert Scott in 1866 and the seating and screen are Victorian.

An extraordinary object lurks in the chancel, the memorial to Thomas Langton Freke (d.1769), attributed to the elder John Bacon. Its theme is the defeat of Death, with a relief representing Christ rising over His own recumbent skeleton. This rib cage is picked out in iron, a composition with a gruesome realism more characteristic of Spanish Baroque. It is an extraordinary object to find in the Northampton countryside.

LOWICK
St Peter ****
Octagonal tower, medieval glass, Greene effigies

Lowick church is a hidden masterpiece of English Perpendicular. Its village lies off the beaten track south of Oundle, and the church is detached even from the village, alone in a field. The tower with its octagonal top stage is visible for miles around, a forest of pinnacles topped by golden weathervanes. From a distance they seem to flutter in the sun, like pennants summoning us to some forgotten Tudor tournament. By the time of the tower's completion, in the 1470s, octagons were in fashion in these parts, as at neighbouring Fotheringhay.

The church was built by the Greene family, of the adjacent Drayton House. They built sumptuously. As we climb up the hill from the south-east, we are presented with a lavish 15th-century chancel and chapel, with Panel tracery in the large windows, that have to be supported by heavy buttresses. Inside, all is light. The architecture is conventional Perpendicular. A large coat of arms crowns the chancel arch and a Victorian screen bars the transept chapel. The sedilia, with lovely ogee arches, must have been retrieved from an earlier church. But these are preliminaries to Lowick's treasures, its medieval glass and its monuments.

The glass is in the upper half of the north aisle windows. It runs along the length of the aisle, an orderly progression of the most vivid colour. How it survived the iconoclasts is a mystery. The narrative is of the Tree of Jesse, showing the Old Testament origins of Jesus. In the right-hand window can be seen a knight holding a church, presumably an early donor. The windows have been dated to the 1320s and were thus, like the sedilia, reset in the new church.

The monuments form a familiar contrast of medieval serenity and Georgian bombast. Between the north-east chapel and the nave lie Ralph Greene (d.1417) and his wife. This is one of the finest alabaster tombs in England. The effigy dates from the creative burst in English art at the turn of the 15th century and is the only one in existence for which a contract survives. This is from Greene's wife to two Derbyshire carvers named Thomas Prentys and Robert Sutton, for 'a counterfeit of an esquire all armed for battle'. The pair lie in effigy with tiny lierne-vaulted canopies above their heads. Her headdress and coat illustrate the wilder shores of contemporary fashion. He wears chainmail and armour but has removed his gauntlet to hold his wife's hand in death. The work is stiff yet moving.

We now move to the south chapel. In the centre lies a monument to Edward,

Earl of Wiltshire, who died in 1499 and was a Greene grandson. Again the effigy is of the highest quality. The knight wears a Lancastrian 'SS' collar and has tiny bedesmen under his feet. Opposite is an extraordinary Westmacott monument of 1843 to the Duke of Dorset. A white tomb chest carries not an effigy or even a medallion but the duke's cloak, shield and coronet, with an angel holding a text. The title became extinct with his death, so perhaps the iconography is appropriate. In the north-east chapel we find a cosy group of Lady Mordaunt (d.1705) resting on a skull. She lies with her second husband, Sir John Germain, who is in old-fashioned armour with his legs in an awkward pose.

MIDDLETON CHENEY
All Saints **
Early Morris glass, greenery-yallery window

The ironstone is redder here than to the south, and the spire of the church is narrower. The church sits on a rise above the village, with loud gargoyles and paired pinnacles as at King's Sutton. The interior was scraped by George Gilbert Scott in what seems to have been a devastating tour of the Midlands in the 1860s, though the aisle walls remain limewashed.

The joy of the church is its Victorian glass, commissioned by the rector of Middleton Cheney in the 1860s, William Buckley. He was a friend of Burne-Jones and through him of the early Morris partnership. The church ranks with Selsley (Gloucs) and Scarborough (Yorks, N) as a gallery of Morris glass of this period. The designs are vivid and the poses full of vigour, with a minimum of clutter round the figures. The glass, produced by the Powell factory, has a luminosity that seems to trap and then transmit light at greater brilliance.

As at Selsley, most of Morris's early colleagues worked on the Middleton Cheney project. The chancel east window includes panels by Burne-Jones, Morris himself, Webb, Madox Brown and a Jewish member of the partnership, Simeon Solomon, who contributed the Tribes of Israel and Abraham and Moses. St Catherine was modelled, as usual, on Morris's wife Janey, an Oxford bargee's daughter whom he had recently married and who was to cause such turbulence among the Morris partnership. In the east window of the south aisle is Morris's own magnificent Annunciation.

Finest of all is the dazzling west window by Burne-Jones, portraying the Fiery Furnace. This swirling work was exhibited at the Grosvenor Gallery and allegedly inspired Gilbert's reference to 'greenery-yallery' in his opera, *Patience*. These are not the lines of Pre-Raphaelitism but of full-blown Art Nouveau. Almost as vivid is the small sunburst in the east gable window of the nave.

NORTHAMPTON
All Saints **
Wren-style rebuild after fire

The church cuts a dash in the centre of this despoiled county town. There are few finer late 17th-century churches outside London. Its pink stone portico lifts the spirit at the top of the hill from the dreary southern approach road. Like Wren's London masterpieces, All Saints was the result of a fire (in 1675). The church was rebuilt in 1676–80, probably the work of Henry Bell of King's Lynn.

The mighty portico dates from 1701. On its parapet is a statue of Charles II and inside the portico a memorial to John Bailes, famous for living in three centuries, born under Elizabeth I and dying under Queen Anne at the age of 126. The original tower survives, sitting happily above the unfluted Ionic columns. There is no pediment and thus none of the aesthetic complication usually associated with placing a tower atop a portico. The north and south elevations are lively, eccentric designs, classical in form yet with Plate tracery. This is bold English Baroque.

The interior is reached through the medieval tower. The nave is centrally planned, and is reminiscent of a number of Wren's designs. A central dome is marked by four giant Ionic columns, and surrounded by vaults superbly plastered by Edward Goudge. The east end was Victorianised in 1864 and 1888. The enormous pulpit and tester were moved from their dominant position before the chancel arch, and the arch itself was remodelled. The pulpit remains in the church, now sadly displaced and truncated.

The reredos was also replaced. Portions of the old one are dotted round the back of the gallery, with two paintings, of Moses and Aaron, against the west wall. Why not put them back? The pews of the civic dignitaries and mayoral chair of 1680 survive, and in the north aisle is a throne used when the church court sat in the church. Behind it is an old cupboard which contains the Nativity figures, alarmingly lifesize should you be tempted to open the door.

NORTHAMPTON
St Peter **
Rare Norman carvings

Desperate efforts are being made to keep this fine Norman church open, despite its redundancy. It sits in a bleak corner of the city centre, neglected but with a proud dignity looking out over the ring road. The tower is short but the nave is remarkably long, a length that appears original despite restoration. In other words, this is a rare early church with no exterior division between nave and chancel. There is blind arcading in almost continuous flow along both tower and clerestory, with some excellent corbel monsters. That no patron sought to demolish and rebuild St Peter's throughout the Middle Ages testifies to its status as an urban 'mother church', or minster for the surrounding parishes.

The interior is a basilica, noble and completely Norman but with such cathedral-like features as alternating arcade piers. Its most prized detail is the carving of the pier capitals, of extraordinary decorative force. Some have simple scrollwork, some have vivid figures of beasts and faces, some clearly hark back to the volutes and leaves of Ionic and Corinthian classicism. They are most unusual and are said to be the work of a lodge of seven masons. During the Puritan period, since the 'icons' on the capitals could not be demolished, they were simply caked in plaster and thus preserved.

The chancel is the product of George Gilbert Scott's restoration in 1850. He pushed the east wall back to create a sanctuary, installing a pattern of neo-Norman east windows based on a set at St Cross, Winchester (Hants). The 14th-century font is a fine work of crocketing.

[CCT]

OUNDLE
St Peter *
Needle spire

Oundle is an attractive ironstone town whose twin glories are its school and its church. The steeple of the latter rises spectacularly above the lanes and alleys of old Oundle. If Northampton steeples were categorised like those of Somerset, Oundle would be of the Wells school, that is with vertical elements dominating horizontal.

The composition is of tower rising to battlements concealing the shift to spire, the whole soaring upwards in a continuous thrust. The buttresses cling tight to the corners, while the bell-openings are elongated and slender. The needle spire has snail crockets climbing its angles and three tiers of lucarnes, a complete 14th-century masterpiece seldom bettered by the later architects of Perpendicular.

We enter through a magnificent porch to find a rather dull interior. The church is essentially Decorated, one of the arcade stops having a modern head of a bishop in 'National Health' glasses. There is a superb Decorated window in the usual place for such insertions, the south aisle, but the modern placing of the altar breaks up the geometry of the interior and cuts off the chancel. There are good Decorated sedilia and a Perpendicular pulpit and brass lectern.

PASSENHAM
St Guthlac **
Classical choir furnishings and murals

Guthlac was a Saxon courtier turned hermit, but the church owes its distinction to a later courtier, Sir Robert Banastre. He was head of household to James I and Charles I and was reportedly an out-and-out villain. The church guide says proudly that he 'features in local ghost stories'. At least he rebuilt the chancel of his church in 1626 and, as an ardent Anglo-Catholic, installed the furnishings that are its principal glory. These were recently restored.

The church lies isolated from the village of Deanshanger and is prettily grouped amid trees with adjacent manor house and tithe barn. The nave and tower base are 12th century, solid and strong, with three bold saints' niches surviving on the west wall. The interior is much as it would have been in the 17th century, replete with woodwork in a chaste classical style unusual for its period.

The style marks a decisive break with the fussily decorated classicism of most of the Jacobean furnishings. In the nave are box pews in olive green, and the west gallery has a full entablature supported on Ionic columns, formerly the chancel screen. The superb pulpit, an amalgam of earlier pieces, includes the emblems of the Stuart union: rose, thistle, harp and fleur-de-lis. The last represents land which the Kings of England still claimed in France.

The chancel is all Banastre's work, presumably executed by or to the designs of court craftsmen, with the name of Inigo Jones inevitably connected to any work of this date. It has a wagon roof and contains choir stalls and murals, discovered under whitewash in 1954. The decoration is of the highest quality, especially the woodwork.

The furnishings which Bishop Cosin installed at Sedgefield and elsewhere in County Durham probably belong to the 1630s, that is a decade later than Passenham. Here the choir stalls are medieval in arrangement, with Gothic panelled fronts and fine misericords. But, as with Cosin's work, the dominant style is classical. Most splendid are the choir stall backs, with full coupled columns and image niches in which statues would once have stood and should be filled again.

On the wall above, the classical architecture is repeated in paint, with pilasters dividing niches depicting four Old Testament prophets to the north and four New Testament evangelists to the south. The roof represents the sky. This is how every English chancel might have looked had the Anglo-Catholic tradition remained in the Laudian ascendant. Passenham survived the Civil War, the Georgians and the Victorians under a blessed coat of whitewash.

RAUNDS
St Peter **
Early Gothic steeple, medieval murals

The church lies up a steep incline from the village, its tower one of the finest of those guarding the Nene valley west of Northampton. This is a complete Early Gothic structure, with blind lancet arcading offering three stages of upward movement. At the top of the tower, rebuilt in 1826, large broaches effortlessly shift the rhythm from square tower to octagonal spire. This form was repeated a hundred times by Victorian architects in the Kentish ragstone Gothic churches supplied to the stucco estates of West London.

The nave is a simple work of five Decorated bays but with an understandably powerful tower arch. The windows are a lexicon of Decorated tracery, the finest being the chancel east window, a marvel of Geometrical design of *c.*1275. It also contains glass worthy of the architecture, by Kempe, with agitated flowing lines and gentle colours. Next to it is a curious Tudor window let into the south wall, full of heraldic and decorative glass. Old armour is on display in the south aisle.

Raunds is best known for its murals. These fill the north wall above the arcade and the east wall above the chancel arch. They are well preserved and portray the parable of the 'three living and the three dead kings'. Such warnings, usually of the mortality of the mighty, were favourite themes of medieval artists and are here married to a depiction of the Deadly Sins.

In her work on church iconography (*see* Introduction) Maisie Anderson discusses Raunds at length, and I can do no better than quote her: 'At the west end ... the little group of sins in the dragons' mouths portrays acts whose extreme familiarity inclines men to condone them. Yet as the eye travels down those branching dragons' bodies into the giant form of Pride, and through her limbs to their true place of origin, Hell, these petty vices are seen in the awful perspective of eternity. A few paces eastwards and our glance falls on a second allegory [three living and three dead], seizing first upon the rabbit and the hunting dogs, still clearly visible, and then ... the Kings in their careless enjoyment of the chase, and lastly their horrible vision of their Deaths.'

Over the tower arch is a 15th-century clock, with angels and the donor kneeling behind. As was then customary, its circuit is 24 hours.

ROTHWELL
Holy Trinity ***
Ironstone and limestone walls, chancel grotesques

Rothwell is one of the county's most attractive small towns, once second only to Northampton in size. The church is tucked apologetically behind the market square, but once discovered apologises for nothing. It lost its spire in 1660 but compensates in being the longest church in the county. The tower base is massive, its ironstone and limestone layered like a honey sandwich. The scale of the church is that of a benefice of the Abbey of Cirencester in the 13th century, the golden stone glorious in an evening sun.

The nave is tall and airy, a marvellous space dominated by lofty Transitional arcades with stiff-leaf capitals, and high Perpendicular transepts that once extended further north and south. The massive crossing piers have capitals of foliage and faces. Sun streams into the nave. The ironstone seems able to absorb the light and glow with it, a quality shared with Somerset's Ham stone. In the nave stands an unusual font, with shafts and an odd outer shelf round its bowl.

The chancel too is Transitional and aisled, but with lower arcades. Part of the south chancel aisle has been demolished and the line of the old arches can be detected on the exterior. Looking up we can see the relics of the old Norman clerestory row with a higher Perpendicular clerestory above. This looks odd. Rothwell is like a Russian doll of one church inside another. The choir is dark and rich with stalls and misericords. The roof corbels are of dogs and hares on the north side and people on the south – mankind facing the animals? The north side of a church was always the Devil's side.

Under the south aisle is an ossuary or bonehouse, discovered when an 18th-century gravedigger fell through into the old chamber and found himself surrounded by 1,500 skeletons of his forebears. The bones have been reordered, but unlike the ossuary at Hythe (Kent), this one is not easy of access. Rothwell has a fine tradition of monumental masonry. On the south side of the church are superb gravestones with elaborate lettering, the slate in excellent preservation.

STANFORD ON AVON
St Nicholas ****
Stone and wood carving, medieval glass, Cave monuments

This superb church lies to the east of the William-and-Mary Stanford Hall, a house designed by Smith of Warwick. It has been home of the Caves and their descendants, the Brayes, to this day and their monuments fill the church. The churchyard is a meadow whose gate firmly warns us to keep out the sheep. The windows alternate graceful Intersecting and a swaying Reticulated tracery. The steeple lacks a spire, the crude tower pinnacles forming a sort of apology.

The interior is mostly clear of pews. With the chancel, it offers a gallery of church furnishing, glass and sculpture as complete as that of any small parish church. The nave arcades are limestone arches with no capitals, just a continuous, sweeping arc. The stone carvers were confined to the spandrels. Others were at work round the south aisle piscina and others still on the Decorated font.

Stanford is rich in woodwork. The chancel roof beams are apparently Norman in origin, while the dark oak wall panelling is 16th century, from the former Stanford Hall. The sanctuary chairs are Flemish, their backs portraying Stations of the Cross, and the altar was that used by William Laud, vicar here in 1607 before his ascent to Canterbury. Gnarled choir stalls display poppy-heads and misericords. Indeed all the furnishings are pre-Victorian. Even the church doors have medieval woodwork. The organ case in the west gallery is Tudor, said to have been removed by Cromwell from Whitehall Palace after the execution of Charles I and acquired by Thomas Cave. How many such treasures are dispersed unrecorded in England's parish churches?

The Stanford monuments commemorate generations of Caves, a parade of gentry from the Middle Ages to the 19th century, courtiers, soldiers, priests, scholars, custodians of the heart of England. There are 15 tombs scattered round the church with an enjoyable juxtaposition of styles. Nothing charts the changes in English taste over the centuries so much as funerary sculpture. From wealth and pomposity to misery, piety and gloom, Stanford recalls it all.

The monuments are in a chronological jumble, and the more delightful for that. In the south aisle, the tomb of the medieval priest who built the church (Alan de Aslaghby) lies under a fine Decorated recess. Against the west wall is a mid-Victorian marble monument to Sarah, Baroness Braye (d.1862), by Mary Thornycroft. The effigy lies asleep with dead lilies in her hand. A friend watches over her, while her children are angels in the sky. She herself gathered the coloured stones from Italy that form the paving before her tomb.

Across the nave on the north-west wall is another large Victorian piece by Westmacott. Robert Otway Cave (d.1844) sleeps with his head affectedly on his hand. A women weeps as she inscribes his praises, his books lying dishevelled by his side. Next is an extraordinary memorial by Felix Joubert of 1896, to Edmund Verney, who fell in the Zulu wars. Next door are the recumbent effigies of Margaret Cave and her husband (c.1600) lying as if on shelves, one above the other.

The chancel monuments include a panel to Thomas Otway Cave (d.1830), in which piety and pain are on full display. His wife weeps while an angel cruelly extinguishes a huge torch in the earth. A fine Jacobean monument in red-streaked marble next to the sanctuary celebrates Sir Thomas Cave (d.1613). It is oddly linked by a scroll to a cenotaph to his eldest son Richard, who died on a visit to Italy at the age of nineteen. He was clearly much favoured.

I cannot write of Stanford's glass, reputedly the best in the county, as it was being restored during my visit. Photographs inside the south door show that it includes early 14th-century as well as later heraldic windows. Among the former is a rare depiction of the Virgin, most such depictions being destroyed by iconoclasts. Stanford retains a fine collection of cobwebs. The habitat of the noble spider is, like the stones themselves, a symbol of the passage of time.

WARKTON
St Edmund **
Montagu tombs by Roubiliac and Adam

Warkton is a scattered village on the outskirts of Kettering, its church separated by a wide meadow. The building is architecturally undistinguished, apart from a fine tower. But Warkton was lucky to be chosen as the mausoleum of the Montagus of neighbouring Boughton (now owned by the Dukes of Buccleuch). The big house was built in the manner of Versailles by the 1st Duke of Montagu (d.1709) on his return from France as ambassador. His son the 2nd Duke, 'Planter John', laid out some 70 miles of avenues connecting the house to the villages round it.

The 2nd Duke demolished the chancel of Warkton church in 1748 and rebuilt it as a private chapel, this being a time when most chancels were in disuse. Four superb monuments dominate the interior, presenting a study in contrasting, some might say deteriorating, styles of funerary sculpture. The sequence begins on the left with the 2nd Duke's own memorial by Roubiliac. He was the most celebrated sculptor working in 18th-century England and was, appropriately, a Frenchman. The Duke died in 1749 and the monument was erected in 1752. It is an allegorical work, with a putto hanging a medallion of the Duke on his tomb, while below his wife holds his discarded coronet and shield. The composition is full of movement and rococo asymmetry.

Directly opposite is the monument to John's wife, Mary Churchill (d.1753), daughter of the Duke of Marlborough. It too is by Roubiliac. Here the style is reminiscent of Poussin rather than Boucher. The urn moved to centre-stage in the mid-18th century. Three Fates watch as putti garland it with flowers. The next tomb, to the left of the altar, is quite different. It is a memorial to the 2nd Duke's daughter, Mary (d.1775), famous for her generosity to the poor. The architectural frame is a familiar coffered apse by Robert Adam, while the sculpture is by P. M. van Gelder. Whereas the architecture is restrained, the sculpture is a bold allegorical composition charged with emotion. Opposite and half a century on, inspiration seems to have departed the Montagu sculptors. Thomas Campbell presents Elizabeth, Duchess of Buccleuch (d.1827), seated between an angel and a woman writing. They look like characters posing for an early photograph. It is a shock to turn back to the Roubiliacs.

The church guide makes no mention of this remarkable collection of 18th-century art, instead directing visitors to the graveyard outside, where 'stones bear the names of the humble village families that have lived in Warkton for centuries'. What plodding political correctness.

WARMINGTON
St Mary *
13th-century wooden roof, Green Men bosses

This is Northamptonshire squat rather than soaring. Warmington's church sits comfortably in the middle of its village, the tower low and lucarnes uncommonly big, as if someone had grasped a taller structure and squashed it short. The dedication is taken seriously. The Madonna's lily can be seen over the vaulted porch and everywhere inside. The building is Early Gothic, with later Decorated work only in the tracery of the south wall and clerestory.

Inside, the arcades are graceful, resting on large plinths and rising to Transitional capitals, some with lilies. Above is a great rarity, a wooden vault of the 13th century, with nine Green Men for bosses running down its crest. This emblem is usually displayed singly in churches, like a watching devil from the woods. To find nine of them given such prominence is an indication of the potency of these 'men' to 13th-century designers. Bold corbel heads and undercut stiff-leaf capitals decorate the vault shafts.

The screen to the north chapel has linenfold panelling. The pulpit is 15th century, recalling that at Fotheringhay, with what appear to be the old dado panels of a screen worked into its sides. In the east wall of the chancel is a rough 13th-century sculpture, apparently showing the deadly sin of Wrath piercing herself with a sword.

WELLINGBOROUGH
St Mary, Knox Road ****
Comper's masterpiece interior

The church lies along the eastern skyline of Wellingborough near the station. Here in a suburb of a lifeless Midlands town is the masterpiece of Sir Ninian Comper and one of the most splendid large church interiors of the 20th century. It is well supported and in good hands, but there can be few such unknown and unobtrusive monuments in this book.

Comper regarded St Mary's as his favourite church and wished to be buried here with his wife, though a grateful nation sent him finally to Westminster Abbey. The church was begun in 1908 under the patronage of the spinster Misses Sharman, daughters of a local landowner. It did not reach its present state until the 1950s. The plan is simple Perpendicular with transepts and full-length aisles, based on St Patrice in Rouen. The exterior is uninteresting.

The north-west door opens to a waft of incense, for the church has always been Anglo-Catholic. The first impression is sensational, intended, in Betjeman's words, 'to force even the atheist to his knees'. The interior is crowded with the inspiration of European Gothicism down the ages. The volume is vast, filled with waving fan vaults and dripping pendants above a sumptuous golden sanctuary, a sort of fantastical King's College Chapel, Cambridge.

The nave has eight bays of ironstone piers with concave sides, as at Northleach (Gloucs), and unorthodox capitals of Comper's own design. The painted roof decoration was never completed. Over the rood screen can be seen the black-and-white paint scheme intended for the arcade, while the western nave bays show the blue-and-gold paint intended for the vault. Finishing both should be a challenge to any conservationist.

Moving eastwards, the inspiration is increasingly Italianate. The rood screen has gilded Doric columns and exquisitely decorated spandrels and loft. It is surmounted by golden angels each with six folded wings and crowned above with a Christ in Majesty, based on the Christ Pantokrator in the apse of the Capella Palatina in Palermo. It is, said Comper, 'as much Italian as English and English as Italian'. The intricate ironwork of the screen is repeated in the filigree patterning round the north chapel.

The sanctuary is protected by a palisade of screens, angels, bridges and painted surfaces. The altar shelters under a ciborium with gilded Corinthian columns, crowned by cherubs and a Resurrection. They are brought forward into the church in the manner of San Clemente in Rome. The font is magnificent, surrounded by an octagonal screen with gilded dolphins. Of other furnishings there are few. The thin pulpit seems to disapprove of anyone preaching in such a church.

The interior of St Mary's has a remarkable completeness. Not every critic has liked it. Comper had his detractors and the vicar's bitter opposition to the eclectic nature of the fittings led Comper to resign twice during construction. But even Pevsner, ultra-Modernist in his taste for 20th-century architecture, was won over. He wrote that St Mary's 'glistens and reveals and conceals to one's heart's delight'. Its day has yet to come.

Northumberland

Northumberland is England's northernmost county, and one of the wildest and least populated. With Co. Durham, it saw Christian colonisation from Iona in the 7th century, of which era the only substantial relic is the crypt at Hexham. Wars with the Scots and military expenditure in the 12th and 13th centuries left a clearer mark on its churches. Above all, Northumberland is uniquely a county of Early Gothic. Almost all the churches in this list boast surviving features of this period. The characteristic soaring lancet beneath a steep gable is best displayed, in a small scale, at Ovingham and Corbridge, but few churches in the north of England equal the spectacular interior and monastic relics of Hexham.

The county has almost no Decorated work and Perpendicular appears only under Percy patronage at Alnwick and Warkworth. Over both churches hangs the ghost of Harry Hotspur. But this is more a county of churches in their settings, of black stone, blowing trees and Roman and Saxon carvings. Like Cornwall this is England at its extremes.

Alnwick ***
Berwick-upon-Tweed *
Bywell *

Corbridge **
Hexham ****
Holy Island **

Norham **
Ovingham *
Warkworth ***

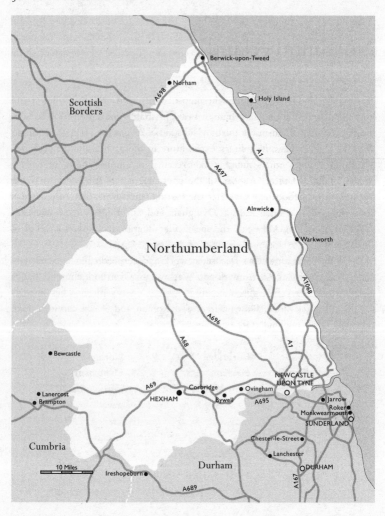

ALNWICK
St Michael ***
Hotspur capital

Alnwick was a fortress of the north against the Scots, as Ludlow was of the west against the Welsh. The town was engrossed in the Wars of the Roses, as home of the Percys, Earls of Northumberland. The most famous of the clan, the volatile Harry Hotspur, had died at Shrewsbury in 1403 in revolt against Henry IV. As Queen Margaret and her Lancastrians restlessly challenged the House of

York from the north, the town was for decades a place of armies, fugitives and vengeance. The church owes its Perpendicular character, rare in the far north, to Margaret's husband, Henry VI. In a desperate bid for support, in 1464 he granted the town a port and tolls for the rebuilding of the church.

The church lies on the northern outskirts of the town, high on a bluff overlooking the river, its churchyard crowded with memorials and yews. The south-west tower is keep-like with heavy stepped diagonal buttresses. The main south elevation is a surprise: a wall of Perpendicular glass, a feature that is rare in northern churches. The spacious interior comprises two building periods. The nave is 14th century and dark, the chancel 15th century and light. Both are aisled, but the chancel has taller arcades, wide aisles and big east windows bursting free of the squat nave. There is no crossing to modulate the passage from the one to the other.

Most famous of Alnwick's carvings are the capitals of the chancel piers. These include the 'Hotspur' capital with the Percy badge, a crescent and fetter-lock. At the south-east corner of the chancel is a turret, probably both a priest's room and a lookout. Under the tower is a statue said to be of Henry VI, but with a new head. Opposite is a huge 14th-century chest with unusual figurative relief carving, a work of magnificent quality.

BERWICK-UPON-TWEED
Holy Trinity *
Rare Commonwealth church

Berwick retains the aura of a frontier town. It was walled and barricaded against Picts, Scots, Jacobites and any insurrection threatened from north of the border. To retain its loyalty, successive English kings declared it a 'free town' and not part of any county, or even country. The Crimean War was declared on behalf of England, Scotland and Berwick. The walls are almost intact, pierced only by Victorian railway builders.

While the heart of the town lies down the slope towards the river and sea, on the hill next to the castle and barracks is one of England's architectural curiosities. Holy Trinity, though planned and authorised by Charles I, was one of the few churches built under Cromwell, by the then garrison commander, Colonel George Fenwick. The previous medieval church could not possibly hold the growing population. Cromwell, so tradition has it, was consulted over its appearance, at least to the extent of forbidding a tower.

Fenwick appeared eager to put on a display of metropolitan style. He brought up a London mason, John Young, and the church, which was completed in 1652, is similar to the then 'latest' City church of St Katharine Cree completed in 1631. The product of this strange fusion of politics, theology and fashion is a curious amalgam of classical form and Gothic detail. The exterior is in local red sandstone, not only without a tower but with no pitched roof either. The dumpy effect is scarcely relieved by crenellated aisles and a clerestory.

In the 19th century two odd turrets and cupolas were erected on the west front. The Gothic east and west nave windows were classicised, and a Tuscan west doorway and an eastern chancel were added. All the windows are now Venetian, even when, as in the original clerestory, they sit inside the original Gothic hood moulds. Where did these masons think that their marriage of styles was heading?

The interior is altogether more classical, with arcades of columns and round arches. In the often dark northern light, made darker by Victorian stained glass, it is an austere place. Even the pulpit lacks the usual Jacobean levity, and is a thoroughly Roundhead furnishing. The choir stalls have unusual arcading. The galleries have gone except in the west, and the most exotic insert is an early reredos by Lutyens. His overall style is severely classical but the details display refreshing touches of Art Nouveau.

BYWELL
St Andrew, St Peter *
Saxon crosses

We might be in Hampshire. Here by the River Tyne is an old manor house set in a park with castle, farm, great trees and, for reasons unknown, not one but two churches, situated immediately next to each other, like the Swaffhams of Cambridgeshire. St Andrew has the finer tower, of Saxon date, and a more or less pure Saxon structure. Inside is a collection of carved coffin lids and cross fragments but the rest is dull.

St Peter is set in a wild churchyard, filled with the giant tombstones in which Northumberland abounds. Were these Viking descendants larger than the old British stock, or do northerners just like to be remembered as big? St Peter's interior is friendly and domestic. The nave is narrow but high, in the Saxon style. It is given a touch of class by the presence of transepts and a smart Victorian pulpit and lectern. The chancel arch is low and takes us into a pure Early Gothic chancel. Here prosperity asserts itself in a fine triple lancet east window and a mosaic reredos. The Decorated north chapel has glass by Wailes. The other glass is acceptable and appears to be at least school-of-Morris.

The church has modern pews and poppyheads. In the aisles are more Saxon carved slabs and fragments of crosses. How confident were these ancient carvers, how tentative the modern ones.

CORBRIDGE
St Andrew **
Saxon tower with Roman arch

Like many towns in the far north, Corbridge has the feel of a garrison. The church is happily located on the side of the old market square, the walls filled with Roman masonry from the nearby camp of *Corstopitum*. In the churchyard is a rare early priest's dwelling, a tower house of Roman stones. It was built in the 14th century to protect the priest from incessant Scottish raids.

The church has a pure Saxon west tower of the 8th and 11th centuries. The main body shares with most of its neighbours the dark fenestration of Early Gothic, set about a much earlier Saxon core, compared with which the Gothic additions must have seemed all sweetness and light. The entrance is through a crude Norman doorway with zigzag cut into the rough blocks of stone. Even cruder is the massive tower arch, apparently taken in its entirety from the Roman camp. Most impressive is the view east of the 13th-century chancel arch. This is a fine work. It rises from a cluster of shafts which somehow lose their confidence, die into a second stage and then recover to soar upwards.

On all sides are lancets, tall and thin, lending a graceful verticality to the interior even where, as in the east wall, they are heavily restored. Only the south transept has been permitted larger openings, on its east side, though it seems hardly worth the effort since the stained glass is so dark.

Despite my reservations on this score, we have to take Corbridge glass at face value. The church would have been filled with such glass originally and the 'modern' work was intended to replicate the atmosphere of the old. There is an admirable guide to the glass but no documentary evidence of a single one of the designers. We must assume that much of it is by Wailes, who worked extensively in the county, and in this style.

HEXHAM
Priory ****
Saxon crypt, canons' night staircase, 'Dance of Death'

This splendid church asserts itself uncompromisingly in the centre of the old fortress town, presenting its gate and walls to the market square. In the Middle Ages this was turbulent country. The 7th-century foundation by St Wilfrid was plundered and burnt by the Vikings. It was refounded in 1113 as an Augustinian priory but attacked by the Scots under William Wallace at the end of the 13th century, when the nave was destroyed and not rebuilt.

After the Dissolution the citizens used the chancel as a church. The eastern bay of the chancel collapsed in the 19th century and a road was then driven through the monastic ruins. It was not until 1905 that thought and money were given to building a proper nave and restoring dignity to the composition. The priory buildings have long gone.

The architect of the new work, which included both a nave and a new east wall facing the market, was Temple Moore. He apparently used the Decorated style so as not to appear to be copying anything in the original church. The result is really two contrasting churches at Hexham, the old church to the east comprising the magnificent crossing and chancel, and Moore's rather cold and scholastic nave to the west.

The east end of Hexham is the apotheosis of Early Gothic in a parish church. We enter it as the canons would have done, by a passage known as a slype at the end of the south transept. It linked the church with the monastic buildings to the south. The entrance thus gives directly on to the interior in the most dramatic possible fashion. The transept is dominated by the priory's famous night staircase, once leading directly to the canons' dormitory from which they could troop down for nocturnal services. This is one of the finest monastic relics in an English church. Above this stage rise two tiers of superb lancets: the lower tier is plain with blind arcading, the upper is fenestrated with rich shafts and mouldings. They form a wonderful group, a completely developed Gothic that would make a perfect set for a medieval film. Above both transepts are 15th-century roofs with bosses intact.

The view east from the crossing is dominated by the chancel arch. Beneath is a complete 16th-century screen and rood loft. It is the work of one of the last priors, Master Thomas Smithson, whose term ended just before the Dissolution in 1524. The dado panels still carry paintings of saints and bishops of Hexham and Lindisfarne. Also on the screen are a Visitation and a poignant Annunciation. On a wall of the sanctuary is another remarkable survival of medieval art, a Dance of Death, the best preserved in England. Centrepiece of the choir is the frith stool, or bishop's throne, one of only two dating from the Saxon period and carved from a single block of stone. Frith means peace, and the stool symbolises Wilfrid's right to grant sanctuary up to a mile from the seat. This right was abolished in 1624.

In the north choir aisle is the chantry chapel of Prior Leschman, Smithson's predecessor, who died in 1491. The chamber is guarded by a crude figure believed to be St Christopher. The prior's tomb chest is adorned with stone carvings which, as Pevsner comments, are barbaric and 'surprisingly inappropriate for their purpose'. Some are of almost Aztec primitiveness and ferocity. One is of a fox preaching to geese, familiar satire on the clergy, but why on a prior's tomb? The effigy of the prior is abstract and has, most unusually, his cowl drawn down over his eyes.

Temple Moore's nave is handsome rather than moving. Even the best 20th-century architecture cannot re-create the mystery of the Middle Ages. Beneath it is the old Saxon crypt, a tunnel-vaulted chamber built partly of Roman stones with carved ornaments and inscriptions. Its arch reputedly dates from the 7th century. Like all such small places, Hexham crypt has a remarkable power of calm.

The church possesses many relics of Celtic and Roman occupation. In the south transept is the tombstone of a Roman soldier, Flavinus, riding his horse above a cowering British native. He was twenty-five years old and had seen seven years' service in these parts. Hexham is admirably lit.

HOLY ISLAND
St Mary **
Off-shore setting, Gospels museum

This is not a remarkable church but is a remarkable site. No traveller down the Northumbrian coast will miss it. From the coast, a sandy spit reaching out into the North Sea seems a curious place for a settlement, low-lying and hard to defend. Yet here St Aidan arrived from Iona to found the famous monastery of Lindisfarne at the invitation of the local king in 635. The loneliness and privation of life here in the Dark Ages is unimaginable. Perhaps it was this that inspired the creation of one of the greatest works of early European art. Recent scholarship has cast doubt on Lindisfarne's claim to authorship of the Gospels, written c.700, that bear its name. In 1997 Professor David Dumville of Cambridge claimed that the only likelihood was that the Gospels were from the north-east. Such doubts do not diminish the fine museum celebrating the Gospels – which are in the British Museum in London but should be here – at the entrance to the church.

Lindisfarne was destroyed by the Danes and not refounded until the late 11th century by the Bishops of Durham. The Norman priory is now a ruin, but a spectacular one. Its sandstone walls, fashioned into pink sponge by the wind and rain rolling in from the sea, look like coral sculptures. St Mary's church is equally rugged. The exterior seems to have been built to deter no enemy but the elements. The west front facing the sea is massively buttressed, with a tall lancet arch supporting a small 18th-century bellcote.

The interior is part Norman, part Early Gothic, with an oddly elongated chancel. The north aisle was, and is, traditionally reserved for fishermen while their womenfolk occupy the nave. Many of the furnishings take the Lindisfarne Gospels as their theme, including the kneelers and the fine carpet on the floor of the chancel. This was woven locally and is based on the 'carpet page', an abstract design used to illustrate St Mark's Gospel.

The church cannot be visited from the mainland except at low tide. Mistake the times and you will have to spend the night on the island.

NORHAM
St Cuthbert **
Giant Norman arcades

Norham is not quite the northernmost church in England – Berwick has that distinction – but it is closest to Scotland. It is sited in wild country from which we can look across the River Tweed to the border. Church and castle were both built *c.*1165 on the site of St Aidan's crossing of the Tweed, on his way to found Lindisfarne. Both became strongholds of the Bishops of Durham against the Scots. The church retains the form of the Norman foundation and even has fragments of Celtic carving, fashioned into a block of statuary next to the font. Although the church was heavily restored by Ignatius Bonomi in 1846, hamfistedly in the case of the oblong tower, enough original work remains to convey grim northern fastness.

This characteristic is most evident in the exterior of the chancel, a fine sequence of five bays of nook-shafted windows with wall buttresses between them, running the full height of the building. The windows on the south side are ornate, with zigzag and beakhead, while those on the north are simple round-headed openings. The east bay of the chancel is restored Gothic, the Norman bay having been destroyed when fortified by Robert Bruce during a siege of the castle in 1320.

Norman is again displayed inside, particularly since Bonomi reopened the old arcades which had been walled up in the 17th century. These arcades are the glory of the interior. The south arcade has round Norman piers with water-leaf capitals and what are said to be the widest Norman church arches in England. The north arcade has octagonal piers, some with water-leaf capitals. The whole nave is a worthy outpost of mighty Durham. Behind the lectern is a mason's mark said to be identical to one in Trondheim in Norway.

Norham's saviour, if restoration is salvation, was the Victorian vicar, William Gilly, from 1831 to 1855. He brought from Durham Cathedral some of Bishop Cosin's 17th-century furnishings, including a richly carved pulpit, lectern and stall. Under the tower is a superb carved coat of arms of Charles II. The chancel south wall contains a Decorated tomb recess with a knight's effigy. This was found by the Victorians under mud in the nave.

OVINGHAM
St Mary *
Early Gothic interior

The Tyne valley is rich in churches of the 13th century, and perhaps lucky to have lacked the late-Gothic wealth to rebuild them. They are luckier still in the deference of their Victorian restorers, and in having, in the Newcastle designer William Wailes, a sensitive interpreter of Gothic Revival glass.

Ovingham church dominates its village opposite Prudhoe Castle. Its tower is Saxon with bell-openings in the Bywell style, two arches with a small circular opening above. But this is a dumpy, defensive work compared with the superbly proportioned nave, transepts and chancel. Indeed the pleasure of Ovingham, which suffers from a rather frigid interior atmosphere, lies principally in this balance of components, their scale perfectly complemented by long lancet windows. Northumberland is truly the county of the lancet.

The nave is of four bays, and both transepts have west aisles. This gives an exciting sense of spaciousness. Each transept has no fewer than four lancets along its eastern wall. The arcading throughout is superbly modulated. The glass is here mixed, with some by Wailes and some Kempe-ish work in the nave north wall. Ovingham was the birthplace of the naturalist engraver, Thomas Bewick. The guide includes one of his charming vignettes, of village boys playing on the churchyard gravestones.

WARKWORTH
St Lawrence ***
Norman chancel, Perpendicular aisle

England's northernmost settlements benefit from an absence of surrounding suburban sprawl. Town rises from country, not from a no-man's-land of estate development. Nowhere is this more true than at Warkworth. The castle, when approached from the north, rises on a mound hard by the North Sea, defying Scot, Lancastrian and Hanoverian alike.

The castle stands above the sloping main street, down which it glowers at the old church at the far end, like a château on the Dordogne. The church itself lies in a meadow by the River Coquet, with grass running down to the water. Warkworth Hermitage lies on the other side. Old cottages cluster close around. This was the refuge of Shakespeare's Harry Hotspur, the Percy hothead and scourge of Henry IV: 'Out of this nettle, danger, we pluck this flower, safety.'

We should consider Warkworth a 'modern' church by north-east standards. It is Norman rather than Saxon, and Perpendicular rather than Early Gothic. The nave and chancel are wholly Norman, while the tower belongs to *c.*1200.

The openings are mere slits, to keep out the Scots and the wind. The south aisle is later, as is the sturdy 14th-century stone spire with crude broaches.

Warkworth has two distinct elements. Its first claim to attention is the pure late-Norman chancel. This is rib-vaulted with zigzag decoration, and appears to be influenced, like many churches in this county, by Durham Cathedral. The deep-splayed windows have nook-shafts. The Victorians scraped the chancel, leaving it somewhat bleak, but it possesses superb Queen Anne altar rails.

The 'second' Warkworth is the south aisle, facing across the nave to the blank Norman north wall like a dancer under stage lights. It boasts a Decorated arcade and Perpendicular windows. Some medieval glass survives in the aisle east window, including a picture of St Hilda of Whitby.

In the nave is a stone effigy of a knight of c.1330. He lies holding his heart in his hands under a Gothic canopy.

Nottinghamshire

Nottinghamshire is an oddity. Of all Midlands counties it slides most easily into its neighbours. The north is like Yorkshire, the west Derbyshire, the east Lincolnshire and the south Leicestershire. Nottinghamshire is where South meets North, yet without shaking hands. They nod as they pass. It is often a dull, suburban county with a ruined county town of Nottingham. Yet in Blyth and Worksop we can still find the ghosts of great Norman priories. Newark steeple vies with Lincolnshire's finest. The Decorated carving in the chancel at Hawton is some of the best in any parish church. As for endearing Holme, on the banks of the mighty Trent, its motto speaks for half the churches of England: 'It is the sheepe hath payed for all.'

The county was renowned nationwide for the quality of its alabaster and for the masons who worked it. This can be seen in tomb effigies throughout the county, notably at Ratcliffe, Willoughby, Clifton and, most superb, Strelley. The delicacy of their late-medieval workmanship, especially in reproducing armour and garments, was not equalled until the marble carvers of the 18th century. The finest landscape in the county lies to the north, in the Dukeries. Although much of their glory is departed, it survives in one of England's great Victorian churches, Bodley's Clumber.

Blyth ***
Bunny *
Clifton **
Clumber ****
Coddington *
East Markham *

Egmanton **
Hawton ***
Holme *
Kingston on Soar *
Newark-on-Trent ****
Nottingham: St Mary *

Ossington *
Ratcliffe on Soar *
Strelley ***
Willoughby on the
  Wolds **
Worksop **

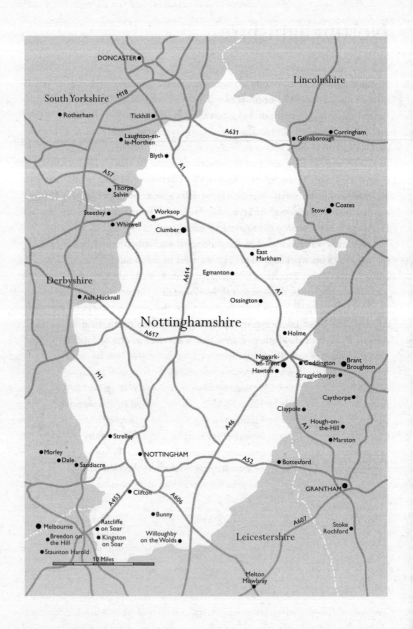

BLYTH
St Mary and St Martin ***
Giant mural of Last Judgement

Blyth is a village on what was once the Great North Road and boasted a Norman priory, church and great house. The composition suffered a terrible fate in the 1970s, when Blyth Hall was demolished and replaced with an estate of luxury villas. Where once were cedars and oaks are now manicured lawns with barking guard dogs. Only to the south-east does the old village retain some dignity.

The Benedictines of Rouen built the original church shortly before 1100, but parochial activities encroached throughout the medieval period. First a large south aisle for the parish was built *c.*1290, as wide as the Norman transept and as high as its clerestory. Then the priory was curtailed during the Anglo-French wars early in the 15th century and the church was bisected by a great wall near the crossing. The nave west of the wall was also given over to the parish and a new west tower was built. Finally the priory along with the monastic east end of the church was demolished at the Dissolution. From the outside the present church thus looks Gothic.

This does not prepare us for the interior. Blyth is the kind of place to which a D. H. Lawrence hero might take a girl to terrify her with tales of damnation. Even the phlegmatic Pevsner agrees that there is 'nothing like Blyth to get a feeling for early Norman grimness'. The nave is a truncated Norman relic. The blocks of stone are laid slapdash on each other, without thought of nip and tuck. The capitals have virtually no decoration beyond a simple scroll and an occasional monster's head.

We cannot justly call this architecture grim, since we have little record of its original decoration. Areas of walling at the east of the nave, bearing white paint with counterfeit masonry joints in red, show that the fabric was meant to be plastered and painted. Centuries have not added to such buildings but taken away from them, reducing walls to the crudest geology.

The east wall inserted by the crossing at the start of the 15th century is the exception. Since its restoration in 1987, the Last Judgement at Blyth has turned out to be one of the largest and most complete medieval murals in the country. This, coupled with the remains of saints on the old screen panels, constitutes a remarkable gallery of Gothic art.

The mural is in a variable state of repair and is best understood from the excellent guidebook in the church. We can make out a red-haired Christ at the top, sitting on a rainbow. There are angels with flowing wings on either side. Below are apostles with haloes. In the centre, the dead rise from coffins, naked except for the crown worn by a king. The king's coffin is decorated, the others plain. The work is not sophisticated, 'probably done by a travelling artist' says the guide, but is remarkable for its size.

The south aisle is spoiled by Victorian glass, apart from a stylish west window by Kempe. In the north aisle is a monument to Edward Mellish (d.1703), builder of Blyth Hall, lying stiffly on his side with a fine double chin.

BUNNY
St Mary *
Tomb of wrestling baronet

The appeal of the church and its surrounding village is linked to that of its famous patron, Sir Thomas Parkyns. He lived from 1663 to 1741, a polymath, eccentric, philanthropist and sportsman, and devoted the bulk of his life to the improvement of the Bunny estate, following his father's death in 1684. Parkyns collected coffins, wrote a Latin grammar for his children and designed farms, cottages, a school, an inn and almshouses for the people of the estate. His hobby was what he called Cornish Hugg wrestling, earning himself the nickname the 'wrestling baronet'. Towards the end of his life he rebuilt Bunny Hall, near the church, with a stone coat of arms blazoned across its tower. Most of Parkyns's work survives, despite the encroaching sprawl.

The church is big, with a tower and needle spire in the Lincolnshire style. Most of the windows are Decorated, with graceful Intersecting tracery. The magnificent porch has a barrel vault and little Perpendicular windows. The interior, scraped by the Victorians, is rather bleak but the friendlier chancel retains its limewash, with Decorated sedilia and an elaborate traceried piscina. Decorous memorials to various Parkynses adorn the walls. One, of a woman weeping over an urn, is to the last Sir Thomas, who died in 1806. He so loved hunting that, even when bedridden in old age, he had himself dressed in the pink to watch the hounds from his window.

The memorial of the wrestling baronet, which he designed himself in 1715, stands at the back of the north aisle. It must be the only church monument depicting a man poised for a throw, and shows Sir Thomas standing, as he put it, 'in a bruising position, even in an encounter with Master All-bones, alias Death'. Beside him lies a figure on the ground, who has clearly failed this encounter. The inscriptions, in Latin, Greek and English, recount: 'That time at length did throw him it is plain / Who lived in hope that he should rise again.'

CLIFTON
St Mary **
Clifton family tombs

There were Cliftons at Clifton since time without memory. Wide Clifton Grove ran to the big house along the top of the bluff overlooking the Trent. The house was still in the family's ownership after the Second World War, and the north transept of the church is full of its memorials. Today, Nottingham suburbia has crept up on hall and church from all sides. The hall is now an outpost of Nottingham Trent University.

The church sits on a mound between the hall and its stables, and is remarkable for the Clifton tombs and modern furnishings. The plan is cruciform, with a long chancel and central tower. Attractive Decorated tracery fills the south transept windows, shaped as angel wings. The inside has a Norman nave as its core, with arcades of chunky piers but small aisles. The capitals are decorated with water-leaf and human faces. The chancel roof retains painted bosses, including, over the chancel arch, a rare 'spitting Jew' with a cleft tongue. He might be spitting at the east window glass, which is peculiarly horrid.

The 20th century contributed extensive furnishings by Ronald Sims in 1975–9. These include the sanctuary, relocated in the crossing and dominating the nave, and the choir stalls which unusually fill the far west end of the nave. Sims designed the altar and candelabra, the glazed chancel screen and a setting for Bodley's fine Victorian reredos.

The north transept contains a Royal Flush of Cliftons (mostly named Gervase) through the Middle Ages and into the 18th century. There are Cliftons in alabaster, brass, stone and slate. Two of the earliest Clifton monuments lie against the north wall. One is an alabaster knight, an early Sir Gervase, with his head on a peacock. At his feet lies the wife of a 15th-century descendant, Alice Nevill, an elongated figure with a serene face in a long-sleeved gown and with a lamb at her feet.

In the centre of the transept lies a 16th-century Sir Gervase, 'the Gentle', with a wife on either side. He died in 1587 and the three lie in prayer, gorgeously apparelled with high ruffs. One wife has eleven rings and the other eight. Like the Ratcliffe and Strelley alabaster effigies, this monument commemorates Tudor fashion as much as a great family. The monument to a subsequent Sir Gervase who married seven times is on the west wall, with his first three wives remembered in a pile of bones portrayed through the window of a charnel house beneath.

CLUMBER
St Mary ****
Bodley's neo-Gothic masterpiece

The descendants of Bess of Hardwick created the Dukeries, a belt of architectural magnificence east of Hardwick in the environs of Sherwood Forest. Their descendants mostly destroyed that magnificence. The seat of the Dukes of Newcastle, Clumber House, was demolished between the two world wars. The majestic park remains in the care of the National Trust and contains the finest avenues in the Midlands.

Nobody had the courage to demolish the church. It was commissioned by the delicate and devout Anglo-Catholic 7th Duke, nephew of the patron of All Saints, Margaret Street in London and patron of Comper's work at Egmanton. On his own estate he determined to give Bodley free rein, at the then huge cost of £30,000. The duke was just twenty-two at the time of the commission in 1886, Bodley was sixty. They eventually quarrelled over Bodley's expenditure (which rose to £40,000) and the work was completed by others, but Bodley continued to regard Clumber as his finest creation.

The plan of the church is symmetrical and cruciform. The exterior soars upwards, the nave windows are set high, and the tower turns octagonal before ascending as a spire. The model is Patrington (Yorks, ER). The stone is white which, according to Bodley, 're-echoes the silvery gleam of the cold English sky', with red Runcorn sandstone dressings. Seen from the south down by the lake, Clumber Chapel is a truly spectacular work of art.

The Runcorn stone used sparingly outside is used throughout the interior, warm and rich when lit by sun or candlelight. The nave is handsome but austere, the duke separating his estate workers from the majesty of the Mass beyond the chancel screen. The chancel is almost as long as the nave, and considerably grander, flanked by side chapels. Its stalls were designed and carved by Ernest Geldart, a priest and craftsman who completed the furnishing of the church after the duke had fallen out with Bodley. (Geldart also designed the astonishing Hispanic reredos at St Cuthbert, Philbeach Gardens, in London.) But Bodley had time to design the pulpit, lectern and superb screen with intricate Perpendicular tracery. His too is the organ case, at a giddy height above the chancel.

The contract for the stained glass at Clumber went to Kempe, favoured artist (over Morris) of the Anglo-Catholic movement. The church contains some of his most refined work. The east window is a Crucifixion, surrounded by the works of Christ and, below, a depiction of Adam and Eve copied from Dürer. Its architectural detail mirrors that of the niches and canopies that fill the sanctuary. The west window is a Tree of Jesse.

The north transept contains a classical monument by Westmacott to Georgiana, wife of the 4th Duke. The Regency style, complete with angelic messengers, would, as the guidebook says, 'have astonished and dismayed' the 7th Duke.

CODDINGTON
All Saints *
Morris chancel and glass

The little church at Coddington was rebuilt by Bodley in 1865. Only the Perpendicular tower peers over the steep-pitched nave and aisle roofs as a reminder of a former structure. Bodley had recently completed his first big commission at Selsley (Gloucs). He again turned to the rising partnership of William Morris and friends for help. It is their work that merits a visit.

The capitals on the north arcade have little owls peering out over the congregation. Morris's work is concentrated in the chancel, where he designed the painted ceiling and wall panels. He also supplied, in place of sedilia (or perhaps as sedilia), a magnificent settle with a gilded canopy in his most sophisticated West End taste.

The east window is a Crucifixion by Morris and Burne-Jones, the latter normally contributing the overall design and drawing the figures. It displays the muted colours of Morris's early period, allowing daylight to illumine what would otherwise be a dark chamber. Morris at this stage greatly admired 15th-century Flemish glass.

The bottom panel includes a lovely vignette of the Annunciation by Burne-Jones. The same lightness can be seen in the south chancel window, depicting St Cecilia with her harp. On a sunny day the trees outside may be seen dancing to her music. A more vivid example of the firm's work is the John the Baptist in the west wall of the tower. The remaining Morris commissions are in the south aisle, mostly much later. They include saints by Madox Brown, and Kings David and Samuel by Burne-Jones. What gems to find hidden in the Nottinghamshire countryside.

EAST MARKHAM
St John *
15th-century female brass

The church sits on the outskirts of its village, the splendid tower and stepped sequence of tower, nave and chancel more East Anglian than east Midlands. The exterior is battlemented and has a full complement of gargoyles. Eight pinnacles and gargoyles spring from the top of the tall tower, like stone jets of water. A strange Gothic statue occupies a niche in the south side, and a small John the Baptist survives, or has been inserted, in the south porch niche. The chancel gargoyles include a monster in armour with an axe and another with its hand in its mouth.

Yet the appeal of this church lies in its orderly proportion and the happy lightness of the interior. Betjeman, with typical hyperbole, called East Markham the 'cathedral of the Trent valley'. The walls have been vigorously scraped and restored. Arcades of four tall Perpendicular bays rise to a generous clerestory which is not aligned with the arcade beneath. The tower arch is astonishingly high, with concave piers and the same castellated capitals as the arcade piers.

The appeal of East Markham lies in its atmosphere and fittings. The font is unusual, supported by small flying buttresses. It would also have had a Comper screen, had it not been a for a quarrel between the patron, the Duke of Newcastle, and the churchwardens at the turn of the century. The screen went to Egmanton. Medieval stained glass survives in the east window of the south aisle but the remaining glass is Victorian.

The church has one of the best brasses in the county, of 1419 to Dame Milicent Meryng, in long flowing dress and with a headdress of wide cowls. A tomb chest of Sir John Markham stands against the north wall of the chancel. He was famous as the judge who signed the deposition of Richard II.

The churchyard at East Markham stretches out to the fields to the south, a peaceful spaciousness rare in a county so given over to suburbs.

EGMANTON
St Mary **
Revivalist Comper interior

Egmanton had been the site of a medieval shrine of Our Lady, a fact that appealed greatly to the Duke of Newcastle (*see* Clumber) in 1896. He revived the ancient cult and employed Comper to restore the church to its former glory. Comper duly converted a much altered 12th-century church into a glowing casket of colourful woodwork, candles and statuary. By 1900 the church was in effect under the Roman Catholic rite.

As usual with Comper, the screen (once intended for East Markham) steals the show. It is a gem of Gothic Revival, with ribbed coving under the loft and fine panels of saints in red and gold. Above is a rood group beneath a canopy of honour. The pulpit is a curiosity, an open wooden frame apparently copied from one in Ghent. Above the south door is a splendid organ case modelled on that in Freiburg Cathedral, with wide doors that open to reveal the pipes.

The chancel contains a high altar and a tabernacle to the Virgin, accompanied by furnishings in colours of almost garish intensity. There are statues of the

Virgin galore. Egmanton induced contrasting responses from its visitors. It left Henry Thorold, author of the county's *Shell Guide*, breathless with delight: 'the whole place is soaked in the prayers of the faithful'. Pevsner admired Comper's designs 'as pieces of medieval revival . . . but as pieces of contemporary art, they are of course valueless'.

HAWTON
All Saints ***
Decorated Gothic sanctuary carvings

Seen from the main Newark to Nottingham road, Hawton's tower rises pleasingly across open fields. Eight pinnacles crown an ogee bell-opening, while swaying trees dance attendance. There is a splendid west door and the clerestory windows are unusually large. To outward appearances, this is a Perpendicular church of the sort widely financed by 15th-century grandees, in this case Sir Thomas Molyneux and his son in about 1480.

However, a walk round the outside shows that the Molyneux family were adapting an already remarkable Decorated church, dating from the turn of the 14th century. This is shown in the steep-pitched roof and Geometrical tracery to the side windows. The east window is grander, with seven lights below curvilinear tracery, lines whirling upwards, wayward yet under control. Ogees tilt and shoot off at angles, forming the shapes of figs, oranges, daggers, hearts, smiles and tears, English Gothic at its most joyful.

The nave interior need not concern us long: simple, scraped and clean with pleasant oak benches, medieval in the aisles. The screen is original and old glass survives in the Lady Chapel window. What sets Hawton apart is the carving in its chancel. Scholars debate whether its craftsmen came from Ely, York or Southwell, with a preference for the last. What is uncontroversial is the quality of the work.

The chancel walls are adorned with a complete liturgical sequence: tomb and Easter Sepulchre on the north side, piscina and sedilia on the south. Although these have been damaged over the years, and were filled with straw and plaster until the 19th century, they still possess the vitality of their creation. Only the sepulchre at Heckington (Lincs) is of comparable quality in a parish church.

The north side carvings lie under a unified frame, within which each component is distinct. To the left is a priest's doorway carved with small heads of a king and a bishop. In the middle is the tomb recess, supposedly for Sir Robert de Compton, the effigy dated 1308 and possibly moved from elsewhere in the church. The sepulchre itself is a complete tableau. At the base are the four Roman soldiers asleep, like characters from Piero della Francesca's San Sepolcro *Resurrection*. Above is Christ rising from the tomb, with the three Marys come to anoint His body. Above is the Ascension, with Christ's feet disappearing into the clouds and St Peter holding his keys. The scenes are framed in the most ornate form of arch, a cusped nodding ogee, Gothic art at its most inventive.

The south wall balances the north, displaying the piscina and sedilia. Here images of saints are set amid a profusion of naturalistic carving. The mix of sculpted figures with foliage and fruit is rare. Below, magnificently carved, are two eucharistic symbols, the pelican in her piety and grape-pickers. Nor has anybody thought to fill the east window with stained glass. A beech tree waves its shadow over these leaves of stone, from which they might indeed have gained inspiration.

HOLME
St Giles *
Tudor furnishings

Nothing protects a church like being in a cul-de-sac by a river. St Giles lies in a hamlet by the Trent, a 15th-century wool merchant's penance, with a chantry to save his soul in Heaven and a porch for his reputation on earth. The merchant, John Barton, came from Lancashire, presumably following his sheep towards the markets of the east. It is said that an inscription in his house bore the simple message: 'I thanke God and ever shall / It is the sheepe hath payed for all.'

The steeple is a dumpy version of a Northamptonshire style. Tiny broaches and lucarnes support a cock for a weathervane. The walls look tumbledown and the porch, despite its ostentatious gable, is crumbling. However, it has a splendid row of shields above the door and a mullioned window for the priest's room above. The shields are of the Barton family and include sheep and two bales of wool. So many Midlands churches seem poor little rich ones. Holme was a rich little poor one.

Holme's interior has been much battered by age, but to stand in its chancel is to experience a rare thing, a space scarcely touched since the 16th century. The nave has a single three-bay arcade opening into a south aisle with ancient benches, whose poppyheads seem to be nodding in all directions. Simple carved screens divide off the chancel and chapel, brightly restored and one with a modern rood above it. At this point Holme changes mood. Chancel and south chapel are separated by Barton's tomb. This has carved effigies of Barton (d.1491) and his wife with, below, a skeleton granted almost as grand a space as the 'living' corpses above. The chapel has fine niches with fragments of Gothic carving and rich corbels. The roof is embellished by coloured figures and symbols, including the rebus of Barton: a bar and a tun (barrel).

The joy of this chapel lies in its woodwork, which includes lavishly proportioned benches of petrified wood, with reading desks and carved poppyheads.

Birds, lizards, dogs and angels appear to have been hacked by their carvers from living trees and left to mellow with age. Running my fingers over the benches at Holme is the nearest I have come to feeling time. The glass is mostly heraldic, a kaleidoscope of medieval fragments and including 16th-century figures from Beauvais. The windows are cool and enjoyable, and do not hide the sky.

KINGSTON ON SOAR
St Wilfrid *
Babington Chantry

Some treasures are found in the most unexpected places. Kingston is a rebuilt church of 1900 whose exterior hardly rates a second glance, yet it houses the extraordinary Babington memorial, as flamboyant a show of Tudor pomp as the tower at Layer Marney (Essex) or the Bedingfield tombs at Oxborough (Norfolk). The only indication of this outside is the mild enrichment of the south chapel wall and roof.

The Babington family were courtiers and prominent Catholics. A later Sir John Babington was involved in the plot to depose Elizabeth in favour of Mary Queen of Scots, for which treason he was executed and the family ruined. This chantry, however, was founded earlier in the century, by Sir Anthony in *c.*1540. Such chantries were soon to be suppressed, half-heartedly by Henry VIII and whole-heartedly under Edward VI in 1547. Here the tomb itself is missing. What survives is its magnificent canopy, a majestic frame to an unmarked grave.

The canopy has a wide Tudor arch, with a fan vault from which heavy pendants drop. It is supported by four piers, their shafts covered in hexagonal panels. The huge capitals are decorated with babies holding barrels, the Babington rebus (baby plus tun). Between the east piers is a lovely carved relief of the Last Judgement, damaged but still discernible. Buildings rise behind the blessed and the damned. A benign God sits on top and the jaws of Hell are open wide at the bottom. A strip of arabesque here is the only glimpse of the Renaissance on the monument. The canopy was once topped with the coat of arms of Henry VIII, removed as too heavy for the structure.

NEWARK-ON-TRENT
St Mary ****
Decorated tower and civic nave, Dance of Death painting

Newark and Grantham still soar over the east Midlands as they did in the Middle Ages. Grantham may have the finer steeple, but Newark outclasses it as a medieval church. Built over the two centuries of Perpendicular ascendancy after the Black Death, it piles high above its constricted urban site. A style so often dull is here exhilarating, the vistas majestic, the furnishings rich. As the country towns of England emerge from relative depression, these vast churches must revive as centres of cultural and civic activity.

The plan to rebuild the former church took shape in 1310. It began with the completion of the old Early Gothic tower and south aisle in the prevailing Decorated style. The tower thus starts at the bottom with 13th-century blind arcading and trelliswork – but with a Perpendicular window inserted. It rises to Decorated bell-openings under a crocketed gable. The parapet barely interrupts the broaching, as square turns to octagon at the foot of the spire. This spire soars to 236 ft, 50 ft shorter than Grantham.

The rest of the church was not finished until the early 16th century. By then Newark boasted sixteen guild and chantry chapels, two of which survive either side of the high altar. Though battered by Reformation and Civil War, Newark was not as altered in the 19th century as was Grantham. The walls are un-scraped, apart from a patch above the chancel arch, and the roofs gloriously painted. The north side windows are mostly clear but the heavy colouring of the south windows is a blight, despite fine pieces by both Kempe and Wailes.

The nave is a wonder of proportion. Pevsner attributes this to the old Decorated plan, giving the aisles breadth, while the later masons added height. The vista thus extends horizontally and vertically. The chancel is marked by a fine Perpendicular screen and contemporary stalls and misericords. Glowing at its heart is a Comper masterpiece, a reredos of 1937, commissioned to cover a 19th-century one. On either side are the surviving chantries, now rather bare. Outside the south chantry is a fragment of a medieval Dance of Death, once so frequent in English churches but now rare. The panel carries the familiar warning, 'As I am today, so you will be tomorrow.'

The Lady Chapel contains a row of 15th-century sedilia above which the Victorians placed a mosaic of Van Eyck's *Adoration of the Lamb*. The east window of the Holy Spirit Chapel brings together Newark's surviving medieval glass in a composition of Old and New Testament stories. Next to it rises John Hardman's vast memorial east window to Prince Albert. The northern chapel is dedicated to the Sherwood Foresters regiment and is decorated by Caröe.

Back in the nave, Newark's font was desecrated by iconoclasts. The base is medieval while the bowl is of 1660, with Cavalier heads in a classical setting. Next to it is the Markham monument of 1601. Anne Markham is pictured sur-rounded by her children under a knot of drapery, set in the purest of classical frames.

NOTTINGHAM
St Mary *
Art Nouveau door

Terrible things have been done to Nottingham by its burghers since the Second World War. At least the area round St Mary's retains some sense of the earlier city, with town houses, workshops and former lace factories crowding the foot of the busy town church. It is still happily enclosed and its bells ring confidently over the rooftops.

The church is Perpendicular throughout, with so much window that little of its superstructure can be termed a wall. The plan is cruciform with a fine central tower topped by eight pinnacles and no spire. The exterior is in the richest of taste, the prominent transepts adorned with panelled battlements, crocketed pinnacles and north and south windows spanning their entire width. The stone is grey and, where restored in the 19th century, hard and cold.

The visitor enters by the south porch, an eroded remnant of a former church. It is like being greeted by a kindly old janitor before entering an austere school-room. The porch enfolds a superb work of art, a door by Henry Wilson of 1904. This takes the form of a bronze relief of Christ with the Virgin, crowned by a sumptuous Pietà. It is an Art Nouveau masterpiece and worth seeing even if the church is locked and you can get no further.

The interior is undeniably impressive. Its vastness derives from the height of the crossing vault and the generosity of the clerestory windows. Arcade piers glide upwards in a single unbroken sweep. The chancel has startlingly bright 1960s colouring and a spectacular Bodley & Garner reredos and chancel screen.

The window glass is, for the most part, a Victorian gallery by the accepted masters: Hardman, Heaton & Butler, Clayton & Bell and Burlison & Grylls. The best work is by Kempe in the south aisle. A modern organ has been clamped to the east wall of the south transept. The organist sits in it like a rock-climber on a perilous overhang.

OSSINGTON
Holy Rood *
Woodland setting, Georgian monuments

Ossington Hall was demolished in the 1960s and the family moved to the rectory. The estate remains wild and isolated, approached along drives through dark woods. Round a bend in one of these lies the church, on a hillside over-looking a lake. The churchyard is overgrown and thick woodland encroaches on every side. Yet nothing could be more urbane than the Georgian tower with columns and cupola and the handsome pedimented south door. The architect in

1782 is said to have been Carr of York, though there is no documentary evidence for this.

The interior is a classical rectangle with three arches forming a chancel arch. The church contains two fine tombs. First is a Jacobean monument to William Cartwright (d.1602). He kneels facing his wife beneath a flourish of entablature, while 'below stairs' kneel their twelve children in rows, like terracotta Chinese warriors. At the back of the church is Nollekens's monument to the Denisons, Leeds wool merchants who acquired the Ossington estate in 1749. The statues are of William and his brother Robert, leaning on pedestals in casual poses, like characters in a West End club. Later generations of Denisons have kept the church in good repair but defaced its east end with ferocious modern glass, shutting out the glorious woodlands.

RATCLIFFE ON SOAR
Holy Trinity *
Sacheverell tombs

The church lies in the shadow of Britain's biggest power station, nestling between the access road and the M1. It is reached down a lane, an ancient dyke protecting it from the flood plain where the Soar joins the Trent. The churchyard is delightfully overgrown and the Decorated east window seems to draw its mullions from the long grass beneath.

Ratcliffe's exterior is robust. The south side has paired lancets in the chancel and two beefy Reticulated windows in the aisle. The interior is equally unrefined. The walls escaped Victorian scraping and are limewashed. The original 15th-century roofs are unceiled and there is no stained glass. The chancel rises one step and the sanctuary two, the chancel being slightly longer than the nave. An old stone altar was recovered and reinstated after the Reformation, while the Reformers' altar table stands in the south aisle.

The tombs may not be as fine as Strelley's or those of the same family, the Sacheverells, at Morley (Derbys), but they form a charming group. Most are in good condition, of Nottingham alabaster carefully restored in 1973. There are four in all. The oldest is against the north wall and is of Randulfus Sacheverell (d.1539), his wife Cecily beside him. He is bareheaded and in full armour under a wide canopy. Gothic niches guard the heads and feet; these would once have contained statues and candles. The next tomb is of his son, Sir Henry (d.1558), but the decoration of the tomb has only a slight hint of classicism, in the corner balusters. Another Henry died in 1580. His children stand round the chest in solemn dignity within plain frames. Female fashion has moved from medieval austerity to full Elizabethan dress, with a high ruff collar.

The final tomb against the south wall is of the next Henry (d.1625). The man lies alone, though in anachronistic armour and with his helmet under his head. Two babies are portrayed beneath him, indicating infant deaths, and his one surviving daughter. This was to be the last of that Sacheverell line. Above are Henry's three wives, who failed to supply a male heir, each kneeling at a prayer desk. Only here is the change in style decisive. The canopies are classical, with Corinthian columns. The figures now are more coarse, the faces all alike. Dresses are full and severe, the headgear sweeping back in long falls. These ladies seem to offer an ominous welcome to the Stuart age.

STRELLEY
All Saints ***
Strelley tombs

Forget Nottingham and try to forget the M1. The lane leading to the village says 'Strelley Only' and means it. Suddenly suburbia slides behind us and wide fields, woods, cottages and pink walls take over. This is Mansfield stone, to the Midlands what Ham stone is to Somerset. It softens and erodes, as if the long-gone sea were still washing over it. The church sits on a hillside, with the old hall immediately beyond. Strelleys lived here throughout the Middle Ages; twelve generations in succession were knighted. They ceded the manor to the Edges, mayors of Nottingham, in the 17th century. Descendants of Edges lived on, changing names through the female line, until 1978 when old Miss Edge died. She had failed to keep at bay both open-cast mining and the M1. The old hall was sold for commercial use and a version of England came to an end.

A new church was begun on the site by Sir Sampson de Strelley in 1356 shortly after the Black Death, possibly in thanks for his survival. It was probably complete by 1400 and only the base of the tower remained from the former building. The battlemented walls rise like castle ramparts and are a museum of local geology, with stone, brick and mortar slapped into place as and when required. The interior by contrast is high, noble and richly adorned. It suggests not an English parish church but a French private chapel.

The nave is of just three bays, with a high Victorian clerestory, but attention is concentrated on the chancel. To Pevsner this is 'the most complete example in Nottinghamshire of the riches of art which a generous and pious family would bestow on the church of its manor'. The chancel is approached through a Perpendicular screen, the best in Nottinghamshire. It is tall, heavy and dark, with openwork coving. In the centre of the chancel and in pride of place is Sir Sampson himself, peacefully lying hand in hand with his wife and awaiting the Resurrection. The date is *c.*1410. His neck rests on a helmet crowned with the head of a strangled Saracen. This familiar medieval motif implied crusader valour, but was also the Strelley crest. His wife has a wide headdress, allegedly 'Phoenician' in style. Her feet rest on two puppies.

Against the north wall is an even finer tomb, of John de Strelley and his wife Sanchia, of a century later. Husband and wife no longer hold hands but lie in prayer. The quality and ingenuity of the Nottingham alabaster carving is outstanding. The lady's face is serene. The knight wears armour, with the Saracen's head under his neck. The ensemble is full of late-Gothic life. Under his feet, resting on an amiable lion, are two tiny mourners with rosaries. Similar figures nestling with a lion are found at Harewood (Yorks, W) and Lowick (Northants). A child nestles on either shoulder of Sanchia, twins who died in infancy. A puppy plays in the folds of her dress. The tomb lies inside a recess with a superb sculpted surround. The upper register has Abraham gathering souls into his bosom and, once again, the Strelley Saracen. Other Strelley tombs include incised floor plates, some of alabaster, one of brass.

One of the choir misericords is a rarity, a Green Woman, her limbs turning to leaves. The only other Green Women I know are at Ludham (Norfolk) and Clare (Suffolk). The guide proposes this one as a sheela-na-gig, a female fertility symbol with obscure pornographic connotations.

The Victorian restoration of Strelley kept faith with the original. Both the chancel and the south transept, now the Lady Chapel, are panelled and have fine reredoses. The glass in the Lady Chapel includes medieval fragments. That in the north aisle is mostly Flemish of the 16th century. Its roundels form a children's scrapbook of domestic and religious scenes, one being of an obscure saint called Ugbertus.

WILLOUGHBY ON THE WOLDS
St Mary and All Saints **
Willoughby tombs, 'rose' Madonna

The church is architecturally of little account, a friendly place with a stone Midlands spire, Transitional arcade and an apology for some stiff-leaf on one pier capital. The reason for a visit lies in the north chapel, the Willoughby tombs. Four are early and of stone. Another, of a Sir Richard who died in 1369, lies under the dividing arch. A second Sir Richard (d.1362) lies along the north wall and is more important. Experts are intrigued by a rare tomb of this date portraying a judge in a high-collared cloak rather than armour and in being tonsured, that is bald on top of his head but with hair at the sides. In other words, the figure looks suspiciously like a portrait, which 14th-century effigies almost never were.

Even more exciting is the free-standing alabaster tomb in the middle of the chapel. This is of Sir Hugh Willoughby (d.1445) and his wife Margaret. His feet are on a magnificent frowning lion, hers on two puppies. The carving, though somewhat battered, is of high quality. He wears a rare item of armour known as a salet or light fighting helmet, like a metal sou'wester.

At the west end of the tomb chest is a small Trinity, and at the east end a Madonna. The latter, though eroded, is a miniature masterpiece. The Virgin's figure has a delicate face with a large crown, tilted over the Child in her arms. Her sceptre has flowered into a rosebush and is shown with the Holy Dove alighted on it. The fingers are carved with a Baroque sense of movement, as are the folds of the garments. This gem appears in no guidebook, but is noted by Maisie Anderson (*see* Introduction) as 'the supremely beautiful Queen of Heaven, whom men reverenced with warm, romantic devotion and who inspired innumerable poems, legends and paintings of tender loveliness'.

WORKSOP
Priory Church **
Norman west front and nave

Worksop has an unhappy name and unhappy setting. It claims the title of capital of the Dukeries, but its old priory was dissolved and the ruins endured the familiar fate, of decay and demolition, with the parish making what use it could of what remained. This includes an extravagantly long Norman nave and a fine west front with two bold towers. To the east was a detached and ruined Lady Chapel, and this chapel has since been joined to the nave by a modern crossing tower and sanctuary. The marriage of new and old is more of convenience than love, yet the church is full of interest.

The entrance is approached across a wide green from which authority has banished all gravestones. Praise be that some wildness survives to the east of the church. Here the old priory extended to almost three times the length of the present nave. The nave exterior reminds me of a dachshund on its back with its hind legs in the air. But there are fine doorways on all sides of the church and in the south porch can be seen an original Sherwood Forest yew door covered in Norman ironwork. This is a superb piece.

The Norman nave seems even longer inside than outside. The piers of the ten bays are alternately octagonal and round. The arches are adorned with late Norman dogtooth and the capitals have primitive stiff-leaf. The atmosphere lightens with the idiosyncratic gallery and clerestory, but the walls are scraped and battered and the seating is ugly. Eastwards, the crossing and sanctuary are mostly 20th century, completed in 1974 by Laurence King. They are Modernist to the point of bleakness, with stark stained glass of the Virgin and Child divided not by by tracery but by two huge cement mullions.

The transepts are more deferential, forming a careful transition to the south-east Lady Chapel which stands behind a modern screen. Here only the walls and windows are original. The chapel is lit by lancet windows of the purest proportions. This is 'late' Early Gothic, with moulded capitals rather than stiff-leaf. Sadly the vault was never built. The chapel has a painted altarpiece.

13. Ranworth's debonair St Michael, Norfolk

14. Weeper on Burford's Tanfield tomb, Oxfordshire

15. Poley 'swagger' at Boxted, Suffolk

16. The 'soaring' south arcade at New Shoreham, Sussex

Oxfordshire

Oxfordshire is a county in between. It links the Thames valley to the Midlands and the Chilterns to the Cotswolds. The churches reflect this border status. To the west, creamy Cotswold stone composes St Mary, Oxford, Chipping Norton and the superb church at Burford. The county's best work is to the north, in the brown Midlands ironstone (or marlestone) which, in Clifton-Taylor's words, knows how to 'soak up and store the sunshine'. This stone was the canvas for the 14th-century north Oxfordshire carvers of Adderbury and Bloxham, and was later worked at the same churches by the great Perpendicular architect, Richard Winchcombe.

To the south, the quite different character of the Thames valley yielded the Early Gothic splendour of Uffington, Dorchester's majestic choir and the redbrick charm of Ewelme. Elsewhere, Oxfordshire is a county of individual pleasures, enhanced by the addition of a slice of Berkshire in the 1990s. The Normans left the carved tympanum at Church Hanborough and the exotic zigzag decoration of Iffley. The Goths left the knight's effigy at Dorchester, the glass at Kidlington and the murals at South Newington. The Jacobean era brought the royal pew at Rycote, the Fettiplace monuments of Swinbrook and the swaggering Spencers of Yarnton. Yet the county has its subdued delights: little Widford by the Windrush, the lost farmyard chapel of Shorthampton and the pretty 20th-century interior of Compton Beauchamp.

Abingdon ***
Adderbury ***
Bloxham ****
Broughton **
Burford *****
Charlton-on-Otmoor *
Childrey *
Chipping Norton ***
Chislehampton *
Church Hanborough **
Compton Beauchamp **

Dorchester ****
East Hagbourne *
Ewelme ***
Faringdon ***
Hanwell **
Horley **
Iffley ***
Kidlington **
North Moreton **
Oxford: St Mary ***
Radley *
Rycote **

Shorthampton *
Shrivenham **
South Newington **
Sparsholt *
Stanton Harcourt **
Swinbrook **
Thame **
Uffington ***
Wheatfield *
Widford *
Yarnton ***

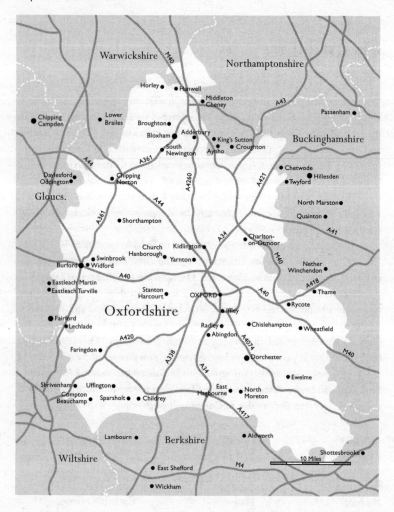

ABINGDON

St Helen ***

Five-aisled nave, Lily Crucifix ceiling

This is a big, confident Thames church, wealthy in its guilds and ideally positioned between town and river. The approach down East St Helen's was admired by Celia Fiennes in the 17th century and remains, as then, a tableau of cottages, roof and tower. The old priest's house survives, and the churchyard is enveloped by almshouses. The Long Alley almshouse was built in the 15th century by the Guild of the Holy Cross, which also financed the enlargement of the church. Near to it is a pumphouse for the organ, the last such engine in England. This is one of the county's best church closes, handsomely placed on the banks of the Thames.

The river bank gives a view of Abingdon's celebrated five east end gables. The nave with four aisles, built or rebuilt in the 15th and 16th centuries, is second only to Great Yarmouth (Norfolk) in width. The inside is darkened by 19th- and 20th-century glass, some of which should urgently be removed. Henry Woodyer renewed the chancel in 1873 and added a fine Gothic screen. The neo-Norman font, by a local artist, was considered sufficiently good to be shown at the 1851 Great Exhibition.

Abingdon's treasure is the painted ceiling of the Lady Chapel, dating from the late 14th century. The chapel was built by the Guild of Our Lady which, with the help of a papal indulgence in 1391, also financed the painting of the ceiling. Four years' relief from Purgatory was assured for donors. The panels portray the Tree of Jesse, which forms a decorative frieze beneath a parade of kings and prophets. Each panel is set in an ogee frame. The kings are splendidly crowned, the prophets having Jews' caps. The ceiling includes a rare Jesus on a Crucifix of a lily, found elsewhere at Godshill (Hants/Isle of Wight) and at Long Melford (Suffolk).

The colours and costumes in the Abingdon ceiling evoke the glory of Perpendicular Gothic under Richard II, a time of wealth and brief peace, when the English court considered itself a match for any in Europe. No work of art so well conveys the luxury of a medieval borough at the turn of the 15th century. The ceiling has been admirably restored.

ADDERBURY
St Mary ***
14th-century stone carvings

Adderbury and its neighbour Bloxham are the twin glories of north Oxfordshire. 'Bloxham for length, Adderbury for strength, King's Sutton [Northants] for beauty,' goes the local saying. At the turn of the 15th century, the manor and church at Adderbury were appropriated by New College, Oxford, who built a magnificent new chancel in 1408–19. It was a time of economic recession, between the death of Richard II and the resumption of the French wars under Henry V. This was the age of Shakespeare's England in turmoil 'bound in with inky blots and rotten parchment bonds'. Church building all but ceased, but not here.

Adderbury's original documents survive as a rare record of medieval church finances. Local tithes were diverted to pay for the rebuilding of the chancel for more than a decade. Its carving commemorates, not the tithe-payers, but New College's founder, William of Wykeham (d.1404). His head and coat of arms appear on the parapet above the east window. Inside, on a roof corbel and a window stop, he is depicted wearing the mitre of the Bishop of Winchester and distinguished by the mole on his chin. He is paired with a king, variously identified as Richard II or Edward III. Master mason of the chancel was Richard Winchcombe. His reward was a commission to build the Divinity School in Oxford.

The rest of the church is earlier, a Decorated structure adorned by the north Oxfordshire school of carvers and with a magnificent tower and spire. The carvings here, as at Bloxham and Hanwell, seem a far cry from Winchcombe's courtly Perpendicular. Both inside and out, their gallery of vernacular art is in line of descent from the friezes of Elkstone (Gloucs) and Kilpeck (Herefs). Animals, grotesques and humans tumble along the cornice line. On the north side, music is the theme, bagpipes, harp, violin, drum, organ and other instruments of the medieval orchestra.

The same hand, or hands, continues inside. Heads start out at us from every corbel, poking from arch, corner and capital. A woman is blowing a fire with bellows, a man is shearing sheep. Devils and angels seem part of the daily life of 14th-century Adderbury, in these happy days before the Black Death. A pier divides each aisle from the transept: on the north capital are women in medieval wimples, on the south one are knights linking arms. They are assumed to indicate the sides of the church on which men and women sat.

By the 18th century the church was badly dilapidated, and the interior suffers from 19th-century restoration. Work was carried out on the chancel in the 1830s, including the replacement of all the window tracery. It was followed by a brave attempt by the Gilbert Scotts, father and son, to restore the western parts. Both strove to respect the Gothic original. The tower has a carillon which plays a different tune each day. Saturday's is 'Home Sweet Home'.

BLOXHAM
St Mary ****
Window carvings, Milcombe Chapel, Burne-Jones glass

Bloxham is a steeple, a window and a chapel. The steeple is a work of art in itself, early 14th century and the finest in Oxfordshire. Bloxham church, with its adjacent school, enjoyed royal patronage until the Dissolution, when it passed to Eton College. The octagon and spire rise 200 ft, almost sheer from the road.

Every surface of the tower is carved. Below the parapet is a frieze of men and beasts, which continues along the north aisle and recalls similar work at Adderbury. The west doorway arch has carvings of the apostles in small niches, with a Last Judgement at the apex. The masons seem to have usurped all convention and set free their imaginations. The brown marlestone is badly eroded, in part by its proximity to the main road, and some carvings are Victorian replicas. In which case, I cannot see what is served by letting the others crumble to nothing. New ones should surely take their place, true to the Victorian practice. If the statues at Chartres can be replaced, why not at Bloxham?

The inside of the church is not easy to read: essentially a 14th-century Decorated structure encasing Norman and Early Gothic features, but with spectacular additions in the Perpendicular period. The south doorway is part-Norman. The nave arcades are Early Gothic, the stone dark and often undressed. The double arch that divides the north aisle from the transept has a superb capital adorned with heads, arms and shields. Most remarkable of the windows is that at the west end of the north aisle, where the tracery is carved with figures both inside and out. This rare practice, also found at Dorchester, must have been intended to complement the story told in the window glass. It here illustrates the Bible in a stone wheel with Christ at its hub.

Roughly a century later came a burst of Perpendicular patronage, probably from the hand of the same Richard Winchcombe as worked at Adderbury. If so, to him we owe the three great windows inserted in the east end of the aisles, and the Milcombe Chapel, a classic of early 15th-century Perpendicular. The contrast with the chancel east window and with the rest of the building is complete. Areas of Panel tracery support large expanses of clear glass. Mullions soar from floor to ceiling. Light floods in past the delicate concave piers of the arcade, like a conservatory tacked on to a gloomy stately home. The chapel was later taken over by the Thornycroft family and contains a number of their monuments. Sir John Thornycroft (d.1725) lies in effigy, smug with his books, as if this room had been built for his personal and eternal use.

The last phase of Bloxham's development came with Street's restoration and the employment of Morris & Co. for the glass. The chancel interior is largely Street, as are the pulpit, choir stalls and marble reredos. The chancel east window glass is an early masterpiece by Morris, Burne-Jones and Webb. It depicts saints, angels and King Alfred set before the Heavenly City. The colours are bold and the effect dramatic. Even more lovely is the vividly coloured window of St Christopher in the south wall of the chancel. It was executed in 1920 to a Burne-Jones design.

BROUGHTON

St Mary **

Contrasting medieval tombs

One of the finest medieval manor houses in the Midlands is happily offset by a church and tower guarding its approach. The stone is a soft Northamptonshire marle, richer than that of the Cotswolds but fast eroding. Broughton church is almost entirely of the early 14th century, contemporary with the rebuilding of the house by Sir John de Broughton. The tower has a broach spire and west doorway, enriched with an ogee arch and ballflower decoration. The windows are mostly early Decorated, with Geometrical and Intersecting tracery.

At some stage in the same century the roofs of the nave and the single, south aisle were raised and given Perpendicular clerestories. The chancel is separated from the nave by a rare stone screen of about 1330, heavily restored in the 19th century. This produces the effect of two large chambers, nave and aisle, of roughly equal proportions. Broughton is an impressively ancestral church, darkly medieval and a match in grandeur for the great house next door.

The chief attraction of Broughton is its tombs. The best is hidden behind a later work in the south aisle, probably that of the rebuilder of the church and house, Sir John (d.1315). An exuberant Decorated work under a wide canopy, it was restored and richly coloured by the Victorians and surely is more true to the spirit of the original than the church's other bleached memorials. Yet it suffers from being overshadowed by the adjacent canopied Perpendicular tomb, supposedly for Edward Fiennes. The Perpendicular window behind was presumably installed to illuminate this later work. The result is rather a mess, of the sort in which English churches delight.

Broughton manor passed to William of Wykeham in 1376 and through the female line to the Fiennes, who hold it to this day under the family name of Twistleton-Wykeham-Fiennes, Barons Saye and Sele. The Wykehams are represented by two alabaster effigies in the chancel, together though not of man and wife. The lady is of the early 15th and the man of the late 15th century. They offer a contrast in styles, she stiff and 'early', he with vigorous features suggesting truth to life.

BURFORD

St John *****

Merchants' guild chapel, Red Indian memorial, Kempe glass

Burford is queen of Oxfordshire, a paragon and museum of the English parish church. It stands where the Thames basin folds into the Cotswolds. Here wealthy medieval cloth merchants exchanged bills of trading, and poured much of the profit into God's House. The spire can be seen rising over the little town from along the Windrush valley, yet it contrives to vanish from within the town, to be found hidden down a lane at the foot of the High Street.

The charm of Burford church lies in personal rather than civic ostentation. No consortium of patrons was ever gathered to rebuild it afresh, as in most wool towns of the Cotswolds and East Anglia. The church is thus a work of accretion. Chapels were added when persons or guilds so decided. The tower is a Norman survival, as is the west door. The panelled and pinnacled entrance porch has three storeys of chambers, almost as grand as that at Cirencester (Gloucs), and modern statues in its niches. To its left runs the Guild of Merchants Chapel, erected c.1200 as a separate building. It was remodelled and joined to the main structure in the late 15th century.

Burford's interior is a maze of low arches, surprising vistas, chapels and shrines. The church counted nine separate altars and six incumbent priests at the start of the 16th century. After the Reformation, the chapels and chantries were converted for use as family pews and mausoleums. St Thomas's Chapel, between the south transept and porch, became the Corporation Pew. The chantry chapel in the north aisle became the Lord of the Manor's Pew. The large Guild of Merchants Chapel became the resting place for the Sylvesters, among the richest of Burford's 16th-century merchants. The last Sylvester commemorated here died in 1904.

In the nave north aisle, a superb classical memorial recalls Edmund Harman (d.1569), Henry VIII's barber and courtier. Harman married a Sylvester after acquiring the local Hospital of St John after the Dissolution. His memorial, completed before his death, carries the first known depiction in England of the Indian inhabitants of the New World, believed to have been copied from a Flemish book. The connection with Harman is unknown, though the intention was probably to indicate the cosmopolitan reach of the town's trade. Spotlit on the turret wall opposite the south transept chapel is a primitive carved panel dated c. AD 160. It is of three figures and a horse, said to allude to the Celtic fertility goddess Epona. Alternatively it may be a Flight into Egypt or Christ's Entry into Jerusalem, surviving from a Saxon church.

The north chancel chapel contains the celebrated Tanfield monument, erected by the wife of Sir Lawrence Tanfield, a prominent judge, in 1628. The couple were unpopular in Burford and, on Tanfield's death, the church refused his widow permission for a memorial, one having already been refused at Westminster Abbey. She was adamant that her husband should have a tomb appropriate to his status, and marched her workmen in undaunted. They erected six Corinthian columns, arches, obelisks and the Tanfield coat of arms above effigies of the couple lying in prayer. For good measure, Lady Tanfield added her own verse: 'So shall I be / With him I loved / And he with me / And both us blessed. / Love made me poet / And this I writt. / My harte did doe it / And not my witt.' The church let them be.

Burford was later the scene of greater strife. In May 1649 Cromwell imprisoned a group of Leveller mutineers in the church for three nights, after which they were to be shot. When three had been executed, Cromwell relented and forced the rest to submit to a recanting sermon by their own leader. One of the prisoners, Anthony Sedley, scratched his name on the font. A more drastic assault on the church came in the 19th century with its restoration by Street. After he had already rebuilt the chancel roof, William Morris arrived from nearby Kelmscott to protest. The vicar, W. A. Cass, retorted: 'The church, Sir, is mine and if I choose to, I shall stand on my head in it.' The infuriated Morris later founded the Society for the Protection of Ancient Buildings.

That said, the vicar, or perhaps the architect, was sufficiently moved to refrain from meddling with the nave. The roof was retained but the manorial pew was restored as a chapel of St Peter. Nor could Morris have objected to the use of the young Charles Kempe for the glass in eight of Burford's windows. The west window installed in 1869 portrays the Tree of Jesse and incorporates medieval fragments. It is full of the colours, animated figures and foliage of the Pre-Raphaelite school. Facing it above the crossing arch is a large painted crucifixion by Clayton & Bell in the style of Piero della Francesca.

The churchyard has a set of bale-tombs almost as good as those at Painswick (Gloucs). These stone chests of about 1700 are topped by 'bales', possibly representing cloth, and carved with cherubs and skulls. They crowd the path like a congregation discussing the sermon after church.

CHARLTON-ON-OTMOOR
St Mary *
Carved screen, boxwood cross

Charlton is an isolated village in the ancient marsh of Otmoor, its church set on a mound above the surrounding damp. Thatched and stone-tiled cottages protect it on all sides. The strong tower, like that of neighbouring Islip, has pinnacled battlements that can be seen for miles. The interior is well-proportioned Decorated Gothic, and comfortingly warm with limewash.

The window at the east end of the south aisle has 13th-century Plate tracery, while in the chancel the windows north and south have 14th-century curvilinear, pleasantly enlivened by splashes of original stained glass. The east window is even later, with a hint of Perpendicular Panel tracery. Charlton's woodwork is exceptional. The late 17th-century altar rails are apparently from the former chapel at Queen's College, Oxford.

The church's treasure is its screen, *c.*1500, one of the finest in the county. The lights are divided by colonnettes decorated with zigzag and lozenges, and have striking tracery in their heads. Above is the coving of the old loft, with flowing tracery crowned by a vine-leaf frieze. Where the rood would once have stood is now a cross formed of boxwood branches. The box is installed fresh on May Day and is renewed in September.

CHILDREY
St Mary *
Norman lead font, memorial brasses

A line of remarkable churches shelter in the lee of the Berkshire Downs, overlooking the Vale of the White Horse. After Faringdon, Childrey is the most prominent, its mound offering sweeping views north to the Cotswolds. The village is decorated with a duckpond, thatch and glebe house with ancient walls. Two big houses stand next to the churchyard whose evergreens frame the view. One is Cantorist House, named after the priests who occupied some portion of it. The other is Rampanes Manor, home of the Fettiplaces, whose tombs adorn the church's south transept. They subsequently moved to Swinbrook, near Burford, home to some of the oddest tombs in England. There are other family tombs at East Shefford (Berks).

Childrey's interior is at first a disappointment. The light is gloomy and the architecture not distinctive: no aisles and no chancel arch. But the contents are excellent. The north transept was being restored on my visit but includes 16th-century stained glass. Pride of Childrey is its Norman font, a lead tub decorated with apostles dressed as abbots. Norman fonts normally prefer monsters or abstract patterns to human faces.

The south transept was converted in 1526 by William Fettiplace as a chantry honouring the Holy Trinity, St Catherine and the Blessed Virgin. Two decades later such chantries were banned. The surviving stained glass and the corbels none the less continue to commemorate the Fettiplace lineage.

The chancel is screened and contains medieval wooden stalls with poppy-heads. On the floor is an outstanding series of brasses. One, to Joan Strangbon, includes an unusual portrayal of the Trinity, with God embracing the Crucifixion. Another excellent piece celebrates William and Elizabeth Fynderne (d.1444) under an architectural canopy. On the south wall are three Early Gothic sedilia, on the north a 15th-century Easter Sepulchre. The latter unusual canopy combines the Decorated forms of an ogee arch with cusps and crockets, with panelling in the Perpendicular style on the wall behind.

In the churchyard a philosophical inscription warns, 'The world is wise and full of crooked streets. Death is the market place where all men meet. If life was merchandise as men could buy, the rich would live and the poor would die.'

CHIPPING NORTON
St Mary ***
'Woolgothic' nave, Decorated tracery

The church lies beneath the old town towards the river, unobtrusive like St Mary, Burford. Not even the wool tycoons had the courage to move their ancestral churches to more prominent sites. Chipping Norton was a fine Decorated church and the customary 15th-century rebuilding was limited to the nave and north aisle, under the patronage of a wealthy clothier, John Ashfield. His additions were outstanding, even in the Cotswolds. The clerestory is almost all window, a glasshouse rising above the older roofs below. On a winter's evening its candlelight must have glowed out across the fields.

The church is a patchwork of periods. The tower is a late Georgian rebuild, the porch a rare vaulted hexagon. But pride of place goes to the virtuoso east window of the south aisle. This is an astonishing piece. Its lights rise to enclose a large central tulip, beautifully counterpointing the arch of the window. The tracery contains no fewer than 98 separate openings. The window, which appears too big for its wall, is reputed to have come from a dissolved monastery at Bruern, not far away. It is painful to imagine what splendid glass must once have adorned this great work. Other south aisle windows are also Decorated.

The interior space is breathtaking. As at Northleach (Gloucs), the nave is tall. In the four bays of Perpendicular arcades, only the tiniest concave capitals can be detected at the springing point of the arches. The clustered shafts of the piers become little more than decorative ribs between the encompassing glass. Above the chancel arch is a 'Cotswold' east window. Though the glazing is unstained it is opaque, making the interior unnecessarily gloomy on a less than bright day. Of all clerestories to head the campaign back to natural light, Chipping Norton should be in the forefront.

The rest of the church is an anticlimax. Clerical chancels were often neglected by mercantile patrons, and Chipping Norton was no exception. But it contains good fragments of earlier structures, including an arcade with stiff-leaf carving on the north side. There are deep Early Gothic window recesses and a charming squint. The churchyard is refreshingly wild in this now somewhat tame environment, its 18th-century chest tombs tumbling down the hillside. A gaunt mausoleum, overgrown with creeper, leans against the north wall of the church.

CHISLEHAMPTON
St Katherine *
Georgian interior

This charming church does not require a lengthy entry. Set between two gateposts across a lawn from the road is an unspoiled Georgian chapel of 1762, now in the care of the Churches Conservation Trust. To the right is Chislehampton House, whose architect was a Londoner named Samuel Dowbiggin. It is not known whether he also designed the church.

The building is a simple stuccoed preaching box, surmounted by an attempt at a swan-necked pediment with corner urns and a top-heavy clocktower with bellcote. It has a modest dignity, like a Massachusetts college chapel. The interior is unaltered Georgian. The walls are articulated by pilaster strips and arches which contain large round-headed windows on the south side. The modest chancel is no more than a shallow recess. Box pews and a west gallery on columns are all in place, as are the candle brackets, chandeliers and wooden reredos with text boards. The pulpit is 17th century, surviving from an earlier church.

All is most decorous. Betjeman honoured the church with a charming poem in support of its restoration in 1952. He wrote of November worship by the light of Chislehampton's candles: 'How gracefully their shadow falls / On bold pilasters down the walls / And on the pulpit high. / The chandeliers would twinkle gold / As pre-Tractarian sermons roll'd / Doctrinal, sound and dry.' [CCT]

CHURCH HANBOROUGH
St Peter and St Paul **
Landmark steeple, Norman tympanum

Church Hanborough's soaring limestone spike can be seen across fields from every point of the compass. The church is set on an incline from the high street, guarded by drystone walls and with yew and privet fussing round its skirts. The spire has eight faces. When a low sun is chased by clouds, each face seems to light up in turn. One moment the spire is a gilded lighthouse, the next dark, almost sinister.

Church Hanborough's most treasured work is the Norman tympanum over the north door. This portrays St Peter with his key, the lion of St Mark and a Lamb of God, and appears to have escaped Victorian restoration. With its roll-mouldings and zigzag decoration, the carving is simple and childlike. The lion appears to be holding a stone but a hand reaches down from Heaven to restrain it.

Inside, the arcades are remarkable: three bays of slender octagonal piers with concave faces extending from base to capital. These are well complemented by a Perpendicular screen extending the width of the church and uniting nave and aisles in one space. The access stair is still visible, as are slots for a tympanum board which would have completely divided nave from chancel. Half way up the west wall of the nave, two faces sneer down on the congregation. Above is a squint for the bellringers to keep watch on the progress of the service.

COMPTON BEAUCHAMP
St Swithun **

Martin Travers restoration

The road beneath the scarp of the Berkshire Downs is as fine as any in the Home Counties, with the valley of the upper Thames stretched out to the north. Tucked into a fold of the hill runs a lane down to Compton House, Georgian with an imposing gate and outhouses. A track to the right leads up to the old church. The exterior has whitewashed walls with stone dressings and a small alpine tower. The porch suggests a church much cared for, with an upholstered bench.

The interior is antiquarian rather than antique, refashioned for a modern enthusiast for the Anglo-Catholic rite, the local grandee, Samuel Gurney. The church is a double-cell with small north and south extensions. The effect is of a private chapel adjacent to a big house, charming and idiosyncratic. Gurney's most obvious introduction is the vine-leaf decoration on the walls of the chancel by Lydia Lawrence in 1900. She was a member of the Kyrle Society, committed to 'brightening the lives of the people' by painting buildings with flowers and planting flowers in cottage gardens. The birds and insects were added in 1967. The glass of the east window behind contains a small medieval Annunciation.

Gurney also employed Martin Travers at Compton Beauchamp between 1925 and 1950. The reredos is by him, and above the chancel arch is his 1920s rood group. A statue of St Swithun holding the church in his hand is by Travers, as is the small west chapel under the tower and the font cover, a Doric octagon.

Travers designed screens to the small transept chapels, that to the north being dedicated to Jesus the Good Shepherd. It contains a large painting on this theme by Noel Paton. On the altar is a small carving by Ulrica Lloyd, apparently fashioned from a Sumerian paving stone excavated in 1948.

Two 18th-century memorials face each other across the nave: one to Anne Richards is complete with skull and crossbones, the other is to her mother Rachel. A smaller and more dignified plaque is to their housekeeper, Mary Cooper, who was 'distinguished by the practice of almost every Virtue and became strictly entitled to the commendation of truly good and faithful servant'.

DORCHESTER
Abbey of St Peter and St Paul ****
Carved window tracery, lead font, 'action effigy' of knight

Dorchester was once a capital of England. Its writ ran north to the Humber, even to Northumbria. St Birinus brought Christianity here and founded a cathedral in the 7th century. But the See departed first for Winchester and then for Lincoln, leaving Dorchester as an abbey. The church is set on a curving high street next to the juvenile Thames, still surrounded by fragments of the medieval abbey which are buried in walls and poke up through shrubbery.

The first impression of the interior is gloomy. We enter through the south nave aisle, added c.1340 for use as a parish church. Its altar had to be raised and set off-centre, above a burial vault for graves disturbed during the building. A large faded wall painting survives. The aisle is enlivened by a variety of sculpture. A Norman lead font is decorated with eleven apostles. They are either minus Judas or, since one appears to be Christ, also minus Doubting Thomas. Lead was used to avoid holy water escaping by seeping through the stone. Such fonts are rare. The designs have been traced to workshops in the Bristol area, possibly under the influence of Carolingian craftsmen in Germany. On a nearby corbel, attached to one of the arcade piers, a devil blows his horn to awaken the canons to service.

The celebrated 'action effigy' of an unknown knight in the south aisle dates from c.1280. The figure is portrayed in the act of drawing his sword, his back and limbs contorted into life. The sculptor seems struggling to escape the stone, to transmit some urgent message.

Dorchester's glory is its chancel and the stylistic variations on a Decorated theme. North and south chapels are divided from the choir by arcades of shafted piers. The north chapel contains excellent Geometrical tracery, but this is surpassed by the windows of the chancel, three masterpieces of c.1340, when English Decorated was at its climax.

The first, in the north side, is a rare Tree of Jesse window, the tree expressed not only in stained glass but in the carving of the mullions. Each one is bent to form the branches of a tree, crowded with sculpture and rising from the body of Jesse carved on the sill beneath. There are stained glass figures in each light. The statues of Christ and Mary are gone from the upper tiers and the walls no longer add their own painted contribution to the effect. Is it beyond possibility that this might be re-created? But the composition is still majestic, stone and glass in restless dialogue.

The second, east window is more conventionally Reticulated, but the tracery is again decorated with carvings, here showing scenes from the Life of Christ. The window fills the east wall, with rich ballflower decoration round the outer frame. The central support and rose window are not original but the work of Butterfield in his 1846 restoration. The glass is a mixture of medieval above and Victorian below.

The third, south window demonstrates Gothic losing the flow of Decorated and moving towards Perpendicular. The large panels have even frames of stone, steady and rather austere, and on the transom stand figures carrying St Birinus's bier. Beneath are magnificent sedilia and a double piscina, their pinnacles, crockets and canopies carved with animals and figures. In the back of each seat is a small window set with reputedly the oldest stained glass in England, some of it dating from the 13th century, possibly imported from a church in France.

The rest of the church is hardly less eventful. In the chapel of St Birinus is a lovely medieval glass roundel, of the saint against a vivid blue background. It is like a picture from an illuminated missal.

EAST HAGBOURNE
St Andrew *
Triceps carving, medieval Nativity window

The ancient village is formed round an old cross, drawn up as guard of honour to the church. The tower is stone, crowned by a curious medieval sanctus bell-turret. These turrets were usually placed on the chancel roof, so the priest could announce the sanctus service without having to move to the tower. The guide declares this to be one of only two such turrets in England that are located on the tower.

The interest of East Hagbourne lies in the sum of its parts, a typical country church that has evolved piecemeal over the centuries. The nave has three bays with an Early Gothic south arcade and a Decorated north. The chancel arch has two extraordinary corbels: on the left is a lion, on the right a triceps or three-headed carving. Faces gaze down on all sides, including in the spandrels of the north arcade. The nave roof is Perpendicular with painted bosses, one of them in the form of a striding man. The pulpit is also Perpendicular.

A precious 14th-century window survives in the north aisle, a Nativity scene with the Virgin and Child in a domestic setting, with a shepherd gazing at them over his crook. The church is well stocked with statues of varying taste. Behind the font in the south aisle is a handsome memorial to John Loder of 1755. The swirling lines are almost Art Nouveau. The church has contrived to keep hold of its 14th-century sanctuary knocker, on the north door.

EWELME
St Mary ***
Tudor almshouse setting, Chaucer memorials

A gleam of flint, a dash of herringbone and red English bond: Ewelme is medieval England at its most huggable. The church is of a piece with its setting, amid almshouses and school, rectory and village, in a cleft in the Chiltern foothills. A stream below yields copious watercress. The almshouses sit round a quadrangle that is as calm as a monastic cloister, linked by a covered stair to the church door. The almsmen were required to pray several times daily for the souls of the monarch and their benefactors. They were not allowed to stray from the precinct for more than an hour, nor can they have found much cause from this lovely place.

Ewelme belonged to Thomas Chaucer, son of the poet, and then to his daughter Alice, who married William de la Pole, the future Duke of Suffolk. The foundation at Ewelme was their creation under licence from Henry VI in the 1430s. De la Pole, descendant of a Hull merchant, had worked his way into the young king's favour and was later showered with honours and land. His house has gone, but the school, almshouses and church survive as unaltered examples of 15th-century patronage. At the time of its construction, brick was a novel and costly material, made by hand. Ewelme was inspired by Eton, where another of Henry VI's schools was being built under Suffolk's supervision.

The de la Poles' East Anglian influence pervades the church. It is seen in the flint walls, the love of light, the high wooden roof and rich detail. The interior might be the Great Hall of a 15th-century gentleman's house. There is no architectural divide between nave and chancel, only a screen of filigree lightness. The Perpendicular font cover has gables and crockets, rising over 10 ft and capped by a statue of St Michael, with a huge rose as the counterweight. This cover is similar to that at Ufford (Suffolk) and was presented by the 2nd Duke of Suffolk in 1475.

Between the chapel and the chancel lies the tomb of Alice de la Pole, Duchess of Suffolk (d.1475). It is a dazzling work of late-Gothic carving, ranking with Warwick's Beauchamp Chapel and possibly by the same hand. The alabaster figure lies elongated and stiff, attended in death by 48 weepers, angels and monks in alabaster, stone and wood. Four are merely puffing up her pillow. A cadaver is represented beneath the tomb, with wrinkled breasts. It gazes up at its own frescoed ceiling. Above rise ogees, pinnacles and crockets, tier upon tier, still with some original paintwork. An Order of the Garter adorns the duchess's arm. Queen Victoria is alleged to have enquired of Ewelme how the Garter should be worn by a lady.

Next door lies the tomb of Alice's father, Thomas Chaucer (d.1434), and his wife Matilda. It is topped by a fine brass and surrounded by medieval heraldic shields. Chaucer was a distinguished politician and courtier, with John of Gaunt as an uncle. Other brasses can be found under the matting on the nave and aisle floors. In the chancel is a Baroque memorial to Francis Martyn (d.1682), a local Parliamentarian who had the good taste, and perhaps courage, to lock the church against the depredations of his own troops during the Civil War.

FARINGDON
All Saints * * *
Transitional carvings, 16th-century tombs

Few Thames valley churches have a lovelier setting. All Saints hugs the crest of a ridge overlooking the wide upper Thames valley, on a site which local legend gives to King Alfred's castle and possibly even to his burnt cakes. In front lies Faringdon's triangular 'square', with the old town hall and market place beneath it. Behind are the great pines of Faringdon House and garden, once home of the eccentric Lord Berners and still blessed with his multi-coloured dyed doves.

The church exterior is not equal to its surroundings, partly because it lost its tower and spire in the Civil War. The long, low outline calls for a stronger vertical emphasis than the lancets of the chancel or the sweeping gable of the south transept. The Norman windows of the nave are restored and severe. Even on a spring day with the graveyard sprinkled with wild flowers, there is an austerity to Faringdon church.

Yet the interior is full of incident, much of it Norman or only a little later. The south door is covered with ironwork of c.1200. The Norman nave must have been intolerably dark until relieved by the Perpendicular windows set into the north aisle. The clerestory window openings are plain, in contrast to the arcades, which display stiff-leaf capitals and mouldings. Beyond the nave almost everything belongs to a later date. The crossing has Transitional pointed arches with a varied array of leaves mingled with trumpet-scallops on its capitals. The early 13th-century chancel is lit by eleven majestic lancets. Against its south wall are sedilia, with three cinquefoil canopies adorned with crockets, almost obscenely florid in this solemn space.

Faringdon's transepts depart in all directions. The north transept is 13th century while the baptistery, south transept and chapel are Victorian. The restorers carved new 'Norman' capitals and shifted doors and windows with abandon. They did not relieve the darkness of the lancet windows, indeed exacerbated it with stained glass. In the north transept, charity boards record the pledges of the local welfare state. Here the revenues of Faringdon Port are allocated to the 'impotent and the poor'. Few locals can have gone needy in a rich parish such as this.

The Unton tombs recall the patrons of this generosity. The memorial to Sir Thomas Unton (d.1533) and his wife, complete with family pets, has conventional effigies, but the chest displays tentative classical forms, with round arches, shell heads, slender columns and wreaths. It is one of a number of early 16th-century English tombs that echo that of Henry VII in Westminster Abbey, as at Bodmin (Cornwall) and Tickhill (Yorks, S). The later wall tombs of Sir Edward Unton (d.1583) and Sir Henry Unton (d.1596) have full classical columns. The latter's wife kneels in prayer on the floor, in Elizabethan costume. Succeeding the Untons were the Pyes, also with a chapel to themselves. Their 18th-century memorials are even more self-congratulatory. Henry Pye manifested a 'gracefulness of person, affability of his demeanour, a courtesy and politeness in his manners, an open benevolence and generosity in his disposition, which plainly denoted him the True English Gentleman'.

HANWELL
St Peter **
North Oxfordshire carvings

Hanwell is a fine composition of hillside village, rectory, castle and church. This was Puritan country, much fought over in the Civil War. The castle, one tower of which survives, was built by the Cope family under Henry VII. Sir Anthony Cope (d.1614) spent time in the Tower of London for his radical Puritanism, but lived to receive James I at Hanwell. His parson was John Dod, as radical as his benefactor, whom Cope was forced by the Church authorities to sack. Worshippers came from throughout the district to hear him preach and he continued to live in the village. Dod lived on through the Civil War. A story tells how Cavalier soldiers put him in a tree and demanded he 'preach himself out of it'. He did.

Hanwell's most prominent works are the carved capitals of the arcades, works of the 14th-century north Oxfordshire school. These depict men and women peering down at the congregation, arms linked, often with minstrels among their number. Other, more battered images line the corbel-table on the exterior of the chancel, including a mermaid and a woman chasing a fox which has stolen her goose (sometimes interpreted as a bishop taking tithes). The windows embrace every type of English tracery, Plate, Geometrical, Intersecting, Reticulated and Panel. The chancel floor was raised in the 1770s to enable later Copes to insert a mausoleum beneath it. This gives a fine view back towards the nave, but cuts off the sedilia. The tomb of Sir Anthony Cope and his wife is next to the altar.

HORLEY
St Etheldreda **
St Christopher mural

The church lies on the Warwickshire border, built of a golden ironstone so crumbly that we could take away handfuls in our pocket. The east end is Norman, with a central crossing tower and rounded window openings. In the west end, the best features are three Early Gothic doorways with shafts of lighter stone. Inside, the nave arcades are remarkably tall, with carved corbels that include a laughing horse and a bearded man, apparently whistling. The large Intersecting east window is a tour de force of vertical lines, rising like palm fronds to create lozenges of differing proportions.

Horley's prize is the great mural of St Christopher adorning the north wall. It is one of the largest and best preserved medieval depictions of this saint, a splendid survival. While the artistry is naive (*c.*1450) the directness of the image, with peasants in the field and fish in the stream, is delightful. The saint is asking why the boy is so heavy. The boy replies, 'Yey I be hevy no wonder ys for I am ye Kinge of Blys.' Might this be a relic of old Oxfordshire grammar? There are other painted fragments on the walls.

The church was restored in 1915 and again by Lawrence Dale in 1950. The latter inserted a new metal screen, rood and loft, as well as scenes from the life of St Etheldreda on the pulpit. The guide says that the figure of St John on the rood is a likeness of Dale himself. The saints' statues round the walls are twee compared with the robust medieval carvings. More in keeping are the fine 17th- and 18th-century chests, chairs and tables that line the aisles and chancel. A large Georgian organ, built for domestic use, lies inside the south door and is apparently still playable.

IFFLEY
St Mary ***
Norman interior and exterior carving

Iffley church is hidden downstream of Oxford amid the sprawl created by the Cowley car works. It lies in an oasis of cottages and chestnut trees, billowing with springtime blossom. Above the trees rises the celebrated, sturdy tower. Closer to, we see one of England's favourite Norman churches, heavily restored and with later insertions, but essentially as built in the 12th century. The church plan retains the original features of crossing tower, chancel and unaisled nave. Only the west and east ends have been reconstructed, largely to rectify un-sympathetic 17th-century alterations. The large west window is Victorian but based on archaeological evidence.

The joy of Iffley is in the detail, in the chunky, barbaric richness of door and window surrounds. These are mostly carved with zigzag and beakhead over roll-moulding, creating a jazzy effect of monsters with huge beaks biting into long rolls of bread. In among these creatures are fighting horsemen, Samson and signs of the zodiac. Most elaborate, and apparently most original, is carving round the south doorway.

The interior is dominated by mighty tower arches with more zigzag, foliage and roll-moulding, the decorative effect enriched with Purbeck marble shafts. These shafts are more characteristic of Early Gothic building and show Iffley bordering on Transitional. Indeed the chancel was partly rebuilt in the 13th century and has a rib vault and shafted lancet windows characteristic of Early Gothic. It also displays naturalistic carving, dragons, rosettes and a nesting bird, a glorious burst of exuberance. This exuberance is reflected in John Piper's glass installed in 1995 in the south-west window, given posthumously by his widow and composed of birds against a dark blue background.

I last saw Iffley with an Easter wedding in progress. The air was filled with the scent of flowers, the organ was booming through the open doorway, and the gathering had thick Oxfordshire accents, now a rarity in this part of the county.

KIDLINGTON
St Mary **
Early misericords, medieval east window

From the delicate water meadows of the Cherwell, Kidlington's steeple rises above a shoreline of Cotswold stone, the spire known as 'Our Lady's Needle'. Round it clusters what survives of a medieval settlement on the fringes of Otmoor, now almost overwhelmed by housing estates and the M40. The church was a collegiate foundation, cruciform and big. The stone inside and out is Cotswold at its most golden. Rebuilt in Early Gothic style, it was further altered in the 1330s with the addition of a south aisle and curvilinear window tracery. The wealth of the enlarged church is indicated by the south porch, with its ogival arch and ballflower decoration.

Inside, the view from the crossing is splendid, especially on a sunny day with rays of light darting in from all angles. The chancel 'weeps' slightly to the right, not the normal direction, and retains a collegiate appearance. There are choir stalls of the highest quality. The plain misericords have been dated to the 13th century, making them among the oldest in England. The panelled stall fronts are later, carved with heraldic devices. A panel has the rebus of Kidlington: a lamb, a small fish and a tun or barrel.

Kidlington's greatest treasure is its 14th-century east window glass. It was collected in 1831 from other windows in the church, reinserted here and put in more coherent form in 1951. The faded King with Prophets, probably from a Tree of Jesse, in the second row up is said to be 13th century and thus very early. The central panels of the Trinity and the Crucifixion are restored; no less fine is the picture of the Virgin being taught to read by St Anne. The chancel south window has heraldic motifs.

A window in the north wall of the nave offers a startling contrast, a copy of the Reynolds window of the Graces in New College, Oxford, a sentimental theme beloved of 18th-century glaziers (e.g., Worstead in Norfolk, and Ledbury in Herefordshire).

Some of Kidlington's empty niches have been filled with statues by a local sculptor, Walter Richie, in a style apparently derived from Eric Gill. They seem as mawkish as the Reynolds window, but perhaps they will seem less so with time. At least the effort has been made. Kidlington leads the way in what should be a national campaign to fill church niches.

NORTH MORETON
All Saints **
Medieval glass

This simple vale church lies in a secluded village of timbered and thatched cottages in the lee of Didcot's giant cooling towers. The manor was acquired in the late 13th century by Miles de Stapleton, a baron who served as Steward to the Household to Edward I and died at Bannockburn in 1314. He left his mark on North Moreton in some of the most extensive medieval glass in a small parish church in England.

The church tower is squat and made of bands of flint and stone. Within, the remains of an earlier Norman church are visible in the drums of the arcade piers. However, most of the work is Decorated, best displayed in the imaginative window tracery. There is graceful Y-tracery in the chancel, and in the south aisle is a lovely 'tear-drop' window, with old glass in its upper lights.

All eyes lead to the south chapel. It was probably rebuilt in the decade after 1299 when Miles de Stapleton founded a chantry chapel. With a low-pitched roof and lofty windows running almost the full height of the walls, it dominates the interior. The east window is of five lights rising to rare 'fish-scale' tracery. This, together with a piscina of extraordinary richness, puts North Moreton in the vanguard of 14th-century Decorated architecture. We must assume that Stapleton's position at court enabled him to commission the workshops of leading masons from Westminster Abbey.

The original glass is now faded and the faces are mostly blank, but the composition is still superb, with dominant reds and blues. The scenes depicted are from the lives of St Peter, St Nicholas, St Paul and the Virgin Mary, with the

Passion as the central panel. The architectural settings, mostly Gothic canopies, are meticulous in their detail. Garments and figures flow with life. A favourite story in the St Nicholas panel has boys being cut up and put in a curing tub, the saint then making them whole again. We also see him offering dowries to a poor man to prevent his daughters becoming prostitutes.

OXFORD
St Mary ***
Enriched tower, 'Raphael' south porch, Gandhi boss

No town church in England can have a finer setting than St Mary's. It forms a bulwark between the shops of the High and the university enclave to the north. Despite the accretion of centuries, no element is out of place, everything in warm Cotswold stone.

The former church porch on to the High is defined by the much-photographed broken pediment and barley-sugar columns. Built by John Jackson in 1637, its possible derivation is the Raphael cartoons acquired by Charles I in 1623. The bullet holes in the statue of the Virgin were made by Cromwell's soldiers as they swept through this strongly Royalist town. The statue's survival is a miracle. The only sadness is that this porch is no longer the entrance to the church, which is from the north.

The bulk of St Mary's stands out over central Oxford with its famous tower and mass of pinnacles and battlements crowning the nave. The tower is Decorated Gothic, encrusted with canopied, crocketed and ballflowered niches which cling like supplicants round the skirts of the spire. This is one of England's richest steeples, the more spectacular when we climb to wander among the pinnacles on top and look down on central Oxford.

The rest of the church is mostly late 15th-century Perpendicular. The interior is something of an anticlimax and is of historic rather than architectural interest. St Mary's was the centre of university ceremony until the building of Wren's Sheldonian Theatre to the north. A two-storey building in the north-east corner of the church housed the first university library and Congregation House. The nave saw such public events as the Marian trials in 1554–5 of Latimer, Ridley and Cranmer. It was here in 1744 that Wesley preached his sermon attacking the sloth of the unreformed university, and declared afterwards, 'I am cleared of the blood of these men.' A century later in 1833, Keble and Newman began their Anglo-Catholic crusade from the same pulpit, precipitating the Tractarian Movement to which so many churches in this book owe their building or restoration. The throne-like pews at the rear of the nave are still used by the senior figures of the university, attended by poppyheads that look like vegetables in an advanced state of decay.

The chancel stalls are original, so is the reredos, although its statues are Victorian, of saints commemorating the Oxford Movement. They are particularly fine, but why could the same carvers not have filled the clerestory niches? Stained glass blocks any view out to the High. The north chapel predates the current church and was built by Adam de Brome, founder of Oriel College. It houses the Chancellor's throne, where he once performed as local magistrate. A lovely Pugin window fills the east end of the south aisle. The west window is Kempe at his most histrionic.

St Mary's retains its roof bosses and has added to them over the years. In the north side of the west gallery, and not to be missed, is a boss of Gandhi sitting cross-legged.

RADLEY
St James *
Wooden arcade, 16th-century glass

Radley has one remarkable feature that sets it apart from other parish churches: a south arcade composed of four vast tree trunks. Coming across them one gloomy autumn day I felt I had entered a forest clearing. The reason for this form of support is obscure. The church was an outpost of St Helen, Abingdon. At the time of its restoration in 1902, traces of wooden nave arches and a wooden chancel arch were found. There are wooden arcades in Shropshire and Cheshire in the absence of local brick or stone, but few in the south. Tradition holds that at the time of rebuilding in 1290, an abbot had a vision in which he was told to 'seek pillars in the forest'. It may have been the abbey treasurer talking. Today these ancient blackened piers seem primitive and dramatic.

Most of the rest of the church is Perpendicular or 20th century. But the Norman font is an unusually delicate work, with a filigree canopy which rumour suggests may once have graced the Speaker's chair in the House of Commons. The grandiloquent misericords have been traced to 17th-century carvers in Cologne; they were presented to the church in 1847. The reredos is Gothic Revival of 1910. Next to the altar is a fine monument by Nicholas Stone to Sir William Stonhouse, whose father acquired the manor from Elizabeth I. He and his wife are represented lying in full Jacobean dress, with a quiverful of children round the chest, some wrapped in cloths to indicate infant death.

The church has stained glass of the 16th century, a small riot of crowns, shields, lions and unicorns, with the identifiable arms of Henrys VI, VII and VIII and what is said to be a portrait of Henry VII. At the back of the church is an embroidered map of the village, worked by the Women's Institute.

RYCOTE
St Michael **
Canopied royal pew

Rycote is a domestic chapel of the mid-15th century, memorable for the survival of a complete set of 17th-century furnishings, its private pews without equal in England. The chapel was founded in 1449 as a chantry for the adjacent house by the lord of the manor, Richard Quatremayne. The tower is battlemented and contains a priest's room, still with its medieval fireplace. The more ornate doorway is on the north side, facing the house. Nothing outside has been altered.

The interior is less a church than a museum of Jacobean woodwork. It is overwhelmed by the two principal pews, both ornately canopied and integral with the screen. The north pew was probably inserted for the Norreys family some time after the Reformation. It is in the form of a cubicle with classical arcading supporting a canopy of lavish Islamic-looking fretwork which contains a musicians' gallery. The old rood loft staircase was adapted to give access to this gallery. Opposite stands an even grander work, the pew reputedly built for a visit by Charles I in 1625 and reminiscent of a pavilion for a Mughal emperor. It is composed of a dainty arcade and colonnade supporting an ogival canopy, with crocketed ribs and arabesque cornice. How it must have appeared when fully decked for Carolean worship can only be imagined.

The pulpit too has a canopy and arcading, and unusually for the date is square in shape. A later reading desk sits beneath it. At the west end of the chapel is a Jacobean gallery with Ionic columns. In 1682, a later proprietor, the Earl of Abingdon, restored the disused chancel. A black-and-white pavement was laid, and a handsome Corinthian reredos and a twisted communion rail were installed. The chapel is now in the custodianship of English Heritage and access conforms to its rigid opening hours.

[EH]

SHORTHAMPTON
All Saints *
Farmyard setting, wall paintings

Shorthampton has the humblest of churches. It appears on few road atlases and lies at the end of a cul-de-sac off the road to Chadlington, leading from the Charlbury to Burford road. The building is surrounded by a farm on an eminence over the Evenlode valley. This is Oxfordshire's most secret place.

The structure is simple to read: a 12th-century chamber with a chancel added probably in the 13th century. The pointed chancel arch is scarcely bigger than a doorway. In the 15th century the nave was widened to the south under a new roof. Since the old chancel was not widened, a curious squint had to be cut through its wall so extra worshippers could see the service. The south windows are Perpendicular. The only subsequent additions were a 19th-century porch to keep out the draught and a Georgian rebuilding of the chancel, including a new east window. This frames what the church guide calls 'the loveliest of all altar-pieces, green fields and the good earth'.

Of furnishings, the 18th-century box pews survive, large for the squire, long for the farmers, with benches at the back for peasants and servants. The pulpit is a Georgian two-decker with wig-stand. Corbel heads include a lady wearing a headdress, a monk and a bearded man, granted immortality in this gallery of village worthies. The walls are dotted with enough fragments of wall paintings to convey the richness of a past interior. These include a saint teaching a child to read, a Last Judgement and Jonah and the whale. Even the squint has a Miracle of the Clay Birds. To the farmers and woodsmen of the Evenlode such intimate art must have been a dazzling treasure.

SHRIVENHAM
St Andrew **
Eccentric Tuscan arcade

Shrivenham church unfolds itself languidly down a lime-shaded lane from the main street. It is one of England's few complete churches of the reign of Charles I, rebuilt by Lord Craven after 1638 from the carcass of an earlier building, of which only the tower remains. Shrivenham is a good example of the ambivalence of ecclesiastical taste well into the 17th century. The exterior is conventional late Perpendicular Gothic and could date from two centuries earlier.

Inside is a different matter. The first impression is that Inigo Jones paid a flying visit, told a local builder to try Tuscan and then vanished. The arcades of both nave and chancel have classical columns and round arches. Even the window lights are grouped under round heads, despite being Gothic outside. The massive wooden roof rests on Jacobean posts and corbels which are not aligned with the arches beneath. The columns are encircled by candleholders, like garters. The pulpit and tester are magnificent, with marquetry and fretwork. The pulpit has false perspective and panels. All this is splendidly wilful.

The classical arcade is rudely interrupted by the tower, still on crossing arches that are unashamedly Gothic. The chancel and side chapels are richly decorated. The chancel has three old chandeliers and a reredos with strange undulating openwork along its top. This looks most effective silhouetted against the east window. There is no stained glass, but lozenges that are alternately clear and tinted green.

Fine ironwork screens close the side chapels, which are filled with classical memorials to the Barrington family. These include works by James Wyatt, Richard Westmacott and John Flaxman. The Barringtons, descended from a Cromwellian officer, have retained their link to the church to the present day.

SOUTH NEWINGTON
St Peter ad Vincula **
Virgin and Child mural

This odd little church sits by the A361, with an eccentric porch in golden stone and sheltering the best wall paintings in Oxfordshire. The exterior is charming, with a battlemented tower and an array of Decorated tracery rare in so small a church. The porch is an architectural pastiche of the Mad Hatter's headgear. Huge pinnacles and battlements crown a diminutive base that is far too small for them. The exterior is covered in gargoyles and monsters.

The interior is an architectural jumble. Some arches are Norman, others Early Gothic with nailhead decoration, others Decorated. The chancel is light and airy. Box pews survive, as does a severe pulpit. But the joy of South Newington is on its walls. The best paintings are in the north aisle, earlier than those in the nave and dating from the 1340s. They owe their bold colouring to being not fresco but oil on plaster. The most prominent, above the old north door, is of the murder of Becket. This familiar scene of early medieval piety is singularly horrific, with Becket's head spouting blood as the sword cleaves it in two. Few such images survive, since Henry VIII was particularly opposed to the Becket cult (*see* Brookland in Kent).

Adjacent is another murder, that of Thomas of Lancaster, rebel against Edward II and venerated by his supporters as a saint. Further east is the church's most outstanding work, a Virgin and Child, its figures delicate and its colouring strong. The composition, deserving front rank in English medieval art, is surrounded by foliage and attended by images of donors. There are lesser pictures in the window splays. The windows themselves contain fragments of medieval glass. Paintings on the north wall of the nave, depicting the Passion, are of poorer quality.

SPARSHOLT
The Holy Rood *
Easter Sepulchre, wooden tomb effigies

On a rainy day Sparsholt presents a grim appearance. A huge yew darkens the approach. The broach spire seems to have arrived from a different county and the Norman door has austere iron scrollwork. Inside there is a decayed air, as if this were the home of a protected species of bat. Yet Sparsholt is a delightful church with the most spectacular view down the nave into the chancel. Solid pews lead the eye to a wooden screen of bold ogees beneath a Decorated chancel arch. The east window, of five lights capped by four tiers of Reticulated tracery, is a superb Victorian re-creation of what was believed to have existed before a 16th-century rebuilding.

The fine chancel has a complete set of 14th-century ritual sculptures: Easter Sepulchre, piscina, sedilia and founder's tomb with a knight with crossed legs. Equally rare is the screen to the south transept, with what appear to be Early Gothic cinquefoil arches. The screen leads into the curtained transept, where the Victorian stained glass is so dark that little can be seen without the use of electric light. The effort is worth it. Here lie wooden effigies, two women under canopies in the south wall, the other a man. They are of Sir Robert Achard (d.1353) and his two wives, Joanna and Agnes. The latter's tomb has men-at-arms as weepers round its chest and was probably intended for Sir Robert himself. The effigies would once have been coated in paint and gold leaf. Much eaten by worms, they remain strangely beautiful.

The nave windows contain fragments of medieval glass. On one of them is graffiti saying, 'Joseph Tuff cleaned some of these windows and that's enough.' He apparently tired of the job. On the north wall of the chancel is a stone cut for a game of Nine Men's Morris, the rules of which are in the church guide. The game dates from the 14th century or earlier.

STANTON HARCOURT
St Michael **
Harcourt monuments

The manor was seat of the Harcourts from the 12th to the 18th century, when they were elevated to Nuneham Courtenay and their old house was demolished. The house's kitchen range alone survives, and is to Pevsner 'one of the most complete medieval domestic kitchens in England and certainly the most spectacular'. The chapel tower also stands, peering incongruously over the churchyard wall.

The church is Norman cruciform. A walk clockwise round its exterior reveals as much of its history as does the interior. The middle stage of the tower is Norman, the belfry stage Perpendicular. The chancel and transepts are Early Gothic, with tall lancet windows. The south chancel chapel is Perpendicular, the nave once again Norman. The interior is remarkable for its 13th-century chancel, which has a triple lancet east window with clustered shafts and stiff-leaf capitals. On the north wall is a tomb chest and effigy with a finely carved Decorated canopy in Purbeck marble. This is variously identified as the shrine of St Edburg, or the tomb of Maud, Lady Harcourt of *c.*1400. The mid-13th-century screen is one of the earliest in England.

The lightweight Perpendicular of the Harcourt Chapel south of the chancel is attributed to William Orchard, master builder of Oxford's Magdalen College tower. Here and elsewhere in the church lie memorials galore. There are Harcourts military, judicial and political, Harcourts Gothic, Renaissance and Baroque, Harcourts in marble, alabaster and brass, rampant and recumbent, mourned by cherubs, angels, bedesmen, wives and offspring. Stanton Harcourt is a monument to the art of monument.

The sequence might have continued to the present day, but in 1756 Simon Harcourt, dilettante and man of letters, left for Nuneham and high fashion. Dark, medieval Stanton became just another parish church.

SWINBROOK
St Mary **
Fettiplace and Mitford tombs

Swinbrook and the adjacent Widford merit inclusion for their setting alone. They are located half a mile apart along a grassy slope of the Windrush valley near Burford, linked by a popular footpath. Swinbrook sits surrounded by Cotswold stone houses and gently undulating fields. There is no traffic to drown the birdsong, only the trumpet blast of the Fettiplace tombs.

The church is Decorated and Perpendicular, with a late Georgian tower. The latter was built in six weeks in 1822 and, as the guide says, is 'not beautiful but interesting'. The church contains Transitional nave arcades and a crossing with incised capitals. There are medieval misericords and, in the south aisle, a window composed of fragments of ancient glass shattered by a wayward wartime bomb. The pieces were recomposed by the vicar.

The tombs are among the most eccentric in England. Little is known of the Swinbrook Fettiplaces (*see* Childrey) but they clearly meant their church to remember them. There are two monuments along the north chancel wall, each with three effigies lying on shelves. The six have been compared to merchandise in a shop, passengers travelling steerage on a steamer, or a congregation of the dead, awakened to watch something important on television.

The monument on the left was erected by Sir Edmund (d.1613) and includes effigies of himself, his father and grandfather. The surround is a grand affair with fluted Corinthian columns, segmental pediment and much surface enrichment. The figures are identical, with stylised hair, moustaches and beards. They are wearing armour and swords, and lie prim and formal with heads resting on hands, their elbows on cushions. They might be the lovelorn subjects of a Spenser poem.

On the right is the monument to Edmund Fettiplace (d.1686) and his father and uncle. More than fifty years have passed. The framework, with three knights reclining on shelves, is similar to the earlier tomb. However, life has been breathed into them. They are relaxed and lounging. Left arms are draped, dandy-like, on raised knees and gauntlets are held casually in right hands. They wear soft cravats not stiff ruffs, and the hair is long and curled. These faces appear to be sculpted from life. Here the mason signed his name, William Bird of Oxford.

In the churchyard are the graves of another famous local family, the Redesdales. They include Nancy and Unity Mitford. The latter's unhappy life is summed up with 'Say not the struggle naught availeth.' + Diana Mosley
  née Mitford
+ Alexander Mosley
  son of Diana + Mosley

THAME
St Mary **
Medieval choir stalls, Williams tomb

The mellow stone tower rises above trees well away from the town centre across a cricket field. Decorated and Perpendicular windows lighten the walls and, to the north, the church is protected by a close of a prebendary and cottages. The interior is airy and spacious. The central position of the tower permits light to pour in from each point of the compass. The west window is 17th century, but still Perpendicular in style. The nave arcades are Decorated, rising to a fine roof with carved angels, one playing a mandolin.

The chancel woodwork is excellent: tables, chairs, benches and chests, with linenfold panelling everywhere. The choir stalls, brought from Thame Abbey at the Dissolution, are panelled and the pretty screen has uprights carved with lozenges and cusped arches. In the middle of the chancel sits the tomb of Lord Williams (d.1559), Thame's leading citizen and benefactor. He lies in a cloak over his armour with a chainmail codpiece, his wife also cloaked but over a chemise. Their feet rest on a dog and a horse. The couple, carved from alabaster, lie on a Renaissance chest, repaired after damage in the Civil War. They form a splendid pair.

UFFINGTON
St Mary * * *
Immaculate Early Gothic interior

Uffington is celebrated for its unity of style, that of the Early Gothic 13th century. It looks perfect on a warm day, with steep shingled roof, lancet windows and octagonal tower basking in sunlight. To stand under the crossing tower and gaze up at the undulating lines of its arches and vaults is to see medieval architecture at its most pure. The church owes its survival to the generosity of its founder, Abbot Fabritius of Abingdon. There was no compelling need for later expansion, though the church was extensively restored by the Saunders family in the late 17th century.

Of the exterior, the most changed parts are the nave and tower. The former lost and then regained its steep roof, the tops of the windows being sliced in the process. The spire was lost in a storm in the 18th century and not replaced. Instead, the octagonal tower was raised by one storey. The three doorways on the south side of the church are all grandly treated. Even the priest's door in the chancel has a tiny porch. The nave porch niches have found modern figures and good ones. They are of Alfred the Great and St George and were carved by Heidi Lloyd in 1975.

The character of the interior is entirely that of an early 13th-century collegiate foundation. The (clerical) chancel and transepts are rich in decoration, the (parochial) nave simple and bleak. The style is dictated by ubiquitous lancet windows, the only later insertion being a Decorated window in the south side of the chancel, illuminating what would have been the clerk's desk.

The chapels in the transepts are a puzzle. They are perfectly Early Gothic in form, except for their extraordinary windows. These are composed entirely of straight lines, with mullions intersecting the heads at an acute angle. They can scarcely be original and probably belong to the restoration in the 1670s. The chancel has a stately progress of arches and shafts, breaking the line of the walls with superb trefoiled sedilia. There is a blessed lack of modern stained glass.

Uffington is spare of furnishings, which are mostly Victorian or modern. A handsome classical monument to Edward Archer of 1603 fills the north transept wall. Here too is a monument to Thomas Hughes, judge and author of *Tom Brown's Schooldays*, who was brought up in the village. The local primary school, founded by the Saunders family next to the churchyard, taught 'Tom Brown' before the latter set off for Rugby. An effigy of John Saunders of 1638 gazes down from the wall of the south transept. John Betjeman, resident for a time at Wantage, was a churchwarden at Uffington and loved it deeply.

WHEATFIELD
St Andrew *
Parkland setting, Georgian interior

Heaven preserve the little places. Wheatfield is a charming building, set on a parkland slope dotted with oak, cedar and beech beneath the Chiltern escarpment and just visible from the M40. It was the first of my 'thousand churches', and will always be a favourite.

Wheatfield House was destroyed in 1814, its brick stables now lying ruined in the lee of the hill. Only the church lives on, a medieval structure part-converted by the Rudge family after they bought the manor in 1727. It then passed to the Spencers, so ubiquitous in the Midlands. The church is not Georgian but Georgianised. Seen from a distance, the 18th-century fenestration and parapet sit easily within the medieval frame. The unknown architect did not want, or could not afford, to obliterate all sign of the past. A classical entrance porch was added at the west end. The thick walls of the nave were pieced by four round-headed Georgian windows. Squint holes and scratched sundials can still be seen on the west end. Old bootscrapers remain in place.

The inside is flooded with light, splashing across the peach-coloured stucco wash. The box pews remain. The Rudge/Spencer pew is longitudinal with a carved frieze carrying the Rudge family arms, and looks directly across the nave to a two-decker pulpit. The other pews face towards the altar. Looking down on this decorous scene is a huge 1739 memorial to John Rudge by Scheemakers, in 'landed-gentry Baroque'.

In the chancel floor is a tablet to an 18th-century rector, a Mr Clerke, who was 'zealous in the defence of the Established Church, yet was charitable and indulgent to those who conscientiously differed from him in opinion'. A memorial records deaths during the Great War. Of fourteen Wheatfield men lost, five were Hollands and two were Spencers – villagers and gentry devastated alike.

WIDFORD
St Oswald *
Roman pavement

There is little to say about Widford except that those who visit it never forget it. The church lies across a meadow in the Windrush valley and can be reached only on foot. It seems to have risen from the earth round it, ready at a moment's neglect to sink again without trace. Its stone is the same as that of its drystone churchyard wall, which serves no purpose but to keep out sheep.

Beneath the chancel floor is the mosaic of a Roman villa in a remarkable state of preservation. Who decided to build a church here and whether it was on the site of an early Christian shrine is a mystery. The church is a single-cell structure of the 13th century. The only indication of any divide between nave and chancel is a small bellcote above a trace of a ridge. The interior is without architectural adornment.

The essence of Widford is simplicity. The pulpit appears to be made from the old screen. The box pews are Georgian, the communion rail Jacobean. On the walls are extensive and apparently early wall paintings. This is a church to visit at peace.

YARNTON
St Bartholomew ***
Spencer tombs, ancient glass

Most churches speak a dominant language. Yarnton's is Jacobean. Most of the building is Norman or Early English, but over its solid tower and warm stone walls hovers the spirit of the 17th century. Yarnton Manor was among the largest Jacobean houses in the county, now much reduced. Its gables and porch with fluted pilasters and obelisks serve as a backdrop to the churchyard, which is filled with battered tombs. By the gate is an old cross, at which travelling friars stopped to conduct services.

Yarnton is a monument to the taste and generosity of an Oxfordshire village. The Spencers transformed the old church in 1611–16, erecting a tower, a porch and a chapel containing a mausoleum for themselves. The monument to Sir William Spencer (d.1609) is attributed to the Dutch carver, Jasper Hollemans, who worked for the Spencers at Great Brington (Northants). It is a canopied tomb chest, rich, brash and vulgar, with strapwork filling every space. Yet there are affecting details, such as delicate veins on praying hands and winsome children in attendance round the base.

The adjacent memorial to Sir Thomas Spencer (d.1684) is a shallow wall monument and a complete contrast. From the roast beef of old England we move to a Restoration fop. Sir Thomas's hose is neatly rolled at the knee, his shoe is high-heeled, his hand rests effeminately on his hip. Son and wife look on, adoring; four daughters are relegated as mere supporters. The representation of family groups was popular under Charles I, but was unusual in the reign of Charles II, who had no legitimate children.

Light floods the chapel from high Perpendicular windows, enriching the red roof and spilling into the church through a splendid carved screen. In the middle of the chapel stands a wooden funeral bier, as if awaiting the arrival of yet more Spencers.

Yarnton is full of treasures collected mostly on the Continent by a local benefactor, Alderman William Fletcher, in the late 18th century. The reredos consists of four 15th-century alabaster panels of the Nottingham school, showing Bible scenes, including a Pietà. Two of this set were taken from Yarnton in the 1860s, and are now in the Victoria and Albert and British Museums. A seventh has been lost. Fletcher also brought stained glass from Flanders and France. In the chancel windows is a set of quarries depicting guests uttering homilies at the funeral of Reynard the Fox, representing the Devil. They are excellent survivors of this once common art form.

The church has admirable modern kneelers showing the pub, manor, farm, railway junction and even the electricity pylons. All Yarnton is under its knees.

Rutland

The best things come in small parcels. England's littlest county, famously independent, has more good churches per square mile than any other. The countryside was rich and agricultural, and was profitably located on the drovers' routes east–west and north–south across central England.

The characteristic Rutland church building is that of the transition from Norman to Early Gothic. This brief period of English architecture, roughly 1180–1200, is displayed in half the county's fifty or so churches, yielding a local style of faintly pointed arches with scallop and water-leaf capitals. This era is preceded by one great monument, the chancel arch at Tickencote, one of the most lavish 12th-century compositions in any English church, its carving a rival to Kilpeck (Herefs). The later Gothic period is best represented by steeples, most splendid at Ketton, Langham and Oakham. The last has another Rutland treasure, the pier capitals with carvings of the Bible story.

Of the post-Reformation age, the Harington tombs at Exton are exceptional, with Gibbons's superb Campden monument in a class of its own. But for joyful eccentricity nothing can beat the Earl of Harborough's chapel at Teigh, designed for himself as preacher.

Brooke **   Lyddington *   Tickencote ***
Empingham *   North Luffenham *   Tixover *
Exton ***   Oakham **   Whissendine *
Ketton *   Stoke Dry **
Langham *   Teigh **

BROOKE
St Peter **
Early classical furnishings, Norman hinges

This charming church is set in a hollow in the wolds in a village of fudge-brown cottages. Only round the church have crude modern houses been allowed to spoil the visual coherence. The tower peeping over the side of the contour from the approach road is built of chunks of ashlar, ironstone and whatever rubble came to hand.

The interior is the familiar Rutland mix, a Norman body clothed in an Elizabethan jacket. The rebuilding took place in 1579, well after the Reformation and a rare date for such activity. The Brooke estate had been acquired by Sir Andrew Noel after the Dissolution and he built his new house and church at the same time, possibly using the same craftsmen. He may have intended the north chapel as his family mausoleum, but sadly this function passed to Exton, acquired by the Noels shortly afterwards, where the memorials show the glory of which

Brooke was deprived. Little was done to the church in subsequent centuries. Brooke leaps from Norman arch to Elizabethan as if Gothic had never existed.

We enter through the south door, a Transitional arch of the most ostentatious carving. The old Norman nave has a north arcade of three bays, but Noel rebuilt the chancel, north aisle and chapel, and chancel arcade with rounded arches and capitals which are more or less Doric. Such classical forms are rare in 16th-century churches. He also installed a complete set of furnishings, the glory of the present church. The nave and aisle are divided from chancel and chapel by emphatic screens, virtually wooden walls, with balusters much like classical columns. Box pews fill the nave, and in the chancel are boxed stalls. The communion rails also with balusters and the simple pulpit with small tester are Jacobean.

In the north chapel is the one Noel monument which evaded removal to Exton. It is a 1619 alabaster memorial to Charles Noel, son of the builder of the house and church. Despite its date he is clad in ancient armour, like a medieval knight asleep in his private chantry. At the back of the church is a Norman font on blind arcades and a chest hewn from a solid log. The Norman hinges on the north door are extraordinary, even sinister. They are shaped like giant fishbones, centipedes or spiders, according to taste.

EMPINGHAM
St Peter *
'Rocket' steeple

The best Midlands towers are on slopes, as if pinning their churches to the hillside. Empingham is a magnificent specimen, rising directly from the steep village street. Strong Early Gothic buttresses summon up their energy to launch the spire into space, with pinnacles as fuel pods. There is no Rutland dumpiness to Empingham tower. It soars.

Entry to the church is by the west door under the tower, as if to emphasise the latter's importance. The doorway arch is beautifully composed of shafts decorated with rings and ballflower, capped by tiny ogival crowns. Inside we find the customary Rutland Transitional, a Norman south arcade and Early Gothic north one, for once unscraped and in soft limestone with whitewash.

The chancel has Intersecting tracery in its east window, refreshingly free of stained glass. The round-arched sedilia and piscina group is in good repair. The principal surprise is the north transept, with high Perpendicular windows and fragments of medieval glass. The tracery is wayward, the designer distorting his panels into daggers, a Decorated form rarely seen in the stern production lines of Perpendicular. On the floor are Norman stone coffin tops. The nave seating is ugly modern schoolroom but the flowers, on my visit, were spectacular.

EXTON
St Peter and St Paul ***
Telescopic tower, Gibbons monument

The tower is first glimpsed through the trees of the estate owned by the Noel, Campden and Gainsborough families. The church has a private drive leading into a clearing in the woods, attended only by the ruins of the former Jacobean house and a farm. On all sides are the trappings of landed wealth. To the west and north runs the park of a later big house. Cedars and pines dot a landscape across which sheep move in clouds. The church tower and aisles were restored by Pearson in a fierce yellow stone after the tower was hit by lightning in the 19th century. His hand lies heavy on the window tracery.

At first view the tower seems telescopic, as if each component were waiting to be stretched from above. The more we look the more carefully it is balanced. A square tower is topped by heavy battlements and corner turrets, between which rise a narrower octagonal stage, again battlemented, which thrusts the eventual spire into the air. The composition is fussy but not unsuccessful. The rest of the exterior is ugly, the lead roofing all too visible above Pearson's stone.

Exton is not for architecture but for monuments. 'There are no churches in Rutland and few in England in which English sculpture from the 16th to the 18th centuries can be studied so profitably and enjoyed so much as at Exton,' says Pevsner emphatically. The family line is Harington-Noel-Campden-Gainsborough, each hyphen adding wealth and nobility down the ages. Yet the monuments reflect the style of the age rather than the dignity of those remembered. They fill every corner of the church.

At the west end of the south aisle lies the tomb of John Harington (d.1524), a lovely alabaster work. A lion and a bedesman are at his feet and his wife Alice is by his side, pet dogs nibbling her dress. In the chancel is Harington's grandson James (d.1592) and his wife Lucy. They had eighteen children, eleven of whom survived. In the south transept is the monument erected by his son, John, to his father-in-law, Robert Kelway (d.1580). He lies in lawyer's rather than soldier's costume within a classical frame. Three young people kneel in prayer before the father's effigy. The design is conventional but the carving exceptional, especially the ribbonwork.

We now move to the west end of the north aisle, to see the Haringtons' granddaughter, Anne, on a classical chest of black and white marble. The date is 1627, when most such tombs were florid Jacobean compositions of kneeling families. This monument is extraordinary for its period. The woman wears a shroud hanging loose round her body. She lies serene and natural in death.

Next comes Exton's most celebrated work, the huge wall monument dated

1686 to the 3rd Viscount Campden at the east end of the north aisle. It is in marble by Gibbons. Swags, garlands, urns and curtains adorn a classical frame flanked by obelisks and crowned with a broken pediment. The viscount stands in the niche with his fourth wife, both wearing Roman dress and divided by an urn. Previous wives and their progeny are recorded in the relief panels beneath. (It was important to be the last wife of a Stuart grandee.) The monument would not look out of place commemorating an 18th-century pope in St Peter's, Rome. What a delight to find in an English country church.

KETTON
St Mary *
Setting of tower, gravestone calligraphy

English churches derive their character as much from their situation as their architecture. St Mary's sits high above a bend in the village street, where it slopes down towards the stream. The contour of the street and churchyard wall thrusts the steeple upwards. Here is a church that truly crowns its settlement.

The essence of Ketton lies in this steeple, within and without. Located over the crossing it was heavily restored by the Victorians and lacks the patina of antiquity, but the composition is superlative. The work is typical of most Midlands towers, a bell-stage of Early Gothic and a stone spire erected in the 14th century. The bell-stage has three shafted twin-openings with dogtooth on each face, and is not capped by a parapet but moves smoothly into the broaches of the spire. This tapers gracefully upwards, defined by ribs and broken by lucarnes on alternating faces, each with its own diminutive Decorated tracery. There are statues in the niches. The proportion and adornment are faultless. The splendid west doorway has zigzag and is flanked by a pair of blind arches.

Inside, the atmosphere is dictated by a nave restoration by George Gilbert Scott and chancel restoration by T. G. Jackson. We are left only with the original proportions of the Early Gothic structure, spacious and lofty. The roof has a series of grandiloquent Victorian hammerbeams, vividly repainted in the 1950s. The angels are big enough to be ships' figureheads.

Some visitors have objected to the rearrangement of the gravestones into a fence along the churchyard path. It is not oppressive, and enables us to admire the pale Ketton stone and handsome calligraphy. The fence offers a charming gallery of memorial lettering, a much neglected field of craftsmanship, one largely unique to the British Isles.

LANGHAM
St Peter and St Paul *
Churchyard horticulture, south façade

The delight of this church is its 'stage set' south façade to the road, and a superbly maintained churchyard. The latter merits a star in itself: rows of yews dividing flower beds and rose bushes, and a magnolia keeping guard over the south porch. To the east is an inspired touch, untended grass rising to the height of the gravestones, a wild prairie in the midst of a manicured Rutland village. There should be a society for good churchyard practice, which could use Langham as a model.

The south side is a sequence of tower, clerestory, aisle, porch, transept aisle and transept, all in Rutland ironstone punctuated with ashlar. The windows are 14th-century transitional from Decorated to Perpendicular. Every buttress is pinnacled and every roof battlemented. Ballflower ornament pops up all over, notably round the Reticulated window. The apexes of the porch and transept roofs have tiny ogival crenellations with crosses. The east wall of the transept has excellent Intersecting tracery. In the south transept is a good incised slab to John Dickinson (d.1535).

The clerestory continues round the east wall of the nave above the chancel arch. This does little to enliven a bare interior. There is a small flurry of excitement in the form of an aisle to the south transept, apparently preceding the Perpendicular rebuilding. The glass is clear, affording charming views of the trees outside.

LYDDINGTON
St Andrew *
Acoustic jars, modern carvings

The Bede House survives from the ancient palace of the Bishops of Lincoln, another of their many stopping places on their slow progress northwards. As at Buckden (Hunts), they seem to have been happy for anything to postpone their arrival in their distant and possibly inhospitable seat at Lincoln.

Lyddington today is an immaculate ironstone village. Not a leaf or roof tile is out of place. It would seem an offence to break a blade of grass – except in the churchyard, which is left refreshingly unkempt by the Bede House. The church itself is large and handsome, with a wilfully eccentric tower. Large buttresses frame the west door, rising in rich ironstone to an odd spirelet. This appears to have been ordered three sizes too small, or to have shrunk in the rain.

The interior is described by the *Shell Guide* as 'heartless Perp'. Others might consider it graceful Perp or even serene Perp, but it is rather frigid. A large, well-proportioned nave of slender piers and high roof leads to a chancel ruthlessly scraped by Ewan Christian in 1890. The walls might be those of a 'rustick inglenook' in a pub lounge.

Yet the church has intriguing survivals. Round the chancel arch are wall paintings, including a finely robed king, possibly representing Edward the Confessor. There is an original rood screen, and the altar is surrounded on four sides by a Laudian rail. Dating from 1635, this is unusual in itself and even more unusual in its scale.

Equally rare, high in the chancel walls, are openings for acoustic jars, believed to improve the quality of sound from the choir below. Has anyone tested this thesis? Modern restorers have fashioned two delightful stops to the chancel arch. One is of a ferocious Green Man, the other the bespectacled figure of the 20th-century Bishop of Peterborough, Bill Westwood.

NORTH LUFFENHAM
St John *
Elaborate sedilia, medieval glass

Away from the bleakness of Rutland Water and the tat of the local RAF station lies a gentle group of farm, manor, rectory and church on the slopes of a hill dropping down to the River Chater. North Luffenham qualifies as an archetypal Rutland church. The tower is of the 'dunce's cap' type, made ponderous by a jutting stair turret and nave aisles that embrace its base. The chancel appears bigger than the nave.

The Transitional interior is scraped but otherwise not over-restored, with fine angels surviving in the Perpendicular roof. More interesting is the chancel, almost as long as the nave, and as high. Its style is Decorated and its windows wayward even by 14th-century standards. None is the same, as if the masons were given no patterns but left to their own devices. Even the window openings are of different shapes.

North Luffenham has two remarkable works of art. One is the finest sedilia in the county, with trefoil heads under cusped ogee arches, set in a ballflowered square frame. This decorative motif was a speciality of the early 14th century, no course of stone left unpunctuated by a flower. The other glory of the church is the medieval glass in the north wall, showing three saints of willowy posture standing beneath huge, elongated canopies. There are donors' shields above and beneath. The east window is a variation on the same theme by Kempe.

OAKHAM
All Saints **
Narrative carved capitals

Oakham is a charming small county town wholly dominated by its church, castle and school. The church tower is magnificent. Rutland steeples are often too thickset to soar, but not Oakham's. The tower rises in six stages, attended by angle buttresses with no fewer than 14 steps. Three medieval statues survive in the niches on the west front above a flowing Decorated window. The spire is conventional with three tiers of lucarnes above a pierced parapet and pinnacles.

The interior is that of a large town church. The heaviness of the restoration by George Gilbert Scott is relieved by the vigour of his chancel and by a crossing full of light and surprise. Most precious are the Decorated nave arcades, with superbly carved figurative capitals in a continuous programme, like the windows at Fairford (Gloucs). On the north side they depict the Fall of Man and on the south His Redemption and the Coronation of the Virgin. These are interspersed with such vernacular features as a Green Man and Reynard the Fox. Copies of these carvings should be made so that they can be appreciated at ground level.

The chancel is Scott's work. Its Decorated-style east window looks odd alongside the Perpendicular tracery of the side chapels. But the arcades and roof are of a piece, the latter brightly repainted in the 1890s.

STOKE DRY
St Andrew **
Norman bell-ringer carving, Digby tombs

Rutland is a chameleon county. For all its smallness it can take on the colouring of a fen, plain or hill. At Stoke Dry we might be in rolling Dorset. A homely porch and modest ironstone tower cling to the edge of a slope opposite a farm. Above the porch is a room with an oriel window, which might be a child's cottage bedroom.

The interior is as much an antique shop as a church. A Norman fragment survives in the shafts of the chancel arch. The carver, rather than concentrate on the capitals, has also covered the support with beasts and flowers. On the south side a man pulls on a bellrope while the Devil cowers beneath. This form, says Pevsner, is 'extremely rare in England though occasionally met with in France'. He traces the source to a Gloucester candlestick. The nave is of three bays with Reformation texts visible in the clerestory above. The furnishings are yeoman style, the pews roughly hacked from trees, with crude poppyheads. The ill-fitting screen is a ghost of a once lovely original. In the south aisle lies an incised slab of Jaquetta Digby (d.1496). She wears a pomander and is defaced by later graffiti carved into the alabaster by vandals, a crime tempered by age.

The chancel paraphernalia includes an ancient bier, some old Bibles and prayer books, and a jolly Elizabethan tomb of Kenelm Digby (d.1590), grandfather of the Gunpowder Plotter. The alabaster effigies are fine, but for some reason the family weepers are smiling, even the infant in swaddling clothes. The Digbys were recusants and, like the Sacheverells at Morley (Derbys), felt entitled to use their manorial church for Catholic services, assuming that it would one day return to Rome. As a result, the Digby south chapel was at one point surrounded by brick and wood screens. Inside the chapel is the part-Gothic, part-classical tomb of Everard Digby (d.1540). Here too are crude wall paintings of St Edmund and St Christopher. The former is being punctured with arrows by Danes in funny hats.

One implausible rumour holds that the Gunpowder Plot was hatched over the porch at Stoke Dry church. A more plausible one is that a rector locked a witch in there to die of starvation.

TEIGH

Holy Trinity **
Georgian west wall with gallery pulpit

This delicate Georgian church sits in a rugged farming hamlet like a Jane Austen maiden deposited by a coachman at the wrong inn. A 14th-century rector of Teigh was a Folville, a notorious Leicestershire bandit family. He was seized from the church by the county sheriff and decapitated for murder on the spot. This seems unlikely to happen here today.

The present church was designed by George Richardson in 1782 for Robert Sherrard, 4th Earl of Harborough, wealthy clergyman and enthusiastic church-builder. Richardson also built a church for him at Stapleford (Leics). The medieval tower was retained but the rest is entirely 18th century, completed in 1789. The church comprises nave and chancel in one, its exterior in a soft silvery stone. The interior is arranged in the collegiate form favoured by the late Georgians, with pews set lengthwise down the sides. The walls are pink and the plaster ceiling sky blue with darker blue panels and ribs. The reredos has simple Gothic panelling and a Flemish 17th-century painting as altarpiece.

The surprise is at the west end. Here the central bay has an extraordinary pulpit set above the doorway, flanked by two subsidiary reading desks. These burst like opera boxes from beneath Gothic canopies. High above them soars a *trompe l'oeil* window, filling the tower arch and suggesting trees and sky behind the preacher's head. The wall is not mere whimsy but a confident Gothic composition, using wood, plaster and paint to theatrical effect. It is the only church I know where the entire congregation would have had to face west to hear the sermon and readings.

A small mahogany font set into the wall is contemporary with the church, and originally attached to the altar rails. It is a dainty classical object of a quality that suggests Robert Adam or William Chambers. The stained glass is deplorable in a church that demands to be united with the soft Rutland skies outside. The churchyard has excellent gravestones in local materials.

TICKENCOTE
St Peter ***
Norman chancel arch

Tickencote lies on a slope leading down to the River Gwash beneath the course of the old Ermine Street, later the Great North Road. Millions must have tramped this way, diverting from the road to visit the old church and gaze in wonder at its famous chancel arch. It would be good to think that respect for this architectural piety is what prevented later ages from destroying it.

Tickencote's history is full of vicissitude. The church in the 18th century comprised a Norman chancel but a Gothic nave. This was dilapidated, and in 1792 the local Wingfield family commissioned a restoration of the entire church from S. P. Cockerell. The resulting style is hard to define. Cockerell rebuilt the chancel at least from the lower stages up, freely interpreting the eroded Norman remains, but he left the celebrated chancel arch intact. He also gave the church a completely new neo-Norman nave. As a result the exterior looks artificial. Although we are told that he respected the work of the original, the details of the 'wedding-cake' east front seem playful variations on the theme of the interior. High in the gable are square-headed windows with wild surrounds.

The spectacle that greets us on opening the door is breathtaking. The great arch at Tickencote is like is a peacock's tail, comprising every motif of Norman art. A fan of seven bands rests on five shafts. The sequence of bands includes beakheads, crenellation, odds and ends of faces and much zigzag. The carvings are the forte of the composition, a mass of animals, heads and monsters. The origin of many of these figures is obscure, perhaps Roman, perhaps Saxon, perhaps Viking. 'Once the floodgates of fancy were opened,' says the guide, 'a full tide of grotesque imagery poured through.'

Historians have suggested that the arch was once the exterior entrance to a small chapel, before a nave was built. This thesis is supported by the billet hood round the outside and the stepping back of the shaft bases. We must be grateful that the later nave preserved the carving from the weather and is in good condition.

Cockerell's restored chancel now has a a six-part vault with ribs, covered in zigzag, rising to a rare Norman stone boss. Above the chancel is an 'in-house' priest's chamber. The Norman font is hard to see in the shadow of the arch, but has beautiful intersecting arches with carved heads.

TIXOVER
St Luke *
Family pew, Swiss glass

This isolated church lies across a muddy field well away from the present village. An earlier village lay in the woods to the north. The land was owned by the monks of Cluny until the suppression of foreign abbeys by Henry V. The French monks would recognise it today. The church sits four-square in its old enclosure, with a massive tower and tiny chancel.

The antiquity of the foundation is immediately evident in the small Norman openings in the tower. The church walls are high and the windows tiny. Pevsner dates these windows to the Tudor period, but the guide treats them as rare instances of early 13th-century square heads. This would be unusual, especially with stone mullions that look decidedly Tudor. Either way, the windows are charming. The interior has simple, two-bay arcades with Norman arches and capitals to the south, and pointed arches with stiff-leaf to the north. The Norman tower arch has splendid carved capitals.

A fine Jacobean monument commorates Roger Dale (d.1623) and his wife and two daughters. They sit either side of a prayer desk in a frame that seems too sophisticated for this deserted, muddy spot. In the south aisle is a family pew, with behind it some pretty 16th-century glass, most of it apparently from Switzerland. The church is lit by candles and heated by an old stove. The overgrown churchyard merges into surrounding woods and fields, as if nature were about to seize the old stones back for its own.

WHISSENDINE
St Andrew *
Clerestory statues

The big church rises on a hill overlooking its village, hurling itself full tilt into the 14th century with a fine Rutland tower. If Whissendine only had Oakham's spire, it would be a superb creation. The bell-stage alone has fine blind arcading and tracery, though the need for a staircase resulted in irregular bell-openings to west and south. The whole composition is topped by a strange pierced parapet, as at Oakham.

The interior of Whissendine has been heavily restored and the walls brutally scraped. The chancel is gloomy, with an architectural reredos by Kempe.

Perpendicular lies heavy on aisles, transepts and clerestory. But the arcade piers are a delight, apparently Decorated but with a wilful variety of capitals, including stiff-leaf. They may be reused from an earlier building. The delicate piers lean outwards, to be propped up by later arches on the north side. These give the nave a slightly drunken aspect.

Whissendine has a complete set of medieval statues of saints and kings in its clerestory niches. These are rare, since Reformation soldiers took pride in shooting such icons from their perches. The statues sit on grotesque corbels. There are also two excellent corbel heads guarding the east wall of the nave. The screen in the south aisle has Elizabethan doors. It was removed by George Gilbert Scott from St John's College Chapel, Cambridge, which he was rebuilding at the time. St John's loss is Rutland's gain.

Shropshire

Shropshire is a little-explored county. Its rolling hills form a northern climax to the Marches and its castles are a reminder of the threat of marauding Welsh throughout the Middle Ages. Wood and water brought it the birth of the Industrial Revolution at Coalbrookdale, but this prominence soon passed to the Midlands and South Wales. Today Shropshire's rich valleys and deep red sandstone villages and towns are still beyond the reach of Midlands sprawl.

The security needs of the Marcher lords left Shropshire many churches either attached to castles or with towers of keep-like proportions, as at Stokesay, Lydbury North and Claverley. The county's dominant church is that of Ludlow, rebuilt in the 15th century as a cathedral to Marcher wealth and retaining its superb collection of medieval glass. At Shrewsbury, the old abbey was restored by J. L. Pearson and St Mary's has been excellently conserved and reopened.

Melverley is a gem of timber-framing and Minsterley offers Baroque sophistication from the Thynnes of Longleat. Tong displays some of the finest alabaster tombs in England, of the Vernons. Langley and Heath offer a contrast, tiny moorland chapels lost in Shropshire fields.

Acton Burnell **
Bromfield *
Burford **
Claverley ***
Heath **
Kinlet *
Langley *
Leebotwood *

Llanyblodwel **
Ludlow *****
Lydbury North *
Melverley **
Minsterley **
Shrewsbury:
  The Abbey ***
  St Chad **

Shrewsbury:
  St Mary ****
Stokesay *
Tong ***

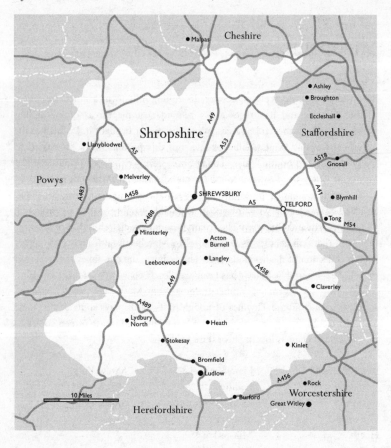

ACTON BURNELL

St Mary **

Castle setting, Elizabethan tomb

The ruined castle is more a fortified manor, built of bright red sandstone and standing immediately behind the church. Robert Burnell (d.1292) was Lord Chancellor to Edward I and Bishop of Bath and Wells. He entertained the king here in 1283, when Edward is reputed to have held an early 'parliament' on the site. A decade earlier Burnell had built the church, a beautifully proportioned Early Gothic work, but with emerging traces of the new Decorated style, possibly by craftsmen from the king's court. The small tower is a Victorian addition, overpowered by the great cedars and yews of the estate. The church has a decorated corbel-table round most of its eaves.

The interior is simple and bare, with lancet windows and a high-beamed post-medieval roof. The east end is best, the chancel and transepts greeted by three gracefully pointed arches. The chancel east window is filled with Geometrical tracery, a foiled circle resting on three lesser circles above lancets. This and other features of the church echo work at Wells during Burnell's episcopacy. The other chancel windows are no less distinctive, lancets with shafted rere-arches and trefoil heads. The piscina is similarly embellished. Everything is decorated in Purbeck marble and stiff-leaf carving and looks sumptuous.

Despite his fame, Burnell was, says the guide, 'immoral in his private life' and never again 'did the family or the village come into the limelight'. None the less, the north transept contains a brass for Sir Nicholas Burnell (d.1382) and an outstanding monument to a Burnell successor at the castle, Sir Richard Lee (d.1591). The tomb is a late Elizabethan tour-de-force in alabaster, carved all over with strapwork. Richard's nine daughters line the back of the tomb, while his three sons stand at his head and feet. Every detail is finely executed, with a tiny puppy crawling out of Lee's discarded gauntlet.

Opposite is a more conventional monument to Sir Humphrey Lee (d.1632) by Nicholas Stone. The floor is covered with exquisite medieval tiles on which we appreciate being permitted to walk.

BROMFIELD
St Mary *
Painted Restoration chancel

As the River Teme made its way through the upper Marches, it watered farms and sustained tithes for many Saxon religious houses. At Bromfield, almost within sight of Ludlow, a group of lay canons in the 11th century founded a college and received a charter from Edward the Confessor. In 1155 this became a Benedictine priory and remained one until the Dissolution.

The village is now desecrated by the A49, but the church is guarded by tall Scots pines on either side of the lychgate. Across the churchyard is the priory gatehouse and farm buildings that modestly replicate neighbouring Stokesay. For a clue to the church's history we must wander to the south side. Here is a surprise, the ruins of the 16th-century mansion built over what would once have been the south transept. This is the house that Charles Foxe built for himself inside the carcass of the old priory which he acquired at the Dissolution. He converted the chancel into his dining-room with a bedroom above. The house was destroyed by fire a century later but left its mark on the church to this day.

The interior of Bromfield is so gloomy that even on a sunny day the lights need to be turned on to see the contents. Little of the Norman building remains beyond its generous proportions. What is seen is mostly Early Gothic, a tall nave with original roof timbers and a truncated north aisle. Facing it on the south wall is a mural coat of arms of Charles II, one of the largest I know.

The nave is swamped by the chancel. Without the benefit of lights, what might be the ceiling of a faded Venetian palace must lurk in the shadows. This is Foxe's old dining parlour, restored as a chancel after the fire in 1658. The ceiling of putti prancing across the sky is not of Foxe's time, but was a fantasy installed when the chamber was once again a chancel. Originally the walls were similarly painted. The ceiling is well described by the guide as 'the best specimen of the worst period of ecclesiastical art'. The artist was one Thomas Francis in 1672.

The later altar and reredos are worthy of this setting, and there is a Jacobean pulpit with panels carved in relief. The best that can be said for the enveloping glass is that it is mostly by Kempe. That in the north aisle lancets is of high quality.

BURFORD

St Mary **

Cornewall monuments, Aston Webb alterations

Burford is a rare church, worth seeing for the quality of its Victorian restoration. It forms one of many Teme-side groupings, of big house, rectory and farm. The house's garden is open to the public and, with neighbouring Tenbury Wells, forms a lovely corner of old Shropshire.

Burford's massive tower, overlooked by chestnut trees, might be that of a Suffolk church. It is the outward face of Aston Webb's comprehensive rebuilding for the Rushout family in the 1880s. He went on to design those emblems of imperialism, Admiralty Arch, the front range of Buckingham Palace and the Victoria and Albert Museum, and must have looked back on Burford as a modest first step. He was a young man and still an enthusiast for Arts and Crafts Gothic.

Burford's interior is of simple nave and chancel. Artificial light is needed to see the chancel, revealing a superbly crafted screen, roof and organ case, the last a fine acquisition from a Belgian monastery. Webb's roof is made up of Perpendicular panels supported by ten angels, the easternmost being seraphim, the remainder cherubim. Beneath is a frieze of the arms of the two families that owned Burford since the Middle Ages, the Cornewalls (until the 1720s) and the Rushouts (until the 1950s). Four huge brass chandeliers by Webb hang over nave and chancel, and the marble chancel floor is also by him.

This Rushout ostentation would have been appreciated by their predecessors, the Cornewalls. The latter's restored monuments are the treasures of Burford, especially that to Edmund Cornewall (d.1508) in the centre of the chancel. He was just twenty on his death but wears the armour of a knight. His head is bare but rests on a helmet, with a crudely carved lion at his feet. The effigy is of wood rather than stone. This moving tribute to a young man was erected by his wife Anne.

Against the north wall is another effigy, this time of a grander figure, Princess Elizabeth (d.1426), daughter of John of Gaunt and wife of an earlier Cornewall. The tomb and effigy are brightly painted. The face is probably the work of a local craftsman portraying a noble lady in her prime. Within the sanctuary is a rare triptych memorial. The centrepiece has three portraits of 16th-century Cornewalls and the wings show saints and heraldry. Like the triptych at Lydiard Tregoze (Wilts), this was a popular form of family commemoration in the Tudor period, though vulnerable to destruction. This one is dated 1588 and signed by an artist with the splendid name of Melchior Salaboss.

The glass in Burford is mostly by Powell & Sons, good work that partly redeems the darkness of the wretchedly scraped walls. When will the lime-washers return?

CLAVERLEY
All Saints ***
Medieval murals, verger's waking-up pole

The setting is the most picturesque of Shropshire's picture villages, with plaster and timbering on all sides and rolling hills in the distance. This is country of dark red earth and stone, reflected in the oft-restored walls of the church. The tower is like a castle keep. The exterior and interior are in every way eccentric. The north side of the nave is of a markedly different period from the south side. The latter is interrupted by an internal tower, and the chancel is quite different again.

Claverley's north arcade is of Norman arches pierced through earlier walls. In the aisle behind is a charming clutter of church furniture, memorials, hatchments, Commandments boards and old screen fragments; it might be an ecclesiastical antique shop. Above on the nave wall is a celebrated mural of the early 13th century recalling the Bayeux Tapestry. It shows pairs of knights in armour, fighting either on horseback or on foot. The mural scholar, Professor Tristram, debated whether this represented a specific battle, but decided it was an allegory of the seven Christian Virtues fighting the seven pagan Vices.

The south arcade is Early Gothic, its capitals evolving from water-leaf to stiff-leaf with attendant beasts. This arcade is interrupted by, of all things, the tower and an organ. The former has one of its buttresses projecting into the nave, with a curious alcove that is reputedly a penitent's seat, or medieval 'sin bin'.

The chancel is virtually a second church, spaciously rebuilt in the 14th century. Its south chapel contains a tomb chest of Sir Robert Broke (d.1558) and his two wives, in alabaster with no fewer than sixteen children. The effigies retain traces of original colour and gilding. Here are also memorial slabs to the Gatacre family, long of this parish.

One of the charity boards records a legacy of eight shillings a year to be paid to a verger to awaken anyone seen sleeping during the service. The last holder of this office, who died in 1777, used a pole with a fox's brush at one end for waking ladies. The bare end was used for men.

HEATH
Undedicated **
Isolated hillside setting

Heath Chapel is near impossible to find on the slopes of hidden Corve Dale. Perhaps that is why it has survived almost untouched for some nine centuries. If Gothic or later masons ever stumbled across Heath, they ignored it. Yet the fact that a stone church can have been built here at all shows how populated these hills were in the 12th century. After desertion in the plague-ridden 14th century, the parish has remained stable at roughly seven farms and forty people ever since.

The chapel sits in a field between Abdon and Clee St Margaret, a double cell with flat buttresses and tiny round-arched window openings. Only the south door and chancel arch show signs of ornament, rather elaborate for such a place. Two pairs of restored shafts rise to two orders of arches, one of them with zigzag decoration. The door hinges appear to be Norman.

The interior is as built, except for the insertion in the 17th century of the window behind the pulpit to help the preacher read his notes. The carpentry is spatchcock. Tie-beams hold up the roof. The pulpit and pews have been reassembled from old bits of wood. The guide suggests that the rectory pew now in the chancel is composed of the rood beam. Medieval wall paintings and biblical texts are said to be hiding beneath the whitewash. These have yet to be restored, an exciting prospect.

KINLET
St John *
Medieval tombs

The church lies on the side of a hill that sweeps up to the façade of Kinlet Hall, now a prep school. The village has gone, the only locals being the ghosts in the churchyard and rooks in the high trees. The tower is of grey stone, softened by an evening sun to the colour of honey. The chancel priest's door has a splendid medieval hinge.

This is a church of monuments. On either side of the chancel are tombs of the medieval Blounts, that on the south side of Sir Humphrey (d.1477) and on the north side of Sir John (d.1531). Both are in armour, their wives in dress of the late 15th century. The weepers are charming. Overshadowing both is the Blount Chapel, with the superb Elizabethan tomb of Sir George Blount (d.1584). It is a two-tier design, with a cadaver in the tomb chest seen through trefoil arches. Above, man and wife kneel side by side, facing out as if from a family pew, beneath a canopy with more Gothic arches forming a pelmet. The tomb was erected by Sir George's nephew, presumably to thank his uncle for having chosen him as heir against his daughter, whom he had disinherited for marrying against his wishes.

The south transept chapel contains a lovely alabaster carving of a Trinity, with God the Father holding the crucified Christ in His lap. Next to it is an effigy of a medieval woman of the time of Henry V, exquisitely carved and with a baby at her side. She is believed to be Isobel, last of the Cornewalls of Kinlet.

LANGLEY
Undedicated *
Deserted chapel in field

Most churches in this book are in some sense of today, used for regular worship and centres of parochial life. Langley belongs to English Heritage and was the first church to be taken into 'state' care. Though still consecrated and therefore qualifying for this list, it shows little sign of use. Langley has long lost any human settlement and has returned to commune with its landscape. I visited it one early evening when the spirits of the gloaming were awakening. Sheep nibbled round the walls and the door hung loose.

The chapel lies in a meadow off a lane near Ruckley. It belonged to the now vanished Langley Hall, house of the Lee family. One window suggests a 13th-century foundation, but the building as we see it is dated 1564 or 1601, depending on which graffiti are to be believed. The structure is therefore mostly post-Reformation. The charm of Langley is not its antiquity as such, but that its oldness seems so pure. Through this door would have stomped the Lee family, their servants and farm workers from the 16th century to the 20th.

The church is single-cell with a small weatherboarded bellcote and windows of different periods, including Y-tracery in the east one. The interior has furnishings apparently dating from the late-Tudor, early-Jacobean period. They include rough benches with poppyheads, a family box pew, a musicians' bench, a portable lectern and a strange pulpit. This last is a panelled box with floor, walls and a ceiling, but with two sides half open. The sanctuary arrangement is Protestant, with a simple table surrounded on three sides by benches for communicants. The place holds an aura of a lost and primitive faith.

[EH]

LEEBOTWOOD
St Mary *
Medieval murals, original furnishings

The church lies on a mound with spectacular views to the Long Mynd. Leebotwood was the burial church of the Corbetts of Longnor, though why they decided not to use their church at neighbouring Longnor itself is not clear. This spot is peaceful, with medieval wall paintings only partly revealed. Its furnishings are those of rough hands and heavy boots, untouched by the Victorian period. There is no proper chancel. This is a people's church, with the monuments to the Corbetts crowded into the sanctuary, as if for protection from the peasants.

Outside and in, Leebotwood church is meek. The bell-tower is an early 19th-century addition. The roof's tie-beams are painted and one has dramatic dragons visible from the gallery. Another beam once served as support for the screen, with two columns surviving from a later insertion. The nave furniture is all of the 18th century, with a three-decker pulpit surrounded by a flurry of box pews. Inside the pews are old kneelers in the form of leather-covered stools.

On the north wall is a medieval painting of remarkable vividness, discovered in 1976. Mary and Christ are shown receiving gifts with angels in attendance.

LLANYBLODWEL
St Michael **
Eccentric Victorian's hobby church

The Welsh Marches are seldom so lovely as where the River Tanat crosses the border through steep wooded valleys west of Oswestry. This is really Wales and the place names profess it. Llanyblodwel is a tiny village down a cul-de-sac leading to the river. An old pub stands by the narrow bridge. Black-and-white houses start out of the trees.

The church stands on the other side of the stream next to a large Georgian mansion. Over the doorway is a Victorian inscription which reads, 'From lightning and tempest, from earthquake and fire, Good Lord deliver us', a strangely alarmist plea in this tranquil spot. The church was founded by the Normans, possibly their first to the west of Offa's Dyke. Blodwel appears to refer to a 'bloody wold' or battlefield, with *llan* being the Welsh for a saint's church. The present structure is an eccentric rebuilding by the early-Victorian incumbent, John Parker. He designed it himself in the 1840s, together with the vicarage and school. Even the guide admits that the outcome 'will horrify some and amuse others'. It is in no sense a scholarly work, rather hobby architecture, a Gothic Portmeirion.

Most noticeable is the tower. This was borrowed by Parker from Freiburg Cathedral in Germany. The form, a swelling cone rising to a point, with window openings all the way up, is unusual and not unpleasing. The design was intended for strength on a difficult site. When it was unveiled in 1856, Parker wrote that it was exactly as he had hoped, 'with a degree of scientific and geometrical grandeur'. Unlike other gentlemen parsons of the period, Parker was not indulging a rich man's whim. His church was ruinous and he appears to have proceeded piecemeal when money was available. The south wall is entirely his design, with Early Gothic windows and dormers, spiced by an original Norman doorway. The interior is more bizarre, a mass of dark woodwork and painted decoration appropriate to an Edwardian summer-house.

At the core of the church is an old Perpendicular arcade dividing nave from north aisle. This has been stencil-painted in brown and cream and covered in curlicues. There are texts on the walls and even the window openings are embellished. The ceiling is divided by a grid of panels with painted sections and an occasional hammerbeam with pendant, elaborately carved. In the north chapel hangs a Baroque tablet of 1752 by Rysbrack to Sir John Bridgeman, a professional flourish amid these amateur theatricals.

LUDLOW
St Laurence *****
Medieval Palmers' glass, Pietà bench-end, civic tombs

Ludlow is the most appealing of English hill towns. It was a wealthy political and commercial centre throughout the Middle Ages and was seat of the Lord President of the Council of the Marches. The town was to the Welsh borders what Berwick was to the Scottish, except that it was as often a centre of rebellion as protection against one. The castle was headquarters of the Mortimers, descendants of the Conquerer's brother and later Earls of March. In the Wars of the Roses they were again powerful magnates, backbone of the Yorkist cause. Their castle is a still a frontier fortress, looking out towards the dark hills of Wales.

The church is worthy of this status, the 'cathedral of the Marches'. Never collegiate, it sheltered the fraternities of a proud town, notably of its Pilgrims' (or Palmers') Guild. Members of this guild rebuilt and enriched the church in the 15th century. Their cruciform church and crossing tower is big from a distance and even bigger close to, crammed on its hilltop site and near invisible down an alley from Drapers Row. Only at the door of the porch can the scale of the aisles, chancel and tower be appreciated, yet by then we are too close to take in the whole.

Before raising their tower, Ludlow's citizens had already erected the hexagonal south porch. This strange shape is shared only with Chipping Norton (Oxon) and St Mary Redcliffe, Bristol. The interior is Perpendicular in every sense. The nave arcades are lofty and noble. The tower arch forms a massive tribute to the tower above, sweeping upwards to touch the almost flat roof. Though much of the Victorian restoration, especially the nave furnishing, is severe, the original chapels, woodwork and medieval stained glass are excellent.

Ludlow's climax is formed by the three great chambers of the chancel and its flanking chapels. The north chapel was that of the Palmers, a select band of citizens wealthy enough (and brave enough) to be able to afford the pilgrimage to Jerusalem. They were the jet-set travellers of their age. Up to six priests were financed to sing masses for the souls of departed Palmers. Though the church had no college of priests, its endowed chantries gave it a large clerical establishment. The chapel is lucky to retain its Tudor altar canopy and panelling, and even luckier to retain most of its glass.

This glass rivals that of Great Malvern (Worcs) and Fairford (Gloucs). The east window portrays the Ludlow Palmers in blue costume on pilgrimage to the Holy Land. There St John the Evangelist gives them a ring to bring back to King Edward. On their return they meet the king and are fêted by their fellows in Ludlow. In the north wall is the Annunciation window, a masterpiece of 15th-century glass. The three lower panels are particularly fine, portraying St Catherine, St John the Baptist and St Christopher against a golden background. To the south is the Lady Chapel, adorned with Commandment and charity boards. It contains another glass treasure, the medieval Tree of Jesse window much restored by Hardman & Co., but apparently true to its original fragments. The wooden pegs are not for top hats but for fire buckets.

The contents of the chancel are of the highest quality, windows, glass, roof, bosses and monuments. Most remarkable are the stalls, 32 in all. In 1447 the Palmers are recorded as buying 100 planks of oak for them, though many of the poppyheads and misericords must be older. One poppyhead is of a complete Pietà. A visitor is quoted in the guide as remarking, 'With a few strokes the carver has given her face such a look of suffering as you do not find even in 16th-century painting.' The Ludlow misericords, for which there is a separate guide, are important both as works of art and for their iconography. The favourites depict the wiles of women, from mermaids to the dishonest ale-wife, the hag and the witch. One woman is disappearing bottom-up into the jaws of Hell. Such anti-feminism was a favourite medieval theme. Why?

The reredos is a Victorian reconstruction from fragments of a Decorated original. Astonishingly the chancel windows, dating from the 1430s, survived into the 19th century, when they were restored by a Shrewsbury glazier who renewed roughly half the glass. The east window tells of the tortures of St Laurence. The south-east window depicts six of the Ten Commandments, again a rare survival of a once-common theme. 'Thou shalt not covet thy neighbour's house' is a splendid work, including a castle besieged by archers.

Ludlow's principal monuments were all erected in the chancel at the turn of the 17th century and in varying styles. That to Ambrosia Sydney (d.1574), daughter of the President of the Council of the Marches, has a wallplate with tablets set into the Perpendicular panelling of the chancel wall. That to Sir Robert Townshend, built in 1581, lends a splash of colour; the classical chest with fluted Ionic columns is set within a Gothic canopy. Sir Robert, although a Roman Catholic, was grand enough to merit burial in the sanctuary of his civic church. His children stand round the base in contemporary costume like so many dolls.

The various guidebooks to Ludlow church are so admirable that they deserve mention as part of the pleasure of visiting it. They are generous with quotations from old records and early visitors, and include a plan of the pre-Reformation chantries, some fifteen in all. David Lloyd's official guide also offers a glimpse of church life down the centuries. A church court prosecuted a man for being a 'common swearer and drunkard' and another for 'selling drink during divine service'. A woman was accused of being 'illegally pregnant', and 'William Crumpe for his usuall departure out of church in sermontime'.

LYDBURY NORTH
St Michael *
Arts and Crafts restoration

The village is sandwiched between the Long Mynd and the Forest of Clun, but its church is no mere filling. The tower is a 13th-century Marches bastion, tacked on to a massive Norman nave and chancel. There are no aisles, the walls standing rock-solid in their field. They defy any marauding Welsh to do their worst.

The pleasure of the interior is atmospheric, enhanced by early 20th-century restoration by J. T. Micklethwaite. His generation was more sensitive to the qualities of old English churches than were the Victorians. Apart from the arch to the south transept, it is hard to tell modern from medieval. Windows, arches, stone carvings and roof braces all have the timeless quality of English vernacular craftsmanship. Micklethwaite also restored the old schoolroom above the south transept, a rare survival which is reached by a small outside staircase.

The north transept is now in use as a Roman Catholic chapel, an admirable ecumenism.

The church's best work is the screen, with delicate tracery in the heads of the openings and a pierced dado. Above is a plastered tympanum, entirely covered with the Creed and the Commandments, dated 1615. The box pews are prettily carved with ball finials. Micklethwaite's light fittings are stylishly Art Nouveau.

MELVERLEY
St Peter **
All-wood church with Jacobean fittings

At the end of a lane leading down to the River Vyrnwy is what appears a black-and-white manor house. It is a church rebuilt on the site in 1406, after Owain Glyndwr had burnt its predecessor at the start of his rebellion against the Bolingbroke usurpation. The churchyard runs down to the river under the shadow of Breidden Hill across the Severn. The church is celebrated as one of Britain's few timber-framed churches. Whatever the Middle Ages may have thought of the superiority of stone or brick, the poorer materials of wood, wattle and daub have an endearing appeal, especially when guarded by two massive yew trees.

The interior is as domestic in appearance as the exterior. It is divided into three cells by two open timber screens, that to the east forming a rood screen and that to the west incorporating a gallery, probably inserted in 1588. Most of the furnishings are Jacobean, including pulpit, altar table and chairs. The lectern has a chained Bible. Melverley is all of a piece, a building with the texture of rich Shropshire ale mellowed in oak. A plaque on the churchyard gate announces that Melverley was 'Britain's most motivated village 1991', awarded for restoring the church.

MINSTERLEY
Holy Trinity **
Baroque west front, maidens' garlands

The year of the Glorious Revolution, 1688, was an unusual time to be building a country church. The reason had more to do with the history of the Thynne family than of the nation. The Thynnes, later Marquesses of Bath, lived at Longleat in Wiltshire but owned land in the Marches. They had seen their Caus Castle, north-west of Minsterley, destroyed in the Civil War. Female members of the family had traditionally lived there, but decided to move to Minsterley Hall, where they required a new church commensurate with their status. An architect, William Taylor, was duly sent from London.

The result, completed in 1689, is a curious box with a weatherboarded bell-cote above a west front in 'artisan's Baroque'. It would do credit to a William and Mary grammar school. This front is the building's showpiece. Pilasters rise to an open segmental pediment of stone on brick. This frames a centrepiece of door, window and clock, linked in a vertical strip and elaborately carved. In the lintel of the doorway are reliefs of cherubs, skulls, cross-bones and hour glasses. The Thynne ladies might have been living in the distant wilds of Shropshire, but they meant to live and die in style.

The interior is as simple as the exterior, a six-bay space with no chancel divide and round-headed windows. The east window has attractive Y-tracery. The Victorians inserted tinted glass to shut out the world, and with it any view of the superb redwoods in the churchyard. Most spectacular of the furnishings is the pulpit tester, overpowering the lesser pulpit below. Testers were intended to project the sound of the preacher's voice. Perhaps the Thynnes were hard of hearing.

Minsterley has a rare collection of maidens' garlands. These hang in incongruous plastic bags along the front of the gallery, but a replica can be inspected at close quarters in a case by the bookstall. The garlands were made to commemorate the death of a girl before she had married, and were also known as virgins' crowns, or crants. They were mounted on rods and hung over the relevant family pew. The garlands are made of wood, with attached paper flowers, ribbons and white gloves, this last as a challenge to any who would defame the reputation of the dead girl. A reference in *Hamlet* to Ophelia is much cited: 'Yet here she is allowed her virgin crants, / Her maiden strewments and the bringing home / Of bell and burial.' The Minsterley garlands date from the 18th century.

SHREWSBURY
The Abbey of the Holy Cross ***
Pearson restoration of Norman church

Until the 18th century, the entry into Shrewsbury from the south was dominated by the Benedictine abbey of the Holy Cross. Founded in 1083 by the Marcher potentate Roger de Montgomery, its status was further enhanced by the acquisition of the relics of St Winefride in 1136. Time and Dissolution wrought terrible damage on this structure, and then in 1836 Thomas Telford drove his new road to Holyhead through what remained. Telford's road now passes under the south wall of the church. Of the monastery only an eerie refectory pulpit survives in an adjacent car park.

What might then have declined into a parochial 'stump' of a monastic church was saved by Pearson in the 1880s. His re-creation of the old crossing and his building of a new chancel was masterful. Norman core and Gothic Revival are clear and distinct, yet neither jars the other. The exterior is noticeable for its power and bulk, forming a mountain of red sandstone on the outskirts of the town. The west front has a 12th-century lower stage, with a magnificent late 14th-century window above the old Norman doorway. Seven lights rise to Perpendicular panel tracery, fracturing into Decorated reticulation. An ogee hood then carries the upward thrust of the window to a statue of Edward III between belfry openings. Above this should be a spire; the brief Tudor battlement is a disappointment.

Inside, we are immediately overawed by the nave, the western bays in a light Perpendicular, the eastern bays and the chancel arch in elephantine Norman, solid, weighty and devoid of ornament. The lofty crossing was restored by Pearson, who also built new transepts and chancel in his favourite Early Gothic style, with lancet windows and a stone vault. The chancel is bare but for Pearson's fine triptych reredos.

The church is rich in furnishings, many brought from other churches in the town. In the north aisle are fragments of the old shrine of St Winefride and a collection of 16th- and 17th-century tombs of Shrewsbury worthies. The west window glass is a Georgian replica of the original heraldic panes.

SHREWSBURY
St Chad **
Hilltop setting, circular Georgian plan

St Chad's, on a bluff above the Severn, is one of the most original of England's classical churches. The exterior is of local grey stone rather than the customary Shropshire red. It was built above the old town quarry in 1790–92, replacing an earlier building in the town centre. Some parishioners wanted neo-Gothic, but a radical faction secured the contract for George Steuart, architect of the great Shropshire house of Attingham, outside the town. The location involved the demolition of a portion of city wall. Both conservationist and stylistic passions ran so high as to lead to riots in the town. Georgian Shrewsbury took its architecture seriously.

The outcome is a superb structure, especially from the outside. A Doric portico is surmounted by a three-stage tower which changes from square to octagon to circle, with a small dome. Seen from the west, the composition is uncommonly strong. The portico does not dominate the tower as often with such marriages, but merely adorns the entrance. Steuart then had to link this vertical feature to the circular nave. This he did by means of an oval foyer, yielding a well-modulated sequence of chambers.

The entrance hall might be that of a country house. It contains a curving oval staircase that sweeps upwards to the gallery, as at Attingham. Beyond is the body of the church, a wide, galleried amphitheatre supported on superimposed Ionic and Corinthian columns, the latter wildly elongated. The plasterwork is excellent and the upper space is lit by big round-headed windows. The organ pipes filling the western portion of the gallery merge gracefully with the columns. Box pews form concentric circles below.

The chancel is flanked by large columns, but the most prominent feature of St Chad's is unquestionably the Venetian east window. The glass is a virulently coloured copy of a Rubens Deposition, executed by a local stained glass artist named David Evans in the 1840s. Four more works by Evans were commissioned for elsewhere in the church. The pulpit is a fine brass work in the style of the Arts and Crafts movement.

SHREWSBURY
St Mary ****
Norman Transitional arcades, medieval glass

Since its rescue by the Churches Conservation Trust and the restoration of its glass, St Mary's has re-emerged as one of the great churches of the Marches. Its 222-ft spire dominates the old part of the town and its architecture offers a full range of Norman and Gothic design. The stained glass is as remarkable as that of Ludlow or Great Malvern (Worcs).

The church holds court in an attractive close. The west tower wall carries a plaque commemorating a steeplejack named Robert Cadman who, in 1739, plunged to his death while walking a tightrope strung from the tower across the Severn to Gaye Meadow. The exterior of sandstone and ashlar is easily read, with Norman tower and porches, Early Gothic transepts with lancet windows, Perpendicular in the aisles, and a large south-east chapel in the Decorated style.

The interior contrives to be both majestic and intimate. The nave is of the Transitional style, c.1200. The arcades display rounded (Norman) arches above (Early Gothic) shafted piers. The same period is evident in the capitals: Norman scallop and trumpet in the tower arch, the stiffest of stiff-leaf in the south arcade, and free Early Gothic stiff-leaf with peering heads in the north arcade. Above rises a magnificent panelled roof of c.1500, with giant fleurons as bosses and angels with musical instruments. To the east the chancel arch is pointed but with two Victorian twin-light openings above it, a splendid composition.

Proceeding east we reach the transepts, both of them Early Gothic with high lancets, but with earlier Norman work intruding everywhere. The splendid glass in the chancel's east window is one of the most complete Tree of Jesse windows in the country, albeit brought here after the collapse of old St Chad's in the 18th century.

This window dates from the high-point of the Decorated period, 1330–50. Newer glass has been added at the top and the sides but most is original and excellently restored. Jesse lies at the foot of the composition, his tree rising and encircling the characters of the Old and New Testaments. Below him is Edward III, flanked by the donor, Sir John de Charlton, and members of his family.

The remaining glass in the church is almost all from the collection acquired by a Victorian vicar of St Mary's, William Rowland (1828–52), from various churches on the Continent. The glass is of remarkable quality. The Trinity Chapel has two windows of 16th-century Belgian glass. In the north window of the chancel are 14 panels of the life of St Bernard from Altenberg Abbey, near Cologne. The aisles contain three 1479 windows from Trier Cathedral and delightful panels from the Netherlands.

All these are 15th and 16th century and sit far more happily in this architecture than would the Victorian glass in so many town churches. They combine biblical, mythical and domestic scenes, much as did the artists of the later Golden Age, the Dutch 17th century. To wander from one window to the next is to see scenes and faces that might be taken from Dürer, Hieronymus Bosch or Bruegel. This is Shrewsbury's Old Master gallery, set in glass.

Only in the east window of the Trinity Chapel does Rowland assert his own talent: its two side lights were designed by a local man, David Evans, while the centre light and wheel window are by Powell & Sons, superbly Art Nouveau in swirling lines of vivid blues and reds. At its foot is a depiction of the town. [CCT]

STOKESAY
St John *
Canopied pews, semi-wild churchyard

My visits to Stokesay always coincide with thunderstorms. One minute bright sunshine is beaming on walls, gatehouse, keep and church. The next, sheets of driving rain come pouring out of Wales and turn the road from Ludlow into a black ravine. The church could not ask for a more dramatic setting. The castle walls abut the churchyard and a path leads from the one to the other.

The church took a direct hit during the Civil War siege of the castle, which demolished most of its south side. The building was ruined for ten years, but the nave and tower were rebuilt in 1654, without aisles but with a bold black-and-white ceiling. The chancel was rebuilt ten years later. The wood furnishings installed at the time mostly survive to this day, as do the biblical texts on the walls. The pulpit text is, 'As new born Babes, desire ye sincere milk of ye Word that ye may grow thereby.' Stokesay has a complete set of box pews, a pulpit with reader's desk and two austere canopied private pews. These are more like courtroom cages than the upholstered rectory parlours beloved of the later Stuarts. They are covered in handsome panelling.

Few churches have been so blighted by modern glass, which here fills the south windows of the nave and thus prevents worshippers from enjoying the view up to the castle. Given that the guidebook admits that these windows 'darken the nave unduly . . . and make it somewhat oppressive', why not remove them? Against the exterior south wall is a Renaissance tomb of the Bough family, its pilasters worn thin from being used for the sharpening of crossbow bolts.

The churchyard is managed as 'semi-wild', with a reputed 88 species of wild flowers on display.

TONG
St Bartholomew ***
Vernon alabaster tombs

Behind lie the horrors of the west Midlands, the M54 and the M5. Ahead lies Ironbridge and the Wrekin. But at Tong is a collection of village tombs to match those of the Russells at Chenies (Bucks) or the Spencers at Great Brington (Northants). The Vernons lived at Haddon Hall in Derbyshire, but the family and its descendants owned Tong from the 15th to the 18th centuries and here they chose to be buried.

The church is of hard pink sandstone, mostly rebuilt in 1409 by Lady Isabel de Pembrugge in memory of her relatives. It is thus an aristocratic foundation, dedicated to the memorial needs of the departed rich. The exterior is stately, with a short but dignified octagonal tower and spire. The interior is as it was left by the 15th century, the windows mostly clear, the arch-braced roofs original, the bosses worthy of a cathedral.

The tombs form a dramatic sequence across the crossing and south chapel. They cover a complete stylistic span of the late Middle Ages, from early 15th century to late Elizabethan. Almost all the earlier tombs are of alabaster and would have come from the workshops of Derbyshire or Nottingham. The difference between the effigies did not reflect the appearance of the subjects, rather the evolution of contemporary dress and heraldry.

Against the north-west crossing pier is the tomb of Richard Vernon (d.1517). His son is portrayed at the foot while along the chest are hooded weepers. Beyond that and under the south crossing arch is Tong's masterpiece, the tomb of an earlier Richard (d.1451) and his wife Benedicta of Ludlow. The historian of medieval alabaster, Arthur Gardner, gives this tomb his palm: 'perhaps the finest and most imposing of all the alabaster knights that have come down to us'. The headdresses are magnificent, the fingers encrusted with rings. Two angels, beautifully carved, fuss over the positioning of the woman's pillow. The faces are crisply carved and beautiful. This is the Middle Ages brought vividly to life.

Beyond in the south aisle is the extraordinary monument, now rearranged, to Sir George Vernon's son-in-law, Sir Thomas Stanley (d.1576), and his wife, with their son underneath. As Earls of Derby, the Stanleys were patrons of Shakespeare and the lengthy epitaph on the tomb was reputedly by him. The epitaph ends, 'Not monumental stone preserve our Fame / Nor sky aspyring pyramids our name / The memory of Him for whom this stands / Shall outlive marble and defacers Hands / When all to tyme's consumption shall be geaven / Standley for whom this stands shall stand in Heaven.' It is hardly the Bard's best but is reasonably well authenticated.

South of this tomb is the enriched archway leading to the Golden Chapel, built and endowed by Sir Henry Vernon in 1510. In the archway is Sir Henry's tomb with that of his wife Anne. He was guardian to Henry VII's son Arthur, Prince of Wales, the first husband of Catherine of Aragon. The tomb and chapel display the final flowering of English Gothic. Crests and heraldry adorn the heads, bedesmen and dogs attend the feet. Four niches rise above the arch, while within is a graceful fan vault. Sir Henry's son, Arthur (d.1517), is shown in a wall memorial with a bust, reading a book beneath a gilded canopy. The bust later became a common form of commemoration for a scholar, but it was still unusual at this date.

Tong contrived to declare itself the burial place of Dickens's Little Nell. According to the guide, this was the lucrative invention of a recent verger, who would show visitors a relevant stone in the churchyard.

Somerset

Somerset is one of the finest counties for churches. As against the titans of East Anglia and Yorkshire, its architecture may lack depth, notably in the Early Gothic and Decorated periods, but throughout the 15th and early 16th centuries, huge sums were spent on refurbishing naves and rebuilding towers. The waterways of the Somerset Levels, like those of the Fens, enabled boats to bring stone to every mason's yard and wood to every carver's workshop. Wealth extended far beyond the great monasteries, to embrace clothiers, merchants and farmers. Money for church-building thus expanded beyond the collegiate foundations who were principal patrons of the chancels, to embrace the mercantile and civic patronage of naves, aisles and, above all, towers.

In Somerset, the golden age of Perpendicular meant golden. The county lies at the southern end of England's limestone belt, from Lincolnshire across the Midlands to the Cotswolds. Here the building stone turned from 'blue lias' and cool white Mendip in the north to the glorious Ham stone of the south. The latter is the loveliest building material in England. A restored niche in the porch of Long Sutton shows it glowing in ochre, orange and cream, a confection of sand, earth and sea shell.

From this combination of lias and Ham, Somerset fashioned its famous towers. Of the two dozen best steeples in England, half are in Somerset. Scholars from F. J. Allen and Kenneth Wickham to Pevsner and Clifton-Taylor have sought to classify them, roughly into the 'vertical' Wells school and the 'horizontal' Taunton or Quantock school. The finest combine qualities of both, as at Kingston St Mary, Isle Abbotts, Chewton Mendip and Leigh-upon-Mendip. These structures, with their buttresses, bell-opening tracery and crowns, rank with Nottinghamshire alabaster as England's finest contribution to medieval art.

After the towers, the naves and chancels of Somerset churches can seem an anticlimax. The county has three excellent Norman interiors at Stogursey, Stoke sub Hamdon and Compton Martin. Early Gothic is limited to the Carthusian foundation at Witham, and Decorated chiefly to the windows of Huish Episcopi. But the richness of Perpendicular is glory enough: not only the towers, outside and inside, but such works as the north aisle at Isle Abbotts, the windows of Crewkerne and the porch at Yatton.

The county's woodwork is superlative. Nothing in East Anglia can compare with the roofs at Somerton, Martock and Shepton Mallet. Nothing in Devon can equal the bench-ends at North Cadbury and Trull or the screen at Dunster.

The local style of gargoyle known as 'hunky punk' – named after a short creature squatting on its hunkers – adorns the upper stages of many Somerset towers. Nor did the Reformation stem the flow of patronage. New donors left fine roofs at Axbridge and East Brent, and the Jacobean screen and pulpit at Croscombe.

Yet the true pleasure of Somerset churches lies in the experience of visiting them. They invite us into a landscape of warm contours and gentle villages, into the cloister garden at Dunster, the old manor at Brympton and the wooded combe of Culbone. They offer the perfection of English building set in the perfection of English countryside.

Axbridge ***
Banwell **
Batcombe *
Bath ****
Bishop's Lydeard **
Brent Knoll **
Bruton **
Brympton ***
Cameley **
Chewton Mendip *
Compton Martin **
Crewkerne ****
Croscombe ***
Crowcombe **
Culbone *
Curry Rivel **
Dunster ****
East Brent **

Evercreech *
Glastonbury **
Goathurst *
High Ham **
Huish Episcopi ***
Ilminster ***
Isle Abbotts ****
Kingsbury Episcopi **
Kingston St Mary **
Leigh-upon-Mendip *
Long Sutton **
Lullington **
Martock ***
Mells ***
Muchelney *
North Cadbury **
North Petherton *
Norton sub Hamdon **

Oare *
Queen Camel **
Selworthy ***
Shepton Mallet ***
Somerton ***
Stogumber ***
Stogursey ***
Stoke Pero *
Stoke sub Hamdon **
Swell *
Taunton: St Mary
   Magdalene ***
Trull **
Wells: St Cuthbert
   ***
Westonzoyland ***
Witham Friary *
Yatton **

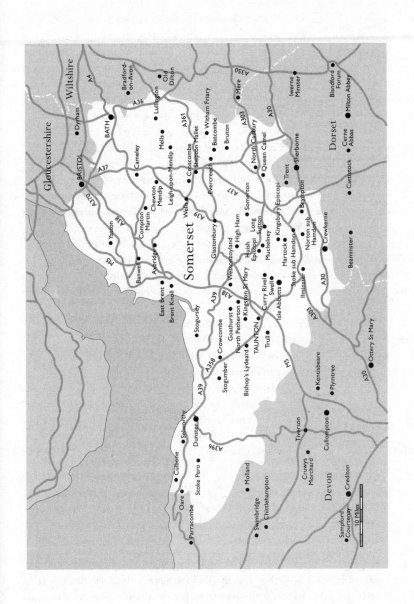

AXBRIDGE
St John ***
17th-century ceiling

Axbridge is now bypassed by the main road from Wells to the coast. On a quiet day it could be a settlement in the Umbrian hills. The main street opens out into a square of old houses with jettied upper floors. The church presides over a corner of this square, into which its steps pour like a glacier of stone. The walls are crowned with pierced parapets worthy of a bishop's palace.

The church was rebuilt at the turn of the 15th century and its size is only evident inside. The building is cruciform, with a crossing tower. But the Gothic shell is packed with 17th-century fittings. The astonishing nave ceiling was installed in 1636 by a local craftsman, George Drayton, who also designed the similar roof at East Brent. It is in the form of a plastered wagon roof but is decorated like a stone vault with cusped ribs and pendants, all painted a deep Italian blue with white trimmings.

This is not so much a church, more the banqueting hall of a Royalist courtier, 'a self-conscious or romantic allusion to the past,' says Pevsner. Adding to the conviviality are corbel heads from an earlier roof, alternately bearded and clean shaven. More-sober ceilings adorn the aisles, transepts and nave. The crossing has a fine early fan vault.

The view east from the nave is splendid. The chancel is guarded by handsome Arts and Crafts screens, restored in 1888 by J. D. Sedding. The height of the aisles floods these intersecting spaces with light, and the Gothic and Art Nouveau motifs seem perfectly in harmony.

Axbridge is well supplied with monuments of those who would have enjoyed its ceiling in its prime. In the south chancel aisle is a memorial to Anne Prowse (d.1668) with mermaids in attendance, primitive, chocolate-box Carolean, voluptuous from a voluptuous age. Next door is a more accomplished wall monument to Thomas Welsh (d.1678). He is graced with stars, cherubs, garlands and pillars.

BANWELL
St Andrew **
Annunciation lily, porch rood loft

Mendip churches are earnest places, unlike their glamorous sisters down on the Levels. The stone is darker and the settings more forbidding. Banwell is a church clad in a cassock, with a stovepipe hat for a tower. The churchyard is enclosed with houses. On my visit a magnificent magnolia was blooming against a backdrop of black yews. Traffic rushed past on its way to the sea.

The west wall of the tower is lightened by a rare surviving Annunciation with a lily in relief. The lily was known by medieval scholars as 'the happiest of herbs', representing the rod of Jesse brought by the Angel Gabriel to the Virgin, with Christ as its flower. In Long Melford (Suffolk) and Godshill (Hants/Isle of Wight), the Crucifixion takes place on a lily.

The interior of Banwell offers some hint of the theatricality of pre-Reformation ceremonial. Over the doorway in the south porch are the remains of a rare external rood loft. Its purpose is obscure but it presumably greeted the Easter procession with singers and music as celebrants arrived at the church, unless it was a lesser rood for those not permitted for whatever reason to enter. Inside, the capitals of the Perpendicular arcades carry gilded flowers. The clerestory has a frieze of wooden trefoils embracing the windows, like the 'gods' in a theatre. The roofs are excellent: that in the nave enriched with angels and foliage bosses while the chancel roof is panelled, carved, decorated and painted. The pulpit is a refined work of stone dating from the late 15th century, with a most ornate wine-glass stem.

Banwell has one of Somerset's best screens, erected in 1522, with a deep cornice and fan-vault coving on both east and west faces. The benches and much of the west gallery survive from the 16th century. They need to be filled with people, lit with candles and entertained with music and a medieval mystery play. Roll on the day.

BATCOMBE
St Mary *
Late Somerset tower

The view of the church rising above its village is incomparable. We pass a scatter of cottages on a slope, then a manor with cedars, high walls and hedges, then a rectory and pub. Finally one of the last of Somerset's mighty towers looms over us. It is worth visiting for this view alone.

The tower was built *c.*1540, at the same time as Chewton Mendip and possibly by the same designer. It is thick-set and heavy, yet falls within the 'vertical' Wells group, with a strong Perpendicular accent. Slender buttresses peter out before reaching the top while bell-openings continue as panelling into the stage below. The roof has no pinnacles and ends rather abruptly. Above the west window is a fine carving of Christ with three angels on either side.

The interior is a disappointment, apart from the fine panelled arch and fan vault inside the tower. The restored chancel contains an Elizabethan brass to Philip Bisse, whose family acquired the manor about the time of the building of the tower and later contributed to the porch. Batcombe is surrounded by glorious trees. None is visible from inside, which is dark with Victorian glass, except in the chancel whose old plain glass apparently comes from King's College, Cambridge.

BATH
Abbey ****
West front 'ladders', old and new fan vaults

Bath Abbey is a parish church and has been since its completion in the 19th century. It closes the east end of a piazza around which are the ancient façades, roofs and alleys of the old part of the town. This is close-grained townscape, the abbey offering thrilling glimpses of flying buttresses and walls of glass from the adjacent lanes. It is my favourite Bath, dating from before the arrival of the Georgian swells.

After the departure of the Romans, a Saxon abbey stood on this site and then a Norman one. Not until the end of the medieval period was a Gothic church erected, in 1499, allegedly the result of an episcopal dream. Bishop Oliver King claimed to have seen an olive tree and a king's coronet (clearly indicating his name). Ladders rose from this tree, with angels ascending and descending. A voice commanded 'a king to restore the church'.

Not a man to doubt such a vision, King commissioned Robert and William Vertue, the royal master masons, who were later to work at Windsor and Westminster Abbey. They promised him 'the finest vault in England'. Progress, however, was slow and only the walls and part of the choir had been built by the time of the Dissolution. But the west front had been given its celebrated frame of turrets with ladders, portraying King's dream. They are a charming conceit.

After the Dissolution the abbey was looted and the church given to the parish. The nave was covered by a simple roof and the choir used for services. Houses soon enclosed the building and the north aisle became a public thoroughfare. The church remained in this incomplete state throughout the days of Bath's Georgian glory.

Only in 1864 did a new rector, Charles Kemble, begin a reconstruction, mostly at his own expense. George Gilbert Scott virtually rebuilt the nave and aisles, replicating Bishop King's choir fan vaulting and buttressing. The building that we see today is thus mostly a Victorian replica of a Tudor design. The failure of modern restorers to replace the eroded statutary on the west front is disappointing, given the completeness of Scott's work on the architecture.

The first impression of the interior is of an awesome unity. The crossing and transepts are hardly noticed as the vault carries the eye from west to east in one great sweep. The nave has five bays, the chancel an identical three; both are aisled. The diminutive one-bay crossing and transepts are almost apologetically narrow. To the east a vast window rises the full height of the wall, with only transom and mullions for support. This is 'conservatory' Perpendicular at its most glassy.

This interior is not to every taste. Ruskin referred to Bath's 'icy regularity'. Betjeman called the abbey 'barren and unmysterious' and not as effective as King's College Chapel, Cambridge, or St Mary Redcliffe, Bristol. Pevsner dismissed the interior as 'impressive in a wholly unpicturesque way. The light is even.' It is true that the nave is tall and thin, almost a cavern, and the transepts certainly so. The crossing arches break the rhythm without yielding any upward thrust and the Victorian stonework is too clean cut.

Yet I like Bath. First, it is a true Tudor church. Records show that Scott meticulously respected King's intention. Each nave detail is a copy of one from the chancel. The result may be Victorian in archaeology but it is medieval in inspiration and style. And the vault is superb. By day the soaring ribs might be tropical palms brought back by early 16th-century explorers. Illuminated at night they become Tudor ladies fluttering their fans while pages with heraldic tunics peep through the gaps. This vault, a final flourish of English Gothic, is both orderly and exotic. When filled with music during the Bath Festival, it takes wing and flies.

In the south transept is a jolly 17th-century memorial to Lady Waller of 1633, with her husband gazing at her from a half-seated position. Richard 'Beau' Nash is commemorated in the south aisle, modestly, as a servant of the city rather than as an aristocrat. Most of the memorials are wall tablets to visitors in the 18th and early 19th centuries. They fill every inch of wallspace. Here Jane Austen might have wandered, collecting names and circumstances for her characters.

BISHOP'S LYDEARD
St Mary **
Taunton tower, carved benches

Not all the diocesan wealth of Somerset went to glorify Wells Cathedral. Some glorified the episcopal estates. Among these 'episcopi' churches is Bishop's Lydeard. Its tower is an outlier of the fine Taunton group, guarding the approach to the vale between the Quantocks and the Brendons. This is red earth country, where masons worked the deep ochre stone as though they were fashioning architecture from mahogany.

The tower is distinct from the church, surviving triumphant while the Victorians corrupted the nave below. Its red stone complements the deep green of the churchyard yews and the open hills of the Quantocks beyond. Built c.1450, it is one of the earliest of the Taunton towers, a form that reached its climax at Isle Abbotts. It is characterised by a careful balance of width to height, with gracefully set-back buttresses and an abundance of pinnacles. A large five-light west window fills the lowest stage, then two stages with smaller windows and finally double belfry openings. Enrichment increases with the height.

The rest of the church is heavily restored. The window tracery is Victorian while the glass is 20th century, darkening what should be a sun-filled space. The 16th-century screen is splendid, with fan-vaulted coving, recoloured by Comper and given a new rood. Equally remarkable is Comper's reredos with gilded canopy.

Lydeard has excellent benches, complete with ornamented backs, fronts, ends and even some original colouring. Subjects include a medieval sailing ship, a windmill, dogs chasing rabbits and the usual emblems of the Passion. Lydeard's two Green Men are charming characters.

BRENT KNOLL
St Michael **
Bench-end cartoons, Civil War monument

Brent Knoll forms a mound above the Bridgwater flood plain. Like many mounds, it has a church dedicated to St Michael to protect it from the Devil. The two Brent churches, Brent Knoll and East Brent, are architecturally similar. Both have tall ashlar towers and rich north aisles with pierced parapets, presumably built by the same or rival patrons. Brent Knoll is set into the side of the hill, as a result of which the chancel became so unstable as to require complete rebuilding in the 19th century.

The church is mostly Perpendicular, with an elegant nave and six-bay north arcade. The north aisle has a roof with lavish sculpted panels, huge bosses and angels, a miniature of those at Martock or Somerton. Fine woodwork is also displayed in the profusion of bench-ends. They depict an extraordinary ecclesiastical satire, with a fox in bishop's clothing. The target is assumed to be the Abbot of Glastonbury, owner of the manor, yet it is hard to imagine such an attack in the abbot's own church. A more likely candidate is Bishop Richard Fox, who arrived at Bath and Wells in 1492 and was widely unpopular, not least at Glastonbury. The first panel has the fox dressed as a bishop addressing a flock of animals. In the second panel, the animals have taken revenge on the fox, stripped him and put him in the stocks. In the third he has been hanged by a group of geese. It is a savage cartoon, whether born of rage or of wit.

On the south wall is a memorial to John Somerset (d.1663). His story was typical of a landed gentry tossed and turned by the Civil War. He was tormented by troops of both sides, by rebellious locals and by his own sense of duty, which he could never quite place. He is described in the guide as 'no soldier, no valiant man at arms and no great hero, but a simple country gentleman who was held in high esteem by the people of the district'. His is an early example of a monument with busts, in contrast to the full-length effigies of earlier tombs. Underneath, he appears to be rising from the dead to greet his second wife in a desert.

BRUTON
St Mary **
Powerful tower, Georgian chancel

Here is a fine Somerset tower in a classic Somerset setting. The church sits on the bend of a steep hill known at The Plox. Its tower rises on a mound where a marker indicates a flood in June 1917 reaching the doorstep. If this is true, the lower part of the town must have been completely inundated.

The church and tower are Perpendicular, the latter strongly vertical and of the Wells group, with slender buttresses rising to simple pinnacles. The west side is much enriched: a hooded west door, then a Perpendicular window, then three saints' niches, then a window and two more niches. The tall belfry stage has pierced stonework on each side to let the sound cry out across the valley. This is Somerset architecture at its most powerful. The north porch has its own, earlier tower, now rising like a subordinate and rather sad parasite. When the Victorians restored Bruton they honoured both towers by leaving them alone.

The interior is scraped and darkened, with a bold original roof. However, the chancel is an astonishing irruption, inserted in 1743 by the Berkeley family, lords of the manor. It could be a proprietary chapel for the Medici. The plaster roof has garlands of leaves for ribs and bright gilding on bosses and corbels. The east end has no window but a large plaster reredos, with the Berkeley arms set above the altar. In the north wall of the chancel is the tomb of an earlier Berkeley, Sir Maurice (d.1581). The alcove is crowded with his first and second wives, in effigy alongside him. Opposite is a bust of William Godolphin (d.1636), attributed to Hubert Le Sueur, sculptor of the equestrian monument to Charles I in Trafalgar Square.

To the south of the church is a cricket field and then a hillside sloping up to a ruined dovecote on the horizon. An express train occasionally races across this sublime landscape, but Bruton's tower and bells are a match for it.

BRYMPTON
St Andrew ***
Country house setting, stone screen

The manor of Brympton D'Evercy was in single family ownership for generations. In the 1980s it was put on the market, and publicised as a 'house without hope'. Yet it was bought by the Weekes family and is cared for as well as ever. The gates are opposite a farm on the road from Odcombe to Yeovil and firmly marked private, but there is a right of way to the church.

Brympton is the best of English house-and-church compositions. The approach round a bluff in the hillside presents a superb spectacle of gates, lawn, herbaceous border and Tudor façade, all in the warmest Ham stone. The 17th-century rear of the house can be seen from the churchyard, above a terrace made familiar in the (1995) television version of *Pride and Prejudice*.

The church is not grand, but small and friendly. A medieval range links it to the main house, variously identified as a dower house or a chantry. The church has no tower but carries a rare bell-cage set high over the west end. The northern chantry chapel is curious, with battlements added to an earlier pitched roof like paper crowns round a lamb cutlet. The fenestration suggests a Perpendicular extension of the former Decorated transept.

Inside nothing jars. The cruciform plan allows light from windows of all periods to dance across the interior. The Victorian scraping can be forgiven, for there is no stone so delicious as Ham. The screen is also stone, a rarity, with decorated spandrels. These have dragons on their far side and a splendid Green Man facing the nave. Above is a painted rood beam. The lectern appears to be composed of the twisted balusters of a former altar rail. In the south transept are wall plaques to later occupants of the manor, the Ponsonbys, neat and in a row.

The north chapel is full of medieval activity. Old priests, knights and their ladies lie against walls, much bashed and restored. One is holding his heart. Medieval glass starts out of the windows, enough to be more than just decorative. Filling the space between the chapel and the chancel is the tomb of the Sydenhams, former owners of the house, covered in colourful heraldry and surmounted by Sydenham rams. Outside the east wall of the church the gravestones are in the form of a regiment of box hedges, an unusual memorial.

CAMELEY
St James **
Unmodernised interior, box pews

No Somerset pyrotechnics here, no long vistas, soaring aisles or noble monuments. This is a church left alone on its mound when the village of Cameley moved to neighbouring Temple Cloud in the 18th century to benefit from the new turnpike. St James's was declared redundant in 1976 but has since reopened for occasional services. It struggles to call itself 'not a museum . . . but still hallowed by worship'. I know few churches where building, churchyard and surrounding fields and streams are more in harmony.

The tower is a surprise. It rejects the cold 'blue' Mendip limestone of which the rest of the church is built in favour of red sandstone. Out of keeping with the rest of the building, it might have been sent from afar to protect a local secret. Inside, all is atmosphere. The church guide protests that the place is 'humble, functional and devoid of airs and graces'. It is right. This might be the parlour of the local squire.

Centuries of settlement have splayed the walls outwards. A narrow Norman chancel arch is flanked by solid walls which show clear signs of blocked-up arches, probably the remains of side chapels. Over the chancel arch are fragments of the Ten Commandments, booming down on the congregation. But why is a crab painted on the north wall? Is it a sign of the zodiac? The nave is filled with box pews, so many and so different that they might have been designed for particular families. One, allocated to 'Samuel Oliver', is behind the preacher's back. Two others face him across the nave and others are beneath the gallery. Cameley was well supplied with gentry.

Along the south wall of the nave is a prominent gallery erected 'for the free use of the inhabitants, 1819'. This was shortly before a new church was built at Temple Cloud. Old hatpegs are still in place. Memorials record local families with splendid names such as Cadwallader and Mogg.
[CCT]

CHEWTON MENDIP
St Mary Magdalene *
Tower and setting

Of all distant views of Somerset towers, none is more evocative than that of Chewton, set in a fold in the rolling Mendips. Walk these hills and you see it constantly poking up over a contour, then disappearing, like an adult playing boo with a child. I have seen Chewton tower darting through clumps of trees, looming out of mists and soaring across meadows. Within the village it is enclosed by slopes that swoop down on it from every side.

The tower is the fourth highest on a church in the county (after Taunton, Wells and Glastonbury), and the last to be completed, in 1541. It is also one of the best. Chewton can thus claim to be the summation of this great tradition in English architecture. The design is similar to contemporary Batcombe and takes its cue from Wells. The Wells masons were masters of the vertical line, carrying the eye upwards through buttress, mullion and pinnacle. At Chewton, the door, window, saint's niche, twinned lower stage and twinned bell-stage all merge into each other in perfect balance. The buttresses peter out beneath the battlements in a flurry of pinnacles, but the battlements, as if not to be outdone, take over with jutting corner turrets and pinnacles of their own.

The church was not finished until well into the Reformation. A sign of the wealth and continued confidence of the community was the interior fan vault supporting the tower. When Chewton restored it in the 19th century, it stripped the interior of much of its character. The north doorway is a Norman survival with a round arch, zigzag decoration and scalloped capitals to the shafts. The chancel is mostly restored Early Gothic, with stiff-leaf decoration on the arcade dividing it from its aisle.

COMPTON MARTIN
St Michael **
Norman interior, ancient dovecote

Compton Martin is one of just three Norman churches in Somerset (with Stogursey and Stoke sub Hamdon). It was home of St Wulfric in the 12th century, a priest who enjoyed the good things of Norman life until he met a beggar, returned to his parish and asked the lord of the manor, William Fitzwalter, to build him a hermit's cell. The lord obliged, adding as afterthought an expensive penitent's shirt of chainmail. The shirt was too long, but the power of the saint's prayers enabled the shirt to be cut with scissors as if it were cloth.

The exterior is dominated by an austere Mendip Perpendicular tower. The interior core of the church is much as in Wulfric's day, an enclosure of chunky Norman arches and zigzag ribs. Even the Norman clerestory survives. One of the south arcade piers has twisted barley-sugar fluting of a style borrowed from Durham Cathedral. This may survive from some other building previously on the site. A Perpendicular arch incongruously divides Norman nave from Norman chancel, its right-hand pier distorted under the weight of the roof. The earlier masons would have ridiculed the effeminate Goths for inserting an arch that could not stand the strain. The Norman chancel is composed of two low bays with rib vaulting. The effect is of a castle undercroft, cool and intimate.

There is not much more to Compton Martin. The chancel is decorated with fine corbel heads and bosses, including Norman animals. The nave bosses are fierce and red. The chancel vault hides, of all things, a Norman dovecote built for the priest's use. The only other 'built-in' dovecote I know is at Elkstone (Gloucs).

CREWKERNE
St Bartholomew ****
Perpendicular window tracery, 'clean and unclean' doors

Crewkerne church was rebuilt at the turn of the 16th century. It is a church of vistas and perspectives. From the high ground to the west we see an embattled minster rising proud from a frame of trees. The grand west front is symmetrical, with windows, octagonal turrets and low-pitched roofs, and with battlements in balance above a doorway of ogee arch and niches. This is attributed to William Smyth of Wells and is considered by Kenneth Wickham the best in the county. Yet the view from the north gate is quite different. Here a horizontal sequence of six-light windows reaches almost to the ground. To the north-east we see no fewer than seven right angles, as transept, chancel, chancel aisles and chapel jostle for wall space.

The window tracery of Crewkerne is among the most complex Perpendicular work of any church in England. The style, lacking the flamboyance of Decorated, is sometimes regarded as tedious, yet at Crewkerne it blossoms into ceaseless invention. Mullions rise and split and replicate and cusp, demanding a pullout section to themselves in the church's admirable guide. Even more exciting is the effect these great windows have on the interior spaces. The church is cruciform and the crossing forms a dark sanctuary, from which transepts and aisles seem to spin outwards in search of the light.

This plan has all the exhilaration of German High Baroque. The view diagonally from the south aisle is of a forest of piers through which, on a sunny day, the fall of light on Ham stone, whitewashed walls and oak roofs is incomparable. The short aisled nave is a square of three bays with a high wagon roof. Both transepts are deep, but the north fragments into chapels and secluded chambers of high windows, carved screens and altars. The corbel heads in the crossing include an excellent Green Man, gazing down as though he were the presiding genius of the place.

The north end of the north transept is the Woolminstone Chapel, after the home of the Merefield family, whose banner hangs here. Next to it, behind modern screens, is the children's chapel with a classical altar. The chancel is dominated by Victorian and 20th-century furnishings, with a Ham stone reredos of the Last Supper. On either side of the sanctuary are two doorways, once thought to represent the unclean to the left (with spandrels of pigs) and the cleansed to the right (with angels). However, the guide suggests that boars were the arms of the local Courtenay family, and the angels were just angels.

CROSCOMBE
St Mary ***
Jacobean fittings, medieval treasury

Croscombe pronounces its s. The church sits on a Mendip slope above a green valley, its grey tower pinning the village to the hillside. Remove all the Mendip towers and I wonder if this bleak limestone range might not slide gently into the Glastonbury plain. The tower is over 100 ft, with a rare Somerset spire. Under the west end is a curious treasury room with barred windows, looking like the village lock-up, which purpose it once served. The 15th-century vestry above the treasury was the meeting place of the village's medieval guilds, listed as the Yonglens (young men), Maidens, Webbers (weavers), Fullers, Hogglers (labourers), Archers and Wives. Is the last the earliest known Women's Institute? Records give the exact amounts each was expected to contribute to candles and other expenses in the church.

Croscombe's glory postdates them. The church is the frame inside which are some of the richest Jacobean furnishings in England, gift not of local guilds but of the Fortescue family. Woodwork of the period is on all sides and in the roofs. Here are nave pews, chancel stalls, pulpit and tester, a pair of clerks' desks, parclose and rood screens. All belong to *c.*1616, the date on the pulpit, except for the chancel roof, which is later. All are lavishly carved.

The rood screen is sensational, two tiers of dainty Ionic columns supporting beams with arches and pendants. The piece is crowned by a coat of arms flanked by obelisks and scrollwork, taking the place of the medieval rood. It almost touches the roof. The purpose of a screen at this period would be to emphasise the monarch as head of the Reformed Church and to shield the congregation from the then-defunct sanctuary beyond.

The adjacent pulpit, whose tester has a full classical entablature, carries the arms of the Bishop of Bath and Wells. It ranks with the City of London's best. The nave roof bosses represent the 15th-century Palton family together with emblems of the weavers. An elderly 'saint of the loom' has a male and female weaver kneeling by rolls of cloth. Only East Anglia could equal these Somerset communities for ecclesiastical conspicuous consumption.

CROWCOMBE
Holy Ghost **
Octagonal font, Green Men bench-ends

Crowcombe is a place of bliss. A neat village arrays itself on the slopes of the Quantocks. The Court is grandly secluded up its drive, the walls thick with rose and wistaria. The church presents a sumptuous south elevation. Having lost its spire in the 18th century, a Somerset nave is left to speak for itself and does so with eloquence. The three-bay south aisle forms a superb Perpendicular composition, as tall as the two-storey porch, which has a richly decorated priest's room and is fan vaulted.

Crowcombe's interior is high, light and full of art. The font is one of the best in Somerset, panelled Perpendicular with pendants under an octagonal bowl decorated with biblical scenes. The church retains early 16th-century bench-ends, especially strong on foliage. Green Men are everywhere. One appears to have mermen growing out of his ears. Another could include the earliest depiction of tomatoes in this country, brought to England after the Spanish conquest of Peru. Green Men are also shown consorting with fish, indicating the importance of the sea even to these inland settlements.

The rood screen is early 18th century and appears to be part of a single design with the pulpit. The north transept forms a memorial chapel to the Carew family, its walls crowded with monuments and hatchments.

CULBONE
St Culbone *
Smallest church, woodland setting

The church can justly claim to be the smallest (in floor area), most isolated and most picturesque in England. The South-West Coast Path passes it, but those visiting by car must turn off the A39 opposite the Culbone pub and drive down a narrow track and park where they can. There follows a 1½-mile walk through steep woods of walnut and oak, glorious on a summer's day with the sea glinting through the trees, darkly mysterious and dripping with water in winter.

These hills once supplied wood for Porlock's shipyards but the settlement was always poor and remote. In the 14th century it was used as a colony for French prisoners, in 1544 as a leper colony and in 1720 again as a prison colony. The victims were ferried in by boat and left to fend for themselves in the woods. The lepers were not even allowed into the village, but a small leper window in the north wall of the church recalls that they were not denied at least a sight of the Sacrament.

Today the combe may be a happier place, yet it is deserted but for a small house sometimes serving tea to walkers. The church has a 19th-century spike of a tower. The tiny double-cell, 35 ft long, divides into nave and minute chancel, each with a wagon roof. The east end is restored. A small, probably Saxon window carved from a single block of sandstone can be seen outside the south wall of the chancel, with a face grinning atop a pillar dividing the two window lights. The tall proportion of the nave also suggests a Saxon original as does the primitive font bowl.

The nave retains box pews, including a Jacobean squire's pew for the now-ruined Ashley Combe House. What can this place have been like then? One of the pews at the front has some reused linenfold panelling, similar to that which forms the dado of the screen. The church is candlelit. The whole place, with a magical stream dancing past and with woods threatening to engulf the little graveyard, is entrancing.

CURRY RIVEL
St Andrew **
Manorial tombs

Incredible, writes the rector, that so small a village community can have constructed such a magnificent building. Even in its prime, Curry Rivel cannot have merited the superb windows which adorn the south wall of its church. For once a Somerset nave overshadows its tower, rebuilt here by the Victorians in blue lias rather than Ham stone.

The manor was owned in the 13th century by the de Lorty family. In the Wars of the Roses the manor passed to the Lancastrian Beaufort family and the church to the Yorkist canons of Bisham Abbey (Berks). This was Shakespeare's sceptr'd isle 'of inky blots and rotten parchment bonds'. Both the Beaufort portcullis and the Prince of Wales's feathers appear in the frieze over the porch entrance.

Whatever the motives of its builders, Curry Rivel shows a fine face to its village. The porch has a big Perpendicular window to its upstairs parvise and fan vaulting inside. The aisle windows almost fill the wallspace between the buttresses, and are divided into four by the main mullion and a transom, in a design of perfect poise. The interior is unusually open, with tall arcades, an equally tall chancel arch and big east window. The guide records a debate over whether to fill this window with stained glass, thankfully resolved against. The window has some heraldic fragments and a roundel from Canterbury Cathedral. The trees outside are thus drawn into the chancel and made part of its architecture. A similar naturalism prevails in the foliated bench-ends, and in the bosses and cornice carving of the original screens, which survive in both the aisles. These are an unusual design with uprights in two different planes.

The north chapel is a step back in time to the late 13th century. Canopies of diminishing sizes cover battered effigies, probably of de Lortys. The floor has memorial slabs of local families connected with the church after the Reformation, including Speke, Powell and Jennings. It is to Jennings that we owe the oddest monument in Curry Rivel, the Jacobean tomb of Marmaduke Jennings, who died in 1625, and his son Robert, who died five years later. They lie together in prayer wearing not armour but huge boots and jerkins.

DUNSTER
St George ****
Longest screen, cloister garden

The view of Dunster from the coast road is rightly praised. The castle on its rock and the church tower lie against a backdrop of deep green Exmoor combes. The tumbling contours might be those of a Dutch Renaissance painting. Within the town, the church is well hidden behind the swoop of the main high street. It was once part of a Benedictine priory, its red sandstone exterior expressing strength rather than elegance. To the north of the church is the former cloister garden, surely the most delightful church garden in England. It is reached from the north transept or from a side road by the priory dovecote, a secret place filled with summer flowers.

The church's plan is cruciform. Fragments of the Norman priory can be detected on the west face of the crossing arch and in a restored west door. This was the church founded by William de Mohun, courtier of the Conqueror, as a gift to the monks of Bath. He was, he said, 'pricked by the fear of God'. There is no evidence that the great church planned by the monks with this gift ever extended beyond the present crossing.

The rest of the present church is Perpendicular, the divide between the monastic and civic church being the cause of lengthy litigation. The feud, typical of many churches at the end of the Middle Ages, pitted a distant monastic authority and its local agent, the prior, against an increasingly prosperous and assertive town. At one point the townspeople imprisoned the monks in the east end of the church. A settlement in 1498 found largely in favour of the parish.

The church was then split in two, a division clearly visible today. The townspeople constructed a long rood screen across the nave, three bays west of the crossing, to demarcate their own space. By then, they had crammed their own tower on top of the monks' Norman one, and completely surrounded the monastic chancel with aisles, transepts and chapels. They even tied up the bell-ropes so the monks could not sound their services. The screen which the town constructed is one of the finest in the West Country and reputedly the longest in

England – or 'anywhere' hazards the guide. It is of 15 bays and stretches across the entire interior, nave and aisles. A choir can still allegedly perform on top. The bays between this screen and the crossing have choir stalls and candelabra, replacing the choir, which was still occupied by the monks to the east.

Other screens have been reused to divide the chapels. The south transept chapel has part of the original rood screen, of superlative quality. The archway, seen down the south aisle, has a curious double curved arch, apparently the result of a remodelling to enable monks to process side by side. Behind are the monuments to the Luttrells, successors to the Mohuns as lords of Dunster from 1376. The one dedicated to George and Thomas, dating from 1613, is the only case I know of two couples sharing a single composition. Three of the four are recumbent, but George kneels behind his wife, presumably the last alive at the time. On the floor by the east wall is an incised alabaster memorial to Elizabeth Luttrell of 1493.

Dunster's chancel was 'authentically' restored by Street. The church has a fine collection of medieval muniment chests scattered about the aisles. In the tower is a carillon, one of the few examples in England of this delightful instrument.

EAST BRENT

St Mary **

Carolean ceiling, carved bench-ends

This charming church and spire is set into the side of Brent Knoll amid a beautifully tended churchyard. On my visit flowers seemed to be exploding on all sides. The tower is slender for Somerset, its stone severely eroded by the sea wind but crowned by a ribbed spire. Each stage still has its carving, with three tiers of Gothic statuary intact. Though barely visible, they enable East Brent to claim itself as a rare example of a 15th-century tower completely unrestored and in its original appearance.

The interior is approached through a traceried Gothic porch. Its principal treasure is the nave ceiling inserted in 1637, a year after a similar one at Axbridge and presumably by the same hand. It has the same Gothic maze of cusped tracery with pendant bosses in plaster. This was once coloured but has, for some reason, recently been whitewashed over. East Brent, like Brent Knoll, has a north aisle grander both inside and out than the rest of the church. Its flat wooden roof is less spectacular than that of the nave, with angel carvings and giant acanthus bosses.

The church's bench-ends are superb, and include an Annunciation with Gabriel and Mary under tall Gothic canopies, an ox of St Luke richly ornamented and a pelican 'in her piety', feeding her babies in a basket. East Brent's other treasure is a complete 15th-century Passion cycle in the glass in the east window of the north aisle. It is Flemish work, strongly architectural with feathered angels in the tracery bars.

EVERCREECH
St Peter *
Wells group tower, repainted roof

The church is set in the heart of the village opposite a fine old village cross. The tower rests on its laurels as Clifton-Taylor's Somerset favourite, 'a gem ... of exquisite refinement, one of the most perfect in all England'. I would not go that far. The Ham stone is heavily restored. The edges are crisp and the surface rather bare. But Evercreech is a superb example of the Wells group, of the vertical line dominating the horizontal. The west façade has just one thin string course beneath the soaring bell-openings. The entire belfry stage is the same height as the lower stages, a beautifully balanced composition. The eye is led in uninterrupted flow from ground to pinnacles. Nave and aisle parapets are pierced.

The interior is a valiant effort of 1843 to re-create the atmosphere of a Perpendicular interior. At the time, jolly Regency-style galleries were inserted, the chancel restored and the south aisle rebuilt. The most vivid survival is the roof of 1548, restored and recoloured in the 1960s on the basis of paint traces. If this is what a Perpendicular roof looked like, and we have no reason to doubt it, the effect was dazzling. Bright red, blue, white and gold predominate, above fine corbel heads, more Hindu shrine than sedate English nave.

On the outside of the nave is a row of extravagant Victorian gargoyles. They apparently resulted from a quarrel between the stone mason from Wells and the local vicar, the publican and two women. The latter are depicted respectively as a monster, a monkey and two cats.

GLASTONBURY
St John **
Mythical setting, 15th-century glass

Glastonbury in the tourist season is the capital of 'alternative' England. Shops in the High Street seem determined to regress to the dawn of English Christianity, and before. The famous knoll rises over the ruins of the Abbey, with its own tower on top. Until the 19th century, the parish church did not even face on to the street, being divided by a row of houses. In their place now flowers a Glastonbury Thorn, the holy thorn of St Joseph of Arimathaea. As every pupil and tour guide knows, he landed at Glastonbury from the Holy Land, bringing with him the Holy Grail (or cup), with the aim to convert Britain. The spot later became Avalon, burial place of King Arthur, and thus the rootstock of a myriad myths and spells. In their honour, a sprig of the holy thorn is sent by the vicar each year to the Queen.

St John's is first and foremost a tower, another Somerset spectacular and the second tallest in the county. Originally over the crossing, it was rebuilt at the west end after 1403. The design is of the Wells group, with vertical rather than horizontal emphasis. The buttresses and pinnacles are particularly soaring, but stop most emphatically at the crown. This is of such richness that its shafts and pinnacles seem to have been crowded out at the corners, where they stand free as pure ornament. The battlements are two-decked and pierced.

As so often in Somerset, the interior is something of an anticlimax. This is town-church Perpendicular. The roof is plain, albeit with fine bosses. Most of the furnishings were inserted by George Gilbert Scott in the 19th century, including the pulpit, font and chancel roof. Best survivor is the 15th-century glass reassembled in the north chancel window, for once in a coherent pattern. The images include saints and, along the bottom, kneeling donors. The east window of the south transept depicts some of Glastonbury's less fanciful legends.

At the west end of the church are two huge carved modern statues, one of the Virgin, the other of the risen Christ. They are by Ernst Blensdorf, who fled Germany and settled in Somerset in 1933 after the Nazis had destroyed all his work. They are powerful but may not be to every taste.

GOATHURST
St Edward *
Halswell monuments, child with broken flower

The lanes that lead from the 'shore' of the Somerset Levels up on to the Quantocks are among the loveliest in the county. They wind back and forth between high hedges, with sudden views over low moorland to the sea. Against the hillside stand many fine mansions, including the perfect William and Mary cube of Halswell House, its grounds dotted with Grecian follies. At the foot of the estate stands the Halswell family church of Goathurst.

The 14th-century tower is modest by Somerset standards, but with beautiful pierced bell-openings. The interior is initially undistinguished, despite the fine tester to the Jacobean pulpit, ablaze with flames of gold. This dates from 1690 and was lost for some time until recovered in 1910 from the attic of a local farm.

The church's principal treasures commemorate the Halswell, then Tynte families, occupants of the big house into the 20th century. The south transept has an Elizabethan-style plaster ceiling of the Regency period, with a border composed of family shields. On the east wall is a case containing a helmet and armour, traditionally carried at family funerals. Old Bibles and prayer books survive on the big house pew which, though ceded to the church, retains its private door.

The principal tomb is in the north chapel, to Sir Nicholas Halswell (d.1633), with his wife by his side. This is a strong Jacobean work, plain but with effigies with bold faces, attended by six sons and three daughters. Adjacent is a collective memorial to various descendants of Sir Nicholas through his grand-daughter Jane, who married John Tynte. In the corner is a 19th-century monument of little Isabella Kemeys, another family name, who died aged three. By an Italian, Raffaele Monti, it is in the ultra-realist style designed to move the spectator to tears. The child lies on a pillow, a broken flower in her hand. The nave contains two Georgian memorials, by Rysbrack and by Nollekens. In the churchyard are two magnificent Wellingtonias.

HIGH HAM
St Andrew **
Gargoyles, fan-vaulted screen

High Ham sits among woods on a mound above Sedgemoor and the River Cary. The church is an aristocratic building. A Gothic gateway links the churchyard wall to the grounds of the old vicarage. As at Curry Rivel, the tower is less remarkable than the rest of its church. This comprises a chancel rebuilt by the rector John Dyer in 1476, at the same time as the nave was rebuilt by the manorial authority, Glastonbury Abbey, with contributions from local farmers. The work was completed within a year. It is an example of co-operation be-tween lay and clerical patrons at a time when, as at Dunster, conflict was more usual.

The exterior roof is drained by huge gargoyles. They include fiddlers, pipers, trumpeters and a monkey playing with a child. In the niche on the porch is a St Andrew reading a book, an admirable medieval carving. The interior has further carvings. A nave of five bays with shafted piers rises to a roof of chunky angels, apparently singing from songsheets. Some look like High Court judges.

High Ham's glory is its screen, with two tiers of traceried panels. The mullions have slim shafts crowned by fan vaults, with an exquisite foliage frieze. It seems to burst from the bounds of the modest chancel arch. Some original glass is swamped by garish Victorian work.

HUISH EPISCOPI
St Mary ***
Taunton group tower, Burne-Jones window

Huish Episcopi is among the aristocrats of Somerset towers. It beckons across Thorney Moor to its sister tower at Kingsbury, in blue lias with Ham stone dressings. The pattern is of the Taunton group, with horizontal friezes of quatrefoils dividing its stages. The twin openings of the belfry are perforated, as is the single opening of the lower stage. The whole is liberally decorated with pinnacles which project from the pierced and battlemented parapet. Remove each stage and set it on the ground and it would form a perfect Gothic gazebo. The tower was chosen to appear on the 9p stamp in 1972.

Huish has been twice rebuilt. A fire in the 1300s left only the large porch standing, its doorway with zigzag carving still reddened by the heat. The interior is complex in plan, with a north transept and truncated south aisle backing on to the porch. This aisle is intriguing, guarded by two big arches opening to wide Perpendicular windows. Its east window is a superb late work by Burne-Jones, depicting the Adoration of the Magi. Opposite is a little quatrefoil roundel of Christ on the Cross, set into the west wall.

A complete contrast is offered by the north transept, a rare survival of Somerset Decorated Gothic. The north window takes time even for an enthusiast to 'read'. Three lights rise to a head with two trefoils and a final quatrefoil. These trefoils are supposedly contained within circles, but instead permit two mouchettes to penetrate them from the bottom. What can the mason have been seeking to portray? The window marks a mid-point between Geometrical and Reticulated tracery. The nave wagon roof is painted blue, based on medieval paintwork found during restoration. The stencilling is Victorian.

Huish was reputedly the model for Plumstead Episcopi in Trollope's *The Warden*, but since Trollope's cathedral was supposedly Salisbury and Hiram's Hospital supposedly St Cross, Winchester, this is a game any can play. Long may fact and fiction live in such intriguing harmony.

ILMINSTER
St Mary ***
Wadham tomb

This is a minster in more than name. The church stands on a slope in the centre of the town, a collegiate foundation of the second half of the 15th century. It then had four priests and four chantry chapels under the patronage of Sir William Wadham. The college belonged to Wells, and its rebuilding enabled the masons to start afresh, apparently seeking a microcosm of that cathedral. The crossing tower is of the Wells group, in Ham stone, evenly proportioned and vertical, the recessed bell-openings filling the wallspaces with tracery. Nave, chancel and south transept are plain, but not so the north transept. This contains the Wadham Chapel and is in the richest Perpendicular. Windows completely fill the wallspaces between panelled buttresses, creating what amounts to a glasshouse. Wadham died in 1452 and the transept was his bequest.

The view of the interior from the west door is spectacular, but first requires us to run the gauntlet of the 20th and 19th centuries. The west entrance is through metal and glass swing doors into a glazed narthex, called the Cooper Chapel, below a modern gallery and organ loft. The nave roof was raised in 1825 to take side galleries, since removed. At the same time the arcade was remodelled to three exaggerated arches. This destroyed the rhythm of the 15th-century original. In addition to this woe, stained glass filling the aisle windows has completely shut the nave off from the trees and town outside.

Tempers are restored to the east. The chancel is framed by the lofty vault and arches of the crossing, adorned with a forest of shafts. The early 20th-century reredos, for some reason of Caen stone, was garishly coloured in 1954, by what the guide refers to as an 'artist of repute' (unnamed). The north transept is less exciting inside than out, but contains Ilminster's memorial brasses and the superb tomb chest of Wadham himself and his mother. They are in conventional 15th-century garb, without facial character but in a fine Gothic frame. The nodding ogee arches for absent weepers round the base of the tomb are badly bashed.

More remarkable is the brass to Wadham's descendants, Nicholas and Dorothy, founders of Wadham College, Oxford. They died in 1618 and 1609 respectively, and the brasses are unusual both in their late date and in their expressiveness. Though in anachronistic armour, Wadham raises his hand to his wife and she to him, a human gesture rare in this form of art. At the entrance to the transept, an old Jacobean screen has been fashioned into a family pew.

ISLE ABBOTTS
St Mary ****
Taunton group tower, Perpendicular north aisle

Isle Abbotts is the monarch of the Somerset Levels. As Kenneth Wickham puts it, this remote moorland church 'sits like a queen with her court ranged around her in widening circles ... the heart and core of so much beauty'. The tower overlooks a tiny settlement on an isolated mound in the Levels north of Ilminster. It is attended by pretty thatched cottages, and less pretty council houses. The path to the porch runs deep through the vegetation of the churchyard. On my last visit roses and wild flowers were so abundant as almost to prevent access.

Ham stone did not come cheap. Like many churches Isle Abbotts used it only for decorating its tower, the structure itself being built of blue lias. The contrast between the two is softened by a patina of lichen. The tower is less ornate than Huish and Kingsbury Episcopi nearby, and virtually identical to the earlier Bishop's Lydeard and Kingston St Mary. Wickham attributes it to the same designer or group of designers, variously called the Quantock or Taunton group.

The tower's three stages are distinct, with each stage framing windows and niches. Buttress pinnacles cling close to the tower, pushing it upwards like rockets. The rhythm of fenestration, the pierced battlements and the delicacy of the crown render the structure light, almost floating. No fewer than ten of the tower's original statues survived the iconoclasts. The carving is as fine as the St Andrew at High Ham. The Virgin has flowing hair. The resurrected Christ rises from the tomb with figures tumbling beneath Him. The hunky punks on the tower summit are superb, including a man blowing a bagpipe.

This Somerset church has a body worthy of its head. A walk round the north side reveals an aisle probably added some forty years after the completion of the tower, by that generous patron of late Gothic chapels, Lady Margaret Beaufort. The south side of the church and the chancel are a complete contrast to the north side. They survive from the previous church of *c.*1300 and have grouped and stepped lancets, and windows with Bar tracery.

This contrast is reflected inside. The south wall is solid and heavy and the eye is immediately led across the nave to the glorious four-bay north arcade. Its piers have capitals of foliage and the character of a theatrical proscenium, framing the chapel beyond. On its stage, the actors are beams of sunlight, playing across the warm stone.

The chancel is no anticlimax. It is watched over by a high pulpit and squint punched through the old rood staircase. The piscina has a carved surround. The Norman font has flowers and monsters around its side. Most of the remaining furnishings, including screens, pulpit, benches and heavy studded door, are original. So are the graffiti in the porch which, says the guide, are 'such as are found in Pompeii and Rome'.

KINGSBURY EPISCOPI

St Martin **

Taunton group tower

Kingsbury stands out across the surrounding Somerset Levels, its pinnacled crown peering over clumps of trees, rich but solid. It must have been a beacon in times of flood, protecting its village on the moor with a company of trees. The tower is of the Taunton family, similar to its sister at Huish, but is more lavish, being entirely of Ham stone. The tower has quatrefoil bands and little detached pinnacles on the corners of the crown. In the niches are figures of the donors, the Lambroc and Radbord families. The rest of the church is of blue lias.

The interior of Kingsbury's tower fits the majesty of its exterior. Not one but two panelled tower arches, one framing the other, rise to an immense height, with behind them a fan vault supporting the bell-chamber. The outer archway has buttresses decorated by two tiers of niches, with crockets crawling like monsters up their pinnacles. The rest of the nave is a much-restored work dating from an earlier 14th-century church, lacklustre compared with the lavish innovations of Somerset Perpendicular.

Perpendicular reappears in the chancel and transepts, indeed the entire east end is a virtual greenhouse. So huge are the windows as to leave little room for wall and plenty of scope for trees and sky to join the celebration within. The tops of the windows survived a visitation from Cromwell's troops. The glass has more interest than most such fragments, including Gothic architecture, faces and angels.

KINGSTON ST MARY
**

Tower hunky punks, carved bench-ends

Kingston is not the tallest or the richest or, in its lower stages, the most composed Somerset tower. Yet it rises over its red stone and whitewashed village on the slopes of the Quantocks with classic dignity. Here the Ham stone dresses not the customary blue lias but local sandstone.

The tower shows the familiar Quantock features. Buttresses rise to enriched second and third stages, where pinnacled niches rest on angels' wings and pierced Somerset tracery softens the sound of bells. The stair turret ends in an octagonal crown with more pinnacles and a weathercock. The crown is surrounded with hunky punks, one on the west side identified by Peter Poyntz Wright as a woman in labour, a huge baby emerging from between her legs. Another is of St Michael and another of a 'lion dog'. The tower design is attributed by Kenneth Wickham to the same architect as Isle Abbotts. Since Kingston is later (c.1490) he grants this the accolade as 'the perfected model'. It was also one of Clifton-Taylor's top three Somerset towers. On a sunny evening the Ham stone seems to grasp at the light and turn it a rich gold, while the sandstone glows red as background.

The porch, contemporary with the tower and fan vaulted, is guarded by a gargoyle of a monkey and a hawk. The interior is a surprise. The citizens of

Kingston may have lavished money on their tower but sudden poverty seized them on the inside. The nave is Early Gothic with a plastered wagon roof. The barest of arches interrupts the roof line through to the chancel. Yet disappointment is allayed by Kingston's second marvel, a complete set of 16th-century benches with carved ends. These include hands holding rosary beads, a Tree of Life, variations on a Reticulated tracery theme and a splendid panel of oxen and yokes. They are lit in the evening by an 18th-century brass chandelier.

At the end of the south aisle lies the tomb chest of John de la Warre, who fought at Poitiers and whose family occupied adjacent Hestercombe House from the 14th to the late 19th century. The house is now the Fire Brigade headquarters but has a Gertrude Jekyll garden open to the public. While the church has not benefited from firemen's patronage, it might hope for special attention should it catch fire. At the back of the church near the tower are some fine churchwardens' plaques.

LEIGH-UPON-MENDIP
St Giles *
Elongated tower, panelled roof

Leigh is pronounced Lie. The church tower is supreme in the north-east of the county, a rival to Chewton and Mells and one of Clifton-Taylor's three best in Somerset. A speciality of Leigh is that its fourth stage is marginally taller than the third, lengthening the beat on the way to the crown. This defining feature of the Wells group of towers gives them a verticality that renders any spire unnecessary. The crown itself is exceptionally tall, the pinnacles drawing the eye towards the sky.

The interior is almost an afterthought and is much restored. The nave walls have been scraped and the naked stones repointed with crude cement. The work looks like a botched barn rebuilding job. This is sad, since the stone dressings to the windows, the wall memorials and corbel carvings are excellent and deserve to be offset against limewashed walls, as they would have been originally. At least the glass is mostly clear, allowing the sun to illumine the excellent furnishings, including original pews and bench-ends.

Leigh has an excellent Somerset roof, its panels and bosses a small-scale version of Martock. The beams are heavy and richly carved with fleurons and angels.

LONG SUTTON
Holy Trinity **
Restored Perpendicular pulpit and screen

Long Sutton is inland of the Somerset Levels, where sumptuous churches are thick on the ground. Holy Trinity lies in a rambling churchyard on an eminence with views east to the hills whence came its stone. On the exterior, blue lias contrasts boldly with Ham. Inside the porch is a small Gothic niche of the purest Ham, in which we can see freshly restored the stone's characteristics. Here in the striations can be detected ochre, orange, gold and milk-white, the layers set with tiny grains of sand and shell. I recommend a magnifying glass.

The interior is bright and colourful, spoiled only by the scraping of the walls and their repointing with mortar. Long Sutton has restored woodwork, a pulpit and screen in the brightest of Gothic colours. Both are in red and green picked out with gold. The pulpit on a wine-glass stem has 12 (new) apostles under tiny nodding ogee canopies. The screen, though simple in design, runs across the chancel and aisles and forms a blaze of colour between the deep gold Ham piers. There is an owl in the vine above the central arch. Such owls were sometimes carved on to screens to scare away bats.

The nave roof is open and tie-beamed, but the chancel is ceiled, the two forming a contrast in roofing style. I normally prefer the latter, since this is what the medieval carpenters usually intended. They also preferred their walls plastered with lime rather than exposed stone. The piscina and sedilia are again of Ham, completing a feast of this delicious material.

LULLINGTON
All Saints **
Norman carvings

The estate village of the Duckworths of Orchardleigh seems lost amid the high-hedged lanes of north Somerset. A small green and an old pump mark its 'downtown'. On rising ground beyond stands a structure on which opinions are mixed. Pevsner calls Lullington 'perhaps the most enjoyable Norman village church in Somerset', but Kenneth Wickham castigates it as spoiled by 'the lavish care of an over-zealous squire', with Victorian tiles, pews and glass.

Both are right. Here, as so often elsewhere, the Victorians confronted a church that over the centuries had become a damp, tumbledown, eroded ruin, which they had to restore to meet competition from warm modern chapels. They clearly sought to preserve the remarkable Norman work amid the re-building. Time has mellowed the Victorian imports and stabilised the Norman carvings for another millennium. These carvings are in the north and south doorways, the crossing arches and the font. The south doorway is simple, but the north is spectacular, a complex composition of one spiral and one zigzag shaft rising to beakhead and zigzag arches. These enclose a tympanum of two animals apparently eating from the Tree of Life, while Christ in Majesty sits above under an elongated arch.

Inside, the tower and chancel arches are equally exciting, including carvings of a Green Man, a double-bodied, single-headed ox and a winged lion. The Norman font at the rear of the church also dates from the foundation of the church and is one of the finest in Somerset. It has the customary intersecting arches round the bottom, then a band of flowers, an inscription and a row of monsters round the brim. The Latin inscription translates as 'Sins vanish in the sacred water of this font.' Lullington is a serene spot, its churchyard giving on to orchards and fields in all directions.

MARTOCK
All Saints ***
Carved roof, old fives court

The town used to be called Martock inter Aquas, rising on its mound over the waters of the Somerset Levels. Later the town specialised in glovemaking, and today straggles out along its approach roads. There is no confusion in the centre, which comprises a lovely group of 17th- and 18th-century townhouses with medieval cottages round the church. Martock church is essentially a roof. Whether the carvers of Martock were the same as those of Somerton, or were rivals, we cannot know. Between them they created two masterpieces of English woodwork.

The former church on the site was owned by Mont St Michel in France. It survives in the Early Gothic chancel, with its five-lancet east window. The chancel was the responsibility of the Treasurer of Wells Cathedral, clearly a man of economy. When the central tower was demolished in the 15th century, he did not share the generosity of the ubiquitous Beauforts in rebuilding the nave and west tower.

Martock is one of the few churches in the county not just dressed with Ham stone but entirely built of it. Its soft texture but clean lines are best shown in the quatrefoil piercing of the battlements. Against the nave north wall is a rare item of social history, a disused fives court formed of the old buttresses. The south porch has a star vault with bosses and contains a Decorated niche from an earlier wall.

The interior is among the finest late-Perpendicular works in Somerset. The tower is supported by two panelled arches and two tiers of statue niches, the lower ones now with wooden statues. The nave arcades are beautifully composed, of sweeping arches with minute capitals and traceried spandrels. But all eyes turn upwards. The roof beams seem to take the weight effortlessly from the walls, with a row of vacant niches dividing the clerestory windows. These niches are extraordinary. Each one has a mini-vault and canopy, each one different. Whether they ever carried statues is not known, but the back wall of each now has a figure of an apostle painted on to it.

The roof is in the form of two sloping quilts on either side of a row of king-posts to the central ridge. There are 128 carved panels to each of the six bays. These panels are of a variety of pierced designs. Those who might tire of the flocks of angels that fill the roofs of East Anglian churches will find ceaseless delight in these patterns. The work in rich oak was completed in 1513 and has never been bettered.

MELLS
St Andrew ***
Fan-vaulted porch, Edwardian memorials

Mells offers a feast of views. From a distance the flag weathervanes on the tower seem to flutter over its cluster of trees like pennants on a castle keep. Close to, the same pinnacles join with those of the porch to offset the severe Tudor gables on the adjacent manor. The manor was that of the Horner family, acquired from the Abbots of Glastonbury after the Dissolution. It included rich mineral workings, sometimes wrongly thought to be the 'plum' that 'Jack Horner' pulled out of his Christmas pie. At the end of the 19th century, a later generation of Horners brought an artistic flowering to Mells, adorning village and church with works by Burne-Jones, Lutyens, Eric Gill and Alfred Munnings. The estate passed by marriage to the Asquith family, who converted to Catholicism. Ronald Knox lived at Mells from 1948. Today the manor, still in Asquith hands, is secluded from the churchyard behind high walls.

The church is reached down a rare thing in England, a planned medieval street contemporary with the 15th-century rebuilding of the church. The tower is a Somerset 'four-decker', culminating in a fine crown. Since the lower stages are relatively plain, the tower is best viewed from the south-east, with the highly decorated porch in the foreground. This porch is a superb creation. An ogee canopy to the doorway rises past an upper window to a giant concave-sided gable. This has as its apex an empty saint's niche. If only the Horners could have encouraged Gill to fill it. The porch contains a superb fan vault.

The interior is not as spectacular as the exterior, but is blessed with much late-Victorian and Edwardian art. Under the tower are memorials displaying work by Burne-Jones, Lutyens and Gill. In the north chapel is Munnings's equestrian statue of Edward Horner, who died in the Great War, on a plinth by

Lutyens. Looking down on it is William Nicholson's stained glass window of St Francis, more pleasing than most of this period. The church is littered with curious fragments of Jacobean benches, mostly used as wall panels.

The churchyard has a handsome clipped yew walk, leading to a curiously shaped stile. Round it are the graves of many of the Horner–Asquith set, including Ronald Knox, Siegfried Sassoon and Lady Violet Bonham Carter. The gravestones include some by Lutyens and Gill.

MUCHELNEY
St Peter and St Paul *
Bare-bosomed angels

The 'great island' of Muchelney was host to one of the largest monastic houses of the Somerset Levels. Today the abbey ruins lie spread out dramatically across the fields and are open to the public. Such places in the Middle Ages attracted pilgrims, dignitaries and royal officials, but also a horde of vexatious tenants, vagrants, beggars, thieves and carriers of deadly diseases. As the parish clergy kept the laity outside their chancels, so monks sought to keep unwelcome visitors outside the walls of their monasteries. Hence the many churches 'ad portas', for the comers and goers whom monasteries did not admit to their own churches within their walls.

This building is mostly a reconstruction of the 15th century. The tower is meagre and there are battlements only on the entrance side of the church, away from the abbey. The Ham stone interior is a friendly space. At the time of its building, the abbots appear to have felt the need for some ostentation, to improve relations with the surrounding community. A sign of this is the panelled arches not just to the tower but to the transepts as well. The tower has an excellent fan vault with bosses. In the chancel are battered sedilia with medieval tiles set into the floor.

None of this might be worth a detour were it not for a ceiling that has nothing to do with the abbey. Some time in the early 17th century the entire wagon roof was painted with blue panels, each containing its own angel, full face and scantily clad. Some of these are bare breasted, forming the only 'topless' ceiling in England. A celestial beauty contest appears to be in progress, crude, colourful and great fun. Above the south vestry is an old barrel-organ of 1840 that runs to 25 hymn tunes and 3 chants. In the centre of the nave aisle is a bold octagonal font, with detached shafts at its corners.

NORTH CADBURY
St Michael **
Symmetrical aisles, bench-ends of domestic life

North Cadbury is a mile from the torrent of the A303, but might be a hundred miles. With the adjacent North Cadbury Court it forms an immaculate composition of avenue, trees, grey stone mansion and wide churchyard. This is no accident. The church was the creation of a wealthy Plantagenet lady, Elizabeth Botreaux, in 1420. Her intention was to found a college of seven secular priests, licensed in 1423. For some reason Botreaux's priests never appeared and Cadbury did not become a college. A century and a half later, Sir Francis Hastings rebuilt the old house. The church remains a church, but clearly designed with a medieval college in mind.

The entrance is from the drive to the main house, whose stable wall forms one side of the churchyard. The other side offers a view west over the Somerset Levels. Most unusual for a Gothic church, north and south elevations are identical, offering two sweeps of Perpendicular windows broken by two-storey porches, each set into an aisle. The porches have ogee doorways surrounded by panelling, rising to a saint's niche. Behind are stair-turrets capped by cones similar to that on the tower. I can think of no other instance of such symmetry.

As with many collegiate foundations, the chancel was designed to be grander than the nave. Inside, a large east window is flanked by tall niches for saints' statues, with three windows on north and south walls set high enough to take collegiate stalls. Some of these are now in the aisle; others are in Exeter Museum, which is a pity. The reredos is Gothic with ferocious cusping and colouring.

The pride of the nave is its bench-ends. These are among the most intriguing in the county, since they include not only biblical and mythical scenes, but vivid portraits of individuals. We have a merchant, a labourer, a cleric and two men apparently in the course of an argument, nose to nose. These works seem full of incident and made by carvers intrigued by human physiognomy. To this extent they are Renaissance rather than Gothic. The Virgin and Child might be any harassed mother. St Margaret stands over her dragon which is still vomiting out her garment. Under the tower is a battered tomb chest, with effigies and weeping angels on the sides. The lady is assumed to be Lady Botreaux, with a horned headdress and her feet resting on dogs, symbols of fidelity.

NORTH PETHERTON
St Mary *
Somerset tower tracery, Kempe window

The church lies close to the M5 in flat country near Bridgwater. It has a tower of *c.*1500 as celebrated as any in the county, much copied by admirers as far afield as Probus (Cornwall). The church was a Knights Hospitaller foundation and two realistic effigies of a St John Ambulance man and woman stare down from the tower gallery, an alarming sight if you are in the church alone on a dark evening.

The church is approached from the road across a churchyard converted into a lawn. It retains a fine cross from the time of the church's construction in the late 15th century. Nave and chancel are in eroded Ham stone; the tower is of blue lias, with Ham dressings and crown. The latter is an outstanding work, with a single window in the second stage and a double opening in the bell-stage, surrounded by panelling and pinnacles. All openings have the most lovely Somerset tracery. A fragment of a Pietà remains in one of the statue niches.

The interior has been modernised, though with 20th-century deference rather than Victorian ruthlessness. The woodwork is of *c.*1910 but the bench-ends incorporate old panels. Fragments of the original screen are built into the south gallery. The church has a good Kempe window in the south chapel. The subject is the visit of the Wise Men, amid lush vegetation and with a gathering of angels on a blue background above. Pevsner claims it as one of Kempe's best works, though I could not find his wheatsheaf signature. The church was a stronghold of the Tractarians in the 19th century and remains in that tradition. The guide gives a highly partisan account of British Church history, depicting the Reformation as an unmitigated disaster.

NORTON SUB HAMDON
St Mary **
Arts and Crafts furnishings

Under the lee of Ham Hill is a church that might be a shrine to its famous stone. I came upon Norton early on a summer evening with the sun moving down over the Somerset Levels to the west. As daylight turned to gloaming, the walls changed from biscuit-brown to a strange pink-ochre, then to the 'rose-red' of the poet's Petra. A dovecote guards the entrance to the churchyard, its birds signifying the peace of the place.

The church stands alone against a backdrop of hill and trees, its tower rising to a crown with 16 pinnacles. The tall bell-openings have pretty Somerset tracery. Inside, the tower arch rises the full height of the nave, complementing a wagon roof that carries the eye in a continuous sweep into the chancel. There is no clerestory. The space is warmed by the softness of the stone and peopled with angels and carved bosses. On the other hand, almost all the glass is either stained or opaque, so on a sunny day the interior might be under water.

An unusual late Victorian iron pulpit is clearly by the same hand as the equally rare iron chancel screen. Other screens of stone divide the aisles from the small side chapels. The font of 1904 is by the Arts and Crafts craftsman, Henry Wilson. It is of alabaster on a base of four giant fishes, and might have come from a Roman bath. Also by Wilson is the bold oak screen under the tower arch.

OARE

St Mary *

Moorland setting, Doone legend

We have it on good (fictional) authority that at these altar steps Lorna was shot dead by Carver Doone. From here her groom, John Ridd, rode out on to Black Barrow Down to seek his revenge.

Ever since, Oare has held the magic of that moment in R. D. Blackmore's novel, while Exmoor has carried the curse of the Doones. No amount of scholarly research has revealed any real Doones or Ridds, but these were wild hills at the end of the Civil War, of bandits, smugglers and outlaws. Blackmore was son of a local rector and recorded his visits to the parish in the early 19th century. In his novel he used real places, if not real people's names, thus adding to the verisimilitude of his writing, and intriguing his many enthusiasts.

The church, much restored outside, lies in a fold of the moor, some two miles from the sea. A great bank of heather rises across a valley of oak, pine and gorse, deep purple in autumn. It is at such seasons that Exmoor offers a passable version of paradise.

The building consists of three cells, the chancel having been extended in the 19th century, thus further vexing Doone addicts, who must work out where the 17th-century Lorna would 'really' have been standing when shot. There are no aisles or chapels. The choir is separated from the nave by an unusual wooden chancel arch decorated with large rosettes.

Oare has a full complement of Commandments boards scattered round its walls. There are 18th-century box pews and a pulpit. Next to the pulpit is a large fleur-de-lis commemorating a visit by the Prince of Wales in 1863 to hunt on Exmoor. On the north wall of the nave is a row of memorials to members of the Snow and Spure families, in admirably clear English lettering. The memorial to Nicholas Snow (d.1914) speaks of 'an upright man greatly skilled in wood-craft who served his generation for many years as Justice of the Peace, master of hounds and church warden of this parish'. Next to the door is a relief of Blackmore himself. The inscription reads suitably: 'Insight and humour, and the rythmic roll, / Of antique lore, his fertile fancies sway'd, / And with their various eloquence array'd / His sterling English, pure and clean and whole.'

QUEEN CAMEL
St Barnabas **
Medieval bestiary roof

There was no camel, only a manor owned by successive queens of England on the River Cam, a tributary of the Yeo. The church was built by the monks of Cleeve. After the Reformation the manor was given by Mary I to her chancellor, Sir Walter Mildmay, and the family held it into the 20th century. The church stands at the end of the village street, which forms a guard of honour to the west tower. The old village was burned down on St Barnabas Eve in 1639, allegedly by gypsies in revenge for some slight.

The tower is unique in Somerset in having five stages. While not as rich as many – it was built early, *c*.1380 – the buttressed stair turret finely balances the Perpendicular nave and aisles. A modern statue of St Barnabas stands in the west wall niche. The tower is of Ham dressing blue lias, welcoming us to an interior wonderfully rich in medieval carving.

The early Perpendicular nave is of four bays, the north aisle piers having friezes for capitals. The screen is superb, composed of intricate bays, each with six lights crowned by a deep cornice over ribbed coving. This ostentatious work survived the Reformation, during which it was never dismantled, as is proved by the evidence of paint covering the nail heads. Next to it is a pulpit of similar date, *c*.1500, with nodding ogee niches.

The roofs were commissioned by the monks of Cleeve in imitation of the ceiling of their own refectory, with characters from a medieval bestiary. The 35 bosses in the chancel form a magnificent collection. Two monsters, brightly repainted, gaze down over the screen into the nave, while behind them is a menagerie. Each beast is a metaphor for a liturgical incident: the unicorn is the Nativity, the phoenix the Resurrection, the eagle the Ascension. There is also a camel, a tiger, a hyena, a pelican, a siren and a rare merman. The nave roof is more restrained.

The Victorian eagle lectern rises above a pile of rocks. It was carved from the wood of Edinburgh Castle's drawbridge.

SELWORTHY
All Saints ***
Painted aisle roof, leather reredos

High on the slopes of Selworthy Beacon the limewashed outline of All Saints is visible across the valley of the Holnicote estate from Dunkery on Exmoor. The church overlooks its picture-book village of yellow estate cottages, roses and thatch, with woods of pine and beech rising directly behind. This is a place to be savoured in various climates. In summer it might be in the Italian lakes, in winter the Alps, but in spring, with rainclouds racing in from the Bristol Channel, this could be only in Somerset.

The estate belonged to the Steynings at the time of the church's rebuilding in the early 16th century. Since the 18th century it has been held by Aclands. It was an Acland who, in 1810, constructed the small model settlement known as the Green, directly beneath the church, and Aclands still live in these parts.

The church's principal treasure is the south aisle and its glorious wagon roof, built by the Steynings in the 1530s during an outburst of patronage immediately before the Reformation. The ceiling is white and blue, decorated with angels and bosses carved with the symbols of Christ's Passion. The aisle beneath contains memorials to the Steynings (with various spellings), while Aclands are more modestly commemorated in two memorials by Francis Chantrey against the west wall. Both record deaths in Africa. In the 19th century the Aclands altered the porch, opening the upper storey towards the body of the church, and so created a handsome family pew for themselves.

After the south aisle, the rest of the interior finds it hard to hold its own. A bold classical west gallery contains the organ. The pulpit has Tudor panelling, hour glass and tester above. Most remarkable is the reredos, a Pre-Raphaelite work of 1900 in coloured leather, apparently by a Porlock artist, Philip Burgess.

SHEPTON MALLET
St Peter and St Paul ***
350-panel wagon roof, stone pulpit

Shepton Mallet is a market town on an eastern limb of the Mendips. Its church is a Saxon foundation, with the original Saxon walls forming the core of the present nave. Norman expansion brought aisles with massive arcade piers, creating space sufficient for the needs of the town until the late Middle Ages. The tower was built *c.*1380. Today it rises above the lanes to the east of the market, its unfinished steeple crudely truncated. The exterior carries a zoo of huge gargoyles.

The church interior is dominated by the tall, narrow proportions of the nave and chancel, a Norman space within a Perpendicular auditorium. This narrowness contributes to the impact of Shepton's masterpiece, the wagon roof built in the second half of the 15th century. While the generality of Somerset roofs are not the equal of East Anglia's, those at Martock, Somerton and Shepton are supreme. Shepton's is set high above a Perpendicular clerestory, narrow and immensely long.

The roof consists of 350 small panels, and almost as many bosses. The panels are painted with traceried patterns, each apparently a different design. The large bosses are intricately carved in high relief. A squadron of 18 angels spread their wings in support, attended by reinforcements on the wallplates. Unlike most such roofs, the visible members do not uphold the roof but are nailed to it. The result is a superb vista towards the chancel, an oaken quilt spread out above the rude piers below. I am told that one of the bosses is a Green Man with plants emerging from his eyes as well as his mouth.

No less celebrated is Shepton's stone pulpit of *c.*1530, carved from a single block and decorated with classical as well as Gothic motifs. The tower entrance is adorned with a fine collection of 17th- and 18th-century memorials.

SOMERTON
St Michael ***
Monster roof carvings

The white limestone village sits on an eminence over the River Cary and Sedgemoor. Terraced cottages are long and low, and the high street opens to a village square with a market cross and town hall. This was briefly the county town from the mid-13th to the mid-14th centuries, leading to extensive rebuilding of the church in the Decorated style, earlier than most Somerset churches. Across a spacious churchyard rises an octagonal tower of grey stone with Ham dressings. Within is a majestic work of English craftsmanship, the Somerton roof.

The church is cruciform and has windows from all periods. One in the north transept, only visible outside, is enriched with Y-tracery and further enriched with ogival cusping, a lovely work of early Decorated art. The aisle windows mostly have Reticulated tracery, but the big west window has flowing curvilinear. All this must have been in place when, in *c.*1500, a new roof was prepared by the carpenters of Muchelney Abbey. Its angels hold the arms of the Speke family of Whitelackington, who may have donated the oak.

The roof is supported on tie-beams with short king-posts. The panels are deeply coffered, 640 in all, filled with quatrefoils. The tie-beams are carved with vine trails and the faces of men and angels. Fastened to an east–west purlin on the north side of the roof is a foot-long cider barrel, either carved deliberately with its bunghole pointing down, or left by the original joiner and kept ever since to amuse visitors. On the rafters are Wessex wyverns. These are small at the west end but grow in size as the chancel is approached, until the last pair are giant monsters gnashing their teeth at each other across the king-post. The Book of Revelation tells how 'Michael and his Angels fought against the dragon'. With a cold wind outside and candlelight flickering from the rood, these beasts must have been fearsome.

The bench-ends are vigorous Perpendicular survivals retained on the Victorian benches. The pulpit, communion table and reredos with carved figures are all Jacobean. On the chandelier roundels are inscriptions, 'To God's Glory & the Honor of the Church of England, 1782'. Betjeman claimed that these lines inspired his celebrated *Collins Pocket Guide to England's Parish Churches*.

STOGUMBER
St Mary ***
Sydenham Chapel, 'Morris' chancel

Only the Welsh Marches can rival the charm of the vale that divides the Quantocks from Exmoor. In its midst, the village of Stogumber seems to retire even further from view. Whitewashed cottages, thatched or slated, surround a tranquil churchyard. The view of the church from the south is dominated by its large sandstone gargoyles, by Tudor windows and by the outline of the Sydenham Chapel. From the north, the church is more enclosed. The crumbling tower rises behind a façade encrusted with buttresses, pinnacles, gargoyles and battlements.

The interior is full of light and colour. The arcade bays are a mix of styles with the piers growing wayward as they approach the chancel, many of them richly shafted and with foliage capitals. At the chancel the piers are so thick as to embrace smaller arches, which once would have accommodated an Easter Sepulchre or a founder's tomb. Against the wall of the final arch is a Green Man spouting vegetation. It is all most jolly.

The chancel itself is a surprise. Edward Jones, the vicar from 1871 to 1907, was a keen follower of William Morris and set about repainting the rafters, walls and corbels of his chancel in the Morris style. The result has panache. The walls are covered in rosettes, fruit and tendrils and would pass muster in any Sanderson's catalogue.

To the south lies the 15th-century Sydenham Chapel. It is not part of the church but a proprietary chapel of the family, divided off with an iron screen and with a higher roof than the rest of the church. Between chapel and chancel, as if wanting the best of both afterworlds, is the monumental tomb of Sir George Sydenham (spelt Sidnum) of *c.*1597, with six free-standing Corinthian columns on the chancel side. His two wives are uncomfortably tucked in beside him, his children crammed against the wall at his feet. The design is odd, with two coffered arches supported by a central pier, detaching body from legs like a magician's dummy. One of the children married Francis Drake.

The stone pulpit is Perpendicular, and the pews and bench-ends are original. On a wall at the back of the nave is a plaque to Thomas Rich, its stone frame beautifully carved to look like oak. Most of the nave windows have clear glass, with charming views of village roofs and trees outside.

STOGURSEY
St Andrew ***
Norman crossing and chancel, Verney tombs

Stogursey stands on a plain in the shadow of the Quantocks, yet the church might be in Normandy. It was founded by the Norman Falaise family, later de Courcy, and the church name is a corruption of Stoke Curci. The family granted the land to the monks of Lonlay in Normandy, who built the church *c.*1100. It was seized by Henry V during the French wars in 1414 and granted by Henry VI to Eton College. The village has recently been 're-twinned' with Lonlay and thus the Hundred Years War is finally at an end. When I last visited it, the church was *en fête*, with flags flying and a crafts fair filling pews and chapels.

The church is an ambitious cruciform structure with a crossing tower. The exterior has been prettily plastered, cream with stone dressings, and boasts a rare Somerset spire on its tower. The interior vividly demonstrates the divergent patronage of nave and chancel. While the townspeople rebuilt 'their' nave in the 15th century, the patrons of the chancel, Eton, saw no need for such expense and left the crossing, transepts and aisled chancel in their Norman state. The Norman font is girded by a stone rope, with primitive faces peering out from its sides.

Today we are thankful for Eton's meanness. Stogursey's early 12th-century crossing has four great piers with eight responds supporting mighty arches. The eight capitals are all different. Some evoke Roman, Corinthian or Ionic, some are of human heads or doves. They appear to have escaped scraping or retooling and are wonderful survivals of the earliest period of Norman architecture in England. The two-bay aisled chancel is mostly later, having been extended at the end of the 12th century. It has cylindrical piers with scalloped capitals and heavy dogtooth carvings. In the floor can be made out the semicircular foundation of the earlier apse, repeated in both of the side chapels. The present sanctuary is mostly neo-Norman of 1865, with a reredos of precious stones and saints in roundels.

The south chapel is dedicated to the Verney family of Fairfield. William de Verney (d.1333) lies in an ancient but battered tomb, holding his heart. The tomb of John (d.1472) has niches and weepers in good condition. Other memorials display the evolving styles of 17th- and 18th-century funerary art, beautifully set against white walls.

STOKE PERO
*

Wild Exmoor setting

The poor church does not even merit a dedication. Its settlement lies in a fold of Exmoor where Dunkery Beacon drops suddenly towards Porlock and is reached by a lane between steep heathery banks. Local people were said to have high-pitched voices from having to shout to each other across the combe. The parish had ten farms at the time of Domesday; only one survives. Three parsons in succession perished during the Black Death. Not surprisingly, Stoke Pero was an unpopular living and was often left in the charge of a curate. The parsonage had vanished by 1790.

As so often, the Victorians took matters in hand. In 1897 the lord of the manor, Sir Thomas Acland, rebuilt the church completely, leaving only the huge Norman tower arch, two wooden uprights in the porch and windows on the north wall. Yet this is enough to give Stoke Pero an aura of continuity. Quaint neo-Tudor windows decorate the south wall while the barrel roof holds the arms of the Acland family.

Inside, there are simple benches, some at the back surviving from before the restoration. The pulpit also appears old, with an unusual misericord on which the preacher may rest his knees rather than his bottom. A harmonium sits in the chancel, with candleholders. There is no electricity.

The place may have been poor but it was not ungenerous. Records of 1912 include a letter to the parishioners from the Lord Mayor of London, thanking them for 6s 3d raised for the survivors of the *Titanic*.

STOKE SUB HAMDON
St Mary **
Norman tympanum, 20th-century window

The village of Stoke lies beneath Ham Hill, looking over the rolling moor towards the Blackdown and Mendip Hills. A mile east of the village and set back from the road is one of Somerset's oldest churches, of Ham stone encrusted with lichen. It has a Norman nave and chancel with a 13th-century tower. The slope rises directly behind the churchyard, as if about to engulf it.

The Gothic tower is attached to the north side of the nave and greets us like a face: two lancet bell-openings for eyes, a slit window for a nose and a snarling Perpendicular window for a down-turned mouth below. To the left are more ghosts, the primitive faces of the Norman corbel-table above the chancel wall. Indeed the exterior is dotted with interesting Norman carvings and blocked openings.

Inside the porch a tympanum depicts Sagittarius shooting an arrow at Leo across a Tree of Life. This tree is filled with doves and a Lamb of God. Depending on source, this is meant to be summer shooting winter, good shooting evil, Christ shooting the Devil while mankind looks on from the tree, or perhaps King Stephen shooting Leo, the emblem of Geoffrey of Anjou, whom he had just deposed. It is a delightful design, in appearance as much Eric Gill as Romanesque.

The central feature of the interior is the Norman chancel arch. It has three orders with nailhead, zigzag and billet mouldings, and supports with decorated shafts. The transepts are divided from the crossing by Transitional arches. The crossing is vaulted with corbels of lovely trumpet shapes, deeply carved in scrolls and swirls. The north transept, gloomy with glass, has the longest squint I have seen, like a tunnel cut through rock.

The chancel is brighter. Above the overpowering 20th-century reredos rises a modern memorial window depicting scenes from life in the postwar parish. These include potato farming, glovemaking and quarrying Ham stone. Next door is the Strode monument of 1595, portraying an old man stretched uncomfortably beneath an arched recess as if told to lie still by the undertaker.

SWELL
St Catherine *
Farmyard setting

This is not a great Somerset church, more a place for quiet contemplation. A lane leads down to the Fivehead River from the Curry Rivel road, reaching a medieval hall opposite a grove of poplars. This must once have been the shore of the Somerset Levels flood plain. The church is to the left past the farmyard, sitting tranquil in its enclosure.

The building is little more than a chapel, comprehensively rebuilt in the 1450s with plaster walls and Ham stone dressings. It has no tower, aisles or chapel, merely two cells of equal height. Yet Swell is full of incident: a Norman door thick with zigzag, a Norman font, Perpendicular windows, a panelled chancel arch, a Jacobean-style pulpit and a Laudian altar. The pews are of gnarled elm. An old medieval bell rests its tired drum on the nave floor.

By the visitors' book is a simple appeal, undated but apparently index-linked:

If aught thou hast to give or lend,
This ancient parish church befriend.
If poor but still in spirit willing
Out with thy purse and give a shilling,
But if its depths should be profound
Think of God and give a pound.

TAUNTON
St Mary Magdalene ***
Biggest Somerset tower, giant nave

St Mary, Taunton, has the noblest parish tower in England. It may not appeal to those who prefer the verticality of the Wells group of towers, but for height, grandeur and richness of ornament it is without equal. The approach from the west down Hammet Street is particularly happy, with Georgian terraces symmetrically designed with the tower as a climax. The view from the railway has it aligned with the earlier tower of St James's in a superb townscape composition.

That said, St Mary's tower was so decayed in the 19th century as to require complete rebuilding in 1858–62. It thus shares with St Mark's campanile in Venice and Cologne Cathedral the characteristic of not being the same age archaeologically as it is stylistically. But the rebuilding, by Benjamin Ferrey and George Gilbert Scott, was faithful, even reinstalling the old sculptures. The height is 163 ft, the highest in Somerset. Two stones were employed, red Quantock for the walls and Ham for the dressings. Above the west entrance and nave window are three stages with two perforated openings each, separated by friezes of quatrefoils. In most towers the top tier is the shortest; here it is the longest and panelled. The pierced corner turrets, pinnacles and battlements are so developed as to constitute almost another stage, a coronet of stone. This tower soars by elegance as much as height.

The church was completed in 1514 and is thus contemporary with such masterpieces of late-flowering English Gothic as Magdalen College tower in Oxford and Henry VII's Chapel at Westminster. The interior is a match for the exterior in splendour, though perhaps lacking in detail what it displays in scale. There are double aisles and angel capitals to the arcades. This is a preaching and ceremonial auditorium, with a hundred saints, apostles and angels joining the congregation from the roof above.

Indeed there are angels everywhere. They are on the tower arch, on corbels, capitals and on the king-posts and wallplates of the roof, where they are picked out against the black and blue of the panels. These angels were apparently not gilded until 1968. The roofs throughout are Tudor, that in the south aisle carrying fine bosses. What are claimed to be carvings of Henry VII and Archbishop Wareham face each other across the chancel arch, both looking disagreeable. A ferocious east window in the south aisle portrays ten Somerset worthies, including King Alfred.

TRULL
All Saints **
Pulpit carvings, processional bench-ends

This otherwise modest Perpendicular church in a suburb of Taunton contains some of the county's finest woodwork. The exterior is plain, the south side facing the road adorned with battlements but little else. The interior is unspectacular, but has a rood screen with fan-vaulted coving towards the nave. What is unusual is the survival of a plaster tympanum above the rood beam, as at Parracombe (Devon) a relic of the blocking of the chancel after the Reformation. Removing such tympanums was standard to almost every Victorian restoration.

Trull's treasures are its pulpit and benches. The pulpit probably dates from the early 16th century. It is polygonal and of wood, with saints surviving in ogee niches and with angels above. The saints include John the Evangelist and the four Doctors of the early Church. They are broadly carved in the round, and their draperies fall in stylised folds. The work is charming and full of vitality. More panels form a backing to the pulpit where it is attached to the arcade pier. The composition is extraordinarily rich.

The bench-ends are cruder, but as vigorous as the pulpit. They include priests and citizens taking part in what appears to be a procession, the only known example of this portrayal. The faces are Piccasso-esque. A bench-end in the north aisle is signed Simon Warman and dated 1560. This master carver has been identified in half a dozen Somerset churches, his work typified by an early classical foliage frame. On my visit, children were practising recorders in the chancel, a cacophonous company of angels.

WELLS
St Cuthbert ***
Soaring tower, reredos fragments

As the road over the Mendip escarpment falls towards Wells, it offers a sudden view of a spectacular tower framed by trees, with the old town at its feet. We assume this tower must belong to the cathedral. It is in fact the tower of St Cuthbert's, rival to the cathedral. It represents the wealth of commerce challenging that of the church.

St Cuthbert's is the climactic example of the 'vertical' group of Somerset towers, designed not as a stack of separate stages but as a soaring unity. Seen from south or west, the corner buttresses push upwards like four pylons with the walls strung between them. The buttresses end in pinnacles, short of the crown, at which point new pinnacles take over the upward thrust. The bell-openings are hidden within panels that rise through three stages, though the openings are here without the usual perforations. A second tower once stood above the crossing but collapsed in 1561. Two towers so close together must indeed have outpunched the cathedral.

The interior of St Cuthbert's is appropriately ostentatious. Under the tower is a lierne vault, and the tower arch is panelled. The nave piers are 13th century, with elaborate shafts. Later, the 15th-century masons ingeniously took the old piers, inserted an extra 10 ft at the bottom, replaced the arches and added a clerestory and new roof. This roof is pure show. Where an East Anglian roof would be alive with fluttering angels, glorifying Heaven, St Cuthbert's is rather the ceiling of a merchant's palace. Its angels, heralds, rosettes and shields were vividly restored in 1963.

The rest of the church is an airy volume of aisles, chapels and transepts, a great hall of interlocking space and light. The north and south transepts retain the sad relics of their stone reredoses, so smashed as to have lost unity or meaning. The south one is a Tree of Jesse, so bleak as surely to merit restoration with modern figures. The 1636 pulpit has carving in high relief, and Bible scenes that include Daniel in the lion's den and Jonah and the whale. Under the tower vault is a 17th-century memorial to Luellin, a local benefactor. It shows a small, sturdy man kneeling in prayer on a cushion, a fitting occupant of this merchant's church.

WESTONZOYLAND
St Mary ***
Taunton group tower, roof carvings

The medieval Somerset Levels were dotted with small islands, many of great wealth. Westonzoyland is the 'west town' on the island of Sowy or Zoy. The land is eerily flat, the Quantocks rising like a shoreline in the distance. The Ham dressings on Westonzoyland's blue lias tower catch the sun for miles around.

The church enjoyed a brief but grim fame as a prison after the Battle of Sedgemoor. This was the last pitched battle fought on English soil, in July 1685, between the Duke of Monmouth's rebels and forces loyal to King James. The battlefield is just north of the church. After the rout of the rebels, some 500 survivors, many of them wounded and dying, were herded into the church to spend a ghastly night sleeping on the floor and benches. Outside, gibbets were erected for their hanging the following day. The church had to be fumigated and perfumed afterwards.

The tower is a spectacular example of the Taunton group, a serene composition of pinnacles, pierced bell-openings, decorative battlements and statuary. Angle buttresses soar to detached pinnacles. These carry hunky punk carvings, all unusually based on one theme, that of a dragon.

The tower's glory is matched by that of the roof interior. Tie-beams adorned with angels alternate with collar-beams and pendants. The roofs of aisles and transepts are of equal quality. The remainder of the interior is a study in brown, dark in the roof and the ancient benches, lighter in the 1930s' rood screen, lighter again in the shadows falling through the clerestory on to the limewashed walls. The church carries the initials of Richard Bere, Abbot of Glastonbury 1493–1525, to whom we owe this fine work.

WITHAM FRIARY
St Mary, St John and All Saints *
St Hugh's Carthusian foundation

This little chapel is for Carthusian addicts, and for those tiring of Somerset's Perpendicular plutocracy. Though heavily restored, Witham survives as a fragment of the first Charterhouse to be founded in England by Henry II, in penance for Becket's murder in 1170. The Order was renowned for its vows of austerity, humility and silence. Witham's third prior was St Hugh, a Frenchman sent in 1179 from the Order's headquarters at La Grande Chartreuse in Grenoble. He arrived in neighbouring Selwood, says the guide, a poor settlement of 'resentful peasants, drenching gales and a monastery of wretched wattle huts'. He spent six years here, before his elevation to the See of Lincoln, and built a stone monastery to which he returned annually until his death in 1200. Hugh was a typical 12th-century European administrator, travelling, politicking and preaching. So great was his reputation that he was canonised within twenty years of his death.

The friary was dissolved in 1539, but the lay brothers' chapel continued as the local parish church. In the 19th century it was given a tower that was found to be unstable, and was replaced with the present bellcote and heavy buttresses. It is a simple aisleless structure with an apsidal east end, vaulted throughout. The windows are deeply splayed and round-headed. Three eastern lancets have free-standing Purbeck shafts, Victorian insertions replacing an earlier Perpendicular east window. They are in keeping with the solemn mood of the chancel, as is the stained glass.

The Comper glass in the south window illustrates Hugh's life and good work, notably his affection for his pet swan.

YATTON
St Mary **
South porch, gypsy's grave

The village is dreary, but the Perpendicular church detaches itself and its churchyard from the eastern suburbs and lends majesty to Yatton Moor. The effort is diminished only by Yatton's loss of most of its spire in 1595. The crossing tower now has a truncated stump, oddly mimicked in the adjacent modern chapter house roof. Pride of place goes instead to the west front and south porch. The former is a superb Perpendicular composition of nave doorway and west window, flanked by polygonal turrets and medieval statuary. The porch has a curtain wall of ogival panelling, with a lierne vault inside.

Yatton's interior is supremely harmonious. The five bays of the nave arcades have intricate capitals, the one adjacent to the chancel arch being of a lady in a huge shawl. The wagon roofs are complete throughout, every junction embossed with a rose or starburst, many brilliantly restored. The stone vault beneath the tower is so dominant as to separate the four components of the interior space into compartments which, in Clifton-Taylor's account of this church, 'hardly seem to know each other'.

Most remarkable of these compartments is the north chapel, containing the Newton family tombs. Sir Richard Newton (d.1449), a judge, is commemorated in a fine work of Somerset alabaster. Whether such effigies are likenesses is controversial. Kenneth Wickham considers 'the features too fine and individual to be other than a portrait'. Yet an identical effigy has been found in Bristol, from where this carving probably came. So once again we are probably cheated of 'truth to life'. Equally splendid is the tomb erected by Newton's daughter-in-law, for herself and her husband Sir John (d.1488). This is in stone, the effigies less delicate. Behind them is a medieval relief of the Annunciation. At the back of the church stand two Baroque carvings of saints, from the Bath Abbey organ. They add a dash of class to this fine interior.

In the churchyard is the grave of one of the gypsy Joules family. The inscription reads: 'Here lies Merily Joules / A beauty bright / Who loved Isaac Joules / Her heart's delight.' She died in 1827. Isaac is said to have been so overwhelmed by her loss that he pitched camp by her graveside for fourteen years, until he joined her in death.

Staffordshire

Staffordshire is half hill and half plain, half beautiful and half dull. The hills contain some of the most spectacular scenery of the southern Pennines, the plains offer lush lowlands along the border with Shropshire. There is no distinctive Staffordshire architecture. Norman work is not plentiful, but the doorway to the old priory at Tutbury is a splendid fan of carving. The Goths are best seen in the stiff-leaf capitals at Gnosall and the windows at Clifton Campville. The Perpendicular age is fallow, apart from the fine stained glass at Checkley.

The tempo quickens after the Reformation. The Broughton family restored their church with heraldic glass and the Mavesyns filled theirs with monuments to their prowess. Wren built a rare out-of-town church for the Chetwynds at Ingestre. But it was the Victorians who did Staffordshire most proud, with G. F. Bodley's memorial masterpiece at Hoar Cross and G. E. Street's work at Blymhill and Denstone. Towering over them all is A. W. N. Pugin's great Roman Catholic church for the Earl of Shrewsbury in Cheadle, flagship of the Gothic Revival.

Alstonefield *	Checkley *	Hoar Cross ****
Ashley **	Clifton Campville **	Ingestre **
Blymhill *	Denstone *	Mavesyn Ridware **
Broughton *	Eccleshall *	Tamworth ***
Cheadle *****	Gnosall **	Tutbury ***

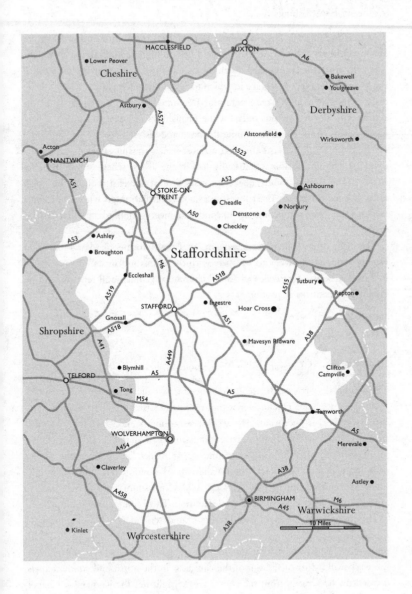

ALSTONEFIELD
St Peter *
17th-century furnishings

This is secluded Peak District, where Derbyshire 'strays' into Staffordshire, or some would say the reverse. Alstonefield lies on high ground above Dovedale. The view from the churchyard down the dale is superb, as indeed is the view in every direction. Here is a place in which to rest and contemplate.

The church has a Norman core and Decorated arcade, but apart from the setting it is worth a detour only for the furnishings of pews and pulpit. These are survivals from the 1630s, filling the nave and aisles. They are uncommonly ornate, with scroll patterns covering not just bench-ends but backs, shelves and dividers. The decoration is markedly less in the aisles, where simple benches survive. The Cotton family pew now rests against the east wall of the north aisle, painted turquoise. Over this towers a magnificent pulpit with subordinate clerk's seat. These furnishings are like museum pieces, set amid bare limewashed walls.

Alstonefield has little other ornament, as if the Reformers had at some point eagerly stripped the walls to compete with the Nonconformists, always strong in these parts. But this was a plain hill church, of yeomen and tenants with no money for chantries or monuments.

ASHLEY
St John **
Gerard memorial, funeral urn by Wedgwood

The church sits on a small rise at the foot of its village, challenging any passer-by to guess its date. The answer is that the entire structure, apart from a 17th-century tower, is Victorian. The work was commissioned by Hugo Meynell Ingram, whose widow Emily later commissioned Bodley to build Hoar Cross in his memory after he died, out hunting. At Ashley he obtained the service of a more modest architect, John Ashdown of London. His brother-in-law, Frederick, carried out further work at Ashley in memory of his own wife in 1904, shortly before he too died while hunting. This is dangerous country.

The church must be experienced rather than described. It is full of sumptuous fittings by Cecil Hare, a follower of Bodley, in 1910. The nave, packed with incident, is just two bays long and dominated by a large organ case jutting from the west wall. Most of the fun of the church is in the north and south chapels, divided off by screens from the choir. To the right lies the Kinnersley Chapel, dedicated to yet more patrons of this much patronised church. The most prominent memorial is to Thomas Kinnersley, by Sir Francis Chantrey in his

'Westminster Abbey' style. The effigy lies in bed, a cameo of his wife behind him.

From this we cross to the Gerard Chapel and a truly monstrous monument. Betjeman claimed it to be the largest Elizabethan work in England, executed 'under the influence' of Hollemans, sculptor to the Spencers and Cavendishes. Sir Gilbert Gerard (d.1592) was an Elizabethan courtier and Attorney-General. He left instructions to his son to build a mortuary chapel, as a pre-Reformation knight would have endowed a chantry. Mother and father lie in splendour, he in armour, she with her dog Talbot at her side. The elder son, Thomas, towers over their heads while the younger son is at the feet. Beneath is a corpse in a funerary shroud. The canopy encloses both effigies and mourners, rising not from the tomb chest as usual, but from the ground, an enormous and independent structure. The whole ensemble looks like something from a Tolkien romance. Yet it is the real thing, in alabaster and dated 1612.

Over the sanctuary arch is a funeral urn in memory of William Chetwynd, another patron of the church. He was an associate of Josiah Wedgwood and his wife, a friend of Queen Charlotte, secured Wedgwood's reputation by recommending his pottery to the court. Wedgwood returned the favour by himself making this urn in his friend's honour. It is in his Etruscan style.

BLYMHILL
St Mary *
Chapel restoration by Street

In such a small village we would expect a modest church, yet Blymhill plays host to a masterpiece of restoration by the Victorian, G. E. Street. In 1856–9 he not only rebuilt the nave of the church but also designed a school and churchyard gateway. His new nave joins a medieval chancel to the old west tower. His work is most visible in the windows, with meticulously varied tracery, and in the stiff-leaf carving of the porch. The attention to detail is also seen in the spandrel of the north-west window, occupied by three finely carved kings. The south porch is adorned by one of the most evocative gargoyles I know. A lion, grossly disproportionate to its task, vomits rainwater into a drainpipe.

The interior hardly pretends at restoration. It is a complete Victorian chapel. The roof is deep and steeply pitched with dormer windows, like that of a Swiss chalet. The screen carvings have doves eating pineapples. The chancel floor is inlaid with alabaster, while black and gilded ironwork guards the north chapel. Pulpit, font, pews, indeed everything appears to have received Street's personal care. Only the stained glass is insipid, most of it by Wailes, some by John Hardman.

BROUGHTON
St Peter *
Late-medieval glass

This pocket battleship of a church sits on a hill above the spectacular black-and-white Broughton Hall. It was rebuilt in 1630–34 by Thomas Broughton as a private chapel to the big house, at a time when no road divided house from church. The outside is short, steeply roofed and with a powerful tower, all in 17th-century Gothic and demonstrating no trace of the classicism by then appearing in such churches as St Paul, Covent Garden (London) or Shrivenham (Oxon). The Staffordshire gentry clearly had no time for such a new-fangled style.

The cheerful Jacobean interior is full of bustle, the more so when I saw it during harvest festival. The walls are plastered, and the font is set into a curious niche under the tower arch. The nave had high box pews reserved for the big house and its staff, to which villagers were not admitted until well into the 18th century. The principal feature of the interior is the glass, most of which appears to have been salvaged and reset by the family from an earlier church at the time of the rebuilding.

The east window is a burst of colour, some of the glass medieval, some later, framing four 15th-century figures in excellent preservation. They depict King David, St George, St Roche and St Andrew. The chancel south window has old glass showing St Mary and St Francis, with local donors below them. On the north side is the Broughton family heraldic glass. The whole is an admirable example of church patronage both before and after the Reformation.

CHEADLE
St Giles RC *****
Pugin's complete 13th-century re-creation

A. W. N. Pugin's St Giles, Cheadle, is the outstanding English church of the 19th century. The patron was the 16th Earl of Shrewsbury, who lived at the neighbouring mansion of Alton Towers. Shrewsbury was rich, liberal and a Roman Catholic. Pugin, also a Catholic and still only twenty-nine, was the architectural impresario of the day. The church commissioned in 1841 for the centre of Cheadle was intended to re-create the architecture of the pre-Reformation church. Since most of the churches in this book have their roots in the same religion, Cheadle shares their form and customary features. The difference is that at Cheadle they were re-created complete, in full colour and splendour. Cheadle was a reaction against both the classical architecture and sparse fittings of the Protestant church, and the frivolous Gothic of the Regency period.

The dark sandstone steeple can be seen from miles around, but within the town it rises as a sudden *coup de théâtre* at the foot of a hill off the High Street. The height is 200 ft and the proportion almost unbearably slender. Buttresses, then pinnacles, then lucarnes cling to the sides of the spire, as if pleading with it to go no higher. Some spires seem reluctant to escape their towers. Cheadle does so joyfully. The west door is almost as dramatic as the steeple, the hinges formed into two huge Shrewsbury lions, covering each door in gold on a red background. Exterior niches are filled with the appropriate statues, including the two St Johns on the east wall.

The interior lacks nothing that the late 13th century would have included. The church has a standard plan with a nave, aisles, baptistery to the west and a chancel with chapels to the east. There is a screen with loft and rood, a Doom painting and saints in niches. In the chancel are an Easter Sepulchre, piscina, sedilia and reredos. The Doom includes the Earl's daughter, Gwendoline, on the right of Christ among those to be saved. Such was the power of patronage.

Not an inch of Cheadle is without paint, carving or gilding. Even the window reveals are meticulously decorated, each shaft picked out in different-coloured patterns, like the leggings of a Carpaccio gondolier. Nor is there any restraint in the materials. The Lady Chapel screen is of brass, as are the candlesticks, the candelabra and even the step treads. The sedilia and Easter Sepulchre shimmer in reds, greens and gold. Coloured tiles from Wedgwood and Minton line the floor.

Decoration reaches crescendo in the south chancel chapel. Metal grilles and symbols of the Eucharist and Lamb of God are everywhere. The pulpit is carved from a single block of stone, the font from one of alabaster. Whether the decoration of a Gothic church of the 13th–14th centuries was truly as rich as this we cannot know. Certainly that was the belief of the Gothic revivalists. Glass mostly by William Wailes fills the windows. Piped church music fills the interior, and delightfully too.

The only disappointment is the pews, dull and uncomfortable.

CHECKLEY
St Mary and All Saints *
Red Indian poppyhead

The chancel at Checkley is a gem of Decorated Gothic. It is reached through a south porch with a doorway of *c.*1300, a sweeping arch on short shafts. The nave is tall and narrow, reflecting the proportions of the old Norman church. The arcade arches are Transitional, their shallow curves contrasting with the arches to the tower and chancel, which are high, slender and beautifully shaped.

Under the tower arch sits the font, a primitive Saxon tub with a donkey on its front panel.

The chancel was dedicated *c.*1320 and has Y- and Intersecting tracery filling large, graceful windows. These are filled with superb 14th-century glass, a rare case of our being able to enjoy glazing contemporary with its building. The east window includes the martyrdom of St Thomas à Becket and is remarkably complete. In the south wall is a window with 17th-century Dutch roundels showing the seasons of the year, fine examples of this genre, like miniature Bruegels.

The chief tomb (*c.*1560) is the ubiquitous Midlands Foljambes, here Godfrey and his wife Margaret. She is wearing voluminous petticoats. It is unusually plain for an Elizabethan monument.

The choir stalls have excellent giant poppyheads, including one of a Red Indian. The Elizabethans were fascinated by the Americas and a similar image can be seen at Burford (Oxon).

CLIFTON CAMPVILLE
St Andrew **
Tower base windows, Vernon alabaster tomb

The setting and steeple are superb. The tower rises with confidence above three giant Decorated windows round its base, where would normally be heavy supporting walls. Of all the church towers that I have compared to rockets, that of Clifton Campville most merits the simile.

The church plan is eccentric, with a nave of three bays and a chancel with a large east window of Reticulated tracery. Running down the south side of both nave and chancel is a long south aisle, while to the north lies a charming, small vaulted chantry chapel. The latter was the manorial pew in the 18th century, with a schoolroom above. The chapel has now been restored with seemly modern furnishings. With so much room in today's churches, and schools so short of the same, it seems a pity that more schools cannot make use of parts of churches. I found a successful instance of this community co-operation in the church at Cliffe (Kent).

Clifton Campville has fine woodwork. The nave roof is Perpendicular with extensive carvings. Of the same age is the screen dividing nave from chancel, though the doors are of 1634. The parclose screens enclosing the Lady Chapel are more remarkable. Four appear to be 14th century, with Intersecting tracery, while the eastern screen is Carolean. Inside this chapel is the tomb of Sir John Vernon (d.1545). This comprises two standard alabaster effigies, but with lively bedesmen round the tomb chest, not the usual staid weepers. The tomb is believed to come from workshops in Burton-on-Trent and is almost identical to others from this inspired source, for instance at Macclesfield (Cheshire).

The Clifton Campville church guide boasts that it is one of the 'finest churches in England'. As an 'off-peak' visitor, I was begrudged entry – but gather the welcome has improved.

DENSTONE
All Saints *
Country chapel by Street

The 1860s must have been an exciting time for young architects. While the youthful Bodley was 'speaking French' at Selsley (Gloucs), the youthful Street was hard at work in Staffordshire in a similar cause. His patron was Sir Thomas Percival Heywood, a Manchester banker.

The result, commissioned in 1860, is a simple yet satisfying Victorian church. The tall apsidal chancel has a roof higher than the short nave, with short buttresses and Plate tracery windows. The stone of the walls, both outside and inside, is subtly banded in grey and pink, the former rough, the latter smooth. As at Blymhill, Street designed a complete 'community kit', with a wall, lychgate, vicarage and school. This was much favoured by generous Victorian patrons. Woodyer designed a similar group at Highnam (Gloucs), as had the great innovator, Butterfield, at All Saints, Margaret Street (London).

The interior is unaltered. There are no aisles and the visual progression from south-west entrance to chancel and distant apse is without jarring notes. Every detail is considered and richly executed. Thus the font is an astonishing variant on a Gothic theme, four angels with their wings outstretched, holding the four Rivers of Paradise; the sculpture is by Thomas Earp. Costly marble is used for the font, chancel screen and the shafts of the chancel windows. The pulpit is of alabaster with marble shafts.

The stained glass is not by Morris but by Clayton & Bell, always an admirable second best. Denstone was Street's favourite small work. My only quibble is with the radiators, which look most un-medieval.

ECCLESHALL
Holy Trinity *
Caröe's memorial chapel

Eccleshall church owes much of its splendour to being adjacent to what was, until the 1860s, the castle of the Bishops of Lichfield. The castle was rebuilt in the 1690s and is now a private house, but the medieval bridge survives across what was the moat. The church is architecturally more significant than its dour appearance at first implies. It describes itself as the most perfect 13th-century church in Staffordshire, yet this is belied by its exterior. The porch, tower top and clerestory are Perpendicular. The long chancel with lancets and the Y-tracery of the south aisle and tower are 13th century, but the south aisle lancets were inserted in a restoration by Street.

The interior is notable for the Early Gothic arcade, a graceful sequence of arches rising above stiff-leaf capitals, some stiffer than others and some looking as if their leaves have suffered an early autumn droop. The chancel is impressively long, as befits the church of bishops. It contains a bishop's throne and is lined with their tombs. None is of particular distinction, though that which Bishop Overton built for himself before his death in 1609 has some presence. He lies in alabaster with his two wives kneeling above and behind him.

To the north of the chancel is the small Lady Chapel converted by W. D. Caröe in 1931. It was a memorial to Mary Lowe, a talented musician who died of meningitis at the age of twenty-one. Her parents refurbished the chapel and donated a new organ between it and the chancel. Both are panelled in delicate limed oak, a pleasing contrast to the surrounding Victorian darkness.

The beautiful reredos and organ case are among Caröe's most intricate works, worthy of the best 20th-century West Country carvers whom he so admired.

GNOSALL
St Lawrence **
Norman and Early Gothic carvings

Gnosall church presents a grand face to the world. It sits at the heart of the village, yet detached on a rise, as if the cottages were built to pay obeisance. The church is cruciform and was previously collegiate. It is rare in the Midlands in having traces of all architectural periods. Indeed to sit against the north wall of the chancel and gaze left and right across its interior is to enjoy a spectacular 'read' of church history.

The tower top is Perpendicular, adorned with pinnacles and delightful carved heads. The interior is dominated by the large Norman crossing, which has survived every alteration to the rest of the church. Its west wall is elaborately carved. Also Norman is the south transept, with a triforium in the west wall. Here too is a charming Early Gothic arch with 'windblown' stiff-leaf carving on one of its piers. The composition is a delight, like a fragment of an Old Master set in a later frame.

The rest of the interior is anticlimax, though pleasantly so. The nave is well lit by its clerestory and blessedly free of too much stained glass. The chancel is dominated by a superb Reticulated east window. The bottom tier of the reticulation takes the form of leaves beneath the bloom of a rose. The symmetry of this pattern is spoiled by the 20th-century glass, depicting saints packed tight, like a football crowd.

HOAR CROSS
Holy Angels ****
Victorian memorial church in Decorated style

Hoar Cross is a masterpiece of the Gothic Revival. Bodley's early churches of
the 1850s and 1860s, such as Selsley (Gloucs) and St Michael, Brighton
(Sussex), were designed in a spare, early French Gothic. Hoar Cross, of 1872, is
from Bodley's middle period, when he had selected English late Decorated as
the zenith of medieval architecture. Here, with his partner Thomas Garner,
he developed the style to new heights, cramming his interior with liturgical
paraphernalia. His client was Emily Meynell Ingram (*see* Ashley), daughter of
Lord Halifax, whose husband of just seven years had been killed in a hunting
accident. She commissioned the church both as his memorial and as a citadel of
Anglo-Catholicism, to which Bodley was also attached.

The church lies at the entrance to the old house, now a health spa, into whose
grounds the churchyard gently merges across a sunken garden. The exterior is a
superb work of Decorated revival, comparing with Bodley's Clumber (Notts).
The tower contrives to soar despite its lack of a spire. The graceful lines of the
window mullions grow restless and break into furious Decorated tracery. The
buttresses all have niche statues.

The inside is Victorian High Gothic with all the trimmings. This was intended
as a church for remembering and worshipping, not for preaching. The gloom of
the nave, which has no clerestory, leads the eye through the crossing and great
screen to the chancel. This is taller than the nave and vaulted, lit by lofty
windows, as though it were an ante-chamber to Heaven. Sedilia line both sides
of the sanctuary, with the walls densely wrought with panelling and saints.
More saints climb up the walls and windows, jostling with ballflower and
nodding ogee arches, then spilling over into the stained glass. While Bodley and
Garner collaborated on the architecture, the internal carving is mostly by
Garner.

The stained glass is by Burlison & Grylls, but to Bodley's design. It depicts
saints in soft colours that do not clash with the wood and stone carving. If
stained glass there must be in an English parish church, it should have this sense
of harmony. The stone reredos is magnificent.

The private chapel contains the tombs of Hugo and Emily. He lies under a
sweeping ogee canopy, she under a flat wooden one, both on alabaster chests.
Angels guard their heads, candles their feet. The ensemble is a superb display of
wealthy Victorian piety.

INGESTRE
St Mary **
Wren interior

Ingestre church is celebrated as Sir Christopher Wren's one church outside London, also one of the earliest purely classical works in the provinces. It is attributed to Wren because he and the landowner, Walter Chetwynd, were fellow members of the Royal Society, and drawings survive of his design, at least for a tower. This is dated some time after Chetwynd applied to demolish the former church in 1671. Ingestre (pronounced gestray by locals) lies at the end of a long drive through what is now a golf course. Pevsner calls the house 'magniloquent', the church 'laconic', apt adjectives. The church sits uncomfortably between the house and the old stables.

The exterior is extremely simple, a familiar classical box with a west entrance topped by a mildly Baroque flourish of coat of arms and clock. The interior is similar to Wren's City churches. The nave has unusual Tuscan arcades and no galleries. The fittings are not as grand as those which survive in, say, St Mary Abchurch (London). But they are intact save for some Victorian lowering of pew heights. The pulpit and screen are beautifully carved. Where the Middle Ages would have placed the rood, the 17th century put a royal coat of arms that is little short of sensational. The east window is Victorian and pestilential.

The glory of the church is the ceiling, which has panelled plasterwork worthy of the City. The central panel in the nave is decorated with high relief flowers, angels and waving fronds. The chancel has a similar design applied to a barrel vault, above a pavement of black and white marble. The church is crowded with monuments to the Chetwynds and their Talbot relatives. Remarkable 17th-century memorial tablets line the chancel walls, while the aisles hold later works, mostly 19th century, including a number by Francis Chantrey. The big house now belongs to Staffordshire Education Department, where nobody seems to know or care about the church.

MAVESYN RIDWARE
St Nicholas **
Chapel of the fighting Mavesyns

Enthusiasts for English eccentricity would put Mavesyn high on their list. The church is half medieval, half Georgian, but also half sane and half mad. The Mavesyns were Normans, their name deriving from 'malvoisin' or 'mauvesin', meaning bad neighbours. The family was true to the appellation. They appear to have been incapable of avoiding fights. They came over with the Conqueror and took land in Staffordshire and Shropshire, plunging into one quarrel after another. The last of the line, Robert Mavesyn, killed his hated neighbour William Handsacre in 1403, then died fighting for Henry IV at Shrewsbury. The descent passed through his daughters to the Cawardens of Cheshire and then the Chadwicks, who survived into the 20th century.

The church that stands today is composed of the north aisle and tower of the old church and of a simple rectangle, which replaced the rest of the building in 1782. The latter is a beautifully proportioned preaching box, a tiny Gothic apsidal sanctuary extending from the east wall with plaster ribs. Having paid our respects to this part of the church we turn to the Mavesyn Chapel in the north aisle. This can best be described as a raucous medieval revel. The chapel's floor and walls are completely covered in tombs, memorials, slabs, panels, hatchments and shields commemorating the bloody (and possibly glorious) history of the Mavesyns.

Which elements are medieval and which the product of a fertile 18th- and 19th-century imagination is obscure. Midlands grandees loved incised alabaster for their tombs. Some of those in the chapel appear to be 16th century, others 17th and some possibly late 18th, dating from the time of the nave rebuilding. One slab, of a Chadwick who died in 1689, is marked 'old deeds, old names we'll preserve, old monuments restore'. But when restored? The slabs which surround the chapel look surprisingly similar in style, like a game of Happy Families.

Against the west wall are two tablets recording the two battles fought by Sir Robert Mavesyn in 1403, the first against Handsacre, the second for the king. Both are accompanied by splendid doggerel: 'He rushed from yonder moat girt walls / With lance and bill and bow. / "Down, down (he cried) with Bolingbroke", / Dares Mavesyn say "No"?' The last of the family line appears to be Mai Hermione Montagu, née Chadwick, who died in Simla in 1985. Sadly she could not be brought back to lie among her ancestors.

TAMWORTH
St Editha ***
Market setting, Burne-Jones glass

The church and tower of this old town form a fine profile from the bypass, and will be even finer when someone removes the high-rise flats erected next to them in the 1960s. Who sanctioned this outrage? The church tower at least puts up a fight. It is a Perpendicular bastion supported by beefy buttresses, rising on a mound overlooking the market place. On market day it is crowded with shoppers drifting in and out for coffee and other purchases, setting a lively example for every town church.

The interior is a delightful jumble. The Decorated nave, rebuilt after a fire in

1345, is wide and airy. The eye is led towards the chancel through an elegant 18th-century iron screen beneath a fragment of a Norman crossing. Above runs a superb uninterrupted clerestory. This produces an elongated perspective towards the east, enhanced by regilded roofs. In the chancel is a collection of stone tombs along the wall, of indeterminate age but a jolly ensemble.

The pride of Tamworth is stained glass by most of the Victorian masters, of sufficient quality to overcome the resulting gloom. There is Wailes in the east window, and elsewhere works by Powell & Sons, Henry Holiday and a large collection of Burne-Jones and Morris. The last is mostly gathered in the north chapel, though there is also a fine Burne-Jones in the south aisle. All this glass is outstanding in its colour and composition. Especially bold are the roses in the top lights in the north chapel.

In the entrance porch is a pompous Restoration monument to John Ferrers (d.1680) and his son. The tomb was apparently commissioned from Gibbons, but the figures are by C. G. Cibber.

TUTBURY
St Mary ***
Carved Norman west front

Tutbury Castle is a ruin hiding behind a 17th-century façade above the River Dove. Its church, surviving from an old Norman priory, sits just below it on the hill. They make a noble pair, especially when floodlit at night. The old priory was wasted at the Dissolution, the church nave being retained for the parish. In the 1860s, Street arrived to put things into a semblance of order, saving the church but leaving both interior and exterior stripped of their antique patina.

Even Street could not detract from Tutbury's glory, as fine a Norman west front as adorns any English parish church. He inserted shafts into the central doorway, added new windows and arcading wherever fancy took him and retooled individual carvings. He might have argued that without his intervention there would be no west front surviving today at all. He has left us the fragment of one, but it is a magnificent fragment.

The best view is from the churchyard, which banks steeply up to the castle amid tombs covered with flowers. The central doorway is an astonishing composition, dated *c.*1150 and reminiscent of the great arch at Tickencote (Rutland). It is of seven orders and includes the customary mouldings of zigzag and beakhead. The outer arch is the first known use in England of alabaster, in which the Midlands was particularly rich. Similar carving is found round the window above, a Gothic insertion flanked by original blind arcading.

The south doorway of the church has more Norman carving, including a boar hunt in its tympanum, though in its eroded state the boar looks more like a hippopotamus. The interior of Tutbury is dominated by the Norman arcades surviving from the priory church, and by the inner face of the west front, the latter almost as richly carved as the exterior. Wavy lines surround the door. The eastern two piers of the nave are round, the rest strangely bloated, as if having had to grow appendages to maintain the height of the towers. These piers march towards the chancel, only to be cut short by an effete Street arch, leading to his new apse. Where there should be trumpets and drums, there is only a tinkle.

Suffolk

Suffolk is an odd place, a landscape of wide coastal marshes and big inland horizons along the Norfolk border. The sandy Breckland, west of Norwich, is still one of the most sparsely populated areas of the south half of England. The county saw its commercial apogee, like the rest of East Anglia, during the late-medieval boom in wool cloth and lay economically dormant until the farming boom of the second half of the 20th century. It is now a peaceful land of attractive small villages and towns, famous, like the fictional Akenfield, for a robustly introverted English ruralism.

Suffolk's Norman churches were mostly rebuilt in the 15th century. There is remarkably little architecture before, say, 1400. But the rebuilding was splendid and only the materials were poor. Even the rich patrons of Lavenham and Long Melford had to make do with flint, either set into the walls whole or knapped to produce a flat surface. This knapping was interspersed with stone to create the 'flushwork' of which Suffolk is supreme, best seen at Southwold and on the superb tower at Eye.

Suffolk's other excellence was in roofs. The engineering masterpieces of Needham Market and Woolpit are equalled only by March (Cambs) while the carved beams at Mildenhall equal Somerset's finest. The county has two outstanding font covers at Ufford and Sudbury and charming bench-ends at Blythburgh. As the Reformation approached, Suffolk carvers turned their attention from religious to family piety. Lavish chantries appeared at Bury St Edmunds and Lavenham. At Long Melford, the Clopton family produced one of the most extravagant family memorials in England, embracing architecture, glass, stone and paint. The Reformation swept away much of this, but left enough for another bout of destruction by Cromwell's iconoclast, William Dowsing, who visited the county in 1643–4.

The fine Howard tombs at Framlingham mark the transition from Gothic to classical forms. After that we may admire the Jennens tomb at Acton and the remarkable collection of Poley monuments at Boxted. But with that the story is over. Of all the great English counties, Suffolk is the most truly medieval. The Georgians and Victorians appear to have pronounced its churches beyond improvement.

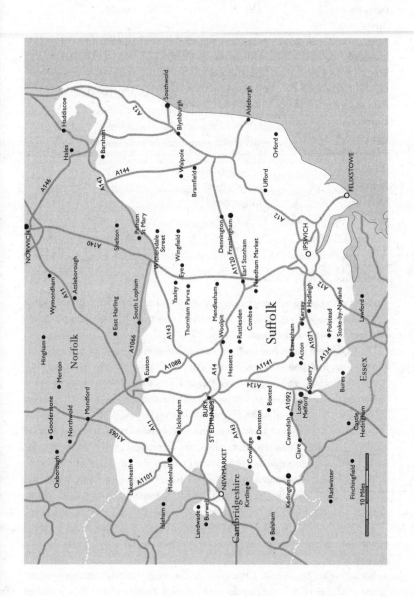

Acton *

Aldeburgh *

Barsham **

Blythburgh ***

Boxted **

Bramfield **

Bures *

Bury St Edmunds:
    St Mary ***

Cavendish *

Clare ***

Combs *

Cowlinge *

Dennington **

Denston ***

Earl Stonham ***

Euston **

Eye **

Framlingham ****

Hadleigh *

Hessett *

Icklingham *

Kedington ****

Kersey *

Lakenheath *

Landwade *

Lavenham ****

Long Melford *****

Mendlesham *

Mildenhall ****

Needham Market **

Orford *

Polstead *

Rattlesden *

Southwold ****

Stoke-by-Nayland ***

Sudbury: St Gregory *

Thornham Parva **

Ufford **

Walpole *

Wingfield **

Withersdale Street *

Woolpit ***

Yaxley *

ACTON

All Saints *

Bures brass, Jennens monument

Acton is a charming village church of *c.*1300 tucked away between the giants of Lavenham and Long Melford. It is architecturally undistinguished but holds two remarkable works of art.

The first is the Bures brass (*c.*1310–20) in the north chapel, widely regarded as the finest and one of the earliest brasses in England. It commemorates Sir Robert de Bures (d.1302) who served Edward I, mostly in Wales. The armour is similar to that in another early brass also dated *c.*1320, of Sir John D'Abernon (d.1277) in the church of Stoke D'Abernon (Surrey).

The armour consists of a long tunic and fine chainmail suit, forms of armour current since the Conquest more than two centuries earlier. However, Sir Robert wears reinforcements at the knee, marking the advent of armour plate which superseded chainmail in the early 14th century. The work shows the Knight with his hands in prayer, the folds in the tunic realistically gathered at the belt. His legs are crossed and his feet rest on a charmingly domesticated lion.

Nearby is a brass to Alice de Bryan (died *c.*1435) in a shroud-like widow's gown and set beneath a canopy. She was probably great-granddaughter to Sir Robert.

Acton's other treasure is a curiosity. In the south chapel, concealed behind vestry paraphernalia, is the monument to Robert Jennens (d.1725), descendant of a Birmingham ironmaster whose family acquired the manor of Acton in 1708. He lies on a mattress in everyday clothes while his wife looks on in grief.

Jennens's son, William, was a celebrated miser who died a bachelor and intestate at the age of ninety-seven. He was reputedly the richest commoner in England; his great house, Acton Place, was subsequently demolished. Litigation over his estate was said to have inspired Dickens's Jarndyce v. Jarndyce in *Bleak House*, though there are other claimants to this notoriety.

ALDEBURGH
St Peter and St Paul *
Britten memorials

Aldeburgh churchyard looks out over the rooftops towards the sea. The charming old town was a place of fishermen and farmers, and is now full of weekend and retirement cottages. But it is forever associated with its distinguished resident, Benjamin Britten, and the festival which he founded here and at Snape Maltings inland. Every church in the district seems to have some festival connection, an admirable reuse of these fine old buildings.

The church's flint exterior was heavily restored after near ruin in the 18th century, its chief curiosity being a processional arch under the south porch with openings on all three sides. The crowded interior, also mostly Victorian, might be seeking warmth from the sea and the bitter east wind outside. The proportions are heavy and there is no clerestory, though a wartime bomb helpfully relieved the windows of most of their stained glass.

The church is to be visited for its rich furnishings, including an altar rail with angels and fine brasswork. The church's principal treasure is the Britten memorial window, by John Piper and Patrick Reyntiens. It depicts his three oratorios, *The Burning Fiery Furnace*, *Curlew River* and *The Prodigal Son*. With brilliant reds and greens it is one of Piper's finest works in this medium.

In the south chapel is a memorial to Lady Henrietta Vernon (d.1786). She looks suitably mortified by the impertinence of death, but consoled by a handsome Adonis ministering to her from above.

The north chapel contains a bust of George Crabbe, Georgian poet and rector of the church. He liked its pre-Blitz darkness, writing: 'Here large plain columns rise in solemn style / You'd love the gloom they make in either aisle, / When the sun's rays, enfeebled as they pass / And shorn of splendour through the storied glass / Faintly display the figures on the floor.' Crabbe must have written that before the arrival of Victorian glass, which shuts out the sky.

BARSHAM
Holy Trinity **
20th-century Gothic revival interior

A small bluff runs east–west along the south bank of the River Waveney, on which sit the towns of Bungay and Beccles, marking the Suffolk–Norfolk border. This is a strange, rather lost England. To the south lies a tract of East Anglia, its villages mostly named after saints, long regarded as untamed and lawless. Barsham church seems untroubled by these neighbours. It sleeps gently in a meadow with, next door, a charming rectory with a Dutch gable.

The church is round-towered and partly thatched. Most remarkable is its east end, with flushwork and window tracery forming a trellis of lozenge patterns. It appears medieval but is now regarded as do-it-yourself Gothic by a Stuart rector, Robert Fleming, in 1633. The interior is a combination of Fleming's restoration and an embellishment by Eden in 1906, on the commission of a later rector, Allan Coates. The result is a delightful nave, chancel and modest two-arch arcade to a north aisle, all decorated in a pink wash. The east window is filled with restrained Kempe glass, restricted to one figure for each of Fleming's lozenges.

The furnishings are mostly by Eden in what might be called his doll's-house style. The screen appears to be part Jacobean, part 20th century, with rood and candles surmounted by a proscenium arch decorated with Adamish motifs. The pulpit has a tester with fine strapwork. The guide says that twice a year a low sun can shine a ray of light onto the figure of Christ through the west tower window.

Eden also fitted out the St Catherine Chapel 'in the style of Henry VIII's reign'. He was adamant that all work should be done by medieval methods, including the use of old adzes for the carved bench-ends. A blue and gold tabernacle protects the altar; an Italian majolica plaque adorns the chapel, with a *trompe l'oeil* background. The glass in the north chapel has roundels surrounded by ribbons, flora and putti who, on closer inspection, appear to be wearing T-shirts and kilts.

BLYTHBURGH
Holy Trinity ***
Angels roof, Seven Sins poppyheads

Blythburgh is queen of the Suffolk coast. My first visit was as a student on a summer evening for an Aldeburgh concert. Unable to get a seat, we lay on the grass outside, trying to hear the recital through the open doors. As the evening drew in, the music seemed to grow and the windows to shimmer with light. Of these coastal churches, Southwold may offer finer architecture, but few can rival Blythburgh's splendid profile, towering at dusk over the marshes of Reydon.

Though the tower is disappointing, the nave exterior is superb, set on a mound with views north-east across the estuary of the River Blyth towards the coast. The flushwork is mostly confined to the buttresses, but the south aisle and porch have a sumptuous pierced parapet of quatrefoils with crowns. The interior is renowned for its roof, lit by a glorious run of 18 clerestory windows. It is simple in construction, a series of rafters interspersed with beams and arch braces. These are beautifully carved with angels facing east and west. Many are riddled with shot, either from Dowsing's Cromwellian iconoclasts or from boys shooting jackdaws. The rafters are still decorated with original paint.

Down below are the famous poppyheads, sadly now fixed to modern pews. These portray the failings of mankind, notably the Seven Deadly Sins, overseen by the virtuous angels overhead. They include Slander with his tongue out, Gluttony with his paunch, Hypocrisy at prayer with his eyes open and, my favourite, Sloth still in bed. The original screen is much restored but the excellent choir stalls retain wooden saints in niches with their emblems. The stalls have holes for inkwells, the chancel having served as a school after the Reformation. The font is, or was, a Seven-Sacrament one but its sacraments were ruthlessly chiselled off by the iconoclasts.

The church has a fine Jack-o'-the-Clock dating from 1682, a figure still found in many churches and used to strike a bell. An old priest's chamber above the porch has been restored and set aside for prayer and peace.

BOXTED
Holy Trinity **
Poley monuments

Boxted House nestles cosily in the bottom of the small valley of the Glem, tributary of the Stour. It has been home to Poleys (pronounced Pooley) for six centuries. The church is virtually the family's private chapel and lies amid fine chestnuts on a hill overlooking the house, as if keeping spiritual watch over it. The medieval church was converted in the mid-17th century, with the addition of a redbrick Poley Chapel. Family pews for the house and its servants were inserted in the north aisle. Both have decorative Jacobean-style screens. The curious gallery in the chancel arch is Victorian – indeed the late 19th-century restoration was so careful that Victorian and Jacobean are barely distinguishable.

Boxted is for Poley monuments. There are Poleys from floor to ceiling, Poleys in wood and stone, Poleys in brass and alabaster and from the Middle Ages to the present day. In Boxted we walk on Poleys, talk of Poleys and, if their ashes are dust, breathe Poleys. For the most part, they are represented by handsome floor stones, rarely noticed features of English churches, beautiful in their calligraphy and dignified in their sentiment. But the two earliest effigies are from the Tudor period, of William and Alice Poley, he dying in 1587, she ten years earlier. He wears armour and she an Elizabethan dress. They are carved from oak, black with age, and lie serene in the light streaming in from their estates outside.

The contrast could not be greater with the occupants of the Poley Chapel opposite. Though Sir John died in 1638 and his wife Abigail in 1652, their memorials were not erected until some time afterwards. Sir John's is dated c.1675 and Abigail's 1725, the Poleys being dilatory in these matters. John Poley was an Elizabethan mercenary who served the kings of both France and Denmark. For the latter he was awarded an honour represented by a gold frog earring. Hence (perhaps) the nursery rhyme, 'a frog he would a wooing go' with its refrain of 'rowley, poley, gammon and spinach'. The four grandees of the neighbourhood are indeed Rowleys (of Stoke), Poleys, Bacons and Greenes. This charming attribution is dismissed in one local guide on the grounds that the song predates this particular Poley, and probably refers to a chicken roll, or *poulet*. I prefer the legend.

Despite fifty years between them, both statues are characteristic English Baroque monuments, the later the more purely classical, with Ionic pilasters replacing the earlier paraphernalia of curtains, consoles and putti. The alabaster statues form a fine 'swagger' pair. Sir John is portrayed with mustachio and pointed beard, one hand on hip and the other lifting his cloak to reveal an armoured leg. Abigail's is more demure, yet a voluptuous figure is evident under a classical toga. On the west wall of the chapel is a lengthy family tree of Poleys from the 14th century to today. The chapel window is full of Poley crests and shields, filtering the sunlight and revealing the old house in the distance.

BRAMFIELD
St Andrew **
Enriched screen, 'second marriage' epitaph

This lovely church still displays an amiable guidebook from the 1940s. Chapters have such headings as, 'A ploughman turns back the pages of history' and 'An acorn falls to the ground'. The building overlooks its village up a road flanked by a crinkle-crankle, or undulating brick wall. The round tower stands separate in the churchyard, apparently defensive and with no sign of an attached nave. The church is Decorated, with steep thatched roof and variegated window tracery.

Dominating the interior is a screen that, for originality, is in the first rank.

The heads of the lights contain ogees and richly ornamented Panel tracery, above which the coving splays outwards in a series of glorious shallow fans. This should be termed rococo Gothic. Sadly only five saints survive in the dado, but these are excellent. On the north side of the chancel is a monument to Arthur and Elizabeth Coke by Nicholas Stone. It was carved in 1629, when most effigies were still lying stiff and supine on slabs of marble. Elizabeth died in childbirth in 1627 and her effigy records that moment. She is shown in bed, reclining on several pillows, with a newborn child poignantly clutched in her arms. Her husband is kneeling by her side, vainly praying for her survival.

Next to the eccentric reredos is a memorial to Bridgett Applewaite. Its epitaph relates that Bridgett, 'after the Enjoiment of the Glorious Freedom of an Easy and Unblemisht Widowhood for four years and upwards, resolved to run the risk of a Second Marriage Bed'. This proved a terrible mistake. 'An Apoplectick Dart (the same Instrument with which Death had formerly dispatcht her Mother) toucht the most Vital part of her Brain', and she duly died 'in terrible convulsions, plaintive groans or stupefying sleep'.

BURES
St Stephen *
De Vere tombs

The village church of St Mary at the bottom of the hill is not to be confused with St Stephen's up above. The latter is hard to find, in a grove a mile to the north-east along a cart track. The church was founded by Archbishop Langton in 1218, believing this to be the spot where St Edmund was crowned king of Anglia in 855. Subsequent history ignored the significance of the venue. For many years it was a barn, but was restored in the 1930s and reconsecrated in 1940.

Steep thatch shelters a single-cell structure, with Early Gothic lancet windows. The church takes the form of a mausoleum for three de Veres, Earls of Oxford, whose memorials are ubiquitous in these parts. The tombs, apparently moved from Earls Colne in Essex, fill the centre of the tiny chamber, forcing the congregation into two rows of chairs on either side. The earliest is of stone, of Roger de Vere (d.1296). He has crossed legs, his feet resting on the family emblem of a boar. The chest, apparently intended for a different tomb, has Decorated ogee arches of about 1330. Some of the weepers survive in a damaged state. The next tomb leaps the Black Death to Thomas de Vere (d.1371). His effigy is of alabaster and the chest also has ogival arches. Most of his weepers survive.

We then skip Richard de Vere (reputed lover of Richard II), who died banished in France in 1392, and reach another Richard de Vere, commander at

Agincourt, with his wife Alice. His tomb is of 1417, Perpendicular with crenellation and angels for weepers. She has a Plantagenet headdress with horns.

These are tombs of the sort we might expect in Warwick or Westminster, not lost on a Suffolk hillside. To Macaulay, the de Veres were 'the longest and most illustrious line of nobles that England has seen'. Yet here they lie alone and unsung, in the humblest of hilltop resting places.

BURY ST EDMUNDS
St Mary ***
Medieval roof carvings, Baret cadaver tomb

This, the parish church of the fine old town of Bury, is architecturally superior to its former sister church of St James next door. But St James's is now a busy cathedral, and St Mary's is left like Cinderella up the road, rather forlorn. The side elevations are bold, with a 14-bay south aisle and the magnificent Notyngham Porch embellishing the north aisle. Inside the porch is a wheel vault with a pendant in which God is ministered to by angels.

The interior has one of the largest and most exhilarating naves in the county. Arcades of ten majestic bays march towards the chancel, each rising on continuous mouldings with only the tiniest of capitals. The unusually wide hammerbeam roof is a marvellous survival. Eleven pairs of angels guard the space below, attended by lesser angels on the wallplates and by saints, martyrs, prophets and kings, 42 figures in all. On the frieze a medieval menagerie takes over, with dragons, unicorns, birds and fish. The east window above the chancel arch is a fiercely coloured version of a pilgrim's badge, depicting the martyrdom of St Edmund. It is by Willement, the early Victorian medievalist whose taste was usually subdued but who here shouts when a murmur might do.

The chancel is a contrast, with a wagon roof decorated a vivid blue. Its wallplate angels and bosses are superb, even if hard to see from below. One is of an angel playing a guitar. Another shows a fox dressed as a bishop preaching to a cock and a hen. In the south aisle is another fine roof, over the chantry of John Baret, merchant of Bury in the 15th century. Its panels, stipulated in Baret's will, celebrate his wealth, piety and Lancastrian sympathies. The stars have little mirrors for twinkling effect. Beneath is Baret's cadaver tomb, actually made before his death to remind him of mortality; these were also known as pardon graves. Baret had obtained papal remission from Purgatory, doubtless at a price, and was eager for his friends to know it.

The south chapel is littered with pleasant brasses. The north aisle by the tower has its memorials spectacularly displayed. They climb up the wall to the ceiling, a valhalla of Bury worthies.

CAVENDISH
St Mary *
Comper reredos with Flemish alabaster

The villages on the Suffolk–Essex border rank with the best of the West Country. Cavendish lies on the upper Stour and is set round a village green. The church is well placed opposite the pub, with a cluster of thatched cottages named Hyde Park Corner as a skirt beneath the tower. Sir John Cavendish was Chief Justice of the King's Bench and had the worst of the Peasants' Revolt of 1381, being beheaded by the rebels. He left £40 for the rebuilding of the church chancel.

Pride of his chancel is the east window, filling its entire elevation with a seven-light wall of glass. This is divided into two three-light arches with a central panelled section towering up between them. Apart from a fragment of medieval glass glowing in the centre of this composition, the trees outside are left to supply the interior with movement, their shadows moving over bright Victorian floor tiles.

The nave was rebuilt a century after the chancel. The interior is whitewashed, high and severe, like many East Anglian churches. There are no roof angels, just coloured bosses, but there is compensation in the furnishings below. These include an Elizabethan eagle lectern of the sort much copied by the Victorians, an active hour glass next to the pulpit, and in the chancel the Purbeck marble chest tomb of Sir George Colt (d.1570). On its top has been carved a graffito of a game known as Alquerque, a complex version of Nine Men's Morris.

The church's principal treasure, against the north wall of the nave, is a fine 16th-century Flemish alabaster of the Crucifixion. This is framed by a Comper reredos and was donated to the church in 1953.

CLARE
St Peter and St Paul ***
Gallery of roof faces, Henry VIII pew

The Norman Earls of Clare were relatives of William the Conqueror and attained great wealth and status. The family was to give its name to County Clare, Clare College and to the first house of the Austin Friars in England, Clare Priory. The estate passed to the Crown in the Wars of the Roses and Henry VIII vested it in each of his wives in turn. It remains an outpost of the royal Duchy of Lancaster, sitting as a gateway to East Anglia from Essex.

For newcomers to the region's churches, Clare is a foretaste of the Perpendicular splendours to come. Seen from almost any angle it floats on the skyline like a great ship, with a small tower for a fo'c'sle and two turrets for masts. In the churchyard are sliced-off yew trees, like bales on the quayside. The aisle windows are so large as to leave little room for wall. The interior is ablaze with light pouring down from the clerestory. Even the west end has a large window, with tracery similar to the great east window at neighbouring Cavendish.

Clare's nave arcades are lavish. When the church was rebuilt in the 15th century the masons reused the piers from the earlier church but inserted four-stepped bases and battlemented capitals to heighten them. The chancel arch and arcades are again earlier survivals, with 14th-century ballflower decoration. A gallery of 15th-century faces look down from above, seeming in perpetual conversation with each other. When Dowsing's iconoclasts visited Clare in 1643 to 'brake down 1,000 pictures superstitious', they tried to shoot down the faces. Bullet holes in the roof indicate the poverty of their marksmanship, or of their guns.

The church retains two fine private pews. In the south aisle is one composed of a former rood screen with splendid tracery incorporating the emblems of Henry VIII and Catherine of Aragon, survivor of the many erected throughout England in honour of the royal nuptials. Most were destroyed a few years later after the Reformation – or after the divorce. Near the door is a more ostentatious gallery pew of the Stuart period. In the chancel are carved Jacobean choir stalls, a rarity. They have richly carved blind arcades, and support poppy-heads and candleholders. The 16th-century eagle lectern was allegedly given by Elizabeth herself (as were most such lecterns). In the east window is some medieval glass that survived Dowsing, depicting the sun and moon.

The south porch has a Green Man boss. One guide suggests that the half face above the door, cut when the aisle was extended outwards into the old porch, may have been a rare Green Woman. The church offers a treatise on Green Men/Women, a mysterious link between medieval Christianity and the myths and legends of the pagan woods. The writer lamely suggests a modern role for the old woodman in the 'unity of mankind with the natural world'. The sundial outside is more workaday. 'Go about your business' it says peremptorily.

COMBS
St Mary *
Medieval glass, animal bench-ends

Suffolk churches seem big even when not especially so. Combs rises on its hillock outside Stowmarket with familiar East Anglian strength. The tower needs no spire to assert itself. The flint walls need no further decoration and can even sustain ugly cement rendering. The churchyard falls away towards the valley bottom, gazing disdainfully at a distant housing estate.

The interior is big and spacious, with high limestone nave walls. A well-proportioned chancel has an elegant ogival window in the north wall and the east window has beautiful Intersecting tracery. The two delights of Combs are its bench-ends and its glass. The benches offer a familiar array of poppyhead figures, as intriguing as at Blythburgh. There are dogs, rabbits, an eagle, a lion and men reading the Bible and at prayer. All are drawn from the biblical passage, 'All ye beasts and cattle, praise ye the Lord.'

Combs's medieval glass was blown out by an explosion five miles away in 1871. After this trauma it was collected in the south aisle, where much of it remains an unresolved jigsaw. The restored composition of some panels depicts the Works of Mercy, including ministering to the thirsty, and scenes from the ever-colourful life of St Margaret. We see the saint as a shepherdess, standing before a King with the Devil on a pedestal, in prison and beating the Devil.

COWLINGE
St Margaret *
Doom painting, Scheemakers monument

Lost in a corner of west Suffolk near the Cambridgeshire border is a church (pronounced Coolinje) blessed, like the best English churches, by the 14th and 18th centuries but spared by the 19th. Its square brick tower was built in 1733 by a lawyer and lord of the manor, Francis Dickins.

The interior carpentry is almost all pre-Victorian and in light oak: nave pews with brass name plates, Georgian pulpit with candleholders, a battered screen and Perpendicular parclose screens round a chapel. Gazing down on it all is a pretty 18th-century gallery under the tower. Nothing seems out of place, not even the stepped benches inside the north door, originally for prisoners at a local 'house of correction' and later used for children.

Over the chancel arch is an extensive Doom painting. This shows, most unusually, St Michael weighing the souls of the dead. The Virgin Mary on the other side is holding a long rod with which she is cheating by tilting the scales in favour of the virtuous. The colours are still strong and are repeated in the arch below.

Dickins's memorial is in the chancel, an urbane intrusion on this scene of vernacular worship. Dickins was a lawyer at the Temple. His tomb claims him as 'seriously religious ... upright without severity in preventing suits and procuring reparation for the injured, ending strife in content'. The accolade was apparently penned by his wife. Not only did he devote his fees to the rebuilding of the tower but also to commissioning a work from one of the finest sculptors of the day, Scheemakers. It is a wall tomb, plain and sober, with ornament limited to a shield of arms in an open pediment in the Palladian taste. Dickins and his wife sit on the tomb chest, proud and comfortable in Roman dress, on either side of a funerary urn. The date is 1747.

DENNINGTON
St Mary **
Sciapod bench-end, parclose screen with lofts

Dennington church stands with all the dignity it can muster in an unshaved churchyard. The tower is massive, the walls are said to be 5 ft thick and their length is prodigious. Such proportions often suggest a disappointing interior. Not at Dennington. This is the church of the Phelip family of Dennington Court, whose head fought at Agincourt and rose to be Lord Bardolph and manager of Henry V's funeral.

The nave is uninterrupted by any screen, granting a noble vista from west to east, under a long wagon roof and with a beautiful Reticulated east window in the distant chancel. Beneath is a mix of medieval benches and later box pews inserted for the gentry, still with upholstered seats. The older seating forms a forest of bench-ends and poppyheads. On one of these is claimed to be the only portrayal of a 'sciapod' in England, a mythical creature that rests from the sun under the shadow of its own massive foot. These most curious of ancient beasts were said to carry fruit at all times to smell, since they died if they breathed contaminated air.

Though the nave has no chancel screen, there are many parclose screens. These have surviving lofts of filigree delicacy, their colour renewed in the 19th century. The tomb of Lord Bardolph (d.1441) and his wife lies in the south chapel, in beautifully restored alabaster. The effigies are superbly carved, with the jewels of her headdress and the buckles on his armour clearly detailed. They are as remarkable for their preservation as for their artistry and they lie bathed in sun from a window presumably inserted for this purpose.

The chancel is Decorated, with foliage capitals on the window shafts. The tracery panels contain old glass depicting architectural motifs, frames for saints lost to the iconoclasts. The sedilia have fine canopies and there is a rare pyx canopy over the altar. The nave still has an old sand table, used in the 19th century to teach children how to write. This was cheaper than the ever breakable slates.

DENSTON
St Nicholas ***
Woodland wallplates, Everard brass

Denston is a Suffolk connoisseur's favourite, to the Suffolk historian Munro Cautley 'the most beautiful and interesting of the smaller churches in the county'. The structure was rebuilt in 1475 as a college by Sir John Howard and John Broughton. A long nave lies along its mound like a beached supertanker, with a diminutive tower as a bridge. The interior is that of a classic late-Perpendicular hall church, with now no divide for the chancel and only a murmur of a capital announcing the curve of its arcade arches.

Like so many East Anglian churches, Denston's character is determined not by stone but by wood and the love that generations of local carvers put into its beautification. This is immediately apparent in the roofs. These are of pale oak, their wallplates carved with hares, hounds and harts in a parade of nature. So joyful is this work that we might guess that the creatures of woods and fields had danced up the church path and leapt on to the walls. Below are benches with carved ends in the nave and box pews in the aisles. The squire's pew has the dimensions of a small drawing-room. Subsidiary pews, presumably for the rectory and larger farms, diminish in size as they progress backwards down the aisle, a class distinction which the Victorians deplored.

With the suppression of chantries, most private chapels became private pews or family mausoleums. Some reverted in the Victorian period or since. Here the chapel to St Nicholas has a window showing his miracles at sea and a bishop holding a model of the church. What passes for the chancel contains carved stalls with traceried fronts and also four misericords. On the floor is a brass to Henry Everard (d.1524) and his wife, a fine example in full Tudor regalia.

When a visitor, James Turner, visited Denston in 1948 he wrote of its condition: 'The box pews were green with wet and slime and the altar cloth was a mass of rat dirt. It is a place of ghosts, of strange sounds when the wind blows, and the ever increasing noise of rats, nibbling as they eat into the woodwork. I suppose the church will eventually fall down.' That could not be said today. English churches may be perpetually in need of help, but none of those listed in this book are falling down, or are ever like to do so.

EARL STONHAM
St Mary ***
Hammerbeam roof carving, triple hour glasses

Some East Anglian churches crouch in their churchyards as if waiting to jump. Others such as Earl Stonham stand bold on an eminence. It is set in rolling country outside Stowmarket and well to the east of its village. The outside has cement rendering, but the clerestory and tower are adorned with flushwork of the highest quality.

The interior is a virtuoso display of Suffolk woodwork. It is cruciform with no aisles, just the deep splays of 14th-century windows and, immediately above them, a Perpendicular clerestory. This lights one of the finest roofs in Suffolk. It is composed of a row of hammerbeams, richly ornamented despite the mutilation of its angels by Dowsing's iconoclasts. The roof continues into the crossing, where it meets Decorated arches to transepts and chancel and then divides in all three directions. This is a wonderfully theatrical effect. In the nave the roof wallplate has three tiers, with angels in the top and bottom tiers. The hammerbeams alternate pendants and angels lying prone. Every member of the roof, even the rafters, is worked with intricate carving – requiring binoculars for detailed study.

The nave is filled with original benches and poppyheads, a silent congregation of nodding trefoils filling every corner. Even the tiny children's benches at the back of the nave have their own poppyheads. Most are local work of 1874. The choir stalls are plainly original, their ends including a man with a bagpipe and a grotesque tricaput of a three-headed monster. Since the old work and that of the Victorian restorers is so similar, we may assume that the latter took inspiration from the former.

The Jacobean pulpit has not one but three hour glasses, plus a holder for a fourth. Sermon length was an obsession of 18th-century congregations or at least of their patrons. Usually the reason was to discipline lazy preachers who were inclined to speak too short a time, not too long. The three glasses measure a quarter, half and three-quarters of an hour. The fourth, presumably for an hour, must have been removed by a prudent congregation.

EUSTON
St Genevieve **
Restoration plaster and woodwork

Do not be deceived by Kent's mock 'church' by the stream, which is really a mill. Euston church lies in the park between the house and the temple on the hill. The site was medieval and its churchyard is a rude intrusion on Kent's picturesque landscape. While landed magnates could move their villages and tenants to suit the whim of their architects, they dared not move God's Acre. Hence Euston's eccentric position. The church was rebuilt in 1676, just after the house, at a time when few country churches were being created. The owner was Lord Arlington, a member of the circle of advisers to Charles II known as the Cabal.

The plain exterior, with round-headed windows and quoins, resembles Wren's City churches. The interior is a virtuoso work of Restoration classicism. The walls and groin vaults are plaster, with restrained but exquisite arabesques in the pilaster strips and with rosettes in the arches. Especially good is the stucco relief in the ceiling of the former Arlington pew.

Euston's forte is its woodwork. The lower walls have plain dados, and the nave is filled with box pews. The pulpit, reredos and screen are boldly carved with high reliefs and openwork. We might indeed be in St Martin within Ludgate (London) or the parlour of a City livery company.

The pulpit is in the style of Gibbons and may be by him, as also might the altar reredos. Memorials of Arlingtons and Graftons fill side chapels and transepts. The south transept window is brown grisaille, but the remaining windows were blessedly relieved of Victorian glass by the modern Duke of Grafton, a notable conservationist, who admirably restored the church in the 1970s.

EYE
St Peter and St Paul **
Tower flushwork, Comper furnishings

Eye tower is one of the most magnificent in this county of fine towers. It stands aloof from the centre of the small town, happily placed at the end of Church Street beyond the black and white former Guildhall. Architectural interest lies in the beauty of the flint flushwork on the west front, its designers imitating on a flat surface the verticality and ornamental subtlety which the masters of Perpendicular achieved in stone. The panels soar upwards to merge into a superbly decorative parapet. The corner buttresses are rounded and look from below like extended telescopes rising the full height of the tower.

The south porch contains a rare dole table with, above it, a poem illustrating the diverse legal uses of medieval porches. The church interior is notable chiefly for its screen and for Comper's enlivening of the furnishings. The 15th-century roof was given new carvings in the 1860s. The new corbel heads on the deep wallplates are hard to distinguish from medieval ones; they appear to be commoners supporting kings, all with lifelike faces. Tinted glass was removed from the clerestory in 1969 and replaced by clear: praise be.

The screen dates from 1480 and retains on its dado some of the most complete paintings of saints in the county. Their faces, undamaged by iconoclasts, are naive but the settings are beautiful, with blue curtains and gold background. St Ursula is particularly jolly, with her virgins sheltering under her mantle. She gazes at Henry VI, who looks like a doll. The original coving survives.

In 1925 Comper touched all this with his wand and brought it to life. To him we owe the screen's restored coving, loft and rood group with attendant seraphim and dragons, all gilded. Above in the roof is a superb gilded canopy of honour. Comper also designed the delicate font cover.

Eye church is in the Anglo-Catholic tradition. A florid 14th-century tomb recess in the north aisle has been converted into a Shrine to Our Lady, with a modern carving of the Virgin and Child, her drapery flowing as if in the wind.

FRAMLINGHAM
St Michael ****
16th-century Howard family mausoleum

Framlingham Castle is among the most picturesque in England, its towers and battlements riding majestically over the Suffolk landscape. Until the 17th century, it belonged to the Dukes of Norfolk, variously of the Mowbray and Howard lines. At the Dissolution, the 3rd Duke lost his ancestral mausoleum of Thetford Priory, and rebuilt the chancel at Framlingham church as the new resting place for his family's remains. He was condemned to death by Henry VIII, but was reprieved when the king died the day before the execution was due to take place. Though uncle of both Anne Boleyn and Catherine Howard and politically reckless, the Duke contrived to die in his bed in 1554. His new mausoleum served its purpose for only a few years, since in 1555 his son, the 4th Duke, married Mary Fitzalan and moved the family's principal seat to her home in Sussex. The tombs at Framlingham are thus from just three decades of the 16th century.

The church exterior is conventional Suffolk Perpendicular, though its tower has an unusually elaborate bell-opening. The flushwork of the clerestory and the pierced lead cresting of the roof are superb. Inside, this roof is no less sensational. The arch braces fall on to hammerbeams, but these are not revealed, being concealed behind an 'aisle' of wooden lierne vaults. This is not a roof of angels and fantasy, more one of virtuoso carpentry.

There is no escaping that this is a church remodelled as the shrine to a great family. Huge open chapels flank the chancel on both north and south sides. These house and celebrate the tombs that now stand splendidly restored and recoloured, offering an array of early classicism unique in England. They are rightly described by the guidebook as 'the last major display of religious imagery in England before the full weight of the Reformation theology made such things impossible'.

Much ink has been spilt over the dates of the four main 16th-century tombs, but the work is now thought to belong to two phases, the 1530s and the 1550s–60s. The effigies are not the strongest feature of the works, interest lying chiefly in the details of the tomb chests beneath them. The first tomb, south of the altar, belongs to the builder of the chapels, the 3rd Duke. The chest probably dates from the 1530s, with the effigies added in the 1550s. The design is unorthodox classical, thick with balusters, colonnettes and double capitals. Yet the saints round the chest are grave figures beautifully carved in shell niches, true Renaissance forms.

Nearby is the tomb of Henry Fitzroy, son of Henry VIII by Catherine of Aragon's lady-in-waiting, Elizabeth Blount. He was created Duke of Richmond and married the 3rd Duke's daughter; alas for Norfolk's ambitions, he died aged seventeen in 1536. The tomb is more chaste and classical than the 3rd Duke's, with Ionic pilasters round the chest, and probably belongs to the mid-16th century. However, the reliefs round the top of the chest, showing scenes from Genesis, including the Expulsion from the Garden of Eden, are probably earlier work moved from Thetford.

The north chapel contains two monuments of a similar date. Against the wall is the small tomb of the infant daughter of the 4th Duke, Elizabeth (d.1565). It is a simple classical chest modelled on that of the Duke of Richmond, crowned by a Gothic ogee canopy, presumably from a former monument. Also in this chapel is the tomb of the 4th Duke's two wives. Its classicism is much the most accomplished, with full columns round the chest, surmounted by beautifully carved consoles.

Next door, the style alters again with the 1614 tomb of an earlier Howard, the Earl of Surrey, beheaded in 1547. The proportions are exaggerated, effigies are boastful and architectural features heavy and distorted. Decorum was re-established with the acquisition of Framlingham from the Howards by Robert Hitcham in 1635. His tomb is a serene black marble slab of 1638, with no effigy and supported by kneeling angels. He lies in the south chapel, apparently happy to be overshadowed by his ducal surroundings.

HADLEIGH
St Mary *
Town steeple, Perpendicular font

Hadleigh is not quite Lavenham, but a fine wool town none the less. The bold spire of the church soars over the façades of the high street, drawing us into a small close. Here the church sits between the old Guildhall and the splendid red-brick tower of the Tudor Dean's Palace. In the East Anglian contest between steeples and naves, Hadleigh is a victory for steeples. The spire is lead-covered, soaring on broaches above the 14th-century tower. On its east face hangs an ancient angelus bell, to summon townspeople to Mass. The guide says this is as old as the tower and could thus be one of the oldest bells in England.

The rest of Hadleigh church was built slowly over the period of the town's greatest wealth. The Perpendicular nave is of five graceful bays, with two more forming the chancel. Hadleigh suffered sorely from a Dowsing visitation. In February 1644 he 'brake down thirty superstitious pictures and gave orders for taking down the rest which were about seventy'. The Victorian glass in the south chapel tells the story of the Hadleigh martyr, Rowland Taylor. He was burned at the stake during the Marian Counter-Reformation in 1555, for having previously ousted a Catholic priest from the church. Even the soldiers guarding him wept at his courage. We must long for a modern Dowsing to dispose of the present glass in the chapel's east window.

In the chancel is a fine bench-end, perhaps representing a wolf but with cloven feet holding St Edmund's head in its jaws. The best work in the church is the Perpendicular font. This is octagonal with delicate blind niches and angels. It has a fine modern cover by Charles Spooner of 1925.

HESSETT
St Ethelbert *
South porch, Christ of the Trades mural

Hessett is a classic Suffolk church, wealthy and well mannered. The tower with its frieze and pierced battlements and the magnificent south porch were the gift of the Bacon family. The Hoo family gave the north aisle, the chancel chapel and the font. Such was the patronage expected of the county's comfortable 15th-century bourgeoisie.

The porch is of mixed stone and knapped flint and has a well-composed entrance, with St George and the Dragon in the door-frame. The church interior is both spacious and gracious. The four Perpendicular bays rise to an original roof. The benches are severe and the ogee lights to the screen have no tracery.

Hessett retains two treasures lost to most medieval churches, a considerable amount of medieval glass and original wall paintings. The glass is fragmentary but plentiful. A window of St Nicholas in the south aisle appears to portray a boy with a golf club. The guide describes this as St James with a fuller's club, used for treating cloth.

Of the paintings, there is a St Christopher unusually located over the south door, with fishes in the river and pictures of the donors underneath. On the north wall are the Seven Deadly Sins in the form of men in the branches of a tree emerging from the mouth of Hell. Here too is a Christ of the Trades, showing the tools forbidden to be used on Sunday lest Christ's wounds bleed. Very few of these admonitory murals survive: *see* Breage (Cornwall).

The tools have been dated to *c.*1430 and may have accompanied a chapel endowed by a local trade guild. The trades depicted include a playing-card maker, possibly indicating a Flemish painter, and a scourge, as used by a schoolmaster or a constable. Sabbatarianism was either strict, or badly in need of strictness, in 15th-century Hessett.

The church owns a fine set of altar cloths, including a rare pyx cloth. Like many church treasures, these were 'lent' to the British Museum and are unlikely to return. Thieves are not alone in stripping churches of their glory. How are they to attract visitors if they cannot keep their treasures?

ICKLINGHAM
All Saints *
Thatched roof, 17th-century fittings

The village has two churches, both medieval and both illustrated on the jolly village sign. All Saints is the more interesting, albeit now redundant, lying picturesquely on a small mound on the village outskirts. An earlier Norman building is recalled in ghostly fragments of Norman windows on the outside of the north wall. The nave is thatched and the roof interior is unceiled, which gives the church a pleasant harvest smell.

The richest feature of the church is its south aisle, with a splendid Reticulated east window and fine statue niches flanking its altar. The church is fitted out in the Churches Conservation Trust's most characteristic 'atmospheric' style, with limewash and 17th-century fittings. The altar rail, pulpit, family pew and bench-ends are crude but seemly.

The font, as Pevsner says, is 'a veritable mason's pattern book' of 14th-century tracery motifs. The windows mostly have clear glass, except in the south aisle and chancel. These retain the upper portions of original windows, showing figures and architectural canopies of unusual completeness.
[CCT]

KEDINGTON
St Peter and St Paul ****
Unmodernised interior, Barnardiston tombs

Kedington comes in the top rank of small English churches. It offers nothing out of the ordinary, nothing jarring or shocking, just consistency of craftsmanship and the harmony of ages. On a sunny day we can sit in the churchyard and watch the shadows glide over tombstones and spread across the chancel wall, as they have done for centuries.

Inside, no inch is without diversion. Nave and aisles contain every component of a parish church, tombs, screens, pews, altars, paintings, all tumbling out of the gloom. Overhead a hammerbeam roof is illuminated by strange sky-lights. The nave piers have 18th-century painted fluting. In each spandrel is a hatchment, most belonging to the local Barnardiston family, grandees of Kedington from the Middle Ages to the 18th century.

The seating forms an extraordinary collection, from small uncomfortable benches at the back to tall family pews at the front. The Barnardiston pew on the left is composed of the battered fragments of the old screen, complete with defaced saints. The tall three-decker pulpit still has its tester, candle, hour glass and wigstand.

At the back of the church is a set of raised children's pews with a boxed-in seat for the teacher, and next to them a musicians' gallery. A Jacobean screen of 1619 guards the chancel, but can be folded back on hinges. The survival of all this in one place is remarkable. It is reminiscent of another Dickensian sort of church, that of Puddletown (Dorset).

The aisles are devoted to Barnardiston tombs, earlier in the south aisle, later in the north. They form a gallery of vernacular monuments from the Middle Ages to the Renaissance and on into the 18th century. There are Barnardistons of 1503, 1584, 1609 and 1610. None is of great quality and the early effigies are battered. The value is in the collection as a whole, a vivid evocation of dynasties past and glories gone. More tombs are in the Barnardiston vault, reached from behind the pulpit and reputedly containing up to fifty coffins. John Betjeman understandably christened Kedington 'a village Westminster Abbey'.

KERSEY
St Mary *
Junk shop of Gothic carvings

Kersey is a Suffolk 'picture village'. Its main street swoops down one side of a small valley, across a ford and then up the other. The church is on a hill at one end.

No tower could ask for a finer setting. Kersey's presents itself to the world as a miniature Stoke-by-Nayland, dominating the landscape north of Hadleigh. The tower flushwork extends to the decoration of the buttresses and the pretty Perpendicular south porch. This has an unusual wooden ceiling of 16 intricately carved panels, elegant as if intended for somewhere grander.

Inside the church, the eye is drawn to a fine half-hammerbeam roof. But the chief interest is in the north aisle. This part of the church is pre-Perpendicular, with a seven-bay arcade of c.1335. The aisle has been curiously mutilated over the centuries – or perhaps endearingly maltreated is more appropriate. Its windows are Decorated, with a four-petal motif in their tracery. Between two of them is a large niche under an ogee arch, presumably meant for a large statue. There are also two niches either side of the altar. All are empty. Between the aisle and the main sanctuary is an excellently canopied sedilia group, heavily restored.

Hovering over the east end of this aisle is a 17th-century plasterwork ceiling, with the arms of the local Sampson and Thorrowgood families. Also displayed are six panels from a rood screen dado, in remarkably good condition. One is of St Edmund, the martyr king and a favourite of 15th-century screen painters, holding an arrow.

Yet the final charm of Kersey's north aisle is its collection of medieval junk. Fragments of painted stonework, corbels, bosses and large lumps of meaningless chalk have been left on every niche and shelf. Who gathered up this detritus of the Middle Ages we do not know. Such relics were usually dispersed after the Reformation, finding their way into house walls or ground down for mortar.

LAKENHEATH
St Mary *
Acrobat bench-end, sedge kneelers

Lakenheath lies across the open country where the Fens merge with the Breckland and where clay becomes infertile sand. This was long an unpopulated area. The skyline is filled only with contorted pines and firs, wandering like cripples into the distance. The landscape is still blighted by ageing and ugly air bases. Lakenheath was one of the biggest American bases in England and the Stars and Stripes still hangs in its honour by a private altar in the south aisle of the church.

Entering St Mary's we are immediately faced with Lakenheath's most remarkable survival. In place of a north arcade pier is a stretch of wall carrying a medieval wall painting of the Tree of Life flanked by saints. One is St Edmund carrying the arrows of his martyrdom at the hands of the Danes. It is well preserved and offers a glimpse of how these churches would have looked when painted throughout. At the foot of the mural are two old bundles of matted sedge from the fens. These are early kneelers.

The church also has fine stone and wood carving. Corbel heads appear to have suffered from the iconoclasts, but the roof angels are big and the benches have superbly carved ends, pierced backs, and deep wooden bases which would once have been filled with straw for warmth in winter.

The Lakenheath bench-ends are celebrated for their originality and domestic themes. The characters include animals, priests, a farmer harvesting his crop and a splendid contortionist. Each presents the carver with the challenge of squeezing the figure into the frame as if it was itself an act of contortion. A unicorn has its horn tucked under its back, while a tiger tries to see itself in a mirror. The iconography of these images remains a mystery.

The font is rare in being 13th century. The bowl is supported on an octagonal stem and detached shafts, with gables and thick stiff-leaf foliage in the panels. Above is a bold wooden cover of 1961. The guide apologises for the shortage of other modern works of art. After the Reformation, it says, 'the villagers, having seen their gifts and those of their forefathers wantonly destroyed, have never again given of their very moderate wealth to the extent of their ancestors'. To use the Reformation to excuse church poverty today is stretching a point.

LANDWADE
St Nicholas *
Estate setting, Cotton tombs

South of Burwell, the land rises towards the chalk ridges of Newmarket. Here the Fen marshes gave way to richer estates. Landwade was acquired by the Cotton family in the 15th century and stayed with them into the 19th, when the Gibsons arrived. The church lies in fields beyond the house, a gracious English setting, part formal avenue with temples, part wilder parkland. A stream flows under a bridge in the garden. The church sits amid trees, the ground in springtime carpeted with snowdrops, crocuses, then daffodils.

The structure is of little architectural interest, that of an unaisled estate church whose window tracery has been renewed and whose exterior is cemented. The inside is more charming, especially when caught with sunlight falling on its limestone and whitewash. The nave has medieval benches with crude poppyheads. Old corbel heads stare down from the restored roof. The heraldic glass is of Cottons, with saints for company. The walls are lit by candles.

The assembled Cotton tombs are a surprise. Behind a Decorated chancel screen lie four Purbeck chests, covered on my visit with dust sheets and mousetraps as if awaiting a celestial removal man. The earliest is in the north chapel, of Sir John Cotton (d.1593) and his wife Isabel. The six-poster canopy is crowned with obelisks and heavy openwork scrolls round a coat of arms. The effigies are stiff but wonderfully rich, his gloves and her lace petticoats beautifully crafted. Traces of gilding survive in the architrave.

In the south chapel is a wall tomb recess, with heavy decoration but no effigy. Here I found a miniature haystack, as if in offering. Against the west wall is another John, who died in 1620, although his tomb is probably of thirty years later. He lies on his side and looks down on his supine wife. A third John (d.1689) rests against the south wall, still on his side and in armour, but bewigged, with his legs crossed and a satisfied grin on his face.

LAVENHAM
St Peter and St Paul ****
Late-Gothic chantries and screens

The old saying gives Lavenham the town, Long Melford the church and
Stoke-by-Nayland the tower. I agree. Now that Lavenham has rid itself of road
markings and overhead wires, it has only to oust parked cars to rival Chipping
Campden in Gloucestershire as the perfect pre-Georgian market town. But the
church is its equal. Many enthusiasts prefer it to Long Melford, finding it less
ostentatious, more serene. To the purist, its tower is more original, its nave
more Perpendicular and its chancel arch more majestic. Against this must be set
its dire Victorian glass, but for that at least there is an easy cure.

The late 15th-century rebuilding of most of Lavenham was undertaken by the
de Veres at the head of a consortium of local families. The building commission
was to celebrate the Tudor triumph at Bosworth, in which the de Veres played a
part. The town contribution came chiefly from the Spryngs, wealthy clothiers
whose arms, with those of the de Veres, are ubiquitous in the church. The
alliance was later cemented when a Spryng married a de Vere, new money
marrying old. The tower was begun at once in 1486, the year after Bosworth,
and building continued through to the 1520s, by when both the Spryng and the
de Vere who had begun the project had died. The Reformation brought work to
a halt, with the chancel not yet rebuilt.

The tower dominates the overall composition and is almost as high as
the nave is long. Its pinnacles were never added. De Vere's porch is a superb
example of early Tudor patronage: the doorway is crowned with the boars of
the de Veres, a rebus from the Latin *verres*, a boar. It has been whitewashed,
which seems oddly garish against the soft flint walls of nave and tower. Its niche
contains modern statues of St Peter and St Paul.

Lavenham's interior is one of the most dramatic in Suffolk. The nave is high
and noble, the roof original but unusually modest in its detail, with bosses only
in the eastern bays. It is as if the designer did not wish to detract from the great
chancel arch, dating from the early 14th century, that is before the rebuilding. It
rises above a Decorated screen of exquisite tracery. Each opening is a flower
burst of fronds topped by an ogee arch, each a work of art in itself.

In the nave aisles stand Lavenham's chief treasures, possibly the finest
parclose screens not just in Suffolk but in the country. In the north aisle is the
former chantry of the younger Thomas Spryng, dated 1523. It is now dedicated
to St Catherine and St Blaise, the latter the patron saint of clothiers, terrifyingly
'combed to death' by the emperor Diocletian. The screen is of the finest tracery,
flamboyant rather than Perpendicular, a riot of naturalism with branches,

tendrils, fronds and crocketing decorating dado, uprights, coving and canopy. The oak is as dark as ebony.

In the south aisle stands the slightly earlier Spourne Chantry. Here the tracery is less fantastic, with each ogee embracing flower petal ribs, but no less fine in its craftsmanship. These two chantries are superb works of early 16th-century craftsmanship.

Beyond stretches the old chancel, forbidding in its gloom: the Decorated tracery surely deserves the light of nature. But the misericords are excellent and include a couple playing home-made musical instruments. There are two chancel chapels. The one to the north commemorates Simon Branch and that to the south, the elder Thomas Spryng. The latter contains Georgian glass reproducing Dutch depictions of the Life of Christ, and a fine Virgin and Child of 1982 by Neil Godfrey.

LONG MELFORD
Holy Trinity *****
Richest East Anglian church, Clopton Chantry, Lily Crucifix, medieval glass

One day we may honour towns created in the 20th century as we now honour Lavenham and Long Melford. For the time being, there is no contest. They both embody the informal yet graceful development of 16th- and 17th-century England. They were not planned, growing up round medieval streets as and when building was needed, yet today they seem all of a piece. Once among the richest towns in Europe, their churches reflected that wealth. Long Melford was blessed with three wool tycoons, the Cloptons of Kentwell, the Cordells of Melford Hall and the Martyns of Melford Place. All left their mark on a church which is a treasure house of English medieval art.

Of a former church on the site, only the nave arcades survive, with piers and capitals of the 14th century. The remainder was rebuilt c.1490 under the ascendancy of John Clopton, the arcades being extended to nine bays. Clopton generosity is recalled throughout the church, with thirty-two members of the family honoured in the north aisle donors' windows. Other names associated with the building include Loveday, Boteler, Smyth, Hyll, Martyn and, as one inscription relates, 'all the well-disposed men of this town'. These donors so dominate the Melford story that we can never escape them.

Like its Cotswold contemporaries, Long Melford is almost all late-Perpendicular, its excitement deriving from contents more than architecture. Nothing at Long Melford is hidden under a bushel. The exterior is stretched out on a rise at the edge of the town, a giant of flushwork, flint and glass. Tudor almshouses frame the churchyard approach. The original tower was destroyed by lightning, replaced in the 18th century and further encased in flint in 1903.

The chancel displays a single lofty window embracing the clerestory, reminiscent of a Tudor banqueting hall. The Lady Chapel has steeply pitched roofs ending in three gables. It is the only chapel of such ambition attached to an English parish church – though Burford (Oxon) is similar – and is surrounded by a sunny ambulatory.

The interior is best appreciated by moving clockwise round the church from the north aisle. The surviving north window glass records a plutocracy that must have deterred even the most determined iconoclast. Second from the left is the 'Alice in Wonderland' glass of Elizabeth Talbot, said to have inspired John Tenniel's drawings for Lewis Carroll. Next to it is a glass of three rabbits sharing three ears, representing the Trinity. The remainder of the north aisle is a roll call of kneeling donors and associated saints and heraldry, God and Mammon in magnificent unison.

At the east end of this aisle is the Kentwell Chapel. Here Sir William Clopton (d.1446), father of John, rests in prayer and calm serenity. Next door is an alabaster relief of the Adoration fixed to the wall, presumably recovered from a ruined reredos. This is the Clopton corner. Family brasses litter the floor. In the east wall is a double squint, cutting through both chapel and chantry wall for a glimpse of the high altar. A passage now leads east through a tiny priest's alcove, containing a fireplace and its own miniature fan vault, into John Clopton's private chantry.

The Clopton Chantry contrasts with the rest of the church. It is a small chapel with a continuous frieze of saints in niches with, round the cornice, John Lydgate's 'Vine of Life' poem in the form of a scroll. The tomb of John Clopton (d.1497) stands in the wall between the chantry and main chancel. It has no effigies, but the vault of the canopy has faded portraits of him and his wife and a well-preserved Christ, apparently walking with a flowing cloak. The chapel east window contains an exquisite and now rare Lily Crucifix, depicting Christ on the leaves of a lily against a sky-blue background (*see* Godshill on the Isle of Wight and Abingdon in Oxfordshire). The clear glass round it reveals a hollybush outside. This chapel would once have been a blaze of colour.

We now enter the chancel, and encounter the Cordell family and the Renaissance. Clopton was a merchant prince of the early Tudor period; Sir William Cordell (d.1580) was a new man, a lawyer-courtier to the Elizabethans. He was a judge and Speaker of the House of Commons. His entertainment of Elizabeth I at Melford Hall set a standard for extravagance that ruined numerous courtiers.

The century dividing Cordell's tomb from Clopton's could hardly be wider. Cordell may still lie in medieval armour with his hands in prayer, but above him rise the columns, coffered arches and Cardinal Virtues of classicism. Justice, Prudence, Temperance and Fortitude watch over him in Roman dress.

Balancing the Clopton Chapel on the south side of the chancel is the Martyn Chapel, notable for early family brasses. From here we reach the separate Lady Chapel. The building was used as a school after the Reformation and a multiplication table is preserved on the east wall. The chapel has the unusual form of a central sanctuary surrounded on four sides by an ambulatory. It is a happy, light-filled place with an old clock on the wall. Today it must be Britain's grandest Sunday school. The verges outside are lined in summer with giant hollyhocks, dancing attendance on well-clipped yews.

MENDLESHAM
St Mary *
Village armoury, font cover

The church rises proud in the centre of its village, the churchyard forming the village green. The tower has a flushwork parapet and the north porch is guarded with pinnacles in the form of wildmen and beasts. This is as well, as the room above contains England's only surviving village armoury. The weapons and armour date from the 15th to the 17th century and were kept for the use of villagers, or at least those in authority, in case of insurrection. Like roods, vestments, wall paintings and statues of the Virgin, these fragments of churches past have almost all vanished, and those that survive are the more precious.

The interior of the church is surprisingly spacious. The Early Gothic nave is six bays long, though the eastern bay appears to be the remains of a crossing. The aisles retain their old roofs, and most of the windows are Decorated. Benches keep their poppyheads, with a wyvern biting its tail near the north door. The pulpit is by a local carver, John Turner, who also executed the unforgettable font cover in 1630. It is a confection of pediments and obelisks on columns, a classical answer to Ufford's Gothic wedding cake.

Today Mendlesham is the highest of Anglo-Catholic churches. Not an altar is undressed and icons and candles crowd every shelf. The south porch has been converted into a chapel of the Holy Cross. It is decorated with modern paintings by Cyril Fraden. These depict the finding of the Cross by St Helena with, says the guide, 'a subsidiary theme of water'. They will not be to every taste. To see the armoury requires an appointment.

MILDENHALL
St Mary and St Andrew ****
Naturalistic roof carvings, east window tracery

Mildenhall lies off the main road to Norwich and is a small market town with an ancient market cross. Unusually for East Anglia, where churches are normally on the outskirts of settlements, the church appears squeezed on to a central site, surrounded by undistinguished buildings and with only a small churchyard.

There are compensations. Fronting the high street is one of England's most remarkable Decorated east windows. Seven lights rise to what might be an 18th-century lace collar wrought in stone. Two pointed lights flank an octofoil, surrounded by 12 quatrefoils. The purpose of this window must have been purely decorative, with the Virgin in the central space and other saints in attendance round her. But oh for the original glass!

The porch, one of the largest in Suffolk, is a theatrical composition. Its upper storey was the village school. Locals recall that, at Easter between the two world wars, children would still throw flowers down on those coming to worship. Inside, the nave is Perpendicular, with inventive Panel tracery in the aisles. The clerestory tracery appears eager to imitate the halo effect of the east window surround. The chancel and adjacent north chapel are mostly Early Gothic, with stepped lancet windows and stiff-leaf capitals.

All eyes turn to the roofs. That in the nave is low-pitched, with tie-beams alternating with hammerbeams. The purpose of this is more decorative than structural. The hammers are carved with large angels, whose outspread wings seem to fill the roof volume. Every member is carved and decorated. But the nave is surpassed by the more visible roofs of the aisles, with some of the finest carving in England. Here the hammerbeams are actually in the form of angels, lying as if peering over the edge of a cliff.

The more elaborate decorative programme is in the north aisle. Here each spandrel is a carved panel, an independent work of art depicting a mix of biblical and domestic scenes. The wall-posts are in the form of saints in niches with angels watching over them. At Mildenhall, the art is not applied to the roof but is integral to it. Here is structure fashioned into art, like the caryatids on the Erechtheum or Red Indian totem poles.

The spandrel designs are reproduced in photographs on the wall below. Many of the figures were defaced in the Reformation and again under the Commonwealth. Records show that a man in 1651 was paid a shilling a day to 'deface all symbols of superstition' in the church, which is odd since they were supposedly removed a century earlier. Angels are full of gunshot as soldiers tried to bring them down without erecting scaffolding. One figure in the north aisle still has the head of a pike embedded in its garment. Despite such injuries the roofs offer a glorious array of religious art.

The tower has a choir loft with a fine fan vault beneath it. The North family have two memorials in the south aisle, one an alabaster effigy of 1620 with children kneeling beneath, the other a contrasting Baroque cartouche.

NEEDHAM MARKET
St John **
Giant hammerbeam roof

Yet another roof. Needham Market church contains one of England's most spectacular works of medieval engineering. Experts shower its wooden hammerbeams with superlatives, though the appeal is more to the head than the heart. The roof is a textbook demonstration of lateral thrust turned into vertical. Unfortunately it lacks a great church beneath.

The building lies in the middle of the town and its exterior is that of a Victorian chapel of cheap ashlar and flint. There is no tower, no aisles, a rather odd bell-turret above the porch and no churchyard. The clerestory might from the outside be a row of weavers' attics. St John's was rebuilt *c.* 1500 and appears to have been bare of chapels, monuments or ornaments. There are medieval poppyheads surviving in the chancel, a Victorian pulpit and a modern screen. The chairs are schoolroom.

The roof is a different matter. It seems to float in the air unattached, not only long and wide, but immensely deep, making a complete chamber in itself. Hammerbeam construction involves each horizontal member resting on a deep wall-post that distributes weight down a wall rather than pushing it out on to buttresses, as with a Gothic arch. The hammerbeam can be single or double and lends itself to splendid carving. The distinctive feature of Needham's roof is its vast height, as if it were a church in itself. It begins with a coving, leading to vertical 'aisle walls', then lean-to 'aisle roofs' rise up to a vertical clerestory, complete with windows. Rising from the hammerbeams are lofty vertical posts which take the role of nave piers. They soar to the dizzy height of the low-pitched nave roof.

To complete this tour-de-force, the roof has spectacular carving. The coving is adorned with angels and fleurons. Pendants on the roof-posts drop below the angels on the beam ends, creating an effect of lightness, as if the beams were suspended from above. Finally the posts are braced by a network of further members, all cambered and crenellated, forming a lattice against the dark wood of the rafters.

This was all covered by a low ceiling in the 18th and 19th centuries, not removed until 1880. It was then that the main hammerbeam angels were inserted or replaced. They have their wings alternately open and closed, as if flapping in the breeze. What Needham Market did to deserve this splendour is unclear.

ORFORD
St Bartholomew *
Perpendicular font

The road from Snape to Orford is as lovely as any in Suffolk. Pines rise out of sandy meadows and the scent in the air changes from marshland to sea. Soon the two Norman towers of Orford rise on the horizon, the castle keep to the right and the church to the left. The town is today more a village, its environs spoilt by retirement bungalows. But the church stands proud on its mound and the ruins of a former chancel lie to the east, with moulded arches and great shafted piers still standing. Traces of the old Norman crossing survive inside in the present chancel. The top stage of the tower fell in the 19th century and was not replaced, with its flushwork parapet, until 1971.

The church consists only of the old 14th-century nave. Though the stonework is whitewashed and rather cold, the undulating mouldings of the Decorated arcades are restful on a hot afternoon. Orford's shadows are a relief from the glasshouses of East Anglian Perpendicular. Most of the furnishings are Victorian or 20th century, but the font is an original Suffolk octagon with much of its carving intact, including a wildman with club, a powerful Trinity and lovely Pietà. The Hampshire carver, Sidney Tugwell, designed the 20th-century screen and choir stalls.

At the west end of the nave is a rough museum which includes old coffin lids, bells, stocks and pictures of the church in various stages of decay and restoration. There is also a floor memorial to Benjamin Britten. Orford saw the first performances of *Noye's Fludde*, *Curlew River*, *The Burning Fiery Furnace* and *The Prodigal Son* (*see* Aldeburgh).

POLSTEAD
St Mary *
Hilltop setting, font cover by Oxford nun

Polstead sits across a small valley beyond Stoke-by-Nayland and is a place of mystery. In the village pond a witch was once 'swum'. The village was also scene of a famous murder, that of a village girl by a local farmer's son, William Corder, in 1827. He had induced her to flee with him to a secret marriage at Bury, but killed her to marry someone else. Such was the celebrity of the case that when Corder was hanged a year later at Bury St Edmunds, 10,000 people turned out to watch. The hangman sold the rope at a guinea an inch and the trial record was bound in Corder's own skin (now at the Bury Museum). Not surprisingly, the village cottages require frequent exorcism.

Polstead church is one of Suffolk's few Norman works. It sits well on a hill, its lead roof recently replaced by one of stainless steel. I remember seeing this roof in its early days from across the valley, shining like a new kitchen utensil. It has mellowed since and the stone spire has been able to reassert itself on the landscape.

The Norman style is immediately visible at the entrance, with a zigzag doorway surround. The arcades are round-arched, except the one supporting the tower, and appear to be of Norman bricks. This greatly excited Pevsner, who concluded that these are among the earliest bricks found in England after the Romans (see Copford in Essex). Many look new, presumably later restorations, but some at least are old; these, together with the brown tufa stones, make Polstead a most exotic relic. To add to its interest, there is a Norman brick clerestory.

The pews have heraldic shields of manorial lords and of the patrons of the living, including St John's College, Oxford. The font is a brick bowl set on 13th-century supports. This is most rare (in my experience unique) and indicates a church too poor and inaccessible to afford stone or lead lining. The modern cover undulates to represent the waters of the Jordan and was made of fibreglass by an Oxford nun. A gauche Jacobean memorial behind the pulpit is to Jacob Brand, lord of the manor, with his hand on his son's head in prayer.

RATTLESDEN
St Nicholas *
Victorian angel roof

Rattlesden, says the Suffolk church historian, Munro Cautley, 'in its restored state approximates more nearly than any in the county to the appearance of a late 15th-century village church'. The operative word is 'approximates'. The church looks out from its slope to rows of bungalows apparently situated so as to cause maximum offence.

Yet the church itself is undeniably handsome, with a tower and conical spire rare in Suffolk and, inside, one of the most spectacular angel roofs. Nowhere have I seen the famous 'wing-flutter' to such effect. Creatures crowd the rafters like birds in a coop, with lesser wings in the aisles. The wood is rich and dark, though it is not original.

Rattlesden roof is not medieval but an 1883 re-creation. It is no less dramatic for that. The angels are all Victorian carvings, a single original in the south aisle having been used as the model. The chancel roof has its hammerbeam enclosed in panelling. Equally impressive are the modern rood screen and parclose screen, by the Devon master G. H. Fellowes Prynne, superb works of early 20th-century craftsmanship. They deserve the same accolades now visited on the 18th-century masters. A screen and loft continue round into the south chapel, incorporating the original loft staircase. A kaleidoscope of medieval glass has been fashioned into a cross in the north aisle.

SOUTHWOLD
St Edmund ****
Flint flushwork exterior, medieval choir stalls, 20th-century font cover

Southwold is the grandest of the galleons that once sailed the length of the Suffolk coast. It has survived while Walberswick, Covehithe and Dunwich disappeared or decayed. The mighty flint tower is an East Anglian classic and its porch a fitting companion. The proportion of tower to nave is harmonious, 100 ft to 144 ft. Nowhere in Suffolk is the subtle interplay of flushwork flint and stone better displayed. What the Somerset masons could fashion from sculpted stone, their Suffolk contemporaries fashioned in the marquetry of knapped flint.

Southwold church sits on the outskirts of the resort, surrounded by a spacious close, and seems to affirm permanence on a constantly shifting coast. The west front is a glory of flushwork. Panelling rises up each buttress, dado and niche. Chequerboard courses and a pseudo-pierced parapet are all created flush with the wall. Round the west window is the simple inscription which translates from the Latin as 'Saint Edmund Pray For Us', each letter under a flushwork crown.

The porch speaks the same language. It has chequerboard stone and flint on its battlements. Two Perpendicular windows light the south wall of the upper chamber and a modern statue of St Edmund fills the niche. The porch is vaulted and the door, with linenfold panelling, is original.

The interior is a hymn to light, enhanced by the clear glass in the windows and by sensitive restoration. Nothing jars. The 19th- and 20th-century work, so often offensive, here preserves or re-creates a stylistic whole, essentially that of the late 15th century. The roof alternates arched braces and angels on hammerbeams. As they reach the chancel area, the angels change from monochrome to vivid colouring, their feathers spread beneath a sky of blue and golden stars.

Below is a forest of screens. The chancel screen has no tracery, the decoration being carried on the painted uprights and the cusped arches. The saints are excellently painted. The 1870s retouching is said to be 'diffident', though Norman Scarfe in the Shell Guide remarks that St Jude was made to seem 'very much like the rector'.

Southwold's choir stalls are among the best in Suffolk, rich especially in their arm-rests, poppyheads and canopies. The rests include finely carved animals and a man with toothache. The benches display the initials of boys who used this as a school until the 19th century.

The present quality of the furnishings owes much to the work of Comper's pupil, F. E. Howard, who visited the church in the 1920s and declared it a 'model of an English church after the Book of Common Prayer'. Howard was an authority on woodwork. He designed the reredos and lectern and restored the 15th-century pulpit. His chief contribution is the font cover. This dwarfs even that of Ufford. It takes off like a rocket, rising 24 ft to be the highest in any English parish church. Next to it stands Southwold Jack, a medieval clock 'smiter' in 15th-century costume.

Southwold possesses a walnut chest covered in intricate tracery and depicting a knight hunting a boar. Those who worry at the plight of the Church of England might note that, when Defoe visited this community in 1722, he found just twenty-seven people in the church, and over 600 Dissenters worshipping elsewhere.

STOKE-BY-NAYLAND
St Mary ***
Mighty flint tower, Tree of Jesse door

Stoke-by-Nayland tower is a masterpiece of English medieval architecture. What it concedes in beauty to the flushwork artistry of Eye it makes up for in sheer power. I have often stood under its west front and felt the huge buttresses about to enfold and crush me. The tower has inspired English landscape artists from Constable to Piper. In John Piper's depiction, it seems to float, disembodied from its surroundings. The individual bricks, stones and flints are made to seem like keys on a piano, crashing out a massive fugue.

The tower's date is controversial, probably the 1470s when almost all Suffolk churches were being rebuilt during (or perhaps ignorant of) the climax of the Wars of the Roses. The diagonal buttresses are immensely deep, forming theatrical flats to the central proscenium, where the west door and three tiers of windows act out their play. The doorway is adorned with the shields and emblems of the chief patrons, the Tendring and Howard families. When bells ring out from this place on a cool autumn evening, all Suffolk stops to listen.

The handsome south porch is earlier than the rest of the church, with restored Decorated windows and a vault with fine bosses. Inside is one of the most remarkable Perpendicular doors to survive from the Middle Ages. This is a Tree of Jesse, carved in solid oak, with strong mullions and a pretty decorated border. Its features are charmingly eroded by the touch of a thousand hands. The porch also contains a map of local rights of way, a facility which might be imitated in rural porches.

The interior is memorable chiefly for its scale, for the high bases of the arcades, the limewash and soft stone. The view west from the chancel arch presents a vision of the tower inside out, with an arch of immense height and refinement. The centrepiece of this majestic vista is the octagonal font, with shields and reliefs of the symbols of the Evangelists. Its steps are carved in the form of seats. The chancel is best left to its gloom. The glass is dreadful and the reredos unworthy of the splendour before it. There are two 17th-century tombs, one of Lady Anne Windsor and another of Sir Francis Mannock.

SUDBURY
St Gregory *
Schorne relic, soaring font cover

I find it hard to choose between Sudbury's three churches, but St Gregory's has the edge, both for its setting on a pleasant green by the river and for its astonishing font cover. The church was founded by Simon of Sudbury, Archbishop of Canterbury, in 1381 as a training college for priests in the town. The chancel is almost as long as the nave. The porch curiously shares a roof with St Anne's Chapel next door.

The interior of St Gregory's was being restored on my visit. The chancel ceiling had already been brilliantly painted, together with a canopy of honour above the rood screen. The chancel retains its stalls, with arm-rests and misericords. Painted panels from the old screen have been reused in some places and one, of the gout doctor 'Saint' John Schorne (*see* North Marston, Bucks), hangs behind a glass screen. Another panel depicts an endearing St Gregory.

The medieval font cover is a remarkable work of carpentry, rivalling and perhaps even surpassing that at Ufford. It soars upwards on a series of crocketed gables, each above openings with transoms and mullions. It has been regilded and recoloured and telescopes when the font is in use. Otherwise Sudbury's most notable feature is the modern lighting brackets in black and gold on the nave arcades, admirably in keeping with the church.

THORNHAM PARVA
St Mary **
Thatched roof, 14th-century retable

Parva by name and parva in fact. The church is a tiny, single-cell building with a thatched roof and even a thatched tower roof, the only one I know. A photograph in the church shows it covered in snow, looking snug and Christmassy.

Thornham Parva has many small treasures and a great one. Almost every window is of a different period. The ancient walls are pierced by a Saxon round window to the west and a small Norman one to the south. The aisleless nave is lit by Perpendicular openings, flooding it with light and illuminating the extensive wall paintings. These tell the favourite Suffolk tale of the martyrdom of St Edmund. The walls are lined with old oil lamps. Also in the nave is an engraved glass window by Laurence Whistler commemorating Lady Osla Henniker-Major. It is in his most whimsical style, carrying the quotation, 'Full many a glorious morning have I seen: Flatter the mountain tops with sovereign eye.'

On the altar is Thornham's glory, a painted retable of *c.*1300, with eight saints on either side of a Crucifixion. The figures are refined and sinuous, with rosettes and vine leaves in the spandrels of their Gothic canopies. This exquisite work is a precious survival in an English country church – and a well-protected one. Most such pictures have been stolen by thieves or museums. The church-yard contains the grave of the architect Sir Basil Spence, adorned with the spare lines of an architect's compass. Next to it is a more cheerful memorial to Mr and Mrs Martins, local musicians, the one a violinist, the other a cellist.

UFFORD
St Mary **
Telescopic font cover

The setting is charming. The village is approached over hump-backed bridges, past meadows and medieval cottages, after which the lane to the church dives between old walls. The tower and porch display magnificent flint flushwork. Inside, the roof has hammerbeams with various portions of angels as decoration, some with original colouring. The remains of the screen are disappointing, but the bench-ends are admirable, with carved panels and poppyheads.

Ufford is celebrated for one stupendous work, an 18-ft font cover rivalled for height only by Southwold and Sudbury. The purpose of these covers was to pro-tect the holy water from theft, since the consecrated water was much favoured for witchcraft. Some churches merely locked their fonts with a flat lid, but others erected elaborate covers, requiring pulleys to lift them during baptisms. Ufford's is so high that it touches the roof. The craftsmen thus had to enable the lower tiers to retract telescopically into the upper ones when the font was in use.

This arrangement is the excuse for a virtuoso display of Perpendicular woodwork. Six tiers of crocketed pinnacles rise towards the roof. When the iconoclast, Dowsing, visited the church in 1643 he was so overawed by the cover that he spared it from destruction, despite likening it to a 'pope's triple crown'. The niches have mostly lost their statues, probably to common thieves, and some have been replaced. The original pelican survives on top.

WALPOLE
The Old Chapel *
Early Dissenting interior

Walpole chapel is testament to the vigour of Independent Nonconformity in the isolated communities of East Anglia. Its congregation was formed in 1649 and converted the old house of *c.* 1570 some 20 years later. The building is said to be the second oldest Dissenting chapel in England, after Longleat in Wiltshire. Though now disused, it is cared for by the Historic Chapels Trust, supported by local friends, and is open to the public.

The chapel lies some way to the east of the main village and is set back from the road in its own graveyard. The walls are plastered and the windows mostly early 17th century. The interior is completely unaltered, although at some point a ship's mast was brought from Great Yarmouth to prop up the central roof. Box pews and benches are arranged round three sides with a gallery above them. The pews seem graduated in importance and some are numbered and have hat pegs. All face a pulpit against the north wall, raised on a dais with seats for elders and Bible reading in front. This arrangement is similar to those in many Anglican churches at the time, but few of the latter are so untouched by the 19th or 20th centuries.

The interior is decorated in cream and brown and has oil lanterns. On the wall is an ancient notice announcing the 'unavoidable postponement' of an ordination service and the holding instead of 'a sermon and tea meeting'.

WINGFIELD
St Andrew **
De la Pole tombs, including 'royal' tomb

The church is beautifully positioned in a small village adjacent to College Farm, both church and farm commemorating the college founded in the 14th century by Sir John Wingfield (d.1361). Of this date is the charming Decorated window tracery of flower petals. The interior of the nave is of little interest, but the chancel and its flanking chapels contain superb relics of medieval patronage. While there is no chancel screen there are two excellent ones to the chapels. The choir stalls survive with poppyheads and simple misericords.

The glory of the church is the two de la Pole tombs in the chancel, both masterpieces of 15th-century carving. The de la Poles rose from Yorkshire merchants to become Dukes of Suffolk and powerful politicians during the Wars of the Roses. Family tombs can be found from Hull (Yorks, ER) to Ewelme (Oxon). The earlier of the chancel tombs, in the south arcade, is of the 2nd Earl of Suffolk, who died in 1415 during Henry V's French campaign.

The arch over the tomb doubles as a canopy, with heraldic motifs, shields, ball-flower and pinnacles. The chest has niches and provides backs for a row of sedilia. The effigies, most unusually for the period, are of wood.

The later monument, of John, Duke of Suffolk (d.1491), and his Duchess stands against the north wall of the chancel. The Duchess was sister to Edward IV, and this superb work qualifies as virtually a royal tomb. The Duke wears some of the most meticulously carved armour of the period and his rough face, careworn with civil war, is regarded as one of the few Plantagenet effigies that might be a portrait. His head rests on a superb Saracen's head.

The chancel north chapel commemorates the Wingfield family, and is guarded by the tomb of the founder, Sir John Wingfield (d.1361). It has a magnificent ogee-arched doorway and a rare upper room for a priest or sacristan. Pevsner finds this arrangement 'Le-Corbusiesque', perhaps for its spartan inconvenience. The south chancel chapel commemorates more de la Poles and is decorated with a lavishness of carving appropriate to the family's status.

WITHERSDALE STREET
St Mary *
Unaltered 'atmospheric' interior

What street? The church lies a mile east of the village up a sloping field with only an ancient farmhouse for company. The elms that greeted Arthur Mee in the 1940s have gone. He also noted medieval benches in an adjacent field, 'two of them with poppyheads, which once held an honoured place in God's house and are now a shelter from the sun for a few of God's sheep'. This is a simple farmers' chapel, perhaps a survival of a village deserted by the plague. Unusually for Suffolk, there is no tower, merely a small bellcote with unbuttressed walls. The building is double-cell with simple nave and chancel, and with lancet and Y-tracery windows that hardly merit the designation Decorated.

The inside demonstrates the familiar 17th-century arrangement of gentry box pews and double-decker pulpit with tester, of the plainest design. Further back are rough Jacobean benches, their ends capped with three balls on newel posts. The benches in the chancel may be those seen by Mee in the field. On the floor are soft pink bricks. The font is exceptional, dating from the 12th century and with complex carving on each of its four sides. Since one has a pointed arch, it may have been recut c.1300.

An old harmonium sits cosily alongside the pulpit, as if on a warm summer's day with no humans within earshot they might converse with each other alone.

WOOLPIT
St Mary ***
Pinnacled porch, six-tiered angel roof

The name has nothing to do with wool but with wolves, a pit for whose capture was apparently located here. The village is composed of charming cottages, but the church tower is an ungainly import. In 1853 the medieval tower and Georgian spire fell in a storm and were rebuilt by a local architect called R. M. Phipson. He chose an ostentatious Northamptonshire style, with pierced parapet and flying buttresses, wrong for these parts.

We should forget the tower and admire the porch. This is of a splendour to rank with that of Northleach (Gloucs). It rises above the height of the aisle behind and is two-storeyed, with five stepped niches, sadly empty. On top is a beautifully pierced parapet. The east wall, where presumably money did not run to stone, is composed of superb flushwork. The inside has a two-bay lierne vault with excellent bosses. This porch is a true 'church without a church'.

The interior is another variation on a theme of Suffolk joinery. The form is simple, a stone Gothic chamber clothed in wood. Here is one of East Anglia's most spectacular roofs, with figures six tiers deep. The double hammerbeam has two rows of angels. The upper hammer is purely decorative, stepping harmoniously towards the crest. Below, the wallplates have two further rows of angels. Finally the wall-posts have saints in canopied niches, supported by angel-corbels. Yet more angels people the aisle roofs, lying horizontally and forming the actual rafters, as at Mildenhall, their heads almost touching in the middle. Although some of these angels are medieval, most are 19th-century replacements.

Over the chancel arch is a lierne-vaulted canopy, once covering the rood. It is painted blue and apparently comes from somewhere else. With the tiny Cotswold window above, it forms with the roof, arch and screen a virtuoso display of English Gothic. Below are benches with carved and pierced ends along the shelf backs. The screen is strong and high, its dado embellished with eight saints, repainted in reds and blues. The eagle lectern is one of the small group of surviving Tudor ones, much imitated by later generations.

A window under the tower arch was designed by the wife of a former curate, an excellent modern work. She should have turned her attention to the windows elsewhere in the church, preferably with a hammer.

YAXLEY
St Mary *
Porch carvings, painted screen

This is a classic Suffolk church set in a sylvan churchyard and putting its best face forward in its porch. In the spandrels over the doorway are two magnificent carvings, one of a man fighting a beast and the other a wildman. Niches await new statues, and why not new donors' arms to go in the shields? There is money in these parts.

Inside, the swagger loses some of its élan. Yaxley is engagingly decrepit. On the bench ends, the poppyheads march in line eastwards until they meet the pulpit and screen that are the church's best features. The pulpit of 1635 is one of Suffolk's grandest, florid with carved panels, backboard and tester. Despite this Jacobean bravura it is sternly inscribed, 'Necessite is laid upon me, yea woe is me if I preach not the Gospel.'

The screen is ostensibly a mess. The rood has gone, as has a superb tympanum visible in a Victorian photograph of the interior. The tracery has also been deprived of its decorative cusping, only the entrance arch retaining a fragment of what must have been a fine work. Beneath are painted panels of saints, primitive in artistry but with patterned backgrounds and gilded surrounds. It is a ghost of a masterpiece. Another ghost hovers above, that of a Doom painting covered in cobwebs.

The chancel east window is made up of fragments of medieval glass attractively set so as not to cut out all sunlight. Some portray butterflies and birds. Over the south door is a curiosity, a 'sexton's wheel' used to mark the feast and fast days of the year.

Surrey

Poor Surrey. It must have the least exciting history of any English county, and its churches agree. Thickly forested and hard of access throughout the Middle Ages, Surrey developed only to the west, along the road to Guildford. Not until the coming of the railway did Downland villages see some dormitory prosperity. This led the Victorians to restore the old chapels, including those along the Pilgrims' Way towards Canterbury. Yet Surrey has its moments. The Norman two-storey chancel at Compton is unique. Dunsfold is a lovely Early Gothic church and at Stoke D'Abernon are two of the best early brasses in England. Henry Woodyer's chancel at Hascombe is a Victorian gem, and the Byzantine treasury at Lower Kingswood is sole representative of its style in this book.

Albury **
Bletchingley *
Chaldon *
Compton **
Dunsfold **

Esher *
Gatton ***
Hascombe ***
Lingfield *
Lower Kingswood ***

Ockham **
Shere *
Stoke D'Abernon ***

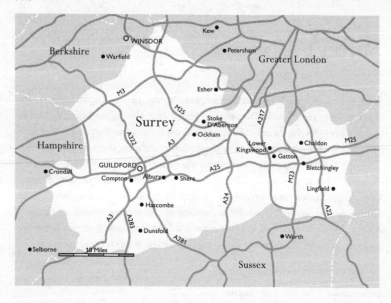

ALBURY
St Peter and St Paul **
Pugin chapel

Albury is a rare jewel in Surrey's dull crown. The church stands in the estate of Albury Park to the east of the village, but was once surrounded by a village of its own. The setting is sylvan and peaceful, with cedars, firs, yews and a river in the distance. The curious cupola on the battlemented tower might mark the folly of an 18th-century grandee.

Instead it marks a church of surprises. The entrance is from the north, through a 15th-century porch with delicately pierced bargeboards. The door itself is a magnificent piece of 13th-century carpentry. It gives on to a wide Early Gothic nave and south aisle, redundant, bare but with a fine old flagstone floor. The crossing tower is Saxon and Norman, with a scraped and semi-ruinous 13th-century chancel beyond. This is all grandly proportioned.

More remarkable is the south transept chapel, designed by A. W. N. Pugin in the mid-19th century as a mortuary chapel for Henry Drummond (d.1860), owner of Albury Park. Drummond was an enthusiastic advocate of Edward Irving's Second Advent movement and made Albury a centre of the Catholic Apostolic Church. In 1840, he built for the movement the now-disused Gothic church that can be seen from the adjacent A25. His memorial here is the tomb against the south wall of the chapel, below a large south window with glass by

Wailes. The chapel is richly decorated, with painted walls and ceiling, a niche with a nodding ogee head, and excellent tiles on the floor. It is an extraordinary contrast with the robust antiquity of the rest of the interior.

Over the south door is a wall painting of St Christopher, well preserved. The saint was traditionally depicted on the wall opposite the main entrance, usually on the north side but here on the south.

[CCT]

BLETCHINGLEY
St Mary *
Clayton memorial

Bletchingley is a Surrey show village. It lies off the A25, under the shadow of the North Downs. The church stands away from the village centre and is, according to the guidebook, 'one of the finest in the country', a bold effort. The best names in Victorian architecture struggled to bring order to a building that dates from the 11th, 13th and 15th centuries. They included Butterfield, Street, Pearson, Comper and Kempe, though not all in person. The cooks were Cordon Bleu, but to invite so many risked spoiling the broth.

Seen from the south, Perpendicular predominates. The battlements, turret porch and Norman tower give the church the air of a castle. The entrance is through the west door, where a small museum celebrates Bletchingley campanology. The original bells were 'melt to infinite fragments' in a fire in 1606; the present ring of eight was cast in 1780. On the floor of the tower is a simple Tudor brass of a man and woman. The chancel reredos is by Street, bold, architectural and with Bishop Wilberforce unashamedly placed among the saints.

Bletchingley's treasure is in the south chapel. There on the east wall, where once would have been a chantry altar, rises the monument to Sir Robert Clayton (d.1707). Clayton was a typical product of 17th-century upward mobility, a City clerk who rose to be a successful bill broker. He foreclosed on the local Evelyn and Peterborough estates and contrived to become owner of the rotten borough of Bletchingley and patron of two MPs.

The monument is in extravagant Queen Anne Baroque. A huge open pediment supported by Corinthian columns and pillars frames the figures of Sir Robert and his wife in the robes of the Lord Mayor and his lady. Underneath is a poignant figure of an only child, a baby son who died in infancy. He wears minutely carved lace, with a pathetic hand held out in imitation of his father. At each side a putto weeps. This work is the only signed piece by a City mason named Richard Crutcher. Sacheverell Sitwell regarded the Clayton monument as 'the most splendid relic of the long past age of periwigs'.

CHALDON
St Peter and St Paul *
Ladder of Salvation mural

Chaldon is a small chapel lost in a fold of the North Downs. Here modest
commuter homes nestle among beech, box and monkeypuzzle. The building is
of no architectural distinction. Inside is a 17th-century pulpit, unusual only in
its date of 1657, during the artistically barren Commonwealth. Facing it is the
basis of Chaldon's fame, a primitive wall painting discovered beneath whitewash in 1870. Dated to about 1200, it is claimed by the guide to be the earliest
in Britain. This is not so, as many in the south-east are earlier, such as Hardham
(Sussex) and Copford (Essex). What is remarkable about Chaldon is its subject,
the Ladder of Salvation rising out of Purgatory, and its fine preservation.

The artistry is gauche, like a child's version of an Egyptian tomb mural.
But the vitality of the figures, especially those down in Hell, and the horror of
the subject matter, makes Chaldon a favourite example of early English art.
This is no genteel Bath Abbey ladder, of angels ascending joyfully to Heaven.
At Chaldon you are roasted, boiled and tormented by the Seven Deadly Sins.
Demons hold up a bridge of spikes over which dishonest workers, deprived of
their tools, have to cross. Above, Heaven is more boring, except for a devil
trying to tip the balances of justice. Christ is shown at the top of the ladder,
spearing the Devil with His cross. The composition is in white, silhouetted on
an ochre background. It is all most jolly.

COMPTON
St Nicholas **
Two-storey sanctuary

Compton sits on the rolling waves of greensand south of the Hog's Back. Its
approach from the road is framed by two cedars looming from the adjacent
Eastbury Manor. These trees are so vast as to merit a visit in themselves. The
church tower and parts of the walls have Saxon masonry. A Sussex broach spire
fits neatly on top, and the sweeping pitched roof, with a clerestory of dormer
windows, suggests a Surrey country cottage. None of this prepares us for the
remarkable interior.

Each Home County seems to have one Norman flagship: Buckinghamshire
has Stewkley, Oxfordshire Iffley, Cambridgeshire Ickleton. Surrey has Compton, and, such is Surrey, we might expect it to be disappointing. Not at all. In
one respect at least, it is unique.

The nave has Norman arcades with variegated capitals. Those decorated with
scallops are big and beefy; those with undercut Early Gothic foliage above a

solid drum are more uncomfortable, like a Sumo wrestler in a tutu. On the inside of the chancel arch is carved graffiti of a knight, apparently late 12th century. The guide suggests that the knight carved this figure on departing for the crusade, with St George's cross next to him. On his return he added St Andrew's cross on top in thanks for his success. Above the chancel arch is a Norman lozenge mural uncovered in 1966. It is unusual since this position was normally reserved for a portrayal of the Crucifixion.

Compton's surprise is the only double-deck sanctuary to survive in England. Seen from the nave it looks most odd, as if the floor has dropped or a movie frame has frozen halfway through its gate. The lower storey has a decorated Norman arch more refined than those in the nave, including tiny nook-shafts. It echoes the chancel arch, and is closed by Jacobean railings. The deeply-splayed east window has some early stained glass, probably dating from the Norman rebuilding of the Saxon church. It shows the Virgin and Child with a flowering sceptre.

Upstairs is the second sanctuary, in a gallery. Archaeology says this was inserted in the walls after construction, with a Norman railing carved from a single piece of wood. This is reputedly the oldest architectural wood carving in an English church. The purpose of the gallery is a mystery. It may have been intended to house a relic, for pilgrims on their way to Canterbury. It may even have been a viewing gallery for this purpose. There is a piscina which indicates a possible later use as a chantry chapel. Even with an original east window, the sanctuary must have been dark and heavy with incense and the smoke of pilgrims' candles.

In the wall of the sanctuary is a tiny window that would have given an anchorite a view of the altar as she prayed in walled-up solitude, her grave already waiting alongside. An excavation in 1906 discovered six skeletons under the spot where the cell would have stood (*see* Shere).

DUNSFOLD
St Mary and All Saints **
Ancient pews, holy well

Dunsfold might seem a contradiction in terms, a lost church in deepest Surrey. It sits on an ancient mound near the Sussex border, as if its village had forgotten it and wandered elsewhere. The church is big for these parts. As a Crown living it was blessed with a more substantial endowment than the Surrey norm. The design was much favoured by William Morris. Like many mid-Victorians he found in the churches of the late 13th century the apotheosis of English Gothic architecture. Dunsfold is a remarkable survival of that period. Pevsner offers it as 'a complete example of what the generation after Westminster Abbey thought suitable for a small and fairly remote village church ... no surplus ornament or display – an architect's building'.

The exterior is characterised by a long chancel, steeply-pitched roofs, Geometric tracery and a clear differentiation of parts. The wall surface has little ironstone chips inserted in the mortar between the stone, a decorative practice known as galleting. Inside, there are no aisles, but there are transepts with the piscinas of former chapels. In the chancel is a graceful sequence of piscina and stepped sedilia, again indicating 13th-century prosperity.

Dunsfold even retains benches contemporary with the time of its building, which means they must be as old as any in England. Seating of any sort was not common in churches until the 15th century. The bench-ends are particularly graceful, deep cusps ending in knobs with holes for carrying lighted tapers. Their lights must have danced down the aisle on a dark evening. At the west end, Dunsfold has a huge wooden tower arch.

Down the lane towards the stream is the local holy well. This has been analysed as similar to the water of Lourdes, rich in chloride and good for the eyes.

ESHER
St George *
Family pew by Vanbrugh

The centrifugal force of Esher's gyratory traffic appears to have spun this little chapel away behind a pub, as if in a fit of pique. How dare such a quaint relic survive in so orderly a suburb? Yet St George's does survive, thanks to the Victorians erecting the bigger Christ Church round the corner – and thanks to the Churches Conservation Trust. Its faintly scruffy charm is an Esher surprise, as is its most remarkable possession, the Newcastle pew.

The 16th-century church fronts the old Portsmouth Road with an un-assuming west front. Made of a crumbly chequerboard of stone and clunch, it is topped by a simple gable and wooden bellcote. Inside, St George's cannot decide whether it is a barn masquerading as a chapel, or a chapel masquerading as a barn. The fittings are mostly 18th and 19th century, as are most of the windows. A pretty Doric arcade of wooden columns divides off the north aisle. For some reason the panelled front of a vanished north gallery has been left in place, half way up these columns. There is a three-decker pulpit with a modest tester and a west gallery on fluted columns.

This would be of small consequence but for the arrival in Esher in the early 18th century of John Vanbrugh, who built himself a country house and tower looking out towards London. In the 1720s he sold both to the Earl of Clare, later Duke of Newcastle and prime minister. Clare built himself a new house, appropriately named Claremont, and laid out the grounds (now owned by the National Trust). He was apparently less enthusiastic about spending on a new village church. He merely made sure that when he went to church, he did so in style.

In 1725 the Duke commissioned Vanbrugh to design the Newcastle 'pew', in fact a complete brick extension to the south wall of the church. Inside, the pew sits like a royal box at a provincial rep, looking down on the proceedings with confident superiority. The effect is supremely theatrical. There is an external staircase and the nave is viewed only through an opening, framed by two rows of Corinthian columns surmounted by a pediment.

The pew was later divided into two sets of three boxes, the occupants of Esher Place sitting to the left and of Claremont to the right. Each side has its own fireplace and the seats behind are for the servants. The pew was used in the early 19th century by Princess Charlotte, George IV's heir, and her husband Prince Leopold. She would have succeeded as monarch (rather than William, then Victoria) had she not died in childbirth at Claremont in 1817. Queen Victoria worshipped here on visits to her Uncle Leopold, before he left Esher to become King of the Belgians.

Despite this distinguished past, St George's lacks monuments above the average. A large sculpted triptych to Charlotte and Leopold by a local sculptor, F. J. Williamson, stands against the west wall of the aisle. The three scenes show Charlotte on her deathbed, Leopold on becoming King of the Belgians, and the royal couple giving charity to the poor of Esher. Round the aisle walls the pictures of Charlotte, Claremont and Esher form a gallery of local history. It is sad that so attractive a building in the centre of the town cannot be permanently open as a museum to its past.

[CCT]

GATTON
St Andrew ***
Treasure trove of Continental furnishings

Gatton is a Surrey original. Sandwiched on the side of the Downs above the M25 is the mansion of Gatton Park, now the Royal Alexandra and Albert School. Ornamental grounds with cedar and pine look out southwards towards the Weald. Trees shelter sedate school buildings while the house, rebuilt after a fire in 1934, clatters with the noise of children.

Between the two is a disorderly folly, the church of St Andrew. It was built by the young Lord Monson in 1834, shortly after he had bought the estate and started to reconstruct the house. Lord Monson was a passionate Conservative who voted against the Reform Bill in 1832 when even the Duke of Wellington abstained. One reason was that the Act abolished Monson's rotten borough at Gatton, which the reformer William Cobbett called 'a very rascally spot of earth'. Monson was described as 'a little figure of a man or rather of a child, shy and silent, through embarrassment at his diminutive size and feeble body'. As a collector, however, he gained a more imposing stature.

The neo-Gothic church barely qualifies as serious architecture. The *Shell Guide* refers to the porch as 'a castle from a model train set and the tower is of starved proportions'. Inside, Gatton is Surrey's Old Warden (Beds), a church taken in hand by a Grand Tourist with money to spend and good contacts in the European antiques trade. Lord Monson's agents brought him enough choir stalls, panels and glass to transform his church into a gallery of delights. The result is not really a 19th-century English church, more a Flemish collegiate chapel of the 16th century.

Four rows of stalls from Ghent face each other across the nave. The panelling behind and the canopies above are from Louvain. The communion rails are from Tongres, the delicate chancel panelling from Burgundy. The pulpit, with a superb Descent from the Cross, is probably Flemish (surely not by Dürer as suggested in the guide, though perhaps 'after' him). The door beneath came from Rouen and this leads up to a gallery. Above hangs the standard of the Redhill and Reigate Branch of the Old Contemptibles Association (disbanded), like Hogarthian roast beef looking down on the Continental foppery below.

Opposite in the north transept is the Monson family pew. It has upholstered chairs and benches and a large fireplace. The pew has its own side entrance as well as the only example I know of a private covered way, leading out across the churchyard towards the house. This passage is sadly ruined. On the wall is a memorial to Sir Jeremiah Colman (of mustard fame) and his wife, who acquired Gatton from the Monsons in 1880.

The glass in Gatton is mostly Flemish and French. The altar carries a rare portrayal of the feast of Passover, of 1500. In the south wall of the nave, a French window shows Mary telling her cousin of her pregnancy. The landscape background is vividly realistic. Kempe supplied the excellent Colman memorial window in the south wall of the chancel, its angel wings of the most gorgeous peacock feathers.

HASCOMBE
St Peter ***
Complete Victorian decorative scheme

Hascombe's location in the sandy hills south of Godalming is what a *Country Life* advertisement would call 'important and agreeable'. The country is pictur-esque with dunes, bracken and Scots pine. Here the Edwardian architects Edwin

Lutyens, J. D. Coleridge and F. W. Troup hid commuter mansions amid gardens by Gertrude Jekyll. Newcomers to these estates would have been invited to worship in a dazzling work of Gothic revival, under the stern Canon Vernon Musgrave.

Musgrave arrived from Cambridge in 1862 to a small country parish that can have offered little intellectual stimulus. He was one of many wealthy Victorian clergymen who found a decrepit church and devoted their lives and fortunes to its revival. Early pictures of Hascombe show an Early Gothic chapel with high box pews and a screen. Musgrave was an Ecclesiologist, shocked at the liturgical inappropriateness of his new church: 'high pews barricading each man off from his neighbour in solitary exclusiveness ... unseemly stove ... windows robbed of glass, filled with bricks and mortar ... little, insignificant uncared-for altar with its shabby covering all but hidden from sight'. Musgrave set to work. He paid for the chancel himself and persuaded four local landowners to finance the rest. Within two years of his arrival he opened the first stages of his new building.

His architect, Henry Woodyer, was a fellow spirit. A pupil of Butterfield, he was responsible for many restorations in Surrey, where his practice was based. At Hascombe he was able to create a church of his own, a work to match his earlier masterpiece at Highnam (Gloucs). The simple perfection of the exterior, with its lancet and Plate tracery windows and apsidal east end, echoes a previous church on the site, but the interior was transformed.

The nave received its mural of the Miraculous Draught of Fishes after 1883 and must have been quite plain before then. This working of a theme round an entire nave is rare in an English parish church of any period (see Garton, Yorks, ER). On the east wall the six disciples draw in their net which, laden with fishes, runs the length of the north and south walls to the west window. Here the miracle is repeated in stained glass as the Ship of the Church. The nave is lit by simple paired lancets divided by slender Purbeck shafts. Almost all the glass in the church is by Hardman & Powell.

The chancel screen is a survivor of the old church, restored, brightly painted and with panels of saints inserted in its dado. The chancel itself glows with colour. Every inch of wall and ceiling is decorated, even the window splays. The rafters, cusped and gilded, spread out from the apse like a giant fan, as if trying frantically to cool the heat below. The dominant colours of the reredos, which Woodyer thrusts up into the roof space, are red and gold. The walls are covered with either murals or mosaic. Angels trumpet from the embroidered altar frontal.

This decoration proceeded piecemeal as money was available, and was not complete until the end of the century. Happily Musgrave lived to see his creation finished. He died in 1906 after forty-four years in the parish, and is commemorated, in medieval style, by a brass in the chancel floor. He attended to every detail of his building, including the design of gravestones in the church-yard and the clipping of the yew that forms the lychgate. He also wrote a guide-book so that visitors 'need not ask questions of accidental persons and be imperfectly or erroneously answered'. Hascombe needs to be seen with lights, the switch being under the stair.

LINGFIELD
St Peter and St Paul *
Cobham tombs

The town sits on a hill with a bracing air more of Sussex than of Surrey. The church hides in an enclave to the south, facing out over East Grinstead towards Ashdown Forest. A parade of Tudor houses frames the entrance to a church-yard of tomb chest and yews. Lingfield is rural Surrey's most successful attempt at cutting a dash.

The Perpendicular church has a modest broach spire with a heavily buttressed tower. The interior is spacious. The nave and aisle are equally proportioned, so that without furnishings it would be hard to tell which is which. Pevsner wonders if Lingfield is a case of a true double nave, one collegiate and the other parochial. The wagon roofs lack decoration: not even an angel, a boss or a carved corbel. The Perpendicular screens have mediocre tracery, the pews are modern, the pulpit humble. Only the misericords are reasonably exciting. What was it about Surrey patrons that left their churches so poor?

Not all is poverty stricken, however. The patrons at least guarded their own glory. The tombs of Sir Reginald Cobham (d.1446) and his wife lie prominently in front of the altar. On the Day of Judgement there was to be no question which Lingfield resident was first in line for consideration. While the alabaster faces are stylised, the armour, clothing and hairstyles are beautifully realistic. The sculptor gives free rein to his imagination in the Saracen crest on the helmet under Lord Cobham's head, a small masterpiece of Gothic carving. At the couple's feet are a wyvern and a sea-dog.

The Cobham family bestrode the Surrey–Kent border in the Middle Ages, with more spectacular tombs in Cobham (Kent). They typified the romantic warrior knights of the Hundred Years War, who liked to believe they were fighting a Christian crusade against the infidel, when they were mostly fight-ing the French and each other. (The Saracen's head emblem was symbol of the crusader commitment.) In the north chapel is a work of an earlier period, the tomb of the 1st Lord Cobham, who died of the plague in 1361 after serving the Black Prince at Crécy and Poitiers. The effigy is primitive in execution but vividly coloured, a Saracen at his feet.

LOWER KINGSWOOD
St Sophia, the Wisdom of God ***
Neo-Byzantine treasure house

This extraordinary church is encountered in a suburb on the Banstead Downs. Commuters on the A217 must pass it every day without knowing that inside this redbrick box amid holly and pine is a Byzantine shrine, somehow detached from Constantinople and dropped into the Home Counties. The guide claims it to be stylistically unique in England.

Kingswood was unusual in having as parishioners two Victorian archaeologists, Edwin Freshfield and Sir Henry Bonsor. In 1892 they ordered a church in the Byzantine style from the architect Sidney Barnsley. Externally the most remarkable feature is the bell-tower in the churchyard. This is based on a sketch by Freshfield of a tower in a village in Bulgaria, and has a strange domed top with exaggerated gargoyles. The exterior is broadly Byzantine with, at the west end, a narthex and a Diocletian window. The studs in the west door are from the 6th-century Roman church of St Demetrius in Salonica, which seems a sad removal.

The interior is a cross between a place of worship and an archaeological museum. A nave with arcades of massive columns leads to an apsidal chancel. This apse dominates the church and is of astonishing richness, coated in a variety of marbles – greens, greys, reds and whites – each quarried from specific parts of the Byzantine empire. Above is a complete mosaic of gold leaf with a charming frieze of flowers. On either side of the apse are bastions of marble, supporting twin domed pulpits of ebony inlaid with mother-of-pearl.

The nave is a simpler affair, with a wooden wagon roof painted by Barnsley himself. The aisles and the west wall have fragments of 5th- and 6th-century Byzantine capitals. Set into the west wall is the baptistery, again dressed in precious marble, the font of Egyptian alabaster. Over it hangs an ostrich egg, commemorating the birth of a Freshfield grandson. Adorning the adjacent Freshfield seats are a lion and unicorn, to remind worshippers that this is after all an Anglican church. They look understandably startled.

OCKHAM
All Saints **
Seven-lancet window, Ockham's 'razor'

Ockham does not welcome visitors. The key must be found from the hall porter at the Hautboy Hotel a quarter of a mile up the road. I was almost tested on Ockham's 'razor' to obtain it. The church sits amid trees in the lee of Ockham Park, a redbrick mansion designed by Hawksmoor but destroyed by fire in

1948. It has since been rebuilt in the same style. The outbuildings are original and the ensemble remains happily aloof from enveloping commuterland.

The church is renowned for its distinguished son, William of Ockham, a Franciscan intellectual born c.1284. A rationalist sceptic, he was a (distant) precursor of the Reformation and indeed of logical positivism. His distinction between reason and faith led to a summons to the Inquisition in Avignon. He escaped and found refuge for the rest of his life in Munich, where he is believed to have died of the plague. His famous 'razor' – the maxim that every hypothesis should be sliced to its essentials, or 'Keep It Simple Stupid' – is printed on a mug on sale in the church. William is also celebrated in a small stained glass window.

The 13th-century east window is almost as famous, and is evident from the car park. With Blakeney (Norfolk), Ockham has one of only two windows of seven stepped lancets surviving in England. Inside and out there is a charm to these soaring sword-like shapes, filling the eastern gable of the church. The exterior stonework suggests that they replaced three earlier windows that were even deeper. They make the Decorated and Perpendicular tracery in the side windows seem heavy handed.

Ockham's interior is full of curiosities. In the chancel, seven lancets are separated by Purbeck shafts with stiff-leaf capitals. The glass is by Powell & Sons, 1875. Pale blue is used where Morris & Co. might have better used green, but the effect is restrained and serene. The saints are picked out in clear glass with red backgrounds.

Off the north aisle lies the King Chapel, mausoleum for the 18th-century owners of Ockham Park. It is dominated by a monument to the 1st Lord King (d.1734), Lord Chancellor of England. It was a good time to die. English monumental sculpture was at its apogee and King was able to call on the services of Rysbrack for a splendid conversation piece of himself and his wife resting against a large urn. King was upwardly mobile: 'his genius superior to his birth, he rose to be Lord Chancellor before being felled by a paralytic disease'.

Back in the north aisle by the organ is a carved medieval bracket in the form of a girl's head, a tiny work of accomplished loveliness. The south windows contain much old glass, including Flemish work next to the pulpit. A pane in the chancel is inscribed by a Georgian glazier, 'W. Peters new leaded this in 1775 and never was paid for the same.'

SHERE
St James *
15th-century brass, anchorite cell

Shere is Surrey's most picturesque village, sheltered in a hollow between the North Downs and the greensand ridges. The prettiness of the village is corrupted only by the litter of cars that fill its narrow lanes. The church stands bold – for Surrey remarkably bold – with a Norman tower that would once have beckoned pilgrims down from the Canterbury Way along the Downs above. The spire is emphatically broached. The church was proud enough of its history to withstand too much Victorian restoration.

Shere has Norman west and south doorways and a spacious interior beneath its original scissor-truss roofs. The old church was soon extended and the crossing and east end are Gothic of different periods. The arch between the south chapel and aisle has polished stone shafts, suggesting that someone had money to spend. The east window tracery is Decorated, its beauty marred by ferocious Victorian glass. Otherwise the pleasures of Shere are mostly in the details. The font is a handsome late-Norman work. In the crossing is a modern statue of St James, carved by John Cobbett. A bandy-legged and slightly dotty brass of Lord Audley (d.1490) adorns the floor of the chancel.

The church has a fine collection of kneelers in ochre and green, showing the flora and fauna of the adjacent North Downs. Perhaps it was these Downs that enticed the anchorite of Shere, Christine Carpenter, to leave her cell in the wall of the church in 1332, after three years of pious incarceration. Anchorites were the holiests of hermits, walled in to await death only if a bishop considered them sufficiently sincere. To leave a cell was unthinkable. The woman later repented her departure and the bishop ordered 'that the said Christine shall be thrust back into the said re-enclosure ... that she may learn at your discretion how nefarious was her committed sin'. The sin is undisclosed but the remains of the cell can be seen outside the north chancel wall. The church lychgate is by Lutyens.

STOKE D'ABERNON
St Mary ***
Vincent monuments, D'Abernon brasses

Here on the banks of the River Mole, Surrey seems to collapse in a mess of motorways and suburban sprawl. The village and church of Stoke D'Abernon are poorly signposted but an enclave of manor house and churchyard clings to the river bank, an oasis of civility. Some wealth did penetrate into the wooded land south of the Thames during the Middle Ages. There was a settlement here from Roman times. Stoke D'Abernon can even lay claim to have seen the first recorded honeymoon in English history, of Henry III's tutor with the daughter of the Earl of Pembroke. The event took place in 1189 and is related in a French poem, 'L'Histoire de Guillaume le Marechal'.

Stoke church was heavily restored by the Victorians and the interior is dull at first sight. But patience is rewarded with a gallery of church art of all periods, including medieval glass and two of the earliest brasses in England. The nave is dominated by the pulpit, donated by the local Vincent family in 1620, on Sir Francis becoming a baronet. It has grotesque monsters as supports, each with a single female breast, and a fine tester with its original iron ties. In the same style is the hour-glass holder on the adjacent wall.

To the north of the chancel is the Norbury Chapel, built by Sir John Norbury (an earlier owner of the manor) after the Battle of Bosworth, in which he took part. Many such chapels were built to greet the end of the Wars of the Roses and the hoped-for dawn of Tudor peace. The chapel windows are filled with heraldic glass, mostly of the manorial lords of Stoke. Their surnames changed seven times, the result of inheritance through the female line.

Two large, crude but most enjoyable Jacobean monuments fill the north and east walls. To the east is Sarah, Lady Vincent (d.1608). The lines of her hair, ruff and sleeves are meticulously carved, and the horizontal folds of her dress defy gravity. Her parents-in-law, Sir Thomas Vincent and his wife, died only a few years later but their tombs show a stylistic change. The elder Lady Vincent is portrayed as more relaxed, her draperies falling naturally. A small memorial on the wall portrays old Sir John Norbury himself incongruously depicted in 17th-century armour.

Stoke's greatest treasures are the brasses under a carpet on the chancel floor. The left-hand brass is of Sir John D'Abernon, who died in 1277. It has been dated by its armour to c.1320, making this possibly the earliest extant brass in England (but see Acton, Suffolk). He is clad still in 13th-century crusader chain-mail with a surcoat and shield filled with Limoges enamel. His feet, with cruelly spiked spurs, rest on a curiously shaved lion which is biting his lance. Although he is in full knightly regalia, his legs are uncrossed, a symbolism now regarded as obscure and unrelated to crusader status. This is the only known case of a spear in a military brass. Next door lies Sir John's son, who died in 1327. The figure is more sophisticated, the armour plated and the belt and robe more ornamental. They form a magnificent pair.

Stoke has a fine collection of glass, mostly gathered from elsewhere in England and from Europe. There is no great variation in style since most north European glaziers at the time were Flemish. The east window is a masterpiece from the now-ruined Costessey Park in Norfolk, originally from Cologne. It depicts the Crucifixion with donors on either side in vivid maroon and red costumes.

Sussex

Sussex faces across the Channel to Normandy. It was the venue for the Conquest of 1066, but saw Norman missionaries and masons penetrating its Downs and coastal plains well before then. As a result, the transition from Saxon to Norman is hard to date. Edward the Confessor's nave at Worth is clearly Saxon, as are the great arch at Bosham and the Rhenish steeple at Sompting. But Norman carvers fashioned the charming capitals at Steyning and the doorway at Climping, while the Cluniac outpost at Lewes appears to have influenced the fresco-artists of Clayton and Hardham.

Sussex was never a wealthy county and, as a result, these early churches survived where richer medieval communities would have rebuilt. The Goths were not generous to Sussex. The Norman–Gothic transition is displayed in the choir at New Shoreham, and stone shipped from Caen was mixed with local flint for the fine chancel and Decorated tombs at Winchelsea. But Gothic Sussex is notable chiefly for its Downland chapels, among the smallest and most charming in England, as at Didling and Up Marden. A distinctive characteristic of the county is the shingled spire, made of wooden laths often covering an earlier structure, as at Playden and West Grinstead.

The Reformation passed with little change in tempo. The 18th century contributed modest Glynde, Warminghurst's Queen Anne screen and the fine monuments at Ashburnham. It was not until the 19th century that the railways brought Sussex wealth and population. These are best demonstrated in the two spectacular Brighton churches of St Michael's and St Bartholomew's.

Arundel *
Ashburnham **
Bishopstone *
Bosham **
Boxgrove ***
Brighton:
  St Bartholomew ***
  St Michael ****
Clayton **
Climping **
Coombes *

Cuckfield *
Didling *
Etchingham *
Glynde *
Hardham **
New Shoreham ***
Old Shoreham *
Penhurst *
Playden *
Rotherfield **
Rye **

Sompting **
Southease *
South Harting **
Steyning ***
Up Marden *
Warminghurst **
West Grinstead **
Winchelsea ***
Worth **

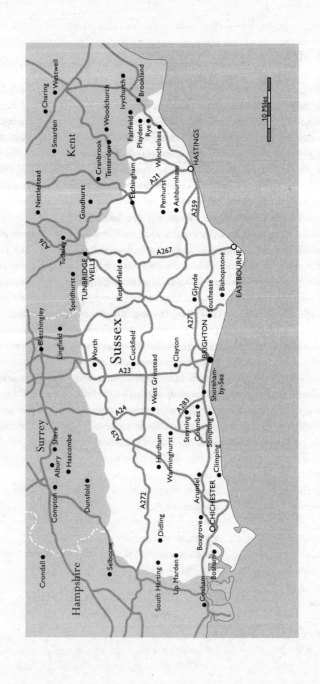

ARUNDEL
St Nicholas *
Stone pulpit, view of Fitzalan tombs

Arundel parish church begins as an anticlimax. On one side rises the mighty castle of the Dukes of Norfolk, towering over the town and the Arun valley. On the other rises the Roman Catholic cathedral of St Philip Neri. Together they form a landscape reminiscent of Bavaria or the Dordogne. The church hardly gets a notice. Built in the 1380s, its east end was intended for a college of priests and a mausoleum for the Fitzalans (see Framlingham, Suffolk). The west end was for the parish. After the Reformation, the Fitzalans remained Roman Catholic, and the divide between chancel and nave became a monument to Christian faction. As founders of the original college, the family claimed the chancel as their own, a claim contested by the vicar but vindicated in the High Court in 1879.

As a result the Fitzalans, by then Dukes of Norfolk, built a dividing wall between chancel and church. This wall was removed in 1969, leaving only the previous barrier, a grille of old Sussex ironwork, and a new sheet of glass. In 1977 an inter-denominational service took place in both halves of the church and with the grille open. But it remains locked to this day, and the chancel tombs can be inspected only by paying to enter the castle grounds. This is sad since the patrician/plebeian division is also architectural. The Fitzalan Chapel, viewed through the grille, is a splendid Perpendicular chamber with a Victorian oak roof which replicates the original stone vault. The tombs below are equally splendid, given added hauteur by being visible only at a distance.

We must content ourselves with the nave, with conventional 14th-century arcades and a choir now positioned under the crossing tower. The stalls include excellent modern poppyheads depicting animals straining upwards, as if seeking escape. Most remarkable of the furnishings is the pulpit. This is of stone, Perpendicular and with a canopy, looking like a private chantry from which the congregation has woken the priest and demanded a sermon.

In the north aisle is a window containing a picture of a swallow, emblem of the town of Arundel. The name was based on the Norman word for a swallow, *hirondelle*. There are also fragments of wall paintings, including a faded wheel of the Seven Deadly Sins.

ASHBURNHAM
St Peter **
Ashburnham monuments

Few churches can have a more splendid approach than Ashburnham. An avenue from the A271 leads through thickly wooded slopes of oak and bracken. Rides branch off at odd angles. Round a bend stretches a lake with a bridge, leading to what was once the great house but is today replaced by a mean conference centre. Beyond lie the original 18th-century stables and the church. The ensemble is marred only by the lack of a strong architectural focus.

Ashburnhams reputedly defended Dover against William the Conqueror and continued to occupy this land into the 20th century. The most distinguished family member, John, lived a turbulent generation from 1603 to 1671. He was courtier to Charles I and was imprisoned under the Commonwealth. After the Restoration he rebuilt his local church 'on a noble scale and in the ancient style'. Hence the Perpendicular Gothic, and hence the east end raised above a family vault and flanked by two chapels. These contain a total of 45 Ashburnham coffins. According to the guide, the last member of the family, Lady Catherine Ashburnham, who died in 1953, conveniently took the last available space in the vault.

The church is thoroughly Gothic yet has a classical doorway. The unaisled interior has clear window glass, and light floods over the cream walls, blue ceiling, box pews, gallery and panelled pulpit. On the south wall is an extraordinary Flemish frame round a set of biblical texts. This was apparently once the reredos. All eyes turn to the chancel, rising dramatically up the slope of the hill, and to the chapels on either side. Only the north is of interest, containing two of Sussex's best Restoration tombs: of John Ashburnham, builder of the church, and his brother William.

Though only four years apart (1671 and 1675), the tombs mark a watershed in English memorial sculpture. John's tomb has him lying dressed in armour alongside his two wives, their hands in prayer in the medieval style. Beneath are their children as weepers and above rises a formal Renaissance canopy with an ornate open pediment.

William's tomb could not be more different. Though only a few years later, this is High Baroque and with a named artist, John Bushnell, sculpting a grief-stricken man. He gazes up at the image of his adored wife, Jane, Countess of Marlborough, carried off by an angel in death. The tomb is surrounded by four pedestals; on one rests her coronet, on another his helmet. The chapel also contains a bust of Bertram Ashburnham, displaying nothing but a Victorian stiff upper lip.

BISHOPSTONE
St Andrew *
Saxon–Norman remains

The church sits well in a combe of the Downs high above Seaford and the sea. It dates from the assiduous South Coast church-building of the 10th and 11th centuries. The date-conscious Pevsner puzzles over which arch, window and quoin is Saxon or Norman, but Bishopstone is a good example of a Sussex church where the divide is almost meaningless, such was the flow of influence across the Channel both before and after the Conquest.

Broadly speaking, the nave and south porch are Saxon, the north aisle and east end are Norman, while the tower is both. The tower has four stages and a pyramid cap, the latter resting on a corbel-table lined with monsters. The outside walls are immaculately restored, each stone sparkling and each flint scrubbed clean. The mostly Saxon porch is certainly big enough to have been, as claimed, a transept chapel. It has long-and-short work. A sundial in the gable is inscribed to 'Eadric' and marked into four 'tides of the day'.

Inside the tower is a fine Saxon–Norman chamber rising the height of the first two tower stages. Here are the deep splays, lofty proportions and round arches of the 12th century, with no Victorian intrusions. This space is almost a chapel in itself. On one wall hangs a Norman coffin lid, curiously decorated with three circles of rope, a cross, a lamb and two doves drinking. There are three further spaces opening off the nave, gloomy for lack of later windows.

The choir is Transitional, with pointed arches above scalloped and stiff-leaf capitals. Enough apparently survives of the old sanctuary in the present restoration for us to assume the restorer was respecting the spirit of the original. It has a vault and blind arcading with zigzag carving, a village church decked out in finery as if expecting a distinguished ecclesiastical visitor.

BOSHAM
Holy Trinity **
Saxon arch, maritime churchyard

Bosham is Sussex at its most ancient, set amid a large enclosed harbour ideal for the flat-bottomed boats of the Roman and Saxon navies. This was one of the earliest recorded Christian settlements in the south of England: Bede mentions it as a home of Irish missionaries in the 7th century. Here (if not at Southampton) Canute allegedly showed his nobles that even a king could not hold back the tide. Harold sailed from Bosham for Normandy before the fateful Conquest, probably worshipping under the great arch before taking ship. The arch appears in the Bayeux Tapestry, and is one of the noblest spans in early English architecture. It rises on piers adorned with roll-mouldings, curving into an arch the shape of a horseshoe. The shape might be Roman, even Moorish. No additions or alterations have dimmed its majesty.

Bosham's aisled nave and deep chancel are Early Gothic. Both are more refined than the arch yet hover under its shadow. The five lancets of the east window have Purbeck shafts. Beneath the south aisle is a small crypt, probably an old charnel house, with a strong vault. Later ages contributed little, apart from the restored Decorated tracery in the aisle windows. The interior seems of a piece with its royal genesis. On a quiet evening, when the yachtsmen have departed and the wind is heard in the sycamores, the shouts of arriving Saxons and the clatter of armour might almost be heard through the door.

The spacious churchyard runs down to the water across the Quay Meadow, filled with wild flowers. The gravestones have been almost completely defaced by the sea air but one, dated 1759 to Thomas Barrow, has been well cleaned and recut by local craftsmen. More such restoration, please.

BOXGROVE
Priory of St Mary and St Blaise ***
De la Warre chantry, painted vault

Boxgrove Priory was founded from Normandy in 1117 and maintained by the de la Hayes of Lessay in France. Via the de la Warre line, this Anglo-Norman family kept its link with the Priory through to the Dissolution and is remembered in the de la Warre chantry, Boxgrove's most prominent monument.

Despite its 'English' additions, Boxgrove's exterior looks unmistakably French, with steeply-pitched roofs, flying buttresses and pyramidical tower cap. The building is surrounded by monastic ruins, with remains of the priory buildings and the original nave lying to the west and north. Before the Dissolution, the old nave had served as the parish church, divided from the crossing and chancel by a stone screen visible at the present west end. Set into it are the remains of the doorways that gave access from the lay to the monastic half of the building. The present porch gives directly into the late 12th-century crossing. Its thick piers and semicircular arches of Caen stone are now flooded with light from later windows. The transepts are dark places, with heavy wooden galleries, the northern one strangely inaccessible except by ladder.

East of the crossing runs what was the great chancel and is now the nave, built in the early 13th century. The east end has high lancet windows and black Purbeck marble shafts, set amid white stone. Each pier of the main arcades is different. The rhythm is immaculate, wide rounded arches enclosing two pointed ones within, rising to a clerestory. The rib vaulting is decorated with early 16th-century painting by Lambert Bernard of Chichester. Its rococo floral pattern includes Tudor roses and de la Warre heraldry. The second boss from the altar is so crafted that each of eight faces comes complete with two eyes, yet there are only eight eyes in all.

On the right of the nave stands the de la Warre chantry of 1532. This superb chamber takes its colonnette motifs from an early French *Book of Hours*, acquired by Thomas West, 9th Lord de la Warre. The architecture of the chantry is pure Gothic, but the lavishly carved decoration is a mix of Gothic and classical, including putti as supporters for some of the heraldic shields. Relief carvings display a Dance of Death and a man climbing a tree with a maiden waiting at its foot. The vault has carved pendants. There are angels and putti everywhere. Within a few years of this chantry being built the Priory was dissolved and chantries abolished. Although the de la Warres purchased the building, they later exchanged it for property in Hampshire, and so lost their link with Boxgrove.

The church is rich in other works of art. A reredos by George Gilbert Scott fills the east end. Victorian glass in the south aisle lancets is in the Arts and Crafts style, by Mary Lowndes. A more bizarre 20th-century contribution is the tomb chest for Admiral Nelson-Ward of 1937. He is laid out in the manner of a medieval knight, but in full naval uniform.

BRIGHTON
St Bartholomew, Ann Street ***
Biggest nave, Henry Wilson sanctuary

No 19th-century ecclesiastical grandee was more extravagant or exotic than Father Arthur Wagner. Son of the vicar of Brighton, he was himself ordained, accused of popery, summoned to the ecclesiastical court and even assaulted. From his own pocket, he built five new churches in the town. He was a doyen of what Betjeman called 'London, Brighton and South Coast' Anglo-Catholicism, at a time when the coastal resort saw its most spectacular expansion. He died in 1902.

St Bartholomew's was his crowning glory or, to some, his folly. I can still recall my first sight of it, riding over the smoky railway terraces above The Steyne like a Cunard liner steaming through a fog. The surrounding roofs have since been cleared and replaced by the brand-new New England Quarter. Yet the great west gable, with its giant rose window set in bands of patterned brick, is a stunning affirmation of architectural and religious self-confidence.

The church was designed under Wagner's instructions by a local architect named Edmund Scott, and built in 1872–4. The interior is huge. It has the highest nave of any parish church in England, rising 135 ft from the floor and given added verticality by not having aisles or chancel. One visitor described it to me as a set for *Aida*, with the congregation awaiting a triumphal procession of elephants, soldiers and slaves to emerge at any moment from behind the high altar.

The walls are of unadorned brick with faint diapering, soaring past nine bays of clerestory windows to a roof that seems lost in the clouds. The chancel was never built, and a plan by the Arts and Crafts designer, Henry Wilson, to pierce the east wall and construct a huge apse with a Christ in Majesty beyond was never effected. The east wall is now filled with a large and dull cross.

In 1895 instead, Wilson designed the present sanctuary within the nave. It is his masterpiece, comprising a marble ciborium 45 ft high, guarded by two magnificent candlesticks. Beneath is an Art Nouveau altar rail of brass with blue enamel insets. Behind is a later, dazzling mosaic mural. Wilson also designed the Lady Altar of beaten silver and copper and the green marble font and pulpit. St Bartholomew's remains firmly in the Anglo-Catholic tradition and boasts that its choir sings 'nearly fifty different settings of the Mass, usually in their original language'.

BRIGHTON
St Michael, Victoria Road ★★★★
Bodley Lady Chapel, Burges nave with Nicholls carvings

St Michael's is what historians would call 'important'. Built over a period of thirty years to designs by two masters of Victorian architecture, Bodley and Burges, its huge volume contrives to bury itself in the hillside. The church lurks gloomy amid the dazzling stucco of the Montpelier neighbourhood. Rarely can so imposing a building have made itself so invisible.

The plan is virtually a square, but was not always thus. The first church on the site was designed for Charles Beanlands, yet another of the many wealthy Cambridge graduates who took holy orders in the 1840s. He came to Brighton under the influence of the Wagners (*see* St Bartholomew's, above) and met the young Bodley, whose father was a doctor in the town. In 1858 he commissioned Bodley to design a new church on a confined site off Dyke Road. Bodley was at the time applying his French Gothic enthusiasm to a church at Selsley (Gloucs), with the aid of his friends in the Morris partnership. St Michael's was to be in a fashionable part of Brighton, its pews individually rented by parishioners.

Bodley's church survives as the south aisle of the present building, with a sub-ordinate aisle of its own. It is clearly distinct from the larger nave and north aisle which the flamboyant Burges designed in 1865 but which was not built until 1893. Bodley was a severe Gothicist in search of what he called 'refined beauty and restrained power'. His early works are brought to life by his friends, the William Morris partnership. At St Michael's they painted the chancel ceilings and supplied the stained glass. The jewel of the 'old church' is the Lady Chapel, with its chequerboard floor, white panelled ceiling and delicate reredos. The windows by Burne-Jones, Webb and Morris, including Burne-Jones's superb Flight into Egypt, are masterpieces of the partnership's early period.

To pass from Bodley to Burges is to pass from a French motet to a Handel oratorio. We leave polychrome brick in favour of the stone of a noble abbey. From the outside, Burges's addition is so overwhelming that the present south aisle looks a mere addendum. Why Burges was commissioned to extend Bodley's church is unclear, but we know that Bodley was upset – perhaps understandably so. The result, however, is spectacular. Massive Gothic arcades with coupled columns rise to a triforium knitted by multiple shafts into the clerestory. It bears a close resemblance to the east end of Canterbury Cathedral, where French Gothic forms were first introduced into England. Three huge lancets light the chancel, above which hovers a gilded rood beam.

Burges's glass was not as good as the Morris work in the south aisle, but the north windows are competent pieces by Kempe. Burges's best work was in collaboration with his carver Thomas Nicholls, who realised his more grandiose designs. The sculpture of St Michael and the dragon at the west end is by Nicholls, as presumably are the lush 'Indian Mutiny' capitals to the chancel arch. The choir stalls are by Burges and the misericords by Nicholls, including such delights as boxing frogs and a grasshopper riding a snail. The reredos is a later work by Romaine Walker, not designed until 1902.

CLAYTON
St John **
Norman wall paintings

Clayton is an arch and a painting. The Saxon–Norman church huddles under its Downland slope away from the Brighton road. It has somehow survived both a railway tunnel and a motorway, as it survived Reformation and Victorian restoration. On the hill above are two windmills, Jack and Jill, and a path leads across the churchyard up to the South Downs Way.

Clayton was too poor for aisles, too poor to rebuild its ancient chancel arch and too poor, when ordered to destroy its wall paintings, to do more than whitewash over them. They were rediscovered at the end of the 19th century and rival those of Kempley (Gloucs) as relics of Norman mural art. They frame a magnificent 11th-century chancel arch, with thick slabs of stone for capitals. The walls of both nave and chancel are of Saxon origin, though as elsewhere in Sussex the Saxon–Norman distinction is moot. The windows are mostly Early Gothic lancets. The chancel was entirely restored by the Victorians.

The wall paintings were once thought to be the work of the priory at Lewes,

English headquarters of the monastic citadel at Cluny, in its day the biggest church in Christendom. Today, the frescos surviving in so many Sussex churches are accepted as works of indigenous artists, Clayton and Hardham being their principal memorials. That said, there is a similarity between the Clayton Christ in Majesty over the chancel arch and a drawing in the scriptorium at Cluny. The style is variously attached to Saxons and Byzantines, to Cluniacs and non-Cluniacs. Church art was never so 'European' as in the 12th century.

The theme is of souls progressing eastwards along the nave walls towards the chancel arch and the Day of Judgement, where Christ dispenses love and justice. As in most Romanesque art, the figures are elongated and swaying, crowded into the available space and surrounded with strong scroll borders. Both processions begin with an angel blowing a trumpet. There were presumably more terrifying images further west, now defaced. The impression of the interior of Clayton is of a distant, almost Mediterranean, culture far removed from that of north Europe.

Despite copies of the drawings at ground level to help us understand the paintings, they are indistinct. They have lost their capacity to instil fear.

CLIMPING
St Mary **
Norman carved doorway

The Saxons and early Normans built simple chapels high on the Downs, but they built grand churches by the sea. These stone structures would once have towered over their settlements. Today they are overwhelmed by miles of coastal development. Climping church sits on the outskirts of Littlehampton, protected by a lychgate big enough to admit a coach and four and guarded by a magnificent yew. It has a large, stocky tower with a Norman doorway and, above, a Norman window like none other in Britain. Both appear original and unrestored.

The doorway arch is astonishing, surrounded by dogtooth and zigzag, with an inner arch that is a giant trefoil. The window above looks like a starburst, its surround broken by exaggerated zigzag. These are the work of imported French carvers working Caen stone with panache. The door forms a closed entrance into a south transept. Within half a century of the tower's completion in *c.*1170 a new Early Gothic church was built alongside it.

The contrast with the wild early doorway could not be greater. The rest of Climping's exterior and interior is the epitome of early 13th-century decorum. Lancet windows punctuate every wall. The arches of the south arcade keep perfect time as they progress towards the crossing and the chancel. The lovely east wall of deep-set lancets displays what Pevsner calls 'divine harmony made visible in masonry'. This was the new international Gothic, here in vivid contrast to the extravagant display of Romanesque.

Climping is for sitting in and marvelling. There is little else to see. The Perpendicular pulpit is simple and strong. An ancient Crusader chest lies in the south transept, a rare survivor of those ordered to be put in churches to collect money for those wishing to join the crusades. There are fine Georgian headstones in the churchyard, with excellent lettering. Over the wall and across a field is the dreary architecture of Ford open prison. Do prisons have to be so ugly?

COOMBES
*
Norman wall paintings

Like many Downland chapels, Coombes seems to have been too insignificant to merit a dedication. It lies on a hillside overlooking the River Adur, reached through a farm, over a stile and across a field. Merely getting to Coombes church is a pleasure. Was it a hermit's cell? Was there some rudimentary settlement clinging to the hillside and grubbing a living from the chalk soil?

The church has a long, low unbroken roofline. The tower fell in the early 18th century and the west end is so buried into the hillside that the ground covers the wall up to the window sill. The Norman interior is divided by a simple chancel arch. Various windows have been blocked and others inserted over many centuries, though apparently not the 19th or 20th.

Coombes's treasure is its 12th-century wall paintings of the Lewes Cluniac school, of which examples also survive at Clayton and Hardham. They make up in vividness what they lack in extent. Just two colours, red and yellow, were used with black and white, yet they yield a multitude of shades.

The figures at Coombes include doubting Jews, a lion of St Mark above the arch and a single monster that is worth any detour to witness. He crouches like a caryatid under the chancel arch, his mouth open in agony and his body fiercely contorted under the weight of the architecture, wonderfully alive to his onerous predicament.

CUCKFIELD
Holy Trinity *
Roof restoration by Bodley and Kempe

Cuckfield is pure Sussex, all flint, red tiles and white wooden fences. The church close is protected from traffic by an old grammar school and by the backs of houses along the high street. Yew and pine adorn a churchyard which looks south to the Weald. The tower has a shingled broach spire and battlements above a frieze, while a deep roof embraces both nave and aisles. The interior is dominated by this roof, a 15th-century wagon with tie-beams so sweeping as to render the small clerestory windows largely decorative. The church was restored by Bodley in 1855 and painted by his pupil, Kempe, who also designed much of the stained glass.

Kempe's decoration of the roof is a delight, covered in red and white roses interspersed with flowers and leaves. It is supported by brightly coloured angels on the corbels, all singing hallelujah, indicated by the helpful scrolls that each holds like modern subtitles. The nave arcades are of different periods. The south with round piers is 13th century, the north is 14th century with hexagonal ones. The first pier on the south side is oval for no obvious reason.

Bodley was gentle with Cuckfield. Screen and fittings are seemly and the glass less offensive than most. The east window, by Hardman & Co., is vividly Gothic and the Clayton & Bell south aisle window glows with dark blue and red skies. In the chancel is an eccentric memorial to Charles Sergison (d.1732). Truth leans on a sarcophagus in front of an obelisk, holding a medallion of Sergison in one hand and in the other a mirror into which she is gazing at herself. Sergison was, says the inscription, 'a gentleman of great capacity and penetration, exact judgment, close application to business, strict in everything'. He looks it.

DIDLING
St Andrew *
Setting in Downs field

The churches of the Sussex Downs merit a book to themselves. They are the simplest religious structures in England, begun by pious Saxons and Normans and mostly left alone in their poverty even by the Victorians. While Didling has no speciality apart from its benches, its setting at the end of a lane on a sweeping north slope of the Downs is incomparable. This solitude has given it the title of 'the shepherd's church', and sheep still graze its boundary.

The building has a continuous barn-like roof and no break between nave and chancel. Priest and congregation must always have been as one. From the Saxon period there remains only the font, a rough-hewn lump of stone. The rest of the church dates from the early 13th century. The remarkable bench-ends are gnarled and old, with holders for candles, their backs an 18th-century luxury. The windows are Early Gothic, the rough-carved pulpit Jacobean, the altar rails slightly later. Yet all merges into one timeless whole.

Didling was in a state of neglect in the 16th century and derelict in the 19th, but was restored and reopened in 1872. It is still in use, candle-lit in winter since there is no electricity. By the gate is a huge yew which narrowly escaped felling in the 19th century. The woodmen were stopped by a passing parishioner as they began work. The axe marks can still be seen on its base.

ETCHINGHAM
The Assumption and St Nicholas *
Cistercian stalls and misericords

The church lost its manor to the railway in the 19th century. More dignity was lost to the need for extensive buttressing. Yet this old Cistercian foundation of the 14th century, beautifully set in its churchyard, is a good example of a monastic church adapted to present-day worship. The chancel, built for the canons, is longer than the parochial nave, which has aisles and is square in plan. Under the crossing, arches of differing heights, lit by shafts of coloured light from fragments of ancient glass, play tricks with the eye. The interior is sparse, attributed by the guide to its Cistercian antecedents. The Order's aversion to ornament appears to have preserved it from 17th-century iconoclasts.

Thus the chancel's one comfort, choir stalls with misericords, survive intact. They are unusual. The carved scenes are not compressed under the bracket but spread across the whole underside of the seat. The themes are traditional and include a fine fox preaching to geese, normally a satire on a bishop. Old glass has been collected in the east window of the north aisle, and a number of brasses survive on the chancel floor.

GLYNDE
St Mary *
Intact Georgian interior

The church stands on the brow of a hill, prominent across the valley that divides it from the South Downs. Next door, the Elizabethan flint house of Glynde Place (distinct from opera-lovers' Glyndebourne a mile to the north) shows its back to the road. Two fine wyverns guarding its entrance can be seen from the churchyard.

Glynde's owner in the 18th century was Richard Trevor, Lord Bishop of Durham, who inherited the house in 1743 after a cousin was killed in a duel. He was a fastidious and elegant prelate, dubbed by George II 'the beauty of holiness'.

The bishop's architect for his local church was the little-known Thomas Robinson. Though Georgian (of 1763) it has no portico or tower and is more in the style of a century before. The entrance front has a porch flanked by two niches. The pediment holds the bishop's coat of arms. The path to the door is lined with headstones covered in lichen, drawn up like guardsmen at a wedding.

The interior is an immaculate Georgian composition, continuing the exterior theme of quiet elegance. In the words of the guide it 'conforms to the architectural precision that a prince of the church and a great landowner could no doubt command'. The ceiling has mildly rococo decoration. There is no chancel, only a small enclosure round the altar. The box pews, pulpit and reading desks are all of their original height. The walls are most unusually covered in fabric, now rather faded. It is the only church I know with this feature.

The windows once contained clear glass but in the 1870s the church authorities decided that this was old-fashioned and commissioned Kempe to put stained glass in the windows. This is not his usual parade of saints in Gothic settings, but what Pevsner deplores as a 'grossly ill-chosen Holbein style of fat Renaissance decoration'. The frames are filled with swags, pillars and scrolls and the church is suffused with a yellow-brown light. This is most unlike the usual Kempe.

HARDHAM
St Botolph **
Cluniac wall paintings

This wayside chapel on a side road near the A29 contains 12th-century wall paintings comparable with those at Clayton, the work of Cluniac artists from Lewes, sometimes called the Lewes School. They are severely faded, but their restoration has been masterly, creating an interior of great charm, a survivor of what must have been hundreds of south-coast chapels of the pre-Gothic era.

Hardham is a tiny double-cell Norman building, the nave divided from the chancel by a plain arch. Apart from a Victorian clock turret and porch, little appears to have changed since the artists returned to Lewes. The paintings cannot be easily discerned, although the installation of electric light helps and the guide is indispensable.

The sequence of biblical and mythological scenes covers the whole church. It starts with a well-preserved Adam and Eve on the far side of the chancel arch. The naked figures are in the Anglo-Norman style, elongated with strong bodies and small heads. The faces are portrayed boldly, as in a Matisse. Across the arch Eve is shown milking a huge cow while Adam looks down from a tree.

An Annunciation can be made out on the west side of the chancel arch overlooking the nave. On the north wall is a Flight into Egypt and, in the lower portion, St George fighting infidels, rather than a dragon. Given the date of the paintings, this must be an early re-creation of the First Crusade scene in which St George arrives in time to save the Crusader army. Other scenes on the lower part of this wall show St George's various tortures, including breaking on the wheel. This superb gallery of Norman art awaits further conservation, long overdue.

NEW SHOREHAM
St Mary ***
Contrast of Norman and Early Gothic styles

New Shoreham is a giant church, begun by the Normans in *c*.1130. It was constructed to serve the new harbour that was to replace Old Shoreham, then silting up inland. The tower still dominates the little town, especially from the harbour and beach, but we must imagine the original church as twice the present size. Legend holds that its first patron, Philip de Braose, intended it as a monastery to celebrate his return from the First Crusade in 1103. For some reason he had to flee the country before completing his monastic foundation, leaving the port only with a magnificent church. Shoreham was thus always a parish church, ranking with (but predating) such other great seaport foundations as Boston (Lincs) or St Mary Redcliffe, Bristol (Gloucs).

The original building was cruciform. The old nave became ruinous and was demolished in the 17th century, leaving just one bay. We can see surviving only the crossing and transepts of *c*.1130, and the superb choir and upper tower which were begun half a century later, *c*.1180. The appeal of the church derives from the contrast between these two periods of building, Norman and Transitional. New Shoreham is a textbook of comparative 12th-century style.

The glory of the church is the choir interior. Seen from the west end, it is framed by the high arches of the crossing, whose piers have capitals clearly in an earlier and heavier Norman style. These piers presumably date from de Braose's church. The choir was apparently designed as a unity, which is extraordinary since each side displays strongly contrasting late Norman and Early Gothic motifs, the 'Transition' in microcosm. The north arcade piers are alternately round and octagonal, with stiff-leaf capitals and moulded arches rising to the slightest of points. These are attributable to masons from Canterbury, where the same pattern had recently been introduced from France (in the 1170s).

The south arcade opposite is more evidently Early Gothic, with embryonic clustered shafts rising to moulded arches with a hint of a point. On this side, a continuous shaft rises the full height of the wall, reaching to the springing of the vault. This feature unites arcade, gallery and clerestory in one composition, while the earlier north side merely piles one storey heavily on another. Thus does Norman sit and Gothic soar, yet at New Shoreham they contrive to sing in harmony. The vault and east windows are also Early Gothic. The church is unusually bereft of furnishings, as if seaborne marauders had at some point stripped it bare.

OLD SHOREHAM
St Nicholas *
Norman figure carvings

Before the construction of the A27 bridge over the River Adur, Old Shoreham's location was sublime. Set on a mound above the old harbour, where the river pierces the Downs to reach the sea, the church looked across the sweep of valley to where Lancing chapel rose on the opposite bluff. The view has been ruined by the insensitive siting of the road.

No matter, the church survives. It is a Saxon foundation dated to the 9th century, and must have looked on with despair and envy as the river silted up and New Shoreham rose on the coast. The circular extent of the old graveyard – sometimes associated with a pre-Christian place of worship – can still be made out, as can traces of ancient stonework in the church walls. Yet the Normans did not ignore the old church. Indeed its chief interest today lies in its Norman additions, especially the mighty crossing arches supporting the tower.

These are not so much Norman restored as Norman thoroughly cleaned behind the ears. In 1840 the Camden Society, Cambridge's version of the Oxford Movement (*see* Introduction), adopted Old Shoreham with gusto. On a visit in the 1840s they declared it so ruinous that a visitor might 'imagine he was descending into the dungeon of a criminal rather than going into the House of the Lord'. As a result, there was far more 'Norman' in Old Shoreham after 1840 than there was before.

That said, the crossing tower is real Norman and the crossing arches form an archaeological sanctuary at the heart of the restored church. The details of the capitals and corbels are superb. Here we can see a woman's face, a monster, a shell, a rosette, a cat and an elf, all still evocative after centuries of decay and restoration. The rest of the church is pseudo-Norman, a Victorian architectural collage. But without such a rescue there would presumably be nothing at Shoreham today but a ruin.

PENHURST
St Michael *
Placid woodland setting

Sussex can seem England's most private county. Penhurst is one of its most private churches. It is found at the end of a long winding lane, deep in rolling wooded countryside. The manor house has fashioned a pond from its moat and a farm has converted its barns into studios. The church nestles quietly between them, amid a carpet of daffodils in springtime. A visitor in 1946 came upon the church, 'desolate and forlorn, still ringing its solitary bell to bid a small band of worshippers'. That band must be even smaller today, but Penhurst is anything but forlorn. Rural prosperity has revived and restored it. The church is welcoming and warm, a charming discovery well off any beaten track.

The building's age is immaterial. The tower has a Sussex cap and the interior appears undisturbed since the 17th century. The nave has old box pews and a Jacobean pulpit under a king-post roof. An arch to the chancel is guarded by a crudely carved Perpendicular screen. The chancel has a wagon roof, with fragments of heraldic glass in the east window. They depict manorial donors attended by the usual angels. In the north chapel, now the vestry, are two fine poppyheads standing alone and detached from their seats. In this place they represent the household gods of peace and continuity.

PLAYDEN
St Michael *
Carved aisle screens

The shingled spire is visible from across Romney Marsh, guarding the northern approach to Rye above the Royal Military Canal. The church with a Norman tower is hidden from its village behind a screen of trees and a spacious churchyard. The steep tiled roof sweeps low over the aisles, supported on thick buttresses.

The interior is happily unrestored, with a Norman arcade of rounded arches on moulded capitals. The Victorians appear to have left the nave roof ceiled and unmolested. The view from the west end, from nave to crossing to chancel, is from darkness to light. Two screens guard the crossing, one Perpendicular to the chancel, one Decorated to the north aisle. The north aisle screen has flamboyant tracery with much ogee work, remarkably sophisticated for so rudimentary a setting. It is believed to have been donated by a kindly patron from a dissolved monastery.

The chancel has three bays of windows with clear glass. One of them contains a delicately engraved memorial to the men of HMS *Barham*, sunk in 1941. Under the crossing tower stands a wonderfully battered ladder to the bell-chamber, dating from the 17th century.

ROTHERFIELD
St Denys **
Pulpit eagle, Perpendicular font cover

The dedication is attributed to a cure obtained by a Saxon nobleman from monks at St-Denis near Paris in the 8th century. The big church has a rare Sussex battlemented tower with a shingled needle spire rising 135 ft. It soars over a well-preserved village, facing west towards Ashdown Forest and north over the Weald towards Tunbridge Wells. From the churchyard the tower and two-storey porch appear as tough customers, ready for imminent assault. The stone is strong and smooth in contrast with Sussex's ubiquitous flint.

The interior is generously proportioned, with an especially wide chancel. The nave retains box pews, which rise at the back as in a theatre. There are fragments of paintings on most walls, including a Doom above the chancel arch and St Michael weighing souls. Dated to *c.*1300, the saint's wings are half folded; his hand points to the heavier end of the scales, normally reserved for sin. Clive Rouse explains in his study of such murals, 'If you wished to impress crude and simple people, crude methods had to be employed to bring home the enormity of sin and its penalties, the rewards of the just and the uncertainty of life.'

The 17th-century pulpit is particularly rich, having apparently been made for an archbishop of York whose daughter married the local rector. The two wings of a giant eagle spread across its back, as if to help the preacher take flight. The tester is decorated above and below with openwork. Separated from the font, a Perpendicular cover of 1533 is decorated with the arms of the Nevilles and with early Renaissance panels.

Rotherfield has an east window by Morris & Co. of 1874. This radiates an eerie light across the Early Gothic chancel. For once Morris's design overpowers Burne-Jones's graceful figures, who seem lost in a dense forest of foliage. On the north wall is a painting of the village, dating from the early 20th century.

RYE
St Mary **
Tranquil town setting

Rye's church rises over the walled hill town, its tower looking out towards Romney Marsh and the sea. Medieval houses enclose the churchyard to the south. Lamb House, once home of Henry James, lies down a lane to the west. To the north, the town tiptoes close to the north transept to glimpse its large clock with an 18th-century surround and model boys to strike the quarter hour. The huge pendulum of this clock swings over the crossing inside, with a 16th-century mechanism which is one of the oldest working in England. The church has made itself a focus of the town's tourism, a role other resorts should imitate.

The cruciform church was already substantial in the Norman period, owned by the monastery of Fécamp in Normandy. Both transepts have blind arcading and are studded with Norman fragments outside and in. The much-restored nave has Norman piers and arches with dogtooth decoration, which become more pointed as they move west. The east end has two large Early Gothic chapels. The church was sacked by the French in 1377, some of Rye's citizens afterwards being hanged and quartered for failing to put up sufficient resistance. Rebuilding continued under the stimulus of further French raids, but no raid and no rebuilding was as drastic as that of the Victorians.

Rye church is well furnished but heavily restored. The windows are dark, their glass blotting out most views of the lovely close. Were the windows only clear, this setting would superbly infuse the interior. The glass in the south transept is by Powell & Sons of 1928. The west window is also from Powell's, and was donated in 1937 by the novelist and mayor of Rye, E. F. Benson. He kneels in mayoral robes in the bottom right-hand corner, medieval style. There is a Burne-Jones in the north aisle.

SOMPTING
St Mary **
Rhenish tower, Saxon carvings

Sompting's celebrated steeple is visible from the trunk road that now separates it from its village. Those who regard Saxon architecture as the work of forest primitives should see Sompting. It possesses England's supreme Saxon steeple, surpassing even Earls Barton (Northants) in sophistication. Four gables are set on a tower, the roof between them pushed upwards and downwards to form four lozenges. The result is known as a 'Rhenish helm', familiar in some north European countries to stop snow from forming on roofs. The tower is articulated by a vertical strip at each corner and in the centre of each face, topped by a corbel. The roof is as soaring as any Gothic spire, reminding us that the Saxons too were 'Goths'. It has been dated to c.1000, before the pre-Conquest penetration of Sussex by Normandy's church-builders.

Assuming the arches of the tower interior are of a similar date, their capitals are among the earliest manifestations of English architectural carving, retaining faint echoes of ancient Corinthian and Ionic orders. The Sompting capitals appear to display an art still rooted in a Roman past, before discovering new sources of inspiration in natural, human and abstract forms. These capitals look like throw-backs, a Saxon 'classical renaissance' that never flowered.

The rest of Sompting is mostly late Norman, dating from the donation of the church to the Knights Templar in 1184. They added a north transept and a southern chamber, originally inaccessible from the church but now opened by a Victorian archway. Both have rib-vaulted chapels and arches with scalloped capitals, demonstrating the lavishness associated with this most privileged of knightly orders. In the 14th century the Templars were dissolved in favour of the Hospitallers (*see* The Temple, London), who, in the form of St John Ambulance, still have a room in the church. The interior is scrubbed and restored, and rather characterless.

SOUTHEASE
*

Downland setting, chancel arch beam

The little chapel at Southease merits a visit for its setting alone. The village lies at the end of a cul-de-sac beyond Rodmell, where the River Ouse cuts through the South Downs between Lewes and Newhaven. The building is pinned to a slope above the village green by a west tower, unusual outside East Anglia, with a conical shingle spire. Behind is a tree-framed manor house. The church roof is coated with an array of lichens.

The Norman church has mislaid both its chancel and its aisles, possibly ruined and demolished after the Black Death. Fragments of Norman work litter the walls both outside and inside. The charm of the church derives from an attempt in the 15th century to create a new chancel under the existing roof at the east end of the old nave.

This was achieved by the device of inserting a wood, lath and plaster chancel arch, presumably above a now-vanished rood screen. This arch is a graceful structure, dividing the interior in two. The remains of Reformation texts can be made out on the spandrels of the arch. The other walls reply with pale shadows of old wall paintings. This is another case of paintings too fragmentary to have meaning as art, and unconvincing as decoration. They should be repainted in an approximation of the original style where this can be plausibly attempted, as the Victorians would have done.

An old Jacobean pulpit looks down on three rows of box pews. On the day of my visit, the church had been so filled with wild flowers that its walls appeared to be growing up out of the meadow. It needed only for its lovely old Georgian chamber organ to break into Sussex song.

SOUTH HARTING
St Mary and St Gabriel **
Cowper tombs, Gill memorial

This big medieval church seems eager to drag its village back into the dark woods which, at this point, clothe the Downs on every side. The great house of Uppark lies just over the hill. A vivid copper spire dominates the main street. The walls are of any material that came to hand: flint, stone, brick, rubble and cement rendering. The church outside and inside is remarkably casual. The nave arcades look as if a local mason had run up some rudely chamfered arches on octagonal piers, without bothering with capitals.

All is uplifted by Harting's splendid Tudor roofs, inserted after a fire in 1576. The chancel roof is a complex structure of tie-beams with ornamental pendants, the other roofs more simple barn-like structures. Together they form a remarkable set.

In the south transept is another Tudor spectacular, a set of tombs of the Cowper family, reminiscent of the eccentric group at Swinbrook (Oxon). John Cowper and his wife lie on their sides in full Elizabethan rig, semi-prone with elbows on cushions and holding books. The father kneels above, facing the wall, as if praying for their souls. Next to them is a shattered 17th-century stone figure of Sir Richard Caryll, brought in from his private chapel, which once stood outside the transept wall. Opposite stands a charming bronze of a mother and child of 1985, by Karin Jonzen. Harting's modern kneelers include a series depicting local butterflies.

In the churchyard is a tall, slender memorial to the dead of the Great War by Eric Gill. Simple reliefs, including one of St George and the Dragon, surround the base beneath the names of those who died. It sits well among the old stones and lofty trees.

STEYNING
St Andrew ***
Norman carvings, Renaissance reredos

The church could hardly be less like its village. The latter is picturesque and delicate, a Sussex delight. The former is a bruiser of a building, surviving from the 9th century when Steyning was a seaport on the River Adur. As the resting place of St Cuthman, it was donated by Edward the Confessor to the Norman monks of Fécamp (who also held Rye) before the Conquest.

After the Conquest, the monks demolished the Saxon church and built the core of what we see today, shipping their stone up the Adur from Caen in France. Their tower, crossing and choir were demolished after the Reformation, leaving just today's nave for the use of the parishioners.

The present tower is a 16th-century structure built on to the west end. The nave is magnificent, as if the Norman masons were freed of episcopal supervision and left to take the Norman style wherever their imagination led them. The chancel arch of c.1100 survives from the earlier crossing, more Saxon than Norman, its capitals with unusual Celtic frond motifs.

The nave arcades and clerestories are of fifty years later, richly confident and a gallery of Norman art. Here are the familiar zigzag and dogtooth, scallops, trumpets and volutes, but also fantasies of human and animal grimaces, sculptures expressing joy and fear. Best are the inventive abstract patterns of the arcade capitals, densely carved and with a verve that makes them the best of their time in Sussex.

There is one splendid furnishing at Steyning, the reredos of 48 carved panels, dated 1522 and taken from the old rectory. Most of the panels are of abstract scrollwork, but one contains the coat of arms of Henry VIII. The remarkable work of local craftsmanship gives out a warm glow at the end of the chancel.

UP MARDEN
St Michael *
Woodland setting

Sussex's Downland churches were founded by missionaries penetrating dense upland forests to convert pagan settlements. They would have been wood-framed, with wattle and daub walls and thatched roofs. The rebuilding of these churches must have seemed a huge architectural advance, known to have begun under both Saxon and Norman patronage well before the Conquest of 1066. Continental masons brought French stone and French styles even to the poorest and most inaccessible places. These churches remained isolated, at least until 19th-century restoration. Some survived even that.

Of this group Up Marden is special, a church that appears still to hold its original *genius loci*. It owes some of its renown to the eulogy written by Ian Nairn in the Sussex volume of the Pevsner series. He granted it an aura, 'as tangible as any moulding, the slow, loving, gentle accretion century by century ... incredibly moving whether one is Anglican or not, whether one is religious or not'.

We have no record of a Saxon foundation on the site, this church being apparently Early Gothic in origin. But, like all these downland chapels, Up Marden exists in a time and place of its own. The early missionaries knew what they were about.

The church is reached down a track beside a house. It is virtually devoid of architecture, with thick walls and deep-set single lancet windows. The plan is double-cell, divided by an old arch of indeterminate date, underpinned by the Tudors. The church would have been vividly painted, so the present whitewash is anachronistic. Equally out of place is the fussy Victorian Gothic pulpit. Yet the brick floor, box pews and wooden benches are a study in tranquillity. Outside, the crazily tilting headstones of the Padwick and Pinnix families enliven the churchyard. On a summer evening we can imagine ancient peasants climbing from the fields below, to find comfort and hope of salvation in their place of holiness.

WARMINGHURST
Holy Sepulchre **
Queen Anne fittings

Warminghurst is a small village, protected from fame by being near impossible
to find. A side road reaches it north-west from the village of Ashington. The
church, now redundant, sits on a knoll bounded by an old wall next to a farm.
Chanctonbury Ring, a celebrated clump of trees on the South Downs, can be
seen from the churchyard. The exterior is an Early Gothic single-cell with a
'splay-foot' spirelet hung with tiles.

The exterior belies the extraordinary interior. This greets us with a Queen
Anne screen dividing nave and chancel, composed of three classical arches
topped by a giant tympanum. Here the queen's coat of arms is painted with
exaggerated panache against a dramatic background of drapery, like the
proscenium of a village theatre.

This may have been a Royalist assertion on the part of a new lord of the
manor, James Butler. In 1702 he bought the adjacent house of the Quaker,
William Penn, who had drafted the earliest constitution of the State of Pennsylvania at Warminghurst (though Buckinghamshire makes a similar claim, and
boasts Penn's grave at the Meeting House at Jordans). Butler demolished Penn's
house, so as 'not to leave a trace of the old Quaker'.

The screen is complemented by a fine arched roof and irregular paved floor.
Three Georgian hatchments of the Butler family hang on the north wall.
Eighteenth-century pinewood box pews fill the entire nave. Beneath the pulpit,
the clerk's elmwood chair was plainly tailor-made for a vast posterior. Next to
it is a pretty lectern designed to fit on the corner of the pew.

Georgian wall memorials to the Benet and Riches families complete what
seems not a rural place of worship but a chapel of ease to the local landed
gentry.
[CCT]

WEST GRINSTEAD
St George **
Yeoman pews, Rysbrack monument

West Grinstead church is like an old Sussex farmer in a tweed coat. The church
occupies a site on the banks of the River Adur, in open Weald with the South
Downs rising in the distance. No village survives, just an old Jacobean house
and rectory for company. Yet this rich landscape once yielded enough farms to
fill the pews installed and named in the early 19th century. The churchyard is

full of sycamore, oak and yew, with headstones and paths meandering towards the woods. In the centre stands a familiar Sussex spire, shingled and broached, above a long nave roof. The 15th-century timber porch is so cosy it might be a country cottage in miniature.

The interior is a rustic jumble. Old benches, bits of organ, cassocks and hymn books are scattered here and there. So too is the architecture. In the middle of the south aisle is the base of what must have been a massive Norman tower, with high arches, scallops and stiff-leaf capitals. Great things must once have been envisaged for West Grinstead. In comparison, the nave arcade to the south aisle is almost diminutive, formed of three neat Early Gothic arches. The walls are pierced with deeply splayed windows.

The naming of local farms on the pew backs dates from the 1820s and is a rare survival. Here we read fine old Sussex place names such as Hobshorts, Sunt, Grinders, Freezers, Figland, Brightams and Buckells, their locations all still traceable on a map helpfully pinned to the wall. The chancel is panelled, probably with Continental woodwork introduced in the early 19th century. The pulpit retains its tester. A fragment of a St Christopher can be made out on the wall near the north door.

The surprise of the church is the irruption into this rusticity of a group of 18th-century memorials, to the Burrells of West Grinstead and the Powletts of Champions. The 1746 Powlett monument is by Rysbrack and shows man and wife in Roman dress leaning on an urn before an obelisk. A bust of Merrik Burrell of 1787 has its face bashed off; it is surely capable of restoration. The Norman arches look down disapprovingly.

WINCHELSEA
St Thomas ***
14th-century tombs, 20th-century glass

Winchelsea must tire of comparison with Rye. It too was sacked by the French, deserted by the sea and bypassed by the Industrial Revolution. But in the 1280s it rebuilt itself inland on higher ground on a rectangular town plan. This left it with open streets which today lack any sense of presence or intimacy. Winchelsea today seems a suburb rather than a town. The church was built under the patronage of Edward I to be grander than Rye's, but is detached across a large churchyard. It never seems quite able to hold hands with its surrounding streets.

But enough carping. What we see today are the chancel and side chapels of a once huge and magnificent church. This was sacked (yet again) by the French soon after it was built, and as a result the west elevation appears as a row of gabled blank walls, like a set of barns. Only from behind, to the east, can we see windows with Decorated tracery, heavily cusped in the Kentish style and dating from the end of the 13th century.

The interior, even in its fragmentary state, is formidable. This was a foundation intended to dazzle the French. Slender piers with Purbeck shafts and rings soar upwards, as if in search of stone vaults to support. Windows with more Purbeck shafting fill every wall. In the sanctuary, the piscina and sedilia might be those of a cathedral.

Winchelsea's glory is its medieval tombs. These line the walls of both aisles. Those along the north wall commemorate a knight, a lady and a gentleman, of black Sussex 'marble' under crowded arches. The effigies may have been brought from a vanished former church. The canopies are Decorated at its most lavish. Giant leaves fill the trefoils, the cusping splendidly exaggerated. This chapel also has a 17th-century Madonna and Child.

Opposite, in the south aisle, are the two Alard tombs, even richer than those in the north aisle. They are reputedly of two Wardens of the Cinque Ports, Gervase and Stephen Alard. They lie in prayer, with carved panelling on the chests and in the alcoves, below canopies with nodding ogees covered in swirling foliage. From its depths stare a Green Man, a lion and angels galore. This is a superb display of English carving.

Now for the windows. Winchelsea saw one of England's most comprehensive programmes of modern glazing, by Douglas Strachan in the 1930s as a memorial to the Great War. Work began in the north aisle and extended round the whole church. The theme is of the elements of earth, fire and water, dark, vivid and sentimental. They wholly dominate the church, which means that if one dislikes them they spoil it. The work is dramatic and perhaps a future generation will show more enthusiasm for it than I can muster.

WORTH
St Nicholas **
Giant Saxon arches

Worth the name and worth the detour, from the horrors of Crawley, the M23 and the Gatwick sprawl. The rescue of this pre-Conquest church from Victorian restorers and from a recent fire puts it in the front rank of Saxon structures. Archaeologists have dated 95 per cent of Worth to before the 11th century. It is an extraordinary building to find, even as an abbey, in what can have been no more than a simple forest clearing. The foundation was probably by Edward the Confessor as an outpost of the abbey at Chertsey.

The church lies in a valley surrounded by woods, though motorway noise spoils the peace of the churchyard. The steep tiled roof, Victorian broach spire and cottagey Tudor porches ill-disguise its past. From below the eastern apse, we might be looking up at the tower of a Teuton castle. Characteristic of a Saxon building are the pilaster strips topped by a horizontal string course, and the nave windows of two lights divided by a column upright. All openings are high off the ground since these buildings would also have been places of sanctuary from attack. Subsequent builders brought more light into the interior with two Decorated and a Perpendicular window. The tower was added by Anthony Salvin in 1871, amid much debate over whether to alter the old church more drastically, a debate in which the conservationists scored an early victory.

They thus preserved the three great Saxon crossing arches that dominate Worth's interior. The arch to the chancel is one of the largest extant, a massive semicircle set on two square abaci. These seem far distant from the developed Saxon–Norman capitals of the south coast. Salvin also restored the chancel, retaining the cool simplicity of the old apse. Less cool is the nave. A fire in 1986 destroyed the Victorian roof and the new one conceals fierce downlighters which glare on to bright whitewash and modern benches. Here the atmosphere is of a photographer's studio rather than a Saxon church, at least softened by two splendid 17th-century chandeliers. The church has a 13th-century font, curious for the date in showing no trace of Gothic design but instead a double Maltese cross.

Warwickshire

Warwickshire must once have been one of the loveliest counties in the Midlands, linking the valley of the Avon and Forest of Arden to the rolling hills of Leicestershire. Today it suffers grievously from the gash of the Birmingham conurbation. Despite recent efforts to rescue the city centre from some of Europe's worst postwar rebuilding, this is a visually barren landscape. In Birmingham and its satellite west Midlands towns there are a few interesting Victorian churches, but they are bleak and inaccessible. The county's second city, Coventry, was sorely bombed and far more sorely replanned, but at least Holy Trinity has a fine setting next to the cathedral.

Away from Birmingham, and especially in the valley of the Avon, the country is still lush and the building materials vary from rich honeyed ironstone to dark russet sandstone. Here are two of England's finest Perpendicular works: Stratford-upon-Avon, with its great chancel and the tomb of the Bard, and Warwick, whose Beauchamp monument is a supreme work of late-medieval art. Otherwise, Berkswell has a charming Norman crypt, Merevale has splendid medieval glass and Wootton Wawen is an archaeologist's treasure trove.

Astley **
Berkswell ***
Birmingham:
  St Martin **
Burton Dassett **
Coventry:
  Holy Trinity **

Hampton Lucy **
Lapworth **
Lower Brailes *
Lower Shuckburgh *
Merevale **
Preston on Stour *
Solihull *

Stratford-upon-Avon
  ****
Warwick *****
Wootton Wawen ***

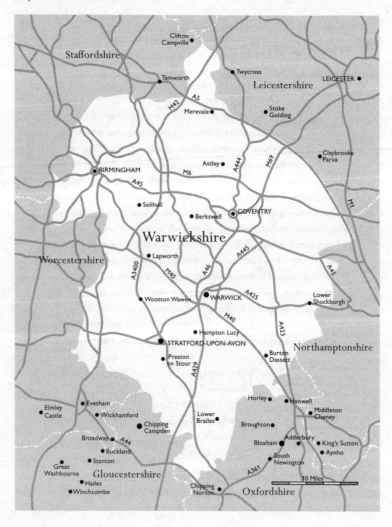

ASTLEY

St Mary **

Jacobean conversion of ruined chancel

The castle was home of Lady Jane Grey. The Elizabethan house subsequently built on the site is now ruined, its bridge and moat pathetic relics of what was, until the Second World War, a fine mansion. The church next door is a rarity, one of the few 1,000 best churches still urgently needing restoration. On my visit, storm-tossed tiles littered an overgrown churchyard. There was broken glass everywhere. The adjacent village seemed to have turned its back on the place in embarrassment.

The exterior is spectacular. Tower and chancel are early 17th century but the core is a three-bay Decorated nave. This nave was itself once the chancel of a large collegiate church whose nave and crossing tower were lost after the Dissolution. It had been built on the eve of the Black Death in 1343 by Sir Thomas Astley. A later occupant of the castle, Richard Chamberlaine, decided in 1607 to restore what was by then a ruin, rebuild the tower at the west end, convert the former chancel into a nave and add a new chancel in the Gothic style to the east end.

This arrangement is not wholly successful. From the west, the aspect is of an Oxford college chapel gone to seed. The nave still looks like a chancel, with longitudinal seating and choir stalls. The new chancel beyond is more a private chapel, with a Gothic plaster ceiling. On either side soar three big windows with Decorated tracery: two of these are tear-drop and one fleur-de-lis on the north side, the converse on the south side, typical 14th-century wilfulness. The east wall, above the arch to the new chancel, carries the tracery of the old Perpendicular east window, now blank.

The walls round these windows are peeling, although intermittently covered with post-Reformation biblical texts. In the window heads is medieval glass, jumbled but colourful. The effect is rich and eerie. Some of the nave stalls carry misericords of *c.*1400. These are simple in themselves but their backs have rare paintings of prophets and apostles on a black background with their scrolls overwritten by iconoclasts. Medieval tombs of the Grey family grouped inside the entrance look as dejected as the rest of the church. There is something splendid about this place.

BERKSWELL

St John ***

Norman crypt, Thompson woodwork

The setting is immaculate: lane, old wall, roses, fir trees and the Dutch gable of the old rectory. The church presents a pink Norman chancel to the road, like a jolly face freshly shaved. Midlands sandstone is a relief for travellers from the cold limestone of the north Cotswolds. The picture is completed by a half-timbered south porch with a cottagey chamber above. This used to be the village school, a pleasant place in which to learn.

The interior is darkened by the presence of a big south gallery and by Victorian scraping. But Berkswell is full of surprises. A series of steps rises from the west end towards the sanctuary, lending it much mystery. The north arcade and the chancel are Norman. The chancel is pure and unspoilt, with a charming arrangement of small east windows. The screens are Perpendicular but much of the woodwork was inserted by that ubiquitous carver, Robert Thompson of Kilburn (in North Yorkshire), between 1926 and 1946. He made stalls, pulpit, north aisle altar and the font. There are nine examples of his famous mouse signature, fun for children to find scattered about the church.

A door in the north aisle leads down to the crypt, one of the most remarkable in any Midlands parish church and ranking with those of Repton (Derbys) and Lastingham (Yorks, N). It has a unique octagonal ante-chamber and both spaces are rib vaulted. The crypt is late Norman, c.1150, and was reputedly the burial place of St Mildred, Bishop of Worcester, or of a quite different St Mildred (no relation). It was later a burial vault for the Eardley Wilmots, lords of the manor, and forms a serene contrast with the rich furnishings above. The church is well endowed with hatchments and charity boards. The latter are apparently still active, with trustees administering to the poor of the parish as their 18th-century forebears were bidden to do. Outside the churchyard is an old well, used for ancient baptisms.

BIRMINGHAM
St Martin, Bull Ring **
Defiant city centre Gothic, Burne-Jones window

Other than the cathedrals, St Martin's is the only church of note in central Birmingham. It once towered over the old Bull Ring market place, dramatically clinging to a hillside. Today the site is desperate, squeezed between what survives of the market and an inhuman whirl of urban roads and concrete blocks. Rescue is planned, but the cost of rectifying the horrors of the 1960s and 1970s will be huge. For the moment, St Martin's is a beacon in a wilderness.

The church was rebuilt in 1873–5 on the basis of the Gothic original to the designs of a local architect, J. A. Chatwin, who had worked with Barry and A. W. N. Pugin at the Palace of Westminster. He designed with panache. Though the building is dark and its red sandstone exterior hard on the eye, Gothic detail and the ubiquitous gargoyles and other exterior carvings shout defiance at their surroundings. The interior is impressive, a sweep of Decorated arches with foliated capitals. When it can catch the sun, the sandstone radiates a pink glow. The hammerbeam roof is based on that of Westminster Hall.

The richest part of the church is the aisled chancel, a lofty chamber, its arcades heavily cusped. Chatwin held that Gothic meant carving. St Martin's is encrusted with heads, animals and flowers, much of it salvaged from the previous church. Three 14th-century monuments to the de Bermingham family flank the chancel. An alabaster effigy on the south side, apparently of an ecclesiastical Bermingham, is beautifully executed and has well-preserved angels on its tomb chest. The reredos is also of alabaster, a set of fine biblical reliefs. The south transept contains a window by Burne-Jones, with Christ and the evangelists, and Old Testament kings and prophets – the Pre-Raphaelite familiars on magnificent parade.

BURTON DASSETT
All Saints **
Hillside setting by holy well

This is a wild spot at the watershed of three Englands. To the north lies the valley of the Avon, on its way west to the Severn. To the south over Edge Hill is the Cherwell, tributary of the Thames. To the east stretches the great Northamptonshire plain towards East Anglia. The point is marked by a sudden jumble of steep hillocks, as if England's tectonic plates had yet to sort out some geological dispute. Until recently the only sound was of a handful of sheep. Now the M40 thunders past. Only an old watch tower and the church on the hill stand guard over the turmoil.

The church lies not along the contour but properly 'oriented' to the east. This must have caused its builders no end of trouble. The tower at the downhill end is massive, while the chancel is buried in the hillside. The structure dates from the 13th century, when the local de Sudeley family prospered under Henry III and were granted rights of 'Court Leet, Gallows, Cuckstool, Pillory and Assize'. The powers sound awesome. The church interior is Early Gothic, its spaciousness assisted by five sets of steps leading up the gradient to the altar. The north arcade capitals carry carved animals, a delightful zoological variant of the neighbouring Oxfordshire work, seen at Adderbury. There is stiff-leaf on the Transitional chancel arch.

The church is decayed yet not shabby. Much of its internal plaster is original, reminder of what most churches were like before Victorian scraping. There are extensive wall paintings, notably above the chancel arch. According to the guide these are appearing gradually 'and miraculously' over time as the Reformation whitewash falls away. The chancel is totally bare, even its sedilia devoid of decoration. The east window has graceful Y-tracery, and the rest of the windows are free of Victorian glass. They are thus open to the trees and the sky.

Next to the church is a holy well set into the hillside. Such wells were discredited after the Reformation and most were dismantled (or secularised). This structure is Victorian, but recalls the faith of medieval travellers in the healing powers of nature – or at least of cleanliness.

COVENTRY
Holy Trinity **
Majestic Blitz survivor, Marler Chapel

A fragment of medieval Coventry survives immediately west of the cathedral. The townscape is intimate, the infilling unobtrusive and crowded lanes take over from the bleak piazzas of the postwar city. Holy Trinity's spire complements that of the ruined St Michael on the Coventry skyline, the latter one of the finest in England. To have two such churches next to each other suggests a medieval wealth that few cities can have matched. Holy Trinity rises 237 ft, but is still topped by St Michael.

The exterior is conventional Perpendicular, mostly of red sandstone refaced by the Victorians. The interior is also heavily restored, but not so as to destroy the grand proportions and cruciform plan. Parts of the sandstone are still scorched pink from the Blitz firestorm. The tower crossing interrupts a high, four-bay nave with a south aisle, two north aisles and a superb panelled roof. This leads the eye towards a chancel that is even longer than the nave, giving the interior space an exhilarating visual drama. Like the nave, it has three aisles, most splendid of which is the northernmost containing the Marler Chapel. This was endowed by a wealthy Coventry merchant in the 1530s and its dark oak roof is original.

The furnishings of Holy Trinity are mostly Victorian. In the sanctuary are exotic sedilia, like a sofa with a cluster of pinnacles as a central canopy. The walls are painted with Victorian murals. In the choir are old stalls from the dissolved Whitefriars, with excellent misericords. It may seem unfair to complain of the quality of glass in Coventry, its previous work having been destroyed by bombs, but the postwar replacements are mostly dire, including Comper's east window. The old brass lectern is a Commonwealth survivor, the head used for collecting money through its beak and the tail for disgorging it.

HAMPTON LUCY
St Peter **
Picturesque neo-Gothic setting

The spectacle begins to the east, from the road past Charlecote Park. The church rises like a cathedral across the water meadows, set about with trees in a perfect fusion of architecture and landscape. The tower is Perpendicular with elongated pinnacles, the chancel a polygonal apse with crocketed gables that rise above its roofline: La Sainte-Chapelle transported from Paris to a Warwickshire village.

The church was commissioned by the Lucys of Charlecote and built in 1822 by one of their number, the rector Sir John Lucy. He presided over the church from 1815 to 1874, another wealthy Victorian divine to whom we owe the revival of church architecture. The nave was designed by Henry Hutchinson and the tower by Thomas Rickman, Gothicists of a different stamp from A. W. N. Pugin and the Ecclesiologists. It was Rickman who classified the styles of English Gothic as 'Early English', 'Decorated' and 'Perpendicular'. (I prefer Early Gothic to Early English – *see* Introduction.) He was an eclectic Gothicist, with a strong sense of the picturesque, who welcomed such modern materials as cast iron.

Hampton Lucy is the most successful of Rickman & Hutchinson's many churches. The first impression is austere. The beauty of the building lies in a graceful nave leading the eye towards the choir and apsidal sanctuary. The latter is the work of George Gilbert Scott, who completed the church in 1856. The nave has a wealth of Decorated-style carving rising from the ground to a plaster ribbed vault.

The chancel arch reveals canopied Gothic choir stalls and a handsome iron altar rail. The apse has a complex lierne vault. There is stained glass through-out, that in the clerestory rendering the interior eerily dark. The rose window in the west wall is almost invisible except in the brightest sunlight. The east window glass is by Thomas Willement and is regarded by his admirers as among his masterpieces. I prefer a colourful yet ungarish window in the north aisle, dedicated to John Lucy. The tracery in some of these windows is cast iron.

LAPWORTH
St Mary **
Pilgrim chapel over road, Eric Gill statue

Lapworth church can be seen from all points of the compass, yet is reached with difficulty owing to the line of the canal. The building stands on a small hill and has an unusual plan. Tacked on to its west end is a two-storey porch over what was once the road. The upper chamber was probably a chapel in which sacred relics were shown to pilgrims as they passed or took shelter underneath. The open archway at ground level was thus a passageway. This road may also explain the location of the tower, which is detached to the north instead of being built into the west front as normal.

This confusion yields an exterior full of interest. Apart from the Victorianised chancel, the nave and aisles are Perpendicular with battlements, pinnacles and much carving. Recent restoration has replaced only the most eroded stonework, leaving a spatchcock surface much beloved of modern conservers. It looks like a face covered in sticking plaster, and presumably always will. The clerestory appears brand new.

The interior is mostly Early Gothic, the arcades having bold chamfered arches on round piers. The westernmost arch on the north side has an endearing distortion, where the mason appears to have misjudged the width of his arch in bridging the gap, like a signwriter who has left too little space for the end of his message. Beneath is a 14th-century font with strange faces peering from beneath the bowl. The clerestory is in the richest Perpendicular, with a fine wooden roof on posts embossed with dragons and other beasts.

In the north chapel hangs a memorial by Eric Gill to Florence Bradshaw of 1928. The Virgin and Child are in a poignant pose, predating his more robust later style. The nave west window is filled with heraldic glass.

LOWER BRAILES
St George *
Font with Decorated tracery

Lower Brailes calls itself the 'cathedral of the Feldon', the name of this region of Warwickshire. The church is tall and long, built in the local red-brown stone that is almost as rich as Somerset's Ham stone. The tower appears to have the consistency of gingerbread. The building was extensively restored in 1649 during the Commonwealth, to repair damage suffered from the quartering of Royalist troops in the church during the Civil War. This work was repeated in 1879 and is being repeated again today. The stone does not enjoy longevity.

The rebuilding of Lower Brailes church straddled the plague years of the mid-14th century, although fragments of a 13th-century church survive in the south aisle and arcade. There are also monster heads on the fine corbel-table. The nave is six bays long with a magnificent clerestory of 12 windows, as long as Stratford's. The church's masterpiece is the east window, its Reticulated tracery indicating a date before the Black Death. This has five lights and four decks of quatrefoils, neatly framed by the gabled roofline. This window appears to be the inspiration for the panels of the font, each one treated with blind tracery.

The charm of the interior lies in its volume and atmosphere. A 15th-century tomb brought in from the churchyard lies just inside the door, the effigy variously identified as a vicar or a crusader.

LOWER SHUCKBURGH
St John *
Rogue 'Crimean' interior

This church is for addicts of Victorian eccentricity. From the outside, Lower Shuckburgh looks like an endearing chapel, all yellow stone and funny windows with an odd hexagonal Midlands steeple. It was built by the local lord of the manor, George Shuckburgh, in 1864 on his return from the Crimea. This is strange since there is another church extant near the hall, containing the Shuckburgh monuments. The architect of the new church was J. Croft, whose only other church was in Lincolnshire. He appears to have been instructed to make the interior faintly oriental, reminiscent of the Crimea.

The interior is curious. The arcades appear not to support the roof, which has small hammerbeams. Every arch is in bright red brick or imitation brick, with 'double dogtooth' serrated edges. The arches are Saracenic in shape, with cement dressings and white plaster walls. The windows are either lancet or Decorated, 'wildly improbable', says Pevsner, 'nor is it easy to find much in the Gothic 19th century to match the sheer ugliness of Croft's tracery'. The arcade piers are hollow, as is much of the brick.

On the other hand the vaults of the tower arch and the chancel have great panache, covered in tiny tiles of lozenge and other shapes, and unmistakably Moorish in style. The same is true of the benches, which have flaring poppy-heads. The result is colourful and jolly. It might be the chapel of a progressive public school, with the congregation teetering on the brink of anarchy.

MEREVALE
Our Lady **
Stained glass Tree of Jesse

The church huddles next to the gatehouse of the Dugdale mansion of Merevale, on a hill overlooking Atherstone. This is old industrial Warwickshire, with the coal mines of Baddesley to the north. It was the site of a Cistercian abbey, the present church being the chapel at its gate. Such churches were necessary for visitors and servants, since most Cistercian abbeys were strictly private. There is no tower. The Early Gothic nave is a short, windowless foyer of two bays whose aisles have been demolished and arcades filled in. The luxurious chancel is 16th century but its south aisle has 'teardrop' 14th-century windows. The guide suggests that the chancel was rebuilt *in situ* to receive the gifts, glass and memorials of donors to the abbey.

The chief reason for visiting Merevale is its excellent glass (to which there is an exemplary guide), especially the east window's Tree of Jesse. Though the window is Perpendicular, the glass dates from the 1330s, probably moved from the old abbey after the Dissolution. Of the five main lights the upper two-thirds are filled with figures linked by the fronds of the tree, wonderfully lively and as good as any surviving from the earlier Middle Ages. The bottom panels are Victorian re-creations that admirably fit the pattern. There is also good glass by Burlison & Grylls, including a window in the south chapel commemorating a Dugdale killed while helping rescuers during the Baddesley mine disaster of 1882. It depicts another holocaust, the Burning Fiery Furnace.

Against the west wall is a rood screen, originally across the chancel arch. The church is rightly proud of its working Snetzler organ of 1777, one of the few on which, the churchwarden assures me, 'Handel did not play'.

PRESTON ON STOUR
St Mary *
West family monuments

The Midlands is nowhere finer than in the lush, rolling acres of the Stour valley. Preston was remodelled in 1848 as an estate village by the lord of the manor, James Roberts-West. His predecessor, James West, was Secretary to the Treasury, a job that brought him enough money to acquire the manor in 1747. West restored the adjacent Alscot Park in a Gothic style and continued with the church, using the same builder as for the house, Edward Woodward of Chipping Campden. The original design (dated 1752) was luxuriant, with a spire and flying buttresses, battlements and pinnacles. In the event West was only able to rebuild the chancel and restore the rest. Howard Colvin, in his dictionary of architects, remarks that Preston is 'none the less remarkable as one of the earliest 18th-century Gothic churches, and the only one of its kind known to have been designed by a mason with a traditional background, not an architect'.

Outside, the church looks medieval. We climb the slope from the village green through an avenue of yews and with a view over the Stour valley on all sides. The interior is like an 18th-century family chapel. Woodward's nave retains the old timbered roof with original bosses but is lit by new side windows. The effect is light-hearted. At the west end is a Georgian gallery with the hatchments of the Alston-Roberts-West family. Beneath are panels of needlepoint illustrating village scenes, including a bright red phone box.

The chancel is unashamedly Georgian, with painted arches and ogees on stalls, wall panelling, windows and iron railings. The earliest memorials predate the Wests, a bold Jacobean group of Nicholas Kempe (d.1624) and his two wives overlooking the altar. The Wests double- and treble-barrelled their surname as the generations progressed. Eighteenth-century Wests died classical, assisted by angels and mourning women. Nineteenth-century Wests died Gothic. Twentieth-century ones were Modernist. Two bold instances of the last group adorn the nave, one a scroll within a lancet of 1988, the other a primitive crucifix of 1978.

SOLIHULL
St Alphege *
Crypt chapel, Kempe glass

As I left Solihull church a white Cadillac covered in roses rolled into view, carrying the next bride of a busy weekend of weddings. Solihull is plutocratic Midlands. The steeple of the church fills the vista down the old village street, pedestrianised at the core of the suburb. The red sandstone church hangs on to the edge of a hill, dominating the lower part of the town.

The interior was scraped by the Victorians with a ferocity that only the most careful modern lighting can alleviate. Bare roughcast limestone, never meant to be exposed, distracts the eye from the fine ashlar of the arcades. Solihull could surely afford a coat of plaster. The church is self-confident Early Gothic and Perpendicular, deeply carpeted, richly furnished and well chapelled. The nave has a fine collection of hatchments, including some of tapestry in frames.

To the north of the chancel lies St Alphege's chantry chapel. Beneath it a stairway leads down to a dark crypt with a low rib vault and its original simple stone altar. It contrasts with the lushness of the rest of the church and is a most subdued chamber. Solihull's outstanding treasure is the Kempe glass. The south aisle contains a Resurrection window of ten lights, the lower ones rich in landscape and human movement typical of Kempe's mature style. The west window is also by him, strongly architectural and a contrast to the Wailes work in the chancel.

STRATFORD-UPON-AVON
Holy Trinity ****
Perpendicular chancel, Clopton Chapel, Shakespeare's tomb

Were the name of Stratford not associated with a certain playwright, it would be noted for its church. Holy Trinity stands with St Mary, Warwick, as one of the glories of the county. It is peacefully away from the town's centre, upriver from the theatre and the main Shakespearean attractions. From the river walk, the chancel rises ghostly white on the bank, a pavilion of stone and glass with enriched window surrounds. From the churchyard, the impression is different, of a solid Early Gothic and Decorated tower and 18th-century spire, and transepts with Decorated windows. In the churchyard is a fine avenue of pollarded limes, as in many churchyards representing biblical tribes and apostles.

The church welcomes tourists seeking Shakespeare's tomb, and reasonably requests a small fee to enter the chancel to see it; there is no charge for the rest of the church. The aisle windows display a variety of Decorated tracery, maybe due to wayward masons or wayward patrons. The south aisle is the more ornate, being the chapel of Stratford's college of St Thomas. Its corbels include a monstrous bull. The college prospered in the 15th century and was responsible in 1480 for the rebuilding of the chancel and nave clerestory, hence the soaring nave superstructure of vertical panelling and twelve windows each side. The roof has bosses and the tie-beams rest on little castellated corbels. The view east is given added drama by a Victorian *coup de théâtre*, the organ case by Bodley above the crossing arch, carved with tracery and crockets, a tremendous Gothic flourish.

In the nave is the dark green and white marble pulpit donated by an Edwardian benefactor, Sir Theodore Martin, in honour of his wife, the actress Helen Faucit. She is said to be depicted in the carving of St Helena. Behind Tudor screens in the north aisle lies the Clopton Chapel. This was built for Hugh Clopton, who, like many medieval clothiers, grew rich, moved to the City of London, became Lord Mayor and was buried there, in 1496. His tomb chest therefore stands empty and the chapel houses a number of his less eminent descendants.

William Clopton (d.1592) and his wife lie against the north wall. He is armoured, in medieval fashion, and both hold small prayer books. Behind are their children, those who died at birth wrapped in swaddling clothes. The adjacent tomb of their son-in-law, George Carew, Earl of Totnes (d.1629), is a fine composition by Edward Marshall, chief mason to Charles II. Carew was Master in Ordnance for James I and the emblems of his office decorate the chest. The guide reports this as 'the finest Renaissance tomb in Europe', a bold claim.

Stratford's chancel 'weeps' to the north. It is as glorious within as without. North and south walls are filled with transomed Perpendicular windows, niches and memorials. The roof angels hold shields of Warwickshire families; the niche statues on the east wall are supported on giant insects. Under the choir stalls, misericords include the popular depiction of a wife beating her husband, pulling his beard and kicking his crotch, as well as a naked woman riding a stag.

Shakespeare's tomb is by the sanctuary rail, with its famous curse: 'Bleste be the man that spares these stones, and curst be he that moves my bones.' Above is the 'sunburnt' portrayal of him by Gerard Johnson, a memorial sculpted for his wife shortly after his death in 1616 and thus said to be the most plausible likeness. It has the half-length bust popular at the time for scholars. He gazes benignly out at his admirers, quill and paper in hand. Barely a line in the guide-book omits his name. We see the font in which he would have been baptised, the Bible he would have heard read and the register of his birth and his death.

WARWICK
St Mary *****
Beauchamp Chapel and tombs

Warwick church rises over the roofs of the old town, higher even than the castle. There is no finer testament to the status of the parish churches of medieval England than their use as mausoleums by the nation's most illustrious families. The family in this case was Beauchamp. The church was a pre-Conquest foundation and became part of the college of the Newburgh Earls of Warwick. It was the advent of Beauchamps to that earldom in the 14th century that marked St Mary's rise to glory. Thomas Beauchamp (d.1369) was an original Knight of the Garter. His son, also Thomas, died in 1401, and another son, Richard, in 1439. Their tombs in the Beauchamp Chapel embrace the flowering of English late Gothic. The tomb of Richard is one of the masterpieces of medieval art.

First, the west tower. This was rebuilt in the early 18th century along with the nave after the Great Fire of Warwick in 1694. It projects from the west front, rising sheer from the pavement above an open arch. The composition forms a magnificent climax to views from all over the town. Though sometimes attributed to Wren, it was the work of an architect named William Wilson, working with the 'Smith of Warwick' brothers. The design does not find universal favour. It is criticised for the identical scale of each of its stages, depriving it of vertical tension. Warwick's tower sits rather than soars.

The first impression of the interior is of a German hall church, with aisles the same height as the nave. All three spaces are vaulted. The piers are Gothic like huge palm trees, but the capitals are almost Corinthian, with acanthus leaves. At the west end is an intrusive tower arch, inserted but not needed when the tower was relocated further west over the street, to avoid further settlement. In the south aisle are bread shelves for 32 poor men and women.

Beyond the nave lies the Middle Ages. It starts to the north of the chancel in the Norman crypt, a large vaulted space containing one of only two ducking stools said to survive in England. The other is at Leominster (Herefs). Above is the chapter house with the tomb of Fulke Greville (d.1628). The Grevilles, barons Brooke, emerged from the wool plutocracy of Chipping Campden in the Middle Ages, to be granted Warwick Castle by James I and eventually the revived earldom of Warwick, which they retain (though without the castle) to this day.

The panelled chancel is early Perpendicular at its most graceful. The vault has unusual flying ribs, found in Bristol and other cathedrals but probably unique in a parish church. In the middle of the chancel is the tomb of the first earl, Thomas, holding the hand of his wife Catherine. Thomas fought at Crécy when just seventeen, and then at Poitiers, and was guardian of the Black Prince. Round the chest are 36 mourning relatives in a superb parade of 14th-century alabaster carving. To the north of the chancel is the vestry, with the sacristy above, its windows looking down on the chancel beneath. Warwick in its heyday was a treasury of relics, boasting fragments of the Manger, the True Cross, the Burning Bush and Thomas à Becket's hair shirt.

To the south we enter the curious Dean's Chapel, a casket of late-Perpendicular panelling and plaster fan vaults with pendants. It was inserted among the buttresses of the Beauchamp Chapel, which was originally a free-standing building. This latter chamber is normally approached from the south transept and is the only medieval chantry that stands comparison with Henry VII's chapel at Westminster. It is complete, spectacular and to some acerbic critics (such as Pevsner) even rather vulgar. To the modern eye it is also spoiled by the Gothic reredos of 1775, whose whitewashing remains a garish intrusion.

The centrepiece is the Beauchamp tomb with its gilded bronze effigy and strange semicircular cage protecting it. Richard Beauchamp was a towering figure of the late Middle Ages. He was confidant of Henry V, was present at his death at Vincennes and was appointed guardian of the infant Henry VI, whose disastrous reign spawned the Wars of the Roses. Richard was duly authorised by 'the king in council' to 'chastise us from time to time according to his good advice'. He later became governor of the king's domain in France, dying in Rouen in 1439.

Within ten years Richard's line had died out and his wealth passed by marriage to the Nevilles, the combined Beauchamp–Neville wealth making them the most powerful magnates in England. Warwicks were no longer king-servers, but often mischievous 'king-makers'. Old Beauchamp is thus a romantic figure, last of a generation of medieval noblemen who won renown for loyalty to their king and country abroad, rather than in civil war at home. His will stated that he be interred 'within the collegiate church of Our Lady in Warwick . . . a chapel of Our Lady well faire and goodly built, within the middle of which chapel I will that my tomb be made'.

The chapel was begun in 1442 but not completed until 1464, at the then phenomenal cost of £2,481. Contracts for the tomb are extant, including for Purbeck marble from Corfe. The effigy, an 'image of a man armed' but not thought to be a likeness, was executed by a London craftsman, John Essex of St Paul's, from a model by John Massingham. According to the historian, John Harvey, Massingham was 'a by no means unworthy contemporary of Donatello'. Essex was later to work on Henry VI's tomb. Beauchamp lies with his feet facing the altar, his hands parted half in prayer, half in wonder, to enable him on resurrection to see the Virgin on the vault boss. He is attended by his family emblems, the griffin and the bear. The face, hands and armour are superbly fashioned, yet the setting and pose remain stiff and medieval. The weepers cast in brass stand, Burgundian style, in carved Gothic niches round the chest. Each is identified by the adjacent heraldry, including the robed figure of 'Warwick the Kingmaker', a gallery of 15th-century sculpture.

Facing Beauchamp's tomb rises the great east window, also designed by Massingham. To relieve and adorn the expanse of Perpendicular tracery, he carved figures in the window frame. The glass, by the court glazier John Prudde, survives and is outstanding. Prudde 'jewelled' his glass, inserting precious stones into halos and garments, for instance in the halo of the Virgin Annunciate. Saints, angels, biblical characters are piled high to the roof, flanked by their parallels in coloured stone. Above flows the rich curvilinear vault.

Nor is this the end. Another century yields three Renaissance tombs of the Dudleys, Earls of Warwick in a new creation by Henry VIII. One of these, Ambrose Dudley (d.1590), lies on a simple alabaster chest next to Richard. Another Dudley, Robert, Earl of Leicester (d.1588), favourite of Elizabeth I, lies with his wife Lettice against the north wall. This Tudor tomb would rate pride of place were it not in such company. Heraldry climbs the wall with increasing pomp. The chapel's original choir stalls are meek in comparison. As we retreat from the chapel through the screen into the nave, England seems to fall silent, like the doors closing on *Henry V*.

WOOTTON WAWEN
St Peter ***
Saxon core, attic of ancient furnishings

Pronounced Wootton Warn, the church is a dash of wildness in urbane surroundings. It also reminds us that English architecture embraces a whole millennium. On first view, the building is as baffling outside as in. Buttresses jut out at odd angles. Saxon windows peek from hidden corners. The south-east corner appears to have a tithe barn attached to it, yet one with Decorated windows. On entering we are told that this is not one church but three churches, which adds to the confusion.

Each age has subtracted little but added something to Wootton Wawen. At the heart of the church a Saxon crossing survives, now a secret sanctuary with modern stained glass in its north wall by Margaret Traherne, who designed the Chapel of Unity window at Coventry Cathedral. The north wall of the nave is Norman. The chancel and south aisle are Early Gothic. But these are the less interesting parts of the church.

We now move through to the large south-east chapel – the apparent tithe barn. Here the church presents an atmospheric jumble of walls and windows, vistas and secluded corners, run-down but not dejected and filled with the impedimenta of Wootton citizens over the centuries.

The south-west chapel, reached through the vestry from the south aisle, is a museum in itself. Its complex history can be traced in the guidebook. Why the 14th-century builders decided to extend what would have been a side chapel eastwards and on such a scale, when so much else awaited rebuilding, is a mystery. Presumably a patron offered money for a specific purpose. The chapel east window is filled with flowing Decorated tracery, as are the two south windows beneath the steeply pitched roof.

The walls of the chapel have traces of wall paintings and a clutter of 17th- and 18th-century monuments. The most eccentric is to Francis Smith (d.1605), lying uncomfortable but surrounded by fine Jacobean strapwork. Here too is an old clock, two parish chests and some faded hatchments.

A Perpendicular screen divides the chapel from the chancel, with its unusual east window tracery. The latter I would term curvilinear Perpendicular (surrounded by 'double-leaf strip'). The east windows have fragments of medieval stained glass but are mostly clear. The trees outside wave in unison with the tracery. Medieval bench-ends have Gothic panels, as do the old tombs of the Harewells. These are of the 15th and 16th centuries, with alabaster effigies.

The rest of Wootton is like an attic in which anything of interest is helpfully labelled: an old book case, a lost carving, a fragment of a charter, faded photographs of Victorian vicars. It contrasts delightfully with the 'best kept churchyard' outside, and the road crashing past to Birmingham.

Wiltshire

This is a county of open, sweeping hills and cosy valleys. With its relics of Stonehenge and Avebury, the region is believed to have been one of the most populated in England in prehistoric times. Yet Wiltshire is strangely poor in church patronage. Its uplands were too barren for wool wealth and its forests too dense for passing trade. The finest building was within the penumbra of the great Early Gothic cathedral at Salisbury.

That said, Wiltshire has examples from all periods of medieval architecture. The Saxons left the curious survival of St Laurence, Bradford-on-Avon, and the Normans the chancel at Devizes and England's best 12th-century carving at Malmesbury. Thirteenth-century Salisbury extended its patronage to Bishops Cannings and Potterne and the 14th-century bishops of Winchester responded with the splendid church at Edington. Not to be outdone, the townspeople of Salisbury commissioned the great Doom mural in St Thomas's, shortly before the Reformation forced its concealment.

The county's monuments are few but rich, including the fine Renaissance tomb at Lacock and the Golden Cavalier of Lydiard Tregoze. The Georgian interior at Mildenhall, with its twin pulpits, was an early church to entrance the young John Betjeman, then at Marlborough. Even more eccentric is the shrine from Santa Maria Maggiore in Rome, which turns up as a pulpit in Wilton.

Alton Barnes *
Amesbury * *
Avebury *
Bishops Cannings * * *
Bishopstone * *
Bradford-on-Avon:
   Holy Trinity *
   St Laurence * *
Chippenham *
Cricklade * *

Devizes * * * *
Edington * * * *
Great Chalfield *
Great Durnford *
Lacock * * *
Lydiard Tregoze * * *
Malmesbury * * * *
Mere * * *
Mildenhall * * *
Old Dilton * *

Potterne * *
Purton *
Salisbury:
   St Thomas * * *
Steeple Ashton * * *
Tisbury *
Urchfont *
Wilton * *

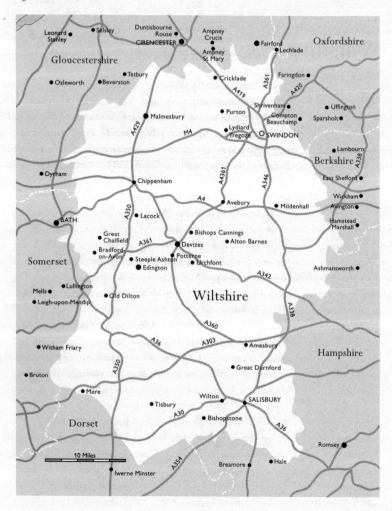

ALTON BARNES

St Mary *

Farmland setting, Saxon fragments

The appeal of Alton Barnes and its neighbour Alton Priors lies partly in their juxtaposition. They lie in muddy fields on either side of a small stream, with the old manor at a distance. Alton Barnes might be a Sussex Downland chapel. The exterior shows fragments of a Saxon foundation, including large upright stones embedded in the wall and long-and-short quoins at the west end.

The tall, narrow nave is Saxon in its proportion, while the chancel was rebuilt in 1748. Though much restored, the interior is cosy, with Georgian panelling and pews in the nave and with a triple-decker pulpit. An ancient harmonium backs on to them, facing the chancel with a tray for its candle. So small is the space that preaching in Alton Barnes must be more like a private conversation with the congregation.

At the west end of the church is a gallery with biblical texts on its panels. Above rises a strong, barnlike roof. In contrast, the chancel ceiling is vivid blue. A window in the south wall of the chancel has small quarries of glass engraved in 1992 and depicting local farmland scenes. This is an enchanting place.

AMESBURY
St Mary and St Melor **
Early Gothic tower, Decorated chancel

Amesbury is the town for Stonehenge and is rich in history and legend. It is said that Queen Guinevere came here to repent her marital sins and eventually to die. Here Henry II founded one of his many priories in penance for Becket's murder and sent into exile his queen, Eleanor, who remained until released by his successor, Richard Lionheart. The priory comprised over 100 monks and nuns in the 14th century. It was granted to the Seymour family after the Dissolution, when Jane Seymour became Henry VIII's queen. Though the convent buildings were demolished, the church passed to the town for parochial use.

The building is worthy of this history. It sits boldly in a glade beyond the main street, cruciform with an Early Gothic crossing tower and lofty lancets. The core is Norman, but this is encased in later extensions. The nave shows fragments of all periods, with two Decorated capitals on the south arcade piers and fine Perpendicular roofs in the nave and aisle. Off the north transept is a small Early Gothic chapel with a ribbed vault and a piscina.

The glory of Amesbury is the chancel, a screened chamber appropriate to an abbey. Two wonderful 14th-century windows have been inserted among the earlier lancets, one with Reticulated tracery, the other with a version of Intersecting. The east window is free of stained glass and thus offers trees and sky as a reredos. A facsimile of the Amesbury psalter is displayed in the nave while the north transept contains the remains of the old abbey clock, dating from the 15th century.

AVEBURY
St James *
Norman font, Perpendicular screen

Avebury is neolithic man come to town. Here old and new, sacred and profane are vividly juxtaposed. Although medieval iconoclasts smashed many of the standing stones and buried them, the survivors seem to wander round the village like dinosaurs released from a pen. The Saxons regarded the ring of stones as pagan and evil, and deliberately placed their church outside the rim. Today it happily balances the village, manor and stone circle. It has a 15th-century tower, Saxon nave and Norman aisles, with arcades and chancel rebuilt in the 19th century. Saxon openings survive in the west wall, and a Norman south doorway offers a lovely composition of foliated capitals and a zigzag arch beneath an empty saint's plinth.

The nave is short, of just two bays, its space further enclosed by a restored rood screen that bars more than a glimpse of the chancel. The screen is a superb work of modern restoration. The traceried loft survives from the 15th century, while the coving and lower parts are a 20th-century re-creation or are much restored. The saints portrayed along its dado are echoed in the Victorian reredos.

Avebury has a fine Norman tub font. The lower section is formed of conventional intersecting arches, but the upper section is more ambitious, with serpents trying to bite the cloak of a bishop. The heathen were never far from the fount of Christianity.

BISHOPS CANNINGS
St Mary ***
Early Gothic carvings, penitent's pew

The spire forms a splendid focus in the Vale of Pewsey. I saw it once from the Marlborough Downs, caught by a ray of sun in a storm. It shot upwards like the vision of a Wiltshire druid. The church is often compared with Salisbury Cathedral, whose bishops founded and built it before they began work on their cathedral. It is thus Early Gothic cruciform, but is otherwise unlike Salisbury. The most prominent external features apart from the spire are tall lancet windows lighting the transepts and the east and west ends. The (later) vaulted porch has a magnificent portal of *c*.1300, adorned with Decorated ballflower.

The nave interior is a superb example of Early Gothic architecture at the moment, towards the end of the 12th century, when it was emerging from its Norman origins. The arcade piers carry some trumpet and some stiff-leaf capitals and rise to gently pointed arches. The journey from nave to crossing is from pre-Gothic gloom to Early Gothic half-light, culminating in an elegant grove of piers and chamfered arches. Stiff-leaf clings to the capitals as if sprouting naturally from the stone. The north transept has become a vestry but the south has a charming chapel with Elizabethan furnishings, honouring the Ernle family. Near the crossing is a rarity, a carrel or penitential pew beneath a huge painted hand which warns the occupant of vanity, mortality and sin. The work appears to be 17th century. Worshippers allegedly volunteered to sit in it to ponder their evil ways.

The vaulted chancel is almost as long as the nave, but lower because of the weight of the stone vault. The crossing arches must therefore adjust to different heights east and west, forming a rich collection of joins for students of Gothic building. The east window glass is by Wailes in 1860, designed in Early Gothic style. Attached to the north side of the chancel is a two-storey sacristy or priest's house, complete with chimney. This was a substantial dwelling for its time.

BISHOPSTONE
St John **
Decorated windows

St John's was left behind when its village moved along the valley after the Black Death, and it is now mostly surrounded by fields. The neighbouring rectory is said to have been the home of Trollope's Archdeacon Grantly. The canopy to the priest's door certainly suggests obeisance to that fierce ecclesiastic. Otherwise all is tranquillity, here in the secluded Ebble valley.

The church is chiefly of interest for its window tracery, offering three versions of 13th- and 14th-century Decorated, a luxury reflecting the status of the patrons, the bishops of Winchester. The west window has three lights surmounted by elongated trefoils. The chancel and transepts have tracery encompassing a fleur-de-lis. Elsewhere the window ribs are bent into flowing curves. Trefoils are distorted. Arches are inverted into ogees. In the south transept is conventional Reticulated tracery beneath an ogee arch, a grander work probably for a private chantry. At this point on the exterior is an unusual shelter with vaulted roof.

The chancel is stone vaulted, with bosses and corbels of flowers, leaves and carved figures, some crouching as if under the weight of their arches. The sedilia are beautiful, each seat with its own mini-vault. Bishopstone's early Victorian rector, George Augustus Montgomery (d.1843), was a prominent benefactor of his church. He donated new stalls, pulpit, reredos and vestry door. The pulpit panels, as often in early 19th-century churches, are assembled from antiquarian fragments, including one of tooled leather representing the Garden of

Gethsemane. Montgomery's tomb in the south transept is by A. W. N. Pugin. Could these be the shades of Trollope's archdeacon?

BRADFORD-ON-AVON
Holy Trinity *
Tombs by Nost and Rysbrack

While St Laurence opposite bears modest witness to the earliest days of Christianity, Holy Trinity is a busy place of worship appropriate to this lovely market town. Though fragments of a Norman structure are evident in the chancel, it is mostly Perpendicular, a large town church whose spacious interior is filled with memorials to the burghers of Bradford-on-Avon.

The interior comes in four parts. The nave is magnificently roofed with wooden bosses and has fine Flemish glass in its south wall windows. The nave is divided from the north aisle by an arcade restored in the 19th century, including inscribed ribbons wrapped round one of the piers, an eccentric touch that I have not seen elsewhere. The east bay of the nave is now formed into a choir and is startlingly modern: off-white floor tiles give the area the feel of a corporate foyer. Such insertions rarely succeed, but here the proportions and colours are muted and the furnishings do not jar. It will mellow with time.

The chancel is a High Church sanctuary with six broad steps leading to the altar. Candles flicker on all sides. The walls are lined with medieval tombs under Decorated canopies. Another tomb, to Charles Steward (d.1698), is by John Nost, a swaggering statue in a round-headed archway with weeping putti and skulls. A more restrained Rysbrack opposite is to Anthony Methuen (d.1737) with no effigy. Three decades on, the deceased prefers to rest inconspicuous inside a sarcophagus.

BRADFORD-ON-AVON
St Laurence **
Rediscovered Saxon chapel

There are bigger and more beautiful Saxon churches in England than St Laurence, but few seem so thoroughly ancient, despite or because of its urban setting. The church was discovered in 1856 after previously being converted into a school, a house and then a warehouse. In among these buildings, the then vicar of Holy Trinity opposite, Canon Jones, noticed fragments of carved angels and researched their origins. George Gilbert Scott's medievalist clerk of works, James Irvine, was summoned for advice and pronounced the building 11th century. Pevsner and the church guide disagree over which parts are early or late Saxon, and who did what during the Victorian restoration. The general view is that the church was built by St Aldhelm at the turn of the 8th century and much rebuilt in the late 10th and early 11th centuries.

St Laurence is unique among Saxon churches in never having suffered subsequent alteration, chiefly because the Normans abandoned it in favour of the adjacent Holy Trinity. The church has a small nave, tiny chancel and one surviving transept or porticus. The exterior is decorated with attractive blind arcading and simple pilasters. The interior is tall, dark and impressive, dominated by a narrow Saxon arch with carved 'flying' angels surviving from the rood. It is also bare. It would benefit from some bold soul taking a deep breath and reinstating the candles, shrines, altars and screens with which it must once have been crammed.

CHIPPENHAM
St Andrew *
Town setting, 13th-century chest

The church is finely sited on a hill at the top of the high street. The tower dominates the guildhall and old quarter of the town, safe from the horrors of Chippenham's modern ring road. The tower, of golden limestone, rises in three stages to an open parapet, above which rises a short but graceful spire. This is mainly of 1633. The inside is even later, most of it the result of a Victorian rebuilding in 1875. Neither alteration has destroyed the church's status as repository of the history of a great cloth town, even as its modern inhabitants race past to the supermarket.

The charm of St Andrew's is in the details. The south transept baptistery once formed the chapel, probably on an upper floor, of the old Clothiers' Guild of St Katherine. It now contains a Christopher Whall memorial window to three local boys killed in the Great War. In the south chapel is a low-relief stone effigy of a woman, dating from the 13th century. At the rear of the same aisle is a 17th-century kneeling monument to Sir Gilbert Prynne with his wife and an array of children beneath, some holding skulls indicating death in infancy.

In the Victorian north aisle, with fearsome corbel heads, is a magnificent and rare piece of medieval woodwork. The 13th-century chest is decorated with scenes from a medieval bestiary, including unicorns, leopards, a stag and various domestic animals. No less splendid is the baroque organ case rising at the east end of the aisle. It is dated 1752 and was by Seede of Bristol.

CRICKLADE
St Sampson **
Tudor heraldry

The crossing tower of Cricklade dominates both the small crossroads town and its surrounding countryside. It was added to the old church after the Reformation by John Dudley, Duke of Northumberland and Lord Protector under Edward VI. It thus constitutes one of the last great extravagances of Perpendicular church architecture. It did Northumberland little good. He was beheaded by the Catholic Queen Mary for trying to secure the succession for his daughter-in-law, the Protestant Lady Jane Grey. But his tower remained, a rare example of mid-16th-century church-building.

The tower is massive rather than graceful. It has polygonal corner turrets capped by battlements and small spires. The upper stages are panelled, the effect being of strength and weight. The interior is mostly deferential to the central vault beneath this tower, a dazzling work. The lierne ribs have some 60 bosses, emblazoned with Dudley's arms and badges, including the bear and ragged staff of his secondary title, Earl of Warwick. Pevsner found it a 'bleak' version of a Spanish church under a Catholic monarch, which cannot have been Dudley's intention at all. It is a bravura Tudor performance, but could benefit from some further jollity.

The nave has both Norman and Early Gothic features. The west window is composed of tall lancets with two circles above them. The glass, by Kempe, depicts his usual saints. In the churchyard is a Gothic cross that once stood in the main street.

DEVIZES
St John ****
Norman chancel carving, 15th-century chantries

Devizes is my first choice as the quintessential English country town. It lies beneath the Wiltshire Downs, its name derived from 'ad divisas', or the division of two regions. The parish church stands over a small valley from the castle, both created in *c.*1130 by Roger, Bishop of Salisbury and Chancellor to Henry I. He might still recognise them. St John's lies down a medieval lane behind the town hall, framed by an old gate and lamp-bracket. The scene is closed by the heavy Norman crossing tower and north transept.

The east end should first be inspected from outside. Here Roger's original chancel east wall survives with its windows and buttresses. While most chancels were rebuilt and embellished in the Gothic period, Devizes was for some reason overlooked. By the 15th century, the laity were dominating church patronage and their interest was not in spending money on chancels. At Devizes the Beauchamp and Lamb families donated chantries for the sake of their own souls. These stand on either side of the chancel, which is left as a poor relation sandwiched in between. Of the two chantries, Beauchamp is the more ostentatious, with lofty pinnacles, carved battlements, panelled buttresses and an ornamental priest's door. Beauchamps were rarely outshone.

The interior of St John's is an essay in stylistic contrast, between Perpendicular nave and Norman chancel. The former is refined and English, the latter brash and French, two nations in not altogether happy juxtaposition, joined by a chancel arch above which hang two flags as if of two monarchs. (They are Wiltshire's regimental colours.) The 'English' nave is heavily restored, graceful but rather mass-produced. Its best feature is the set of corbel faces in the aisles. There is no clerestory, making the interior gloomy on a dark day.

The 'French' chancel wins the day, tunnel-like, a stage-set for a Norman drama of incense, hooded monks and drawn swords. Seen from the nave, it is a forest of shafts, rising to a low rib vault. This frames the extraordinary east end, a riotous tableau of blind arcading, intersecting arches and zigzag carving. The poppyheads on the choir stalls stand to attention in the foreground.

The two side chapels bring us back to the 15th century. Their ceilings are of a Moorish refinement and their windows are ablaze with glass. The north, Lamb, chantry is now a vestry, but the south, Beauchamp, chapel of the same 1480s date forms a florid contrast to the Norman work, with its panelled arches and 5-light traceried windows. A reminder of the Normans are the corbel heads surviving high on the north wall. These carvings, of Kilpeck (Herefs) grotesqueness, would previously have been outside the old church. They smirk down on the effete Tudor rosettes, angels and saints like devils peeping in on Heaven.

The glass in St John's is mostly awful, but the organ case in the north transept is a 17th-century masterpiece, in the style of Grinling Gibbons.

EDINGTON
St Mary, St Katharine and All Saints ****
Post-Reformation ceilings, memorial by Chantrey

Edington is a surprise, a rich and ostentatious church in otherwise retiring Wiltshire. It sits on a platform beneath the Salisbury Plain escarpment, survivor of a priory whose fishponds can be seen below in the valley. The priory was built for Augustinian canons by William Edington, a local man who became Bishop of Winchester. The date of the foundation was 1351–2, shortly after the Black Death. The bishop had been at Winchester for six years and was soon to start the cathedral's great Perpendicular nave, to be completed by his successor, William of Wykeham. Some reports suggest that Wykeham may have had a hand in Edington, or at least his master mason, William Wynford. Either way, Edington is a coherent work of late Gothic art, completed in ten years at a time of stylistic transition from Decorated to Perpendicular.

Bishop Edington was rich and was spending his own money on what amounted to a private foundation. He was able to build fast and to his own taste. Windows were now being expanded to support ever more elaborate religious and heraldic glass. Yet there appears to be a class distinction between the windows in the chancel, which are still Reticulated, and those in the nave, which are Perpendicular. Whether this reflected differing requirements for heraldic glass as between clergy and parishioners, or was merely a matter of slightly different dates, is not clear. Certainly the chancel has intricate pinnacles on its buttresses, the nave mere battlements.

Although the interior is almost all of the 1350s, its richness lies in ceilings inserted in the 17th and 18th centuries, and in its prolific, mostly modern, High Church furnishings. The nave roof has coloured quatrefoil panels, similar to those at Axbridge (Somerset). The tower crossing is no less surprising, a plaster fan vault in maroon and white. Both date from c.1663. By the time we reach the chancel – the view impeded by a heavy Tudor screen – the ceiling has changed again, to a delicate Gothic of 1790. These three roofs return to Edington some of the colour that the Reformation must have stripped away.

The chancel retains its canopied niches, two of them with headless evangelists. They have carved corbels, and the chancel walls seem crowded with heads. Angels, cherubs, sprites, soldiers, merchants, old men and women peer down from every corner. This is surely a portrait gallery of the 14th-century priory community, each figure a character in itself. The 1930s neo-Gothic reredos is by Randoll Blacking. In its right niche is a statue of George Herbert with a mandolin, recalling his time as incumbent at Bemerton near Salisbury.

The chancel contains two fine monuments. The first is a tomb for Lady Anne Beauchamp and her husband, Sir Edward Lewys (d.1630). It shows him clad in medieval armour, with recumbent praying effigies and kneeling children, an old-fashioned design for its date. Newer motifs are the stone curtains drawn back to reveal a cherub holding a coronet over the couple. The dogs' tongues have been painted red. The second is a memorial by Francis Chantrey to Simon Taylor (d.1815), depicting him at the moment of death attended by two women. The guide graciously assures us this 'must be allegorical because he was a bachelor'.

In the south transept lies a 15th-century ecclesiastic, his colours vividly restored. Upon the canopy and chest appear the motifs of a sprig of bay and a tun barrel, supposedly a rebus of his name, Beckington. Two medieval effigies inside the south door come from poor Imber church nearby, used for target practice on Salisbury Plain by the British army. The east window of the Lady

Chapel contains a rare 14th-century Crucifixion. Edington's font has a handsome Jacobean cover.

Behind the exquisite pulpit hangs the Taylor benefactions board, setting out the charitable entitlement of each of the deserving poor. Loaves 'of the best wheaten bread' were to be distributed after morning service to six men and six women over the age of fifty, not living in the same house and resident in the parish five years or more. There was also one pound for an annual sermon at Easter 'suited to the capacity of children', plus cakes for teachers and scholars. The Easter bread and cakes are still distributed. The church has an active music life. Worship and art have here walked hand in hand for centuries.

GREAT CHALFIELD
All Saints *
Manorial setting, Tropenell Chapel

Manor, farm and church stand amid the meadows of this lush countryside, gazing at each other in mutual admiration. Not a stone seems out of place. The one trace of the present day is a genteel notice indicating that this is National Trust property. The manor was embellished by the Tropenell family in 1452, and is a rare pre-Tudor house open to the public. The Tropenells extended the little church across what was their front courtyard, adding the bellcote to the west end. The setting of Great Chalfield is worth any detour.

The interior is that of a family chapel, despite having in miniature all the components of a parish church. There is a 14th-century nave with a 17th-century three-decker pulpit and a screen to the chancel. To the south is the Neale family chapel of 1775 (now the vestry), and the Tropenell Chapel of c.1480. Here the family sat in splendour, with a squint enabling them to see the altar. The chapel has a wagon roof and the remains of a mural of the Martyrdom of St Katharine. The stone screen carries five painted family shields. On either side of the chapel altar are two splendid armchairs. Who would ever have sat in them?

The church is apparently occupied by protected bats, though the only creature present during my visit was a pleasantly lazy bumble bee attending to a display of wild flowers on the altar. The pulpit is candle-lit and candles also fill the Georgian chandelier above the nave.

GREAT DURNFORD
St Andrew *
Riverside setting

Great Durnford sits on the banks of the Avon, lost to the world. Many of these riverside churches appear to have been Saxon shrines located on pagan sites. Durnford shows two Norman doorways, both with curious green and white chequerboard tympanums. The interior is spacious, with a large Norman chancel arch with zigzag moulding. Though heavily restored, the arch has beautiful capitals of a dove and an owl. There are also fragments of wall paintings.

Durnford's character lies in its furnishings. The communion rail alternates the normal twisted balusters with flat openwork ones, repeated above as finials. An old Jacobean family pew has been divided up and set along the east wall of the nave. The pulpit is poor. Like the wooden lectern, it is presumably the work of a local joiner. Most of the seating is Tudor, upright for the gentry in the main part of the nave, crude benches for servants and peasants at the back.

In the nave are two Gothic tomb recesses, one ogival. The chancel contains two monuments to members of the Younge family, one of 1607, the other of 1710, a study in comparative classicism. The font is Norman, with interlaced arches. This is a peaceful church that seems detached from the 20th century. It was a particular favourite of John Betjeman.

LACOCK
St Cyriac ***
Sharington tomb, Baynard brass

Lacock is the sort of village tourists like to put in their pocket and take home. It is guarded enough to survive the summer crowds, and even reincarnation as Meryton in the BBC TV's *Pride and Prejudice*. Medieval houses, some stone, some half-timbered, lead to an open space above which sits St Cyriac's church. The exterior is cosy and eventful. Chapels and transepts leap in odd directions, each guarded by a gargoyle. Set into the south transept is a Jacobean priest's house of three storeys. Tomb chests gambol across the churchyard.

Lacock's interior is mainly Perpendicular, a lofty chamber of tall, three-bay nave with a high crossing and transepts. It is like an ancient minster with some of its limbs chopped off and others stitched on in their place. North of the chancel is the magnificent Lady Chapel of *c*.1430 with a lierne vault and pendants. The arches and springers retain much of their floral and heraldic colouring and include a lady in a dress, a dog and a grim-faced man. The window tracery is a delightful heap of quatrefoils.

Against the north aisle wall stands the tomb of Sir William Sharington (d.1553). He was a Tudor magnate who acquired Lacock Abbey from the Augustinians at the Dissolution and made it into his home. His daughter married a Talbot and the house stayed in that family until 1958, when it passed to the National Trust. The tomb is dated 1566, yet is Early Renaissance in character, covered in relief carving of putti, dolphins and cartouches.

In the south transept is a brass to Robert Baynard (d.1501) and his wife Elizabeth. To those who find brasses a frigid form of memorial, this diminutive couple is a pleasant surprise. He is in armour and she in a flowing dress. At their feet are their thirteen sons and five daughters. Lacock's chancel is modern, redecorated at the start of the 20th century in Arts and Crafts Gothic, as a memorial to the photographer, William Fox Talbot, resident of adjacent Lacock Abbey. Nowhere does it mention the word photography, a craft of which he was virtual inventor. Nor could I see any trace of a photograph in the church.

LYDIARD TREGOZE
St Mary ***
St John mausoleum, Golden Cavalier statue

Forget Swindon and the fact that Lydiard Tregoze is just five minutes from the M4. Visit the great house of the St John family, now a local museum and conference centre. Ignore the crowds, walk to the house and ask the custodian for the key to the church. This lies at the back of the Palladian mansion, in what would previously have been a medieval complex of outbuildings, alleys and a village. From the exterior, the building is unremarkable and the entrance through the west door offers nothing more unusual than an aisled Gothic nave with a blush-pink wash on its walls. The seating is Jacobean, Georgian and Victorian and includes the family pew beneath the Jacobean pulpit.

The chancel is divided from the nave by a colourful Jacobean screen surmounted by the Stuart coat of arms, and from the south by a Tuscan colonnade. Peer beyond the screen into the south chancel chapel, and strange shapes start to emerge from the darkness. Here lies a treasure trove of Carolean art, the inspiration of one man, Sir John St John Bart, Stuart courtier and obsessional family genealogist. His mausoleum obeys no plan. Its tombs are casually littered in what amounts to a private chapel. Were it to be removed lock, stock and barrel to the Victoria and Albert Museum in London it would cause a sensation.

Sir John lived from 1586 to 1648, turbulent years for an English grandee. Although he was a strong Royalist in the Civil War, his five sons fought on both sides. The three who supported the king all died, the two who fought for Cromwell survived. As a result, there is an air of tragedy to these ostentatious spaces, as of a man aware of his mortality and eager that plaster and stone should defy it. The monuments were mostly erected in the 1630s at a time when

Sir John was also remodelling the chapel with painted ceiling and marbled columns.

In the south aisle is the oldest monument, to Sir John's grandparents and erected by his father in 1592. It reflects the purer classicism of the late Elizabethans, and is a beautifully calm work. Another memorial, in the south chapel above the door, is a 'conversation piece' to Sir John's sister, who married a notorious Stuart tax farmer, Sir Giles Mompesson. Nearby is a masterpiece of early 17th-century art, Sir John's own monument carved in 1634 and attributed to Samuel Baldwin. It is a vast eight-poster with a grandiose canopy and three exquisitely carved alabaster effigies. His effigy is flanked by his two wives and attended by eight of his thirteen children. His first wife, Anne, holds her last baby, after whose birth she died of exhaustion.

Against the north wall is Lydiard's prize, the Golden Cavalier monument to Sir John's son Edward (d.1645), one of the three who died in the Royalist cause. It has a standing effigy in a curtained canopy. The contrast with his father's monument could hardly be greater. The statue was originally painted black to simulate marble, but was subsequently gilded. The young man holds a fey pose, armoured but with boots and long hair. The pedestal contains a scene from the cavalry charge in which he died. The ensemble is theatrical and reverential, a shrine to a favoured son.

Next to it, on the chancel wall, is the St John triptych. The outer panels comprise a gigantic family tree. The central panel has a picture of Sir John's parents kneeling on a sarcophagus, with himself and his wife standing to the left, the stars of the show. The memorial was begun in 1615, when Sir John would have been just twenty-nine. Such family memorials are rare. (There is one in Burford church in Shropshire.) The tree was continued by later members of the family.

MALMESBURY
The Abbey ****
Romanesque figure sculpture, King Athelstan's tomb

Seen from the north across the Avon, Malmesbury sits like a ruined galleon. Holes gape in its superstructure, turrets are gaunt in the wind, flanks bear the scars of old battles. Yet from the town side the view is totally different. A close unfolds gracefully from the high street. Across the churchyard rises the large porch inside which is one of England's outstanding compositions of Anglo-Norman art.

The church lies in the remains of a Benedictine abbey whose spire was once as high as that of Salisbury. The abbey church was built c.1170, but its crossing tower collapsed in the early 16th century, destroying the chancel and crossing.

Then in the 17th century the Gothic west tower fell, taking with it the three west bays of the nave. This fall was catastrophic and what survives today is a truncated section of the Norman nave. Approaching from the south, we can clearly see the relics of the old west front and the fragments of the south transept.

But there is still the famous porch. The outer entrance has a Norman portal of eight arches, including three of sculptured reliefs set in roundels. These depict the Creation and scenes from the Old Testament and from the Life of Christ. Such stories were often portrayed in wall paintings or stained glass. Here they are executed in stone. The inner doorway is crowned with a tympanum showing Christ on a rainbow supported by angels in a flowing embrace. Even more remarkable is the carving along the interior walls of the porch, six on each side portraying the apostles at Pentecost, with an angel flying overhead. They are shown seated in exaggerated poses with sinuous draperies. St Peter has had his feet knocked off by iconoclasts, to prevent worshippers from kissing them. These are big, highly expressive works which Pevsner relates to Burgundian work of *c*.1130. They are great treasures in what is now the parish church of a small town.

The interior is a lovable hybrid. The surviving arcades are late Norman, with multi-scalloped capitals, cylindrical piers and slightly pointed arches. Above is a splendid Norman gallery. A few splashes of naturalistic foliage on the capitals of the wall shaft mark the point at which the later, Decorated Gothic builders took over, adapting the clerestory and constructing a lierne vault. The vault has magnificent bosses, some human but most foliage, recently repainted. Looking down from the south gallery is an abbot's oratory, like an opera box.

The abbey's proudest possession is the tomb of the Saxon King Athelstan (d.939), grandson of Alfred the Great. He is acknowledged as first king of all the Britons, achieved by defeating both the Scots and the Norsemen of York. The monument is Perpendicular, though the head and the lion are later replacements. A stone screen in the south aisle encloses the chapel of another famous scion of Malmesbury, the 8th-century St Aldhelm. He was a scholar and writer of Latin riddles who owned, so it was said, a finer library even than the Venerable Bede. He was beneficiary of the Roman Abbot Hadrian's visit to Britain in 668, which led to the revival of Roman studies at Canterbury, whence Aldhelm came to Malmesbury as abbot.

Above the porch is a museum of some of the abbey's treasures. These include illuminated manuscripts and prints of the abbey at various stages of its decay and restoration. In the south aisle is an unusual Burne-Jones window made after his death by Morris & Co. It portrays Faith, Courage and Devotion in glamorous armour against a background of green lozenges. Another window celebrates England's earliest aviator, an 11th-century monk named Elmer. He made himself wings, took off from one of the abbey towers and broke both his legs.

MERE

St Michael ***

Restored rood screen, medieval glass

Mere is a strange, lost place. It is an old coaching station comforted by surrounding hills but, because of a bypass, deserted by the hordes streaming to the south-west. The church tower still rises confidently behind the main street, its tall pinnacles visible from miles around. Beneath is laid out a church that splendidly marries the two great ages of English church architecture, the 15th and the 19th centuries. The porch has a ribbed stone vault with abstract carved bosses, spotlit at night. In a niche outside is a rare 12th-century statue of St Michael killing a dragon, St George having no monopoly on such heroism.

The interior is a museum of delights. Old galleries were cleared from the nave in 1855 but sober Commonwealth pews (of 1640) were left in place, raised on wooden platforms for warmth. In the 1880s, Mere was blessed by antiquarian restorers who revealed parts of the old church concealed at the Reformation. They restored the rood screen with a new loft, a cross, and figures of St Mary and St John. The screen is the best in Wiltshire. The chancel is an amalgam of Tudor, Victorian and 20th-century carving on the choir stalls, presenting a continuous display of craftsmanship. To the north is the Still Chapel of *c.*1325; to the south the finer Bettesthorne chantry, founded *c.*1350 by 'John of Mere', whose brass lies on the floor. A Purbeck marble tomb divides this chapel from the chancel, said to be of a 15th-century Berkeley, to whom the Bettesthornes were related by marriage.

Mere has excellent stained glass. In the Bettesthorne chantry are four 14th-century lights showing St Christopher, St Nicholas, St Martin and a pope. They have a delicacy of gesture and drapery typical of the late Middle Ages. The best Victorian windows are at the west end of the north and south aisles, both by Henry Holiday. He worked for Powell & Sons at the end of the 19th century and was much influenced by Burne-Jones. The churchyard includes a trim avenue of 'twelve apostles'. A house in the close was for chantry priests, a sign of Mere's medieval prosperity.

MILDENHALL
St John ***
Regency interior, double pulpit

The name is pronounced and often written as Minal. The church lies in the Kennet valley, just a mile from the outskirts of Marlborough, and has one of England's most eccentric Regency interiors. John Betjeman, an Old Marlburian, said that to visit Minal was to 'walk into a church of a Jane Austen novel'.

The exterior is modest. Traces of a Saxon window survive in the tower, which also holds a sundial said to be seven minutes ahead of Greenwich (as in Wiltshire it should be). The nave arcades are Norman, as is most of the chancel arch. But the architecture is of little interest. Minal's appeal dates from 1815 when the churchwardens and other villagers, enriched by the Napoleonic war boom, decided to repair their ruinous place of worship.

They financed a virtuoso display of woodwork, completely refurnishing both the nave and chancel. Their patronage is recorded under the gallery: 'This church deeply in decay has been rebuilded generously and piously at their own expense by . . .' and there follow such stout Wiltshire names as Oakley, White, Watts, Cox, Young, Wentworth, Halcomb, Hutchings and Woodman. This was no noble patronage, nor was it the work of a wealthy rector down from Cambridge, installing antiques gathered from the Continent. This was a church of and by local people.

The box pews are shoulder high, from which only heads are visible to the surrounding congregation. The pulpit and reading desk are identical twins, glaring down on the congregation on either side of the arch. Such twin fittings are rare (compare Leighton Bromswold, Hunts), and symbolised the equality of preaching and liturgy in the three centuries between the Reformation and the Tractarians. The testers have delicate neo-Jacobean tops forming a splendid frame to the arch.

The chancel reredos is a flame of woodwork rising up over the east window. The west end is even more spectacular. A sumptuous gallery with a concave centre echoes the circular baptistery below. The joinery throughout is immaculate. The prevailing motif is the leaf, one on each of the pew backs, turned left or right at its tip.

OLD DILTON
St Mary **
Unaltered 18th-century interior

The little church of Old Dilton, now redundant, abuts on to a byway in a settlement most of whose inhabitants moved long ago to Dilton Marsh. A railway races past, but the churchyard is peaceful, overgrown with wild flowers. Apart from a pleasant little bell-tower and spirelet with 'flute' openings, the Perpendicular exterior is unremarkable.

The interior might be that of a Georgian meeting house, more Dissenter than Anglican. The altar is a table against the east wall. The chancel is differentiated from the nave by a tympanum, adorned with the arms of George III. Stand beneath the three-decker pulpit and you will notice that each pew faces you. This was a church for preaching, not for liturgy. The pews were restored in the 1950s and fill the church with 18th-century oak, a few panels making use of medieval fragments. Some narrow and uncomfortable benches survive at the back for the poor.

The gallery on the north side of the old chancel has a fireplace, having once been the village schoolroom. The church contains a few memorials; one to William and Elizabeth Budd records the sad deaths of all their children, at the ages of 9, 18, 26 and 32. A charity board for a local clothier, John Wilkins, tells of his bequests for the poor.

[CCT]

POTTERNE
St Mary **
Complete Early Gothic interior

Potterne's crossing tower soars over a bend in the Devizes road. Below its embanked churchyard stands a row of medieval houses. It is a magnificent edifice for so small a village, softened on my last visit by a field of glorious snowdrops. The church is a rarity, an almost intact Early Gothic church with a complete set of lancet windows and steeply pitched roofs. Here the 12th-century bishops of Salisbury owned the manor and established a college of priests. When they departed the manor, there was no cause to rebuild what was already a sizeable church. Only the tower bell-openings and battlements are later, incongruously updating what is otherwise an immaculate work of 'lancet Gothic'.

The interior has the spaciousness of a cruciform collegiate foundation. Crossing arches sweep from roof to floor with barely a pause for a capital. Potterne is worth a visit for these alone. The east window is a triple lancet, flanked by two blind lancets, divided by Purbeck shafts. The roofs of the transepts are decorated with rosettes and stars, the products of chantry patronage. The west wall is decorated with two panels from an 18th-century screen, portraying Moses and Aaron.

Under the west window is a Saxon tub font with a Latin inscription round its rim. Taken from Psalm 42, it translates: 'As a deer longs for the running brooks, so longs my soul for you, O God.' In the north wall of the nave hangs an ancient door, much battered and patched but still with a Gothic trefoil top. It looks like a monk in his habit.

PURTON
St Mary *
Christ of the Trades mural

A lovely structure of honey-coloured stone and tiled roofs, the church sits in a village of thatched cottages next to a manor house. The churchyard is full of yews and ancient tomb chests. Most remarkable is the presence of both a crossing tower, with spire, and a west tower. This rarity is nowhere explained, but presumably results from the parishioners wanting their own bell-tower while the clerical authorities wanted to keep the crossing tower separate, as at Wymondham (Norfolk). Or perhaps the crossing tower could not sustain the weight of bells. Either way, the west front is busy with niches and an ornamented crown.

The spacious nave and crossing are flooded with light from the generous Perpendicular south aisle. The nave walls are dappled with medieval wall paintings. One of these is a rare depiction of Christ of the Trades, illustrating the body of Christ bleeding when workers fail to observe the Sabbath and showing the tools forbidden to be used on that day (*see* Breage, Cornwall). The west gallery survives, decorated with fragments of an old screen. The south chapel window has delightful flowing Decorated tracery and some medieval glass.

The chancel was restored by Butterfield in the 19th century, with two bold saints' niches in the east wall filled with modern statues. A stolen Flemish reredos has recently been recovered.

SALISBURY
St Thomas ***
Complete medieval Doom

While the dean and chapter were sitting secure in their close, the burghers of Salisbury busied themselves in the market place. This big town church was begun as a place of worship for masons working on the 13th-century cathedral. Rebuilt in the mid-15th century it bears the emblems of the townsmen who paid for it: Godmanstones, Hungerfords, Swaynes, Ludlows and Nichols. The tower is, or was before extension, detached on the south side of the church, presumably to prevent any collateral damage in the event of collapse. The church is not an obvious rival to the cathedral, like St Cuthbert in Wells (Somerset) or St Mary Redcliffe in Bristol (Gloucs). Yet a chance of history preserves above its chancel arch the most complete Doom mural in England.

St Thomas's nave and aisles are richly Perpendicular. Thin piers rise to foliated capitals. Windows, mostly clear glass, look over the market buildings outside. The roofs are sumptuous, especially that of the nave, with crested and painted beams and over 100 angels in various locations. The south chapel, built by William Swayne in *c.*1450, has a primitive mural of Nativity scenes on its north wall, and a fine classical reredos and wrought-iron screen. Its windows hold fragments of medieval glass, including the Virgin apparently tending a garden of lilies.

Now for the Doom, commissioned to fill the wall above the chancel arch some time after 1470. The figures are familiar, Christ in Judgement with the apostles, the blessed on the left, the damned on the right. A gruesome prince of darkness is to the right of the arch with an ale-wife beneath him. This being a town church, bishops (not merchants) are noticeable among those entering the vicious Jaws of Death. The two saints at the foot of the composition are St James, patron of pilgrims, and St Osmund. The guide points out that the demons lack the customary instruments of torture.

The work was painted over in 1593 (well after the Reformation), then discovered and restored in 1881. The repainting was sufficiently drastic for Pevsner to decry its quality. Yet we know from pre-restoration drawings that the composition is original, and the details are familiar from other 15th-century murals. Though the colour has faded, the completeness is remarkable, as is the presence of trees, buildings and landscape as a backdrop.

In the north aisle is the coat of arms of Elizabeth I, with lion and dragon supporters, which would have hung above the chancel arch when the Doom was whitewashed over. In the south Lady Chapel and behind the classical panelling are two alabaster memorials to members of the Eyre family (*c.*1628). Both are painted to resemble the oak below. When I was last in St Thomas's, a winter sun was sliding through the west windows. Suddenly a ray of light, fractured by stained glass, set fire to the Jaws of Hell, an effect surely intended by their creator.

STEEPLE ASHTON
St Mary ***
Roof pinnacles, lierne vault carvings

From the north, the church seems to float on the horizon like a fairy castle awaiting a tournament. The roof is a mass of turrets, pinnacles and battlements, in the most ostentatious Perpendicular style. The church was rebuilt after 1480, but the rebuilding did not extend to the Early Gothic chancel, which survived until the 19th century. It too was then rebuilt. Admirers have counted 70 pinnacles and twice that number of external carvings. Steeple Ashton lost its spire in a storm in 1670. It was never replaced, but the loss seems of little account.

The south porch is of two storeys with a lierne vault. Above its door is a sternly conservative quotation from Proverbs: 'Fear thou the LORD and the KING and meddle not with them that are given to CHANGE.' The Virgin looks down from the vault boss in apparent terror. The porch is mirrored by a similar one on the north side. Inside, Steeple Ashton has magnificent vaults. Clusters of Perpendicular shafts support a lierne vault above the chancel, chapel and aisles. The nave roof is of wood and plaster, the ribs starting of stone but soon turning to painted wood. The width of the piers suggests that a stone vault was intended here too, though few English parish churches could afford stone vaults throughout.

No such parsimony applied to the private chantry aisles. They were commissioned by two late 15th-century clothiers, the north by Robert Long, the south by Walter Leucas. They gave them superb lierne vaults. The ribs rise from Gothic niches, empty but filled with wild flowers on my visit. Equally splendid is the collection of carved heads with which the vaults are adorned. They are everywhere, heads grinning or gloomy, bearded or clean shaven, showing off jackets and hair styles or grimacing in mockery. Not a corbel or springer is without one. This gallery of Gothic art lacks a proper guide.

TISBURY
St John *
Crossing carvings, Arundell Chapel

This long, low, cruciform church crouches on the banks of the River Nadder with the old town spread up the hill above it. The Wiltshire Brewery has been restored next door and this, together with Tisbury's plentiful Nonconformist chapels, gives the town a mildly industrial aura. The top of the crossing tower is in tiers, like a recessed telescope, rebuilt in the Georgian period after its predecessor collapsed, a bad habit of Wiltshire towers.

Successive generations have played tricks on the interior. The crossing is Norman with Transitional arches. The trumpet capitals are incomplete, as if the masons had suddenly realised they were out of date and departed Tisbury in embarrassment to work elsewhere. The west wall of the tower descends low into the church, doubtless the result of heightening the nave by adding a clerestory in the 15th century, leaving the ghost of an old gable, window and bell-opening visible over the chancel arch. The nave has a good 15th-century wagon roof with embryonic hammerbeams carved with angels. Its south aisle contains a window celebrating those rarely noted servants of the parish church, the choirboys.

Beneath the chancel is a mausoleum to the Arundell family. On its floor is a memorial to Anne, an Arundell who married the 2nd Lord Baltimore and gave her name to Annapolis in the Maryland colony as he did to the colony's biggest city. The wife of a later Arundell, Blanche Somerset, was famous in Cavalier annals for her hopeless defence of Wardour Castle against the Parliamentarians in 1643.

URCHFONT
St Michael *
Chancel vault carvings

The first thing we notice is the beautiful Intersecting tracery in the south transept window, beaming its welcome over a churchyard crowded with classical tomb chests. The stone is weathered with lichen, the porch heavily buttressed, the chancel roof crowned with fleur-de-lis. Everything looks enjoyable and eccentric.

The exterior is a Perpendicular casing of an earlier inside. The chancel arch is Early Gothic with stiff-leaf capitals. The transepts are Decorated, both with superb windows of *c.*1320. Best of all is the stone-vaulted chancel. This has ribs worthy of a cathedral chapel. They cross back and forth, forming lozenge patterns with corbel heads and carved bosses at the junctions. Pevsner relates this work to the aisles at Bristol Cathedral. The central bosses represent St Michael and a dragon, Abraham and a ram, a pelican and a mermaid with dragons – a chamber of delights.

In the chancel is a memorial to Robert Tothill by Scheemakers of 1753, with busts and weeping putti in attendance. There is a terrible Victorian east window of Christ appearing to dance the twist.

WILTON
St Mary and St Nicholas **
Italian furnishings, French medieval glass

Even the most determined enthusiast for Victorian revivalism must find Wilton's exterior off-putting. It was created in 1841–5 by the Russian-born dowager Countess of Pembroke with her son, Sidney Herbert. They determined that Lombardic Romanesque, not French Gothic, was to be the preferred successor to Regency classicism. They chose as architects the partnership of Wyatt & Brandon. Despite the enormous cost, eventually exceeding £60,000, the result was not widely imitated. A. W. N. Pugin and the Oxford and Cambridge Goths triumphed.

Lady Pembroke set the church on a north–south axis, as in Russia. She also made it big, disregarding the intimacy and the soft limewashes that charm so many Italian churches. Wilton nave is high and its stone hard and yellow. The revivalism is aggressive, each derivation copied then inflated. However, the arcaded passage between tower and church and the various doorways are undeniably magnificent.

Equally lavish are the furnishings within. If the eye can avoid the gigantism of the arcades and the west gallery, it should concentrate on the font, the pulpit and, above all, the stained glass. The black columns supporting the arches of the chancel aisles set the tone of magnificence. They were acquired from a Roman temple of the 2nd century BC. The font was the gift of the Herberts' governess, who must have been a lady of means. Copied from a Baroque original, it is of black marble carved to represent vine leaves, a wonderfully flowing composition.

More black marble adorns the pulpit, its twisted columns coated in mosaic from the shrine of Santa Maria Maggiore in Rome. It dates from the 13th century. The shrine had been removed from Santa Maria, acquired by Horace Walpole for Strawberry Hill and bought by Herbert from Walpole's estate. His mother wanted to use it for the altar, but was prevented by an outraged bishop. The resulting pulpit glows in its corner of the nave, a relief from the ponderous pillars and capitals towering over it. But would Santa Maria not want to have it back?

The effigies of Sidney Herbert and his mother are in the chancel, designed by T. H. Wyatt and resting on Romanesque tomb chests. Many of the church's doors contain English and Flemish Renaissance panels. Altar rails, pavements, carpets and candelabra were donated by local organisations eager to make the church the most splendid of its day. The mosaics that fill the apse are by Gertrude Martin and the guide tells us that each of Christ's eyeballs required twenty pieces of stone.

Wilton has a superb collection of stained glass, medieval work from France, Germany and the Netherlands. The finest is in the apse, including rare 12th-century pieces acquired by those vultures of the French Revolution, the peripatetic antique dealers. These come from the abbey of St-Denis outside Paris, from Rouen and even from La Sainte-Chapelle in Paris. The fragments include the Flight into Egypt and the Prodigal Son. Similar relics from St-Denis can be found in Twycross (Leics).

Worcestershire

With each passing year, the dark stain of the west Midlands spreads further into Worcestershire. Yet the county remains predominantly rural, covering the middle reaches of the Severn valley and the Vale of Evesham, with the Malvern Hills to the west. Here were three Benedictine foundations at Evesham, Pershore and Great Malvern, all Saxon and rebuilt by the Normans. Evesham is no more, but the other two retain traces of their 12th-century magnificence. Pershore displays one of England's most graceful Early Gothic chancels, well restored and extended by George Gilbert Scott. Malvern, tucked into a fold of its hill, is pre-eminent for its Perpendicular exterior and magnificent medieval glass.

The county is blessed in the wealth of monuments to its noble families, to the Coventrys at Croome, the Reeds at Bredon, the Savages at Elmley and the Russells at Lower Strensham. These would be masterpieces in any county. Attached to the ruined mansion at Great Witley is the finest Baroque church interior in England, decorated by James Gibbs for the Foleys, early ironmasters.

At Dodford, the Bromsgrove Arts and Crafts Guild displayed their excellent wood carving, in line of vernacular descent from the medieval masters. Their work, in turn, can be seen tucked under the choir seats at Ripple, some of the best misericords in England.

Besford *
Bredon **
Broadway *
Chaddesley Corbett **
Croome D'Abitot ***
Dodford **

Elmley Castle **
Evesham **
Great Malvern ****
Great Witley ****
Holt **
Lower Strensham *

Pershore ****
Ripple *
Rock **
Wickhamford *

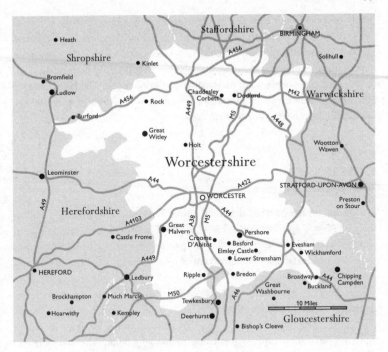

BESFORD
St Peter *
Timber-framed church, wooden window tracery

Besford is described in the guide as the only timber-framed church left in England. A number of others survive, including in neighbouring Shropshire and Cheshire, but Besford is a fine example of the style, its interior concealed within a Victorian casing. The timber frame is 14th century, indicated by the ogival arch to the north doorway and the rare Decorated tracery made of wood that can be found in the west window. So accustomed are we to stone tracery that to see it of any other material comes as a shock.

The Victorians reordered much of the interior and experts can enjoy working out which parts are new and which come from elsewhere in the medieval building. The decorative elements of the screen are mostly original, and the loft is still in place. Within living memory children were allowed to sit here during services. The tie-beams and posts of the nave roof appear original, while the panelling round the walls is from the old box pews. High on the chancel wall is an old helmet, together with gauntlets and a sword.

The tomb chest in the chancel is of young Richard Harwell (d.1576), whose family held land both here and in Oxfordshire. His alabaster effigy is formal but excellently carved, with large, puffed-up legwear. The chest has a classical egg-and-dart moulding oddly married to a Gothic tracery rim. An even more remarkable monument stands by the nave door, a triptych in poor repair commemorating three nephews of Harwell who all died young. The faded pictures are variants on a theme of mortality. The work is late 16th century and the inscription describes the death of children.

BREDON
St Giles **
Norman porch, Reed tomb

Bredon sits on the bank of the Avon above Tewkesbury with Bredon Hill to the east. This is splendid countryside. A manor house, rectory, tithe barn and thatched cottages pay court to a fine church, dominated by a spire which rises sheer and slender from a diminutive central tower. The spire is 14th century and a rare sight in these parts.

The church is Norman in its basics, evident in the turreted west front, the doorways on all three sides of the nave, and the most unusual vaulted Norman north porch. The tower arch is Norman Transitional, still with zigzag moulding and trumpet-scallop capitals but rising to a slight point. The style changes abruptly in the later nave arcades, Perpendicular to the north and Early Gothic to the south. The south aisle was built by the lords of Mitton manor, the Reeds, in the early 13th century and is of great beauty. Its south wall has four paired lancet windows, with Purbeck marble shafts.

These admit a gentle, even light, illuminating the church's treasure, the Reed monument against the west wall. Even the austere Pevsner allows this to be 'superb'. The tomb is of Sir Giles Reed (d.1611), his family holding the manor since the 14th century. His effigy and that of his wife are of the most intricate alabaster carving, portrayed in the richest of clothes. Above rises a canopy on columns, with symbols of death including putti extinguishing torches in skulls, and a crest flanked by obelisks. At their heads and feet their children kneel in prayer beneath their own miniature canopies. This is restrained yet luxurious, with little of the bombast typical of tombs of this period.

The chancel is a museum of medieval art. Easter Sepulchre, piscina and sedilia are in place, with Decorated cusping to the arches. The sanctuary steps are faced in medieval tiles carrying the arms of numerous great families of the day. To the right of the steps is an unusual 14th-century coffin lid with a relief carving of a man and woman peering out over the arms of a crucifix. The guide suggests they may be Reeds and the Cross of Thorns a reference to Glastonbury.

On the north wall of Bredon chancel is a memorial to Bishop Prideaux of

Worcester (d.1650), toppled by Cromwell for having been chaplain to Charles I. When asked later how he was coping with the resulting poverty he replied: 'I have too great a stomach for ... I have eaten a great library of excellent books, a great deal of linen, much of my brass, some of my pewter and now I am come to eat my iron.'

BROADWAY
St Eadburgha *
Medieval and Jacobean woodwork

This well-mannered church turns its back on the famous village, as if appalled at its capitulation to tourism. The building lies a mile to the south along the lane leading up to Snowshill. The old church, as it is known, is where medieval travellers crossing the Cotswolds from Moreton or Campden descended into the vale. A new track down the escarpment in the 15th century shifted the village to its present position, leaving the church marooned in what is now countryside.

The dedication is rare. St Eadburgha was Alfred the Great's granddaughter to whom sainthood came without too much hardship when, as a child, she was offered jewels or a Bible as a gift and she chose the latter. The church stands alone in its acre, separated from an adjacent house by a spectacular yew hedge. The exterior is mostly Perpendicular, and the crossing tower is perfectly balanced by nave, chancel and transepts. Collyweston tiles crown Costwold stone walls. The gravestones are thick with lichen.

The church is cruciform and the interior thus benefits from transverse light spreading through its central spaces. On a sunny day, warmth splashes on to stone piers and arches and brings to life the Norman arcades with scallop and trumpet capitals and Transitional arches. The crossing arches are Perpendicular, with chamfers that run sheer from floor to apex. Further light comes from square-headed Perpendicular windows in the aisles, unusually small but unsullied by Victorian glass.

St Eadburgha's woodwork is the product of various restorations. The pulpit and choir stalls have been pieced together from former 14th-century benches. The altar rail is Jacobean and the reredos is formed from a Flemish chest. It portrays eight saints with their emblems set beneath Gothic arches.

The church memorials commemorate Sheldons and Savages, leading Broadway families after the Reformation. The Savages hailed from Elmley Castle, where their memorial is one of the treasures of the county. On my last visit, Broadway church was filled with candles and lilies, apparently in preparation for an evening wedding.

CHADDESLEY CORBETT
St Cassian **
Decorated chancel, 'Herefordshire' font

We leave the sprawl of the Midlands and its chains of motorways and enter the Severn Vale. The first picture village west of the M5 is Chaddesley Corbett, with a church equal to its setting and presenting a fine Decorated east window to the street. An ogee-headed tomb recess on the outside of the south wall indicates patrons of substance. The interior seems at first sight to be gloomily dominated by Butterfield's scraped walls and high roof. The north aisle windows are impossibly dark, though the glass of the Perpendicular south aisle windows is lighter. This aisle's east window includes lovely 20th-century stained glass vignettes, depicting the wild flowers of the neighbourhood.

The atmosphere changes in the chancel, Decorated and the best of its size in Worcestershire. With the adjacent chapel, it commemorates the ownership of the Chaddesley manor by the Corbett family throughout the Middle Ages. The only medieval Corbett monument, now in the south aisle, has a knight with his legs crossed and about to draw the sword, like the effigy in Dorchester (Oxon). The chancel has a complete set of aumbry, saints' niches, piscina and sedilia, all in soft pink stone. Beneath the niches are Green Men. The aumbry has a trefoil arch under an ogee hood. The chancel chapel has earlier Y-tracery windows with clear glass and jolly 17th-century wall memorials.

Chaddesley's Norman font is by the Herefordshire School of carvers and is in superb condition and glowing with vigour. The rim and base are plaited like a loaf of bread. The plaiting motif continues in the tails of the dragons round the bowl. Why such a motif should adorn a font is customarily explained as the dragon symbolising the evil from which baptism will save the child.

CROOME D'ABITOT
St Mary ***
Coventry family tombs

A Gothic tower peers over the trees across a meadow from the main road. Approaching on foot we see a superb panorama unfolding: the grounds and north façade of Croome Court school, forming on my last visit an immaculate backdrop to a stately cricket match. Beyond, stretches apparently unsullied countryside to the Malvern Hills.

The church, which is now redundant, was built in 1763 for the 6th Earl of Coventry, who filled it with an outstanding collection of family monuments. The architect of the exterior is believed to have been Lancelot 'Capability' Brown, the landscape gardener who had already designed the big house. The style is a most accomplished Georgian Gothic. The interior is attributed to Robert Adam, with three magnificent roundels floating down the centre of the nave ceiling. The openings have ogee arches. The furnishings all appear to be original, including pulpit, pews, panelling and altar rails. The pulpit has feathery foliage on its tester.

The walls of both nave and chancel comprise a Coventry family mausoleum, from the 17th to the 19th centuries, of great interest to iconographers of the period. The earliest, to the 1st Lord Coventry (d.1639) is attributed to the workshop of Nicholas Stone. He is shown in the robes of the Keeper of the Great Seal, with the mace and bag of his office before him, flanked appropriately by figures of Justice. The decorated capitals and unorthodox canopy herald the Baroque of the later 17th century.

The 2nd Lord (d.1661) with his lady are commemorated by identical tombs on opposite sides of the chancel, both with twisted columns. She died in childbirth and is portrayed with a swathed baby in her arms and her other children kneeling at her feet. The tomb of the 4th Lord (d.1687), next to her on the north side, is by Gibbons and has exquisite detailing. He is flanked by figures of Hope and Faith and is appealing to the latter, presumably for salvation. [CCT]

DODFORD
Holy Trinity and St Mary * *
Bromsgrove Guild masterpiece

Do not be deterred by the grey stone and pebbledash exterior. Dodford lies in rolling country just west of Bromsgrove where, in 1848, Feargus O'Connor founded a settlement of Chartist political radicals, with a small mission church. The church's fortunes were transformed half a century later in 1902 when a young curate from the neighbouring town, Walter Whinfield, inherited a fortune from his father. He determined to give Dodford a proper church and parsonage.

He was lucky to be so near to Bromsgrove. Its local branch of Morris's Arts and Crafts Guild was nationally celebrated and flourishing under Walter Gilbert. It appears to have been Gilbert who recommended to Whinfield an unknown architect working in Reginald Blomfield's London office, Arthur Bartlett. The favour was returned by Bartlett, who used local Guild workers for his decoration. Gilbert had attracted round him a group from all over Europe, and this church is a museum of their work, comparable with Lethaby's Brockhampton (Herefs). Building began in 1906 and was completed two years later.

The church is set round a dog-leg colonnade and cloister, overlooked by a wayward rose window and outdoor pulpit. Whinfield used this pulpit at least for the first summer. The interior is severe, reminiscent of an Ivy League college chapel in America, its cream-washed walls marred by batteries of wall heaters. Interest lies in the craftsmanship, especially the wood carving.

This covers every feature of the building, including gutters and rainwater heads, roof ribs, bench-ends, organ case, altar rails, reredos and pulpit. The subjects are those familiar from medieval churches: saints, Bible scenes, motifs drawn from nature and from the domestic life of the countryside.

Most noticeable are the panels of the ceiling ribs, representing the fruits of Dodford. The front bench-end recalls John Bungay, first child born in the Chartist village in 1849. An Italian carver, Celestino Pancheri, is given credit for the pulpit, the altar rails, and the magnificent organ case and gallery. He came to Bromsgrove through an advertisement placed by the Guild in a Paris newspaper. The altar rails, also by Pancheri, include a handsome carving of a lion eating honey.

There is little stained glass at Dodford, though the pieces in the transept rose window are vivid and appealing. The guide points out that, since the theme of Dodford is the wonder of nature, the windows should 'let the sunlight in, to connect the church to the countryside beyond'. This should be a motto for every restorer of church windows.

ELMLEY CASTLE
St Mary **
Savage and Coventry monuments

The church lies in the shadow of an ancient Beauchamp castle, one of many owned by that mighty tribe. It is composed of an embattled nave sandwiched between an ancient chancel and a square tower. The porch has carvings of a rabbit and a pig set into its wall.

The interior is dreadfully scraped, but no matter. Elmley's treasures lie in the north transept, the alabaster memorial to Sir William Savage (d.1616) and his family. The faces are serene, the folds of the gilded costumes immaculate and the ensemble rich and simple. Each is individualised, the woman carrying her child in her arms, its little fist clutching a purse of gold. At their feet are supporting emblems, lions and a stag with an arrow through its neck. Sir William's four grandsons kneel, three in prayer, one in a gesture of fealty. There is no superstructure. The message lies in the alabaster alone.

Opposite is the Coventry memorial by William Stanton, father of the sculptor of the great Lytton memorials of St Mary, Knebworth (Herts). A lavish baroque canopy with Grecian attendants crowns a statue of the 1st Earl of Coventry (d.1699) reclining on one arm. His pomposity contrasts with the quiet repose of the effigies opposite. The tomb is obviously modelled on that of the 1st Baron at Croome, where we might have expected to find it. The monument is here for a curious reason. It was brought here by his second wife, who had remarried a Savage when her stepson, the 2nd Earl, had refused to allow the statue to be placed in the church at Croome. He objected to her describing herself in her inscription as of noble family. She was, he said, the daughter of 'one Richard Grimes, a mean person, by trade a turner'. He protested to the College of Heralds at such a solecism being allowed on his father's monument and duly kicked his father out of Croome. Its loss is Elmley's gain.

At the rear of the nave is the base of an Early Gothic font with fierce dragons cavorting round its foot, a superb work. A 17th-century sundial stands in the churchyard.

EVESHAM
All Saints **

Bell-tower, Lichfield chantry chapel

Evesham Abbey church has gone but the abbey precinct encompassed two churches, All Saints and St Lawrence, as well as a magnificent bell-tower. They form a fine composition overlooking the Avon. The old Benedictine abbey was founded by Egwin, Bishop of Worcester, in the early 8th century. When going to Rome to see the Pope, he had his feet manacled and the key thrown into the Avon, presumably as a penance to impede his journey. The key reappeared inside a fish that was served to him when in Rome. This must rank as one of history's most astonishing coincidences. The abbey he duly founded on his return survived until the Dissolution.

Most of the buildings we see today are the works of a later abbot, Abbot Lichfield. Most prominent of these is the bell-tower of 1513, lavishly panelled and magnificent on the edge of the park. It was always a detached structure. A work of solidity and grace, it contains a peal of 13 bells that ring out regularly over the Vale. A carillon performs every three hours during the day. All Saints next door is a busy, jolly church, mostly Perpendicular and recognisable by its tall needle spire. The entrance is directly opposite the half-timbered Abbot Reginald Gateway, from which visitors enter into a Tudor north-west porch. This is decorated with quatrefoils containing symbols of the marriage of Henry VII's first and short-lived heir, Prince Arthur, to the unfortunate Catherine of Aragon. Inside the porch is a large roof boss of the Sacred Wounds, encircled by a Crown of Thorns. Beneath the tower is a carving of the horned Moses, a wonderfully flowing work.

The church interior is lit by a pair of Cotswold windows (*see* Gloucs) above the chancel arch. Off the south aisle is the chantry of Abbot Lichfield. His tomb vanished during the Commonwealth, but vandals were unable to remove the chapel's charming fan vault and pendant. The Victorian glass that fills the windows of All Saints is unusually good, tracing the ecclesiastical history of Evesham, albeit at the price of preventing any view of the architecture outside.

Next to All Saints is the redundant church of St Lawrence [CCT]. The best feature of the heavily restored interior is another relic of Abbot Lichfield's era, a sumptuous south chapel with panelled roof, fan vault and pendant.

GREAT MALVERN

The Priory Church ****

Hillside setting, Norman nave arcades, medieval wall tiles and stained glass

The former Benedictine priory of Great Malvern, now the parish church, nestles cosily in a fold of the Malvern Hills. It is nearly invisible until we are upon it, when it erupts like a volcano from the side of the hill. The tower and exterior are of extraordinary richness. Even the turrets on the tower battlements have pierced finials. Night-time floodlights throw the tower panelling into relief and offer a superb display of Perpendicular grandeur, from the chancel to the theatrical north porch. And this is just the setting. Malvern contains some of the finest medieval glass in England, to rank with that at Ludlow (Salop) and Fairford (Gloucs).

The first impression of the nave interior comes as a shock after the exterior. The arcades are severely Norman, the cylindrical piers rising to unadorned capitals and arches. The walls above are of solid masonry, more Cistercian than Benedictine. Only in the Perpendicular clerestory are we granted some of the light of day. The nave roof is a George Gilbert Scott re-creation of a 15th-century original. The eye, however, is swiftly drawn eastwards. There are no screens in Malvern and the volume of the nave continues through the vaulted and panelled crossing into the chancel, to reach a climax in the great east window. This is a tunnel of architecture.

Once reached, the chancel is a complete contrast to the nave. It is in panelled Perpendicular, its walls little more than decorative frames for the windows and, like the tower, influenced by Gloucester Cathedral. Beneath are medieval choir stalls with superb misericords. These include an almost complete set of the Labours of the Months, forming a parade of medieval secular life.

Also in the chancel is the alabaster memorial to John Knotsford (d.1589), one of the beneficiaries of the dissolution of the priory. He respected the church, and his daughter was proud to have him commemorated here. Malvern's unique collection of medieval wall tiles, the largest in the country, adorns the rear of the screens round the sanctuary.

Now for the glass. I know of no church which so well displays the majesty as well as the intimacy of medieval glazing. From a distance, the effect is kaleido-scopic rather than narrative, a shimmering refraction of pure colour. Malvern's glass dates from the end of the 15th century, the colouring soft and complex and slightly earlier than that at Fairford. Some of the original background has gone and there is much Victorian repair and insertion, so that sometimes the theme of each window is clear, sometimes a jumble of restoration. But the inten-tion is intact, of presenting biblical and other scenes in a strong architectural framework.

Of the dominant east window, a third is thought to be original. Much is jumbled, but the Crucifixion and apostles are clear. The north transept window contains an exceptionally rare depiction of the Coronation of Mary (particular target of iconoclasts) in a wide halo of blue sky with stars. This gift to the priory by Henry VII was designed by the royal glaziers in 1501. The glass in the south chancel aisle is of Old Testament scenes and includes the much reproduced Expulsion and the Burning Bush. The west window is also medieval and is a copy of the east window at Exeter Cathedral.

Malvern's glass has been the subject of much study, to which the bookshop supplies an admirable guide.

GREAT WITLEY
St Michael ****
Gibbs interior, Georgian painted glass, Rysbrack monument

Every church has its moment. I caught Great Witley on a wild December evening with the sun setting over the wooded hills to the west. It might have been in Transylvania. The vast ruin of the old house next door was already fill-ing with nocturnal ghosts. The church, in the midst of Evensong, was a casket of light and sound. I saw coloured glass as it is rarely seen, lit from the inside at dusk to the accompaniment of a choir.

Witley Court was created by the Foleys, early ironmasters, in the 17th century. In the 1730s it was expanded for Thomas Foley and a new church was built next door. Determined to do it proud, he imported the fittings, pictures and windows bought at the famous 1747 auction of the Duke of Chandos's Canons estate in Edgware. The old village was moved a mile away to the pres-ent Great Witley. Foleys went and Dudleys came, and Victorian Witley became one of the most spectacular mansions in the Midlands. But all fortunes wane. Witley was sold in 1920 and in 1937 a fire rendered the house uninhabitable. Its contents were plundered by vandals and it is now in the care of English Heritage.

The church survived through the care of the once-spurned villagers, for this was never just the preserve of the big house but always the local parish church.

The architecture, by an unknown hand, is Baroque, with cupola, urns and balustrades bold against the skyline, and windows flanked by pilasters. This hardly prepares us for the Italianate extravaganza inside. Great Witley possesses the only full scheme of Baroque decoration of any church in England, certainly of any outside London.

The interior is the work of James Gibbs and reflects his training in Rome under Carlo Fontana, the leading Baroque architect of the day. Walls and ceiling are covered in lavish gilded relief decoration. Although it looks like stucco it is mostly of papier-mâché, a technique employed to reduce weight across so wide a ceiling. The craftsmen were Italians, who worked extensively in English country houses in the early 18th century. Set into the ceiling are paintings on canvas by Antonio Bellucci. The central panel shows the Resurrection in dramatic foreshortening. It is as if Christ were struggling to ascend from the roof of Great Witley itself.

The ten windows depicting Bible scenes came from Canons. They were possibly by another Italian, Francisco Slater, although executed in enamel and signed by a Yorkshireman, Joshua Price. They arrived by wagon in 38 sections and form a complete biblical narrative round the church, the best collection of 18th-century glass extant. The benches, font cover and pulpit are Victorian but were intended to complement the Baroque above, replacing more staid Georgian predecessors. The organ case is a Canons original and seems about to burst forward from the west wall. It was one of the instruments at which Handel is believed to have played his Chandos anthems.

We turn almost in relief to the gigantic Rysbrack memorial to the 1st Lord Foley, completed in 1735 and thus before the fitting out of the church. The cost was an astonishing £2,000. It is reputedly the tallest such monument in England and is a masterpiece of the genre. The conventional obelisk is crowded with tiers of figures, their poses and flowing costumes completing the Baroque effect.

HOLT
St Martin **
Norman doorways, pulpit by 'a lady'

Holt Castle was built to defend this part of the Marches against the Welsh, its country deliberately left uncultivated as a barrier of wildness. The land did not see a plough until the 16th century. Subsequent history has done little to tame it. The village moved north to the main road and the church was left in its field opposite an old Tudor gatehouse, attended by waving cedars. It is a lonely spot to encounter on a winter evening.

Most counties have at least one Norman survivor and Holt is Worcestershire's. The building material is pink sandstone, which brought out the best in the Norman carvers. Only the tower and Lady Chapel are later, the tower being Perpendicular with an oddly jutting upper stage and frilly latticework to its bell-openings. Both south and north doorways are Norman, the south with capitals including a Green Man and a monster biting its tail. Inside the survival continues. The north wall is massive and blank, apart from small round-arched windows high up. The chancel arch has zigzag decoration and the font is also Norman with monsters' heads.

The south aisle was built as the Talbot Chapel in the mid-14th century in the Decorated style. Curiously, the arcade which divides it from the nave and chancel is round-arched, as if the masons were keen to respect the character of the rest of the church. It is most unusual for any work of this date (c.1360) not to have pointed arches. The pulpit and lectern were the work of the wife of a Victorian rector and again respect the Norman tradition. *Building News* wrote of them patronisingly in 1858, 'We refuse to criticise them as they are the work of a lady and it is pleasing to find them [ladies] taking an interest in these matters.'

LOWER STRENSHAM
St John *
Russell monument by Stanton

The church stands in noble isolation from its village on a bluff overlooking the River Avon. Canal boats and a lock lie beneath its east wall. They may escape the visitor, since to the south is a fiendish intrusion of motorway interchanges (M5/M50) and service stations. Such throbbing, roaring, hissing surroundings have marooned the church. Its tower leans a full foot away from the nave and has had to be firmly propped. On my visit, the church, which is officially redundant, was being prepared for its first service in six years, gaily decked in Christmas decorations.

The building is architecturally dull, but is filled with superb woodwork. Nothing seems to be in its original place. The wide wagon roof has an old angel lashed to one of its tie-beams, as if on the point of flight. Linenfold panelling from the screen appears round the walls. The benches are early 16th century, the two-decker pulpit and high family pew are Georgian. The west gallery rises on carved posts and is adorned with 23 saints from the old rood screen loft. These saints are under canopies with what appear to be their original colours. Everywhere is dark, rich wood.

The chancel is filled with memorials to the Russells, manorial lords from the 14th to the 18th centuries. These include floor and wall brasses and an alabaster memorial to Sir Thomas Russell (d.1632) and his wife, with the usual strapwork and classical surround, but with the tomb chest open to show the coffin, in an adaptation of the medieval display of the cadaver.

Opposite is a fine work by Edward Stanton commemorating Sir Francis Russell (d.1705). Stanton was a master of theatrical Baroque, best known from the Lytton monuments at St Mary, Knebworth (Herts). His father William carved the Coventry tomb at Elmley Castle and both tombs employ a similar symbolism of salvation. Here his subject lies, as usual, semi-prone, his hand raised in a supplicant gesture. He looks back towards the wife he must leave. She points up towards his heavenly crown, carried aloft into the clouds by putti. The church is lit by candles.

[CCT]

PERSHORE
The Abbey ****
Early Gothic chancel vault, crossing tower lantern and monuments

Pershore is a pretty town on the banks of the Avon, its former abbey set back from the Georgian main street across a wide green. From the outside it might be just another Dissolution fragment, a ghost of past majesty left for the benefit of the townspeople. But here the Reformers at least left not a nave but a chancel, with a sumptuous crossing and tower.

Norman Pershore was of the same period and stylistic group as Gloucester and Tewkesbury, that is begun within a generation of the Conquest. The exterior shows scattered dogtooth, a Norman corbel-table on the south transept, blind arcading and a pair of vigorous 20th-century buttresses to keep it all upright. The tower is later, with Decorated bell-openings and pinnacles. So too is the chancel, with its lofty lancet windows and effete Victorian apse.

Pershore's interior is superlative, one of the most beautiful in the county. The inside of the tower was opened up in George Gilbert Scott's 1860s restoration so that the internal stone panelling could be seen. To Scott, Pershore's lantern was bettered only at Lincoln. He replaced the old ringing-chamber with a platform floating in space, reached by a spiral staircase. It looks surreal.

The south transept is substantially Norman, but its interest lies in the monuments. These include the tombs of a knight and an abbot and, against the west wall, a strangely elongated memorial to Thomas Haselwood. The charity boards are of unusual detail. One refuses charity to any 'who are given to excessive drinking, or are whoremongers, common swearers or pilferers or otherwise scandalous'. This must have excluded many candidates.

The chancel was rebuilt in the Early Gothic style after a fire destroyed the Norman chancel in 1223. Its principal beauty lies in its arcades and high clerestory, and in the richness of the lierne vault, erected half a century later at the dawn of the Decorated period. The triple shafts of the clerestory arches embrace a wall passage below the windows. The vault ribs rise from shafts beginning in the spandrels of the main arcades, themselves composed of luxuriant clusters of shafts. The effect is of a soaring forest of ribs.

The capitals are superb, displaying a variety of stiff-leaf, some of it wrought into knots, some 'windblown', all a delight to the eye. No less dazzling are the star-patterned vaults, the liernes creating scissor shapes and given 'ploughshare twists' for 3-D effect. The bosses include Green Men and a 'laughing boss'. They are hard to see against a scraped ceiling that yearns for limewash.

The east wall of the church was restored by Scott, who inserted an apse. His thin Victorian east lancet thus enjoys a dominant position, pointing upwards to a triple lancet above. The insertion is entirely successful, new architecture enhancing old. Perhaps a future generation will open the upper windows to complete the clerestory circuit. There is so much adjustment of this sort, which need not be controversial, awaiting restorers in English churches.

In the south aisle are windows by John Hardman, tracing Pershore's history, culminating in a depiction of Queen Victoria. This is the best sort of narrative glass, unashamedly medieval in style and set in a dominant blue.

RIPPLE

St Mary *

Misericords of the Labours of the Months

The approach to Ripple church presents a superb tableau. To the left stands the old rectory of 1726, five bays wide by six deep. To the right is the church itself, surrounded by an old wall with a scatter of gravestones. It is powerfully built, of thick Norman walls, lancet windows and a sweep of steep tiled roofs. The 18th-century tower is almost absurdly delicate in comparison.

The north porch contains an Early Gothic doorway with stiff-leaf carving on its main shafts. This carving rises and spreads over the adjacent shafts, an inventive gesture by an imaginative medieval mason. The interior is of limited architectural interest. The Early Gothic chancel has splayed windows oddly adorned with 18th-century memorials. One window has pretty fragments of 16th-century faces set into clear glass. The west window is a fine work by Kempe, flowing with figures and canopies.

Ripple's treasures are semi-buried, some of the most enjoyable carved misericords in England. The 16 seats date from the 15th century and appear to be locally produced, rather than imported from a dissolved monastery as was the case with many chancel fittings in parish churches. While not outstanding as art, they are detailed and uninhibited, craftsmen depicting their own community at work. The subjects are familiar, the four seasons and the twelve labours customarily associated with the months of the year. Most show two figures going about their business, cutting corn, ploughing and collecting wood. The moon has a man's face in it and the crops are blessed by a woman in a flowing dress. April is for bird scaring, July is for loaf measuring (Lammas), November for pig-killing and December for sitting by the fire. These evocations of medieval life are more engaging than anything in stone or brass – and here are admirably lit.

ROCK
St Peter and St Paul **
Norman Herefordshire School carvings

Rock is a small village buried in the Wyre Forest which divides the Severn from the Teme. Here Norman masons came up from Herefordshire to build a church for Roger of Tosny, grandson of Ralph of Normandy. The latter had fought with William I at Hastings and been rewarded with land in the Marches. He gave Rock to monks from back home, apparently to compensate them for having carelessly burnt their town in a raid. Whether they considered this a fair exchange we do not know.

Today the tower, nave and chancel step pleasingly down the slope of the churchyard. The north wall is articulated with flat buttresses. Between them is a curious grouping of paired Norman arches, one with a window, one blank. This appears to be no more than a decorative whimsy. Indeed Rock is a most sophisticated church of its period. The north entrance doorway has three orders of columns and arches with zigzag decoration under a deep gable. The door itself has excellent metalwork, while the main chancel arch inside is a superb work, with a centaur and the heads of humans and monsters decorating its capitals.

The carvings are familiar from those of the Herefordshire School to the south. They have caused much scholastic debate. Pevsner's sources claim that this is 'by far the finest example of Norman decorative sculpture in the county'. The expert in Norman carving, Professor Zarnecki, believes Rock 'to be the work of a Herefordshire mason, very close to Shobdon'. The guidebook asserts that the capital motifs are 'part allegorical in accordance with the taste of the Cluniac monks, and partly Celtic fantasy' while in Pevsner the doorway 'was done locally after the Herefordshire master had left'.

After this excitement, the south aisle is merely intriguing, with a Perpendicular arcade of concave octagonal piers and capitals, graceful in the nave and stumpy in the chancel. In the south chapel is an old altar slab with a consecration cross, set on a modern base like a large pillow. This was the Coningsby family chapel, a chantry before the Reformation and a chapel/mausoleum afterwards. The 16th-century tomb chest of an early Coningsby remains at the back of the chapel. The family died out two centuries later when a young Coningsby heir died, choking on a cherry stone.

WICKHAMFORD
St John *
Washington arms, Sandys monuments

This outwardly modest church is hidden at the far end of its village below the Evesham–Broadway road, with a fine Tudor manor for company. The structure is unremarkable, the stark late-Gothic tower not completed until 1686. The appeal of the church is due to the patronage of the Sandys family, which bought the estate in 1594. A Sandys was treasurer of the Virginia Company and may have taken local villagers to found a colony there. A colleague of Samuel Sandys, Royalist governor of Evesham during the Civil War, was Colonel Henry Washington. His widow married a Sandys and his daughter Penelope is commemorated in the chancel with the famous coat of arms of the stars and stripes. These arms were carried to America by other members of the family and are noted also at Great Brington (Northants) and Maldon (Essex). The coat of arms above the chancel arch displays the Sandys's Royalist sympathy. They are of James I, overpainted for Charles II and again for James II.

The nave is filled with high box pews decorated with linenfold panelling, more ornate towards the pulpit. The panels nearest the east of the nave and those of the three-decker pulpit are thought to be Flemish. The gallery and much of the church were restored in the 1940s by George Lees-Milne, father of the literary James. A memorial to the former is in the nave, beautifully lettered by Reynolds Stone. The gallery is faced with three Baroque carvings from a London church. Similar carvings crown the font.

The chancel is dominated by the extraordinary Sandys twin monuments. The two men, father and son, both died in 1626 and are portrayed lying head to toe, with their wives by their sides. The son is a little lower than the father while the children are relegated to the chests. The carving of the figures, clothes and faces is excellent, sadly unattributed. The crests with obelisks on top are comparatively restrained for the period. The two canopies combine in four arches on five columns. Everywhere is the Sandys griffin. To the right of the altar is a revealed fresco of the Virgin and Child, of great antiquity and probably 13th century.

Yorkshire, East Riding

The East Riding of Yorkshire was thought so unimportant that the 1970s boundary commissioners renamed it Humberside. Such was local fury that they restored the old name a decade later. South of the county is the city of Kingston upon Hull, set in a landscape lacking topographical charm. North rise the splendid Cleveland Hills, but most of them are in North Yorkshire.

East Riding's treasures divide between the steeples of the Humber estuary and the twin glories of the small town of Beverley. The former are tremendous works, including the 'navigation' towers of Hedon, Howden, Hull and Patrington. The architecture of the medieval Humber was a match for that of the Fens and is less appreciated only because of its comparative inaccessibility. Supreme among these churches is the 'Queen of Holderness', Patrington, a harmonious work of Decorated Gothic and one of the loveliest parish churches in England.

Beverley's Minster and St Mary's are two churches of the first rank, testifying to the wealth of this country town and tracing the story of English Gothic from earliest days to its Perpendicular climax. The Minster's Percy tomb is a masterpiece of medieval carving while St Mary's is said to have 600 medieval roof bosses. Nor were the Victorians ungenerous to the East Riding. George Gilbert Scott performed a spectacular act of restoration at Bridlington. J. L. Pearson created his most soaring spire for Lord Hotham at South Dalton, and a smaller church for Hotham's agent at Scorborough. G. E. Street adorned Garton-on-the-Wolds with the best Victorian Gothic murals in England, now a model of 20th-century restoration.

Beverley:
  The Minster *****
  St Mary ****
Boynton **
Bridlington ***
Burton Agnes *

Garton-on-the-Wolds
  ***
Hedon **
Howden ***
Hull ***
Lockington *

Patrington *****
Scorborough *
South Dalton ***
Welwick *
Winestead *

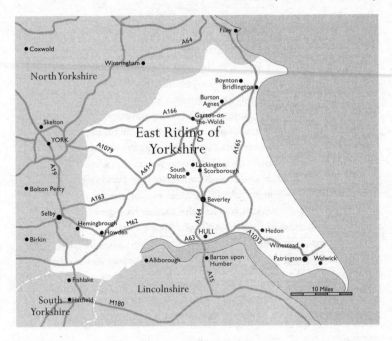

BEVERLEY
The Minster *****
Perpendicular west front, continuous vault, Percy tomb,
Hawksmoor font cover

There are many candidates for 'best' non-cathedral church in England, but Beverley most often takes the palm. Like Selby (Yorks, N), Tewkesbury (Gloucs) and Christchurch (Dorset), it ranks architecturally with the cathedrals and thus with the best Gothic churches in Europe. Although neglected for episcopal status at the Dissolution it was luckier than, say, Waltham Abbey (Essex) or Malmesbury Abbey (Wilts) in surviving mostly intact when transferred to parochial use. It lost only its chapter house. Beverley is thus a church no different in status from many other 'war wounded' of the Reformation. Its glory is a measure of the astonishing spectacle that ecclesiastical England must have presented at the start of the 16th century.

The town of Beverley boasts not one but two churches of the highest quality, the Minster and St Mary's. In the 14th century it was taxed as the eleventh richest town in England. Today it is a modest market town, but the Minster and St Mary's are well cared for, and the town deserves congratulation for sustaining what must be an immense burden on so small a population.

The best view of the Minster is from the south, over the famous and much threatened meadow. From here Beverley displays itself as a paragon of church architecture, a golden ship on a sea of green. To the east rise the twin transepts flanking the chancel, still French in character with Early Gothic lancets, turrets and blind arcading of the 1230s. The crossing tower collapsed in the 13th century and was not replaced. The eye moves westwards past another pair of transepts to the nave. Here ten bays of Decorated tracery windows are punctuated by flying buttresses and pinnacles. The tracery is superb, like a row of tulips rising from the window sills. After Early Gothic and Decorated we reach Perpendicular at the west front and the twin towers. To Clifton-Taylor, they surpass the west front of any English cathedral. Four buttresses are encrusted with panelling and statuary, helping the great windows to lift the whole composition skywards. The Victorians had the courage to recarve the statues and refill the niches, a task so often beyond our fastidious age.

The interior of Beverley is remarkable for its visual unity. The stylistic sequence is simple. The chancel, the two sets of transepts and the crossing are Early Gothic of the 13th century. The nave is Decorated of the 14th century, while the west end is 15th-century Perpendicular, flooding the nave with light. The vault is astounding, travelling the entire length of the nave and chancel with barely a nod to the crossing as it passes. A visitor walking from east to west thus moves from early collegiate gloom to later civic light.

The chancel with its transepts, aisles and retro-choir is an exotic world of arcades, Purbeck marble and voluptuous stiff-leaf carving. In the north aisle wall is a double-flight staircase leading to the former chapter house. Opposite stands the jewel of Beverley, the Percy tomb. It is thought to commemorate Lady Eleanor Percy and is dated (by the heraldry) to c.1340, the climax of the Decorated period. The canopy over the tomb is embellished with an astonishing decorative display. The gable encloses a giant nodding ogee, which rises above a large cusped cinquefoil. Foliage and angels rise and fall from every surface. At the apex, an enthroned Christ receives the soul of the departed emerging from a shroud, crowned by a huge confection of leaves and fruit. The wonders of nature pay homage to God in one of the supreme artefacts of Gothic art.

The adjacent choir is no less flamboyant. The screen continues the Decorated style of the Percy tomb, as do the wooden sedilia opposite. They are wood carving of the highest quality. The 16th-century choir stalls are a later insertion, with no fewer than 68 misericords. The 18th-century flooring of the choir is *trompe l'oeil*, to give an illusion of raised stepping stones. The medieval glass was blown out in a great storm in 1608, but was collected and installed in the east window in 1725. Although much restored, it glows with medieval intensity. The exquisite retro-choir once sheltered the Shrine of St John of Beverley.

Beverley has two pairs of transepts. The east ones are dark with Victorian glass. The west ones are aisled and more open, the sun bursting through their clerestories. The nave is altogether lighter. The Early Gothic design of the chancel was continued into the new nave by the Decorated masons, but Purbeck marble was abandoned and the windows updated. The later erection of the Perpendicular west end with its great window must have drastically altered the chief source of light and thus the balance of the composition. When built, the nave and chancel at Beverley would have been dark, with lancets at each end and the light slanting laterally from side windows.

The treasures of the nave include the sturdy Norman font topped by a later cover of scrolls and cherub heads, carved in 1726 by the Thornton family of York, who also were responsible for the fine reliefs on the west door. Both the font cover and the doors were probably to designs by Hawksmoor. Their dark oak marries well to gold limestone. The west window glass is a virtuoso piece by Hardman & Co.

The Minster, like St Mary's, was a centre of medieval musical life. The nave is alive with carvings of musicians, said to be 70 in all. They drip from capitals, cling to hood moulds, hide in corners and stare down from eaves, as if waiting to come to life and help fill this fine church with sound.

BEVERLEY
St Mary ****
Perpendicular west front, minstrels' capital, kings of England ceiling

If Beverley had no Minster, St Mary's would still draw crowds to the town. The church sits at the north end of a maze of 'gates' or streets, now Georgian but once medieval. It was founded in the 12th century for the patrons of an already busy market and drew its prosperity from the merchant guilds. The pinnacled transepts and crossing tower and the panelled west front with its polygonal turrets might belong to another minster rather than a parish church. The south porch greets visitors with gilded vaulting and grotesque carvings, its door a sombre Norman survivor.

The interior is the best that late-medieval money could buy, the nave arcades having been rebuilt after the central tower collapsed into the nave in 1520. These new arcades are curiously low-slung, an effect balanced by their length and the scale of the clerestory. On a pier on the north side is the 'minstrels' capital', presumably donated by the relevant guild as its contribution to the post-collapse rebuilding. These five minstrels, with idiosyncratic costumes and hairstyles, might be England's first pop group. They represent a vocation that must have been as popular, and lucrative, as its successor today. Beverley was famous for its music in the Middle Ages, with 34 carvings in St Mary's on musical themes. Above the nave is the first of St Mary's many fine roofs, sky-blue with stars.

The transepts bring us to the pre-collapse parts of the church. Here are zigzag arches, Intersecting window tracery and ceilings lit by diagonal shafts of light from transept aisles. The choir stalls retain their misericords, 28 in all and easily visible. There is an admirable elephant and castle, and satirical references to doctors, priests and bishops as apes, foxes and monkeys. Above rises the splendid chancel ceiling, originally mid-15th century and depicting the kings of England, actual and putative. The sequence runs from the legendary 'founder' of Britain, the Trojan immigrant Brutus, to Henry VI. In 1939 a restorer decided to paint George VI over the top of Brutus's son, Lochrine. In fact, the whole ceiling is a Victorian reproduction of 1863, made by tracing the originals and copying the colours. Some of the old panels are in the church museum. The ceilings of St Mary's have a reputed 600 carved bosses.

In the north-east chancel aisle is St Michael's Chapel, with Reticulated east window tracery swirling round a giant tulip. Above is an outstanding tierceron ribbed vault. On the wall is a carving of a rabbit with a pilgrim's bag, said to be the original for Carroll's White Rabbit. Above the chapel and reached by a charming Gothic staircase is the old priests' room, now a museum of objects gathered from church and town. These include stocks, scold's bridles and a rare maiden's garland, carried over the coffin of a dead girl to indicate her virginity.

St Mary's contains good Victorian glass, and not too much of it. The east window is by Clayton & Bell and that at the west end is by Hardman & Co., to a design by A. W. N. Pugin.

BOYNTON
St Andrew **
Carr of York interior, Strickland tombs

The Elizabethan traveller, William Strickland, was the first European to bring a turkey back from the New World, a bird which duly appeared on the family crest. His church at Boynton is all turkey. The bird is everywhere. Even the lectern is a turkey. The big house and grounds are still in the hands of a Strickland descendant, and the church keeps guards over the approach to its gates.

Apart from its tower, the church was rebuilt after a serious fire in the mid-18th century. The architect of the new work was John Carr of York, who was working at the house at the time. While the exterior of the nave is a simple Georgian brick box, the interior is a delightful variation on a Gothic theme. Carr's inventiveness produced an unusual plan, with the sanctuary embraced by screens east and west and a mortuary chapel beyond. This pleasantly breaks the rhythm of the interior. Light floods through wide leaded windows.

The furnishings include olive-green box pews, not in their original position facing each other across the central aisle but rearranged facing east in 1910. The vicar had complained that 'the existing mode of seating keeps people from church. They cannot bear the strain of being stared at by persons sitting on the opposite side.' They also had to bear the Stricklands gazing down at them from the family pew in the west gallery. This gallery is carried on columns with charming fluted capitals, and reached by a curving staircase of the sort that Carr might have designed for the big house itself.

The mortuary chapel is dominated by two 17th-century Strickland memorials rescued from a previous church. The man's monument is garlanded with flowers, the woman's with symbols of war. There must, as the saying goes, be some mistake. In the nave is a Norman tub font decorated with intersecting arches.

BRIDLINGTON
The Priory ***
Nave arcades, incised Tournai slab

The Priory of Bridlington once outshone both Beverley Minster and Selby (Yorks, N) and ranked in the county of Yorkshire second only to York. Its last prior joined the Pilgrimage of Grace to protest against the Reformation and was promptly executed, his priory suffering savage destruction. Of the church only the nave remained to be passed to the parish. Yet even the nave is a mighty building. Today it stands aloof from the Victorian seaside resort, in what is known as the Old Town.

Seen from the south-east, the destroyed crossing is still visible, a congealed wound of fallen masonry. The church exterior, however, is dominated by its western aspect, in particular the top storeys of the west towers, added by George Gilbert Scott in the 1870s. The one is squared off above the bell-stage, the other rises to a pinnacled and battlemented crown, as if seeking to reassert the priory's former glory. The two towers enclose reputedly the biggest Perpendicular window in Yorkshire, oddly designed on two distinct planes. Beneath this window is a west doorway whose ogee gable rises up over the window, covered in elaborate crocketing. A similar richness is shown in the capitals of the north porch, with the heads of a king, queen and archbishop peering from deeply carved stiff-leaf.

The interior is a single space, that of the former Early Gothic nave with ten bays of arcading. The north arcades rise to a triforium and clerestory in the Decorated style, 'which has no peer in the country', says the guide with splendid hyperbole. On the south side, the aisle has no windows where the prior's lodging once adjoined it, and higher windows, where the cloister once lay. Above is an unusual triforium with tracery in two planes. The parclose screens are modern. So too is the pulpit panelling and tester, added in the 1960s and demonstrating the continued vigour of church wood-work. The east window is a Tree of Jesse, by Wailes in his best early-medieval style.

Beneath the west window are displayed carved bosses and capitals salvaged from the old priory, forming an excellent collection of 12th-century art. Most precious of all is the slab of black Tournai marble, incised with the outline of a Byzantine church and believed to commemorate the founder of the Priory, Walter de Gant. The church is similar in design to one depicted on the Bayeux Tapestry.

BURTON AGNES
St Martin *
Griffith tombs

The grouping of house, manor, vicarage and church on the side of the Wolds is a happy one. The genial church is approached through a dense tunnel of yew trees. The nave has the familiar asymmetry of Norman north arcade and Early Gothic south one, the Norman strong and powerful, the Gothic refined and sensitive. They glare at each other like man and wife across a dinner table.

This domestic scene is disrupted by a large pew inserted by the Boyntons of Burton Agnes in the north arcade in 1730, probably at the same time as box pews were erected in the nave. The chancel is Victorian, rebuilt by the vicar, Archdeacon Robert Wilberforce, in the 1840s in honour of his father, the social reformer. The latter's face is carved on a corbel on the north wall of the chancel.

The Boynton family died out in 1989. Their chapel contains fine tombs, including a bizarre wall monument honouring Sir Henry Griffith (d.1654). The canopy has curtains drawn back and tied, to reveal not effigies but cold, black coffins. The tomb chest has reliefs of gruesome skulls and bones. Nothing in English design is more bizarre than the changing taste in commemorating death. Griffith's ancestor, Sir Walter (d.1481), is commemorated in an alabaster tomb, attended by 14 saints and angels in excellent repair.

GARTON-ON-THE-WOLDS
St Michael ***
Restored Victorian murals

Garton is two churches in one. The first church stands proud of its village, with a bold west tower buttressed like a castle keep. The exterior is predominantly Norman. The doorways have round arches, the windows tiny slits and the roof rises steeply from a corbel-table. This church was extensively restored by Pearson in the 1850s, with that ubiquitous Yorkshireman Sir Tatton Sykes as patron. Pearson rebuilt the chancel in the Norman style on the basis of archaeo-logical remains, as he did the more spectacular Stow (Lincs).

The second church is inside and is astonishing. In 1872 Garton passed from Pearson's care to that of Street, a more radical Victorian restorer. He initiated a comprehensive scheme of decoration, entirely coating the interior in murals. They cover the nave and chancel, not excluding the splays of the windows and the roof beams. They were executed by the firm of Clayton & Bell, who were also responsible for the stained glass. Murals and glass form a single iconographic programme, with Old Testament scenes in the nave and New Testament in the chancel. The style is Early Gothic with a Byzantine flavour, though no pretence is made of copying medieval originals. These rugged figures, despite medieval costumes, are unmistakably Victorian. The colours are pastel shades of pinks, blues and browns. The spirit paint technique was the same as that used at Highnam (Gloucs).

Pearson returned to work at Garton in 1878 and evidently liked what he saw, engaging Clayton & Bell to paint murals in his later masterpiece, St Augustine, Kilburn (London). Pevsner commented that, 'Despite the money lavished on the church, the residents of Garton were stubbornly Methodist in the 19th century.' Garton was the first recipient of a grant from the Pevsner Memorial Trust, for the restoration of its murals. The visitor thus sees them in pristine condition. I can list a hundred churches that would benefit from like treatment.

HEDON
St Augustine **
Early Gothic transept, Decorated font

The town is in a sad place, across the marshes from the looming gas plants of the Humber estuary. It was founded by the Norman lords of Holderness and, like Barton upon Humber (Lincs), was prosperous until silt and Hull stole its trade in the 13th century. Incorporated as a borough in 1170, Hedon still enjoyed two MPs until the 1832 Reform Act. It has a church to match this historic status.

Hedon calls itself 'King of Holderness', to Patrington's 'Queen'. It must have been a shotgun marriage. Where the latter is a delicate beauty, Hedon is a heavyweight. It looms up behind the Georgian terraces in the village centre like a creature from a different age. The tower, though Perpendicular, is as gloriously rugged as the rest of the church and is similar in form to the tower of Hull. The church is cruciform with an Early Gothic chancel and transepts. Its showpiece is the north transept exterior, where three tiers of lancets rise above the ground floor entrance. The nave is early Decorated.

The interior of Hedon is gloomy, streaked by scraping and much abused by centuries of alteration. Hardly a surface round the central crossing is without scars of demolished aisles, chapels or roofs, intriguing for church archaeologists. The north transept is like an architectural quarry. Dogtooth, stiff-leaf and blind arcading leap from the darkness in unexpected places. In the nave an old pulpit and tester frown down on Victorian benches. Stained glass keeps out any relieving sun. But Hedon has a magnificence that renovation might ruin. In the south aisle is a Gothic gem, a Decorated font covered in ogees and blind tracery, original and perfect.

HOWDEN

Minster of St Peter and St Paul ***
Decorated west front, stone screen

Howden was once owned by the bishops of Durham and was the site of the biggest horse fair in England. It lent its name to the surrounding 'Howdenshire'. Soon Hull, Goole and Selby stole its thunder. After the Dissolution of the collegiate church in 1540, Howden's chancel and chapter house were unused, and gradually decayed. The chancel vault collapsed in 1696 and the chapter house vault shortly afterwards. These ruins survive to the tops of their walls, set in a charmingly decrepit garden.

The church's west end continued in use by the parish. The crossing tower is Howden's pride, Perpendicular with high bell-openings and a further stage suggesting that the patrons were out to rival Boston. The Decorated west front is no less splendid, with three windows divided by buttresses crowned with four delightful openwork turrets. The buttresses contain saints in niches. The interior lost its balance when it lost its chancel and the nave is scraped, high and dark. The transepts are jollier and a crossing pier carries a lovely statue of the Virgin with a dove, dating from the 14th century.

In the south transept is a chapel known as the Saltmarshe chantry. This contains a number of medieval effigies, including a knight in chainmail (c.1322), round which children play during nursery school. More church transepts should be put to this admirable purpose. Also in the chapel is an empty wooden coffin, which was used for the parish poor as a temporary container to carry them to the graveside. The corpse would be tipped directly into the grave in a shroud. Outside is a bier with 'white walls' to its wheels. They take death seriously in Howden.

The church possesses a great rarity, a pulpitum or stone screen which once divided the collegiate east from the parochial west (as at Milton Abbey, Dorset). It has four big niches, containing medieval statues salvaged from the ruins behind. It now serves as a grand reredos. In the centre is a wooden altar carved after a fire in 1929, by Robert Thompson of Kilburn in North Yorkshire. His signature, a tiny mouse, derives from his father warning him not to be 'poor as church mice' when he was young. He never forgot the mouse.

HULL
Holy Trinity ***
Perpendicular tower, de la Pole tomb

The hinterland of Hull is an unattractive sprawl, often shrouded in mist rolling up the Humber from the North Sea. Yet a miracle has preserved the Old Town round Holy Trinity church. If a further miracle could bury the mad highway of Castle Street, then Hull could once more relate to its waterfront. Even today Holy Trinity's tower rises proud of the surrounding tower blocks, set amid well-restored streets and with a proper sense of urban enclosure. The west front overlooks the square, lacking only the courage to open its west door and invite wanderers in the square to come inside.

The church is one of the biggest in England by floor area, and the tower is one of Yorkshire's finest. Four large openings fill each face, the ogee hoods to the top stage pushing through, and even above, the openwork parapet. The nave exterior might be a Gothic supertanker lying at anchor. The 14th-century transepts are supposedly the first post-Roman use of brick for a large building in England. From the east the church is mostly Decorated, the east window having lovely tulip tracery. From the west we see a virtuoso display of Perpendicular glazing.

The interior of Holy Trinity instils awe purely by virtue of its size, albeit diminished by the incoherent insertion of Victorian and modern glass. Were the glass to some consistent programme, as in the Middle Ages (or in some Victorian churches), this might be less distracting. Instead we have a gallery in which nobody has thought how best to hang the pictures. More convincing, indeed spectacular, are the painted ceiling panels and lierne ribs of the crossing roof.

The aisles are filled with the customary trappings of civic patronage. The medieval de la Poles grew to wealth on the Dutch trade, later becoming Earls of Suffolk and prominent in the Wars of the Roses. Their chantry was in the south transept, but family monuments litter East Anglia and even Oxfordshire (*see* Ewelme). The finest of their tombs is a flowing Decorated work in the south choir aisle, with alabaster effigies of *c.*1370. The interior was refurnished in the 19th century. The screen round the choir has no fewer than 29 bays with tracery and forms a warm enclosure at the church's heart.

LOCKINGTON
St Mary *
Chapel of rival manorial claimants

The church lies at the end of the village by a farm in the flat country north of Beverley. Its exterior is of stone patched with brick. Tower, nave, south chapel and chancel seem disjointed from each other, as if attached by accident rather than design. There is extensive Norman work and the chancel has a fine Reticulated east window.

The chief interest of this church lies in the south chapel, monument to an ancestral feud. Its present decoration is said to result from a dispute between two local families in the 1630s, the Estofts and the Moysers, both claiming the Lordship of the Manor. In the middle of the chapel is the altar tomb of Mary Moyser, who died in 1633. She lies unusually on her side with her four sons in attendance beneath and angels and Virtues aloft. The inscription indicates that she inspected and approved this monument before she died.

So much for the Moyser claim. The chapel was subsequently painted in a defiant spirit, wall panels entirely filling the chapel and setting out the pedigree of her rivals to the manor, the Estofts. There are no fewer than 173 coats of arms, a formidable feat of heraldry, emphatically staking the Estoft claim. This claim was eventually recognised by the High Court in 1641, but the case was resumed in the 18th century on the grounds of 'bad title'. The manor was eventually awarded to a Mr Jarret of Beverley.

PATRINGTON
St Patrick *****
Octagonal tower top, Decorated carvings throughout

Patrington church calls itself 'Queen of Holderness' and rightly so. It is queen too of what I regard as the finest era of English Gothic, the final flowering of the Decorated style in the early 14th century before the Black Death. If we knew the names of the creators of these churches, they would be as celebrated as the masters of the Flemish and Italian trecento. Here we know only that a 'Robert de Patrington' went on to become master mason at York Minster in 1369. Certainly, if a single creator was responsible for this church, he ranks among the masters of English art.

Patrington lies in one of England's appendices, the Holderness peninsula beyond Hull. Its splendour indicates that this must, at very least, have been prosperous farming and trading country in the Middle Ages. Today, anticipation of this paragon of beauty must be sustained across flat farmland past chemical works on the far side of Hull. The church is cruciform with a nave and aisled transepts, but is an aesthetic unity. It was begun at the end of the 13th century, its spire completed in the mid-14th. The stone is a pale, silvery limestone. The window tracery is Reticulated and other forms of curvilinear, the openings divided outside by boldly pinnacled buttresses which seem to act as braces to the whole composition. The bare tower has corner pinnacles on open bases. These support an arcaded octagon which embraces the base of the spire, a device of great delicacy. The proportion of the steeple in relation to the nave and transepts seems perfect.

Of non-monastic churches, only St Mary Redcliffe, Bristol (Gloucs), has an interior that is equal to Patrington. The space is not big, but perfectly proportioned. From the west end, arcades rise and fall in even waves towards the crossing. There the transept aisles turn an orderly avenue into a forest of waving trees. Clustered piers shatter the sun's rays into shards of light and spread a patina of shadows on the stone. An extra bay beyond the crossing and before the chancel arch gives the perspective added depth. This effect, surely deliberate, is a gesture worthy of the Baroque.

The capitals of these piers are no longer the freehand carving of the earlier, 13th-century Decorated. They are still foliate, but the leaves are now tight bunches, like posies. Richer carving is found at the crossing and transepts. The south crossing arch is an architectural adventure. A staircase to the tower emerges high above the south-east pier, crossing the transept arch on corbels and disappearing again above the south-west pier. These corbels are astonishing works, their masons apparently released from the restraint of the pier capitals. Grotesque faces peer down at us from the gloom: monks, animals, villagers, an entire community come to inspire the carvers. Today they would instead pose for a group photograph. Off the transept is a small apsidal Lady Chapel that is a jewel in itself. It has a stone vault and stone reredos, with a carved pendant marking the join to the transept.

Equal exuberance is shown in the carvings in the chancel. Patrington has a complete surviving set of Easter Sepulchre, piscina and sedilia. The Sepulchre is strongly architectural, high rather than wide. It retains its sleeping soldiers and an intact image of Christ with angels. Of the same 14th-century period are the rood screen and the 12-sided font with arcaded bowl.

Later alteration has been kind to the church. The reredos by J. Harold Gibbons, of 1936 in exquisite gilded Gothic, respects its setting. Victorian stained glass is spare, leaving the thin Holderness daylight to penetrate every corner of the interior. Monuments do not intrude. This is a church that I would love to have seen as built. Such is its purity, I find it hard to imagine it covered in murals and liturgical clutter.

SCORBOROUGH
St Leonard *
Early Pearson Gothic essay

This sister church to neighbouring South Dalton was built for James Hall, Lord Hotham's agent and tenant on the Scorborough estate. He used the same architect, Pearson, as at South Dalton but spent only a fifth of what Hotham spent on his church. Built in 1857–9, Scorborough is a simple rectangle with an accomplished steeple. The spire emerges from its tower accompanied by spirelets whose effect is elegant but deprives the composition of South Dalton's soaring quality.

Scorborough was Pearson's first major church, the architect having previously worked only on restoration. It is more decorative in manner than his mature, ascetic style. He loved the coloured shafts and doubled arches of Early Gothic, the opportunity to decorate every plane and every curve. The capitals are crowded with stiff-leaf. The shafted window openings, especially in the chancel, are complex and full of incident. The roof corbels are extraordinarily rich while the east window by Clayton & Bell is seemly.

Enthusiasts for Pearson's work prefer Scorborough to South Dalton, finding it a more scholarly and decorative Gothic. Yet even here, Pearson seemed unable to invest his churches with a lightness of touch, let alone with joy. For me he is the Archdeacon Grantly of Victorian architects. I find it a church for addicts, for comparing and contrasting. It stands to attention rather than dances.

SOUTH DALTON
St Mary ***
Pearson masterpiece, soaring spire

The spire rises above the trees from a distance, described in the guidebook as 'an arrow in the breast of the Wold'. Even from afar, this famous spike is serenely proportioned, one of the loveliest Victorian steeples in England, rivalled for slenderness only by A. W. N. Pugin's Cheadle (Staffs). So careful is the engineering that there is no need of buttressing, nor is the geometrical shift from square tower to octagonal spire concealed by any parapet. Four enriched spirelets suffice to change the tempo. This is the young Pearson at his most immaculate.

The church was commissioned by the 3rd Lord Hotham in 1858. The family had been prominent Hull Parliamentarians in the Civil War but retreated from both Hull and Beverley to concentrate on rural rather than commercial aggrandisement. Hotham, who succeeded to the title in 1814 and died in 1870, amassed 18,000 acres in the East Riding. Pearson was already handling Norman and Gothic restorations throughout the north-east, and was designing a church for Hotham's agent at neighbouring Scorborough (*see* above). He was the ideal choice and money appeared to be no object, the building costing £25,000.

The body of the church pays dutiful homage to its steeple. The nave and chancel are short but powerful supports. The south transept, chapel and porch are all set high on a plinth that increases the sense of verticality. Pearson's biographer, David Lloyd, points out that the roofs are of different slopes, contriving an irregular series of planes to create an 'effect of uplift from solid earth to heaven'.

The interior is austere, despite the chancel being liberally adorned with stiff-leaf. Bench-ends are decorated with flowers and sleeping dragons. The one prominent monument is to an earlier Hotham, Sir John (d.1689). It is attributed to C. G. Cibber and is evidently derived from the Cecil monument in Hatfield (Herts). Kneeling Cardinal Virtues support a slab on which lies the effigy, while below lies his skeleton. The east window is by Clayton & Bell.

WELWICK
St Mary *
Decorated wall tomb

We are in Holderness on the north shore of the Humber and beyond even Patrington on the way to Spurn Head. This rolling country has big, fogbound skies and seems closer to the Netherlands than to England. The church is on a mound at the entrance to the village, yet seems to shrink from recognition. A bare area in the north-east of the churchyard was allegedly the plague pit. Even today, no burials are conducted there.

Only the clerestory and chancel windows offer a measure of external dignity, the former with Y-tracery, the latter Reticulated. The east window is a beautiful work, with tracery like opening tulips. Its companion in the south wall is most odd, having grown a fourth light like an amoeba about to separate. The guide suggests it was built for a poor-sighted incumbent who was having trouble reading his service.

The inside is white and spacious. Four Decorated bays with clear window glass give it the atmosphere of a summer-house on a sunny day. There are old tiles on the floor and a deeply coved chancel screen. The pulpit still has its tester of 1618. The principal treasure of Welwick is the wall tomb set into the south aisle. Its origin is obscure, yet it is a work of the most elaborate Decorated carving: the recess arch has wavy cusping and a cornucopia of fruit and flowers. Above is a relief canopy of foliated arcading. The craftsmanship is on a par with

Patrington and may be by the same hand. The cause of this excitement was probably the tomb of William de la Mare, Provost of Beverley.

WINESTEAD
St Germain *
Hildyard monument

St Germain, Bishop of Auxerre, visited England in the mid-5th century, allegedly to help Christian Britons refute the heresies of Pelagius. I hope that the Holderness serfs appreciated his metaphysical aid. The church lies down a track from a side road, half-hidden in a grove of yews. Beyond are the remains of an ancient manor, abandoned and its moat drained after the owner's daughter drowned in it.

The church is short, with high roofs and no tower. The approach passes a north wall almost devoid of fenestration. The interior was reordered by Temple Moore in the 1890s, like a child throwing everything into the air and seeing where it landed. The old box pews became coloured wall panelling. Family pews became a screen. Neo-Jacobean bench-ends were inserted. The roof was renewed with heraldic shields. Only the pulpit and screen appear to have needed no replacement. The screen has fan-vaulted coving.

Temple Moore built the south mausoleum for the Hildyard family monuments. Chief of these is to Sir Christopher Hildyard (d.1602), who lies on his back in armour in medieval fashion with his hands in prayer. Other Hildyard memorials include a fine 18th-century cartouche. On the floor are tablets removed from the old family mausoleum. Among the tombstones in the churchyard is an incongruous apparition, an insipid angel guarding members of the Bailey family. It is of the 1880s by a sculptor named J. J. Castello from Lisbon.

Yorkshire, North

with York

North Yorkshire is good country for churches. The Dales and North York Moors may not have been rich and the monasteries of Fountains, Bolton, Byland and Rievaulx must have used resources that might elsewhere have gone to parish churches. But the monasteries left handsome relics for parochial conversion. The lowlands of the Vale of York were and still are a fertile farming district, and therefore fertile in churches.

Oldest of the monasteries was Lastingham, founded from Lindisfarne. That closed as early as the 12th century, but still remains in the form of its crypt and exotic capitals. More splendid are the Dissolution relics of Selby and Bolton Abbey, the former a complete church and one of the finest in the north of England. Both are new refugees to North Yorkshire from the old West Riding.

Less recognised gems are the fragments of an Early Gothic nave at Nun Monkton and the curious 19th-century reinstatement of Early Gothic at Skelton, outside York. The Perpendicular churches of the Vale are architecturally disappointing, best on display at Thirsk and Coxwold, but the county's surviving furnishings are magnificent. The Fitzalan alabaster monument at Bedale and the classical Fauconberg memorials at Coxwold are masterpieces. Here also are two of England's most extraordinary family pews, theatrical at Wensley, drawing-room at Croft-on-Tees. Whitby, wild on its cliff top, is a favourite of all lovers of Georgian furnishing.

North Yorkshire is strong in Victorian churches. The young G. F. Bodley brought Morris and Burne-Jones to Scarborough. William Burges produced not one but two spectacular works for the family of the Marquess of Ripon, at Studley Royal and Skelton near Ripon. At Croft-on-Tees we can fantasise that Lewis Carroll found the White Rabbit.

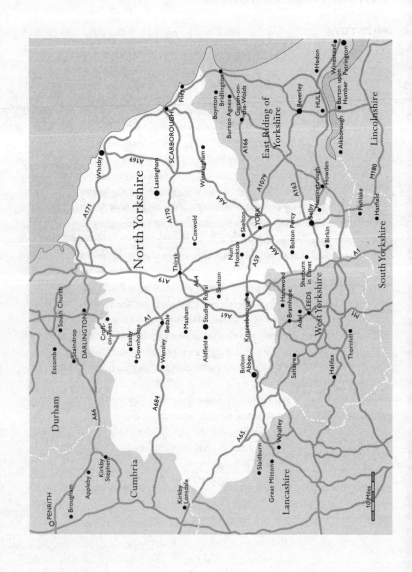

ALDFIELD
St Lawrence *
Rustic interior

Any visitor wishing to experience the full range of Anglican liturgy need only walk the mile from Burges's High Church extravaganza at Studley Royal to neighbouring Aldfield, on the outskirts of the Fountains estate. The foundation is medieval, and an earlier church had a tower. The building became derelict and was reconstructed in about 1782. It could be taken for a Methodist chapel. Apart from a small bellcote, the only ecclesiastical note on the exterior is a Decorated east window that survives from the old church.

The interior is a pure evocation of Protestant worship. Original box pews fill a small rectangular chamber, with a single transept facing the three-decker pulpit. This makes the pulpit seem even more central to the worship of the church, as in a Methodist chapel. The windows have Y-tracery, the plaster ceilings have Gothic ribs and biblical texts hang either side of a small altar. An organ fills the west wall. That is all. Outside, invading willowherb seems ready to carry the small churchyard off into the surrounding country.

BEDALE
St Gregory **
Fitzalan monuments

A strong church in every sense, St Gregory's rises at the end of the curving high street, alight in spring with a vivid blend of dark yew and bright forsythia. Its tower is a rare example of one fortified for defensive rather than decorative purposes, erected after Bannockburn in 1314 by the Fitzalans. It contains refuge rooms and even traces of a portcullis over the stairs. The battlements are embellished with eight pinnacles. I last saw it with the cross of St George flying from its mast, as if all Wensleydale were being summoned to a crusade.

The interior is dominated by windows, some Decorated, some Perpendicular, some Victorian Early Gothic. The chancel east window came from neighbouring Jervaulx Abbey at the Dissolution. The most exotic tracery is in the windows that fill the east ends of the aisles. That in the north aisle is of a form found elsewhere, says the guide, only in a church on the Rhine. The nave is as odd as the windows. The north arcade has a selection of late Norman capitals, its arches covered in nailhead and nutmeg motifs.

Bedale's chief interest lies in the Fitzalan monuments. That of Sir Brian (d.1306) with his wife, at the back of the nave, is one of the earliest known uses of alabaster for a tomb effigy. He is in chainmail with crossed legs. She, however, is of stone and has freely flowing garments, well demonstrating the agitated movement of early 14th-century sculpture. From the same period is the dramatic mural of St George and the Dragon on the north aisle wall. The church has a fine crypt and the headstones in the churchyard are magnificent.

BIRKIN
St Mary *
Norman interior with apse

The church is visible from a distance, sitting pretty but alone in the Aire valley. The landscape is dominated on every horizon by the cooling towers of England's biggest concentration of power stations, steaming sentinels of energy. The church is a Norman chapel with a rare apse and a corbel-table of monsters and demons, all well preserved. Apart from the top of the tower and the 14th-century south aisle, this is a complete Norman survival, the openings enriched with shafting, medallions and zigzag decoration.

The interior has been sorely scraped, but the Norman form is still evident. The tower arch answers to the chancel arch, and the apsidal chancel lies to the east as a distant and secretive chamber. In the chancel north wall is a knight lying cross-legged, with his heart in his hands. The east window of the south aisle has some brightly coloured medieval glass. Otherwise most of the windows are clear. Birkin has an 18th-century pulpit with tester.

BOLTON ABBEY
St Mary and St Cuthbert ****
Early Gothic doorway, botanical reredos

Bolton shares with Fountains Abbey a landscape as picturesque as any in England. Ruskin's verbose account is often quoted: 'Noble moorlands extend above, purple with heath and broken into scars and glens ... an instinctive apprehension of the strength and greatness of the wild northern land. It is to the association of this power and border sternness with the sweet peace and tender decay of Bolton Priory that the scene owes its distinctive charm.' The ensemble of house, village, park and priory is immaculately conserved.

The history of the Augustinian priory is important. The east end of the church, including its crossing, transepts and choir, decayed after the Dissolution and is now a ruin. A new west tower begun in 1520 by the last prior, Prior Moone, was left unfinished and the Early Gothic nave behind it was converted in 1539 into a parish church. Bolton, like Milton Abbey (Dorset), was a grandiose monastic project cut short by the Reformation, with the local parish given whatever the masons had completed so far. What we see today is an archaeological curiosity, half ruin, half unfinished tower, set amid lawns, trees and the slopes of distant hills. The west tower was intended to be spectacular, judging by the two huge buttresses and a west window that is crowned with an ogee arch that now rises impressively into space.

This tower base has been given a modern roof and bell-turret, and forms an entrance porch which also protects the old 13th-century west front. 'A historical calamity', says the guide, 'has been transformed into a glorious antechamber to the House of God.' The doorway is a masterpiece of Early Gothic design, its clustered shafts and chamfered arches rising to a beautifully balanced point. The doorway is surrounded by blind arcading which covers every part of the elevation. Even the door hinges are lovely works of what I call Gothic rococo.

The interior, despite the loss of the east end, is most satisfying. To the south runs a sequence of six Early Gothic twinned lancets, embellished with dogtooth and filled with A. W. N. Pugin glass. They tell the Life of Christ in 36 panels, within a controlled swirl of abstract patterns that form a wall of light and colour. The north arcade opposite is of four giant bays with deep-set but spacious clerestory windows above. At the west end of this north aisle is a brilliantly coloured small window depicting St Cuthbert.

The sanctuary is Victorian, with as backdrop the east wall inserted at the Reformation to fill the old crossing arch. It was rebuilt by Street in 1877 and is dominated by his stone panelled reredos. This was painted by two local craftsmen, Thomas Bottomley and his apprentice, R. G. Greenwood. It depicts Pre-Raphaelite Madonna lilies, alternating with symbolic biblical plants, barley, olive, vine, passion flower, rose and palm. It forms a wonderful climax to the interior but was once considered too secular and was covered with a curtain. The dark Perpendicular roof is alive with golden angels. One of the bosses is a gruesome Green Man, with one branch emerging from his mouth, the other from his eye.

BOLTON PERCY
All Saints *
Rare medieval glass of the Virgin

The church sits on the Yorkshire plain next to the remains of a river crossing. The gatehouse of an ancient manor lurks next door among the trees. The early 15th-century church is big and grey, its white limestone interior darkened by age and stained glass, but saved from impenetrable gloom by some clear windows in the south aisle. The Jacobean box pews are complete, with charming knobs as poppyheads. There are two pulpits, one early 17th and one early 18th century, the former austere, the latter more flamboyant, its tester supported on an Ionic column.

The church's principal treasure is the glass in the east window. This presents a complete medieval set of saints and bishops with, as its centrepiece, a rare depiction of the Virgin Mary. The cult of the Virgin had been strong in the 15th century and she thus became (with Thomas à Becket) a principal target of the iconoclasts. Though the faces are stylised and the surrounds include much Victorian insertion, the forms and colours of the original figures are wonderfully bold.

COXWOLD
St Michael **
Octagonal tower, Fauconberg monuments

Coxwold lies on the edge of the North York Moors, the gateway to England's most splendid landscape with abbeys, those of Byland, Newburgh and Rievaulx. The church is nobly sited at the end of the wide village street, the bold battlements of its east end rising like the wall of a castle keep. The distinctive Perpendicular west tower is an unusual octagon from base to crown. The structure is altogether odd. The lower stages are bare of niches or tracery, adorned only with the rhythmic stepping of angle buttresses. Yet the pierced parapet above is phenomenally ornate. This was a tower designed to be seen from a distance.

The interior of Coxwold comprises a nave, wide, unaisled and Perpendicular. A low arch leads to a Georgian chancel rebuilt to house the Fauconberg monuments. The nave's box pews, some with their original locks, were installed by Laurence Sterne, author of *Tristram Shandy* and occupant of the local Shandy Hall. He was vicar here in 1760–68 and is buried in the churchyard. Sterne's partitions, which meant that only the preacher could see into the pews during services, were later regarded as too exclusive. In 1906 carpenters cut 18 ins from the bottoms of the pews and removed the lowest deck from the pulpit, in the general interest of church democracy. Above the chancel arch is a fine George II coat of arms with the Fauconberg arms flanked by feathers on either side.

The chancel is so crowded with monuments that the communion rail has been extended down the centre, like a feeding trough. It gives, says the guide, 'a sense of togetherness'. The Belasyse family, later Viscounts Fauconberg, acquired the Newburgh estates on the Dissolution and their descendants are here to this day. The tomb of Sir William (d.1603) is against the north wall, the chest surrounded by a spreading canopy of columns, strapwork and obelisks lauding the pedigree and virtue of the house of Belasyse. The monument rises almost to the roof and retains much of its black, gold and red colour.

Opposite is the chaste tomb of Sir William's grandson, Thomas, 1st Viscount Fauconberg (d.1652). This was carved by Nicholas Stone, and shows a man and wife soberly at prayer under a classical canopy with two pediments. It includes the endearing inscription, 'Every man is a bubble. All flesh is grass.'

The monument to Thomas, 1st Earl Fauconberg (d.1700), thought to be by John Nost, is now attributed to Gibbons. Thomas married Cromwell's daughter Mary and served as a diplomat under both the Commonwealth and the Stuart Restoration. A figure representing worldly goods, in contemporary dress and proffering an earl's coronet, is rebuffed by Thomas, wearing Roman costume, in favour of a heavenly crown held aloft by putti. Both figures are in full dress wigs.

CROFT-ON-TEES
St Peter ***
Milbanke pew, Lewis Carroll inspiration

This splendid church lies on the Yorkshire/Durham border marked by a bridge over the River Tees. The church is best known as the boyhood home of Lewis Carroll, whose father was rector of Croft from 1843 to 1868. It is hard not to see in Croft's eccentricities the spur to young Carroll's imagination. On his memorial plaque stands the White Rabbit. Local lore even holds that the phrase, 'I'm late, I'm late for a very important date' derives from the men of Croft rushing across the bridge to benefit from the later opening hours of the tavern on the Yorkshire side.

Eccentricity starts with the building material, which is the softest of pink stone, and continues with the proportions. The chancel is large, the nave smaller and the tower diminutive, as if like Alice in Wonderland it had experienced shrinkage from east to west. The interior is wholly dominated by the insertion during the Restoration of a 'pew' for the Milbanke family of Halnaby. Not even the theatrical pew at Wensley is as big. It fills a complete bay of the nave like a royal box at the opera, and towers over even the pulpit. The pew is carried on Doric columns and is reached by its own private staircase, with banisters and two landings. The interior is upholstered and has curtains to be drawn should the occupants tire of the service below.

Behind the pew lurks a large classical monument, presumably to the Milbanke responsible for the pew, Sir Mark (d.1680). It is surrounded by a railing and is crowned with a simple funeral helm. In the same chapel is a fragment of a Saxon cross shaft decorated with animals and birds in scrollwork, dating from the early 9th century.

Croft chancel admirably demonstrates what fun even the least sophisticated Decorated carvers could have with the standard furnishings of the liturgy. Here are a piscina, an aumbry and sedilia executed in robust vernacular style, displaying human faces, angels, trees, rabbits and a pig feeding on corn, as well as the usual ballflower designs. Were these the inventive figures that inspired the young Carroll? Is that a Mad Hatter above the middle arch?

There is a memorial plaque to Carroll in the church, depicting the White Rabbit and including a verse that he wrote in reflecting on his youth: 'I'd give all wealth that years have piled, / The slow result of life's decay, / To be once more a little child / For one bright summer day.'

DOWNHOLME
St Michael *
Dales setting

Here, if anywhere, is an entry justified by a church's location. On the back road from Leyburn to Richmond, a small chapel lies lost in a valley, surrounded only by dales, fields and drystone walls. A scattering of sheep and cows is serenaded by curlews, peewits and (mostly) crows. The church is well maintained and the stone exterior suggests more than a primitive dale chapel. There is Decorated tracery, including an excellent Reticulated east window. Under the eaves is a rough but distinctive corbel-table. Two wires connect the bell rope to the bellcote.

Inside, all is quiet dignity. There is a three-bay Transitional arcade to an unusually wide north aisle. This holds two hatchments that are far too big for the church and must surely have come from elsewhere. Next to them is an equally grand George III coat of arms. The church is decorated in a soft cream rendering. It is a place of remarkable peace.

EASBY (nr Richmond)
St Agatha **
Saxon cross, medieval murals

Easby is a picturesque ruin under the shadow of the town and mighty castle of Richmond. The church is not a fragment of a monastery but a lay church that once stood next to the old gatehouse to the abbey. The abbey decayed but the church preserved both its old cross and its wall paintings. The entrance is reached down a tunnel of holly and oak, leading into a no less tunnel-like porch.

The interior is curious rather than beautiful. The nave is tall and narrow, clearly of Norman proportions. Zigzags have been painted on the three arches of the south arcade. Easby chancel contains two treasures. The first is a facsimile of Easby Cross, a ghost of the original now in the Victoria and Albert Museum. The two versions should, of course, be exchanged.

The cross, at least in facsimile, is a fine work of *c.*800. Apart from the usual scrolls inhabited by fauna, there are saints' busts in relief attending on Christ. The form is derived, according to Pevsner, from 'the obelisk of Theodosius at Istanbul, probably via ivory diptychs. The richness of the scrolls indicates Carolingian influence from the Continent.' Was Europe ever so cosmopolitan as during this ancient cultural Common Market?

The other treasure is the Easby murals. These date from the mid-13th-century and were restored by the stained glass firm of Burlison & Grylls in the 19th century. As was customary, the north wall is Old Testament, the south wall New Testament. Every character is in place. The murals are complemented by the east window, which has two medieval stained glass figures, thankfully surrounded by clear glass and a view of the sky outside.

FILEY
St Oswald **
Norman tower, Transitional nave, Boy Bishop memorial

The church is positioned on a hill north of Filey, Scarborough's sedate Edwardian sister. There is nothing sedate about its architecture. The sea crashes beneath the churchyard to the east and a deep ravine runs to the south, crossed by a footbridge. St Oswald's was built to defy the North Sea gales and guide ships to the beach. The crossing tower is massive, as are the transepts and chancel. All still boast Norman windows or Early Gothic lancets. The corbel-table survives.

The interior is dark, the darkness of Transitional architecture and Victorian glass (albeit well lit by spotlights). The nave is composed of five bays, including the piers of a west tower that was never completed. The crossing arches have clustered piers and are orderly and dignified. A single capital by the south door is decorated with swirling stiff-leaf. In the south aisle of the nave is a rare, and crude, statue of a Boy Bishop. These youths were elected by their friends to act as mock bishop at the medieval feast of St Nicholas in December. This memorial is to a boy who died 'in office', possibly in the late 13th century.

The Victorian vicar of Filey was a famous walker, striding out from his church to reach both Venice and Rome on different occasions. The sundial outside the chancel priest's door is inscribed in Greek rather than Latin, believed to be a unique use of the language for this purpose.

HEMINGBROUGH

St Mary **

England's oldest misericord, modern wood carvings

This church, located midway between the glories of Selby and Howden (Yorks, ER), looks as if it is shouting to be noticed by each. The prominent steeple is almost 200 ft tall. While the tower is modest, the spire seems to shoot upwards like a rocket from behind its parapet, with no lucarnes or other interruptions. The spire is twice the height of the tower and the rest of the cruciform church serves chiefly as its launch pad.

The interior is a friendly jumble of styles. Two nave bays are Norman and two bays Early Gothic. The crossing arches are big and the transepts correspondingly spacious, but why does the north transept have a west aisle that is so narrow as to be useless? In other words, the inside is as eccentric as the outside is exciting. Large Perpendicular north and south windows and clear glass in the clerestory flood the nave with light.

The chancel is heavily Victorianised. It has fine wood carving, including screens and stalls which boast a single misericord of *c.*1200, probably the oldest to survive in England. The south chapel has big windows and a funeral helm and gauntlets. Its modern furnishings and screen are by Thompson of Kilburn, who expands on his mouse motif to include a wealth of squirrel poppyheads.

Excellent carving continues in the nave, which has an extensive set of bench-ends. Under the tower are four relief panels of monsters, carved with great relish, probably once part of the parish chest or bench-ends. Some carvings are 15th century, some 19th and some modern. The craftsmanship of the ages seems to have merged into one continuous and triumphant tradition.

On the north wall outside, a recent carver has produced a gargoyle in the shape of a horrific dolphin.

KNARESBOROUGH
St John ***
Hillside setting, Slingsby monument

Seen from below and at the right angle, Knaresborough might be a fortress town on the Dordogne. Steep cobbled streets lead up from the river gorge to the market square. Names such as Bond End, Water Bag Bank and Precious Street abound. In the 19th century the railway drove its track through the middle of the town next to the church, cutting off the latter with a station and level crossing. As a result, St John's sits aloof from the centre. The best view is from the river, where the tower with its 'candle-snuffer' spike piles up over the roofs of the waterside houses.

The interior is full of incident. The chancel has a fine Reticulated east window, a Victorian copy of an original window said to be hidden in a local summer-house. On either side of the chancel are fine chapels. St Edmund's to the south is entered through an ornate Early Gothic arch, multi-shafted and with simple stiff-leaf capitals. It appears to have come from a different, altogether grander church. Inside are fine sedilia with ogee arches and a simple modern altar.

The Slingsby Chapel contains monuments to that family, including that of Sir William (d.1634). It is an early example of a standing effigy in naturalistic pose conveying bodily weight, and every inch the cavalier. His head rests on his hand, his arm on his sword and his other hand on the Slingsby crest. It is attributed to Epiphanius Evesham. Emma Slingsby died in 1899 and was said to be last of a line stretching back to the Conqueror. But I notice that there is a memorial here to a Major Slingsby, who gave money to the church and died in 1962.

At the back of the south aisle is a lovely Morris & Co. window, not too dark, designed by Madox Brown.

LASTINGHAM
St Mary ****
Norman crypt with ancient capitals

The crypt at Lastingham is among England's special places. I first visited it on a damp autumn evening when the moor outside was cold and still. Solitude itself had crept inside the church, descended to the crypt and knelt to pray.

The ghosts were those of the age of Bede, St Cedd, St Chad and the earliest missionaries to the north. On a small lectern I found Eliot's stern lines: 'You are here to kneel where prayer has been valid ... Here the intersection of the timeless moment is England and nowhere. Never and always.' Some churches are a challenge to the faithful; Lastingham is a challenge to the faithless.

The church lies in a picturesque fold in the North York Moors. A monastery of Lastingham was founded by St Cedd in 654 as an outpost of Bishop Aidan's at Lindisfarne. The following year St Cedd travelled south to found the surviving church of Bradwell (Essex) and was succeeded as abbot by his brother St Chad. It was abandoned during the Viking period, rebuilt after the Conquest with the present crypt dedicated to St Cedd, but deserted again in 1088. Lastingham has been a parish church since the 13th century.

The crypt is unique in England in its complexity, having two aisles, a small chancel and an apse. It is reached down steps from the nave and is low and cell-like. The Norman piers and capitals in the crypt are like dwarfs with the heads of grown men. The 11th-century carvers of these capitals knew the relics of the Roman empire. They knew the classical orders even if they interpreted them freely, for instance taking Ionic volutes and turning them into rams' horns. This is the most intriguing of all architectural transitions: Norman Romanesque at its most Roman.

The main church presents different exterior aspects. When seen from the east and below, it is of massive proportions. From the west, the higher west end is more domestic and has a Perpendicular tower. The interior is composed of the 11th-century aisled chancel and crossing. The nave planned at that time was never constructed, and instead the crossing is closed by a west wall erected in the 13th century. Yet the sequence of arcades and arches progressing towards the eastern apse is spectacular, enhanced by Pearson in his 19th-century restoration. He added groin vaults and clerestory lancets.

Lastingham has few furnishings of interest. It does not need them.

MASHAM
St Mary *
Wyvill monument

Masham is a peaceful market town that has, as yet, miraculously survived suburbanisation. The wide market square might be that of a French *bastide*. Tucked away to the east of the square lies the church, its unusual octagonal belfry and spire rising above a strong Norman tower.

Outside the south porch is an earlier relic, the round shaft of a Saxon cross. Its figures are eroded beyond recognition, leaving an eerie piece of archaeology rising out of a refreshingly unkempt churchyard.

The interior is dominated by the wide Perpendicular nave. There are six bays on the north side and, for some reason, only five on the south. Masham was so restored by the Victorians that it is hard to distinguish new from old. Yet its furnishings are remarkable. In the north aisle stands a Jacobean monument to Sir Marmaduke Wyvill, conventional in style but superb in execution. Husband and wife lie on cushions, propped on their elbows, while their children 'weep' below. In the spandrels are allegorical figures of Death and Mortality, putti blowing bubbles.

A painting of the Madonna and Child over the tower arch is by John Blakey (in 1994) and was paid for by the Yorkshire brewers, Theakstons. It used a sixteen-year-old local beauty as a model and is framed by the word 'Mary' translated into numerous foreign languages.

NUN MONKTON
St Mary **
Charming village setting, Early Gothic arcading

A duckpond in a wide green, a tall maypole, a 17th-century mansion and the relics of an old priory form one of Yorkshire's best-known picture villages, at the end of a cul-de-sac outside York. The church is further isolated at the end of an avenue of trees. It is a relic of a Benedictine convent of notoriously leisurely habits. The nuns were criticised for wearing furs and jewellery, for liaisons with the local clergy and for enjoying good food and wine. Shortly before the Dissolution, the prioress no less had to be forbidden by her bishop from 'holding candle-lit dinners', in particular 'alone with one John Monkton'.

When the Dissolution came, the buildings were mostly demolished. What survived, to be later restored by the Victorians, is a fragment of the old nave, including some of the best wall arcading of any northern church to survive from the 13th century.

The west front exterior is exquisite, formed of an elaborate doorway with five orders of colonnettes. The capitals display the earliest evidence of stiff-leaf decoration, sign of the transition from Norman to Gothic. Above are niches with, in one of them, a portion of a 13th-century statue. Inside, the church is aisleless and the lower walls are plain, However, the arcading along the upper level of the walls is dazzling. The walls are double-thickness with a passage at sill level, as if this were a cathedral. Arches and shafts frame the lancet windows, which are divided by smaller twin arches. The composition is simple, orderly but immaculate.

The east wall is a Victorian structure, with stepped lancet windows. These contain superb works of Morris glass by Burne-Jones of 1873. They were recently restored and reinstated in 1998.

SCARBOROUGH
St Martin **
Bodley church with Morris windows

The young Bodley had a happy association with the seaside resorts of England, whether in Yorkshire or Sussex. In Brighton (St Michael's) his father was a local doctor; in Scarborough his patron was also a parental friend. The building towers over the centre of the resort. The architecture is early French Gothic, cold and uninviting, but the church is to be visited for its glass.

This was commissioned in the fruitful early 1860s, when Bodley was already employing the new William Morris partnership at Selsley (Gloucs) and Brighton. At Scarborough, begun in 1861, the partnership turned an undistinguished structure into a gallery of Pre-Raphaelite art. Every window and much of the wall decoration is by the firm and the unity of style is immediately apparent.

The east window Crucifixion is by Madox Brown, the west rose window is by Burne-Jones and Morris himself, and angels by the partnership fill the clerestory. The aisle windows are uncluttered and their images of saints are strong, dark and striking. The windows do not sit flat against the line of the wall, like much Victorian and later glass, but glow from their recesses. As was Morris's intention, they illumine the interior like medieval windows, using shadow as well as light.

The partnership also decorated much of the structure. The east wall bears a mural of the Adoration by Burne-Jones and angels by Morris himself. Morris and Philip Webb contributed the painted ceilings. Best of all is the pulpit, described by Pevsner as 'a Pre-Raphaelite gem'. Its ten panels were designed by Rossetti, Morris and Madox Brown. I hope no avaricious museum curator takes a fancy to it.

SELBY
The Abbey *****
Norman nave, chancel stiff-leaf, east window tracery with medieval glass

Selby is subordinate only to Beverley Minster (Yorks, ER) and York Minster among the giants of Yorkshire. Comparing Selby and Beverley is one of the joys of English church visiting. Beverley's glory is promiscuous and loud. Selby's is that of a stately old lady, retired to the country with her dignity and memories intact.

Like York, Selby rests on just 3 ft of sand above the water table. This has led to tower settlement, drastically distorting the arches of the nave. The early builders had to let the structure settle on beams of wood sunk into the water. As a result, the centre of the abbey suffered extensive collapse in the 17th century. The roof was also destroyed in a fire in 1906, when the bells in the central tower melted and poured in a molten stream down into the church. A vast operation of reconstruction took place, including stone cleaning both inside and out. Today's church is in excellent condition.

Seen from the road to the south, its nave and Norman tower are low and powerful. To the east the sacristy and chancel erupt in a forest of 14th-century buttresses, pinnacles and flowing tracery, culminating in the famous Decorated east window. This is a swirl of flamboyant tracery, losing discipline as it rises and finding order only in the tulip-shaped oval at the top.

To the west beyond the nave stands the serene group of west front and towers, the lower storey Norman, the upper Early Gothic and the rather stumpy towers Victorian. The façade is divided from Selby market place by a small parking area, trees and a lawn. It would benefit hugely by having the market extended directly to the foot of the abbey and the west door opened to the public. The planning of England's small towns is too aloof: the Italians and French handle these things better.

Selby's nave interior is Norman and Early Gothic, a mighty work of eight bays rising in three tiers, becoming later as we move westwards, and upwards. The alternating piers are unmistakably copied from Durham Cathedral. The two eastern shafts have trellis decoration. The capitals throughout are rich and varied, scalloped, figurative, moulded and foliate. The north gallery is Transitional with water-leaf capitals and detached shafts. The south gallery and clerestory are Early Gothic. In the final bays the carvers can contain themselves no longer and burst into water-leaf. The post-fire roof includes a number of bosses saved from the wreckage. One can see why Pevsner regarded the Selby nave as 'to be warmly recommended to students'.

The chancel is Decorated and dates from the late 13th and early 14th centuries. The piers are adorned with elaborate foliage capitals, the leaves deeply undercut but tightly bunched, as at Patrington (Yorks, ER). Here the leaves are ubiquitous, turning aisles and arcades into arbours of vegetation. The arcade spandrels carry saints standing to attention. Above them rise a clerestory and passage adorned with carving and ogival arches. The roof begins on stone springers, but soon turns to wood and carries heavy gold bosses at its ridge.

All this is but a guard of honour for the chancel's east window, whose extraordinary tracery we noted outside. The work is more remarkable for retaining its medieval glass. Though much restored and with numerous Victorian surrounds to the original images, Selby's Tree of Jesse window is a masterpiece of English stained glass. It was saved from the 1906 fire when, at the last moment, the wind changed direction. Today it glows with a different fire, that of medieval artistry living on into the present day.

The chancel sedilia, four in number, are works of soaring filigree stonework. They have been attributed to the celebrated architect of early Perpendicular, Henry Yevele. The font cover of a similar date and design was luckily rescued from the fire. Stalls and other furnishings at Selby were not so fortunate. The awful chairs should be removed from the nave when not in use.

SHERBURN IN ELMET
All Saints **
Janus cross sliced in two

Elmet was an ancient British kingdom that emerged after the Roman occupation but disappeared into Northumbria under the Saxons. It lives on in Yorkshire romanticism and in the name of the church that crests the wave of a hill above the River Ouse. Its white limestone tower is balanced by a long chancel with a steep roof. Inside are big Norman nave arcades, heavily retooled by the Victorians but still with individual capitals, some showing scallops, some leaves. The chancel is Early Gothic.

The most remarkable survival in Sherburn is a fragment of a rare 15th-century stone crucifix which carries carving on both front and back and was thus known as a Janus (or two-faced) cross. One side shows the emblems of the Passion, the other Christ's seamless coat and the dice. The cross survived iconoclasm and was found in the ruins of a chapel located in the churchyard. A dispute between the vicar and a churchwarden as to who owned it ensued, and was resolved by a judgement of Solomon. The cross was sliced in half, one face being carried off to the local manor of Steeton Hall, where it suffered considerably. The two halves have been brought back into the church, but hung apart in the south aisle chapel. Why not restore them as one?

The church tower has been in continuous need of support, witness the heavy buttresses intruding into the nave. Beneath the tower is a large west window filled with vivid heraldic glass. Sherburn has an early 16th-century chantry chapel to St Martin, enclosed to the east of the porch.

SKELTON (nr Ripon)
Christ the Consoler ***
Burges memorial to dead aristocrat

There are many Skeltons in Yorkshire. This one is near Newby Hall on the banks of the River Ure, south of Ripon. In the estate grounds is a memorial church to a young man who, in 1870, visited Greece as part of his classical education, was captured by brigands and held for ransom. The British consul in

Athens informed his parents, but before a deal was reached and an appropriate sum despatched, the boy was killed.

Thus died Frederick Grantham Vyner, fourth son of Henry Vyner of Newby Hall in the County of Yorkshire, and of Lady Mary, daughter of Lord Grantham (who also inherited an earldom) one-time owner of Newby, Baldersby and Studley. The money for Frederick's ransom was redirected from the brigands to build a church in the grounds of Lady Mary's seat at Newby. The architect chosen was William Burges, who also designed a church in the same year at neighbouring Studley Royal for Lady Mary's daughter.

Whereas Studley is an evocation of High Church joy, Skelton is unashamedly a shrine. At Studley, Burges designed a church as the focus of a picturesque landscape. At Skelton his theme was the deepest tragedy. Hence the dedication and memorial atmosphere which, to this day, permeates the place. The church was finished in 1876 and lies in a clump of dark evergreens, accessible by a lane from the village to Newby Hall. The south door and east end are overwhelmed by huge beech trees, weeping tears of leaves in sympathy with the architecture.

The church is the customary Burges variation on a French Gothic theme. This involves Plate tracery and a rose window, with a weighty spire and corner spirelets rising over the trees. Chancel, nave and tower are in perfect balance. The interior is similar in style to Studley, colour in the nave being confined to the stained glass in the windows. The walls and arcades are of funereal white stone and the shafts of black Purbeck marble. Above the chancel arch is an extraordinary decorative feature, a complete Adoration in high relief. Burges was not only an accomplished artist but worked closely with his principal carver, Thomas Nicholls. The stained glass throughout was designed by Burges and made by the London firm of Saunders & Co.

The low-vaulted chancel contrasts with the tall, cool nave. It glows with restrained colour, the walls lined with coloured marble and decorated by clustered shafts with stiff-leaf capitals and ballflower around the window. It is enriched with glass, metalwork, painting and sculpture. Nicholls's work is again on display in the organ loft. A gallery for the organist is supported by beasts and birds, while angels uphold the pipes, carrying cymbals and tambourines. Here sadness is allowed to give way to joy, crucifixion to resurrection.

[CCT]

SKELTON (nr York)
St Giles *
Restored Early Gothic remnant

This Skelton is a small village just off the Thirsk road, north of York. At first the church looks like a Victorian cemetery chapel, set under trees in a dormitory village. Yet it is an exemplar of Early Gothic style, and of its careful restoration by a Regency enthusiast. Skelton, according to the guide, 'was a source of inspiration to the architects of the 19th-century Gothic Revival ... Here for once we can look at a medieval architect's design, carried out in accordance with his original intentions and left virtually free from later alteration.'

This historical deference was that of the nineteen-year-old Henry Graham, son of a York rector, who took on the task of rescuing the small church in 1814. His material was an Early Gothic work, founded in 1247, as an outpost of York Minster. Local legend held that it was built of stone left over from the Minster. Its design is similar to that of the Minster's south transept. Graham studiously restored what he found of the old church, his only addition being a plaster ceiling that was later removed in 1883 in a further restoration by Ewan Christian. The 13th-century structure appears to have been planned as the core of a much bigger cruciform church, with what is now the two-bay nave as the crossing. It is hard otherwise to explain the mighty arches and scale of the interior spaces.

St Giles is all Early Gothic. The south doorway carries restored 'windblown' stiff-leaf capitals. The windows are lancets, apart from a circle in the west gable and an almond-shaped window above the triple lancet in the east. Even the small bellcote is 13th century. The atmosphere of the interior is 19th century, despite its architectural authenticity. Too much has been retooled to look original and the stained glass is unprepossessing. The restorers did not think to reinstate the wall paintings or furnishings that might have made St Giles seem less bare. That said, this is a remarkable work of archaeology. Graham died at the age of twenty-four in 1819.

Skelton churchyard is a nature sanctuary. The grass is roughcut, as should be every churchyard, and the guide lists its flora and fauna.

STUDLEY ROYAL
St Mary ****
Joyful Burges in Fountains Abbey setting

The church that William Burges built in 1870–78 for the Marquess and Marchioness of Ripon may not be to every taste, but for those who hold that the Victorians at their best were the equal of the 13th and 14th centuries,

Studley Royal is a masterpiece. It sits at the far end of the landscaped estate of Fountains Abbey, now owned by the National Trust, closing the central avenue of what remains the definitive work of 18th-century English picturesque. The house has gone, so Burges's steeple must carry the climax to the composition. It does so with panache.

Landowners everywhere were erecting churches in the 1860s and 1870s. Lady Ripon was daughter of Lady Mary Vyner (and sister of the murdered boy at neighbouring Skelton). She commissioned the architect working for her mother, albeit to a more cheerful task. Lord Ripon was, or was to become, Viceroy of India, Grand Master of the Freemasons and an early Christian Socialist. He also converted to Roman Catholicism. Lady Ripon was the moving spirit behind the church, on which £50,000 was to be spent. The foundation stone was laid in the same year, 1870, as Skelton but the church was not opened until 1878. Burges was a gentleman architect with a private income and time to spend on detail. He was not racing from commission to commission like Scott, Street or Pearson and enjoyed working for a few grand patrons, such as the Butes in South Wales and the Ripons in Yorkshire. He was not a devout man and his approach to Gothic was, as the guide says, 'romantic, visual and scholastic rather than moral'.

The exterior is in Burges's familiar muscular style. At night, the silhouette against the sky can seem like a giant rhinoceros, with the tower as its horn. The building is heavily buttressed, the chancel windows enriched and the doors emboldened with splendid Gothic ironwork.

The interior is one of Burges's most successful compositions. The nave is a study in white stone and black Purbeck marble. Colour comes from the glass, not garish or over-elaborate and admitting enough light to give depth to Burges's shadows. Facing each other across the nave are the great organ, always a Burges speciality, reached by a spiral staircase, and the memorial tomb to the Marquess, executed in the finest marbles.

The chancel bursts into colour. Its dominant feature is the window tracery on two planes, possibly inspired by the Angel Choir at Lincoln Cathedral. The walls have shafts using differing marbles and are adorned with murals. The theme of the decorative scheme is the Book of Revelation. The sanctuary has an extraordinary gilded and painted dome with imagery of angels, music, trumpets, glory and Heaven. The floor mosaics depict the Garden of Eden and the building of Jerusalem. Not an inch is left undecorated, and there is a great rose window as a climax in the east wall.

The building is best seen with bright sunlight streaming through Burges's glass and dancing with the angels on his walls. The church, reached by a foot-path across the park, is in the care of English Heritage.

[EH]

THIRSK
St Mary *
Perpendicular exterior, Lister Bower window

Nothing in the unassuming town of Thirsk quite prepares us for its church. Lanes drift north from the market square and peter out towards the river. Suddenly the view is closed by St Mary's, presenting its entire south flank to a bend in the road. This exterior is the best feature. The west tower is massive with heavily stepped buttresses. The nave clerestory rises high above a long south aisle enclosing the chancel. All these elements are decorated with pierced crenellation. The result is immensely bold, a fortified bastion in sandy stone whose blackness throws its recesses into relief.

The porch, with a parvise above, is full of arrow-sharpening slits. The original 15th-century door is covered in gnarled Perpendicular tracery. Thirsk was reconstructed after 1430 and restored by Street in 1876. The resulting interior is spectacular in its Perpendicular proportions, if disappointing in its details. Best of the latter are the parclose screens and a fine roof complete with ornamental bosses. The chancel arch is plainly Victorian and the east window, designed by Lady Walsingham and her daughters in 1844, is dire.

Light relief is supplied by the 1932 Lister Bower memorial window at the west end of the south aisle. Designed by Douglas Strachan, it portrays Sir Robert Bower as St George slaying the dragon, with his own crest on the shield. Subsidiary scenes illustrate his diverse career as 'the Happy Warrior', including his leadership of the local regiment, membership of the Red Cross and service in Nigeria. Such enjoyable bombast is sadly missing from demure modern memorials.

WENSLEY
Holy Trinity **
Scrope–Bolton pew

Wensley struggles to uphold its title of 'Queen of Wensleydale'. It is rather the dale's retired lady-in-waiting. The church gazes sleepily across the rounded slopes of the dale, its exterior of soft sandstone with flat buttresses carrying the shields of local families. Large Yorkshire headstones fill the churchyard.

The interior is a total surprise, a space of high drama. A tall three-bay nave gives way to a neat Early Gothic chancel, but not before being interrupted by a family pew as astonishing as the one at Croft-on-Tees. It belongs to the Bolton family, once Scropes and Dukes of Bolton, now humbler Lords. It was installed by the 3rd Duke for a Restoration opera singer, Lavinia, with whom he was infatuated. She insisted, in return for accepting his on-first-sight proposal, that he acquire the opera box from which he experienced his *coup de foudre*. This he duly did. The box is sumptuous, with two bays looking out over the nave as if from the Grand Tier at Covent Garden.

Behind the Bolton pew is a fragment of the Scrope family screen moved from Easby Abbey after the Dissolution. Its entrance carries a large framed hatchment of George III. On the obverse are the arms of the Scropes, reputedly the oldest in the land after those of the Royal Family.

The whole ensemble is wildly self-regarding and a joy to behold. The rector in his modest pulpit must have quaked beneath his lordship's gaze. Seen from the box, the nave takes on the appearance of the first monastic act of *Don Carlos*.

Wensley has other delights. The chancel is older and brighter than the nave, its Early Gothic windows shafted and with dogtooth ornament. On the chancel floor is a Flemish brass of 1395, of a priest in full robes. A reliquary from Easby by the door purports to be the only one surviving in England, made for the remains of St Agatha. (Bodmin in Cornwall also has one.)

WHITBY
St Mary * * * *
Hilltop setting, box pews and galleries

The steep climb from the old port of Whitby is the most exhilarating approach to any church in England, especially on a stormy evening (of which there are many). The town lies in a cleft below. Fishing boats chug past the breakwater. The air is loud with seagulls. Ahead rises the old abbey, the archetypal Gothic ruin chosen by Bram Stoker as the setting for Count Dracula's landfall in Britain.

St Mary's sits between town and abbey, alone on its eminence. The short tower, dark stone walls and battlements stand defiant against the North Sea. Yet the friendly windows seem eager to warm the souls within. This is a big-hearted church. It has never been rebuilt or stripped and each generation has been greeted with another pew, gallery or extension until the place seems to burst at every seam. The result could be treated as part folly, part museum, part large parlour. The church contains one of the most complete sets of pre-Victorian furnishings in England.

The fabric retains fragments of Norman and Early Gothic rebuilding and appears outwardly a pre-Reformation structure. A closer look reveals that many if not most of the windows are 18th century, while the extensions, porches and external stairs are of any period or none. The charm of the church lies inside, and this almost defies description. An obviously nautical congregation produced woodwork that might include every portion of a ship from quarterdeck to fo'c'sle. The roof is low and the pillars are like deck supports. The regular pushing out of aisles and transepts on all sides and the insertion of galleries wherever space permitted reduced the interior to a delightful confusion.

The focus of the church is the triple-decker pulpit, with candleholders and tester, erected in 1778. There are two ear-trumpets fixed behind, relic of a 19th-century vicar's deaf wife. In front of the pulpit is a large stove, still used, with a flue that rises to the ceiling. Behind, and astride what is strictly the chancel arch, is the 17th-century Cholmley Pew, a gallery on twisted columns whose occupants would have looked down on to the back of the preacher's head. The remaining pews and galleries were built at various times in the 18th and early 19th centuries. The sanctuary is completely hidden but has a window by Kempe.

The churchyard is crowded with monuments to those lost at sea, sailors, fishermen, Royal Navy seamen and lifeboatmen. They seem sad memorials since few are able to record a burial.

WINTRINGHAM
St Peter *
Jacobean furnishings, medieval glass

The Wolds Way passes the gate of Wintringham church on the outskirts of the Cholmley family's estate village. Its Perpendicular tower offers walkers a welcome beacon and promise of shelter against the weather. The chancel has a Norman corbel-table. The nave roof is most odd: where there would normally be battlements is a delightful series of stone heads popping up along the parapet, like schoolboys playing hide and seek.

The interior has a complete set of furnishings, left alone by Temple Moore's Victorian restoration. They are mostly Jacobean, including bench-ends with carved posts, a pulpit, tester, reader's desk and poor box. Temple Moore's contribution was the screen and choir stalls, but incorporating old misericords, one of which is a fine Green Man. The poppyheads are griffins.

Wintringham has the best glass in North Yorkshire. Thirty-two medieval saints fill the tracery lights of the aisle windows, the rest of which are clear. They are believed to be Flemish and date from the 14th century. They form a sunny gallery against the sky, brightening the church even on the gloomiest day.

York

York has England's finest set of medieval town churches. It has also been successful in bringing them back to life, a success that has eluded the two other provincial 'church cities', Norwich and Bristol. Though much damaged by time and war, they remain a wonderful complement to York Minster, evoking some sense of an English city in the late Middle Ages, each neighbourhood owing allegiance to an often tiny place of worship, enclosed by lanes and alleys. Above all, York's churches were careful of their medieval stained glass during the Second World War, storing it and then reinstating it as one of the best collections of civic glass in the country.

All Saints, North Street **   St Martin-le-Grand **
All Saints, Pavement *   St Michael-le-Belfrey *
Holy Trinity, Goodramgate *

ALL SAINTS
*North Street ***
Pricke of Conscience window

The church lies in a bleak corner of the city, west of the Ouse. It is over-shadowed by the modern Viking Hotel and car park, which have done more damage to York's townscape than the Vikings ever did. The church, which tilts away as if in disgust towards a row of medieval cottages, is marked by a strange tower with octagonal belfry and 120-ft spire of white limestone.

The interior is more complex than at first appears and has been admirably restored after a fire. It began as an aisleless Norman cell, but the accretions of five centuries have turned it into a seven-bay aisled rectangle. The chancel is marooned in the centre, encased in Perpendicular screens of 1906 and crowned by a small hammerbeam roof, unusual for Yorkshire. This is painted like a funfair roundabout, with angels in flesh tones and golden wings. The pulpit of 1675 is wooden resting on a stone base.

The medieval stained glass of All Saints is the best in York. The east window depicts 'all saints', including St Anne teaching the Virgin to read. The most celebrated panels are towards the east end of the north aisle. The Pricke of Conscience sequence of *c.*1425 portrays the fifteen signs of the end of the world, expected to occur in 1500, then still some way in the future. The donors kneel beneath in hope of salvation. The work is attributed to John Thornton, designer of the Minster's east window, and is based on a poem by a 13th-century hermit, Richard Rolle.

Next to it is the Corporal Acts of Mercy window. A man in a beard and ermine coat visits the sick, tends a man in the stocks, clothes the naked and feeds the hungry. Here is a one-man welfare state in microcosm. It illustrates daily life in the 15th century as vividly as any Burgundian Book of Hours. Other windows were comprehensively restored by Wailes, but include much original glass.

ALL SAINTS
Pavement *
Octagonal lantern, Crucifixion window

This jolly church is blessed with the best tower in York, topped by an open octagonal lantern in which a light used to burn to guide travellers into the city. This purpose is puzzling, given the church's proximity to the lofty Minster. The lantern has a crown of delicate stonework. It was built *c.*1400.

The interior is composed of a Perpendicular nave with aisles, and a crossing forming a chancel. The original chancel was demolished in 1782 to make way for a market, at a time when chancels were disused (or less profitable than markets).

The church's treasures include a 17th-century pulpit on a goblet stem with a tester, and some finely lettered mayoral boards. There are also banners, swords and other memorabilia appropriate to a regimental chapel. The church has superb glass, both medieval and Victorian. The east windows are excellent works by Kempe, with his typical figurative vitality.

The west window is a reconstruction using glass of *c.*1370, brought from the city church of St Saviour's after the war. It includes a Crucifixion, a splendidly colourful version of this scene not often found surviving in medieval glass. The roofs of the city are partly visible through the clearer panes, a rare pleasure in a town church.

HOLY TRINITY
Goodramgate *
Hidden setting

No town church can be more exquisitely secluded than this. Holy Trinity, with its battered tower, is reached down a number of tiny alleys in the heart of the old quarter. It is redundant only in name, a place of quietness amid hubbub. The exterior is unpretentious, with Decorated and Perpendicular windows. The interior is filled with a jumble of 17th- and 18th-century furnishings, the pulpit a two-decker. Nothing in Holy Trinity seems to have been planned. Even the floor undulates with the lie of the soil beneath, while pews seem to have been run up as and when spare panelling from earlier parts of the church became available.

Again it is the glass that gives a York interior its lustre. The east window depicts the piety and prosperity of its donor in the late 15th century. It was given by the rector, John Walker, a prominent member of two wealthy guilds, those of Corpus Christi and of St George & St Christopher. He is portrayed kneeling by the body of Christ while round him saints perform the requisite miracles. Another window shows St Ursula embracing a pope, with a king and the virgins to be martyred with her.

The list of parochial mayors includes the name of George Hudson, 'the railway king'. His palace in London's Knightsbridge, now the French Embassy, could hardly be further in spirit from this little church.

[CCT]

ST MARTIN-LE-GRAND
Coney Street **
St Martin window

The church announces its presence to the street with a Perpendicular tower and a garish Victorian clock, manned by a painted figure of a sailor. It was thoroughly bombed in the Second World War and George Pace's 1960s' reconstruction is only of the tower and south aisle. His work shows both decorum and flair. The remainder of the ruin was intended as a garden of contemplation but is closed.

Pace's restoration is strong on colour. He has put coloured bosses in the roof, bright colours in Harry Stammers's east window depicting the flames of the Blitz, and dazzling colours on the memorial to Sir William Sheffield (d.1633). The former west window was removed for safe keeping during the war and is now restored in a special screen facing the south entrance. This depicts the life of St Martin, and was the donation of Robert Semer in 1437; he appears at the bottom of the composition.

The St Martin window, as it is known, is among the best-preserved examples of late Gothic glass in England. It is apparently without Victorian accretions and is superbly displayed. How did it escape a museum?

ST MICHAEL-LE-BELFREY
Minster Yard *
Baroque reredos

As York churches go, St Michael's is pompous. It shelters under the lee of the Minster like a footman waiting at the door of the big house. Though an ancient foundation, the church was rebuilt in the early 16th century, squat and rather fat. The west turret can do no better than imitate the lantern of All Saints, Pavement, and is dwarfed by the stepped gables connecting nave and aisle roofs. The guide boasts that this is the finest church of the reign of Henry VIII anywhere. It is good, but not that good.

The interior is light and spacious, but the eye is drawn at once to the large Baroque reredos. This is so dominant that when I left the church I could hardly remember whether the rest of the interior was not classical as well. The reredos is tall and grand, with four Corinthian columns and a segmental pediment. The work is by William Etty, erected in 1712 and fronted by a fine communion rail with projecting semicircular gates, complementing the form of the pediment. These would do credit to the finest Wren work in London. Of the same date is a delicate coat of arms of Queen Anne.

In the south aisle is a monument to Robert Squire (d.1709) and his wife, Priscilla. It is of a type known as a reredos tomb, and a comparison with Etty's piece demonstrates why. St Michael's glass is excellent, testament to wartime care. The east window is formed of medieval fragments from the earlier church. Most of the other windows are probably Flemish and are contemporary with the 1530s' rebuilding. Standing saints vie with kneeling donors for glory at the glaziers' hands. In the south aisle there is a fine St George and the Dragon. In the north aisle, a set of glass panels illustrates the romantic story of Thomas à Becket's parents, his father eloping with the daughter of his heathen captor during a pilgrimage to the Holy Land.

Near the entrance is the baptismal record of Guy Fawkes, a local boy made bad.

Yorkshire, South

The new administrative county of South Yorkshire was carved mostly from the old West Riding. Sadly it brought with it few fine churches. The landscape is that of the Don valley running down from the High Peak of the Pennines to the wide Humber basin. The stone is mostly limestone blackened by soot, except where a strong sun can peel back the covering. The church settings derive most of their character from their bleakness.

Ecclesfield proclaims itself as the minster of the moors north of Sheffield; Tickhill with its magnificent tower dominating the South Yorkshire plain better deserves a grandiloquent title. The best work in the county is at Rotherham, its bold tower struggling to hold the old town centre together. Fishlake church has an excellent Norman doorway and Laughten-en-le-Morthen a magnificent spire. The county's most unusual treasure is Tickhill's Fitzwilliam tomb of 1533, illustrating in one piece the transition from Gothic to classical style, and from the Middle Ages to the Reformation.

Arksey *
Doncaster: St George *
Ecclesfield **
Fishlake **

Hatfield *
High Bradfield *
Laughton-en-le-
   Morthen *

Rotherham ***
Silkstone *
Thorpe Salvin *
Tickhill ***

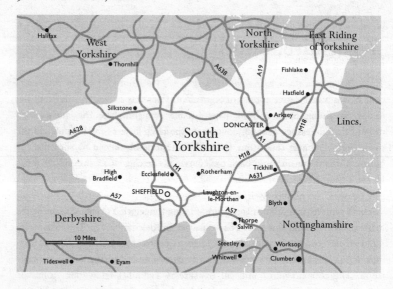

ARKSEY

All Saints *

Norman interior, Cooke memorial

The church and almshouses form an oasis in the suburbs of Doncaster, where they are surrounded by former colliery estates. Finding the church is the more delightful for the dreariness of seeking it. The Norman cruciform building of creamy limestone has been filled out with chantries and chapels. The interior has an antiquated aura that George Gilbert Scott failed to destroy when he restored it while working on St George, Doncaster. It has the enjoyable diagonal views that came with a cruciform plan. The dating of the nave, aisles and crossing is confusing since nothing seems to match. The crossing is rich in shafted Early Gothic piers, while Norman work survives on the north side.

The pews were restored by Scott, using old ones as models for facsimiles where necessary. The pulpit looks Jacobean, though dated 1634, but the tester with its elaborate scrolls is similar to the font cover, dated 1662. In the north transept is a superb 17th-century bust of Sir George Cooke, his lace ruff and wig beautifully carved. The Cooke family has been associated with the church to this day.

DONCASTER
St George *
Scott's biggest town church, Victorian glass

The huge structure which George Gilbert Scott gave Doncaster after the former church was burnt down in 1853 is unmissable. When seen from the railway or the encompassing motorways it rises over the town centre as majestic as any medieval predecessor. The deep sandstone crossing tower is a virtual replica of the Perpendicular tower lost in the fire. The closer we get to the church, however, the more disappointing it becomes. Its setting is miserable, besieged by traffic and stripped of townscape. The exterior is alarmingly unkempt. The place desperately needs environmental first aid.

Yet Doncaster is a Scott masterpiece. He was expected to reproduce the old Perpendicular tower, and this he did. But for a mid-Victorian architect to build the rest of the church in what was to him the debased late-Gothic style was too much. The rest of the church is therefore early Decorated, with Geometrical tracery in the windows.

The interior is big. The arcades have stiff-leaf carving and the chancel has medallions of saints. The south choir aisle, known as the Forman Chapel, is rich in its decoration. What the church does possess is good Victorian glass: a fine east window by Hardman & Co., a giant of eight lights 44 ft high, and work by Wailes and Clayton & Bell. Why not gather other glass from Yorkshire's too-gloomy churches and open a stained glass museum here? Do something!

ECCLESFIELD
St Mary **
Black stone exterior, Hardman window

Black the hillside, black the houses, black the tombstones and, except on the sunniest of days, black the church. There is nothing so grim as Yorkshire limestone streaked with dirt. Yet this is a powerful church dating from days when Ecclesfield might look down on Sheffield and claim itself the principal settlement of Hallamshire. It improbably declares itself 'Minster of the Moors'.

The exterior is Perpendicular and would be almost delicate were it not for the coldness of the stone. The plan is cruciform, the tower square and the roofs battlemented throughout. The interior is spacious and grand, with aisles running the length of nave and chancel. I like the suggestion in the guide that the mismatching of arcade piers was 'to stop the builders getting bored'. The nave has a new roof but the roofs of the aisles and chancel chapels are original, with tie-beams and big bosses.

Best of the furnishings is the excellent rood screen. This has tall openings and deep coving, and behind it are remains of medieval stalls and misericords. On one of these is a superb carving of a medieval monk, a gem to find in such a place.

The glass is Victorian but mostly of good quality. The east window is a Crucifixion in vivid picture-book colours by George Hedgeland, completely dominating the east end of the church. There is a bright Hardman & Co. window in the south aisle, followed by two to its west by Kempe and by lesser practitioners of the gloomy art. The effect of the clashing styles is jarring and overwhelmingly dark. Even the vicar admits that more light might be welcome.

FISHLAKE
St Cuthbert **
Carved Norman doorway, Decorated font

This is flat country beyond Doncaster, where trade once poured down the rivers Ouse and Aire to the Humber and the coast. Trade has receded, leaving waterways lined with empty factories, housing estates and plucky farmers. Fishlake is surrounded by dykes. Yet for so small a church it has a magnificent exterior with a handsome white Perpendicular tower and west window of five tall lights.

The principal treasure is immediately apparent, a Norman south doorway with few equals in the north of England. It appears to be unrestored and, though eroded, is still evocative. There are four orders of columns rising to capitals enriched with leaves and faces. The lavishly worked arches include medallions carved with seated figures, fighting angels and heads surrounded with greenery. This an exciting relic of the former church, when these marshes must have been thick with woodland and when a carver needed only to look up from his work for inspiration.

The interior is surprisingly spacious, given that the arcades are Transitional and the walls not so much scraped as grouted to the point of collapse. There is a mercifully generous clerestory and west window. The chancel east window has tracery that swirls upwards and then appears to lose itself in confusion.

Fishlake has a fine Decorated font with nodding ogee niches and saints. It is singled out by Norman Pounds in his study of English fonts as 'a work of great beauty'.

HATFIELD
St Lawrence *
Tudor tower, Oughtibridge monument

The level country between Doncaster and Scunthorpe is unprepossessing and can bear little relation to its appearance when Hatfield was first founded.

The church was big for the Normans, and is still big today. Its glory is its tower, rising over the central crossing as a beacon to all dwellers in flat country. The builder was a member of the Savage family of Macclesfield, bailiffs of Hatfield in the reign of Henry VII. The Savage arms adorn the tower, which has a lantern.

The best thing to do inside is look upwards. The interior is dominated by the central space created by the tower, carrying the arms of a Savage who rose to be Archbishop of York (in 1501). The raised chancel has been scraped, but its roof and the roofs of the side chapels are excellent, with many original bosses. The screen also survives, still with its loft coving with lierne vaults and with strange faces in its side panels. These look like Red Indians on totem poles.

In the south transept stands an eccentric memorial to William Oughtibridge of 1756. He is attended in death by disgruntled angels above, and by large chrysanthemums beneath. What on earth is this all about? To add to the eccentricity of the work, it is signed by T. Oughtibridge, who was presumably a relative of the deceased. In the south aisle are a magnificent Norman chest and Kempe windows.

HIGH BRADFIELD
St Nicholas *
Peak setting

The old church was founded under the priors of Ecclesfield in the manor of Hallam, later known as Hallamshire. It sits on the side of a hill, looking out across Strines Moor to Derwent Edge and Black Tor. We are four miles from the outskirts of Sheffield, yet we might be a hundred. On a sunny day the view is glorious, enjoyed by the weatherbeaten gargoyles peering from under toppling pinnacles. The guide is right to make its frontispiece not the church but the view from the porch.

There is little to say of the interior, except that it forms a warm contrast to the wildness outside. The oddest feature of the nave is that some crazed iconoclast has hacked off all the pier capitals. What so offended his gaze? The nave and aisle roofs avoided such attention and are fine Perpendicular works with bosses. The chancel steps up the slope of the hill, as does the sanctuary beyond, a dramatic architectural effect. An old vestry with a fireplace is left curiously sunk on the right.

The reredos is of medieval wood brought from an abbey in Caen by a benefactor in 1887. It was installed by the Sheffield carver, Arthur Hayball, whose daughter executed the figure of Christ in one of the pulpit panels. The superb eagle lectern is American and was given first prize at the Philadelphia Exhibition of 1876. Bits of 16th-century glass survive in the north aisle but most is Victorian, not all of it bad.

LAUGHTON-EN-LE-MORTHEN
All Saints *
Soaring tower with Saxon base

The name refers variously to a low-town or a law-town, and Morthen is either a wasteland/moor or a morth-eng, a place of death. The latter is more exciting and is lent substance from the possibility that this is the site of the Battle of Brunanburgh (937) between Athelstan and the Danes. What is clear is that a solid church of the Saxon period was built here, which bequeathed us the fine ironstone north doorway at the foot of the tower. It was preserved when a new tower was constructed in the late 14th century. The latter work has been linked to William of Wykeham, who held the Prebend of Laughton in addition to his many responsibilities in the south.

The tower is the glory of Laughton and among the finest in Yorkshire, soaring over the surrounding countryside. Square lower stages give way to an octagonal lantern. The needle spire is supported by two tiers of flying buttresses, one springing from the tower and the other from the pinnacles, as if steadily squeezing the square into an octagon. This is a work of great aesthetic ingenuity.

The interior of the tower is stone vaulted. The rest of the church is largely Perpendicular, relieved from dullness only by the lavish carved angels decorating the nave arcades. They are huge, 2 ft high, and must have dominated the church when coated in medieval paint.

ROTHERHAM
All Saints ***
Roof bosses, Wise Men poppyheads

All Saints is more than a fine church, it is the visual fulcrum for Rotherham's town centre. The crocketed spire rises over the civic square to its north, a relationship spoilt only by a barricade of public lavatories (which must go). The square, which is now pedestrianised, should somehow be merged with the church close, as at Tamworth (Staffs). Town markets belong in proximity to their churches, so that the activity of the one can be fused with the grandeur of the other. Bleak churchyards so often act merely as moats.

All Saints is a polished work of Perpendicular Gothic. Its centrepiece is a sturdy crossing tower with clasping pinnacles and crocketed ribs to its spire. The rest of the exterior is rightly deferential. The crispness of the stone is due to restoration in the 18th century and again by George Gilbert Scott in the 1870s. The result can seem black and forbidding in anything but the sunniest weather.

The interior is sophisticated and full of colour. The nave arcades have curious flat pseudo-capitals, the foliage presaging Art Nouveau. The original roof bosses are big and well restored, leading to an immense 1420 fan vault under the tower. The chancel is a work of stylistic accretion, from Early Gothic through Decorated and Perpendicular (notably the roof) to Victorian. The sedilia have ogee arches and the stalls have charming poppyheads of the Three Wise Men. The chamber is rich and dark.

The church has recently been fitted with an new altar beneath the tower and new stalls in both crossing and nave. These are traditional in style, but their fresh limewood looks fiercely white in colour. The wood is expected to mellow in time. In the south transept, now a coffee bar, are 18th-century memorials, including a lugubrious work by John Flaxman. The organ is by Johann Snetzler of 1777, with a superb black and gold case. The keyboard still has Snetzler's typical reversal of the white and black keys.

SILKSTONE
All Saints *
Memorials to inventor and to a pit disaster

Silkstone is spread across a Yorkshire hillside, where it bespeaks North Country coal mines, grime and the wrath of God. The church sits impressively self-confident in its dell, surrounded not by pitheads or city streets but by the rolling countryside between Barnsley and Penistone. Its stone is black, its mortar washed white by the elements. Bold embattlements defy all comers. On my visit the sun was shining and a garden party was being prepared in the vicarage. Such are the kaleidoscopic moods of the mighty county of Yorkshire.

The church tower was built by the Cluniac priory of Pontefract. The aisle walls are supported outside by unusual flying buttresses, rising through bold gargoyles as at Halifax (Yorks, W). The interior is spacious and is lucky to retain parts of the original screens, elaborately Perpendicular. The nave pews retain the names of their 19th-century subscribers and the vicar can list those families which continue to live in the village. Silkstone's most distinguished monument is to Sir Thomas Wentworth (d.1675), a bravura work. He lies carved mostly realistically in marble yet lying on his back in the medieval style. More original is the memorial to Joseph Bramah (d.1814). He was a master inventor whose creations included a flushing lavatory, a fountain pen, an unpickable lock and a fire engine.

In the pleasantly overgrown churchyard is a grimmer memorial, to twenty-six children lost when a pit in which they had taken shelter was flooded with storm water. The inscription records that they were 'suddenly summoned to appear before their Maker. So reader remember, every neglected call of God will appear against thee on the Day of Judgement.' This is stern stuff. The guide consoles us that this is 'a theology no longer accepted by the Church'.

THORPE SALVIN
St Peter *
Carved Norman font

Thorpe Salvin comes complete with a fine ruin, that of an Elizabethan manor house which forms a stark backdrop to the churchyard. The church itself stands on a hill opposite a farm, where the keyholder demanded I stand back and receive 'a good looking over in case you've come for the silver'. The exterior is homely, with chancel and north chapel tacked on to one end, and a tower tacked on to the other as if an afterthought.

The core of the interior is a large Norman church with two big round arches to the north aisle and a more sophisticated arch to the chancel. The tower arch – which appears intended for a much larger tower – is already Transitional. There are pretty Decorated windows in the chancel and north chapel, the latter with lily tracery. This end of the church has been so brutally scraped that the chapel walls look like the outside of a barn.

The jewel of the church is the Norman font. It sits poked away at the back and is not easy to see. A foliate frieze round the bowl frames charming domestic scenes. Two are of baptism and four represent the seasons, with a man sowing, harvesting, hunting and resting (in winter). They are well preserved and simple, in a style common across Europe in the 12th century.

TICKHILL
St Mary ***
Ornamented tower, early classical tomb chest

The silvery tower of Tickhill rises over the south Yorkshire plain, where a tangle of motorways race north from the Nottinghamshire border. This has always been travelling country. Tickhill Castle once guarded the Great North Road. Today this is a dull, half-developed landscape, but the church guidebook contrives a fine view of Tickhill tower, appearing to show it lost in countryside.

The church is built of the silver/white limestone familiar in the region. When black it is ugly but when clean, even in a grey light, it has an ethereal quality all of its own. At Tickhill the silver is delicately wrought by the stone carvers. The Perpendicular exterior has pinnacles on every available upright. Its particular glory is the tower crown. The bell-stage is set back and the ogee hoods to the bell-openings rise into the battlements, where they are greeted by tiny gables linking each crenellation.

Although the north chapel is Decorated, the interior is mostly grand Perpendicular. The arcades are early examples of the style, and the rhythm of the steep arches still demonstrates 'decorative' undulation. The interior is relatively bare. (Oh, for some of the original Perpendicular colour in these churches!) There is a gratifying amount of medieval glass surviving in the south aisle and Kempe windows in the north-east chapel.

Tickhill's principal treasure is the alabaster tomb of Sir Thomas Fitzwilliam, moved from the old friary. The effigies, much bashed, are medieval in style, but the chest beneath is adorned with the early classical forms of wreaths, putti and shell-heads. It was probably commissioned by Sir Thomas's wife, Lucy (d.1534). Her son by her second marriage, Sir Anthony Browne (d.1548), has an almost identical tomb at Battle Abbey in Sussex. Sir Anthony was part of an embassy to France in 1533 and these tombs are in the French style popular at the court of Henry VIII. Like the contemporary tomb of Henry VII in Westminster Abbey, they are among the earliest manifestations of classicism in English church art.

Yorkshire, West

The old West Riding lost its finest churches to North Yorkshire in the last (surely the final) round of modern boundary revision. West Yorkshire's share of the Pennines includes splendid country round Haworth, but few good churches. Most of the county is composed of the conurbations of Leeds, Bradford, Halifax and Huddersfield. Herein we must find its pleasures.

Ledsham has a Saxon tower and Adel a remarkable set of Norman carvings. The mausoleum church of Harewood has the best group of alabaster monuments in the north. The two Leeds churches offer a fine contrast in post-Reformation styles, St John's with one of the boldest Jacobean screens in England and St Peter's as an essay in evangelical Gothic Revival. For the rest, all is modesty: the charming altar rail at Halifax, Bramhope's simple Puritanism and the Savile memorials at Thornhill. As for the witch of Ledsham, such tales put flesh on the stones of an old church, even if the flesh sometimes creeps.

Adel **	Harewood ***	Leeds: St Peter **
Bramhope *	Ledsham **	Saltaire *
Halifax: St John **	Leeds: St John ***	Thornhill **

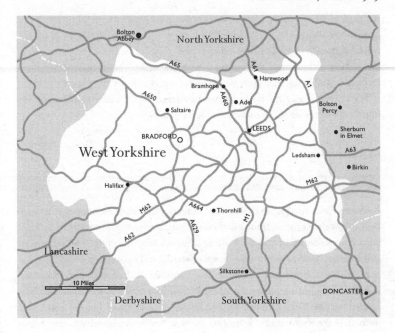

ADEL
St John **
Norman doorway and chancel arch

'Adel, *see* Leeds,' says Pevsner. Leeds would be happy to claim it, but the church sits in a rural backwater next to a cricket field and the big city is nowhere seen or heard. Only the stonework carries the familiar Yorkshire badge, blackness. Adel is that so-called rarity, a surviving Norman church left untouched by the Goths. It was not, however, neglected by the Victorians and some of its carving has been recut *in situ* or replaced. But even if Norman is sometimes hard to tell from 19th century, Adel remains one of the finest works of Romanesque art in the North.

The exterior presents a double-cell surrounded by a complete corbel-table of human heads and beasts. The carvings at the top of the west gable appear to be original. The south doorway is so deep as to be virtually a porch. At the time of its creation it must have been magnificent, four orders of roll-mouldings, zigzag and beakhead. Above in the gable is a barely decipherable Adoration of the Lamb. The modern door has a well-preserved bronze sanctuary ring, of a monster about to swallow a man.

The interior is dominated by the spectacular chancel arch. One capital has the

Baptism of Christ, with a flying angel holding Christ's clothes while the water rises to his waist. The beast beneath the angel is the Devil trying to drink the water of the River Jordan. The other capital is a Crucifixion. The outer rim of the arch is of beakhead decoration. The guide complains that 'whether these faces are swallowing their prey or spitting it out is impossible to decide'.

The church is scraped but is warmed by large 18th-century paintings on the north wall of the nave. The font cover is by Eric Gill.

BRAMHOPE

*

Atmospheric Commonwealth chapel

By the entrance to a garish commercial hotel is a low stone building with a small bellcote. We pass through the hotel's automatic doors, enter the luxurious foyer and enquire for the key to the 'Puritan Chapel'. We then dodge parked Jaguars and Bentleys and make our way into the woods, and to another world.

Bramhope Chapel is one of the few churches built during the Common-wealth, in 1649, intended as a specifically Puritan place of worship. It was erected by the local grandee, Robert Dyneley, who found himself in trouble soon after the Restoration for defying the new Anglican authorities. The church was later converted into an Anglican chapel of ease. It forms an interesting contrast with Staunton Harold (Leics), built at a similar date but by a High Church Anglican patron.

The exterior is as simple as a barn, yet the interior could not be called severe. The warm wood, white walls and timbered roof proclaim comfortable domestic worship. These all belong the post-Dyneley period, when the interior was altered and given new fixtures and fittings. For instance, there would have been no font in the original interior, the present one being dated 1673. The other fittings are probably contemporary with it, including the box pews and the pulpit. This is a complete three-decker with tester and candleholders. Some of the pews carry the names of those for whom they were reserved and two are even upholstered. The Puritans would have sat on rough benches.

This is a church recognisably of its time, reflecting the religious shifts of 17th-century England. The rudimentary altar at the east end now serves as a desk for the visitors' book and for a transcription of baptisms, marriages and burials at Bramhope from 1560 to 1890. The chapel is redundant, and is owned by the local council. Strictly I should exclude it from my list, but Bramhope could, I assume, still be used for Nonconformist worship. It stands as a memorial to a time when England's Protestant sects sought uniformity but found only discord.

HALIFAX
St John, Church Street **
Baroque rail, Commonwealth windows

With the Calder valley, Dean Clough Mill, Piece Hall and its children's museum, Halifax has emerged as one of West Yorkshire's more dynamic towns. The church sits opposite the museum, still surrounded by half-hearted urban renewal. It could at least receive the honour of a clean. The guidebook bravely pictures the tower rising defiantly against a backdrop of high-rise blocks.

The church was rebuilt by a rich vicar named Wilkinson in 1438, with a particularly magnificent chancel. It is Perpendicular, well proportioned, battlemented and pinnacled and with buttresses carrying giant gargoyles. A large sundial adorns the south wall. The interior has no nave clerestory and this, combined with the scraping of the walls and much stained glass, means that the lights must be turned on, even on the brightest of days. The nave was reroofed in the 17th century and painted with the arms of the tribes of Israel and the tribes of Halifax, great families both. The handsome pews are also 17th century, but were lowered by 2 ft in the 19th. In the middle of the nave rises the font cover, a masterpiece of Perpendicular woodwork that survived the Commonwealth by being hidden in a private house. On the north wall is a memorial which, instead of the customary weeping damsel, has a weeping willow.

The focus of attention in the chancel is a William and Mary altar rail, a work worthy of a royal palace, with intertwined balusters on acanthus leaf bases. The reredos is modern, by the ubiquitous Thompson of Kilburn, with his signature of a mouse to delight children. The chancel aisles have a rare set of Commonwealth windows. These were permitted by the Puritan Church authorities on condition that they did not contain coloured glass, the only permitted decoration being abstract patterns created by the leading. These patterns are of great beauty, and were sadly not imitated by later generations. Near the door is Old Tristram, a coloured wooden effigy of a beggar who used to haunt the church precincts collecting alms for the poor. He collects still, in a more sheltered place.

HAREWOOD
All Saints ***
Wars of the Roses mausoleum

Harewood church is in the grand tradition of aristocratic burial places. Like most English magnates, the lords of Harewood laid themselves to rest not in some private mortuary but in the church of their local community, yet with an ostentation that left no doubt of their status. Today, the church lies, partly hidden by trees, off the drive to Harewood House, and is in the care of the Churches Conservation Trust. It is, as the guide admits, 'cold and stark', a bleak but impressive evocation of 15th-century architecture. It would form a dramatic epilogue to a film of the Wars of the Roses, when men slaughtered each other daily and women inherited great wealth.

The church was built c.1410 as a conventional Perpendicular box. Inside, lying like ships at anchor, are its treasures, the six alabaster tombs of the related Aldburgh, Redman and Gascoigne families, most dating from the 15th and 16th centuries. The tombs have often been moved and it seems sad that recent restoration has not set them in chronological order. This would help visitors to follow the story of the families and the changes in monumental style.

The two heiresses to the Harewood estate, and builders of the church, Elizabeth and Sybil Aldburgh, lie on either side of the chancel with their husbands (the one dying in 1425, the other in 1426). The men are in heavy armour, the women in astonishing headdresses. An earlier tomb in the south aisle of Sir William Gascoigne (d.1419) with his wife is more serene. Both effigies are robed, he in the official dress of the Lord Chief Justice and with a beautifully carved purse at his side. Later Gascoigne tombs in the north aisle are more elaborate and in better repair. The women wear veils over their heads, fitted under the chin, indicating widowed status. The men are less heavily armoured.

The finest couple are Sir Edward Redman and his wife Elizabeth (effigies c.1510). His face is strong and well carved, a rare case of a medieval monument that is regarded as probably a likeness. On the lion under his feet is a similar bedesman to that on John de Strelley's tomb at Strelley (Notts), probably indicating the endowment of a chantry. The woman's eyes, most unusual for medieval effigies, are closed.
[CCT]

LEDSHAM
All Saints **
Saxon tower, Bolles and Hastings memorials

The church is attractively located at the foot of its village, the picturesque tower and spire rising above a cluster of cottages. The tower offers a cross-section of church architecture, Perpendicular at the top, Norman at the bell-stage but unmistakably Saxon below. The Saxon south doorway in the tower base has a vine scroll surround. This is Victorian but is apparently based on original evidence and thus grants Ledsham the title of oldest building in West Yorkshire. The tower walls are covered in ghostly outlines of blocked Saxon windows and doors. The limestone top sits like a silver cover on a primitive reliquary.

The interior is scraped and dark, but enlivened by the tombs and tales of two remarkable ladies buried within. Their story begins with Henry Witham, who acquired the estate after the Reformation but lost his heir, William, in 1593 when a spell was laid on him by a local witch, Mary Pannel. For this she was executed at York, one of numerous claimed 'last executions' for witchcraft in England. Witham's daughter, Mary Bolles, proved to be almost as eccentric as Pannel, and was said to have also practised the black arts. This did not stop Charles I creating her a baronetess in 1635, one of the few ever created.

Before her death in 1662, Lady Mary ordered that her body be embalmed and not buried until six weeks after her death, while money and food be supplied to her kin, friends and servants 'to entertain other persons, ordinary and extra-ordinary'. Lady Mary's tomb in the church shows her recumbent in a shroud, white marble on a black tomb. Her ghost makes regular appearances in the village.

The estate passed to the Lewis and then Hastings families. Sir John (d.1677) and Lady Lewis are commemorated as reclining figures on a sarcophagus, she in an unusually low-cut dress. Their descendant, Lady Elizabeth Hastings, was a celebrated 18th-century philanthropist, disposing of the wealth that her family had amassed in the East Indies trade. She patronised churches in Leeds, schools in Ledsham, missionaries to the East Indies and clergymen every-where. Retreating in her twenties from her many London suitors to the quiet of Ledsham Hall, she never married and became a paragon of distant virtue to London society. She died in 1739 at the age of fifty-seven, after an operation without anaesthetic for breast cancer.

Her memorial by Scheemakers has her resting on her sarcophagus reading a book, her half-sisters on either side. Her name is still revered in the district.

LEEDS
St John ***
17th-century screens and fittings

St John's is tucked away across a scruffy garden just north of the Headrow. It was built in 1632–4 by the cloth merchant, philanthropist and virtual founder of modern Leeds, John Harrison. He paid for the town's grammar school, its market cross and numerous charities. Finding the old parish church severely overcrowded, he financed a new church higher up the town and set twenty almshouses round it. Harrison appears to have been a moderate in all things, contriving to straddle every shift in religious persuasion prior to the Civil War, and thus having trouble surviving it. The church respected both the advocates of the Sacrament and those of the Word. It boasts an emphatic screen dividing sanctuary from nave, yet also a fine preaching pulpit against the north wall. There is a lengthy discussion of liturgical history in the guide.

St John's, like many 17th-century churches (such as Staunton Harold in Leicestershire), is probably Gothic survival rather than Revival. It is rectangular in plan, its exterior plain, Perpendicular and uninspiring. There are no aisles but a double nave with a central arcade. What sets the church apart is its complete set of contemporary fittings, Jacobean in style and lavishly carved. The twin screens by Francis Grundy have the most superb cresting of strapwork and royal arms. Comparable screens in the church at Croscombe (Somerset) are earlier, plainer and more classical.

The wooden roofs have arches with openwork in the spandrels over the screen and ceiling panels with plaster reliefs. The two-decker pulpit is complete, with a backplate flanked by eagles, symbols of St John the Evangelist. The walls are panelled and the nave is filled with pews which have lost their doors but are otherwise complete. All this woodwork is covered with arabesques, grotesques and strapwork.

The church was condemned to destruction in the 1860s, stimulating an early preservationist campaign involving the young Richard Norman Shaw, George Gilbert Scott and A. J. Beresford Hope. Like the vicar of Burford (Oxon), with whom William Morris had such trouble, the churchwardens were furious at outside interference. They demanded of the preservationist, why they should have to keep a church as a mere 'curiosity ... to satisfy the morbid taste of anyone who can admire the debased architecture of the seventeenth century'? Shaw's faction won, and he himself was commissioned to carry out the restoration. This he did so successfully that it is hard to know what is 17th century and what are his own insertions. It was a style of architecture that he spent much of his career reviving. A stained glass window depicts Harrison ordering the building of the church, which is now in the care of the Churches Conservation Trust.

[CCT]

LEEDS

St Peter **

Gothic Revival interior

Leeds parish church is in a 'drab setting near railway' says Betjeman and 'a half derelict dead end' says Pevsner. When I first visited it on a wet, black winter evening, I expected either to be run down by a train or fall into the canal next door. Instead a choir practice was under way and the choristers were singing from their dark stalls, lit by red reading lamps. They offered a spectacle of serenity amid squalor. Today the railway's arches are alive with traders. Canal warehouses have been converted into a hotel and restaurant, and the Royal

Armouries Museum has arrived up the road. Canalside Leeds is on the mend.

St Peter's was created by another of Yorkshire's energetic Victorian vicars, Dean Walter Hook. He arrived in 1837, determined to reverse the decline in Anglicanism in the face of Leeds's booming Nonconformist chapels. He was appalled at the semi-dereliction of the former St Peter's and immediately set about building a new church. The design was to be Gothic, by Dennis Chantrell, and 'a standing sermon'. Hook raised the £26,000 cost himself. Wide galleries would enable 2,000 people to hear him preach. The choir was refounded, an 18th-century Bristol organ obtained and Samuel Wesley brought from Exeter as organist. Hook's tradition of daily choral worship continues to this day.

The church appears conventional early 19th century, mixing Perpendicular and Decorated styles, but many corners were cut to save money. The wide galleries have panelled fronts not of wood but of painted plaster. The finials on the pulpit are of papier mâché and there are plaster vaults over the crossing and chancel. Such features – galleries, plaster vaults, false materials – were anathema to the subsequent Gothic revivalists. Hook was more to their taste in his emphasis on the liturgy and sacraments. The church has a long chancel with a raised sanctuary. The extraordinary pulpit and organ case survive and the church is rich in stained glass and monuments, some of them rescued from the medieval church.

A tall Anglo-Saxon cross stands near the sanctuary. Behind it is a rare painted Elizabethan table tomb depicting an early Leeds lawyer, Thomas Hardwick, with his wife and family. Round the chancel walls are 1870s mosaics of the apostles by the Venetian firm of Salviati. The reredos is by Street and the Lady Chapel reredos by Eden. At the back of the church is a fine marble font by Butterfield.

SALTAIRE
United Reformed Church *
Classical rotunda in formal 'new town'

Saltaire is Britain's grandest model town. It was named after Sir Titus Salt, who in 1850 moved his alpaca and mohair works from Bradford to green fields near Shipley and built an estate for his workers round them. The houses were of a comfort and spaciousness then unknown in the mill towns of Yorkshire. The commercial and civic buildings, including a town hall and Institute, have been restored to their honey-coloured stone. Saltaire is more urban than later 'garden suburbs' and more exciting. At its centre, in the park near the canal, is Salt's old Congregational church, the best building in the town.

Victorian Anglicanism was so strongly identified with Gothic architecture that Nonconformists (and Roman Catholics) were drawn to contrasting styles. Saltaire church was built by the estate architects, Lockwood & Mawson, as richly classical. The main front, viewed down an avenue of trees from the road, has a semicircular portico crowned by a circular tower. Projecting from the left side is Salt's own domed mausoleum.

The interior is a spacious classical preaching box lit by large opaque windows in white and green. Above each of the five bays is the initial S for Salt. The Corinthian columns are of scagliola and the walls are cream, pink and pale blue.

The furnishings are sumptuous. Large pews are raised on wooden plinths and a bold pulpit holds centre stage, where an Anglican church would place the altar. Behind sits the organist, with the organ pipes rising like a reredos. This is clearly a church for preaching and hymn singing. The two huge lanterns which hang in the nave might have been borrowed from Brighton Pavilion.

In the porch is a bust of Sir Titus himself, looking most contented.

THORNHILL
St Michael **
Savile tombs and medieval glass

This is a friendly church in warm sandstone, afflicted only by the adjacent road into Dewsbury. The scenery was once that of the mill-and-farm country between Leeds and Huddersfield. Uncontrolled redevelopment has dulled it, but Thornhill contains a quiet reminder of Yorkshire's pre-industrial days. The Savile Chapel dates from the second half of the 15th century, high point of English chantry endowment. Its monuments form a remarkable family sequence from 1447 to 1931.

The Saviles were not grandees but middle-rank gentry; they chose their memorial styles in keeping with the age. Three of the tombs, which lie in the north chapel, are Gothic and three classical. The Goths win the prize. Sir John Thornhill (d.1321) is portrayed with an effigy of a cross-legged knight in chainmail. His head, plainly a modern insertion, stares out incongruously from beneath a medieval visor, like an actor in fancy dress. The tomb of Sir John Savile (d.1481) is a superb alabaster work, with its weepers still intact.

My favourite monument is that of his son and namesake who died in 1504. His effigy is of that unusual funerary material, wood, with his two wives on either side. Although a primitive, almost fairground, carving it is strangely moving. The later tombs are more self-regarding. Maximilian Colt's effigy of Sir George Savile (d.1622) is magnificent, his curls as immaculate as the embroidery on his cushion. A small effigy of a naked baby holding up a font bowl is the last monument, commemorating a Lord Savile who died in 1931.

The windows of the Savile Chapel comprise an almost complete set of 15th-century donor's glass. Though the colours are faded, the outlines are still visible and new pieces have been inserted from medieval windows elsewhere to restore the original effect. The Tudor chancel has an east window containing a 16th-century Tree of Jesse, as accomplished as the best Flemish work.

This theme brought out the best in late medieval artists, representing as it did the beginning and the end of the Christian story.

Index of artists

Index of places